New Venture Creation

ENTREPRENEURSHIP FOR THE 21ST CENTURY

FIFTH EDITION

New Venture Creation

ENTREPRENEURSHIP FOR THE 21ST CENTURY

Jeffry A. Timmons, A.B., M.B.A., D.B.A.
Franklin W. Olin, Distinguished Professor of Entrepreneurship

Director, The Price-Babson College Fellows Program
Franklin W. Olin, Graduate School of Business
Babson College
Babson Park, Massachusetts

Irwin
McGraw-Hill

Boston   Burr Ridge, IL   Dubuque, IA   Madison, WI   New York
San Francisco   St. Louis   Bangkok   Bogotá   Caracas   Lisbon
London   Madrid   Mexico City   Milan   New Delhi   Seoul
Singapore   Sydney   Taipei   Toronto

IRWIN/McGraw-Hill
*A Division of **The McGraw-Hill** Companies*

NEW VENTURE CREATION: ENTREPRENEURSHIP FOR THE 21ST CENTURY

This book is printed on acid-free paper.

5 6 7 8 9 0 CSI/CSI 9 3 2 1

ISBN 0-256-19756-3

Vice president/Editor-in-chief: *Michael W. Junior*
Publisher: *Craig S. Beytien*
Sponsoring editor: *Karen M. Mellon*
Development editor: *Sarah Reed*
Marketing manager: *Kenyetta Giles*
Senior project manager: *Mary Conzachi*
Production associate: *Debra R. Benson*
Freelance design coordinator: *JoAnne Schopler*
Supplement coordinator: *Rose M. Range*
Compositor: *Carlisle Communications, Ltd.*
Typeface: *10/12 New Caledonia*
Printer: *Courier Stoughton, Inc. (CSI)*

Library of Congress Cataloging-in-Publication Data
Timmons, Jeffry A.
    New venture creation : entrepreneurship for the 21st century /
Jeffry A. Timmons.—5th ed.
        p.   cm.
    Includes bibliographical references and index.
    ISBN 0-256-19756-3
    1.   New business enterprises—Handbooks, manuals, etc.
 2.   Entrepreneurship—Handbooks, manuals, etc.   I.   Title.
HD62.5.T55   1999
658.1′1—dc21
                                                    98-43156
                                                      CIP

http://www.mhhe.com

DEDICATION

To Michie P. Slaughter, Cofounder and First President (1991–98) of The Kauffman Center for Entrepreneurial Leadership, Ewing Marion Kauffman Foundation, Kansas City, Missouri. Colleague, Friend, Partner, and Mentor. All of us who support the entrepreneurial mission in America and the world are forever grateful for your pioneering leadership and superb contributions to our collective dream. Because of your personal effort, entrepreneurship education and research have been dramatically advanced at all levels. Enjoy your well-earned retirement!

About the Author

Since the late 1960s the author has been one of the pioneers in the development of entrepreneurship education and research in America. He is recognized as a leading authority internationally for his research, innovative curriculum development, and teaching in entrepreneurship, new ventures, entrepreneurial finance, and venture capital. He is somewhat of an academic heretic, having resigned tenure twice, as well as resigning two endowed chairs. In 1994 he resigned the Harvard endowed professorship he held since 1989 to return to Babson College, which he had joined in 1982, and in 1995 was named the first Franklin W. Olin Distinguished Professor of Entrepreneurship. Earlier he became the first to hold the Paul T. Babson professorship for two years, and subsequently became the first named to the Frederic C. Hamilton professorship, from which he resigned in 1989 to accept the Harvard chair. *Business Week's 1995 Guide to Graduate Business Schools* rated professor Timmons as a "best bet" and among the top 10 professors at Harvard Business School. *Success* magazine (September 1995) in a feature article called him "one of the two most powerful minds in entrepreneurship in the nation." Michie P. Slaughter, president of the Ewing Marion Kauffman Foundation's Center for Entrepreneurial Leadership of Kansas City, the world's leading philanthropic venture supporting entrepreneurship, calls him "the premier entrepreneurship educator in America." Gloria Appel, president of the pioneering entrepreneurship philanthropic venture in the United States, The Price Institute for Entrepreneurial Studies, noted "he has done more to advance entrepreneurship education than any other educator in America." In 1995, the Price Institute and Babson faculty and friends endowed The Jeffry A. Timmons professorship in recognition of his contributions to Babson and the field.

In 1985 he conceived of and launched The Price-Babson Fellows Program, aimed at improving teaching and research by teaming highly successful entrepreneurs with an itch to teach with experienced faculty. In May 1995 *INC*. magazine's "Who's Who" special edition on entrepreneurship research called him the Johnny Appleseed of entrepreneurship education and concluded that this program has "changed the terrain of entrepreneurship education." The program was the winner of two national awards in 1994. During the past decade he helped launch several new initiatives at Babson, including the Babson-Kauffman Foundation entrepreneurship conference, The CEL/Kauffman Foundation challenge grant, the Price challenge grant, business plan competitions, and a president's seminar. He helped attract leading faculty and chaired the annual Babson Entrepreneurship Conference. In 1997 he led an initiative to create what is believed to be the first need-based full-tuition scholarships for MBA students in the nation: The Price-Babson Alumni Scholars. With a $900,000 challenge grant from the Price Institute, the total pool will reach at least $3 million. Since the graduate school rankings began in 1994, Babson's entrepreneurship program was named first in the nation by *US News & World Report, Success,* and *Business Week.* Babson has been ranked the number-one undergraduate business program in America for several years by the *U.S. News & World Report* annual ratings. In 1995 the Franklin W. Olin Foundation made the largest gift ever received by a U.S. business school to Babson, $30 million.

In 1989 he became the first to hold a joint appointment at Babson and Harvard and was named the first occupant of the MBA class of 1954 professorship in new ventures at the Harvard Business School. At Harvard his entrepreneurial finance course became one of the most over-subscribed MBA courses. He proudly notes it became the most difficult course to get into—and to get out of—in the spring of the second year of the MBA program. He also taught in the YPO president's seminar at Harvard.

At Babson he devotes his efforts to the Price-Babson fellows program and a new joint initiative funded by the Kauffman Center for Entrepreneurial Leadership and Babson. This includes a new venture and growth capital institute and other research and curriculum development activities, including the entrepreneurial management program for emerging company CEOs and a leadership development initiative to assist Native Americans seeking economic self-determination and community development. Since 1995 he has assisted Haskell Indian Nations University in Lawrence, Kansas, and other tribal colleges, to develop entrepreneurship curricula and video and written cases on Native American entrepreneurs.

Earlier, at Northeastern University in 1973, he launched what is believed to be the first undergraduate major in new ventures and entrepreneurship in the country and later created, headed, and taught in the executive MBA program. Both programs exist today.

A prolific researcher and author, he has written nine books, including this leading text on the subject, *New Venture Creation*, which has been rated by *INC.*, *Success*, and *The Wall Street Journal* as a "classic" in entrepreneurship, and has been translated into Japanese. In 1996 and 1998, *INC.* featured the book's fourth edition as one of the top ten "must read" books for entrepreneurs. *Venture Capital At The Crossroads*, with Babson colleague William D. Bygrave, (1992), is considered the seminal work on the venture capital industry and is also translated into Japanese. Earlier he wrote *The Entrepreneurial Mind* (1989), *New Business Opportunities* (1990), *Planning and Financing a New Business* (1990), *The Insider's Guide to Small Business Resources* (1982), *The Encyclopedia of Small Business Resources* (1984), and has contributed chapters to other books, including *The Portable MBA-Finance* (1992) and *The Portable MBA-Entrepreneurship* (1994 and 1997). He has authored over 100 articles and papers which have appeared in numerous leading publications, such as *Harvard Business Review* and *Journal of Business Venturing* and numerous teaching cases. In 1995, he began to develop a new audiotape series on entrepreneurship, working with Sam Tyler, producer of the *In Search of Excellence* series for PBS with Tom Peters, in collaboration with the Center for Entrepreneurial Leadership at The Kauffman Foundation. He has also appeared in the national media in the United States and numerous other countries and has been quoted in *INC.*, *Success*, *The Wall Street Journal*, the *New York Times*, the *Los Angeles Times*, *Business Week*, *Working Woman*, *Money*, *USA Today*, and has had feature articles in *The Boston Globe* (1997), *Success* (1994), and *Rolling Stone* (1997).

Dr. Timmons has earned a reputation for "practicing what he teaches." One former graduate and software entrepreneur interviewed for the *Rolling Stone* article put it succinctly: "When going to his classes I couldn't wait to get there; and when I got there I didn't ever want to leave!" For over 25 years he has been immersed in the world of entrepreneurs and startup companies. A cofounder, investor, and advisor of several private companies, he has also served, since its inception, on the board of the Center for Entrepreneurial Leadership at the Ewing Marion Kauffman Foundation in Kansas City, where he conceived of the Kauffman fellows program and serves as dean of faculty. The aim of this innovative fellowship program is to create for aspiring venture capitalists and entrepreneurs what the Rhodes scholar and White House fellows programs are to politics and public affairs. In 1994 and 1996, he served as a national judge for the annual Ernst and Young/CNN/USA *Today* entrepreneur of the year awards.

Earlier he became the first outside member of the board of Cellular One in Boston at its inception and was a cofounder and director of Cellular One in Maine and New Hampshire, a company that was sold in 1989. He serves on the boards of BCI Advisors, Inc. (five growth capital funds with nearly $900 million under management), and Atlantic Investment Advisors, Inc., a Boston money management firm owned by Hambrecht and Quist. He was a founding shareholder and director of the Boston Communications Group, a venture capital-backed leading cellular service firm, which completed an IPO in June 1996 (NASDAQ: BCGI); he worked with national directors of Ernst and Young's National Entrepreneurial Services group from 1985 to 1996, Internet Securities, Inc., the first such firm on the Net, Web Enable, The National Foundation for Teaching Entrepreneurship (NFTE), three venture capital funds, Chase Venture Partners, Spectrum Equity Partners, and others.

He received his MBA and doctorate from Harvard Business School, where he was a National Defense Education Act fellow and is a graduate of Colgate University, where he was a Scott Paper foundation scholar. He has served as a Colgate Trustee since 1991. He lives on his 470-acre farm in New Hampshire with his wife and partner of 33 years, Sara, and winters at Bray's Island Plantation near Savannah. They are proud parents of twin daughters, Jesseca, a bilingual teacher in the Denver schools, and Samantha, a third-year medical student at Wake Forest University. He enjoys the outdoors; fly fishing; hunting with Annie, his Elhew pointer; and golf. He is active in the Henry's Fork Foundation, Wildlife Conservation Trust of New Hampshire, serves as an officer and director of Timber Owner's of New England, and is a member of numerous other wildlife and nature organizations, including The Nature Conservancy, Trout and Quail Unlimited, Atlantic Salmon Federation, and Ruffed Grouse Society.

A Book for the E-Generation and the 21st Century

Never in the history of the nation has the entrepreneurial spirit been more alive. The explosive growth of the Internet since the last edition in 1994 has rapidly become what I call the great equalizer and great liberator of the entrepreneurial process. Unlike any previous generation, the new E-Generation is creating new and growing businesses in unprecedented numbers, with stunning quality and impact on the economy. As a student of this phenomenon for nearly four decades, beginning as a student in the early 1960s, I see no end in sight. Nearly, ten years has passed since the entrepreneurial revolution toppled the Berlin wall, and brought an end to totalitarian governments and centralized, government-controlled economies. The far-reaching consequences are still being felt around the world, among all age groups.

At Babson College the most revolutionary MBA program ever was created in the 1990s. The old functional model of separate courses without integration of marketing, finance, operations, human resources, quantative methods, and the like was totally abandoned. In its place a completely new approach based on the model of the entrepreneurial process in *New Venture Creation* was created. Now in its sixth year, the new program has been a rave success with students and employers alike. Such an approach sets the new standard for management education in the 21st century and makes obsolete most other programs.

As we enter the new millennium, three major challenges emerge. First, larger corporations will desperately seek to think, act, and perform in more entrepreneurial ways. The marketplace for top talent and ideas poses no other choice: They either have to adjust to and invent entrepreneurial ways or they will be replaced by competitors and upstarts.

Second, sustainability in new ventures will require that they include strategies and practices that are ecologically and environmentally sane and sensible. Finally, the coming E-Generation faces the ultimate and most demanding juggling act: How to simultaneously balance the insatiable requirements of marriage, family, new venture, service to the community, and still have time for one's own pleasure and peace.

Silver Anniversary Edition

Although I was quite certain there was something very big about to happen as I first prepared the manuscript for the first edition 25 years ago, I had no idea just how gigantic this entrepreneurial revolution would be. At the time few envisioned the profound potential of such a revolution both in education and in management.

Take, for instance, my original proposal and manuscript for *New Venture Creation*. In the Fall of 1974 the manuscript was flatly rejected by two of the largest and most credible business, economics, and management publishers in the nation. Their reasoning shows why many large companies become bureaucratic, risk averse, and afraid of innovating. They seem afraid to lead, until it is such a sure thing that it is too late to do anything but follow. Consider these quotes from the editors' rejection letters:

"Unless you plan to make this a 'new and up-to-date' manuscript I don't think the published book would have much of a market." (Of course, I was planning to write an 'old and out-of-date' book.)

"We've had to ask ourselves if there is a substantial market out there. . . Unfortunately our reading is in the negative. We have not been able to assure ourselves of a market for your project to justify commercial publication."

To be fair it was understandable that these publishers had difficulty seeing a market. After all, at the time, we estimated that there were at most 50–75 colleges and universities around America that offered courses in new ventures or entrepreneurship. It is most revealing how little vision they had of the potential of this field.

As Mark Twain so eloquently put it: "I was seldom able to see an opportunity, until it ceased to be one." Fortunately, the *first* edition of *New Venture Creation* was published in the United States, by a fairly small, at the time, and very entrepreneurial publisher: Richard D. Irwin, Inc., of Burr Ridge, Illinois, now part of the McGraw–Hill Companies. Editor Robert Dame was the only one who could see the future opportunity.

Since that time there has been a thunderous entrepreneurial revolution in America and now, the world, as you shall see in Chapter 1. Over this past 25 years entrepreneurship has become the fastest growing field in American business and engineering schools. In 1999, over 1,100 colleges and universities will offer courses in this field. Perhaps 200 endowed professorships exist, and more than 50 centers of entrepreneurship have sprung up. *New Venture Creation* is in its fifth edition (1999) and is believed to be the largest-selling book for these courses in the United States.

As we shall explore in Chapter 1, innumerable shifts in the U.S. economy and society can be seen as a direct result of this revolution. Take, for instance, the starting jobs of recent college graduates. In the 1960s and early 1970s about one in four went to work in one of the 500 largest companies in the country. Today, that number has changed radically, to one in fourteen. Similarly, 25 years ago fewer than one million women owned businesses in America, and they worked predominantly for themselves. Today, women employ considerably more people than the 12 million who work for America's 500 largest companies. In the 1970s only $50 million to $100 million of venture capital was invested each year in the United States. Today, that has risen to as much as $12 billion annually. Codes developed by the U.S. government that define and track new technologies, processes, and products developed by American companies are at least ten years behind today's actual developments. To make matters more perplexing, ten years ago about 2,600 new products were introduced in America. Today that number is more than 26,000! On top of all this, the power of the microprocessor chip has been doubling each 18 months for the past 30 years, and continues.

Dawn of a New Entrepreneurial Era Worldwide

The 21st century is here for all practical purposes, and the new millennium will usher in a new entrepreneurial era. It will spark the creation and development of enterprises and a new equity base not known previously. The glimpses of change we have seen in America are very likely to occur around the world. The surge of the entrepreneurial process worldwide can no longer be turned back. People in every nation have enormous entrepreneurial qualities: a very competitive spirit, willing team players and builders, a play-for-long-haul perspective, and they value results and relationships. The innovative and creative spirit is finding its way into nearly all world markets. It is daunting to imagine the future economic power of so many emerging and developed nations, such as China and Japan, once this entrepreneurial genie gets out of the bottle. *New Venture Creation* may play a role here: It was translated into Japanese in 1997.

A Book About the Entrepreneurial Process: Start-to-Finish-to-Restart

New Venture Creation is a book about the actual process of getting a new venture started, growing the venture, successfully harvesting it, and starting again.

There is a substantial body of knowledge, concepts, and tools that entrepreneurs need to know, prior to and while taking the startup plunge and after, if they are to get the odds in their favor. Accompanying the explosion in entrepreneurship has been a significant increase in research and knowledge about the entrepreneurship process. Much of what was known previously has been reinforced and refined, some has been challenged, and numerous new insights have emerged.

New Venture Creation has been the product of experience and considerable research in this field, rooted in real-world application, nearly two decades of research, and refinement in the classroom. The fifth edition updates and refines the best of the first four editions and includes new insights that have emerged.

As before, the design and flow of the book are aimed at creating knowledge, skills, awareness, and involvement in the process, and the critical aspects of creating a new venture and then making it grow. In a pragmatic way—through text, case studies, and hands-on exercises—the book guides students in discovering the concepts of entrepreneurship and the competencies, skills, know-how and experience, attitudes, resources, and networks that are sufficient to pursue different entrepreneurial opportunities. No doubt about it: There is no substitute for the real thing—actually starting a company. But short of that, it is possible to expose students to many of the vital issues and immerse them in key learning experiences, such as the development of a business plan.

The book is divided into five parts. The first three parts detail the driving forces of entrepreneurship—the opportunity recognition, the team, and resource requirements. Part I addresses the process by which *real* opportunities—not just ideas—can be discovered and selected. This section concerns opportunities around which higher potential ventures can be built, where the risks and trade-offs are acceptable, and where entrepreneurs will be able to exit their businesses profitably and when they want to, rather than when they have to or, worse, not at all. It also helps in crafting a personal entrepreneurial strategy. Once an entrepreneur knows how winning entrepreneurs think, act, and perform, then he or she can establish goals to practice emulating those actions, attitudes, habits, and strategies. This section asks entrepreneurs to think of the process of becoming an entrepreneur, much as a coach of an athlete would in preparing for a winning season, and also to consider the following: What are my real talents, strengths, and weaknesses and how can my talents and strengths be exploited (and my weaknesses minimized)? What are the opportunities to use my strengths and to capitalize on the competition's weaknesses?

Part II concerns the team and what makes entrepreneurs tick—how they think and act—and what they do to get the odds of success in their favor.

Part III is about resources and developing a business plan.

The next two parts concern some details. Part IV concerns entrepreneurial finance and the process of financing new ventures. Part V talks about startup, strategies for success and managing rapid growth, and harvest issues.

New Venture Creation seeks to enable entrepreneurs to immerse themselves in the dynamics of launching and growing a company and to address the following practical issues:

- What does an entrepreneurial career take?
- What is the difference between a good opportunity and just another idea?
- Is the opportunity I am considering the right opportunity for me, now?
- Why do some firms grow quickly to several million dollars in sales but then stumble, never growing beyond a single-product firm?
- What are the critical tasks and hurdles in seizing an opportunity and building the business?
- How much money do I need and when, where, and how can I get it—on acceptable terms?
- What financing sources, strategies, and mechanisms can I use from prestart, through the early growth stage, to the harvest of my venture?

- What are the minimum resources I need to gain control over the opportunity, and how can I do this?
- Is a business plan needed? If so, what kind is needed and how and when should I develop one?
- Who are the constituents for whom I must create or add value to achieve a positive cash flow and to develop harvest options?
- What is my venture worth and how do I negotiate what to give up?
- What are the critical transitions in entrepreneurial management as a firm grows from $1 million to $5 million to $25 million in sales?
- What are some of the pitfalls, minefields, and hazards I need to anticipate, prepare for, and respond to?
- What are the contacts and networks I need to access and to develop?
- Do I know what I do and do not know, and do I know what to do about it?
- How can I develop a personal "entrepreneurial game plan" to acquire the experience I need to succeed?
- How critical and sensitive is the timing in each of these areas?
- Why do entrepreneurs who succeed in the long term seek to maintain reputations for integrity and ethical business practices?
- Why do entrepreneurship and entrepreneurial management seem surrounded by paradoxes, well known to entrepreneurs, such as:
  — Ambiguity and uncertainty versus planning and rigor?
  — Creativity versus disciplined analysis?
  — Patience and perseverance versus urgency?
  — Organization and management versus flexibility?
  — Innovation and responsiveness versus systemization?
  — Risk avoidance versus risk management?
  — Current profits versus long-term equity?

New Cases, Chapters and Major Revisions

This edition is a major overhaul and enhancement with several new 1990s cases and updates on earlier cases and textual material to capture the new financial and technological context and global competitive environment of the 1990s. A special effort was made to include cases that capture the dynamic ups and downs new firms experience over an extended period of time. By grappling with decisions faced in new companies over both the first year or two and the next 5 to 20 years, you begin to develop a much broader and richer perspective on the often turbulent and unpredictable nature of the entrepreneurial process. These include the following:

Michael Healey is a new case and a sequel to the PC-Build series of cases. The series continues to track the saga of two Babson MBAs whose award-winning business plan leads to a new venture. By the mid-1990s the company has grown to several million in sales and is seeking to raise capital for growth. This leads to a unique reverse proposition by the company from which Healey is seeking capital: It wants PC-Build to acquire one of its divisions.

Roxanne Quimby is a remarkable entrepreneur who lives a near-subsistence, bare-bones existence in the remote woods of Maine, with a beekeeper. Her creative ideas and entrepreneurial spirit lead her to create a new business around beeswax products and derivatives. The company faces rapid and profitable growth and poses a major issue of relocation to North Carolina.

Gary and George Mueller conduct a second-year MBA field research project at Harvard Business School under the author's supervision to examine publishing opportunities in Eastern Europe in the early 1990s. The resulting business plan poses a major decision for both: Should we start the venture or pursue other highly lucrative and attractive opportunities, including going to Harvard, Yale, or Stanford Medical Schools.

Wayne Postoak introduces readers to Native American entrepreneurship in the great plains. He is a remarkable teacher and highly successful basketball coach at Haskell Indian Nations University, America's only four-year university for Native Americans. He struggles with his own ambitions and wants to be able to afford college education and medical school for his own children. Entrepreneurial opportunities for Native Americans in the 1990s are very limited, yet Postoak uses his entrepreneurial ingenuity to identify opportunities and to develop a strategy that today has built a $10 million-plus business.

Internet Securities is an exciting new case about two recent MBAs who conceive of, launch, and raise venture capital for a new business on the Internet. It explores how and why the Internet is reshaping the way business is being conducted and is creating innumerable opportunities for the coming E-Generation of information-age entrepreneurs.

Fax International Japan is a sequel case to the Fax International series which examines how the founders pursued their opportunity in international faxing in Japan, including finding financial backers, developing strategic alliances, and acquiring the license to do business. This is an excellent look at 1990s global entrepreneurship in action in the telecommunications industry.

Paul J. Tobin rises from army private to MBA to self-employment to president of Cellular One in Boston. Seeing so many opportunities in the wireless telecommunications industry in the late 1980s and early 1990s, he decides to create his own company. The case examines his journey, how he identified opportunities, developed strategies, and raised venture capital to build the business. Unfortunately, the strategy is flawed and the company must be re-created or go under.

Boston Communications Group, Inc. is a series that examines the process of orchestrating and managing the harvest of a telecommunications company in the mid-1990s, either through a strategic sale to the likes of GTE or an initial public offering (IPO). The cases provide an intimate look at the anatomy of valuation and pricing of an IPO, the role and selection of underwriters, and the nature of the robust and tumultuous capital markets in mid-1996.

Quick Lube Franchise Corporation is a sequel to the Jiffy Lube International case series. One of the young founders of Jiffy Lube acquires franchise rights and builds a chain of 44 outlets in the late 1980s and early 1990s while completing an MBA evenings at Babson College. The case examines the issues of determining when to harvest the investment, the company's valuation, and its complex negotiations process with Pennzoil.

Several new or substantially revised chapters bring this edition into the new century of the Internet, information age, and fundamentally new capital and equity markets. These include:

- **The Entrepreneurial Revolution** (new Chapter 1), which documents the radical transformation of the U.S. economy at the hands of entrepreneurs over the past generation and the burgeoning revolution in education, organization, and management alike.

- **The Entrepreneurial Process** (new Chapter 2) is a major revision and enhancement of the core conceptual model of the entrepreneurial process, utilizing Netscape to illustrate its analytical power and practical use.

- **Entrepreneurs and the Internet: The Great Equalizer** (new Chapter 5) examines the explosive growth and impact of the Internet on opportunities for entrepreneurs.

- **Quick Screen** is a new tool (Chapter 4) that can be used to conduct an initial screen and due diligence of an idea that might be an opportunity. This is a dehydrated version of the detailed Venture Opportunity Screening Guide (VOSG) which can save time and effort.

- **Opportunity Identification and Search** criteria and sources, particularly utilizing the Internet, have been added to Chapter 5.
- **The Business Plan** (Chapter 11) has received a major overhaul to communicate its use by both entrepreneurs and investors and the reality that the plan is obsolete the moment it comes out of the printer.
- **Updates and Revisions** of key facts, charts, tables, and data to provide the latest information available at the time of publication.
- **Chapter Summary** is a new addition at the end of each chapter to provide a succinct closure and review of the most important points in the chapter.
- **Study Questions** are also a new addition to each chapter to enable you to focus on key issues, test your knowledge, and organize important material and insights presented in the chapter.
- **Mind Stretchers** are another new addition at the end of each chapter to pose some thought-provoking ideas for readers. For instance: How many millions might it cost you over your entrepreneurial career if you fail to digest the lessons and wisdom from this course and in *New Venture Creation?*

Supplements

- **New Web Site** for NVC will contain old cases not included in the 5th edition, special material from the old edition's appendices that are timeless and valuable, links to entrepreneurship sites, new mind stretchers, and a bulletin board for updates on all the cases and entrepreneurs as time progresses. Visit the site at www.mhhe.com/timmons.
- As with the fourth edition, the fifth edition offers an Instructor's Manual and Test Bank to adopters of the text. The manual includes teaching notes, case summaries and exercises, additional resources, and transparency masters.

- A computerized test bank (Computest) is also available in Windows and Macintosh formats.

The Roots of New Venture Creation

An Approach with Real World Results

New Venture Creation is the most practical and comprehensive book of its kind available for aspiring and existing entrepreneurs. Its focus is on determining *the risks and rewards of entrepreneurship, the difference between an idea and an opportunity, and how to get the odds in your favor.* It will help you to compress and accelerate the learning process without compromising quality, and, if diligently adhered to, may save you sizable sums of 'unwanted tuition.'

The model, approaches, and processes in the book have been used by several hundred thousand entrepreneurs, students, private investors, venture capitalists, and managers in larger companies who are in search of the entrepreneurial dream. Previous editions of the book have received accolades and recognition as one of the leading books on entrepreneurship in the world. In October, 1987, *The Wall Street Journal* praised it as a "textbook classic," as did *Success* magazine in 1994. In 1996 and again in 1998, *INC.* magazine featured the book on its top-ten must-read books for entrepreneurs.

Every new class of Kauffman fellows, the highly coveted two-year post-graduate and work fellowship in venture capital and high-growth ventures sponsored by the Kauffman Center for Entrepreneurial Leadership, receives an inscribed copy of the book from the author, who serves as dean of the program. Their assignment: Read it cover to cover, or again, since many have had it as former MBAs.

Jeffry A. Timmons
Woodland Hill Farm
Greenfield, N.H.
August, 1998

The Spirit of Crazy Horse Lives.

Acknowledgments

This silver anniversary of the original manuscript for the book celebrates over 30 years of intellectual capital acquired through research, case development, course development, teaching, and practice. The latter has included risking both my reputation and my wallet in a wide range of ventures, involving former students and others. All of this was possible because of my incredibly supportive wife Sara and my daughters, Jesseca and Samantha, throughout this journey. It also was made possible by the support, encouragement, thinking, and achievements of many people: colleagues at Babson and Harvard, former professors and mentors, associates, entrepreneurs, former students, and many friends who till this soil. The major upgrades in the last (4th) edition were made possible in large part by the superb assistance of my former Harvard research associate Christine C. Remey. Since that edition, Christy has worked in a venture capital firm, a consulting firm, and then graduated with an MBA with honors from Harvard Business School in 1998.

The original book (1977) stemmed from research and concepts developed in my doctoral dissertation at Harvard Business School, and later with work with the coauthors of the earlier editions. My course development work and research in new ventures at Northeastern University in the 1970s, and in new ventures and financing entrepreneurial ventures at Babson College in the 1980s contributed heavily to the evolution of the book. Since 1989, my research in venture capital and my course development work in the entrepreneurial finance MBA elective at Harvard have enabled me to make major additions and improvements in this edition, especially in the venture-financing chapters.

I have drawn intellectual capital from many roots and contributors, and I have received support and encouragement, as well as inspiration. To list them all might well take a chapter by itself. I wish to express special thanks to those who have been so helpful in recent years, especially my colleagues and all of my MBAs at Harvard Business School who have been a constant source of encouragement, great inspiration, and friendship. I would also like to thank Dean John H. McArthur, Associate Dean Thomas R. Piper, and Warren F. Mcfarlan, my research dean. Thanks to all my colleagues in entrepreneurial management, but especially William Sahlman for his superb work in entrepreneurial finance, much of which is evident in this edition, and Howard Stevenson for his tremendous support and encouragement.

This edition of the book was made possible by the tremendous support of Babson College and the wonderful $30 million gift by the Franklin W. Olin Foundation to build the new Olin Graduate School and to fund the author's chair. Now retired, former president William F. Glavin was both the key in convincing me to return to Babson College full-time in 1995 and a huge supporter of all my work. Other key supporters of this project at Babson were Allan Cohen, Bob Holmes, new MBA Dean Tom Moore, Bill Nemitz, my partner Bill Bygrave, and many other Babson colleagues. New president Lee Higdon has been totally supportive of this effort as well. A very special thanks is also in order to Arthur M. Blank for his support and gift to build the new Blank Center for entrepreneurship at Babson.

Nancy Godfrey, my partner in the Price-Babson College Fellows Program and its annual symposium for entrepreneurship educators (SEE), has raised the bar once again in working with me as project editor to revise the book. Besides doing a highly professional and thoroughly competent job in all respects, she is, as always, a great partner to work with. Without Nancy we could not accomplish all we do at Babson. Gail Daniels has also been of tremendous help in freeing both me and Nancy from other distractions to work on the project. Rebecca Voorheis and Andrea Alyse both assisted with this project as research assistants.

Special thanks to professor Steve Spinelli for his invaluable insights and translations of the Timmons model and for contributing the case on his own company. Steve has also been a partner in the SEE initiative and in my work with Native American Tribal Colleges. Professor Julian Lange, one of Babson's Internet gurus, generously contributed the chapter on the Internet.

Several new cases are only possible because of the collaboration of sharing entrepreneurs: Mike Healey, Wayne Postoak and Cheryl Chuckluck, Roxanne Quimby, Gary and George Mueller, Paul Tobin and Fritz VonMeiring, Doug Ranalli and Shae Plimley.

One of the most inspiring and rewarding sources of my energy for this project, and the entire entrepreneurial mission, is the 700-plus alumni, from 150 universities in over 30 nations, who are my partners and colleagues in the Price-Babson fellows program. In 1999 we will celebrate the 15th year of our annual symposium for entrepreneurship educators. Gloria Appel, president of the Price Institute for Entrepreneurial Studies, has been a phenomenal partner, friend, mentor, and supporter over these 15 years and continues to inspire my work.

Since 1991 my colleagues and dear friends at the Kauffman Center for Entrepreneurial Leadership in Kansas City continue to be a source of both inspiration and support and have become America's leading foundation with the mission of accelerating entrepreneurship in America. What a joy to find others who care so much about entrepreneurship: the late Ewing Marion Kauffman (Mr. K.), Michie Slaughter (retired), Kurt Mueller, Bob Rogers, Lou Smith, and board members Bert Berkeley, Pat Cloherty, Bob Compton, Cliff Illig, Willie Davis, salmon-fishing partner Mike Herman, Tony Maier, and Jim McGraw. The team at the Kauffman Center has been outstanding and a joy to work with since 1991: Ray Smilor, Marilyn Kourilsky, Steve Roling, Trish Costello, Mary McElroy, Dave Lady, and others. No organization in America is doing more to advance education, research, policy, thinking, and practice than the Kauffman Center.

Great inspiration for this continuing work comes from my Native American colleagues who are the very first to create entrepreneurship curricula and centers in America's 30 tribal colleges. Since the early 1990s I have been working with a sizable and growing group of faculty who see the potential in entrepreneurship education as a viable long-term strategy for community economic development while remaining true to native cultures. Their professionalism, creativity, and keen humor are only exceeded by their ingenious, bootstrapping abilities. Special thanks to the leaders of the first U.S. center for tribal entrepreneurial studies and first associate's degree at Haskell Indian Nations University in Lawrence, Kansas: Bob Martin, Cheryl Chuckluck, Don Bread, Marilyn Bread, and faculty. Michele Lansdowne at Salish-Kootenai Tribal College in Montana has been a leading innovator in developing video cases of Native American entrepreneurs in the storytelling tradition. Lisa Little Chief Bryant at Rosebud in South Dakota has been a major contributor to this effort as well. Florence Stickney of San Francisco State University has led groundbreaking efforts at Pine Ridge Reservation, South Dakota, to bring entrepreneurship education into the schools. At the Cherokee Reservation in Oklahoma, Charles Gourd has been the prime mover in helping to bring entrepreneurship education to the middle schools through the breakthrough work and support of Marilyn Kourilsky at the Kauffman Center. Finally, I get great inspiration from all my faculty colleagues who are part of the C.I.R.C.L.E. initiative (Community Innovation and Creative Learning and Renewal through Creative Learning and Entrepreneurship) with Haskell Indian Nations University and the tribal colleges.

The relevance and richness of the cases and new material in the book can be traced in no small way to my involvement with both ventures and venture funds. My colleagues at BCI Growth Capital (Don Remey, Hoyt Goodrich, Bart Goodwin, Bill Spencer, Ted Horton, Matt Gormley, Steve Ely, Peter Wild, and Mark Hastings) have contributed ideas and new cases to the book. Brion Applegate and Bill Collatos, and their associates at Spectrum Equity Investors have been generous with their time and ideas in contributing a new case and coming to classes. Mitchell Blutt and former student Brett Ingersoll at Chase Capital Partners have been a source of encouragement and support.

The third and fourth editions benefited from my long association with Ernst and Young (1985–96), as I worked with five national directors to help shape and develop the strategy and professional development programs for the firm in Entrepreneurial Services. Ernst and Young is now far and away the dominant player in this field.

In addition to all of those acknowledged and thanked in the previous editions, a special thanks and debt of appreciation is due to all my current and former students from whom I learn and by whom I inspired with each encounter. I marvel at your accomplishments and sigh in great relief at how little damage I have imparted—usually!

I would like to extend a special thanks to those professors who have reviewed previous editions of *New Venture Creation*, as they have helped to shape the direction of the text. Thanks, especially, to those who reviewed the fourth edition in preparation for this fifth edition:

Terry W. Noel, University of Colorado, Boulder
Sally A. Martin Egge, Cardinal Stritch College
Bryan C. Toney, Georgia Institute of Technology
Sonny S. Ariss, University of Toledo
William B. Relf, University of LaVerne
Louis D. Ponthieu, University of North Texas

Finally, I want to express a very special thank you to Mary Conzachi, Senior Project Manager at McGraw-Hill Higher Education Group, for her highly competent and professional effort in advancing the revision.

J.A.T.

Table of Contents

The Opportunity

One often hears, especially from younger, newer entrepreneurs, the exhortation: "Go for it! You have nothing to lose now. So what if it doesn't work out. You can do it again. Why wait?" While the spirit reflected in these comments is commendable and while there can be no substitute for doing, such itchiness can be a real mistake unless it is focused on a solid opportunity.

Most entrepreneurs who start businesses, particularly the first time, run out of cash at a faster rate than they bring in customers and profitable sales. While there are many reasons for this, the first is that they have not focused on the right opportunities. Unsuccessful entrepreneurs usually equate an idea with an opportunity; successful entrepreneurs know the difference.

While there are boundless opportunities for those with the entrepreneurial zest, the fact of the matter is that a single entrepreneur will be able to launch and build only a few good businesses—probably no more than three or four—during his or her energetic and productive years. (Fortunately, all you need to do is grow and harvest one quite profitable venture whose sales have exceeded several million dollars. The result will be a most satisfying professional life, as well as a quite financially rewarding one.)

How important is it, then, that you screen and choose an opportunity with great care? Very important. It is no accident that venture capital investors have consistently invested in no more than 1 percent, in recent years, of all the ventures they review.

As important as it is to find a good opportunity, each good opportunity has its risk and problems as well. The perfect deal has yet to be seen. Identifying risks and problems before you start so steps can be taken, early on, to eliminate them or reduce any negative effects in another dimension of opportunity screening.

Chapter One

The Entrepreneurial Revolution

"We are in the midst of a silent revolution—a triumph of the creative and entrepreneurial spirit of humankind throughout the world.

I believe its impact on the 21st century will equal or exceed that of the Industrial Revolution on the 19th and 20th."

Jeffry A. Timmons
The Entrepreneurial Mind, 1989

Results Expected

Upon completion of this chapter you will have:

1. Examined evidence of the radical transformation of the U.S. economy and the profound impact of this entrepreneurial revolution on the nation and the world as it has become America's "secret economic weapon."

2. Learned how entrepreneurs and their growing companies are the engine of job creation, innovation, and new industries, and how venture and growth capital fuels that engine.

3. Discovered how the entrepreneurial revolution has led to the demise of "Brontosaurus Capitalism" as these new and smaller firms have replaced the old established companies.

4. Learned why the American Dream is more alive and well than ever in our nation's history and is ready for the E-Generation now.

The Entrepreneurial Revolution

During the last 30 years, America has unleashed the most revolutionary generation the nation has experienced since its founding in 1776. This new generation of entrepreneurs (the E-Generation) has altered permanently the economic and social structure of this nation and the world, and has set the "entrepreneurial genetic code" for future generations. It will determine more than any other single impetus how the nation and the world will live, work, learn, and lead the next century and beyond.

Consider the impact 70 founders/mega-entrepreneurs have had as their companies transformed industries and the economy. These luminaries have been honored by induction in The Academy of Distinguished Entrepreneurs at Babson College and include the likes of: Craig R. Benson (Cabletron Systems, Inc.), Arthur M. Blank (The Home Depot, Inc.), Richard Branson (Virgin Group of Companies), Ely R. Callaway (Callaway Golf), Willie D. Davis (All-Pro Broadcasting, Inc.), Paul Fireman (Reebok), Ewing Marion Kauffman (Marion Laboratories, Inc.), Sandra L. Kurtzig (Ask Computer Systems, Inc.), Patrick McGovern (International Data Group), William McGowan (MCI Communications, Inc.), Heinz Nixdorf (Nixdorf Computer AG), Kenneth H. Olsen (Digital Equipment Corporation), Anita Roddick (The Body Shop), Frederick W. Smith (Federal Express, Inc.), Thomas G. Stemberg (Staples, Inc.), and Robert A. Swanson (Genentech, Inc.). Just consider, *if you combined the sales of all these companies they would be as large as the economy of the 10th largest country in the world!*

The E-Generation and the Death of Brontosaurus Capitalism

If Washington, Adams, Jefferson, Franklin, and their contemporaries in the Continental Congress were alive today they would be stunned at the magnitude and diversity of this modern generation of entrepreneurial leaders. During the last quarter of the 20th century entrepreneurs and innovators have radically transformed the economy of America and the world. Amazingly, over 95 percent of the wealth in America today has been created by this E-Generation of revolutionaries since 1980. By 1997, one of every three households in America—37 percent or 35 million households—includes someone who has had a primary role in a new or emerging business.[1] Uniformly, the self-employed report the highest levels of personal satisfaction, challenge, pride, and remuneration. They seem to love the entrepreneurial game for its own sake. They love their work because it is invigorating, energizing, and meaningful. Entrepreneurs, as they invent, mold, recognize, and pursue opportunities, are the genius and energy behind this extraordinary value and wealth creation phenomenon: *the entrepreneurial process.*

What may be more important, in my assessment, we are just at the dawn of a new age of entrepreneurial reasoning and at the dawn of the age of equity creation whose impact in the next century will dwarf what we have experienced in the last quarter century.

What is the evidence of this profound, radical transformation of the nation and the economy? What is the magnitude of these volcanic changes? How is entrepreneurship changing the way people live, work, learn, and lead? What are the implications for the young, as well as older people, who aspire to self-sufficiency, economic independence, and a self-determined way of life, which are embedded in entrepreneurship?

Entrepreneurship: America's Secret Economic Weapon

> "It ain't what you don't know that hurts you. It's what you know that ain't true!"
>
> Robert Solow, Nobel Prize Winner

Up until quite recently it was widely held in the popular press and media that huge, dominant firms were the key to America's strong economy. After all, in the post-World-War-II global seller's market these companies did become giants, and by the 1960s and 1970s seemed to be impervious to competitors and invincible to upstart firms. Legendary among these giants was IBM, with a 70 percent-plus market share and more cash on its balance sheet than the combined sales of the rest of the computer industry! Everyone knew the obvious truth: Invincible IBM was here forever and would only get stronger. Few if any observers and analysts, even those with the wildest imaginations, envisioned what was about to happen.

When Bill Gates founded Microsoft in the late 1970s, IBM dominated everyone. Yet, by the late 1980s and early 1990s, IBM again stunned the business world with its shocking slide at the hands of upstarts like Apple Computer, Lotus Development Corporation, Dell Computer, Gateway 2000, Microsoft, and others. Its staff size shrank by nearly half; its stock—long Wall Street's most coveted—plummeted, and it was in disarray. It had become a victim of the entrepreneurial revolution. As Robert Solow would say: "It's what you know that ain't true that hurts you!"

The mountain of evidence which destroys other long-held "truths" about the nature of the U.S. economy is profound. From job creation to innovation, from the creation of wholly new industries to risk capital formation, from competitiveness and productivity to social renewal through private and not-for-profit initiatives, entrepreneurial leaders and the entrepreneurial process have and continue to redefine the American and world economy. Consider the following changes.

Job Creation Twenty years ago MIT researcher David Birch began to report his landmark findings in his seminal work "The Job Creation Process" (1979). The results defied all previous notions that the large established businesses were the backbone of the economy and the generator of new jobs. In fact, one Nobel Prize-winning economist gained his award by "proving" that any enterprise on the face of the planet with fewer than 100 employees was irrelevant to the study of economics and policy making. Birch surprised researchers, politicians, and the business world with just the opposite conclusion: It was the new and growing smaller firms that created 81.5 percent of the net new jobs in the economy from 1969–1976.[2] This general pattern has been repeated yearly. Since 1980, for instance, America has created over 34 million new jobs (Europe had basically stagnant job creation during this period), but the Fortune

---

[1] "Economic News" *The Small Business Advocate,* February 1997 (Washington, DC, Office of Advocacy, SEA), p. 4.
[2] Birch, David L "The Job Creation Process," unpublished report, MIT Program on Neighborhood and Regional Change prepared for the Economic Development Administration, U.S. Department of Commerce, Washington, DC, 1979.

500 lost over 5 million jobs. From 1993–96 alone, eight million new jobs were created. Who creates these jobs? Just 5 percent of the young and fastest growing companies created 77 percent of these jobs, and 15 percent of them accounted for 94 percent of all these net new jobs.

When one considers the history of Microsoft, a start-up in the late 1970s, these job creation findings are not quite so surprising. In 1980, for instance, Microsoft had just $8 million in revenue and 38 employees. By the end of 1997, its sales were $6.5 billion, it had over 21,000 employees, and the total market value of its stock was $151.4 billion—the sixth largest among public companies in the world—compared to downsized IBM's $89.6 billion market cap.

One can readily see the far-reaching change in employment patterns caused by this explosion of new companies beginning in the mid to late 1960s. At the time, approximately one in four persons went to work for a Fortune 500 company. As recently as 1980, the Fortune 500 employed 1 in 5 members of the work force. Yet by the late 1990s, that number was just 1 in 14. This same pattern tells the story of the explosive growth of new centers of technology and entrepreneurship throughout the country. It is impossible to name a new high-growth area, starting with Silicon Valley and Boston, and extending to The Research Triangle of North Carolina; Austin, Texas; Denver/Boulder, Colorado; Indianapolis, Columbus, and Ann Arbor; or Atlanta, Georgia, without observing this same job creation phenomenon from new and growing smaller companies.[3]

Twenty years later innumerable research studies have examined and reexamined the job creation statistics. The ultimate conclusion is the same, as reported in the most comprehensive study as recently as 1995:

> After twenty years, it seems safe to say that, on average, firms with less than 100 employees create the majority of net new jobs in the U.S. economy.[4]

New Venture Formation Job creation in America is driven by the birth and growth of companies. A generation ago it is estimated that only about 200,000 new firms of all types were launched yearly in the nation. By the mid-1970s, this number had tripled, and as recently as the prior edition of this book (1994), most statistics compiled by the government and other researchers reported that about 1.1 to 1.2 million new enterprises were created each year in America. This five-fold increase surely explains the robust job creation during this same period.

Yet in August 1996, research sponsored by The National Federation of Independent Businesses concluded that the annual number of start-ups of all kinds was more likely 3.5 million. This is a remarkable finding with enormous implications. If America's population had grown as fast we would be a nation of over two billion people today. After all, if new and growing companies are the engine of job creation, and there are more than three times as many new firms each year as previously believed, then job creation in the new century will be even more robust. Couple this finding with our own discovery that the federal government's statistical coding of categories of companies and technologies is at least 10 years behind what is actually happening in the economy.[5] This may explain the continuing surprise by most economists and observers of the robust economy of the 1990s, and their endless upward revisions of underestimated forecasts of growth.

Classical entrepreneurship means new venture creation. But it is much more, as you shall discover throughout this chapter and book. It is arguably the single most powerful force to create economic and social mobility. Because it is opportunity-centered and rewards only for talent and performance—and could care less about religion, sex, skin color, social class, national origin, and the like—it enables people to pursue and realize their dreams, to falter and to try again, and to seek opportunities that match who they are, what they want to be, and how and where they want to live. No other employer can make this claim.

Take *women and entrepreneurship*, for instance. Consider what has happened in a generation. In 1970, women-owned businesses were generally limited to small service businesses and employed less than one million persons nationwide. They represented only 4 percent of all businesses. By 1991, women-owned businesses employed 12 million people, more than all the Fortune 500 companies combined. Today they constitute over 35 percent of all businesses and employ more than 18 million people. Increasingly, women start businesses at a faster pace than men, and a growing portion are high-potential, higher growth companies. According to the 1992 Census of Business there were 6.4 million women-owned businesses, double the number in 1987. Pick up any issue of *Fortune, Business Week, Forbes, Inc., Success* or *Fast Company* and you will read stories of remarkable women—and men—who are creating, reinventing, and transforming companies of all kinds into multimillion dollar successes.

A similar pattern has emerged for minority groups as well, with African Americans realizing significant

3 "The Valley of Money's Delight," *The Economist*, March 29, 1997, pp. 5–20.
4 Kirchhoff, Bruce A "Twenty Years of Job Creation: What Have We Learned?" Small Business Foundation of America, Washington, DC, 1995, p. 19.
5 Bygrave, William D & Timmons, Jeffry A *Venture Capital At The Crossroads* (Cambridge, MA: Harvard Business School Press), 1992.

gains. Since 1980, for instance, the number of African American families with incomes over $50,000 a year has quadrupled. A recent study by *NEXT STEP*, published in Philadelphia, PA, notes that directly there are over 621,000 African-American business owners with combined annual revenue of $32 billion; approximately 706,000 Asian-American business owners with combined revenues of $1.0 trillion; and 1.5 million Hispanic business owners with combined annual revenue of $200 billion.[6]

American Dream: For the Young at Start

Aspiring to work for oneself is deeply embedded in American culture, and has never been stronger. A 1994 Gallup Poll survey (crafted by Dr. Marilyn Kourilsky and sponsored by the Kauffman Center for Entrepreneurial Leadership, Ewing Marion Kauffman Foundation in Kansas City [see pages 12–13 for a description of this extraordinary philanthropic foundation devoted to accelerating entrepreneurship in America, and at their web site for entrepreneurs: *www.entreworld.com*]) showed just how lively and robust the American Dream is today. A national random sample of high school seniors were asked a number of questions about their future career aspirations. Seventy percent said they wanted to own their own business. A generation earlier this was less than 10 percent. Further, 86 percent said they wanted to know more about entrepreneurship. Reflective of today's transformed economy, half of their parents said they would like to own their own business. Among corporate managers laid off as a result of downsizing, 70 percent are over 40 years of age, and one-fifth are starting their own company. Other recent studies show that at any one time about 7 percent of the adult population is attempting to start a business of some kind.

More recently, Roper Starch polled the founders of *Inc.* magazine's 500 fastest-growing firms in America between 1992 and 1996 and compared their responses with 200 high-level executives of Fortune 500 companies. Among the survey's conclusions:

- More than 90 percent of the *Inc.* 500 founders and 80 percent of the executives said smaller entrepreneurial companies have become role models for the way business should operate.
- Sixty-nine percent of the entrepreneurs, but only 40 percent of the executives, agreed with the statement: "I love what I do for a living."
- Asked what would they do if they could live their lives over, more than one-third of the corporate executives said they would choose to run their own company.

Employees seem to win more respect at young growing companies.[7]

Sir Winston Churchill probably was not thinking about the coming Entrepreneurial Generation when he wrote in his epic book, *While England Slept*, "The world was meant to be wooed and won by youth." Yet this could describe perfectly what has transpired over the past 30 years as young entrepreneurs in their twenties conceived of, launched, and grew rapidly new companies that, in turn, spawned entirely new industries. Consider just a few of these twenty-something entrepreneurs (*Exhibit 1.1*):

There are many more, lesser known, but just as integral a part of the entrepreneurial revolution as these exceptional founders. You will come to know and appreciate some of them in this book.

Take, for example, Doug Ranalli and Shae Plimley, who, along with technical expert Tom Sosnowski created UNIFI in 1991. Still in their twenties, Doug, a former student of the author, and his wife conducted research to identify opportunities for high growth. Result: the creation of a company in 1991 that would become the MCI of international faxing. As the fifth edition went to press, they had raised $270 million in 13 separate rounds of financing and expanded company revenues beyond $100 million, heading for $200 million.

Roxanne Quimby is a very different but extraordinary entrepreneur. Enjoying a basic subsistence living on a small farm in the backwoods of Maine, she conceived of an idea to develop natural products from bee's wax and other natural things. Her new business began slowly and was very fragile, but today is a thriv-

---

EXHIBIT 1.1

Mega-entrepreneurs Who Started in Their 20s

Entrepreneurial Company	Founder(s)
Microsoft	Bill Gates & Paul Allen
Netscape	Marc Andressen
Dell Computers	Michael Dell
Gateway 2000	Ted Waitt
McCaw Cellular	Craig McCaw
Apple Computers	Steve Jobs and Steve Wozniak
Digital Equipment Corporation	Ken and Stan Olsen
Federal Express	Fred Smith
Genentech	Robert Swanson
Polaroid	Edwin Land
Nike	Phil Knight
Lotus Development Corporation	Mitch Kapor

---

[6] "Diversity: The Bottom Line for Small Business", *Inc.*, Special issue: The State of Small Business 1998, p. 126.
[7] *Fast Company* "Building a Company Is the New American Dream." *The Boston Globe*, Oct. 1, 1997, p. D4.

ing business relocated to North Carolina and exceeding $15 million in annual sales.

Jack Staack had worked his way up, after dropping out of school, to the mail room and the factory floor at an International Harvester Plant in Springfield, Missouri, in the early 1980s when it was announced that the plant would likely close. He and a handful of colleagues pooled $100,000 of their own money and borrowed $8.9 million from a local bank—note the 89:1 leverage—and bought the plant for ten cents a share to try to save the business and their jobs. The plant was failing, with $10 million in revenues. Today the business does nearly $150 million, is quite profitable, has a share price over $40, now rebuilds engines shipped to the United States by Mercedes, and has led to the startup of over 30 additional businesses.

Michael Healey and Bob Loftblad, also former students, were in their twenties as second-year MBAs at Babson College in 1990 when they began work on a business plan to create a new do-it-yourself computer kit venture. Their plan won the annual Douglass Prize as the best in the competition in 1991 and became the basis for launching their company. Today the company exceeds $10 million in sales.

Paul J. Tobin also began his entrepreneurial career while in his twenties after completing his MBA. His first venture, U.S. Glass, a glass replacement business in New England, was moderately successful, but taught him many lessons and only whetted his appetite to be on his own. After selling his company to his partners, he became a marketing manager for a major satellite communications company. A few years later John Kluge selected him as CEO to launch Cellular One in Boston. Kluge's Metro Media Corporation had won the first cellular license for eastern Massachusetts. This became a launching pad to raise venture capital to acquire his own cellular licenses in Maine and New Hampshire, which became Cellular One. The company acquired its licenses at $9 "per pop" or per capita, and was sold in 1989 for $147 per pop—for a 132 percent internal rate of return for the venture capital investors, and an infinite return for him and his cofounders, as they invested their time and talent only. This team founded Boston Communications Group, Inc. to create roaming and other services for the cellular industry, and had an initial public offering in June 1996 (NASDAQ: BCGI).

Another former MBA candidate at Babson, Ann Stockbridge Sullivan developed a business plan while still a student to build a retirement community in Kennebunkport, Maine. She succeeded in raising $6 million of capital, achieved a 97 percent occupancy rate in the first year and has had a two-year waiting list since July of 1993.

Wayne Postoak, a Native American, was a young professor and highly successful basketball coach at Haskell Indian Nations University, in Lawrence, Kansas, in the 1970s. Haskell is the only national four-year university for Native Americans, with students from nearly 200 tribes throughout North America. Haskell also launched the first Center for Tribal Entrepreneurial Studies in 1995. Mr. Postoak had young children, each with aspirations for a college education and medical school, which he knew he could not afford on his coaching and teaching salary. He decided to launch his own construction firm, which today employs nearly 100 people and has sales above $10 million. (Note that only about 3 percent of all businesses in the country exceed $10 million in annual sales.)

Doug Mellinger is another member of the coming E-Generation of entrepreneurs. Frustrated by the inability to attract software programmers to PRT, Inc., a Manhattan body shop in 1989, and by his clients' unwillingness to go to such countries as India and Malasia, he conceived of an idea to invent a place and a country where programmers would want to come, work, and stay, and that would appeal to customers as well. By 1994, some 400 programmers from around the world had come to Barbados to work for PRT.

In 1982, John Coleman, a weatherman for ABC-TV, was frustrated that the weather coverage was brief during a typical news hour. How could such a complex and dynamic phenomenon affecting every person on the planet be given only three minutes! He thought the weather could be covered continuously on a dedicated TV channel—a radical idea at the time. The Weather Channel was born. It lost $6 million the first year and, typical of the entrepreneurial process, it took six years to turn a profit. But by 1997, it had 62 million subscribers and was an extraordinary success.

Formation of New Industries   This E-Generation of economic revolutionaries has become the creators and leaders of entire new industries, not just a few outstanding new companies. From among the staggering raw number of startups emerge the lead innovators and creators that often become the dominant firms in new industries. This is evident from the twenty-something list above. *Exhibit 1.2* is a partial list of entirely new industries, not in existence a generation ago, that are today major sectors in the economy.

These new industries have transformed the economy. In the true creative birth and destruction process first articulated by Joseph Schumpeter, these new industries replace and displace older ones. David Birch reported how this pace accelerated from the 1960s to the 1990s. Then, it took 20 years to replace 35 percent of the companies then on the list of Fortune 500 companies. By the late 1980s, that replacement took

EXHIBIT 1.2

New Industries Launched by the E-Generation

Personal Computers	Voice Mail Information Technology Services
Biotechnology	Cellular Phone Services
Wireless Cable TV	CD-ROM
Fast Oil Changes	Internet Publishing and Shopping
PC Software	Desktop Computing
Desktop Information	Virtual Imaging
Wireless Communications	Convenience Foods Superstores
Healthy Living Products	Digital Media and Entertainment

place every five years, or nearly 30 new faces each year, and in the 1990s, it occurred in three to four years. This outcome is the downsizing and rightsizing of large companies we commonly hear about today. A generation earlier virtually no one predicted such a dramatic change. How could this happen so quickly? How could huge, cash-rich, dominant firms like IBM and so many of their counterparts in the Fortune 500 of the 1960s and 1970s get toppled from their perch by upstart newcomers?

Consider the following example, which is typical of how this has occurred. The author, in 1984, became the first outside member of the partner's committee (effectively, the Board of Directors) at the launch of Cellular One in Boston and eastern Massachusetts. We had one competitor: NYNEX, the cash-rich, multibillion-dollar phone giant. The FCC ruled that both firms could initiate service on January 1, 1985, which they did. Compare the strategies of the two firms. NYNEX built twice as many microwave transmission towers at a cost of $500,000 each, and it is estimated spent two to three times as much on advertising and promotion of their new service as did Cellular One. They also had a substantially larger staff.

But what Cellular One lacked in size, cash, towers, and marketing budget it made up for in entrepreneurial ingenuity and strategies. For instance, NYNEX initially had one service and installation center, near its headquarters in the center of downtown Boston (narrow, one-way streets with very limited and expensive parking). Cellular One opened multiple service and installation centers on the famous Route 128, America's Technology Highway, which circumscribes the greater Boston area. It was a marketing and service battle, not a hardware (translate more towers) battle. This pattern repeated itself for each of the next five years, as NYNEX replaced its Mobile Communications president each year. And each year

Cellular One won three customers for each one that NYNEX gained.

This pattern continues to repeat itself time and again in industry after industry, which accounts for the pace and magnitude of the demolition of the old Fortune 500 group of yesteryear.

The capital markets certainly note the future value of these up-and-comers, compared to the old giants. Take, for instance, the Big Three automakers, giants of the prior generation of the 1950s and 1960s. By year-end 1996, they had combined sales of $372.5 billion, employed 1,106,000 but had a market capitalization (total value of all shares of the company) of $103 billion, or just 28 cents per dollar of revenue. Intel, Microsoft, and Cisco had 1996 total sales of $33.6 billion, employed just 80,000 but enjoyed a market cap of $270 billion. That's 2.7 times the value of the Big Three and $8.04 per dollar of revenue, or nearly 29 times the Big Three.[8]

This pattern of high market value characterizes virtually every new industry that has been—and continues to be—created by the new E-Generation. *Exhibit 1.3* shows the size and impact of some of these other upstarts of the past generation.[9]

Innovation At the heart of the entrepreneurial process is the innovative spirit. After all, from Ben Franklin to Thomas Edison to Steve Jobs and Bill Gates, the history of the country shows a steady stream of brilliant entrepreneurs and innovators. For years it was believed by the press, the public, and policymakers alike that research and development taking place in large companies after World War II and driven by the birth of the space age after Sputnik in 1957 was the main driver of innovation in the nation.

This belief turned to myth—similar to the earlier beliefs about job creation—as the National Science Foundation, U.S. Department of Commerce and

[8] *The Economist,* March 29, 1997, p. 19.
[9] The author wishes to thank Dr. Ralph Sorenson, President Emeritus, Babson College, for sharing these and other data from his presentation, "What Japan Can Learn from Entrepreneurship in America," Kobe, Japan, May 21, 1997.

EXHIBIT 1.3

The Impact of Entrepreneurship on American Giants Old and New[10]

	Sales 1996, $b	Employees 1996, '000	Market Capitalization Mid-March '97, $b
General Motors	164.1	647	43
Ford	147.0	345	38
Chrysler	61.4	114	22
Total	**372.5**	**1,106**	**103**
Intel	20.8	49	116
Microsoft	8.7	21	120
Cisco	4.1	10	34
Total	**33.6**	**80**	**270**

Source: Company reports, Datastream.

others began to report research in the 1980s and 1990s that surprised many. They found that since World War II *small entrepreneurial firms have been responsible for half of all innovation and 95 percent of all radical innovation* in the United States. Other studies showed that research and development at smaller entrepreneurial firms was more productive and robust than at large firms: Smaller firms generated twice as many innovations per R&D dollar spent as the giants; twice as many innovations per R&D scientist as the giants; and 24 times as many innovations per R&D dollar versus those megafirms with more than 10,000 employees.

Clearly, smaller entrepreneurial firms do things differently when it comes to research and development activities. This innovative environment accounted for the development of the transistor and then the semiconductor. Today, Moore's Law—the power of the computer chip will double every 18 months at constant price—is actually being exceeded by modern chip technology. Combine this with management guru Peter Drucker's Postulate: A tenfold increase in the productivity of any technology results in economic discontinuity. Thus, every five years there will be a tenfold increase in productivity. Author George Gilder recently argued that communications bandwidth doubles every 12 months, creating an economic discontinuity every three to four years.[11] It does not take a lot of imagination to see the profound economic impact of such galloping productiv-

ity on every product use and application one can envision. The explosion in a vast array of opportunities is imminent.

It is just this innovation cylinder of the entrepreneurial engine of America's economy that has led to the creation of major new inventions and technologies. *Exhibit 1.4* is a summary of some of these in the 20th century.

Venture and Growth Capital   Venture capital has deep roots in our history, and its evolution to today's industry is uniquely American. This private risk capital is the rocket fuel of America's entrepreneurial engine. Classic venture capitalists work as coaches and partners with entrepreneurs and innovators at a very early stage to help shape and accelerate the development of a company.[12] The fast-growth, highly successful companies backed by venture capital investors read like a "Who's Who of the Economy": Apple Computer, Lotus Development Corporation, Compaq Computer, Staples, Intel, Netscape, Yahoo, Sun Microsystems, Genentech, and thousands of others. Typical of the legendary investments that both created companies and lead their new industry are the following:

- In 1957, General George Doriot, father of modern American venture capital, and his young associate Bill Congelton at American Research & Development (ARD) invested

[10] *The Economist*, March 29, 1997.
[11] I am indebted to Mr. Robert Compton, a colleague on the Board of Directors of the Kauffman Center for Entrepreneurial Leadership, for bringing my attention to these economic discontinuities arguments.
[12] Bygrave, William D & Jeffry A Timmons, *Venture Capital at the Crossroads*, Harvard Business School Press, 1992.

EXHIBIT 1.4

Small Companies' Innovations Can Lead to Major New Industries: Major inventions by US small firms in the 20th century

Acoustical suspension speakers	Aerosol can	Air conditioning
Airplane	Artificial skin	Assembly line
Automatic fabric cutting	Automatic transfer equipment	Bakelite
Biosynthetic insulin	Catalytic petroleum cracking	Continuous casting
Cotton picker	Fluid flow meter	Fosin fire extinguisher
Geodesic dome	Gyrocompass	Heart valve
Heat sensor	Helicopter	Heterodyne radio
High capacity computer	Hydraulic brake	Leaning machine
Link trainer	Nuclear magnetic resonance	Piezo electrical devices
Polaroid camera	Prefabricated housing	Pressure sensitive cellophane
Quick frozen foods	Rotary oil drilling bit	Safety razor
Six axis robot arm	Soft contact lens	Sonar fish monitoring
Spectographic grid	Stereographic image sensoring	

Source: State of Small Business.

$70,000 for 77 percent of the founding stock of a new company created by four MIT graduate students, led by Kenneth Olsen. By the time their investment was sold in 1971, it was worth $355 million. The company was Digital Equipment Corporation, and became the world leader in minicomputers by the 1980s.

- In 1968, Gordon Moore and Robert Noyce teamed with Arthur Rock to launch Intel Corporation with $2.5 million, and $250,00 from each of the founders. Intel is the leader in semiconductors today.

- In 1975, Arthur Rock, in search of concepts "that change the way people live and work," invested $1.5 million in the startup of Apple Computer, Inc. The investment was valued at $100 million at Apple's first public stock offering in 1978.

- After monthly losses of $1 million and more for 29 consecutive months, a new company that launched the overnight delivery of small packages turned the corner. The $25 million invested in Federal Express was worth $1.2 billion when the company issued stock to the public.

In the 50 years since the founding of American Research & Development by General Doriot, the U.S. venture capital industry has accounted for thousands of such investments. This value creation has had a hugely disproportionate impact on the formation of new industries and the economy.

In 1997, over $10 billion of new capital was placed in venture capital partnerships, the largest amount in the 50-year history of the institutional venture capital industry, to bring the industry total pool to about $60 billion. While minuscule compared to the over $9 trillion of wealth in the nation's equity markets, and the $100-plus billion private equity market, its relative impact has been dramatic. Numerous studies have illustrated this impact. One study of venture-capital-backed companies found that the 235 responding firms had been in existence for an average of 1.9 years, for the years 1985 through 1989 had created 36,000 new jobs, had $786 million in export sales, had $726 million in research-and-development expenditures, and had $170 million in corporate tax payments. The average firm employed 153 people, with $3.3 million in export sales, invested $3.1 million in R&D, and paid $723,000 in taxes. These firms' contributions to the economy far outstrip the majority of small businesses and giant corporations.[13]

A good depiction of the long gestation period for these upstart companies, whose collective expansions blossom into entire new industries is shown in *Exhibit 1.5*, the semiconductor industry, and *Exhibit 1.6*, the minicomputer industry, led by the original investment in Digital Equipment Corporation by General Doriot in 1957. Note that even in these fast-paced, emerging technologies it took nearly 10 years before the industry really took off. Second, the venture capital investments came in during these very early years. Virtually every other new industry since, from biotechnology to personal computers to PC software to wireless communications to the Internet, would follow this pattern.

---

[13] Ibid., p. 3

EXHIBIT 1.5

Semiconductor industry: Cumulative number of venture capital investments and industry shipments

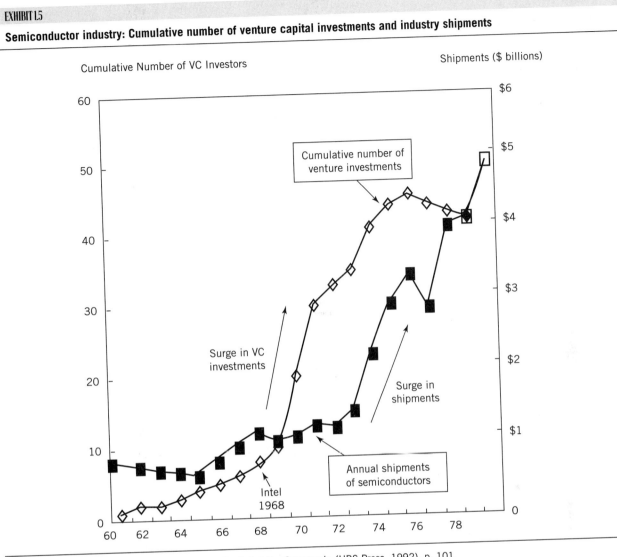

Source: Bygrave, W D and J A Timmons, *Venture Capital at the Crossroads,* (HBS Press, 1992), p. 101.

In addition to the $10 billion of venture capital, moderately wealthy to very wealthy individuals represent a total pool of about $60–80 billion which they invest in new ventures. These "Angels," as they are called, like the venture capitalists, bring far more than money to the entrepreneurial process. As successful entrepreneurs themselves, they bring experience, learning curves, networks, wisdom, and maturity to the fledgling companies in which they invest. As directors and advisors they function as coach, confidant, mentor, and cheerleader. Given the explosion of the entrepreneurial economy in the past 25 years, there is now a cadre of harvested entrepreneurs in the nation that is 20 to 30 times larger than that of the past generation. This pool of talent, know-how, and money plays an enormously important role in cultivating and accelerating the current and coming E-Generations.

Leadership: Giving Back to the Community   What may surprise readers most of all is the little known and largely ignored story of American entrepreneurs as philanthropists and creative community leaders. One cannot find a new building, classroom, athletic facility, or endowed professorship at any university in the nation without discovering it has been funded, the vast majority of the time, by a harvested company founder who wants to give back. The largest gifts and the greatest proportion of donors among any groups giving to university capital campaigns are successful entrepreneurs. In fact, at one time half of the total endowment of MIT was attributed to gifts of founder's stock.

This same pattern also characterizes local churches, hospitals, museums, orchestras, and schools. The bulk of the financial gifts to these institutions is from successful entrepreneurs, such as Ted Turner's $1 billion

EXHIBIT 1.6

Minicomputer Industry: Cumulative number of startup companies and industry shipments

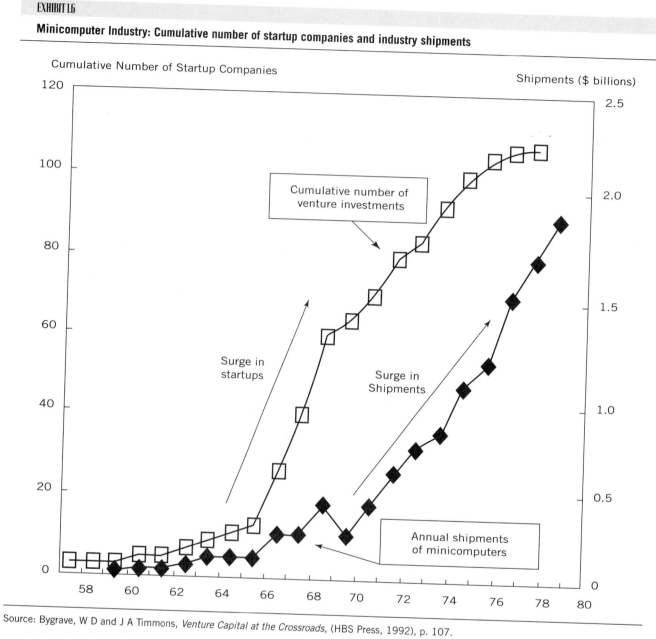

Source: Bygrave, W D and J A Timmons, *Venture Capital at the Crossroads,* (HBS Press, 1992), p. 107.

gift over 10 years to the United Nations, which he announced in 1997. As important as their money is the time and creative leadership they devote to these community institutions. Talk with any person from another country who has spent enough time in America to come to see these entrepreneurial leaders active in their communities, and they will convince you just how unique this is. America's leading foundations were all created by gifts of the founders of great companies: Ford, Carnegie, Kellogg, Mellon, Kauffman.

It has been the author's great honor and privilege to have known and to have worked with Ewing Marion Kauffman and his team in the creation and development of The Kauffman Center for Entrepreneurial

Leadership in Kansas City, at The Ewing Marion Kauffman Foundation—now among the 15 largest foundations in the country, approaching $2 billion in assets. Its vision is clear: self-sufficient people in healthy communities. The Kauffman Center's mission is at the core of the entrepreneurial revolution: *accelerating entrepreneurship in America.*

Mr. K, as he was affectionately known, was probably best known outside Kansas City as owner of the Kansas City Royals (which he has given to the city). In 1950, he quit his top sales job because of his treatment by the president of the company for which he worked. "The year before," Mr. K says, "I made more money than the president so he cut back my commission. The next year I made more money than he did again, so he cut back my territory. So I quit and started Marion Labs in my basement." His entrepreneurial genius created Marion Laboratories, Inc. which grew to $1 billion in revenues, $6.5 billion in market cap, and had over 300 millionaires among its 3,400 employees. Mr. K grew the company on three principles: (1) Treat people as you would want to be treated. (2) Share the wealth with those who contribute to its creation. (3) Give back to the community.

The Entrepreneurial Revolution Accelerates and Broadens

The 30-year journey just traveled provides impressive evidence that the entrepreneurial revolution is for real. When I completed my doctoral program about 30 years ago, entrepreneurship research, curricula, and programs were basically nonexistent. My dissertation was, to the best of my knowledge, the first one at Harvard Business School to have the word "Entrepreneurial" in the title. One could count on one hand the number of universities where such a course was taught, and these were a few elite graduate schools. At the time of original publication of *New Venture Creation* (1977), it was estimated that only 50 to 75 colleges and universities in America offered even a single course in new ventures and entrepreneurship.

The 'revolution' in higher education has changed all that. Today well over 1,000 colleges, universities, and community colleges offer such courses, and many of them offer majors in entrepreneurship or entrepreneurial studies. Innumerable entrepreneurial initiatives among not-for-profit foundations and organizations, such as the Kauffman Foundation, are further accelerating, expanding, and deepening this trend.

Consider, as further evidence, that during the five years since publication of the fourth edition of this book we have witnessed the following:

- The Kauffman Foundation has been joined by other new and established foundations in supporting entrepreneurship, including The Franklin W. Olin Foundation, The Reynolds Foundation, The Ted & Vivian Johnson Foundation, The Koch Foundation, and The Manchester Craftsman's Guild in Pittsburgh, and others.
- In 1994, the United Nations General Assembly passed a unanimous resolution endorsing and encouraging all emerging and developed nations to pursue entrepreneurship as a policy.
- In 1996, National Public Radio, with the encouragement and support of the Kauffman

Center for Entrepreneurial Leadership, for the first time began to cover entrepreneurs and entrepreneurial companies in their daily programming on "All Things Considered."

- The national Girl Scouts and Boy Scouts in 1997 created, with the help and support of the Kauffman Center, the very first Scout merit badges in entrepreneurship. The badge symbol: a hand reaching for a star.
- In 1997, the national Public Television Broadcasting System showed a new film "The Entrepreneurial Revolution," produced by Sam Tyler and John Nathan for the Kauffman Center and PBS.
- Entrepreneurship education is now gaining a foothold in and out of schools for grades K–12 in at least 30 states. At least eight states have passed legislation requiring such education, and the Federal Department of Education has approved the first curriculum, YESS/Mini-Society, created by the Kauffman Center.
- Haskell Indian Nations University in Lawrence, Kansas, created the first Center for Tribal Entrepreneurial Studies, and is now partnering with numerous tribal colleges around the nation to develop appropriate entrepreneurship curricula for Indian Country.
- *USA Today,* CNN, NASDAQ, and Ernst & Young have teamed up to sponsor the annual nationwide Entrepreneur of The Year awards for America's top ventures.
- Major national media from CNN, CNBC, Bloomberg TV and Radio, and leading business publications now cover the entrepreneurial beat regularly. A new magazine, *Fast Company* is capturing the space between start-up companies and large corporations by chronicling how the entrepreneurial revolution and the application of entrepreneurial thinking is now permeating and transforming both midsize and large firms, to avoid becoming another downsize statistic.
- Gallup and Roper Starch polls show an unprecedented level of interest in entrepreneurship among young people and adults.
- The Kauffman Fellows Program was created in 1994 as a direct result of research from our book *Venture Capital at the Crossroads* (HBS Press, 1992). Its aim was to offer to young people with an interest in entrepreneurship, venture capital, and growth companies a two-year, post-graduate and work fellowship that would become to the entrepreneurial world

what the Rhodes Scholars and White House Fellows are to the world of politics and international affairs.

- The National Foundation for Teaching Entrepreneurship (NFTE) has significantly expanded its out-of-school educational programs in the inner cities to help youths seeking self-sufficiency and self-respect through entrepreneurship.

- The entrepreneurial revolution is truly more global than ever as the NASDAQ expands to Europe and Eastern Europe and Asia. Both *New Venture Creation* and *Venture Capital at the Crossroads* have been translated into Japanese.

- In 1996, it was reported that 83 percent of the *Forbes* 400 wealthiest individuals were the first generation of wealth in their families, compared to just 40 percent 10 years earlier.

- The capital markets for new and emerging companies have exploded with record numbers of initial public offerings and trading levels.

- The number of new products in America was estimated at 26,000 in 1996, a tenfold increase from 1986, thus confirming Moore's Law and Drucker's Postulate.

As a student, researcher, observer, and participant in The Entrepreneurial Revolution over the past thirty years, I can honestly say that this pattern appears to grow larger and faster each year.

Entrepreneurs: America's Self-Made Millionaires

No one can be surprised to learn that the founders of great companies such as Apple Computer, Inc., Federal Express, Staples, Intuit, and Lotus Development Corporation become millionaires when their companies become publicly traded. What may be surprising is that the vast majority of the new generation of millionaires are invisible to most Americans, and do not at all fit the stereotype one derives from the press and media. The authors of *The Millionaire Next Door*, Thomas J. Stanley and William D. Danko, share some new insights into this group:

[T]he television image of wealthy Americans is false: The truly wealthy are not by and large ostentatious but, rather, are very persistent and disciplined people running ordinary businesses.[14]

The profile of these 3.5 million millionaires (net worth of $1 million or more)—out of 100 million households in the nation—is revealing: they accumu-

lated their wealth through hard work, self-discipline, planning and frugality, all very entrepreneurial virtues. Two-thirds of them still working are self-employed. They are not descendants of the Rockefellers or Vanderbilts. Instead, they are truly self made: over 80 percent are ordinary people who have accumulated their wealth in one generation. They live below their means, would rather be financially independent than display high social status and don't look like most people's stereotype of millionaires. What may also surprise is they get rich slowly: the average millionaire is 57 years old. Their businesses are not the sexy, high-tech, Silicon Valley variety, rather they have created and own such businesses as: ambulance service, citrus farm, cafeteria, diesel engine rebuilder, consulting service, janitorial service, job training school, meat processor, mobile home parks, pest controller, newsletter publisher, rice farmer and sandblasting contractor.[15]

The implications of this new study are quite significant and encouraging for the vast majority of entrepreneurs. Clearly, the American Dream is more alive and well than ever, and more accessible than ever. One clearly does not have to be born to wealth, attend prep school and go to an elite ivy league school to become successful. Further, the study seems to confirm what has been articulated in all editions of *New Venture Creation*: a combination of talent and skills, the opportunity for you, matched with the needed resources, applied with the entrepreneurial mindset is key. And there have never been more opportunities to pursue an entrepreneurial dream.

Dawn of the New Age of Equity Creation

We are at the dawn of the new age of equity creation in America and the world. Entrepreneurs create value and realize that value through the creation of equity through ownership. In a nutshell, the entrepreneurial process is about making the pie bigger. The evidence of this new age is dramatic.

The U.S. capital markets have been an integral and resilient part of this revolution in entrepreneurship. The market response to the 15-fold increase in the number of new firms and 30-fold leap in the availability of venture capital has been a similar explosion in the capital markets. Total capital raised for all U.S. businesses, for instance, has increased from less than $50 billion in the late 1960s to surpass $1 trillion for the first time in 1993. (See Exhibit 1.7.) In just 15 years, 1982–1997, the U.S. stock markets have mushroomed at an unprecedented pace as the Dow Jones Industrial Average catapulted from 777 in August

---

14 "The Millionaire Next Door," *Success Magazine,* March 1997, pp. 45–51.
15 Ibid., pp. 46–48.

EXHIBIT 1.7

Total U.S. Capital Raised

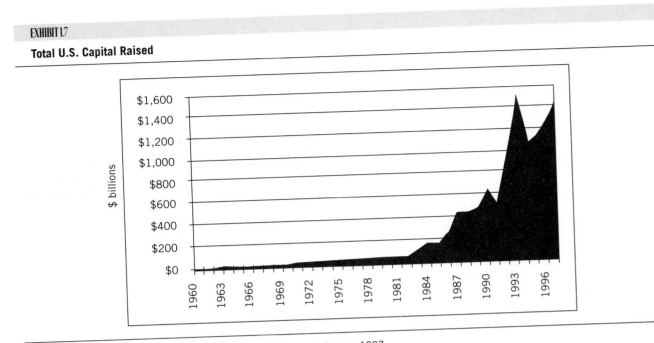

Source: The Carlyle Group, *Economic and Investment Environment*, January 1997.

EXHIBIT 1.8

The Stock Market Explosion

	August 1982	August 1997
DJIA	777	8,000+
Number of equity Mutual Funds	320	2,800+
Number of Investment Clubs	4,000	32,000
Net Cash Flows into Mutual Funds*	$−2 b	$+193 b

*for the prior 12 months

EXHIBIT 1.9

U.S. Stock Markets—Average Daily Trading

	# of Shares		$ Value	
	1980	1997	1980	1997
NYSE	44.9 m	513 m	$ 1.5 b	$ 22.1 b
NASDAQ	26.4 m	696 m	$ 0.3 b	$ 17.3 b

Source: SIA Research Department.

1982 to 8,500+ in early 1998, and the number of mutual funds grew from 320 to 2,800. (See Exhibit 1.8.)

This capital markets eruption is also evident from the nearly 15-fold to 30-fold increase in the average daily trading volume on the New York Stock exchange and the rapid maturation of the NASDAQ exchange for emerging companies (*Exhibits 1.8 and 1.9*).

By 1998, these numbers increased about another 30 percent. Not surprisingly, the value of all equity underwritings also grew about 15 times, while initial

EXHIBIT 1.10

U.S. Stock Markets: $ Value 1980 vs. 1996

	1980	1996
IPOs	$ 1.4 b	$ 41.6 b
Total Underwritings	$ 57.6 b	$ 953.6 b
All Equity	$ 16.0 b	$ 152.5 b

Source: SIA Research Department.

public offerings (IPOs) skyrocketed, increasing by nearly 40 times from 1980 to 1996 (*Exhibit 1.10*).

The implications of all this are profound for aspiring entrepreneurs and the nation. The overall wealth of the nation, expressed as a U.S. household balance sheet, grew from $550 billion in 1970, to about $9 trillion by the end of 1997. What may astonish some is that over 95 percent of the nation's wealth has been created since 1980, a direct result of this entrepreneurial revolution. We are now beginning to see this result duplicated in the rest of the world.

Building an Entrepreneurial Society

The entrepreneurial spirit and process is truly America's secret economic weapon. The opportunity exists as never before in the history of the nation to capture this national asset and to build upon this unique national capacity. Thanks to Ewing Marion Kauffman and the Kauffman Center for Entrepreneurial Leadership, a great deal has been done to educate Americans of all ages, as well as our legislators and policymakers throughout government. The Center's mission, "Accelerating Entrepreneurship in America," drives this ambitious effort.[16]

The Poorer Get Richer   More than any other aspect of our society and economy, entrepreneurship is the great equalizer and mobilizer of opportunity. It is indifferent to race, religion, sex, or geography. It rewards performance and punishes shabbiness and ineptness. No other institutional process offers the chance for self-sufficiency, self-determination, and economic improvement than the entrepreneurial process. We saw earlier the profile of America's millionaires: they are by and large self-made entrepreneurs. Even the *Forbes* 400 wealthiest persons list reflects this trend: 86 percent of the 1996 list were self-made.

Yet, one of the most durable debates in American society is our love-hate relationship with wealth and income distribution. Our heritage as a land of opportunity came to be known as "Horatio Alger Stories," as these 120 novels after the Civil War portrayed ordinary boys rising from rags to riches in a generation. All too often, however, one hears that 'the rich get richer' and, by implication, the poor must be getting poorer. But if this is true, and the middle class is eventually encroached upon, the political repercussions will be heard round the world.

Create Equal Opportunities Not Equal Incomes   What has been lost historically in this debate is that equal incomes are neither desirable nor possible. What counts most is that opportunities are available for anyone who wants to prepare and to compete. The entrepreneurial process will take over and result in economic expansion and accompanying social mobility. A recent study at The Federal Reserve Bank of Dallas provides valuable insight.[17] In one experiment in the 1970s, for instance, three groups of Canadians, all in their twenties, all with at least 12 years of schooling, volunteered to work in a simulated economy where the only employment was making woolen belts on small hand looms. They could work as much or as little as they liked, earning $2.50 for each belt. After 98 days, the results were anything but equal: 37.2 percent of the economy's income went to the 20 percent with the highest earnings. The bottom 20 percent received only 6.6 percent.[18]

Entrepreneurship = Economic and Social Mobility
What is the evidence on this richer–poor income distribution debate? The authors of the Federal Reserve study would agree with the earlier case presented here showing the radical transformation of the American economy as a result of the entrepreneurial revolution. Their data also show this is still the land of opportunity. Indeed, income mobility in America from 1975–1991 shows that a significant portion of those in the lowest quintile in 1975 had moved up, including 29 percent all the way to the top quintile (*Exhibit 1.11*). In terms of absolute gain, the data, adjusted for inflation, showed the poor are getting richer faster (*Exhibit 1.12*).

The study concluded with this important summation:

> Striving to better oneself isn't just private virtue. It sows the seeds of economic growth and technical advancement. There's no denying that the system allows some Americans to become richer than others. We must accept that. Equality of income is not what has made the U.S. economy grow and prosper. It's opportunity . . .

[16] Michie P Slaughter, March 1996, "Entrepreneurship: Economic Impact and Public Policy Implications," for the Library of Congress Congressional Research Service, (Kansas City, MO: Kauffman Center for Entrepreneurial Leadership, Inc.).
[17] Cox, Michael W and Richard Aim, "By Our Own Bootstraps: Economic Opportunity and the Dynamics of Income Distribution," 1995 Annual Report, (Dallas, TX: The Federal Reserve Bank), pp. 2–23.
[18] Ibid., p. 5.

EXHIBIT 1.11

Moving on Up

Income Quintile in 1975	Percent in Each Quintile in 1991				
	1st	2nd	3rd	4th	5th
5th (highest)	.9	2.8	10.2	23.6	62.5
4th	1.9	9.3	18.8	32.6	37.4
3rd (middle)	3.3	19.3	28.3	30.1	19.0
2nd	4.2	23.5	20.3	25.2	26.8
1st (lowest)	5.1	14.6	21.0	30.3	29.0

EXHIBIT 1.12

The Poor Are Getting Richer Faster

Income quintile in 1975	Average Income in 1975	Average Income in 1991	Absolute Gain
5th (highest)	$45,704	$49,678	$3,974
4th	22,423	31,292	8,869
3rd (middle)	13,030	22,304	9,274
2nd	6,291	28,373	22,082
1st (lowest)	1,153	26,475	25,322

Figures are in 1993 dollars.

Our proper cultural icon is not the common man. It's the *self-made* man or woman.[19]

As a nation, at all levels of government, we need to create and encourage policies and practices that are more friendly to the entrepreneurial process. We need to take advantage of this great national asset and secret economic weapon to foster and ensure the mobility of opportunity just described.

Chapter Summary

This chapter has set the stage for the remainder of the book. We have seen that:

1. The Entrepreneurial Revolution is here to stay, having set the genetic code of the U.S. and global economy for the 21st century, and having sounded the death knell for Brontosaurus Capitalism of yesteryear.

2. Entrepreneurs are the creators, the innovators, and the leaders who give back to society, as philanthropists, directors and trustees, and who, more than any others, change the way people live, work, learn, play, and lead.

3. Entrepreneurs create new technologies, products, processes, and services that become the next wave of new industries.

4. Entrepreneurs create value with high potential, high growth companies which are the job creation engines of the U.S. economy.

5. Venture capital is a unique feature of the U.S. economy which provides the fuel for the skyrocketing engines that are high-potential, high-growth companies.

6. America and the world are at the dawn of a new age of equity creation, as evidenced by a 10- to 30-fold increase in our capital markets in just 15 years.

7. Entrepreneurs are realizing the value they have created in unprecedented numbers; over 95 percent of the wealth in America today has been created since 1980.

8. America's 3.5 million millionaires are mostly self-made entrepreneurs.

9. In America, the "poorer get richer" as a result of the entrepreneurial process.

10. Building an entrepreneurial society for the 21st Century and beyond is the highest priority for the E-Generation.

19 Ibid., p. 18.

Study Questions

Can you answer the following?

1. How has America's and the world's economy changed over the past generation, and why?

2. How have the number of new venture formations in the U.S. changed in the past 30 years? Why has this happened? Why will this pattern continue into the 21st century?

3. From where do the new jobs in America derive, and why?

4. Explain the extent to which large versus new and emerging companies contribute to all innovations. To radical innovations.

5. When was the vast majority of wealth created in America, and by whom: (a) Carnegies, Vanderbilts, and Rockefellers before 1990. (b) Automobile, food, and real-estate magnates after 1900 but before 1970. (c) Founders of companies since 1970.

6. Who are the millionaires today?

7. Can you name some exceptional companies whose founders were in their twenties when they launched their company?

8. What role has venture capital played in this economic transformation?

9. It is often argued that "the rich get richer; the poor get poorer." How and why has the entrepreneurial revolution affected this old stereotype? What are its implications?

10. What has happened to large and established companies of yesteryear as a result of this surge by entrepreneurial upstarts?

MIND STRETCHERS

Have You Considered?

1. As a citizen, what policies are needed to encourage and build an entrepreneurial society?

2. How will opportunities and the availability of capital change in the new century as a result of this economic and social revolution? How can one be best prepared for this?

3. Many, if not most people, prefer predictability to unpredictability. Yet, the entrepreneurial process is inherently rather chaotic, unpredictable and unplannable. Who will succeed and who will falter in this dynamic process? What skills and mindsets are required?

4. If this revolution continues at its pace of the past 25 years, or a 10- to 15-fold increase, at your 25th college or graduate school reunion what will be the Dow-Jones Industrial and the NASDAQ Average? How many businesses and jobs will there be? How many new industries that no one has thought of today? What if this pace is 50 percent faster or slower?

Exercise—A Visit with an Entrepreneur

Over the years, students have found it valuable to interview entrepreneurs who have, within the past 5 to 10 years, started firms whose sales now exceed $1 million and which are profitable. Through such an interview, you can gain insight into an entrepreneur's reasons, strategies, approaches, and motivations for starting and owning a business. Gathering information through interviewing is a valuable skill to practice. You can learn a great deal in a short time through interviewing if you prepare thoughtfully and thoroughly.

The Visit with an Entrepreneur Exercise has been used by students to interview successful entrepreneurs. While there is no right way to structure an interview, the format in this exercise has merit because it is chronological and it has been tested successfully on many occasions. A breakfast, lunch, or dinner meeting is an excellent vehicle.

Select two entrepreneurs and businesses about which you would like to learn the most. This could be someone you see as an example or role model in a field to which you aspire, or which you know the least but are anxious to learn. At a minimum, interview two entrepreneurs in order to contrast a high-potential (e.g. $5 million revenue plus) and a lifestyle business (usually much smaller, but not necessarily).

Create a Life-Long Learning Log

Create a computer file, or acquire a notebook or binder where you can begin to record your goals, triumphs and disappointments, and lessons learned. This can be done as key events happen or on some other frequent basis. The author has kept such a log since his graduate school days, usually when key life events have occurred, times of crises, and at year's end to sum up accomplishments and new goals. The record of personal insights, observations and lessons learned can provide valuable anchors during times of difficult decisions, as well as very interesting reading—for you at least.

A Visit with an Entrepreneur

STEP 1

Contact the person you have selected and make an appointment.

Be sure to explain why you want the appointment and to give a realistic estimate of how much time you will need.

STEP 2

Identify specific questions you would like to have answered and the general areas about which you would like information. (See the interview in Step 3). Using a combination of open-ended questions (general questions about how the entrepreneur got started, what happened next, and so forth), and closed-end questions (specific questions about what his or her goals were, if he or she had to find partners, and so forth), will help keep the interview focused and yet allow for unexpected comments and insights.

STEP 3

Conduct the Interview.

Recording the interview can be very helpful to you later and is recommended unless you or the person being interviewed objects to being recorded. Remember, too, that you most likely will learn more if you are an interested listener.

The Interview

Questions for Gathering Information

- Would you tell me about yourself before you started your first venture?

    Who else did you know while you were growing up who had started or owned a business, and how did they influence you? Anyone later, after you were 21 years old?

    Were your parents, relatives, or close friends entrepreneurial? How so?

    Did you have role models?

    What was your education/military experience? In hindsight, was it helpful? In what specific ways?

    Did you have a business or self-employment during your youth?

    In particular, did you have any sales or marketing experience? How important was it, or a lack of it, to starting your company?

When, under what circumstances, and from whom did you become interested in entrepreneurship and learn some of the critical lessons?

- Describe how you decided to create a job instead of take a job by starting your venture.

    How did you spot the opportunity? How did it surface?

    What were your goals? What were your lifestyle needs or other personal requirements? How did you fit these together?

    How did you evaluate the opportunity in terms of the critical elements for success? The competition? The market? Did you have specific criteria you wanted to meet?

    Did you find or have partners? What kind of planning did you do? What kind of financing did you have?

    Did you have a start-up business plan of any kind? Please tell me about it.

    How much time did it take from conception to the first day of business? How many hours a day did you spend working on it?

    How much capital did it take? How long did it take to reach a positive cash flow and break-even sales volume? If you did not have enough money at the time, what were some ways in which you bootstrapped the venture (bartering, borrowing, and the like). Tell me about the pressures and crises during that early survival period.

    What outside help did you get? Did you have experienced advisors? lawyers? accountants? tax experts? patent experts? How did you develop these networks and how long did it take?

    How did any outside advisors make a difference in your company?

    What was your family situation at the time?

    What did you perceive to be the strengths of your venture? Weaknesses?

    What was your most triumphant moment? Your worst moment?

    Did you want to have partners or do it solo? Why?

- Once you got going:

  What were the most difficult gaps to fill and problems to solve as you began to grow rapidly?

  When you looked for key people as partners, advisors, or managers, were there any personal attributes or attitudes you were particularly seeking because you knew they would fit with you and were important to success? How did you find them?

  Are there any attributes among partners and advisors that you would definitely try to avoid?

  Have things become more predictable? Or less?

  Do you spend more time, the same amount of time, or less time with your business now than in the early years?

  Do you feel more managerial and less entrepreneurial now?

  In terms of the future, do you plan to harvest? To maintain? To expand?

  In your ideal world, how many days a year would you want to work? Please explain.

  Do you plan to ever retire? Would you explain.

  Have your goals changed? Have you met them?

  Has your family situation changed?

  What did you learn from both success and failure?

  What were/are the most demanding conflicts or trade-offs you face (e.g. the business vs. personal hobbies or a relationship or children)?

  Describe a time you ran out of cash, what pressures this created for you, the business, your family, and what you did about it. What lessons were learned?

  Can you describe a venture that did not work out for you and how this prepared you for your next venture?

Questions for Concluding

- What do you consider your most valuable asset—the thing that enabled you to make it?

- If you had it to do over again, would you do it again, in the same way?

- As you look back, what do you feel are the most critical concepts, skills, attitudes, and know-how you needed to get your company started and grown to where it is today? What will be needed for the next five years? To what extent can any of these be learned?

- Some people say there is a lot of stress being an entrepreneur. What have you experienced? How would you say it compares with other "hot seat" jobs, such as the head of a big company, or a partner in a large law or accounting firm?

- What things do you find personally rewarding and satisfying as an entrepreneur? What have been the rewards, risks, and trade-offs?

- Who should try to be an entrepreneur? And who should not? Can you give me any ideas there?

- What advice would you give an aspiring entrepreneur? Could you suggest the three most important lessons you have learned? How can I learn them while minimizing the tuition?

- Would you suggest any other entrepreneur I should talk to?

- Are there any other questions you wished I had asked, from which you feel I could learn valuable lessons?

STEP 4

Evaluate what you have learned.
Summarize the most important observations and insights you have gathered from these interviews. Contrast especially what patterns, differences and similarities exist between lifestyle and high-potential entrepreneurs. Who can be an entrepreneur? What surprised you the most? What was confirmed about entrepreneurship? What new insights emerged? What are the implications for you personally, your goals, career aspirations?

STEP 5

Write a Thank you Note.
This is more than a courtesy; it will also help the entrepreneur remember you favorably should you want to follow up on the interview.

Preparation Questions

1. What are the strengths and weaknesses of the entrepreneurs, individually and as a team?
2. What is the opportunity?
3. Would you invest in the entrepreneurs if you were convinced that the opportunity was sound? Why or why not?
4. What are the critical skills and resources necessary to succeed in the business?
5. What should the entrepreneurs do and why?

In early 1993, at age 31, J. C. Egnew was employed as vice president of manufacturing by Wilderness Products, Inc., a large tent producer. He was responsible for the overall planning and administration of the company's manufacturing operations. The company's sales were about $12 million per year, and it employed over 350 people at three plants. Although the company was growing, Egnew began to encounter basic differences of opinion and philosophy with the owners and top management of the company, particularly over issues of new product development and expansion. Prompted by these differences, Egnew became increasingly intrigued with the possibility of starting his own tent-manufacturing company. He discussed his ideas with a co-worker, John F. Moore, the sales service manager.

Wilderness Products had experienced substantial growth in unit volume and dollar sales, but Egnew was troubled about its apparent lack of concern for profits. Drawing from his business school training, he also observed other problems in the company:

> There is not one page of formal planning. There is no real organization—everyone is just doing his own thing. And the techniques being used to manage the company aren't keeping up with the rate of growth. They may be appropriate for a $3–6 million tent manufacturer, but not one doing $36 million.

There were still other problems with the way the company was being managed. As Egnew put it:

> If I ask the production manager, the sales manager, and the president what our capacity is and for a sales forecast, I get three very different answers. The company is very sales oriented in a seller's market. So we fill up with orders which require too much overtime to produce, and we end up with missed delivery schedules and unprofitable sales. It has gotten to the point where I honestly feel that something is way out of balance.

During the three years since joining Wilderness Products, Egnew had gained experience in, and knowledge of, the tent-manufacturing industry. He felt that there was a substantial national market for tents and that his current employer was not competing as effectively as it could. In particular, he felt that there was significant potential to manufacture and market a line of camping tents and accessories having broad-based consumer appeal. He felt that such trends as more discretionary income and more leisure time were favorably affecting consumer demand for tents. Two-thirds of heads of households surveyed by the University of Michigan agreed that camping is the best vacation a family can take. The U.S. Travel Data Center reported that camping was the nation's second most popular vacation activity in 1991. Hiking was first.[1]

Egnew's operating experience in the industry was confirming the impact of these trends. During the previous four years, for example, the six major tent manufacturers had been continually delinquent to customers because they were unable to keep pace with the growing market. Poor deliveries prevailed in this period, while production by the "big six" was expanding at an annual rate of 20 percent. Egnew also knew that strong retail demand had led to a severe erosion of product quality as a result of haphazard industry expansion.

In response to the situation, Egnew decided to try to convince the management that a coordinated plan was needed to pull the business together and make it profitable. During evenings and weekends he and Moore drew up what they considered a sensible long-range plan, and Egnew then discussed the plan with his employer. "I got them to agree to it, but in six months it all went out the window." He concluded: "I didn't have what it takes to convince them to run the business the way I wanted to."

This left him with what he felt were three principal alternatives:

1. Quit and get another job.
2. Get the president fired.
3. Start his own tent manufacturing company.

Egnew had little net worth and only three years in the business. He was married and had a son. His salary of $78,000 per year provided him with a comfortable standard of living. He wondered whether he wasn't kidding himself, whether it was realistic to go out on his own, and how he might pursue the idea since he had never started a company previously.

Determined to resolve their future, Egnew and Moore agreed to meet again for an entire weekend to decide on a strategy.

[1] Tom Huggler, camping editor. "The *Compleat* Camper," *Outdoor Life*, June 1993, p. 59.

Personal Backgrounds

J. C. Egnew.   J. C. Egnew was born and raised in Indiana. He recalled some of his attitudes, which he attributed to his upbringing:

> My dad was a teacher, but a farmer at heart. I remember his thoroughness—"If you're going to do something, do it well." He believed in sticking with things. Both my parents developed in me a high regard for my individual freedom.

This independence apparently also included emancipation from the classroom and attraction to the world of work and basketball. By the time Egnew was 16 he was working full-time after school. He noted: "I learned a sense of self-responsibility and how to support myself. I made most of my own decisions concerning school and other things. I found work a lot more interesting than school."

In addition to working full-time in high school, Egnew also played basketball. His schoolwork suffered. "I always did what I had to do to get by, and I wasn't sure I wanted to go to college." He graduated from high school 401st in a class of 439 students.

Following graduation from high school, Egnew entered the University of Evansville, where he received his bachelor of science in mechanical engineering in 1984. He described himself as a loner during college, without a large circle of friends. He became very interested in the cooperative education program, which allowed students to alternate between full-time schooling and work. During co-op he worked for NASA in Huntsville, Alabama, rising from the rank of GS-3 to GS-5 in two years. He graduated in the lower third of his class after an erratic academic performance that included both dean's list and probation. He summed it up: "I hated to take tests, and I was not a crammer."

After graduation he joined NASA in Huntsville as a flight systems test engineer, GS-7, and rose to GS-9 by July 1986. He served as lead test engineer responsible for the conduct of hardware development test programs. This included coordinating and directing about 20 engineers and technicians in formulating, conducting, and evaluating tests and test results. In July 1986, he was promoted to production test manager for NASA and moved to Bay St. Louis, Mississippi. His responsibilities included the supervision of flight vehicle tests. By August 1989, he had risen to GS-13. He commented on his work:

> I enjoyed getting involved in things where there was no established solution. I liked to find the solutions. I especially liked the new position since it involved work that hadn't been done before. But in about two years most of the problems were solved and it got boring. So I decided to return to school for my master's in industrial management at the University of Tennessee, Knoxville.

John F. Moore.   John Moore was born and raised in Columbus, Ohio, one of two sons of a navy career officer who had worked his way up through the ranks. Though his father ran the house "like the commander of a ship," he was quite permissive with his two sons. "He taught us right from wrong. But what he really gave me was the motivation to do things on my own."

In high school John Moore was captain of the swimming, baseball, and football teams. At the same time he worked about 15 hours a week after school in a shoe store, and each summer he worked full-time paving driveways. He graduated in the lower third of his high school class, noting that "I did what I had to do to stay eligible and graduate." His considerable athletic promise earned him a full baseball scholarship to Ohio State University. The lure of fraternity life, particularly its social activities, detracted further from his less-than-enthusiastic interest in academics. Repeated academic probation caused him to lose his scholarship, so he entered the navy in April 1982. He was honorably discharged in April 1986.

In July 1986, Moore joined North American Rockwell Corporation as a materials requirements analyst, and in early 1989 he became supervisor in the Support Operations Division. In September 1989, he returned to college and met with greater academic success: "Once I went back, I got A's and B's and even won an honors medal in physics."

Upon graduating in June 1991 with a BS in Industrial Management from the University of Tennessee, Knoxville, Moore returned to North American Rockwell for three months as logistics staff assistant in Bay St. Louis, Mississippi. In October 1991, after much urging by J. C. Egnew, he joined Wilderness Products, Inc., as sales service manager.

At Wilderness, he was responsible for customer service, inventory control, transportation, and warehouse activities. This included factory sales to key "house accounts," developing product mix and initiating marketing plans, supervising 30 employees in office areas and transportation and warehousing facilities, and purchasing some accessory products and equipment.

Discussions between Egnew and Moore

In early 1993, Egnew and Moore began a series of thoughtful discussions about what their future might hold. The first topic they raised was a very basic one: the reasons that each of them had for wanting to start his own business. Egnew felt that

> as long as my professional talents are being challenged, I have an opportunity to grow, and the rewards for my contributions are commensurate with the marketplace, I'm happy. Everybody likes to have their future tied to a winner. Nobody likes to be in a losing operation. I have begun to look at alternatives. I see tremendous opportunities in the tent business that aren't being properly taken care of. I feel that there is room for another firm. Now I'm trying to decide what to do next.
>
> I never really think about the chance to make a big killing. If I'm on target in 5, 8, or 10 years, at the end of that time I'll be able to do what I want to do. I'll have a new

sense of freedom, a sense of independence to do my own thing. Ownership and growth will provide the real rewards. We all dream about making something happen. If you succeed in building your own business, there's no question about who's responsible.

Moore shared similar views:

> J. C. is the only one at Wilderness doing anything with any principles in mind or using what we learned in school instead of just shooting from the hip. If we could get organized, we could do it. I feel that I have been exposed to the business. It is dynamic, something new every day, and I like this. I am excited by the challenge of doing it ourselves. I keep thinking to myself, we can do it!

In addition to the challenge, both men appreciated the need to make a total commitment to the business if it was to be a success. Egnew believed that

> the commitment to go into business is made when you sever whatever ties you have and say "my livelihood is dependent on this enterprise"—that's when the commitment is made. If the two or three people aren't willing to use most of their key assets for the business, then I wouldn't touch them. So the commitment is also shown when you get everybody to put their bucks in. That's when it all starts.

He also believed that starting salaries were a useful measure of commitment and that investors were right to expect personal and financial commitment from the key team members:

> Starting salaries should be lean. A new business needs every possible advantage it can find. If key personnel won't make sacrifices up front, then they won't make them when it gets tough. You should be prepared to make a substantial personal commitment to your business if you haven't already done so. I would be naive to think, "Well, I have this fine educational background, and I have some pretty relevant experience—after all, I'm putting my professional reputation on the line here. What else can you ask for?" "But if the milk turns sour," an investor would point out, "all you have to do is move to some place as far away as southwest Texas and get a 10 percent or 20 percent salary increase in a new job and you're off and running again, while we're sitting here holding all the empty baskets." That's when it really hit me. If I were investing money in a new business and the two or three key people weren't able to make a significant commitment based on their personal assets, then I sure wouldn't be willing to commit a dime to them. That's the commitment that makes you work a little bit harder and makes you determined that you're going to find a way to succeed. Any investor with sense is going to look for this kind of commitment.

Risks and Rewards

Next, Egnew and Moore discussed their attitudes about risks and rewards in starting a new business. Egnew began:

> If we were to start our own business, I wouldn't waste much time thinking about "What if it doesn't work out?" My thinking is positive. If we can ever afford to blow something, now

is the time—we are young and have no heavy debts. The idea or dream of having your own business is one many people have, and here is our opportunity. We are frustrated with the way things are going at Wilderness, the opportunity for a better way to do things looks real, and we have a chance to build something.

Moore's comments reflected his confidence in Egnew's optimism:

> If we decide to go ahead, I won't have time to worry or think about not making it. I don't feel that it's that much of a risk when we sit here talking about it, I am so hyped up thinking it could work. I guess if we'd both been fired from Wilderness and had to start our own company, I would do a bit more worrying. Whenever I am ready to throw in the towel, J. C. keeps the momentum going. It looks like an opportunity to make a lot of money. Wilderness went public in 1972, and one owner with 7 percent of the stock made $1,800,000. I feel J. C. has it all together, more than any other person I've ever met. I have tremendous respect for him. I am willing to gamble on a good guy, and therefore I feel it is a good gamble.

Taking the Plunge—Or Not

By spring 1993, J. C. Egnew and John F. Moore had continued to investigate the idea of starting their own tent-manufacturing business. Recognizing the difficulties of starting a new venture and their own inexperience in business, they began to assess their entrepreneurial and management strengths and weaknesses, and to analyze the feasibility of the new business idea. Time was also becoming a serious factor and Egnew and Moore were faced with a serious dilemma: how to start their business in time to take advantage of the 1994 spring market.

From their previous business training, both Egnew and Moore were aware of the high failure rates of new businesses. Egnew expressed his opinions on this issue:

> Most new companies begin with an idea for a new product or service. Few of them survive, and rarely, if ever, does one excel on the strength of the product alone. You have to put it all together. You can't just have a great idea that's better than anything on the market and have a winner. You also need an organization and a plan. Getting the movement going is the hardest thing. That's what makes a startup so risky. All these things have to get moving at the same time—it's like the inertia of a large train. You've got to devote a lot of energy just to get things going.

Part of the process of taking the plunge included assessing the opportunity. Although committed to the venture psychologically, they did not want to launch a venture that had a poor chance of succeeding. A principal aim of their initial work was to determine whether any major flaws existed in their idea and to decide whether the business was worth pursuing. *Exhibit A* summarizes the industry and financial data Egnew and Moore have gathered to investigate the potential for their new tent-manufacturing business.

More Dilemmas

Their preliminary investigation provided Egnew and Moore with a substantial amount of data. Since they began their investigation, several more weeks had passed. They wondered whether their idea was worth pursuing.

Certain developments, previously unknown to them, emerged from their investigations. First, they found that the industry was closed to outsiders, making it very difficult to get useful market information. Second, they found that the sales of the major canvas suppliers for tents had been declining steadily in recent years, as synthetic fabrics, such as nylon and polyester, became the material of choice. Third, they discovered, to their surprise, that no new U.S. firms had entered the tent business in the past five to six years, in spite of what they estimated as a growing, seller's market. Further, they learned that a handful of small tent manufacturers had actually failed and gone out of business during this period. There had also been significant inroads by offshore manufacturers who imported into the United States.

The Entrepreneurial Process

If Egnew and Moore did start this tent company, what would make them successful? Between the two of them there seemed to be the basic know-how of the business, but was that enough? Were they missing an important element of the business? Or several key competencies? Would there be a need for a third or fourth founder? Who should make up their board? These were constant concerns of both Egnew and Moore as they commuted, worked, and relaxed after work.

At times both Egnew's and Moore's thoughts wandered off into the pursuit of the dream, but there were so many issues they had to confront first. For instance, how would the management of Wilderness react to their resignations? If there was a negative reaction, then they wondered if Wilderness would be an obstacle to their company. After all, Wilderness did have established supplier relationships, lines of distribution, and recognition in the marketplace. With all these attributes, Wilderness could be a valuable ally or a large destructive competitor.

Additionally, questions were emerging as Egnew and Moore wrote Sara Reed, their advisor (see *Exhibit A*). How much money did they need to get this business off the ground? How much more money would they need to operate the business, until it was self-sustaining? When would their tent company be self-sustaining? Where should they be looking for investors? Who would be likely to invest? Were Egnew and Moore willing to give up some equity? Were there assets they could use to secure bank loans? So many things had to be decided on quickly, because the 1994 spring market was quickly approaching.

EXHIBIT A

To:	Sara Reed	June 10, 1993
From:	J. C. Egnew	
	John Moore	
Re:	Feasibility Information for a New Tent Manufacturing Company	

The Industry

The significant tent-producing companies in the continental United States are ranked below, based on 1993 sales:

Kellwood Company:	
Sears	30,000,000
Wentzel	24,000,000
	54,000,000
Hettrick (Olin Corporation)	45,000,000
Wilderness Products	30,000,000
National Canvas Products	21,000,000
Coleman	12,000,000
Eureka Tent and Awning	9,000,000
Other	9,000,000
Total	180,000,000

The Thomas Register lists a good many other firms in the tent business. Most of these firms are small mom-and-pop operations consisting of those who custom produce (make to order) awnings and tents and other canvas items such as show tents and circus-type carnival tents. Others are primarily in the repair business. Some of these have a national market, while others have a regional market only.

Approximately 10 percent of this total tent market consists of tents designed for specific uses (e.g., mountain climbing and backpacking). This factor will limit the general tent market potential for the coming year to $162 million (not accounting for an anticipated 1994 growth factor of 20 percent in the market as a whole).

Following is an estimated geographic breakdown of the national tent market that is based on observed industry sales patterns:

	Percent
New England states	22%
Metropolitan New York City	13
Mideast (New York, Pennsylvania)	8
Midwest (Corn Belt, Plains)	26
Central Atlantic Coast	4
Southeast	9
Southwest	6
Far West (Coastal)	8
Other	4
Total	100% ($180,000,000)

It has been an industry practice for retailers to start taking deliveries of tents after January 1 since tents are not usually Christmas items. To encourage early order commitments and deliveries, the industry has been allowing "net April 1st" payment terms on tents delivered prior to April. Because delivery service has been poor in the past, it is not unusual for customers to place orders in October and November for tents desired in March or April. Projected sales trends by month for the total tent market follow:

Month	Percent of Annual Sales
January	16%
February	21
March	15
April	11
May	10
June	6
July	4
August	2
September	3
October	3
November	4
December	5
Total	100%

The Competition

Listed below is a comparison of prices among three of the industry leaders for some of the main types of tents available to the consumer. Profit margins do not vary significantly from one type of tent to another.

Prices of the Major Products for Three Competitors (1993 published prices)

Style	Size	Wilderness	Hettrick	National
Cabin	7 × 7	$ 90.80	$NA	$ 99.60
	8 × 10	120.00	142.05	151.74
	9 × 12	143.85	167.25	175.44
	10 × 16	167.85	197.70	NA
Cabin-screen	10 × 16	209.25	230.40	NA
Umbrella	7 × 7	65.70	63.00	71.46
	9 × 9	96.75	110.40	123.36
Canopy	10 × 10	38.25	NA	45.51
	12 × 12	46.35	47.25	55.20
Screenhouse	10 × 10	86.85	100.95	NA
Pup tent	5 × 7	14.25	13.35	15.54
	5 × 7	32.40	31.50	30.00
Jvc. umbrella	7 × 7	26.25	27.75	33.48
Tri. awning	8 × 10	41.25	47.40	51.60
	8 × 12	49.05	54.60	55.80

NA means not offered by that competitor.
All prices listed are for the season and are expected to increase from 10% to 12% on the average for the upcoming season.

The next table presents a comparison of the number of models of each type of tent produced by some of the leading manufacturers.

Comparison of the Number of Models* Offered by Five Major Tent Producers

Company	Cabin	Umbrella	Play	Canopy and Screen	Awnings	Nylon	Other
Wilderness:							
Regular	20	4	5	8	9	6	2
Special	32	3	2	9	2	—	—
Hettrick:							
Regular	12	4	9	7	10	2	6
National	9	6	17	6	14	1	4
Coleman	18	2	2	3	—	1	13
Eureka	9	9	14	11	31	7	13

*Includes ice tents, "flies," wind curtains, etc.

Financial Considerations

The following is a summary of industry practices relating to the manufacture and sale of tents.

Accounts receivable:	75% of all sales prior to April 1 billing. Further, 50% of the accounts will be paid on or before April 1, 35% will be 30 days past due, 10% will be 60 days past due, and 5% will be 90 or more days past due when paid.
Inventories:	Monthly inventories will peak in February and be at a minimum level in June.
Work in process:	20% of monthly production.
Finished goods:	9.3% of monthly sales.
Accounts payable:	80% of monthly purchases.
Cost of goods sold:	76% of sales.
Gross profit:	24% of sales.
General, selling, and administration:	Industry average is 15% of sales.

## Chapter Two

The Entrepreneurial Process

"Who can be an entrepreneur you ask?

Anyone who wants to experience the deep, dark canyons of uncertainty and ambiguity; and who wants to walk the breathtaking highlands of success. But I caution, do not plan to walk the latter, until you have experienced the former."

An Entrepreneur

Results Expected

Upon completion of this chapter you will have:

1. Developed a definition of entrepreneurship and the entrepreneurial process that spans life-style to high potential ventures.

2. Examined the practical issues you will address and explore throughout the book.

3. Learned how entrepreneurs and their financial backers get the odds for success in their favor, defying the pattern of disappointment and failure experienced by many.

4. Examined The Timmons Model of the entrepreneurial process, how it can be applied to your entrepreneurial career aspirations and ideas for businesses, and how recent research confirms it validity.

5. Analyzed the proposed startup of PC Build, Inc. by two about-to-graduate students.

Demystifying Entrepreneurship

Entrepreneurship is a way of thinking, reasoning, and acting that is opportunity obsessed, holistic in approach, and leadership balanced.[1] Entrepreneurship results in the creation, enhancement, realization, and renewal of value, not just for owners, but for all participants and stakeholders. At the heart of this process is the creation and/or recognition of opportunities,[2] followed by the will and initiative to seize these opportunities. It requires a willingness to take risks—both personal and financial—but in a very calculated fashion in order to constantly shift the odds to your favor, balancing the risk with the potential reward. Typically, entrepreneurs devise ingenious strategies to marshall their limited resources.

Today, entrepreneurship has evolved beyond the classic startup notion to include companies and organizations of all types, in all stages. *Thus, entrepreneurship can occur—and fail to occur—in new firms and in old; in small firms and large; in fast and slow growing firms; in the private, not-for-profit, and public sectors; in all geographic points; and all stages of a nation's development, regardless of politics.*

Entrepreneurial leaders inject imagination, motivation, commitment, passion, tenacity, integrity,

---

[1] This definition of entrepreneurship has evolved over the past two decades from research at Babson College and the Harvard Business School; and has recently been enhanced by Stephen Spinelli, Jr., John H. Muller, Jr., Term Chair at Babson College.

[2] Timmons, J A, D F Muzyka, H H Stevenson and W D Bygrave, "Opportunity Recognition: The Core of Entrepreneurship," in *Frontiers of Entrepreneurship Research* (Babson Park, MA: Babson College 1987), p. 409.

teamwork, and vision. They face dilemmas and must make decisions despite ambiguity and contradictions. Very rarely is entrepreneurship a get-rich-quick proposition; rather, it is one of building—and continually renewing—long-term value and durable cash-flow. The result of this value creation process, as we saw in Chapter 1, is that the total economic pie grows larger and society benefits.

Classic Entrepreneurship: The Startup

The classic expression of entrepreneurship is the raw startup company, an innovative idea that catapults as a high growth company. The best of these become entrepreneurial legends: Netscape, Amazon.Com, Sun Microsystems, Home Depot, McDonald's, Compaq Computer, Intuit, Staples, and hundreds of others have become household names. In addition to the entrepreneurial leadership qualities noted above, success usually involves building a team with complementary skills and talents, the ability to work as a team, and sensing an opportunity where others see contradiction, chaos, and confusion. It also requires the skill and ingenuity to find and control resources—often owned by others—to pursue the opportunity. And it means making sure the upstart venture does not run out of money when it needs it the most.

Entrepreneurship in Post–Brontosaurus Capitalism: Beyond Startups

As we saw in Chapter 1, the upstart companies of the 1970s and 1980s have had a profound impact on the competitive structure of American and world industries. Giant firms, such as IBM (knocked off by Apple Computer and then Microsoft), Digital Equipment Corporation (another victim of Apple Computer and recently acquired by Compaq Computer Corporation), Sears (demolished by upstart Wal-Mart) and AT&T (knocked from its perch first by MCI, and then by cellular upstarts: McCaw Communications, Inc., Cellular One, and others), once thought invincible, have been dismembered by the new wave of entrepreneurial ventures. The resulting downsizing during the 1980s was still going strong by the end of 1997, as the top 10 job cuts alone amounted to 65,700 jobs, led by Kodak (10,000), Woolworth (9,200), Citicorp (9,000) and International Paper (9,000).[3]

As autopsy after autopsy was performed, a fascinating pattern emerged, showing, at worst, total disregard for the winning entrepreneurial approaches of their new rivals, and at best, a glacial pace in recognizing the impending demise and changing course.

"People Don't Want to Be Managed. They Want to Be Led!"[4]

These giant firms can be characterized, during their highly vulnerable periods, as hierarchical in structure with many layers of review, approvals, vetos, and decision making. Their tired executive blood conceived of leadership by *managing and administering* from the top down, a quite custodial set of assumptions about what the E-Generation was in search of for meaningful careers. This is in stark contrast to Ewing M. Kauffman's powerful insight: "People don't want to be managed; they want to be led!" These stagnating giants tended to reward people who accumulated the largest assets, budgets, number of plants, products, and head count, rather than rewarding those who created or found new business opportunities, took calculated risks and occasionally made mistakes, and did so with bootstrap resources. While very cognizant of the importance of corporate culture and strategy, their pace was glacial: The research on dozens of giant companies in the 1970s–80s concludes that typically it took *six years* for a large firm to change its strategy and *10 to 30 years* to change its culture.

To make matters worse, they had many bureaucratic tendencies, particularly arrogance. They shared a blind belief that if they followed the almost sacred best-management practices of the day they could not help but prevail. It is noteworthy that during the 1970s–80s, these best-management practices did not include entrepreneurship, entrepreneurial leadership, and entrepreneurial reasoning. If anything, these were considered dirty words in corporate America. Chief among these sacred cows was: Stay close to your customer. What may shock you is the recent conclusion of two Harvard Business School professors:

> One of the most consistent patterns in business is the failure of leading companies to stay at the top of their industries when technologies or markets change . . . But a more fundamental reason lies at the heart of the paradox: leading companies succumb to one of the most popular, valuable management-dogmas. They stay close to their customers.[5]

Reminiscent of the case in Chapter 1, where upstart Cellular One in Boston dramatically outper-

[3] Mathias, Edward J, "Economic & Investment Environment-1997," January 1998, (Washington, D.C.: The Carlyle Group), p. 119.
[4] The author's favorite quote from Ewing M Kauffman, founder of Marion Laboratories, Inc., The Ewing Marion Kauffman Foundation, and Kauffman Center for Entrepreneurial Leadership, Kansas City, MO.
[5] Bower, Joseph L and Clayton M Christensen, "Disruptive Technologies: Catching the Wave," *Harvard Business Review*, Jan.–Feb, 1995, p. 43.

formed giant NYNEX, the authors explain how this heretical outcome can happen.

> When they do attack, the [new] entrant companies find the established players to be easy and unprepared opponents because the opponents have been looking up-markets themselves, discounting the threat from below.[6]

One gets further insight into just how vulnerable and fragile the larger, so-called well managed companies can become, and why it is the newcomers who pose the greatest threat. This pattern also explains why there are tremendous opportunities for the coming E-Generation even in markets that are currently dominated by large players. Professors Bower and Christensen summarize it this way:

> The problem is that managers keep doing what has worked in the past: serving the rapidly growing needs of their current customers. The processes that successful, well-managed companies have developed to allocate resources among proposed investments are incapable of funneling resources in programs that current customers explicitly don't want and whose profit margins seem unattractive.[7]

Coupled with what we saw in Chapter 1 regarding how many new innovations, firms, and industries have been created in the past 30 years, it is no wonder that Brontosaurus Capitalism has found its Ice Age.

Signs of Hope in a Corporate Ice Age

Fortunately, for many giant firms, the entrepreneurial revolution may spare them from their own Ice Age. One of the most exciting developments of the decade is the response by some large, established U.S. corporations to the revolution in entrepreneurial leadership. After nearly three decades of experiencing the demise of giant after giant, corporate leadership, in unprecedented numbers, are launching experiments and strategies to recapture their entrepreneurial spirit and to instill the culture and practices we would characterize as entrepreneurial reasoning. The E-Generation has too many attractive opportunities to work in truly entrepreneurial environments to have to work for a brontosaurus.

Increasingly, we see examples of large companies who are adopting principles of entrepreneurship and entrepreneurial leadership in order to survive and to renew. A new magazine, *Fast Company*, is setting the new standard in entrepreneurial journalism. Stories document how large firms are applying what we

would call entrepreneurial thinking in pioneering ways to invent their futures, including companies like Harley-Davidson Motorcycles ($1.35 billion revenue), Marshall Industries ($2.2 billion), and Science Applications International Corporation (SAIC) in San Diego.[8] Most large brontosaurus firms could learn valuable lessons on how to apply entrepreneurial thinking from companies such as these.

Metaphors

Improvisation. Quick, agile thinking. Resourcefulness. Inventiveness. Whatever the adjective to describe the behavior, innumerable metaphors from other parts of life can describe the complex world of the entrepreneur and the entrepreneurial process. From music it is jazz, with its uniquely American impromptu flair. From sports many metaphors exist: the Michael Jordan dominance and flair, the broken-field running of Terrell Davis or Barry Sanders, the wizardry on ice of Wayne Gretzky, freestyle snowboarding, a downhill run on skis, or the creativity and competitiveness of Tiger Woods.

Perhaps the game of golf, more than any other, replicates the complex and dynamic nature of managing risk and reward and all the intricate mental challenges that are faced in entrepreneuring. No other sport at one time demands so much physically, is so complex, intricate, and delicate, and is simultaneously so rewarding and punishing; and none tests one's will, patience, self-discipline, and self-control like golf. This is what entrepreneurs face as well. And if you think that the team concept isn't important in golf, remember that the 1997 American Ryder Cup team, which failed to work together as a team, lost to the Europeans.

An entrepreneur also faces challenges like a symphony conductor or a coach who must blend and balance a group of diverse people with different skills, talents, and personalities into a superb team. On many occasions it demands all the talents and agility of a juggler who must, under great stress, keep many balls in the air at once, making sure if one comes down it belongs to someone else.

The complex decisions and numerous alternatives facing the entrepreneur also have many parallels with the game of chess. As in chess, the victory goes to the most creative player, who can imagine several alternative moves in advance, and anticipate the possible defenses. This kind of mental agility is frequently demanded in entrepreneurial decision making.

---

[6] Ibid., p. 47.
[7] Ibid.
[8] *Fast Company*, June–July 1997, pp. 32, 79, and 104.

Still another parallel can be drawn from the book *The Right Stuff*, later made into a movie. The first pilot to break the sound barrier, Chuck Yeager, describes what it was like to be at the edge of both the atmosphere and his plane's performance capability, a zone never before entered—just like the first-time entrepreneur.

In the thin air at the edge of space, where the stars and the moon came out at noon, in an atmosphere so thin that the ordinary laws of aerodynamics no longer applied and a plane could skid into a flat spin like a cereal bowl on a waxed Formica counter and then start tumbling, end over end like a brick . . . you had to be "afraid to panic." In the skids, the tumbles, the spins, there was only one thing you could let yourself think about: what do I do next?[9]

This feeling is frequently the reality on earth for entrepreneurs who run out of cash!

Regardless of the metaphor or analogy you choose for entrepreneurship, each is likely to describe a creative, even artistic, improvised act. The outcomes are often either highly rewarding successes or painful and visible misses. Always, urgency is on the doorstep.

Entrepreneurship = Paradoxes

One of the most confounding aspects of the entrepreneurial process is its contradictions. Because of its highly dynamic, fluid, ambiguous, and chaotic character, its constant changes frequently pose paradoxes. What follows is a sampling. Can you think up some that you have observed or heard about?

An opportunity with no or very low potential can be an enormously big opportunity. One of the most famous examples of this paradox is Apple Computer Corporation. Founders Steve Jobs and Steve Wozniak approached their employer, Hewlett-Packard Corporation, with the idea for a desktop, personal computer and were told this was not an opportunity for HP, so they started their own company. Frequently, business plans rejected by some venture capitalists become legendary successes when backed by another investor. Intuit, maker of Quicken software, for example, was rejected by 20 venture capitalists before securing backing.

In order to make money you have to first lose money. It is commonly said in the venture capital business that the lemons, or losers, ripen in two-and-a-half years, while the plums take seven or eight years to ripen. A startup, venture-backed company typically loses money, often $10–25 million and more, prior to sustaining profitability and going public, usually at least five to seven years later.

In order to create and build wealth one must relinquish wealth. Among America's most successful growing companies, the founders aggressively dilute their own ownership in order to create ownership throughout the company. By rewarding and sharing the wealth with the people who contribute significantly to its creation, owners motivate others to make the pie bigger.

In order to succeed one first has to experience failure. It is a common pattern that the first venture fails, yet the entrepreneur learns and goes on to create a highly successful company. Jerry Kaplan teamed with Lotus Development Corporation founder Mitch Kapor to start the first pen-based computer. After $80 million of venture capital investment the company was shut down. Kaplan went on to launch On-Sale, Inc., and Internet Dutch-auction, which exploded in growth and went public in 1996.

Entrepreneurship requires considerable thought, preparation and planning, yet is basically an unplannable event. The highly dynamic, changing character of technology, markets, and competition make it impossible to know all your competitors today, let alone five years hence. Yet great effort is invested in attempting to model and envision that future. The resulting business plan is inevitably obsolete when it comes off the printer. It is important to remember that this is a creative process—like molding clay. You need to make a habit of planning and reacting as you constantly reevaluate your options, blending the messages from your head and your gut, until this process becomes second nature.

In order for creativity and innovativeness to prosper, rigor and discipline must accompany the process. For years hundreds of thousands of patents for new products and technologies lay fallow in government and university research labs because there was no commercial discipline.

Entrepreneurship requires a bias toward action and a sense of urgency, but also demands patience and perseverance. While his competitors were acquiring and expanding rapidly, one entrepreneur's management team became nearly outraged at his inaction. This

---

[9] Tom Wolfe, *The Right Stuff* (New York: Bantam Books, 1980), pp. 51–52.

entrepreneur reported he saved the company at least $50–100 million during the prior year by just sitting tight, a lesson learned from the Jiffy Lube case series from *NVC*, which he studied during a week-long program for the Young Presidents Organization (YPO) at Harvard Business School in 1991.

The greater the organization, orderliness, discipline, and control, the less you will control your ultimate destiny. Entrepreneurship requires great flexibility and nimbleness in strategy and tactics. One has to play with the knees bent. Over-control and an obsession with orderliness are impediments to the entrepreneurial approach. As the great race car driver, Mario Andretti said: "If I am in total control, I know I am going too slow!"[10]

Adhering to management best practice, especially staying close to the customer, that created industry leaders in the 1980s, became a seed of self-destruction and loss of leadership to upstart competitors. We discussed earlier the study of "disruptive technologies."

In order to realize long-term equity value, you have to forgo the temptations of short-term profitability. Building long-term equity requires major continuing reinvestment in new people, products, services, and support systems, usually at the expense of immediate profits.

No doubt about it. The world of entrepreneurship is not one that is neat, tidy, linear, consistent, and predictable, no matter how much we might like it to be that way.[11] These paradoxes illustrate just how contradictory and chaotic this world can be. To thrive in this world one needs to be very adept at coping with ambiguity, chaos, and uncertainty, and at building management skills that create predictability.

The Higher Potential Venture: Think Big Enough

One of the biggest mistakes aspiring entrepreneurs make is strategic: They think too small. Sensible as it may be to think in terms of a very small, simple business as being both more affordable, more manageable, less demanding, and less risky, the opposite is true, judging by the facts. Not only are the chances for survival and success lower in these small, job-substitute businesses, even if they do survive, they are less financially rewarding. As one founder of numerous businesses put it: unless this business can pay you at least five times your present salary, the risk and wear and tear won't be worth it.

Consider one of the most successful venture capital investors ever, Arthur Rock. His criterion for searching for opportunities is very simple: *Concepts for businesses that change the way people live or work.* His home-run investments are legendary, including Intel, Apple Computer, Teledyne, and dozens of others. Clearly, his philosophy is to think big.

Today an extraordinary variety of people, opportunities, and strategies characterize the approximately 30 million enterprises of all kinds in the nation; proprietorships, partnerships and corporations. We saw earlier in Chapter 1 the unprecedented number of 3.5 million new businesses created per year in the United States, and that in 37 percent of the 35 million households in the country someone had a primary role in a new or small business. A 1997 Dun & Bradstreet report estimated the total number of corporations in 1996 at 9,900,088.[12] Over 90 percent of these had revenues of less than $1 million annually, while 863,505 reported revenues of $1–25 million, or just over 9 percent of the total. Of these, only 296,695 grew at a compounded annual growth rate of 30 percent or more for the prior three years, or about 3 percent. Similarly, just 3 percent—1 in 33—exceed $10 million in sales, and only .3 percent—1 in 333—exceed $100 million in revenue.

Not only can nearly anyone start a business, a great many succeed. While it certainly may help, a person does not have to be a genius to create a successful business. As Nolan Bushnell, founder of Atari, one of the first desktop computer game companies in the early 1980s, and Pizza Time Theater, has said: "If you are not a millionaire or bankrupt by the time you are 30 you are not really trying!"[13]

While we saw earlier the stunning number of mega-entrepreneurs who launched their venture during their twenties, the rigors of new ventures may favor the "young at start." But age is no barrier to entry. One study showed that nearly 21 percent of founders were over 40 when they embarked on their entrepreneurial careers, the majority were in their 30s, and just over one-quarter did so by the time they were 25. Further, numerous examples exist of founders who were over 60 at the time of launch, including one of the most famous seniors, Colonel Harland Sanders, who started Kentucky Fried Chicken with his first social security check.

[10] My special thanks to Professor Stephen Spinelli for this wonderful quote.
[11] See Howard H Stevenson, *Do Lunch or Be Lunch*, 1998, Harvard Business School Press, (Cambridge, MA.), for a provocative argument for predictability as one of the most powerful of management tools.
[12] "High Growth Companies," for the Kauffman Center for Entrepreneurial Leadership, Kansas City, MO 1997.
[13] In response to a student question at Founder's Day, Babson College, April 1983.

Overall New Business Failure Rates

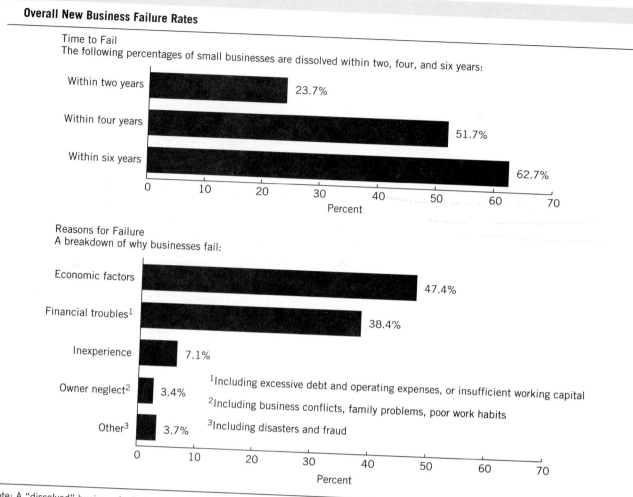

Time to Fail
The following percentages of small businesses are dissolved within two, four, and six years:

Within two years — 23.7%

Within four years — 51.7%

Within six years — 62.7%

Percent

Reasons for Failure
A breakdown of why businesses fail:

Economic factors — 47.4%

Financial troubles[1] — 38.4%

Inexperience — 7.1%

Owner neglect[2] — 3.4%

Other[3] — 3.7%

[1]Including excessive debt and operating expenses, or insufficient working capital
[2]Including business conflicts, family problems, poor work habits
[3]Including disasters and fraud

Percent

Note: A "dissolved" business includes those that are voluntarily shut down as well as those forced to file for bankruptcy.
Source: *The Wall Street Journal*, October 16, 1992, p. R7.

Smaller Means Higher Failure Odds

Unfortunately, the record of survival is not good among all firms started.

For the vast majority of new businesses in the country, the odds of survival definitely are not in their favor. While government data, research, and business mortality statisticians may not agree on the precise failure and survival figures for new businesses, they do agree that failure is the rule, not the exception.

Complicating efforts to obtain precise figures is the fact that it is not easy to define and identify failures, and reliable statistics and databases just are not available. However, the Small Business Administration estimated in 1983 that, for every three new businesses formed, two close their doors.[14]

There is also wide variation in failure rates across industries. In 1991, for instance, even though retail and services accounted for two of nine categories reported in *The State of Small Business*, they accounted for 61 percent of all failures and bankruptcies in that year.[15]

Exhibit 2.1 is a distillation of a number of studies of failure rates over the last 50 years. Illustrated are the facts that (1) failure rates are high and (2) although the majority of the failures occur in the first two to five years, it may take considerably longer for some to fail. This picture is supported by the findings of several different studies.[16]

To make matters worse, most people think that the failure rates are actually much higher. Since most would argue that actions are governed, more often than not, by perceptions rather than facts alone, this

[14] *The State of Small Business: A Report of the President, Transmitted to the Congress,* March 1983 (Washington, DC: Small Business Administration, 1983).
[15] *The State of Small Business 1992,* p. 128.
[16] Summaries of these are reported by Albert N Shapero and Joseph Giglierano, "Exits and Entries: A Study in Yellow Pages Journalism," in *Frontiers of Entrepreneurship Research: 1982,* ed. K Vesper, et. al. (Babson Park, MA: Babson College, 1982), pp. 113–41; and Arnold C Cooper and Carolyn Y Woo, "Survival and Failure: A Longitudinal Study," in *Frontiers of Entrepreneurship Research: 1988,* ed. B Kirchhoff, et. al. (Babson Park, MA: Babson College, 1982), pp. 225–37.

perception of failure, in addition to the dismal record, can be a serious obstacle to aspiring entrepreneurs.

Still other studies have shown significant differences in rates of survival and failure among different types of businesses. For instance, just 3 of 21 Dun & Bradstreet categories accounted for 70 percent of all failure and bankruptcies: retail trade, construction, and small service businesses. Further, 99 percent of these had fewer than 100 employees. Through observation and practical experience one would not be surprised by such reports. The implications for would-be entrepreneurs are important: Knowing the difference between a good idea and a real opportunity is vital. This will be addressed in Chapter 3.

A certain level of failure is part of "creative self-destruction" described by Joseph Schumpeter. It is part of the dynamics of innovation and economic renewal, a process which requires both births and deaths.

More important, it is also part of the learning process inherent in gaining an entrepreneurial apprenticeship. If a business fails, no other country in the world has laws, institutions, and social norms that are more forgiving. Firms go out of existence, but entrepreneurs survive and learn.

This daunting evidence poses two important questions for aspiring entrepreneurs. First, are there any exceptions to this general rule of failure, or are we faced with a punishing game of entrepreneurial roulette? Second, if there is an exception, how does one get the odds for success in one's favor?

Getting the Odds in Your Favor

Fortunately, there is a decided pattern of exceptions to the overall rate of failure among the vast majority of small, marginal firms created each year. Most smaller enterprises that cease operation simply do not meet our notion of entrepreneurship: They do not create, enhance, or pursue opportunities that realize value. They tend to be job substitutes in many instances. Undercapitalized, unmanaged, and often poorly located, they soon fail.

Threshold Concept

Who are the survivors? The odds for survival and a higher level of success change dramatically if the venture reaches a critical mass of at least 10 to 20 people and $2–3 million in revenues, and is pursuing opportunities where there is growth potential. *Exhibit 2.2* shows that based on a cross-section of all new firms, one-year survival rates for new firms jump from

approximately 78 percent for firms having up to 9 employees to approximately 95 percent for firms with between 20 and 99 employees.

A 1991 study found that "empirical evidence supports the liability of newness and liability of smallness arguments and suggests that newness and small size make survival problematic;" the authors inferred that "perceived satisfaction, cooperation, and trust between the customer and the organization [are] important for the continuation of the relationship. High levels of satisfaction, cooperation, and trust represent a stock of goodwill and positive beliefs which are critical assets that influence the commitment of the two parties to the relationship."[17] It is interesting that the authors of this study noted that "smaller organizations are found to be more responsive, while larger organizations are found to provide greater depth of service. . . . The entrepreneurial task is to find a way to either direct the arena of competition away from the areas where you are at a competitive disadvantage, or find some creative way to develop the required competency."[18]

After four years, as shown in *Exhibit 2.3*, the survival rate jumps from approximately 37 percent for

EXHIBIT 2.2

One-Year Survival Rates by Firm Size

Firm Size (employees)	Survival Percent
0–9	77.8%
10–19	85.5
20–99	95.3
100–249	95.2
250+	100.0

Source: Michael B Teitz et al., "Small Business and Employment Growth in California," Working Paper No. 348, University of California at Berkeley, March 1981, p. 42.

EXHIBIT 2.3

Four-Year Survival Rates by Firm Size

Firm Size (employees)	D&B Study (1969–76)	California Study (1976–80)
0–19	37.4%	49.9%
20–49	53.6	66.9
50–99	55.7	66.9
100–499	67.7	70.0

Sources: David L Birch *MIT Studies*, 1979–1980; and Michael B Teitz et al., "Small Business and Employment Growth in California," Working Paper No. 348, University of California at Berkeley, March 1981, table 5, p. 22.

[17] S Venkataraman and Murray B Low, "On the Nature of Critical Relationships: A Test of the Liabilities and Size Hypothesis," in *Frontiers of Entrepreneurial Research: 1991*, p. 97.
[18] Ibid., p. 105–6.

EXHIBIT 2.4

Percentage of New Small Firms Surviving Six or More Years*

Industry	All Classes (percent)	Zero Growth 0%	Low Growth 1–4%	Medium Growth 5–9%	High Growth +10%
Total, All Industries	39.8%	27.5%	66.3%	75.5%	78.4%
Agriculture, Forestry, Fishing	43.1	35.0	74.7	80.7	82.8
Mining	39.1	27.1	67.8	61.5	57.0
Construction	35.3	24.1	65.0	72.2	74.3
Manufacturing	46.9	27.0	66.9	73.5	76.0
Transportation, Utilities, Communications	39.7	25.7	68.5	72.4	75.6
Wholesale Trade	44.3	28.3	66.5	74.9	77.2
Retail Trade	38.4	27.1	62.7	74.4	76.8
Finance, Insurance, Real Estate	38.6	28.7	68.7	76.4	78.5
Services	40.9	28.7	69.1	79.4	83.5

*Ranked by number of jobs created from 1976–86.

Source: U.S. Small Business Administration, August 29, 1988; B D Phillips and B A Kirchhoff, "An Analysis of New Firm Survival and Growth," *Frontiers in Entrepreneurship Research: 1988*, ed. B. Kirchhoff et al., pp. 266–67.

firms with fewer than 19 employees to about 54 percent for firms with 20 to 49 employees.

Although any estimates based on sales per employee vary considerably from industry to industry, this minimum threshold translates roughly to a threshold of $50,000 to $100,000 of sales per employee annually. But highly successful firms can generate much higher sales per employee.

Promise of Growth

The definition of entrepreneurship implies the promise of expansion and the building of long-term value and durable cash flow streams as well.

But, as will be discussed later, it takes a long time for new companies to become established and grow. A Small Business Administration study, summarized in *Exhibit 2.4*, covering the period from 1976 to 1986, found that two of every five small firms founded survived six or more years but that few achieved growth during the first four years.[19] The study also found that survival rates more than double for firms which grow, and the earlier in the life of the business that growth occurs, the higher the chance of survival.[20]

Other data also confirm this exception. A study done by *INC.* shows that, between 1982 and 1987, the average growth in sales of the *INC.* 500 was 96 percent per year. The study also finds that, of the 7 million corporations in the United States, approximately 7 percent (just under 500,000 firms) grew over 20 percent per year and just over 1 percent (approximately 80,000 firms) grew 50 percent per year.

Some of the true excitement of entrepreneurship lies in conceiving, launching, and building firms such as these.

Venture Capital Backing

Another notable pattern of exception to the failure rule is found for businesses which have attracted startup financing from successful private venture capital companies. Instead of the 70 percent to 90 percent failure rate shown when all types of new firms are considered, these new ventures enjoy a *survival* rate nearly that high.

Studies of success rates of venture capital portfolios, summarized in *Exhibit 2.5*, show that in the portfolios of experienced professional venture capital firms, typically about 15 percent to 20 percent of the companies will result in total loss of the original investments and, further, that it is unusual for the loss rates for portfolios of experienced venture capital firms to exceed 30 percent to 35 percent and for the loss rates to fall below 10 percent.[21]

[19] Bruce D Phillips and Bruce A Kirchhoff, "An Analysis of New Firm Survival and Growth," in *Frontiers in Entrepreneurship Research: 1988*, p. 266–67.
[20] This confirms this exception to the failure rule noted above and in the original edition of this book in 1977.
[21] J A Timmons et al., *New Venture Creation* (Homewood, IL: Richard D Irwin, 1977), pp. 10–11; E B Roberts, "How to Succeed in a New Technology Enterprise," *Technology Review* 2, no. 2 (1970); C Taylor, "Starting-Up in the High Technology Industries in California," commissioned by the Wells Fargo Investment Company, 1969; R B Faucett, "The Management of Venture Capital Investment Companies," Sloan School master's thesis, MIT, 1971; and R B Faucett, "Venture Capital: Fact and Myth," Foothill Group, 1972.

EXHIBIT 2.5

Studies of Success Rates of Venture Capital Portfolios

	Success Rates (percent)
Venture Capital Journal survey (1983)—232 portfolio companies and 32 venture capital firms	85%
International venture capital firm results (1972–88)—$60 million funds in U.S., U.K., Canada, and Belgium	85
Wells Fargo Bank study (1972)—279 high-technology firms	65
Studies by MIT and other studies	80–82

According to *Venture Economics* (1988), more than one-third of 383 investments made by 13 firms between 1969 and 1985 resulted in an absolute loss. More than two-thirds of the individual investments made by these same firms resulted in capital returns of less than double the original cost. Nevertheless, the returns on a few investments have more than offset these disappointments. *Venture Economics* reports, for example, that 6.8 percent of the investments resulted in payoffs greater than 10 times cost and yielded 49.9 percent of the ending value of the aggregate portfolio (61.4 percent of the profits).[22] Even higher returns have been achieved by such spectacular successes as Apple Computer, Lotus, Digital Equipment, Intel, Compaq, and the like.

It is clear that venture capital is not essential to a startup, nor is it a guarantee of success, as is evident in the following statistics: only 5 percent of the *INC.* 500 have venture funding and merely 1 percent of all new companies have venture funding. Consider, for instance, that "in 1987—a banner year—venture capitalists financed a grand total of 1,729 companies, of which 112 were seed financings and 232 were startups. In that same year, 631,000 new businesses incorporations were recorded.[23]

This compelling data has led some to conclude that there is a threshold core of 10 percent to 15 percent of new companies which will become the winners in terms of size, job creation, profitability, innovation, and potential for harvesting (and thereby realizing a capital gain). Eventually, from among these 10 percent to 15 percent of all new firms emerge the "winning performers."[24] As shown in *Exhibit 2.6*, the top 25 percent among all medium-sized companies achieved records of growth from 1978 to 1983 that exceeded the growth of the top quarter of the economy, the top quarter of the Fortune 500 and firms classified as "excellent companies."

Not Only the Insights of Venture Capitalists

Harvested entrepreneurs by the tens of thousands have become "Angels" as private investors in the next generation of entrepreneurs. Many of the more successful have created their own investment pools and compete directly with venture capitalists for deals. Their operating experiences and successful track records provide a compelling case for adding value to an upstart company. Take, for example, highly successful Boston entrepreneur Jeff Parker. His first venture, Technical Data Corporation, was the first to enable Wall Street bond traders to conduct daily trading with a desktop computer. Parker's software on the Apple II created an entirely new industry in the early 1980s.

After harvesting this and other ventures, he created his own private investment pool in the 1990s. As the Internet explosion occurred, he was one of the early investors to spot opportunities in startup ventures. In one case, he actually persuaded the founders of a new Internet firm to select him as lead investor, instead of offers from some of the most prestigious venture capital firms in the nation. How could this be? According to the founders, it was clear that Parker's unique entrepreneurial track record and his understanding of their business would add more value than the venture capitalists at startup.

Private investors and entrepreneurs like Parker have very similar selection criteria to the venture capitalists: they are in search of the high-potential, higher growth ventures. Unlike the venture capitalists, however, they are not constrained by having to invest so much money in a relatively short period of time that they must invest it in minimum chunks of $3–5 million or more. Thus, such private investors are prime sources for less capital-intensive startup and early stage businesses.

---

[22] Cited in W A Sahlman, "Structure of Venture-Capital Organizations," *Journal of Financial Economics* 27 (1990), p. 483.
[23] Amar Bhide, "Bootstrap Finance: The Art of Start-Ups," *Harvard Business Review* (November–December 1992), p. 110.
[24] Donald K Clifford, Jr., and Richard E Cavanagh, *The Winning Performance* (New York: Bantam Books, 1985), p. 3.

EXHIBIT 2.6

Compound Annual Growth Rates, 1978–83

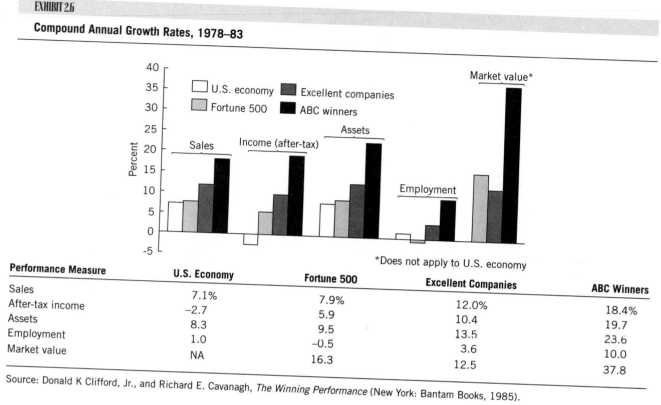

Performance Measure	U.S. Economy	Fortune 500	Excellent Companies	ABC Winners
Sales	7.1%	7.9%	12.0%	18.4%
After-tax income	–2.7	5.9	10.4	19.7
Assets	8.3	9.5	13.5	23.6
Employment	1.0	–0.5	3.6	10.0
Market value	NA	16.3	12.5	37.8

Source: Donald K Clifford, Jr., and Richard E. Cavanagh, *The Winning Performance* (New York: Bantam Books, 1985).

If anything, this overall search for higher potential ventures has become even more evident in recent years. The new E-Generation appears to be learning the lessons of these survivors, venture capitalists, private investors, and founders of higher potential firms. Certainly, hundreds of thousands of college students now have been exposed to these concepts for over two decades, and their strategies for identifying potential businesses are mindful and disciplined about the ingredients for success. Unlike 20 years ago, it is now nearly impossible not to hear and read these principles whether on television, in books, on the Internet, or in a multitude of seminars, courses, and programs for would-be entrepreneurs of every sort.

Find Financial Backers and Associates Who Add Value

One of the most distinguishing disciplines of these higher potential ventures is how the founders identify financial partners and key team members. They insist on backers and partners who do more than bring just money, friendship, commitment, and motivation to the venture. They surround themselves with backers who can add value to the venture through their experience, know-how, networks, and wisdom. Key associates are selected because they are smarter than the founder, are better at what they do than the founder, and raise the overall average of the entire company. This theme will be examined in detail later on.

Option: The Lifestyle Venture

For many aspiring entrepreneurs, issues of family roots and location take precedent. Accessibility to a preferred way of life, whether it is fly fishing, skiing, hunting, hiking, music, surfing, rock climbing, canoeing, a rural setting, the mountains, you name it, simply is more important than how large a business one has, or the size of one's net worth. Others vastly prefer to be with and work with their family and spouse and live in a nonurban area they consider very attractive. Take Jake and Diana Bishop, for instance. Both college educated with masters' degrees in accounting, they gave up six-figure jobs they both found rewarding and satisfying on the beautiful coast of Maine. Why? They decided to return to their home state of Michigan for several important lifestyle reasons. They wanted to work together again in a business (which they say was the best former period of their marriage). It was important to be much closer than the 14-hour drive to Diana's aging parents. They also wanted to have their children—then in their twenties—join them in the business. Finally, they wanted to live in one of their favorite areas in the entire country, Harbor Spring, on the northwest tip of the state on Lake Michigan. They report never to have worked any harder in their 50 years, nor have they been any happier. They are growing their rental business more than 20 percent a year, making an excellent living, and creating equity value. If done right, it turns out that one can have a lifestyle business and actually realize higher potential.

Yet it is generally known that couples who give up successful careers in New York City to buy an inn in Vermont or New Hampshire to avoid the rat-race last only six to seven years. They discover the joys of self-employment; including seven-day, 70–90 hour work weeks, chefs and day help that don't show up, roofs that leak when least expected, and occasional guests from hell. The grass is always greener, so they say.

The Timmons Model: Where Theory and Practice Collide in the Real World[25]

What is going on here? How can aspiring entrepreneurs—and the investors and associates who join the venture—get the odds on their side? What do these talented and successful high-potential entrepreneurs, their venture capitalists and private backers do differently? What is accounting for their exceptional record? Are there general lessons and principles underlying their successes that can benefit aspiring entrepreneurs, investors, and those who would join a venture? If so, can these lessons be learned?

These are the central questions of the author's lifetime work, originating during MBA and doctoral work in the late 1960s. Over the past 30 years, beginning with doctoral research, I have been immersed as a student, researcher, teacher, and practitioner of the *entrepreneurial process*. As a founding shareholder and investor of several high-potential ventures (some of which are now public), as a director and advisor to ventures and venture capital funds, and as a charter director and advisor to the Kauffman Center for Entrepreneurial Leadership at the Ewing Marion Kauffman Foundation, I have applied, tested, refined, and tempered academic theory as fire tempers iron into steel: in the fire of practice.

Intellectual and Practical Collisions with the Real World

Throughout this period of evolution and revolution, *New Venture Creation* has adhered to one core principle: In every quest for greater knowledge of the entrepreneurial process and more effective learning there must be intellectual and practical collisions between academic theory and the real world of practice. The standard academic notion—That may be all right in practice, but does it work in theory?—is simply not acceptable. This integrated, holistic balance and juggling act is at the heart of what we know about the entrepreneurial process and getting the odds in your favor.

Value Creation: The Driving Forces

The conclusion to those central questions has boiled down to this: a core, fundamental entrepreneurial process accounts for the substantially higher success pattern among higher potential ventures. Despite the great variety of businesses, entrepreneurs, geography, and technology, time and again central themes dominate this highly dynamic entrepreneurial process. What are these driving forces?

- It is *Opportunity* driven.
- It is driven by a *Lead Entrepreneur* and an *Entrepreneurial Team*.
- It is *Resource Parsimonious and Creative*.
- It depends on the *Fit and Balance* among these.
- It is *Integrated and Holistic*.

These are the controllable components of the entrepreneurial process that can be assessed, influenced, molded and altered, thereby changing in positive ways the risk-to-reward equation. Throughout the careful due diligence process conducted by prospective investors, and by the founders, these themes are the focus in analyzing the risks and trade-offs and determining what can be changed, added, deleted, or reconfigured to improve the fit and balance and thereby get the odds in one's favor.

First, we will elaborate on each of these themes to provide a blueprint and a definition of what each means. Then using Netscape as an example, we will illustrate the holistic, balance, and fit aspects.

Change the Odds: Fix It, Shape It, Mold It, Make It

The driving forces underlying successful new venture creation are illustrated in *Exhibit 2.7*.[26] The process starts with opportunity, not money, not strategy, not networks, not the team, not the business plan. Most genuine opportunities are much bigger than either the talent and capacity of the team or the resources available to the team at the outset. The role of the lead entrepreneur and the team is to juggle all of these key elements in a dynamic, moving environment. Think of a juggler bouncing up and down on a trampoline that is moving on a conveyor belt at unpredictable speeds and directions, while trying to keep all three balls in the air. That is how dynamic it can be. The business plan provides the language and

---

[25] I succumb to the urging of my colleagues, especially Professor Stephen Spinelli, and refer to the conceptual framework as they do.
[26] I am greatly appreciative to Babson College Professor Stephen Spinelli for his contribution to this section. The graphical depiction of the Timmons Model, the notion of balance, and a number of enhancements to describe and explain it since the 4th edition of *New Venture Creation* have all been contributed by Professor Spinelli.

EXHIBIT 2.7

Timmons Model of the Entrepreneurial Process

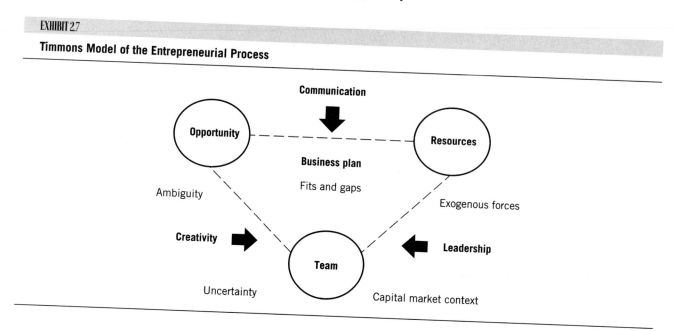

code for communicating the quality of the three driving forces and of their fit and balance.

The lead entrepreneur's job is simple enough: he or she must carry the deal by *taking charge of the success equation*. In this dynamic context, ambiguity and risk are actually your friends. Central to the homework, creative problem-solving and strategizing, and due diligence that lies ahead is analyzing just what are the fits and gaps that exist in the venture. What is wrong with this opportunity? What is missing? What good news and favorable events can happen, not just the adverse? What has to happen to make it attractive and fit me? What market, technology, competitive, management and financial risks can be reduced or eliminated? What can be changed to make this happen? Who can change it? What are the least resources necessary to get this the farthest? Is this the right team? And so on. By implication, if one can determine these answers, make the necessary changes and additions, figure out how to fill the gaps and improve the fit, and/or attract key players who can add such value, then the odds for success rise significantly. In essence, the entrepreneur's role is to manage and redefine the risk–reward equation.

The Opportunity   At the heart of the process is the opportunity. Successful entrepreneurs and investors know that a good idea is not necessarily a good opportunity. In fact, for every 100 ideas presented to investors in the form of a business plan or proposal of some kind, usually just 1 or sometimes 2 or 3 ever get funded. Over 80 percent of those rejections occur in the first few hours; another 10 to 15 percent are rejected after investors have read the business plan

carefully. Less than 10 percent attract enough interest to merit thorough due diligence and investigation over several weeks, and even months. Those are very slim odds. Countless hours and days have been wasted by would-be entrepreneurs chasing ideas that are going nowhere. An important skill, therefore, as an entrepreneur or an investor, is to be able to size up quickly whether serious potential exists, and to decide how much time and effort to invest.

John Doerr is a 48-year-old partner at one of the most famous and successful venture capital funds ever, Kleiner, Perkins, Caulfield & Byers, and by all accounts, the most influential venture capitalist of his generation, according to *Fast Company*. During his 18-year career he has been the epitome of the revolutionaries described earlier who have created new industries as lead investor in such legends as Sun Microsystems, Compaq Computer, Lotus Development Corporation, Intuit, Genentech, Millennium, Netscape, and Amazon.Com. Regardless of these past home-runs, Doerr insists:

> There's never been a better time than now to start a company. In the past, entrepreneurs started businesses. Today they invent new business models. That's a big difference, and it creates huge opportunities.[27]

Exhibit 2.8 summarizes the most important characteristics of good opportunities. Underlying market demand—because of the value-added properties of the product or service, the market's size and 20+ percent growth potential, the economics of the business, particularly robust margins (40 percent or more), and free cash flow characteristics—drives the value creation potential.

[27] "John Doerr's Start-Up Manual," *Fast Company*, February–March 1997, pp. 82–84.

EXHIBIT 2.8

The Entrepreneurial Process is Opportunity Driven

Opportunity

Market demand is a key ingredient to measuring an opportunity:

- Is the customer reachable?
- Customer payback less than one year
- Market share and growth potential equals
- 20 percent annual growth, 20 percent + and durable?

Market structure and size:

- Emerging and/or fragmented?
- $50 million + with a $1 billion potential?
- Proprietary barriers to entry?

Margin analysis helps differentiate an opportunity from an idea:

- Low cost provider? (40 percent gross margin)
- Low capital requirement versus the competition?
- Break even in 1–2 years?
- Value added increase of overall corporate P/E ratio?

These criteria will be described in great detail in Chapter 3 and can be applied to the search and evaluation of any opportunity. In short, the greater the growth, size, durability, and robustness of the gross and net margins and free cash flow, the greater the opportunity. The more *imperfect* the market, the greater the opportunity. The greater the rate of change, the discontinuities, and chaos, the greater are the opportunities, as we saw with Moore's Law and Drucker's Postulate in Chapter 1. The greater the inconsistencies in existing service and quality, in lead times and lag times, and the greater the vacuums and gaps in information and knowledge, the greater the opportunities.

Resources: Creative and Parsimonious

One of the most common misconceptions among untried entrepreneurs is that you first have to have all the resources in place, especially the money, in order to succeed with a venture. Thinking money first is a big mistake. Money follows high potential opportunities conceived of and led by a strong management team. Investors have bemoaned for years that there is too much money chasing too few deals. In other words, there is a shortage of quality entrepreneurs and opportunities, not money. Successful entrepreneurs devise ingeniously creative and stingy strategies in marshalling and gaining control of resources (*Exhibit 2.9*). Surprising as it may sound, investors and successful entrepreneurs often say one of the worst things that can happen to an entrepreneur is to have *too much money too early.*

EXHIBIT 2.9

Understand and Marshall Resources, Don't Be Driven by Them

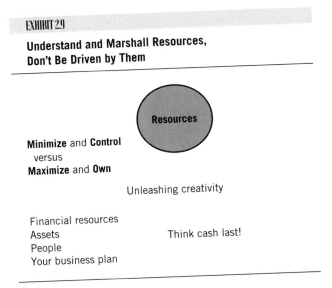

Resources

Minimize and **Control**
versus
Maximize and **Own**

Unleashing creativity

Financial resources
Assets   Think cash last!
People
Your business plan

The best example of this the author has ever encountered is the late Howard Head, who developed the first metal ski, Head, which became the market leader, and then the oversize Prince tennis racket, two totally unrelated technologies—a rare feat. Head left his job at a large aircraft manufacturer during World War II and worked in his garage on a shoestring budget to create his metal ski. It took over 40 different versions before he succeeded in developing a ski that worked and could be marketed. He insisted that one of the biggest reasons he finally succeeded is that he had so little money. He argued that if he had complete financing he would have blown it all long before he evolved the workable metal ski.

Bootstrapping is a way of life in entrepreneurial companies and can create a significant competitive advantage. Doing more with less is a powerful competitive weapon, as we saw in Chapter 1 as upstart Cellular One outperformed NYNEX three-to-one, with one-half to one-third the resources. Their approaches are to minimize and control the resource, not necessarily own the resource. Whether it is assets for the business, key people, the business plan, or startup and growth capital they *think cash last.* Such strategies have a wondrous effect on the company in two ways: a discipline of leanness, where everyone knows that every dollar counts and permeates the firm; and, the principle of CYE—Conserve Your Equity—becomes a way of maximizing shareholder value. The resource dimension will be discussed later, along with the business plan, in Chapters 10 and 11.

The Entrepreneurial Team

There is little dispute today that the *entrepreneurial team* is a key ingredient in the higher potential venture. Investors are captivated "by the creative brilliance of a company's head entrepreneur: A Mitch Kapor, a Steve Jobs, a Fred Smith . . . and bet on the superb track records of the management team working as a group."[28] Venture capitalist John Doerr reaffirms father of American venture capital General George Doriot's dictum: I prefer a Grade A entrepreneur and team with a Grade B idea, over a Grade B team with a Grade A idea.

In the world today, there's plenty of technology, plenty of entrepreneurs, plenty of money, plenty of venture capital. What's in short supply is great teams. Your biggest challenge will be building a great team.[29]

Famous investor Arthur Rock articulated the importance of the team over a decade ago. He put it this way: "If you can find good people, they can always change the product. Nearly every mistake I've made has been I picked the wrong people, not the wrong idea."[30]

Finally, as we saw earlier, the ventures with more than 20 employees and $2–3 million in sales were much more likely to survive and prosper. In the vast majority of cases, it is very difficult to grow beyond this without a team of two or more key contributors.

Exhibit 2.10 depicts the important aspects of the team. Make no mistake about it, these teams invariably are formed and led by a very capable entrepreneurial leader whose track record exhibits both accomplishments and many of the qualities that the team must possess. A pacesetter, culture-creator, and player/coach; the lead entrepreneur is central. The ability and skill in attracting other key management members and then building the team is one of the most valued capacities investors look for. The founder who becomes the leader does so by building heroes in the team; by a philosophy that rewards success and supports honest failure, that shares the wealth with those who help create it; and by setting high standards for both performance and conduct. We will examine in detail the entrepreneurial leader and the new venture team in Chapters 6, 7, and 8.

Importance of Fit and Balance

Rounding out the model of the three driving forces is the concept of fit and balance. Note that the team is positioned at the bottom of the triangle in *Exhibit 2.7.* Imagine the founder, entrepreneurial leader of the venture standing on a large ball, grasping the triangle over her head.[31] The challenge is to balance the balls above her head, without toppling off. This imagery is helpful in appreciating the constant balancing act from the outset, since rarely, if ever, are the three ingredients matched. When envisioning a company's future using this imagery, the entrepreneur can ask herself,

---

[28] William D Bygrave and Jeffry A Timmons, *Venture Capital at the Crossroads,* (Boston: Harvard Business School Press, 1992), p. 8.
[29] *Fast Company,* Feb.–Mar. 1997, p. 84.
[30] Arthur Rock, "Strategy vs. Tactics from a Venture Capitalist," *Harvard Business Review,* November–December 1987, p. 63–67.
[31] My thanks once again to Professor Spinelli for this imagery.

EXHIBIT 2.10

An Entrepreneurial Team Is the Key Ingredient for Success

An entrepreneurial leader
- Learns and teaches—faster, better
- Deals with adversity, is resilient
- Exhibits integrity, dependability, honesty
- Builds entrepreneurial culture and organization

Quality of the team
- Relevant experience and track record
- Motivation to excel
- Commitment, determination, and persistence
- Tolerance of risk, ambiguity, and uncertainty
- Creativity
- Team focus of control
- Adaptability
- Opportunity obsession
- Leadership
- Communication

What pitfalls will I encounter to get to the next boundary of success? Will my current team be large enough, or will we be over our heads if the company grows 30 percent over the next two years? Are my resources sufficient (or too abundant)? Vivid examples of the failure to maintain a balance are everywhere, such as when large companies throw too many resources at a weak, poorly defined opportunity. The Ford Motor Company's launching of the Edsel is just one example from a very large list.

Exhibit 2.11(a) through (d) show how this balancing act evolved for Netscape from inception through the initial public offering to today. While the drawings oversimplify these incredibly complex events, they help us to think conceptually—an important entrepreneurial talent—about the company building process, the strategic and management implications in striving to achieve balance, the leads and lags, the inevitable fragility of the process.

Clearly, the Internet was a huge, rapidly growing, but elusive opportunity. Mark Andressen had no significant capital or other resources to speak of. There was no team. One can envision how quickly such a mismatch of ideas, resources, and talent could quickly topple out of the founder's control, and, most likely, fall into the hands of someone who could turn it into a real opportunity. Visually, the process can be appreciated as a constant balancing act, requiring continual

EXHIBIT 2.11(a)

Netscape—Journey through the Entrepreneurial Process At Startup, a huge imbalance

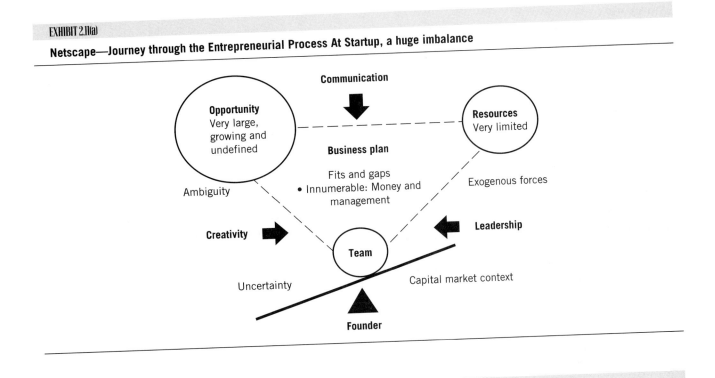

EXHIBIT 2.11(b)

Netscape—Journey through the Entrepreneurial Process At venture capital funding, toward new balance

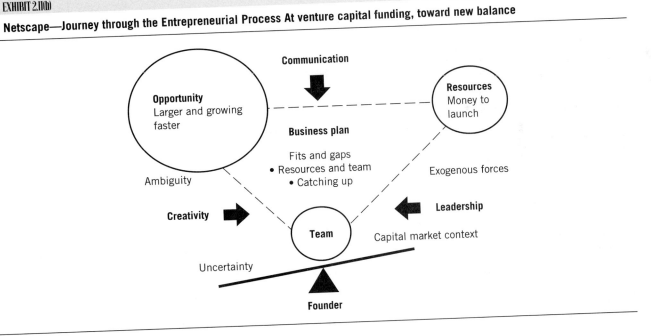

assessment, revised strategies and tactics, an experimental approach. By addressing the types of questions necessary to shape the opportunity, the resources, and the team, the founder begins to mold the idea into an opportunity, and the opportunity into a business, just as you would mold clay from shapeless form to a piece of artwork.

At the outset, founder Marc Andressen would have seen something like the first figure, Exhibit 2.11(a), with the huge Internet opportunity far outweighing the team and resources. Needless to say, the gaps were major. Enter venture capitalist John Doerr, et. al., the first venture capitalist to vividly see the size and potential of the opportunity. He had great faith in Andressen, and knew he could fill the resource gaps and help build the team, both with inside management and outside directors and professional advisors. This new balance 2.11(b) creates a justifiable investment. The opportunity is still huge and growing, and competitors are inevitable 2.11(c). To fully exploit this

EXHIBIT 2.11(c)

Netscape—Journey through the Entrepreneurial Process At IPO, a new balance

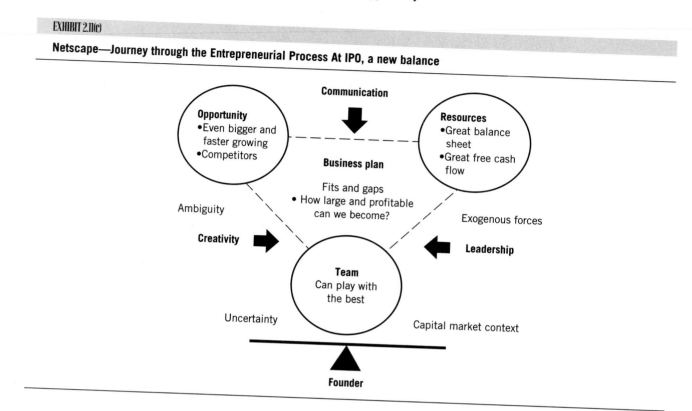

EXHIBIT 2.11(d)

Netscape—Journey through the Entrepreneurial Process Today, toward a new imbalance

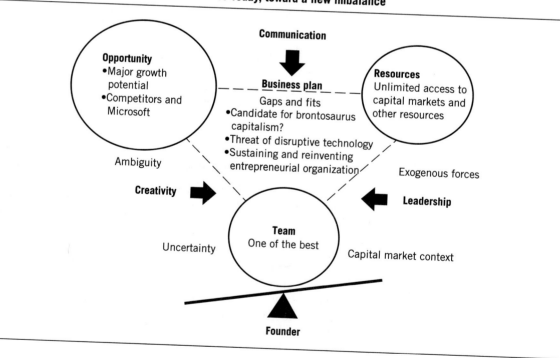

opportunity, attract a large and highly talented group of managers and professionals, and to create even greater financial strength vs. competitors, the company must complete an initial public stock offering (IPO).

Netscape today, 2.11(d), is larger, stronger in people and resources, but faces new challenges. As we saw in Chapter 1 there is an overwhelming tendency for even the best and brightest of new firms—from IBM, to Digital Equipment Corporation to Apple Computer—to erode over two or more decades into Brontosaurus Capitalism. Can Netscape sustain and reinvent its entrepreneurial roots and organization, as the opportunity continues to mushroom and competition for markets, people, and technology are greater than ever? Will it become blindsided and eclipsed by a new disruptive technology, just as Apple Computer and Microsoft bludgeoned IBM and Digital Equipment. Is Netscape today a new candidate for the next installment of Brontosaurus Capitalism, and if so, when will this occur? These, of course, are questions that rob management and the board of directors of much sleep.

This iterative entrepreneurial process is both logical and trial and error. It is both intuitive and consciously planned. It is a process not unlike what the Wright brothers originally engaged in while creating the first self-propelled airplane. They conducted over 1,000 glider flights before succeeding with the Wright Flyer. These were the trial and error experiments that led to the new knowledge, skills, and insights needed in order to actually fly. Entrepreneurs have similar learning curves.

The Fit issue can be appreciated in terms of a question: this is a fabulous opportunity, but for whom? It is well known that some of the most successful investments ever were actually turned down by numerous investors before the founders received backing. Time and again, there can be a mismatch between the type of business, the chemistry between founders and backers, or a multitude of other factors that can cause a rejection. Thus, how the unique combination of people, opportunity, and resources come together at that particular time and space may be the most important factor in a venture's ultimate chance for success. How else could one explain Intuit's 20 rejections by sophisticated investors for startup funding?

The potential for attracting outside funding for a proposed venture depends on this overall fit, and how the investor believes he or she can add value to this fit, improve the fit, risk–reward ratio and odds for success. *Exhibit 2.12* shows the possible outcomes.

Importance of Timing   Equally important is the timing of all these entrepreneurial events. Each of these unique combinations occurs in real time, where the hourglass drains continually, and may be friend, foe or both. Decisiveness in recognizing and seizing the opportunity can make all the difference, particularly when the sand disappearing from the hourglass is cash. In fact, there is no such thing as a perfect time for an opportunity. Most new businesses run out of money before they can find enough customers and the right team for their great idea. Opportunity is a moving target.

EXHIBIT 2.12

Fit of Entrepreneur and Venture Capital

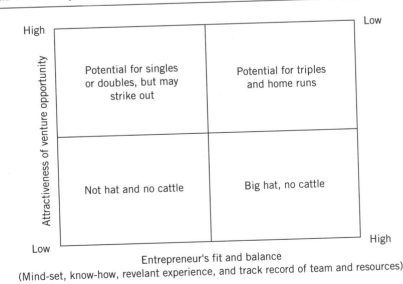

Recent Research Supports the Model

The Timmons Model originally evolved from doctoral dissertation research at the Harvard Business School about new and growing ventures. Over nearly three decades it has evolved and has been enhanced by ongoing research, case development, teaching and the author's hands-on experience in high-potential ventures and venture capital funds. The fundamental components of the model have not changed, but their richness and the relationships of each to the whole has been enhanced steadily, as they have become better understood. Numerous other researchers have examined a wide range of topics in entrepreneurship and new venture creation. The bottom line of all this is that the model, in its simple elegance and dynamic richness, harnesses what you need to know about the entrepreneurial process, and getting the odds in your favor. As each of the chapters, and accompanying cases, exercises, and issues elaborates the process and addresses individual dimensions, a detailed framework and explicit criteria will emerge. If you engage this material fully you cannot help but improve your chances.

Quite recently, a major new research effort was conducted by the National Center for Entrepreneurship Research at the Kauffman Center for Entrepreneurial Leadership with a specific focus on 906 high-growth companies.[32] These findings provide important benchmarks of the practices in a diverse group of industries, among a high performing group of companies who were regional and national award winners in the Ernst & Young LLP Entrepreneur of the Year Program. These firms increased their sales from 1994 to 1996 on average by 28 percent, compared to an increase of just 15 percent for the Fortune 500 companies. One-third of these firms have less than $10 million in sales, most were in the $25–75 million range, were quite profitable, one-fifth had fewer than 49 employees, and over half had 50 to 499 employees. Over half had less than $9.9 million in assets, and about half had assets of $3 to $49.9 million.

Most significantly, these results reconfirm the importance of the model and its principles: the team, the market opportunity, the resource strategies, most of the individual criteria, and the concept of fit and balance, and the holistic approach to entrepreneurship.

Summarized in *Exhibit 2.13* are the 26 leading practices identified in four key areas: Marketing, Financial, Management and Planning. (A complete version of the study is available from the National Center for Entrepreneurship Research, Kauffman Center for Entrepreneurial Leadership, Kansas City, MO 64112.)

Entrepreneurial Reasoning: The Entrepreneurial Mind[33] in Action

Most research about entrepreneurs has focused on the influences of genes, family, education, career experience, and so forth, but no psychological model has been supported. Successful entrepreneurs seem to be of both sexes and in every imaginable size, shape, color, and description. Perhaps one Price–Babson College fellow phrased it best when he said, "One does not want to overdo the personality stuff, but there is a certain ring to it."[34]

However, the real question is, *What do successful entrepreneurs do?* That is, how do they think, what actions do they initiate, and how do they go about starting and building businesses? The result is what counts, and by understanding the attitudes, behaviors, management competencies, experience, and know-how that contribute to entrepreneurial success, one has some useful benchmarks for gauging what to do and what to do differently.

Successful entrepreneurs share common attitudes and behaviors. They work hard and are driven by an intense commitment and determined perseverance; they see the cup half full, rather than half empty; they strive for integrity; they burn with the competitive desire to excel and win; they are dissatisfied with the status quo and seek opportunities to improve almost any situation they encounter; they use failure as a tool for learning and eschew perfection in favor of effectiveness; and they believe they can personally make an enormous difference in the final outcome of their ventures and their lives.

Those who have succeeded speak of these attitudes and behaviors time and again.[35] For example, two famous entrepreneurs have captured the intense commitment and determined perseverance of entrepreneurs. Wally Amos, famous for his chocolate chip cookies, said, "You can do anything you want to do."[36] And John Johnson of Johnson Publishing Company

[32] Donald L Sexton and Forrest I Seale, "Leading Practices of Fast Growth Entrepreneurs: Pathways to High Performance," (Kansas City, MO.: Kauffman Center for Entrepreneurial Leadership, 1997).

[33] See Timmons, *The Entrepreneurial Mind* (1989).

[34] Comment made during a presentation at the June 1987 Price–Babson College Fellows Program by Jerry W Gustafson, Coleman–Fannie May Candies Professor of Entrepreneurship, Beloit College, at Babson College.

[35] See the excellent summary of a study of the first 21 inductees into Babson College's Academy of Distinguished Entrepreneurs by John A Hornaday and Nancy Tieken, "Capturing Twenty-One Heffalumps," in *Frontiers of Entrepreneurship Research: 1983*, pp. 23–50.

[36] Made during a speech at his induction in 1982 into the Academy of Distinguished Entrepreneurs, Babson College.

EXHIBIT 2.13

Leading Practices

Leading marketing practices of fast growth firms

- Deliver products and services that are perceived as highest quality to expanding segments.
- Cultivate pace-setting new products and services that stand out in the market as best of the breed.
- Deliver product and service benefits that demand average market or higher pricing.
- Generate revenue flows from existing products and services that typically sustain approximately 90% of the present revenue base while achieving flows from new products and services that typically expand revenue approximately 20% annually.
- Generate revenue flows from existing customers that typically sustain approximately 80% of the ongoing revenue base while achieving flows from new customers that typically expand revenue flows by about 30% annually.
- Create high-impact new product and service improvements with development expenditures that typically account for no more than approximately 6% of revenues.
- Utilize a high-yielding sales force that typically accounts for approximately 60% of marketing expenditures.
- Rapidly develop broad product and service platforms with complementary channels to expand a firm's geographic marketing dimensions.

Leading financial practices of fast growth firms

- Anticipate multiple rounds of financing (on average every 2.5 years).
- Secure funding sources capable of significantly expanding their participation amounts.
- Utilize financing vehicles that retain the entrepreneur's voting control.
- Maintain control of the firm by selectively granting employee stock ownership.
- Link the entrepreneur's long-term objectives to a defined exit strategy in the business plan.

Leading management practices of fast growth firms

- Use a collaborative decision-making style with the top management team.
- Accelerate organizational development by assembling a balanced top management team with or without prior experience of working together.
- Develop a top management team of three to six individuals with the capacity to become the entrepreneur's entrepreneurs.
- Align the number of management levels with the number of individuals in top management.
- Establish entrepreneurial competency first in the functional areas of finance, marketing and operations.
- Assemble a balanced board of directors comprised of both internal and external directors.
- Calibrate strategies constantly with regular board of directors meetings.
- Involve the board of directors heavily at strategic inflection points.

Leading planning practices of fast growth firms

- Prepare detailed written monthly plans for each of the next 12 to 24 months and annual plans for three or more years.
- Establish functional planning and control systems that tie planned to actual performance and adjust management compensation accordingly.
- Share with employees periodic planned versus actual performance data that is directly linked to the business plan
- Link job performance standards that have been jointly set by management and employees to the business plan.
- Prospectively model the firm based on benchmarks that exceed industry norms, competitors and the industry leader.

(publisher of *Ebony*) expressed it this way: "You need to think yourself out of a corner, meet needs, and never, never accept no for an answer."[37]

It seems that entrepreneurs who succeed possess not only a creative and innovative flair and other attitudes and behaviors but also solid general management skills, business know-how, and sufficient contacts. *Exhibit 2.14* demonstrates this relationship.

Inventors, noted for their creativity, often lack the necessary management skills and business know-how. Promoters usually lack serious general management and business skills and true creativity. Administrators govern, police, and ensure the smooth operation of the status quo; their management skills, while high, are tuned to efficiency as well, and creativity is usually not required. Although the management skills of the

[37]Made during a speech at his induction in 1979 into the Academy of Distinguished Entrepreneurs, Babson College.

EXHIBIT 2.14

Who is the Entrepreneur?

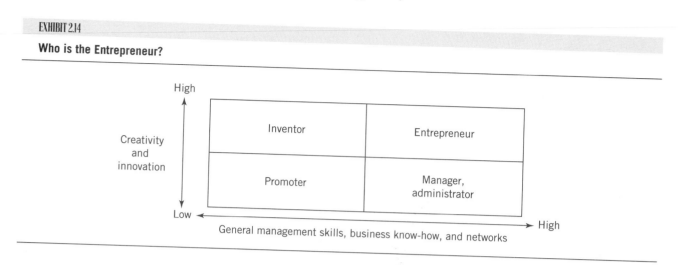

manager and the entrepreneur overlap, the manager is more driven by conservation of resources and the entrepreneur is more opportunity-driven.[38]

Apprenticeship: Acquiring the 50,000 Chunks

During the past several years, studies about entrepreneurs have tended to confirm what practitioners have known all along: That some attitudes, behaviors, and know-how can in fact be acquired and that some of these attributes are more desirable than others.[39]

Increasingly, evidence from research about the career paths of entrepreneurs and the self-employed suggests that the role of experience and know-how is central in successful venture creation.[40] Evidence also suggests that success is linked to thoughtful preparation and planning.[41] This is what getting the 50,000 chunks of experience is all about.

Most successful entrepreneurs follow a pattern of apprenticeship, where they prepare for becoming entrepreneurs by gaining the relevant business experiences from parents who are self-employed or through job experiences. They do not leave acquisition of experience to accident or osmosis. As entrepreneur Harvey "Chet" Krentzman has said, "Know what you know and what you *don't* know."

Role Models

Further, there is no more powerful teacher than a good example. Numerous studies show a strong connection between the presence of role models and the emergence of entrepreneurs. For instance, one recent study showed that over half of those starting new businesses had parents who owned businesses.[42] The authors summarized it this way:

> People who start companies are more likely to come from families in which their parents or close relatives were in business for themselves. These older people were examples, or "models," for the children. Whether they were successful or not probably didn't matter. However, for the children growing up in such a family, the action of starting a new business seems possible—something they can do.

Myths and Realities

Folklore and stereotypes about entrepreneurs and entrepreneurial success are remarkably durable, even in these informed and sophisticated times. More is known about the founders and the process of entrepreneurship than ever before.

However, certain myths enjoy recurring attention and popularity. Part of the problem is that while generalities may apply to certain types of entrepreneurs and particular situations, the great variety of founders tend to defy generalization. *Exhibit 2.15* shows myths about entrepreneurs that have persisted and realities that are supported by research.

Studies have indicated that 90 percent or more of founders start their companies in the same marketplace, technology, or industry they have been working in.[43] Others have found that founders are likely to have from 8 to 10 years of experience, and they are

[38] Timmons, Muzyka, Stevenson, and Bygrave, "Opportunity Recognition: The Core of Entrepreneurship," pp. 42–49.
[39] See studies cited in footnote 59.
[40] Karl H Vesper, "New Venture Ideas: Don't Overlook the Experience Factor," *Harvard Business Review*, reprinted in *Growing Concerns: Building and Managing the Smaller Business*, ed D E Gumpert (New York: John Wiley & Sons, 1984), pp. 28–55.
[41] See Robert Ronstadt's and Howard Stevenson's studies reported in *Frontiers of Entrepreneurship Research: 1983.*
[42] A Cooper and W Dunkelberg, *A New Look at Business Entry* (San Mateo, CA: National Federation of Independent Businesses, March 1984).
[43] A good summary of some of these studies is provided by Robert H Brockhaus, "The Psychology of the Entrepreneur," in *Encyclopedia of Entrepreneurship*, ed. C Kent, D Sexton, and K Vesper (Englewood Cliffs, NJ: Prentice-Hall, 1982), pp. 50–55.

EXHIBIT 2.15

Myths about Entrepreneurs

Myth 1—Entrepreneurs are born, not made.
Reality—While entrepreneurs are born with certain native intelligence, a flair for creating, and energy, these talents by themselves are like unmolded clay or an unpainted canvas. The making of an entrepreneur occurs by accumulating the relevant skills, know-how, experiences, and contacts over a period of years and includes large doses of self-development. The creative capacity to envision and then pursue an opportunity is a direct descendent of at least 10 or more years of experience that lead to pattern recognition.

Myth 2—Anyone can start a business.
Reality—Entrepreneurs who recognize the difference between an idea and an opportunity, and who think big enough, start businesses that have a better chance of succeeding. Luck, to the extent it is involved, requires good preparation. And the easiest part is starting up. What is hardest is surviving, sustaining, and building a venture so its founders can realize a harvest. Perhaps only one in 10 to 20 new businesses that survive five years or more results in a capital gain for the founders.

Myth 3—Entrepreneurs are gamblers.
Reality—Successful entrepreneurs take very careful, calculated risks. They try to influence the odds, often by getting others to share risk with them and by avoiding or minimizing risks if they have the choice. Often they slice up the risk into smaller, quite digestible pieces; only then do they commit the time or resources to determine if that piece will work. They do not deliberately seek to take more risk or to take unnecessary risk, nor do they shy away from unavoidable risk.

Myth 4—Entrepreneurs want the whole show to themselves.
Reality—Owning and running the whole show effectively puts a ceiling on growth. Solo entrepreneurs usually make a living. It is extremely difficult to grow a higher potential venture by working single-handedly. Higher potential entrepreneurs build a team, an organization, and a company. Besides, 100 percent of nothing is nothing, so rather than taking a large piece of the pie, they work to make the pie bigger.

Myth 5—Entrepreneurs are their own bosses and completely independent.
Reality—Entrepreneurs are far from independent and have to serve many masters and constituencies, including partners, investors, customers, suppliers, creditors, employees, families, and those involved in social and community obligations. Entrepreneurs, however, can make free choices of whether, when, and what they care to respond to. Moreover, it is extremely difficult, and rare, to build a business beyond $1 million to $2 million in sales single-handedly.

Myth 6—Entrepreneurs work longer and harder than managers in big companies.
Reality—There is no evidence that all entrepreneurs work more than their corporate counterparts. Some do, some do not. Some actually report that they work less.

Myth 7—Entrepreneurs experience a great deal of stress and pay a high price.
Reality—No doubt about it: Being an entrepreneur is stressful and demanding. But there is no evidence that it is any more stressful than numerous other highly demanding professional roles, and entrepreneurs find their jobs very satisfying. They have a high sense of accomplishment, are healthier, and are much less likely to retire than those who work for others. Three times as many entrepreneurs as corporate managers say they plan to never retire.

Myth 8—Starting a business is risky and often ends in failure.
Reality—Talented and experienced entrepreneurs—because they pursue attractive opportunities and are able to attract the right people and necessary financial and other resources to make the venture work—often head successful ventures. Further, businesses fail, but entrepreneurs do not. Failure is often the fire that tempers the steel of an entrepreneur's learning experience and street savvy.

Myth 9—Money is the most important start-up ingredient.
Reality—If the other pieces and talents are there, the money will follow, but it does not follow that an entrepreneur will succeed if he or she has enough money. Money is one of the least important ingredients in new venture success. Money is to the entrepreneur what the paint and brush are to the artist—an inert tool which, in the right hands, can create marvels. Money is also a way of keeping score, rather than just an end in itself. Entrepreneurs thrive on the thrill of the chase; and, time and again, even after an entrepreneur has made a few million dollars or more, he or she will work incessantly on a new vision to build another company.

Myth 10—Entrepreneurs should be young and energetic.
Reality—While these qualities may help, age is no barrier. The average age of entrepreneurs starting high potential businesses is in the mid-30s, and there are numerous examples of entrepreneurs starting businesses in their 60s. What is critical is possessing the relevant know-how, experience, and contacts that greatly facilitate recognizing and pursuing an opportunity.

Myth 11—Entrepreneurs are motivated solely by the quest for the almighty dollar.
Reality—Entrepreneurs seeking high potential ventures are more driven by building enterprises and realizing long-term capital gains than by instant gratification through high salaries and perks. A sense of personal achievement and accomplishment, feeling in control of their own destinies, and realizing their vision and dreams are also powerful motivators. Money is viewed as a tool and a way of keeping score.

Myth 12—Entrepreneurs seek power and control over others.

(Continued)

Reality—Successful entrepreneurs are driven by the quest for responsibility, achievement, and results, rather than for power for its own sake. They thrive on a sense of accomplishment and of outperforming the competition, rather than a personal need for power expressed by dominating and controlling others. By virtue of their accomplishments, they may be powerful and influential, but these are more the by-products of the entrepreneurial process than a driving force behind it.

Myth 13—If an entrepreneur is talented, success will happen in a year or two.

Reality—An old maxim among venture capitalists says it all: The lemons ripen in two and a half years, but the pearls take seven or eight. Rarely is a new business established solidly in less than three or four years.

Myth 14—Any entrepreneur with a good idea can raise venture capital.

Reality—Of the ventures of entrepreneurs with good ideas who seek out venture capital, only 1 to 3 out of 100 are funded.

Myth 15—If an entrepreneur has enough start-up capital, he or she can't miss.

Reality—The opposite is often true; that is, too much money at the outset often creates euphoria and a spoiled-child syndrome. The accompanying lack of discipline and impulsive spending usually lead to serious problems and failure.

Myth 16—Entrepreneurs are lone wolves and cannot work with others.

Reality—The most successful entrepreneurs are leaders who build great teams and effective relationships working with peers, directors, investors, key customers, key suppliers, and the like.

Myth 17—Unless you attained 600+ on your SATs or GMATs you'll never be a successful entrepreneur.

Reality—Entrepreneurial IQ is a unique combination of creativity, motivation, integrity, leadership, team building, analytical ability and ability to deal with ambiguity and adversity.

---

likely to be well educated. It also appears that successful entrepreneurs have wide experience in products/markets and across functional areas.[44]

Studies also have shown that most successful entrepreneurs start companies in their 30s. One study of founders of high-tech companies on Route 128 in Boston from 1982 to 1984 showed that the average age of the founders was 40.

It has been found that entrepreneurs work both more and less than their counterparts in large organizations, that they have high degrees of satisfaction with their jobs, and that they are healthier.[45] Another study showed that nearly 21 percent of the founders were over 40 when they embarked on their entrepreneurial career, the majority were in their 30s, and just over one quarter did so by the time they were 25.

What Can Be Learned?

For nearly 30 years, the author has been engaged as an educator, cofounder, investor, advisor and director of new, higher potential ventures. Many of these have been launched by former students and most of the cases in the book are about those founders. One of my most vivid memories is when the great Texas real estate entrepreneur Trammel Crow was inducted into Babson College's Academy of Distinguished Entrepreneurs. The instant we met he put his arm around me and said: "Perfesser. Do you mean to tell me you think you can actually teach someone to be an on-

tree-pre-newer!" My response was straightforward: "Mr. Crow, What I think you are really asking me is; am I preposterous enough to believe that in 35 to 40 hours of class time, during a single semester, that I can convert the average student into the economic equivalent of a Picasso or a Beethoven!? Mr. Crow, I think we both know the answer to that question." He laughed and smiled, and said he reckoned he did.

New Venture Creation will immerse you in the dynamics and realities of launching and growing life-style to higher potential ventures. Through the text and multipart cases about real, college- and graduate school-age, and young entrepreneurs, you will face the same situations these aspiring entrepreneurs faced as they sought to turn dream into reality. The cases and text, combined with the book's Website including supporting materials and exercises, will enable you to grapple with all of the conceptual, practical, financial, and personal issues entrepreneurs encounter. It will focus your attention on developing answers for the most important of these questions, including:

- What does an entrepreneurial career take?
- What is the difference between a good opportunity and just another idea?
- Is the opportunity I am considering the right opportunity for me, now?
- Why do some firms grow quickly to several million dollars in sales but then stumble, never growing beyond a single-product firm?

---

[44] Over 80 studies in this area have been reported in *Frontiers of Entrepreneurship Research* (Babson Park, MA: Babson College) for the years 1981 through 1997.

[45] Stevenson, "Who Are the Harvard Self-Employed?" p. 233.

- What are the critical tasks and hurdles in seizing an opportunity and building the business?
- How much money do I need and when, where, and how can I get it—on acceptable terms?
- What financing sources, strategies, and mechanisms can I use from prestart, through the early growth stage, to the harvest of my venture?
- What are the minimum resources I need to gain control over the opportunity, and how can I do this?
- Is a business plan needed? If so, what kind is needed and how and when should I develop one?
- Who are the constituents for whom I must create or add value to achieve a positive cash flow and to develop harvest options?
- What is my venture worth and how do I negotiate what to give up?
- What are the critical transitions in entrepreneurial management as a firm grows from $1 million to $5 million to $25 million in sales?
- What is it that entrepreneurial leaders do differently which enables them to achieve such competitive breakthroughs and advantages, particularly over conventional practices, but also so called 'best practices'?
- What are the opportunities and implications for 20th century entrepreneurs and the Internet, and how can these be seized and financed?
- What do I need to know and practice in entrepreneurial reasoning and thinking in order to have a competitive edge?
- What are some of the pitfalls, minefields, and hazards I need to anticipate, prepare for, and respond to?
- What are the contacts and networks I need to access and to develop?
- Do I know what I do and do not know, and do I know what to do about it?
- How can I develop a personal "entrepreneurial game plan" to acquire the experience I need to succeed?
- How critical and sensitive is the timing in each of these areas?
- Why do entrepreneurs who succeed in the long term seek to maintain reputations for integrity and ethical business practices?

There is no question in my mind that we can significantly improve the quality of decisions students make about entrepreneurship, and thereby also improve the fit between what they aspire to do and the requirements of the particular opportunity. In many cases, those choices lead to self-employment or meaningful careers in new and growing firms, and increasingly, in post-Brontosaurus Capitalism, in large firms that "get it." In other cases, students join larger firms whose customer base and/or suppliers are principally the entrepreneurial sector. Still others seek careers in the financial institutions and professional services firms which are at the vortex of the entrepreneurial economy: venture capital, private equity, investment banks, commercial banks, consulting, accounting, and the like.

Regardless of their decisions, my view of entrepreneurship is that it need not be an end in itself. Rather, it is a pathway that leads to innumerable ideas and opportunities, and opens visions of what young people can become. You will learn some skills, and how to use those skills appropriately. You will learn how to tap your own and others' creativity, and to apply your new energy. You will learn the difference between another good idea and a serious opportunity. You will learn the power and potential of the entrepreneurial team. You will learn people skills. You will learn that happiness is a positive cash flow. You will learn how entrepreneurs finance and grow their companies, often with ingenious bootstrapping strategies that get big results with minimal resources. You will learn the joy of self-sufficiency and independence. You will learn how entrepreneurial leaders make this happen, and give back to society. You will discover anew what it is about entrepreneurship that gives you sustaining energy and the fuel for your dreams.

One of the best perspectives on this comes from Professor Jerry Gustafson, Coleman–Fannie May Chair, Beloit College, Beloit, Wisconsin, who was probably the first professor at a liberal arts college to create an entrepreneurship course:

> Entrepreneurship is important for its own sake. The subject frames an ideal context for students to address perennial questions concerning their identity, objectives, hopes, relation to society, and the tension between thought and action. Entrepreneurship concerns thinking of what we are as persons. . . . Furthermore, of it nature, entrepreneurship is about process. One cannot discuss entrepreneurship without encountering the importance of goal-setting, information gathering, persistence, resourcefulness, and resiliency. It is not lost on students that the behaviors and styles of entrepreneurs tend to be socially rewarded, and these are precisely the behaviors we wish to see the students exhibit in the classroom.[46]

———————
[46] Professor Jerry Gustafson, "SEEing is Not Only About Business", *PULSE*, 1988, (Babson Park, MA: Price-Babson Fellows Program).

A Word of Caution: What SATs, IQ Tests, GMATs and Others Don't Measure

It was always a shock to my second-year Harvard MBA students when I shared the following data about alumni whose careers were followed for nearly 25 years. Regardless of the measure one applies, among the very top of the class were graduates who were both highly successful and not very successful at all. At the bottom of the class were alumni who became outrageously successful, and others who accomplished little with their lives and exceptional education. The middle of the class achieved all points on the continuum of success. How could this be? Indeed, I recall as a doctoral student a research study showing that a combination of GMAT score and undergraduate GPA together accounted for only 11 percent of the variance in class rank in the MBA program.

Amazing as it may seem, America's brightest fared poorly in the recent Third International Mathematics and Science Study comparing high school seniors from 20 nations, according to the *New York Times*. In a competition between the world's most precocious seniors, those taking physics and advanced math, the Americans performed at the bottom. The article noted:

> After decades of agonizing over the fairness of S.A.T. scores, the differences between male and female mathematical skills, and gaps in I.Q. between various races and ethnic groups, the notion of intelligence and how to measure it remains more political than scientific, and as maddeningly elusive as ever.[47]

In short, there are many different kinds of intelligence, a much greater bandwidth than most researchers and test architects ever imagined. The dynamic and subtle complexities of the entrepreneurial task require its own special intelligences. How else would one explain the enormous contradiction inherent in business and financially failed geniuses?

One only need consider the critical skills and capacities that are at the heart of entrepreneurial leadership and achievement, yet are not measured by the IQ tests, SATs, GMATs and the like that grade and sort young applicants with such imprecision. It is no wonder that a number of excellent colleges and universities eliminated these measures, or placed them in a proper perspective. Obviously, this should not be construed to read: Entrepreneurship is for dummies. Quite the opposite is true. Indeed, intelligence is a very valuable and important asset for entrepreneurs, but by itself is woefully inadequate.

Consider the skills and capacities not measured by these tests:

- Leadership skills
- Interpersonal skills
- Team building and team playing
- Creativity
- Motivation
- Learning skills (vs. knowledge)
- Persistence and determination
- Values, ethics, honesty and integrity
- Goal-setting orientation
- Self-discipline
- Frugality
- Resourcefulness
- Resiliency and capacity to handle adversity
- Ability to seek, listen, and use feedback
- Reliability
- Dependability
- Sense of humor

Clearly, just being very smart won't help much if one doesn't possess numerous other qualities (see Chapters 6, 7 and 8: "The Entrepreneurial Mind," "The Entrepreneurial Manager," and "The New Venture Team," respectively, for an elaboration on these other qualities). A fascinating article by Chris Argyris, "Teaching Smart People How to Learn," is well worth reading to get some powerful insights into why it is often *not* the class genius who becomes most successful.[48]

Chapter Summary

1. We began to demystify entrepreneurship by examining its classic startup definition, and a broader, holistic way of thinking, reasoning, and acting that is opportunity obsessed and leadership balanced.

2. Entrepreneurship has many metaphors and poses many paradoxes.

3. Getting the odds in your favor is the entrepreneur's perpetual challenge, and the smaller the business the poorer are the odds of survival.

4. Thinking big enough can improve the odds significantly. Higher potential ventures are sought by successful entrepreneurs, venture capitalists, and private investors.

5. The Timmons Model is at the heart of spotting and building the higher potential venture, and understanding its three driving forces: opportunity, the team, and resources; the concept of fit and balance is crucial.

---

[47] "Tests Show Nobody's Smart About Intelligence," *The New York Times*, March 1, 1998, p. 4–1.
[48] Chris Argyris, "Teaching Smart People to Learn," *Harvard Business Review*, May–June 1991.

6. Recent research on 906 CEOs of fast-growth ventures nationwide add new validity to the model.

7. There are many myths and realities about entrepreneurship that provide important insights for aspiring entrepreneurs.

8. Entrepreneurship can be learned; it requires an apprenticeship.

9. A word of caution: IQ tests, SATs, GMATs, LSATs and others do not measure some of the most important entrepreneurial abilities and aptitudes.

Study Questions

1. Can you define what is meant by classic entrepreneurship, post-Brontosaurus Capitalism entrepreneurship, the high-potential venture, the threshold concept, cover your equity, bootstrapping of resources, fit, and balance? Why and how are these important?

2. How many additional metaphors and paradoxes about entrepreneurship can you write down?

3. "People don't want to be managed, they want to be led." Explain what this means, and its importance and implications for developing your own style and leadership philosophy.

4. What are the most important determinants of success and failure in new businesses? Who has the best and worst chances for success, and why?

5. What are the most important things you can do to get the odds in your favor?

6. What criteria and characteristics do high-growth entrepreneurs, venture capitalists, and private investors seek in evaluating business opportunities? How can these make a difference?

7. Define and explain The Timmons Model. Apply it and graphically depict, as in the Netscape example, the first five years or so of a new company with which you are familiar.

8. What are the most important skills, values, talents, abilities, and mind-sets one needs to cultivate as an entrepreneur?

MIND STRETCHERS
Have You Considered?

1. Who can be an entrepreneur? When?

2. Over 80 percent of entrepreneurs learn the critical skills they need after age 21. What does this mean for you?

3. In your lifetime the odds are that such leading firms today such as Microsoft, Netscape, Dell Computer, American Airlines, McDonald's, and American Express will be knocked off by upstarts. How will this happen? Why does it present an opportunity? And for whom?

4. What do you need to be doing now, and in the next 12 months to get the odds in your favor?

5. Can you list 100 ideas, and then pick out the best 5 that just might be an opportunity? How can these become opportunities? Who can make them opportunities?

Case
PC–Build, Inc.*

Preparation Questions

1. Evaluate the PC-Build™ business plan and the opportunity.[1]

2. Should Michael Healey and Robert Lofblad start the business?

3. Would you invest in the business? Join the venture?

4. What should the founders do?

"We won!" Elation flooded Mike Healey's head with the announcement that he, Bob Lofblad, and their team had won the 1992 MBA Douglass Prize at Babson College for the best proposed business among dozens of business plans submitted to the competition. It was not the $5,000 award plus the engraved watch that were most important. Was this award the confirmation of nearly a year-long effort to determine whether PC-Build was a serious business opportunity or just another good idea? After all, the panel of judges was made up of experienced and successful entrepreneurs who thought that PC-Build was the best idea of the lot. Mike and Bob wondered if the panel's support was a positive indicator of how the market would assess PC-Build's potential.

---

* Research Associate Christine C Remey prepared this case, under the supervision of Professor Jeffry A Timmons, as the basis for class discussion rather than to illustrate either effective or ineffective handling of an administrative situation. Reprinted with permission from Michael Healey and Robert Lofblad.

[1] PC-Build™ is a registered trademark of Discovery Curve, Inc.

Graduation was less than a month away, May 1992. Mike thought it was a bit scary: Should we really try to launch this business? Most people say starting a business right out of school is too risky. While most classmates were headed for regular jobs, Mike had not spent time at the placement office. He wondered if this was the right time and place to take the plunge. He was confident about the idea, the market potential, and his team—but some major issues still needed to be resolved. Among them, how much capital would be required to get started? As Mike thought about the capital requirements, he commented to Bob, "I do not think that this venture will require that much capital, because the only thing we plan to buy new is lunch!" Yet, he continued to wonder: How could he raise money and on what terms? Who might invest in the company? If everything worked out, the upside was not hard to figure out. But what if it did not work out? Could he get another job? What would his family and friends think? How would he handle all that? What follows is the original business plan for PC-Build Computer Kits.

Executive Summary

Discovery Curve Corporation was formed in October 1991 and incorporated in Massachusetts in February 1992. Discovery Curve's primary line of business is the manufacture and sale of IBM-compatible personal computer kits, sold as PC-Build Computer Kits. These kits are targeted at the home hobbyist and educational institutions, such as computer camps and adult continuing education. This market niche targets the computer users who "want to get their hands dirty." There are similar kits for a variety of industries, including stereo equipment and automobiles. The founders believe an opportunity exists in the personal computer (PC) industry for four main reasons:

- Technological standardization.
- Changing consumer attitudes toward PCs.
- Definite market opportunity.
- Sleepy competitors.

As a result of these conditions, there is a unique opportunity to provide high-quality PC kits at affordable prices.

The Company differentiates itself from its direct competition by being a full-service provider of an integrated learning experience. PC-Build kits will be far more than the "box of parts" favored by our competition. Competitors target users whose primary goal is saving money. We target those who love to experiment and learn.

The total market size for build-it-yourself computers in 1991 was estimated to be $70 million, roughly 66,000 units. PC-Build's Year 1 projected sales volume is 1,500 units, about $1.2 million. This represents a very conservative 1.43 percent market share. The company's break-even volume is 749 units of its lowest priced kit. Gross margins are 28–35 percent.

Initial market research has been encouraging. The company has 10 education proposals under review and has received orders from several individuals. Preliminary supplier selection is complete, and the company has secured production/administrative facilities in Wellesley, Massachusetts.

Management has done exhaustive research into the industry, the product, and the market. The company is proceeding according to schedule. Discovery Curve, Inc., is seeking $100,000 to implement the plans described herein. The 3,000 shares of common stock offered for $33 per share will represent 30 percent of PC-Build.

The Industry and the Company and Its Product

The personal computer (PC) industry has undergone tremendous growth in the last 10 years. Advances in microprocessor technology have put mainframe power in the price range of the individual. The acceptance of PCs has been fueled by a boom in available software. As a result, PCs have become commonplace in the office, at school, and at home. Worldwide sales of PCs were 24 million units ($10.4 billion) in 1990.

In the late 1970s and early 1980s, a large number of PC kits were available. As industry sales grew, the kits died off. Profitability for the manufacturer came from volume production. Kits were a low-volume niche product. Many PC makers, notably Apple and Dell, switched from selling kits to selling finished products because the margins and volumes were higher. As of today, there are only two national manufacturers of complete PC kits.

The industry can be split into two general product segments, IBM compatible and Apple. *IBM compatible* refers to all MS-DOS–based PCs that are 100 percent compatible with IBM. This group accounts for over 80 percent of industry sales; the rest go to Apple and some smaller segments.

The IBM-compatible segment has developed a unique pecking order. Any major technological change is usually released by a major player, such as IBM or Intel. Within weeks, all major clone makers follow suit. The result is that previous versions of hardware are bumped down and begin to drop in price. This pecking order is not limited to fully assembled PCs. The same pattern is evident in components such as hard disks and monitors.

Opportunity Rationale

There are three main reasons why an opportunity exists for PC-Build: Technological standardization, changing consumer attitudes, and an identified neglected market segment.

PC-BUILD COMPUTER KITS—BUSINESS PLAN
A DIVISION OF DISCOVERY CURVE, INC.
Table of Contents

Technological Standardization. All IBM compatibles are based on Intel's microprocessor technology. Intel has become the dominant producer of central processing units (CPUs). The clones also use the same standard layout for their main circuit boards. By doing so they can claim 100 percent compatibility and easily accommodate any add-in hardware, such as a modem.

Standardization has created machines that are relatively simple to assemble. All complex engineering is done on the board. Boards simply plug into a slot. A typical PC is made up of only 11 major components. A working PC can be easily assembled by an ordinary individual. This ease can be enhanced by making some structural changes to the typical PC chassis and by creating detailed assembly instructions.

Common circuit board designs have given rise to a booming original equipment manufacturing (OEM) business. Most PC manufacturers, including IBM, do not build all their components in house. Most components are subcontracted out, leaving the PC maker the task of assembly and testing. PC-Build will be able to pick and choose suppliers based on their price, quality, warranty, and delivery terms.

PC-Build also gains a "free-engineering" factor because of this standardization and pecking order of new releases. PC-Build kits will not be the leading edge in PC technology. Instead, they will lag one generation behind. For example, PC-Build will be marketing a 286 PC as its low-end product. This computer is not leading edge, but is standard in the market. By waiting until a standard develops in the marketplace, PC-Build has its systems engineered for free. (Please refer to the "Technological Surfing" section on p. 55 for a detailed explanation of this logic.)

Changing Consumer Attitudes. PCs are everywhere—in the home, the office, and at school. The number of different distribution channels available underscores PCs' acceptability. Even the *Home Shopping Channel* sells PCs.

Changing consumer attitudes affect PC-Build in two ways. First, consumers are no longer loyal to brand names. Buying a big name is no longer an issue. Second, the PC itself is no longer a mystery. This second change can best be seen by examining recent trends with add-in hardware. This area used to be a major contributor to a retail computer store's profits. People would bring their PCs into the store to have the component added by a technician. The volume of this business has been steadily declining. Many consumers are simply buying the add-in and installing it themselves.

Market Opportunity. After considerable research and analysis the founders of PC-Build are convinced that the kit segment of the PC market is being inadequately served. The market leader offers an overpriced, low-quality product. The entire industry ignored the educational learning aspect of a "Do It Yourself" (DIY) computer. All competitors treat kits in one of two ways:

- Minor side business: These companies' main line of business is selling assembled PCs. Kits represent a side business that merits no serious investment.
- Cash cow: The main competitor, Heathkit, is a small subsidiary of Bull, the French conglomerate. The company puts minimal effort into the product in terms of quality and marketing support.

The Company

The opportunity for a new manufacturer to enter the personal computer kit industry was conceived in February 1991. The company will begin operations in 1992, with the first product available in May 1992. Initially, the company intends to sell all products directly, eventually expanding to retail DIY electronics stores.

The Product

A full line of 100 percent IBM-compatible, MS-DOS–based personal computer kits will be produced. These kits are designed for a nontechnical individual who possesses some knowledge of computers. No soldering or wiring is required. All an individual needs is a few basic tools and a desire to learn.

The computer kit will be supplemented with a fully illustrated instruction manual and video cassette. Both will be fully integrated, designed to walk the customer through the assembly. The instruction manual will also explain the basics of how a computer works.

All kits will come with a 30-day money-back guarantee and a one-year warranty on parts. Customers will be given access to PC-Build's toll-free technical support line, available Monday through Friday 9 AM to 5 PM EST. Each kit comes complete with MS-DOS 5.0 and PC-Build's proprietary DOS starter program, Quickstart™.[2]

Quickstart is an interactive program designed to configure and test the assembled computer. Quickstart automatically tests the assembly, configures the hard disk, and loads MS-DOS. It also contains an interactive tutorial that explains the basics of Microsoft's MS-DOS.

Product Line. The Company will initially offer three main products. These products are intended to appeal to a broad range of home hobbyists and computer users.

- *B2000 Basic Kit.* Designed for the budget conscious consumer who wants a simple, inexpensive kit. Ideal for the head of household who wants to build a computer as a family experience. Priced at $699. Kit includes:

  80286-based motherboard (16 MHz).

  20 MB hard disk.

  Floppy/hard disk controller.

  Parallel/serial/game port card.

  Keyboard.

  Cabinet and power supply.

  Instruction manual and video.

  1 MB Ram.

  5¼-inch and 3½-inch floppy disk drives.

  VGA monitor card.

  MS-DOS 5.0

  Monitor not included.

Note: The 286 motherboard may be replaced with a 386SX/16 board by May.

- *SX3000 Super Kit.* Designed for the more computer literate customer who wants a technically superior machine. This is ideal for the individual who understands the basics of computers and wants to "get his/her hands dirty." Priced at $899. Kit includes:

---

[2] Quickstart™ is a registered trademark of Discovery Curve, Inc.

80386/SX-based motherboard (20 MHz).

44 MB hard disk.

Floppy/hard disk controller.

Keyboard.

Cabinet and power supply.

Instruction manual and video.

2 MB RAM.

5¼-inch and 3½-inch floppy disk drives.

Parallel/serial/game card.

VGA monitor card.

MS-DOS 5.0.

Monitor not included.

- *SX4000 Deluxe Kit.* Designed for the power computer customer who wants a big machine. This is ideal for the individual who understands and uses computers frequently, and wants to build a "rocket." Priced at $1,500. Kit includes:

  80486/SX-based motherboard (20 MHz).

  120 MB hard disk.

  Floppy/hard disk controller.

  Keyboard.

  Cabinet and power supply.

  Instruction manual and video.

  4 MB RAM.

  5¼-inch and 3½-inch floppy disk drives.

  Parallel/serial/game card.

  VGA monitor card.

  MS-DOS 5.0

  Monitor not included.

- *Custom Kit.* This option is designed for consumers having an in-depth understanding of the various PC components who seek to build a custom kit. PC-Build has designed its components and manufacturing operations in such a way that customer orders can be processed economically. All custom kits include MS-DOS 5.50, 5 ¼-inch and 3 ½-inch floppy disk drives, disk controller card, keyboard, cabinet, power supply, parallel/serial/game card, instruction manual and video. Individuals can choose their own:

  Motherboard (286, 386, or 486 based, various MHz speeds).

  Amount of RAM (1–8 MB).

  Hard disk size (20–110 MB).

  Monitor (monochrome, VGA black and white, VGA color, or Super VGA).

- *Monitors.* The company will offer a full line of monitors. All monitors are VGA based and are compatible with the aforementioned kits. Models and prices are as follows:

Black and white VGA (800 × 600 resolution)	$125
Color VGA (800 × 600 resolution)	275
Super color VGA (1024 × 768 resolution)	400

Computer Education Service. The company will offer additional service to the computer education market. Training materials designed to supplement the instructional manual will be available as part of our education services. In addition, the company will offer the service of original equipment manufacturer (OEM)-certified instructors for $200 per session. The company will waive this fee for volume purchases.

Additional Business. Discovery Curve's founders will continue to offer services in programming, consulting, and documentation development. Both founders have excellent industry reputations and have established consulting arrangements with several companies. The exact amount of this additional income is difficult to predict, but is estimated in the range of $25,000 to $35,000 annually.

Competitive Advantages. PC-Build will strive to offer the best quality kit on the market. No other competitor has its combination of design, service, and instruction. This gives the company four main competitive advantages:

- *Quality.* All components are from recognized suppliers, such as Intel and Seagate. An unconditional one-year warranty covers all parts.

- *User friendliness.* PC-Build kits have been designed with the customer in mind. The instruction manual will have complete instructions on assembly and computer operations. PC-Build is the only company to offer a video that details the assembly process.

- *Service.* No other competitor offers a 30-day money back guarantee and access to a toll-free technical support line. Our custom product line gives an individual the ability to design the exact kit he or she wants.

- *Affordability.* PC-Build's prices are 10–15 percent below a comparable fully assembled PC. This creates a perception of true savings.

Technological Surfing. PC-Build kits will not be the leading edge in PC technology. The company will follow a policy of always lagging one generation behind. This gives the company four main advantages:

- Proven hardware.
- Easy access to suppliers.
- A recognizable standard.
- Lower cost components.

Please note that PC-Build is fully aware of the fact that by not offering a leading edge kit, we are eliminating a segment of the home hobbyist market. However, we feel this loss is outweighed by the savings in engineering, warranties, and material costs.

The primary reason an individual buys a kit is the desire to build and learn about computers, not to buy the most expensive leading-edge technology. New technologies will be introduced based upon our new technology screening system (see "Future Products" section on p. 65).

Entry and Growth Strategy. The company will begin selling to educational institutions first. The first target will be computer education camps in operation throughout the United States. PC-Build plans to offer its products beginning in June 1992. There are several reasons why this market was chosen first:

- No competition.
- High volume.
- Proven customer interest.
- Minimal up-front marketing costs.

No competitors are offering PC kits to computer education camps. Initial contacts with these camps have been encouraging. Several camps are considering purchases. Personal selling will continue to be the main marketing approach. PC-Build has identified all the potential customers in this category and can contact them directly.

Another key reason for targeting this market first is the fact that a product can be developed and introduced relatively quickly. A video instruction tape is unnecessary for computer camps. The initial product and instructional manual will be production ready by June (See "Overall Project Schedule" section on p. 68).

PC-Build will target the home hobbyist market in November. PC-Build has chosen the direct marketing channel to reach the home market. We feel this channel is important because it gives us a greater degree of control over pricing, quality, and volume. PC-Build will advertise in publications that our target market members read, such as *Popular Electronics*. The intent of these advertisements is to provoke them to call our toll-free sales line for more information. Our telemarketing staff can then personally sell the product.

Eventually, PC-Build will expand to retail outlets, specifically do-it-yourself (DIY) stores. There are over 500 such stores in the United States (excluding Radio Shack). Radio Shack (Tandy Corporation) has stated that they will not offer a kit through their retail outlets. They feel it will cannibalize assembled PC sales.

We feel that by going direct first we achieve two main goals: (1) establishing the PC-Build name and (2) creating a direct marketing organization. Experience in the PC industry has shown that companies have successfully expanded from direct marketing into retail, but not the reverse.

Expansion Opportunities. The most natural expansion route for the company is add-on sales. As soon as a significant customer base is developed, the company will begin offering add-in boards, such as modems and sound cards. Our customers are perfect prospects for these types of products; they are comfortable with PCs and have a proven track record of purchasing high tech toys.

Market Research and Analysis

As indicated above, PC-Build will have two primary target segments, the home hobbyist PC user and educational institutions. The following is a description of the major characteristics of each:

The *home computer user* is somewhat price sensitive but concerned about quality and service. Home computers are typically purchased at a computer store or a department store. However, a substantial percentage is sold through nontraditional channels such as mail order. Currently 15 percent of all personal computers sold for home use were purchased through mail order. This percentage is expected to increase over the coming years. Buyers are overwhelmingly male. Home computers are mainly used for word processing, computer games, education, and database management/filing. The age groups, listed in order of dominance: 35–44, 25–34, 45–55, and 18–24. Our targeted customers are predominantly male and fall into the 18 to 44 age group. Thus, PC-Build's customers range from college-aged kids to dads wanting to build PCs as a family product.

Educational institutions refer to schools, colleges, or businesses that specialize in computer training. The most promising segment is the computer camp. There are 252 accredited summer camps offering computer learning programs. Over 90 percent of these camps are run during the summer months. The camps offer courses on programming, computer games, microelectronics, and so on. Students pay a flat fee for the camp. Fees range from $700 to $2,000 per week. A PC kit is a natural extension of their program. Camps will have the option of incorporating the cost of the kit into their tuition, or charging an additional fee. The following camps are potential customers:

- TIC Computer Camps, Washington, DC.
- High Tech Educational Camps, Woburn, Massachusetts.
- FutureKids, Franchised throughout the United States.

The education market also includes all vocational schools, technical colleges, and other tertiary educational institutes that offer computer training programs, workshops, and courses. There are over 10,000 such institutions in the United States. Approximately 10 percent of them offer computer assembly training. The company is currently negotiating with:

- Computer Learning Centers, Somerville, Massachusetts.
- MIT-Lowell Institute School, Cambridge, Massachusetts.
- UMass, Lowell, Amherst, and Boston, Massachusetts.
- PRA Computer Training Center, Marlboro, Massachusetts.

Educational institutions can be thought of as a distribution channel. They funnel our products to the end user. The value-added they provide is personal instruction. PC-Build will offer volume discounts to these institutions, as well as access to trainers and teaching materials.

Whether they are a channel or customer is a minor point; they are an untapped market. Many institutions we spoke to had considered the concept, but could not find a product. Until now.

Market Size. 1990 Total U.S. sales of products that can be considered kits are estimated at $70 million. The company derived this estimate by analyzing total personal computer sales, direct competitor sales, and indirect competitor sales.

Worldwide sales of all types of personal computers in 1990 are 24 million units. Most forecasts project 8–10 percent annual growth for the next several years. The U.S. home market is a small portion of this total market, with 5.5 million units sold in 1990. This segment is expected to grow faster than the overall industry growth rates, with industry sources projecting 15–30 percent growth rates.

Direct competitor sales in 1990 were approximately $20 million. Indirect competitor sales were $50 million. Indirect competition refers to companies that offer all the components needed to build a PC, but not as a kit, and limited instructions.

Estimated Market Share and Sales

PC-Build's estimated market share and sales volumes are presented in *Exhibit A*. The first year's sales figure is based on bulk sales of 200 units to the education market during summer (i.e., summer camps) and 250 units sold during the Christmas season. The remainder of the volume is spread out throughout the year. Given these assumptions, our market share (of total amount of kits and pseudo kits sold) will be less than 2 percent of the entire market. This market share is projected to increase to 4 percent by 1996. Sales growth is estimated to be 20 percent per annum after the second year.

Market Trends

It is estimated that the home market consists of 94 million households; penetration of the home market therefore reached 5.6 percent in 1990. The inherent potential for growth within this segment is revealed by the low level of market penetration. This growth potential applies to PC-Build since our kits are targeted toward the home users.

Given the increased computer literacy, the introduction of user friendly software, and the increased usage of computers for business and education, the home market is expected to continue growing. Sales projections for 1994 reach 7.4 million units for this segment.

EXHIBIT A

PC-Build: Market Analysis

	1991	1992	1993	1994	1995	1996
Unit sales (in 000s):						
Total PCs	10,500	11,400	12,400	13,400	14,600	15,900
PCs for home use	5,500	6,000	6,500	7,000	7,700	8,300
PCs sold as kits and pseudokits	61	66	72	77	85	91
Dollar sales (in millions):						
Total PCs	$31,800	$34,500	$37,500	$40,700	$44,200	$48,000
PCs for home use	$16,700	$18,100	$19,700	$21,300	$23,200	$25,200
PCs sold as kits and pseudokits	$ 65	$ 70	$ 75	$ 81	$ 88	$ 96
PC-Build sales forecasts:						
Units		1,200	2,200	2,600	3,200	3,800
Dollars (in millions)		$1.0	$2.0	$2.5	$3.0	$3.6
PC-Build market share:						
Units		1.82%	3.08%	3.38%	3.78%	4.16%
Dollars		1.43%	2.67%	3.09%	3.41%	3.75%

Notes: Total market growth expected at 8% per year.
Home Sales represent approximately 50% total market sales. Kits sales were estimated by looking at total market sales and competitor sales (both direct and indirect competitors).

EXHIBIT B

Major Competitors

Competitor Type	Annual Sales	Pricing Strategy	Market Share	Distribution Channel	Major Strength/Weakness
Heathkit, direct	$10 million	Highest	15%	Direct	Size & name; ignored market changes
ATS, direct	3 million	High	5	Direct	Only Apple kit; side business
Microtech, direct	1 million	Low	1	Retail	Custom service; side business
DTK, indirect	15 million	Medium	23	Retail	Supplier to local PC makers
JDR, indirect	5–6 million	Medium	10	Direct	Established PC maker, no complete kit
Jameco, indirect	5–6 million	High	10	Direct	Poor quality PCs disguised as kits
Microlabs, indirect	5 million	Low	5	Both	Good quality parts, no complete kit

In the long run the viability of the PC is dependent upon factors such as the development of:

- Software programs.
- Multimedia applications.
- Online information systems and personal service systems.
- Integrated home management networks controlling, for example, communications and security systems.

Competition

Two PC kits are available nationally. Atlanta Technical Specialists builds an Apple-based kit that retails complete for $1,100 to $2,000. Heathkit sells an IBM-compatible PC that retails for $1,000 to $1,800.

Some regional companies manufacture IBM kits as a side business. The quality is poor in terms of both the hardware and the instruction materials. Also, a large number of companies do not sell all components needed to build a PC. *Exhibit B* is a breakdown of our major competitors.

Direct Competitors. The largest competitor is Heathkit. The company was one of the pioneers in the PC industry in the 1970s. They subsequently became part of Zenith Data Systems in the early 1980s. Both are now wholly owned subsidiaries of the French conglomerate Groupe Bull. The Groupe Bull purchase has been a disaster for Zenith Data Systems. Revenues are down by more than $1 billion. Heathkit is a small fraction of Bull's business and has been ignored. The products are high priced and offer limited options. Custom models are not offered. Heathkit's main strength is its market leader position. However, its main weakness is its apathy toward the market. The company no longer advertises nationally and its direct sales offices only sell Zenith systems.

Atlanta Technical Specialists (ATS) is a relatively new player in the market. They began offering their Apple-based kits only two years ago and have seen their kits sales climb to $3 million in that time period. The company markets kits which are high quality and high priced. The high prices reflect the relatively higher cost of Apple computers versus IBM. The company's main strength is the quality of its kits. They supply Apple with some of their components and developed kits as an expansion in that business. ATS's main weakness is their reliance on Apple. Apple machines constitute only 10 percent of the over-the-counter market; IBM compatibles are the recognized standard.

Indirect Competition. These companies merit special attention for two main reasons. First, the sheer volume of the component sales is an indication of the size of this neglected market. Second, their product offerings are often poor in quality and are not user-friendly. Instruction manuals are nonexistent; customers are often left to fend for themselves. Often these companies are unaware they are even serving the do-it-yourself PC segment. For example, DTK manufactures a variety of computer components, including motherboards, video cards, and disk controllers. According to the company, their main customers are local manufacturers who assemble and sell their systems complete. (See *Exhibit C* for product comparisons.)

However, we discovered several local manufacturers who market DTK components as a kit, offering a bare-bones shell (consisting of a case, power supply, and motherboard) plus a selection of components. These companies advertise a "customer kit you can build yourself." PC-Build adds significant value over the competition by offering a complete kit, with superior quality and service. Our kits are priced competitively, further accenting our value for the dollar.

Ongoing Market Evaluation

Continuous market evaluation is crucial to the long-term viability of the company. New product introduction by industry leaders and sales levels of existing technologies will be monitored closely. These figures form the basis of PC-Build's pricing and technology decisions. We are a niche player, receiving our cues from the market leaders.

EXHIBIT C

Competitor Product Analysis

Company	Product	Price	Warranty	Technical Support	30 day guarantee	Manual	Video
PC-Build	286 Standard	$ 825	One year	Yes	Yes	Yes	Yes
	386 Super	999	One year	Yes	Yes	Yes	Yes
	Custom kits	1,200	One year	Yes	Yes	Yes	Yes
Heathkit	286-based kit	929	One year	Yes	No	Yes	No
	386-based kit	1,200	One year	Yes	No	Yes	No
Microtech	386-based kit	1,149	Six months	Yes	Yes	No	No
ATS	Mac-based kit	1,699	One year	Yes	No	Yes	No
DTK	Parts only	850	One year	Yes	No	No	No
Jameco	Parts Sales	779	Limited	Yes	No	No	No

Competitors' products and market strategies will naturally be under close scrutiny. The company will subscribe to all industry periodicals and associations, and will make extensive use of board members and personal contacts.

The Economics of the Business

The continuing trend in PC price reduction is expected to continue for the next several years. The actual downward pressure on prices stems from two main forces: competitive price pressure and declining material costs. The combination of these factors has reduced industry margins, down from an average of 35 percent in 1985 to under 30 percent today. PC-Build has a projected gross margin of 28–35 percent.

Our higher margins are due to labor savings. Labor generally is 20 percent of the total product cost. PC-Build computers have relatively low levels of labor. Only a portion of this savings is passed on to the consumer, the rest goes to PC-Build. A PC-Build kit is priced 10–20 percent below a comparable assembled PC. Refer to the marketing section for a detailed explanation of pricing logic. For a detailed breakdown of actual unit cost for the basic kit, see *Exhibit D*. These costs are based on volume purchases from our suppliers.

One of the key elements to PC-Build's continued profitability is our ability to purchase quality components at the lowest possible cost. To increase our relative bargaining position, PC-Build will have at least three alternative suppliers for all components, except the operating system.

PC-Build has a master license agreement with Microsoft Corporation. Microsoft is paid a flat fee ($32) for every MS-DOS–based system we sell. In return, PC-Build can incorporate DOS into its proprietary software programs.

We fully expect downward pressure on our prices. As overall PCs prices continue to fall, kits will be expected

EXHIBIT D

Cost Estimates

Component	Unit Cost
Chasis	$ 30.00
Power supply	31.00
Motherboard	58.00
MB RAM memory	10.00
I/O Port	9.00
Monitor card	35.00
Monitor	86.00
Keyboard	21.00
Floppy drives	88.00
Hard drive	140.00
Disk controller	9.00
Software cost	40.00
Video cost	7.00
Documentation	5.00
Shipping/handling	0.00
Total cost	$569.00

Note: Cost estimates include supplier quantity breaks.

to follow suit. By selling directly, we will have a greater degree of control over when we reduce prices and by how much. Suppliers will be expected to follow suit with component price reductions. Overhead will be kept at a minimum via the following:

- Operations management.
- Free engineering factor.
- Extensive use of subcontractors.
- Early automation.

PC-Build does not assemble PCs in house; therefore, fixed costs are naturally lower. Our operations are mainly for packing and shipping. The main fixed costs will be for rented space.

EXHIBIT E

Supplier Selection Criteria

Criterion	Specific Target	Description
Price	10–15% less than industry average	Suppliers must offer prices that are less than industry standard. This standard will be calculated based on public sources.
Discounts	Quality based	PC-Build will strive for high-volume purchases. Suppliers are required to offer additional discounts at quantities of 100, 250, and 500 units.
Quality	Zero defect target	Each supplier must embrace some type of quality management program. Annual defects cannot exceed 2% of purchases.
Delivery	Same week delivery	Average order-processing time should range from one to two weeks.
Expandability	N/A	Suppliers who can easily meet orders of up to 1,000 units will be given priority.
Technology	N/A	PC-Build will be expanding to EDI* ordering within two years. All suppliers should have or be planning EDI.
Terms	30 days	PC-Build expects credit terms from all suppliers.
Obsolete stock	Negotiable	Suppliers should have some type of buyback provision for obsolete components.
Warranty	One year	All suppliers *must* offer a one-year warranty.

*EDI stands for electronic data interchange.

As mentioned, PC-Build will make extensive use of its suppliers. In the beginning, all components will be sources outside the company; no internal manufacturing will be done. There is an abundance of component suppliers in the marketplace. PC-Build has developed a supplier certification process to ensure good supplier selection. *Exhibit E* outlines our supplier selection criteria. By waiting until a new standard develops in the marketplace, PC-Build gets its systems engineered for free. Suppliers have developed expertise with the new technology and it has been market tested.

PC-Build's entire operations will be computerized from the beginning. Order processing, manufacturing, accounting, and purchasing will be automated. The toll-free phone network will be managed by a voice messaging service. By automating in the initial stages of the corporation PC-Build can grow without significant additions to administrative overhead.

Exhibit F lists first-year fixed costs and details the PC-Build break-even point. Under the most conservative scenario, the company will break even after selling 1,300 units, with an average gross profit of 30 percent. This projection is *very* conservative. It assumes that all sales are for the B2000, and no higher priced kits are included. Based on our sales forecast, we should break even within the first 10 months of operations.

The company produces a positive cash flow from operations within two months, but returns to negative cash flows two months later. (See *Exhibit G* for pro forma cash flow statement.) This is due to the highly cyclical nature of sales to computer education camps. The company will be spending a minimum amount on advertising, development, and salaries, yet can achieve significant unit sales.

However, camp sales are highly cyclical, occurring only during the summer months. As the summer ends, the initial marketing effort toward the home hobbyist begins. Home sales will also be cyclical, peaking during Christmas and late spring (graduation, beginning of summer). The company will have continuous positive cash flow from the operations after the seventh month.

Marketing Plan

Overall Marketing Strategy

The company's overall marketing strategy will be to appeal to our target markets' demonstrated desire to experiment and learn. PC-Build will be the company of reference for personal computer kits on the MS-DOS platform. The company will establish this position by means of a two-pronged marketing attack:

- Heavy personal selling and advertising in the education channel. This means high-school level computer science curricula and computer camps. Penetration of this market segment has already begun and will be the primary focus of the company's early efforts. This segment will provide the volume needed to fund the early stages of the product adoption phase in the home hobby market.
- The home hobby market is represented by single-unit sales to end users either directly or through a distribution channel.

PC-Build will differentiate itself by emphasizing the user-friendly, high-quality service and documentation approach that marks the success of our corporate cousins in the ready-to-serve PC market.

EXHIBIT F

PC-Build: Cost Analysis and Break-Even Levels

| | Cost Analysis | | | |
| | Fixed and Semivariable Costs | | | Fixed Costs Only |
	Start-up	Six Month	One Year	One Year
Office	$ 0	3,000	$ 6,000	$ 6,000
Inventory	15,000	15,000	15,000	15,000
Advertising	15,000	40,000	61,500	50,000
Wages	0	45,000	105,000	80,000
Phone	1,550	4,525	6,800	3,000
Equipment	4,300	4,300	4,300	4,300
Insurance	1,333	8,000	8,000	8,000
Software	1,700	9,700	9,700	9,700
Video	5,500	5,500	5,500	5,500
Printing	4,500	4,500	6,500	4,500
Other	1,700	4,700	7,700	1,700
Total	$50,583	$144,225	$236,000	$187,700

Break-Even Points—First Year,
Conservative Scenario

Costs	Units
Fixed Only	733
Fixed and Semivariable	922

Varied Product Sales	
Fixed Only	430
Fixed and Semivariable	540

Note: Conservative scenario is low-priced-product sales only. Varied sales mix is split evenly between models.

Pricing

Prices start at $699 for the basic 286-based kit and vary according to the central processing unit (CPU), options, and quantities ordered. Prices will be in the low-average range for the content (CPU, options) category, but margins will be above average because of our sourcing and the absence of labor cost for assembly. The price will play a role in positioning the product as a premium value kit. This means that the company's customers will not consider us to be low-budget; rather, they will perceive that they paid a fair price for value received.

"Clone makers" have traditionally gone after market share on the basis of price competitiveness. By purchasing cheap parts in quantity, achieving efficiencies in mass assembly, and distributing in the less-expensive mail-order channel, they have been able to arrive at a cost structure that allows them to undercut the major PC players. The early entrants to this market cycle have been successful, but with low barriers to entry this market is getting crowded. Margins are shrinking as players cut their prices to maintain the gaps between their offerings and those of the major players. Thus, the business is poised on the brink of a shake-out—commodity pricing is putting the clone makers in a hard-to-win situation.

Sales Tactics

Personal selling will be the method of choice for sales to our multiple unit educational and camp customers. This sales effort will be effected by the president and the vice president for product development. An in-house telemarketing staff (one person initially) will close sales and manage inquiries generated by advertisements in general and specialty magazines.

Service and Warranty Policies

The company will include in the price of the kit a 30-day money-back guarantee, and a one-year parts replacement warranty. These types of guarantee mechanisms have become standard in the larger mail-order clone industry, but 30-day money-back guarantees are not standard among our direct competition in PC kits. The components used in the kits are covered by manufacturers' warranties and are tested prior to leaving the factory. Statistically, failure rates of these types of electro-mechanical components have been fairly low, around 3 percent. The company forecasts a much lower (1 percent) component failure rate for the kits because of the following:

- Standard, tested technology.
- Supplier certification process screens for high quality suppliers.
- In-house total quality management program.

EXHIBIT 6

PC-Build: Pro Forma Monthly Cash Flow—Year 1

	Start-up	Month 1 Jul. 1992	Month 2 Aug. 1992	Month 3 Sept. 1992	Month 4 Oct. 1992	Month 5 Nov. 1992	Month 6 Dec. 1992	Month 7 Jan. 1993	Month 8 Feb. 1993	Month 9 Mar. 1993	Month 10 Apr. 1993	Month 11 May 1993	Month 12 June 1993
Sales	$ 0	$ 61,875	$ 82,500	$ 82,500	$123,750	$165,000	$103,125	$ 61,875	$ 61,875	$ 61,875	$ 61,875	$ 82,500	$123,750
Units		75	100	100	150	200	125	75	75	75	75	100	150
Purchases	15,000	41,775	55,700	55,700	83,550	111,400	69,625	41,775	41,775	41,775	41,775	55,700	83,550
A/R collections	0	0	60,328	80,438	80,438	120,656	160,875	100,547	60,328	60,328	60,328	60,328	80,438
A/R payments	7,500	7,500	41,775	55,700	55,700	83,550	111,400	69,625	41,775	41,775	41,775	41,775	55,700
Office	0	500	500	500	500	500	500	500	500	500	500	500	500
Advertising/ promo	15,000	1,500	1,500	5,000	5,000	7,000	5,000	1,500	1,500	5,000	7,000	5,000	1,500
Wages	0	5,000	5,000	7,000	9,000	9,000	10,000	9,000	9,000	9,000	10,000	11,000	12,000
Commissions	0	0	0	0	0	0	0	0	0	0	0	0	0
Utilities	0	0	0	0	0	3,506	0	0	0	3,919	0	3,500	0
Phone	1,750	500	500	500	500	500	550	550	550	550	550	550	550
Equipment	4,300	338	400	400	525	650	463	338	338	338	338	400	525
Insurance	6,000	0	0	0	0	0	0	0	0	0	0	0	0
Software	9,700	0	0	0	0	0	2,000	0	0	0	0	0	0
Video	5,500	0	0	0	0	0	0	0	0	0	0	0	0
Warranty exp.	0	0	0	0	0	0	0	0	0	0	0	200	0
Printing	4,500	0	0	0	0	0	0	0	0	0	0	0	0
Other	1,700	500	500	500	500	500	500	500	500	500	500	500	50
Cash needs	−55,950	−15,838	10,103	10,788	8,663	15,400	30,413	18,484	6,116	−1,303	−384	−7,147	9,113
+ Carry over	90,000	34,050	18,213	28,316	39,103	47,766	63,166	93,578	112,063	118,178	116,875	116,491	109,344
Ending Cash	$ 34,050	$ 18,213	$ 28,316	$ 39,103	$ 47,766	$ 63,166	$ 93,578	$112,063	$118,178	$116,875	$116,491	$109,344	$118,456
Cash flow from operations	−55,950	−71,788	−61,684	−50,897	−42,234	−26,834	3,578	22,063	28,178	26,875	26,491	19,344	28,456

(Continued)

EXHIBIT 6 (concluded)

Pro Forma Monthly Cash Flow—Year 2

	Month 1 July 1993	Month 2 Aug. 1993	Month 3 Sept. 1993	Month 4 Oct. 1993	Month 5 Nov. 1993	Month 6 Dec. 1993	Month 7 Jan. 1994	Month 8 Feb. 1994	Month 9 Mar. 1994	Month 10 Apr. 1994	Month 11 May 1994	Month 12 June 1994
Sales	$165,000	$247,500	$123,750	$206,250	$247,500	$247,500	$123,750	$82,500	$103,125	$165,000	$165,000	$185,625
Units	200	300	150	250	300	300	150	100	125	200	200	225
Purchases	111,400	167,100	83,550	139,250	167,100	167,100	83,550	55,700	69,625	111,400	111,400	125,325
A/R collections	120,656	160,875	241,313	120,656	201,094	241,313	241,313	120,656	80,438	100,547	160,875	160,875
A/P payments	83,550	111,400	167,100	83,550	139,250	167,100	167,100	83,550	55,700	69,625	111,400	111,400
Office	833	833	833	833	833	833	833	833	833	833	833	833
Advertising/promo	3,000	5,000	7,000	8,000	9,000	8,000	3,000	3,000	5,000	7,000	8,000	3,000
Wages	12,000	14,000	15,000	15,000	16,000	17,000	14,000	14,000	14,000	14,000	14,000	14,000
Commissions	3,300	0	0	0	7,425	0	0	0	7,013	0	0	0
Utilities	600	600	600	600	600	600	600	600	600	600	600	600
Phone	650	900	525	775	900	900	525	400	463	650	650	713
Equipment	0	0	0	0	0	2,000	0	0	0	0	0	0
Insurance	6,000	0	0	0	0	2,000	2,500	0	0	0	0	0
Software	0	0	2,000	0	0	2,000	0	0	2,000	0	0	2,000
Video	50	50	50	50	50	50	75	75	75	75	75	0
Warranty exp.	0	0	2,000	0	0	2,000	0	0	2,000	0	0	2,000
Printing	500	500	500	500	500	500	500	500	500	500	500	500
Other												
Cash needs	10,173	27,592	45,704	11,348	26,535	40,329	52,179	17,698	−7,746	7,264	24,817	25,729
+ Carryover	118,456	128,629	156,221	201,925	213,273	239,808	280,138	332,317	350,015	342,269	349,532	374,349
Ending cash	$128,629	$158,221	$201,925	$213,273	$239,808	$280,138	$332,317	$350,015	$342,269	$349,532	$374,349	$400,078
Cash flow from operations	38,629	66,221	111,925	123,273	149,808	190,138	242,317	260,015	252,269	259,532	284,349	310,078

Notes: 30-day collection on all receivables (ignores MC/Visa payment).
30-day collection on all payables.
Start-up funds are detailed in business plan.
To be conservative, all sales are forecasted as low-end products (Basic kit w/B&W VGA).
One-half of initial inventory will be purchased on cash terms.
Cyclical sales indicated by surges before Christmas and summer.
A/R collections reflect 2.5% discount for MC/VISA purchases.
Payroll reflects additional hirings per schedule.
Phone charges are minimum of $150 per month plus $2.50 per sale.
Initial software/video/manual production will be 1,000 units.
Minimum $15,000 cash balance is added for unforeseen expenses.
Warranty costs include postage and handling of replacement parts.
Commissions are 1% of sales and are paid quarterly.

EXHIBIT H

First-Year Advertising Budget

Publication	Circulation	Ad Price	Number of Ads	Total
Popular Electronics	152,000	$2,200	4	$ 8,800
Popular Science	750,000	6,200	4	24,800
Discover	450,000	5,400	2	10,800
Electronic Learning	87,000	2,325	2	4,650
PC Home Journal	500,000	5,500	2	11,000
Computer Buyer's	Special Issue	3,000	1	3,000
Total advertising				$63,050
Initial press releases				2,000
Trade shows				5,000
Grand total				$70,050

Advertising and Promotion

Advertising and promotion strategy is linked directly to the channel being targeted. End-user sales will be sought with print advertisements in several periodicals. The choice of periodical is very important to the success of the advertising campaign because of the specialty nature of our product. While mainstream computer magazines may be a part of our customers' reading "diet," hobbyists have their own subculture and sources of information in which we must appear to gain acceptance by the early adopter and hard-core hobbyists. See *Exhibit H* for a list of magazines which the company feels adequately reach our target audience. The print campaign will have two primary focuses driving it:

- Create awareness of the company and its products.
- Sell boxes.

The company will endeavor to obtain low-cost or free promotion in the form of news reports or endorsements from industry luminaries. Press releases will be distributed regularly, as will copies of the instruction video and a video of young campers having fun putting together the standard kit.

Distribution

As time progresses and unit volume grows, the company's main channel of distribution will evolve from direct sales to retail. As a small, unknown company, we would have limited leverage with retailers and be forced to accept lower margins. Further, research has shown that the competition and the early mail-order PC success stories have gone direct first and retail later and not vice versa. Dell, for example, made its mark as a high-quality mail-order supplier and then began selling through retailers. On the flip side, industry giant IBM abandoned its plans.

The move to retail will come when the company's market position is such that it can sustain itself in that realm. Among the factors contributing to the decision to make the move will be sales volume (demand), the financing situation and other company economics, and the existence of a suitable strategic partner to be the primary retail distributor.

Design and Development Plans

The development process is ongoing. To date, an initial prototype has been completed and is fully functional. The Quickstart program is complete and operational. Several key development tasks still must be completed:

- Final system specification.
- Final prototype production.
- Video production.
- Supplier selection/certification.
- Manual development.

These items are not mutually exclusive. The order in which they are listed is the order in which they must be completed. A certain amount of work can be done concurrently, but the system specifications must be completed before any other work can be finished. *Exhibit I* is a general breakdown of time and money required for each task.

EXHIBIT I

Development Plans

Task	Money Required	Time
System specifications	0	Eight weeks
Supplier selection	$ 500	Four weeks
Prototype production	1,500	Two weeks
Manual development	4,000	Six weeks
Video production	5,500	Six weeks

Please note: PC-Build kits will be FCC Class B certified. FCC certification means the product is suitable for home use. We have located several suppliers who have Class B certification for the cabinet/motherboard configurations. In addition, all suppliers' components must be Class B certified.

Future Products

PC-Build will upgrade its kits based on a predefined technology-screening system. This system can best be illustrated by applying it to the next level of Intel chip, the 486DX. This system will be applied to all new technologies, not just to Intel chips. PC-Build will begin offering 486DX-based kits when the following criteria have been met:

1. *Demonstrated market acceptance.* The new chip should account for at least 20 percent of new PC sales before it will be considered by PC-Build. This 20 percent hurdle ensures market acceptance and significant volume to push unit costs within PC-Build's customer's price range. 486DX sales only account for 10 percent of current unit volume.

2. *Reliable supplier base.* All new motherboard suppliers must meet supplier certification requirements. Existing suppliers will be reevaluated with respect to their new motherboard. A limited number of 486DX suppliers meet PC-Build's selection criteria.

3. *Unit cost decreases.* The price difference between the new technology versus PC-Build's current technology must not exceed 30 percent. Currently, 486DX-based motherboards are 85 percent more expensive than 486SX-based boards.

Proprietary Issues

The company is seeking and is in the process of copyrighting the following:

- Instructional video.
- Instructional manual.
- Computer set-up program.
- Advertising copy.

The company name, logo, model names, and Quickstart program will all be registered trademarks of the corporation.

Manufacturing and Operations Plan

PC-Build has located its main facilities in Wellesley, Massachusetts. This location was chosen for three main reasons: (1) cost, (2) location, and (3) expandability.

Discovery Curve has signed a 14-month lease for 1,500 square feet at $1,000 a month. This includes heat, electricity, furniture, and the use of an existing phone system.

Actual production is relatively simple. PC-Build's operations are essentially for packing and shipping; all other production is subcontracted. No major fixed investment in manufacturing is required other than for assembly, storage, and staging equipment. The initial 1,500 square feet can support production of up to 500 units per month. A bigger storage area and extra shipping bays will be needed if capacity exceeds this level.

Manufacturing Policy

Manufacturing will be done using a multipurpose assembly line. All three products can be produced quickly using the same line. Inventory will be located at multiple points along the assembly line. (See *Exhibit J.*) Operations seek to leverage the standardization of PC-Build's production lines. Actual production and ordering will be controlled by integrated software. (*Exhibit K* details actual work flow.)

Production and inventory control will follow the basic principle of materials requirements planning. The company will strive to develop and maintain a zero defect rate for its products. This philosophy will be extended to our suppliers. Total quality management is essential to our business. A rejected part will result in an unfinished kit, hence an angry customer.

Operating Cycle

Because PC-Build sells direct, the operating cycle is fairly short. (See *Exhibit L.*) In the best-case scenario, cash is converted within three days after purchase payment. This would be the case if we had a massive demand surge and were producing for back orders. In the conservative scenario, cash is converted within 33 days of initial purchase payment. This is the most likely scenario, since PC-Build is expecting to hold some inventory to meet unexpected demand.

Management Team

Michael Healey, President. Mr. Healey has several years of experience in manufacturing and computer systems. He has served as a project manager for large-scale automation projects. At Automatic Data Processing (ADP) Corporation, he managed new customer implementation of Distribution 2000, ADP's business application software. At Nixdorf Computer Corporation, as an international business consultant, he was the US contact for all activities related to COMET, Nixdorf's worldwide

EXHIBIT J

PC-Build: Operations Flow

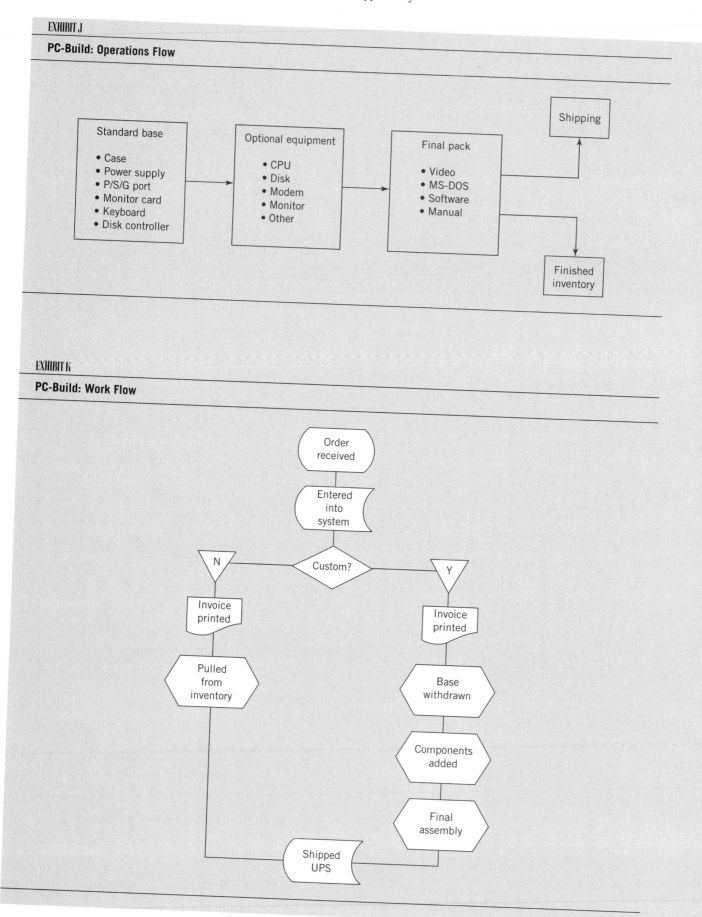

EXHIBIT L

PC-Build: Cash Conversion

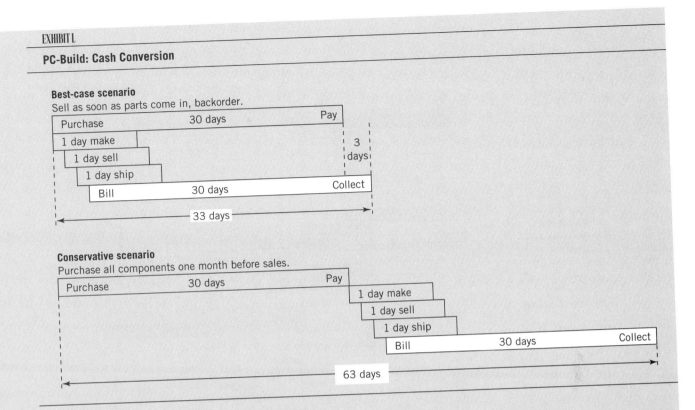

Best-case scenario
Sell as soon as parts come in, backorder.

Conservative scenario
Purchase all components one month before sales.

---

business application software. He successfully developed a series of training materials for the product and has taught both software and hardware courses. He has built several personal computers for customers in the Boston area. Mr. Healey received his master of business administration degree in international business from Babson Graduate School of Business in May 1992. He received his bachelor's degree in management from the University of Massachusetts School of Management in 1986.

Robert P. Lofblad, Vice President, Development and Support. Mr. Lofblad has over 10 years of experience working with personal computers. He has written programs for a variety of applications, from financial analysis to computer games. At Bank Leu in Zurich, he designed an automated system for tracking client positions in derivative securities. At the Boston Company in Boston, he was marketing systems liaison and designed the user interface for the company's telemarketing control system. He has performed systems analysis and design for several local companies, including TBC Funds Distributor, W. A. Wilde Co., Eight Oars, and Corob Corporation. Mr. Lofblad received his master of business administration degree in high-technology marketing from Babson Graduate School of Business in May 1992. He received his bachelor's degree in management information systems from Providence College in 1986.

Mr. Healey and Mr. Lofblad will each receive a year-end bonus, based on pre-tax earnings. This bonus will be based on percentage ownership. (See *Exhibit M* for ownership percentages.)

EXHIBIT M

Compensation/Ownership

Name	Annual Salary	Percent Ownership
Robert Lofblad	$30,000	25%
Michael Healey	30,000	40

Future Team Members

In addition to the two principals, one other key person has committed to PC-Build's program. John Healey will oversee the development and implementation of all educational materials for the education segment. Mr. Healey will also serve on the review committee for the manual development. Mr. Healey has a BS in mathematics and computer science and a masters in education from the University of Lowell. Due to the seasonal nature of educational camp sales, Mr. Healey will continue his full-time teaching position at Trinity Catholic in Newton.

Board of Directors

PC-Build currently has plans for a board of directors of four to seven members. Current members: Kevin Glynn, vice president of sales and marketing, Glynn Electronics; Robert Lofblad, PC-Build; Michael Healey, PC-Build; Paul Storiale, former president, Omni Bank of Connecticut; and one directorship is reserved for representation of equity investors.

Overall Schedule

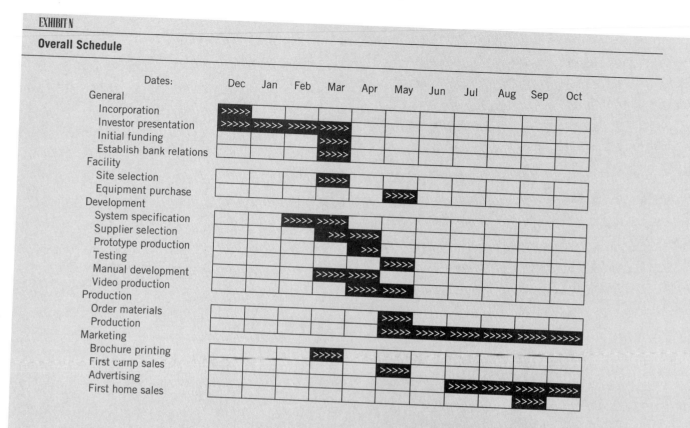

Dates:	Dec	Jan	Feb	Mar	Apr	May	Jun	Jul	Aug	Sep	Oct
General											
Incorporation	>>>>>										
Investor presentation	>>>>>	>>>>>	>>>>>	>>>>>							
Initial funding				>>>>>							
Establish bank relations				>>>>>							
Facility											
Site selection				>>>>>							
Equipment purchase						>>>>>					
Development											
System specification			>>>>>	>>>>>							
Supplier selection				>>>	>>>>>						
Prototype production					>>>						
Testing						>>>>>					
Manual development				>>>>>	>>>>>						
Video production					>>>>>	>>>					
Production											
Order materials						>>>>>					
Production						>>>>>	>>>>>	>>>>>	>>>>>	>>>>>	>>>>>
Marketing											
Brochure printing				>>>>>							
First camp sales						>>>>>					
Advertising						>>>>>					
First home sales							>>>>>	>>>>>	>>>>>	>>>>>	
									>>>>>		

Supporting Professional Staff. PC-Build is represented by James Dangora, of Dangora Associates, as general counsel.

Overall Project Schedule

See *Exhibit N.*

Critical Risks, Problems, and Assumptions

- *Educational sales fail to materialize:*

  Evaluation: Given the size of the educational market (summer camps) and the interest already expressed in this regard, it is unlikely that sales to this segment of the education market will fail to materialize.

  Contingency: PC-Build's survival is not contingent upon the highly cyclical sales of this market. The company aims to derive its main income from the steady demand from home hobbyists. If this market produces no sales at all in the first year, the company can still be profitable.

- *Price cutting continues in market:*

  Evaluation: Price cutting has become commonplace in the PC industry. Older technologies often become commodities. Companies that simply compete on price are constantly seeing margins erode. However, as end user prices of older technologies drop, suppliers follow suit.

  PC-Build has a differentiated product and will therefore not engage in the price wars of the commodity sellers. However, the company realizes that the declining price of the technology does affect PC-Build. The price of our products is partly based on projected labor savings. Our product must be priced below the market price of fully assembled machines. (See *Exhibit O.*)

  Contingency: PC-Build has developed a pricing policy regarding model price reductions. We will reduce prices when the price differential between our kits and a fully assembled substitute drops to 15 percent. PC-Build can sustain price cuts of up to 15 percent on its current prices and still remain in our target gross margin range, 30–40 percent.

- *Swift response from competition (particularly Heathkit):*

  Evaluation: response to our product offering will come from other niche players such as Heathkit. Given the recent purchase of Zenith Data systems by Groupe Bull and the financial difficulties of the former, it is unlikely that Zenith will embrace and support this minuscule and poorly run fraction of Bull's business.

  Contingency: PC-Build will have an established lead over any competitor, seeking to introduce

EXHIBIT O

Pricing Sensitivity Analysis

Markup Levels	Price	Percentage of Sales		
		Basic kit with B&W VGA monitor:		
20% margin	$711.25	Target price	$825.00	
25% margin	758.67	Unit cost	569.00	69.97%
30% margin	812.86	Gross margin	256.00	31.03
35% margin	875.38			
40% margin	948.33			

video-aided education or sales to education institutions. The market entry strategy intentionally avoids direct confrontation with competitors. Within a short time span, our product will be complete and our sales network established. The company will be in a strong position within two years. However, if there is a massive response from a number of large competitors, PC-Build could consider using our strong position as the basis for a quick harvest.

■ *Higher-than-expected sales volume:*

Evaluation: The educational institution is a new channel. There is no market data on the potential sales of computer kits to this segment. We have used extremely conservative figures for this market. Higher-than-expected sales volume is a real possibility.

Contingency: The company should financially be able to meet any unexpected demand from the education market. Computer camps will place orders after they receive applications from new campers. The company can secure interim financing based on these orders. Main capacity is 500 units. The real challenge will be for our suppliers, getting large orders to us in a short period of time. One of the key elements of our supplier selection criteria is the ability to meet demand quickly.

■ *Lower-than-expected sales volumes:*

Evaluation: Given the size of our market, the superiority of our product, and our conservative approach in determining our market share, it is unlikely that our actual sales volume will be substantially less than the volumes estimated.

Contingency: The company already has a low break-even point of 749 units per year. This figure was calculated by using our lowest selling product only. The super and custom kits have approximately the same gross margin percent as the basic kit, but contribute significantly more dollars. A large portion of first-year fixed costs, such as hirings, are based upon our sales

projection. If sales fail to materialize, the company can cut back on non-essential fixed costs. This reduces our break-even point to 521 units. Sales can be less than half of the current forecast (1,200 units) and the company will still make money.

■ *Shut out of supplier network:*

Evaluation: The standardization of the layout of circuit boards has led to a booming OEM business. Entry is easy, and small firms can stay competitive by providing service and support and by pricing competitively. Several manufacturers supply industry giants such as IBM and Compaq, yet few exclusive supply arrangements exist. OEMs benefit from having multiple customers in that demand risk is dispersed and product life is extended. The relative bargaining power of customer groups also remains less threatening. Additionally, overseas suppliers are marketing their products more aggressively in the United States. The industry trend toward less concentration and more internationalization is expected to continue as worldwide competition increases. Being shut out of the supplier network is highly unlikely.

Contingency: If a shutout occurs, PC-Build can source components from non–U.S.-based manufacturers interested in breaking into the U.S. market. Another option would be to license older technologies and manufacture components in-house. The viability of this alternative depends on the circumstances then at hand.

■ *Delays in design or manufacturing:*

Evaluation: Several key development tasks must still be completed. The execution of the first phase of our planned entry strategy depends on the completion of the following key development tasks:
—Final system specification.
—Final prototype production.
—Video production.
—Supplier selection/certification.
—Manual development.

These tasks must be completed in the order listed. The estimated time frame for completion is 14 weeks. Currently 24 weeks remain before the planned roll-out in June 1992. Allowing for double the planned normal production lead-time, 22 weeks remain. A buffer of eight weeks thus remains in the event of manufacturing delays. A delay is not anticipated.

Contingency: In the event of a delay extending beyond this period, PC-Build will be rolled out in November of 1992 in accordance with its planned entry into the home hobbyist market. The final development tasks necessary to enter this market can be completed simultaneously and will take up to a maximum of 12 weeks. This leaves us with an additional 16 weeks to complete the initial tasks. Since the company's survival is not dependent upon the education market, a delay, however disappointing, will not be fatal.

The Financial Plan

Detailed financial forecasts for the first several years of operations have been created utilizing figures from sales forecasts, pricing strategy, detailed cost estimates, overhead budgets and hiring schedules. (See *Exhibits P* through *S* and *Exhibit U* for these forecasts.) All projections are based in 1991 dollars. PC-Build's fiscal year is from July 1 to June 30.

Break-even Analysis

The worst-case scenario break-even point for the company is 1,300 units. We felt this is a very conservative figure. This figure was calculated by using the dollar contribution of our lowest priced product only.

The SX3000, SX4000, and custom kits have approximately the same gross margin percent as the basic kit, but contribute significantly more dollars. The actual sales mix does not affect fixed costs; therefore, to be conservative we used the lowest contributor. If PC-Build simply achieves an even sales mix of all three products, the break-even point drops to 521 units. (See *Exhibit R.*)

Balance Sheet

PC Build's proposed financial plan provides excellent financial strength and liquidity. Company operations are designed to be lean and to reflect this in the balance sheet. (See *Exhibit S.*) Accounts receivable payments do not represent a significant risk for the company; most payments will be made using Visa or Mastercard (MC).

EXHIBIT P

Initial Capital Equipment

Capital Equipment

	Cost
Three personal computers	$ 1,800
Two printers	500
Fax machine	450
Phone system	1,000
Phone lines	300
Production equipment	2,000
Software	8,000
Total equipment	$14,050

Other Expenses

	Cost
Brochure printing	$500
Documentation printing	4,000
Software production	1,500
Software copying	200
Video production	3,500
Video copying	2,000
Prototype system	2,000
Initial inventory	15,000
Initial advertising	15,000
Travel/entertainment	5,000
Other	2,250
Total	$50,950

Additional working capital estimate: (derived by examining sales forecast cash conversion cycle, and desired minimum cash balance of $15,000)	34,000
Total funds needed	
	$99,000

70

EXHIBIT 0

Pro Forma Income Statement, Years 1–5

	Year 1	Percent	Year 2	Percent	Year 3	Percent	Year 4	Percent	Year 5	Percent
Gross sales	$1,237,500	100.00%	$2,000,000	100.00%	$2,500,000	100.00%	$3,000,000	100.00%	$3,600,000	100.00%
Less discounts	49,500	4.00	80,000	4.00	100,000	4.00	120,000	4.00	144,000	4.00
Net sales	1,188,000	96.00	1,920,000	96.00	2,400,000	96.00	2,880,000	96.00	3,456,000	96.00
COGS	853,500	68.97	1,379,394	68.97	1,724,242	68.97	2,069,091	68.97	2,482,909	68.97
Gross profit	334,500	27.03	540,606	27.03	675,758	27.03	810,909	27.03	973,091	27.03
Office	6,000	0.48	10,000	0.50	12,000	0.48	12,000	0.40	12,000	0.33
Advertising	61,500	4.97	69,000	3.45	100,000	4.00	110,000	3.67	120,000	3.33
Wages	105,000	8.48	173,000	8.65	198,950	7.96	238,740	7.96	286,488	7.96
Commissions	11,880	0.96	19,200	0.96	24,000	0.96	28,800	0.96	34,560	0.96
Utilities	6,350	0.51	7,200	0.36	9,000	0.36	10,800	0.36	12,960	0.36
Phone	6,800	0.55	8,050	0.40	10,063	0.40	12,075	0.40	14,490	0.40
Depreciation	2,679	0.22	3,250	0.16	4,107	0.16	4,800	0.16	5,760	0.16
Insurance	8,000	0.65	8,000	0.40	8,800	0.35	9,400	0.31	10,000	0.28
R&D	1,700	0.14	2,500	0.13	3,500	0.14	5,000	0.17	5,000	0.14
Travel/entertainment	5,700	0.46	8,000	0.40	10,000	0.40	12,000	0.40	14,000	0.39
Printing	5,500	0.44	6,500	0.33	7,500	0.30	8,500	0.28	9,500	0.26
Other	7,700	0.62	6,000	0.30	5,000	0.20	6,000	0.20	7,200	0.20
EBT	105,691	8.54	219,906	11.00	282,838	11.31	352,794	11.76	441,133	12.25
Income tax	31,707	2.56	65,972	3.30	84,851	3.39	105,838	3.53	132,340	3.68
Projected net profit	$ 73,984	5.98%	$ 153,934	7.70%	$ 197,987	7.92%	$ 246,956	8.23%	$ 308,793	8.58%

Note: All figures are displayed before management bonuses/profit sharing (see "Compensation and Dividends" section).

EXHIBIT R

PC-Build: Break-Even Analysis (1 Year)

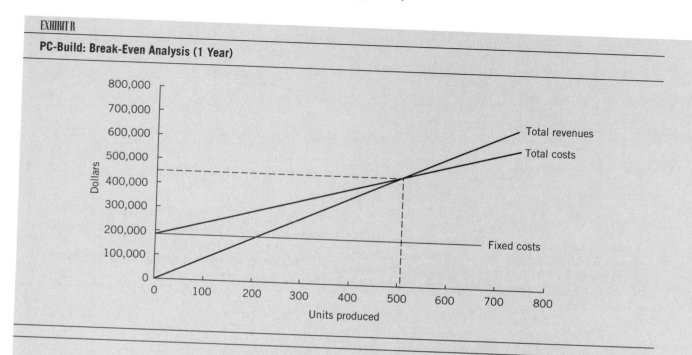

EXHIBIT S

Pro Forma Balance Sheets

			Fiscal Years Ended June 30, 1992–1994			
	1992	Percent	1993	Percent	1994	Percent
Current Assets						
Cash	$118,456	33.82%	$310,078	49.83%	$400,000	46.48%
Accounts Receivable	123,750	35.33	185,625	29.83	235,000	27.31
Inventory	92,000	26.26	107,040	17.20	195,000	22.66
Total Current Assets	334,206	95.41	602,743	96.87	830,000	96.44
Fixed Assets						
Computer system	14,000	4.00	14,000	2.25	25,000	2.90
Manufacturing equipment	2,000	0.57	4,000	0.64	5,000	0.58
Furnitures/fixtures	2,750	0.79	4,750	0.76	5,750	0.67
Less: Depreciation	(2,679)	−0.76	(3,250)	−0.52	(5,107)	−0.59
Net Fixed Assets	16,071	4.59	19,500	3.13	30,643	3.56
Total Assets	$350,278	100.00%	$622,243	100.00%	$860,643	100.00%
Current Liabilities						
Accounts Payable	$ 83,550	23.85%	$125,325	20.14%	$154,916	18.00%
Accrued Expenses	83,744	23.91	160,000	25.71	170,823	19.85
Total Current Liabilities	$167,294	47.76%	$285,325	45.85%	$325,739	37.85
Equity						
Capital stock	$ 10,000	2.85%	10,000	1.61%	10,000	1.16%
Paid-in surplus	99,000	28.26	99,000	15.91	99,000	11.50
Retained earnings	73,984	21.12	227,918	36.63	425,905	49.49
Total equity	182,984	52.24	336,918	54.15	534,905	62.15
Total liabilities and equity	$350,278	100.00%	$622,243	100.00%	$860,643	100.00%

The company has intentionally set high working capital requirements as a buffer against unforeseen contingencies. Balance sheet assumptions are:

- 30 day terms on receivables and payables.
- Accounts receivable reflect a 2 percent payment of MC/Visa.
- No significant debt financing.
- Inventories turn 6–12 times per year.

Income Statement

Company sales are forecast to increase from $1.2 million in 1992 to $3.6 million by 1996. First-year net profit is only $93,014, which represents 8.5 percent of sales. This figure is expected to climb steadily over the next five years, mainly through realization of economies of scale with respect to direct marketing, operations, and product development. Net profit margins are 14 percent by 1996.

Cash Flows

Equity capital raised at start-up should be enough to finance PC-Build's operations. The company expects positive cash flow from operations after seven months of operations. However month-to-month cash flows are subject to cyclical swings, particularly during the off months, January–March. The company intends to limit expenditures during this time period, minimizing the negative impact on cash balances.

Proposed Company Offering

PC-Build was incorporated in February 1992, with 20,000 shares of common voting stock authorized. The company issued 6,500 shares to the founders in exchange for their initial contributions.

The company is planning to issue an additional 3,000 shares to outside investors at $33 per share. The common stock sold will represent 30 percent of the outstanding stock. Any future stock issues will be offered to current shareholders first.

Offering: All partners and the outside investor receive common stock in return for effort and investments in the proportions described in *Exhibit T*.

Dividend Payments. The company will pay dividends during the first profitable year. Dividends will be paid on a quarterly basis, and will be equal to 25 percent of projected after-tax profits.

EXHIBIT T

Proposed Offering

Name	Percent Ownership	Number of Shares
Robert Lofblad	25%	2,500
Michael Healey	40	4,000
Board Members	3	300
Outside Investors	30	3,000

Note: The shares being offered to all the investors are restricted securities and may not be sold readily.

EXHIBIT U

Hiring Schedule

	Responsibilities	Hire Dates
Initial staff:		
M. Healey	President	Start-up
B. Lofblad	Tech support/development	Start-up
Part-time telemarketer	Sales/sales support	Start-up
Variable staff:		
Trainers	Computer camp training	Seasonal
Sales and marketing:		
Unknown	Director sales/marketing	January 1993
Telemarketer (2)	Sales/sales support	November 1992
Outside sales	Sales	March 1993
Technical/administrative support:		
B. Batra	Production/development	Part-time
Tech Support		April 1993
Secretary		June 1993
Operations:		
Assembly		December 1992
Shipping		May 1993

Note: Projections are based on sales forecasts in cash flow. The company will adjust hiring based on actual sales.

Chapter Three

The Opportunity: Creating, Shaping, Recognizing, Seizing

I was seldom able to see an opportunity, until it ceased to be one.

Mark Twain

Results Expected

At the conclusion of this chapter, you will have:

1. Examined the roles of ideas, pattern recognition, and the creative process in entrepreneurship.
2. Defined the differences between an idea and an opportunity.
3. Examined opportunity via a zoom lens on the criteria used by successful entrepreneurs, angels, and venture capital investors in evaluating potential ventures.
4. Identified sources of information for finding and screening venture opportunities.
5. Generated some new venture ideas and your personal criteria using the Idea Generation Exercise.
6. Analyzed the Roxanne Quimby case.

Opportunity through a Zoom Lens

As incomprehensible as 39 rejections may be for many, the original proposal by founder Scott Cook to launch a new software company called Intuit was turned down by that many venture capital investors before it was funded. Thousands of similar examples illustrate just how complex, subtle, and situational (at the time, in the marketspace, the investor's other alternatives, etc.) is the opportunity recognition process. If the brightest, most knowledgeable, and most sophisticated investors in the world miss opportunities like Intuit, we surely can conclude that the journey from idea to high-potential opportunity is elusive, contradictory, and perilous. Think of this journey as occurring on a highly flexible, pliable, three-dimensional relief map that is rapidly undulat-ing on all axes. The journey consists of full sunshine and straight, smooth superhighways, as well as twist-ing, turning, up-and-down narrow passages that lead to breathtaking views. Along the way you also will en-counter tornadoes, dust storms, hurricanes, and vol-canoes. All too often you seem to run out of gas with none in sight, and flat tires come when you least ex-pect them. This is the entrepreneur's journey.

Transforming Caterpillars into Butterflies

This chapter is dedicated to making that journey more friendly by focusing a zoom lens on the oppor-tunity. This chapter shares the road maps and bench-marks used by successful entrepreneurs, venture capitalists, angels, and other private equity investors in their quest to transform the often shapeless caterpillar of an idea into a spectacular butterfly of a venture. Finally, this chapter examines the role of ideas and pattern recognition in the creative process of entrepreneurship.

You will come to see the criteria used to identify higher-potential ventures as jumping-off points of the opportunity continuum, rather than mere end points. One to 10 out of 100 entrepreneurs create ventures that emerge from the pack. Examined through a zoom lens, these ventures reveal a highly dynamic, constantly changing work in progress, not a pat formula or items on a checklist. This highly organic and situational character of the entrepreneurial process underscores the criticality of determining *fit* and balancing *risk and reward*. As the author has argued for three decades: The business plan is obsolete as soon as it is printed! It is in the shaping process that the best entrepreneurial leaders and investors add the greatest value to the enterprise, and creatively transform what may appear as a mundane caterpillar of an idea into a magnificent butterfly of a venture.

The Role of Ideas

Ideas As Tools

It is worth emphasizing again that *a good idea is nothing more than a tool in the hands of an entrepreneur.* Finding a good idea is the *first* step in the task of converting an entrepreneur's creativity into an opportunity.

The importance of the idea is most often overrated, usually at the expense of underemphasizing the need for products or services, or both, which can be sold in enough quantity to real customers.

Further, the new business that simply bursts from a flash of brilliance is rare. What is usually necessary is a series of trial-and-error iterations, or repetitions, before a crude and promising product or service fits with what the customer is really willing to pay for. After all, Howard Head made 40 different metal skis before he finally made the model that worked consistently. In fact, with surprising frequency, major businesses are built around totally different products than those originally envisioned. Consider these examples:

- F. Leland Strange, the founder and president of Quadram, a maker of graphics and communications boards and other boards for microcomputers, told the story of how he developed his marketing idea

into a company with $100 million in sales in three years.[1] He stated that he had developed a business plan to launch his company, and the company even hit projected revenues for the first two years. He noted, however, that success was achieved with completely *different* products than those in the original plan.

- Polaroid Corporation was founded with a product based on the principle of polarizing light waves, a discovery by Dr. Land that he patented. Polarized head lamps, it was reasoned, would have the compelling safety feature of reducing head-on collisions caused at night by "blinding" by oncoming lights. Conceivably, such polarized lamps could be installed by car manufacturers in every vehicle manufactured. However, the company grew to its present $2 billion-plus size through a quite different application of the original technology—instant photography.

- IBM began in the wire and cable business and later expanded to time clocks. Sales in the 1920s were only a few million dollars a year. Its successful mainframe computer business and then its successful personal computer business emerged much later.

As one entrepreneur expressed it:

Perhaps the existence of business plans and the language of business give a misleading impression of business building as a rational process. But, as any entrepreneur can confirm, starting a business is very much a series of fits and starts, brainstorms and barriers. Creating a business is a round of chance encounters that leads to new opportunities and ideas, mistakes that turn into miracles.[2]

The Great Mousetrap Fallacy

Perhaps no one did a greater disservice to generations of would-be entrepreneurs than Ralph Waldo Emerson in his oft-quoted line: "If a man can make a better mousetrap than his neighbor, though he builds his house in the woods the world will make a beaten path to his door."

What can be called the great mousetrap fallacy was thus spawned. Indeed, it is often assumed that success is possible if an entrepreneur can just come up with a new idea. And, in today's changing world, if the idea has anything to do with technology, success is certain—or so it would seem.

The truth of the matter is that ideas are inert and, for all practical purposes, worthless. Further, the flow

---

[1] Keynote address at the 1984 Babson Entrepreneurship Research Conference, cosponsored by the School of Management, Georgia Institute of Technology, April 23–25, 1984, Atlanta, Georgia.

[2] Joline Godfrey, *Our Wildest Dreams: Women Entrepreneurs, Making Money, Having Fun, Doing Good* (New York: Harper Business, 1992), p. 27.

of ideas is really quite phenomenal. Venture capital investors, for instance, during the investing boom of the 1980s, received as many as 100 to 200 proposals and business plans each month. Only 1 to 3 percent of these actually received financing, however.

Yet the fallacy persists despite the lessons of practical experience noted long ago in the insightful reply to Emerson by O. B. Winters: "The manufacturer who waits for the world to beat a path to his door is a great optimist. But the manufacturer who shows this 'mousetrap' to the world keeps the smoke coming out his chimney."

Contributors to the Fallacy

One cannot blame it all on Ralph Waldo Emerson. There are several reasons for the perpetuation of the fallacy. One is the portrayal in oversimplified accounts of the ease and genius with which such ventures as Xerox, IBM, and Polaroid have made their founders wealthy. Unfortunately, these exceptions do not provide a useful rule to guide aspiring entrepreneurs.

Another is that inventors seem particularly prone to mousetrap myopia. Perhaps, like Emerson, they are substantially sheltered in viewpoint and experience from the tough, competitive realities of the business world. Consequently, they may underestimate, if not seriously downgrade, the importance of what it takes to make a business succeed. Frankly, inventing and brainstorming may be a lot more fun than the careful and diligent observation, investigation, and nurturing of customers that are often required to sell a product or service.

Contributing also to the great mousetrap fallacy is the tremendous psychological ownership attached to an invention or, later, to a new product. This attachment is different from attachment to a business. The intense and highly involved personal identity and commitment to an invention or new widget tends to weaken or preclude entirely realistic assessment of the other crucial aspects of the business. While an intense level of psychological ownership and involvement is certainly a prerequisite for creating a new business, the fatal flaw in attachment to an invention or product is the narrowness of its focus. The focal point needs to be the building of the business, rather than just one aspect of it, the idea.

Another source of mousetrap myopia lies in a technical and scientific orientation, that is, a desire to do it better. A good illustration of this is the experience of a Canadian entrepreneur who founded, with his brother, a company to manufacture truck seats. The entrepreneur's brother had developed a new seat for trucks that was a definite improvement over other seats. The entrepreneur knew he could profitably sell the seat his brother had designed, and they did so. When they needed more manufacturing capacity, one brother was not as interested in manufacturing more of the first seat, but he had several ideas on how to improve the seat. The first brother stated: "If I had listened to him, we probably would be a small custom shop today, or out of business. Instead, we concentrated on making seats that would sell at a profit, rather than just making a better and better seat. Our company has several million dollars of sales today and is profitable."

The Best Idea

Consider the following examples, which drive home the point that having the best technology or idea by itself often does not make the critical difference in success:

- UNIVAC had the early elegance and technology lead over IBM in computers, but it was never able to seize the emerging, significant opportunities in the computer industry.

- In 1967 and 1968, a lead investor, Fred Adler, received over 50 business plans from entrepreneurs who proposed to start minicomputer firms. Several minicomputer companies were started at that time, and several of the firms actually had a better idea in the form of more advanced technology than the one that most attracted Adler's attention. Data General's lead entrepreneur and his team had an entrepreneurial flair and market focus, which Adler bet on.[3] In 1988, the company had sales of $1.3 billion.

- In 1969, the then-fledgling Cullinet, Inc., raised $500,000 in the then-hot new issues market. Two years later, the firm had spent this initial capital, and according to its founder, John Cullinane, still had a payroll of $8,500 to meet. Cullinane said the money had been spent unwisely through "programmer anarchy." He turned the company around by firing his programmers since, he said, they did not understand what happiness was. "Happiness," Cullinane said, "is a satisfied customer."[4] He then developed customer-anchored software products and a plan for growth that led to a substantial venture capital investment during a lean time for venture capital.

---

[3] The story of the entrepreneurial culture at Data General was told in a best-seller by Tracy Kidder, *The Soul of a New Machine* (Boston: Little, Brown, 1981).
[4] Speaking at his induction in 1984 into the Babson College Academy of Distinguished Entrepreneurs.

- Finally, Lotus and its product, Lotus 1-2-3, the first integrated package for the personal computer to include spreadsheet, graphics, and database management capabilities, is a good example. Critics and reviewers have since reported that some new software products are indeed more elegant and sophisticated than Lotus 1-2-3, but new entrants probably require $5 million and up to fund the marketing necessary to launch new software products and gain attention and distribution in this tumultuous marketplace.

Being There First

Further, having the best idea first by no means is a guarantee of success. Again, just ask Adam Osborne, or Dan Bricklin, who was first with the spreadsheet software VisiCalc.

Also, unless having the best idea first also includes the capacity to preempt other competitors by capturing a significant share of the market or by erecting insurmountable barriers to entry, being there first can mean proving for the competition that the market exists to be snared.

Pattern Recognition

The Experience Factor

Since ideas are building tools, one cannot build a successful business without them, as one could not build a house without a hammer. In this regard, experience is vital in looking at new venture ideas. Those with experience have been there before.

Time after time, experienced entrepreneurs exhibit an ability to recognize quickly a pattern—and an opportunity—while it is still taking shape. Herbert Simon, winner of the 1978 Alfred Nobel Prize in Economic Sciences and currently the Richard King Melon University Professor of Computer Science and Psychology at Carnegie-Mellon University, described the recognizing of patterns as a creative process that is not simply logical, linear, and additive. He says that the process often is intuitive and inductive, involving the creative linking, or cross-association, of two or more in-depth "chunks" of experience, know-how, and contacts.[5] Simon contends that it takes 10 years or more for people to accumulate what he calls the "50,000 chunks" of experience, and so forth, that enable them to be highly creative and recognize patterns—familiar circumstances that can be translated from one place to another.

Thus, the process of sorting through ideas and recognizing a pattern also can be compared to the process of fitting pieces into a three-dimensional jigsaw puzzle. It is impossible to assemble such a puzzle by looking at it as a whole unit. Rather, one needs to see the relationships between, and be able to fit together, seemingly unrelated pieces before the whole is visible.

Recognizing ideas which can become entrepreneurial opportunities stems from a capacity to see what others do not—that one plus one equals three, or more. Consider the following examples of the common thread of pattern recognition and creating new businesses by linking knowledge in one field or marketplace with quite different technical, business, or marketing know-how:

- A middle manager employed by a larger company was on a plant tour of a small machinery manufacturer, a customer, in the Midwest. A machinist was mechanically cutting metal during a demonstration of a particular fabricating operation. Shockingly, the machinist accidentally sliced his hand in the cutting machine, removing two fingers. Instantly, the manager recognized that the application of new laser technology for this cutting operation was a significant business opportunity which would make it possible to eliminate such horrible accidents as he had just witnessed. He subsequently launched and built a multimillion-dollar company. Here linking the knowledge of the capabilities of lasers to an old, injury-prone metal-cutting technology yielded an opportunity.

- During travel throughout Europe, the eventual founders of Crate & Barrel frequently saw stylish and innovative products for the kitchen and home that were not yet available in the United States. When they returned home, the founders created Crate & Barrel to offer these products, for which market research had, in a sense, already been conducted in Europe. This knowledge of consumer buying habits in one geographical region, Europe, was applied to a previously untapped consumer market in another country, the United States.

- Howard Head had been an aeronautical design engineer working with new light metal alloys to build more efficient airfoils during World War II. Head transferred knowledge of metal bonding technology from the aircraft manufacturing business to a consumer product, metal skis, and then to another, tennis rackets. In the first case, although he had limited skiing experience, he had concluded that if he could make a metal ski, there would be a signif-

---

[5] Herbert A. Simon, "What We Know About the Creative Process," in R. L. Kuhn (ed.), *Frontiers in Creative and Innovative Management,* 1985, Cambridge, MA, Ballinger Publishing Co. (pp. 3–20).

icant market as a result of the limitations of wooden skis. His company dominated the ski industry for many years. In talking about his decision to develop the oversized Prince tennis racket after he saw a need for ball control among players learning tennis, Head said, "I saw the pattern again that had worked at Head Ski. . . . I had proven to myself before that you can take different technology and know-how and apply it to a solution in a new area."[6] He set about learning the physics of tennis rackets and surfaces and developed the Prince racket.

- In Texas, a young entrepreneur launched a modular home sales business in the late 1970s. First, he parlayed experience as a loan officer with a large New York City bank into a job with a manufacturer of mobile and modular homes in Texas. This enabled him, over a three-year period, to learn the business and to understand the market opportunity. He then opened a sales location in a growing suburb about 25 miles from booming larger cities. By studying his competitors and conducting an analysis of how customers actually went about purchasing new modular homes, he spotted a pattern that meant opportunity. Customers usually shopped at three different locations, where they could see different models and price ranges, before making a purchase decision. Since his market analysis showed there was room in the city for three or four such businesses, he opened two additional sites, each with a different name and with different but complementary lines. Within two years, despite record high interest rates, his business had nearly tripled to $17 million in annual sales, and his only competitor was planning to move.

Enhancing Creative Thinking

The creative thinking described above is of great value in recognizing opportunities, as well as other aspects of entrepreneurship. The notion that creativity can be learned or enhanced holds important implications for entrepreneurs who need to be creative in their thinking. Most people can certainly spot creative flair. Children seem to have it, and many seem to lose it. Several studies suggest that creativity actually peaks around the first grade because a person's life tends to become increasingly structured and defined by others and by institutions. Further, the development in school of intellectual discipline and rigor in thinking takes on greater importance than during the formative years, and most of our education beyond grade school stresses a logical, rational mode of orderly reasoning and thinking. Finally, social pressures may tend to be a taming influence on creativity.

There is evidence that one can enhance creative thinking in later years. Take, for instance, a group called Synectics of Cambridge, Massachusetts, one of the first organizations in the early 1950s to investigate systematically the process of creative thinking and to conduct training sessions in applying creative thinking to business. Underlying the Synectics approach to developing creativity were the following theories:[7]

- The efficiency of a person's creative process can be markedly increased if he or she understands the psychological process by which the process operates.
- The emotional component in the creative process is more important than the intellectual, and the irrational more important than the rational.
- The emotional, irrational elements need to be understood in order to increase the probability of success in a problem-solving situation.

The author participated in one of these training sessions, and it became evident during the sessions that the methods did unlock the thinking process and yielded very imaginative solutions.

Approaches to Unleashing Creativity

Since the 1950s, a good deal has been learned about the workings of the human brain. Today, there is general agreement that the two sides of the brain process information in quite different ways. The left side performs rational, logical functions, while the right side operates the intuitive and nonrational modes of thought. A person uses both sides, actually shifting from one mode to the other (see *Exhibit 3.1*). How to control modes of thought is of interest to entrepreneurs, and they can, perhaps, draw on two interesting approaches.

More recently, professors have focused on the creativity process. For instance, Michael Gordon stressed the importance of creativity and the need for brainstorming in a recent presentation on the elements of personal power. He suggested that creative visualization could be enhanced by using the following 10 brainstorming rules:[8]

1. Define your purpose.
2. Choose participants.
3. Choose a facilitator.

---

[6] Keynote address at the first annual Entrepreneur's Night of UCLA Graduate School of Business, April 18, 1984, Westwood, California.
[7] William J. J. Gordon, *Synectics* (New York: Harper & Row, 1961), p. 6.
[8] Michael Gordon, "Why Personal Power?" Presented at the Price-Babson Reflect, May 1992. Reprinted with permission from Michael Gordon.

EXHIBIT 3.1

Comparison of Left-Mode and Right-Mode Characteristics

L-Mode	R-Mode
Verbal: Using words to name, describe, and define.	*Nonverbal:* Awareness of things, but minimal connection with words.
Analytic: Figuring things out step-by-step and part-by-part.	
Symbolic: Using a symbol to *stand for* something. For example, the sign + stands for the process of addition.	*Synthetic:* Putting things together to form wholes.
	Concrete: Relating to things as they are at the present moment.
Abstract: Taking out a small bit of information and using it to represent the whole thing.	*Analogic:* Seeing likenesses between things; understanding metaphoric relationships.
Temporal: Keeping track of time, sequencing one thing after another, doing first things first, second things second, etc.	*Nontemporal:* Without a sense of time.
Rational: Drawing conclusions based on *reason* and *facts*.	*Nonrational:* Not requiring a basis of reason or facts; willingness to suspend judgment.
Digital: Using numbers as in counting.	
Logical: Drawing conclusions based on logic; one thing following another in logical order—for example, a mathematical theorem or a well-stated argument.	*Spatial:* Seeing where things are in relation to other things, and how parts go together to form a whole.
	Intuitive: Making leaps of insight, often based on incomplete patterns, hunches, feelings, or visual images.
Linear: Thinking in terms of linked ideas, one thought directly following another, often leading to a convergent conclusion.	*Holistic:* Seeing whole things all at once; perceiving the overall patterns and structures, often leading to divergent conclusions.

Source: Betty Edwards, *Drawing on the Right Side of the Brain* (Boston, MA: Houghton Mifflin, 1979), p. 40.

4. Brainstorm spontaneously, copiously.
5. No criticism, no negatives.
6. Record ideas in full view.
7. Invent to the "void."
8. Resist becoming committed to one idea.
9. Identify the most promising ideas.
10. Refine and prioritize.

Team Creativity

Teams of people can generate creativity that may not exist in a single individual. Continually, the creativity of a team of people is impressive, and comparable or better creative solutions to problems evolving from the collective interaction of a small group of people have been observed.

A good example of the creativity generated by using more than one head is that of a company founded by a Babson College graduate with little technical training. He teamed up with a talented inventor, and the entrepreneurial and business know-how of the founder complemented the creative and technical skills of the inventor. The result has been a rapidly growing multimillion-dollar venture in the field of video-based surgical equipment.

Students interested in exploring this further may want at this time to do the Creative Squares exercise at the end of the chapter.

Sources of Opportunities

Source	Percent of Companies
Work activity	47%
Improving an existing product/service	15
Identifying an unfilled niche	11
Other sources	16

Source: Adapted from John Case, "The Origins of Entrepreneurship," INC., June 1989, p. 54. The survey involved 500 of the fastest growing companies.

When Is an Idea an Opportunity?

If an idea is not an opportunity, what is an opportunity?[9] *An opportunity has the qualities of being attractive, durable, and timely and is anchored in a product or service which creates or adds value for its buyer or end user.*

For an opportunity to have these qualities, the "window of opportunity" is opening and remains open long enough. Further, entry into a market with the right characteristics is feasible and the management team is able to achieve it. The venture has or is able to achieve a competitive advantage (i.e., to achieve leverage). Finally, the economics of the venture are rewarding and forgiving and allow significant profit and growth potential.

To repeat, opportunities that have the qualities named above are anchored in a product or service

---

[9] See Jeffry A. Timmons, *New Business Opportunities* (Acton, MA: Brick House Publishing, 1989).

that creates or adds value for its buyer or end user. The most successful entrepreneurs, venture capitalists, and private investors are opportunity-focused; that is, they start with what customers and the marketplace want and do not lose sight of this.

The Real World

Opportunities are created, or built, using ideas and entrepreneurial creativity. Yet, while the image of a carpenter or mason at work is useful, in reality the process is more like the collision of particles in the process of a nuclear reaction or like the spawning of hurricanes over the ocean. Ideas interact with real-world conditions and entrepreneurial creativity at a point in time. The product of this interaction is an opportunity around which a new venture can be created.

The business environment in which an entrepreneur launches his or her venture is usually given and cannot be altered significantly. Despite the assumptions individuals make about social and nonprofit organizations, they too are subject to market forces and economic constraints. Consider, for instance, what would happen to donations if it were perceived that a nonprofit organization was not reinvesting its surplus returns, but instead was paying management excessive salaries. Or what if a socially oriented organization, like the Body Shop, concentrated all its efforts on the social mission, while neglecting profits? Clearly, dealing with suppliers, production costs, labor, and distribution are critical to the health of these social corporations. Thus, social and nonprofit organizations are just as concerned with positive cash flow and generating sufficient cash flows, even though they operate in a different type of market than for-profit organizations. For-profit businesses operate in a free enterprise system characterized by private ownership and profits.

Spawners and Drivers of Opportunities

In a free enterprise system, *opportunities* are spawned when there are changing circumstances, chaos, confusion, inconsistencies, lags or leads, knowledge and information gaps, and a variety of other vacuums in an industry or market.

Changes in the business environment and, therefore, anticipation of these changes, are so critical in entrepreneurship that constant vigilance for changes is a valuable habit. It is thus that an entrepreneur with credibility, creativity, and decisiveness can seize an opportunity while others study it.

Opportunities are situational. Some conditions under which opportunities are spawned are entirely idiosyncratic, while, at other times, they are generalizable and can be applied to other industries, products, or services. In this way, cross-association can trigger in the entrepreneurial mind the crude recognition of existing or impending opportunities. It is often assumed that a marketplace dominated by large, multibillion-dollar players is impenetrable by smaller, entrepreneurial companies. After all, how can you possibly compete with entrenched, resource-rich, established companies? The opposite can be true for several reasons. A number of research projects have shown that it can take 6 years or more for a large company to change its strategy, and even longer to implement the new strategy since it can take 10 years or more to change the culture enough to operate differently. For a new or small company 10 or more years is forever. When Cellular One was launched in Boston, giant NYNEX was the sole competitor. From all estimates they built twice as many towers (at $500,000 each), spent two to three times as much on advertising and marketing, in addition to having a larger head-count. Yet, Cellular One grew from scratch to $100 million in sales in five years and won three customers for every one that NYNEX won. What made this substantial difference? An entrepreneurial management team at Cellular One.

Some of the most exciting opportunities have actually come from fields the conventional wisdom said are the domain of big business: technological innovation. The performance of smaller firms in technological innovation is remarkable—95 percent of the radical innovations since World War II have come from new and small firms, not the giants. In fact, another study from the National Science Foundation found that smaller firms generated *24 times as many innovations* per research and development dollar versus firms with 10,000 or more employees.

There can be exciting opportunities in plain vanilla businesses that might never get the attention of venture capital investors. The revolution in microcomputers, management information systems (MIS), and computer networking has had a profound impact on a number of businesses that had changed little in decades. Take, for instance, the used-auto-wreck and used-auto-parts business, which has not changed in decades. Yet, Pintendre Auto, Inc., saw a new opportunity in this field by applying the latest computer and information technology to a traditional business that relied on crude, manual methods to track inventory and find parts for customers.[10] In just three years, he built a business with $16 million in sales.

---

[10] Barrie McKenna, "More than the Sum of its Parts," *The Globe and Mail*, February 23, 1993, p. B24.

Other regulatory and technology changes can radically alter the way you think about the opportunities because of the economics of sales and distribution for many customer products, from fishing lures to books to cosmetics to sporting goods. By the mid-1990s, there will be 500 or so cable television channels in America versus 40 to 50 for most markets in 1993. A number of new companies up to $100 million in sales have already been built using "infomercials." A 30-minute program can be produced for $50,000 to $150,000 and a half hour of air time can be purchased today for about $20,000 in Los Angeles or for about $4,000 in smaller cities. Compare that with a $25,000+ cost of a full-page advertisement in a monthly magazine. With a large increase in the number of channels, the cost and market focus will undoubtedly improve. Traditional channels of distribution through distributors, wholesalers, specialty stores, and retailers will be completely leapfrogged. Entrepreneurs will find ways to convert those funds previously spent on the profit margin that went to the distribution channel (30 to 50+ percent) to their infomercial marketing budget and to an increased gross margin for their business.

Consider the following broad range of examples that illustrate the phenomenon of vacuums in which opportunities are spawned:

- Deregulation of telecommunications and airlines led to the formation of tens of thousands of new firms in the 1980s, including Cellular One and Federal Express.

- Microcomputer hardware in the early 1980s far outpaced the development of software. The development of the industry was highly dependent on the development of software, leading to aggressive efforts by IBM, Apple, and others to encourage software entrepreneurs to close this gap.

- Many opportunities exist in fragmented, traditional industries that may have a craft or mom-and-pop character and where there is little appreciation or know-how in marketing and finance. Consider such possibilities as fishing lodges, inns, and hotels; cleaners/laundries; hardware stores; pharmacies; waste management plants; flower shops; nurseries; tents; and auto repairs.

- In our service-dominated economy (where 70 percent of businesses are service businesses, versus 30 percent just 25 years ago), customer service, rather than the product itself, can be the critical success factor. One study by the Forum Corporation in Boston showed that 70 percent of customers leave because of poor service and only 15 percent because of price or quality. Can you think of your last "wow" experience with exceptional customer service?

- Sometimes existing competitors cannot, or will not, increase capacity as quickly as the market is moving. For example, the tent industry, as seen in the Outdoor Scene case earlier, was characterized by this capacity stickiness in the mid-1970s. In the late-1970s, some steel firms had a 90-week delivery lag, with the price to be determined, and foreign competitors certainly took notice.

- The tremendous shift to off-shore manufacturing of labor-intensive and transportation-insensitive products in Asia, Eastern Europe, and Mexico, such as computer-related and microprocessor-driven consumer products, is an excellent example.

- In a wide variety of industries, entrepreneurs sometimes find they are the only ones who can perform. Such fields as consulting, software design, financial services, process engineering, and technical and medical products and services abound with examples of know-how monopolies. Sometimes a management team is simply the best in an industry and irreplaceable in the near term, just as is seen with great coaches with winning records.

Exhibit 3.2 is a summary of the major types of discontinuities, asymmetries, and changes that can result in high-potential opportunities. Creating such changes, by technical innovation (PCs, wireless telecommunications, Internet servers, software), influencing and creating the new rules of the game (airlines, telecommunications, financial services and banking, medical products) and anticipating the various impacts of such changes is central to the opportunity recognition process.

Big Opportunities with Little Capital

Within the dynamic free enterprise system, opportunities are apparent to a limited number of individuals—and not just to the individuals with financial resources. Ironically, successful entrepreneurs like Howard Head attribute their success to the discipline of limited capital resources. Thus, in the 1990s, many entrepreneurs have been learning the key to success is in the art of bootstrapping, which "in a startup is like zero inventory in a just-in-time system: It reveals hidden problems and forces the company to solve them."[11] Consider the following:

- A 1991 study revealed that of the 110 startups researched, 77 percent had been launched with

---

[11] Amar Bhide, "Bootstrap Finance," *Harvard Business Review,* November–December 1992, p. 112.

EXHIBIT 3.2

Summary of Opportunity Spawners and Drivers

Root of change/chaos/discontinuity	Opportunity Creation
Regulatory changes	Cellular, airlines, insurance, telecommunications, medical, pension fund management, financial services, banking, tax and SEC laws
10-fold change in 10 years or less	Moore's Law—computer chips double productivity every 18 months: financial services, private equity, consulting, Internet, biotech, information age, publishing
Reconstruction of value chain and channels of distribution	Superstores—Staples, Home Depot; all publishing; autos; Internet sales and distribution of all services
Proprietary or contractual advantage	Technological innovation: patent, license, contract, franchise, copyrights, distributorship
Existing management/investors burned out/undermanaged	Turnaround, new capital structure, new breakeven, new free cash flow, new team, new strategy; owners' desires for liquidity, exit: telecom, waste management service, retail businesses
Entrepreneurial leadership	New vision and strategy, new team equals secret weapon; organization thinks, acts like owners
Market leaders are customer obsessed or customer blind	New, small customers are low priority or ignored: hard disk drives, paper, chemicals, mainframe computers, centralized data processing, desktop computers, corporate venturing, office superstores, automobiles, software, most services

$50,000 or less; 46 percent were started with $10,000 or less as seed capital. Further, the primary source of capital was, overwhelmingly, personal savings (74 percent), rather than outside investors with deep pockets.[12]

- In the 1930s, Josephine Esther Mentzer assisted her uncle by selling skin care balm and quickly created her own products with $100 initial investment. After convincing the department stores rather than the drug stores to carry her products, Estee Lauder was on its way to a $3 billion corporation.[13]
- Putting their talents (cartooning and finance) together, Roy and Walt Disney moved to California and started their own film studio—with $290 in 1923. Today, the Walt Disney Co. has a market value exceeding $16 billion.[14]
- While working for a Chicago insurance company, a 24-year-old sent out 20,000 inquiries for a black newsletter. With 3,000 positive responses and $500, John Harold Johnson published *Jet* for the first time in 1942. In the 1990s, Johnson Publishing publishes various magazines, including *Ebony*.[15]

- With $100, Nicholas Graham, age 24, went to a local fabric store, picked out some patterns, and made $100 worth of ties. Having sold the ties to specialty shops, Graham was approached by Macy's to place his patterns on men's underwear. So Joe Boxer Corporation was born and "six months into Joe Boxer's second year, sales had already topped $1 million."[16]

Real Time

Opportunities exist or are created in real time and have what is called a window of opportunity. For an entrepreneur to seize an opportunity requires that the window be opening, not closing, and that it remain open long enough.

Exhibit 3.3 illustrates a window of opportunity for a generalized market. Markets grow at different rates over time and as a market quickly becomes larger, more and more opportunities are possible. As the market becomes larger and established, conditions are not as favorable. Thus, at the point where a market starts to become sufficiently

[12] Edward B. Roberts, *Entrepreneurs in High Technology: Lessons from MIT and Beyond* (New York: Oxford University Press, 1991), p. 144, Table 5–2.
[13] Teri Lammers and Annie Longsworth, "Guess Who? Ten Big-Timers Launched from Scratch," *INC.*, September 1991, p. 69. © 1991 by Goldhirsh Group, Inc., 38 Commercial Wharf, Boston, MA 02110.
[14] Ibid.
[15] Ibid.
[16] Robert A. Mamis, "The Secrets of Bootstrapping," *INC.*, September 1991, p. 54.

EXHIBIT 3.3

Changes in the Placement of the Window of Opportunity

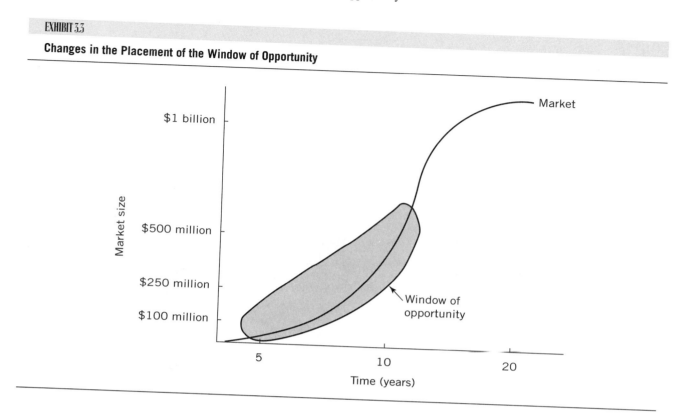

large and structured (e.g., at 5 years in *Exhibit 3.3*), the window opens; the window begins to close as the market matures (e.g., at 15 years in the exhibit).

The curve shown describes the rapid growth pattern typical of such new industries as microcomputers and software, cellular car phones, quick oil changes, and biotechnology. For example, in the cellular car phone industry, most major cities began service between 1983 and 1984 for the very first time. By 1989, there were over 2 million subscribers in the United States, and the industry continued to experience significant growth. In other industries, such as a mature industry, where growth is not so rapid, the slope of a curve would be less steep and the possibilities for opportunities fewer.

Finally, in considering the window of opportunity, the length of time the window will be open is important. It takes a considerable length of time to determine whether a new venture is a success or a failure. And, if it is to be a success, the benefits of that success need to be harvested.

Exhibit 3.4 shows that for venture-capital-backed firms, the lemons (i.e., the losers) ripen in about two and a half years, while the pearls (i.e., the winners) take seven or eight years. An extreme example of the length of time it can take for a pearl to be harvested is the experience of a Silicon Valley venture capital firm that invested in a new firm in

1966 and was finally able to realize a capital gain in early 1984.

Another way to think of the process of creating and seizing an opportunity in real time is to think of it as a process of selecting objects (opportunities) from a conveyor belt moving through an open window, the window of opportunity. The speed of the conveyor belt changes, and the window through which it moves is constantly opening and closing. That the window is continually opening and closing and that the speed of the conveyor belt is constantly changing represent the volatile nature of the marketplace and the importance of timing. For an opportunity to be created and seized, it needs to be selected from the conveyor belt before the window closes.

The ability to recognize a potential opportunity when it appears and the sense of timing to seize it as the window is opening, rather than slamming shut, are critical. That opportunities are a function of real time is illustrated in a statement made by Ken Olsen, the president and founder of Digital Equipment Corporation, in 1977: "There is no reason for any individual to have a computer in their home." Nor is it so easy for even the world's leading experts to predict just which innovative ideas and concepts for new business will evolve into the major industries of tomorrow. This is vividly illustrated by several quotations from very famous in-

EXHIBIT 3.4

Lemons and Pearls

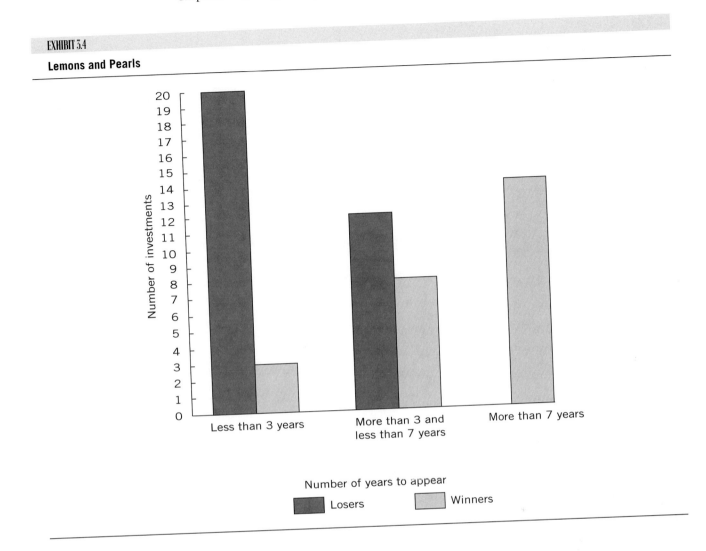

novators. In 1901, two years before the famous flight, Wilbur Wright said, "Man will not fly for 50 years." In 1910, Thomas Edison said, "The nickel-iron battery will put the gasoline buggy . . . out of existence in no time." And in 1932, Albert Einstein made it clear: "There is not the slightest indication that nuclear energy will ever be obtainable. It would mean that the atom would have to be shattered at will."

Relation to the Framework of Analysis

It is also important to remember that successful opportunities, once recognized, fit with the other forces of new venture creation. This iterative process of assessing and reassessing the fit among the central driving forces in the creation of a new venture was shown in *Exhibit 2.7* in Chapter 2. Of utmost importance when talking of opportunity recognition is the fit of the lead entrepreneur and the management team with an opportunity. Good opportunities are both *desirable to* and *attainable by* those on the team using the resources that are available.

In order to understand how the entrepreneurial vision relates to the analytical framework, it may be useful to look at an opportunity as a three-dimensional relief map with its valleys, mountains, and so on, all represented. Each opportunity has three or four critical factors (e.g., proprietary license, patented innovation, sole distribution rights, an all-star management team, breakthrough technology). These elements pop out at the observer; they indicate huge possibilities where others might see obstacles. Thus, it is easy to see why there are thousands of exceptional opportunities that will fit with a wide variety of entrepreneurs, but that might not fit neatly into the framework outlined in *Exhibit 3.5.*

EXHIBIT 3.5

Criteria for Evaluating Venture Opportunities

Criteria	Attractiveness	
	Highest Potential	**Lowest Potential**
Industry and market		
Market:	Changes way people live and work	Incremental improvement only
	Market driven; identified; recurring revenue niche	Unfocused; one-time revenue
Customers	Reachable; purchase orders	Loyal to others or unreachable
User benefits	Less than one-year payback	Three years plus payback
Value added	High; advance payments	Low; minimal impact on market
Product life	Durable	Perishable
Market structure	Imperfect, fragmented competition or emerging industry	Highly concentrated or mature or declining industry
Market size	100+ million to $1 billion sales potential	Unknown, less than $20 million or multibillion sales
Growth rate	Growth at 30–50% or more	Contracting or less than 10%
Market capacity	At or near full capacity	Undercapacity
Market share attainable (Year 5)	20% or more; leader	Less than 5%
Cost structure	Low-cost provider; cost advantages	Declining cost
Economics		
Time to breakeven/positive cash flow	Under 1½–2 years	More than 4 years
ROI potential	25% or more; high value	Less than 15–20%; low value
Capital requirements	Low to moderate; fundable	Very high; unfundable
Internal rate of return potential	25% or more per year	Less than 15% per year
Free cash flow characteristics:	Favorable; sustainable; 20–30% or more of sales	Less than 10% of sales
Sales growth	Moderate to high (+15% to +20%)	Less than 10%
Asset intensity	Low/sales $	High
Spontaneous working capital	Low, incremental requirements	High requirements
R&D/capital expenditures	Low requirements	High requirements
Gross margins	Exceeding 40% and durable	Under 20%
After-tax profits	High; greater than 10%; durable	Low
Time to break-even profit and loss	Less than two years; breakeven not creeping	Greater than four years; breakeven creeping up
Harvest issues		
Value-added potential	High strategic value	Low strategic value
Valuation multiples and comparables	Price/earnings = 20 + $x_\$$; 8–10 + $x_\$$ EBIT; 1.5–2 + $x_\$$ revenue: free cash flow 8–10 + $x_\$$	Price/earnings $\leq$ 5x, EBIT $\leq$ 3–4x; revenue $\leq$ .4
Exit mechanism and strategy	Present or envisioned options	Undefined; illiquid investment
Capital market context	Favorable valuations, timing, capital available; realizable liquidity	Unfavorable; credit crunch
Competitive advantage issues		
Fixed and variable costs	Lowest; high operating leverage	Highest
Control over costs, prices, and distribution	Moderate to strong	Weak
Barriers to entry:		
Proprietary protection	Have or can gain	None
Response/lead time	Competition slow; napping	Unable to gain edge
Legal, contractual advantage	Proprietary or exclusivity	None
Contracts and networks	Well-developed; accessible	Crude; limited
Key people	Top talent; an A team	B or C team
Management team		
Entrepreneurial team	All-star combination; free agents	Weak or solo entrepreneur
Industry and technical experience	Top of the field; super track-record	Underdeveloped
Integrity	Highest standards	Questionable
Intellectual honesty	Know what they do not know	Do not want to know what they do not know

(Continued)

EXHIBIT 3.5 (concluded)

	Non-existent	One or more
Fatal-flaw issue		Surprises, as in *The Crying Game*
Personal criteria		
Goals and fit	Getting what you want; but wanting what you get.	Linear; on same continuum
Upside/downside issues	Attainable success/limited risks	Comfortable with status quo
Opportunity costs	Acceptable cuts in salary, etc.	Simply pursuing big money
Desirability	Fits with lifestyle	Risk averse or gambler
Risk/reward tolerance	Calculated risk; low risk/reward ratio	Cracks under pressure
Stress tolerance	Thrives under pressure	
Strategic differentiation		Low
Degree of fit	High	B team; no free agents
Team	Best in class; excellent free agents	Perceived as unimportant
Service management	Superior service concept	Rowing against the tide
Timing	Rowing with the tide	Many substitutes or competitors
Technology	Groundbreaking; one of a kind	Slow; stubborn
Flexibility	Able to adapt; commit and decommit quickly	Operating in a vacuum; napping
Opportunity orientation	Always searching for opportunities	Undercut competitor; low prices
Pricing	At or near leader	Unknown; inaccessible
Distribution channels	Accessible; networks in place	Unforgiving, rigid strategy
Room for error	Forgiving strategy	

Screening Opportunities

Opportunity Focus

Opportunity focus is also the most fruitful point of departure for screening opportunities. The screening process should not begin with strategy (which derives from the nature of the opportunity), with financial and spreadsheet analysis (which flow from the former), or with estimations of how much the company is worth and who will own what shares.[17]

These starting points, and others, usually place the cart before the horse. Perhaps the best evidence of this phenomenon comes from the tens of thousands of tax-sheltered investments that turned sour in the mid-1980s. Also, as has been noted, a good number of entrepreneurs who start businesses—particularly those for whom the ventures are their first—run out of cash at a faster rate than they bring in customers and profitable sales. There are lots of reasons why this happens, but one thing is certain: These entrepreneurs have not focused on the right opportunity.

Over the years, those with experience in business and in specific market areas have developed rules of thumb to guide them in screening opportunities. For example, one such rule of thumb was used by a firm with approximately $1 billion in sales in evaluating startups in the minicomputer industry in the mid-

1980s. This firm believed, based on an analysis of performance data relating to 60 computer-related startups in the United States from 1975 to 1984, that one leading indicator of the progress of new firms and a good boundary measure of positive performance and a healthy start was sales per employee of $75,000 or more. To this firm, sales of less than $50,000 per employee signaled serious trouble. While there is always the risk of oversimplification in using rules of thumb, it is true also that one can miss the fundamentals while searching for subtleties.

Screening Criteria: The Characteristics of High-potential Ventures

Venture capitalists, savvy entrepreneurs, and investors also use this concept of boundaries in screening ventures. *Exhibit 3.3* summarizes criteria used by venture capitalists to evaluate opportunities. These criteria are used by this group to evaluate a select group of opportunities that tend to have a high-technology bias. As will be seen later, venture capital investors reject 60–70 percent of the new ventures presented to them very early in the review process, based on how the entrepreneurs satisfy these criteria.

However, these criteria are not the exclusive domain of venture capitalists. The criteria are based on plain good business sense that is used by successful

---

[17] See J. A. Timmons, D. F. Muzyka, H. H. Stevenson, and W. D. Bygrave, "Opportunity Recognition: The Core of Entrepreneurship," in *Frontiers of Entrepreneurship Research: 1987*, ed. Neil Churchill et al. (Babson Park, MA: Babson College, 1987), p. 409.

entrepreneurs, private investors, and venture capitalists. Consider the following examples of great little companies built without a dime of professional venture capital.

- Paul Tobin, who built Cellular One in eastern Massachusetts from ground zero to $100 million in revenue in five years, has started Roamer Plus with less than $300,000 of internally generated funds from other ventures. Within two years, it grew to a $15 million annual sales rate and was very profitable.

- Another entrepreneur started a small specialty publishing company with minimal capital and grew it to over $12 million in highly profitable sales by 1987. While looking for acquisitions, he discovered that valuations were at an all-time high. Instead of buying, he decided to sell. In 1988, he sold his small firm for over $70 million.

- Morris Alper & Sons was a third-generation, small, traditional food brokerage business with around 40 employees when the founder's grandson joined the firm in the early 1970's. By 1993, financed entirely by internally generated cash flow, they have grown to nearly 350 employees. The company has become an integrated marketing services firm whose clients are 70 of the largest consumer food product companies in North America.

- In 1983, Charlie Butcher, at age 66, had to decide whether to buy out an equal partner in his 100-year-old industrial polish and wax business with less than $10 million in sales. This niche business had high gross margins, very low working capital and fixed-asset requirements for increased sales, substantial steady growth of over 18 percent per year, and excellent products. The result was a business with very high free cash flow and potential for growth. He acquired the company with a bank loan and seller financing, and then he increased sales to over $50 million by 1993. The company continues to be highly profitable. Charlie vows never to utilize venture capital money or to take the company public.

The point of departure here is opportunity and, implicitly, the customer, the marketplace, and the industry. *Exhibit 3.5* shows how higher and lower potential opportunities can be placed along an attractiveness scale. The criteria provide some quantitative way in which an entrepreneur can make judgments about industry and market issues, competitive advantage issues, economic and harvest issues, management team issues, and fatal flaw issues and whether these add up to a compelling opportunity. For example, *dominant* strength in any one of these criteria can readily translate into a winning entry, whereas a flaw in any one can be fatal.

Entrepreneurs contemplating opportunities that will yield attractive companies, not high-potential ventures, can also benefit from paying attention to these criteria. These entrepreneurs will then be in a better position to decide how these criteria can be compromised. As outlined in *Exhibit 3.3*, business opportunities with the greatest potential will possess many of the following, or they will dominate in one or a few that the competition cannot come close:

- ***Industry and market issues***
  Market. *Higher potential* businesses can identify a market niche for a product or service that meets an important customer need and provides high value-added or value-created benefits to customers. Customers are reachable and receptive to the product or service, with no brand or other loyalties. The potential payback to the user or customer of a given product or service through cost savings or other value-added or value-created properties is one year or less and is identifiable, repeatable, and verifiable. Further, the life of the product or service exists beyond the time needed to recover the investment, plus a profit. And the company is able to expand beyond a one-product company. Take, for example, the growing success of cellular car phone service. At prevailing rates, one can talk for about $25 an hour, and many providers of professional services can readily bill more than the $25 an hour for what would otherwise be unused time. If benefits to customers cannot be calculated in such dollar terms, then the market potential is far more difficult and risky to ascertain.

  Lower potential opportunities are unfocused regarding customer need, and customers are unreachable and/or have brand or other loyalties to others. A payback to the user of more than three years and a low value-added or value-created also makes an opportunity unattractive. Being unable to expand beyond a one-product company also can make for a lower potential opportunity. The failure of one of the first portable computer companies, Osborne Computer, is a good example of this.

  Market structure. Market structure, such as evidenced by the number of sellers, size distribution of sellers, whether products are differentiated, conditions of entry and exit, number of buyers, cost conditions, and sensitivity of demand to changes in price, is significant.

  A fragmented, imperfect market or emerging industry often contains vacuums and asymmetries that create unfilled market niches—for example, markets where resource ownership, cost advantages, and the like can be achieved. In addition, those where information or knowledge gaps exist and where competition is profitable, but not so strong as to be overwhelming, are attractive. An example of a market with an information gap is that of the experience a Boston entrepreneur encountered with a large New York company that wanted to dispose of a small, old office building in downtown Boston. This office building, because its book value was about $200,000, was viewed by the financially oriented firm as a low-value asset, and the company wanted to dispose of it so the resulting cash could be put to work for a higher return. The buyer, who had done more homework than the out-of-town sellers, bought the building for $200,000 and resold it in less than six months for over $8 million.

Industries that are highly concentrated, that are perfectly competitive, or that are mature or declining industries are typically unattractive. The capital requirements and costs to achieve distribution and marketing presence can be prohibitive, and such behavior as price cutting and other competitive strategies in highly concentrated markets can be a significant barrier to entry. (The most blatant example is organized crime and its life-threatening actions when territories are invaded.) Yet, revenge by normal competitors who are well-positioned through product strategy, legal tactics, and the like, also can be punishing to the pocketbook.

The airline industry, after deregulation, is an example of a perfectly competitive market and one where many of the recent entrants will have difficulty. The unattractiveness of perfectly competitive industries is captured by the comment of prominent Boston venture capitalist William Egan, who put it this way: "I want to be in a nonauction market."[18]

Market size.   An attractive new venture sells to a market that is large and growing (i.e., one where capturing a small market share can represent significant and increasing sales volume). A minimum market size of over $100 million in sales is attractive. Such a market size means it is possible to achieve significant sales by capturing roughly 5 percent or less and thus not threatening competitors. For example, to achieve a sales level of $1 million in a $100 million market requires capturing only 1 percent of the market. Thus, a recreational equipment manufacturer entered a $60 million market that was expected to grow at 20 percent per year to over $100 mil-

lion by the third year. The founders were able to create a substantial smaller company without obtaining a major market share and possibly incurring the wrath of existing competitors.

However, such a market can be too large. A multibillion-dollar market may be too mature and stable, and such a level of certainty can translate into competition from Fortune 500 firms and, if highly competitive, into lower margins and profitability. Further, an unknown market or one that is less than $10 million in sales also is unattractive. To understand the disadvantage of a large, more mature market, consider the entry of a firm into the microcomputer industry today versus the entry of Apple Computer into that market in 1975.

Growth rate.   An attractive market is large and growing (i.e., one where capturing a good share of the increase is less threatening to competitors and where a small market share can represent significant and increasing sales volume). An annual growth rate of 30 percent to 50 percent creates new niches for new entrants, and such a market is a thriving and expansive one, rather than a stable or contracting one, where competitors are scrambling for the same niches. Thus, for example, a $100 million market growing at 50 percent per year has the potential to become a $1 billion industry in a few years, and if a new venture is able to capture just 2 percent of sales in the first year, it can attain sales in the first year of $1 million. If it just maintains its market share over the next few years, sales will grow significantly.

Market capacity.   Another signal of the existence of an opportunity in a market is a market at full capacity in a growth situation—in other words, a demand that the existing suppliers cannot meet. This situation was precisely the case for Outdoor Scene, the company profiled in Chapter 1. Not only was there a 20 percent growth rate, but the other manufacturers were at full capacity. Timing is of vital concern in such a situation, which means the entrepreneur should be asking himself or herself, Can a new entrant fill that demand before the other players can decide to and then actually increase capacity?

Market share attainable.   The potential to be a leader in the market and capture at least a 20 percent share of the market is important. The potential to be a leader in the market and capture at least 20 percent can create a very high

[18] Comments made during a presentation at Babson College, May 1985.

value for a company that might otherwise be worth not much more than book value. For example, one such firm, with less than $15 million in sales, became the dominant factor in its small market niche with a 70 percent market share. The company was acquired for $23 million in cash.

A firm that will be able to capture less than 5 percent of a market is unattractive in the eyes of most investors seeking a higher potential company.

Cost structure.   A firm that can become the low-cost provider is attractive, but a firm that continually faces declining cost conditions is less so. Attractive opportunities exist in industries where economies of scale are insignificant (or work to the advantage of the new venture). Attractive opportunities boast of low costs of learning by doing. Where costs per unit are high when small amounts of the product are sold, existing firms that have low promotion costs can face attractive market opportunities.

For instance, consider the operating leverage of Johnsonville Sausage. Their variable costs were 6 percent labor and 94 percent materials. What aggressive incentives could management put in place for the 6 percent to manage and to control the 94 percent? Imagine the disasters that would occur if the scenario were reversed!

A word of caution from Scott W. Kunkel and Charles W. Hofer, who observed that

Overall, industry structure . . . had a much smaller impact on new venture performance than has previously been suggested in the literature. This finding could be the result of one of several possibilities:

1. Industry structure impacts the performance of established firms, but does NOT have a significant impact on new venture performance.

2. The most important industry structural variables influencing new ventures are different from those which impact established firms and thus research has yet to identify the industry structural variables that are most important in the new venture environment.

3. Industry structure does NOT have a significant DIRECT impact on firm performance, as hypothesized by scholars in the three fields of study. Instead, the impact of industry structure is strongly mitigated by other factors, including the strategy selected for entry.[19]

- **Economics:**
    Profits after tax.   High and durable gross margins usually translate into strong and durable after-tax profits. Attractive opportunities have potential for durable profits of at least 10–15 percent, and often 15–20 percent or more. Those generating after-tax profits of less than 5 percent are quite fragile.

    Time to breakeven and positive cash flow. As mentioned above, breakeven and positive cash flow for attractive companies are possible within two years. Once the time to breakeven and positive cash flow is greater than three years, the attractiveness of the opportunity diminishes accordingly.

    ROI potential.   An important corollary to forgiving economics is reward. Very attractive opportunities have the potential to yield a return on investment of 25 percent or more per year. After all, during the 1980s, many venture capital funds achieved only single-digit returns on investment. High and durable gross margins and high and durable after-tax profits usually yield high earnings per share and high return on stockholders' equity, thus generating a satisfactory "harvest" price for a company. This is most likely true whether the company is sold through an initial public offering or privately or whether it is acquired. Given the risk typically involved, a return on investment potential of less than 15–20 percent per year is unattractive.

    Capital requirements.   Ventures that can be funded and have capital requirements that are low to moderate are attractive. Realistically, most higher potential businesses need significant amounts of cash—several hundred thousand dollars and up—to get started. However, a business that can be started with little or no capital is rare, but they do exist. One such venture was launched in Boston in 1971 with $7,500 of the founder's capital and grew to over $30 million in sales by 1989. In today's venture capital market the first round of financing is typically $1 million to $2 million or more for a startup.[20] Some higher potential ventures, such as those in the service sector or "cash sales" businesses, have lower capital requirements than do high-technology manufacturing firms with continual large research and development expenditures.

---

[19] Scott W. Kunkel and Charles W. Hofer, "The Impact of Industry Structure on New Venture Performance," *Frontiers of Entrepreneurship Research: 1993.* Reproduced with permission.
[20] J. A. Timmons, W. Bygrave, and N. Fast, "The Flow of Venture Capital to Highly Innovative Technological Ventures," a study for the National Science Foundation, reprinted in *Frontiers of Entrepreneurship Research: 1984,* ed. J. A. Hornaday et al. (Babson Park, MA: Babson College, 1984).

If the venture needs too much money or cannot be funded, it is unattractive. An extreme example is a venture that a team of students recently proposed to repair satellites. The students believed that the required startup capital was in the $50 million to $200 million range. Projects of this magnitude are in the domain of the government and the very large corporation, rather than that of entrepreneurs and venture capitalists.

Internal rate of return potential.   Is the risk reward relationship attractive enough? The response to this question can be quite personal, but the most attractive opportunities often have the promise of—and deliver—a very substantial upside of 5 to 10 times the original investment in 5 to 10 years. Of course, the extraordinary successes can yield 50 to 100 times or more, but these truly are exceptions. A 25 percent or more annual compound rate of return is considered very healthy. In the early 1990s, those investments considered basically risk free had yields of 3 to 8 percent.

Free cash flow characteristics.[21]   Free cash flow is a way of understanding a number of crucial financial dimensions of any business: the robustness of its economics; its capital requirements, both working and fixed assets; its capacity to service external debt and equity claims; and its capacity to sustain growth. We define unlevered free cash flow (FCF) as earnings before interest but after taxes (EBIAT) *plus* amortization (A) and depreciation (D) *less* spontaneous working capital requirements (WC) *less* capital expenditures (CAPex), or $FCF = EBIAT + [A + D] - [+ \text{ or } - WC] - CAPex$. EBIAT is driven by sales, profitability, and asset intensity. Low-asset-intensive, high-margin businesses generate the highest profits and sustainable growth.[22]

Gross margins.   The potential for high and durable gross margins (i.e., the unit selling price less all direct and variable costs) is important. Gross margins exceeding 40–50 percent provide a tremendous built-in cushion that allows for more error and more flexibility to learn from mistakes than do gross margins of 20 percent or less. High and durable gross margins, in turn, mean that a venture can reach breakeven earlier, an event that preferably occurs within the first two years. Thus, for example, if gross margins are just 20 percent, for every $1 increase in fixed costs (e.g., insurance, salaries, rent, and utilities), sales need to increase $5 just to stay even. If gross margins are 75 percent, however, a $1 increase in fixed costs requires a sales increase of just $1.33. An example of the cushion provided by high and durable gross margins is provided by an entrepreneur who built the international division of an emerging software company to $17 million in highly profitable sales in just five years (when he was 25 years of age). He stresses there is simply no substitute for outrageous gross margins, by saying, "It allows you to make all kinds of mistakes that would kill a normal company. And we made them all. But our high gross margins covered all the learning tuition and still left a good profit."[23] Gross margins of less than 20 percent, particularly if they are fragile, are unattractive.

Time to breakeven—cash flow and profit and loss (P&L).   New businesses that can quickly achieve a positive cash flow and become self-sustaining are highly desirable. It is often the second year before this is possible, but the sooner the better. Obviously, simply having a longer window does not mean that the business will be lousy. Two great companies illustrate that a higher potential business can have a longer window. For instance, Pilkington Brothers, an English firm that developed plate glass technology, ran huge losses for over two-and-a-half years before it was regarded as a great company. Similarly, Federal Express went through an early period of enormous negative cash flows of $1 million a month.

- ***Harvest issues:***
  Value-added potential.   New ventures that are based on strategic value in an industry, such as valuable technology, are attractive, while those with low or no strategic value are less attractive. For example, most observers contend, a product technology of compelling strategic value to Xerox was owned, in the mid-1980s, by a small company with about $10 million in sales and showing a prior-year loss of $1.5 million. Xerox purchased the company for $56 million. Opportunities with extremely large capital commitments, whose value on exit can be severely eroded by unanticipated circumstances, are less attractive. An example would be nuclear power.

---

[21] For a more detailed description of free cash flow, see "Note on Free Cash Flow Valuation Models: Identifying the Critical Factors that Affect Value," HBS 288-023, Harvard Business School, 1987.

[22] William A. Sahlman, "Sustainable Growth Analysis," HBS 9-284-059, Harvard Business School, 1984.

[23] R. Douglas Kahn, president, Interactive Images, Inc., speaking at Babson College about his experiences as international marketing director at McCormack & Dodge from 1978 through 1983.

Thus, one characteristic of businesses that command a premium price is that they have high value-added strategic importance to their acquirer: distribution, customer base, geographic coverage, proprietary technology, contractual rights, and the like. To illustrate, such companies might be valued at four, five, even six times (or more) last year's *sales,* whereas perhaps 60 to 80 percent of companies might be purchased at .75 to 1.25 times sales.

Valuation multiples and comparables. Consistent with the above point, there is a large spread in the value the capital markets place on private and public companies. Part of your analysis is to identify some of the historical boundaries for the valuations placed on companies in the market/industry/technology area you intend to pursue. The rules of thumb outlined in *Exhibit 3.3* are variable and should be thought of as a boundary and a point of departure.

Exit mechanism and strategy. Businesses that are eventually sold—privately or to the public—or acquired usually are started and grown with a harvest objective in mind. Attractive companies that realize capital gains from the sale of their businesses have, or envision, a harvest or exit mechanism. Unattractive opportunities do not have an exit mechanism in mind. Planning is critical because, as is often said, it is much harder to get out of a business than to get into it. Giving some serious thought to the options and likelihood that the company can eventually be harvested is an important initial and ongoing aspect of the entrepreneurial process.

Capital market context. The context in which the sale or acquisition of the company takes place is largely driven by the capital market context at that particular point in time. Timing can be a critical component of the exit mechanism because, as one study indicated, since World War II, the average bull market on Wall Street has lasted just six months. For a keener appreciation of the critical difference the capital markets can make, one only has to recall the stock market crash of October 19, 1987, or the bank credit crunch of 1990–1992. In fact, by the end of 1987, the valuation of the Venture Capital 100 index dropped 43 percent and private company valuations followed. Initial public offerings are especially vulnerable to the vicissitudes of the capital markets; here the timing is vital. Some of the most successful companies seem to have been launched when debt and equity capital were most available and relatively cheap.

■ *Competitive advantages issues:*
Variable and fixed costs. An attractive opportunity has the potential for being the lowest-cost producer and for having the lowest costs of marketing and distribution. For example, Bowmar was unable to remain competitive in the market for electronic calculators after the producers of large-scale integrated circuits, such as Hewlett-Packard, entered the business. Being unable to achieve and sustain a position as a low-cost producer shortens the life expectancy of a new venture.

Degree of control. Attractive opportunities have potential for moderate-to-strong degree of control over prices, costs, and channels of distribution. Fragmented markets where there is no dominant competitor—no IBM—have this potential. These markets usually have a market leader with a 20 percent market share *or less.* For example, sole control of the source of supply of a critical component for a product or of channels of distribution can give a new venture market dominance even if other areas are weak.

Lack of control over such factors as product development and component prices can make an opportunity unattractive. For example, in the case of Viatron, its suppliers were unable to produce several of the semiconductors that the company needed at low enough prices to permit Viatron to make the inexpensive computer terminal that it had publicized extensively.

A market where a major competitor has a market share of 40 percent, 50 percent, or, especially, 60 percent usually implies a market where power and influence over suppliers, customers, and pricing create a serious barrier and risk for a new firm. Such a firm will have few degrees of freedom. However, if a dominant competitor is at full capacity, is slow to innovate or to add capacity in a large and growing market, or routinely ignores or abuses the customer (remember "Ma Bell"), there may be an entry opportunity. However, entrepreneurs usually do not find such sleepy competition in dynamic, emerging industries dense with opportunity.

Entry barriers. Having a favorable window of opportunity is important. Having or being able to gain proprietary protection, regulatory advantage, or other legal or contractual advantage, such as exclusive rights to a market or with a distributor, is attractive. Having or being able to gain an advantage in response/lead times is important since these can create barriers to entry or expansion by others. For example, advantages in response/lead times in technology, product innovation, market innovation, people, location, resources, or capacity make an opportunity attractive. Possession of well-developed, high-quality, accessible contacts that are the products of years of building a top-notch reputation and that cannot be acquired quickly is also advantageous. In fact, there are times when this competitive advantage may be so strong as to provide dominance in the marketplace, even though many of the other factors are weak or average. An example of how quickly the joys of startup may fade if others cannot be kept out is the experience of firms in the hard disk drive industry that were unable to erect entry barriers in the United States in the early to mid-1980s. By the end of 1983, some 90 hard disk drive companies were launched, and severe price competition led to a major industry shakeout.

If a firm cannot keep others out or if it faces already existing entry barriers, it is unattractive. An easily overlooked issue is a firm's capacity to gain distribution of its product. As simple as it may sound, even venture-capital-backed companies fall victim to this market issue. Air Florida apparently assembled all the right ingredients, including substantial financing, yet was unable to secure sufficient gate space for its airplanes. Even though it sold passenger seats, it had no place to pick the passengers up or drop them off.

- **Management team issues:**
  Entrepreneurial team.   Attractive opportunities have existing teams that are strong and contain industry superstars. The team has proven profit and loss experience in the same technology, market, and service area, and members have complementary and compatible skills. An unattractive opportunity does not have such a team in place or has no team.

  Industry and technical experience.   A management track record of significant accomplishment in the industry, with the technology, and in the market area, with a proven profit, and lots of achievements where the venture will compete is highly desirable. A top-notch management team can become the most important strategic competitive advantage in an industry. Imagine relocating the Chicago Bulls or the Phoenix Suns to Halifax, Nova Scotia; do you think you would have a winning competitor in the National Basketball Association?

  Integrity.   Trust and integrity are the oil and glue that make economic interdependence possible. Having an unquestioned reputation in this regard is a major long-term advantage for entrepreneurs and should be sought in all personnel and backers. A shady past or record of questionable integrity is for B team players only.

  Intellectual honesty.   There is a fundamental issue of whether the founders know what they do and do not know, as well as whether they know what to do about shortcomings or gaps in the team and the enterprise.

  Fatal-flaw issues.   Basically, attractive ventures have no fatal flaws; an opportunity is rendered unattractive if it suffers from one or more fatal flaws. Usually, these relate to one of the above criteria, and examples abound of markets which are too small, which have overpowering competition, where the cost of entry is too high, where an entrant is unable to produce at a competitive price, and so on. An example of an entry barrier's being a fatal flaw was Air Florida's inability to get its flights listed on reservation computers.

- **Personal criteria:**
  Goals and fit.   Is there a good match between the requirements of business and what the founders want out of it? A very wise woman, Dorothy Stevenson, pinpointed the crux of it with this powerful insight: "Success is *getting* what you want. Happiness is *wanting* what you get."

  Upside/downside issues.   An attractive opportunity does not have excessive downside risk. The upside and the downside of pursuing an opportunity are not linear, nor are they on the same continuum. The upside is easy, and it has been said that success has a thousand sires. The downside is quite another matter, since it has also been said that failure is an orphan. An entrepreneur needs to be able to absorb the financial downside in such a way that he or she can rebound, without becoming indentured to debt obligations. If an entrepreneur's financial exposure in launching the venture is greater than his or her net worth—the resources he or she can reasonably draw upon, and his or her alternative disposable earnings stream if it does not work out—the deal may be too big. While today's bankruptcy laws are extremely generous, the psychological burdens of living through such an ordeal are infinitely more painful than the financial consequences. An existing business needs to consider if a failure will be too demeaning to the firm's reputation and future credibility, aside from the obvious financial consequences.[24]

---

[24] This point was made by J. Willard Marriott, Jr., at Founder's Day, Babson College, 1988.

Opportunity cost. In pursuing any venture opportunity, there are also opportunity costs. An entrepreneur who is skilled enough to grow a successful, multimillion-dollar venture has talents that are highly valued by medium- to large-sized firms as well. While assessing benefits that may accrue in pursuing an opportunity, an entrepreneur needs to take a serious look at other alternatives, including potential "golden handcuffs," and account honestly for any cut in salary that may be involved in pursuing a certain opportunity.

Further, pursuing an opportunity can shape an entrepreneur in ways that are hard to imagine. An entrepreneur will probably have time to execute between two to four multimillion-dollar ventures between the ages of 25 and 50. Each of these experiences will position him or her, *for better or for worse,* for the next opportunity. Since it is important for an entrepreneur, in his or her early years, to gain relevant management experience and since building a venture (either one that works out or one that does not) takes a lot more time than is commonly believed, it is important to consider alternatives while assessing an opportunity.

Desirability. A good opportunity is not only attractive but also desirable (i.e., a good opportunity fits). An example of an intensely personal criterion would be the desire for a certain lifestyle. This desire may preclude pursuing certain opportunities (i.e., certain opportunities may be opportunities for someone else). The founder of a major high-technology venture in the Boston area was asked why the headquarters of his firm were located in downtown Boston, while those of other such firms were located on the famous Route 128 outside of the city. His reply was that he wanted to live in Boston because he loved the city and wanted to be able to walk to work. He said, "The rest did not matter."

Risk/reward tolerance. Successful entrepreneurs take calculated risks or avoid risks they do not need to take; as a country western song puts it: "You have to know when to hold 'em, know when to fold 'em, know when to walk away, and know when to run." This is not to suggest that all entrepreneurs have the same risk tolerance; some are quite conservative while others actually seem to get a kick out of the inherent danger and thrill in higher risk and higher stake games. The real issue is fit—recognizing that gamblers and overly risk averse entrepreneurs are unlikely to sustain any long-term successes.

Stress tolerance. Another important dimension of the fit concept is the stressful requirements of a fast-growth high-stakes venture. Or as President Harry Truman said so well: "If you can't stand the heat, then stay out of the kitchen."

- **Strategic differentiation:**

  Degree of fit. To what extent is there a good fit among the driving forces (founders and team, opportunity and resource requirements) and the timing given the external environment?

  Team. There is no substitute for an A-quality team, since the execution and the ability to adapt and to devise constantly new strategies is so vital to survival and success. A team is nearly unstoppable if it can inculcate into the venture a philosophy and culture of superior learning, as well as teaching skills, an ethic of high standards, delivery of results, and constant improvement. Are they free agents—clear of employment, noncompete, proprietary rights, and trade secret agreements—who are able to pursue the opportunity?

  Service management. A few years ago, the Forum Corporation of Boston conducted research across a wide range of industries with several hundred companies to determine why customers stopped buying these companies' products. The results were surprising; 15 percent of the customers defected because of quality and 70 percent stopped using a product or service because of bad customer service. Having a "turbo-service" concept that can be delivered consistently can be a major competitive weapon against small and large competitors alike. Home Depot, in the home supply business, and Lexus, in the auto industry, have set an entirely new standard of service for their industries.

  Timing. From business to historic military battles to political campaigns, timing is often the one element that can make a significant difference. Time can be an enemy or a friend; being too early or too late can be fatal. The crux is to row with the tide, not against it. Strategically, ignoring this principle is perilous.

  Technology. A breakthrough, proprietary product is no guarantee of success, but it certainly creates a formidable competitive advantage (see *Exhibit 3.6*).

  Flexibility. Maintaining the capacity to commit and decommit quickly, to adapt, and to abandon if necessary is a major strategic weapon, particularly when competing with larger organizations. Larger firms can typically take six years or more to change basic strategy and 10 to 20 years or more to change the culture.

EXHIBIT 3.6

Major Inventions by U.S. Small Firms in the 20th Century

Acoustical suspension speakers	Fluid flow meter	Nuclear magnetic resonance
Aerosol can	Fosin fire airinguisher	Plezo electronic devices
Air conditioning	Geodesic dome	Polaroid camera
Airplane	Gyrocompass	Prefabricated housing
Artificial skin	Heart valve	Pressure-sensitive cellophane
Assembly line	Heat sensor	Quick frozen foods
Automatic fabric cutting	Helicopter	Rotary oil drilling bit
Automatic transfer equipment	Heterodyne radio	Safety razor
Bakelite	High capacity computer	Six-axis robot arm
Biosynthetic insulin	Hydraulic brake	Soft contact lens
Catalytic petroleum cracking	Learning machine	Sonar fish monitoring
Continuous casting	Link trainer	Spectographic gird
Cotton picker		Stereographic image sensoring

Source: Small Business Association.

Opportunity orientation. To what extent is there a constant alertness to the marketplace? A continual search for opportunities? As one insightful entrepreneur put it, "Any opportunity that just comes in the door to us, we do not consider an opportunity. And we do not have a strategy until we are saying no to lots of opportunities."

Pricing. One of the most common mistakes of new companies, with high-value-added products or services in a growing market, is to underprice. A price slightly below to as much as 20 percent below competitors is rationalized as necessary to gain market entry. In a 30 percent gross margin business a 10 percent price increase results in a 20–36 percent increase in gross margin and will lower the break-even sales level for a company with $900,000 in fixed costs to $2.5 million from $3 million. At the $3 million sales level, the company would realize an extra $180,000 in pre-tax profits.

Distribution channels. Having access to the distribution channels is sometimes overlooked or taken for granted. New channels of distribution can leapfrog and demolish traditional channels; take for instance, direct mail, home shopping networks, infomercials, and the coming revolution in interactive television in your own home.

Room for error. How forgiving is the business and the financial strategy? How wrong can the team be in estimates of revenue, costs, cash flow, timing, and capital requirements? How bad can things get, yet be able to survive? If some single engine planes are more prone to accidents, by 10 or more times, which plane do you want to fly in? High leverage, lower gross margins, and lower operating margins are the signals in a small company of these flights destined for fatality.

Gathering Information

Finding Ideas

Factors suggest that finding the right idea that is a potential opportunity is most often a matter of being the right person, in the right place, at the right time. So how can you increase your chances of being the next Anita Roddick of The Body Shop? There are numerous sources of information that can help generate ideas.

- ***Existing businesses.*** Purchasing an ongoing business is an excellent way to find a new business idea. Such a route to a new venture can save time and money and can reduce risk as well. Investment bankers and business brokers are knowledgeable about businesses for sale, as are trust officers. It is worth noting, however, that the very best private businesses for sale are not advertised by brokers, and the real gems are usually bought by individuals or firms closest to them, such as management, directors, customers, suppliers, or financial backers. Bankruptcy judges have a continual flow of ventures in serious trouble. There can be some excellent opportunities buried beneath all the financial debris of a bankrupt firm.

- ***Franchises.*** Franchising is another way to enter an industry, by either starting a franchise operation or becoming a franchisee. This is a fertile area. The number of franchisors nationally now stands at over 2,000, according to the International Franchise Association and the Department of Commerce, and franchisors account for well over $300 billion in sales annually and nearly one-third of all retail sales.[25] The following sources can provide a useful start for a search in this field:

Franchise Opportunity Handbook, U.S. Department of Commerce.

The Franchise Annual Handbook and Directory, edited by Edward L. Dixon.

Franchising: Proven Techniques for Rapid Company Expansion and Market Dominance, by David Seltz.

Franchising World, published by the International Franchise Association.

Franchising Today, published by Franchise Technologies.

Listings of opportunities and ads in such publications as *INC.*, *Venture*, and *The Wall Street Journal*.

International Franchise Handbook.

Databases, such as Dialog and CompuServe.

- **Patents.** Patent brokers specialize in marketing patents that are owned by individual inventors, corporations, universities, or other research organizations to those seeking new commercially viable products. Some brokers specialize in international product licensing, and, occasionally, a patent broker will purchase an invention and then resell it. Although, over the years, the patent broker's image has been tarnished by a few unscrupulous brokers, acquisitions effected by reputable brokers have resulted in significant new products. Notable among these was Bausch & Lomb's acquisition, through the National Patent Development Corporation, of the United States rights to hydron, a material used in contact lenses. Some patent brokers are:

MGA Technology, Inc., Chicago, Illinois.

New Product Development Services, Inc., Kansas City, Missouri.

University Patents, Chicago, Illinois.

Research Corporation, New York, New York.

Pegasus Corporation, New York, New York.

National Patent Development Corporation, New York, New York.

- **Product licensing.** A good way to obtain exposure to a large number of product ideas available

from universities, corporations, and independent investors is to subscribe to information services, such as the *American Bulletin of International Technology*, *Selected Business Ventures* (published by General Electric Company), *Technology Mart*, *Patent Licensing Gazette*, and the National Technical Information Service. In addition, corporations, not-for-profit research institutes, and universities are sources of ideas:

Corporations. Corporations engaged in research and development develop inventions or services that they do not exploit commercially. These inventions either do not fit existing product lines or marketing programs or do not represent sufficiently large markets to be interesting to large corporations. A good number of corporations license these kinds of inventions, either through patent brokers, product-licensing information services, or their own patent-marketing efforts. Directly contacting a corporation with a licensing program may prove fruitful. Among the major corporations known to have active internal patent-marketing efforts are the following:

- Gulf and Western Invention Development Corporation.
- Kraft Corporation, Research and Development.
- Pillsbury Company, Research and Development Laboratories.
- Union Carbide Corporation, Nuclear Division.
- RCA Corporation, Domestic Licensing.
- TRW Corporation, Systems Group.
- Lockheed Corporation, Patent Licensing.

Not-for-profit research institutes. These nonprofit organizations do research and development under contract to the government and private industry as well as some internally sponsored research and development of new products and processes that can be licensed to private corporations for further development, manufacturing, and marketing. Perhaps the most famous example of how this works is Battelle Memorial Institute's participation in the development of xerography and the subsequent license of the technology to the Haloid Corporation, now Xerox Corporation. Some nonprofit research institutes with active licensing programs are:

- Battelle Memorial Institute.
- ITT Research Institute.

---

[25] See also David E Gumpert and Jeffry A Timmons, *The Encyclopedia of Small Business Resources* (New York: Harper & Row, 1984).

- Stanford Research Institute.
- Southwest Research Institute.

Universities. A number of universities are active in research in the physical sciences and seek to license inventions that result from this research, either directly or through an associated research foundation that administers its patent program. Massachusetts Institute of Technology and the California Institute of Technology publish periodic reports containing abstracts of inventions they own which are available for licensing. In addition, since a number of very good ideas developed in universities never reach formal licensing outlets, another way to find these ideas is to become familiar with the work of researchers in an area of interest. Among universities that have active licensing programs are:

- Massachusetts Institute of Technology.
- California Institute of Technology.
- University of Wisconsin.
- Iowa State University.
- Purdue University.
- University of California.
- University of Oregon.

- ***Industry and Trade Contacts.***
    Trade shows and association meetings. Trade shows and association meetings in an industry can be an excellent way to examine the products of many potential competitors, meet distributors and sales representatives, learn of product and market trends, and identify potential products. The American Electronics Association is a good example of an association which holds such seminars and meetings.

    Customers. Contacting potential customers of a certain type of product can help determine what their needs are and where existing products are deficient or inadequate. For example, discussions with doctors who head medical services at leading hospitals might lead to product ideas in the biomedical equipment business.

    Distributors and wholesalers. Contacting people who distribute a certain type of product can yield extensive information about the strengths and weaknesses of existing products and the kinds of product improvements and new products that are needed by customers.

    Competitors. Examining products offered by companies competing in an industry can show whether an existing design is protected by patent and whether it can be improved or imitated.

- ***Former employers.*** A number of businesses are started with products or services, or both, based on technology and ideas developed by entrepreneurs while they were employed by others. In some cases, research laboratories were not interested in commercial exploitation of technology, or the previous employer was not interested in the ideas for new products, and the rights were given up or sold. In others, the ideas were developed under government contract and were in the public domain. In addition, some companies will help entrepreneurs set up companies in return for equity.

- ***Professional contacts.*** Ideas can also be found by contacting such professionals as patent attorneys, accountants, commercial bankers, and venture capitalists who come into contact with those seeking to license patents or to start a business using patented products or processes.

- ***Consulting.*** A method for obtaining ideas that has been successful for technically trained entrepreneurs is to provide consulting and one-of-a-kind engineering designs for people in fields of interest. For example, an entrepreneur wanting to establish a medical equipment company can do consulting or can design experimental equipment for medical researchers. These kinds of activities often lead to prototypes that can be turned into products needed by a number of researchers. For example, this approach was used in establishing a company to produce psychological testing equipment that evolved from consulting done at the Massachusetts General Hospital and, again, in a company to design and manufacture oceanographic instruments which were developed from consulting done for an oceanographic research institute.

- ***Networking.*** Networks can be a stimulant and source of new ideas, as well as a source of valuable contacts with people. Much of this requires personal initiative on an informal basis; but around the country, organized networks can facilitate and accelerate the process of making contacts and finding new business ideas. Consider, for example, in the Boston area, a high-density area of exceptional entrepreneurial activity, several networks have emerged in recent years, including the Babson Entrepreneurial Exchange, the Smaller Business Association of New England (SBANE), the MIT Enterprise Forum, the 128 Venture Group, and the Boston Computer Society. Similar organizations can be found in all of the United States, for example, the American Women's Economic Development Corporation in New York City; the Association of Women Entrepreneurs; the Entrepreneur's Roundtable of the UCLA Graduate Student Association; and the Association of Collegiate Entrepreneurs at Wichita State University.

Shaping Your Opportunity

You will need to invest in some thorough research to shape your idea into an opportunity. *Data available about market characteristics, competitors, and so on, is frequently inversely related to the real potential of an opportunity;* that is, if market data are readily available and if the data clearly show significant potential, then a large number of competitors will enter the market and the opportunity will diminish.

The good news: Most data will be incomplete, inaccurate, and contradictory, and their meaning will be ambiguous. For entrepreneurs, gathering the necessary information and seeing possibilities and making linkages where others see only chaos are essential.

Leonard Fuld defined competitor intelligence as highly specific and timely information about a corporation.[26] Finding out about competitors' sales plans, key elements of their corporate strategies, the capacity of their plants and the technology used in them, who their principal suppliers and customers are, and a good bit about the new products that rivals have under development is difficult, but not impossible, even in emerging industries, when talking to intelligence sources.[27]

Using published resources is one source of such information. Interviewing people and analyzing data also is critical. Fuld believes that since business transactions generate information which flows into the public domain, one can locate intelligence sources by understanding the transaction and how intelligence behaves and flows.[28]

This can be done legally and ethically. There are, of course, less-than-ethical tactics, which include conducting phony job interviews, getting customers to put out phony bid requests, and lying, cheating, and stealing. Entrepreneurs need to be very careful to avoid such practices and are advised to consult an attorney when in doubt.

Note that the sources of information given below are just a start. Much creativity, work, and analysis will be involved to find intelligence and to extend the information obtained into useful form. For example, a competitor's income statement and balance sheet will rarely be handed out. Rather, they most likely must be derived from information in public filings or news articles or from credit reports, financial ratios, and interviews.[29]

Published Sources

The first step is a complete search of materials in libraries and on the Internet. You can find a huge amount of published information, databases, and other sources about industry, market, competitor, and personnel information. Some of this information will have been uncovered when you search for ideas. Listed below are additional sources that should help get you started.

Guides and Company Information

Valuable information is available in special issues of *Forbes, Inc., The Economist, Fast Company,* and *Fortune* and in the following:

- Compact D/SEC
- Compustat
- Thomas Register
- Directory of Corporate Affiliations
- Standard & Poor's Register of Corporations, Directors, and Executives
- Standard & Poor's Corporation Records
- Dun & Bradstreet Million Dollar Directory
- Dunn's Million Dollar Disc Plus
- Moody's Manuals
- World Almanac
- Worldscope

Valuable Sites on the Internet

- Entreworld (*http://www.entreworld.org*)—the web site of the Kauffman Center for Entrepreneurial Leadership, Ewing Marion Kauffman Foundation.
- Fast Company (*http://www.fastcompany.com*)
- Securities Data (*http://www.securitiesdata.com*)
- Ernst & Young (*http://www.ey.com*)
- Global Access—SEC documents through a subscription-based web site. *http://www.disclosure/com*
- INC online (*http://www.inc.com*)
- Success online (*http://www.successmagazine.com*)

---

[26] Leonard M. Fuld, *Competitor Intelligence: How to Get It; How to Use It* (New York: John Wiley & Sons, 1985), p. 9.
[27] An excellent resource is Fuld, *Competitor Intelligence.* See also David E. Gumpert and Jeffry A. Timmons, *The Encyclopedia of Small Business Resources* (New York: Harper & Row, 1984); "How to Snoop on Your Competitors," *Fortune,* May 14, 1984, pp. 28–33; and information published by accounting firms, such as *Sources of Industry Data,* published by Ernst and Young.
[28] Fuld, *Competitor Intelligence,* pp. 12–17.
[29] Ibid., p. 325.

Journal Articles via Computerized Indexes

- Dow Jones News
- FirstSearch
- Ethnic News Watch
- LEXIS/NEXIS
- New York Times Index
- Reuters Business Briefings
- Searchbank
- Uncover (http://uncweb.carl.org)
- ABI/Inform
- Wall Street Journal Index

Statistics

- Profiles in Business and Management
- USA Countries
- Zip Code Business Patterns
- Stat-USA (http://www.stat-usa.gov)
- http://www.census.gov (This is the URL for the U.S. Census Bureau that is listed in statistics and financial and operating issues.)
- http://www.census.gov/stat-abstract (This is the URL for the Statistical Abstract of the United States that is listed in statistics and financial and operating issues section.)
- Knight Ridder . . . CRB Commodity Year Book
- Manufacturing USA
- Economic Census
- Economic Statistics Briefing Room (http://www.whitehouse.gov/fsbr/esbr.html)
- Federal Reserve Bulletin
- Survey of Current Business
- Labstat (http://stats.bls.gov/labstat.htm)
- DRI (aka Citibase)
- International Financial Statistics
- Reuterlink PC
- Bloomberg Database

Projections and Forecasts

- Proquest Direct
- Computer Industry Forecasts
- Guide to Special Issues and Indexes to Periodicals
- Value Line Investment Survey

Market Studies

- LifeStyle Market Analyst

Consumer Expenditures

- The Official Guide to American Incomes
- Consumer Expenditure Survey

Other Sources:

- Wall Street Transcript
- CIRR: Company & Industry Research Reports
- Brokerage House reports
- Company annual reports

Other Intelligence

Everything entrepreneurs need to know will not be found in libraries, since this information needs to be "highly specific" and "current." This information is most likely available from people—industry experts, suppliers, and the like.

Summarized below are some useful sources of intelligence.

- ***Trade associations.*** Trade associations, especially the editors of their publications and information officers, are good sources of information.[30] Especially, trade shows and conferences are prime places to discover the latest activities of competitors.

- ***Employees.*** Employees who have left a competitor's company often can provide information about the competitor, especially if the employee departed on bad terms. Also, a firm can hire people away from a competitor. While consideration of ethics in this situation is important, certainly the number of experienced people in any industry is limited, and competitors must prove that a company hired a person intentionally to get specific trade secrets in order to challenge any hiring legally. Students who have worked for competitors are another source of information.

- ***Consulting firms.*** Consulting firms frequently conduct industry studies and then make this information available. Frequently, in such fields as computers or software, competitors use the same design consultants, and these consultants can be sources of information.

- ***Market research firms.*** Firms doing the market studies, such as those listed under published sources above, can be sources of intelligence.

- ***Key customers, manufacturers, suppliers, distributors, and buyers.*** These groups are often a prime source of information.

───────────
[30] Ibid., pp. 46 and 48.

- **Public filings.** Federal, state, and local filings, such as filings with the Securities and Exchange Commission (SEC) or Freedom-of-Information Act filings, can reveal a surprising amount of information. There are companies that process inquiries of this type.

- **Reverse engineering.** Reverse engineering can be used to determine costs of production and sometimes even manufacturing methods. An example of this practice is the experience of Advanced Energy Technology, Inc., of Boulder, Colorado, which learned first-hand about such tactics. No sooner had it announced a new product, which was patented, when it received 50 orders, half of which were from competitors asking for only one or two of the items.

- **Networks.** The networks mentioned in Chapter 2 as sources of new venture ideas also can be sources of competitor intelligence.

- **Other.** Classified ads, buyers guides, labor unions, real estate agents, courts, local reporters, and so on, can provide clues.[31]

Chapter Summary

1. Ideas are a dime a dozen. Perhaps one out of a hundred become truly great businesses, and of those 1 in 10 to 15 become higher potential businesses. The complex transformation of an idea into a true opportunity is akin to a caterpillar becoming a butterfly.

2. High-potential opportunities invariably solve an important problem, want, or need that someone is willing to pay for now. In renowned venture capitalist Arthur Rock's words: "I look for ideas that will change the way people live and work."

3. There are decided patterns in superior opportunities, and recognizing these patterns is a skill aspiring entrepreneurs need to develop.

4. Rapid changes and disruptions in technology, regulation, information flows, and the like cause opportunity creation. The journey from idea to high-potential opportunity requires navigating an undulating, constantly changing, three-dimensional relief map while inventing the vehicle and road map along the way.

5. Some of the best opportunities actually require some of the least amount of capital, especially via the Internet.

6. The best opportunities often don't start out that way. They are crafted, shaped, molded, and reinvented in real time and marketspace. Fit with the entrepreneur and resources, the timing, and the balance of risk and reward govern the ultimate potential.

7. The highest-potential ventures are found in high-growth markets, with high gross margins, and robust, free cash flow characteristics, because their underlying products or services add significantly greater value to the customer, compared with the next best alternatives.

Study Questions

1. What is the difference between an idea and a good opportunity?

2. Why is it said that ideas are a dime a dozen?

3. What role does experience play in the opportunity creation process, and where do most good opportunities come from?

4. List the sources of ideas that are most relevant to your personal interests, and conduct a search using the Internet.

5. What conditions and changes that may occur in society and the economy spawn and drive future opportunities? List as many as you can think of as you consider the next 10 years.

6. Evaluate your best idea against the summary criteria in Exhibit 3.3. What appears to be its potential? What has to happen to convert it into a high potential business?

7. Draw a value chain and free cash flow chain for an existing business dominated by a few large players. How can you use the Internet, desktop computer, and other information age technology to capture (save) a significant portion of the margins and free cash flows?

MIND STRETCHERS
Have You Considered?

1. Steve Jobs, founder of Apple Computer, was 10 years old when he built his first computer. Colonel Sanders was 65 years old when he started Kentucky Fried Chicken. What is an opportunity and for whom?

2. Most successful existing businesses are totally preoccupied with their most important, existing customers and therefore lack the peripheral opportunity vision to spot new products and services. How is this happening where you work? Is this an opportunity for you?

3. The most successful ventures have leadership and people as the most important competitive advantage. How does this change the way you think about opportunities?

4. Who can you work with during the next few years to learn a business and have the chance to spot new opportunities outside the weak peripheral vision of an established business?

[31] Fuld, *Competitor Intelligence*, pp. 369–418.

Preparation Questions:

1. Who can be an entrepreneur?
2. What are the risks, rewards and tradeoffs of a lifestyle business vs. a high potential business—one that will exceed $5 million in sales and grow substantially?
3. What is the difference between an idea and an opportunity? For whom? What can be learned from Exhibits C and D?
4. Why has the company succeeded so far?
5. What should Roxanne and Burt do, and why?

"Our goal for the first year was $10,000 in total sales. I figured if I could take home half of that, it would be more money than I'd ever seen."

-Roxanne Quimby

Introduction

Roxanne Quimby sat in the president's office of Burt's Bees newly relocated manufacturing facility in Raleigh, North Carolina. She was surrounded by unpacked boxes and silence from the unmoving machines with no one there to operate them. Quimby looked around and asked herself, "Why did I do this?" She felt lonely and missed Maine, Burt's Bees' previous home. Quimby had founded and built Burt's Bees, a manufacturer of beeswax-based personal care products and handmade crafts, in central Maine and was not convinced she shouldn't move it back there. She explained:

When we got to North Carolina, we were totally alone. I realized how much of the business existed in the minds of the Maine employees. There, everyone had their mark on the process. That was all lost when we left Maine in 1994. I just kept thinking 'Why did I move Burt's Bees?' I thought I would pick the company up and move it and everything would be the same. Nothing was the same except that I was still working 20-hour days.

Quimby had profound doubts about this move to North Carolina and was seriously considering moving back to Maine. She needed to make a decision quickly because Burt's Bees was in the process of hiring new employees and purchasing a great deal of manufacturing equipment. If she pulled out now, losses could be minimized and she could hire back each of the 44 employees she had left back in Maine, since none of them had found new jobs yet. On the other hand, it would be hard to ignore all the reasons she had decided to leave Maine in the first place. If she moved Burt's Bees back, she would face the same problems that inspired this move. In Maine, Burt's Bees would probably never grow over $3 million in sales, and Quimby felt it had potential for much more.

Roxanne Quimby and the Founding of Burt's Bees

The Black Sheep

"I was a real black sheep in my family," Quimby said. She had one sister who worked for AMEX, another sister who worked for Charles Schwab, and her father worked for Merrill Lynch. She was not interested in business at all, though, and considered it dull. Quimby attended the San Francisco Art Institute in the late 60s and "got radicalized out there," she explained. "I studied, oil painted, and graduated without any job prospects. I basically dropped out of life. I moved to central Maine where land was really cheap—$100 an acre—and I could live removed from society."

Personal politics wasn't the only thing that pushed Quimby below the poverty line. While in college, Roxanne's father discovered she was living with her boyfriend and disowned her, severing all financial and familial ties. Her father, a Harvard Business School graduate and failed entrepreneur, did give her one gift—an early entrepreneurial education. At the age of five, Roxanne Quimby's father told her he wouldn't give her a cent for college but would match every dollar she earned herself. By her high school graduation Quimby had banked $5,000 by working on her father's numerous entrepreneurial projects and selling her own handmade crafts.

In 1975 Quimby and her boyfriend married and moved to Guilford, Maine—an hour northwest of Bangor. They bought 30 acres of land at $100 an acre and built a two-room house with no electricity, running water, or phone. In 1977 Quimby had twins and her lifestyle became a burden. She washed diapers in pots of boiling water on a wood-burning stove and struggled constantly to make ends meet with minimum wage jobs. Her marriage broke apart when the twins were four. Quimby packed up everything she owned on a toboggan and pulled the load across the snow to a friend's house.

The money-making skills her father forced her to develop allowed Quimby to survive. She and her children lived in a small tent and Quimby made almost $150 a week by working local flea markets—buying low and

© Copyright Jeffry A. Timmons, 1997. This case was written by Rebecca Voorheis, under the direction of Jeffry A. Timmons, Franklin W. Olin Distinguished Professor of Entrepreneurship, Babson College. Funding provided by the Ewing Marion Kauffman Foundation. All rights reserved.

selling high. She also held jobs waitressing. Quimby described, "I always felt I had an entrepreneurial spirit. Even as a waitress I felt entrepreneurial because I had control. I couldn't stand it when other people controlled my destiny or performance. Other jobs didn't inspire me to do my best, but waitressing did because I was accountable to myself. Eventually I got fired from these jobs because I didn't hesitate to tell the owners what I thought. I had a bit of an attitude."

In 1984 Quimby began to question her lifestyle and realized she had to make a change. She explained, "I decided I had to make a real income. I started to feel the responsibility of having kids. I had waitressing jobs but there were only three restaurants in town and I had been fired from all three. That's when I hooked up with Burt."

A Kindred Spirit

Like Roxanne Quimby, Burt Shavitz had also dropped out of life in the early 70s. A New York native and ex-photographer for *Life* and *New York* magazines, Shavitz lived in an 8′ by 8′ house (previously a turkey coop) on a 20-acre farm in Dexter, Maine, which he purchased in 1973. Shavitz, a beekeeper with 30 hives, sold honey off the back of his truck during hunting season. He earned maybe $3,000 a year, which was exactly enough to pay property taxes and buy gas for his pickup truck.

When Roxanne first saw Burt, who she described as a "good-looker," she knew she had to meet him. In an article in Lear's magazine Quimby said, "I pretended I was interested in the bees, but I was really interested in Burt. Here was this lone beekeeper. I wanted to fix him, to tame the wild man."[32] When Quimby and Shavitz met in 1984, the bond was immediate. Quimby talked about Shavitz's role at Burt's Bees;

I convinced Burt into this enterprise. He has always believed in my vision, but unlike me he's emotionally detached and uninvolved. Therefore, he has some great ideas and is more likely to take risks. He's my main sounding board and gives me a lot of moral and psychological support. I never could have done this without him. In all this time, there's never been a conflict between us. The chemistry has always been there. We're just really on the same wavelength. We've been through a lot together that would have broken other relationships. I've always been the motivator and the one involved in day-to-day operations, but very rarely does he disagree with me. He's kind of my guru.

In the beginning of their fast friendship, Burt taught Roxanne about beekeeping and Roxanne discovered Burt's large stockpile of beeswax. Quimby suggested making candles with the beeswax. She took her hand-dipped and -sculpted candles to a crafts fair at a local high school and brought home $200. She remembers, "I had never held that much money in my hand." Burt's Bees was born.

Quimby and Shavitz pooled $400 from their savings to launch a honey and beeswax business. They purchased some household kitchen appliances for mixing, pouring, and dipping. A friend rented them an abandoned one-room schoolhouse with no heat, running water, windows, or electricity for $150 a year—the cost of the fire insurance. Neither of them had a phone so they convinced the local health food store to take messages for Burt's Bees. Quimby traveled to fair after fair around the region, sleeping in the back of a pickup truck and making a few hundred dollars a day. She set what seemed like an impossible goal for the first year's sales—$10,000. That year, 1987, Burt's Bees made $81,000 in sales.

Burt's Bees' Early Success

Burt's Bees' big break came in 1989 at a wholesale show in Springfield, Massachusetts. The owner of an upscale boutique in Manhattan bought a teddy bear candle and put it in the window of his store. The candle was a hit and the boutique owner barraged the health food store with messages asking for new shipments. Quimby began hiring employees to help with production and expanded the product line to include other handmade crafts and beeswax-based products like lip balm. In 1993, Burt's Bees had 44 employees.

Quimby explained her transformation into a businessperson;

After a while, I realized I just liked it. I liked buying and selling things well, adding value. I had no security issues because I'd been living at the bottom for so many years. I knew if worse came to worse and the business failed, I could survive. I'd seen the worst and knew I could handle it. I'd never been trapped by the need for security or a regular paycheck. I loved the freedom of starting a business, of not knowing how it would turn out. It was this big experiment and whether it succeeded or failed totally depended on me. I realized the goal was not the most interesting part; the problems along the way were. I found business was the most incredibly liberating thing. I never would have thought that before. The only rule is that you have to make a little bit more than you spend. As long as you can do that, anything else you do is OK. There are no other opportunities that have as few rules.

Not only did Roxanne Quimby have a passion for business, she also had a talent. Since the beginning of Burt's Bees in 1987, the company had never once dipped into the red, had always turned a profit, and its profits had always increased [see *Exhibit A*]. A number of large national retailers stocked Burt's Bees' products including L.L. Bean, Macy's, and Whole Foods Market Company. By 1993, Burt's Bees had sales representatives across the country and sold its products in every

---

[32] John Bentham, "Enterprise," *Lear's*, March, 1994, pp. 20–21.

EXHIBIT A

Burt's Bees Sales, 1987–1993.

Year	Sales
1987	$81,000
1988	$137,779
1989	$180,000
1990	$500,000
1991	$1,500,000
1992	$2,500,000
1993	$3,000,000

state. By all accounts, Burt's Bees' products were a success. Quimby explained their appeal:

> We sell really well in urban areas. People in urban areas need us more because they can't step out the front door and get freshness or simplicity. Our products aren't sophisticated or sleek. They're down-home and basic. Everyone has an unconscious desire for more simplicity and our products speak to that need.

The company was not only profitable, it was totally debt-free. Burt's Bees had never taken out a loan. Quimby didn't even have a credit card. When she applied for one in 1993, by then a millionaire, she had to get her sister to co-sign because she had no credit history. She was strongly averse to going into debt. Quimby explained:

> I've never taken on debt because I don't ever want to feel like I can't walk away from it this afternoon. That's important to me. A monthly payment would trap me into having to explain my actions. I love being on the edge with no predictability, no one to report to. Anyway, there was no way a bank would have given me the money to start Burt's Bees. I could just see myself with some banker trying to explain, 'I've never had a job or anything but could you give me some money because I have this idea about beeswax.'

Quimby was so debt-averse and cash-aware, she refused to sell products to any retailer that didn't pay its bill within the required 30 days. This meant turning down orders from retailing powerhouses like I. Magnin and Dean & Deluca. In 1993, with about $3 million in sales, the company wrote off only $2,500 in uncollected debts. In the same year, Burt's Bees had $800,000 in the bank, and pretax profits were 35 percent of sales.

The Move

The Costs of Doing Business in Maine

The main impetus for the move was the excessive costs associated with Burt's Bees' location in northern Maine. These costs were:

1. **High transport costs:** "Our transport costs were ridiculously high," said Quimby. Because of its vast distance from any metropolitan areas, shipping products to distributors and receiving materials were astronomically expensive. Burt's Bees was almost always the last stop on truckers' routes.

2. **High payroll taxes:** Burt's Bees was being taxed about 10 percent of its payroll by the state of Maine. Payroll taxes were so high because unemployment in Maine hovered around 20 percent.

3. **Lack of Expertise:** In 1993, Burt's Bees had 44 employees who were all "welfare moms." Quimby said, "They brought a set of hands and a good attitude to work, but no skills." Everything was made by hand. Burt's Bees' most popular product, lip balm, was mixed with a household blender then poured from teapots into metal tins. "When we received a shipment of containers or labels, we had to break down the pallets inside the truck because no one knew how to operate a forklift. Everything was inefficient and costly. There weren't any people with expertise in Maine," Quimby explained. For a while, Quimby aggressively recruited managers from around New England. When they came up to Guilford to interview and realized how isolated the town was, though, they would turn down any offer Quimby made.

Roxanne Quimby moved the company to free Burt's Bees from these constraints and liberate it to grow. Since beginning operations in 1987, Burt's Bees struggled to keep up with demand. Quimby had no time to focus on broad management issues since she spent most of her time pouring beeswax along with the other 44 employees in order to fill distributors' unceasing orders. She explained;

> The business had developed a life of its own and it was telling me it wanted to grow. But it was growing beyond me, my expertise, my goals, and definitely beyond Maine. If I kept it in northern Maine, I would have stunted its growth. But the business was my child in a way and as its mother I wanted to enable it to grow. The business provided a great income and I could have gone on like that for a while. But I knew it had a lot more potential than $3 million. At the same time, I knew $3 million was the most I could do on my own. I was working all of the time and there was no one to lean on or delegate to. My lack of formal business training really began to bite me. I didn't even know about payroll taxes. We would get fined for missing tax deadlines we didn't even know existed.

Why North Carolina?

Roxanne Quimby felt she had to move the company away from Maine. But to where? She didn't want to live in a big, bustling city, but the new location had to be central. Quimby explained how she finally chose North Carolina as Burt's Bees' new home:

I had a map of the United States in my office with pins where all of our sales reps were. I used to always look at that map—when I was on the phone, doing paperwork, or just sitting at my desk—until one day I noticed North Carolina. It just seemed central, well placed. And, it turned out, a large percentage of the country's population lives within a 12-hour drive of North Carolina. One of my biggest worries about moving was telling Burt. I said to Burt one day, "We need to move and it looks like North Carolina is the place to go." Burt said, "OK, Roxy" and I thought to myself, "Thank God Burt is always on my wavelength."

Burt got on the phone with a representative at the North Carolina Department of Commerce and told him about Burt's Bees. Burt and Roxanne were pleasantly surprised to learn North Carolina was extremely aggressive about recruiting new companies to the state and was eager to attract Burt's Bees, even though it was quite a bit smaller than other companies locating in the "Triangle"[33] The North Carolina Department of Commerce sent Burt's Bees a software program which Quimby used to plug in financial information and calculate the estimated taxes Burt's Bees would pay in North Carolina. The estimated taxes were significantly less than those they were paying in Maine.

Perhaps more compelling, though, was the large supply of skilled labor in North Carolina. If Burt's Bees moved, it would be able to hire an ex-Revlon plant engineer to establish and operate its manufacturing processes. Quimby also had a lead on a marketing manager in North Carolina with experience at Lancome, Vogue, and Victoria's Secret's personal care products division.

As a next step, the North Carolina Department of Commerce invited Roxanne and Burt to visit North Carolina for a three-day tour of the Triangle area and available manufacturing facilities. "You should have seen the look on the representative's face when he picked us up from the airport," Quimby laughed. "Burt has this deep, gruff voice, so he must have sounded very different on the phone than he looks. Burt is 62, has crazy white hair to his shoulders and a long white beard, is really tall, and pretty much looks like he just walked out of the woods of Maine." She continued to say, "The representative recovered really well, though, and took us around the whole area for three days. He showed us tons of plants and real estate. He made us a great offer and we were impressed."

When they got back to Maine, Quimby called the Maine Department of Commerce to give it a chance to keep Burt's Bees in the state. "If they had offered us half the deal North Carolina did," Quimby said, "I would have taken it." The Maine Department of Commerce asked Roxanne to call back in a couple of months because the person in charge of business recruiting was out on maternity leave. Quimby marveled, "We were the second largest employer in the town and they didn't respond to us at all. We finally heard from the Governor of Maine when he read an article about us in *Forbes*[34] which mentioned we were leaving the state. By then it was too late. The move was only a few days away and we had already signed a lease on the new manufacturing facility."

Trimming the Azalea Bush: The Economics of the Move

Roxanne Quimby likened Burt's Bees' move to transplanting an azalea bush in full bloom. She said, "I realized I had to trim and prune radically to allow it to survive." In Maine, Burt's Bees biggest resource was cheap labor—people on the production line were paid $5 an hour. Therefore, most of Burt's Bees products were very labor-intensive and production was totally unautomated. All of its products, from birdhouses to candles to baby clothes, were handmade.

In North Carolina, though, the company's biggest resource was skilled labor. But skilled labor is expensive and Burt's Bees wouldn't be able to keep making its labor-intensive handmade items. Quimby would have to automate everything and change Burt's Bees' whole product line to focus on skincare products [see *Exhibit B*, for industry employment statistics]. She explained, "Our products in Maine were totally unrelated production-wise, but they were related in the sense that each product communicated down-home values and simplicity. In North Carolina, though, we would have to get rid of all the handmade products and that was pretty much everything. We had to automate."

When Quimby arrived in North Carolina she sat down to evaluate the product line and decided to focus on skincare [for general industry statistics, see *Exhibit C* and D]. Skincare products require only blending and filling, which is very straightforward, and machinery can do almost everything. "To justify the move to North Carolina from a cost- and manufacturing-perspective, we would have to make more 'goop'," Quimby stated. "I looked at my list of prospective new products and there wasn't anything on the list that we made in 1988."

Quimby planned on retaining Burt's Bees environmental ethic by excluding any chemical preservatives and using primarily all-natural ingredients in its skincare products. Still, though, Burt's Bees would have to become an entirely new company and abandon the product line responsible for the company's early success.

Not only would the product line have to be overhauled, Roxanne realized she and Burt couldn't remain the sole owners of the company if she wanted it to grow.

---

[33] The "Triangle" area in North Carolina includes Chapel Hill, Raleigh, and Durham and is the home of Research Triangle Park, a large high-tech business park similar to Silicon Valley in California or Route 128 in Massachusetts.

[34] "Dear Dad," by Dana Wechsler Linder. *Forbes*, December 6, 1993, pp. 98–99.

EXHIBIT B

Occupations Employed by Standard Industrial Classification (SIC) 284: Soap, Cleaners, and Toilet Goods.*

Occupation	% of Industry Total, 1994	% Change to 2005 (projected)
Packaging & filling machine operators	8.5	−30.1
Hand packers & packagers	6.3	−20.1
Assemblers, fabricators, & hand workers	5.7	16.5
Sales & related workers	4.9	16.5
Freight, stock & material movers, hand	3.6	−6.8
Secretaries, ex legal & medical	3.5	6.0
Chemical equipment controllers, operators	3.0	4.8
Industrial machinery mechanics	2.7	28.1
Machine operators	2.6	2.6
Industrial truck & tractor operators	2.6	16.5
Chemists	2.5	28.1
Crushing & mixing machine operators	2.5	16.4
General managers & top executives	2.5	10.5
Traffic, shipping & receiving clerks	2.2	12.1
Marketing, advertising & PR managers	2.0	16.5
Science & mathematics technicians	1.8	16.5
Bookkeeping, accounting & auditing clerks	1.8	16.5
Maintenance repairers, general utility	1.7	4.8
Inspectors, testers & graders, precision	1.6	16.5
General office clerks	1.6	−.7
Order clerks, materials, merchandise & service	1.5	13.9
Machine feeders & offbearers	1.5	4.8
Clerical supervisors & managers	1.5	19.1
Professional workers	1.4	39.7
Industrial production managers	1.4	16.4
Stock clerks	1.4	−5.3
Managers & administrators	1.3	16.4
Adjustment clerks	1.2	39.8
Accountants & auditors	1.2	16.5
Management support workers	1.1	16.4
Engineering, mathematical & science managers	1.1	32.2
Truck drivers light & heavy	1.0	20.1

Manufacturing USA: Industry Analyses, Statistics, and Leading Companies: 5th edition, volume 1, ed. Arsen J. Darnay. Gale Research Inc. (1996), p. 837.

EXHIBIT C

General Industry Statistics for SIC 2844: Toilet Preparations.*

Year	Establishments		Employment			Compensation		Production ($million)			
	Total	With 20≤ employees	Total (000)	Production workers (000)	Production hours (mill)	Payroll ($mill)	Wages ($/hour)	Cost of materials	Value added by manufacture	Value of shipments	Capital investment
1988	687	277	64.9	40.5	78.1	1,551.3	9.08	4,445.1	12,053.2	16,293.6	292.6
1989	676	282	63.6	39.4	75.4	1,615.5	9.69	4,758.2	11,979.2	16,641.9	313.7
1990	682	284	63.6	38.1	74.3	1,620.6	10.14	4,904.6	12,104.2	17,048.4	280.4
1991	674	271	57.4	35.6	69.8	1,616.3	10.81	5,046.3	12,047.4	18,753.5	299.5
1992	756	305	60.1	37.2	75.6	1,783.3	10.82	5,611.3	13,167.2	19,706.4	507.3
1993	778	299	61.7	38.6	79.7	1,857.8	10.59	6,152.6	13,588.8	19,736.0	472.6

**Manufacturing USA*, p. 833. Source: 1982, 1987, 1992 *Economic Census; Annual Survey of Manufactures,* 83–86, 88–91, 93–94. Establishment counts for noncensus years are from *County Business Patterns.*

EXHIBIT D

Comparison of Toilet Preparations Industry (SIC 2844) to the Average of All U.S. Manufacturing Sectors, 1994.*

Selected Measurement	All Manufacturing Sectors Average	SIC 2844 Average	Index
Employees per establishment	49	77	157
Payroll per establishment	$1,500,273	$ 2,397,065	160
Payroll per employee	$ 30,620	$ 31,191	102
Production workers per establishment	34	47	137
Wages per establishment	$ 853,319	$ 1,061,646	124
Wages per production worker	$ 24,861	$ 22,541	91
Hours per production worker	2,056	2,062	100
Wages per hour	$ 12.09	$ 10.93	90
Value added per establishment	$4,602,255	$17,781,454	386
Value added per employee	$ 93,930	$ 231,375	246
Value added per production worker	$ 134,084	$ 377,541	282
Cost per establishment	$5,045,178	$ 8,648,566	171
Cost per employee	$ 102,970	$ 112,536	109
Cost per production worker	$ 146,988	$ 183,629	125
Shipments per establishment	9,576,895	26,332,221	275
Shipments per employee	195,460	342,639	175
Shipments per production worker	279,017	559,093	200
Investment per establishment	$ 321,011	$ 654,570	204
Investment per employee	$ 6,552	$ 8,517	130
Investment per production worker	$ 9,352	$ 13,898	149

*Same as previous.

Since the inception of Burt's Bees, Roxanne and Burt held 70 percent and 30 percent of its stock, respectively. The truly talented employees Quimby hoped to attract would want shared ownership of the company and would be highly motivated by stock rewards. Quimby knew sharing ownership would mean feeling accountable to others and having to justify her sometimes unorthodox decisions. Accountability was exactly what she had fought so hard to avoid her whole life, and Quimby's autonomy was partly a cause of her success.

Conclusion

Quimby walked around the empty North Carolina factory. She tried to imagine the empty space filled with machinery and workers, humming with activity and production. Her mind kept reflecting back to the old schoolhouse in Maine, though. Was her ambiguity about this move merely a temporary sentimentality or should she listen to her instinct, which hadn't failed her to date? She had to make a decision soon. As she saw it, Quimby had three choices:

1. **Stay in North Carolina:** Quimby could mentally and financially commit to the North Carolina move and try to get over her doubts. Burt's Bees had promising leads in North Carolina on a plant manager from Revlon and a Sales and Marketing manager with experience at Lancome, Vogue, and Victoria's Secret. Quimby's expertise deficit could largely be solved with these two experts.

2. **Move back to Maine:** Quimby could halt all purchasing and hiring and move back to Maine where most of her ex-employees could be hired back. There would be some sunk costs involved, but they could be minimized if she acted quickly. Additionally, Burt's Bees could keep its original product line that made the company so successful in the first place. The governor of Maine said to call him if she changed her mind about North Carolina. She could pursue a deal with the state of Maine to mitigate Burt's Bees' tax, transport, and employment costs.

3. **Sell the Company:** Although it might be difficult to attract a buyer at only $3 million in sales, Burt's Bees had received quite a bit of attention in the industry and would be an enticing purchase to many prospective buyers. Quimby knew she didn't want to be at Burt's Bees forever and said, "I feel like at some point, this business isn't going to need me anymore. My child will grow up and want to move away from its mother. There are other things I want to do which are next on my list." Quimby dreamed about living in India and working with rural women on product design, production, and marketing of their handmade crafts. If she sold Burt's Bees, this dream could become an immediate reality.

Exercise

Creative Squares

STEP 1

DIVIDE YOUR GROUP BY (1) SEPARATING INTO A NUMBER OF GROUPS OF THREE OR MORE PERSONS EACH AND (2) HAVING AT LEAST FIVE INDIVIDUALS WORK ALONE.

STEP 2

SHOW THE FOLLOWING FIGURE TO EVERYONE AND ASK THE GROUPS AND THE INDIVIDUALS TO COUNT THE TOTAL NUMBER OF SQUARES IN THE FIGURE. Assume that the figure is a square box on a single flat plane. In counting, angles of any square must be right angles, and the sides must be of equal length.

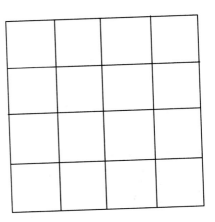

STEP 3

DISCUSS THE CREATIVE PROCESS BY WHICH THE GROUPS AND THE INDIVIDUALS REACHED THEIR ANSWERS.

Idea Generation Guide

Before beginning the process of generating ideas for new ventures, it is useful to reflect on an old German proverb that says, "Every beginning is hard." If you allow yourself to think creatively, you will be surprised at the number of interesting ideas you can generate once you begin.

The Idea Generation Guide is an exercise in generating ideas. The aim is for you to generate as many interesting ideas as possible. *While generating your ideas, do not evaluate them or worry about their implementation.* Discussion and exercises in the rest of the book will allow you to evaluate these ideas to see if they are opportunities and to consider your own personal entrepreneurial strategy.

And remember—in any creative endeavor there are no right answers.

Exercise

Idea Generation Guide

NAME:

DATE:

STEP 1

GENERATE A LIST OF AS MANY NEW VENTURE IDEAS AS POSSIBLE. Thinking about any unmet or poorly filled customer needs you know of that have resulted from regulatory changes, technological changes, knowledge and information gaps, lags, asymmetries, inconsistencies, and so forth, will help you generate such a list. Also, think about various products and services (and their substitutes) and the providers of these products or services. If you know of any weaknesses or vulnerabilities, you may discover new venture ideas.

STEP 2

EXPAND YOUR LIST IF POSSIBLE. Think about your personal interests, your desired lifestyle, your values, what you feel you are likely to do very well, and contributions you would like to make.

STEP 3

ASK AT LEAST THREE PEOPLE WHO KNOW YOU WELL TO LOOK AT YOUR LIST, AND REVISE YOUR LIST TO REFLECT ANY NEW IDEAS EMERGING FROM THIS EXCHANGE. See discussion about getting feedback in Chapter 18.

STEP 4

JOT DOWN INSIGHTS, OBSERVATIONS, AND CONCLUSIONS THAT HAVE EMERGED ABOUT YOUR BUSINESS IDEAS OR YOUR PERSONAL PREFERENCES:

4

Screening Venture Opportunities

Entrepreneurs need to think big. You are going to end up exhausted in building a company. So you might as well end up exhausted and rich!

Patricia Cloherty, first woman president
of the National Venture Capital Association,
President, Patricof and Co.

Results Expected

At the conclusion of this chapter, you will have:

1. Examined two screening methodologies—Quick Screen and the Venture Opportunity Screening Guide (VOSG)—which can help you to determine whether your ideas are potential opportunities.

2. Applied the opportunity criteria from Chapter 3 to your ideas and begun to assess the probable *fit* with you, your team, and resources, and the *balance of risk and reward.*

3. Begun to consider with more creativity and depth what you need to do to improve both the *fit* and the *risk and reward relationship.*

4. Determined whether your best idea at this time has sufficient potential to pursue the development of a thorough business plan.

5. Concluded whether you believe you can sufficiently alter the idea and your strategy to create a *good fit* and an *attractive risk:reward balance* for you and your investors.

6. Analyzed the "Gary and George Mueller" case.

Screening Venture Opportunities

Time is the ultimate ally and enemy of the entrepreneur. You will not have enough time in a quarter, a year, or a decade to pursue all the ideas for businesses you and your team can think of. Perhaps the cruelest part of this paradox is: you *have* to find and make the time for the good ones. To complicate the paradox, *you do not have a strategy until you are saying no to lots of opportunities.* This is part of the punishing and the rewarding aspects of entrepreneurship: many will try, many will fail, some will succeed, and a few will excel. It is estimated that in 1999 as many as 3.5 to 4 million new enterprises of all kinds will be launched in the United States, or about 300,000-plus each month. Of those, only 10 to 15 percent will prove to be good opportunities that will achieve sales of $1 million or more.

Four Anchors

This chapter will put you in the trenches, engaging in the first of many struggles to determine whether your good idea is truly a good opportunity. Ideas that turn into good businesses are not accidents. Consistent with the model in Chapter 2 and the opportunity criteria in Chapter 3, the superior businesses have four anchors:

1. They create or add significant value to a customer or end user.
2. They do so by solving a significant problem, or meeting a significant want or need, for which someone is willing to pay a premium.
3. They therefore have robust market, margin, and moneymaking characteristics: They are large enough (at least $50 million), have high growth (at least 20 percent), high margins (at least 40 percent), strong and early free cash flow (recurring revenue, low assets and working capital), high profit potential (at least 10–15 percent after taxes) and offer attractive realizable returns for investors (at least 25–30 percent IRR).
4. They are a good *fit* with the founder(s) and management team at the time and in the marketplace and with the risk/reward balance.

QuickScreen

If most sophisticated private equity investors and venture capitalists invest in only 1 to 5 out of 100 ideas, then one can see how important it is to focus on a few, superior ideas. The ability to quickly and efficiently reject ideas is a very important entrepreneurial skill. Saying no to lots of ideas directly conflicts with one's passion and commitment for a particular idea. This chapter provides two methods to make this struggle more manageable. The first, QuickScreen, should enable you in an hour or so to conduct a preliminary review and evaluation of an idea. Unless the idea has the four anchors, or you are confident it can be molded and shaped so that it does, you will waste a lot of time on a low-potential idea. The first section (pages 115 to 117) is a tearout of the QuickScreen, which can be reproduced for your own use.

Venture Opportunity Screening Guide (VOSG)

The second section (pages 118 to 156) is the complete Venture Opportunity Screening Guide (VOSG). Completing the VOSG may take 20 to 30 hours or more. Typically, this effort is reserved for the two or three very best ideas you have at this time. Over a one- to two-year period, the author has known entrepreneurs who have conducted the research and analysis necessary for the VOSG on as many as 8 to 10 good ideas before determining which one is attractive enough, given the four anchors, to develop a complete business plan.

Whether or not an entrepreneur plans to seek venture capital or an outside private investor to pursue an opportunity, it is vital to have a realistic view of the project's vulnerabilities and realities, as well as its compelling strengths. Often, the *iterative process* of carefully examining different ideas through many eyes, within and outside your team, triggers creative ideas and insights about how the initial business concept and strategy can be altered and molded to significantly enhance the value chain, free cash flow characteristics, and risk/reward relationships, and thus the *fit*. This process is central to value creation and the development of higher potential ventures. It is far from cut and dried.

This early seed stage is also a marvelous time for a "trial marriage" with prospective team members. This work can be detailed, tedious, and downright boring. Finding out now who can deliver what; who has the work ethic, consistency, and reliability; and whether you can work together will save a lot of money and headaches later on.

Ultimately, the *fit* issue boils down to this: do the opportunity, the resources required (at their cost), the other team members (if any), the timing, and balance of risk and reward *work for me?*

Exercise
QuickScreen

I. Market and Margin Related Issues

Criterion	Higher Potential	Lower Potential
Need/want/problem	Identified	Unfocused
Customers	Reachable and receptive	Unreachable/loyal to others
Payback to users	<One year	>Three years
Value added or created	IRR 40% +	IRR<20%
Market size	$50–100 million	<$10 million or >1 billion
Market growth rate	+20%	Less than 20%, contracting
Gross margin	40%+ and durable	Less than 20% and fragile
Overall potential:		
1. Market	higher _____ avg _____ lower	
2. Margins	higher _____ avg _____ lower	

II. Competitive Advantages

	Higher Potential	Lower Potential
Fixed and variable costs	Lowest	Highest
Degree of control	Stronger	Weaker
Prices and cost		
Channels of supply & distribution	None	Strong
Barriers to entry		
Proprietary advantage		
Lead time advantage (product, technology, people, resources, location)		
Service chain		
Contractual advantage		
Contacts and networks		
Overall potential		
1. costs	higher _____ avg _____ lower	
2. channel	higher _____ avg _____ lower	
3. barriers to entry	higher _____ avg _____ lower	
4. timing	higher _____ avg _____ lower	

III. Value Creation and Realization Issues

	Higher Potential	**Lower Potential**
Profit after tax	10–15% or more and durable	<5%; fragile
Time to break even	< 2 years	> 3 years
Time to positive cash flow	< 2 years	> 3 years
ROI potential	40–70% +, durable	< 20%, fragile
Value	High strategic value	Low strategic value
Capitalization requirements	Low–moderate; fundable	Very high; difficult to fund
Exit mechanism	IPO, acquisition	Undefined; illiquid investment
Overall value creation potential		
1. Timing	higher _____ avg _____ lower	
2. Profit/free cash flow	higher _____ avg _____ lower	
3. Exit/liquidity	higher _____ avg _____ lower	

IV. Overall Potential

	Go	No Go	Go, if . . .
1. Margins and markets			
2. Competitive advantages			
3. Value creation and realization			
4. Fit: "O" + "R" + "T"			
5. Risk/Reward Balance			
6. Timing			
7. Other compelling issues: must know or likely to fail			
a.			
b.			
c.			
d.			
e.			

Venture Opportunity Screening Guide

The Venture Opportunity Screening Guide (VOSG) is based on the screening criteria discussed in Chapter 3.

As you proceed through the VOSG, you will come to checkpoints. At each checkpoint, you can evaluate whether to proceed with your evaluation, change the definition of your opportunity in some way, or abandon it. When you pass all checkpoints in the VOSG, the extent of your opportunity's attractiveness should be much more apparent. Rarely is it simply cut and dried, however. Most of the time, there will be considerable uncertainty and numerous unknowns and risk involved even at this point. What the process can do is help you to understand those uncertainties and risks in making your decision and to devise ways to make them acceptable for you. If they cannot be made acceptable, then you keep searching.

Deciding where your opportunity falls will take a considerable amount of work. Plan to spend at least 20–30 hours in completing the VOSG. Depending upon the nature of your opportunity and your knowledge and access to critical information, completing the VOSG may require more effort, but probably not less. While this time commitment may seem large, the amount of time ultimately consumed in evaluating an opportunity by trial and error is almost always greater, and the tuition is much higher.

Every venture is unique. Operations, marketing, cash flow cycles, and so forth, vary a good bit from company to company, from industry to industry, and from region to region or country to country. As a result, you may find that not every issue pertinent to your venture will be covered in the VOSG or that some questions are irrelevant. Here and there, you may have to add to the VOSG or tailor it to your particular circumstances.

We suggest that you and each of the members of your team fill out a VOSG.

As with other exercises in the book, feel free to make as many Xerox copies of the VOSG as you need.

Venture Opportunity Screening Guide

Name:

Venture:

Date:

STEP 1

Briefly Describe Your Vision, the Opportunity Concept and Strategy.   What is your vision for the business? What is the value creation proposition? What is the significant problem, want or need that it will solve? Why is this important enough that a customer or end-user will pay an above average to a premium price for it? Why does this opportunity exist, now, for you? Can you describe the concept and your entry strategy in 25 words or less?

STEP 2

Fill in the Venture Opportunity Profile below by Indicating for Each Individual Criterion Where Your Venture Is Located on the *Potential* Continuum.   Make an *x* to indicate your best estimate of where your idea stacks up. Be as specific as possible. (If you have trouble, relevant trade magazines and newsletters, other entrepreneurs, trade shows, fairs, or other sources can help.)

Venture Opportunity Profile

Criterion	Highest Potential	Lowest Potential
Industry and Market		
Market: Need	Market driven; identified; recurring revenue niche	Unfocused; one-time revenue
Customers	Reachable; purchase orders	Loyal to others or unreachable
User benefits	Less than one year payback	Three years plus payback
Value added	High; advance payments	Low; minimal impact on market
Product life	Durable	Perishable
Market structure	Imperfect, fragmented competition or emerging industry	Highly concentrated or mature or or declining industry
Market size	$100 + million to $1 billion sales potential	Unknown, less than $20 million or multibillion sales
Growth rate	Growth at 30 to 50% or more	Contracting or less than 10%
Market capacity	At or near full capacity	Undercapacity
Market share attainable (Year 5)	20% or more; leader	Less than 5%
Cost structure	Low-cost provider; cost advantages	Declining cost
Economics		
Profits after tax	10–15% or more; durable	Less than 15%; fragile
ROI potential	25% or more; high value	Less than 15 to 20%; low value
Capital requirements	Low to moderate; fundable	Very high; unfundable
Internal rate of return potential	25% or more per year	Less than 15% per year
Free cash flow characteristics	Favorable; sustainable; 20–30 + % of sales	Less than 10% of sales

(Continued)

Economics

Criterion	Higher Potential	Lower Potential
Sales growth	Moderate to high (15 + % to 20 + %)	Less than 10%
Asset intensity	Low/sales $	High
Spontaneous working capital	Low, incremental requirements	High requirements
R&D/capital expenditures	Low requirements	High requirements
Gross margins	Exceeding 40% and durable	Under 20%
Time to breakeven—cash flow	Less than 2 years; breakeven not creeping	Greater than 4 years; breakeven creeping up
Time to breakeven—P&L	Less than 2 years; breakeven not creeping	Greater than 4 years; breakeven creeping up

Harvest Issues

Criterion	Higher Potential	Lower Potential
Value-added potential	High strategic value	Low strategic value
Valuation multiples and comparables	p/e 20 + ×; 8–10 + × EBIT; 1.5 – 2 + × revenue free cash flow 8–10 + ×	p/e = 5 ×, EBIT = 3–4×; revenue = .4
Exit mechanism and strategy	Present or envisioned options	Undefined; illiquid investment
Capital market context	Favorable valuations, timing, capital available; realizable liquidity	Unfavorable; credit crunch

Competitive Advantage Issues

Criterion	Higher Potential	Lower Potential
Fixed and variable costs	Lowest; high operating leverage	Highest
Control over costs, prices, and distribution	Moderate to strong	Weak
Barriers to entry: Proprietary protection	Have or can gain	None
Response/lead time	Competition slow; napping	Unable to gain edge
Legal, contractual advantage	Proprietary or exclusivity	None
Contacts and networks	Well-developed; accessible	Crude; limited
Key people	Top talent; an A team	B or C team

(Continued)

Management Team

Criteria	Positive	Negative
Entrepreneurial team	All-star combination; free agents	Weak or solo entrepreneur
Industry and technical experience	Top of the field; super track record	Underdeveloped
Integrity	Highest standards	Questionable
Intellectual honesty	Know what they do not know	Do not want to know what they do not know

Fatal-Flaw Issue

Criteria	Positive	Negative
	Non-existent	One or more

Personal Criteria

Criteria	Positive	Negative
Goals and fit	Getting what you want; but wanting what you get	Surprises
Upside/downside issues	Attainable success/limited risks	Linear; on same continuum
Opportunity costs	Acceptable cuts in salary, etc.	Comfortable with status quo
Desirability	Fits with lifestyle	Simply pursuing big money
Risk/reward tolerance	Calculated risk; low R/R ratio	Risk averse or gambler
Stress tolerance	Thrives under pressure	Cracks under pressure

Strategic Differentiation

Criteria	Positive	Negative
Degree of fit	High	Low
Team	Best in class; excellent free agents	B team; no free agents
Service management	Superior service concept	Perceived as unimportant
Timing	Rowing with the tide	Rowing against the tide
Technology	Groundbreaking; one-of-a-kind	Many substitutes or competitors
Flexibility	Able to adapt; commit and decommit quickly	Slow; stubborn
Opportunity orientation	Always searching for opportunities	Operating in a vacuum; napping
Pricing	At or near leader	Undercut competitor; low prices
Distribution channels	Accessible; networks in place	Unknown; inaccessible
Room for error	Forgiving strategy	Unforgiving, rigid strategy

STEP 3

Assess the External Environment Surrounding Your Venture Opportunity.   Include the following:

- An assessment of the characteristics of the opportunity window, including its perishability:

- A statement of what entry strategy suits the opportunity, and why:

- A statement of evidence of and/or reasoning behind your belief that external environment and the forces creating your opportunity, described in **Step 1** and in the Venture Opportunity Profile, fit:

- A statement of your exit strategy and an assessment of the prospects that this strategy can be met, including a consideration of whether the risks, rewards, and trade-offs are acceptable:

CHECKPOINT: Before you proceed, be sure the opportunity you have outlined is compelling and you can answer the question, why does the opportunity exist now? It is just possible you ought to abandon or alter the product or service idea behind your venture at this point. The amount of money and time needed to get the product or service to market, and to be open for business, may be beyond your limits. Remember, even in the abundant venture capital market of the mid-1980s, only 1–3 percent of all ventures received funding. Remember, also, that the first round of financing is typically in the $1 million to $2 million range and, to raise over $5 million, you need a truly exceptional management team and a concept whose potential rewards are large compared to the risks and vulnerabilities to obsolescence and competition.

STEP 4:

Assess the Attractiveness of Your Venture Opportunity by Applying Screening Criteria.   Include the following:

- What is the critical problem, want, or need your product or service will solve?

- Why is this a critical problem?

- Who will pay a premium price, compared with alternatives, if you can address this problem or want?

- What is the underlying value creation proposition: how and why will it pay for itself, yield major benefits/advantages, etc.?

- A brief description of the market(s) or market niche(s) you want to enter:

- An exact description of the product(s) or service(s) to be sold and, if a product, its eventual end use(s). (If your product(s) or service(s) are already commercially available or exist as prototypes, attach specifications, photographs, samples of work, etc.)

- An estimate of how perishable the product(s) or service(s) are, including if it is likely to become obsolete and when:

- An assessment of whether there are substitutes for the product(s) or services(s):

- An assessment of the status of development and an estimate of how much time and money will be required to complete development, test the product(s) or service(s), and then introduce the product(s) or service(s) to the market:

Development Tasks		
Development Task	**Dollars Required**	**Months to Complete**

- An assessment of any major difficulties in manufacturing the product(s) or delivering the service(s) and how much time and money will be required to resolve them:

- A description of the necessary customer support, such as warranty service, repair service, and training of technicians, salespeople, service people, or others:

- An assessment of the strengths and weaknesses, relative to the competition, of the product(s) or service(s) in meeting customer needs, including a description of payback of and value added by the product(s) or service(s):

- An assessment of your primary customer group:
  —A description of the main reasons why your primary group of customers will buy your product or service, including whether customers in this group are reachable and receptive and how your product or service will add or create value, and what this means for your entry or expansion strategy:

—A list of 5 to 10 crucial questions you need to have answered and other information you need to know to identify good customer prospects:

—An indication of how customers buy products or services (e.g., from direct sales, either wholesale or retail; through manufacturers' representatives or brokers; through catalogs; via direct mail; etc.):

—A description of the purchasing process (i.e., where it occurs and who is ultimately responsible for approving expenditures; what and who influence the sale; how long does it take from first contact to close, to delivery, and to cash receipt; and your conclusions about the competitive advantages you can achieve and how your product or service can add or create value):

- An assessment of the market potential for your venture's product or service, the competition, and what is required to bring and sell the product or service to the customer. (Such an analysis need not be precise or comprehensive but should serve to eliminate from further consideration those ventures that have obvious market difficulties.) Include the following information:

  —An estimate, for the past, present, and future, of the *approximate* size of the *total* potential market, as measured in units and in dollars or number of customers. In making your estimates, use available market data to estimate *ranges* of values and to identify the area (country, region, locality, etc.) and data for each segment if the market is segmented:

Total Market Size				
Year				
19	20	20	20	20

Sales of Units/
Number of Customers

Sales in Dollars

Sources of Data:

Researcher:

Confidence in Data:

—An assessment of the type of market in terms of price, quality, and service; degree of control, and so on; and your conclusions about what approaches are necessary to enter, survive, and win:

- An assessment, based on a survey of customers, of how your customers do business, and of what investigative steps are needed next:

	Customer Survey		
	Customer		
	No. 1	**No. 2**	**No. 3**
Nature of Customers			
Business or Role			
Reactions:			
Positive			
Negative			
Questions			

Specific Needs/Uses

Acceptable Terms—Price, Support, etc.

Basis of Purchase Decisions: Time Frame

Who Makes Decision

Dollar Limits

Substitutes/Competitive Products or Services Used

Names of Competitors

Competitive Products

Substitute Products

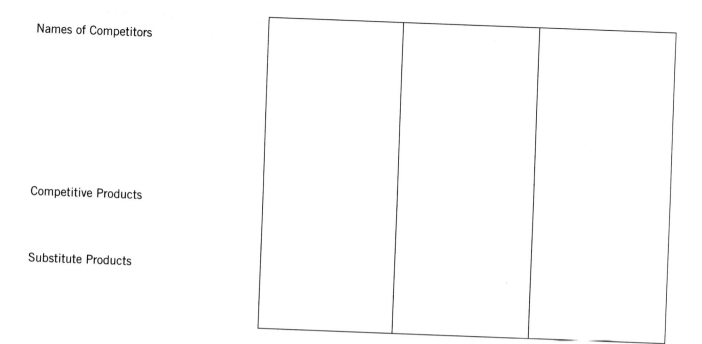

No.	Customers Surveyed
	Name

- An assessment of how your product or service will be positioned in the market, including:
  —A statement of any proprietary protection, such as patents, copyrights, or trade secrets, and what this means in the way of a competitive advantage:

—An assessment of any competitive advantages you can achieve in the level of quality, service, and so forth, including an objective description of any strengths (and weaknesses) of the product or service:

—An assessment of your pricing strategy versus those of competitors:

| | Pricing Strategy | | |
	Highest Price	Average Price	Lowest Price
Retail			
Wholesale			
Distributor			
Other Channel			
Manufacturing			

—An assessment of where competitors in your industry or market niche are in terms of price versus performance/benefits/value added:

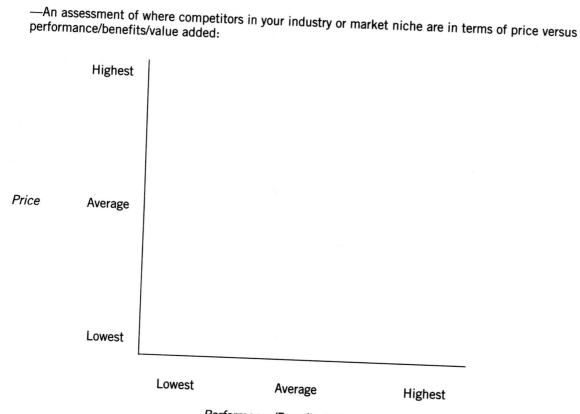

—An indication of how you plan to distribute and sell your product or services (e.g., through direct sales, mail order, manufacturers' representatives, etc.) and the likely sales, marketing, and advertising/trade promotion costs:

—A distribution plan for your product(s) or service(s), including any special requirements, such as refrigeration, and how much distribution costs will be as a percent of sales and of total costs:

- Map the value chain for your product or service (i.e., indicate how your product or service will get to the end user or consumer, the portion of the final selling price realized in each step, and the dollar and percentage markup and the dollar and percentage gross margin per unit).

  (Note that the value chain below is constructed for a generalized consumer product and needs to be modified for your particular product or service.)

Value Chain

| Components (Materials & Labor) | → | Manufacturer or Service Provider | → | Distributor | → | Wholesaler | → | End User |

Price/Unit:
  Dollars
  Percent

Markup/Unit:
  Dollars
  Percent

Gross Margin:
  Dollars
  Percent

■ A realistic estimate of approximate sales and market share for your product or service for your market area which your venture can attain in each of your first five years:

Product/Service Sales and Market Share

	Year				
	1	2	3	4	5
Total Market: Units Dollars					
Est. Sales: Units Dollars					
Est. Market Share (percent):					
Est. Market Growth: Units Dollars					

Source of Data:

Researcher:

Confidence in Data:

CHECKPOINT: Consider whether you suffer from mousetrap myopia or whether you lack enough experience to tackle the venture at this stage. It is possible that if your venture does not stand up to this evaluation, you may simply not be as far along as you had thought. Remember, the single largest factor contributing to stillborn ventures and to those who will ripen as lemons is lack of opportunity focus. If you were unable to respond to many of the above questions, or do not have much of an idea of how to answer them, it is possible that you need to do more work.

■ An assessment of the costs and profitability of your product or service:

Product/Service Costs and Profitability

Product/Service:

Sales Price:

Sales Level:

	Dollars/Unit	Percent of Sales Price/Unit
Production Costs (i.e., labor and material costs) or Purchase Costs		
Gross Margin		
Fixed Costs		
Profit before Taxes		
Profit after Taxes		

- An assessment of the minimum resources required to "get the doors open and revenue coming in," the costs, dates required, alternative means of gaining control of (but not necessarily owning) these, and what this information tells you:

Resource Needs

	Minimum Needed	Cost ($)	Date Required	Probable Source
Plant, Equipment, and Facilities				
Product/Service Development				
Market Research				
Setup of Sales and Distribution (e.g., brochures, demos, and mailers)				
One-Time Expenditures (e.g., legal costs)				
Lease Deposits and Other Prepayments (e.g., utilities)				

Overhead (e.g., salaries, rent, and insurance)

Sales Costs (e.g., trips to trade shows)

Other Start-up Costs

TOTAL

COMMENTS

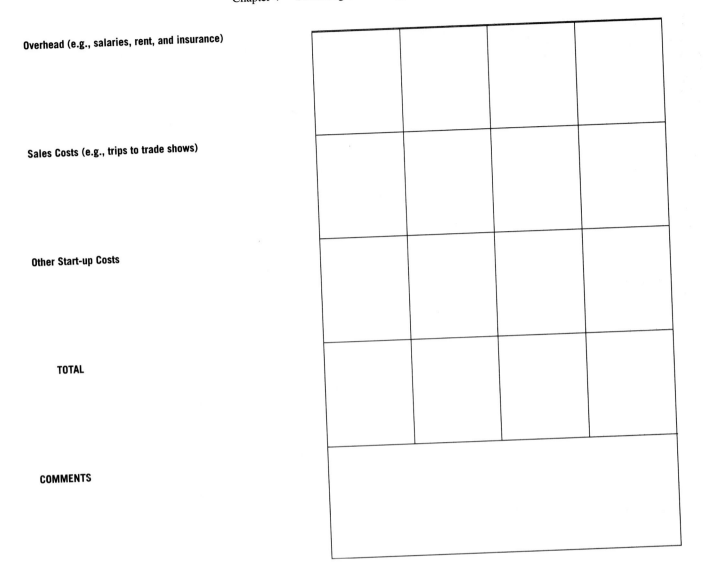

- A rough estimate of requirements for manufacturing and/or staff, operations, facilities, including:
  —An assessment of the major difficulties for such items as equipment, labor skills and training, and quality standards in the manufacture of your product(s) or the delivery of your service(s):

—An estimate of the number of people who will be required to launch the business and the key tasks they will perform:

—An assessment of how you will deal with these difficulties and your estimate of the time and money needed to resolve them and begin saleable production:

- An identification of the cash flow and cash conversion cycle for your business over the first 15 months (including a consideration of leads/lags in getting sales, producing your product or service, delivering your product or service, and billing and collecting cash). Show as a bar chart the timing and duration of each activity below:

Cash Flow, Conversion Cycle, and Timing of Key Operational Activities

Development of
Forecasts

Manufacturing

Sales Orders

Billing:

  Invoice

  Collect

Selling Season

1   2   3   4   5   6   7   8   9   10   11   12   13   14   15

Months

- A preliminary, estimated cash flow statement for the first year, including considerations of resources needed for start-up and your cash conversion cycle:

- An estimation of (1) the total amount of asset and working capital needed and peak months and (2) the amount of money needed to reach positive cash flow and the amount of money needed to reach breakeven, and an indication of the months when each will occur:

- Create a break-even chart similar to the following:

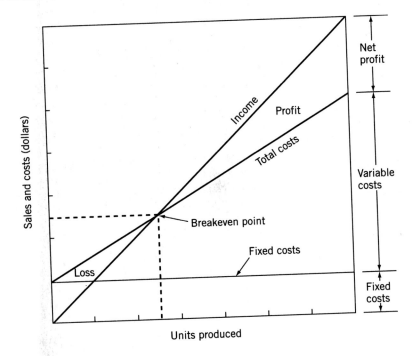

- An estimate of the capital required for asset additions and operating needs (and the months in which these will occur) to attain the sales level projected in five years:

- A statement of how you intend to raise capital, including all types (e.g., venture capital, financing raised through asset lenders, financing against inventory, receivables, equipment, and real estate), when, and from whom:

- A statement of whether you intend to harvest your venture, how and when this might occur, and the prospects. (If you do not intend to harvest the venture, include instead a statement of the prospects that profits will be both durable and large enough to be attractive.)

- An assessment of the sources of value, such as strategic, to another firm already in the market or one contemplating entry and an indication if there is a logical buyer(s) of your venture:

- An assessment of how much it would take to liquidate the venture if you decided to exit and whether this is high:

CHECKPOINT: Reconsider if your venture opportunity is attractive. Beware of compromising on whether your opportunity has forgiving and rewarding economics. For example, are you convinced that the amount you need to raise is reasonable with respect to the venture's potential and risk? Are others convinced? If they are not, what do you know that they do not (and vice versa)? Most start-ups run out of cash before they secure enough profitable customers to sustain a positive cash flow. Your preliminary estimates of financial requirements need to be within the amount that an investor, venture capitalist, or other lender is willing to commit to a single venture or that you can personally raise. Even if your idea is not a candidate for venture capital financing, it is worth looking at your venture in this way.

■ An assessment of competitors in the market, including those selling substitute products:

Competitor No.	Name	Products/Services That Compete Directly	Substitutes

■ A profile of the competition:

Competitor Profile

	Competitor No.			
	1	2	3	4
Estimated Sales/Year ($)				
Estimated Market Share (%)				
Description of Sales Force				

Marketing Tactics:

  Selling Terms

  Advertising/Promotion

  Distribution Channel

  Service/Training/Support

  Pricing

Major Strengths

Major Weaknesses

- A ranking of major competitors by market share:

No.	Competitor	Estimated Market Share

■ A Robert Morris Associates statement study:

RMA Study

RMA Data for Period Ending	Estimates for Proposed Venture				
Asset Size Number of Statements	**Under $250M**	**$250M and Less than $1MM**	**$1MM and Less than $10MM**	**$10MM and Less than $50MM**	**All Sizes**
Assets: 　Cash 　Marketable securities 　Receivables net 　Inventory net 　All other current 　　Total current 　Fixed assets net 　All other noncurrent 　　Total	%	%	%	%	%
Liabilities: 　Due to banks—short-term 　Due to trade 　Income taxes 　Current maturities long-term debt 　All other current 　　Total current debt 　Noncurrent debt, unsubordinated 　　Total unsubordinated debt 　Subordinated debt 　Tangible net worth 　　Total					
Income data: 　Net sales 　Cost of sales 　Gross profit 　All other expense net 　Profit before taxes					
Ratios: 　Quick 　Current 　Fixed/worth 　Debt/worth 　Unsubordinated debt/capital funds 　Sales/receivables 　Cost sales/inventory 　Sales/working capital 　Sales/worth 　Percent profit before taxes/worth 　Percent profit before taxes/total assets Net sales/total assets					

M = thousand.
MM = million.

- An assessment of whether there are economies of scale in production and/or cost advantages in marketing and distribution:

- An assessment, for *each* competitor's product or service, of its costs and profitability:

Competitor Costs and Profitability			
Product/Service			
Sales Price			
Sales Level			

For Each:

	Dollars/Unit	Percent of Sales Price/Unit
Production Costs (i.e., labor and material costs) or Purchase Costs		
Gross Margin		
Fixed Costs		
Profit before Taxes		
Profit after Taxes		

- An assessment of the history and projections of competitors' profits and industry averages:

Competitor Profits—Historical and Projected					
Industry Average	Competitor				
	1	2	3	4	

Profits (percent of sales)

Past Two Years

Current Year

Projected Next Two Years

Sales/Employee

Profit/Employee

- A ranking of competitors in terms of cost:

No.	Competitor

- A profile for the current year of your competitors in terms of price and quality and of market share and profitability. Place competitors (using small circles identified by names) in the appropriate locations in the boxes below:

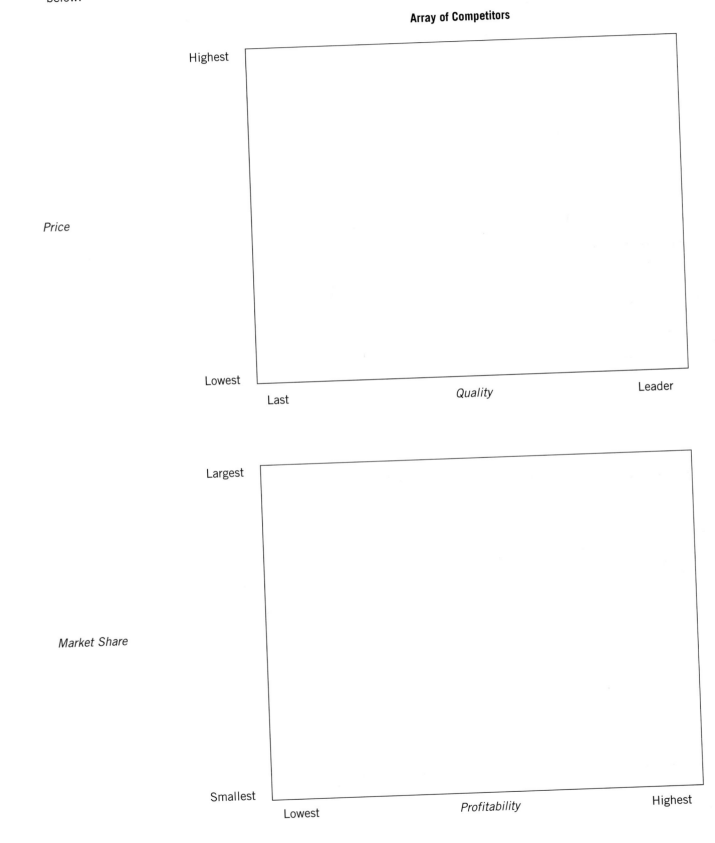

Array of Competitors

- An assessment of the degree of control in the market (including that over prices, costs, and channels of distribution and by suppliers, buyers, etc.) and the extent to which you can influence these or will be subject to influence by others:

- An assessment of current lead times for changes in technology, capacity, product and market innovation, and so forth:

- An assessment of whether your venture will enjoy cost advantages or disadvantages in production and in marketing and distribution, and an indication of whether your venture will have the lowest, average, or highest costs of production, marketing, and distribution:

- An assessment of other competitive advantages which you have or can gain, how you would secure these, and what time and money is required, including:
  —An indication of whether your product or service will benefit from, or be subject to, any regulations and of the status of any copyrights, trade secrets, or patents or licenses and distribution or franchise agreements:

—An indication if you enjoy advantages in response and lead times for technology, capacity changes, product and market innovation, and so forth:

—An indication if you enjoy other unfair advantage, such as a strategic advantage, people advantage, resource advantage, location advantage, and so on:

—An assessment of whether you think you can be price competitive and make a profit, or other ways, such as product differentiation, in which you can compete:

- A ranking of your venture in terms of price and quality and of market share and profitability relative to your competitors. Add your venture to the Arrays of Competitors above:

- An assessment of whether any competitors enjoy competitive advantages, such as legal or contractual advantages:

- An assessment of whether any competitors are vulnerable, the time period of this vulnerability, and the impact on market structure of their succumbing to vulnerabilities:

CHECKPOINT: Do you have sufficient competitive advantage? Remember, a successful company sells to a market that is large and growing, where capturing a small market share can bring significant sales volume, where it does not face significant barriers to entry, and where its competition is profitable but not so strong as to be overwhelming. Further, a successful company has a product or service that solves significant problems that customers have with competitive products, such as poor quality, poor service, poor delivery, etc., and a sales price that will enable it to penetrate the market.

- An assessment of your partners and/or management team, including:

    —An evaluation of whether the founders and/or the management team are sufficiently committed to the opportunity and how much they are personally willing to invest in time, money, personal guarantees, and so forth:

    —An assessment of whether the founders and/or the management team possess the industry knowledge, experience, know-how, and skills required for the venture's success; if additional personnel is necessary and if these can be attracted to the venture; and if anyone on the team has managed previously what you are trying to undertake:

    —An assessment of whether the founders and/or management team have the necessary vision and entrepreneurial zest and whether they will be able to inspire this in others:

—An assessment of the level of trust felt among the founders and/or management team:

—A statement about who will do what—roles, responsibilities, and tasks:

—A statement about the contributions each founder and team member is expected to make:

—A statement about who will get what salary, what benefits, and what ownership share:

> **CHECKPOINT:** Can do? Remember, the team is a primary force driving successful entrepreneurial ventures. It is important to question the assumptions on which your team has been shaped; for example, equal salaries and stock ownership can indicate that assumptions as to tasks, roles, and responsibilities are naive. Someone on your team needs to be experienced and competent in these areas, or the team needs to be able to attract someone who is.

STEP 5

Include Any Other Vital Issues or Considerations That Are Unique to Your Venture Opportunity and That Have Not Been Covered in the VOSG.   For example, a location analysis is necessary for retail establishments or real estate:

STEP 6

Assess Whether Your Venture Opportunity Has Any Fatal Flaws:

STEP 7

List Significant Assumptions (Assumptions about Customer Orders, Sales Projections, etc.), Including:

- A consideration of significant trade-offs that you have made:

- A consideration of the major risks (unreliability of customer orders; overoptimistic sales projections; inability to achieve cost and time estimates; underestimating the magnitude, intensity, and vindictiveness of competitors' responses; etc.):

STEP 8

Rank Assumptions According to Importance:

STEP 9

Evaluate the Downside Consequences, If Any, When Your Assumptions Are Proved Invalid; How Severe the Impact Would Be; and If and How These Can Be Minimized, Including:

- The cost and consequences of (1) lost growth opportunities and (2) liquidation or bankruptcy to the company, to you, and to other stakeholders:

STEP 10

Rate the Risk of the Venture as High, Medium, or Low:

STEP 11

List Chronologically the 10 to 15 Most Critical Actions You Need to Take During the Next Six Months and the Hurdles That Need to Be Overcome in Order to Convert Your Idea Into a Real Opportunity.   It is a good idea to have another person review what you have listed and adjust the list, if warranted.

Date	Action

STEP 12

Make a Week-by-week Schedule of Key Tasks to Be Performed, When They Are to Be Performed, and by Whom.   Break larger tasks into their smallest possible components. Be alert for conflicts.

Week No.	Task	Date Completed	Person Responsible

CHECKPOINT: It is important to take a hard look at the assumptions you have made, both implicit and explicit, and to assess the risk of the venture. Time and again, first-time entrepreneurs overestimate sales and delivery dates and underestimate costs, effort, and time required to execute the opportunity and to reach a positive cash flow. Also, while each new business has its risks and problems, as well as its opportunities, difficulties need to be identified as soon as possible so they can be avoided or eliminated or their impact minimized.

STEP 13

Return to **STEPS 1** and **2** to Refine Your Opportunity Summary and Make Any Adjustments to Your Venture Opportunity Profile.   Attach to your VOSG a list of the names, addresses, and phone numbers of relevant sources of industry and market data.

CHECKPOINT: Your responses to the "venture opportunity screening guide" will help you to determine whether you want to continue with your venture and develop a complete business plan. If your venture has passed, a crucial question to consider before proceeding, is, what do I want to get out of the business? You will want to think twice about whether the venture provides a strong fit with your personal goals, values, and needs, is what gives you energy, leads you down the path you want to be on and to further and even better opportunities. Remember, you are what you do. If you have been able to complete the guide, are satisfied that most of the results are positive, and if the answers to the personal issues are yes (see Part VI), then *go for it.*

STEP 14

Four Anchors Revisited.   You should have a much sharper sense of the extent to which your good idea exhibits the four anchors described at the beginning of the chapter. As you proceed you need to constantly consider the following, since creative insights that can make a significant difference can occur at any time:

1. How can the value proposition be enhanced and improved?
2. What can be changed, added, modified, or eliminated in order to improve the *fit?*
3. What can be done to improve the value chain and the free cash flow characteristics?
4. What can be done to enhance the risk/reward balance?

Case

Gary and George Mueller

Preparation Questions:

1. Evaluate the opportunity facing Gary Mueller in 1994 and his business plan.

2. What fund-raising strategy would you recommend?

3. How would you value a startup company?

4. What should the professor say? What should Gary do?

Gary Mueller sat in his usual seat in the sky deck of his Entrepreneurial Finance class. The last class of his career at a rather well-known East Coast business school had just ended and his professor, who had just received a standing ovation amid calls of "O Captain, My Captain,"[1] left the room for the final time. In addition to Entrepreneurial Finance, Gary had conducted an independent study project with this professor, who had heard about his job search many times: he would probably hear about it again.

Gary had come to business school to figure out how to recognize great business opportunities. His family background predisposed him to entrepreneurship; Gary had fond memories of wandering around his grandfather's manufacturing business, visiting his dad's packing plant in Pennsylvania, and working in his mother's store. These experiences not only made him feel comfortable with the risk of entrepreneurship, but were also a source of passion for becoming an entrepreneur.

The quest for a golden opportunity seemed within reach. Gary had evaluated numerous opportunities and had narrowed the field to two. Now it was time to graduate and decide which life to live next.

Privatizing Eastern Europe

Before business school, Gary spent two years working on privatization and economic reform in eastern Europe and the former Soviet Union. This work made him realize the potential of setting up a business in Russia. He recalled discussing business ideas while having dinner with a reporter for the *Financial Times* who said, "Every sentence written about eastern Europe contains clues to a business opportunity."

Toward the end of his work in eastern Europe, Gary looked into several startup possibilities. He spent two months researching the possibility of setting up a food packaging company in Russia. The company would be a subsidiary of his father's packaging company in Pennsylvania. The dearth of packaging in Russia, the potential market, the availability of supplies, and the cost structure of the business made the idea appealing. They pursued the opportunity further, even entering talks with a partner, but ultimately decided that the risk of investment in Russia at that time was too high. Instead of setting up a business, Gary returned to the States to attend business school.

Gary remained intrigued by business opportunities in eastern Europe. He closely followed business development in the region and continued to explore business ideas. For summer employment after his first year in graduate school, he looked for positions with small companies or startups in eastern Europe, eventually joining a group doing privatization in Poland. This gave him a chance to get a good overview of the region's economic transformation and establish contacts for the future.

In addition to working on the privatization of several companies, Gary looked at possible investments for a $100 million fund the company was setting up in Poland. He had meetings with representatives from a wide array of industries and prepared extensive investment memoranda on these opportunities. The summer experience further convinced him that the timing was right for entrepreneurship in eastern Europe.

The Final Year

During Gary's second year, he invested most of his job search time looking at opportunities in eastern Europe. An offer to go back to his summer employer was his fallback option in case he did not pursue an entrepreneurial opportunity.

His search in the fall was wide ranging, from working with owners of newly established firms in eastern Europe to startup ideas. In terms of new businesses, he looked into setting up a bottled water company in Poland, but quickly realized that the business was too capital intensive. From the bottled water idea, he developed the following criteria for business opportunities in emerging economies:

1. Low fixed costs

2. Low variable costs going forward

3. Low asset intensity

4. Quick to break-even

5. Proven business rather than completely new idea

6. High market potential

© Copyright Jeffry A. Timmons, 1996. This case was written by Gary Mueller. For purposes of class discussion, it has been edited by Dan D'Heilly and Andrea Alyse under the direction of Jeffry A. Timmons, Franklin W. Olin Distinguished Professor of Entrepreneurship, Babson College. Funding provided by the Ewing Marion Kauffman Foundation. All rights reserved.

[1] From "O Captain, My Captain!" by Walt Whitman.

Ventures that met these criteria would be far more attractive for a young entrepreneur. With low fixed costs, it would be possible to get startup capital from friends and family. It also limited any venture's downside. Low variable costs going forward would keep the burn rate low in the critical early stages and give the company more financial flexibility. Also, a company with low asset intensity, such as publishing or online services, would require less cash to fuel its growth. As Gary's uncle said, such companies have the potential to "mint money."

Gary also wanted a business where he could quickly tell how things were going. Any business which entailed setting up a manufacturing facility, for example, would not only involve high fixed costs, but may also take a year before starting production and a longer time before reaching break-even. In an uncertain environment such as eastern Europe, Gary wanted to know as soon as possible if the business was going poorly. He also felt that a shorter time to break-even would make it easier to adapt and change business focus if it was necessary.

Gary thought it was important to look for proven businesses. It is usually easier to transplant a business idea from one place to another, rather than starting something completely new. Gary had been impressed by several cases and examples he studied where entrepreneurs in other countries had simply mimicked what worked in developed countries. For example, in eastern Europe successful startups included English language publications, restaurant franchises, and copy centers.

Finally, Gary wanted a business with a large market potential. While a bagel shop in Prague might be a successful business, he felt that such an idea did not have the potential upside to make it interesting.

These criteria made it easier for Gary to screen possible opportunities as he headed into his final semester at business school. One by one he had eliminated possibilities. In January, two new opportunities arose.

Opportunity Knocks

Gary had dinner with a fellow second-year student who told him that his dad, Ludwig Gelobter, had recently launched a magazine in eastern Europe. He thought there might be an opportunity for Gary with this startup operation. Gary called Ludwig the next day, and they talked about his magazine and the possibility of working together.

Born in Poland, Ludwig emigrated to America as a youth. When the Soviet Union loosened its grip on eastern Europe in the early 1980s, Ludwig had been one of the first wave of entrepreneurs back into Poland. He had run an export-import business since 1986, and in 1991 he cofounded the magazine, *What, Where, When* in Warsaw.

After several telephone conversations, Gary flew to New York for a meeting. They discussed the magazine and a variety of other business opportunities in the eastern block. At the end of the day, Ludwig asked Gary to put his ideas in writing.

On the plane back to Boston, Gary thought about the opportunity to work with Ludwig Gelobter. They got along well during this visit, and Gary thought that he would probably be a valuable mentor in eastern Europe. This was particularly important because his friend had described his father as "difficult." Gary also liked the publishing business, and thought the *What, Where, When* magazine niche might be a good entry point into eastern European markets. Gary had a rough draft for Ludwig (see *Exhibit A*) before the plane touched down.

Ludwig responded to Gary's letter (see *Exhibit B*) saying he wanted Gary to work for him full-time; half as general manager of the magazine, and half on new business opportunities. He suggested Prague as a base, which Gary found very appealing. Ludwig also included his thoughts about compensation and suggested they arrange a trip to eastern Europe to visit his operations.

What, Where, When Magazine

After the fall of the wall, Ludwig had noticed a dearth of periodicals in Poland (see *Exhibit C*). He also realized that it was a struggle for a westerner to obtain basic information about what was going on in Warsaw. Even for him, someone who spoke fluent Polish, it was not easy to navigate in the new climate.

One night in the fall of 1990, while he was in his room at the Warsaw Marriott, Ludwig thought of the idea to start a magazine aimed at western businesspersons which would provide an assortment of information about what to do in Warsaw. He talked to a friend, Nicholas Andrechevski, the publisher of the second largest Polish daily newspaper, and Nicholas said he would look into it. A month later, Ludwig and Nicholas met again and decided to launch the *What, Where, When* magazine. They formed a joint venture, with each party owning 50 percent of the equity.

The magazine was put together based on the model of similar magazines in the west, such as *New York Magazine*, the *Where* magazines, or *Time Out* in London. It served as a combination business directory, arts and entertainment guide, restaurant directory, and tourist guide. Articles were written about Polish culture, upcoming events, and other interesting features about the city or the people. Articles and information were featured in English, Polish, and German.

Revenue was 100 percent advertising driven, compared to industry standards of 80 percent advertising and 20 percent subscription/newsstand sales. This revenue came from targeting businesses that wanted to reach western businesspersons and tourists. The primary advertisers were restaurants, professional service firms, hotels, airlines, car rentals, and other companies catering to affluent travelers in Poland.

EXHIBIT A

Gary Mueller
90 Putnam St. #2
Cambridge, MA 02139
Tel/Fax: 617-497-7673

March 8, 1994

Ludwig Gelobter
Crystal Publishing

Dear Ludwig:

I hope you've enjoyed your trip to Poland and Russia. No lost limbs, I trust. On this side of the ocean I have been thinking about our conversations and feel that the opportunity to work for you in some capacity is very appealing. I see several options (and combinations of options):

1. **Manager Role.** I could serve as an on-the-ground manager/overseer for your publishing company. Areas of focus would include improving cash flow, expanding the advertising base (especially from German and other international companies looking to advertise across your network of magazines), and expanding the business. In this position I would also help with long-term strategy.

2. **Business Development Role.** I would help you look for business opportunities that complement your existing operations. This could include looking for other publishing or business opportunities that could be started up with little or no capital and benefit from the network of offices you have developed.

   One such idea I mentioned when we talked on the phone was to become the eastern European sales representative for a telephone company called Telegroup, a leading international phone service repackager. It is possible to use their service from anywhere in the world, including eastern Europe. Their price from the Czech Republic to the States, for example, is about 40 percent cheaper than that of the Czech phone company, or AT&T direct. They also offer lower rates to any country you dial, such as Germany or Japan. Our cut would be 10 percent of revenues we generate in an annuity form. So if we signed up people who made a total of $100K worth of phone calls to the United States per month (the office in Warsaw I worked in with only 6 U.S. professionals made about $10K worth of phone calls to the United States monthly), we would make $10K per month. The representative in France now makes about $30K/month, and Paris has the same number of U.S. ex-pats as Prague—40,000. Apparently the best way to get ex-pats to sign up is to advertise in English publications. In France, single full-page ads in the English dailies each generated about 300 customers (at an average revenue per month of $150). Your magazine might be the perfect way to reach such customers and it's an easy sell if you can publish rates 40 percent below AT&T or the local carrier.

3. **Advisor Role.** As you know I have several other offers to work in privatization or investment management in eastern Europe. It may be possible to negotiate an offer with one of these companies whereby I'm able to spend time working for you. I could serve as an advisor/consultant who helps with the items mentioned above, but still work for another company.

   There are certainly more options and combinations of options, but I think that this would be a good starting point. All have their appeal. If I were to work in more of a 'full-time' role for you, you would have a man on the ground to devote his energy to increasing revenue and profitability, expanding the business and looking for other opportunities. In the other options where I do not work for you full time, your current business would not have me as a full-time expense, but would still get some of the benefits of me working for you.

   In terms of remuneration, for an option where I work for you full-time, I think the following might serve as a starting point:

   - Salary: $35–40K
   - Profit sharing: 5–10 percent (depending on the current numbers)
   - Options: A fair percentage vested quarterly (depends on current numbers)
   - Commissions: The amount above a fair price per page (say $1,300 for Poland)
   - New Business: Sharing of revenue or profit or equity of new businesses

   The cash flow characteristics of the Telegroup idea are extremely appealing. For essentially no additional fixed costs, we may be able to develop say $5–10K cash flow per month. An option for remuneration of this idea, based on my time invested and using your office as the base, might be that we split the revenue between us.

   For the more part-time option, we could use commissions and some small remuneration as a basis. The upside could be in the form of profit sharing or options if certain profit levels or targets are passed.

   These are my initial thoughts. I look forward to talking to you further about them. I hope things went well in LA.

Sincerely,

Gary

EXHIBIT B

March 19, 1994

Gary Mueller
Cambridge, MA
Via FAX 1 617 497 7673

Dear Gary:

Thanks for your fax of March 8th. In fact, things in LA went rather poorly. Hopefully, just another demonstration of the cyclical nature of that business.

I am very pleased at your interest in working with me in Eastern Europe. I thought we got along well during our meeting in February, and believe that working as a team would have interesting possibilities.

I have tried to combine the ideas you put forward with some of my own thoughts, and want to make you the following proposal:

1) I would prefer to have you working with me in a full-time capacity. Thus, the Manager Role you suggest could be a good start. However, as you know, I already have a number of other business activities and projects. I am always seeking to leverage my time and situation, so, a Business Development Role would certainly be a part of your activities. Let me advance some specifics . . .

   A) You would be headquartered in Prague

   - It is more centrally located
   - I have access to an apartment there
   - It is the site of the magazine which I believe will be the most profitable in the group, but also one where the most managerial and sales help is needed right now.

   B) You would act as my associate vis-à-vis the magazine operations. I would want some type of commitment, e.g. a one year contract. Your activities would include . . .

   - Assist in organizing and improving local sales
   - Major focus on group and international marketing
   - Review feasibility of international distribution
   - Participate in organizing new magazines in places like Budapest, Sofia, etc.

   C) My long-term strategy 2 to 3 years down the road, is either to sell out to a larger publishing group, or bring our own group public. It will be your task to analyze the possibilities and to begin our preparation in this direction.

2) As mentioned above, leveraging my time is always on my mind. I am ready to work with you on any new business ideas, and am prepared to design a suitable generous, profit sharing plus equity structure.

   As I mentioned in our discussions I am very interested in learning more about the specifics and technical aspects of the Telegroup deal. Clearly using our magazines and offices, both in terms of direct advertising, barter possibilities, contracts, etc. would give us a low cost entry into this field, and, if the projections can be even partially realized, it would be a sorely needed cash generator.

   Here are some potential problems to be addressed in this project.

   - I am only a, plus/minus, 50 percent owner of the magazines. While I have no obligation to share my other initiatives with my magazine partners, I cannot take advantage of them either. We would have to devise a fair, arms-length, compensation system for the local offices.
   - Since the majors are already advertising with us, or will be sooner or later, we cannot become so identified with one service provider as to lose those revenues.

3) As far as your entrepreneurial interests are concerned, I am more than willing to allow those full scope. I too have some ideas which I have not had the time and/or funds to pursue, and would see our association as useful in this regard.

   One of your first entrepreneurial tasks might well be the raising of some debt or equity capital to allow us to take advantage of opportunities, and grow the business in a faster and more effective manner.

4) Compensation, given my present cash-flow situation, I must limit my fixed cash obligations as much as possible. Here are my thoughts:

   - Basic Salary: 25K
     Plus reasonable travel expenses, and possibly an apartment in Prague.

- Assuming the "Telegroup" project materializes, a division of profits 50/50. Always keeping Number 2 above in mind.
- Commissions: 10 percent of international sales
- Profit sharing: 10 percent of my share
- Options/equity: To be discussed, but available
- New business: Sharing of revenue, profit, or equity of new business on equal terms.
- Finders fee: 5 percent in cash or equity for any initial funds raised.

Clearly there will be many details and much planning to be done. We must agree on the broad principles first, but I am prepared to do what I can to get you on board quickly. Please let me know what you think of the above, and how you wish to proceed.

I am leaving for Europe Tuesday evening. My itinerary covers Prague, Warsaw, Sofia and Bucharest, with a possible stop in Budapest. I will be back in the New York area on the evening of April 10th (another auction) and will stay until April 15th.

Monday, the 11th, will be an all day inspection as this is to be a big auction. I am likely to be free Tuesday, but my friend/client from Central America will be arriving Tuesday evening, so the balance of the week is tied up.

However, I will certainly be available by phone, both these next two weeks and in New York. And I can always stay over a day or two after the 15th if necessary. Perhaps we can meet in New York again. Depending on the state of affairs in Europe I will probably be going back there, perhaps as soon as April 20th. If your schedule permits it, and our talks have advanced sufficiently, you may want to join me then for say 7 to 10 days.

Regards,

Ludwig

P.S. Enclosed is an unaudited balance sheet from Warsaw for the calendar year ending 12/31/93. I hope you can make some sense of these numbers, as they are Polish accounting principles. For example, we are apparently allowed to amortize all of our "Startup costs/losses" pre-tax.

EXHIBIT C

The Publishing Opportunity in Eastern Europe

I. Overview

The upheaval in Eastern Europe over the previous four years has spawned a flurry of free-market activity. Across industries, formerly state-owned companies, after rounds of privatization, now operate in the private sector. Foreign companies have entered the market, launching joint ventures or wholly owned subsidiaries. And entrepreneurial ventures have sprung up to take advantage of the new opportunities.

Within this context of rapid change, the publishing industry, like most other industries, has undergone a tremendous transformation. Before the fall of the Communist regimes, publishing was extensively controlled—even more so than most industries because of its political importance. But the fall of the wall launched the political and economic transformations in the east. The formerly state-owned and controlled publishing industry was liberalized. New publishing companies emerged—some entrepreneurial startups, other subsidiaries or joint ventures of western companies. As a result, new publications of all sorts sprung up across the former Eastern Bloc.

Now newsstands and bookstores in Eastern Europe are beginning to resemble those in the West. Newspapers are no longer controlled by the state—they are published by independent, privately held companies. Foreign books, which used to circulate in limited numbers in the communist regimes, are now ubiquitous. Shakespeare and Stephen King are readily available. Magazine proliferation is similar—customers can choose from *Business Week* to local versions of *People,* from children's magazines to *Playboy.*

While the size of the publishing market in eastern Europe is about the same size now as it was just before the revolutions, the growth in the share of that market held by new private sector ventures has been phenomenal.

EXHIBIT C   (Continued)

The Publishing Opportunity in Eastern Europe

II. The Publishing Industry in Eastern Europe—History

In the former Eastern Bloc, publishing was tightly controlled by the state. Usually the State Media Ministry or Cultural Ministry would select appropriate material for the population to read, and the state-controlled companies (cooperatives) would publish only that material. Supply was regulated by the central ministry, distribution was through state-owned channels, and for books, the final point of sale was almost invariably at state-owned book stores.

Most eastern block countries had far fewer publishers than western countries, and advertising agencies were virtually nonexistent. In Poland, for example, prior to 1989 a total of only 60 publishers, printers and distributors existed and only one advertising agency served the entire industry (Laidler, 1993).

The breadth of publication was also extremely limited. This was especially true in magazines and newspapers. Typically only a handful of newspapers existed for the entire country. Nearly all western newspapers and magazines were banned. Even western scientific publications took years to receive. In book publishing, breadth was also more limited than in the West.

Distribution was through a central subscription and distribution monopoly. The government distribution office would tell the publisher how many subscribers it had, and thus how many issues to print. It would not tell the publisher who its actual readers were or where they lived (Evans, 1993). In Poland, for example, all authorized publishers were required to send their print runs to one of two distributors, Skladnica Ksiegarska for books or Ruch for magazines and newspapers. For books, the distributor would supply the 18 wholesalers who, in turn, supplied the state-owned retail bookstores (Laidler, 1993).

High literacy coupled with extensive bans formed the basis for the dramatic change in the publishing industry after the revolutions swept eastern Europe in 1989 and 1990.

III. Publishing in Eastern Europe

1. The Market in the West

The publishing industry covers the actual putting together of a book or magazine or other publication. Publishers guide the publishing process, taking the editorial content and advertising, if any, through the editing, layout and other stages, and are usually the company which markets the final product. The veritable printing of the pages though, is part of the printing industry. Advertising is often considered a separate industry from publishing.

The size of these industries are considerable. The world printing industry, for example, is $400 billion; the U.S. share of the industry is $117 billion, or 2 percent of GNP; and Europe is $74 billion. The publishing industry in the United States is smaller, and its size depends on what is included in the figure. The book, magazine and newspaper publishing industry, for example, represents about $60 billion, or 1 percent of GNP. Print advertising is about a $63 billion industry, or 1 percent of GNP (U.S. Statistical Abstracts, 1993).

2. Market Size and Growth in Eastern Europe

It is difficult to get exact figures for the publishing and printing industries in eastern Europe, but estimates put the publishing industry at just over $1 billion and the printing industry around $2.7 billion (Simpson, 1992; figures do not include the former Soviet Union). The size of the print advertising industry is difficult to determine, but is probably between one and three billion dollars.

A comparison of the size of the printing and publishing markets in the three leading eastern European countries with the size in the United States reveals that Poland and Hungary are still far below the United States in terms of percent of GNP for those industries. In the United States, printing and publishing represent 2 percent and 1 percent of GNP, respectively. In Poland, they represent 0.09 percent and 0.05 percent, respectively—about half the level in the United States. In Hungary, printing represents 0.7 percent and publishing 0.6 percent of GNP. This gap represents potential for further growth for these industries in Hungary and Poland, if development in these countries mirrors that in the States.

As noted above, the growth since the beginning of the transition has come from the new private-sector companies. While in most eastern European countries the size of the publishing and printing markets are about the same size they were at the beginning of the transformation, private companies now predominate in the market. As mentioned above, in Poland, the growth in book volume of the private sector between 1990 and 1992 was nearly 1,000 percent. Growth in the private sector will most likely continue, though probably at rates of 25 percent to 50 percent during the next few years (various conversations).

TABLE 1

Country Analysis

	Growth	Market Publishing	Size Printing	Private Sector % GNP	Political Stability	Assoc. of Printers
Poland	5%	$350 Mil.	$615 Mil.	60%	High	8
Hungary	0%M	$250 Mil.	$263 Mil.	45%	High	9
Czech	2%	$300 Mil.	$ 1 Bil.	40%	High	7
Russia	−20%	−$500 Mil.	$ 16 Bil.	−20%	Low	8
Bulgaria	−10%	−$ 50 Mil.	$360 Mil.	Low	Med	6
Romania	−15%	−$ 50 Mil.	$465 Mil.	Low	Med	4

TABLE 2

Segment Analysis

	Seg Size	Grow	Cmpt'n	Distrib Ease	Pub. Power	New Title Intro Ease	Cust Loyalty	Ad Rev % of Rev
Magazines	Lg	H	M–H	L–M	M	H	M–H	80%
Newspapers	Lg	L	H	H	H	L	H	50–90%
Newsletters	Sm	H	L	L	H	L	H	Varies
Other	Sm	H	L–M	L–M	H	L–H	L–H	Varies

3. Newspaper and Magazine Markets in eastern Europe

As in the West, the market may be broken down into five major segments: 1) books, 2) magazines, 3) newspapers, 4) newsletters, 5) other specialty publications. In the U.S. publishing industry, book publishing totals $24 billion, magazines about $10 billion, and newspapers about $35 billion (Halverson, 1993). The size of the other segments are difficult to determine.

It is also difficult to determine the exact size of the periodical industry in eastern Europe. In Poland, the size of the newspaper and magazine market is probably about $150 million, not including advertising. As in the West, advertising usually makes up between 30 and 90 percent of the revenues of the periodical. Thus, in Poland the advertising associated with periodical publishing is probably around $250 million.

In Poland, over 4,000 periodical titles exist ("Polish Press Market", *PAP Newswire*, 1992). Over 70 dailies and 20 national newspapers are in circulation ("Polish Press Market," *PAP Newswire*, 1992). The market, though, is still highly fragmented. *Wprost* and *Polityka*, weeklies in Poland whose formats resemble *Newsweek* and *Time*, are among the 10 most popular magazines, but their regular readers represent only 2 percent of the total number of people reading Polish periodicals, according to the Pentor Institute. Throughout eastern Europe, only about half the magazines launched then are still being published, according to Chicago-based international publishing consultant Lee B. Hall (Johnson, 1993).

The range of newspapers is also considerable and has begun to resemble the range in the West. In Poland, for example, newsstands typically have between 10 and 20 newspapers. The variety is also extensive, from the serious, a la the *Wall Street Journal*, to the tabloids, similar to the *National Enquirer* in the United States. The two largest dailies, *Gazata Wybczal* and *Rzeczpospolita*, are serious, traditional newspapers. Many of the most popular weekly newspapers are tabloids, such as *Nie* (No), *Skandale* (Scandals), *Super Skandale bez kurtyny* (Super-scandals without a curtain) and *Noweskandale* (New scandals).

Just as entry into the market has been extensive during the last four years, so has exit. Similar to the western periodical market, most new entrants actually fail. In the west, the failure rate is well over 70 percent, and while it is unclear what the exact percentage is in eastern Europe, the figure is likely just as high. An example of a high profile failure was the first Polish daily in color, *Glob 24*. After just months of publication, the newspaper went bankrupt.

The market for newspapers also mirrors that in the west in terms of its generally regional basis, except for a few leading national newspapers. Most newspapers are based in the city where they have their largest circulation. Describing the regional nature of the Polish newspaper market, one article notes: "Poland is a country of regional newspapers . . . Polls indicate that 40 percent of readers read regional newspapers more or less regularly, while little more than 20 percent are regular readers of nationwide newspapers" (Bartyzel, 1993).

EXHIBIT C (Continued)

The Publishing Opportunity in Eastern Europe

As with books, the periodical market has seen extensive western entrance. German Publishers, for example, translated about 7 million copies per month of German publications for the Polish market in late 1992 (Bartyzel, 1993). The most popular were the bi-weeklies *Tina* and *Bravo* and the monthlies *Dziewczyna* (Girl) and *Popcorn*. Their cheap price, their target marketing to specific audiences (young people, women, narrow groups of hobbyists) and their simple formulas made them quite successful (Bartyzel, 1993). Even though German publishers were discouraged from buying periodicals during the privatization process (largely because of historical reasons), they now own a substantial number of newspapers and magazines.

The one Polish magazine publisher of magazines able to keep up with the westerners is Prozynski and Co. It sells nine periodicals, most of which are monthlies such as *Poradnik domowy* (Household Guidebook), *Cztery kety* (Four Corners) and periodicals for children (Bartyzel, 1993).

Other western publishers have come into eastern Europe in full force. *BusinessWeek, PC World, PC Magazine, Scientific American, Playboy, Cosmopolitan,* and numerous other western periodicals are now published across eastern Europe. They are published under a variety of arrangements, including licensing agreements, joint ventures and wholly owned subsidiaries. The section that follows on western houses in eastern Europe will feature some of those companies and publications.

Distribution The current distribution system still suffers because the inadequate system during the command era has yet to be replaced by a well-functioning western-style distribution system. While it is getting better in Eastern Europe, especially Poland, the Czech Republic and Hungary, it is still a problem. In order to reach subscribers of magazines, for example, it is necessary to use the postal service. The post though, remains unreliable and many issues never end up where they are sent.

It is estimated that hundreds of distributors and dozens of book wholesales operate today in the new market economies of eastern Europe. In Poland, hundreds exist, but of those, 18 wholesale centers have 90 percent of the book trade market. The publisher still has little power in the value chain. Distributors in Poland mark up the price by 30 percent to 40 percent. In Hungary about 10–12 major distributors exist and had a total turnover of about HUF 200 million in 1992.

The situation in other eastern European countries is similar, although as one heads further east, distribution becomes even more difficult. In Russia, for example, periodical publishers have no subscriber lists to rent out because the formerly state-owned distribution monopoly owned the lists, and at the present time the government monopoly will not rent them out. Part of the delivery monopoly has been privatized, but even with this change the Russian mail service is so inadequate that distribution remains a major obstacle.

In Poland, the formerly state-owned distributor Ruch is still responsible for the sale of most periodicals, but has been overwhelmed organizationally by the flood of new titles. Under the law, and unlike private distributors, Ruch is forced to accept all periodicals for distribution. As of 1993 about 10 other periodical distribution firms had strong market presence. They usually refuse to distribute less popular periodicals and as a result, they have fewer and fewer Polish publishers as preferred suppliers.

Market information from distributors is still difficult to obtain, but the situation is getting better. Macek Machnacz, director of Jard Press, the largest private distribution firm in Poland, noted that substantial information is now available for the publisher about the publication. He stated, though, that too few publishers make use of this information. He also discussed the nature of the increasingly competitive market: "It's true that this market is very cramped but it doesn't mean that all vacancies are already occupied."

Price and Costs Coupled with the increase in new publishers and the availability of an array of new titles and publications, prices have increased dramatically. Book prices in Poland, for example, have tripled. But even though they have tripled, Polish books are still less expensive than books in the West, where paperbacks cost from 5 to 10 dollars. The average price for a paperback in Poland is 50,000 to 100,000 zlotys (about two and a half to five dollars).

During the initial part of the transition, much of the printing, especially of western authors and new publishing companies, was done in the west. Phantom Press in Poland, for example, initially sent its books to be printed in the United Kingdom. It did so because its unit cost of $0.17 per book (on orders averaging 40,000) was cheaper than having the books printed in Poland. And the quality was better. Ludwig Gelobter, who started International Publishing and the magazine *What, Where, When* (see below), initially sent the magazine to be printed in Berlin. In Germany, his unit costs were about $0.40 for his 48-page glossy magazine, to which he had to add transportation and tariffs. Harlequin had its books printed in either Germany or the United Kingdom. Total unit costs (printing, transportation, distribution, tariffs, etc.) for Harlequin were about $0.40 in 1991, when they printed abroad.

Now publications in Poland, Hungary and the Czech Republic are increasingly printed in eastern Europe. In general, because of lower labor and transportation costs, printing in eastern Europe is about 25 to 40 percent less expensive than in the West, (Gelobter, conversations; Wotjak, conversations). For Harlequin, when they started to print in Poland in 1992, unit costs dropped to $0.33. Ludwig's glossy 48-page magazine cost about $0.30 per unit to print in Poland.

IV. Western Houses in Eastern Europe

Western publishing houses have become dominant, if not the dominant, players in eastern Europe. While many hesitated at first, they are now heading full-force into the former Eastern Bloc. Some, such as IDG, Robert Hersant, Ringier, Gannett and Maxwell now own several publications. The following, while by no means exhaustive, gives a broad overview of western houses' activities in eastern Europe:

- **IDG Communications.** IDC launched a Russian edition of *PC World* in 1988 in a joint venture with Radio iSviaz, a state-owned publishing company. The company now publishes 18 magazines in the former East Bloc. But problems abound. IDG often has problem getting paper. According to one IDG executive: "In some countries, we were limited to 50,000 copies because of paper allocations. For us, it was not hard to distribute, but to distribute for the demand that was there" (Johnson, 1993). One amusing problem happened with the premier issue of *PC World* in Russia. The issue had 30 advertising pages. But when the first issue came back from the press, only three of the 30 ad pages were actually in the issue. The "technical problem" was with the Russian editor, who had cut out the ads to make room for more substance. He thought the ads were "unattractive and unnecessary" (Johnson, 1993).

- **McGraw-Hill, *Business Week* International** The Polish edition of *BusinessWeek,* launched in April 1992 with an initial circulation of 10,000, was at 25,000 by July 1993. The Russian edition was launched in September 1990 with an initial circulation of 50,000, and is now at 60,000. However, parent company McGraw-Hill stopped publishing the Hungarian edition last year because of lack of advertising and problems with its publishing partner. Ad revenue is now $600,000 per year for the Russian edition.

- **Publisher Jurg Marquard Group** (JMG) of Zug, Switzerland acquired majority ownership in the second largest Polish newspaper, *Express Wieczorny,* in 1993. Jurg Marquard, owner and founder of the publishing group, commented on the acquisition: "This acquisition provides us with the opportunity to participate in the most significant moment in recent history, the opening of Eastern Europe to open and free publishing." *Express Wieczorny* is published in Warsaw and is considered one of the most influential daily newspapers in Poland ("Jurg Marquard," *Business Wire,* 1993).

  JMG formed a 50/50 joint venture in Poland called Fibak Marquard Press with Wojtek Fibak's Noma Press. The joint venture now operates a printing plant in Katowice which prints 19 newspapers and 17 other publications, including *Sports, Panorama,* and *Nowe Echo.* The plant employs approximately 1,000 workers ("Jurg Marquard," *Business Wire,* 1993).

  JMG has had publishing operations in Eastern Europe for many years. In Hungary, the company is the majority stock holder in *Magyar Hirlap,* the second largest daily newspaper. In addition, the company owns possibly the most modern newspaper printing plant in Hungary, Marquard Color Print. The Jurg Marquard Group also has operations in the Czech and Slovak Republics, Romania, Bulgaria and Russia ("Jurg Marquard," *Business Wire,* 1993).

- **Ringier.** Swiss media giant Ringier AG launched a new daily in Czech called *Blesk* after extensive market research and a $500,000 promotional campaign. *Blesk* was launched in 1992 and within one year had become the number-one daily with sales of 500,000 copies.

- **Playboy.** One of the most successful magazines in eastern Europe is *Playboy*. It currently licenses to publishers in Hungary and the Czech Republic and has a joint venture in Poland. In the licensing deals, Playboy International provides the structure and the foreign publishers provide the time, energy and capital. Advertising is done at both levels. The eastern European editions sell on average between 275 and 300 ad pages per year, and circulation ranges from 40,000 to 80,000.

- **General Media International.** Another company using the licensing approach, General Media International publishes *Penthouse* in eastern Europe. The magazine was launched in Russia in 1992 with an initial circulation of 300,000. Amusingly, a dual pricing structure was established by newsstands: one to look and one to buy. GMI has launched a Czech edition and is in discussions about Polish and Hungarian versions. In contrast to the success of *Penthouse,* GM's launch of *Omni* in Russia in 1990 was a complete failure; *Omni* is no longer published in Russia.

- **Rodale Press.** The U.S. company Rodale Press was one of the first publishers in post-Communist Russia with the farming magazine *Novii Fermer.* But because of a complicated way to earn hard currency to support the magazine which involved setting up a meat processing plant, the venture ran into problems. Distribution was also extremely difficult. From an initial circulation of 50,000, production was cut back in 1993 to a circulation of 40,000. Currently, Rodale is working with a number of private distribution companies to develop more efficient distribution systems in Russia.

- **Ziff.** *PC Magazine,* published by Ziff, now has Russian, Czech, Hungarian and Polish editions. The magazine is widely distributed and is in a niche that has grown quickly over the past three years.

- **Maxwell.** Maxwell owns a number of dailies in Hungary. One of the most successful, the newspaper *Magyar Hirlap,* was sold to the Swiss publisher Marquard in 1992.

These advertisers were reached by a direct sales force in each city, who received up to 10 percent commission. The sales force had expanded dramatically in the past year, and now totaled eight in Warsaw, six in Prague, five in Bucharest, three in Lodz, and three in Krakow.

The production process of the magazine included three main steps: 1) design and layout; 2) printing; and 3) distribution. For the first part, design and layout, much of the magazine stayed the same from issue to issue. The centerfold was always a map of the city, and several pages contained the same information about the city from issue to issue. Advertising was then allotted the appropriate number of pages. Other pages were filled with stories or features that fit the style of the magazine.

Layout for the first magazine was done in the United States. Ludwig brought the relevant information and advertisements, and a layout company prepared the films. The films were taken to Germany for printing. The initial run was 35,000 copies. The magazines were then trucked to Warsaw for local distribution.

Once in-house design and layout was completed, disks were sent to the printer. Printing had originally been done in Germany, but was now done locally. Print runs were 50,000 for the Warsaw and Prague issues, and 35,000 for the other cities.

Distribution was through hotels, airline offices, travel agents, tourist offices and directories, and car rental agencies. Ludwig managed to convince nearly every prominent hotel in Warsaw to put the magazine in their hotel rooms, so that visitors would have a readily-accessible city guide. It was not a difficult sell: the magazine was, after all, free to the hotels, and gave their guests relevant information. Ludwig hired one person to ensure that distribution was taken care of properly.

The basic financials for the Warsaw magazine are shown in *Exhibit D.* Net profit of only $10K for 1993 was partly due to the fact that the Warsaw office absorbed many of the startup costs for the other magazines, such as initial layout work and administration. For the first months of 1994, the Warsaw magazine was running a net income of just under $10K per month.

As far as the other magazines were concerned, the two other Polish magazines and the Bucharest magazine had reached positive cash flow. Prague was still a net consumer of cash, but was projected to reach positive cash flow in the summer of 1994.

For major cities, the advertising price per pages was about $1,200 for local advertisers, and about $2,000 for international advertisers. The inside covers were $3,000 and the back cover was $5,000. Based on Ludwig's initial expenses, this gave him a break-even of 12 to 14 pages. By the third issue, the magazine had reached positive cash flow. Warsaw currently had about 30 pages of advertising per issue, yielding revenues of $45K per month. Based on this recent performance, Ludwig expected yearly revenues of slightly over $500K. He expected net income to be around $100K. Ludwig thought that the other magazines had the potential to follow Warsaw's path.

EXHIBIT D

Annotated Income Statement for Warsaw Magazine

($000s)	1993	1994*
Revenue	350	500
COGS		
Labor	100	130
Printing	150	165
Rent/Office	30	40
Gross margin	70	165
Depreciation	20	20
General Administration	40	45
Net Income	10	100

*estimated

One of the problems the startup faced was currency devaluation. Inflation in Poland was well over 50 percent, but it was difficult to constantly raise prices. The value of his advertising revenues one year down the road would amount to about half the present value in real terms, and several customers had prepaid for an entire year. What made the issue particularly troublesome was that his printing bills were paid in German marks.

Despite this problem, the magazine continued to operate with a positive cash flow during the first year. Ludwig improved and expanded the magazine. He quickly increased the number of pages to 48, and professionalized the layout. He moved the production to Poland and bought a Macintosh II to do layout in-house. His staff had grown to 12 people by the end of 1993.

Ludwig also launched the *What, Where, When* magazine in other Polish cities and eastern European countries. In 1993, he moved forward with two new Polish offices, Krakow and Lodz. Both were funded by the flagship Warsaw office. Also, cash from the Warsaw magazine funded the first issues of the Prague and Bucharest versions of the magazine, which were launched in the beginning of 1994.

Ludwig planned to continue expanding his business. He set up a joint venture in Sofia with the intention of publishing the first magazine by the fall of 1994. He also pursued negotiations with a potential partner in Budapest. In the established cities, his goal was to improve cash flow and leverage *What, Where, When* into other magazine publishing opportunities.

The Eastern European Operations

After negotiating a more specific understanding, Gary flew to eastern Europe for a tour of Ludwig's operation. Gary thought that a business trip to eastern Europe would allow them to become better acquainted, in addition to providing insight into the nature of the publishing opportunity. As the overnight train from Munich pulled into Prague, Gary found himself awash in memories of his adventures in the former Eastern Bloc. The spires of Prague also rekindled pleasant thoughts about this city. Getting off the train, he changed money and took the subway to the Forum Hotel to meet Ludwig.

At the Forum, Ludwig welcomed him and they discussed the coming day's events. On the agenda was a trip to the lawyer's office, visiting the magazine's office, a meeting with a layout editor, and a visit with one of Ludwig's customers from his export-import business. The day went quickly, a series of meetings and glimpses into the workings of his business in Prague. Before long, they had boarded the 9:20 PM train to Warsaw.

The two days in Warsaw followed a similar pattern. Most of his time was spent in the magazine office, and Gary had an opportunity to talk with staff members: the general manager, the production manager, the layout staff, the advertising manager and several advertising reps. He saw the production of the magazine, and had a chance to review financial statements. He also had a chance to attend the semiannual board meeting and meet Ludwig's Polish partner, Nicholas. Gary observed that although Ludwig was always a powerful man, he was even more so when in his own element.

At the end of two days, Ludwig flew on to Bucharest. Gary spent one more day in Warsaw before flying back to the States. That day he met with several other people about another business opportunity he had been exploring. Most important, he met Rafal Sokól, a broker and analyst who had previously worked on the Warsaw Stock Exchange.

An Online Financial Information Service for Eastern Europe

It was also in late January that a second serious business idea began to gather momentum. In the fall, he had thought about the opportunity to set up some type of online service for eastern Europe. But he felt his initial idea, to start a Polish information service covering business opportunities, had limited potential. After his first entrepreneurial finance class though, he revisited the idea. The case that day had been about an online financial service company called Technical Data Corp. The second case was about another online company called BRC. Gary decided to reevaluate the opportunity for an online financial information service in eastern Europe (see Exhibit E).

The recent growth in the eastern European stock markets made the idea attractive. In Poland, total capitalization was now $3 billion and daily volume had reached $200 million. In the Czech Republic, total capitalization was a spectacular $15 billion, with daily volume at $15 million. This was coupled with the fact that a total of $6 billion in foreign investment had poured into the two countries.[2] Into Czech equities alone, $350 million had moved eastward.[3] In Poland, Pioneer Mutual now had a $1 billion fund. An array of other funds had been set up in the two countries in the $100 million range. The growth in the private sector, about 12 percent in Poland, and the returns in the stock markets, over 700 percent in Poland, were additional reasons for the rush into these countries.

Reuters and Telerate had entered into the eastern European markets, but they only provided real-time stock quotes and limited news stories. These companies viewed themselves more as wire services and had historically focused on real-time information. No one provided a comprehensive online financial information service for the eastern block. In fact, no database service existed which had information on the publicly traded companies in the Czech Republic or Poland. Gary thought a need existed for a Bloomberg-style information service.

Gary contacted several fund managers and analysts whose portfolios included companies in the eastern block. They all indicated that most of their information came from daily newspapers and word of mouth. Some said that they would pay for information about the eastern block online. In the future such information would become increasingly necessary. Others indicated that most of the investing in Czech and Polish equities was speculative by unsophisticated investors. As such, they thought an online information service was not needed, yet it might be needed in the future.

While his background was not in information services, Gary thought he had the background to set up a business in eastern Europe. He had helped set up an office in Moscow, and was even entrusted to run the company's office in Poland during the summer when the managers were traveling.

In part due to his lack of experience, he felt the most important aspect would be team building and marshaling human resources. He had seen how important this was in his family's entrepreneurial ventures. So from the beginning he sought to build a team which would bring together players with the right experience, skills, and attitudes.

The first person he called was his brother, George, who was a research engineer at Carnegie Mellon University and had extensive experience with advanced systems integration and programming. George, who had expressed entrepreneurial yearnings in the past, was intrigued. After looking into the idea, his brother said that it was feasible from the hardware and software perspectives. Because of recent strides in computer technology and the dramatic decrease in price, it should be possible to get the hardware for around $25K, and the software could be developed by adapting an off-the-shelf database program for about $4K.

[2] Sosnowski, Warsaw Voice, May 8, 1994
[3] Mastrini, Reuters, May 2, 1994

Gary also pursued contacts with individuals who had experience in the online financial information industry. Fortuitously, the father of a fellow business school friend had just retired from Reuters. Gary did a Nexis search on Robert Reid and learned that he had been a senior VP in charge of Instinet, an off-the-big-board trading service that Reuters offered. Before that, he was a Senior VP at the NYSE. His friend put Gary in touch with his father, and Reid helped Gary think through the idea. He said he thought the idea was a good one, and that he certainly could envision the upside of such a service. He also said that while Reuters was in the market, they were not in the database business. They would not likely compete in the intended niche.

Most important to Gary, Reid indicated his willingness to serve as an advisor to the company, and potentially as a director. Their conversations were long and involved, and Reid seemed excited about the idea. During the course of the following weeks, Reid sent Gary a couple of packets of pertinent information in the mail.

Gary talked to others in the online industry, such as Jerome Rubin, the founder of Lexis/Nexis, who was now the head of the News in the Future Project at MIT. He confirmed that the technology these days was "cheap and simple." He said it was possible to get a standard retrieval program inexpensively and have a programmer adapt it. Several others in the online industry who he talked to were basically in agreement with Rubin.

A key part of the team would be a Polish partner. During Gary's April trip to Poland with Ludwig, he dedicated his last day to meetings for the online service. In addition to meeting with the head of the trading system at the stock exchange and analysts at one of the funds in Poland, he also met with potential partners. In his last meeting he met the cousin of a former Polish colleague, Rafal Sokól. Sokól was formerly at the Warsaw Stock Exchange, and now in a financial consulting partnership. The partners produced a daily column on the Polish Stock Market for the most popular financial daily.

Gary was impressed with Sokól, and his partner Szafirowski. They were smart, knowledgeable, young, ambitious, and they spoke good English. It was decided that they should continue to talk, to fax each other additional information about themselves and the opportunity, and to meet again in three weeks in Poland.

When Gary got back home, he talked to Reid and his brother George about Sokól and Szafirowski. George had done more research on the technical side of the business. He had spoken at length with friends who worked in the Real-time Financial Information Lab which had been endowed by Reuters, Bloomberg, Knight-Ridder and others. He talked to another friend who owned his own database consulting company and ordered sample kits from several database companies. After these talks and research, George had put together a summary of the technical requirements of the business based on several different options.

George had also talked to one of the programmers working for him, Jae Chang, who was one of the best programmers George had ever known. Chang was excited about the startup idea and said that he would be willing to work for next to nothing, in exchange for equity. George even managed to get him a job for the summer programming the interface of a new Internet node at Carnegie Mellon, an experience which would be directly applicable to the online service—the Internet would be one of the channels of information dissemination for the service.

Gary realized business school would soon come to an end. Since returning from Warsaw he had written an outline and an executive summary of the business plan. He had talked extensively to his uncle, who had launched or owned seven different businesses, and now was a substantial supporter of new ventures and young entrepreneurs. After looking at the outline, his uncle said that Gary had his first $50K if he needed it. His parents would put in another $50K. Gary and his brother could add $30K together. Based on his projections, he thought that this amount could get him up and running for at least nine months. Gary wondered if he was crazy to even consider going into business in competition with billion dollar firms like Bloomberg and Rueters, but he had done his homework and he didn't see a fatal flaw—yet.

Commencement

As the clapping in class came to an end, Gary's thoughts turned again to what lay ahead. It was time to make a decision. Gary felt that he could develop the financial information service idea further without additional capital investment. But was he being unrealistic about his ability to create a world-class service when he was a rookie in the industry? On the other hand, Ludwig had an opportunity at the magazine that was ready to grow, and he was also eager to support Gary in developing new ventures. Ludwig was expecting a call within the next few days; Gary wondered what he should do.

Emerging Markets Online—Financial Information

A. Strategy

Emerging Markets Online will provide financial information covering the Polish and Czech stock markets and public companies. The target market will be domestic and international brokers, traders, investors and others working with Eastern European equity markets. Information will be available online, on diskette, on CD-ROM, and via fax.

Emerging Markets Online's (EMO) strategy and focus will be similar to Bloomberg in the United States. EMO will target analysts, brokers, and institutional investors by providing a database of fundamentals, news, press releases, and analyst reports. Fundamental information (Income Statement, Balance Sheet, Ratios, etc.) will come mainly from public sources, such as monthly and quarterly reports, which are readily available in Poland and the Czech Republic. EMO will include news stories from Polish and Czech daily newspapers and newsletters in the database. In other countries, news stories from daily and weekly sources are included in databases in exchange for commission. Analyst reports will also be put online in a similar exchange for commission. EMO will avoid direct competition with Reuters and Telerate in the real-time stock quote arena. The service will be similar to Bloomberg in developed markets.

Even though EMO will offer a service similar to Bloomberg, emerging markets are perceived to be an area of weakness for Bloomberg.[4] Bloomberg currently has a relative dearth of information on emerging market equities because they are focused on developed markets. As one venture capitalist who covers the online industry said, "Bloomberg right now has so much on their plate; they are concerned with the big markets like Japan and London." The markets EMO will cover, while large for an entrepreneurial venture, are too small for a company like Bloomberg to warrant attention at this time.

EMO will have an additional advantage because the expensive human capital will be working primarily for equity. EMO will have a much lower break-even than established online companies, permitting it to reach positive cash flow before the industry becomes more competitive in three years.

B. Opportunity

- **Volume explosion:** Daily stock market volume in Poland up to $200 million. Currently, the daily volume of the Polish stock exchange has surpassed many western European exchanges and is almost as large as the Toronto exchange. The total capitalization is larger than China and approaching smaller, more developed markets. The following provides an overview of the two main markets:

	Total Cap	Daily Vol.	Number of Cos.	'93 Perform.	'93 GNP
Czech	$14 bil.	$ 15 mil.	1330	97%	+5%
Poland	$ 6 bil.	$200 mil.	27	783%	+3%

This leap in the size of the eastern European markets mirrors the growth in the capital flows to emerging market stock markets in general:

- International portfolio investment in emerging markets is now $56 billion, up 56 percent from the year before, and up from $7.5 billion in 1989 (Austin, 1994).
- 9.5 percent of international equity assets allocated to emerging markets in 1993, up from 2.5 percent in 1989 (survey of 30 international institutional investors, IFC, 1993).
- Total market cap of $740 billion in 1992 for group of 25 emerging markets (IFC, 1993).
- Number of companies listed on emerging stock markets now represents roughly 40 percent of the world total (IFC, 1993).
- Pension funds, endowments and foundations now own global equities worth $170 billion, and plan to raise this to $300 billion in the next three years (Financial Times, 1993).
- All 24 emerging stock markets tracked by the World Bank's International Finance Corp. showed greater returns in 1993 than the Standard & Poor's 500 Index (Bailey, 1994).

---

[4] "Technology: Reuters vs. Bloomberg," *Asia Money and Finance*, March, 1993, pp. 63–64.

EXHIBIT E (Continued)

Emerging Markets Online—Financial Information

- **Total capitalization growth:** Poland now $6 billion and Czech $14 billion. The Polish market now has about $200 million in daily volume and the Czech market should grow considerably in volume this year. The total capitalization of the two markets is about $21 billion. Over the course of the next two to three years, about 400 Polish companies should be privatized and listed on the Polish stock exchange. This will tremendously increase the total capitalization of the market and the inflow of capital into the market.

- **No online database service provides in-depth financial information:** The demand for financial information in the United States had driven tremendous industry growth over the past ten years. The market for online services in the United States is now between $15 billion and $35 billion, depending on the estimate, of which one-third to one-half is financial online services.[5] The industry has been growing at 30 percent annually and is expected to continue to grow at 20+ percent per year in the future. The demand for such information is evident by the growth in demand in the investment community for services such as Reuters, Dow Jones, Telerate, Bloomberg, Knight-Ridder, and a slew of smaller companies. The number of online financial information services in the United States now totals 160, up 30 from last year alone.[6] The growth in the size of the market is also partly due to price insensitive customers. Investment managers will readily pay $80K per month each for a broad range of services.
   Poland and the Czech Republic are still low on the online information curve. Analysts now mostly glean information from newspapers and publicly released financial information. This is similar to Mexico before the late 1980s and developed countries before the 1980s. Eastern Europe is on the cusp of the development of the online information industry; it should follow a similar trend as more capital flows into the country and as the equity markets become more sophisticated.

- **Relatively price-insensitive customers:** 200 licensed Polish brokers each trade about $6 million per month; Pioneer in Poland has a $1 billion equity fund. Brokers, institutional investors, and related business are typically price insensitive with respect to critical information. Revenues of more than $250 per month for an information service should be readily achievable.

- **Success of comparables in other emerging markets:** Emerging markets have followed the same trend in the financial information market. As capital flowed into the country, and as the market became more sophisticated, demand for information increased, and online financial information services grew tremendously. In Mexico in 1985, for example, a newspaper, El Norte, set up one of the first online information services covering Mexican financial information. That company now has 2,200 customers and averages about $2K in revenue from each customer, or $4.4 million per month. This is despite the fact the Reuters and Telerate were already in the market when the company started, and that several other domestic and international providers, such as Bloomberg, are now on the scene. Other emerging markets such as Hong Kong have followed a similar trend of moving from relatively low sophistication of information provision to higher sophistication.

- **Quick to Positive Cash Flow:** Low asset intensity (typically 0.15); quick to break even.

- **Easily technologically feasible:** Compare to accessibility of Internet around the world. In terms of software, it is now possible to adapt an off-the-shelf database program in a matter of a couple of months with one or two programmers. The program will be configured so that fundamental information may be accessed and graphed in a manner similar to Bloomberg. The program will also be able to run text searches for news items, and retrieve analyst reports. Because of our technical team's extensive involvement in programmer circles, it will be possible to minimize the costs of the adaptation by hiring the top undergraduate programmers during the summer inexpensively.

Software Program:	$2,000
Programmer Adaptation:	$3,000
Total Software costs:	$5,000

C. Basic Financials

The online industry, like the software industry, is characterized by low asset intensity, typically in the range of 0.1 to 0.2. Once an online service is up and running, the cost of adding an additional customer is low. After break-even is reached, then such companies have great free cash flow characteristics, often with over 50 percent of additional revenue flowing through to the bottom line. (see *Table 3*)

[5]Multimedia, "*The Economist,* October 16, 1993; Ellis, Booker, "Online Services," *Computerworld,* August 24, 1992.
[6]Levin, Jayne, "Online Investment Services Are Exploding," *The Washington Post,* April 11, 1993.

Startup costs are also relatively low, as outlined above. Hardware and software should cost under $30K if purchased. "Loaned" or leased equipment will lower hardware costs even more. Other startup costs will be kept below $20K, keeping the total up-front costs below $50K.

Initial capitalization for hardware, software and 6 mo. working capital:	$100K
Burn rate for one year:	$5K/mo.
Revenue projections for end of year one: 20 customers @ $250/Mo.	$5K/mo.
Revenue projections for year 5 based on comparable countries:	$6 million
(based on a conservative 500 customers @ $1,000/Mo.	

Thus, the company's minimum burn rate in the first 6 months will be $3,750. Even with a higher burn rate of $6,000 per month, the company will be able to operate about nine months without revenue until it is out of cash.

In terms of revenue, it is assumed that the company will have no revenue for the first six months. After that point, the company expects to add 10 customers per month. Customers will be given one month of free usage to try the system. After this period, it is expected that 50 percent will retain the service, with an average monthly bill of $250. With these conservative projections, both cash flow and EBIT will turn positive in month 12. The total operating cash outflow will have been less than $45K.

After one year, the company should show excellent cash flow characteristics. In year two, an estimated average of 50 customers at $500 per month will generate $25K per month in revenue, or $300K per year. Of that, it is estimated that about 20 percent should flow through to the bottom line. In year three, an average of 200 customers at $500 per month will generate $1.2 million in sales, with a net income of $220K. A 20x multiple would put the value of the company at $4.4 million.

- **Exit Strategy.** EMO will be set up with an exit strategy of three to five years in mind. By ensuring that the system remains flexible and compatible with other services, EMO will be a prime acquisition target for any of the larger online services. Reuters, for example, has a business development department which focuses on such acquisitions. One individual in the department, a graduate of the Harvard Business School, said that $5 million to $10 million acquisitions are common in his department.

D. Prospective Management Team

Gary Mueller worked on privatization in Poland and Russia; attended Harvard Business School and Harvard College.

Robert Reid, former Sr. VP, Reuter's; head of Instinet, an online NYSE equities trading system; former Sr. VP, NYSE.

George Mueller, Research Engineer, Carnegie Mellon University; extensive experience in advanced system integration and software engineering.

Jae Chang, extensive programming experience; rewrote Carnegie Mellon's Internet interface; Carnegie Mellon University computer and electrical engineer.

Rafal Sokól, Partner, Conmar Investors. Worked on Polish Stock Exchange. Extensive experience as analyst of Polish equities. Publishes column in leading financial newspaper.

Krzysztof Szafirowski, Partner, Conmar Investors. Investment advisor on Polish equities. Publishes column in leading Polish financial newspaper.

Jeff Grady, Manager, Copernicus Fund in Poland. Manager, first western consulting company in Poland. Four years work experience in Poland.

Walter Wilkie, founder and owner of seven companies. Board Member, various companies.

TABLE 3

Emerging Markets Online—Proforma Income Statement

		Sept '94	Oct	Nov	Dec	Jan '95	Feb	Mar	Apr	May	Jun	Jul	Aug
Rev		0	0	0	0	0	0	0	1250	2500	3750	5000	6250
COGS	Programmer	625	625	625	625	625	625	625	625	625	625	625	625
	Data Entry	1960	1960	1960	1960	1960	1960	1960	1960	1960	1960	1960	1960
	Expenses	1200	1200	1200	1200	1200	1200	1200	1200	1200	1200	1200	1200
	Office	500	500	500	500	500	500	500	500	500	500	500	500
	Other	300	300	300	300	300	300	300	300	300	300	300	300
	Total	4585	4585	4585	4585	4585	4585	4585	4585	4585	4585	4585	4585
Gross		−4585	−4585	−4585	−4585	−4585	−4585	−4585	−3335	−2085	−835	415	1665
Depreciation		833	833	833	833	833	833	833	833	833	833	833	833
SGA		500	500	500	500	500	500	500	500	500	500	500	500
EBIT		−5918	−5918	−5918	−5918	−5918	−5918	−5918	−4668	−3418	−2168	−918	332
Cash Flow	EBIT	−5918	−5918	−5918	−5918	−5918	−5918	−5918	−4668	−3418	−2168	−918	332
	+ Depr	833	833	833	833	833	833	833	833	833	833	833	833
	+ NWC	0	0	0	0	0	0	0	0	0	0	0	0
	− CapEx	0	0	0	0	0	0	0	0	0	0	0	0
	FCF	−5085	−5085	−5085	−5085	−5085	−5085	−5085	−3835	−2585	−1335	−85	1165
	Total Cash	−5085	−10170	−15255	−20340	−25425	−30510	−35595	−39430	−42015	−43350	−43435	−42270

Assumptions:

Costs

Programmer Wages	500/mo
Programmer:	625/mo
Total Cost	
Data Entry	4 people
DE Wages	350/mo
Total DE Cost	1,400/mo
Office	500/mo
Phone	300/mo
Supplies	400/mo
Travel	500/mo
Other	300/mo
Total Other	$2,000/mo
SGA	$500/mo

Revenues

Months until customers	6
New customers/month	10
Months free usage	1
Retention of free customers	50%
Avg. Monthly rev/customer	$250

Depreciation

Total fixed costs	$30,000
Deprec period	3 years
Deprec/mo—straight line	$833

Chapter Five

Entrepreneurs and the Internet: The Great Equalizer*

JULIAN E. LANGE

"Man will not fly for fifty years."

Orville Wright, 1901
To his brother, Wilbur

Results Expected

At the conclusion of this chapter, you will have:

1. Examined the roots and evolution of the Internet and how it is creating opportunities for a new generation of Netrepreneurs.
2. Identified the capabilities and potential benefits of the Web for new and existing businesses.
3. Explored the leading Web sites that can assist entrepreneurs.
4. Extended your consideration of potential venture opportunities vis-á-vis the Internet now and in the future.
5. Examined in detail a case about two brothers who conceived, seed funded, and launched a new venture on the Internet.

The Great Equalizer

Not since the introduction of the personal computer and application software has any technology or medium of commerce and communication so quickly and so radically altered the landscape of enterprise, worldwide. The Internet and the legions of innovative Netrepreneurs have and continue to change the way people live, learn, work, and do business. More than the microcomputer, biotechnology, and wireless telecommunications revolutions, the Web revolution is affecting all peoples and all nations so that we will never be the same.

What is most stunning and exhilarating for aspiring and existing entrepreneurs alike is that the Internet is, indeed, the great equalizer. Like its predecessor, the personal computer, it creates equal access and the power to create, identify, and pursue opportunities on an equal footing with the giants. As importantly, the perilous initial seed stage of many Internet ventures can be successfully navigated with startup capital of less than $100,000. Once a venture has demonstrated feasibility, workability, and the beginnings of a customer base, then securing follow-on capital, through customers, strategic partners, angels, or venture capitalists, becomes possible.

*The author is extremely appreciative to Professor Julian E. Lange, our Internet guru at Babson College's Arthur M. Blank Center for Entrepreneurship, for contributing the text for this chapter.

The Internet has captured the imagination of the world. It is the new frontier of the millennium. It has grown from a little known communication vehicle for scientists and "techies" to a tool that provides access to a seemingly limitless array of information to anyone with a computer, a modem, and a telephone line. Virtually all manner of information is available on the Internet—including stock market quotations, product literature, government statistics, news stories, and video clips from the latest movie releases—all just a few mouse clicks away. But what are the opportunities for entrepreneurs on the Internet? How realistic are they and how can they be identified and developed? How are they likely to change over time?

This chapter will provide an in-depth introduction to one of the two or three most significant developments for entrepreneurs in the past twenty-five years: the Internet. We will explore what tools are available, how to use them, and how to get connected to the Internet. Those readers who are already Internet-savvy may want to turn to the section on "How an existing business can benefit from the Internet," which explores the *why* of being on the Internet and looks at how it can be used to further the goals of existing businesses as well as provide opportunities for the development of new products and services. The Internet is incredibly dynamic. The Internet is changing so rapidly that it is a challenge to keep up. This chapter offers a way of doing that by providing specific references to Internet sites and institutions that you should visit often.

What Is the Internet and Where Did It Come From?

Although the term Internet ("the Net") is familiar to most people, the exact definition may be unclear. The Internet is a vast array of networks connecting millions of other computer networks and individual computers around the world. Estimates of the total number of users vary, but at the time of this writing it is believed to be in excess of 100 million. The Net is growing at an astonishing rate, with the number of users increasing by 10 to 20 percent every month (*Exhibit 5.1*). The number of hosts in Exhibit 5.1

EXHIBIT 5.1

Internet Hosts: 1989–1997

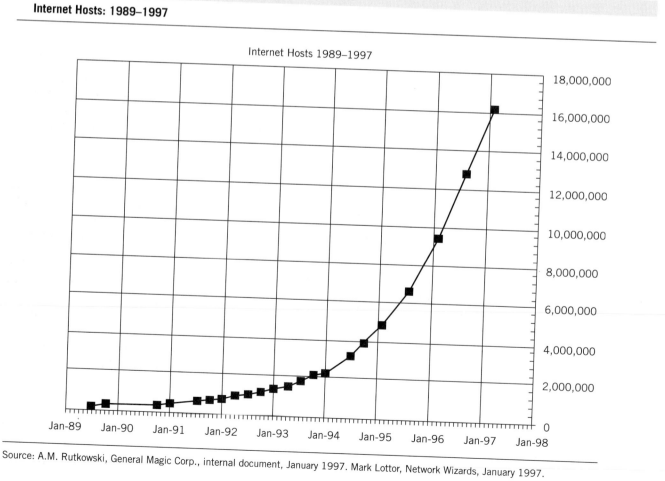

Internet Hosts 1989–1997

Source: A.M. Rutkowski, General Magic Corp., internal document, January 1997. Mark Lottor, Network Wizards, January 1997.

refers to the number of computers acting as servers; that is, computers with which other computers can connect to exchange data. There are approximately 10 users for each host computer. Although the growth rate will inevitably decrease, there is no denying the recent phenomenal growth in the number of hosts and users: a 1,600 percent increase over the past four years.

Once connected to the Internet, a user can communicate with a computer across the room or across the globe with equal facility. Familiarity with computers and the Internet presently provides a competitive advantage to entrepreneurs, but such knowledge will soon be a necessity for conducting business effectively.

The Internet began almost 30 years ago as a project sponsored by the Department of Defense. In the depths of the Cold War, it was thought essential to have a network that could connect key military and scientific computers in the United States. Such a network would be useful as a means of exchanging information in the scientific community as well as in the event of a nuclear disaster. To fulfill this mission, the ARPANET was born, funded by the Defense Department's Advanced Research Projects Agency. It was initially modest in scope, involving only a handful of scientific sites at major research universities, and it remained the province of academics and the military into the early 1980s. The military portion of the network was split off in the mid-1980s, but there were still significant restrictions on commercial use because the network continued to be funded by the government. Ordinary nontechnical users were discouraged from using the network because of the often-obscure "computerese" commands that needed to be learned in order to use what was by now known as the Internet. The user interface was also text-based, consisting of line after line of computer jargon, devoid of the point-and-click ease of use of the Apple Macintosh or Microsoft Windows-based personal computers.

That was all changed by the introduction of the World Wide Web (the Web). A group of scientists led by Timothy Berners-Lee of CERN, the European Particle Physics Laboratory, decided that it would be desirable to develop a user interface that incorporated graphics, sound, and video as well as text, and would also link data from various sources around the world on a single screen of information. Subsequently, in the early 1990s, the National Center for Supercomputing Applications at the University of Illinois sponsored the development of the first computer program, called a browser, which implemented these ideas and provided nontechnical users with a graphic tool that ushered in the age of multimedia on the Internet.

Internet Basics: Principal Features

There are a variety of tools and applications available to users that facilitate information acquisition and exchange on the Net. These tools provide a means to create an Internet presence for an entrepreneurial business that can enhance its growth and effectiveness. If you are new to the Net, you should take some time to get accustomed to the environment. Browse the computer section of a good bookstore and you will find a plethora of introductory how-to books about the mechanics of navigating the Net.

We will give you a general overview of the tools so that you can determine which ones seem relevant to your needs. You do not have to learn every tool or technique all at once. Do some Net surfing—exploring the different tools and Net destinations. See what others are doing and get familiar with the territory. Then, you will be better able to see the possibilities that the Internet offers for your business and, being entrepreneurial, some of you will no doubt invent new capabilities for your business and others.

E-mail

Perhaps the most familiar and universal business tool of the Internet age is electronic mail, or e-mail. Although used by relatively few people 10 years ago, today there are more than 50 million e-mail users worldwide. (As with most of the demographic statistics mentioned here, this number will no doubt increase by the time you read this.) E-mail permits users to send text messages to recipients anywhere in the world. Most systems also permit the sending of attachments containing data in binary form. Such data may include spreadsheet files, database files, word processing documents, and even sound or video files, and allows the sharing of documents in their original format, so that they can be edited or added to by others. In addition to e-mail sent by direct connection to the Internet, there are many e-mail users who exchange electronic messages through online providers like America Online or Compu Serve as well as within systems proprietary to a particular company. Most of these latter systems also have connections to the Internet, allowing users to correspond electronically with users outside their own e-mail system.

E-mail provides a low-cost, simple, and direct way to exchange information. It has all the advantages of voice mail in terms of convenience and time shift—allowing you to leave and retrieve messages when convenient for you—as well as having the additional benefit of being content rich. Rather than a brief summary voice-mail message, you can send someone a complete document or spreadsheet analysis, which they can then work on and respond to while you are doing something else. E-mail also provides a simple way of telling recipients more about you and your company through the use of signature files. Signatures consist of a few extra lines of text that can be appended to every message that you send. These messages should contain essential information, such as your company name, street address, zip code, telephone and fax numbers, as well as your e-mail address and a short description of your company's product or service. Signatures should be kept to a few lines to be effective; they are a useful tool in creating awareness of you and your company.

The World Wide Web

The immense upsurge of interest in the Internet is no doubt directly related to the growth of the World Wide Web (the Web). The Web is the part of the Internet that allows the use of multimedia—graphics, audio, and video, as well as text. The Web also makes extensive use of hyperlinks that permit the user to jump from the document being viewed to another document that may reside on another computer in a different city or possibly on a different continent.

In order to access the Web, you will need to use a program called a *browser*. Browsers permit you to view Web documents that have been created especially to incorporate the Web's multimedia capabilities. Such documents are constructed using a computer language called HTML—hypertext markup language. Hyperlinks transform Web documents into dynamic vehicles for displaying related information in a variety of forms. For example, many businesses have created Web sites called *home pages*, in which they present information about their companies of interest to customers, potential customers, suppliers, employees, shareholders, job applicants, the press, and others. Through the use of hyperlinks, electronic visitors to your home page can jump to other areas they may wish to explore (and which you may want to encourage them to explore) about your company, such as product descriptions, job responsibilities and pictures of key employees, tech support information, or a message from the president.

Equally important, you can gather data about the visitor that can be useful in gaining feedback about your products or services, both through directly surveying visitors or simply gathering information about the time of their visit, which parts of the home page they viewed, and how long they stayed. This interactive aspect of the Net is one of its essential features and potentially the most important reason to include the Web in your business strategy. Keeping close to customers and the marketplace has emerged as an important theme for businesses in the 1990s, and the Web and the Net in general provide many excellent opportunities for doing so.

The leading browsers are Netscape's Navigator and Microsoft's Internet Explorer. The browsers are rapidly incorporating add-on features and capabilities far beyond their original versions, such as linkages to online newspapers and search engines and data security features. At this writing Netscape has the largest share of the market (estimated at approximately 50 percent in 1997), but the competition from Microsoft (with approximately 39 percent of the market, including 16 percent through America Online) is getting very intense. Versions of both browsers can be downloaded free as of this writing from the homepages of Netscape and Microsoft (listed below). Since the competition will no doubt continue to intensify and the vendors will continue to add features and content to their offerings, you should download and try out both products and decide which best meets your needs. You may choose to use both.

The success of Netscape's browser in capturing a huge market share is a good example of the new possibilities opened up by the growth of the Internet. Netscape attained its market share by giving its product away via the Internet. The cost of distribution was negligible to Netscape and primarily borne by the users, in terms of paying for the connection and the download time. This strategy made Netscape the de facto browser standard. Prior to the growth and widespread use of the Internet, the introduction of a new product and attempt to create a standard was a costly and time-consuming process involving significant marketing and distribution costs. But Netscape's experience proved that the growth of the Internet has created new alternatives for marketing and distributing products. Microsoft is counter-attacking using a similar strategy. They are encouraging users to download Internet Explorer without charge from a variety of Internet sites, and it has become an integral part of Windows98.

Telnet

Telnet is an Internet tool that allows you to use your computer to log on to a remote computer; that is, a computer other than your own somewhere else in the Internet system. To do so, the Telnet program turns your computer into a terminal, a device capable of communicating with other computers over a network.

In order to log on, you need to have a valid account and password on the remote computer. When you log on, you can use most of the capabilities of the remote computer. You can access directories, files, and programs, and perform most of the operations that you normally perform on your own computer. But you will only be able to access those files that would normally be available to you. For example, if you log on to your company's computer and are not cleared to access the payroll records, you will be restricted from doing so when you log on remotely as well.

A second important restriction is that you may not be able to run programs very efficiently from a remote computer. The reason for this is technical and has to do with the limited bandwidth of a remote log-in. Bandwidth can be thought of as the diameter of the pipe through which you are accessing the remote computer. The amount of data that can be transferred over telephone lines using even the fastest modem is far less than that which can be transferred internally on your own computer or even over your business's local area network (LAN). Consequently, most programs will run too slowly when accessed remotely using Telnet. Nevertheless, Telnet remains a very useful tool for reading e-mail, accessing files, and uploading and downloading them.

Telnet is a tool that does not require you to be connected to the Web. However, the bad news is that you need to use what is called a command line interface (a series of "computerese" instructions). The good news is that they are the same instructions that you are accustomed to using when you log on to the computer normally. For example, if you are logging on to your office computer during a business trip to read your e-mail, you use the same commands to access your mail as you do when you are in the office.

FTP

Often, the administrators of a computer installation do not want outsiders to log on and roam around the system, but are happy to have remote users access certain data files. The tool for this sort of situation is called file transfer protocol (FTP). It is a means of allowing you to upload and download files from other computers on the Net. The computers on the Net contain vast numbers of files, and it is important to be able to transport those files to your computer in order to view their contents and work with them. FTP permits you to do this by following a series of instructions presented to you by the remote computer. FTP is often used in conjunction with a program called Archie, which facilitates FTP searches through an index of FTP files and servers throughout the Net. You do not need to be on the Web to use FTP, but since most Web browsers include an FTP capability, you might prefer to use the browser interface.

Many educational institutions, government agencies, libraries, and businesses maintain FTP sites to facilitate the downloading of files. And in keeping with the interactive theme of the Internet, FTP allows uploading of files to remote computers. FTP facilitates the sharing of information among large numbers of users. While sharing is a truly useful aspect of the Internet, it is also important to add a word of caution about viruses. When downloading files from an unfamiliar source, you should always check them for viruses. You can do so fairly easily by purchasing one of the several commercial antivirus programs. You should also determine whether the source of the downloaded files scans them for viruses. While many sites have such a policy, it is a good idea to check the files yourself.

Gopher

Gopher is an Internet tool that enables users to locate and download files of interest on a wide variety of topics. It is a non-Web-based system that employs menus and keywords to guide the user. Gopher can be utilized in conjunction with additional application tools to enhance the search process. For example, through the selection of key words, a program called Veronica can be used to narrow a search to the gopher servers on the Web most likely to contain the information that the user is seeking. As with other non-Web tools, a gopher capability is offered with most browsers, and the graphical browser environment is preferred by many users.

The original gopher program was developed at the University of Minnesota. Whoever named the program *gopher* no doubt had a double meaning in mind: The obvious meaning is that the program will fetch data, or be a "go-fer." A second meaning, perhaps less obvious outside the confines of the University of Minnesota and its sports rivals, is the reference to the burrowing animal that also happens to be the mascot of the University of Minnesota's sports teams. The program certainly facilitates the task of burrowing through the Internet for information relevant to the user's request.

Usenet

Usenet is a system of discussion groups centered around a particular news topic of interest to its members. There are approximately 10,000 such newsgroups in existence involving millions of people. You need to use a program called a *newsreader* to access Usenet. There are many such programs available to be downloaded from the Net. Additionally, many browsers contain newsreaders. You can locate newsgroups of interest by consulting references such as the various Internet yellow pages compilations published and updated frequently and available in the computer section of your favorite bookstore. You can also search for various newsgroups or mailing lists on the Net itself (for example, see http://www.liszt.com).

After you have joined a newsgroup through use of your newsreader, you will receive messages posted (i.e., sent to) the newsgroup. Newsreaders have the ability to filter the messages, and you can follow what are called *threads* (messages related to a particular topic). There are two basic types of newsgroups, *moderated* and *unmoderated*. In unmoderated groups, all messages posted to the group are forwarded to all members of the group. As the name implies, in moderated groups posted messages are first reviewed by a moderator for relevance, and some messages are screened out through this process.

While newsgroups vary in content and focus, there are certain unwritten but generally understood rules governing their use. The most important rule from the standpoint of business users is that advertising is not considered acceptable by many newsgroups. Not all groups ban advertising. This is particularly true of business-oriented groups, but you should check out the group's policy before posting any advertising-oriented material. Most groups have a file called FAQ, which stands for frequently asked questions, that covers the major ground rules of the group. You should read that file before beginning to contribute to the group.

If advertising is permitted, it is important to understand that the kind of advertising that is welcome on the Net is high in information content and very low in hype—soft sell versus hard sell. You should be forewarned that violating this rule is considered an unacceptable intrusion by newsgroup members and will result in your being *flamed,* that is, sent a large number of unpleasant messages pointing out your error. Since the purpose of advertising is to win new customers, activities that violate the sensitivities of newsgroup members are worth taking pains to avoid.

Mailing Lists

Mailing lists are similar to newsgroups, but with some important differences. Mailing lists utilize e-mail as the medium for exchanging ideas. You join a mailing list by "subscribing" to the list. Subscribing is a simple matter of sending your e-mail address and a request to be included on the list to the list administrator, which usually is a program called a listserver. Cancelling your electronic subscription is just as easy— simply send a request to the listserver to delete your name from the subscription list. Mailing lists are unmoderated and you do not need special software to read the postings. Perhaps because of the ubiquitousness of e-mail, there are many more mailing lists than newsgroups. The rules for advertising through mailing lists are the same as those for newsgroups. Be sure to check whether any advertising at all is acceptable, and then follow the custom. If you do advertise, try to include as much content as possible in your posting.

IRC

Internet Relay Chat (IRC) is a kind of instantaneous newsgroup. This tool allows the user to send electronic messages concerning particular topics of interest to other users with those interests. But, unlike newsgroups, the messages and responses take place in real time. Participants may be from anywhere in the world (and often are), and the response time for communication is limited only by the other electronic traffic in the channel. The messages and responses are public and include anyone who has joined the chat. At present, the business use of this tool has been limited, given the public nature of the communications, but that is changing. There are mechanisms for holding private chat sessions with invited participants only, and this aspect of the IRC capability allows business participants to hold conference calls for which there is a written record of what was said and who said it. There are also commercial firms that set up and moderate such conference calls, and the use of this feature is likely to grow in the future.

Search Engines

Search engines are tools that allow the user to search for information on topics of interest. A number of such tools have been developed for the World Wide Web, including:

lycos: http://www.lycos.com

altavista: http://www.altavista.digital.com

magellan: http://www.mckinley.com

excite: http://www.excite.com

webcrawler: http://www.webcrawler.com

yahoo: http://www.yahoo.com

infoseek: http://www.infoseek.com

InterNIC Whois facility: http://www.internic.net

These tools can be reached directly from your Web browser. Some browsers have incorporated several search engines in their menu systems, making it that much simpler to use them. For example, Netscape's Navigator presents a choice of several different search engines including Lycos, Yahoo, Excite, Altavista, and Infoseek. You can then enter a one-word or several-word description of the information that you are seeking, and the search engine will process the request, often almost instantly, and display a series of choices that best match your request. The choices are presented as a list of hyperlink references. If one looks interesting, you can click on the text and jump directly to the location of that item on the Net and view and retrieve the file for storage on your computer.

For example, in writing this chapter, it was important to include data on the number and growth rate of users on the Internet. Using Netscape Navigator, we clicked on the search tool (in this case the Lycos search engine) and then entered *Internet statistics* as the topic we were researching. A number of hyperlinked references appeared. After checking out several, we located the home page of General Magic, Inc., which contained an item called *Internet trends.* We then viewed Internet trends, which consisted of a series of presentation slides describing the growth of Internet host computers and domain names (unique user names). Next, using the Lycos engine and refining our search to *Internet statistics genmagic,* we found a reference to the underlying Microsoft Powerpoint file that had generated the presentation slides. The site, maintained by General Magic, is an FTP site, which means that by hyperlinking to that site, we could download the file directly into our computer. This process took just a few minutes. It illustrates the power of the search engines, and also how you can get up-to-date information right now while you are reading this chapter.

Several of the search engines have expanded their business model to offer a variety of additional services to attract users including news, weather, financial information, chat groups, free e-mail, and games. These firms, including Lycos, Yahoo, and Excite, are now referred to as *portals* to the Web and have become attractive acquisition candidates or strategic partners for larger media companies that want to gain access to the rapidly growing online community.

Getting Connected: Online Services versus Direct Connections

There are two basic ways to set up your Internet connection:

- A direct Internet connection through an Internet service provider (an ISP).
- A connection through an online service.

Choosing which alternative is best for you depends on a number of factors, including the amount of time you expect to spend on the Internet per month, your potential usage of other features that online services offer, and whether you intend to transact business using the Internet or at least have your own home page presence.

The more extensive you expect your Internet usage to be, the more beneficial it is to have a direct connection. The cost of such a connection depends upon the service provider. A simple direct connection can vary from $15-$30 per month, before any additional charges for a home page presence. Online services' monthly fee structure usually includes a minimum charge for a given number of hours of connect time both to the service and to the Internet through the service. If you will be connecting to the Internet for more than a few hours per month, you should carefully compare the relative benefits and costs of a direct connection through an ISP with the use of an online service. While opinions vary on this issue, many people find a direct connection to be faster, in terms of both making the initial connection and throughput of data while you are connected. Some of the online services have their own browsers, but most are now also providing versions of Netscape Navigator and Microsoft Internet Explorer for Net surfing while connected through their services.

As a counterbalance to these considerations, it is important to keep in mind that the online services offer many other features besides connection to the Internet. These services offer e-mail capabilities, flashy user interfaces, easy menu-based access to news, financial and company data, and technical and customer support from myriad hardware and software companies. Perhaps their most popular offerings are their *forums,* which are similar to usenet newsgroups in their focus on a wide variety of topics of interest to their users. The online services are working very hard to justify their added value to their customers, and no doubt will continue to offer enhanced capabilities as a means of attracting users. Additionally, most of these services have home pages that are accessible directly through the Internet as a means of attracting new users.

The choice ultimately becomes one of your willingness to experiment and create your own Internet experience versus having menus and services packaged for you. You may in fact decide to do both for a time while you are determining your ultimate strategy. The key point to remember is that the more you explore the Internet, the greater the probability that you will understand the current opportunities it provides to support and grow your business, and more importantly, the greater the chances that you will see *new* possibilities to develop Internet opportunities for your current business and perhaps for a new Internet business as well.

Staying in Tune with the Internet Culture

While considering how best to use the Internet in your business, it is important to take heed of the culture of the Net. Just as companies have their individual cultures that entail norms of behavior, standard operating procedures and the like, the Internet too has a distinctive and sometimes demanding set of rules of conduct, in part stemming from its origin as a scientific and technical medium for exchanging ideas and information. First among these is that "content is king." This is important to remember for both positive and negative reasons. Whether you are posting a comment to a newsgroup or designing your home page, Internet users are focused on content and have little patience for fluff and communications which they deem to be a waste of their time—particularly in the case of newsgroups, where your message will go out to hundreds or thousands of users. They are often intolerant of the mistakes of new users, but you shouldn't let that discourage your explorations.

You should never send a general advertising message to thousands of users on a mailing list (a procedure known as *spamming*). Users do not like their e-mail boxes filled up with the electronic equivalent of junk mail.

Does this mean that you can never advertise on the Internet? Not at all, it just means that you need to get to know its customs and act accordingly. The growth of the Web has somewhat blurred the distinction between information, advertising, and entertainment and this is likely to continue to evolve. More and more users new to the Net do not come from the original "techie" community and will no doubt affect the Internet culture over time. Business users are also clearly amenable to sales and advertising, and they will exert additional influence in shaping the future of the Net. Nevertheless, it is likely that the maxim "content is king" will continue to dominate the Net culture for some time. Your experience with all of the exciting possibilities of the Net will be dramatically improved if you tailor your initiatives to the opportunities presented by the Net's unique culture.

How an Existing Business Can Benefit from the Internet

Three outstanding characteristics about successful entrepreneurs are that they are fast, focused, and flexible.[1] In many ways the Internet holds out the promise of making the playing field more level for startups and smaller, emerging businesses. An attractive, compelling home page is often judged on its own terms and can appear to be the work of a much larger established company. An Internet presence can also help businesses get closer to customers and other stakeholders like suppliers, investors, and professional services providers. Certain tasks, like requests for product literature, can easily be automated, and thus contribute to a company's reputation for a fast response capability.

Before you commit to setting up an Internet presence, it is important to put the decision into perspec-

tive. The Internet should be considered as one possible avenue for achieving your company's objectives. It is important to specify those objectives clearly and to think through how your Internet strategy is consistent with and complementary to your overall business strategy. An Internet presence will cost both money and effort. It is a potentially high maintenance activity and not one to be undertaken lightly. But it also has an intangible benefit as well: that of positioning your business as a cutting edge company conversant with the latest technology. When deciding on a Web presence, the following checklist will be helpful:

- What are your company's business objectives, short term and long term?
- What resources are realistically available?
- Can the company make a long-term commitment to this effort?
- What is the likely benefit/cost ratio of the overall effort or of distinct components?
- What results can be reasonably expected at particular cost and effort levels?
- What is the realistic time frame to accomplish the task?

Some of the traditional business tasks that are being supplemented through an Internet presence include:

- Customer service/support.
- Technical support.
- Data retrieval.
- Public and investor relations.
- Selling products or services.
- Obtaining advice/information.

All of the tools we discussed in the previous section are important for deciding on the type and extensiveness of the Web presence that you desire. Having an FTP site can enhance your value to customers. Some companies even start their own newsgroups. Almost all provide for e-mail communication with company stakeholders. As usual, things are changing so quickly on the Net that Internet presence is quickly coming to mean having your own Web site or home page. While maintaining an FTP site is still useful for many companies as a means of distributing data, such capabilities are fast being included as part of the Web site presence. Let's look at some of these activities in more detail.

Customer Service/Support

There are a number of customer support activities that can be accomplished quickly and efficiently us-

---

[1] Jeffry A. Timmons, *New Venture Creation, 4th. ed., rev.,* (Burr Ridge, Ill: Irwin, 1994).

ing a Web site. Current and new product literature, upgrade information, and short descriptions of common problems and solutions can all be handled easily. It is important to remember that one of the great strengths of the Internet is that it is an *interactive* medium. While you are expeditiously addressing customers' needs, you can also gather information about your customers. This can be done by tracking the number of customers who visit particular areas of your Website and by directly surveying visitors. Surveying should be done with caution, however, lest the questions become a nuisance and discourage customers from visiting your site. Survey participation should be optional, and surveys should be short and to the point. One popular feature is a customer feedback capability in which customers can e-mail their comments to the appropriate executive at your company. Not only does this capability empower customers, it also provides a very useful channel for learning more about how your products are being received in the marketplace. Website support will not completely replace human contact, but it can greatly reduce the number of issues that require the intervention of your staff.

As an example, look at Netscape's home page (*Exhibit 5.2*). If you type in Netscape's address on your browser (http://home.netscape.com), you will see product descriptions, new product announcements, statements concerning major sales to large customers, and communications from key executives.

You will also see some value-added features designed to keep you coming back to the site. There is a What's Cool? and What's New? area with hyperlinks to any of those sites that interest you. There is also an area for downloading evaluation copies of product add-ons (called *plug-ins*). The site is visually attractive and attention getting. Netscape also follows the most important rule of Website design: New content is being added at frequent intervals to give users a reason to return to the site often.

Microsoft's home page is equally compelling (*Exhibit 5.3*). There are hyperlinks to a download page for upgrades for its browser, an essay by Microsoft's co-founder on Internet censorship, and a host of hyperlinks to products, support, guides, downloads, the Microsoft Network, and a general statement describing the company. These two home pages illustrate many of the possibilities of communicating with customers on a Web site. The sites are content rich, address competitor's products directly in a content-based advertising context, and provide users with the opportunity to download products free of charge without human intervention and the costs associated with it, thus transferring much of the cost of distribution from the product developers to the users. This look at the "browser wars" is an example of how quickly the competitive landscape can change on the Internet, aided and abetted by the capability for almost instantaneous product distribution.

EXHIBIT 5.2

Netscape Home Page

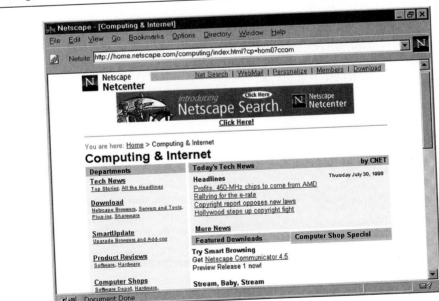

EXHIBIT 5.3

Microsoft Home Page

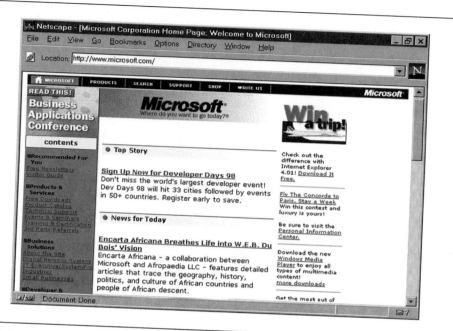

Technical Support

Tech support is another fruitful area to be considered for inclusion on your Web site. If your company sells technology-based products, customers will frequently have questions concerning installation and proper product functioning. Customers downloading a word processor document file describing the problem and solution in detail can handle many such questions. This Web site feature means that your company is open 24 hours a day to solve customer problems. This procedure can also save dollars by reducing the amount of time that tech support reps spend on simple questions and allows your staff to focus their efforts on more complex problems.

Many companies maintain tech support capabilities on forums offered by the online services. These provide for the downloading (and sometimes uploading) of software, e-mail discussions by users, and a facility for asking questions of company tech support reps and receiving answers by e-mail. But companies are moving in greater numbers to developing their own Web presence for these purposes in addition to, or perhaps instead of, use of the online forums.

Data Retrieval

There are many types of information that can be useful in growing your business. These include data on:

- Customers
- Competitors
- Industry trends
- Suppliers
- Economic conditions
- Financial data
- Forecasts

The Internet is a vast repository of such information. The challenge is discovering how to find the data you want.

We have already seen how a Web presence offers opportunities for useful interactions with customers. Feedback from customers about products and observing what product information they are requesting provides data on customer preferences. Data on competitors is readily available by visiting their home pages (if they have them). As illustrated in the comparison of Netscape's and Microsoft's home pages, there is much to be learned about competitors' positioning of products and approach to marketing by frequent observations of their home pages.

There are many sources on the Internet for gathering "traditional" data on industry trends and economic conditions. Among the best places to look are the Websites of academic libraries. For example, the Babson College Library Navigator (http://www.babson.edu/library/index.html) contains lists of sources (both online and otherwise) for industry analyses, overviews, and forecasts, industry statistics, brokerage house reports, trade association data, and market research reports.

The FedWorld Web site (http://www.fedworld.gov) is a central source of U.S. government data maintained by the Commerce Department. The Securities and Exchange Commission's EDGAR database (http://www.sec.gov/edgarhp.htm) is a good source for any filings that public companies are required to make with the S.E.C., including such items as annual and quarterly reports and initial public offerings. Additionally, you can check on the constantly changing environment for IPOs (Initial Public Offerings) by visiting NASDAQ's home page (http://www.nasdaq.com). If you want to check on the progress of legislation, you can find the full text of pending bills at http://thomas.loc.gov (named for Thomas Jefferson, a champion of public education and dissemination of information).

You should also be aware that many business newspapers and periodicals are going online. For example, the *Wall Street Journal* has an online electronic edition, *The Wall Street Journal Interactive Edition* (go to http://www.wsj.com to subscribe), which features in-depth coverage of topics from the regular paper edition. The service requires a paid subscription, with a discount for current subscribers to the paper edition. The use of hyperlinks simplifies the process of locating and retrieving the data from all of these sources.

You can also check on information about companies or individuals through the InterNIC (the Internet Network Information Center), the organization that maintains the set of unique domain names on the Internet. A domain name is part of the URL (Uniform or Universal Resource Locator). For example, if your Internet address is jsmith@yourcompany.com, your domain name is yourcompany.com. It is a good idea to register your preferred domain name with the InterNIC as soon as possible, in order to preserve the simplest way for people to locate you. The current charge is $50 per year for two years paid in advance. Be forewarned that you will not be able to register trademarked names like fedex.com. But if someone gets there first and takes your preferred name, you will be out of luck. You should consider listing your Web site here as well as with the various search engines listed earlier if you decide to have a home page.

You should also be aware of the data available through the online services. Easy access to proprietary databases is one of the strengths of the on-line services. For example, the following are some of the data sources available through Compu Serve:

- The Disclosure II database is a convenient source of data on public companies.

- Iquest offers access to more than 450 databases containing information concerning business, government, and research, as well as sports and entertainment.
- Magazine Database Plus provides for the retrieval of full text articles from more than 150 publications.
- Newspaper Archives is a service that provides access to more than 55 full-text U.S. and U.K. newspapers.

These sources entail usage charges over and above the usual connect-time fees, sometimes charging by the hour and sometimes by the article or report. One trend to watch is the availability of these data sources directly through the Web. As users sign up for direct Web connections in greater numbers, many database providers are presenting their wares on the Web as well as through online services. This trend continues to challenge the online services to develop new value-added services in order to justify their existence.

Public Relations and Investor Relations

It is just a small jump from customer service and tech support activities to the realm of public and investor relations. CEOs of companies with Web sites often use the home page as a vehicle for conveying the company culture and leadership position (or hoped-for leadership position) in an industry. The product literature and the public statements on company vision (for example, Marc Andreessen's statement on Netscape's home page in Exhibit 5.2 and Bill Gates' statement on Microsoft's home page in Exhibit 5.3) can easily be read by securities analysts as well as the company's other constituencies. The Internet provides a very inexpensive way to distribute product announcements and collateral marketing materials, and its instantaneous availability is a plus for analysts and investors seeking the information.

Selling Products and Services

The potential for selling goods and services on the Web is one of its great fascinations for entrepreneurs. It levels the business playing field for many companies. Since the Web is a virtual world, the argument goes, to paraphrase the movie *Field of Dreams,* "if you build it they will come." The potential is certainly great, but as with most things, it's not quite so easy as one might hope. Let's look at some of the issues and choices.

The basic decision involves whether your company wants to open its own Web site storefront (using an Internet Service Provider's server or the company's own server) or open a store in another company's virtual mall. Both strategies involve up-front costs, but being in the cyber-mall usually entails payments of a percentage of sales in addition to monthly rent, similar to a physical mall. Your decision rests partly on whether you think that a stand-alone site will attract sufficient traffic or whether you will benefit from the spillover traffic from other sites in a mall. The decision depends very much on the design of the mall by the developer. Ideally, you would want the demographic profile of mall shoppers to be very similar for as many of the sites as possible, thus encouraging virtual shoppers to follow the hyperlinks among mall Web sites.

Alternatively, you can choose to rent "virtual space" from an Internet Service Provider and go it alone. You don't even have to build the site yourself unless you are adept at programming, and even then you would do well to hire a professional Web site developer to implement the software and concentrate your efforts on refining and attracting the primary target audience. You can also form strategic alliances with other Web sites and pay them a small commission for referring prospective customers to your site via hyperlinks.

An Example: The Internet Fashion Mall

Ben Narasin is the founder and CEO of the Boston Preparatory Company, a manufacturer of high-quality, affordable men's sportswear. From his vantage point in the fashion industry, Narasin saw an opportunity to develop a virtual mall for the fashion industry. Targeting both the mass market and the fashion trade, the Internet Fashion Mall (IFM) affords visitors access to leading fashion houses, magazines, and stores. Within a year of its startup, the Internet Fashion Mall was averaging 5 million hits (page views) a month from customers and potential customers, a figure that has grown to more than 10 million hits a month in 1998. IFM is a classic example of a knowledgeable entrepreneur seizing an opportunity to apply new technology to a field with which he or she is already familiar. As you read this chapter, IFM's story is being written. Why not visit IFM yourself and see what you think? (http://www.fashionmall.com)[2]

Factors to Consider in Designing Your Commercial Web Site

Because Web sites are an electronic and software creation, a potential customer is just a mouse click and a split second away from leaving your site for another.

Consequently, you should follow a few simple principles in implementing your Web site storefront:

- Make sure your Web site is content rich with products geared to pique the interest of your target customer(s).
- Make sure the content changes frequently so that your customers and potential customers will want to return often to your site.
- Design your hyperlinks to keep the customers at your site, particularly at the beginning of their visit. It does not make sense to fill your first Web page with hyperlinks to an area of their interest at some other site. They may never return.
- Be sure to incorporate a means of interaction with your site visitors. Do not be overbearing about it. Initial surveys often turn off visitors, and you should generally allow visitors to bypass surveys if they choose. Alternatively, you can hold a contest, have visitors solve a puzzle or even guess the answers to trivia questions and thus engage their attention and encourage them to return to the site.
- Include an e-mail response mechanism so that you can get feedback from your customers.
- Install some form of tracking software, so that even if visitors decline to participate in surveys and puzzles, you will be able to determine which areas of your site hold the most interest for your customers.
- Make sure to register your Web site on as many search engines and catalogues as possible. If you are offering your site through an Internet Service Provider, make sure that your site is on its "What's Cool?" and/or "What's New?" hyperlink connection.
- Consider redesigning and updating the user interface periodically, in order to add novelty to the experience of the virtual customers.

Security and Payment Issues

Many people have been reluctant to send private payment data over the Internet (for example, credit card and bank account numbers). Part of this apprehension is based on the inherent openness of the Internet, deriving from its origins as a medium for the free exchange of information. Additionally, there have been numerous instances in which computer hackers have broken into systems, many times as a prank but sometimes with the intent to use the information to fraudulently purchase goods and services. Fortu-

---

[2]For further information on IFM, see the case "Internet Fashion Mall, LLC," Babson Park, MA 02457–0310: Center for Entrepreneurial Studies, 1997.

nately, these issues are being dealt with in a number of ways. However, it is important to point out that, despite claims to the contrary, someone skilled and determined enough to do so can defeat most security systems. The real question is what is an acceptable level of security—how much security is enough?

One of the simpler methods of facilitating the ordering of products from Web sites and CyberMalls is to have customers call an 800 number and give their payment information over the telephone. This brings up an interesting question of just how secure traditional telesales transactions are. In fact these transactions are only as secure as the honesty and care with which the payment information is treated. In the early days of mail-order selling, similar security concerns were raised about this process, but over time the public has become comfortable with it despite the occasional problem.

Some innovative technical solutions are emerging. The browser producers are developing and implementing methods to protect the privacy of Web-based communications. Netscape's Navigator, for example, warns the user if information is being transmitted on a nonsecure channel. You can then decide whether to proceed with the transaction. The development of the security technique called the Secure Sockets Layer Protocol offers the promise of a user-friendly solution to the security issue. Additionally, companies such as CyberCash (http://www.cybercash.com) and Digicash (http://www.digicash.com) have developed alternative systems for protecting users while facilitating transactions. These latter systems generally involve your opening an account with the company and establishing a secure, encrypted means of identifying yourself as the person who wants to effect an online transaction. Once this is done, verification of your identity becomes a simple matter. Open Market, Inc. (http://www.open-market.com) is another company working in this area. Hence, the security issue is rapidly being addressed and is much less likely to be a stumbling block to online sales in the future.

Cutting Costs

Revenue-increasing activities are not the only way to use the Internet to enhance your business. Reducing the costs of providing essential support services will also improve the bottom line. As an example, consider FedEx's experience with package tracking.

As part of its operations strategy, FedEx installed a system of bar-coding packages and entering them into portable devices which would convey the information to its data processing system. A customer could then call a support line to check on whether a package had been delivered and if not, what its estimated time of arrival was. In 1996, FedEx instituted a Web-based tracking system. Using a browser, a customer could jump to FedEx's Website (http://www.fedex.com/cgibin/track_it), enter the package number, and observe the progress of the item through the various steps on the way to its ultimate destination. It has been estimated that FedEx will save more than $10 million a year through this system, since each tracking inquiry costs approximately $6.00, and the volume of inquiries exceeds 140,000 per month. The beauty of the system is that FedEx has transferred the cost of the transaction to the customer (who needs to have a computer and the appropriate software), while improving the quality of its customer service at a negligible incremental cost. And the impact on the bottom line is far from trivial.

Another development to watch in the category of cost cutting and improving efficiency is the growth of *intranets*, the use of Internet technology and protocols for *internal* communications within private companies. While this trend is at a relatively early stage in its development, the growth of intranets promises to have a great impact on intracompany operations.

Obtaining Advice/Information

In addition to the data sources that we have explored above, the Internet offers a number of opportunities for entrepreneurs to obtain advice and practical know-how about management and general business issues. Through online forums, newsgroups, mailing lists, and dedicated Web sites, entrepreneurs have many resources to use. The following list represents a sample of these resources:

- Babson's Arthur M. Blank Center for Entrepreneurship Home Page (http://www.babson.edu/entrep/index.html). Babson College has long been a leader in entrepreneurship, and the home page describes the various programs, courses, outreach activities, research, and teaching initiatives being undertaken at Babson. As mentioned previously, the Babson Library Navigator (http://www.babson.edu/library/index.html) is an outstanding source of materials helpful to entrepreneurs in starting and growing their businesses.

- The Ewing Marion Kauffman Foundation Home Page (http://www.emkf.org) is a very useful Web address for entrepreneurs. In addition to the ongoing programs described on its home page, the Kauffman Foundation's EntreWorld Internet site has been designed to provide a wealth of useful information for both practicing and aspiring entrepreneurs (http://www.entreworld.org). Its search engine is an outstanding tool for locating a wealth of practical information for entrepreneurs.

- The NetMarquee Website (http://www.nmq.com) specializes in providing resources for emerging businesses and family businesses. The site includes news articles, guest columnists, hyperlinks to University-based entrepreneurship and family business centers, and a search engine for articles of interest to entrepreneurs and executives of family businesses.

- The Lowe Foundation (http://www.lowe.org) has a Website that provides valuable information for entrepreneurs.

- The U.S. Small Business Administration gopher (gopher://www.sbaonline.sba.gov) contains a great deal of information concerning SBA programs, as well as general resource materials for small businesses.

- The entrepreneurship gopher at St. Louis University (gopher://avb.slu.edu) has several top ten lists for entrepreneurship resources tailored for practicing entrepreneurs, students, and journalists.

- Newsgroups and mailing lists are an additional source of entrepreneurship information. The Liszt Directory of E-Mail Discussion Groups (http://www.liszt.com/) contains a search engine through which you can locate both mailing lists and usenet newsgroups focused on entrepreneurship. Once having subscribed to a few mailing lists or having joined some newsgroups, those discourses will lead to further sources elsewhere on the Net. In addition, when you first set up newsgroups on your browser, you can join a few newsgroups for new users (for example, news.announce.newusers, news.newusers. questions, and news.answers) which can point you in the direction of newsgroups of interest.

- The MIT Enterprise Forum (http://web.mit.edu/entforum/www/) and the MIT Entrepreneurs Club (http://www.mit.edu:8001/activities/e-club-home.html) are sites with a number of hyperlinks to information about starting new businesses, venture capital, and business plans.

- Various forums on the commercial on-line services (for example, Compu Serve and America Online) cater to entrepreneurs' interests. On Compu Serve, use the keyword "go Entrepreneur small business square." On America Online, take a look at the area accessed by the keyword "inc online."

- Additional Web sites of interest to entrepreneurs include:

  Wall Street Journal Interactive Edition (subscription): http://www.wsj.com

  Library of Congress: http://www.loc.gov

  Ziff-Net (computer magazine, news, and software source): http://www.zdnet.com/home/filter/main.html

  On-line bookstore: http://www.amazon.com

  CNN Interactive: http://www.cnn.com/

  AT&T 800 Directory: http://www.tollfree.att.net/dir800

  Telephone directory: http://www.switchboard.com

  Real Audio (source of streaming audio program): http:www.realaudio.com

  White House: http://www.whitehouse.gov

  Postal rates: http://www.usps.gov/consumer/rates.htm

  Land's End (mail order retailer): http://www.landsend.com

  City Net (information on various cities): http://city.net

  Internet Shopping Network: http://internet.net

  Travelocity: http://www.travelocity.com

Internet–related Opportunities for the Creation of New Businesses

The rapid growth of the Internet has resulted in an environment where opportunities abound for entrepreneurs to create software and hardware products and goods and services to meet market needs.

Netscape is one of the most dramatic examples of the achievement of enormous success by Internet software entrepreneurs. The company was created to develop a commercial version of the mosaic browser created at the National Center for Supercomputing Applications. Barely 18 months after its founding, the company launched a successful IPO that put its market value at more than $2 billion. While Netscape's experience is not the norm, there are numerous opportunities for software applications relating to the Internet, including:

- The development of new plug-ins—programs which provide additional features like sound capability to browsers.

- The creation of tools for Internet software developers.

- The development and refinement of increasingly powerful search engines.

- The implementing of enhancements to compression technology.

- The creation of consumer applications (for example, do-it-yourself home pages).

- The development of telephony capabilities for the Net.

- The creation of advanced security and encryption techniques.

Opportunities also exist in creating advances in the hardware necessary to provide Internet capabilities to companies and individuals. Advances in multimedia capabilities demand accompanying hardware improvements in the throughput of data. Areas where creative entrepreneurs can make significant contributions include:

- The development and refinement of high-speed modems.
- Advances in network technology.
- Improved cable technology.

A third area of opportunity lies in providing services to Internet users. Among those services are:

- Creating and maintaining Websites.
- Developing virtual malls.
- Providing technical and design consulting services to Internet users.
- Furnishing of services by Internet Service Providers for direct connections to the Net.

Leadership (entreworld.org), NetMarquee (nmq.com) and teneron.com, the leading document publisher and designer for emerging companies.

7. Information and e-mail overload and anarchy will continue to pose some of the greatest challenges to Internet users.
8. To date, it remains to be seen just how viable various business models will be on the Web.

Study Questions

1. When and how was the Internet developed?
2. Why has its use exploded so rapidly and what does this mean for future opportunities?
3. What existing services and channels of distribution could be far more economic in capital requirements, operating infrastructure and variable costs via the Internet?
4. List the principal tools and applications on the Internet.
5. Can you define the following: e-mail, www.com., Telnet, FTP, gopher, usenet, search engine?
6. How and why can the Internet be beneficial to new and existing businesses?
7. Identify and visit three of the most-used Web sites for entrepreneurs.

Chapter Summary

1. The Internet is changing the way people live, work, learn, and do business at a faster and more pervasive pace than computers, PCs, biotechnology, and wireless communication.
2. For entrepreneurs, the Internet is the great equalizer, creating unlimited opportunities for entrepreneurs with limited resources.
3. Some of the most extraordinary entrepreneurial ventures ever have been during the 1990s and Internet driven: Netscape, YAHOO!, Amazon.com, Infoseek, to name just a few.
4. Existing channels of retail sales and distribution are being transformed radically by the Internet, such as Amazon.com and book selling.
5. Existing businesses can benefit with a variety of applications via the Internet, such as customer service and support, sales and order processing automation, data retrieval, investor relations, purchasing and the like.
6. Leading Web sites for entrepreneurs include: the Babson College home page (babson.edu/entrep/index), the Kauffman Center for Entrepreneurial

MIND STRETCHERS

Have You Considered?

1. Look through the yellow pages for your community. What businesses are least and most likely to exist in 10 years as a result of the Internet?
2. Interview three founders of Internet ventures: What is the underlying economic and business model and how can they become profitable?
3. How do Internet businesses add or create value? Why? For whom?
4. K-Tel's stock price leaped from the teens to the 80s immediately following their announcement that they would begin business on the Internet. It soon retreated to the 20s price range. Why is this so? What does it mean?
5. E-mail and information overload on the Internet poses the following great business opportunities: _____ (Fill in the blank.)

Internet Securities, Inc.

Preparation Questions:

1. Evaluate Internet Securities, Inc., as of 1995.
2. How have the opportunities changed over the past year? Why?
3. What fund raising strategy would you recommend?
4. What should the professor say? What should the Muellers do?

June 1994 graduation was less than two months away as Gary Mueller put the finishing touches on his second-year independent research report at the Harvard Business School. In early February 1994 he and his brother George identified several ideas for entrepreneurial businesses in Eastern Europe, such as food packaging in Russia and acquiring a publishing business in Poland, and were discussing which, if any, might make sense for them. At the time, George was with the Field Robotics Center at Carnegie Mellon University, in Pittsburgh. With his dual engineering degree he had a sharp picture of the technological aspects, while Gary saw emerging opportunities in international information arbitrage. George had been attending Carnegie Mellon business school classes at night in entrepreneurship so he and Gary decided to develop a business plan together as part of their MBA studies.

The conclusions Gary and his brother George were coming to were mind-boggling: There appeared to be so many entrepreneurial opportunities in Eastern Europe and the old Soviet block that it was hard to know where to begin. (See *Appendix A*.) On the surface at least, it also looked like it would be hard to miss. But the lessons he had learned both working in Eastern Europe and in taking the Entrepreneurial Finance course were sobering: slam-dunks are few and far between.

By the spring of 1995, they had made some progress with their business idea and had raised $135,000 of their own capital and from family and friends, as well as a lot of sweat equity, in their attempt to launch the venture. One thing was clear: The business plan that had evolved over the past several months showed promising opportunities in the business publishing and information field (see Appendix A for the Internet Securities Business Plan).

Gary was now contemplating the next phase of the company's financing and development. It appeared that for as little as $300,000–$400,000, Internet Securities could achieve its ambitious growth objectives. He was about to meet with his professor who had supervised the project, and wanted to make sure he had the right questions. Is this a real opportunity? What will it take? How can it be financed? What is the company worth? What should the two founders be prepared to give up to attract outside capital? How might a deal be structured? What if it doesn't work out? These and a myriad of related issues made for a head-spinning morning as the office door opened. "Good morning, Gary!"

Background

Following his graduation from Harvard College, 1988, summa cum laude in biology, Gary went on to a Fulbright Scholarship to travel and work in Germany and the Eastern Block. Subsequently, he turned down admission to the medical schools at Harvard, Yale, Stanford, and others to instead join Graham Allison at the John F. Kennedy School of Government at Harvard to work on privatization projects in Eastern Europe. These were heady days following the fall of the Berlin Wall, and the subsequent liberation from 75 years of centralized, government mandated and (mis)managed economies throughout the Eastern Block. With market-based economies springing up, enabling democracy to bloom, the opportunities for new ventures seemed endless. Not a day went by without hearing of a new company, a new idea, another entrepreneur taking the plunge. Early success stories only fueled the flames of excitement, possibilities, and entrepreneurial dreams. Gary imagined this must have been what it was like one hundred years ago in America as a new nation began to acquire its entrepreneurial and industrial legs. He knew that after obtaining his MBA he wanted to be a part of this renewal in Eastern Europe.

The area of keenest interest to the Muellers was the business data and information vacuum that existed in the just-emerging capital markets and free market economies, particularly in Poland and Russia. Much of this opportunity stemmed from Gary's firsthand experience and knowledge of these two countries. As the Eastern Block embarked upon privatization and market economies, foreign capital, large corporations seeking to establish market access, newcomers, financial institutions, professional services, and consulting organizations all converged on these countries. Whether providing or using capital, or having clients that did so, these players faced serious data and knowledge gaps, adversely affecting the risk–reward ratio in accepting and serving client companies, making investments, and backing entrepreneurs trying to gain market entry.

© Copyright Jeffry A. Timmons, 1996. This case was written by Gary Mueller. For purposes of class discussion, it has been edited by Dan D'Heilly and Andrea Alyse under the direction of Jeffry A. Timmons, Franklin W. Olin Distinguished Professor of Entrepreneurship, Babson. Funding provided by the Ewing Marion Kauffman Foundation. All rights reserved.

The Mueller's field research had explored a wide range of business publishing ideas that might fill the many gaps which existed. Many of these seemed plausible, particularly since little or no competition existed. Yet, he was constantly aware of other would-be entrepreneurs doing market research, exploring alliances, and searching for the concept that could become a major business in Eastern Europe. It seemed that legions of the wannabes of the entrepreneurial world were flocking to the same opportunities the Muellers had set their sights on.

Internet Use Explodes

Since his grade school days, George had been intimately involved in the use of a personal computer, and then the Internet. He continued to focus his interests in this area at Carnegie Mellon. He and Gary were keenly aware that the Internet was beginning to experience explosive growth in the United States and worldwide. The rate of growth only seemed to be exceeded by the optimism and frenzy among corporations and venture capital investors alike to get in on the ground floor. Many sensed that this could be the next big technology breakthrough, similar to the explosion in microcomputers in the early 1980s, and biotechnology in the early 1990s.

These discussions in the spring of 1994 led to a clear sense that there was an opportunity to exploit commercial technology. At this point, hardware prices had been falling 40 percent per year making it possible to launch an information technology firm at extremely low cost. Here was a technology strategy which they concluded could give a significant competitive edge to a new entrant: Rapidly integrate off-the-shelf personal computer technology rather than spend large sums of money and time to research and develop their own proprietary systems and graphical user interface. George explained:

> We are betting on low-cost computers with off-the-shelf products and shareware. Our server technology, Linux, will provide the same functionality and power as very expensive server systems. Jae Chang, our key technical person, has convinced us that this is the technical way to go. It is open to the public, yet there are perhaps 50,000 to 200,000 users or more of this operating system now (spring of 1994). We believe this would allow us to expand in an incredibly cheap manner. It looks like we could open an office for under $10,000 in hardware and software costs.

Most corporate competitors would think they had to spend $150,000–$200,000 for a complete system with hardware, database, distribution and file server, and software.

Jae was key to the success of the new company. George reflected on what he called Jae's "incredible startup mentality:"

> He is one of the most frugal and hard working people I had ever met. He had a monthly living budget of $426 in living expenses, of which $330 went for rent! He did this for 6 months. He is very hard working: 24 hours a day, seven days a week. He would sleep in his office 5 days in a row if he had to.

George noted how important this was since their startup budget did not include salaries for the founders for the first 13 months.

Venture Capital Frenzy

It was well known in the venture capital and entrepreneurial communities that such breakthrough opportunities as envisioned by the Muellers were the fountainhead of early-stage investments that would become industry legends: DEC in the 50s; Apple Computer in the 70s; Lotus Development in the 80s; biotechnology and telecommunications in the 90s. Careers and fortunes were made and lost on such spectacular investment opportunities. Every venture capital investor knew it, and it only made the race between greed and fear even more intriguing and exciting. After all, if you found the equivalent of the next Apple Computer at startup, you would become a venture capital legend at warp speed, not to mention wealthy as well.

Such a climate fueled both ambition and speculation. Valuations for Internet companies were showing a rapid increase in the early 1990s. (see *Exhibit A*). The capital markets were signaling a clear bet: There will be some major companies built, and major fortunes won—and lost—around the emergence of the Internet. What was not so clear was just what those businesses would be, and how entrepreneurs would capture the potential revenue streams and rents. Yet, for those with a recent memory, the frenzy sounded like the familiar ring in the hard-disk drive industry in the early and mid-1980s. While downright scary for private equity investors, this was purely good news for entrepreneurs like Gary and George. This could not be a better time to find capital in search of the next mega home-run investment.

Life is Tradeoffs

With his track record and experience in Eastern Europe, and his excellent performance in the MBA program, Gary was a very attractive candidate for the both the consulting and investment banking industries, and he had been contacted by some of the leaders. Classmates' stories of six-figure starting salaries and substantial starting bonuses made these jobs look virtually risk-free, compared to a startup, not to mention doing so right out of school. Time had run out on the four excellent offers he had secured, and he had to turn them down just at a time when the hope and promise for his new venture far outweighed tangible results.

EXHIBIT A

H&Q Internet Index

Index Components

Ticker	Company
COMS	3Com
ADBE	Adobe Systems
AOL	America Online
ASND	Ascend Communications
BBN	Bolt Beranek & Newman
BBTK	Broadband Technologies
BVSN	BroadVision
CNWK	C:Net, Inc.
CAML	Camelot
CSCC	Cascade Communications
CKFR	Checkfree
CHKPF	Check Point Software Technologies
CSCO	Cisco Systems
CMGI	CMG Information Services
CSRV	CompuServe
CU	CUC International
CYCH	Cybercash
DWTI	Dataware Technologies
DTOP	Desktop Data
EDFY	Edify
EXCA	Excalibur Technologies
XCIT	Excite
FFOX	Firefox Communications
FTPS	FTP Software
FULCF	Fulcrum Technologies
GANDF	Gandalf Technologies
GVIL	Global Village Communication
INDV	Individual
INFO	Infonautics
SEEK	Infoseek
INTU	Intuit
LCOS	Lycos
MAIDY	M.A.I.D. PLC
MACR	Macromedia
MECK	Mecklermedia Corp.
NETC	Netcom On-Line Com. Services
NETM	Netmanage, Inc.
NSCP	Netscape Communications
OMKT	Open Market
OTEXF	Open Text
PRMO	Premenos Technology
PSIX	PSINet
QDEK	Quarterdeck
RAPT	Raptor Systems
SCUR	Secure Computing
SGI	Silicon Graphics
SWEBF	SoftQuad International
SPYG	Spyglass
SSW	Sterling Software
SUNW	Sun Microsystems
SRVC	SunRiver
USRX	U.S. Robotics
USOR	U.S. Order
VRTY	Verity
VOCLF	VocalTec
YHOO	Yahoo

Closing Prices for 10/28/96 — H&Q Internet — Down Jones — Nasdaq Composite

(Chart: y-axis 40–120, x-axis Dec-94, Mar-95, Jun-95, Sep-95)

Source: Hambrecht & Quist, (http://www.hamquist.com/research/stats/indices/compnet.html)

Both George and Jae Chang faced equally difficult choices. George would have to give up his well-paid, prestigious position at one of the world's leading robotics centers. To make matters worse, he was over halfway toward completion of his MBA, but he could not realistically attempt to complete the program and do what was necessary to be a major equity holder and cofounder of the new business. Jae was "the most talented programmer I had encountered at Carnegie Mellon," according to George, "and had other very attractive offers." He too decided to take the plunge with the Muellers.

As the door opened to the office Gary wondered what advice his professor might have. He also pondered whether he could really pull this off:

Do I really want to ask my family and some friends to put their own after-tax, hard-won cash into my startup company nearly halfway around the globe? I feel a tremendous commitment to George and Jae, given what they have had to sacrifice.

Other conflicting demands raced through his mind as he had a flashback to one of the professor's favorite George Bernard Shaw quotes: "Any darned fool can start a love affair; but it takes a real genius to end one successfully!" He reflected that getting started may well be the easiest part of the journey.

Excerpts from the Internet Securities Business Plan

I. Executive Summary

Internet Securities Incorporated ("ISI") offers a truly unique opportunity to invest simultaneously in the tremendous growth of Emerging Markets and the Information Revolution. ISI is an electronic content provider, offering financial and business information on Poland and Russia. The IS service is available both via the Internet and direct dial-up. The content on the service includes news, corporate financials, prospectuses, and analyst reports, as well as industry, money market, fixed income and macroeconomic information. Currently, ISI's database is the most comprehensive source of information covering the Polish markets; a majority of the information is available *only* via ISI online.

ISI intends to expand its business model to additional selected emerging markets and seeks financing for geographic expansion and working capital.

Investment Highlights

- **Prominent, Enthusiastic Customers and Suppliers.** Large multi-national investment banks already use the product regularly. Only two months after the launch of the service in March 1995, major customers include: Citibank, CS First Boston, and the European Bank for Reconstruction and Development. These customers have responded enthusiastically, with comments such as: "This is what we are looking for . . . an outstanding resource,"[3] and "This service is excellent!"[4] Suppliers also include highly-regarded firms, such as *The Financial Times*.

- **Internet Information Revolution.** The Information Revolution is here now on the Internet, which is growing in number of users and overall revenues at well over 100% annually.[5] In this rapidly growing industry, content providers are considered to occupy the highest value-added segment. One expert summed up the general sentiment: "Content is King."[6] As a content provider on the Internet, ISI is well-posed to be at the forefront of this revolution and bring it to emerging markets.

- **Emerging Market Information.** The ISI service covers the fast-growing emerging market segment of the financial services industry—private capital inflows to Emerging Markets have grown annually at 45%, from $40 billion to $175 billion, during the last four years.[7]

- **Leading-edge Service and Technology.** ISI delivers, around the world in seconds, documents in their original format, complete with graphics, charts and corporate logos. The unique ISI service is extremely user-friendly, fully searchable, based on an open architecture and compatible with all the major computer operating systems.

- **First-mover Advantage.** ISI already has the most comprehensive financial and business information service in Poland and it will be the first such service to cover Central and Eastern Europe, and Russia.

- **Low-cost Model.** Internet Securities can produce a superior product while operating on a significantly lower cost structure that competing services (such as Bloomberg, Investext or First-Call) by leveraging the Internet, off-the-shelf software, and recent hardware developments.

The Internet Securities Product

ISI offers a unique online financial and business information service which currently covers Poland and Russia. The information on the service includes news, company financials, prospectuses, industry data, macroeconomic information and analyst reports. In Poland the IS Service is the most comprehensive of its kind.

The IS service is based on advanced technology that enables immediate world-wide retrieval of documents in their original format, including graphics, charts and corporate logos. The service is extremely user-friendly and requires no technical expertise. The entire database of text, spreadsheets, and graphs is searchable in both English and the local languages. ISI employs an open architecture enabling users to download items directly from the service to their personal computer. Access to the service is either via direct dial-up or the Internet.

The Company

ISI was founded in June, 1994, by Gary and George Mueller (brothers) to exploit the opportunities for content providers on the Internet. With the idea of providing an emerging market financial and business information service, the company initially focused on one specific emerging market—Poland. During the course of the following year the company created the service, signed its first customers, became operational in three countries, and grew to a team of 16 full- and part-time employees/consultants in its Warsaw, London and Pittsburgh offices.

---

[3] Dr. Frank Ryan, Head of Research, The European Bank for Reconstruction and Development, 1995.
[4] Douglass Craig, International Finance Corporation, comment sent by e-mail, 1995.
[5] *Business Week*, 1994.
[6] Richard Patterson, *Wired*, May 1995.
[7] Godel Aksa, March 3, 1995.

Mission

ISI's mission is to be the premier provider of online financial and business information on selected emerging markets.

Strategy

ISI's strategy is to:

- Provide in-depth Financial and Business Information
- Focus on Specific Emerging Markets
- Move Early into Selected Emerging Markets
- Exploit the Worldwide Scope of the Internet
- Deliver a More Powerful and User-friendly Service

Management and Advisors

- Gary Mueller. Over four years experience in privatization, transactions and private enterprise in Poland and Russia. Received both a BA and MBA, Harvard University.

- George Mueller. Three years experience in advanced systems integration as a robotics engineer. Received a BS in Electrical and Computer Engineering from Carnegie Mellon University.

- Jeffry Timmons. Currently holds the *MBA Class of 1954 Professor of New Ventures* and the *Frederic C. Hamilton Professor of Free Enterprise Development* chairs at the Harvard Business School. Internationally recognized for his work in entrepreneurship, new ventures, and venture capital.

- Robert Reid. Over 16 years experience in the on-line financial information industry. Senior Vice President, Reuters, head of Instinet; Senior Vice President, NYSE; Vice President, Bridge, Inc.

- Rafal Sokol. Four years experience with the Polish capital markets at the Polish Stock Exchange and a private financial services consultancy. Undergraduate economics, Warsaw School of Economics.

- Jae Chang. Experience in networking software development at Intel and Carnegie Mellon University's Robotics Institute. BS, Computer and Electrical Engineering, Carnegie Mellon.

- Mike Hayward. Experience with Unix, databases, networking, and security at ConnectSoft and Intel. BS, Mathematics and Computer Science from Carnegie Mellon University.

Customers Include:

- Citibank
- CS First Boston
- Kleinwort Bensen
- EBRD
- KPMG
- Goldman Sachs

Financials

ISI revenues are from:

- Selling the service to customers on a subscription or usage basis.
- Selling advertising on its service.

Currently, ISI charges $500 per month for a fixed-rate subscription and has two variable rate options. ISI charges $1000/month for a full advertisement on the service.

ISI has a low break-even of 40 accounts per country. ISI has another very attractive financial feature—low asset intensity. Thus, similar to magazines, increasing the top line substantially impacts the bottom line.

	Actual	Projections			
	Q1 1995	1995	1996	1997	1998
Sales	$3550	$227,000	$1,330,000	$2,853,000	$5,388,000
Net Profit	(48,005)	(406,000)	(121,000)	620,000	1,044,000
# Subscriptions	10	135	375	577	897
Avg Monthly Rev/Subscript.	$255.00	$312.50	$375.00	$437.50	$500.00
# Adverts	1	6	12	18	20
Avg Monthly Rev/Advert	$1000	$750	$1250	$1750	$2250
# Employees	7	18	24	27	30
# Offices	3	6	8	9	10

Statistics

	April 1995
# Data Providers	31
# Documents on Service	16,250
# Files/Week Added (avg)	750
# Server Hits/Month	49,840
# Unique User Visits/Mo	834
# Mirrored Servers	3

Investment Opportunity

ISI is offering equity participation for an investment of $500,000 with an option for an additional $500,000 to be used for geographic expansion and working capital.

ISI intends to sell the business to a strategic investor in three to five years.

II. Mission & Strategy

A. Mission

ISI aims to be the premier provider of on-line financial and business information on selected emerging markets.

B. Strategy

Internet Securities Incorporated's (ISI) strategy is to:

1. Provide in-depth Information

Reliable information is notoriously scarce in emerging markets. ISI fills an unoccupied niche by providing customers with:

1) A unique assortment of difficult-to-find primary and secondary emerging markets data in a centralized, proprietary on-line database service.
2) "Exclusives"—data which are either available in online format *only* from ISI, and/or translations or presentations available only from ISI.

2. Focus on Specific Emerging Markets

ISI will focus on particular emerging markets where data is difficult to obtain and demand for such information is high. ISI will initially focus on Central and Eastern Europe and Russia, and will eventually expand to other selected markets.

3. Move Early into Selected Markets

ISI seeks to move quickly into emerging markets to build up first-mover advantages. Early entrance will make ISI known as the leading (or a leading) provider of online financial and business information in the selected markets. In Poland, ISI now has the most in-depth service, with over three-quarters of its material not available on any other online service.

Relatively few online financial services exist in emerging markets. Reuters, Bloomberg, Telerate and Disclosure all have information on emerging markets, but the amount of in-depth information is limited. ISI will fill the niche of an in-depth source of financial and business information in these markets. In Poland, for example, no other service fills such a niche. In the words of one Polish broker, "you have no competition."[8]

4. Exploit the World-wide Scope of the Internet

ISI is a business conceived to exploit the world-wide scope of the Internet. ISI uses the latest commercially available networking technologies along with the Internet infrastructure to deliver information to customers around the world, to develop and maintain its service, and to run its own internal operations. In this way, ISI does not need expensive proprietary networks relied upon by established information providers.

At the same time, ISI sells its service via direct dial-up, which allows customers to avoid using the Internet to access the service. Thus, while ISI uses the Internet, it does not rely on the Internet.

5. Deliver a More Powerful and User-friendly Service

ISI's unique service makes information retrieval easy by means of its extremely user-friendly interface, easy-to-use tools, comprehensive searching ability and open architecture. The system is capable of delivering information in a format identical to its printed version, including text, charts, graphs, logos, pictures, and even video.

III. The Product

The following section describes the IS product and service in detail. However, words cannot compare to an actual demonstration. Consult Appendix A for instructions on arranging for a demonstration (or, for those already Internet capable, a self-demonstration).

A. Overview

ISI provides a unique, proprietary, online data product for users of Polish and Russian financial and business information. The IS service offers users instant access to corporate financial statements, business and financial news, brokerage reports, money market and fixed-income information, macroeconomic data, prospectuses and a range of other financial and business information on these selected emerging markets. Currently, the ISI service in Poland is the most in-depth of its kind, with over 75 percent of the information available online only via ISI.

[8] Rafal Lys, BGZ, 1995.

The IS service is based on advanced networking technology. ISI delivers, in seconds around the globe, documents in their original format. Brokerage research reports, for example, are available in a format identical to their printed version, including graphics, charts and corporate logos. All of this is within an extremely user-friendly, easy-to-use point-and-click system (see Appendix N for printouts of the service). The database consists of text, spreadsheets, graphs, logos and pictures, all of which is searchable in both English and the local languages. The open architecture of the service enables users to download text and spreadsheet documents directly to their own computer.

Users may access the service via either direct dial-up or the Internet. For direct dial-up, ISI installs software (which is fully Windows, Macintosh or Unix compatible) on the end-user's computer. The user then simply 'points and clicks' to access the service. On the Internet, users go to the IS World Wide Web address (www.securities.com) and then access the service in the same manner.

ISI intends to expand its business model to additional selected emerging markets. The geographic scope of ISI could range from Central and Eastern Europe and the Commonwealth of Independent States or extend to countries in Latin America, Asia and Africa, as well.

B. The Product's Content

Types of Information   ISI's goal is to provide a deeper and broader assortment of up-to-date information from selected emerging markets than is available from any other information service. The broad categories of information include:

- *Company Financial Information.* Basic financial statements (income statement, balance sheet, ratios, etc.) for public companies from both public and private sources. Data for unlisted companies and select private companies will also be provided as available. Much of this information is made available to the user in spreadsheet format.

- *Newspaper and Other Periodical Articles.* ISI has signed agreements with nearly all the leading news periodicals in Poland, including the most highly respected business, financial and economic newspaper (*Nowa Europa*, the Polish equivalent to the *Financial Times*) and the leading investor's newspaper. Stories from these periodicals are gathered and posted to the ISI database on a daily or weekly basis. (In the case of *Nowa Europa*, English articles are now put in the evening before they are published). (See Appendix F for an example of a Data Provider agreement.)

- *Analyst Reports.* Agreements (seven as of 4/10/95) have been made with leading brokerages covering the geographic focus markets. These brokerages include their company, market and other reports on the IS service in exchange for advertisement, commission, or a discount on the service. Users can perform keyword searches on analyst reports just as on any information on the service. The most significant data-provider agreement is with CS First Boston, the leading investment bank in the Eastern and Central Europe and Russian markets. (See page 198 for a discussion of ISI's arrangement with CS First Boston.)

- *Macroeconomic Data.* Spreadsheet or tabular formatted basic economic statistics, cross-sectional and historical, acquired from government and private sources.

- *Prospectuses.* Live and historical prospectuses for offerings within the geographic focus areas are posted for online perusal. The SEC regulations now allow U.S. customers to access live prospectuses online.

- *Fixed-Income.* Daily updates of the Bill and the Bond market, as well as the Commercial Paper market. Sources include the top banks, such as ING and Bank Handlowy.

- *Surveys, General Reports and Other Useful Resources.* General reports on countries and industries from supranational organizations or major financial market press such as the *Financial Times*.

Data Providers   Data providers include the press, government bodies, banks and financial institutions, private companies and research organizations that are capable of supplying the types of data described above.

Data providers are recruited both from the geographic focus areas (in-country) and in the developed financial markets. In-country data providers are particularly important in that they are difficult to access from western financial centers, such as London and New York, and represent opportunities for ISI to gain exclusive agreements. Developed market data providers provide summary analysis and brand name credibility.

A list of data providers (as of 4/10/95) is provided in Appendix M.

C. The Product's Features

Benefits to Data Users   The IS service currently provides unique benefits and features that are not available from other information services. They are as follows:

- *Deep and Broad Assortment of Relevant Data.* As with any distribution channel, one of the primary services rendered by ISI is the assembly of goods and services specific to a set of customer interests. ISI is the first and only online information service that specializes in financial data for the emerging markets of Eastern and Central Europe and Russia. No other information provides such a centralized compilation of relevant data.

- *Exclusive Content.* As of 3/28/95, for three-quarters of its data providers, the IS service is the only online channel. ISI plans to increase both the amount of information available only through ISI and the number of exclusive providers. The CS First Boston arrangement may represent a very significant exclusive arrangement (description follows).

- *Presentation.* The IS service has a leading-edge, easy-to-use, graphical user interface. Windows, Mac, or Unix compatible, the software offers point-and-click navigation, and an intuitive search mechanism for conducting keyword searches of the entire database. Compared to other systems (such as Lexis/Nexis) the ISI system is very easy to learn and use, even for infrequent users.

- *Original Format.* Information on the IS service is available in a format identical to the printed version, including graphics, charts and corporate logos. Thus, research reports, corporate information, and even the *Financial Times* Survey on Poland are presented in a format as they appear in print.

- *Open Architecture.* The service is on an open system platform that features automatic downloading of data into spreadsheets and word processing programs on the user's computer. Many other financial information services either do not permit similar manipulations (e.g. Bloomberg) or do not offer such extensive data downloading.

- *Searchability.* The service enables users to search the entire database of text, spreadsheets, graphs and other files to locate information of interest. The search engine was developed in-house to provide users with an easy to use means of searching, pulling up, printing and saving articles from the service.

- *Native Language Support.* ISI offers data users the ability to find material both in English and in native languages. This enables users to get a variety of information, including information from local sources not available in English.

- *Flexible Access.* Because the IS service does not require dedicated terminals, leased lines or special equipment, the customer can access the service from any computer, modem and telephone line. Clients may even dial in from their portables when traveling. This presents a significant cost and flexibility advantage over fixed-terminal services. This feature also has kept costs low during the growth phase of the company.

- *Relatively Inexpensive.* Relatively means both in comparison to traditional data sources (periodicals, fax services, primary data-gathering) and in comparison to other less-focused information services, where the customer would have to pay for the entire service just to gain access to the small fraction of the data relevant to their interests.

Benefits to Data Providers

- *Wide, inexpensive, fast distribution over a new channel.* Internet distribution reaches customers that data providers would not ordinarily reach. Online format

further amortizes their fixed investment in assembling data without incurring significant variable costs (printing etc.). Distribution via the Internet also enables the information to be disseminated much faster; in the case of some information, such as prospectuses, the information can be available one week before it is available in printed form.

- *Presentation/exact reproduction.* The IS service enables data providers to distribute their information electronically in the same visual format that it would be distributed on paper. This is the primary reason why CS First Boston has decided to include its reports on the service. The quality of the printouts and the presentation of the service is shown in Appendix N.

- *Marketing services.* Data providers can piggyback on ISI's marketing efforts, in that they are listed in the ISI marketing materials and promoted as part of IS service.

- *Subscription/advertising revenues.* Several data providers have cited the possibility of obtaining advertisements and additional subscriptions from ISI's users as one reason to put their information on the service.

- *Databasing and Electronic Archiving.* In many cases, including prominent Western sources such as CS First Boston, the data provider does not have adequate electronic storage of its own information. Even when electronic archives are kept, they are often not searchable or readily accessible. ISI enables data providers to access their archival information readily and easily.

Differentiation   Although ISI will enjoy a first mover advantage in its market niche, ISI anticipates that as these financial markets develop, the challenge to differentiate versus competitors will increase. ISI anticipates that the Assortment advantage will likely diminish, especially if there are any new entrants to the market. Similarly, the Presentation and Data Manipulation advantages are imitable. In order to preserve its first mover advantage, ISI will differentiate itself by: 1) moving faster than competitors into new markets in order to continue being regarded as the leading emerging markets information source, and 2) by adding exclusives, with the following priority:

- New information not available anywhere else, in any media
- Formats or translations not available from sources other than the IS service
- Information not available online except through the IS service

Note that not all the information needs to be exclusive—just a large enough fraction of the total material to create a barrier to switching away from ISI to a competing service.

D. Supply Agreement with CS First Boston (*Pending Legal Approval*)

CS First Boston   CS First Boston is ranked by *Institutional Investor* magazine as the number one broker and provider of research and services in Eastern Europe (here, this includes Russia). They are considered to be the brand leader for advice. For Eastern European activities alone, they market their research and brokerage services to 1,400 companies worldwide.

Proposed Terms   The terms of the arrangement between ISI and CS First Boston currently pending legal approval are as follows:

- CS First Boston will list its Eastern European (Poland, Czech, Hungary and Russia) emerging markets reports on the IS service. There are three types of reports: Industry reports, Company reports and Market Overviews. Reports will be available on-line at the same time as they are published in other formats.
- The relationship is for two years with a 12 month notice for termination.
- ISI is the exclusive World Wide Web (i.e., Internet) source, although not the only online source. CS First Boston also lists its reports on First Call and MAID.
- The reports will only be available to CS First Boston clients. General ISI subscribers will not be able to access the reports until their status as a CS First Boston client has been confirmed.

Implications for Subscription Sales   ISI also stands to benefit from increased subscription sales as CS First Boston intends to market ISI to their customer list. CS First Boston plans to add the current copy to upcoming reports:

> *CS First Boston East European Research Available on the Internet*
>
> From this week, we are making our research available to those of our clients who use "Internet Securities," a new information service specializing in providing information on East European markets, through the Internet. "Internet Securities" can be reached on www.securities.com.
>
> This service will allow clients to download the research at will, in an almost identical form to that in which it is printed, including all graphs and tables. The service will also allow subscribers to send messages to CS First Boston research staff, and to search the reports for key words. We consider that "Internet Securities" is an excellent information service for Eastern Europe, and are pleased to add distribution via this service to our list of client services.

CS First Boston estimates that, of their 1,400 corporate customers who have an active interest in ISI's geographic focus areas, 200 may be interested in subscribing to the IS service. Based on this estimate, the revenue potential for ISI at current subscription rates (excluding set-up fees) is approximately $1.2 million.

Even though the CS First Boston material is only available to CS First Boston clients, the presence of the name on ISI screens and menus will help market the service more generally. Having the imprimatur of a highly respected (market leading) financial institution is likely to have a positive impact on subscription sales.

E. Distribution

Distribution of the ISI information service is primarily online. The IS service is made available to customers through direct dial-up or via the Internet, using standard desktop computing equipment. The Internet currently extends to each of the Eastern European countries. An Internet node will be established in each ISI sales, technical and geographic focus market location to host the service in local areas, maximize network speed and reduce downtime.

The Internet is also instrumental for maintaining ISI's product. ISI collects data from its data providers both over the Internet and through direct dial-up. The data is assembled at ISI's headquarters in Pittsburgh, Pennsylvania and then mirrored back to each location via the Internet. ISI employees, located in various countries, use the Internet (e-mail and Internet chat sessions) as the primary vehicle for intracompany communications and file transfer.

The Internet dramatically decreases the costs of ISI's operations. As an example, ISI has had conference chat sessions on the Internet that have included Poland, the United Kingdom and the United States. An hour-long conference costs ISI a few dollars.

Reliable Internet access is a critical success factor for ISI. In order to function smoothly, ISI must be confident that the local Internet access providers in every relevant market have minimal downtime (i.e., the time which the local service is not accessible).

In Poland, ISI has entered into a joint venture (Internet Technologies, Inc.) to ensure that Internet access will be adequate. In exchange for assistance in setting up the necessary network, ISI has a minority equity stake (35 percent) in Internet Technologies, Inc. Without a capital contribution on the part of ISI, the joint venture enables ISI to control the reliability of access to the Internet and to run its service locally on the Internet Technologies server. This is a very attractive arrangement for ISI, for which reliable Internet access is reason enough to enter into such an arrangement.

Please consult Appendix D: Joint Venture with Internet Technologies, Inc., for further details.

F. The Product's Geographic Focus

Internet Securities currently provides an extensive service covering financial data in one market, Poland. It has begun operations in Russia and currently offers one of the leading providers of Russian financial information. ISI's development will continue in selected geographic focus markets, as follows:

- Phase I: Poland and Russia, with special emphasis on Poland (January 1995–June 1995)
- Phase II: Deeper Russian coverage; inclusion of Czech Republic and Hungary (June 1995–December 1995)
- Phase III: Expansion to other Emerging Markets (January 1996 and onward)

ISI's business model is transferable across many emerging markets. In a conservative scenario, expansion may be limited to Eastern and Central Europe and the Commonwealth of Independent States. Or, ISI's scope could include countries in Latin America, Asia and Africa.

Geographic Focus Market Selection: Phase 1   The focus on Poland in Phase I is for the following reasons: 1) increasing investor interest in the Polish market; 2) growth of the Polish economy and relative stability of the Polish government; 3) familiarity of ISI principals with the Polish privatization and capital markets development process; 4) manageable size of the business model for Poland.

After a period of depressed interest, Poland is gaining favor with investors. A recent United Nations study indicates that Poland attracts 24 percent of initial foreign direct investment (FDI) to Central and Eastern Europe and the Commonwealth of Independent States, accounting for $4.1 billion at the end of 1994. Poland is second only to Hungary (attracting 27 percent) and ahead of Russia (15 percent), Kazakhstan (14 percent) and the Czech Republic (8 percent). Recent leadership changes indicate that privatization activity is likely to accelerate in mid to late 1995,[9] and bullish reports on the Polish economy are appearing more frequently.[10]

ISI's prioritization of Russia over Hungary and the Czech Republic reflects investor interest in potentially large, volatile (and unstable) market, and that information on Russia is extremely difficult to find. The aforementioned U.N. study indicates that Russia draws 31 percent of total foreign investment for long-term projects worth more than $10 million, second only to Kazakhstan (39 percent) and far outstripping Hungary, which draws 8 percent.[11]

Geographic Focus Market Selection, Phase 2 and 3
ISI will balance customer demand with available resources (in particular, useful in-country contacts and staff availability) to determine markets suitable for expansion. After Poland and Russia, ISI plans to expand to the Czech Republic and Hungary.

Long-term non-European targets include India, Turkey, and East Asian countries.

IV. Customers

Overview

ISI's customers consist of sophisticated players in the worldwide capital markets. Information is a key component to the success of investment and business strategy no matter where in the value chain a customer is participating: sales, origination, trading, venture capital, consulting, or fund management. Price is not a primary concern of these customers; pertinent, timely data is.

Capital flows to emerging markets have grown considerably over the past few years. For example, international portfolio investment in emerging markets has grown at 65.3 percent (CAGR) over the last four years.[12] Overall private capital flows to emerging markets have increased 45 percent (CAGR) per year over the last four years.[13] Developing markets often offer higher yield, but they are also riskier as well. In such an environment, timely information is imperative to achieve higher returns. ISI provides information on emerging markets in an easy-to-use format using technologically advanced systems. Target customers are a diverse group of brokers, traders, corporate finance professionals, institutional investors, venture capitalists, management consultants and corporate executives. Ancillary customers include corporate advertisers who may purchase advertising space on the system. Initial customer feedback has been exceedingly positive, and each customer group's diverse characteristics have been addressed by ISI's capabilities.

A. Customers

Since its initial launch in February 1995, ISI has had a very strong response from prominent customers. As of April 20, 1995, major customers include:

- CS First Boston
- Citibank
- Kleinwort Bensen
- KPMG
- European Bank for Reconstruction and Development

Preliminary feedback has been exceedingly positive, and customers generally feel that ISI is providing a valuable service as demonstrated in Box IV. Customer references are available upon request.

9 "Pole Leadership Changes Clear Privatization Path," *The Wall Street Journal* [Europe], 3/27/95.
10 *Financial Times Survey: Poland, Financial Times*, 3/28/95.
11 "Kazakhstan, Russia First for Investment," *Financial Times*, 3/24/95.

12 Austin et al., 1994
13 Godel Aksa, 1995

What ISI's Target Customers are Saying

"This is what we are looking for . . . an outstanding resource."

—Frank Ryan, Head of Research, EBRD

"The economist saw these reports on the service and were simply amazed."

—Peter Johnston, Researcher, CS First Boston

"This service is unique. You have no competition. This service is needed here for investment."

—Rafal Lys, Chief Investment Advisor, BGZ

"This is impressive. I installed the software in no time, used it for half an hour, then had a partner check it out. When he looked at the information on the service, he said, 'This is the most comprehensive information I have encountered since working in the region.' "

—David Saef, Analyst, Schooner Capital

"I log in about twice per day. The service is great. It gives me up-to-date financials and I can do searches on various topics."

—Mariusz Kolecki, Analyst, Kleinwort Bensen

"You will have many users in the Bank."

—Anna Oakeshout, Researcher, EBRD

"This service is excellent! It's precisely the sort of real content service which the Internet needs."

—Douglass Craig, International Finance Corporation, (comment sent by e-mail)

"[A service covering Central and Eastern Europe] would be of great use. Information is scanty."

—Douglas Polunin, Manager, Pictet Emerging Market Fund

"Getting information is a very slow process. I have to go to the exchange in person for information, and even then it is not readily available."

—Mark Seasholes, former Poland Analyst, Baring Securities

"With respect to an on-line information service, because of the need, we may even be prepared to invest money. There is a real need for more information."

—David Mathews, Manager, Fleming Investment

Box IV: ISI's Target Customers

Market Segmentation   The IS service is targeted toward domestic and international brokers, traders, fund managers, other investors, consultants, and businesspersons who use financial, market, and business information in the geographic focus areas.

In Phase I the primary emphasis will be on customers in London and Warsaw.

In the future, ISI will target customers in the other emerging market capitals, as well as in developed market financial centers such as New York, Frankfurt, Zurich, Geneva and Vienna. Those cities are the Western centers for Central/Eastern European and Russian financial activities. Also, ISI will target large companies and other investors in Central/Eastern Europe and Russia.

ISI's primary target markets include:

- Brokers
- Institutional investors/fund managers
- Traders
- Corporate finance professionals
- National investment fund managers in Poland

- Consultants
- Venture capitalists

In addition to targeting groups as users, ISI sells advertising space on its service.

Primary Targets

- **Brokers**

  In Poland, a total of 48 brokerage houses exist, each of which have actively traded an average of about $10–50 MM/month on the exchange over the past year. In addition to the array of Polish brokers, four Western brokerages, Creditanstalt, Citibank, Raiffeisen and CS First Boston are licensed in Poland. Other Western investment houses use Polish or the local Western brokerages.

  Brokers in London also sell Polish securities to London-based and other international investment funds, and to other investors. They, just like Polish brokers, are in need of in-depth information on the Polish market. Because of the distance from the market, it is even more difficult for them to get information.

Brokerage house analysts use information to help clients with investment questions. In most markets, premium information and analysis is a key component to the success of a full-service brokerage house.

One aspect of this segment worth noting is that overall volume of foreign securities is growing rapidly. The total volume of foreign equities was $3.8 trillion in 1993, up from $73 billion in 1979, or cumulative annual growth of 33 percent per year. Of this, fixed income volume was $1.8 trillion in 1993, compared to $36.4 billion in 1974, or annual growth of 23 percent per year.[14]

■ Institutional Investors

Many institutional investors now place a percentage of international or emerging market fund capital in Central/Eastern Europe, especially in Poland, Hungary and the Czech Republic. Furthermore, several institutional investors have set up funds which invest solely in Eastern Europe or are based locally. Pioneer, for example, has a $500 MM equity fund in Poland, and numerous other funds that invest in the region are in the $50+ MM range.

Fund managers and analysts also lack information and analysis in the Polish, Czech, Russian and other Central/Eastern European markets. Fund managers demand information about the markets and the equities they invest in. Some managers actively seek out information themselves, while others tend to rely on brokers for their information. Fund managers that rely mostly on their own information sources are prime candidates for subscribing to the service. Others may be able to get brokers to use soft commissions to pay for the service.

ISI has identified a list of funds which have positions in Central and Eastern Europe and Russia (see *Appendix E* for a list of funds investing in Eastern Europe). These fund managers will be a major target in London and elsewhere.

■ Proprietary Traders

Proprietary traders are individuals who trade on the accounts of large banks and financial institutions. They usually have at their disposal a large amount of cash to invest. Many of these individuals focus on emerging markets and are always looking for new opportunities or interesting vehicles. They scan a wide array of information sources to look for such opportunities.

■ Corporate Finance Professionals

Both Western and local banks are at the heart of transactions in Central and Eastern Europe. Because of the transformations of these economies, there is extensive privatization, merger and acquisition activity. Bankers involved in these transactions require extensive information about the company, the industry and the country for preparing the transaction.

■ New Investment Funds

The Polish government has just recently established 15 mutual funds to manage 444 companies. These funds, managed by teams of western and Polish companies, will control over $200 MM in assets each. As investors and asset managers themselves, they will need company, industry, macroeconomic, market and country information. The teams invariably include western partners who, because they are not as familiar with Poland (but are used to online services), are a prime target for the IS service. The 15 funds chosen by the government were operational by spring/summer 1995.

■ Management Consultants

Many industries and companies in ISI's geographic focus are undergoing major reorganization and restructuring, providing management consultants with demand that is estimated to be growing at over 30 percent per year.

Consultants require company, industry, market and economic information for client analysis. Access to information drives their business. Also, similar to financial service professionals, consultants have high bill rates and are usually under significant time pressure.

Western consultancies are prevalent in ISI's first geographic focus. Each of the Big Six accountancies (KPMG, Price Waterhouse, Coopers & Lybrand, Deloitte & Touche, Ernst & Young, and Arthur Andersen), for example, have on average over 100 professionals in their Warsaw office. The Big Six have large consulting departments, and along with the traditional strategic consultancies are increasing their staffing in Warsaw.

■ Venture Capitalists

In scouting for deals, venture capitalists scan a wide array of information. They read extensively about and do research on various companies and industries. In order to make educated investments decisions, they need access to the right information.

The venture capital industry in Central and Eastern Europe has grown from nonexistence to a considerable size in the last five years. Major venture firms, such as Advent International and Schooner Capital, have set up funds focused solely on the region. Others, backed with funds from the EBRD, are moving in quickly.

Additional Targets

■ Corporate Advertisers

ISI is using a newsletter or magazine model to approach banks and companies to include information about their companies in a service section of the database. Just as many industry newsletters and trade magazines have advertisements in addition to in-depth information, ISI is making it possible for companies to advertise on the service.

---

[14] *The Economist*, December 17, 1994.

- **Hotel Business Centers**

  Hotels play a central role in business activity in Poland. Most top hotels offer clients a business center which provides a range of business services. As a means of reaching hotel guests, ISI is offering business centers the opportunity to put the IS service in the center and to advertise the service to clients by placing a brochure in each hotel room.

B. Characteristics of Target Market

Online financial and business information service customers are characteristically:

- Information dependent
- Time-sensitive
- Multiple source users
- Frustrated with existing sources (for Eastern and Central Europe and Russia)

Information Dependence   Information and analysis drives the business of ISI's target customers. It is critical to the $10–50 MM per month in turnover for each licensed Polish brokerage. It is behind each investment decision of the regular million-dollar investments that fund managers make. It forms the basis of consulting studies for companies investing in the region. Pertinent information is of high value to these customers; it is the life-blood of their business.

Time-sensitivity   In addition to the importance of the information, ISI's target customers are extremely time sensitive. Usually they need the information immediately (or sometimes, yesterday). Mailing, or even express courier service, does not suffice. They also are often under significant time pressure to gather information. They will pay a premium to have the information at their fingertips.

Multiple Information Source Usage   ISI's target market do not limit themselves to one information source. They typically use information from a wide range of sources to drive their analysis and provide depth to their accumulation of information. Multiple subscriptions to online services or databases mirrors subscription to a variety of newspapers and newsletters.

Frustration with Current Sources   In developed countries, financial service professionals and consultants usually have access to several online information providers and databases. With emerging markets, use of online services is less ubiquitous. But if these countries follow the development path of more advanced countries, use should parallel the dramatic increase in such services.

The combination of the growth in stock market volume and total capitalization, the development of the bond market, the increasing amount of foreign direct investment, and a dramatic rise in funds poised for investment in these markets, has pushed demand for financial information.

At the same time, inefficient and insufficient information flows impedes investment. Investors report that lack of quality information on which to base decisions is the single greatest factor holding back investment in Eastern and Central European economies. Customer interviews reveal a great deal of frustration regarding data availability, and enthusiasm for the type of service ISI supplies.

C. Sales & Marketing Agreements

Direct Sales   ISI's sales approach is currently largely via direct sales (accounts). ISI's financial model calls for an average of only 7.5 accounts per month for the first year. In both London and in Poland, ISI is located very close to most of its target market (ISI is in the Marriott/LIM center which is the heart of business activity in Warsaw, and is in the middle of the City of London where most of the banks are situated), thereby enabling sales staff to readily and quickly reach the target customers.

Targeted Advertising Offered by Partners   ISI has approached a number of companies to discuss arrangements which will help to promote the ISI service and link ISI with recognized industry leaders. In doing such, ISI looks for free advertising space or promotion of the ISI service by well-known, well respected firms.

- **Financial Times**

  ISI has an arrangement with the Financial Times to promote its service. The agreement is as follows:

  - IS received a 12 column inch advert in the Poland Country Survey published on March 28, 1995 (see Appendix O).
  - IS included the survey (with graphs and photographs) in its service. The survey was available for no charge on the Internet Securities Internet Server for one week. After the first week, it was available to subscribers at the usual ISI billing rates.
  - ISI and the Financial Times are currently working to include future Surveys and other publications on the service.

- The benefits for ISI include:

  - Credibility. Association with one of the leading worldwide financial newspapers and a recognized name.

- **Promotion.** An advert to a readership directly in line with ISI's target customers.
- **Sales material.** Promotional material to include in future sales and marketing material.

- **CS First Boston**
  See above for a description of the agreement terms with CS First Boston to promote the service.

Local Advertising   ISI also has agreements with other data providers to obtain free advertising space in their publications. For example, in Poland ISI currently has an agreement with the Central European Business Weekly, Capital, Gazeta Bankowa and others for free advertising.

D. Pricing Schedule

ISI has three different pricing options for the service:

- **Fixed-Price Introductory Offer.**
  - $500 per month per country
  - Initial three-month period
  - Unlimited usage

- **Option 1: Fixed + Variable Pricing**
  - $200 per month per country
  - Usage costs approximately $0.10 per line ($2–4 per page)
  - Direct dial-up costs of about $20 per hour

- **Option 2: Variable Pricing**
  - No monthly charge
  - Usage costs approximately $0.20 per line ($4–8 per page)
  - Direct dial-up costs of about $20 per hour

Advertising Pricing   Pricing for advertisements starts with a basic listing of the company for $200 per month. A multiple page listing for $1000 per month.

Payment Terms   For both pricing methods, ISI offers discounts for longer payment periods and usage prepayments. This also benefits ISI's short-term cash position.

V. Industry Overview

A. Business Information Services Market Segmentation

The Business Information Services market ($27 billion in sales in the United States in 1993) can be segmented in two ways: 1) by type of data provided and 2) by the industry which uses the data. By combining these two segmentation schemes, the size of ISI's target market may be estimated. ISI participates in this market using advanced technology to provide economic and financial data to clients in the professional services industry (particularly the Wall Street customer segment, including investment bankers, fund managers and brokers). The following analysis characterizes the global opportunity since information technology adoption globally follows directions set in the United States. Because ISI focuses on geographic markets where the digital transformation is by no means mature, ISI can realistically expect to grow considerably faster than the market in developed countries.

Industry Segmentation   There are five major industry segments, which are further subdivided. ISI provides data to the second largest industry segment, the Professional and Intermediate Services Market. This was the fastest growing segment over the five-year historical period, and growth in this segment has also been accelerating whereas growth in all other segments is slowing down. *Exhibit V.1* summarizes the size and growth of the major industry segments in the United States alone.

The Professional and Intermediate Services Industry segment is subdivided into five major customer submarkets. *Exhibit V.2* shows the size and growth of each of these submarkets in the United States. The three financial submarkets (Wall Street, Banks, and Insurance) represent nearly 80 percent of the Intermediate and Professional services market.

Within this segment, the largest submarket (Wall Street) was primarily responsible for the strong segment growth, accelerating its spending 12.4 percent over 1992. Spending was largely a consequence of the increase in transaction activity and underlying growth in the securities markets.

Data Segmentation   The Business Information Services Market can also be segmented by the type of data provided. *Exhibit V.3* shows how the entire $27 billion U.S. market is broken down:

Economic and Financial Data was the second-fastest growing segment in the five-year historical period. It is projected to be the fastest growing segment in the entire business information market through 1998, at 10 percent per year on average.

Cross-Segmentation   Combining these two types of segmentation (industry and type of data) allows us to size the market in which ISI participates.

Exhibit V.4 shows spending in 1993 in the Intermediate and Professional Market by type of data. Within the Wall Street customer submarket, Economic and Financial Data alone represent over $2.2 billion in spending in the United States.

EXHIBIT V.1

1993 Business Information Services Market by Industry in the United States[15]

Industry	$ Millions 1993	% of Market	% CAGR 1988–93	% Change 1992–3
Consumer Goods and Services	$ 8,995	33.2%	6.1%	5.4%
Professional and Intermediate Services	7,911	29.2	7.7	8.0
Financial				
Legal				
Business Data Services				
Basic Industry:	4,631	17.1	6.1	5.5
Construction				
Agriculture				
Industrial				
Distribution	4,441	16.4	6.1	3.9
Wholesale				
Retail				
Related Services				
Government and Nonprofit	1,089	4.0	6.2	4.0
TOTAL	$27,067	100.0%	6.5%	5.9%

[15] Source for this Section: *Business Information Services,* in the Veronis, Suhler & Associates *Communications Industry Report,* 11/94.

EXHIBIT V.2

Intermediate & Professional Industry Submarkets in the US

Sub Markets	$ Millions 1993	% of Market	% CAGR 1988–93	% Change 1992–3
Wall Street	$2,667	33.7%	9.8%	12.4%
Banks	1,792	22.7	6.7	8.1
Insurance	1,509	19.1	5.9	5.9
Business Data Services	858	10.8	6.7	4.6
Legal	1,085	13.8	7.8	3.3
TOTAL	$7,911	100.0%	7.7%	8.0%

EXHIBIT V.3

1993 Business Information Services Market by Type of Data in the US

Data-Type Segment	$ Millions 1993	% of Market	% CAGR 1988–93	% CAGR 1993–98
Marketing	$8,998	33.2%	5.5%	7.0%
Economic & Financial	5,301	19.6	8.5	10.0
Credit Data	3,122	11.5	5.3	6.3
Payroll & Human Resources	3,246	12.0	6.6	7.0
Product & Price Data	1,756	6.5	5.4	5.4
Legal & Regulatory	2,113	7.8	8.7	6.9
Scientific & Technical	1,117	4.1	9.6	7.0
General Business	1,414	5.2	5.2	5.8
TOTAL	$27,067	100.0%	6.5%	7.4%

EXHIBIT V.4

Business Information Services Market in the US
Intermediate & Professional Industry Segmented by Type of Data ($ Millions, 1993)

Sub-Market	Marketing Info. Services	Economic & Financial Data	Credit Data	Payroll & Human Resource	Product & Pricing Data	Legal & Regulatory	General Business	Total
Wall Street	$194	$2,213	$58	$50	$39	$47	$66	$2,667
Banks	594	363	584	97	26	58	70	1,792
Insurance	599	215	420	97	47	63	68	1,509
Business Data Services	185	168	100	163	37	168	37	858
Legal	10	10	30	100	5	915	15	1,085
TOTAL	$1,582	$2,969	$1,192	$507	$154	$1,251	$256	$7,911

Online Information Services in ISI's Geographic Scope

ISI participates in a geographic segment of the industry which is considerably underdeveloped compared to the United States. Central & Eastern European and Russian databases accounted for only 12 of 660, or less than 2 percent of databases in one comprehensive list. In its first target market, Poland, ISI is the only service of its kind. In Russia, one service exists, which is considerably inferior to the IS service.

VI. Competitive Advantages and Risks

A. Sources of Competitive Advantage

ISI has several sustainable competitive advantages:

- *First mover advantage.* IS is the first such service to cover Poland and it will be the first such service to cover Central and Eastern Europe. The IS service is based on proprietary code which took nine months to develop and is continually improving. Relationships with data providers were developed concurrently and ISI currently has contracts ranging from three months to ten years in duration. To create a salable product required the input of five years of full-time equivalents.

- *Unique Team.* The ISI management and employee team has significant accumulated experience in financial information services, computer programing, and knowledge of and contacts in Poland. This combination of business understanding, Harvard Business School network, and Carnegie Mellon technical expertise gives ISI the ability to understand both the target financial industry and the technology to provide a leading-edge service.

- *Strong understanding of the geographic focus markets.* ISI has considerable experience in Poland and Russia and the target customers of emerging market financial and business information.

- *Technological Basis.* ISI draws on top talent from one of the leading technology Universities in the world, and already has in place sophisticated software and systems which enable it to deliver its service at a low cost. ISI is also extremely quick to respond to the explosive growth and development of the Internet.

- *Low-cost operating model.* ISI uses the Internet for many aspects of its business to keep costs very low. ISI currently has "expensive" human capital working for equity; total current salary expenditures amount to $1,600 per month. ISI is extremely judicious about keeping costs to a minimum. For example, two partners in Poland currently share a small one-room apartment which costs the company $200 per month. This is similar to the cost of a hotel room in Warsaw for one night.

- *Highly-trained Talent Pool.* ISI draws on talent from Carnegie Mellon University and Harvard Business School. ISI maintains relationships and contacts at both of these institutions, and will use these contacts to further extend its staff in the future.

B. Risks

There are risks associated with the ISI business model. Many of the business characteristics are "double-edged swords" in that the benefits they provide to ISI are potentially appropriated by competitors and thus not sustainable advantages. However, being aware of these risks is the first step toward managing them and reducing the threat they pose. Following are the risks, in relative order of their "manageability:"

- *Strategic Risk: Low Barriers to Entry.* This is an example of a competitive advantage that "cuts both ways." If this niche turns out to be highly profitable, ISI could attract competitors.

  ISI can create barriers to entry by:

  1) using its position as first-mover to erect "intangible" barriers such as strong reputation with customers and data providers,

  2) continually improving the service in ways that increase the amount of time required to replicate it or create a competing service, or

  3) entering into exclusive or semi-exclusive (i.e., ISI as the only on-line channel) relationships with data providers

- *Strategic Risk: Low Barriers to Switching:* Again, the low cost of the service to customers is a competitive advantage that cuts both ways. By not requiring customers to invest in fixed hardware, ISI does not create a barrier to switching in the same way some other on-line services do.

  ISI will have to erect other barriers to switching, using means such as:

  1) signing long-term contracts with customers (and data providers)

  2) maximizing users' dependency on, familiarity with and loyalty to ISI data, formats, or tools

- *Business Risk: Existence of Large Established Players with Infrastructure in Place.* Information services have been largely fixed cost businesses. The risk is that although large players such as Bloomberg are currently not prioritizing ISI's geographic focus markets, they may do so in the future. This affects ISI's exit strategy: the risk is that the large financial online services will attempt to provide similar data without purchasing ISI.

  ISI's best defense is to:

  1) build and maintain loyal and dependent customers,

  2) closely watch the moves of other online services,

  3) maintain good working relationships with data providers, and

  4) rapidly expand the depth and breadth of the service.

- *Technology Risk:* Security and integrity of data are the primary concerns of an information service company. While diligent hackers are nearly impossible to avoid, the concern is less that someone will steal data and use it, but rather a simple fear of vandalism.

  ISI's best defense is:

  1) good data hygiene and meticulous adherence to security procedures, and

  2) constant monitoring of activity and password protection.

- *Market/Economic Risk: Upheaval in the Investment Community.* 1994 and early 1995 have witnessed instability in the investment services market as have never been seen before. Layoffs at Goldman Sachs, JP Morgan's loss of the AAA debt rating and speculation-driven financial crises at Baring Securities would have been unthinkable two years ago. These developments may lead to cost control measures or increased risk aversion in these markets that may affect price sensitivity and basic demand for ISI's service.

  While these risks are difficult to manage, ISI can address them by:

  1) marketing its service from a cost–benefit perspective

  2) emphasizing efficiency in data gathering and productivity as major benefits that accrue to ISI customers.

- *Political Risk:* Upheaval in the geographic focus markets could shift investment patterns away from ISI's focus market. (Frankly, it is exactly this risk and its associated returns which attracts investors to these markets, creating the niche opportunity for ISI.) The best defense for ISI is diversification across geographic focus markets, certainly within Eastern/Central Europe and Russia and eventually across other emerging markets.

  ISI's major concern here is operational: To ensure the safety of key personnel and to plan for the expatriation of equipment and documents if necessary.

VII. Management

A. Governance

The Board of Directors is currently composed of ISI's two largest shareholders, Mr. Gary Mueller and Mr. George Mueller. The Board meets formally at least once a month, either in person or via conference call. Each Board member has an equal vote, but in cases of ties, Mr. Gary Mueller has the deciding vote. These members are permanent members of the Board. In addition to the Board, the key management team (which includes Mr. Jae Chang, Mr. Mike Hayward, and Mr. Rafal Sokol) meet regularly to discuss the major management issues.

Upon receipt of external financing, ISI plans to expand Board membership to include a representative from each major source of capital. At that time, ISI may also bring in additional member(s) with no capital stake but with substantial expertise in the online business information industry.

The target for Board composition is Management (2 with 4 votes): External Directors (3). After Board expansion, full Board meetings will occur quarterly, with monthly meetings or conference calls as needed.

B. Management Team

Gary Mueller (Management). Mr. Mueller spent over two years working on privatization and fund formation in Poland and Russia. He also spent two years in Germany, actively studying the transformation of the former East Bloc. He is a graduate of Harvard Business School (1994) and Harvard College (1988), and an alumnus of four family-owned businesses.

George Mueller (Management/Development). As an Electrical and Computer Engineer at Carnegie Mellon University (1992), Mr. Mueller has extensive experience in advanced systems integration. In his most recent position he oversaw a multimillion dollar hardware and software project, involving 12 software programmers and hardware designers.

Dr. Jeffry Timmons (Business Advisor). Dr. Timmons currently holds the *MBA Class of 1954 Professor of New Ventures* and the *Frederic C. Hamilton Professor of Free Enterprise Development* chairs at the Harvard Business School. He is internationally recognized for his work in entrepreneurship, new ventures, and venture capital.

Robert Reid, Sr. (Business Advisor). Mr. Reid was a senior vice president at Reuters, in charge of Instinet, an on-line, NYSE equities trading system. During his eight years at Reuters he helped grow Instinet to its present size of 1,100 large institution investor clients. Before Reuters, Reid served as a senior vice president at the NYSE. He also spent five years as a vice president at Bridge Information Systems, where he helped to expand Bridge's online service.

Jae Chang (Management/Development). Mr. Chang, a BS Computer and Electrical Engineering graduate of Carnegie Mellon University (1994), has experience in developing user interfaces and computer networking. He previously worked as a developer at Intel Corporation and at Carnegie's Robotics Institute.

Mike Hayward (Management/Development). Mr. Hayward is a former Software Engineer at ConnectSoft and Intel. Extensive experience with Unix, databases, networking, and security. He received his BS in Mathematics and Computer Science from Carnegie Mellon University (1994).

Rafal Sokol (Management). Mr. Sokol, a former Partner of Conmar Investors, has spent the last four years working in the financial markets in Poland. He was one of three partners at an investment advisory firm that among other things publishes a daily column in the leading financial newspaper in Poland. Prior to setting up his own company, Sokol worked on the Polish Stock Exchange and as an analyst of Polish equities.

Craig Lane (Management). Mr. Lane worked as an International Consultant in Washington, DC, and as an Investment Banker in Warsaw. He received his MBA from Duke University.

Melissa Burch (Operations/Logistics). Ms. Burch, formerly of Apple Computer, Inc. has extensive knowledge of on-line service marketing and data translation. She was the database administrator for both eWorld and AppleLink and worked with over 50 data providers.

Partnership agreements are currently in place for all stakeholder employees (Gary Mueller, George Mueller, Robert Reid, Sr., Jae Chang, Mike Hayward and Rafal Sokol). Employee work and confidentiality agreements are in place for all other employees.

C. Organizational Structure

Geography   ISI is a decentralized organization with global operations. The corporate headquarters and technical center is in Pittsburgh, Pennsylvania, where most of the technical staff responsible for the design and smooth functioning of the IS service are located.

ISI maintains satellite offices overseas in selected Eastern European capital cities (currently Warsaw) and major financial centers (currently London) where its customers and data providers are located. In the satellite offices activities are divided between managing relationships with data providers and sales. In the major financial centers the focus is on sales and marketing. Where necessary, ISI establishes subsidiaries or enters into joint venture arrangements to ensure compliance with local laws and to access local knowledge, language skills and connections.

Reporting Relationships   The following diagram illustrates current reporting relationships at ISI:

The hierarchical nature of organization charts is not very descriptive for ISI. ISI is a very flat, fluid organization which has tremendous flexibility to quickly deploy technical, sales and managerial resources to the places where they are most needed.

Compensation and equity participation. In-country staff are compensated at market rates which, when translated into dollars, are low compared to the cost of similar labor talent in developed markets. As ISI continues to operate, salaries will be kept low, but will rise somewhat from their current levels which average less than $1,000 per month.

D. Revenue and Income Scenarios

2 primary scenarios:

- *Eastern Europe and Russia only.* Conservative.
- *Wider Emerging Markets.* Aggressive.

	EE & RU	Emerging Mkt.
Sales Year 3	$2.9 m	$5.0 m
Net Income Year 3	$0.7 m	$1.3 m

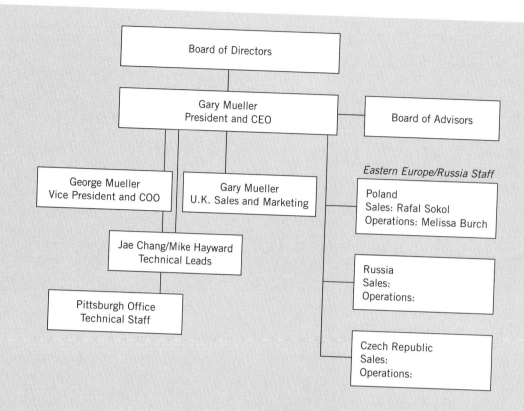

See Appendix J for Pro Formas.

E. Cash Requirements

	EE & RU	Emerging Mkt
Capital Requirement	$514 K	$508 K
Average Burn Rate (year 1)	$34K/Mo	$34K/Mo
Month Cash Flow Pos.	Month 14	Month 13

For more detail, consult Appendix J ("Pro Forma Financial Statements")

F. Valuation

	EE & RU	Emerging Mkt
DCF Valuation	2.5 m	5.5 m
Sales Multiple (of 3x on year 3)	8.7 m	15.0 m
EBIT Multiple (of 8x on year 3)	5.4 m	16.8 m

For more detail, consult Appendix J ("Pro Forma Financial Statements")

IX. Exit Strategy

ISI's target is to exit the business in three to five years via sale to either one of the larger on-line providers or a strategic partner.

Acquisitions are commonplace in the online industry. Companies such as ISI bring larger players in the market new niches and customers, expanded content and product, and enhanced technical skills. For example, Reuters has a business development department that currently has $350 million for acquisitions. Acquisitions of $15 million to $20 million are not uncommon for companies with similar characteristics to ISI. In addition to Reuters, several other online financial information services, such as Telerate, Bloomberg, International Thomson, Maid, Newscorp, are all potential buyers. This market suggests a liquid and attractive acquisition market.

In addition to the online service providers, ISI could also sell to a strategic investor. Recent purchases of "content providers" by communications companies, such as MCI agreeing to buy 13.5 percent of News Corp for $2 billion[16], gives ISI another large pool of potential investors. Acquisition activity in this area, like in the on-

[16] "MCI Agrees To Inject As Much As $2 Billion In News Corp. In Data Highway Venture," Wall Street Journal, 5/11/95.

line industry, has been heavy in the past few years. Also, other companies seeking to understand online information services or electronic publishing are prime potential purchasers.

ISI may be a candidate for acquisition by one of its customers or suppliers as well. A supplier such as *The Financial Times*, may acquire ISI for its technological abilities and understanding of the electronic publishing industry and the Internet. CS First Boston or ING could acquire ISI as a means of strengthening its position in emerging market financial services.

Such a wide array of potential buyers should enable investors to obtain liquidity within three to five years.

A. ISI Demonstration

There are two basic ways for a demo user to access the service: either by directly dialing one of our Points of Presence (POP) or via the Internet. Both methods require the appropriate software and hardware (computer, modem, and phone line), however, the difference is that direct dialing implies that the software is provided by Internet Securities (we assume the user already has the hardware) while access via the Internet typically implies that the user already has the means of accessing the Internet and thus our service without our software.

Thus, for obvious reasons, the easiest and quickest way is via the Internet since the user already has access to our service. All one needs to do is open the Uniform Resource Locator (URL) to "http://www.securities.com/". Access to the publicly viewable side of our service is open to everyone while access to the privileged side of the service is restricted until the user provides a valid username and password which we can provide with a simple phone call.

The other means—the most common—is by having us provide the user with the appropriate software and direct dialing capabilities for use with a modem to connect to our POP. The installation software is mailed out on a couple diskettes. The user simply runs a program which performs the entire installation. Ensuring that the hardware is correctly configured, a click of an icon will start the software and dial the modem to one of our POPs where they can finally access the service directly. For security, the direct dial user must still provide a username and password to access the service. We have mailed out dozens of installation disks in this way, and usually with a bit of extra help on the phone, our demo users have been able to access the service and also quickly and easily navigate through the service. Mastering the interface is as simple as a point and a click.

If you already have the installation software in front of you, then refer to the documentation that came with the software for more detailed instructions. If you would like access to the service, please call us.

B. Economic Opportunities in Eastern Europe and Russia

Various developments in the emerging markets of Eastern Europe and Russia provide opportunities for business in general, and specifically for firms catering to the emerging business-to-business sector in these markets. This includes firms offering administrative services and equipment, communications services, transactions support and information services. Following are a few of the most important relevant trends:

- *GDP Growth*. Poland, the entrance market for ISI, experienced the highest growth in Europe in 1993. GDP rose 3.8 percent in real terms in 1993 and preliminary results for 1994 are even higher at 4.5 percent.[17] Private sector growth is estimated to be 10 percent annually.

- *Stable Macroeconomic and Business Conditions*. Macroeconomic conditions in the three largest economies in eastern Europe—Poland, the Czech Republic and Hungary—now approach their western neighbors. Inflation is under control and decreasing, budget deficits are small, trade policy has been liberated, 60 percent of GNP is in private hands, and a solid legal framework is in place.

- *Foreign Capital Influx*. Foreign direct investment in short and long term projects in Eastern European and former Soviet economies totaled $118 billion at the end of 1994,[18] of which 70 percent was for oil and gas exploration in Russia and Kazakhstan. As the consumer markets develop, the proportion represented by petroleum will decrease.

- *Development and Growth of Capital Markets*. The capital markets are developing quickly. Polish daily volume now $200 million; total market capitalization in Poland is $6 BB; in the Czech Republic it's $14 BB. The daily volume of the Polish stock exchange rivals many western European exchanges, such as Vienna and Helsinki, and is almost as large as the Toronto exchange. The total capitalization in both Poland and the Czech Republic is larger than China and approaching that of smaller, more developed markets. The following provides an overview of the two main markets:

---

[17] *Financial Times Survey: Poland*, page VII.
[18] "Kazakhstan, Russia First for Investment," *Financial Times*, 3/24/95.

	Market Cap.	Daily Vol.	# Cos.	GNP: '93	'94	'95E
Poland	$4 BB	$10 MM	27	4%	5.5%	4.8%
Russia	$15 BB	$7 MM	80	−12%	−15%	−4.0%
Czech	$15 BB	$15 MM	1330	−1.0%	2.6%	4.3%
Hungary	$1.4 BB	$40 MM	40	−2.0%	2.7%	0.5%

Investment Flows to Emerging Markets   This leap in the size of the eastern European markets mirrors the growth in the capital flows to emerging market stock markets in general:

- International portfolio investment in emerging markets now $56 BB, up 56 percent from the year before, and up from $7.5 BB in 1989.[19]
- 9.5 percent of international equity assets are allocated to emerging markets in 1993, up from 2.5 percent in 1989.[20]
- Total market capitalization of $740 BB in 1992 for group of 25 emerging markets.[21]
- Number of companies listed on emerging stock markets now represents roughly 40 percent of the world total.[22]
- Pension funds, endowments and foundations now own global equities worth $170 BB, and plan to raise this to $300 BB in the next three years.[23]
- All 24 emerging stock markets tracked by the World Bank's International Finance Corp. showed greater returns in 1993 than the Standard & Poor's 500 index.[24]
- Continued privatization of economy.
- Over the course of the next two to three years, up to 400 Polish companies will be privatized and listed on the Polish stock exchange. Also, the 15 newly chosen mass privatization mutual funds will be listed on the stock exchange within the next six months. These new listings will tremendously increase the total capitalization of and capital inflow to the market.

C. About the Internet

What is the Internet?   The Internet is essentially thousands (upon thousands) of computers connected together via phone line, cable, or satellite. What began as a means of linking university researchers together, has become the information superhighway connecting not only educational facilities but service organizations, individuals, and businesses worldwide. Internet tools enable rapid transmission and retrieval of data at a very low cost. For example, a stock broker in Australia may order a magazine subscription from a company in the United States, send an electronic mail message to a friend in Germany, gather statistics on a textile business in Malaysia, and at night browse a virtual art gallery in Prague all for the cost of a local phone call.

Growth on the Internet both in terms of connected users and networked computers is growing exponentially. Although there is no precise way to measure growth, some statistics indicate that Internet sites are added at the rate of 40,000 per month while the number of users doubles every five months. By 1997, there will be approximately 175 million users on the Internet. In this climate of rapid expansion, the commercial segment has surpassed all other segments of the Internet market. Companies as diverse as JP Morgan, IBM, MCI, Federal Express, MTV, and LL Bean are now "online".

Currently, 90 percent of all computers on the Internet are in the United States. Lower hardware costs and more fully developed Internet access technology can account for much of this activity. Within the diverse Internet corporate market, the U.S. companies predominate. But the market in Europe is on the verge of tremendous growth. Already in the United Kingdom, Internet growth statistics are following those in the United States, with users growing at over 10 percent to 20 percent per month.

Growth of the Internet Access Industry   A simple hardware setup of a computer and modem is all that is necessary to dial up Internet, but an Internet access provider is also required to connect to the online environment. These companies range from large long distance carriers such as MCI and Sprint, to small, local access providers. Some access companies only provide e-mail; others, such as startups America Online and Compu Serve, offer complete commercial online services, while still others sell full service Internet sites.

It is interesting to note that the new ventures, such as America On-line and Compu Serve, are growing faster than the larger conglomerates. Furthermore, despite the emergence of large providers, small companies continue to proliferate and prosper. In New York City, for example, six local providers exist with between 700 and 3,000 subscribers each. The total revenues for the six online access providers was $10 million in 1993. While revenues of consumer online services (such as e-mail) are

[19] Austin et al., 1994.
[20] IFC, "Survey of 30 international institutional investors", 1993.
[21] ibid.
[22] ibid.
[23] *Financial Times*, 1993.
[24] Bailey, 1994.

growing at 35 percent a month, the average age of the companies is less than three years. Considering growth rates of over 150 percent annually for the industry, valuations of over $10 million seem reasonable.

Growth of the Internet in Europe

These statistics reflect Internet access providers growth in the United States; Europe, east and west, is expected to demonstrate similar patterns. Already in the United Kingdom, Internet growth statistics are following those in the United States, with users growing at over 10 percent to 20 percent per month. Internet access providers in the United Kingdom are showing even greater growth than in the United States: The growth for three of the largest providers combined has been over 400 percent over the last year.

In western Europe, Internet access providers charge up to five times more than in the United States. In Germany, for example, a survey of Internet access providers put the cost per month of basic e-mail services at about $60 and the cost of full Internet access at over $250 per month. The U.K. Internet price schedule is similar to that of Germany.

In Poland, the Czech Republic and Hungary, no western service providers are available locally and only a few domestic Internet access providers exist. In Poland, only one provider actively targets commercial users and its service is primarily in Polish. Without competition the costs for such services are high; with basic e-mail service running about $100 per month and full Internet access at about $400 per month.

Even with the higher Internet service costs and an overall lag in technological sophistication in Eastern Europe, international businesses with Eastern European offices are spurring the demand for e-mail and Internet access. With the influx of western goods, the cost of hardware is beginning to drop to reasonable levels, any company can now have e-mail and Internet access for less than $1000. International businesses are increasingly relying on Internet services as an inexpensive and efficient means of information transfer, and are able to provide the resources to establish the necessary Internet sites in Eastern Europe. Eastern Europe is expected to demonstrate a tremendous growth.

D. Joint Venture with Internet Technologies, Inc.

ISI has entered into a Joint Venture with former banker Rafal Plutecki, to form Internet Technologies (IT). This arrangement represents an ideal partnership for ISI.

The following are the relevant details:

- Plutecki puts up a total of $100K, $30K up front and $7K per month for ten months. The $30K is for equity, the $70K is in the form of a loan to be paid back only when Internet Technologies (IT) is cash flow positive. ISI receives 35 percent of the company.

- Plutecki manages, runs and takes care of IT except for setting it up and training a systems operations person (to be done by Mike Hayward). ISI sets up the server and software, and this is limited to what ISI chooses to do.

- Plutecki buys a Cisco router and Sun Microsystems server in Poland, and obtains the necessary 64KB connection to Eunet (European Internet backbone.)

- Plutecki obtains office space in the Warsaw Marriott. ISI sublets a portion of the space and pays for its phone lines.

- ISI puts the IS service on the IT server so that clients in Poland can dial up a local number and get the service directly. (This also allows ISI to do much of its internal operations activities in Warsaw instead of Pittsburgh if it so chooses).

- ISI brings over (but Plutecki pays for) an undergraduate intern or two to come for the summer.

- If a major problem with the server comes up, ISI provides assistance, which can be in the form of e-mails to IT's systems operations or other people. (This is in ISI's interest anyway, because if the service is "down," both ISI customers and ISI's data providers will be inconvenienced).

- Exit is a buy–sell after three years. (If ISI wants to, after year three, ISI can say it wants to sell its shares to Plutecki. Plutecki names a price, and ISI can either sell all its shares, or buy all of Plutecki's shares at that price; this ensures fair valuation of shares).

## PART TWO

The Founders

Survival odds for a venture go up once sales of at least $1 million are reached and number of employees exceeds approximately 20. Launching or acquiring and then building a business that will exceed 20 employees is more fun and more challenging than being involved in the vast majority of small one- or two-person operations. But perhaps most important, a business of this magnitude achieves the critical mass necessary to attract good people, and as a result, the prospects of realizing a harvest are significantly enhanced.

A leader who thinks and acts with an "entrepreneurial mind" can make a critical difference as to whether a business is destined to be a traditional very small lifestyle firm, a stagnant or declining large one, or a higher potential venture. Practicing certain mental attitudes and actions in a certain way can stimulate, motivate, and reinforce the kind of zest and entrepreneurial culture whose self-fulfilling prophecy is success.

It is almost impossible to take a number of people, give them a single test, and determine those who possess entrepreneurial minds and those who do not. Rather, it is useful for would-be entrepreneurs and others involved in entrepreneurship to study how successful entrepreneurs think, feel, and respond and how those factors that are significant can be developed and strengthened—as a decathlete develops and strengthens certain muscles to compete at a certain level.

Entrepreneurs who create or recognize opportunities and then seize and shape them into higher potential ventures *think and do things differently*. They operate in an entrepreneurial domain, a place governed by certain modes of action and dominated by certain principal driving forces.

External and internal pressures mandate that the entrepreneur be a manager as the venture grows beyond being founder-driven and dominated by the need to survive. The development of competencies as an entrepreneurial manager is critical. Thus, not only do acquired skills and relevant experience position entrepreneurs to see opportunities that others do not see or cannot grasp, these acquired skills and experience are key to achieving longer-term sustained growth and an eventual harvest.

It makes a lot of sense for entrepreneurs to pay particular attention to picking partners, key business associates, and managers with an eye for complementing their own weaknesses and strengths and the needs of the venture. As will be seen, they seek people who *fit*. The reason for this is that not only can a weakness be an Achilles heel for new ventures, but also the whole is almost always greater than the sum of its parts.

For example, Ken Fisher joined Prime Computer in 1975 as president when the company had sales of just $7 million and employed 150 people. In six years the company grew to $365 million in sales and 4,500 employees. Sales grew at a compounded annual rate of 88 percent and net income by 108 percent, while return on shareholder's equity reached a high of 48.8 percent and topped 35 percent for four consecutive years. During his stay, Prime's share price increased 126 times to its 1981 high, just prior to his resignation. He subsequently formed Encore Computer Corporation with two industry leaders. In talking about his experiences, Fisher said a lead entrepreneur needs "an ego that sustains and drives a person to achieve, stress tolerance, controlled empathy, ability to resolve conflicts, keeping everything in perspective between the business and personal life, and least important of all these, intelligence."

Finally, ethics are terribly important in entrepreneurship. In highly unpredictable and fragile situations, ethical issues cannot be handled according to such simplistic notions as "always tell the truth."

Chapter Six

The Entrepreneurial Mind in Thought and Action

Nothing that sends you to the grave with a smile on your face comes easy. Work hard doing what you love. Find out what gives you energy and improve on it.

Betty Coster, Entrepreneur

Results Expected

Upon completion of this chapter, you will have:

1. Examined ways to help you discover whether being an entrepreneur gives you sustaining energy, rather than takes it away.
2. Explored the entrepreneurial mind—the strategies, approaches, attitudes, and behaviors that work for entrepreneurs who build higher potential ventures.[1]
3. Developed concepts for evaluating a personal entrepreneurial strategy and an apprenticeship.
4. Developed an entrepreneur's "creed."
5. Analyzed the "Michael Healey (A)" case.
6. Crafted a personal entrepreneurial strategy.

The Search for Understanding

As was noted in Chapter 2, there is much more behind "walking the breathtaking highlands of success." The lead entrepreneurs who find and seize opportunities and grow higher potential ventures *do* things differently. Recall from *Exhibit 2.14* and the discussion in Chapter 2 that entrepreneurs—in thought and action—are anchored by certain attitudes and behaviors and by the "chunks" of experience, skills, know-how, and contacts they possess. They are thus positioned to see what others do not and seize opportunities and grow higher potential ventures.

Two Principles for Achieving Entrepreneurial Greatness

One of the most extraordinary entrepreneurial success stories of our time is that of the late Ewing Marion Kauffman, who founded and built Marion Labs, a company with $3.06 billion in sales. Kauffman started his pharmaceutical company, now one of the leading companies in the world, in 1950 with $5,000—in the basement of his Kansas City home. Previously, he had been very successful at another company. Kauffman (or "Mr. K." as he preferred) recalled that "the president first cut back my sales commission, then he cut back my territory. So, I quit and created Marion Labs."

---

[1] Jeffry A. Timmons, *The Entrepreneurial Mind* (Acton, MA: Brick House Publishing, 1989).

By 1989, after acquiring Merrell-Dow in 1989 (now Marion, Merrell Dow, Inc.), over 300 people had become millionaires. Thirteen foundations have been created by former Marion associates, and the Ewing Marion Kauffman Foundation is one of only a dozen or so foundations in America with assets of over $1 billion. The two-pronged mission of the foundation is to make a lasting difference in helping youths at risk and encouraging leadership in all areas of American life.

Having had the great privilege and honor of knowing and working with Mr. K., from 1991 until his death in 1993, and continuing the relationship with the Marion Labs management team and now Ewing Marion Kauffman Foundation team, I have come to know and appreciate more each passing year the two core principles that are the cornerstone of the values, philosophy, and culture of Marion Labs and now of the Kauffman Foundation.

- Treat others as you would want to be treated.
- Share the wealth that is created with all those who have contributed to it at all levels.

As simple as these may be, ask yourself the number of organizations you have visited and been a part of that truly, sincerely, and consistently practice these principles. It takes a lot more than lip service or a stand-alone profit-sharing plan to create this entrepreneurial culture. Consider the following unique characteristics at Marion Labs and the Ewing Marion Kauffman Foundation:

- No one is an employee; they are all associates.
- Even at $3.06 billion in sales, there are no formal organizational charts.
- Everyone who meets or exceeds high performance goals participates in a companywide bonus, profit-sharing, and stock option plan.
- Benefit programs treat all associates the same, even top management.
- Managers who attempt to develop a new product and fail are not punished with lateral promotions or geographic relocation to Timbuktu, nor were they ostracized. Failures were gateways to learning and continual improvement.
- Those who will not or cannot practice these two core principles are not tolerated.

The ultimate message is clear: Great companies can be built upon simple but elegant principles, and all

the capital, technology, service management, and latest information technology available cannot substitute for these principles, nor will they cause such a culture to happen. These ideals are at the very heart of the difference between good and great companies.

Leadership and Human Behavior

A single psychological model of entrepreneurship has not been supported by research. However, behavioral scientists, venture capitalists, investors, and entrepreneurs share the opinion that the eventual success of a new venture will depend a great deal upon the talent and behavior of the lead entrepreneur and of his or her team.

The first chapter mentioned that a number of myths persist about entrepreneurs. Foremost among these myths is the belief that leaders are born, not made. The roots of much of this thinking reflect the assumptions and biases of an earlier era, when rulers were royal and leadership was the prerogative of the aristocracy. Fortunately, such notions have not withstood the tests of time or the inquisitiveness of researchers of leadership and management. Consider recent research, which distinguishes managers from leaders, as summarized in *Exhibit 6.1*. It is widely accepted today that leadership is an extraordinarily complex subject, depending more on the interconnections among the leader, the task, the situation, and those being led than on inborn or inherited characteristics alone.

There are numerous ways of analyzing human behavior and so, too, of trying to understand the entrepreneurial mind. The many theories of human behavior have implications in the study of entrepreneurship. For example, for over 35 years Dr. David C. McClelland of Harvard University and Dr. John W. Atkinson of the University of Michigan and their colleagues have sought to understand individual motivation.[2] Their theory of psychological motivation is a generally accepted part of the literature on entrepreneurial behavior and has been used to a considerable extent in actual research, evaluation, and training efforts.

The theory states that people are motivated by three principal needs: (1) the need for achievement, (2) the need for power, and (3) the need for affiliation. The *need for achievement* is the need to excel and for measurable personal accomplishment. A person competes against a self-imposed standard that does not involve competition with others. The individual sets realistic and challenging goals and likes to get feed-

[2] See John W. Atkinson, *An Introduction to Motivation* (Princeton, NJ: van Nostrand, 1964); J. W. Atkinson, *Motives in Fantasy, Action and Society* (Princeton, NJ: van Nostrand, 1958); D.C. McClelland, *The Achieving Society* (Princeton, NJ: van Nostrand, 1961); J. W. Atkinson and N. T. Feather, eds., *A Theory of Achievement Motivation* (New York: John Wiley & Sons, 1966); and D. C. McClelland and D. G. Winter, *Motivating Economic Achievement* (New York: Free Press, 1969).

EXHIBIT 6.1

Comparing Management and Leadership

	Management	Leadership
Creating an agenda	Planning and budgeting—establishing detailed steps and timetables for achieving needed results, and then allocating the resources necessary to achieve these results	Establishing direction—developing a vision of the future, often the distant future, and strategies for producing the changes needed to achieve that vision
Developing a human network for achieving the agenda	Organizing and staffing—establishing some structure for accomplishing plan requirements, staffing that structure with individuals, delegating responsibility and authority for carrying out the plan, providing policies and procedures to help guide people, and creating methods or systems to monitor implementation	Aligning people—communicating the direction by words and deeds to all those whose cooperation may be needed to influence the creation of teams and coalitions that understand the vision and strategies, and accept their validity
Execution	Controlling and problem solving—monitoring results versus plan in some detail, identifying deviations, and then planning and organizing to solve these problems	Motivating and inspiring—energizing people to overcome major political, bureaucratic, and resource barriers to change by satisfying very basic, often unfulfilled human needs
Outcomes	Produces a degree of predictability and order, and has the potential of consistently producing key results expected by various stakeholders	Produces change, often to a dramatic degree, and has the potential of producing extremely useful change

Source: Reprinted with the permission of The Free Press, a Division of Macmillan, Inc. from *A Force for Change: How Leadership Differs from Management* by John P. Kotter. Copyright © 1990 by John P. Kotter, Inc.

back on how well he or she is doing in order to improve performance. The *need for power* is the need to influence others and to achieve an "influence goal" (i.e., the goal of outperforming someone else or establishing a reputation or position according to an externally derived and oriented standard). While it is sometimes easier to see the negative aspects of power motivation, bear in mind that socialized and civilized power needs have played an important role in influencing people and institutions. The *need for affiliation* is the need to attain an "affiliation goal" (i.e., the goal to build a warm relationship with someone else and/or to enjoy mutual friendship).

Research

Other research focused on the common attitudes and behaviors of entrepreneurs. A 1983 study found a relationship between attitudes and behaviors of successful entrepreneurs and various stages of company development.[3] A year later, another study found that entrepreneurs were unique individuals; for instance, this study found that "what is character-

istic is not so much an overall type as a successful, growth-oriented entrepreneurial type. . . . It is the company builders who are distinctive."[4] More recently, a study of 118 entrepreneurs revealed that "those who like to plan are much more likely to be in the survival group than those who do not."[5] Clearly, the get-rich-quick entrepreneurs are not the company builders, nor are they the planners of successful ventures. Rather it is the visionary who participates in the day-to-day routine to achieve a long-term objective and who is generally passionate and not exclusively profit-oriented.

Academics have continued to characterize the special qualities of entrepreneurs. (See *Exhibit 6.2* for a summary of the research.) As a participant in this quest to understand the entrepreneurial mind, in January 1983, Howard H. Stevenson and I spoke with 60 practicing entrepreneurs.[6] One finding was that entrepreneurs felt they had to concentrate on certain fundamentals: responsiveness, resiliency, and adaptiveness in seizing new opportunities.

These entrepreneurs spoke of other attitudes, including an ability "to activate vision" and a willingness

[3] Neil Churchill, "Entrepreneurs and Their Enterprises: A Stage Model," *Frontiers of Entrepreneurship Research: 1983*, ed. J. A. Hornaday et al. (Babson Park, MA: Babson College, 1983), pp. 1–22.
[4] N. R. Smith and John B. Miner, "Motivational Considerations in the Success of Technologically Innovative Entrepreneurs," in *Frontiers of Entrepreneurship Research: 1984*, ed. J. Hornaday et al. (Babson Park, MA: Babson College, 1984), pp. 448–95.
[5] John B. Miller, Norman R. Smith, and Jeffrey S. Bracker, "Entrepreneur Motivation and Firm Survival among Technologically Innovative Companies," ed. Neil C. Churchill et al., *Frontiers of Entrepreneurship Research: 1991* (Babson Park, MA: Babson College, 1992), p. 31.
[6] J. A. Timmons and H. H. Stevenson, "Entrepreneurship Education in the 80s: What Entrepreneurs Say," in *Entrepreneurship: What It Is and How to Teach It*, ed. J. Kao and H. H. Stevenson (Boston: Harvard Business School, 1985), pp. 115–34.

EXHIBIT 6.2

Characteristics of Entrepreneurs

Date	Author(s)	Characteristics	Normative	Empirical
1848	Mill	Risk bearing		
1917	Weber	Source of formal authority	X	
1934	Schumpeter	Innovation; initiative	X	
1954	Sutton	Desire for responsibility	X	
1959	Hartman	Source of formal authority	X	
1961	McClelland	Risk taking; need for achievement		X
1963	Davids	Ambition; desire for independence, responsibility; self-confidence		X
1964	Pickle	Drive/mental; human relations; communication ability; technical knowledge		X
1971	Palmer	Risk measurement		X
1971	Hornaday and Aboud	Need for achievement; autonomy; aggression; power; recognition; innovative/independent		X
1973	Winter	Need for power	X	
1974	Borland	Internal locus of control		X
1974	Liles	Need for achievement		X
1977	Gasse	Personal value orientation		X
1978	Timmons	Drive/self-confidence; goal oriented; moderate risk taker; locus of control; creativity/innovation	X	X
1980	Sexton	Energetic/ambitious; positive setbacks		X
1981	Welsh and White	Need to control; responsibility seeker; self-confidence/drive; challenge taker; moderate risk taker		X
1982	Dunkelberg and Cooper	Growth oriented; independence oriented; craftsman oriented		X
1982	Holy and Hellriegel	Preference for technical versus managerial tasks		X
1983	Pavett and Lau	Conceptual, human, and political competence; technical familiarity in specialized field	X	
1985	MacMillan, Siegel, and SubbaNarisimha	Familiarity with the market; a capacity for intense effort, leadership ability	X	
1986	Ibrahim and Goodwin	Ability to delegate, manage customer and employee relations; interpersonal skills	X	
1987	Aldrich and Zimmer	Networking with people who control important resources and who have relevant skills and abilities	X	
1987	Hofer and Sandberg	Drive to see firm creation through to fruition; ability to clearly communicate goals; ability to motivate others to behave in synergistic manner		X
1987	Schein	Strong management skills with high levels of responsibility and authority; specialist versus general manager		X
1987	Timmons, Muzyka, Stevenson, and Bygrave	Ability to recognize and envision taking advantage of opportunity		X
1989	Wheelen and Hunger	Ability to implement strategy with programs, procedures, budgets, evaluations, etc.		X
1992	Chandler and Jansen	Self-assessed ability to recognize opportunity	X	
1992	McGrath, MacMillan, and Scheinberg*	High individualism; poor distance; uncertainty avoidance; and masculinity		X

Source: James W. Carland, Frank Hoy, William R. Boulton, and Jo Ann C. Carland, "Differentiating Entrepreneurs from Small Business Owners: A Conceputalization," *Academy of Management Review* 9, no. 2 (1984) p. 356; Gaylen N. Chandler and Erik Jansen, "The Founder's Self-Assessed Competence and Venture Performance," *Journal of Business Venturing* 7, pp. 233–36.
*V. McGrath et al., "Elitists, Risktakers, and Rugged Individualists? An Exploratory Analysis of Cultural Differences between Entrepreneurs and Non-Entrepreneurs," *Journal of Business Venturing* 7, pp. 115–35.

to learn about and invest in new techniques, to be adaptable, to have a professional attitude, and to have patience. They talked about the importance of "enjoying and being interested in business," as well as the business as "a way of life."

Many respondents recognized and endorsed the importance of human resource management; one entrepreneur said that one of the most challenging tasks was playing "a leadership role in attracting high-quality people, imparting your vision to them, and holding and motivating them."

Many focused on the importance of building an organization and teamwork. For example, the head of a manufacturing firm with $10 million in sales said, "Understanding people and how to pull them together toward a basic goal will be my main challenge in five years." The head of a clothing manufacturing business with 225 employees and $6 million in sales shared a view of many that one of the most critical areas where an entrepreneur has leverage and long-term impact is in managing employees. He said, "Treating people honestly and letting them know when they do well goes a long way."

A number of respondents felt that the ability to conceptualize their business and do strategic planning would be of growing importance, particularly when thinking five years ahead. Other attitudes they spoke of included a willingness to learn about and invest in new techniques, to be adaptable, to have a professional attitude, and to have patience. They talked about the importance of "enjoying and being interested in business" and also of the business "as a way of life." They mentioned an ability to "activate vision."

Similarly, the ageless importance of sensitivity to and respect for employees was stressed by a chief executive officer of a firm with $40 million in sales and 400 employees: "It is essential that the separation between management and the average employee should be eliminated. Students should be taught to respect employees all the way down to the janitor and accept them as knowledgeable and able persons." At least one company has taken this concept to heart; Ben & Jerry's Homemade Ice Cream Inc. began operations with a covenant that "no boss got more than five times the compensation, including both pay and benefits, of the lowest-paid worker with at least one year at the company."[7] Since its inception, the covenant has been modified to seven to one,

while the company reported $63.2 million in revenue in the first half of 1992.[8]

A consulting study by McKinsey of medium-size growth companies (i.e., companies with sales between $25 million and $1 billion and with sales or profit growth of more than 15 percent annually over five years) confirms that the chief executive officers of winning companies were notable for three common traits: perseverance, a builder's mentality, and a strong propensity for taking calculated risks.[9]

Converging on the Entrepreneurial Mind

Desirable and Acquirable Attitudes and Behaviors

Many successful entrepreneurs have emphasized that while successful entrepreneurs have initiative and take charge, are determined and persevere, and are resilient and able to adapt, it is not just a matter of their personalities, *it is what they do.*[10]

While there is an undeniable core of such inborn characteristics as energy and raw intelligence, which an entrepreneur either has or does not, it is becoming apparent that possession of these characteristics does not necessarily an entrepreneur make. There is also a good deal of evidence that entrepreneurs are born and made better and that certain attitudes and behaviors can be acquired, developed, practiced, and refined—through a combination of experience and study.[11]

While not all attitudes and behaviors can be acquired by everyone at the same pace and with the same proficiency, entrepreneurs are able to significantly improve their odds of success by concentrating on those that work, by nurturing and practicing them, and by eliminating, or at least mitigating, the rest. Painstaking effort may be required, and much will depend upon the motivation of an individual to grow, but it seems people have an astounding capacity to change and learn if they are motivated and committed to do so.

Testimony given by successful entrepreneurs also confirms there are attitudes and behaviors that successful entrepreneurs have in common. Take, for instance, the first 21 inductees into Babson College's Academy of Distinguished Entrepreneurs, including such well-known entrepreneurs as Ken Olsen of DEC,

7 Floyd Norris, "Low-Fat Problem At Ben & Jerry's," *The New York Times*, September 9, 1992, p. D6.
8 Ibid.
9 Donald K. Clifford, Jr., and Richard E. Cavanagh, *The Winning Performance* (New York: Bantam Books, 1985), p. 3.
10 Determining the attitudes and behaviors in entrepreneurs that are "acquirable and desirable" represents the synthesis of over 50 research studies compiled for the first and second editions of this book. See extensive references in J. A. Timmons, L. E. Smollen, and A. L. M. Dingee, Jr., *New Venture Creation*, 2nd ed. (Homewood, Ill.: Richard D. Irwin, 1985), pp. 139–69).
11 David C. McClelland, "Achievement Motivation Can Be Developed," *Harvard Business Review*, November–December 1965; David C. McClelland and David G. Winter, *Motivating Economic Achievement* (New York: Free Press, 1969); and Jeffry A. Timmons, "Black Is Beautiful—Is It Bountiful?" *Harvard Business Review*, November–December 1971, p. 81.

An Wang of Wang Computers, Wally Amos of Famous Amos' Chocolate Chip Cookies, Bill Norris of Control Data, Sochiro Honda of Honda Motors, and the late Ray Kroc of McDonald's. All 21 of the inductees mentioned the possession of three attributes as the principal reasons for their successes: (1) the ability to respond positively to challenges and learn from mistakes, (2) taking personal initiative, and (3) great perseverance and determination.[12] In the 1990s, the following entrepreneurs were inducted into the Academy of Distinguished Entrepreneurs because of their success and by making a world of difference through their work for social change and human development: Paul Fireman of Reebok International Ltd.; Sandra L. Kurtzig of ASK Computer Systems, Inc.; Amar G. Bose of Bose Corporation; John R. Furman of Furman Lumber, Inc.; William G. McGowan of MCI Communications Corporation; Ewing Marion Kauffman of Marion Merrell Dow, Inc.; John C. Merritt of Van Kampen Merritt Holding Corp., Inc.; Anita Roddick of the Body Shop; Leslie H. Wexner of the Limited, Inc.; S. Robert Levine and Craig Benson of Cabletron Systems, Inc.; Arthur M. Blank of The Home Depot; Richard Branson of Virgin Group; Ely R. Callaway of Callaway Golf; Willie D. Davis of All-Pro Broadcasting Company; Leon Gorman of L.L. Bean, Inc.; Leo Kahn of Nature's Heartland; and Robert A. Swanson of Genentech, Inc.

There are "themes" that have emerged from what successful entrepreneurs do and how they perform. In discussing these themes, it is important to emphasize there are undoubtedly many attitudes and behaviors characterizing the entrepreneurial mind and there is no single set of attitudes and behaviors that every entrepreneur must have for every venture opportunity. Further, the *fit* concept argues that what is required in each situation depends on the mix and match of the key players and how promising and forgiving the opportunity is, given the founders' strengths and shortcomings. And, a team might collectively show many of the desired strengths. Even then, there is no such thing as a perfect entrepreneur—as yet.

Six Dominant Themes

A consensus has emerged around six dominant themes, shown in *Exhibit 6.3*:

- *Commitment and determination.* Commitment and determination are seen as more important than any other factor. With commitment and de-

termination, an entrepreneur can overcome incredible obstacles and also compensate enormously for other weaknesses.

- As President Calvin Coolidge stated:

Nothing in the world can take the place of persistence. Talent will not; nothing is more common than unsuccessful men with talent. Genius will not; unrewarded genius is almost a proverb. Education will not; the world is full of educated derelicts. Persistence and determination alone are omnipotent. The slogan "Press on" has solved and solved and always will solve the problems of the human race.

All of the distinguished entrepreneurs referred to earlier said these attitudes were critical. Carl Sontheimer, president and founder of Cuisinarts, Inc., said: "Entrepreneurs come in all flavors, personalities, degrees of ethics, but one thing they have in common is they never give up." Franklin P. Purdue, president of Purdue Farms, Inc., said: "Nothing, absolutely nothing, replaces the willingness to work. You have to be willing to pay the price."

Total commitment is required by almost all entrepreneurial ventures. Almost without exception, entrepreneurs live under huge, constant pressures—first for their firms to survive startup, then for them to stay alive, and finally for them to grow. A new venture demands top priority for the entrepreneur's time, emotions, and loyalty. Thus, being involved in commitment and determination is usually personal sacrifice. An entrepreneur's commitment can be measured in several ways—through willingness to invest a substantial portion of his or her net worth in the venture, through willingness to take a cut in pay since he or she will own a major piece of the venture, and through other major sacrifices in lifestyle and family circumstances.

Entrepreneurs who successfully build new enterprises desire to overcome hurdles, solve problems, and complete the job; they are disciplined, tenacious, and persistent in solving problems and in performing other tasks. They are able to commit and decommit quickly. They are not intimidated by difficult situations; in fact, they seem to think that the impossible just takes a little longer. However, they are neither aimless nor foolhardy in their relentless attack on a problem or obstacle that can impede their business. If a task is unsolvable, an entrepreneur actually will give up sooner than others. Most researchers share the opinion that while entrepreneurs are extremely persistent, they are also realistic in recognizing what they can and cannot do, and where they can get help to solve a very difficult but necessary task.

[12] John A. Hornaday and Nancy B. Tieken, "Capturing Twenty-One Heffalumps," in *Frontiers of Entrepreneurship Research: 1983,* ed. J. A. Hornaday et al. (Babson Park, MA: Babson College, 1983), pp. 23–50.

EXHIBIT 6.3

Six Themes—Desirable and Acquirable Attitudes and Behaviors

Theme	Attitude or Behavior
Commitment and Determination	Tenacity and decisiveness, able to decommit/commit quickly Discipline Persistence in solving problems Willingness to undertake personal sacrifice Total immersion
Leadership	Self-starter; high standards but not perfectionist Team builder and hero maker; inspires others Treat others as you want to be treated Share the wealth with all the people who helped to create it Integrity and reliability; builder of trust; practices fairness Not a lone wolf Superior learner and teacher Patience and urgency
Opportunity Obsession	Having intimate knowledge of customers' needs Market driven Obsessed with value creation and enhancement
Tolerance of Risk, Ambiguity, and Uncertainty	Calculated risk taker Risk minimizer Risk sharer Manages paradoxes and contradictions Tolerance of uncertainty and lack of structure Tolerance of stress and conflict Ability to resolve problems and integrate solutions
Creativity, Self-reliance, and Ability to Adapt	Nonconventional, open minded, lateral thinker Restlessness with status quo Ability to adapt and change; creative problem solver Ability to learn quickly Lack of fear of failure Ability to conceputalize and "sweat details" (helicopter mind)
Motivation to Excel	Goal-and-results orientation; high but realistic goals Drive to achieve and grow Low need for status and power Interpersonally supporting (versus competitive) Aware of weaknesses and strengths Having perspective and sense of humor

- *Leadership.* Successful entrepreneurs are experienced, including having intimate knowledge of the technology and marketplace in which they will compete, have sound general management skills, and have a proven track record. They are self-starters and have an internal locus of control with high standards.

They are patient leaders, capable of installing tangible visions and managing for the longer haul. The entrepreneur is at once a learner and a teacher, a doer and a visionary. The vision of building a substantial enterprise that will contribute something lasting and relevant to the world while realizing a capital gain requires the patience to stick to the task for 5 to 10 years or more.

Recent work by Alan Grant lends significant support to the fundamental "driving forces" theory of entrepreneurship articulated in *Exhibit 2.7.* Grant surveyed 25 senior venture capitalists to develop an entrepreneurial leadership paradigm. Three clear areas evolved from his study: the lead entrepreneur, the venture team, and the external environment influences, which are outlined in further detail in *Exhibit 6.4.* Furthermore, Grant suggested that to truly understand this paradigm, it should be "metaphorically associated with a *troika,* a Russian vehicle pulled by three horses of *equal* strength. Each horse represents a cluster of the success factors. The troika was driven toward success by the *visions* and *dreams* of the founding entrepreneurs."[13]

[13]Alan Grant. "The Development of an Entrepreneurial Leadership Paradigm for Enhancing New Venture Success," *Frontiers of Entrepreneurship Research: 1992.*

EXHIBIT 6.4

The Entrepreneurial Leadership Paradigm

The Lead Entrepreneur	
Self concept	
Intellectually honest	Has a realist's attitude rather than one of invincibility.
	Trustworthy, his/her word is his/her contract.
	Admits what and when he/she does not know.
Pace maker	Displays a high energy level and a sense of urgency.
Courage	Capable of making hard decisions: setting and beating high goals.
Communication skills	Maintains an effective dialogue with the venture team, in the marketplace, and with other venture constituents.
Team player	Competent in people management and team-building skills.
The Venture Team	
Organizational style	The lead entrepreneur and the venture team blend their skills to operate in a participative environment.
Ethical behavior	Practices strong adherence to ethical business practices.
Faithfulness	Stretched commitments are consistently met or bettered.
Focus	Long-term venture strategies are kept in focus but tactics are varied in order to achieve them.
Performance/reward	High standards of performance are created and superior performance is rewarded fairly and equitably.
Adaptability	Responsive to rapid changes in product/technological cycles.
External Environmental Influences	
Constituent needs	Organization needs are satisfied, in parallel with those of the other publics the enterprise serves.
Prior experiences	Extensive prior experiences are effectively applied.
Mentoring	The competencies of others are sought and used.
Problem resolution	New problems are immediately solved or prioritized.
Value creation	High commitment is placed on long-term value creation for backers, customers, employees, and other stakeholders.
Still emphasis	Marketing skills are stressed over technical ones.

Source: Adapted from Alan Grant, "The Development of the Entrepreneurial Leadership Paradigm," unpublished manuscript, Babson College, 1993, Table 4, p. 11.

There is among successful entrepreneurs a well-developed capacity to exert influence *without* formal power. These people are adept at conflict resolution. They know when to use logic and when to persuade, when to make a concession, and when to exact one. To run a successful venture, an entrepreneur learns to get along with many different constituencies, often with conflicting aims—the customer, the supplier, the financial backer, the creditor, as well as the partners and others on the inside. Success comes when the entrepreneur is a mediator, a negotiator rather than a dictator.

Successful entrepreneurs are interpersonally supporting and nurturing—not interpersonally competitive. When a strong need to control, influence, and gain power over others characterizes the lead entrepreneur, or where he or she has an insatiable appetite for putting an associate down, more often than not the venture gets into trouble. Entrepreneurs should treat others as they want to be treated; they should share the wealth with those

who contributed. A dictatorial, adversarial, and domineering management style makes it very difficult to attract and keep people who thrive on a thirst for achievement, responsibility, and results. Compliant partners and managers often are chosen. Destructive conflicts often erupt over who has the final say, who is right, and whose prerogatives are what.

Entrepreneurs who create and build substantial enterprises are not lone wolves and super-independent. They do not need to collect all the credit for the effort. They not only recognize the reality that it is rarely possible to build a substantial business working all alone, but they actively build a team. They have an uncanny ability to make heroes out of the people they attract to the venture by giving responsibility and sharing credit for accomplishments.

In the corporate setting, this "hero-making" ability is identified as an essential attribute of successful entrepreneurial managers.[14] These hero makers, of both the independent and corporate va-

---

[14] David L. Bradford and Allan R. Cohen, *Managing for Excellence: The Guide to Developing High Performance in Contemporary Organizations* (New York: John Wiley & Sons, 1984).

rieties, try to make the pie bigger and better, rather than jealously clutching and hoarding a tiny pie that is all theirs. They have a capacity for objective interpersonal relationships as well, which enables them to smooth out individual differences of opinion by keeping attention focused on the common goal to be achieved.[15]

- *Opportunity obsession.* Successful entrepreneurs are obsessed—with opportunity. They are oriented to the goal of pursuing and executing an opportunity for accumulating resources or money per se. Much has been said about opportunity in the first chapters of this book. The obsession of entrepreneurs is manifested in total immersion in the opportunity. They are discriminating, realizing that ideas are a dime a dozen. They are intimately familiar with their industries, customers, and competition. This obsession with opportunity is what guides how an entrepreneur deals with important issues. It is noteworthy that the Chinese characters for crisis and problem, when combined, mean opportunity.

- *Tolerance of risk, ambiguity, and uncertainty.* Since high rates of change and high levels of risk, ambiguity, and uncertainty are almost a given, successful entrepreneurs tolerate risk, ambiguity, and uncertainty. They manage paradoxes and contradictions.

Entrepreneurs risk money and much more than that—reputation. Successful entrepreneurs are not gamblers; they take calculated risks. Like the parachutist, they are willing to take a risk; however, in deciding to take a risk, they calculate the risk carefully and thoroughly and do everything possible to get the odds in their favor. Entrepreneurs get others to share inherent financial and business risks with them. Partners put up money and put their reputations on the line, and investors do likewise. Creditors also join the party, as do customers who advance payments and suppliers who advance credit. For example, one researcher studied three very successful entrepreneurs in California who initiated and orchestrated actions that had risk consequences.[16] It was found that while they shunned risk, they sustained their courage by the clarity and optimism with which they saw the future. They limited the risks they initiated by carefully defining and strategizing their ends and by controlling and monitoring their means—and by tailoring them

both to what they saw the future to be. Further, they managed risk by transferring it to others.

More recently, in 1990, John B. Miner proposed his concept of motivation–organizational fit, within which he contrasted a hierarchic (managerial) role with a task (entrepreneurial) role.[17] This study of motivational patterns showed that those who are task oriented (i.e., entrepreneurs) opt for the following roles because of the corresponding motivations:

Role	Motivation
1. Individual achievement.	A desire to achieve through one's own efforts and to attribute success to personal causation.
2. Risk avoidance.	A desire to avoid risk and leave little to chance.
3. Seeking results of behavior.	A desire for feedback.
4. Personal innovation.	A desire to introduce innovative solutions.
5. Planning and goals setting.	A desire to think about the future and anticipate future possibilities.

Entrepreneurs also tolerate ambiguity and uncertainty and are comfortable with conflict. Ask someone working in a large company how sure they are about receiving a paycheck this month, in two months, in six months, and next year. Invariably, they will say that it is virtually certain and will muse at the question. Startup entrepreneurs face just the opposite situation; there may be no revenue at the beginning, and if there is, a 90-day backlog in orders would be quite an exception. To make matters worse, lack of organization, structure, and order is a way of life. Constant changes introduce ambiguity and stress into every part of the enterprise. Jobs are undefined and changing continually, customers are new, co-workers are new, and setbacks and surprises are inevitable. And there never seems to be enough time.

Successful entrepreneurs maximize the good "higher performance" results of stress and minimize the negative reactions of exhaustion and frustration. Two surveys have suggested that very high levels of both satisfaction and stress characterize founders, to a greater degree than managers, regardless of the success of their ventures.[18]

[15] Churchill, "Entrepreneurs and Their Enterprises: A Stage Model," pp. 1–22.
[16] Daryl Mitton, "No Money, Know-How, Know-Who: Formula for Managing Venture Success and Personal Wealth, *Frontiers of Entrepreneurship Research: 1984,* ed. J. Hornaday et al. (Babson Park, Mass.: Babson College, 1984), p. 427.
[17] John B. Miner, "Entrepreneurs, High Growth Entrepreneurs and Managers: Contrasting and Overlapping Motivational Patterns," *Journal of Business Venturing* 5, p. 224.
[18] D. Boyd and D. E. Gumpert, "Loneliness of the Start-Up Entrepreneur," in *Frontiers of Entrepreneurship Research: 1982 and 1983,* ed J. A. Hornaday et al. (Babson Park, MA: Babson College, 1983), pp. 478–87.

- *Creativity, self-reliance, and ability to adapt.* The high levels of uncertainty and very rapid rates of change that characterize new ventures require fluid and highly adaptive forms of organization. An organization that can respond quickly and effectively is a must.

Successful entrepreneurs believe in themselves. They believe that their accomplishments (and setbacks) lie within their own control and influence and that they can affect the outcome. Successful entrepreneurs have the ability to see and "sweat the details" and also to conceptualize (i.e., they have "helicopter minds"). They are dissatisfied with the status quo and are restless initiators.

The entrepreneur has historically been viewed as an independent, a highly self-reliant innovator, and the champion (and occasional villain) of the free enterprise economy. More modern research and investigation have refined considerably the ways of focusing on this self-reliance. There is considerable agreement among researchers and practitioners alike that effective entrepreneurs actively seek and take initiative. They willingly put themselves in situations where they are personally responsible for the success or failure of the operation. They like to take the initiative to solve a problem or fill a vacuum where no leadership exists. They also like situations where personal impact on problems can be measured. Again, this is the action-oriented nature of the entrepreneur expressing itself.

Successful entrepreneurs are adaptive and resilient. They have an insatiable desire to know how well they are performing. They realize that to know how well they are doing and how to improve their performance, they need to actively seek out and use feedback. Seeking and using feedback is also central to the habit of learning from mistakes and setbacks, and of responding to the unexpected. For the same reasons, these entrepreneurs often are described as excellent listeners and quick learners.

Entrepreneurs are not afraid of failing; rather, they are more intent on succeeding, counting on the fact that "success covers a multitude of blunders,"[19] as George Bernard Shaw eloquently stated. People who fear failure will neutralize whatever achievement motivation they may possess. They will tend to engage in a very easy task, where there is little chance of failure, or in a very difficult situation, where they cannot be held personally responsible if they do not succeed.

Further, successful entrepreneurs have the ability to use failure experiences as a way of learning.

They better understand not only their roles but also the roles of others in causing the failure, and thus are able to avoid similar problems in the future. There is an old saying to the effect that the cowboy who has never been thrown from a horse undoubtedly has not ridden too many! The iterative, trial-and-error nature of becoming a successful entrepreneur makes serious setbacks and disappointments an integral part of the learning process.

- *Motivation to excel.* Successful entrepreneurs are motivated to excel. Entrepreneurs are self-starters who appear driven internally by a strong desire to compete against their own self-imposed standards and to pursue and attain challenging goals. This need to achieve has been well established in the literature on entrepreneurs since the pioneering work of McClelland and Atkinson on motivation in the 1950s and 1960s. Seeking out the challenge inherent in a startup and responding in a positive way, noted by the distinguished entrepreneurs mentioned above, is achievement motivation in action.

Conversely, these entrepreneurs have a low need for status and power, and they derive personal motivation from the challenge and excitement of creating and building enterprises. They are driven by a thirst for achievement, rather than by status and power. Ironically, their accomplishments, especially if they are very successful, give them power. But it is important to recognize that power and status are a result of their activities.

Setting high but attainable goals enables entrepreneurs to focus their energies, be very selective in sorting out opportunities, and know what to say no to. Having goals and direction also helps define priorities and provides measures of how well they are performing. Having an objective way of keeping score, such as changes in profits, sales, or stock price, is also important. Thus, money is seen as a tool, and a way of keeping score, rather than the object of the game by itself.

Successful entrepreneurs insist on the highest personal standards of integrity and reliability. They do what they say they are going to do, and they pull for the long haul. These high personal standards are the glue and fiber that binds successful personal and business relationships and makes them endure. A study involving 130 members of the Small Company Management Program at Harvard Business School confirmed how important this issue is. Most simply said it was the single most important factor in their *long-term* successes.[20]

---

[19] Cited in Royal Little, *How to Lose $100,000,000 and Other Valuable Advice* (Boston: Little, Brown and Company, 1979), p. 72.
[20] Timmons and Stevenson, "Entrepreneurship Education in the 80s: What Entrepreneurs Say," pp. 115–34.

The best entrepreneurs have a keen awareness of their own strengths and weaknesses and those of their partners and of the competitive and other environments surrounding and influencing them. They are coldly realistic about what they can and cannot do and do not delude themselves; that is, they have "veridical awareness" or "optimistic realism." It also is worth noting that successful entrepreneurs believe in themselves. They do not believe the success or failure of their venture will be governed by fate, luck, or other powerful, external forces. They believe that they personally can affect the outcome. This attribute is also consistent with achievement motivation, which is the desire to take personal responsibility, and self-confidence.

This veridical awareness often is accompanied by other valuable entrepreneurial traits—perspective and a sense of humor. The ability to retain a sense of perspective, and to "know thyself" in both strengths and weaknesses, makes it possible for an entrepreneur to laugh, to ease tensions, and—frequently—to get an unfavorable situation set in a more profitable direction.

Other Desirable (but Not So Acquirable) Attitudes and Behaviors

The list of characteristics that most experts and observers would argue are more innate than acquired is, fortunately, much shorter. Even here researchers debate extensively whether these can be learned or nurtured to some degree. A friend who is a pediatrician provided a very appropriate explanation of the extent to which certain aspects of our personalities and makeup can be changed. It is like working with fine sandpaper on a large and very hard piece of wood. The surface of the wood can be modified by smoothing and refining it, but to alter its shape is an enormous undertaking.

The following five areas are of this nature. While these, too, are highly desirable givens for any aspiring entrepreneur with which to begin, it is possible to find quite successful entrepreneurs that may be lacking some or possess only a modest degree of each of these. Once again, few entrepreneurs—or others—have exceptional capacities in each of these areas. If these describe a particular entrepreneur's innate talents, then he or she possesses a tremendous potential to be harnessed.

- *Energy, health, and emotional stability.* The extraordinary work loads and stressful demands faced by entrepreneurs place a premium on energy and on physical and emotional health. While each has strong genetic roots, they can also be fine-tuned and preserved by careful attention to eating and drinking habits, exercise, and relaxation.

- *Creativity and innovativeness.* Creativity once was thought of as an exclusively inherited capacity, and most would agree that its roots are strongly genetic. But that may be a surprisingly culture-bound notion, judging by the level of creativity and innovation in the United States, compared with other equally sophisticated cultures that are not as creative and innovative. As noted in Chapter 3, a growing school of thought believes that creativity can actually be learned.

- *Intelligence.* Intelligence and conceptual ability are great advantages for an entrepreneur. There is most likely no successful higher potential venture whose founder would be described as dumb or even of average intelligence. But street smarts (i.e., a nose for business), the entrepreneur's gut feel and instincts, and "ratlike cunning"[21] are special kinds of intelligence. Also, there are many examples of school dropouts who go on to become truly extraordinary entrepreneurs.

Take, for instance, the late Colonel Sanders of Kentucky Fried Chicken fame. He has been quoted as saying, "When I got to the point in school where they said X equals the unknown quantity Y, I decided I had learned as much as I could, and decided I needed to quit school and go to work!" Needless to say, this is not intended to encourage anyone to leave school. The point is that an individual may have a kind of intelligence that will serve him or her well as an entrepreneur but not so well in some other situations.

- *Capacity to inspire.* Vision is that natural leadership quality that is charismatic, bold, and inspirational. All great leaders through the ages share vision, as do many truly extraordinary entrepreneurs. It is difficult to get anyone to argue that such exceptional personal qualities are other than inborn. Yet, though an entrepreneur's charisma quotient may be low, he or she is still the leader, and his or her vision is conveyed by the style of leadership. The entrepreneur's goals and values will establish the atmosphere within which all subsequent activity will unfold, and his or her inspiration, regardless of the form it takes, will shape the venture.

- *Values.* Personal and ethical values seem to reflect the environments and backgrounds from which entrepreneurs have come and are developed early in life. These values are an integral part of an individual.

---

21 The author thanks Phillip Thurston of Harvard Business School for this insightful term.

A Look at the Nonentrepreneurial Mind

There also appears to be a nonentrepreneurial mind that spells trouble for a new venture, or can be fatal. There is apparently no research on this topic, other than broad-brush abstractions about "management as the leading cause of failure."

Findings about hazardous thought patterns of pilots that may contribute to bad judgment are intriguing.[22] There may well be some parallels between the piloting task and leading an emerging company. Such feelings as invulnerability, being macho, being antiauthoritarian, being impulsive, and having outer control have been shown by researchers to be hazardous to pilots. To this list have been added three others—being a perfectionist, being a know-it-all, and being counterdependent.

- *Invulnerability.* This is a thought pattern of people who feel nothing disastrous could happen to them. They are likely to take unnecessary chances and unwise risks. This behavior obviously has severe implications when flying an airplane or launching a company.

- *Being macho.* This describes people who try to prove they are better than others and can beat them. They may try to prove themselves by taking large risks, and they may try to impress others by exposing themselves to danger (i.e., they are adrenaline junkies). While it is associated with overconfidence, this thought pattern goes beyond that definition. Foolish head-to-head competition and irrational takeover battles may be good examples of this behavior.

- *Being antiauthoritarian.* Some people resent control of their actions by any outside authority. Their approach is summed up by the following: "Do not tell me what to do. No one can tell me what to do!" Contrast this thought pattern with the tendency of successful entrepreneurs to seek and use feedback to attain their goals and to improve their performance, and with their propensity to seek team members and other necessary resources to execute an opportunity.

- *Impulsivity.* Facing a moment of decision, certain people feel they must do something, do anything, and do it quickly. They fail to explore the implications of their actions and do not review alternatives before acting.

- *Outer control.* This is the opposite of the internal locus of control characteristic of successful entrepreneurs. People with the outer-control trait feel they can do little, if anything, to control what happens to them. If things go well, they attribute it to good luck, and vice versa.

- *Perfectionist.* Time and again, perfectionism is the enemy of the entrepreneur. The time and cost implications of attaining perfection invariably result in the opportunity window's being slammed shut by a more decisive and nimble competitor, or disappearing altogether by a leapfrog in technology. (Being a perfectionist and having high standards are not the same, however.)

- *Know it all.* Entrepreneurs who think they have all the answers usually have very few. To make matters worse, they often fail to recognize what they do *not* know. Good people find good opportunities in other ways.

- *Counterdependency.* An extreme and severe case of independence can be a limiting mind-set for entrepreneurs. Bound and determined to accomplish things all by themselves, without a particle of help from anyone, these entrepreneurs often end up accomplishing very little. But it is all theirs to claim.

The Concept of Apprenticeship

Shaping and Managing an Apprenticeship

When one looks at successful entrepreneurs, one sees profiles of careers rich in experience. Time and again there is a pattern among successful entrepreneurs. They have all acquired 10 or more years of substantial experience, built contacts, possess the know-how, and established a track record in the industry, market, and technology niche within which they eventually launch, acquire, or build a business. Frequently, they have acquired intimate knowledge of the customer, distribution channels, and market through direct sales and marketing experience. The more successful ones have made money for their employer before doing it for themselves. Consider the following examples:

- Apple Computer founders Steve Jobs and Steve Wozniak were computer enthusiasts as preteens and had accumulated a *relatively* lengthy amount of experience by the time they started the company in their mid-20s. In entirely new industries such as microcomputers, a few years can be a large amount of experience.

- Paul Tobin had no prior cellular phone experience when he was picked up by John Kluge to launch Cellular One of eastern Massachusetts—but neither did anyone else! He had had six years of expe-

---

[22] Berl Brechner, "A Question of Judgment," *Flying,* May 1981, pp. 47–52.

rience at Satellite Business Systems in marketing and had previously spent over five years launching and building his own company in a nontechnology business. His learning curves as an entrepreneur were invaluable in the next startup.

- Jeff Parker had worked for 10 years in the bond-trading business at three major investment banks; he had sold, managed, and built a substantial trading business at one of the investment banks. His technical and computer background enabled him to write programs to assist bond traders on the first Apple Computers. He launched Technical Data Corporation with $100,000 in 1981 and built the first on-line computer system for bond traders. A few years later, his company was sold to Telerate for over $20 million.[23]

There are tens of thousands of similar examples. There are always exceptions to any such pattern, but if you want the odds in your favor get the experience first. As was shown in Chapter 2, successful entrepreneurs are likely to be older and to have at least 8 to 10 years of experience. They are likely to have accumulated enough net worth to contribute to funding the venture or to have a track record impressive enough to give investors and creditors the necessary confidence. Finally, they usually have found and nurtured relevant business and other contacts and networks that ultimately contribute to the success of their ventures.

It is fair to say that the first 10 or so years after leaving school can make or break an entrepreneur's career in terms of how well he or she is prepared for serious entrepreneuring. Evidence suggests that the most durable entrepreneurial careers, those found to last 25 years or more, were begun across a broad age spectrum, but after the person selected prior work or a career to prepare specifically for an entrepreneurial career.

Having relevant experience, know-how, attitudes, behaviors, and skills appropriate for a particular venture opportunity can dramatically improve the odds for success. The other side of the coin is that if an entrepreneur does not have these, then he or she will have to learn them while launching and growing the business. The tuition for such an approach is often greater than most entrepreneurs can afford.

Since entrepreneurs frequently evolve from an entrepreneurial heritage or are shaped and nurtured by their closeness to entrepreneurs and others, the concept of an apprenticeship can be a useful one. And there's no doubt that a lot of what an entrepreneur needs to know about entrepreneuring comes from learning by doing. Knowing what to prepare for, where the windows for acquiring the relevant exposure lie, how to anticipate these, where to position oneself, and when to move on can be quite useful.

As Howard Stevenson of the Harvard Business School has said:

> You have to approach the world as an equal. There is no such thing as being supplicant. You are trying to work and create a better solution by creating action among a series of people who are relatively equal. We destroy potential entrepreneurs by putting them in a velvet-lined rut, by giving them jobs that pay too much, and by telling them they are too good, before they get adequate intelligence, experience, and responsibility.

Windows of Apprenticeship

Exhibit 6.5 summarizes the key elements of an apprenticeship and experience curve and relates these to age windows.[24] Age windows are especially important because of the inevitable time it takes to create and build a successful activity, whether it is a new venture or within another organization.

There is the saying in the venture capital business that the "lemons," or losers, in a portfolio ripen in about two and one-half years and that the "pearls," or winners, on the other hand, usually take seven or eight years to come to fruition (see *Exhibit 3.4*). Therefore, seven years is a realistic time frame to expect to grow a higher potential business to a point where a capital gain can be realized. Interestingly, seven years is often described by presidents of large corporations, presidents of colleges, and self-employed professionals as the time it takes to do something significant.

The implications of this are quite provocative. First, time is precious. Assume an entrepreneur spends the first five years after college or graduate school gaining relevant experience. He or she will be 25 to 30 years of age (or maybe as old as 35) when launching a new venture. By the age of 50, there will have been time for starting, at most, three successful new ventures. What's more, entrepreneurs commonly go through false starts or even a failure at first in the trial-and-error process of learning the entrepreneurial ropes. As a result, the first venture may not be launched until later (i.e., in the entrepreneur's mid- to late 30s). This would leave time to grow the current venture and maybe one more. (There is, of course, always the possibility of staying with a venture and growing it to a larger company of $50 million or more in sales.)

---

[23] This example is drawn from "Technical Data Corporation," HBS Cases 283–072, 283–073, Harvard Business School, 1987.
[24] The author wishes to acknowledge the contributions to his thinking by Mr. Harvey "Chet" Krentzman, entrepreneur, lecturer, author, and nurturer of at least three dozen growth-minded ventures over the past 20 years.

EXHIBIT 6.5

Windows of the Entrepreneurial Apprenticeship

Elements of the Apprenticeship and Experience Curve	Age Window			
	20s	30s	40s	50s
1. Relevant business experience.	Low	Moderate to high	Higher	Highest
2. Management skills and know-how.	Low to moderate	Moderate to high	High	High
3. Entrepreneurial goals and commitment.	Varies widely	Focused high	High	High
4. Drive and energy.	Highest	High	Moderate	Lowest
5. Wisdom and judgment.	Lowest	Higher	Higher	Highest
6. Focus of apprenticeship.	Discussing what you enjoy; key is learning business, sales, marketing; profit and loss responsibility.	General management Division management Founder	Growing and harvesting	Reinvesting
7. Dominant life-stage issues.*	Realizing your dream of adolescence and young adulthood	Personal growth and new directions and ventures.	Renewal, regeneration, reinvesting in the system.	

*Adapted from Daniel J. Levinson et al., *The Seasons of a Man's Life* (New York: Alfred A. Knopf, 1978).

Reflecting on *Exhibit 6.5* will reveal some other paradoxes and dilemmas. For one thing, just when an entrepreneur's drive, energy, and ambition are at a peak, the necessary relevant business experience and management skills are least developed, and those critical elements, wisdom and judgment, are in their infancy. Later on, when an entrepreneur has gained the necessary experience in the "deep, dark canyons of uncertainty" and has thereby gained wisdom and judgment, mother nature has begun to recall the vast energy and drive that got him or her so far. Also, patience and perseverance to relentlessly pursue a long-term vision need to be balanced with the urgency and realism to make it happen. Flexibility to stick with the moving opportunity targets and to abandon some and shift to others is also required. However, flexibility and the ability to act with urgency disappear as the other commitments of life are assumed.

A Personal Strategy

An apprenticeship can be an integral part of the process of shaping an entrepreneurial career. One principal task is to determine what kind of an entrepreneur he or she is likely to become, based on background, experience, and drive. Through an apprenticeship, an entrepreneur can shape a strategy and action plan to make it happen. "Crafting a Personal Entrepreneurship Strategy," on the NVC Web site, addresses this issue more fully.

Despite all the work involved in becoming an entrepreneur, the bottom line is revealing. Evidence about the careers and job satisfaction of entrepreneurs all points to the same conclusion: If they had to do it over, not only would more of them become entrepreneurs again, but they would do it sooner.[25] And, they would also do it earlier in their careers.[26] They report higher personal satisfaction with their lives and their careers than their managerial counterparts. Nearly three times as many say they plan never to retire, according to Stevenson, than do managers. Numerous other studies show that the satisfaction from independence and living and working where and how they want to is a source of great satisfaction.[27] Financially, there is no doubt that successful entrepreneurs enjoy higher incomes and net worths than career managers in large companies. In addition, the successful harvest of a company usually means a capital gain of several million dollars or more and, with it, an entire new array of very attractive options and opportunities to do whatever they choose to do with the rest of their lives.

Entrepreneur's Creed

So much time and space would not be spent on the entrepreneurial mind if it was just of academic interest. But they are, entrepreneurs themselves believe, in

[25] Stevenson, "Who Are the Harvard Self-Employed?" *Frontiers of Entrepreneurship Research: 1983*, ed. J. A. Hornaday et al. (Babson Park, MA: Babson College, 1983), pp. 233–54.
[26] Boyd and Gumpert, "Loneliness of the Start-Up Entrepreneur," p. 486.
[27] Robert C. Ronstadt, "The Decision Not to Become an Entrepreneur," in *Frontiers of Entrepreneurship Research: 1983*, ed. J. Hornaday et al. (Babson Park, MA: Babson College, 1983), pp. 192–212; and Robert C. Ronstadt, "Ex-Entrepreneurs and the Decision to Start an Entrepreneurial Career," in *Frontiers of Entrepreneurship Research: 1983*, pp. 437–60.

large part responsible for success. When asked an open-ended question about what they believed are the most critical concepts, skills, and know-how for running a business—today and five years hence—their answers were very revealing. Most mentioned mental attitudes and philosophies based on entrepreneurial attributes, rather than specific skills or organizational concepts. These answers are gathered together in what might be called an entrepreneur's creed.

- **Do what gives you energy—have fun.**
- **Figure out how to make it work.**
- **Say "can do," rather than "cannot" or "maybe."**
- *Illegitimi non carborundum:* **tenacity and creativity will triumph.**
- **Anything is possible if you believe you can do it.**
- **If you don't know it can't be done, then you'll go ahead and do it.**
- **The cup is half-full, not half-empty.**
- **Be dissatisfied with the way things are—and look for improvement.**
- **Do things differently.**
- **Don't take a risk if you don't have to—but take a calculated risk if it's the right opportunity for you.**
- **Businesses fail; successful entrepreneurs learn—but keep the tuition low.**
- **It is easier to beg for forgiveness than to ask for permission in the first place.**
- **Make opportunity and results your obsession—not money.**
- **Money is a tool and a scorecard available to the right people with the right opportunity at the right time.**
- **Making money is even more fun than spending it.**
- **Make heroes out of others—a team builds a business; an individual makes a living.**
- **Take pride in your accomplishments—it's contagious!**
- **Sweat the details that are critical to success.**
- **Integrity and reliability equal long-run oil and glue.**
- **Make the pie bigger—don't waste time trying to cut smaller slices.**
- **Play for the long haul—it is rarely possible to get rich quickly.**
- **Don't pay too much—but don't lose it!**
- **Only the lead dog gets a change of view.**
- **Success is getting what you want: Happiness is wanting what you get.**

Chapter Summary

1. Entrepreneurs come in all sizes, ages, shapes, religions, colors and backgrounds: There is no one single profile or psychological template.

2. Successful entrepreneurs do share six common themes that describe their attitudes and ways of thinking and acting.

3. Rather than being inborn, the behaviors inherent in these six areas can be nurtured, learned, and encouraged, which successful entrepreneurs model for themselves and those with whom they work.

4. Entrepreneurs love competition and actually avoid risks when they can, preferring carefully calculated risks.

5. Most entrepreneurs gain the apprenticeship over 10 years or more after the age of 21 and acquire networks, skills, and pattern recognition ability.

6. The entrepreneurial mind-set can benefit large, established companies today just as much as smaller firms.

7. Most successful entrepreneurs have had a personal strategy to help them achieve their dreams and goals, both implicitly and explicitly.

Study Questions

1. Who was Ewing Marion Kauffman, what did he do, and what was his philosophy of entrepreneurial leadership?

2. What is the difference between a manager and a leader?

3. Define the six major themes that characterize the mind-sets, attitudes, and actions of a successful entrepreneur. Which are most important, and why? How can they be encouraged and developed?

4. Entrepreneurs are made, not born. Why is this so? Do you agree, and why or why not?

5. Explain what is meant by the apprenticeship concept, and why is it so important to young entrepreneurs?

6. What is your personal entrepreneurial strategy? How should it change?

MIND STRETCHERS
Have You Considered?

1. Who can be an entrepreneur, and who cannot? Why?

2. Why has there been a 30-year brain drain of the best entrepreneurial talent in America away from the largest, established companies? Can this be reversed? How?

3. How do you personally stack up against the six entrepreneurial mind-sets? What do you need to develop and improve?

4. If you work for a larger company, what is it doing to attract and keep the best entrepreneurial talent?

5. How would you describe and evaluate your own apprenticeship? What else has to happen?

6. Is Bill Gates an entrepreneur, a leader, or a manager? How can we know?

Preparation Questions

1. Evaluate the progress of PC Build since its founding in 1991 and its current strategy.
2. What is your assessment of the opportunity to acquire EduTech's computer division?
3. Outline in detail a valuation, deal structure, and funding strategy for the EduTech acquisition.
4. What should Healey do?

> "I had a plan in hand asking for $250,000 and they wanted us to *spend* $380,000!"
>
> —Michael Healey

Introduction

The light was brilliant on this late summer evening in 1993, as he drove north on Interstate 84 to Massachusetts after a meeting in East Hartford, Connecticut. PC–Build[28] President Michael Healey tried to make sense of what had transpired during his conversation with EduTech. The original intent of the meeting with EduTech, a large national wholesaler and retailer of educational supplies headquartered in Braintree, Massachusetts, was to request a $250,000 investment from the corporation. EduTech's computer division, established in 1987, was a reseller of PC–Build's build-it-yourself PC kit products. The two companies had a very positive relationship. Healey thought the corporation would be a natural investor, and therefore took this trip to Connecticut to present an investment plan to EduTech's decision makers (see *Exhibit A*).

In an ironic turn of events, EduTech presented a counterproposal during the meeting requesting PC–Build purchase its computer division for $380,000. The proposition was shocking to the PC–Build team. Healey exclaimed, "I had a plan in hand asking EduTech for $250,000 and they wanted us to *spend* $380,000 to acquire their money-losing division with an angry customer base!"

Mike Healey got onto the Massachusetts turnpike headed east toward Boston and resolved to make a decision. What should he do? Should he stick with the original plan and attempt to get another investor to foot the $250,000 necessary to both launch the upgrade business and rejuvenate the PC kit business; recommit to the PC kit market and forget entering the upgrade business, thereby decreasing or eliminating the need for financing; or buy EduTech's computer division?

---

[28] For more information on PC–Build and the company's initial business plan, see Babson case study *PC–Build, Inc.* in *New Venture Creation*, 5th ed. (1999).

EXHIBIT A

Sources and Uses of Expansion Money

Direct Mail (for PC kit products)

Catalog Printing	$26,600	
Catalog Advertisement	$25,000	
Postage	$17,900	
Direct Mail Total		$69,500

Upgrade Business

Additional Hirings	$35,000	
Upgrade Advertising	$30,000	
Inventory/Capital Expansion	$74,550	
Additional Working Capital	$40,950	
Upgrade Business Total		$180,500
Total Funds Needed		**$250,000**

Although PC–Build had several uses for the money, the primary use of new funding would be to finance PC–Build's move into the computer upgrade business. The PC–Build funding proposal stated, "PC–Build is seeking $250,000 in additional funding. The four main uses of the funds are:

1. **Establish an Upgrade Business:** Upgrading a large variety of machines requires a base of knowledge that does not exist anywhere else in the country. The pilot period will be used to work out the bugs, improving the changes of long term success.

2. **Stabilize Daily Cash Position:** There is an immediate need to increase the daily working capital of the company. By increasing our working capital base we will be able to more effectively purchase inventory, hire staff, and take advantage of advertising discounts.

3. **Expand Catalog Operation:** The most promising leads for PC kit customers are still sitting in our database. Inside sales efforts need to be supported with an aggressive direct mail campaign.

4. **Fund Secondary Upgrade Workshop Sites:** Each subsequent upgrade store will require an up-front expenditure. Each additional upgrade workshop site can be thought of as a minicompany with its own investment requirement and break-even point."

EXHIBIT B

Instructional Use of Computers in Elementary and Secondary Schools in the United States: 1985, 1989, and 1992.[29]

	Unit	1985	1989	1992
Computers used for instruction	000's	1,034	2,355	3,536
Schools using computers	percent	86	96	100
Schools with 15 or more computers	percent	24	57	80
Students per computer, median	number	42	20	14
Median hours of use per week	number	17	20	20

Background

Mike Healey first came up with the idea for PC–Build as a second year MBA student at Babson College's F.W. Olin Graduate School of Business. He and Bob Lofblad submitted a business plan for PC–Build to the 1992 MBA Douglass Prize competition for the best proposed business at Babson College. They were thrilled to learn they won. This award gave Healey confidence to forgo the job recruiting process and dedicate himself to launching PC–Build.

PC–Build was founded as a manufacturer and direct seller of build-it-yourself personal computer kits for educational purposes (see *Exhibit B*). Its PC kits were sold through three primary channels:

1. **Catalog:** PC–Build offered a free 16-page product catalog for its three build-it-yourself kits. Most catalog customers were home hobbyists. In early 1993, the catalog was still in the experimental stage. Previously the company relied heavily on the founder's connections for sales.
2. **Educational Institutions:** A growing channel of distribution was the computer courses offered by schools and colleges nationwide. PC–Build would even work with schools to develop their computer assembly curriculum. By early 1993, this was a small but growing segment of PC–Build's business.
3. **Retail:** PC–Build sold to retail distributors and had a small retail operation out of its company office space.

The economics of the PC kit business promised high margins through labor cost savings. While labor costs in computer manufacturing were generally 20 percent of total product cost, customers of the build-it-yourself kit market supplied a large percentage of total labor. Healey realized a kit manufacturing company could pass on a portion of these labor savings to buyers and apply the rest to its bottom line. According to the business plan, PC–Build was expected to break even within the first 10 months of operation at 1,300 units with an average gross profit of 30 percent.

The PC kit market had undergone a dramatic decline in the late 1980s after years of steady growth in the late 1970s and early 1980s—primarily because profitability in the computer manufacturing industry depended heav-ily on volume production and kits were a low-volume niche product. However, Healey believed five changes had taken place in the market which would make PC kits profitable again: 1) technological standardization with the dominance of Intel's central processing units; 2) the widespread use and acceptance of PC technology; 3) declining consumer loyalty to brand names; 4) downward pressure on cost of technology components; and 5) the market leader in the PC kit market offered an overpriced and low-quality product.

The PC Kit and Computer Upgrade Markets

PC–Build was beginning to enter the computer upgrade market in early 1993 and faced a profound dilemma: should the company abandon its original PC kit business, provide both upgrades and computer kits, or recommit solely to the PC kit business (see *Exhibits C1 and C2*)? Comparing the relative sizes of the upgrade and PC kit markets, one might be tempted to drop the PC kit business and focus on upgrades. However, PC–Build could realize a number of economic and marketing advantages by integrating the two businesses. By early 1993, the company had made a conscientious decision to offer upgrade services to its customers, but it still wasn't clear what that meant for the kit business.

The Upgrade Market

Demand for upgrade services was high, but PC–Build didn't have the resources to meet this growing demand. PC–Build's upgrade business was growing rapidly because computers were becoming technologically obsolete faster than ever yet it was still a significant expense to replace old computers with new ones (see *Exhibit D4*).[30]

29 According to *FamilyPC* magazine (1995), the most popular personal computer configuration sold between 1991 and 1993 was a 25-MHz 486SX system with local-bus video, 4MB of RAM, a 0-kilobyte cache, a low-end video board, a 200MB IDE hard drive (IDE is a standard interface hard drive used to talk to a computer), and a double-speed CD-ROM drive. This system was considered "highly upgradable."

30 *Statistical Abstract of the United States, 1995* (115th edition). United States Department of Commerce, Economics and Statistics Adminstration, Bureau of the Census (The National Data Book; Washington, D.C., 1995): p. 169.

Actual and Proforma Income Statements, 1993–1994[31]

	3rd Qtr 1992	4th Qtr 1992	1st Qtr 1993	2nd Qtr 1993	3rd Qtr 1993	4th Qtr 1993	1993 Totals	1994 Totals (est.)
Catalog Sales*	$61,000	$80,000	$108,000	$135,000	$155,000	$200,000	$598,000	$900,000
Upgrade Sales	$0	$0	$22,000	$60,000	$150,000	$200,000	$432,000	$1,500,000
Consulting/Programming	$7,500	$7,500	$1,500	$2,000	$2,500	$3,000	$9,000	$0
Total Sales	$68,500	$87,500	$131,500	$197,000	$307,500	$403,000	$1,039,000	$2,400,000
Cost of Goods Sold	$53,430	$68,250	$99,940	$149,720	$230,625	$302,250	$782,535	$1,776,000
Gross Profit	$15,070	$19,250	$32,700	$47,280	$76,875	$100,750	$257,605	$624,000
Payroll	$6,000	$6,000	$10,000	$15,000	$30,000	$35,000	$90,000	$250,000
Advertising	$10,000	$13,000	$7,500	$10,000	$20,000	$30,000	$67,500	$100,000
Direct Mail Cost*	$2,500	$3,500	$2,100	$5,000	$7,500	$9,000	$23,600	$35,000
Telephone	$1,300	$2,000	$3,800	$4,725	$5,425	$7,000	$20,950	$39,000
Insurance	$2,250	$2,250	$2,250	$2,250	$2,250	$2,250	$9,000	$15,000
Rent	$3,000	$3,000	$2,120	$3,750	$3,750	$3,750	$13,370	$43,370
Office Expense	$1,500	$1,750	$2,000	$2,000	$2,000	$2,000	$8,000	$10,000
Utilities	$0	$0	$0	$250	$300	$350	$900	$30,000
Travel/Ent.	$1,000	$1,000	$1,000	$1,000	$1,000	$1,000	$4,000	$8,500
Other	$1,500	$1,500	$1,500	$1,500	$1,500	$1,500	$6,000	$14,000
Total Expenses	$29,050	$34,000	$32,270	$45,475	$73,725	$91,850	$243,320	$544,870
Net Income (Loss)	($13,980)	($14,750)	$430	$1,805	$3,150	$8,900	$14,285	$79,130

[31] Catalog sales and direct mail costs apply only to PC kit sales.

EXHIBIT 12

Actual and Proforma Balance Sheet, 1993–1994

	3rd Qtr 1992	4th Qtr 1992	1st Qtr 1993	2nd Qtr 1993	3rd Qtr 1993	4th Qtr 1993	1993 Year End	1994 Year End (est.)
Assets								
Cash on Hand	$13,300	$13,730	$6,048	$20,500	$42,640	$58,351	$58,351	$75,000
Accounts Receivable	$7,775	$4,700	$14,561	$31,520	$53,813	$72,540	$72,540	$114,000
Bad Debt Allowance	$0	$0	($146)	($315)	($538)	($725)	($725)	($1,140)
Inventory	$16,141	$16,071	$19,992	$37,641	$58,425	$83,540	$83,540	$103,116
Deposits	$0	($450)	$0	$0	$0	$0	$0	$0
Total Current Assets	$37,216	$34,051	$40,455	$89,346	$154,339	$213,706	$213,706	$290,976
Computer Equipment—Net	$7,465	$10,642	$11,189	$18,000	$22,000	$33,850	$33,850	$84,625
Furniture—Net	$512	$4,197	$4,441	$7,500	$13,500	$17,500	$17,500	$35,000
Total Fixed Assets	$7,977	$14,839	$15,630	$25,500	$35,500	$51,350	$51,350	$119,625
Total Assets	**$45,193**	**$48,890**	**$56,085**	**$114,846**	**$189,839**	**$265,056**	**$265,056**	**$410,601**
Liabilities								
Accounts Payable	$19,513	$24,778	$28,035	$40,424	$62,269	$78,585	$78,585	$95,000
Notes Payable	$0	$0	$3,391	$0	$0	$0	$0	$0
Taxes Payable	$762	$38	$543	$1,000	$1,000	$1,000	$1,000	$1,000
Total Current Liabilities	$20,275	$24,816	$31,969	$41,424	$63,269	$79,585	$79,585	$96,000
Due to Officer	$3,500	$2,500	$2,500	$0	$0	$0	$0	$0
Total Debt	$23,775	$27,316	$34,469	$41,424	$63,269	$79,585	$79,585	$96,000
Equity	$51,658	$71,458	$71,500	$121,500	$171,500	$221,500	$221,500	$271,500
Retained Earnings	($30,240)	($49,884)	($49,884)	($48,079)	($44,929)	($36,029)	($36,029)	$43,101
Total Equity	$21,418	$21,574	$21,616	$73,421	$126,571	$185,471	$187,471	$314,601
Total Liability/Equity	**$45,193**	**$48,890**	**$56,085**	**$114,845**	**$189,840**	**$265,056**	**$265,056**	**$410,601**

Customers also had a hard time finding someone willing to take on upgrade business. Most computer consultants and retailers shied away from upgrades because they could make more money by selling a new system. Old machines also required a great deal of costly troubleshooting on the part of the technical staff while a new machine would work right out of the box. Healey talked about the demand for PC–Build's upgrade services:

> We were being inundated with calls from our customers. They were frustrated with their existing machines, which had become outdated so fast. They wanted new machines but also wanted to save cash. We had the expertise to upgrade their computer systems without purchasing entirely new hardware, but we didn't have the capacity. Being entrepreneurial, we just started performing upgrades without the resources necessary. Demand wasn't just outstripping supply. It was outstripping everything—staff, resources, knowledge, equipment, administration. After a while, we looked at our financial position and realized we really needed money to finance this new business. I had to mail a letter to prospective investors asking for money.

In 1993, the typical PC–Build upgrade customer paid $500 to $600 to fully upgrade her personal computer while PC–Build's average build-it-yourself kit cost $1,500. PC–Build's relative profit margins of PC kits and upgrades were 20–26 percent and 26–30 percent, respectively. According to *Inc.* magazine, "A good upgrade computer may buy you 12 to 18 months of extra life on an old machine; buying a new computer will generally give you two to four years before new software or technology forces you to replace or upgrade again."[32] *InfoWorld* magazine stated that half of all new computer purchases are intended to replace existing PCs.

EXHIBIT D

The following table summarizes the cost benefits in 1993 of upgrading a 286 CPU personal computer versus purchasing a new personal computer with a 486SX CPU.[33]

Item	Upgraded PC	New PC Specifications
Case	Upgrade	New
Motherboard	$320	486SX 25MHz
Memory	$176	4MB RAM
Hard Drive	Upgrade	80 MB
Floppy Drives	Upgrade	2 floppies
Controller Card	Upgrade	IDE
Video Card	Upgrade	VGA
Monitor	Upgrade	VGA Color
Keyboard	Upgrade	Standard 101 Key
Labor Charge	$49	N/C
Total Cost	**$545**	**$1200**

[32] David Goodman, "Working With What You've Got," *Inc.*, Winter 1994, pp. 34–37.
[33] Table from "PC–Build Computer Kits: Expansion Plans and Financing Prospectus," 1993, pg. 3. $1,200 figure is calculated by taking the average price of comparable models as listed in *InfoWorld's Direct Buyers' Guide*, June 1993.

PC–Build hadn't achieved the profits it expected from the PC kit market and had not expanded significantly since the launch date in 1991. "We were still 'Two Guys Inc.'," Mike Healey stated. "The kit market was plodding along, growing at 10 to 15 percent a month. The upgrade market, on the other hand, was growing at a rate of 20 to 30 percent a month. Upgrades were where it was happening."

A PC–Build expansion report stated:

> The upgrade customer is not interested in the utilitarian value inherent in hands-on building. Instead, they are attracted to the economics of upgrading a PC. All IBM compatible PCs (clones) are built around standard architecture. This standardization lets a customer add various components into their PC without worrying about compatibility. It also has the benefit of creating an upgrade path for almost every PC clone ever made. The two most critical elements for success in the upgrade business are developing customer awareness of the concept and mastering the technical requirements of upgrading. Many potential customers don't realize that they *can* upgrade their computers. The natural tendency is towards purchasing a new system. PC–Build's challenge is to make people realize they *can* upgrade their PC. All marketing efforts will be focused on creating this awareness.

The PC Kit Market

Despite the growth of the upgrade market, the PC kit business still served four strategic purposes relative to the upgrade market:

1. **National Exposure:** There were a number of competitors in the upgrade market. However, none of them received the type of national exposure that PC–Build received from its PC kits products. Healey hoped the kits would position PC–Build as a computer expert: "We build them—so we can upgrade them." The geographic distribution of PC kit inquiries would also help define future expansion plans.

2. **Technical Expertise:** Computer kits would force PC–Build to maintain its focus on the technical aspects of PCs. They would also force the company to translate technical jargon into plain English. An expansion report stated, "A large portion of the Company's present success is due to our ability to perform this translation for our customers."

3. **Logistical Synergies:** Both businesses had the same operational characteristics in terms of purchasing, testing, and inventory control. Material cost was directly linked to volume purchases. Increased volume in one division might help lower overall costs for both divisions.

4. **Pricing Benchmarks:** By offering a line of complete PCs in kit form, PC–Build would be able to develop a benchmark for upgrade charges. The company would develop a price point giving the required margin without dampening the economic benefits of an upgrade.

In addition to the above strategic purposes, the PC kit business was still responsible for 75 percent of PC–Build's total revenues in 1993. Healey expected this percentage to decline, though, as the upgrade business grew.

Even though the kit business was stagnant, PC–Build was not sure it had exhausted the potential of the kit market. Sales had grown slowly since the company began shipping its first kits on June 1, 1992, but PC–Build had received national praise in leading computer magazines such as *Computer Shopper, PC–Upgrade,* and *Information Week.* Before PC–Build was founded in February 1992, there were no other companies offering a complete line of high quality kits for home hobbyists and schools. Maybe PC–Build just needed to invest in cultivating the market since it couldn't capitalize on preceding companies that would have developed the consumer base. Perhaps it could create greater opportunity in the build-it-yourself kit market by expanding to retail outlets, offering add-on sales, developing new products, or revitalizing its direct marketing strategy.

By the time PC–Build began providing upgrade service, it was midway through an experiment with catalog sales for its kit products (see *Exhibit E*). PC–Build advertised its catalog in several trade magazines and received an overwhelming response with over 9,000 inquiries in its prospect database. In addition, many of these prospects spread the word about PC–Build. The conversion rate of inquiries into customers was only 1.5 percent compared with 2–3 percent for other catalog retailers, but Healey attributed much of this discrepancy to PC–Build's inability to invest in follow-up mailings or new catalogs due to the big capital outlays necessary for large-scale direct mailings (see *Exhibits F1* and *F2* for a comparison of catalog and upgrade costs). As an offset to the cost of direct mail, though, catalog sales would enable PC–Build to practice just-in-time (JIT) inventory and achieve inventory turnover of three times per month.

Evaluating the Acquisition Opportunity

The Appeal of PC–Build

EduTech wanted to get rid of its computer division because it contributed only a quarter of a million in revenues to a company with total sales of $100 million, distracted from the primary businesses, required a great deal of resources and attention, and was perceived as a nuisance due to customers' unceasing demands for assistance. Healey concisely explained, "They wanted us to buy their nightmares." EduTech's computer division distributed hardware to the education market. Margins at the distribution channel were extremely depressed, though. PC–Build, as a direct seller, might have an advantage EduTech didn't.

Even though the computer division was a "nightmare" for EduTech, the company strongly felt it couldn't just walk away from its customers and wanted to make sure they would be taken care of. Rick Holden, EduTech's president, stated, "Anything we did in the computer division would affect our customers on the wholesale school supplies side. This was a nonfinancial concern that was truly financial in nature." EduTech suspected PC–Build could effectively service its customers.

EXHIBIT E

PC–Build Customer Leads and Sales Generated by Catalog Experiment

Publication	% of Total Leads	% of New Customers
Boston Computer Society	0.42	2.00
Boston Globe	0.50	0.00
Compute	3.72	1.05
Computer Currents	0.54	0.18
Computer Monthly	1.78	0.00
Computer Shopper	1.47	1.70
Computer Craft	4.73	3.10
Electronics Now	0.86	0.00
Info Week	6.38	0.00
Omni	3.68	0.00
PC Computing	8.07	9.54
PC Upgrade	22.27	15.92
Popular Electronics	13.15	11.89
Popular Mechanics	14.06	4.50
Popular Science	5.22	4.52
School Shop	0.59	0.00
Teacher	2.34	0.73
Word of Mouth	3.45	21.13
Other	6.79	23.72

EXHIBIT F1

Annual Catalog Expenditures

Task	Cost
New Catalog Development	$1,500
New Catalog Printing	$12,500
Catalog Postage	$7,500
Supplemental Mailings (4 per year)	$26,400 ($6,600 each)
Supplemental Postage	$15,600 ($3,900 each)
Direct Mail List Purchases (50,000 names)	$4,900
Direct Mail Printing	$7,500
Direct Mail Postage	$6,500
Magazine Advertising	$50,000
Total Annual Expenditures—Catalog Sales	**$132,400**

EXHIBIT F2

Up-front Costs to Establish a Full Upgrade Workshop[34]

Task	Cost
Deposits/Fees	$2,000
Sign	$5,000
Furniture & Workbenches	$4,500
Equipment	$3,350
Workshop Inventory	$10,000
Initial Local Advertising	$10,000
Miscellaneous	$2,000
Additional Working Capital per Store	$7,500
Total Up-front Expenditures per Upgrade Workshop	**$44,350**

[34] According to early estimates (1993), a single upgrade workshop would generate approximately $3 million in sales per year.

As an added plus to EduTech, a large percentage of PC–Build's customers were educational institutions so it was familiar with the market. Equally important, though, PC–Build also had business sector customers. This was a major concern for EduTech, since PC–Build would have to do a lot of "classroom pricing" in the education market and needed private customers in order to finance this discount selling. Holden explained, "A majority of PC–Build's customers were in the education market. But they also had a foundation of business customers, which was attractive because you can't survive by education sales alone. Having business sales in place would provide a cushion to enable education sales. This told us PC–Build would be around to service our customers for a number of years to come."

Obstacles

The disadvantages of the purchase weighed on Healey's mind:

1. PC–Build didn't have $380,000 for the acquisition.

2. EduTech's computer division was losing money and its customers were angry.

3. EduTech had a training division while PC–Build didn't have experience in this area.

4. PC–Build still needed money to finance its upgrade business.

Perhaps the biggest obstacle, though, would be the transition issues of assimilating a division two times larger than PC–Build. "I knew we would have to become an entirely different organization," Healey said. Among other challenges, PC–Build would have to quickly and effectively service a large number of dissatisfied clients and lay off most of the managers in EduTech's computer division while incorporating the technical staff into PC–Build's operations.

Despite these obstacles, Healey couldn't help but be enticed by the proposition. This purchase would bring PC–Build 2,500 customers with 10,000 PCs for its new upgrade business, 10 staff people with eight years of experience each in the industry, a well-known and highly respected name in the education market, and a great deal of equipment. Mike Healey was impressed by the fact that the president of EduTech, who started the computer division in the 1980s when the PC industry was doing well, knew about the benefits of investing in technology and believed in PC–Build's abilities. Another important consideration for Healey was the fact that EduTech wasn't willing to just abandon its customers. Healey couldn't help but ask himself, I wonder if we could make this work.

A Vision for the Future

Healey had a vision for PC–Build as a franchiser of upgrade centers with a nationwide service presence. Healey wasn't sure this vision was anything more than a fantasy, though—or, at the most, decades away. An acquisition of EduTech's computer division could quickly turn this fantasy into reality.

In early 1993, a couple of months before the meeting with EduTech, PC–Build opened what was called "The PC–Build Workshop" where customers could drop off their computers and pick them up a few days later fully upgraded to their specifications. Healey wrote in an expansion plan:

> The Drop-Off service will be the primary sales point emphasized by our marketing materials. On-Site upgrades will eventually be added as our staff expands. The store itself is more akin to an automotive repair shop than computer store like CompUSA or Radio Shack. Floor space is reserved for workbenches, which can be used by customers or PC–Build technicians. The facility can also be used for courses and seminars . . . Once the first Workshop is stabilized and functioning, PC–Build will begin looking at suitable expansion sites, preferably in the Northeast. Once three or four

stores are in place, a final decision will be made regarding future expansion (corporate stores vs. franchises, etc.).

The first store was a pilot project which would help work out the details of billing, operations, pricing, and marketing—and indicate the potential for success. According to conservative estimates, it looked like the first PC–Build Workshop would do approximately $3 million in sales in one year.

Conclusion

Michael Healey pulled up to PC–Build's office in Needham, Massachusetts. Even though the trip was over, he hadn't arrived at a decision and was still a little incredulous about what had transpired at the meeting. His employees were expecting him to walk in and tell them whether EduTech had said "yes" or "no"—not that EduTech had asked PC–Build for $380,000. Healey didn't know what to say when his employees asked the inevitable question: "What are you going to do?" As Mike Healey saw it, he could either 1) write off EduTech as a potential investor and attempt to get the $250,000 from another source; 2) recommit to the PC kit market and pull out of the upgrade market, thereby decreasing or eliminating the need for financing; or 3) find some way to buy EduTech's computer division.

## Chapter Seven

The Entrepreneurial Manager

It's rare to find a leader who can carry a growing company through all its phases. When you get into the $1- to $2-billion range, then you may find leaders with entrepreneurial tendencies; but, in addition, they have real management and people skills.

Peter J. Sprague,
Chairman of the Board,
National Semiconductor Corporation

Results Expected

Upon completion of this chapter, you will have:

1. Studied different views about entrepreneurial managers and discovered that an individual can be both an entrepreneur and a manager.
2. Identified the stages of growth entrepreneurial ventures go through, the domain occupied, the venture modes characteristic of the entrepreneurial domain, and the principal forces acting in the domain.
3. Identified specific skills entrepreneurs need to know in order to manage startup, survival, and growth.
4. Analyzed the "Fenchel Lamp Shade Company" case.
5. Evaluated your own skills and developed an action plan.

The Entrepreneurial Domain

Converging on the Entrepreneurial Manager

There are convergent pressures on being an entrepreneur and being a manager as a venture accelerates and grows beyond founder-driven and founder-dominated survival. Key to achieving longer-term sustained growth, and an eventual harvest, is the ability of an entrepreneur to have or develop competencies as an entrepreneurial manager.

In the past, those studying entrepreneurship and others active in starting new ventures, such as venture capitalists, professors, and researchers, have generally felt that the kind of person with the entrepreneurial spirit required to propel a new venture through startup to a multimillion-dollar annual sales level is different from the kind of person who has the capacity to manage the new firm as it grows from $5 million to $20 million or $30 million in sales. Further, it has long been thought that the entrepreneur who clings to the lead role too long during the maturation process will subsequently limit company growth, if not seriously retard it.

As John Kenneth Galbraith explained in 1971, "The great entrepreneur must, in fact, be compared in life with the male 'apis mellifera.' He accomplishes his act of conception at the price of his own extinction."[1]

---

[1] John Kenneth Galbraith, *The New Industrial State* (Boston: Houghton Mifflin, 1971).

In short, conventional wisdom stated that a good entrepreneur is usually not a good manager, since he or she lacks the necessary management skill and experience. Likewise, it is assumed that a manager is not an entrepreneur, since he or she lacks some intense personal qualities and the orientation required to launch a business from ground zero.

Increasingly, however, evidence suggests that new ventures that flourish beyond startup and grow to become substantial, successful enterprises can be headed by entrepreneurs who are also effective managers. For instance, a 1983 survey by *Inc.* magazine of the heads of the top 100 new ventures showed that the majority of these companies had founders who were still chief executive officers after several years and after their companies had attained sales of at least $10 million (and some as much as $50 million or more). Testing conventional wisdom, two researchers empirically studied the tenure of 54 Fortune 1,000 corporations' founders. They assumed that there are three reasons founders have to adapt: (1) shift from creation to exploitation, (2) shift from passionate commitment to dispassionate objectivity, and (3) shift from direct personal control over organizational actions to indirect impersonal control. Taking into account the growth rate, the timing of the initial public offering, the founder's age, education, and other factors, this 1990 study found the following:

1. "If the firm grows relatively slowly, and the founder is capable of some adaptation, then the firm can apparently become quite large."
2. "Founders with scientific or engineering backgrounds remain in control of the companies they found for shorter periods than do founders whose academic focus was business."
3. The founder's tenure will typically be longer in family dominated firms."[2]

More recently, researchers "observed that many founders can and do manage growth successfully. The applicability of conventional wisdom regarding the 'leadership crisis' in rapid-growth entrepreneurial firms may no longer be valid, if, in fact, it ever was."[3]

These and other data seem to defy the notion that entrepreneurs can start but cannot manage growing companies. While the truth is probably somewhere in between, one thing is apparent: Growing a higher potential venture requires management skills.

Clearly, a complex set of factors goes into making someone a successful entrepreneurial manager.

Launching a new venture and then managing rapid growth involves managerial roles and tasks not found in most mature or stable environments. Further, one of the greatest strengths of successful entrepreneurs is that they know what they do and do not know. They have disciplined intellectual honesty, which prevents their optimism from becoming myopic delusion and their dreams from becoming blind ambition. No individual has all these skills, nor does the presence or absence of any single skill guarantee success or failure. That an entrepreneur knows that he or she needs a certain skill and knows where to get it is clearly as valuable as knowing whether he or she already has it.

Principal Forces and Venture Modes

Companies, whether they are new, growing, or mature, occupy a place in either an administrative or an entrepreneurial domain, an area influenced by certain principal forces and characterized by ways of acting, called venture modes. *Exhibits 7.1* and *7.2* illustrate the entrepreneurial and administrative domains and the dynamic of the principal forces acting in the domains and the dominant venture modes which result.

In the exhibits, the four cells are defined by the stage of the venture (upper axis), the extent of change and uncertainty accompanying it (right axis), and the degree to which a venture is administrative (bottom axis) or entrepreneurial (left axis). Clearly, the entrepreneurial domain is the two upper cells in both exhibits, and the domains are functions both of the change and uncertainty facing a venture and the stage of growth of the venture.

Each venture mode (i.e., ways of acting) for firms in each cell is driven by certain principal forces. These forces are shown in *Exhibit 7.1*. Shown in *Exhibit 7.2* are dominant venture modes characteristic of firms in each cell. Organizations at different stages are characterized by differing degrees of change and uncertainty and are therefore more or less entrepreneurial or more or less administrative. Thus, for example, a new venture in the seed/startup stage, which is characterized by high change and uncertainty, is most entrepreneurial. These firms will be new, innovative, or backbone ventures; will be led by a team; will be driven by their founders' goals, values, commitment, and perceptions of the opportunities; and will minimize the use of resources. At the other extreme is a mature firm, one which is in the maturity stage and characterized by low change and uncertainty, one which is stable or contracting, one

---

[2] George C. Rubenson and Anil K. Gupta, "The Founder's Disease: A Critical Reexamination," *Frontiers of Entrepreneurship Research: 1990*, ed. Neil Churchill et al. (Babson Park, MA: Babson College, 1990), pp. 177–78.
[3] Gary E. Willard, David A. Krueger, and Henry R. Feeser, "In Order to Grow, Must the Founder Go: A Comparison of Performance Between Founder and Non-Founder Managed High-Growth Manufacturing Firms," *Journal of Business Venturing* 7, p. 190.

EXHIBIT 7.1

Dominant Venture Modes

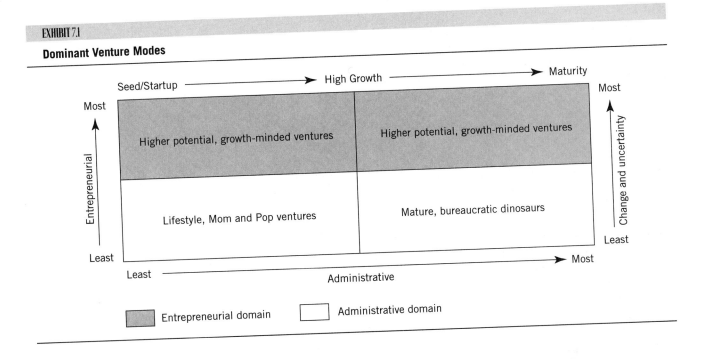

EXHIBIT 7.2

Principal Driving Forces

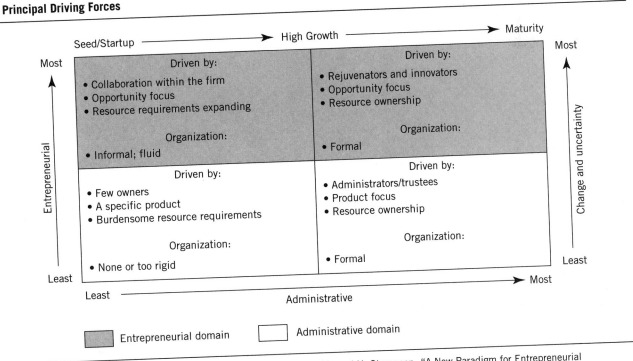

Source: These exhibits are built on work by Timmons and Stevenson: See Howard H. Stevenson, "A New Paradigm for Entrepreneurial Management," in *Entrepreneurship: What It Is and How to Teach It* (Boston: Harvard Business School, 1985), pp. 30–61; and Jeffry A. Timmons and Howard H. Stevenson, "Entrepreneurship Education in the 80s: What Entrepreneurs Say," in *Entrepreneurship: What It Is and How to Teach It,* pp. 115–34.

which is led by an administrator or custodian, one which is driven by resource ownership and administrative efficiency, and one which is reactive. Other firms fall in between.

The managerial skills required of the firms in each cell are more evident upon examination of these principal forces and dominant venture modes. For example, creativity and comprehensive managerial skills are required to manage firms in both cells in the entrepreneurial domain. In the upper left-hand cell, entrepreneurial managers need to cope effectively with high levels of change and uncertainty, whether their management skills can be affectionately labeled MBWA (management by wandering around, of Hewlett-Packard fame), or management by muddling through. Certainly, as the firm enters the high-growth stage, this changes.

Stages of Growth

A Theoretical View

Clearly, entrepreneurship is not static. *Exhibit 7.3* represents a *theoretical* view of the process of gestation and growth of new ventures and the transitions that occur at different "boundaries" in this process.[4] Ventures are sown, sprout, grown, and harvested. Even those successful ventures which are not grown to harvest (i.e., those which have been defined as "attractive") go through stages of growth.

It cannot be stressed enough that this smooth, S-shaped curve in the exhibit is rarely, if ever, replicated in the real world. If one actually tracked the progress of most emerging companies over time, the "curve" actually would be a ragged and jagged line

EXHIBIT 7.3

Stages of Venture Growth, Crucial Transitions, and Core Management Mode

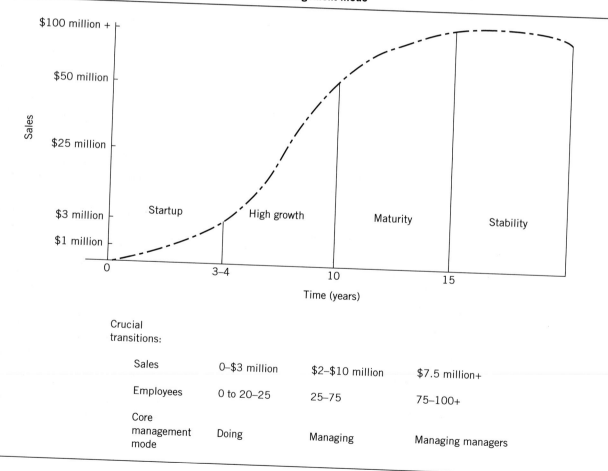

Crucial transitions:			
Sales	0–$3 million	$2–$10 million	$7.5 million+
Employees	0 to 20–25	25–75	75–100+
Core management mode	Doing	Managing	Managing managers

[4] For another useful view of the stages of development of a firm and required management capabilities, see Carroll V. Kroeger, "Management Development and the Small Firm," *California Management Review* 17, no. 1 (Fall 1974), pp. 41–47.

with many ups and downs; that is, these companies would experience some periods of rapid progress followed by setbacks and accompanying crises.

For the purposes of illustration, *Exhibit 7.3* shows venture stages in terms of time, sales, and number of employees. It is at the boundaries between stages that new ventures seem to experience transitions. Several researchers have noted that the new venture invariably goes through transition and will face certain issues.[5] Thus, the exhibit shows the crucial transitions during growth and the key management tasks of the chief executive officer or founders. Most important and most challenging for the founding entrepreneur or a chief executive officer is coping with crucial transitions and the change in management tasks, from doing to managing to managing managers, as a firm grows to roughly 30 employees, to 50, to 75 employees, and then to over 75.

The *startup stage*, a stage that usually covers the first two or three years but perhaps as many as seven, is by far the most perilous stage and is characterized by the direct and exhaustive drive, energy, and entrepreneurial talent of a lead entrepreneur and a key team member or two. Here, the critical mass of people, market and financial results, and competitive resiliency are established, while investor, banker, and customer confidence is earned. The level of sales reached varies widely and may reach several million dollars per year, but sales typically range between $2 million and $20 million. A new company then begins its high-growth stage. The exact point at which this occurs can rarely be identified by a date on the calendar until well after the fact. It is in this stage that new ventures exhibit a failure rate over 60 percent; that is, it is in this stage that the lemons ripen.

As with the other stages, the length of time it takes to go through the *high-growth stage*, as well as the magnitude of change occurring during the period, varies greatly. Probably the most difficult challenge for the founding entrepreneur occurs during the high-growth stage, when he or she finds it is necessary to let go of power and control (through veto) over key decisions that he or she has always had, and when key responsibilities need to be delegated without abdicating ultimate leadership and responsibility for results. But the challenges do not end there. For example, sales of Litton's microwave oven division had reached $13 million, and it had 275 employees. The long-range plan called for building sales volume to $100 million in five to seven years (i.e., growing at 40 percent per year, compounded). The head of the division

said, "Having studied the market for the previous two years, I was convinced that the only limit on our growth was our organization's inability to grow as rapidly as the market opportunities."[6]

From the high-growth stage, a company then moves to what is called the *maturity stage*. In this stage, the key issue for the company is no longer survival; rather, it is one of steady, profitable growth. The *stability stage* usually follows.

Managing for Rapid Growth

Managing for rapid growth involves a management orientation not found in mature and stable environments. (This topic will be addressed again in Chapter 16.)

For one thing, the tenet that one's responsibility must equal one's authority is often very counterproductive in a rapid-growth venture. Instead, results usually require close collaboration of a manager with other people than his or her subordinates, and managers invariably have responsibilities far exceeding their authority. Politics and personal power can be a way of life in many larger and stagnant institutions, as managers jockey for influence and a piece of a shrinking pie in a zero-sum game; but in rapid-growth firms, power and control are delegated. Everyone is committed to making the pie larger, and power and influence are derived not only from achieving one's own goals but also from contributing to the achievements of others as well. Influence also is derived from keeping the overall goals in mind, from resolving differences, and from developing a reputation as a person who gets results, can manage others, and grows managerial talent as well.

Thus, among successful entrepreneurs and entrepreneurial managers, there is a well-developed capacity to exert influence *without* formal power. These people are adept at conflict resolution. They know when to use logic and when to persuade, when to make a concession and when to exact one. To run a successful venture, an entrepreneur learns to get along with many different constituencies, often with conflicting aims—the customer, the supplier, the financial backer, and the creditor, as well as the partners and others on the inside. Similarly, an entrepreneurial manager must operate in a world that is increasingly interdependent. Attempting to advise managers on how to exert "influence without authority," Allan R. Cohen and David L. Bradford assert that "if you are a manager, you not only need to exercise influence

---

[5] L. A. Griener, "Evolution and Revolution as Organizations Grow," in *Trials and Rewards of the Entrepreneur* (Boston: Harvard Business Review, 1977), pp. 47–56; and H. N. Woodward, "Management Strategies for Small Companies," in *Trials and Rewards of the Entrepreneur* (Boston: Harvard Business Review, 1981), pp. 57–66.

[6] William W. George, "Task Teams for Rapid Growth," *Harvard Business Review*, March–April 1977.

skills with your peers and your own boss, but also to help the people who work for you learn to be effective influencers—even of you—since that will free you to spend more of your time seeking new opportunities and working the organization above and around you."[7]

Whereas successful entrepreneurs are interpersonally supporting and nurturing—not interpersonally competitive—successful entrepreneurial managers understand their interdependencies and have learned to incorporate mutual respect, openness, trust, and mutual benefit into their management style. Fundamental to this progressive style of management is the awareness and practice of reciprocity for mutual gain.[8] When a strong need to control, influence, and gain power over others characterizes the lead entrepreneur or the entrepreneurial manager or when he or she has an insatiable appetite for putting an associate down, more often than not the venture gets into trouble. A dictatorial, adversarial, and dominating management style makes it very difficult to attract and keep people who thirst for achievement, responsibility, and results. Compliant partners and managers are often chosen. Destructive conflicts often erupt over who has the final say, who is right, and whose prerogatives are what.

In the corporate setting, the "hero-making" ability is identified as an essential attribute of successful entrepreneurial managers.[9] These hero makers try to make the pie bigger and better, rather than jealously clutching and hoarding a tiny pie that is all

theirs. They have a capacity for objective interpersonal relationships as well, which enables them to smooth out individual differences of opinion by keeping attention focused on the common goal to be achieved.[10]

Exhibit 7.4 characterizes probable crises that growing ventures will face, including erosion of creativity by founders and team; confusion or resentment, or both, over ambiguous roles, responsibilities, and goals; failure to be able to clone founders; specialization and eroding of collaboration; desire for autonomy and control; need for operating mechanisms and controls; and conflict and divorce among founders and members of team. It further delineates issues that confront entrepreneurial managers.

- *Compounding of time and change.* In the high-growth stage, change, amibiguity, and uncertainty seem to be the only things that remain constant. Change, which is constant, creates higher levels of uncertainty, ambiguity, and risk, which, in turn, compound to shrink time, an already precious commodity. One result of change is a series of shock waves rolling through a new and growing venture by way of new customers, new technologies, new competitors, new markets, and new people. In industries characterized by galloping technological change, with relatively minuscule lead and lag times in bringing new products to market and in weathering the storms of rapid obsolescence, the effects of change and time are extreme. For example, the

EXHIBIT 7.4

Entrepreneurial Transitions

Modes/Stages	Doing	Managing	Managing Managers
Sales	0 to $3 million	$3 to 10 million	$10 million or more
Employees	0 to 30	30 to 75	75 and up
Transitions	Characteristics: Founder-driven creativity Constant change, ambiguity and uncertainty Time compression Informal communications Counterintuitive decision making and structure Relative inexperience	Probable crises: Erosion of creativity of founders Confusion over ambiguous roles, responsibilities, and goals Desire for delegation versus autonomy and control	Probable crises: Failure to clone founders Specialization/eroding of collaboration versus practice of power, information, and influence Need for operating controls and mechanisms Conflict among founders

---

[7] Allan R. Cohen and David L. Bradford, *Influence Without Authority* (New York: John Wiley & Sons, 1990), p. 17.
[8] Ibid.
[9] David L. Bradford and Allan R. Cohen, *Managing for Excellence: The Guide to Developing High Performance in Contemporary Organizations* (New York: John Wiley & Sons, 1984).
[10] Neil C. Churchill, "Entrepreneurs and Their Enterprises: A Stage Model," in *Frontiers of Entrepreneurship Research: 1983*, ed J. A. Hornaday et al. (Babson Park, MA: Babson College, 1983), pp. 1–22.

president of a rapidly growing, small computer company said, "In our business it takes 6 to 12 months to develop a new computer, ready to bring to the market, and product technology obsolescence is running about 9 to 12 months." This time compression has been seen in such industries as electronics and aerospace in the 1960s; small computers, integrated circuits, and silicon chips in the 1970s; microcomputers in the 1980s; and telecommunications and biotechnology in the 1990s.

- *Nonlinear and nonparametric events.* Entrepreneurial management is characterized by nonlinear and nonparametric events. Just as the television did not come about by a succession of improvements in the radio, and the jet plane did not emerge from engineers and scientists attempting to develop a better and better piston engine plane, so too within firms events do not follow straight lines, progress arithmetically, or even appear related. Rather, they occur in bunches and in stepwise leaps. For example, a firm may double its sales force in 15 months, rather than over eight years, while another may triple its manufacturing capacity and adopt a new materials resource planning system immediately, rather than utilizing existing capacity by increasing overtime, then adding a third shift nine months later, and finally adding a new plant three years hence.

- *Relative inexperience.* In addition, the management team may be relatively inexperienced. The explosive birth and growth of these firms are usually unique events that cannot be replicated, and most of the pieces in the puzzle—the technology, applications, customers, the people, the firm itself—are usually new. Take Prime Computer as an example. Sales at this manufacturer of minicomputers grew rapidly in five years from $100 million per year to nearly $1.2 billion per year. The average age of all employees in the company was less than 29 years, and the firm was barely 10 years old.

- *Counterintuitive, unconventional decision making.* Yet another characteristic of rapidly growing ventures in the entrepreneurial domain is counterintuitive, unconventional patterns of decision making. For example, a computer firm needed to decide what approach to take in developing and introducing three new products in an uncertain, risky marketplace. Each proposed new product appeared to be aimed at the same end-user market, and the person heading each project was similarly enthusiastic, confident, and determined about succeeding. A traditional approach to such a problem would have been to determine the size and growth rates of each market segment; evaluate the probabilistic estimates of future revenue costs and capital requirements for their accuracy; compare the

discounted, present-value cash flow that will emerge from each project; and select the project with the highest yield versus the required internal rate of return. Such an analysis sometimes overlooks the fact that most rapid growth companies have many excellent alternatives and, more commonly, the newness of technology, the immaturity of the marketplace, and the rapid discovery of further applications make it virtually impossible to know which of any product proposals is best. The computer firm decided to support all three new products at once, and a significant new business was built around each one. New market niches were discovered simultaneously and the unconventional approach paid off.

- *Fluid structures and procedures.* Most rapid-growth ventures also defy conventional organizational patterns and structures. It is common to find a firm that has grown $25 million, $50 million, or even $150 million per year in sales and that still has no formal organizational chart. If an organizational chart does exist, it usually has three distinguishing features: First, it is inevitably out of date. Second, it changes frequently. For example, one firm had eight major reorganizations in its first five years as it grew to $5 million. Third, the organizational structure is usually flat (i.e., it has few management layers), and there is easy accessibility to the top decision makers. But the informality and fluidity of organization structures and procedures do not mean casualness or sloppiness when it comes to goals, standards, or clarity of direction and purpose. Rather, they translate into responsiveness and readiness to absorb and assimilate rapid changes while maintaining financial and operational cohesion.

- *Entrepreneurial culture.* There exists in growing new ventures a common value system, which is difficult to articulate, which is even more elusive to measure, and which is evident in behavior and attitudes. There is a belief in and commitment to growth, achievement, improvement, and success and a sense among members of the team that they are "in this thing together." Goals and the market determine priorities, rather than whose territory or whose prerogatives are being challenged. Managers appear unconcerned about status, power, and personal control. They are more concerned about making sure that tasks, goals, and roles are clear than whether the organizational chart is current or whether their office and rug reflect their current status. Likewise, they are more concerned about the evidence, competence, knowledge, and logic of arguments affecting a decision than the status given by a title or the formal position of the individual doing the arguing. Contrast this with a multibillion-dollar—but stagnant—firm in England. Reportedly, 29 different makes and models of automobiles are used in the firm to signify one's position.

This entrepreneurial climate, or culture, exists in larger firms also. Such a climate attracts and encourages the entrepreneurial achievers, and it helps perpetuate the intensity and pace so characteristic of high-growth firms. *Exhibit 7.5* shows how five companies studied by Rosabeth Moss Kanter range from most to least entrepreneurial. Continuing to study "intrapreneurship" throughout the 1980s, Kanter asserted that the global economy was experiencing the postentrepreneurial revolution, which "takes entrepreneurship a step further, applying entrepreneurial principles to the traditional corporation, creating a marriage between entrepreneurial creativity and corporate discipline, cooperation, and teamwork."[11] This revolution has not made managing any easier; in fact, Kanter suggests that "this constitutes the ultimate corporate balancing act. Cut back and grow. Trim down and build. Accomplish more, and do it in new areas, with fewer resources."[12] Clearly, some corporations will embrace these challenges with more success than others; the following section will shed some light on how "giants learn to dance."[13]

What Entrepreneurial Managers Need to Know

Much of business education traditionally has emphasized and prepared students for life in the administrative domain. There is nothing wrong with that, but education preparing students to start and manage vibrant, growing new ventures cannot afford to emphasize administrative efficiency, maintenance tasks, resource ownership, and institutional formalization. Rather, such a program needs to emphasize skills necessary for life in the entrepreneurial domain. For example, effective entrepreneurial managers need to be especially skillful at managing conflict, resolving differences, balancing multiple viewpoints and demands, and building teamwork and consensus. These skills are particularly difficult when working with others outside one's immediate formal chain of command.

In talking of larger firms, Kanter identifies power and persuasion skills, skill in managing problems accompanying team and employee participation, and skill in understanding how change is designed and constructed in an organization as necessary. Kanter notes:

In short, individuals do not have to be doing "big things" in order to have their cumulative accomplishments eventually result in big performance for the company... They are only rarely the inventors of the "breakthrough" system. They are only rarely doing something that is totally unique or that no one, in any organization, ever thought of before. Instead, they are often applying ideas that have proved themselves elsewhere, or they are rearranging parts to create a better result, or they are noting a potential problem before it turns into a catastrophe and mobilizing the actions to anticipate and solve it.[14]

A recent study of midsized-growth companies having sales between $25 million and $1 billion and a sales or profit growth of more than 15 percent annually over five years confirms the importance of many of these same fundamentals of entrepreneurial management.[15] For one thing, these companies practiced opportunity-driven management. According to the study, they achieved their first success with a unique product or distinctive way of doing business and often became leaders in market niches by delivering superior value to customers, rather than through low prices. They are highly committed to serving customers and pay very close attention to them. For another thing, these firms put great emphasis on financial control and managing every element of the business.

In a book that follows up on the implementation issues of how one gets middle managers to pursue and practice entrepreneurial excellence (first made famous in *In Search of Excellence* by Tom Peters and Bob Waterman), two authors note that some of the important fundamentals practiced by team-builder entrepreneurs—who are more intent on getting results than just getting their own way—also are emulated by effective middle managers.[16] Or as John Sculley, of Apple Computers, explained:

The heroic style—the lone cowboy on horseback—is not the figure we worship anymore at Apple. In the new corporation, heroes won't personify any single set of achievements. Instead, they personify the process. They might be thought of as gatekeepers, information carriers, and teams. Originally heroes at Apple were the hackers and engineers who created the products. Now, more teams are heroes.[17]

[11] Rosabeth Moss Kanter, *When Giants Learn to Dance* (New York: Simon & Schuster, 1989), pp. 9–10.
[12] Ibid., p. 31.
[13] Ibid.
[14] Rosabeth Moss Kanter, *The Change Masters* (New York: Simon & Schuster, 1983), pp. 354–55.
[15] The study was done by McKinsey & Company. See "How Growth Companies Succeed," reported in *Small Business Report*, July 1984, p. 9.
[16] David L. Bradford and Allan R. Cohen, *Managing for Excellence* (New York: John Wiley & Sons, 1984), pp. 3–4.
[17] John Sculley with John Byrne, *Odyssey: Pepsi to Apple . . . A Journey of Adventures, Ideas, and The Future.* New York: HarperCollins Publishers Inc., 1987, p. 321.

EXHIBIT 7.5

Characteristics of Five Companies, Ranging from Most to Least Entrepreneurial

	Companies Studied				
	CHIPCO	**RADCO**	**MEDCO**	**FINCO**	**UTICO**
Percent of effective managers with entrepreneurial accomplishments	71%	69%	67%	47%	33%
Economic trend	Steadily up	Trend up but now down	Upward trend	Mixed	Downward trend
Change issues	Change normal; constant change in product generation; proliferating staff and units.	Change normal in products, technologies; changeover to second management generation with new focus.	Reorganized 2–3 years ago to install matrix; normal product and technology changes.	Change a shock; new top management group from outside reorganizing and trying to add competitive market posture.	Change a shock; undergoing reorganization to install matrix and add competitive market posture and reducing staff.
Organization structure	Matrix	Matrix in some areas; product lines act as quasi divisions.	Matrix in some areas.	Divisional; unitary hierarchy within division; some central officers.	Functional organization; currently overlaying matrix of regions and markets.
Information flow	Decentralized	Mixed	Mixed	Centralized	Centralized
Communication emphasis	Free Horizontal	Free Horizontal	Moderately free Horizontal	Constricted Vertical	Constricted Vertical
Culture	Clear, consistent; favors individual initiative.	Clear, though in transition from invention emphasis to routinization and systems.	Clear; pride in company; belief that talent will be rewarded.	Idiosyncratic; depends on boss and area.	Clear but undergoing changes; favors security, maintenance, and protection.
Emotional climate	Pride in company, team feeling, some burnout.	Uncertainty regarding changes.	Pride in company; team feeling.	Low trust; high uncertainty.	High uncertainty, confusion.
Rewards	Abundant; visibility, chance to do more challenging work in the future, and get bigger budget projects.	Abundant; visibility, chance to do more challenging work in the future, and get bigger budget projects.	Moderately abundant; conventional.	Scarce; primarily monetary.	Scarce; promotion and salary freeze; recognition by peers grudging.

Source: Adapted from Rosabeth Moss Kanter, "Middle Managers as Innovators," *Harvard Business Review*, July–August 1982, p. 103.

Management Competencies

Entrepreneurs who build substantial companies that grow to over $10 million in sales and over 75 to 100 employees are good entrepreneurs *and* good managers. Typically, they will have developed a solid base and a wide breadth of management skills and know-how over a number of years working in different areas (e.g., sales, marketing, manufacturing, and finance). It would be unusual for any single entrepreneur to be outstanding in all areas. More likely, a single entrepreneur will have strengths in one area, such as strong people management, conceptual and creative problem-solving skills, and marketing know-how, as well as some significant weaknesses. While it is risky to generalize, often entrepreneurs whose background is technical are weak in marketing, finance, and general management. Entrepreneurs who do not have a technical background are, as you might expect, often weakest in the technical or engineering aspects, manufacturing, and finance.

What has been stressed throughout this book is the concept of fit. What's important is having a management team whose skills are complementary, not the possession by an individual of a single, absolute set of skills or a profile. The art and craft of entrepreneuring involves recognizing the skills and know-how needed to succeed in a venture, knowing what each team member does or does not know, and then compensating for shortcomings, either by getting key people on board to fill voids or by an individual's accumulating the additional "chunks" before he or she takes the plunge.

Skills in Building an Entrepreneurial Culture

Managers of entrepreneurial firms need to recognize and cope with innovation, taking risks, and responding quickly, as well as with absorbing major setbacks. The most effective managers seem to thrive on the hectic, and at times chaotic, pace and find it challenging and stimulating, rather than frustrating or overwhelming. They use a consensus approach to build a motivated and committed team, they balance conflicting demands and priorities, and they manage conflicts especially adroitly.

These managers thus need interpersonal/teamwork skills that involve (1) the ability to create, through management, a climate and spirit conducive to high performance, including pressing for performance while rewarding work well done and encouraging innovation, initiative, and calculated risk taking; (2) the ability to understand the relationships among tasks and between the leader and followers; and (3) the ability to lead in those situations where it is appropriate, including a willingness to manage actively, supervise and control activities of others through directions, suggestions, and the like.

These interpersonal skills can be called entrepreneurial influence skills, since they have a great deal to do with the way these managers exact influence over others:

- *Leadership/vision/influence.* These managers are skillful in creating clarity out of confusion, ambiguity, and uncertainty. These entrepreneurial managers are able to define adroitly and gain agreement on who has what responsibility and authority. Further, they do this in a way that builds motivation and commitment to cross-departmental and corporate goals, not just parochial interests. But this is not perceived by other managers as an effort to jealously carve out and guard personal turf and prerogatives. Rather, it is seen as a genuine effort to clarify roles, tasks, and responsibilities, and to make sure there is accountability and appropriate approvals. This does not work unless the manager

is seen as willing to relinquish his or her priorities and power in the interest of an overall goal. It also requires skill in making sure the appropriate people are included in setting cross-functional or cross-departmental goals and in making decisions. When things do not go as smoothly as was hoped, the most effective managers work them through to an agreement. Managers who are accustomed to traditional line/staff or functional chains of command are often baffled and frustrated in their new role. While some may be quite effective in dealing with their own subordinates, it is an entirely new task to manage and work with peers, the subordinates of others, and even superiors outside one's chain of command.

- *Helping/coaching and conflict management.* The most effective managers are very creative and skillful in handling conflicts, generating consensus decisions, and sharing their power and information. They are able to get people to open up, instead of clamming up; they get problems out on the table, instead of under the rug; and they do not become defensive when others disagree with their views. They seem to know that high-quality decisions require a rapid flow of information in all directions and that knowledge, competence, logic, and evidence need to prevail over official status or formal rank in the organization. The way they manage and resolve conflicts is intriguing. For one thing, they are able to get potential adversaries to be creative and to collaborate by seeking a reconciliation of viewpoints. Rather than emphasizing differences and playing the role of hard-nose negotiator or devil's advocate to force their own solution, they blend ideas. They are more willing to risk personal vulnerability in this process—often by giving up their own power and resources—than are less-effective managers. The trade-offs are not easy: At the outset, such an approach involves more managers, takes more time, often appears to yield few immediate results, and seems like a more painful way to manage. Later on, however, the gains from the motivation, commitment, and teamwork anchored in consensus are striking. For one thing, there is swiftness and decisiveness in actions and follow through, since the negotiating, compromising, and accepting of priorities is history. For another, new disagreements that emerge do not generally bring progress to a halt, since there is both high clarity and broad acceptance of the overall goals and underlying priorities. Without this consensus, each new problem or disagreement often necessitates a time-consuming and painful confrontation and renegotiation simply because it was not done initially. Apparently, the Japanese understand this quite well.

- *Teamwork and people management.* Another form of entrepreneurial influence has to do with encouraging creativity and innovation, and with taking calculated risks. Simply stated, entrepreneurial managers build confidence by encouraging innovation and calculated risk taking, rather than by punishing or criticizing whatever is less than perfect. They breed independent, entrepreneurial thinking by expecting and encouraging others to find and correct their own errors and to solve their own problems. This does not mean they follow a throw-them-to-the-wolves approach. Rather, they are perceived by their peers and other managers as accessible and willing to help when needed, and they provide the necessary resources to enable others to do the job. When it is appropriate, they go to bat for their peers and subordinates, even when they know they cannot always win. An ability to make heroes out of other team members and contributors and to make sure others are in the limelight, rather than accept these things oneself, is another critical skill.

The capacity to generate trust—the glue that binds an organization or relationship together—is critical. The most effective managers are perceived as trustworthy; they behave in ways that create trust. How do they do this? For one thing, they are straightforward: They do what they say they are going to do. They are not the corporate rumor carriers. They are open and spontaneous, rather than guarded and cautious with each word. And they are perceived as being honest and direct. Also, it is easy to envision the kind of track record and reputation these entrepreneurial managers build for themselves. They have a reputation of getting results, because they understand that the task of managing in a rapid-growth company usually goes well beyond one's immediate chain of command. They become known as the creative problem solvers who have a knack for blending and balancing multiple views and demands. Their calculated risk taking works out more often than it fails. And they have a reputation for developing human capital (i.e., they groom other effective growth managers by their example and their mentoring).

Other Management Competencies

Entrepreneurial managers need a sound foundation in what are considered traditional management skills. Interestingly, in the study of practicing entrepreneurs mentioned earlier, no one assigned much importance to capital asset-pricing models, beta coefficients, lin-ear programming, and so forth, the prevailing and highly touted "new management techniques."[18]

The list below is divided into two cross-functional areas (administration and law and taxation) and four key functional areas (marketing, finance, production and operations, and microcomputers). Technical skills unique to each venture are also necessary.

- **Administration**
  - *Problem solving.* Ability to anticipate potential problems; ability to gather facts about problems, analyze them for *real* causes, and plan effective action to solve them; and ability to be very thorough in dealing with details of particular problems and to follow through.
  - *Communications.* Ability to communicate effectively and clearly—orally and in writing—to media, public, customers, peers, and subordinates.
  - *Planning.* Ability to set realistic and attainable goals, identify obstacles to achieving the goals, and develop detailed action plans to achieve those goals, and the ability to schedule personal time very systematically.
  - *Decision making.* Ability to make decisions on the best analysis of incomplete data, when the decisions need to be made.
  - *Project management.* Skills in organizing project teams, setting project goals, defining project tasks, and monitoring task completion in the face of problems and cost/quality constraints.
  - *Negotiating.* Ability to work effectively in negotiations, and the ability to balance quickly value given and value received. Recognizing one-time versus ongoing relationships.
  - *Managing outside professionals.* Ability to identify, manage, and guide appropriate legal, financial, banking, accounting, consulting, and other necessary outside advisors.
  - *Personnel administration.* Ability to set up payroll, hiring, compensation, and training functions.

- **Law and taxes:**
  - *Corporate and securities law.* Familiarity with the uniform commercial code, including forms of organization and the rights and obligations of officers, shareholders, and

---

[18] Timmons and Stevenson, "Entrepreneurship Education in the 80s: What Entrepreneurs Say," pp. 115–34.

directors; and familiarity with Security and Exchange Commission, state, and other regulations concerning the securities of your firm, both registered and unregistered, and the advantages and disadvantages of different instruments.

—*Contract law.* Familiarity with contract procedures and requirements of government and commercial contracts, licenses, leases, and other agreements, particularly employment agreements and agreements governing the vesting rights of shareholders and founders.

—*Law relating to patent and proprietary rights.* Skills in preparation and revision of patent applications and the ability to recognize a strong patent, trademark, copyright, and privileged information claims, including familiarity with claim requirements, such as to intellectual property.

—*Tax law.* Familiarity with state and federal reporting requirements, including specific requirements of a particular form of organization, of profit and other pension plans, and the like.

—*Real estate law.* Familiarity with leases, purchase offers, purchase and sale agreements, and so on, necessary for the rental or purchase and sale of property.

—*Bankruptcy law.* Knowledge of bankruptcy law, options, and the forgivable and nonforgivable liabilities of founders, officers and directors.

▪ *Marketing:*

—*Market research and evaluation.* Ability to analyze and interpret market research study results, including knowing how to design and conduct studies and to find and interpret industry and competitor information, and a familiarity with questionnaire design and sampling techniques. One successful entrepreneur stated that what is vital "is knowing where the competitive threats are and where the opportunities are and an ability to see the customers' needs."

—*Marketing planning.* Planning skills in planning overall sales, advertising, and promotion programs and in deciding on effective distributor or sales representative systems and setting them up.

—*Product pricing.* Ability to determine competitive pricing and margin structures and to position products in terms of price

and ability to develop pricing policies that maximize profits.

—*Sales management.* Ability to organize, supervise, and motivate a direct sales force, and the ability to analyze territory and account sales potential and to manage a sales force to obtain maximum share of market.

—*Direct selling.* Skills in identifying, meeting, and developing new customers and in closing sales. Without orders for a product or service, a company does not really have a business.

—*Service management.* Ability to perceive service needs of particular products and to determine service and spare-part requirements, handle customer complaints, and create and manage an effective service organization.

—*Distribution management.* Ability to organize and manage the flow of product from manufacturing through distribution channels to ultimate customer, including familiarity with shipping costs, scheduling techniques, and so on.

—*Product management.* Ability to integrate market information, perceived needs, research and development, and advertising into a rational product plan, and the ability to understand market penetration and breakeven.

—*New-product planning.* Skills in introducing new products, including marketing testing, prototype testing, and development of price/sales/merchandising and distribution plans for new products.

▪ *Operations/production:*

—*Manufacturing management.* Knowledge of the production process, machines, manpower, and space required to produce a product and the skill in managing production to produce products within time, cost, and quality constraints.

—*Inventory control.* Familiarity with techniques of controlling in-process and finished goods inventories of materials.

—*Cost analysis and control.* Ability to calculate labor and materials costs, develop standard cost systems, conduct variance analyses, calculate overtime labor needs, and manage/control costs.

—*Quality control.* Ability to set up inspection systems and standards for effective control of quality of incoming, in-process, and finished materials. Benchmarking continuous improvement.

—*Production scheduling and flow.* Ability to analyze work flow and to plan and manage production processes, the ability to manage work flow, and the ability to calculate schedules and flows for rising sales levels.

—*Purchasing.* Ability to identify appropriate sources of supply, to negotiate supplier contracts, and to manage the incoming flow of material into inventory, and familiarity with order quantities and discount advantages.

—*Job evaluation.* Ability to analyze worker productivity and needs for additional help, and the ability to calculate cost-saving aspects of temporary versus permanent help.

- **Finance:**

—*Raising capital.* Ability to decide how best to acquire funds for startup and growth; ability to forecast funds needs and to prepare budgets; and familiarity with sources and vehicles of short- and long-term financing, formal and informal.

—*Managing cash flow.* Ability to project cash requirements, set up cash controls, and manage the firm's cash position, and the ability in identifying how much capital is needed, when and where you will run out of cash, and breakeven.

—*Credit and collection management.* Ability to develop credit policies and screening criteria, and to age receivables and payables, and an understanding of the use of collection agencies and when to start legal action.

—*Short-term financing alternatives.* Understanding of payables management and the use of interim financing, such as bank loans, factoring of receivables, pledging and selling notes and contracts, bills of lading, and bank acceptance; and familiarity with financial statements and budgeting/profit planning.

—*Public and private offerings.* Ability to develop a business plan and an offering memo that can be used to raise capital, a familiarity with the legal requirements of public and private stock offerings, and the ability to manage shareholder relations and to negotiate with financial sources.

—*Bookkeeping, accounting, and control.* Ability to determine appropriate bookkeeping and accounting systems as the company starts and grows, including various ledgers and accounts and possible insurance needs.

—*Other specific skills.* Ability to read and prepare an income statement and balance sheet, and the ability to do cash flow analysis and planning, including break-even analysis, contribution analysis, profit and loss analysis, and balance sheet management.

- **Microcomputers:**

—*Spreadsheet analysis.* Ability to perform spreadsheet analysis using the microcomputer, including databases.

—*Other.* Knowledge of word processing, electronic mail, and so forth, is extremely helpful.

- **Technical skills:**

—*These are unique to each venture.*

As has been said before, not all entrepreneurs will find they are greatly skilled in the areas listed above, and if they are not, they will most likely need to acquire these skills, either through apprenticeship, through partners, or through the use of advisors. However, it is useful to assume that while many outstanding advisors, such as lawyers and accountants, are of enormous benefit to entrepreneurs, these people are not always businesspeople and they often cannot make the best business judgments for those they are advising. For example, in the case of lawyers, their judgments, in many cases, are so contaminated by a desire to provide perfect or fail-safe protection that they are totally risk averse.

Chapter Summary

1. The growing enterprise requires that the founder and his team develop competencies as entrepreneurial leaders and managers.

2. Founders who succeed in growing their firms beyond $10 million in sales learn to adapt and grow quickly themselves as managers and leaders, or they do not survive.

3. Founders of rapidly growing firms defy the conventional wisdom that entrepreneurs cannot manage growing beyond the startup.

4. Ventures go through stages of growth from startup, through rapid growth, to maturity, to decline and renewal.

5. The largest single factor that increases the complexity and difficulty of managing a young company is its rate of growth in orders and revenue.

6. The faster the rate of growth, the more difficult and challenging are the management issues, and the more flexible, adaptive, quick learning must be the organization.

7. Entrepreneurs create and invent new and unique approaches to organizing and managing work.

8. As ventures grow the core management competencies need to be covered by the team.

Study Questions

1. What is the difference between an entrepreneurial manager and an administrator?
2. What do founders do in order to grow their ventures beyond $10 million in sales?
3. Define the stages that most companies experience as they grow, and explain the management issues and requirements anticipated at each stage.
4. What drives the extent of complexity and difficulty of management issues in a growing company?
5. List the main management competencies that need to be addressed as a company grows to exceed $10 million in revenue.
6. Can you compare and describe the principal differences in the leadership, management, and organization between the best growing companies of which you are aware, and large, established companies? Why are there differences?
7. What would be our strategy for changing and creating an entrepreneurial culture in a large, nonentrepreneurial firm? Is it possible? Why, or why not?

MIND STRETCHERS

Have You Considered?

1. It is often said, "You cannot hire an entrepreneur." What are the implications for large companies today?
2. How would you characterize the attitudes, behaviors, and mind-sets of the most effective leaders and managers you have worked for? The worst? What accounts for the difference?
3. Read recent issues of *Fast Company* magazine: What is happening in corporate America?
4. What should the president and the congress do to encourage and accelerate entrepreneurship in America?

Case

Fenchel Lamp Shade Company*

Preparation Questions

1. Does it make sense for Steve and Michele to buy Fenchel?
2. How do you assess the proposed financing plan from both a short-term and a long-term perspective?
3. Would you lend the money required under the terms proposed?
4. What will Fenchel look like in one year? Two years? Five years?

For Steve and Michele Rogers the events of mid-1988 were proceeding at a breakneck pace. They had finally convinced the owners of the Fenchel Lamp Shade Company to sell their business, a process that had lasted well over a year and that had fallen apart more than once. Yet, there were many hurdles to be passed before they could realize their dream of owning their own business. Chief among these was raising the capital required to make the deal work.

While it was exhilarating to think that they would be able to buy Fenchel, Steve and Michele were also painfully aware of the risks. Steve would have to resign from his consulting job at Bain & Company, in Boston, and Michele would have to leave her job in the admissions office at Harvard Business School. They and their two small children would have to move from Boston to Chicago, where Michele would find a new full-time job and Steve would take over responsibility for managing Fenchel. They had no illusions about what it would mean to own and run a small company, one that would be highly leveraged after the deal. On the other hand, that is what they had always wanted to do, and now, it seemed, it would finally be possible.

Background

The search for a business to own had begun for Steve and Michele Rogers while Steve was still in his first year in the MBA program at Harvard Business School (HBS). After careful study, he had decided that he should try to buy a McDonald's franchise. McDonald's was actively seeking African American owners for the Boston area and Steve felt he could find an attractive opportunity with McDonald's help. At the beginning of his second year at HBS, he enrolled in a mandatory McDonald's training program for people interested in owning a franchise. While his classmates ate at the Charles Hotel or

*This case was prepared by William A. Sahlam. Copyright © 1991 by the President and Fellows of Harvard College. Harvard Business School case 291-014 (revised 10-17-91).

flew to New York for meals at Cote Basque, Steve spent 20 hours a week training at a McDonald's store in Lynn, Massachusetts. He did everything from cooking hamburgers to cleaning the lavatories.

After graduating from HBS in June 1985, Steve took a job as a research associate for the Production and Operations Management course at Harvard Business School. Michele, who was pregnant with their second child, was entering her second year at HBS. Steve continued his duties at the McDonald's restaurant. The work was hard and not very glamorous but Steve was committed to the program. Owning a McDonald's franchise and ultimately owning a number of stores would be a lucrative and demanding outcome. In the spring of 1986, Steve began serious negotiations with McDonald's about which store he might be able to buy and the terms. Each McDonald's franchise was priced according to its potential sales volume.

McDonald's suggested that Steve buy a franchise in downtown Boston. After considerable investigation, however, Steve became concerned that the opportunity was not very attractive. The price was too high—on the order of $650,000 for a store with sales of approximately $1 million—given what Steve perceived to be the prospects of the location. McDonald's asking price was based on what Steve thought to be unrealistically optimistic assumptions about what the store could do in the future. After exploring several other store possibilities, and after sometimes heated discussions with McDonald's, Steve finally decided to abandon his two years of training and the related plan to buy a McDonald's franchise.

In the summer of 1986, Steve decided to join Bain & Company, a major international consulting company with headquarters in Boston. After graduation from the MBA program, Michele stayed on at Harvard Business School in the admissions area. Though both were making a lot of money and enjoyed their work, they still wanted to own their own business.

A number of Steve's consulting assignments with Bain took him to the Midwest, where he and Michele had grown up. Steve started the process of trying to find a company to buy in that area. He contacted a number of business brokers, commercial bankers, accountants, and law firms in Chicago, and also began to subscribe to the Chicago papers. Over time he began to receive proposals from his contacts. On his frequent visits to the area, he would meet with representatives of the sellers or visit the company. In total, he saw some 25 companies in early 1987. Discouragingly, none was particularly attractive.

The Fenchel Lamp Shade Company

In May 1987, Steve was contacted by a business broker about the possibility that a lamp shade manufacturing company might be for sale. He had already seen one lamp shade company, which he had rejected because it focused on the highly competitive low end of the market, had terrible management, and was egregiously overpriced. But Fenchel sounded different. They were a manufacturer of premium lamp shades with total sales volume of about $1 million.

Steve flew to Chicago to meet the broker representing the owners and was favorably impressed by what he heard. The company was managed by 65-year-old Kenneth Fenchel, whose father and uncle had founded the company in 1926. The company was owned by Kenneth and his uncle and aunt, who had assumed control when Kenneth's father passed away. Kenneth's uncle was 88 years old and was effectively retired from the business. The company was profitable and had provided the owners with an attractive income stream for many years.

It was also apparent to Steve that the business had not been very aggressively managed. Sales growth had been modest, and Steve was convinced that he could improve the operations of the company.

While Steve's original meeting with the broker representing the Fenchel family was positive, it soon became clear that the Fenchel family was not totally committed to selling the business. Each year they owned Fenchel Lamp Shades, income was very high. Aside from a desire to retire and concerns about health, there was no real pressure to sell.

Also, the Fenchels had placed an $800,000 total value on the company and had insisted that all of the money be paid up front. They were unwilling to consider any kind of seller financing. For Steve and Michele Rogers, this was an unacceptable demand, given the inevitable uncertainties associated with taking over any business. Without seller financing, also, it might be much more difficult to arrange other elements of the financing plan.

Steve's hope of working out a mutually acceptable deal was dashed on December 7, 1987, when Ken Fenchel called to say that he had decided not to sell, and that he intended to take the company off the market. This call came exactly one week after Steve, Ken, and their respective lawyers and accountants had met for over nine hours to finalize the terms of a letter of intent.

While disappointed, Steve and Michele were more committed than ever to buying a company. Moreover, they had decided that Fenchel was perfect for their plans. The company was profitable, generated attractive cash flows, and was affordable. Their conversations with the business broker representing the Fenchels had suggested that there might be another opportunity to buy the company if they were patient. As a result, Steve and Michele suspended their active search for another company.

At the same time, they decided to move to Chicago regardless of the outcome at Fenchel. Steve believed that he would be able to continue his work as a consultant for Bain, which was considering opening a Chicago office, and Michele had arranged to work for James Lowry & Co., a Chicago-based consulting company. They planned to move in mid-summer of 1988.

Back on Track

In April, Steve received a call from the broker representing the Fenchels, who said that it made sense to talk. Ken Fenchel was considering selling the company again. However, a preliminary meeting in May revealed that Ken's uncle was still adamantly opposed to seller financing.

Steve proceeded to line up various potential sources of capital on the assumption that he could work out a reasonable solution to the impasse with the Fenchel family. Steve was convinced that he could get the Fenchel family to take a $75,000 note back for part of the agreed-upon $745,000 purchase price. He and Michele were prepared to invest $50,000 of their own money as a starting point. With respect to the other capital, there were a number of options.

First, Fenchel had certain assets that could be pledged as collateral. Steve intended to apply for a Small Business Administration loan. Under this program, banks agreed to lend money to small businesses, and up to 85 percent of the principal amount of the loan was guaranteed by the U.S. government. Thus, at least some of the risk was passed off on the government, which resulted in significantly lower interest costs.

Steve hoped to gain access to other debt financing by going to certain state and local programs that had been set up to make investments in local businesses. The City of Chicago had such a program from which Steve hoped to raise $100,000. An additional $50,000 would hopefully come from a State of Illinois loan program.

With respect to the remaining capital required, Steve knew that he would have to gain access to some equity-like financing. There were no other assets to pledge, and every lender would insist on some equity base before loaning the money.

One possibility was to go to a MESBIC (Minority Enterprise Small Business Investment Corporation). The MESBIC program was established by the Small Business Administration in 1969 for the purpose of providing long-term financing and management assistance to new ventures started by minorities. MESBICs were private companies that raised equity from individuals or institutions (often commercial banks) and were able to leverage their equity through government guarantees of loans. Under existing regulations, MESBICs could borrow up to four times their equity capital using government guarantees.

The next step was to turn possibilities into realities. The loan request documentation and related business plan prepared by Steve and Michele Rogers is included as Appendix A.

Remaining Issues

Steve and Michele had debated for hours about how much they should pay for Fenchel, how they should get access to the required capital, and what they should do if they were able to buy the company. Now it seemed that they were finally close. That was very exciting, but it was also slightly frightening. As Steve had discovered more than once during his search for a company to buy, being a Harvard MBA was not an automatic ticket to success. In his more cynical moments, he asked himself what he thought a snot-nosed 31-year-old Harvard MBA knew about running a business. On the other hand, he was ready to find out.

Section I: Loan Request Summary

- Loan type: SBA loan.
- Amount: $300,000.
- Borrower: Steven and Michele Rogers.
- Purpose of loan: To purchase Fenchel Lamp Shade Company.
- Total cost of project: $745,000—does not include working capital.
- Other potential funding sources:
  —The Chicago Capital Fund.
  —The Neighborhood Fund.
  —State of Illinois.
- Collateral: Assets of Fenchel Lamp Shade Company and personal guarantees of company's new owners, Steven and Michele Rogers.

APPENDIX A

Fenchel Lamp Shade Company
Loan Request

Section II: Business Plan Summary

Steven and Michele Rogers are attempting to buy Fenchel Lamp Shade Company. Michele will serve as a consultant to the company while Steve works as a full-time owner/operator.

Fenchel is recognized as a leading manufacturer of premium-quality lamp shades in the Midwest. The company has annual sales in excess of $1 million with annual cash flow margins of 15–30 percent. The company is over 61 years old and is owned by Kenneth Fenchel, age 65, and his 88-year-old uncle and 73-year-old aunt. They are selling the business in order to retire.

In 1986, the lamp shade industry had total sales of $70 million, a figure that has been growing at a rate of 5 percent since 1972. There are four identifiable segments in the industry. Fenchel operates in the premium-quality segment (approximately $20 million in 1986 volume) and sells to lamp specialty shops and upscale department stores.

Fenchel sells hard-back and fabric lamp shades. All of the lamp shades are hand made and have wholesale prices of $5 to $35. The company has 65 accounts. Marshall Field's is the company's largest customer, accounting for 10 percent of sales in 1986.

While there are 34 lamp shade manufacturers in the country, competition in the industry is generally restricted to geographical regions due to the extremely high cost of transportation. Most manufacturers are in New York or New Jersey.

The acquirers are both graduates of the Harvard Business School. Steven was born and raised on Chicago's south side where he attended Lewis Champlin grammar school and Englewood high school. He has work experience as a manager, business analyst, and consultant. As the supervisor of customer services with Cummins, he managed eight unionized employees. He also has negotiating and financial analysis experience as a result of working as a purchasing agent with Consolidated Diesel Company and as a business analyst with UNC Venture Capital Company. Finally, his work with Bain as a general management consultant has enhanced his ability to solve business problems through the use of analytical tools and has trained him to be an effective task force leader.

Michele has a strong work history in personnel administration. She has worked for Cummins Engine Company in personnel administration and labor relations, Harvard University in development, and Harvard Business School in admissions. Michele will be employed full-time with James Lowry and Associates, a Chicago-based consulting firm, but will be available for consultation at Fenchel.

John Smith, who has been with Fenchel for 15 years, will continue his position as the supervisor of production. Gerri Wandall, who has been the office manager for the past five years, will also continue in her present position. The diversified labor force at Fenchel will remain after the acquisition. Of the 18 employees, 15 are female, 13 are Black, 2 Hispanic, 2 White, and 1 Asian. Their length of employment with Fenchel ranges from 1 to 21 years.

This combination of characteristics—a loyal and diversified customer base, an experienced and dedicated labor force, and strong cash flow that can meet debt service requirements—makes Fenchel an ideal acquisition candidate.

Section III: Business Plan

The Company

Fenchel Lamp Shade Company is a manufacturer of premium-quality rayon, acetate, and hard-back-covered lamp shades for the replacement market. In addition to diverse materials, Fenchel lamp shades vary by style, shape, and color. All of the lamp shades are made in response to customer orders, with delivery commitments ranging from 4 to 6 weeks.

Fenchel's customers include department stores, independent lamp and shade retail stores, lighting showrooms, and a few (about 2 percent) lamp manufacturers. Of the company's sales, 80 percent are made to customers in the Midwest.

The name *Fenchel* is well regarded in the industry because of the company's strong reputation for high-quality products. To take advantage of Fenchel's strong customer name recognition, customers such as Gatelys and Marshall Field's regularly use the name in their advertisements.

In 1926 Herbert Fenchel (born in 1900) incorporated the company in Chicago. The corporation became a partnership in 1947 when Herbert's wife, Lois Fenchel (born in 1915), joined the company. That same year, Herbert's nephew, I. Kenneth Fenchel (born in 1923), began working for the company as a salesman. In 1957 Kenneth became an equal partner with Herbert and Lois.

For the past five years Kenneth has operated the company alone; Herbert and Lois have been silent partners. For health reasons Herbert and Lois live in Florida six months each year.

The Industry

The domestic lamp shade industry has total annual volume of approximately $70 million spread over 34 manufacturers. The manufacturers are located in seven states; over half of them are in the New York/New Jersey area. The typical manufacturer is a family-owned business with over 25 years of experience in the industry. Since 1972 the industry's compounded annual growth rate has been 5 percent (*Exhibit A*).

The lamp shade industry is seasonal. The slow season is summer, when people usually spend most of their time outdoors and are not making internal home improvements. Less than 15 percent of all sales will be made

EXHIBIT A

Historical Lamp Shade Sales

Year	Lamp Shade Sales*
1972	$36,900,000
1973	42,800,000
1974	43,300,000
1975	41,500,000
1976	37,800,000
1977	51,400,000
1978	55,400,000
1979	58,900,000
1980	53,400,000
1981	59,100,000
1982	41,800,000
1983	45,300,000
1984	65,400,000
1985	70,100,000

*Does not include metal, plastic, or glass lamp shades.
Source: Census Bureau Annual Survey of Manufacturing Value of Product Shipments.

during the months of June, July, and August. The best sales period occurs through the remaining nine months when people typically spend more time inside. The strongest months for sales are before holidays such as Thanksgiving, Christmas, and Easter.

There are four categories of lamp shade manufacturing: lamp manufacturing companies (e.g., Alsy and Stiffel) with internal lamp shade production, independent lamp shade manufacturers that sell primarily to lamp manufacturers, low- to medium-quality lamp shade manufacturers (e.g., Lamp Shade, Inc.) with discount stores as their primary customers, and premium-quality lamp shade manufacturers that sell to lamp specialty shops and upscale department stores. The latter category, which includes Fenchel, is a market of approximately $20 million.

Product Description

Fenchel's products serve the premium-quality segment of the market. Every lamp shade is completely handmade, with all stages of production carefully supervised and inspected. All fabrics are sewn to the frames, not glued. All frames are rust resistant. The trims and folds are bonded to the shade to ensure hand washability. In addition, the lamp shades are wrinkle resistant, glare free, and shadow free. In fact, Fenchel advertises itself as the industry leader of shadow-free lamp shades. All of these characteristics in one lamp shade are very rare, thereby giving Fenchel a reputation for high quality and workmanship. Only two other manufacturers, Silk-o-Lite and Diane, in the New York/New Jersey area, produce lamp shades of similar quality.

Fenchel's lamp shades can be divided into two categories, fabric and hard back. Fabric lamp shades are manufactured using various fabrics on the exterior with satin internal backings. Fenchel sells fabric lamp shades in six different styles, 16 shapes, six materials, four colors, and seven trims. These lamp shades have historically accounted for 63 percent to 74 percent of the company's sales and 64 percent to 76 percent of the company's profits.

Hard-back shades have various fabrics on the exterior and laminated or vinyl internal backings. Fenchel's hard-back lamp shades are distinctive because, unlike competitive products, they are made with more material, which leads to better-defined pleats. In addition, Fenchel's products are made with thicker vinyl or laminated backing and heavier frames than competitive products. The end result is a more durable and beautiful lamp shade. The company's hard-back lamp shades are sold in two different styles and five shapes. These lamp shades have historically accounted for 26 percent to 37 percent of the company's sales and 24 percent to 36 percent of profits.

The wholesale price range of Fenchel lamp shades is $5 to $35. The average selling price is $15. These shades will ultimately be sold by a retailer at prices from $20 to $65.

Fenchel's average wholesale price of $15 compares to $6 for a lamp shade from a low- to medium-quality manufacturer such as Lamp Shades, Inc., which sells primarily to discount department stores.

In addition to producing a standard line of lamp shades highlighted in its catalog (*Exhibit B*), Fenchel accepts custom work. The company will manufacture lamp shades to a customer's specifications or even design an exclusive line for a customer (e.g., Marshall Field's).

Customers

As a manufacturer of premium-quality lamp shades, Fenchel has a stable and loyal customer base. Over 60 percent of their annual sales are to upscale department stores such as Marshall Field's, headquartered in Chicago; the May Company, headquartered in St. Louis; and Lazarus, headquartered in Indianapolis. The only lamp shades sold by these stores are Fenchel's. (In fact, the Marshall Field's State Street store in Chicago has an area on the fourth floor, approximately 12 feet by 12 feet, dedicated entirely to Fenchel lamp shades). The balance of sales are to independent retail stores, lighting showrooms, and lamp manufacturers.

Fifty of Fenchel's 65 customer accounts are located in the Midwest. Some 45 customers account for 80 percent of total sales. The largest customer is Marshall Field's, which operates 25 stores in metropolitan Chicago, Texas, and Wisconsin and accounts for 10 percent of total sales.

Typical orders are $10,000 to $25,000 from department stores and $400 to $2,000 from independent retail stores.

EXHIBIT B

Description of Fenchel Lamp Shades

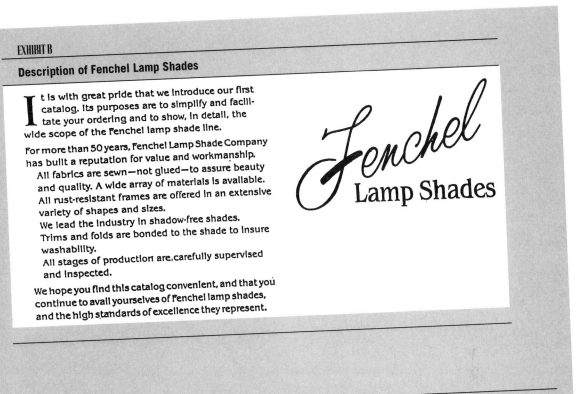

It is with great pride that we introduce our first catalog. Its purposes are to simplify and facilitate your ordering and to show, in detail, the wide scope of the Fenchel lamp shade line.

For more than 50 years, Fenchel Lamp Shade Company has built a reputation for value and workmanship.
All fabrics are sewn—not glued—to assure beauty and quality. A wide array of materials is available.
All rust-resistant frames are offered in an extensive variety of shapes and sizes.
We lead the industry in shadow-free shades.
Trims and folds are bonded to the shade to insure washability.
All stages of production are carefully supervised and inspected.

We hope you find this catalog convenient, and that you continue to avail yourselves of Fenchel lamp shades, and the high standards of excellence they represent.

EXHIBIT C

American Lamp Shade Manufacturers

Lamp Shade Manufacturer	Location	Lamp Shade Manufacturer	Location
1. ABC Lampshade Company.	New York	18. Penn Shade Crafters.	Pennsylvania
2. Artemis Studios.	New York	19. Queen Anne Lampshades.	New Jersey
3. Diane Studios.	New York	20. RLR Industries.	New York
4. Edwards Lamp and Shade Company.	California	21. Robinson Lamp Parts.	New York
5. Else Lamp and Shade Studio.	New York	22. Roseart Lampshades.	New York
6. Elite Lamp Shade Manufacturing.	California	23. Saxe lampshade.	Pennsylvania
7. Gold-Ray Shades.	New Jersey	24. Silk-O-Lite.	New Jersey
8. H. Grabell and Sons.	New Jersey	25. Springel Sales.	Pennsylvania
9. Grabell Industries.	California	26. Standard Shade.	New York
10. Hamilton Corporation.	Illinois	27. Stiffel.	New York
11. Hirks Lane Lamp Parts.	Pennsylvania	28. William B. Venit.	Illinois
12. Lake Shore Studios.	Mississippi	29. Versaponents.	New York
13. Lamp Shades, Inc.	Illinois	30. Frederick Cooper.	Illinois
14. Loumel Corporation.	New Jersey	31. Foss.	California
15. MSWV, Inc.	Illinois	32. Style Craft.	New York
16. Natalie Lamp and Shade Company.	New Jersey	33. Rod International.	Florida
17. Paladin Lampshade.	Pennsylvania	34. Fenchel.	Illinois

Source: Lamp and Shade Institute of America.

Unlike customers for low- to medium-quality lamp shades, Fenchel's customers do not base their purchase decisions on price alone. These customers view product quality and delivery to be just as important as price. Thus, Fenchel's reputation for impeccable quality and service for over 50 years has resulted in a very loyal customer base. For example, Marshall Field's has been a Fenchel customer for 20 years.

Competition

Although there are 34 American lamp shade manufacturers (*Exhibit C*), competition in the industry is regional due to extremely high transportation costs. Lamp shades are bulky but light in weight, which creates strong regional barriers to entry. Those premium-quality lamp shade manufacturers located in the New York/New Jersey area find it cost prohibitive to enter the Midwest region.

The five other lamp shade manufacturers in the Midwest are not competitors of Fenchel because their product focus is the low/medium market.

Silk-o-Lite, a 60-year-old New Jersey firm with sales in excess of $2 million, is Fenchel's closest competitor.

Fenchel's strong reputation for quality and service, combined with prohibitive shipping costs, makes it very difficult for a competitor outside of the Midwest to take away any of Fenchel's market without engaging in predatory pricing.

Marketing and Sales Plan

Fenchel had a 1.3 percent compound annual growth rate in sales from 1983 to 1986. This minuscule rate of growth reflected Kenneth Fenchel's choice not to ag-gressively market the company's products. He did not want sales to grow because it would require more of his time, which he did not want to give at this stage of his life. The business cash flow of approximately $140,000 annually was more than enough to satisfy him, his uncle, and his aunt.

By taking a more aggressive approach in marketing and sales, the company can grow at $100,000 to $500,000 annually. Steven's strategy for growing the company will include a continuation of Fenchel's present marketing practices, such as maintaining the co-op advertising program with 20 department stores, the annual product catalog that is mailed to 200 prospective customers, attending the two annual lamp and lamp shade trade shows (Kenneth will attend one with Steven), and advertising in lamp and lamp shade journals (*Exhibit D*). Steven will also

---

EXHIBIT D

Fenchel Trade Journal Advertising

continue the practice of employing manufacturing representatives, which is common throughout the industry. Fenchel's representatives account for 33 percent of sales. Finally, Steven will service the same 20 in-house accounts that are presently being managed by the owner. Kenneth will visit each of the accounts with Steven for introductory purposes and to assure the customers that product quality and service will be maintained.

In addition, Steven will make several changes. First, he will do a thorough analysis of each form of advertising to gauge effectiveness. The data from this analysis will tell him where advertising dollars should be spent in order to achieve a higher return on investment. Next, he will hire and train more manufacturing representatives in an attempt to increase the number of customers in the independent lamp and lamp shade retail stores and lighting showrooms. Both of these potential customer groups are ideal for Fenchel lamp shades and are experiencing significant growth in affluent suburban areas.

The addition of more manufacturing representatives will be a variable cost since they are entirely compensated via commissions. The present commission system gives a representative 10 percent of any revenues generated. The commission is paid on the 10th of each month following product delivery. Such a system does not encourage the opening of new accounts since the representative gets the same percentage for a new account order as for an order from an existing customer.

Therefore, the third change that Steven will make is to give a one-time bonus for new account orders.

Fourth, he will personally market Fenchel's lamp shades to the premium-quality lamp manufacturers. Opportunities are definitely available in this market, based on the statement of Peter Gershanov, vice president of Frederick Cooper, to Steven that only two lamp manufacturers, Frederick Cooper and Stiffel, make their own lamp shades while the others purchase them from an outside manufacturer. This industry, with sales in excess of $2 billion, is too large to continue to ignore.

He will also seek to increase sales by pursuing untapped accounts in the Midwest, such as Ehr's Lamp Shade Shoppe in Waukesha, Wisconsin, which carries Silk-o-Lite, but not Fenchel, lamp shades.

Other opportunities will come from new kinds of customers not presently served by Fenchel. These potential customers include interior decorating companies, mail-order catalogs, upscale hotels, hospitals, colleges, upscale convalescent homes, and the government.

As a minority-owned company, Steven anticipates opportunities to increase revenue by selling to local, state, and federal government agencies through the 8(a) Set Aside Program (*Exhibit E*).

As a former purchasing agent, minority supplier coordinator, and member of the National Minority Purchasing Council, Steven is aware that many private corporations have minority supplier programs where buyers

EXHIBIT E

SBA Program for Minority Businesses

SBA Seeks Bids for 8(a) Firms, January 1987

Pursuant to Section 8(a) of the Small Business Act (PL95-507), SBA is seeking select set-aside requirements and competitive procurement opportunities on behalf of Illinois 8(a) minority small business in the product and service areas listed below.

Should you have specific set-aside or competitive procurement opportunities in any of the areas listed, SBA would like to receive your set-aside offering letter or IFB solicitation request. Your cooperation and reply will help develop another source of qualified minority small business suppliers. Please direct all information and questions to: *Howard Norris, SBA Assistant Director, Minority Small Business and Capital Ownership Development Division, at (312)353-9098.*

Product and Service areas:

Fabricated Metal Products, Janitorial Services, Computer Programming, Corrugated and Solid Fiber Boxes, Coal, Sand, Gravel-Bulk, Engineering Consulting, Industrial Supplies, Bridge Painting, Pharmaceutical Preparations, Exterminating Service, Mfg. Molding Fabricator Plastic, Computer Related Services, Resilient Floor Laying, Machine Shop Jobbing and Repair, Uniforms, Men's Suit Coats, Mechanical and Piping Construction, Data Entry and Processing, General Construction, Manufacture Light Fixtures, Management and Marketing Consulting, Nonresidential Construction and Excavating, Common Carrier, Heavy Construction, Electrical Construction, Manufacture Railroad Car Equipment, Chemical and Chemical Preparation, Nutritional Consulting, Technical Publications, Asphalt Paving, Reupholstery and Furniture Repair, Lubricant Distribution, Piping, Plumbing and Heating. Manufacture Electronic Components, Special Dies and Tools, Highway-Street Construction, Industrial Garments, Design Engineering and Architecture, Wholesaler of Medical Supplies, Radio and Television Repair, Detective and Protective Services, Concrete Construction, Certified Public Accountants, Real Estate Agents/Managers, Landscaping, Management Consulting, Sewerage Installation, Wholesaler of Metal Products, Lawn and Garden Services, Medal Fabrication, Cleaning Compounds, Dental Equipment Wholesale, Paint Varnish Manufacturing, Technical Writing Consulting, Service Facilities Management, and Garbage and Refuse Collection.

Add us to your bidders list and multiply your response. Send bid request and information to:

Minority Entrepreneur
300 North State Street #3425
Chicago, Illinois 60610.

actively search to buy from minority-owned businesses. He intends to take advantage of such opportunities.

The opportunity to increase sales in upscale department stores will also present itself because of the presence of minority vendor programs in stores such as Bloomingdale's, I. Magnin, and Lazarus (*Exhibit F*). Steven's ability to take advantage of such programs will be enhanced by the efforts of organizations such as the Black Retailers Action Group (BRAG). One of the group's goals, as explained by Mr. J. Thomas, the president of BRAG and also a vice president of Bloomingdale's, "is to increase the volume of dollars spent by major retailers with minority-owned manufacturers." Thus, with Fenchel's excellent reputation it should not be difficult to take advantage of such opportunities.

Another department store opportunity should come from Marshall Field's expansion. On September 18, 1987, the *Chicago Tribune* newspaper reported that "a new Marshall Field's store will open in Columbus, Ohio, next year as the start of an expansion campaign in the midwest." Hopefully, as they expand, their demand for Fenchel lamp shades will increase.

The most important thing about Fenchel's future marketing and sales efforts is that an increase in revenues will occur from selling to customers interested in Fenchel's premium-quality products. The Fenchel repu-

tation for quality, service, and value will not be compromised or sacrificed to increase short-term sales through price discounting.

Facilities

Fenchel is located at 612 S. Clinton Street in Chicago. The operations are in 17,000 square feet of a beautiful open loft space of an industrial building, with 16,000 square feet dedicated to manufacturing and the balance to office space. The rent is $2,841 per month, or $2 per square foot. The lease expires September 31, 1989. The lease is expected to be extended prior to the closing of the business sale.

Operating Plan

The quality control plan will consist primarily of measuring quality throughout each step of the manufacturing process instead of at the end. Each production employee will be held accountable for the quality of his/her value added to the end product. Prior to shipment each lamp shade will have been thoroughly inspected.

The inventory plan will be structured to minimize the amount of inventory carrying cost without threatening raw material availability.

EXHIBIT F

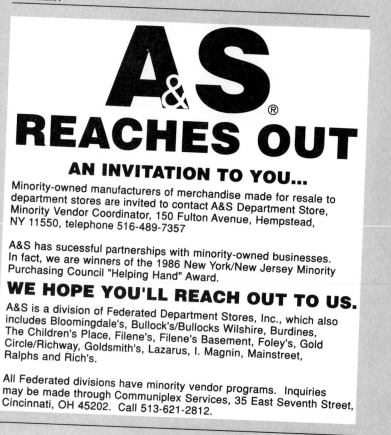

The production plan will remain as it is today. We will continue to manufacture lamp shades to customer orders. Therefore, there will be virtually no finished goods inventory, which can be extremely expensive and vulnerable to obsolescence. As the volume of orders increases, more production employees will be hired to ensure that product quality and delivery commitments do not suffer.

The purchasing plan will be designed to ensure that the number of suppliers is minimized. This will reduce administrative costs and ensure supplier loyalty and commitment. The plan will also require suppliers to consistently deliver raw materials on time, the quality of their materials must consistently meet expectations without rejects, and their costs must always be competitive. Steven's ability to implement such a plan will be enhanced by his previous work experience as a purchasing agent.

Labor Force

Fenchel's labor force of 16 employees (14 production workers and 2 shipping clerks) has been unionized since 1952. The employees are represented by the Warehouse and Mail Order Workers, Local 743, of the International Brothers of Teamsters. There has never been a strike or any kind of work stoppage. The labor contract, which has usually been for two years, expires in June 1988. Kenneth will work with Steven on the new contract.

The workforce is extremely diverse with respect to ethnicity and experience. The ethnic makeup of the employees is 13 Blacks, 2 Hispanics, and 1 Asian. Two of the employees are male. The employees have worked for Fenchel from 1 to 22 years and their ages range from 20 to 70 years old. (Exhibit G).

Employees find Fenchel an attractive place to work because they are treated well and have a very good compensation package. The average hourly wage is $5, with $4.30 per hour as the starting wage. The company's noncontributory benefit plan begins 90 days after a new employee's starting date. Fenchel pays $21 per month for each employee to a pension fund. Each employee also receives $10,000 worth of life insurance and $1 million worth of major medical insurance coverage. The employees also have disability and worker's compensation. The total cost of these benefits is approximately $1.50 per hour.

Management Team

The management team will consist of Steven, the owner of Fenchel, Gerri Wandall, the office manager, and John Smith, the production supervisor.

Steven will be intimately involved in the operations of Fenchel. His work experience (Exhibit H) includes general management duties with Cummins Engine Company, financial analysis with UNC Venture Capital Ltd., and business analysis and problem solving with Bain Consulting, Ltd. Along with this diverse work background, he has a master of business administration degree from Harvard Business School.

With the assistance of Kenneth for three months, Steven plans to immerse himself in learning the lamp shade business and nurturing relationships with customers and employees. His functional responsibilities will include marketing, sales, and purchasing. Finally, his main objective will be to bring in enough revenue to meet payroll, service debt, and maintain and expand the business.

While Steven will oversee the entire operation, the office manager and production supervisor will continue to manage their respective areas. This strategy will minimize disruptions and make the transfer of ownership as smooth as possible.

Gerri, the office manager for the past five years, will continue her present duties of order processing and bookkeeping. Her work in these areas will be enhanced by the introduction of a personal computer.

John, the 53-year-old production supervisor for the past 15 years, will also continue his present duties of managing production operations.

The skills and personalities of this group will complement each other and continue to result in an effective management team. The goals and objectives of the management team will be consistent on-time product delivery, improved product quality, reduced operating costs, labor productivity gains, increased sales and profits, and a happy labor force.

Potential Risks

While Fenchel has a long history of success in the lamp shade business, there are several risks, which can all be managed proactively. The threat of department store consolidation is quite prevalent today. Thus, there is a chance that Fenchel could lose an account such as the May Company if May was purchased

EXHIBIT G

Selected Data on the Fenchel Workforce

Number of Employees	Years With Fenchel
10	1–2
4	4
1	11
2	15
1	22

Number of Employees	Age
3	20–30 years old
3	31–40 years old
2	41–50 years old
10	51–60 years old

EXHIBIT II

Resume of Steven Rogers

Steven Rogers

Education 1983–1985	**Harvard Graduate School of Business Administration** **Boston, MA** Master in Business Administration, general management curriculum. Member of Venture Capital Club and the Afro-American Student Union. COGME Fellow. Resident Director of Wellesley High School "A Better Chance" program.
1975–1979	**Williams College** **Williamstown, MA** Bachelor of Arts. Liberal arts program with a major in history. Deans List. Recipient of Lehman Scholarship, Black Student Leadership Award, and Belvedere Brooks Memorial Medal. Varsity Football. Member of ECAC Division II All-Star Football Team. Treasurer of Black Student Union. Resident Tutor of Mount Greylock High School "A Better Chance" program. Tutor at Monroe State Prison.
Employment Experience 1986–Present	**Bain and Company** Consultant. Case team member on consulting assignments for Fortune 500 corporations in the health care, glassware, electronics, and manufacturing industries. Researched and analyzed financial, market, and productivity data for use in developing and implementing performance improvement strategies. Managed client task forces and teams.
1985–1986	**Harvard Business School** Research Associate. Wrote and published business school case studies concerning various manufacturing businesses. Collected data through statistical analyses, field work, interviews, and library research. Subjects included rubber products, health care, and communications industries.
Summer 1984	**UNC Ventures, Inc.** **Boston, MA** Summer Associated. Assessed the market and return potential of proposals for venture capital financing. Performed detailed investigation of selected ventures; analyzed proposed strategy, market conditions, management qualifications, valuation, and pricing terms. Completed legal synopses, business overviews, and internal rate of return and investment recovery analyses for portfolio companies. Attended UNC Ventures Board of Directors meeting. Visited portfolio companies. Reported directly to the President.
1981–1983	**Consolidated Diesel Company** **Whitakers, NC** Original member of company's start-up team on $450MM project. Commodity Manager of direct and indirect materials. Responsible for $15MM in purchases annually. Negotiated long-term commodity and service contracts. Initiated source selection and approval. Implemented engineering changes. Controlled price increases. Purchased material from foreign suppliers. Consolidated Minority Supplier Program. Interfaced with manufacturing, accounting, finance, engineering, quality, transportation, and marketing. Completed 75% of examinations for National Certified Purchasing Manager certification.
1979–1981	**Cummins Engine Company** **Columbus, IN** Supervisor of Customer Services Parts Department. Trained and supervised eight employees responsible for entering, administering, and expediting parts ordered by distributors. Developed an order entry presentation for visitor orientation program. Coordinated distributor ownership transfers. Supported Marketing's $100MM special parts program.
Personal Background	Head coach, PAL Football team, "A Better Chance" student at Radnor High School in Pennsylvania. Raised in Chicago, Illinois. Guardian of 11-year-old sister for six years. Married with two daughters. NACEL host family. Interests include traveling, reading, and participating in all sports.

---

by another department store that wanted to stock its stores with lamp shades from a company other than Fenchel. To minimize this risk, Steven will continue to keep the customer base diversified and not become too dependent on department stores, in general, or on any specific store. Steven believes it is safe to have the largest customer account be no more than 15 percent of total sales.

Another risk is the threat of a competitor locating in Chicago or the Midwest. The Fenchel reputation will be a very difficult obstacle for any new competitor to overcome. But Steven will not rely solely on Fenchel's name. He will maintain close relationships with customers to ensure that Fenchel's lamp shades completely meet their quality and delivery expectations. He will also manage costs in order to provide the customer with a product that is competitively priced without discounting. Therefore, Fenchel will be able to maintain and grow market share by emphasizing customer service as it relates to quality, delivery, and costs.

Section IV: Historical Financial Statements, Fenchel Lamp Shade

Cash Flow

	1987*	1986	1985	1984
Owner's salaries	$94,000	$96,000	$94,000	$96,000
Owner's automobiles (in Chicago and Florida)	11,976	14,000	12,000	11,500
Life and health insurance	6,000	6,000	4,000	4,000
Owner's personal travel and entertainment	13,000	13,000	11,000	10,000
Herbert and Lois Fenchel's Chicago apartment	9,000	9,000	9,000	8,500
Miscellaneous	2,000	2,000	—	—
Profit	108,366	19,000	(9,291)	(21,000)
Total cash flow	$244,342	$159,000	$120,709	$109,000

*February to December.

Income Statement

	1987*	1986	1985	1984
Net sales	$957,558	$805,869	$789,047	$743,166
Cost of sales:				
Materials	330,252	299,361	332,459	271,454
Direct labor	140,486	115,906	106,474	74,269
Other costs	24,929	20,089	28,783	29,391
Total cost of sales	495,667	435,356	467,716	375,114
Gross profit	461,891	360,513	321,331	368,052
Operating expenses:				
Factory	113,842	114,638	109,944	161,119
Selling	103,559	95,385	83,578	80,451
Administrative	42,124	35,111	43,100	51,253
Total operating expenses	259,525	245,134	236,622	292,823
Income before partners' salaries	202,366	115,379	84,709	75,229
Partners' salaries	94,000	96,000	94,000	96,000
Net operating income	108,366	19,379	(9,291)	(20,771)
Interest and other income	14,060	8,626	9,150	12,646
Net income	$122,426	$28,005	$(141)	$(8,125)

*February to December.

Balance Sheet

	1987	1986	1985	1984
Assets:				
Current assets:				
Cash	$63,759	$18,360	$17,494	$37,143
Accounts receivable	121,789	75,263	71,062	45,839
Allowance for uncollectible accounts	0	(8,000)	(8,000)	(8,000)
Inventories	110,835	57,108	51,637	28,195
Prepaid insurance	9,528	2,440	8,150	6,300
Prepaid rent	2,842	2,842	2,842	2,842
Other prepaid expenses	0	0	0	0
Total current assets	308,753	147,013	142,984	117,261
Investments	81,559	90,503	130,607	129,407
Machinery, furniture, and fixtures, at cost	32,132	32,132	32,132	32,132
Accumulated depreciation	(32,132)	(32,132)	(32,132)	(32,132)
Deposits	790	425	425	425
Total assets	$391,102	$237,941	$274,061	$247,093
Liabilities and Partners' Equity				
Current liabilities:				
Accounts payable	$77,322	$63,111	$58,412	$34,058
Accrued liabilities	29,853	29,932	22,477	21,127
Other expenses	62,220	42,239	48,473	45,113
Total current liabilities	169,395	135,282	129,362	100,298
Partners' equity:				
Balance, beginning of year:	102,659	144,654	146,795	168,564
Net income	122,426	28,005	(141)	(8,215)
Withdrawals	(3,378)	(70,000)	(2,000)	(13,644)
Balance, end of year	221,707	102,659	144,654	146,795
Total liabilities and partners' equity	$391,102	$237,941	$274,061	$247,093

Section V: Projected Financial Statements, Fenchel Lamp Shade Company

Income Statement (best-case scenario)

	1988	1989	1990
Net sales	$1,500,000	$2,000,000	$2,500,000
Cost of sales:			
Materials	555,000	740,000	925,000
Direct labor	195,000	260,000	325,000
Other costs	60,000	80,000	100,000
Total costs	810,000	1,080,000	1,350,000
Gross profit	690,000	920,000	1,150,000
Operating expenses:			
Factory	210,000	280,000	350,000
Selling	150,000	200,000	250,000
Administrative	50,000	55,000	60,000
Total expenses	410,000	535,000	660,000
Income before owners' salary	280,000	385,000	490,000
Owners' salary	50,000	55,000	60,000
Income before debt payments	$230,000	$330,000	$430,000

Balance Sheet (best-case scenario)

	1988	1989	1990
Assets:			
Current assets:			
Cash	$20,000	$25,000	$30,000
Accounts receivable	135,000	180,000	225,000
Allowance for uncollectibles	(8,000)	(8,000)	(8,000)
Merchandise inventories	105,000	140,000	175,000
Prepaid rent	4,250	4,250	4,250
Total current assets	256,250	341,250	426,250
Machinery, furniture, and fixtures, at cost	50,000	50,000	50,000
Total assets	$316,250	$391,250	$476,250
Liabilities			
Current liabilities:			
Accounts payable	$105,000	$140,000	$175,000
Other expenses	75,000	100,000	125,000
Total current liabilities	180,000	240,000	300,000
Long-term debt	550,000	440,000	330,000
Total liabilities	$730,000	$680,000	$630,000

Income Statement (worst-case scenario)

	1988	1989	1990
Net sales	$1,100,000	$1,200,000	$1,300,000
Cost of sales:			
Materials	407,000	444,000	481,000
Direct labor	143,000	156,000	169,000
Other costs	44,000	48,000	52,000
Total costs	594,000	648,000	702,000
Gross profit	506,000	552,000	598,000
Operating expenses:			
Factory	154,000	168,000	182,000
Selling	110,000	120,000	130,000
Administrative	33,000	36,000	39,000
Total expenses	297,000	324,000	351,000
Income before owners' salary	209,000	228,000	247,000
Owners' salary	50,000	60,000	70,000
Income before debt payments	$159,000	$168,000	$177,000

Balance Sheet (worst-case scenario)

	1988	1989	1990
Assets:			
Current assets:			
Cash	$11,000	$12,000	$13,000
Accounts receivable	99,000	108,000	117,000
Allowance for uncollectibles	(8,000)	(8,000)	(8,000)
Merchandise inventories	77,000	84,000	91,000
Prepaid rent	4,250	4,250	4,250
Total current assets	183,250	200,250	217,250
Machinery, furniture, and fixtures, at cost	50,000	50,000	50,000
Total assets	$233,250	$250,250	$267,250
Liabilities			
Current liabilities:			
Accounts payable	$105,000	$110,000	$115,000
Other expenses	55,000	60,000	65,000
Total current liabilities	160,000	170,000	180,000
Long-term debt	550,000	440,000	330,000
Total liabilities	$710,000	$610,000	$510,000

Section VI: Sources and Uses of Funds Tables

TABLE 1

Proposed Sources and Uses of Funds, 1988

Sources of funds:	
Bank (SBA loan)	$300,000
Fenchel trade debt	105,000
City of Chicago	100,000
MESBIC/SBIC	115,000
Fenchel family	75,000
State of Illinois	50,000
Steven and Michele Rogers	50,000
Total sources of funds	$795,000
Use of funds:	
Accounts receivable	$120,000
Inventory	125,000
Machinery, equipment, and patterns	100,000
Noncompete clause (five years)	400,000
Working capital	50,000
Total uses of funds	$795,000

TABLE 2

Terms of Sources of Funds

Source	Amount	Form	Terms
1. Bank Loan.	$300,000	Senior debt	Prime plus 2%
2. City of Chicago.	$100,000	Subordinated debt (second position)	75% of prime 60 monthly payments
3. State of Illinois.	$ 50,000	Subordinated debt (third position)	5% 60 monthly payments
4. Fenchel family.	$ 75,000	Subordinated debt (fourth position)	10% 60 monthly payments of $1,592.95
5. Fenchel trade debt.	$105,000		Normal terms of invoices
6. MESBIC/SBIC.	$115,000	Equity (15–25%); Preferred stock	9% cumulative dividend of $2,600 paid quarterly
			Redeem preferred stock at beginning of Year 4

Managerial Skills and Know–how Assessment

Name:

Venture:

Date:

PART I—Management Competency Inventory

Part I of the exercise involves filling out the Management Competency Inventory and evaluating how critical certain management competencies are either (1) for the venture or (2) personally over the next one to three years. *How you rank the importance of management competencies, therefore, will depend on the purpose of your managerial assessment.*

STEP 1

Complete the Management Competency Inventory on the Following Pages. For each management competency, place a check in the column that best describes your knowledge and experience. Note that a section is at the end of the inventory for **unique skills** required by your venture; for example, if it is a service or franchise business, there will be some skills and know-how that are unique. Then rank from 1 to 3 particular management competencies as follows:

    1 = Critical
    2 = Very Desirable
    3 = Not Necessary

	Competency Inventory				
	Rank	Thorough Knowledge & Experience (Done Well)	Some Knowledge & Experience (So–so)	No Knowledge or Experience (New Ground)	Importance (1–3 Years)
Marketing					
Market Research and Evaluation *Finding and interpreting industry and competitor information; designing and conducting market research studies; analyzing and interpreting market research data; etc.*					

Market Planning

Planning overall sales, advertising, and promotion programs; planning and setting up effective distributor or sales representative systems; etc.

Product Pricing

Determining competitive pricing and margin structures and breakeven analysis; positioning products in terms of price; etc.

Sales Management

Organizing, supervising, and motivating a direct sales force; analyzing territory and account sales potential; managing sales force; etc.

Direct Selling

Identifying, meeting, and developing new customers; closing sales; etc.

Direct Mail/Catalog Selling

Identifying and developing appropriate direct mail and catalog sales and related distribution; etc.

Telemarketing

Identifying, planning, implementing appropriate telemarketing programs; etc.

Customer Service

Determining customer service needs and spare-part requirements; managing a service organization and warranties; training; technical backup; etc.

Distribution Management

Organizing and managing the flow of product from manufacturing through distribution channels to customers, etc.

Product Management

Integrating market information, perceived needs, research and development, and advertising into a rational product plan; etc.

New Product Planning

Planning the introduction of new products, including marketing testing, prototype testing, and development of price, sales, merchandising, and distribution plans; etc.

Operations/Production

Manufacturing Management

Managing production to produce products within time, cost, and quality constraints; knowledge of Manufacturing Resource Planning; etc.

Inventory Control *Using techniques of controlling inprocess and finished goods inventories, etc.*				
Cost Analysis and Control *Calculating labor and materials costs; developing standard cost systems; conducting variance analyses; calculating overtime labor needs; managing and controlling costs; etc.*				
Quality Control *Setting up inspection systems and standards for effective control of quality in incoming, inprocess, and finished goods; etc.*				
Production Scheduling and Flow *Analyzing work flow; planning and managing production processes; managing work flow; calculating schedules and flows for rising sales levels; etc.*				
Purchasing *Identifying appropriate sources of supply; negotiating supplier contracts; managing the incoming flow of material into inventory, etc.*				

Job Evaluation

Analyzing worker productivity and needs for additional help; calculating cost-saving aspects of temporary versus permanent help; etc.

Finance

Accounting

Determining appropriate bookkeeping and accounting systems; preparing and using income statements and balance sheets; analyzing cash flow, breakeven, contribution, and profit and loss; etc.

Capital Budgeting

Preparing budgets; deciding how best to acquire funds for startup and growth; forecasting funds needs; etc.

Cash Flow Management

Managing cash position, including projecting cash requirements; etc.

Credit and Collection Management

Developing credit policies and screening criteria, etc.

Short-Term Financing

Managing payables and receivables; using interim financing alternatives; etc.

Public and Private Offering Skills

Developing a business plan and offering memo; managing shareholder relations; negotiating with financial sources; etc.

Administration

Problem Solving

Anticipating problems and planning to avoid them; analyzing and solving problems, etc.

Communications

Communicating effectively and clearly, both orally and in writing, to customers, peers, subordinates, and outsiders; etc.

Planning

Ability to set realistic and attainable goals, identify obstacles to achieving the goals, and develop detailed action plans to achieve those goals.

Decision Making

Making decisions based on the analysis of incomplete data, etc.

Project Management

Organizing project teams; setting project goals; defining project tasks; monitoring task completion in the face of problems and cost/ quality constraints; etc.

Negotiating *Working effectively in negotiations; etc.*				
Personnel Administration *Setting up payroll, hiring, compensation, and training functions; identifying, managing, and guiding appropriate outside advisors; etc.*				
Management Information Systems *Knowledge of relevant management information systems available and appropriate for growth plans; etc.*				
Computer *Using spreadsheet, word processing, and other relevant software; using electronic mail; etc.*				
Interpersonal Team				
Leadership/Vision/ Influence *Actively leading, instilling vision and passion in others, and managing activities of others; creating a climate and spirit conducive to high performance; etc.*				

Helping

Determining when assistance is warranted and asking for or providing such assistance.

Feedback

Providing effective feedback or receiving it; etc.

Conflict Management

Confronting differences openly and obtaining resolution; using evidence and logic; etc.

Teamwork and People Management

Working with others to achieve common goals; delegating responsibility and coaching subordinates, etc.

Law

Corporations

Understanding the uniform commercial code, including that regarding forms of organization and the rights and obligations of officers, shareholders, and directors; etc.

Contracts

Understanding the requirements of government and commercial contracts, licenses, leases, and other agreements; etc.

Taxes *Understanding state and federal reporting requirements; understanding tax shelters, estate planning, fringe benefits, and so forth; etc.*					
Securities *Understanding regulations of Security and Exchange Commission and state agencies concerning the securities, both registered and unregistered; etc.*					
Patents and Proprietary Rights *Understanding the preparation and revision of patent applications; recognizing strong patent, trademark, copyright, and privileged information claims; etc.*					
Real Estate *Understanding agreements necessary for the rental or purchase and sale of property; etc.*					
Bankruptcy *Understanding options and the forgivable and nonforgivable liabilities of founders, officers, directors, and so forth; etc.*					
Unique Skills *Unique competencies required.*					

PART II—Managerial Assessment

Part II involves assessing management strengths and weaknesses, deciding which areas of competence are most critical, and developing a plan to overcome or compensate for any weaknesses and to capitalize on management strengths.

STEP 1

Assess Management Strengths and Weaknesses:
—Which management skills are particularly strong?

—Which skills are particularly weak?

—What patterns are evident?

—What specific actions can overcome or compensate for each critical weakness?

—What specific actions can be taken on critical strengths?

—What are the time implications of the above actions?

—What areas need to be explored further?

STEP 4

Obtain Feedback. If you are evaluating your management competencies as part of the development of a personal entrepreneurial strategy and planning your apprenticeship, it is recommended you read Chapter 18 and complete the management assessment and feedback exercises in Part V at this time.

STEP 2

Circle the Areas of Competence Most Critical to the Success of the Venture, and Cross out Those That Are Irrelevant.

STEP 3

Consider the Implications for You and for the Venture:
—What are the implications of this particular constellation of management strengths and weaknesses?

Chapter Eight

The New Venture Team

"In the world today, there's plenty of technology, plenty of entrepreneurs, plenty of venture capital. What's in short supply is great teams. Your biggest challenge will be building a great team."

John Doerr, partner,
Kleiner, Perkins, Caulfield & Byers, from
Fast Company, Feb-March, 1997.

Results Expected

Upon completion of the chapter, you will have:

1. Identified and examined the role and significance of teams in building successful new ventures.
2. Examined successful entrepreneurial philosophies and attitudes which can anchor vision in forming and developing effective new venture teams.
3. Identified the critical issues and hurdles, including common pitfalls, faced by entrepreneurs in forming and building new venture teams.
4. Examined issues of reward that new teams face in slicing the equity pie.
5. Analyzed the "Michigan Lighting" case.
6. Developed a reward system for your own venture.

The Importance of the Team

The Connection to Success

Entrepreneurial team building is addressed in light of both the author's experience and recent research that has brought some facts and thoughtful analysis to this least understood aspect of new venture creation.

Accumulating evidence suggests that a management team can make quite a difference in venture success. There is a strong connection between the growth potential of a new venture (and its ability to attract capital beyond the founder's resources from private and venture capital backers) and the quality of its management team.

The existence of a quality management team is one of the major differences between a firm that provides its founder simply a job substitute and the ability to employ perhaps a few family members and others and a higher potential venture. The lone-wolf entrepreneur may make a living, but the team builder creates an organization and a company—a company where substantial value, and harvest options, are created.

Ventures that do not have teams are not necessarily predestined for the new venture graveyard. Yet, building a higher potential venture without a team is extremely difficult. It is true that some entrepreneurs have acquired a distaste for partners and that some lead entrepreneurs can be happy only if they are in complete control; that is, they want employees, not partners, either internally or in outside investors. Take, for instance, an entrepreneur who founded a high-technology firm that grew steadily, but slowly, over

10 years to nearly $2 million in sales. As new patents and technological advances in fiber optics drew much interest from venture capitalists, he had more than one offer of up to $5 million of funding, which he turned down because the investors wanted to own 51 percent or more of his venture. Plainly and simply, he said, "I do not want to give up control of what I have worked so long and hard to create." While clearly the exception to the rule, this entrepreneur has managed to grow his business to more than $20 million in sales.

As was noted in the first chapter, a lot of evidence suggests the team can make quite a difference in venture success.[1] The studies cited indicated that venture capitalists believe teams are important, that the survival rate among venture capital-backed firms was the inverse of national averages, and that returns on these investments were high. A study of 104 high-technology ventures launched in the 1960s reported that 83.3 percent of high-growth companies, which achieved sales of $5 million or more annually, were launched by teams, while only 53.8 percent of the 73 discontinued companies had several founders.[2] This pattern is apparent from an even more recent study of the "Route 128 One Hundred" (i.e., the top firms comprising the new venture phenomenon in the greater Boston area along Route 128).[3] Typically, these firms averaged impressive annual sales of $16 million for ventures up to 5 years old, $49 million for those 6 to 10 years old, and several hundred million for more mature firms. It was found that *70 percent* of these had multiple founders. Among 86 firms, 38 percent actually had three or more founders, 17 percent had four or more, and 9 percent had five or more. One firm was launched by a team of eight.

Not only is the existence of a team important, but so too is the quality of the team. Because of this, venture capital investors have become even more active in helping to shape, and reshape, management teams. One recent study showed a significant shift toward this activity during the boom period in venture capital in the 1980s in contrast with practices in the 1970s.[4] Another study, examining the nature of venture capital investing in highly innovative technical ventures, revealed this role can be quite active.[5]

There is, then, a valuable role that the right partner(s) can play in a venture. In addition, mounting evidence suggests that entrepreneurs face loneliness, stress, and other pressures.[6] At the very least, finding the right partner can serve to mitigate these pressures. The key is identifying and working with the right partner or partners. Getting the right partners and working with them successfully usually involves anticipating and dealing with some very critical issues and hurdles, when it is neither too early nor too late.

Forming Building Teams

Anchoring Vision in Team Philosophy and Attitudes

The most successful entrepreneurs seem to anchor their vision of the future in certain entrepreneurial philosophies and attitudes (i.e., attitudes about what a team is, what its mission is, and how it will be rewarded). The soul of this vision concerns what the founder or founders are trying to accomplish and the unwritten ground rules that become the fabric, character, and purpose guiding how a team will work together, succeed and make mistakes together, and realize a harvest together. The rewards, compensation, and incentive structures rest on this philosophy and attitudes.

This fundamental mind-set is often evident in later success. The anchoring of this vision goes beyond all the critical nuts-and-bolts issues covered in the chapters and cases on the opportunity, the business plan, financing, and so forth. Each of these issues is vital, but each by itself may not lead to success. A single factor rarely, if ever, does.

The capacity of the lead entrepreneur to craft a vision, and then to lead, inspire, persuade, and cajole key people to sign up for and deliver the dream makes an enormous difference between success and failure, between loss and profit, and between substantial harvest and "turning over the keys" to get out from under large personal guarantees of debt. Instilling a vision, and the passion to win, occurs very early on, often during informal discussions, and seems to trigger a series of self-fulfilling prophecies that lead to success, rather than to "almosts" or to failure.

[1] Jeffry A Timmons, "Careful Self-Analysis and Team Assessment Can Aid Entrepreneurs," in *Growing Concerns*, ed. D E Gumpert (New York: John Wiley & Sons, 1984), pp. 43–52.

[2] Arnold C Cooper and Albert V Bruno, "Success among High Technology Firms," *Business Horizons*, April 1977, p. 20.

[3] Jeffry A Timmons and Susan Skinner, research assistant, "The Route 128 One Hundred," working paper, Babson College, Wellesley, MA, 1984.

[4] Jeffry A Timmons, "Discard Many Old Rules about Raising Venture Capital," in *Growing Concerns*, ed. D E Gumpert (New York: John Wiley & Sons, 1984), pp. 273–80.

[5] Jeffry A Timmons, "Venture Capital: More than Money?" in *Pratt's Guide to Venture Capital Sources*, 8th ed. (Wellesley Hills, MA: Venture Economics, 1984), pp. 39–43.

[6] David Boyd and David Gumpert, "The Loneliness of the Start-up Entrepreneur," in *Frontiers of Entrepreneurship Research*, 1982 ed. J A Hornaday et al. (Babson Park, MA: Babson College), pp. 478–87.

Thus, lead entrepreneurs and team members who understand team building and teamwork have a secret weapon. Many with outstanding technical or other relevant skills, educational credentials, and so on, will be at once prisoners and victims of the highly individualistic competitiveness that got them to where they are. They may be fantastic lone achievers, and some may even "talk a good team game." But when it comes to how they behave and perform, their egos can rarely fit inside an airplane hangar. They simply do not have the team mentality.

What are these team philosophies and attitudes that the best entrepreneurs have and are able to identify or instill in prospective partners and team members? These can be traced to the entrepreneurial mind-set discussed in Chapter 5—a mind-set that can be seen actively at work around the team-building challenge. While there are innumerable blends and variations, most likely the teams of those firms that succeed in growing up big will share in common many of the following:

- **Cohesion.** Members of a team believe they are all in this together, and if the company wins, everyone wins. Members believe that no one can win unless everyone wins and, conversely, if anyone loses, everyone loses. Rewards, compensation, and incentive structures rest on building company value and return on capital invested, no matter how small or sizable.

- **Teamwork.** A team that works as a team, rather than one where individual heroes are created, may be the single most distinguishing feature of the higher-potential company. Thus, on these teams, efforts are made to make others' jobs easier, to make heroes out of partners and key people, and to motivate people by celebrating their successes. As Harold J. Seigle, the highly successful, now retired, president and chief executive officer of the Sunmark Companies, likes to put it, "High performance breeds strong friendships!"

- **Integrity.** Hard choices and trade-offs are made regarding what is good for the customer, the company, and value creation, rather than being based on purely utilitarian or Machiavellian ethics or narrow personal or departmental needs and concerns. There is a belief in and commitment to the notion of getting the job done without sacrificing quality, health, or personal standards.

- **Commitment to the long haul.** Like most organizations, new ventures thrive or wither according to the level of commitment of their teams. Members of a committed team believe they are playing for the long haul and that the venture is not a get-rich-quick drill. Rather, the venture is viewed as a delayed—not instant—gratification game in which it can take 5, 7, or even 10 or more years to realize a harvest. *No one gets a windfall profit by signing up now but bailing out early or when the going gets tough.* Stock vesting agreements reflect this commitment. For example, stock will usually be so vested over five or seven years that anyone who leaves early, for whatever reasons, can keep stock earned to date, but he or she is required to sell the remaining shares back to the company at the price originally paid. Of course, such a vesting agreement usually provides that if the company is unexpectedly sold or if a public offering is made long before the five- or seven-year vesting period is up, then stock is 100 percent vested automatically with that event.

- **Harvest mind-set.** A successful harvest is the name of the game. This means that eventual capital gain is viewed as the scorecard, rather than the size of a monthly paycheck, the location and size of an office, a certain car, or the like.

- **Commitment to value creation.** Team members are committed to value creation—making the pie bigger for everyone, including adding value for customers, enabling suppliers to win as the team succeeds, and making money for the team's constituencies and various stakeholders.

- **Equal inequality.** In successful emerging companies, democracy and blind equality generally do not work very well, and diligent efforts are made to determine who has what responsibility for the key tasks. The president is the one to set the ground rules and to shape the climate and culture of the venture. Bill Foster, founder and president of Stratus Computer, was asked if he and his partners were all equal. He said, "Yes, we are, except I get paid the most and I own the most stock."[7] For example, stock is usually not divided equally among the founders and key managers. In one company of four key people, stock was split as follows: 34 percent for the president, 23 percent each for the marketing and technical vice presidents, and 6 percent for the controller. The remainder went to outside directors and advisors. In another company, seven founders split the company as follows: 22 percent for the president, 15 percent for each of the four vice presidents, and 9 percent for each of the two other contributors. An example of how failure to differentiate in

---

[7] Remarks made at a Babson College Venture Capital Conference, June 1985.

terms of ownership impacts a business is seen in a third firm, where four owners each had equal share. Yet, two of the owners contributed virtually everything, while the other two actually detracted from the business. Because of this unresolved problem, the company could not attract venture capital and never was able to grow dramatically.

- **Fairness.** Rewards for key employees and stock ownership are based on contribution, performance, and results *over time*. Since these can only be roughly estimated in advance, and since there will invariably be surprises and inequities, both positive and negative, as time goes on, adjustments are made. One good example is a company that achieved spectacular results in the rather short time period of two years in the cellular car phone business. When the company was sold, it was evident that two of the six team members had contributed more than was reflected in their stock ownership position. To remedy this, another team member gave one of the two team members stock worth several hundred thousand dollars. Since the team was involved in another venture, the president made adjustments in the various ownership positions in the new venture, with each member's concurrence, to adjust for past inequities. In addition, it was decided to set aside 10 percent of the next venture to provide some discretion in making future adjustments for unanticipated contributions to ultimate success.

- **Sharing of the harvest.** This sense of fairness and justness seems to be extended by the more successful entrepreneurs to the harvest of a company, even when there is no legal or ethical obligation whatsoever to do so. For example, as much as 10 percent to 20 percent of the "winnings" is frequently set aside to distribute to key employees. In one such recent harvest, employees were startled and awash with glee when informed they would each receive a year's salary after the company was sold. However, this is not always the case. In another firm, 90 percent of which was owned by an entrepreneur and his family, the president, who was the single person most responsible for the firm's success and spectacular valuation, needed to expend considerable effort to get the owners to agree to give bonuses to other key employees of around $3 million, an amount just over 1 percent of the $250 million sale price. (It is worth considering how this sense of fairness, or lack of it, affects future flows of quality people and opportunities from which these entrepreneurs can choose new ventures.)

A Process of Evolution

An entrepreneur considering issues of team formation will rarely discover black-and-white, bulletproof answers that hold up over time. Nor is it being suggested that an entrepreneur needs answers to *all* questions concerning what the opportunity requires, and when, before moving ahead. Emphasis on the importance of new venture teams also does not mean every new venture must start with a *full* team that plunges into the business. It may take some time for the team to come together as a firm grows, and there will also always be some doubt, a hope for more than a prospective partner can deliver, and a constant recalibration. Again, creative acts, such as running a marathon or entrepreneuring, will be full of unknowns, new ground, and surprises. Preparation is an insurance policy, and thinking through these team issues and team building concepts in advance is very inexpensive insurance.

The combination of the right team of people and a right venture opportunity can be a most powerful one. The whole is, in such instances, greater than the sum of the parts. However, the odds for highly successful venture teams are rather thin. Even if a venture survives, the turnover among team members during the early years probably exceeds the national divorce rate. Studies of new venture teams seeking venture capital show many never get off the ground. These usually exhaust their own resources and their commitment prior to raising the venture capital necessary to launch their ventures. Of those that are funded, about 1 in 20 will become very successful in three to five years, in that they will return in excess of five times the original investment in realizable capital gains.

The formation and development of new venture teams seems to be idiosyncratic, and there seems to be a multitude of ways in which venture partners come together. Some teams form by accidents of geography, common interest, or working together. Perhaps the common interest is simply that the team members want to start a business, while in other cases the interest is an idea that members believe responds to a market need. Others form teams by virtue of past friendships. For example, roommates or close friendships in college or graduate school frequently lead to business partnerships. This was the case with two of the author's classmates in the MBA program at the Harvard Business School. Concluding that they would eventually go into business together after rooming together for a week, Leslie Charm and Carl Youngman have been partners for over 20 years as owners of three national franchise companies, Doktor Pet Centers, Command Performance, and Eye-Natural.

In the evolution of venture teams, two distinct patterns are identifiable. In the first, one person has an idea (or simply wants to start a business), and then three or four associates join the team over the next one to three years as the venture takes form. Alternatively, an entire team forms at the outset based on such factors as a shared idea, a friendship, an experience, and so forth.

Filling the Gaps

There is no simple cookbook solution to team formation; rather, there are as many approaches to forming teams as there are ventures with multiple founders.

Successful entrepreneurs search out people and form and build a team based on what the opportunity requires, and when.[8] Team members will contribute high value to a venture if they complement and balance the lead entrepreneur—and each other. Yet, ironically, while a substantial amount of thought usually accompanies the decision of people to go into business together, an overabundance of the thinking, particularly among the less experienced, can focus on less-critical issues, such as titles, corporate name, letterhead, or what kind of lawyer or accountant is needed. Thus, teams are often ill-conceived from the outset and can easily plunge headlong into unanticipated and unplanned responses to crises, conflicts, and changes.

A team starts with a lead entrepreneur. In a startup situation, the lead entrepreneur usually wears many hats. Beyond that, comparison of the nature and demands of the venture and the capabilities, motivations, and interests of the lead entrepreneur will signal gaps that exist and that need to be filled by other team members or by accessing other outside resources, such as a board of directors, consultants, lawyers, accountants, and so on.

Thus, for example, if the strengths of the lead entrepreneur or a team member are technical in nature, other team members, or outside resources, need to fill voids in marketing, finance, and such. Realistically, there will be an overlapping and sharing of responsibilities, but team members need to complement, not duplicate, the lead entrepreneur's capabilities and those of other team members.

Note that a by-product of forming a team may be alteration of an entry strategy if a critical gap cannot be filled. For example, a firm may find that it simply cannot assault a certain market because it cannot hire the right marketing person. (But it may find it could attract a top-notch person to exploit another niche with a modified product or service.)

Most important, the process of evaluating and deciding who is needed, and when, is dynamic and is not a one-time event. What know-how, skills, and expertise are required? What key tasks and action steps need to be taken? What are the requisites for success? What is the firm's distinctive competence? What external contacts are required? How extensive and how critical are the gaps? How much can the venture afford to pay? Will the venture gain access to the expertise it needs through additions to its board of directors or outside consultants? Questions such as these determine when and how these needs could be filled. And answers to such questions will change over time.

The following, organized around the analytical framework shown in *Exhibit* 2.7, can guide the formation of new venture teams:

- **The founder.** What kind of team is needed depends upon the nature of the opportunity and what the lead entrepreneur brings to the game. One key step in forming a team is for the lead entrepreneur to assess his or her entrepreneurial strategy. (The personal entrepreneurial strategy exercise in Chapter 19 is a valuable input in approaching these issues.) Thus, the lead entrepreneur needs to first consider whether the team is desirable or necessary and whether he or she wants to grow a higher potential company. He or she then needs to assess what talents, know-how, skills, track record, contacts, and resources are being brought to the table; that is, what "chunks" have been acquired. (See the "Managerial Skills and Know-How" assessment in Chapter 6.) Once this is determined, the lead entrepreneur needs to consider what the venture has to have to succeed, who is needed to complement him or her, and when. The best entrepreneurs are optimistic realists and have a real desire to improve their performance. They work at knowing what they do and do not know and are honest with themselves. The lead entrepreneur needs to consider issues such as:
  —What relevant industry, market, and technological know-how and experience are needed to win, and do I bring these to the venture?
  —Are my personal and business strengths in those specific areas that are critical to success in the proposed business?

[8] See J A Timmons, "The Entrepreneurial Team," *Journal of Small Business Management*, October 1975, pp. 36–37.

—Do I have the contacts and networks needed (and will the ones I have make a competitive difference), or do I look to partners in this area?

—Can I attract a "first team" of all-star partners, and can I manage these people and other team members effectively?

—Why did I decide to pursue this particular opportunity now, and what do I want out of the business (i.e., what are my goals and my income and harvest aspirations)?

—Do I know what the sacrifices and commitment will be, and am I prepared to make these?

—What are the risks involved, am I comfortable with them, and do I look for someone with a different risk-taking orientation?

- **The opportunity.** The need for team members is something an entrepreneur constantly thinks about, especially in the idea stage before startup. What is needed in the way of a team depends on the match-up between the lead entrepreneur and the opportunity, and how fast and aggressively he or she plans to proceed. (See the "Venture Opportunity Screening Guide" in Chapter 4.) While most new ventures plan to bootstrap it and bring on additional team members only as the company can afford them, the catch-22 is that if a venture is looking for venture capital or serious private investors, the more it has the team in place in advance, the higher will be its valuation and the smaller the ownership share that will have to be parted with. Some questions which need to be considered are:

—Have I clearly defined the value added and the economics of the business? Have I considered how (and with whom) the venture can make money in this business? For instance, whether a company is selling razors or razor blades makes a difference in the need for different team members.

—What are the critical success variables in the business I want to start, and what (or who) is needed to influence these variables positively?

—Do I have, or have access to, the critical external relationships with investors, lawyers, bankers, customers, suppliers, regulatory agencies, and so forth, that are necessary to pursue my opportunity? Do I need help in this area?

—What competitive advantage and strategy should I focus on? What people are necessary to pursue this strategy or advantage?

- **Outside resources.** Gaps can be filled by accessing outside resources, such as boards of directors,

accountants, lawyers, consultants, and so forth.[9] Usually, tax and legal expertise can best be obtained initially on a part-time basis. Other expertise (e.g., expertise required to design an inventory control system) is specialized and needed only once. Generally, if the resource is a one-time or periodic effort, or if the need is peripheral to the key tasks, goals, and activities required by the business, then an alternative such as using consultants makes sense. However, if the expertise is a must for the venture at the outset and the lead entrepreneur cannot provide it or learn it quickly, then one or more people will have to be acquired. Some questions are:

—Is the need for specialized, one-time or part-time expertise peripheral or on the critical path?

—Will trade secrets be compromised if I obtain this expertise externally?

Additional Considerations

Forming and building a team is, like marriage, a rather unscientific, occasionally unpredictable, and frequently surprising exercise—no matter how hard one may try to make it otherwise! The analogy of marriage and family, with all the accompanying complexities and consequences, is a particularly useful one. Forming a team has many of the characteristics of the courtship and marriage ritual, involving decisions based in part on emotion. There may well be a certain infatuation among team members and an aura of admiration, respect, and often fierce loyalty. Similarly, the complex psychological joys, frustrations, and uncertainties that accompany the birth and raising of children (here, the product or service) are experienced in entrepreneurial teams as well.

Thus, the following additional issues need to be considered:

- **Values, goals, and commitment.** It is critical that a team be well anchored in terms of values and goals. In any new venture the participants establish psychological contracts and climates. While these are most often set when the lead entrepreneur encourages standards of excellence and respect for team members' contributions, selection of team members whose goals and values are in agreement can greatly facilitate establishment of a psychological contract and an entrepreneurial climate. In successful companies, the personal goals and values of team members align well, and the goals of the company are championed by team members as well.

---

[9] See William A Sahlman and Howard H Stevenson, "Choosing Small Company Advisors," *Harvard Business Review*, March–April 1987.

While this alignment may be less exact in large publicly owned corporations and greatest in small closely held firms, significant overlapping of a team member's goals with those of other team members and the overlap of corporate goals and team members' goals is desirable. Practically speaking, these evaluations of team members are some of the most difficult to make.

- **Definition of roles.** A diligent effort needs to be made to determine who is comfortable with and who has what responsibility for, the key tasks so duplication of capabilities or responsibilities is minimized. Roles cannot be pinned down precisely for all tasks, since some key tasks and problems simply cannot be anticipated and since contributions are not always made by people originally expected to make them. Indeed, maintaining a loose, flexible, flat structure with shared responsibility and information is desirable for utilizing individual strengths, flexibility, rapid learning, and responsive decision making.

- **Peer groups.** The support and approval of family, friends, and co-workers can be helpful, especially when adversity strikes. Reference group approval can be a significant source of positive reinforcement for a person's career choice and, thus, his or her entire self-image and identity.[10] Ideally, peer group support for each team member should be there. (If it is not, the lead entrepreneur may have to accept the additional burden of encouragement and support in hard times—one which can be sizable.) Therefore, questions of whether a prospective team member's spouse is solidly in favor of his or her decision to pursue an entrepreneurial career and the "sweat equity" required and of whether the team member's close friends will be a source of support and encouragement or of detraction or negativism need to be considered.

Common Pitfalls

There can be difficulties in the practical implementation of these philosophies and attitudes, irrespective of the venture opportunity and the people involved. The company then may come unglued before it gets started, may experience infant mortality, or may live perpetually immersed in nasty divisive conflicts and power struggles that will certainly cripple its potential, even if they do not eventually kill the company.

Often, a team lacks skill and experience in dealing with such difficult startup issues, does not take the time to go through an extended "mating dance" among potential partners during the moonlighting phase prior to actually launching the venture, or does not seek the advice of competent advisors. As a result, such a team may be unable to deal with such sensitive issues as who gets how much ownership, who will commit what time and money or other resources, how disagreements will be resolved, and how a team member can leave or be let go. Thus, crucial early discussions among team members sometimes lead to a premature disbanding of promising teams with sound business ideas. Or in the rush to get going, or because the funds to pay for help in these areas are lacking, a team may stay together but not work through, even in a rough way, many of these issues. Such teams do not take advantage of the moonlighting phase to test the commitment and contribution made by team members. For example, to build a substantial business, a partner needs to be totally committed to the venture. The success of the venture is the partner's most important goal, and other priorities, including his or her family, come second.[11] Another advantage of using such a shakedown period effectively is that the risks inherent in such factors as premature commitment to permanent decisions regarding salary and stock are lower.

The common approach to forming a new venture team also can be a common pitfall for new venture teams. Here, two to four entrepreneurs, usually friends or work acquaintances, decide to demonstrate their equality with such democratic trimmings as equal stock ownership, equal salaries, equal office space and cars, and other items symbolizing their peer status. Left unanswered are questions of who is in charge, who makes the final decisions, and how real differences of opinion are resolved. While some overlapping of roles and a sharing in and negotiating of decisions are desirable in new venture teams, too much looseness is debilitating. Even sophisticated buy-sell agreements among partners often fail to resolve the conflicts.

Another pitfall is a belief that there are no deficiencies in the lead entrepreneur or the management team. Or a team is overly fascinated with or overcommitted to a product idea. For example, a lead entrepreneur who is unwilling or unable to identify his or her own deficiencies and weaknesses and to

---

[10] Reference groups—groups consisting of individuals with whom there is frequent interaction (such as family, friends, and co-workers), with whom values and interests are shared, and from whom support and approval for activities are derived—have long been known for their influence on behavior. See John W Thibault and Harold H Kelley, *The Social Psychology of Groups* (New York: John Wiley & Sons, 1966).

[11] This has been shown, for example, by Edgar H Schein's research about entrepreneurs, general managers, and technical managers who are MIT alumni. See the *Proceedings* of the Eastern Academy of Management meeting, May 1972, Boston.

add appropriate team members to compensate for these, and who further lacks an understanding of what is really needed to make a new venture grow into a successful business, has fallen into this pitfall.[12]

Failing to recognize that creating and building a new venture is a dynamic process is a problem for some teams. Therefore, such teams fail to realize that initial agreements are likely not to reflect actual contributions of team members over time, regardless of how much time one devotes to team-building tasks and regardless of the agreements team members make before startup. In addition, they fail to consider that teams are likely to change in composition over time. Richard Testa, a leading attorney whose firm has dealt with such ventures as Lotus Development Corporation and with numerous venture capital firms, recently startled those attending a seminar on raising venture capital by saying:

> The only thing that I can tell you with great certainty about this startup business has to do with you and your partners. I can virtually guarantee you, based on our decade plus of experience, that five years from now at least one of the founders will have left every company represented here today.[13]

Such a team, therefore, fails to put in place mechanisms that will facilitate and help structure graceful divorces and that will provide for the internal adjustments required as the venture grows.

Destructive motivations in investors, prospective team members, or the lead entrepreneur spell trouble. Teams suffer if they are not alert to signs of potentially destructive motivations, such as an early concern for power and control by a team member.

Finally, new venture teams may take trust for granted. Integrity is important in long-term business success, and the world is full of high-quality, ethical people; yet the real world also is inhabited by predators, crooks, sharks, frauds, and imposters. It is paradoxical that an entrepreneur cannot succeed without trust, but he or she probably cannot succeed with blind trust either. Trust is something that is earned, usually slowly, for it requires a lot of patience and a lot of testing in the real world. This is undoubtedly a major reason why investors prefer to see teams that have worked closely together. In the area of trust, a little cynicism goes a long way, and teams that do not pay attention to detail, such as performing due diligence with respect to a person or firm, fall into this pit.

Rewards and Incentives

Slicing the Founder's Pie

One of the most frequently asked questions from startup entrepreneurs is: How much stock ownership should go to whom? (In Chapter 13, you will examine in detail the various methodologies used by venture capitalists and investors to determine what share of the company is required by the investor at different rounds or stages of investment.) Consider the recent discussions with Jed, a former student, who is in serious negotiations with none other than John Doerr of Kleiner, Perkins, Caulfield & Byers, to raise funding for a new Internet company. The advice for Jed, and all others is the same.

First, start with a philosophy and set of values that boils down to Ewing Marion Kauffman's great principle: Share the wealth with those who help to create the value and thus the wealth. Once over that hurdle, you are less likely to get hung up on the percentage of ownership issue. After all, 51 percent of nothing is nothing. The key is making the pie as large as possible. Secondly, the ultimate goal of any venture capital backed company is to realize a harvest at a price 5 to 10 times the original investment, and up. Thus, the company will either be sold via an initial public offering (IPO), or to a larger company. It is useful, then, to work backwards from the capital structure at the time of the IPO to be able to envision and define what will happen and who will get what. Most venture capital-backed, smaller company IPOs during the robust capital markets of the late 1990s would have 12 to 15 million shares of stock outstanding after the IPO. Usually, 2.5 to 4 million shares—sometimes more, sometimes less—are sold to the public (mostly to institutional investors) at a price range of $12 to $15 per share. Again, depending on the perceived quality of the company and the robustness of the appetite for IPOs at the time, this can be half or twice as much. Typically, the founder/CEO will own 1 to 3 million shares after the IPO, worth somewhere between $12 million and $45 million. Put in this perspective, it is much easier to see why finding a great opportunity, building a great team, and sharing the wealth with widespread ownership in the team is far more important than what percentage of the company is owned.

Finally, especially for young entrepreneurs in their twenties or thirties, like Jed, this will not be their last

---

[12] J A Timmons presented a discussion of these entrepreneurial characteristics at the First International Conference on Entrepreneurship. See "Entrepreneurial Behavior," *Proceedings*, First International Conference on Entrepreneurship, Center for Entrepreneurial Studies, Toronto, November 1973.
[13] The seminar, held at Babson College, was called "Raising Venture Capital," and was cosponsored by *Venture Capital Journal* and Coopers & Lybrand, 1985.

venture. The single most important thing is that it succeeds. Make this happen, and the future opportunities will be boundless. All this can be ruined if the founder/CEO simply gets greedy and over-controlling, keeping most of the company to himself or herself, rather than create a huge, shared pie.

The Reward System

John L. Hayes and the late Brian Haslett of Venture Founders Corporation have made a major contribution in the area of reward systems, and the following is based on their work.

The reward system of a new venture includes both the financial rewards of a venture—such as stock, salary, and fringe benefits—*and* the chance to realize personal growth and goals, exercise autonomy, and develop skills in particular venture roles. Also, what is perceived as a reward by any single team member will vary. This perception will depend very much upon personal values, goals, and aspirations. Some may seek long-range capital gains while others desire more short-term security and income.

The reward system established for a new venture team should facilitate the interface of the venture opportunity and the management team. It needs to flow from team formation and enhance the entrepreneurial climate of the venture and the building of an effective team. For example, being able to attract and keep high-quality team members depends, to a great extent, on financial and psychological rewards given. The skills, experience, commitment, risk, concern, and so forth, of these team members are secured through these rewards.

The rewards available to an entrepreneurial team vary somewhat over the life of a venture. While intangible rewards, such as opportunity for self-development and realization, may be available throughout, some of the financial rewards are more or less appropriate at different stages of the venture's development.

Because these rewards are so important and because, in its early stages, a venture is limited in the rewards it can offer, the *total* reward system over the life of the venture needs to be thought through very carefully and efforts be made to assure that the venture's capacity to reward is not limited as levels of contribution change or as new personnel are added.

External issues also have an impact on the reward system created for a new venture. It is important to realize that the division of equity between the venture and external investors will affect how much equity is available to team members. Further, the way a venture deals with these questions also will determine its credibility with investors and others, because these people will look to the reward system for signs of commitment by the venture team.

Critical Issues

It is an early critical task for the lead entrepreneur to lead in dividing ownership among the founding team, based on the philosophy and vision discussed earlier. Investors may provide advice but will, more often than not, dump the issue squarely back in the lap of the lead entrepreneur, since whether and how these delicate ownership decisions are resolved often is seen by investors as an important litmus test.

Also, the process by which a reward system is decided and the commitment of each team member to deal with problems in a way which will assure that rewards continue to reflect performance are of utmost importance. Each key team member needs to be committed to working out solutions that reflect the commitments, risks, and anticipated relative contributions of team members as fairly as possible.

A good reward system reflects the goals of the particular venture and is in tune with valuations. If a venture is not seeking outside capital, outside owners need not be considered; but the same issues need to be resolved. For example, if a goal is to realize a substantial capital gain from the venture in the next 5 to 10 years, then the reward system needs to be aimed at reinforcing this goal and encouraging the long-term commitment required for its attainment.

No time-tested formulas or simple answers exist to cover all questions of how distributions should be made. However, the following issues should be considered:

- *Differentiation.* The democracy approach can work, but it involves higher risk and more pitfalls than a system that differentiates based on the value of contributions by team members. As a rule, different team members rarely contribute the same amount to the venture, and the reward system needs to recognize these differences.

- *Performance.* Reward needs to be a function of performance (as opposed to effort) during the early life of the venture and not during only one part of this period. Many ventures have been torn apart when the relative contributions of the team members changed dramatically several years after startup without a significant change in rewards. (Vesting goes a long way toward dealing with this issue.)

- *Flexibility.* Regardless of the contribution of any team member at any given time, the probability is high that this will change over time. The performance of a team member may be substantially more or less than anticipated. Further, a team member may have to be replaced and someone may have to be recruited and added to the existing team. Flexibility in the reward system, including such mechanisms as vesting and setting aside a portion of stock for future adjustments, can help to provide a sense of justice.

Considerations of Timing

Division of rewards, such as the split of stock between the members of the entrepreneurial team, will most likely be made very early in the life of the venture. Rewards may be a way of attracting significant early contribution; however, it is performance over the life of the venture that needs to be rewarded.

For example, regarding equity, once the allocation of stock is decided, changes in the relative stock positions of team members will be infrequent. New team members or external investors may dilute each member's position, but the relative positions will probably remain unchanged.

However, one or more events may occur during the early years of a venture. First, a team member who has a substantial portion of stock may not perform and need to be replaced early in the venture. Or a key team member may find a better opportunity and quit. Or a key team member could die in an accident. In each of these cases, the team will then be faced with the question of what will happen to the stock held by the team member. In each case, stock was intended as a reward for performance by the team member during the first several years of the venture, but the team member will not perform over this time period.

In the case of equity, several mechanisms are available to a venture when the initial stock split is so made that the loss or freezing of equity can be avoided. To illustrate, a venture can retain an option of returning stock to its treasury at the price at which it was purchased in certain cases, such as when a team member needs to be replaced. A buyback agreement is a mechanism to achieve this purpose.

To guard against the event that some portion of the stock has been earned and some portion will remain unearned, as when a team member quits or dies, the venture can place stock purchased by team members in escrow to be released over a two- or three-year period. Such a mechanism is called a stock-vesting agreement, and such an agreement can foster longer-term commitment to the success of the venture, while at the same time, providing a method for a civilized no-fault corporate divorce if things do not work out. Such a stock-vesting agreement is attached as a re-

striction on the stock certificate. Typically, the vesting agreement establishes a period of years, often four or more. During this period, the founding stockholders can "earn out" their shares. If a founder decides to leave the company prior to completion of the four-year vesting period, he or she may be required to sell the stock back to the company for the price originally paid for it, usually nothing. The departing shareholder, in this instance, would not own any stock after the departure. Nor would any capital gain windfall be realized by the departing founder. In other cases, founders may vest a certain portion each year, so they have some shares even if they leave. Such vesting can be weighted toward the last year or two of the vesting period. Other restrictions can give management and the board control over the disposition of stock, whether the stockholder stays or leaves the company. In essence, a mechanism such as a stock-vesting agreement confronts team members with the reality that "this is not a get-rich-quick exercise."

Other rewards, such as salary, stock options, bonuses, and fringe benefits, can be manipulated more readily to reflect changes in performance. But the ability to manipulate these is also somewhat dependent upon the stage of development of the venture. In the case of cash rewards, there is a trade-off between giving cash and the growth of the venture. Thus, in the early months of a venture, salaries will necessarily be low or nonexistent, and bonuses and other fringe benefits usually will be out of the question. Salaries, bonuses, and fringe benefits all drain cash, and until profitability is achieved, cash can always be put to use for operations. After profitability is achieved, cash payments will still limit growth. Salaries can become competitive once the venture has passed breakeven, but bonuses and fringe benefits should probably be kept at a minimum until several years of profitability have been demonstrated.

Considerations of Value

Of course, the contributions of team members will vary in nature, extent, and timing. In developing the reward system, and particularly the distribution of stock, contributions in certain areas are of particular value to a venture, as follows:

- *Idea.* In this area, the originator of the idea, particularly if trade secrets or special technology for a prototype was developed or if product or market research was done, needs to be considered.
- *Business plan preparation.* Preparing an acceptable business plan, in terms of dollars and hours expended, needs to be considered.

- **Commitment and risk.** A team member may invest a large percentage of his or her net worth in the company, be at risk if the company fails, have to make personal sacrifices, put in long hours and major effort, risk his or her reputation, accept reduced salary, or already have spent a large amount of time on behalf of the venture. This commitment and risk need to be considered.

- **Skills, experience, track record, or contacts.** A team member may bring to the venture skills, experience, track record, or contacts in such areas as marketing, finance, and technology. If these are of critical importance to the new venture and are not readily available, these need to be considered.

- **Responsibility.** The importance of a team member's role to the success of the venture needs to be considered.

Being the originator of the idea or expending a great amount of time or money in preparing the business plan is frequently overvalued. If these factors are evaluated in terms of the real success of the venture down the road, it is difficult to justify much more than 15 percent to 20 percent of equity for them. Commitment and risk, skills, experience, and responsibility contribute more by far to producing success of a venture.

The above list is valuable in attempting to weigh fairly the relative contributions of each team member. Contributions in each of these areas have some value; it is up to a team to agree on how to assign value to contributions and, further, to leave enough flexibility to allow for changes.

Compensation and Incentives in High-Potential Ventures

A useful technical note covering the important tax and accounting issues for stock options, incentive stock options, bonuses, phantom stock and the like was developed by the author. It is entitled, "Compensation Incentives in High Potential Ventures" (HBS 9-392-035), available through Harvard Business School Publishing, Soldiers Field Road, Boston, MA.

An excellent CD-ROM has been developed on rewards and compensation in high growth companies by The Kauffman Center for Entrepreneurial Leadership in Kansas City (1-800-489-4900).

Chapter Summary

1. A strong team is usually the difference between a success and a marginal or failed venture, and between a so-so and a great company.

2. Core philosophies, values, and attitudes, particularly sharing the wealth and ownership with those who create it, are key to team building.

3. The fit concept is central to anticipating management gaps and building the team.

4. Numerous pitfalls await the entrepreneur in team building and need to be avoided.

5. Compensating and rewarding team members requires both a philosophy and technical know-how, and can have enormous impact on the odds for success.

Study Questions

1. Why is the team so important in the entrepreneurial process?

2. Describe what is meant by "team" philosophy and attitudes. Why are these important?

3. What are the most critical questions a lead entrepreneur needs to consider in thinking through the team issue? Why?

4. What are some of the common pitfalls in team building?

5. What are the critical rewards, compensation, and incentive issues in putting a team together? Why are these so crucial and difficult to manage?

6. How does the lead entrepreneur allocate stock ownership and options in the new venture? Who should get what ownership and why?

MIND STRETCHERS:
Have You Considered?

1. Think back on teams on which you have been a member or a captain. What were the leadership and coaching principles that characterized the most, and least successful teams?

2. What IS a team?

3. A team may not be for everyone. How do you see the fit between you and the team concept?

4. One expert insists that the only guarantee he can make to a startup team is that in five years at least, one or two members will leave or be terminated? What causes this? Why will your team be different?

5. Ask five people who have worked with you in a team to give you feedback about your team-building skills.

Case

Michigan Lighting, Inc.

Preparation Questions

1. Evaluate the company. How much do you believe the company is worth? Bring to class a written bid of how much you would pay for it if you were Scott and Peterson.

2. What should they do to resolve the ownership situation?

3. How would you finance the purchase of the company?

4. Assume you do purchase the company: What specific actions would you plan to take on the first day? By the end of the first week? By the end of six months? Explain how and why.

Jack Peterson was discouraged by the continuing conflicts with his partner, David Scott, and had sought advice on how to remedy the situation from friends and associates as early as 1976. In 1984, Jack was beginning to believe that he and David had just grown too far apart to continue together. Jack had to find a mutually agreeable way to accomplish a separation. One alternative was for one partner to buy the other out, but they would first have to agree on this and find an acceptable method. David seemed to have no interest in such an arrangement.

During 1984, the differences between the partners grew. The vacillations in leadership were disruptive to the operation and made the employees very uncomfortable.

By early 1985, the situation was growing unbearable. Jack recalled the executive committee's annual planning meeting in January:

> It was a total disaster. There were loud arguments and violent disagreements. It was so bad that no one wanted to ever participate in another meeting. We were all miserable.
>
> What was so difficult was that each of us truly thought he was right. On various occasions other people in the company would support each of our positions. These were normally honest differences of opinion, but politics also started to enter in.

Company Description

Michigan Lighting, Inc. (MLI), manufactures custom-engineered fluorescent lighting fixtures used for commercial and institutional applications. Sales in 1985 were approximately $4.4 million with profits of $115,000.

Most sales are for standard items within the nine major lines of products designed and offered by the company. Ten percent of sales are completely custom-designed or custom-built fixtures, and 15 percent of orders are for slightly modified versions of a standard product. In 1985, CFI shipped 66,000 fixtures. Although individual orders range from one unit to over 2,000 units, the average order size is approximately 15–20 fixtures. Modified and custom-designed fixtures average about 25 per order. Jack Peterson, MLI president, describes their market position:

> Our product-marketing strategy is to try to solve lighting problems for architects and engineers. We design products which are architecturally styled for specific types of building constructions. If an architect has an unusual lighting problem, we design a special fixture to fit his needs. Or if he designs a lighting fixture, we build it to his specifications. We try to find products that satisfy particular lighting needs that are not filled by the giant fixture manufacturers. We look for niches in the marketplace.
>
> Having the right product to fit the architect's particular needs is the most important thing to our customer. Second is the relationship that the architect, the consulting engineer, or the lighting designer has with the people who are representing us. The construction business is such that the architect, engineer, contractor, distributor, and manufacturer all have to work as a team together on a specified project to ensure its successful completion. The architect makes a lot of mistakes in every building he designs, unless he just designs the same one over and over. Consequently, there's a lot of trading that goes on during the construction of a building, and everybody's got to give and take a little to get the job done. Then the owner usually gets a satisfactory job and the contractors and manufacturers make a fair profit. It requires a cooperative effort.
>
> Most of our bids for orders are probably compared with bids from half a dozen other firms across the country. Since a higher percentage of our orders are for premium-priced products, we are not as price sensitive as producers of more commonplace lighting fixtures. It is difficult for a small firm to compete in that market. As many as 30 companies might bid on one standard fixture job.

MLI owns its own modern manufacturing facility, located outside Pontiac, Michigan. Production consists of stamping, cutting, and forming sheet metal; painting; and assembling the fixture with the electrical components which are purchased from outside suppliers. The company employs a total of 104 workers, with 34 people in sales, engineering, and administration, and another 70 in production and assembly.

The company sells nationwide through regional distributors to contractors and architects for new buildings and renovations. Prior to 1983, MLI sold primarily to a regional market. At that time, marketing activities were broadened geographically. This is the primary reason that sales have been increasing over the last few years even during a weak construction market. (See *Exhibit A* for historical sales, earnings, unit sales, and employment.)

EXHIBIT A

Historical Performance

Year	Net Sales	Profit after Tax	No. of Fixtures Shipped	Total Employees	Hourly Employees
1985	$4,412,191	$115,209	66,000	104	70
1984	3,573,579	101,013	58,000	94	58
1983	2,973,780	106,528	52,000	82	52
1982	2,935,721	63,416	54,000	82	50

Background

Michigan Lighting, Inc., was formed in Flint, Michigan, in 1936 by Daniel Peterson and Julian Walters. Each owned one-half of the company. Peterson was responsible for finance and engineering and Walters for sales and design. They subcontracted all manufacturing for the lighting systems they sold.

After several years, differences in personal work habits led Peterson to buy out Walters' interest. Daniel Peterson then brought in Richard Scott as his new partner. Scott had been one of his sheet metal subcontractors. Richard Scott became president and Daniel Peterson treasurer. Ownership was split so that Peterson retained a few shares more than half and all voting control because of his prior experience with the company.

In 1940, MLI began manufacturing and moved its operations to a multifloor 50,000-square-foot plant also located in Flint. The company grew and was quite profitable during the war years and during the following boom in construction of the early 1950s. Peterson and Scott were quite satisfied with the earnings they had amassed during this period and were content to let the company remain at a steady level of about $1 million in sales and about $15,000 in profit after taxes.

Daniel Peterson's son, Jack, joined MLI as a salesman in 1963 after graduating from MIT and then Colorado Business School. Richard Scott's son, David, who was a graduate of Trinity College, became an MLI salesman in 1964 when he was discharged from the service. The two sons were acquaintances from occasional gatherings as they were growing up but had not been close friends.

In 1966, Daniel Peterson had a heart attack and withdrew from management of the business. Although he remained an interested observer and sometime advisor to his son, Daniel was inactive in company affairs after this time. Richard Scott assumed overall responsibility for the management of the company.

Jack Peterson moved inside to learn about other parts of the company in 1967. His first work assignments were in manufacturing and sales service. David Scott joined his father in the manufacturing area a year later. Jack Peterson became sales manager, David Scott became manufacturing manager, and, at Richard Scott's suggestion, another person was added as finan-

cial manager. These three shared responsibility for running the company and worked well together, but major decisions were still reserved for Richard Scott, who spent less and less time in the office.

As the new group began revitalizing the company, a number of employees who had not been productive and were not responding to change were given early retirement or asked to leave. When the man who had been Richard Scott's chief aide could not work with the three younger managers, they ultimately decided he had to be discharged. Richard Scott became so angry that he rarely entered the plant again.

For several years the three managers guided the company as a team. However, there were some spirited discussions over the basic strategic view of the company. As sales manager, Jack Peterson pressed for responding to special customer needs. This, he felt, would be their strongest market niche. David Scott argued for smooth production flows and less disruption. He felt they could compete well in the "semistandard" market.

In 1968, Jack Peterson began to work with an individual in forming a company in the computer field. The company rented extra space from MLI, and MLI provided management and administrative support, helping the new company with bidding and keeping track of contracts. Although David Scott was not active in this company, Jack split his partial ownership in this new company with David because they were partners, and because Jack was spending time away from MLI with the computer company.

In 1969, the fathers moved to restructure the company's ownership to reflect the de facto changes in management. The fathers converted their ownership to nonvoting class A stock, and then each transferred 44 percent of their nonvoting stock to their sons. Daniel Peterson decided to relinquish his voting control at this time in an effort to help things work as the new generation took over. Accordingly, Jack Peterson and David Scott were each issued 50 percent of the class B voting shares.

Due to the demands associated with the startup of the computer company, this new effort began to weaken the relationship between Jack and David. At the same time, David and the financial manager began to have strong disagreements. These seemed to arise primarily from errors in cost analysis, which led the financial manager to question some of David's decisions. There were also differences of opinion over relations with the workforce and consistency of policy. David preferred to control the manufacturing operation in his own way. Jack felt David could be more consistent, less arbitrary, and more supportive of the workforce. When the computer company was sold in 1975, the financial manager joined it as treasurer and resigned from MLI.

Growing Conflict

The departure of the financial manager led to a worsening of the relationship between Jack and David. Jack had been made company president in 1970. Jack recalled the decision:

> Richard Scott had resigned as president and the three of us were sitting around talking about who should be president. David Scott finally said, "I think you should be it." And I said, "Okay."

Yet even after Jack became president, the three managers had really operated together as a team for major decisions. Now, Jack was upset that they had lost an excellent financial manager, someone critical to the operation (partially due, in his opinion, to the disagreements with David). Also, there was no longer a third opinion to help resolve conflicts. Although the financial manager was replaced with an old classmate of David's, the new manager became one of several middle-level managers who had been hired as the company grew.

The pressure of growth created more strains between Jack and David. Sales had reached $1.8 million and had begun to tax MLI's manufacturing capacity. Jack felt that some of the problems could be alleviated if David would change methods that had been acceptable during slacker periods but hindered intense production efforts. David had different views. Both, however, agreed to look for additional space.

The transition to a new factory outside Pontiac, Michigan, in 1977 eased the stresses between the partners. A major corporation had purchased an indirect competitor to obtain its product lines and sold MLI the 135,000-square-foot plant. MLI also entered into an agreement to manufacture some of the other company's light fixtures as a subcontractor. The plant was in poor condition, and David Scott took over the project of renovating it and continuing production of the other company's lines.

Jack Peterson remained in Flint running the MLI operation alone until such time as it became possible to consolidate the entire operation in Pontiac. Jack described this interlude:

> The next year was a sort of cooling-off period. David was immersed in the project with the new factory and I was busy with the continuing operation. David had always enjoyed projects of this sort and was quite satisfied with this arrangement.
>
> Then, in 1978, we hired a plant manager to run the Pontiac plant and David came back to work in Flint. By that

time, of course, a lot of things had changed. All of Flint had been reporting to me. I had somewhat reshaped the operation and the people had gotten used to my management style, which was different from David's.

> David's reaction was to work primarily with the design and engineering people, but he really wasn't involved very much with the daily manufacturing anymore. He developed a lot of outside interests, business and recreation, that took up much of his time.
>
> I was very happy with the arrangement because it lessened the number of conflicts. But when he did come back, the disagreements that did rise would be worse. I guess I resented his attempts to change things when he only spent a small amount of his time in the company.
>
> Then, in 1980, we made the decision to sell the Flint plant and put the whole company in Pontiac. We were both involved in that. Most of the key people went with us. David and I were very active in pulling together the two groups, and in integrating the operations.
>
> That began a fairly good time. I was spending my time with the sales manager trying to change the company from a regional company to a national one and was helping to find new representatives all over the country. David Scott spent his time in the engineering, design, and manufacturing areas. There was plenty of extra capacity in the new plant, so things went quite smoothly. In particular, David did an excellent job in upgrading the quality standards of the production force we had acquired with the plant. This was critical for our line of products and our quality reputation.
>
> This move really absorbed us for almost two years. It just took us a long time to get people working together and to produce at the quality level and rate we wanted. We had purchased the plant for an excellent price with a lot of new equipment and had started deleting marginal product lines as we expanded nationally. The company became much more profitable.

During the company's expansion, a group of six people formed the operating team. David Scott concentrated on applications engineering for custom fixtures and new product design. In addition, there was a sales manager, financial manager, engineering manager, the plant manufacturing manager, and Jack Peterson. Disagreements began again. Jack recounted the problems:

> Our operating group would meet on a weekly or biweekly basis, whatever was necessary. Then we would have monthly executive committee meetings for broader planning issues. These became a disaster. David had reached the point where he didn't like much of anything that was going on in the company and was becoming very critical. I disagreed with him, as did the other managers on most occasions. Tempers often flared and David became more and more isolated.
>
> He and I also began to disagree over which topics we should discuss with the group. I felt that some areas were best discussed between the two of us, particularly matters concerning personnel, and that other matters should be left for stockholders meetings. The committee meetings were becoming real battles.

In 1977, Richard Scott died. Although he had remained chairman of the board, he had generally been inactive in the company since 1968. Daniel and Jack Peterson and David Scott remained as the only directors.

Search for a Solution

When Jack Peterson returned from a summer vacation in August 1985, he was greeted by a string of complaints from several of MLI's sales agents and also from some managers. Jack decided that the problem had to be resolved. Jack sought an intermediary:

> I knew that David and I weren't communicating and that I had to find a mediator David trusted. I had discussed this before with Allen Burke, our accountant. He was actually far more than our accountant. Allen is a partner with a Big Six accounting firm and is active in working with smaller companies. Allen was a boyhood friend who had grown up with David. I felt he had very high integrity and was very smart. David trusted him totally and Allen was probably one of David's major advisors about things.
>
> When I first talked to Burke in March, he basically said, "Well, you have problems in a marriage and you make it work. Go make it work, Jack." He wasn't going to listen much.
>
> Then in early September, I went back to say that it wasn't going to work anymore. I asked him for his help. Allen said that David had also seen him to complain about the problems, so Allen knew that the situation had become intolerable.

Both directly and through Burke, Jack pressured David to agree to a meeting to resolve the situation. Although David was also unhappy about their conflicts, he was hesitant to meet until he had thought through his options.

Jack felt that there were several principal reasons for David's reluctance to meet. Since they couldn't seem to solve their differences, the alternative of having one of them leave the company or become a silent partner glared as a possibility. Jack knew that David's only work experience was with MLI and was limited primarily to managing manufacturing operations he had known for years. Second, Jack thought that David was very uncertain about financial analysis, in which he had little training. Because he had not been directly involved in the financial operations, he was not aware of all the financial implications of his decisions. Jack felt that this made David's task of weighing the pros and cons of alternative courses of action much more difficult. Finally, there was the emotional tie to the company and the desire to avoid such a momentous decision.

As discussion began to result in the possibility that the partners would sell the company, David's reluctance waxed and waned. Just before Thanksgiving, David called Jack, who was sick at home, and said he had decided to fire the financial manager and become the treasurer of the company. David wanted to look at the figures for a year or so, and then he would be able to make a better decision. Jack felt that the financial manager was essential and could not be discharged. He thought that this was really more of an attempt to buy time. After some discussion, Jack convinced David that the financial manager should be retained.

After another month of give and take, Jack and David realized that they had no estimate of the value of the company if it were to be sold. Both felt that this might alter the attractiveness of the alternatives that each was considering.

Valuing the Company

Before making his decision, Jack reviewed the thinking he had done since first considering the idea of buying or selling the company. He began with the company's current position. With the serious discussions going on about the buyout agreement, preparation of the financial statements for 1985 had been accelerated and they were already completed. (These are shown, together with the results of 1984 and 1983, as *Exhibits B* and *C.)*

Jack had also begun developing the bank support he might need to fund a buyout. The company's banker indicated that he would loan Jack funds secured by his other personal assets if Jack was the buyer, but that since he had not worked with David, the bank would decline to finance an acquisition with David as the buyer. In addition, the bank would continue the company's existing line of credit, which was secured by MLI's cash and accounts receivable. The maximum which could be borrowed with this line was an amount equal to 100 percent of cash plus 75 percent of receivables. Both types of borrowing would be at one percent over the prime rate (then about 9 percent).

Jack worked with the financial manager to develop financial projections and valuation assessments. To be conservative, Jack had made the sales projections about 10 percent lower each year than he really thought they would achieve. Because fixed costs would not rise appreciably with modest increases in sales, any improvements in sales volume would directly increase profits. He felt he should consider how these various changes would impact his financing requirements and his assessment.

Jack also had sought out common valuation techniques. By looking through business periodicals and talking to friends, he found that these methods were not necessarily precise. Private manufacturing companies were most often valued at between 5 and 10 times after tax earnings. Book net asset value also helped establish business worth, but was often adjusted to reflect differences between the market value of assets and the carrying values shown on balance sheets. For MLI, this was significant because they had obtained their new plant at an excellent price. Jack felt that it alone was probably worth $200,000 more than the stated book value.

To Jack, the variations in worth suggested by these different methods not only reflected the uncertainty of financial valuation techniques but also showed that a business had different values to different people. His estimate would have to incorporate other, more personal and subjective elements.

EXHIBIT B

Financial Statements

Statement of Earnings

	Year Ended December 31		
	1985	**1984**	**1983**
Net sales	$4,412,191	$3,573,579	$2,973,780
Costs of goods sold:			
Inventories at beginning of year	742,907	593,185	416,512
Purchases	1,599,426	1,275,665	1,109,781
Freight in	19,520	26,595	20,966
Direct labor	430,154	360,568	328,487
Manufacturing expenses	977,229	802,172	673,643
	3,769,236	3,058,185	2,549,389
Inventories at end of year	826,228	742,907	593,185
	2,943,008	2,315,278	1,956,204
Gross profit	1,469,183	1,285,301	1,017,576
Product development expenses	131,746	128,809	102,299
Selling and administrative expenses	1,112,542	915,140	740,801
Operating income	1,244,288	1,043,949	843,100
Other expense (income):	224,895	214,352	174,476
Interest expense			
Payments to retired employee	56,259	37,790	32,416
Miscellaneous	10,000	10,000	20,000
	(923)	(1,551)	(6,193)
	65,336	46,239	46,223
Earnings before income taxes	159,559	168,113	128,253
Provision for income taxes	44,350	67,100	49,000
Earnings before extraordinary income	115,209	101,013	79,253
Extraordinary income—life insurance proceeds in excess of cash surrender value			27,275
Net earnings	$115,209	$101,013	$106,528
Earnings per share of common stock	$19.15	$16.79	$13.17

Assets

	December 31		
Current assets:			
Cash	$51,248	$3,778	$70,520
Accounts receivable:			
Customers	600,361	430,750	318,356
Refundable income taxes	23,001		
Other		2,276	5,289
	623,362	433,026	323,645
Less allowance for doubtful receivables	3,500	3,500	3,500
	619,862	429,526	320,145
Inventories:			
Raw materials	291,790	259,550	277,072
Work in progress	534,438	483,357	316,113
	826,228	742,907	593,185
Prepaid insurance and other	14,208	20,134	26,070
Total current assets	1,511,366	1,196,345	1,009,920
Property, plant, and equipment:			
Buildings and improvements	341,426	325,686	295,130
Machinery and equipment	210,493	173,073	135,419
Motor vehicles	32,578	32,578	29,421
Office equipment	42,866	43,905	36,949
	627,363	575,242	496,919
Less accumulated depreciation	273,284	233,444	185,215
	354,079	341,798	311,704
Land	11,101	11,101	11,101
	365,180	352,899	322,805
Other assets:			
Cash surrender value of life insurance policies (less loans of $19,478 in 1985, $19,590 in 1984, and $19,432 in 1983)	81,978	77,215	72,569
Total assets	$1,958,524	$1,626,459	$1,405,294

(Continued)

EXHIBIT B   (continued)

	December 31		
	1985	**1984**	**1983**
Liabilities and Stockholders' Equity			
Current liabilities:			
Current maturities of long-term debt	$12,184	$10,558	$9,000
Note payable—bank	325,000	200,000	
Note payable—officer		30,000	39,000
Accounts payable	389,582	295,208	313,203
Amount due for purchase of treasury stock			75,000
Accrued liabilities	154,590	116,134	88,957
Total current liabilities	881,356	651,900	525,160
Long-term debt	176,522	189,122	195,710
Stockholders' Equity			
Contributed capital:			
6% cumulative preferred stock—authorized 10,000 shares of $10 per value; issued 2,000 shares	20,000	20,000	20,000
Common stock:			
Class A (nonvoting):			
Authorized 15,000 shares of $10 par value; issued 8,305 shares	83,050	83,050	83,050
Class B (voting):			
Authorized 5,000 shares of $10 par value; issued and outstanding 20 shares	200	200	200
	103,250	103,250	103,250
	892,396	777,187	676,174
Retained earnings	995,646	880,437	779,424
Less shares reacquired and held in treasury—			
at cost: 2,000 shares 6% cumulative preferred stock	20,000	20,000	20,000
2,308 shares Class A common stock	75,000	75,000	75,000
	95,000	95,000	95,000
	900,646	785,437	684,424
Total liabilities and stockholders' equity	$1,958,524	$1,626,459	$1,405,294

Statement of Changes in Financial Position

	Year Ended December 31		
Working capital provided:			
From operations:			
Earnings before extraordinary income	$115,209	$101,013	$79,253
Add depreciation not requiring outlay of working capital	55,978	50,658	44,267
Working capital provided from operation	171,187	151,671	123,520
Extraordinary income from life insurance proceeds			27,275
Capitalized equipment lease obligation		5,295	
Proceeds from cash surrender value of life insurance policies			51,877
Total working capital provided	171,187	156,966	202,672
Working capital applied:			
Additions to property, plant, and equipment	68,259	80,752	47,107
Increase in cash surrender value of life insurance policies—net of loans	4,763	4,646	5,954
Reduction of long-term debt	12,600	11,883	8,995
Purchase of 2,308 shares of nonvoting Class A stock			75,000
Total working capital applied	85,622	97,281	137,057
Increase in working capital	$ 85,565	$ 59,685	$ 65,615
Net change in working capital consists of:			
Increase (decrease) in current assets:			
Cash	$ 47,470	$(66,742)	$ 64,854
Accounts receivable—net	190,336	109,381	(3,548)
Inventories	83,321	149,722	176,673
Prepaid expenses	(6,106)	(5,936)	(4,980)
	315,021	186,425	232,999

(Continued)

EXHIBIT B   (concluded)

Statement of Changes in Financial Position

	Year Ended December 31		
	1985	1984	1983
Increase (decrease) in current liabilities:			
Current portion of long-term debt			
Note payable to bank	1,626	1,558	500
Note payable to officer	125,000	200,000	
Accounts payable	(30,000)	(9,000)	
Amount due for purchase of treasury stock	94,374	(17,995)	104,083
Contribution to profit-sharing trust		(75,000)	75,000
Accrued liabilities			(20,000)
Total	38,456	27,177	7,801
Increase in working capital	229,456	126,740	167,384
Working capital at beginning of year	85,565	59,685	65,615
Working capital at end of year	544,445	484,760	419,145
	$630,010	$544,445	$484,760

EXHIBIT C

Pro Forma Financial Statements

Income Statement Projections (prepared by Jack Peterson)

Historical Percentages			Projected Percentages				Thousands of Dollars		
1983	1984	1985	1986	1987	1988		1986	1987	1988
100.00	100.00	100.00	100.0	100.0	100.0	Net sales	$4,800	$5,100	$5,400
65.80	64.79	66.70	67.0	67.0	67.0	Cost of goods sold	3,216	3,417	3,618
34.22	35.21	33.30	33.0	33.0	33.0	Gross income	1,584	1,683	1,782
28.61	29.28	28.25	28.0*	28.0	28.0	Operating, general, and admin.	1,344	1,428	1,512
5.61	5.93	5.05	5.0	5.0	5.0	Profit before taxes	240	255	270
38.20	39.90	27.80	39.0†	39.0	39.0	Taxes	94	99	105
						Net earnings	$ 146	$ 156	$165

*Projected percentages reflect an assumption that one partner will leave the company, and include a $25,000 cost reduction for the reduced salary requirements of a replacement.
†Effective tax rate.

Personal Financial Considerations

One important consideration was what amount of personal resource each could and should put at risk. Both Jack and David were financially very conservative. Neither of them had ever had any personal long-term debt—even for a house. Jack could gather a maximum of $650,000 of assets outside of MLI that could be pledged to secure borrowing. His bank had already confirmed that he could borrow against those assets. However, for him to put his entire worth at risk to purchase David's share of the company, he would want to be very comfortable that the price was a reasonable one. Jack described his feelings: "You get very protective about what you have outside the company. The problem you always have with a small company is that most of your worth is tied up in it and you may have very little to fall back on if something goes sour. We both have never been big leverage buyers or anything like that."

Besides the element of increased financial risk, there were several other considerations that tempered Jack's willingness to pay a very high price. Since they had moved to the plant in Pontiac, the one-hour commute to work had been a bit burdensome. It would be nice not to have that drive. Jack also felt that he had good experience in the overall management of a business and his engineering undergraduate degree and MBA gave him a certain amount of flexibility in the job market. This was important because, for both financial and personal reasons, he felt he would still have to work if he was no longer associated with MLI.

On the other hand, some factors encouraged Jack to be aggressive. His father cautioned him to be reasonable, but Jack knew his father would be very disappointed if he lost the company, and Jack himself had strong emotional ties to MLI. Jack also developed a point of view that in some ways he was buying the entire company, rather than just half: "I'm sitting here with a company that I have no control over because of our disagreements. If I buy the other half share, I'm buying the whole company—I'm buying peace of mind, I could do what I want, I wouldn't have to argue. So I'd buy a 'whole peace of mind' if I bought the other half of the company."

Finally, Jack considered his competitive position versus David. Although David had not accumulated the personal resources that Jack had, he had a brother-in-law with a private company that Jack knew had the ability to match Jack's resources and might be willing to back David financially. The brother-in-law would also be giving David financial advice in evaluating his alternatives and setting a value for the company. David also probably had fewer job prospects if he sold out. His undergraduate study was in liberal arts and his entire experience was within MLI. Jack also thought David might have some doubts about his ability to manage the company on his own.

The Meeting

After another conversation with Allen Burke, David Scott called Jack Peterson at home one evening: "Jack, I realize that you're right—I can't live in this tense environment any longer. I've spoken with Allen, and he has agreed to meet with both of us to discuss our situation, and to attempt to identify some possible solutions. Would Friday at 9:00 be convenient for you?"

Exercise—Rewards

The following exercise can help an entrepreneur devise a reward system for a new venture. In proceeding with the exercise, it is helpful to pretend to look at these issues from an investor's point of view and to imagine that the venture is in the process of seeking capital from an investor group to which a presentation was made several weeks ago and which is favorably impressed by the team and its plan for the new venture. Imagine then that this investor group would like a brief presentation (of 10 to 15 minutes) about how the team plans to reward its members and other key contributors.

**EXERCISE
REWARDS**

Name:

Venture:

Date:

PART I

Part I is to be completed by each individual team member—*alone.*

STEP 1:

INDICATE WHO WILL DO WHAT DURING THE FIRST YEAR OR TWO OF YOUR VENTURE, WHAT CONTRIBUTIONS EACH HAS MADE OR WILL MAKE TO CREATING A BUSINESS PLAN, THE COMMITMENT AND RISK INVOLVED FOR EACH, AND WHAT UNIQUE CRITICAL SKILLS, EXPERIENCE, CONTACTS, AND SO FORTH, EACH BRINGS TO THE VENTURE. Try to be as specific as possible, and be sure to include yourself.

Team Member	Responsibility	Title	Contribution to Business Plan	Commitment and Risk	Unique/Critical Skills, Etc.

STEP 2:

INDICATE BELOW THE APPROXIMATE SALARY AND SHARES OF STOCK (AS A PERCENT) EACH MEMBER SHOULD HAVE UPON CLOSING THE FINANCING OF YOUR NEW VENTURE.

Team Member	Salary	Shares of Stock (# and %)

STEP 3:

INDICATE BELOW WHAT FRINGE BENEFITS YOU BELIEVE THE COMPANY SHOULD PROVIDE DURING THE FIRST YEAR OR TWO.

Team Member	Vacation	Holidays	Health/Life Insurance	Retirement Plan	Other

STEP 4:

LIST OTHER KEY CONTRIBUTORS, SUCH AS MEMBERS OF THE BOARD OF DIRECTORS, AND INDICATE HOW THEY WILL BE REWARDED.

Name	Expertise/ Contribution	Salary	Shares of Stock (# and %)	Other

PART II

Part II involves meeting as a team to reach consensus on the responsibilities of each team member and how each will be rewarded. In addition to devising a reward system for the team and other key contributors, the team will examine how consensus was reached.

STEP 1:

MEET AS A TEAM AND REACH CONSENSUS ON THE ABOVE TEAM ISSUES AND INDICATE THE CONSENSUS SOLUTION BELOW.

Responsibilities/Contributions

Team Member	Responsibility	Contribution to Business Plan	Commitment and Risk	Unique/Critical Skills, Etc.

Rewards

Team Member	Salary	Shares of Stock (# and %)

Rewards (continued)

Team Member	Title	Vacation	Holidays	Health/Life Insurance	Retirement Plan	Other

STEP 2:

MEET AS A TEAM AND REACH CONSENSUS ON ISSUES INVOLVING OTHER KEY CONTRIBUTORS AND INDICATE THE CONSENSUS SOLUTION BELOW.

Name	Expertise/ Contribution	Salary	Shares of Stock (# and %)	Other

STEP 3:

DISCUSS AS A TEAM THE FOLLOWING ISSUES AND INDICATE ANY IMPORTANT LESSONS AND IMPLICATIONS:
—What patterns emerged in the approaches taken by each team? What are the differences and similarities?

—How difficult or easy was it to reach agreement among team members? Did any issues bog down?

—If salaries or stock were equal for all team members, why was this so? What risks or problems might such an approach create?

—What criteria, either implicit or explicit, were used to arrive at a decision concerning salaries and stock? Why?

## Chapter Nine

Personal Ethics and the Entrepreneur

If you gain financial success at the expense of your integrity, you are not a success at all.

John Cullinane
Founder of Cullinet, Inc., and 1984 Inductee,
Babson Academy of Distinguished Entrepreneurs

Results Expected

Upon completion of this chapter, you will have:

1. Made decisions involving ethical issues and identified and analyzed your reasons for deciding as you did.
2. Discussed with others the ethical implications of the decisions you made and identified how they might affect you, your partners, your customers, and your competitors in the contexts described.
3. Acquired a background, based on history, philosophy, and research, about the nature of business ethics and a context for thinking about ethical behavior.
4. Gained an awareness of the importance of ethical awareness and high standards in an entrepreneurial career.
5. Analyzed the "Wayne Postoak" case.

Exercise—Ethics

In the "Ethics" exercise, decisions will be made in ethically ambiguous situations and then analyzed. As in the real world, all the background information on each situation will not be available, and assumptions will need to be made in order to decide.

It is recommended that the "Ethics" exercise be completed first—before reading the following material, and then revisit it after you have completed the chapter.

Exercise

Ethics

Name:

Date:

Part I

STEP 1:

MAKE DECISIONS IN THE FOLLOWING SITUATIONS.
You will not have all the background information on each
situation; instead, you should make whatever assumptions
you feel you would make if you were actually confronted
with the decision choices described. Select the decision
choice that most closely represents the decision you feel
you would make personally. You should choose decision
choices even though you can envision other creative solutions that were not included in the exercise.

Situation 1. You are taking a very difficult chemistry
course, which you must pass to maintain your scholarship
and to avoid damaging your application for graduate school.
Chemistry is not your strong suit, and because of a just-be-
low-failing average in the course, you must receive a grade of
90 or better on the final exam, which is two days away. A janitor who is aware of your plight informs you that he found the
master stencil for the chemistry final in a trash barrel and
saved it. He will make it available to you for a price, which is
high but which you could afford. What would you do?

_____*(a)* I would tell the janitor thanks, but no thanks.

_____*(b)* I would report the janitor to the proper
officials.

_____*(c)* I would buy the exam and keep it to myself.

_____*(d)* I would not buy the exam myself, but I
would let some of my friends, who are also
flunking the course, know that it is available.

Situation 2. You have been working on some financial
projections manually for two days now. It seems that each
time you think you have them completed, your boss shows
up with a new assumption or another what-if question. If
you only had a copy of a spreadsheet software program for
your personal computer, you could plug in the new assumptions and revise the estimates with ease. Then a colleague offers to let you make a copy of some software which
is copyrighted. What would you do?

_____*(a)* I would readily accept my friend's generous
offer and make a copy of the software.

_____*(b)* I would decline to copy it and plug away
manually on the numbers.

_____*(c)* I would decide to go buy a copy of the
software myself for $300 and hope I would
be reimbursed by the company in a month
or two.

_____*(d)* I would request another extension on an
already overdue project date.

Situation 3. Your small manufacturing company is in
serious financial difficulty. A large order of your products is
ready to be delivered to a key customer, when you discover
that the product is simply not right. It will not meet all performance specifications, will cause problems for your customer, and will require rework in the field; but this, you
know, will not become evident until after the customer has
received and paid for the order. If you do not ship the order
and receive the payment as expected, your business may
be forced into bankruptcy. And if you delay the shipment
or inform the customer of these problems, you may lose the
order and also go bankrupt. What would you do?

_____*(a)* I would not ship the order and place my
firm in voluntary bankruptcy.

_____*(b)* I would inform the customer and declare
voluntary bankruptcy.

_____*(c)* I would ship the order and inform the
customer, after I received payment.

_____*(d)* I would ship the order and not inform the
customer.

Situation 4. You are the cofounder and president of a
new venture, manufacturing products for the recreational
market. Five months after launching the business, one of
your suppliers informs you it can no longer supply you with
a critical raw material since you are not a large-quantity
user. Without the raw material the business cannot continue. What would you do?

_____*(a)* I would grossly overstate my requirements to
another supplier to make the supplier think I
am a much larger potential customer in order
to secure the raw material from that supplier,
even though this would mean the supplier
will no longer be able to supply another,
noncompeting small manufacturer who may
thus be forced out of business.

_____*(b)* I would steal raw material from another firm
(noncompeting) where I am aware of a
sizable stockpile.

_____(c) I would pay off the supplier, since I have reason to believe that the supplier could be persuaded to meet my needs with a sizable under-the-table payoff that my company could afford.

_____(d) I would declare voluntary bankruptcy.

Situation 5.   You are on a marketing trip for your new venture for the purpose of calling on the purchasing agent of a major prospective client. Your company is manufacturing an electronic system that you hope the purchasing agent will buy. During the course of your conversation, you notice on the cluttered desk of the purchasing agent several copies of a cost proposal for a system from one of your direct competitors. This purchasing agent has previously reported mislaying several of your own company's proposals and has asked for additional copies. The purchasing agent leaves the room momentarily to get you a cup of coffee, leaving you alone with your competitor's proposals less than an arm's length away. What would you do?

_____(a) I would do nothing but await the man's return.

_____(b) I would sneak a quick peek at the proposal, looking for bottom-line numbers.

_____(c) I would put the copy of the proposal in my briefcase.

_____(d) I would wait until the man returns and ask his permission to see the copy.

Part II

STEP 1:

BASED ON THE CRITERIA YOU USED, PLACE YOUR ANSWERS TO EACH OF THE ABOVE SITUATIONS ALONG THE CONTINUUM OF BEHAVIOR SHOWN BELOW:

	Duty	Contractual	Utilitarian	Situational
Situation 1				
Situation 2				
Situation 3				
Situation 4				
Situation 5				

STEP 2:

AFTER SEPARATING INTO TEAMS OF FIVE TO SIX PEOPLE, RECORD THE ANSWERS MADE BY EACH INDIVIDUAL MEM-BER OF YOUR TEAM ON THE FORM BELOW. Record the answer of each team member in each box and the team's solution in the column on the far right.

Member Name:						Team Answer
Situation 1						
Situation 2						
Situation 3						
Situation 4						
Situation 5						

STEP 3:

REACH A CONSENSUS DECISION IN EACH SITUATION (IF POSSIBLE) AND RECORD THE CONSENSUS WHICH YOUR TEAM HAS REACHED ABOVE. Allow 20 to 30 minutes.

STEP 4:

REPORT TO THE ENTIRE GROUP YOUR TEAM'S CONCLUSIONS AND DISCUSS WITH THEM HOW THE CONSENSUS, IF ANY, WAS REACHED. The discussion should focus on the following questions:

- Was a consensus reached by each group?
- Was this consensus difficult or easy to achieve and why?
- What kinds of ethical issues emerged?
- How were conflicts, if any, resolved, or were they left unresolved?

STEP 5:

DISCUSS WITH THE GROUP THE FOLLOWING ISSUES:

- What role do ethical issues play and how important are they in the formation of a new venture management team?
- What role do ethical issues play and how important are they in obtaining venture capital? That is, how do investors feel about ethics and how important are they to them?
- What feelings bother participants most about the discussion and consensus reached? For example, if a participant believes that his or her own conduct was considered ethically less than perfect, does he or she feel a loss of self-respect or a sense of inferiority? Does he or she fear others' judgment, and so on?

STEP 6:

DEFINE EACH GROUP MEMBER'S GENERAL ETHICAL POSITION AND NOTE WHETHER HIS OR HER ETHICAL POSITION IS SIMILAR TO OR DIFFERENT FROM YOURS:

Member	Position	Different/ Similar

STEP 7:

DECIDE WHOM YOU WOULD AND WOULD NOT WANT AS A BUSINESS PARTNER BASED ON THEIR ETHICAL POSITIONS:

Would Want	Would Not Want

Overview of Ethics

A good number of successful entrepreneurs believe that high ethical standards and integrity are exceptionally important to long-term success. For example, the author and his colleague, Howard H. Stevenson, conducted a study among 128 presidents/founders attending the Harvard Business School's Owner/President Management program (OPM) in 1983.[1] Their firms typically had sales of $40 million, and sales ranged from $5 million to $200 million. These entrepreneurs were also very experienced, with the average age in the mid-40s, and about half had founded their companies. They were asked to name the most critical concepts, skills, and know-how for success at their companies at the time and what they would be in five years. The answer to this question was startling enough that the Sunday *New York Times* reported the findings: 72 percent of the presidents responding stated that high ethical standards were the single most important factor in long-term success.

Conventional ethical disciplines have been accused of dealing with the business mode by narrowing and defining the scope of inquiry so as to avoid floundering. One author, for instance, *assumed* that "competitors are ethical and engaged in business, rather than jungle warfare."[2]

However, what is ethical and what is not often is not obvious; rather, situations involving ethical issues are often ambiguous. Today, as throughout much of this century, students, business people, and others have received many conflicting signals, as "first artists and intellectuals, then broader segments of the society, challenged every convention, every prohibition, every regulation that cramped the human spirit or blocked its appetites and ambitions."[3]

This discussion has also generated a lot of controversy. As an example, a provocative and controversial article published in the *Harvard Business Review* asserted that the ethics of business were not those of society but rather those of the poker game.[4] The author of the article argued that "most businessmen are not indifferent to ethics in their private lives, everyone will agree. My point is that in their office lives they cease to be private citizens; they become game players who must be guided by a somewhat different set of ethical standards." The author further argued that

personal ethics and business ethics are often not in harmony, and either by negotiation or compromise, a resolution must be reached. The article provoked a storm of response.

Another story that attracted attention was reported by *INC.* magazine in 1989; an interview with Phillippe Kahn of Borland International revealed the following:

INC.: The story goes that Borland was launched by a single ad, without which we wouldn't be sitting here talking about the company. How much of that is apocryphal?

Kahn: It's true; one full-page ad in the November issue of *BYTE* magazine got the company running. If it had failed, I would have had nowhere else to go.

INC.: If you were so broke, how did you pay for the ad?

Kahn: Let's put it that we convinced the salesman to give us terms. We wanted to appear only in *BYTE*—not any of the other microcomputer magazines—because *BYTE* is for programmers, and that's who we wanted to reach. But we couldn't afford it. We figured the only way was somehow to convince them to extend us credit terms.

INC.: And they did?

Kahn: Well, they didn't *offer*. What we did was, before the ad salesman came in—we existed in two small rooms, but I had hired extra people so we would look like a busy, venture-backed company—we prepared a chart with what we pretended was our media plan for the computer magazines. On the chart we had *BYTE* crossed out. When the salesman arrived, we made sure the phones were ringing and the extras were scurrying about. Here was this chart he thought he wasn't supposed to see, so I pushed it out of the way. He said, "Hold on, can we get you in *BYTE*?" I said, "We don't really have to be in your book, it's not the right audience for us." "You've got to try," he pleaded. I said, "Frankly, our media plan is done, and we can't afford it." So he offered good terms, if only we'd let him run it just once. We expected we'd sell maybe $20,000 of software and at least pay for the ad. We sold $150,000 worth. Looking back now, it's a funny story, then it was a big risk.[5]

Commenting on this article, Howard H. Stevenson and Amar Bhide noted that this incident of "early deceit is remembered, if at all, as an amusing prank."[6] But the question remains, How are business people supposed to operate in this capitalist system?

In addition, the law, which one might expect to be black and white, is full of thorny issues. Laws not only have authority but also limitations. In the first place, laws are made with forethought and with the deliberate purpose of ensuring justice. They are therefore

[1] Jeffry A. Timmons and Howard H. Stevenson, "Entrepreneurship Education in the 1980s," presented at the 75th Anniversary Entrepreneurship Symposium, Harvard Business School, Boston, 1983. *Proceedings*, pp. 115–34.
[2] Thomas Garret, *Business Ethics* (New York: Appleton-Century-Crofts, 1966), pp. 149–50.
[3] Derek Bok, "Ethics, the University, & Society," *Harvard Magazine*, May–June 1988, p. 39.
[4] Reprinted by permission of *Harvard Business Review*. An Excerpt from "Is Business Bluffing Ethical?" by Albert Z. Carr, January–February 1968, pp. 145–52. Copyright © 1967 by the President and Fellows of Harvard College.
[5] "Management by Necessity," *INC.*, March 1989, p. 33. Reprinted with permission. Copyright © 1989 by Goldhirsh Group, Inc., 38 Commercial Wharf, Boston, MA 02110.
[6] Howard H. Stevenson and Amar Bhide, "Why Be Honest, If Honesty Does Not Pay?" *Harvard Business Review*, September–October 1990, p. 123.

ethical in intent and deserve respect. However, laws are made in legislatures, not in heaven. They do not anticipate new conditions; they do not always have the effect they were intended to have; they sometimes conflict with one another; and they are, as they stand, incapable of making judgments where multiple ethical considerations hang in the balance or seem actually to war with one another. Thus, from the beginnings of recorded history in Egypt and the Middle East, a code of laws was always accompanied by a human interpreter of laws, a judge, to decide when breaking the letter of the law did not violate the spirit or situation that the law was intended to cover. Great moments in history, religion, philosophy, and literature focus on the legal/ethical dilemma, and debating teams would wither away if the dilemma were to disappear.

Ethical Stereotypes

The 1990s ushered in the "New Era of Entrepreneurship" worldwide. The United States, now as in the past, is seen as providing an inviting and nurturing climate for those wishing to start their own enterprises and reap the rewards. In part, this is because the federal government has encouraged, to a greater degree than in any other country, an atmosphere under which free market forces, private initiative, and individual responsibility and freedom can flourish. Legislation such as antitrust laws, laws regulating labor, and the graduated income tax has not hampered the growth of entrepreneurship in America.

These laws, enacted in response to society's changing perceptions of what constitutes ethical business practices, have had the equally desirable effect of encouraging those in many industries to develop codes of ethics—in large part because they wished to have the freedom to set their own rules, rather than to have rules imposed on them by Congress.

As the ethical climate of business has changed, so has the image of the entrepreneur. The *good* stereotype is personified by Horatio Alger. The *ruthless* stereotype is represented by entrepreneurs doing business in the unfettered economic climate in the 19th century—the era of the Robber Barons, where acts of industrial sabotage, which today we would not condone, were common. The battles of James Hill and Edward Harriman over the rights of railroads, the alleged sabotage by John D. Rockefeller of his competitors' oil refineries, the exploitation of child labor in New England's textile mills and of black labor in the southern cotton plantations, and the promoting of "snake oil" and Lydia Pinkham's tonics leave an unsavory aftertaste in the minds of today's more ethically conscious entrepreneurs.

Yet, thoughtful historians of American entrepreneurship will also recall that regardless of standards by which they are judged or of the motivations attributed to them, certain American entrepreneurs gave back to society such institutions as the Morgan Library and the Rockefeller Foundation. The extraordinary legacy of Andrew Carnegie is another example. (And, of course, these scholars are much more inclined to examine and dissect the ethical behavior of the business sector, rather than that of the clergy, or even of academia itself. In many comparisons, the behavior of the business sector would look quite pure.)

Carnegie's case is also interesting because he described the total change of attitude that came over him after he had amassed his fortune. Carnegie was the son of a Scots weaver and was able personally to amass $300 million in the production of crude steel between 1873 and 1901. As Carnegie himself described, he believed that competition "insures the survival of the fittest in every department." Carnegie also felt that "the fact that this talent for organization and management is rare among men is proved by the fact that it invariably secures enormous rewards for its possessor."[7] So apparently satisfied was Carnegie with the correctness of his view, he did not try to reconcile it with the fact that British steel rails were effectively excluded by a protective tariff equaling over half the production price of each ton of steel rails.[8] That Carnegie's mind was not easy over his fortune, however, is evident from his statement that "I would as soon give my son a curse as the almighty dollar."[9] After 1901, when he sold Carnegie Steel to United States Steel under pressure from a combine headed by J. P. Morgan, Carnegie personally supervised the giving in the United States and Great Britain of more than $300 million—an amount which is equivalent to many billions in today's dollars. Among his gifts to humanity were over 2,800 libraries, an Endowment for International Peace, and the Carnegie Institute of Pittsburgh.

From today's perspective, the entrepreneurs above might be described as acting in enlightened self-interest. However, when the same sort of entrepreneurial generosity is demonstrated today by such people as Armand Hammer of Occidental Petroleum

---

[7] "Introduction to Contemporary Civilization in the West," *The Gospel of Wealth* (New York: Century, 1900), p. 620.
[8] W. E. Woodward, *A New American History* (Garden City, N.Y.: Garden City Publishing, 1938), p. 704.
[9] Ibid., p. 622.

and An Wang of Wang Laboratories and Arnold Hiatt of the Stride Rite Corporation, we are more likely to speak of their acts as philanthropy than as fulfilling their social contract.

Yet, a touch of suspicion still tinges entrepreneurial activity, and the word *entrepreneur* may still connote to some a person who belongs to a ruthless, scheming group located a good deal lower than the angels. In 1975, *Time* suggested that a businessman might make the best-qualified candidate for U.S. president but noted the "deep-rooted American suspicion of businessmen's motives."[10] Quoting John T. Conner, chairman of Allied Chemical and former head of Merck and Company, *Time's* editors added: "Anyone with previous business experience becomes immediately suspect. Certain segments think he can't make a decision in the public interest."[11]

However, in 1988, the prophecy of *Time* was fulfilled when George Bush, an oil entrepreneur, was elected as president of the United States, a revealing conclusion to America's most entrepreneurial decade.

Should Ethics Be Taught?

Just as the 1990s ushered in a new era of worldwide entrepreneurship, the world of business ethics has redefined itself, according to Andrew Stark. Stark asserts that

advocates of the new business ethics can be identified by their acceptance of two fundamental principles. While they agree with their colleagues that ethics and interest can conflict, they take that observation as the starting point, not the ending point, of an ethicist's analytical task . . . Second, the new perspective reflects an awareness and acceptance of the messy world of mixed motives.[12]

The challenge facing this new group of business ethicists is to bridge the gap between the moral philosophers and the managers. The business ethicists talk of "moderation, pragmatism, minimalism"[13] in their attempt to "converse with real managers in a language relevant to the world they inhabit and the problems they face."[14] With this focus on the practical side of decision making, courses on ethics can be useful to entrepreneurs and all managers.

Ethics Can and Should Be Taught

In an article that examines the ancient tradition of moral education, the decline of moral instruction beginning in the 19th century, and the renaissance of interest in ethics in the 1960s, Derek Bok, president of Harvard University, argues that ethics can and should be taught by educational institutions and that this teaching is both necessary and of value:

Precisely because its community is so diverse, set in a society so divided and confused over its values, a university that pays little attention to moral development may find that many of its students grow bewildered, convinced that ethical dilemmas are simply matters of personal opinion beyond external judgment or careful analysis.

Nothing could be more unfortunate or more unnecessary. Although moral issues sometimes lack convincing answers, that is often not the case. Besides, universities should be the last institutions to discourage belief in the value of reasoned argument and carefully considered evidence in analyzing even the hardest of human problems.[15]

It is noteworthy that John Shad, a former chairman of the New York Stock Exchange, gave over $20 million to the Harvard Business School to help develop a way to include ethics in the MBA curriculum. Beginning in the fall of 1988, first-year students at the Harvard Business School are required to attend a three-week, nongraded ethics module called Decision Making and Ethical Values. The cases discussed range from insider trading at Salomon Brothers to discrimination in employee promotions to locating a U.S. manufacturing unit in Mexico. Thomas R. Piper, associate dean, emphasizes that the role of the course is "not converting sinners . . . but we're taking young people who have a sense of integrity and trying to get them to connect ethics with business decisions."[16] J. Gregory Dees, another ethics professor at Harvard, now at Stanford University, stresses that the "primary objective of the course is to get people thinking about issues that are easy to avoid . . . What we want people to leave DMEV with is a commitment to raising these issues in other settings, other courses, and on the job, with [an acceptable] comfort level in doing so."[17]

Since John Shad made his contribution three second-year electives (Moral Dilemmas of Management, Managing Information in a Competitive Context, and Profits, Markets, and Values) have been

---

[10] "Time Essay: New Places to Look for Presidents," *Time*, December 15, 1975, p. 19.
[11] Ibid., p. 19.
[12] Andrew Stark, "What's the Matter with Business Ethics?" *Harvard Business Review*, May–June 1993, p. 46.
[13] Ibid., p. 48.
[14] Ibid.
[15] Derek Bok, "Is Dishonesty Good for Business?" *Business & Society Review*, Summer 1979, p. 50.
[16] John A. Byrne, "Can Ethics Be Taught? Harvard Gives It The Old College Try," *Business Week* (April 6, 1992), p. 34.
[17] Chitra Nayak, "Why Ethics DMEV under The Microscope," *The Harbus*.

added to Harvard's ethics program. The Wharton School has a similar course required of first-year MBA students, *Leadership Skills*, which is a year-long, graded course with a four-week ethics module. The Wharton faculty are hoping to introduce the core literature of business ethics and corporate responsibility, to expose students to discussions, and to stimulate the students to address these moral issues in their other courses. These two programs are part of a larger effort to incorporate ethics, as

over 500 business-ethics courses are currently taught on American campuses; fully 90 percent of the nation's business schools now provide some kind of training in the area. There are more than 25 textbooks in the field and three academic journals dedicated to the topic. At least 16 business-ethics research centers are now in operation, and endowed chairs in business ethics have been established at Georgetown, Virginia, Minnesota, and a number of other prominent business schools.[18]

The Usefulness of Academic Ethics

The study of ethics does seem to have the advantage of making students more aware of the pervasiveness of ethical situations in business settings, of bringing perspective to ethical situations from a distance, and of providing a framework for understanding ethical problems when they arise. Further, the study of ethics has been shown to affect, to some degree, both beliefs and behavior. For example, in a study of whether ethics courses affect student values, value changes in business school students who had taken a course in business ethics and those who did not were examined closely and were plotted across the multiple stages.[19]

The study used a sequence of stages, called the Kohlberg construct, developed by Kohlberg in 1967. These stages are presented in *Exhibit 9.1*. In the Kohlberg construct, being moral in *Stage 1* is synonymous with being obedient, and the motivation is to avoid condemnation. In *Stage 2*, the individual seeks advantage. Gain is the primary purpose, and interaction does not result in binding personal relationships. The orientation of *Stage 3* is toward pleasing others and winning approval. Proper roles are defined by stereotyped images of majority behavior. Such reciprocity is confined to primary group relations. In *Stage 4*, cooperation is viewed in the context of society as a whole. External laws serve to coordinate moral schemes, and the individual feels committed to the social order. One thus subscribes to formal punishment by police or the courts. In *Stage 5*, there is acknowledgement that reciprocity can be in-

EXHIBIT 9.1

Classification of Moral Judgment into Stages of Development

Stage	Orientation	Theme
1	Punishment and obedience	Morality of obedience
2	Instrumental relativism	Simple exchange
3	Interpersonal concordance	Reciprocal role taking
4	Law and order	Formal justice
5	Legitimate social contract	Procedural justice
6	Universal ethical principle	Individual conscience

Source: Adapted from Kohlberg (1967).

equitable. New laws and social arrangements now may be invoked as corrective mechanisms. All citizens are assured of fundamental safety and equality. Cognitive structures at the *Stage 6* level automatically reject credos and actions that the individual considers morally reprehensible, and the referent is a person's own moral framework, rather than stereotyped group behavior. Because most of one's fellows endorse a law does not guarantee its moral validity. When confronting social dilemmas, the individual is guided by internal principles that may transcend the legal system. Although these convictions are personal, they are also universal since they have worth and utility apart from the individual espousing them. Kohlberg's final stage thus represents more than mere conformity with state, teacher, or institutional criteria. Rather, it indicates one's capacity for decision making and problem solving in the context of personal ethical standards. In the study, those who took a course in business ethics showed a progression up the ethical scale, while those who had not taken a course did not progress.

Entrepreneurs' Perspectives

Most entrepreneurs also believe ethics should be taught. In the research project mentioned on page 313, entrepreneurs and chief executive officers attending the Owner/President Management (OPM) program at the Harvard Business School were asked the question: Is there a role for ethics in business education for entrepreneurs? Of those responding, 72 percent said ethics can and should be taught as part of the curriculum. (Only 20 percent said it should not, and two respondents were not sure.)

The most prominently cited reason for including ethics was that ethical behavior is at the core of long-

---

[18] Andrew Stark, "What's the Matter with Business Ethics?" *Harvard Business Review*, May–June 1993, p. 38.
[19] David P. Boyd, "Enhancing Ethical Development by an Intervention Program," unpublished manuscript, Northeastern University, 1980.

term business success, because it provides the glue that binds enduring successful business and personal relationships together. In addition, the responses reflected a serious and thoughtful awareness of the fragile but vital role of ethics in entrepreneurial attainment and of the long-term consequences of ethical behavior for a business. Typical comments were:

- If the free enterprise system is to survive, the business schools better start paying attention to teaching ethics. They should know that business is built on trust, which depends upon honesty and sincerity. BS comes out quickly in a small company.
- If our society is going to move forward, it won't be based on how much money is accumulated in any one person or group. Our society will move forward when all people are treated fairly—that's my simple definition of ethics. I know of several managers, presidents, etc., who you would not want to get between them and their wallets or ambitions.
- In my experience the business world is by and large the most ethical and law-abiding part of our society.
- Ethics should be addressed, considered and thoroughly examined; it should be an inherent part of each class and course . . . ; instead of crusading with ethics, it is much more effective to make high ethics an inherent part of business—and it is.

However, these views were not universally held. One entrepreneur who helped to found a large company with international operations warned: "For God's sake, don't forget that 90 percent of the businessman's efforts consist of just plain hard work."

There is also some cynicism. The 40-year-old head of a real estate and construction firm in the Northeast with 300 employees and $75 million in annual sales said: "There is so much hypocrisy in today's world that even totally ethical behavior is questioned since many people think it is some new negotiating technique."

It would be unfortunate if the entrepreneur did not realize his or her potential for combining action with ethical purpose because of the suspicion that the two are unrelated or inimical. There is no reason why they need be considered generically opposed. Nevertheless, in analyzing ethics, the individual can expect no substitute for his or her own effort and intelligence.

Thorny Issues for Entrepreneurs

Although the majority of entrepreneurs take ethics seriously, researchers in this area are still responding to David McClelland's call for inquiry: "We do not know at the present time what makes an entrepreneur more or less ethical in his dealings, but obviously there are few problems of greater importance for future research."[20] In a recent article, the topics for research were outlined (see *Exhibit 9.2*). Clearly, an opportunity for further research still exists.

Action under Pressure

During an entrepreneurial career, an entrepreneur will have to act on issues under pressure of time and when struggling for survival. In addition, the entrepreneur will most likely decide ethical questions that involve obligations on many sides—to customers, employees, stockholders, family, partners, himself, or a combination of these. Walking the tightrope and balancing common sense with an ethical framework is precarious.

As a way to cope with the inevitable conflicts an entrepreneur will encounter, a first step is developing an awareness of his or her own explicit and implicit ethical beliefs, those of his or her team and investors, and those of the milieu within which the company competes for survival. As the successful entrepreneurs quoted above believe, in the long run, succumbing to the temptations of situational ethics will, in all likelihood, result in a tumble into the quicksand, not a safety net—just ask Ivan Boesky.

An appreciation of this state of affairs is succinctly stated by Fred T. Allen, chairman and president of Pitney-Bowes:

> As businessmen we must learn to weigh short-term interests against long-term possibilities. We must learn to sacrifice what is immediate, what is expedient, if the moral price is too high. What we stand to gain is precious little compared to what we can ultimately lose.[21]

Different Views

Different reactions to what is ethical may explain why some aspects of venture creation go wrong, both during startup and in the heat of the battle, for no apparent reason. Innumerable examples can be cited to illustrate that broken partnerships often can be traced to apparent differences in the personal ethics among

[20] David McClelland, *Achieving Society* (New York: Van Nostrand, 1961), p. 331.
[21] Letter to Editor, *The Wall Street Journal*, October 17, 1975.

EXHIBIT 9.2

Selected Ethical Dilemmas of Entrepreneurial Management

Dilemma: Elements	Issues That May Arise
Promoter: Entrepreneurial euphoria Impression management Pragmatic versus moral considerations	What does honesty mean when promoting an innovation? Does it require complete disclosure of the risks and uncertainties? Does it require a dispassionate analysis of the situation, with equal time given to the downside as well as the upside? What sorts of influence tactics cross the line from encouragement and inducement to manipulation and coercion?
Relationship: Conflicts of interest and roles Transactional ethics Guerilla tactics	Tension between perceived obligations and moral expectations. Changes in roles and relationships: pre versus post venture status. Decisions based on affiliative concerns rather than on task-based concerns. Transition from a trust-based work environment to one that is more controlled.
Innovator: "Frankenstein's problem" New types of ethical problems Ethic of change	Side effects and negative externalities force a social reconsideration of norms and values. Heightened concern about the future impact of unknown harms. Who is responsible for the assessment of risk? Inventor? Government? Market? Breaking down traditions and creating new models.
Other dilemmas: Finders-keepers ethic Conflict between personal values and business goals Unsavory industry practices	Is there a fair way to divide profits when they are not explicitly contracted away? Should the entrepreneur take all the gains that are not explicitly contracted away? Managing an intimate connection between personal choices and professional decisions. Coping with ethical pressures with creative solutions and integrity. Seeking industry recognition while not giving into peer pressure to conform.

Source: Adapted from J. Gregory Dees and Jennifer A. Starr, "Entrepreneurship through an Ethical Lens," in *The State of the Art of Entrepreneurship*, ed. Donald L. Sexton and John D. Kasarda (Boston: PWS-Kent Publishing company, 1992), p. 96.

the members of a management team. So, too, with investors. While the experienced venture capital investor seeks entrepreneurs with a reputation for integrity, honesty, and ethical behavior, the definition is necessarily subjective and depends in part on the beliefs of the investor himself and in part on the prevailing ethical climate in the industry sector in which the venture is involved.

Problems of Law

For entrepreneurs, there are increasingly frequent situations where one law directly conflicts with another. For example, a small-business investment company in New York City became involved in serious financial trouble. The Small Business Administration stated that the company should begin to liquidate its investments, because it would otherwise be in defiance of its agreement with the SBA. However, the Securities and Exchange Commission stated that this liquidation would constitute unfair treatment of stockholders, due to resulting imbalance in their portfolios. After a year and a half of agonizing negotiation, the company was able to satisfy all the parties, but compromises had to be made on both sides.

Another example of conflicting legal demands involves conflicts between procedures of the Civil Service code and the Fair Employment Practice Acts. The code states that hiring will include adherence to certain standards, a principle that was introduced in the last century to curb the patronage abuses in public service. Recently, however, the problem of encouraging and aiding minorities has led to Fair Employment Practice Acts, which require the same public agencies that are guided by Civil Service standards to hire without prejudice, and without the requirement that a given test shall serve as the criterion of selection. Both these laws are based on valid ethical intent, but the resolution of such conflicts is no simple matter.

Further, unlike the international laws governing commercial airline transportation, there is no international code of business ethics. When doing business abroad, entrepreneurs may find that those with whom they wish to do business have little in common with them—no common language, no common historical context for conducting business, and no common set of ethical beliefs about right and wrong and everything in between. For example, in the United States, bribing a high official to obtain a favor is considered both ethically and legally unacceptable; in parts of the Middle East, it is the only way to get things done. What we see as a bribe, those in parts of the Middle East see as a tip, like what you might give the headwaiter at a fancy restaurant in New York for a good table.

"When in Rome . . . " is one approach to this problem. Consulting a lawyer with expertise in international business before doing anything is another. Assuming that the object of an entrepreneur's international business venture is to make money, he or she needs to figure out some way that is legally tolerable under the codes of laws that do apply and that is ethically tolerable personally.

Examples of the Ends-and-Means Issue

A central question in any ethical discussion concerns the extent to which a noble end may justify ignoble means—or whether using unethical means for assumed ethical ends may not subvert the aim in some way. As an example of a noble end, consider the case of a university agricultural extension service whose goal was to aid small farmers to increase their crop productivity. The end was economically constructive and profit oriented only in the sense that the farmers might prosper from better crop yields. However, to continue being funded, the extension service was required to provide predictions of the annual increase in crop yield it could achieve, estimates it could not provide at the required level of specificity. Further, unless it could show substantial increases in crop yields, its funding might be heavily reduced. In this case, the extension service decided, if need be, to fudge the figures since it was felt that even though the presentation of overly optimistic predictions was unethical, the objectives of the persons running the organization were highly ethical and even the unethical aspects could be condoned within the context of the inability of the various groups involved to speak each other's language clearly. The fact that the funding source finally backed down in its demand ameliorated the immediate problem. But if it had not, certainly a danger existed that the individuals in this organization, altruistic though their intentions were, would begin to think that falsification was the norm and would forget that actions that run contrary to one's ethical feelings gradually would build a debilitating cynicism.

Another example is given in the case of a merger of a small rental-service business with a middle-sized conglomerate, where a law's intent was in direct opposition to what would occur if the law was literally enforced. In this case, a partner in the rental firm, shortly before the merger, had become involved in a severe automobile accident, suffered multiple injuries, and was seemingly unable to return to work. The partner also knew that the outlook for his health in the immediate future was unpre-

dictable. Under these circumstances, he was eager, for the sake of his family, to seek some of the stock acquired in the merger and make a large portion of his assets liquid. However, federal law does not allow quick profit taking from mergers and therefore did not allow such a sale. The partner consulted the president and officers of the larger company, and they acquiesced in his plans to sell portions of his stock and stated their conviction that no adverse effect on the stock would result. Still unsure, the man then checked with his lawyer and found that the federal law in question had almost never been prosecuted. Having ascertained the risk and having probed the rationale of the law as it applied to his case, the man then sold some of the stock acquired in the merger in order to provide security for his family in the possible event of his incapacitation or death. Although he subsequently recovered completely, this could not have been foreseen.

In this instance, the partner decided that a consideration of the intrinsic purpose of the law allowed him to act as he did. In addition, he made as thorough a check as possible of the risks involved in his action. He was not satisfied with the decision he made, but he felt that it was the best he could do at the time. One can see in this example the enormous ethical tugs-of-war that go with the territory of entrepreneurship.

An Example of Integrity

That entrepreneurial decisions are complicated also is illustrated in the following example. At age 27, an entrepreneur joined a new computer software firm with sales of $1.5 million as vice president of international marketing of a new division. His principal goal was to establish profitable distribution for the company's products in the major industrialized nations. Stock incentives and a highly leveraged bonus plan placed clear emphasis on profitability, rather than on volume. In one European country, the choice of distributors was narrowed to 1 from a field of over 20. The potential distributor was a top firm, with an excellent track record and management, and the chemistry was right. In fact, the distributor was so anxious to do business with the entrepreneur's company that it was willing to accept a 10 percent commission, rather than the normal 15 percent royalty. The other terms of the deal were acceptable to both parties. In this actual case, the young vice president decided to give the distributor the full 15 percent commission, in spite of the fact that it would have settled for much less. This approach was apparently quite successful because, in five years, this international division grew from zero to $18 million in very profitable sales, and the venture was acquired by a large firm for $80 million. In describing his reasoning, the entrepreneur said his main goal was to create a sense of long-term integrity. He said further:

> I knew what it would take for them to succeed in gaining the kind of market penetration we were after. I also knew that the economics of their business definitely needed the larger margins from the 15 percent, rather than the smaller royalty. So I figured that if I offered them the full royalty, they would realize I was on their side, and that would create such goodwill that when we did have some serious problems down the road—and you always have them—then we would be able to work together to solve them. And that's exactly what happened. If I had exploited their eagerness to be our distributor, then it only would have come back to haunt me later on.

Ethics Exercise Revisited

The following statements are often made, even by practicing entrepreneurs: "How can we think about ethics when we haven't enough time even to think about running our venture?" "Entrepreneurs are doers, not thinkers—and ethics is too abstract a concept to have any bearing on business realities." "When you're struggling to survive, you're not worried about the means you use—you're fighting for one thing: survival."

However, the contemplation of ethical behavior is not unlike poetry—emotion recollected in tranquility. This chapter is intended to provide one such tranquil opportunity.

Through the decisions actually made, or not made, an individual could become more aware of his or her own value system and how making ethical decisions can be affected by the climate in which these decisions are made. However, in the exercise, participants were asked only to answer questions. They were not being asked to carry out an action. Between intent and action lies a large gap, which can only be filled by confronting and acting in a number of ambiguous situations.

Chapter Summary

1. The vast majority of CEOs, investors, and entrepreneurs believe that a high ethical standard is the single most important factor in long-term success.
2. Historically, ethical stereotypes of business persons ranged widely, and today the old perceptions have given way to a more aware and accepting notion of the messy world of ethical decisions.

3. Many leading business schools today have incorporated ethical issues into their curricula.
4. Entrepreneurs can rarely, if ever, finish a day without facing at least one or two ethical issues.
5. Numerous ethical dilemmas challenge entrepreneurs at the most crucial moments of survival, like a precarious walk on a tightrope.

Study Questions

1. What conclusions and insights emerged from the Ethics Exercise?
2. Why have ethical stereotypes emerged and how have they changed?
3. Why is ethics so important to entrepreneurial—and other success?
4. Why do many entrepreneurs and CEOs believe ethics can and should be taught?
5. What are the most thorny ethical dilemmas that entrepreneurs face, and why?
6. Describe an actual example of how and why taking a higher ethical ground results in a good decision for business.

MIND STRETCHERS
Have You Considered?

1. How would you define your own ethics?
2. What was the toughest ethical decision you have faced; how did you handle it, and why? What did you learn?
3. How do you personally determine whether someone is ethical or not?
4. How would you describe the ethics of the President of the United States? Why? Would these ethics be acceptable to you from an investor, a partner, a spouse?

Preparation Questions

1. What roles/titles has Wayne Postoak held? What did he have to do to earn these?
2. What are the strengths and weaknesses of the entrepreneur?
3. Evaluate this business opportunity. What are the opportunities and barriers?
4. What are the critical skills and resources necessary to succeed in this business?
5. Would you invest in this business? Why, or why not?
6. What should the entrepreneur do, and why?

Wayne Postoak

In late 1983, at age 44, Wayne Postoak, a Choctaw Indian, was employed as an instructor in the Biological Science Department at Haskell Indian Junior College (now Haskell Indian Nations University) located in Lawrence, Kansas. Lawrence is approximately 40 miles west of Kansas City and is also the home of the University of Kansas. Wayne had been in the classroom since 1980, but was previously the Haskell basketball coach and recruiter since the early 1970s. During his tenure as coach, the Haskell Indians had the longest winning streak in the history of the school and even beat the JV squad of the University of Kansas. The primary reason he came to Haskell to coach was the administration's support of intercollegiate sports. Eventually the support waned and Wayne ended up teaching in the classroom.

Wayne began to wonder about remaining a teacher because there was a philosophical difference between his approach to education and his supervisor's approach. In addition to this difference was his continued discontentment with not coaching. At the time his eldest son, Darren Wayne, prompted him to consider the future of his children. At the age of 6, Darren Wayne dreamed of becoming a medical doctor. Wayne knew that if he were to help his four children attend college, he could not do so on a teacher's salary. This was ever present in his mind each summer as he, like all other Haskell federal employees, was required to take a summer furlough. During these furloughs, Wayne would supplement his income by completing small construction jobs such as fireplaces and sidewalks.

These summer projects kept him apprised of opportunities within the Lawrence area, and a conversation with a friend in the Anadarko area office of the Bureau of Indian Affairs mentioned the plans to build 36 bridges on the four Indian reservations in Kansas. With his dissatisfaction with his job, the upcoming bridge projects, and his desire to care for his family, Wayne began to look at the possibility of starting his own construction company. At the time of his pondering, he also knew he had accumulated approximately $20,000 in his retirement that could possibly be used to start a company.

The Entrepreneur's Background

Wayne grew up the middle child of six brothers and six sisters in Ardmore, Oklahoma. He originally spoke only Choctaw. When his father was cutting his hair the week before he was to go to school, his mother cried because his beautiful hair was being cut. During his father's explanation for why he was cutting his hair, Wayne was introduced to the English language. To this day, during stressful situations, Wayne tends to translate from Choctaw to English in his mind.

One of Wayne's first role models was Mrs. Crumb, his first grade teacher. There were two Indian children in her class of 21 students. She had the other 19 students learn to say they wanted a drink or wanted to go to the restroom in Choctaw. This helped Wayne and taught him courtesy.

Wayne's father, Sam, was the main role model in his life and owned a masonry company as well as the family truck farm. Because they were below the poverty level, it was surprising to Wayne that his father had acquired over 1,200 acres of land by the time he passed away in the late 1980s.

Early on, Sam trained his sons in bricklaying. When Wayne was only 8 years old, his father gave Wayne and his brothers "assignments" to build walls made of brick. These assignments usually took them 6 to 8 hours each day, so they didn't play like the other kids did. When Sam would come home to check on their assignments, anything less than a "B" would have to be redone. If this required them to do the work at night, he would put up a light bulb for them to see. Sometimes they would finish at 2 or 3 o'clock in the morning. This taught them to do things right without supervision and gave them a skill so they could support themselves, which two of his older brothers eventually did.

Sam also taught his sons about the economy of movement. He showed them that if they laid 500 bricks and took an extra step that was 500 steps. He also showed them that if they cut off the mortar 3 times or tapped the bricks 3 times they would have to multiply that by 500 bricks. Wayne later used this knowledge to consult with other people about different ways to save movements.

This case was written in 1998 by Ms. Cheryl Chuckluck, Director, Center for Tribal Entrepreneurial Studies, Haskell Indian Nations University, Lawrence, Kansas. It has been contributed by, and is used with the permission of Ms. Chuckluck and CTES. The author is most appreciative of Ms. Chuckluck, Mr. Postoak, and CTES.

Wayne also recalls that the family had to wash clothes in some of the streams nearby or in the town washers, when the weather was bad, and then hang them upon the fences near their house. During Wayne's third grade, he and his father were hanging out the clothes to dry when a big, black Chrysler drove up and scattered the clothes with dust. Sam explained to the man, a Mr. Quinn Wicker, that it was hard work to clean the clothes and that it wasn't polite for him to drive up in such a manner.

Mr. Wicker was a businessman from Ardmore who came to buy 20 acres that Sam bought after he had learned that there were plans to drill for oil nearby. Mr. Wicker's manager offered Sam a certain amount of money a couple of times, and Sam counteroffered each time with a larger figure that was only good for that day. Since the manager did not have the authority to accept a larger offer, he had to check with his boss and would come back to Sam the next day. Because Sam stuck to his principle that the offer was only good for that day, Mr. Wicker decided to negotiate directly with Sam. He pulled out a wad of money that turned out to be $3,000. Sam, sensing that Wayne was keenly observing, took Mr. Wicker off to negotiate. Sam did not accept the $3,000 because his land was for sale at $160 per acre, a vastly larger amount than what the other Indians had received for their land. Many of those Indians had unknowingly sold their land for a pittance, and he didn't want Mr. Wicker to take advantage of him. In the end, the land was in the middle of an area where plans were to build a Standard Oil Refinery, and Sam did not sell his land; but he held on to his principle.

Wayne remembers that when he was only six, his father had been an alcoholic, but he had joined a church and never drank again. Wayne understood the discipline his father had, and if he could have that kind of discipline, then he would also develop the behavior. While growing up, team sports also became very important to Wayne and his siblings. They learned how to be a team player and learned the discipline needed to get into shape. His playing ability garnered him scholarships in football, basketball, and baseball. These skills also served him well as a coach.

At the age of 11, Wayne wasn't very accomplished at the production side of construction. His father introduced him to ordering supplies for the company, and it was here that Wayne excelled. During his teenage years, he completed small construction jobs such as fireplaces on his own. Many of his brothers remained in the construction arena. Wayne also enjoyed many aspects of building fireplaces on his own, but he also knew his competencies lay elsewhere.

When he reached 17 years old, Wayne attended the Haskell Institute (now Haskell Indian Nations University) and went into the prevocational program. During his senior year, he was completing six hours of masonry and one hour of English. He also participated in on-the-job training where he could get work and also get school credit. A businessman from downtown Lawrence, Kansas, approached the masonry instructor about building a car wash. The instructor didn't have the time to perform the job, and compared it to what the business owner received from another company. Wayne's estimate was half of the other bid. With the Haskell Institute's equipment, trucks, and subcontractors who were also students, he completed the project in 22 working days (compared to the expected 60 working days) and at half the cost.

Wayne liked the feeling of sharing the work with friends and completing a project. However, the owner thought that they did the job too quickly and that a 17-year-old kid should not be able to make that kind of money. Wayne finally said he couldn't control the student laborers and student subcontractors, so if the building wasn't standing the next day the businessman would just have to build it again. The owner asked if Wayne was threatening him and he said, "I'm not saying anything, I just want to get paid and pay the subcontractors so that it might not happen." The owner paid him $2,800, and he was able to share some of the money with two of his brothers and a sister who were attending Haskell at the time. Thus the first car wash in the midwest was built near the corner of Louisiana and 23rd Street in Lawrence.

While at college Wayne was very shy and withdrew from his speech class three times in a row. He was terrified to complete the required three-minute public speech. Finally he had to complete the class in order to graduate, but with two weeks still remaining before the speech, he couldn't sleep. He did give his speech, and now 100 or so speeches later, public speaking has become easier for Wayne.

Initially, Wayne did not go into the construction industry, but completed college and went into coaching. Eventually he became the coach and recruiter at Haskell Indian Junior College. Wayne identified talent and put together winning teams from 1970 to 1980.

During his time as coach, he taught his teams several important lessons. One of these was to be courteous to others. While they dined, his teams had to say thank you to the waitresses several times and they became known as a courteous group. Those teams were always welcomed back during the following season. He also taught the teams to be courteous with other people's time. Being on time meant that if the basketball team was expected between 4:00 AM and 4:05 AM for a breakfast before a tournament, stragglers arriving after 4:06 AM would find the food line closed, and they'd go hungry. After winning their first game in the tournament, they stayed late (despite growling stomachs) to watch the team they would play the next day. Wayne then would call Don's Steakhouse in Lawrence, and ask them if they could have their meal ready at an exact time. Wayne had a group of hungry boys coming in!

Each time the team traveled, Wayne would tell the team to be ready at 5:00 AM. He went home to get himself ready, and returned at 4:55 AM to find all the students waiting on the bus! They began to check on one another so no one would be late. They learned shared responsibility, and this enhanced their teamwork.

While serving as head coach, Wayne also sold the season tickets to the basketball games to raise funds for the athletic program. At every opportunity he spoke to organizations in Lawrence, and would attempt to sell season tickets to everyone. One season he sold 2,000 tickets to anyone and everyone he could think of—businesses, organizations, and individuals—even though the building could only hold 1,400 people! He knew that not all the people would come to the games, and that the athletic program needed the funds. When he spoke to banks, he would tell them that another bank bought 50 tickets. Wayne challenged them to buy as well, and it worked.

The Industry

During 1983, Lawrence was a town of approximately 65,000 people, when the University of Kansas was in session. Interest rates were high, and reached as much as 19 percent, lessening the feasibility of new construction. Most construction firms in the area were small, and specialized in one area or another. There were only two larger general contractors that had annual sales up to $18 million. At this time there were 22 minority certified construction firms that were mostly specialized, subcontractors in the entire state of Kansas. Many projects were found by attending the Association of General Contractors' monthly cocktail hour. This event was held the evening before the bid letting—mainly for Department of Transportation projects.

During this time, the Affirmative Action law had been passed and was scheduled to be implemented in January 1984. Any construction firm that obtained federal contracts had to utilize a certain percentage of minority-owned subcontractors to be in compliance. In addition to this mandate, there were 36 bridge projects in northeast Kansas available for Indian-owned construction companies because of the Buy Indian Act. (See *Exhibits A-D* for population and employment data for Douglas County, Kansas).

The Risks

As Wayne contemplated what to do, he started to list the risks and unknowns:

- He would have no job, which meant no continuous income.

- He would be undercapitalized for a construction company—he had only $20,000.
- He would have no employees.
- He would have no equipment.
- If he considered the bridge projects, he had no bridge building experience.
- He would have no estimator.

EXHIBIT A

Douglas County, Kansas Population

Year	Population
1980*	67,640
1981	69,574
1982	69,947
1983	69,945

Source: U.S. Bureau of the Census
*Indicates decennial census 10% population counts. Others are population estimates.

EXHIBIT B

Douglas County, Kansas Per Capita Income

Year	Per Capita Income
1980	8,157
1981	8,939
1982	9,188
1983	9,846

Source: Bureau of Economic Analysis (REIS)

EXHIBIT C

Employment and Civilian Labor Force, Douglas County, Kansas

Year	#Employed	Civilian Labor Force
1980	33,214	34,650
1981	33,133	34,506
1982	32,472	34,066
1983	32,421	34,103

Source: Kansas Department of Human Resources

EXHIBIT D

Employment by Industry, Douglas County, Kansas

Year	Total	Non-Farm	Construction	Manufacturing	Transportation	Gov't/G Services
1980	34,655	33,604	1,681	4,908	1,345	10,326
1981	33,777	32,707	1,336	4,743	1,323	9,817
1982	33,595	32,513	1,243	4,527	1,209	9,768
1983	34,102	32,945	1,382	4,447	1,180	9,755

Source: Bureau of Economic analysis (REIS)

## PART THREE

Resource Requirements

Resources to the entrepreneur are like the paint and the brush to the artist. They remain inert until the creative flair engages them with the canvas. There are special attitudes, strategies, and techniques used by successful entrepreneurs in *gaining control over the minimal resources* necessary to pursue an opportunity. Ownership of these resources is not the key. What is vital is control and influence over OPR (other people's resources)—both monetary and nonmonetary. The latter are often far more important than is commonly thought.

Identifying the necessary financial requirements of a startup or emerging firm is a primary task. This includes knowing how much cash the venture will need and when and where to raise it. Developing the appropriate financial statements "without the pain" is something every entrepreneur would like to accomplish. An exercise in Chapter 10 will help entrepreneurs get started. Another significant task is identifying and utilizing effectively various outside resources—di-

rectors, advisors, accountants, attorneys, bankers, and the like. It is important to know where and how the best outsiders can be found, and what needs to be known about selecting, compensating, and working with them.

If the resources are the paint and brush, then the concept of the business plan is the canvas. By itself, it is sterile and bland. What's critical is knowing why, whether, and how to turn one's idea, a team, and resources into an artistic feat in the form of a first-rate business plan that can be used to raise money and resources and to grow the business.

Finally, what do entrepreneurs do when the pace is so quick that there is simply not enough time to prepare a complete business plan? This can happen to an entrepreneur seeking to acquire a business, a license, a franchise, or other rights in a hot seller's market. Knowing what to do and how to develop quickly a "dehydrated" business plan can make the difference between success and disappointment.

## Chapter Ten

Resource Requirements

When it comes to control of resources . . . all I need from a source is the ability to use [the resource]. There are people who describe the ideal business as a post office box to which people send cash.

Howard H. Stevenson
Harvard Business School

Results Expected

Upon completion of this chapter, you will have:

1. Examined the successful entrepreneur's unique attitudes about and approaches to resources—people, capital, and other assets.
2. Identified the important issues in the selection and effective utilization of outside professionals, such as members of a board of directors, lawyers, accountants, and consultants.
3. Examined decisions about financial resources.
4. Analyzed "FAX International" case.
5. Created simple cash flow and income statements and a balance sheet.
6. Discovered the ways in which entrepreneurs turn less into more.

The Entrepreneurial Approach to Resources

Resources include (1) people, such as the management team, the board of directors, lawyers, accountants, and consultants; (2) financial resources; (3) assets, such as plant and equipment; and (4) a business plan. Successful entrepreneurs view the need for and the ownership and management of these resources in the pursuit of opportunities differently from the way managers in many large organizations view them. This different way of looking at resources is reflected in the definition of entrepreneurship given in Chapters 1 and 2—the process of creating or seizing an opportunity and pursuing it *regardless of the resources currently controlled.*[1]

Howard H. Stevenson has contributed to understanding the unique approach to resources of successful entrepreneurs. The decisions on what resources are needed, when they are needed, and how to acquire them are strategic decisions that fit with the other driving forces of entrepreneurship. Further, Stevenson has pointed out that entrepreneurs seek to use the minimum possible amount of all types of resources at each stage in their ventures' growth. Rather than own the resources they need, they seek to control them.

Entrepreneurs with this approach reduce some of the risk in pursuing opportunities:

- **Capital.** The amount of capital required is simply smaller, thereby reducing the financial exposure and the dilution of the founder's equity.

---

[1] This definition was developed by Howard H. Stevenson and colleagues at the Harvard Business School. His work on a paradigm for entrepreneurial management has contributed greatly to this area of entrepreneurship. See Howard H. Stevenson, "A New Paradigm for Entrepreneurial Management," in *Proceedings from the 7th Anniversary Symposium on Entrepreneurship, July 1983* (Boston: Harvard Business School, 1984).

- *Flexibility.* Entrepreneurs who do not own a resource are in a better position to commit and decommit quickly.[2] One price of ownership of resources is an inherent inflexibility. With the rapidly fluctuating conditions and uncertainty with which most entrepreneurial ventures have to contend, inflexibility can be a serious curse. Response times need to be short if a firm is to be competitive. Decision windows are most of the time small and elusive. And it is extremely difficult to predict accurately the resources that will be necessary to execute the opportunity. In addition, the entrepreneurial approach to resources permits iterations or strategic experiments in the venture process—that is, ideas can be tried and tested without committing to the ownership of all assets and resources in the business, to markets and technology which change rapidly, and so forth. For example, Howard Head says that if he had raised all the money he needed at the outset, he would have failed by spending it all too early on the wrong version of his metal ski. Consider also, for example, the inflexibility of a company that commits permanently to a certain technology, software, or management system.

- *Low sunk cost.* In addition, sunk costs are lower if the firm exercises the option to abort the venture at any point. Consider, instead, the enormous up-front capital commitment of a nuclear power plant and the cost of abandoning such a project.

- *Costs.* Fixed costs are lowered, thus favorably affecting breakeven. Of course, the other side of the coin is that variable costs may rise. If the entrepreneur has found an opportunity with forgiving and rewarding economics, then there still will most likely be ample gross margins in the venture to absorb this rise.

- *Reduced risk.* In addition to reducing total exposure, other risks, such as the risk of obsolescence of the resource, are also lower. For example, it is no wonder that venture leasing has been used by biotechnology companies as a way to supplement sources of equity financing.

While some might scoff at the practice, assuming erroneously that the firm cannot afford to buy a resource, the truth of the matter is that not owning one provides advantages and options. This is not to say that these decisions are not extremely complex, involving consideration of such details as the tax implications of leasing versus buying, and so forth.

Bootstrapping Strategies: Marshalling and Minimizing Resources

Minimizing resources is referred to in colloquial terms as bootstrapping, or, more formally, as a lack of resource intensity, defined as a multistage commitment of resources with a minimum commitment at each stage or decision point.[3] Thus, to persevere, entrepreneurs ask at every step how they can accomplish a little more with a little less and pursue the opportunity. Or as Amar Bhide explained, "For the great majority of would-be founders, the biggest challenge is not raising money but having the wits and hustle to do without it."[4]

As was outlined in *Exhibit 6.2*, just the opposite attitude is often evident in large institutions that usually are characterized by a trustee or custodial viewpoint. Managers in larger institutions seek to have not only enough committed resources for the task at hand but also a cushion against the tough times.

Using Other People's Resources (OPR)

Obtaining the use of other people's resources, particularly in the startup and early growth stages of a venture, is an important approach for entrepreneurs. In contrast, large firms assume that virtually all resources have to be owned to control their use, and decisions center around how these resources will be acquired and financed—not so with entrepreneurs.

What is key is having the use of the resource and being able to control or influence the deployment of the resource. The quote at the beginning of the chapter illustrates this mindset perfectly.

Other people's resources can include, for example, money invested or loaned by friends, relatives, business associates, or other investors. Or resources can include people, space, equipment, or other material loaned, provided inexpensively or free by customers or suppliers, or secured by bartering future services, opportunities, and the like. In fact, using other people's resources can be as simple as benefiting from free booklets and pamphlets, such as those published by many of the Big Six accounting firms, or making use of low-cost educational programs or of government-funded management assistance programs.

---

[2] Howard H. Stevenson, Michael J. Roberts, and H. Irving Grousbeck, *New Business Ventures and the Entreprenuer* (Homewood, IL: Richard D. Irwin, 1985).
[3] Ibid.
[4] Amar Bhide, "Bootstrap Finance: The Art of Start-Ups," *Harvard Business Review*, November–December 1992, p. 110.

EXHIBIT 10.1

Hypotheses Concerning Networks and Entrepreneurial Effectiveness

Effective entrepreneurs are more likely than others to systematically plan and monitor network activities.

- Effective entrepreneurs are able to *chart their present network* and to discriminate between production and symbolic ties.
- Effective entrepreneurs are able to *view effective networks as a crucial aspect for ensuring the success of their company.*
- Effective entrepreneurs are able to *stabilize and maintain networks,* in order to increase their effectiveness and their efficiency.

Effective entrepreneurs are more likely than others to undertake actions toward increasing their network density and diversity.

- Effective entrepreneurs set aside time for purely random activities—things done with no specific problem in mind.
- Effective entrepreneurs are able to *check network density,* so as to avoid too many overlaps (because they affect network efficiency) while still attaining solidarity and cohesiveness.
- Effective entrepreneurs multiply, through extending the reachability of their networks, the stimuli for better and faster adaptation to change.

Source: Adapted from Paola Dubini and Howard Aldrich, "Executive Forum: Personal and Extended Networks Are Central to the Entrepreneurial Process," *Journal of Business Venturing* 6, no. 5., (September 1991), pp. 310–12.

How can you as an entrepreneur begin to tap into these resources? Howard H. Stevenson and William H. Sahlman suggest that you have to do "two seemingly contradictory things: seek out the best advisors—specialists if you have to—and involve them more thoroughly, and at an earlier stage, than you have in the past. At the same time, be more skeptical of their credentials and their advice."[5] In addition to networking with family, friends, classmates, and advisors, Stevenson and Sahlman suggest that the human touch enhances the relationship between the entrepreneur and the advisors to the venture.[6] Jennifer A. Starr and Ian C. MacMillan tested their hypothesis that "some entrepreneurs and intrapreneurs employ social assets, such as friendship, liking, trust, obligation, and gratitude to secure resources at prices far lower than the market price, to the significant benefit of their ventures."[7] Yet another group of researchers, Paola Dubini and Howard Aldrich, have contributed to the growing body of knowledge about how these "social assets" may in fact benefit the bottom line of a new venture; see *Exhibit 10.1* for the strategic principals they have identified. However, entrepreneurs should be cautioned that another study "found no evidence . . . that the size of an entrepreneur's personal network or the amount of time invested in developing and maintaining a network affect business survival or performance."[8]

There are many examples of controlling people resources, rather than owning them. In real estate, even the largest firms do not employ top architects full-time but, rather, secure them on a project basis. Most smaller firms do not employ lawyers but obtain legal assistance as needed. Technical consultants, design engineers, and programmers are other examples.

An example of this approach is a company that grew to $20 million in sales in about 10 years with $7,500 cash, a liberal use of credit cards, reduced income for the founders, and hard work and long hours. This company has not had to raise any additional equity capital.

An example of the opposite point of view is a proposed new venture in the minicomputer software industry. The business plan called for about $300,000, an amount which would pay for only the development of the first products. The first priority in the deployment of the company's financial resources outlined in the business plan was to buy outright a computer costing approximately $150,000. The founders refused to consider other options, such as leasing the computer or leasing computer time. The company was unable to attract venture capital, even though, otherwise, it had an excellent business plan. The $150,000 raised from informal private investors was not enough money to execute the opportunity, and the founders decided to give it back and abandon the venture. Would not a more entrepreneurial team have figured out a way to keep going under these circumstances?

---

[5] Howard H. Stevenson and William H. Sahlman, "How Small Companies Should Handle Advisors," in *The Entrepreneurial Venture* (Boston: Harvard Business School, 1992), p. 296. See also a *Harvard Business Review* reprint series called "Boards of Directors: Part I" and "Board of Directors: Part II" (Boston: Harvard Business Review, 1976).

[6] Ibid., p. 301.

[7] Jennifer A. Starr and Ian C. MacMillan, "Resource Corporation Via Social Contracting: Resource Acquisition Strategies For New Ventures," *Strategic Management Journal* 2 (1990).

[8] Howard E. Aldrich and Pat Ray Reese, "Does Networking Pay Off?" (Forthcoming).

Outside People Resources

Board of Directors

Initial work in evaluating the need for people resources is done in the process of forming a new venture team (see Chapter 8). Once resource needs have been determined and a team has been selected, it will usually be necessary to obtain additional resources outside of the venture, in the startup stage and during other stages of growth as well.

The decision of whether to have a board of directors and, if the answer is yes, the process of choosing and finding the people who will sit on the board are troublesome for new ventures.[9]

The Decision   The decision of whether to have a board of directors is influenced first by the form of organization chosen for the firm. If the new venture is organized as a corporation, it must have a board of directors, which must be elected by the shareholders. There is flexibility with other forms of organization.

In addition, certain investors will require a board of directors. Venture capitalists almost always require boards of directors and that they be represented on the boards.

Beyond that, deciding to involve outsiders is worth careful thought. This decision starts with the identification of missing relevant experience, know-how, and networks, and of what the venture needs at this stage of its development, that can be provided by outside directors. Their probable contributions then can be balanced against the fact that having a board of directors will necessitate greater disclosure to outsiders of plans for operating and financing the business. It also is worth noting that one of the responsibilities of a board of directors is to elect officers for the firm, so the decision also is tied to decisions about financing and the ownership of the voting shares in the company.

A survey of entrepreneurial firms showed that one-fourth of the companies responding had no outside directors and 16 percent had only one.[10] Of those who did have outside directors, these companies valued them most for their objectivity. Among the respondents, 93 percent had sales under $25 million, while 58 percent had annual revenues of less than $2 million. Eighty-three percent reported they were profitable. Sixty-four percent said the lead entrepre-

neur owned a controlling equity interest. This might account for a somewhat more sanguine view in the survey results.

Recently, when Art Spinner of Hambro International was interviewed by *INC.*, he explained that

> entrepreneurs worry about the wrong thing . . . that the boards are going to steal their companies or take them over. Though entrepreneurs have many reasons to worry, that's not one of them. It almost never happens. In truth, boards don't even have much power. They are less well equipped to police entrepreneurs than to advise them.[11]

As Spinner suggests, the expertise that members of a board can bring to a venture, at a price it can afford, can far outweigh any of the negative factors mentioned above. In one enterprise for instance, a venture capitalist who first invested in the company sat on the board of directors through the first years of highly successful growth. He made vital contributions in helping to recruit key top management, in giving the firm credibility with potential customers, in being a sounding board and devil's advocate, and in stimulating strategic thinking at a critical time—two years earlier than would have been done otherwise. The director served until it was evident that another kind of contribution was needed—that is, someone who could be valuable in helping in a public offering.[12]

Selection Criteria: Add Value with Know-How and Contacts

Once the decision to have a board of directors has been made, finding the appropriate people for the board is a challenge. It is important to be objective and to select people who are known to be trustworthy. Most ventures typically look to personal acquaintances of the lead entrepreneur or the team or to their lawyers, bankers, accountants, or consultants for their first outside directors. While such a choice might be the right one for a venture, the process also involves finding the right people to fill the gaps discovered in the process of forming the management team.

This issue of filling in the gaps relates back to one of the criteria of a successful management team, intellectual honesty, that is, knowing what you know and what you need to know (see *Exhibit 3.3*). In a recent study of boards and specifically venture capital-

[9] The author is indebted to Howard H. Stevenson of the Harvard Business School, and to Leslie Charm and Karl Youngman of Doktor Pet Centers and Command Performance hair salons, respectively, for insights into and knowledge of boards of directors.

[10] "The *Venture* Survey: Who Sits on Your Board?" *Venture*, April 1984, p. 32.

[11] "Confessions of a Director: Hambro International's Art Spinner Says Most CEOs Don't Know How to Make Good Use of Boards. Here He Tells You How," *INC.*, April 1991, p. 19.

[12] Jeffry A. Timmons and Harry J. Sapienza, "Venture Capital: More Than Money?" in *Pratt's Guide to Venture Capital Sources* (New York: Venture Economics Publishing, 1993), p. 47–53.

ists' contribution to them, entrepreneurs seemed to value operating experience over the financial expertise.[13] In addition, the study reported that "those CEOs with a top-20 venture capital firm as the lead investor, on average did rate the value of the advice from their venture capital board members significantly higher—but not outstandingly higher—than the advice from other outside board members."[14]

Defining expectations and minimum requirements for board members might be a good way to get the most out of a board of directors.

A top-notch outside director usually spends *at least* 9 to 10 days per year on his or her responsibilities. Four days per year are spent for quarterly meetings, a day of preparation for each meeting, a day for another meeting to cope with an unanticipated issue, plus up to a day or more for various phone calls. Yearly fees are usually paid for such a commitment.

Quality directors become involved for the learning and professional development opportunities, and so forth, rather than for the money. Compensation to board members varies widely. Fees can range from as little as $500–$1,000 for a half- or full-day meeting to $10,000–$30,000 per year for four to six full-day to day-and-a-half meetings, plus accessibility on a continuous basis. Directors are also usually reimbursed for their expenses incurred in preparing for and attending meetings. Stock in a startup company, often 2 percent to 5 percent, or options, for 5,000 to 50,000 shares, are common incentives to attract and reward directors.

Additionally, Art Spinner, a director of 11 companies and an advisor to two other companies suggested the following as a simple set of rules to guide you toward a productive relationship with your board:

- Treat your directors as individual resources.
- Always be honest with your directors.
- Set up a compensation committee.
- Set up an audit committee.
- Never set up an executive committee.[15]

New ventures are finding that for a variety of reasons, people who could be potential board members are increasingly cautious about getting involved:

- *Liability.* Directors of a company can be held personally liable for its actions and those of its officers,

and, worse, a climate of litigation exists in many areas. For example, some specific grounds for liability of a director have included voting a dividend that renders the corporation insolvent, voting to authorize a loan out of corporate assets to a director or an officer who ultimately defaults, and signing a false corporate document or report. Courts have held that if a director acts in good faith, he or she can be excused from liability. The problem is, however, that for a director to *prove* that he or she has acted in good faith, especially in a startup situation, is no easy matter. This proof is complicated by several factors, including possibly an inexperienced management team, the financial weaknesses and cash crises that occur and demand solution, and the lack of good and complete information and records, which are necessary as the basis for action. In recent years, many states have passed what is known as the "Dumb Director Law." In effect, the law allows that directors are normal human beings who can make mistakes and misjudgments; it goes a long way in taking the sting out of potential lawsuits that are urged by ambulance chasers.

- *Harassment.* Outside stockholders, who may have acquired stock through a private placement or through the over-the-counter market, can have unrealistic expectations about the risk involved in a new venture, the speed at which a return can be realized, as well as the size of the return. Such stockholders are a source of continual annoyance for boards and for their companies.

- *Time and risk.* Experienced directors know that often it takes more time and intense involvement to work with an early-stage venture with sales of $10 million or less than with one having sales of $25 million to $50 million or more, and the former is riskier.

One solution to liability concerns is for the firm to purchase indemnity insurance for its directors. But this insurance is expensive. Despite the liability problems noted above, the survey mentioned found that just 11 percent of the respondents reported difficulty in recruiting board members.[16] In dealing with this issue, new ventures will want to examine a possible director's attitude toward risk in general and evaluate whether this is the type of attitude the team needs to have represented.

[13] Joseph Rosenstein, Albert V. Bruno, William D. Bygrave, and Natalie T. Taylor, "The CEO, Venture Capitalist, and the Board," *Journal of Business Venturing* 8 (1988), pp. 99–113.
[14] Ibid., pp. 99–100.
[15] "Confessions of a Director," *INC.*, April 1991, p. 119. Reprinted with permission. © 1991 by Goldhirsh Group, Inc. 38 Commercial Wharf, Boston, MA 02110.
[16] "The *Venture* Survey: Who Sits on Your Board?" p. 32.

Alternatives to a Formal Board

The use of advisors and quasi-boards can be a useful alternative to having a formal board of directors.[17] A firm can solicit objective observations and feedback for these advisors. Such informal boards can bring needed expertise to bear, without the legal entanglements and formalities of a regular board. Also, the possible embarrassment of having to remove someone who is not serving a useful role can be avoided. Informal advisors are usually much less expensive, with honorariums of $500 to $1,000 per meeting common. It should perhaps be noted that the level of involvement of these advisors probably will be less than members of a formal board. The firm also does not enjoy the protection of law, which defines the obligations and responsibilities of board members of a formal board.

An informal group of advisors can also be a good mechanism through which a new venture can observe a number of people in action and select one or two as regular directors. The entrepreneur gains the advantages of counsel and advice from outsiders without being legally bound by their decisions.

Attorneys

The Decision

Almost all companies need and use the services of attorneys, entrepreneurial ventures perhaps more so.[18] *INC.* magazine recently conducted a readership poll of approximately 5,000 subscribers and 5,000 lawyers. The typical subscribing company reported it had sales of $5.1 million, with 62 employees. Of these companies, 94 percent reported that they regularly relied on outside legal counsel. In addition, 88 percent of the attorneys who responded considered small business clients important to their practices.[19]

Indeed, it may be necessary for entrepreneurs to possess extensive knowledge of the law in addition to selecting good attorneys. John Van Slyke, a consultant who has also taught at Harvard Business School, thinks it may be wise for entrepreneurs to pursue a law degree, either instead of or in addition to an MBA.[20] He believes that students of entrepreneurship have remained novices about the law and are not aware they are vulnerable. He says:

While lawyers are currently in abundant supply, quality in the profession is so thinly spread that our students are told repeatedly by guest speakers in class that it is vital to *find a good lawyer.* Yet experienced businessmen and women know that legal advice is in fact another form of outside expertise which must be managed effectively. To manage relationships with lawyers effectively, entrepreneurs must know what lawyers do and how they think. Prudent businessmen and women do not delegate wholesale all important legal matters to their lawyers, nor do they allow their lawyers to make many decisions for them. After all, the important signatures on contracts, tax forms, and other legal documents are those of the principals, not the lawyers.[21]

Just how attorneys are used by entrepreneurial ventures depends on the needs of the venture at its particular stage. Size is also a factor. *Exhibit 10.2* summarizes the findings of a survey by *INC.* magazine. Apparently, firms with sales under $1 million use attorneys mostly for contracts and agreements. These companies also use a substantial amount of their attorneys' time for the personal needs of top management, matters surrounding incorporation, and formal litigation. As company size increases, so does the need for advice in such areas as liability, mergers, and benefit plans. It is also noteworthy that contracts and agreements were almost uniformly the predominant use, regardless of the size of the venture.

The following are areas of the law that entrepreneurs will most likely need to get assistance with:

- *Incorporation.* Issues such as the forgivable and nonforgivable liabilities of founders, officers, and directors or the form of organization chosen for a new venture are important. As tax laws and other circumstances change, they are important for more established firms as well. How important this area can be is illustrated by the case of a founder who nearly lost control of his company as a result of the legal maneuvering of the clerk and another shareholder. The clerk and the shareholder controlled votes on the board of directors, while the founder had controlling interest in the stock of the company. The shareholder tried to call a directors' meeting and not re-elect the founder president. The founder found out about the plot and adroitly managed to call a stockholders' meeting to remove the directors first.

- *Franchising and licensing.* Innumerable issues concerning future rights, obligations, and what happens in the event of nonperformance by either a franchisee or lessee or a franchisor or lessor require specialized legal advice.

[17] See the article by Harold W. Fox, "Quasi Boards: Useful Small Business Confidants," in *Growing Concerns*, ed. David E. Gumpert (New York: John Wiley & Sons and *Harvard Business Review*, 1984), pp. 307–16.

[18] The author wishes to acknowledge the input provided by Gerald Feigen of the Center for Entrepreneurial Studies, University of Maryland, from a course on entrepreneurship and the law he has developed and teaches at George Washington University Law School; also John Van Slyke of Alta Research.

[19] Bradford W. Ketchum, Jr., "You and Your Attorney," *INC.*, June 1982, pp. 51–56.

[20] John R. Van Slyke, "What Should We Teach Entrepreneurs about the Law," *Entrepreneurship: What It Is and How to Teach It* (Boston, MA: Harvard Business School, 1985), p. 135.

[21] Ibid., p. 139.

EXHIBIT 10.2

How Attorneys Are Used

Legal Service Used (ranked by total mentions)	Annual Company Sales (percent of respondents)				
	Under $1 Million	$1–2.9 Million	$3–4.9 Million	$5–24.9 Million	$25 Million or More
Contracts and agreements	70%	74%	69%	84%	85%
Personal needs of top management	46	58	56	53	38
Formal litigation	34	50	63	61	91
Real estate and insurance matters	32	35	50	51	56
Incorporation	45	34	39	33	24
Estate planning	23	42	48	44	17
Delinquent accounts	20	33	39	34	21
Liability protection	20	17	22	33	41
Copyrights, trademarks, and patents	21	19	24	28	38
Mergers and acquisitions	12	14	29	32	47
Employee benefit plans	10	26	19	27	27
Tax planning and review	13	17	22	17	12
Employee stock ownership plans	9	15	10	18	21
Franchising and licensing	13	11	14	14	12
Government-required reports	8	6	6	10	12
Prospectus for public offering	2	1	5	2	18
Labor relations	1	2	2	3	3

The need for legal counsel is obvious when it comes to contracts and lawsuits. But the *INC.* survey shows that small business managers also rely on company attorneys for personal problems ranging from tax matters to divorce and estate probate. As company size increases, so does the need for advice in such areas as liability, mergers, and benefit plans.

Reprinted with permission, *INC.*, June 1982. Copyright © 1982 by Goldhirsh Group, Inc., 38 Commercial Wharf, Boston, MA 02110.

- **Contracts and agreements.** Firms need assistance with contracts, licenses, leases, and other such agreements as noncompete employment agreements and those governing the vesting rights of shareholders.

- **Formal litigation, liability protection, and so on.** In today's litigious climate, sooner or later most entrepreneurs will find themselves as defendants in lawsuits and require counsel.

- **Real estate, insurance, and other matters.** It is hard to imagine an entrepreneur who, at one time or another, will not be involved in various kinds of real estate transactions, from rentals to the purchase and sale of property, that require the services of an attorney.

- **Copyrights, trademarks, patents, and intellectual property protection.** Products are hard to protect. But, pushing ahead with development of products, such as software, before ample protection from the law is provided can be expedient in the short term but disastrous in the long term. For example, an entrepreneur—facing the loss of a $2.5 million sale of his business and uncollected fees of over $200,000 if his software was not protected— obtained an expert on the sale, leasing, and licensing of software products. The lawyer devised subtle but powerful protections, such as internal clocks in the software that shut down the software if they were not changed.

- **Employee plans.** Benefit and stock ownership plans have become complicated to use effectively and to administer. They require the special know-how of lawyers so common pitfalls can be avoided.

- **Tax planning and review.** Here, a word of caution is in order. All too frequently the tail of the accountant's tax avoidance advice wags the dog of good business sense. Entrepreneurs who worry more about finding good opportunities to make money, rather than tax shelters, are infinitely better off.

- **Federal, state, and other regulations and reports.** Understanding the impact of and complying with regulations often is not easy. Violations of federal, state, and other regulations often can have serious consequences.

- **Mergers and acquisitions.** There is specialized legal know-how in buying or selling a company. Unless an entrepreneur is highly experienced and has highly qualified legal advisors in these transactions, he or she can either lose the deal or end up having to live with legal obligations that may be costly.

- **Bankruptcy law.** Many people have heard tales of entrepreneurs who did not make deposits to pay various federal and state taxes in order to use that cash in their business. It is likely that these entrepreneurs falsely assumed that if their companies went bankrupt, the government was out of luck, just like the banks and other creditors. They were wrong. In fact, the owners, officers, and often the directors are held personally liable for those obligations.

- **Other matters.** These matters can range from assistance with collecting delinquent accounts to labor relations.

- **Personal needs.** As entrepreneurs accumulate net worth (i.e., property and other assets), legal advice in estate, tax, and financial planning is important.

Selection Criteria: Add Value with Know-How and Contacts

In a survey of the factors that enter into the selection of a law firm or an attorney, 54 percent of the respondents said personal contact with a member of the firm was the main factor.[22] Reputation was a factor for 40 percent, and a prior relationship with the firm, 26 percent. Equally revealing was the fact that fees were mentioned by only 3 percent.

In many areas of the country are attorneys who specialize in new ventures and in firms with higher growth potential. The best place to start is with acquaintances of the lead entrepreneur, of members of the management team, or of directors. Recommendations from accountants, bankers, and associates also are useful. Other sources are partners in venture capital firms, partners of a Big Six accounting firm (those who have privately owned and emerging company groups), a bar association, or the *Martindale-Hubbell Law Directory* (a listing of lawyers).

An attorney, to be effective, needs to have the experience and expertise to deal with specific issues facing a venture. Stevenson and Sahlman state that

> hooking up with the vast resources of a large law firm or Big Six accounting firm may be the best course, but we do not necessarily advise that strategy. You can usually get reasonable tax or estate-planning advice from a big law firm merely by picking up a telephone. The trade-off is that, if you are a small company and they have a dozen General Electrics as clients, you may get short shrift. One-

to two-person firms can have an excellent network of specialists to refer to for problems outside their bailiwick. The point is, you'd better use the specialist when you have to.[23]

For example, one entrepreneur who relocated his business to new office space—in a renovated historical building that was being converted into office condominiums—did not use the two attorneys who handled his other business for the relocation because neither had specific experience in office condominium deals involving historical properties and the complicated tax and multiple ownership issues involved. As with members of the management team, directors, and investors, the chemistry also is important.

Finally, advice to be highly selective and to expect to get what you pay for is sound. It is also important to realize that lawyers are not business people and that they do not usually make *business* judgments. Rather, they seek to provide perfect or fail-safe protection.

Most attorneys are paid on an hourly basis. Retainers and flat fees are sometimes paid, usually by larger ventures. The amount a venture pays for legal services expectedly rises as the firm grows. Many law firms will agree to defer charges or initially to provide services at a lower than normal rate in order to obtain a firm's business. According to the *Massachusetts Lawyers Weekly*, legal fees fall into the following ranges: partners' hourly rates, from $195 to $400; associates' hourly rates, from $80 to $245; and paralegals' rates are between $45 and $165.

Bankers and Other Lenders

The Decision

Deciding whether to have a banker or another lender usually involves decisions about how to finance certain needs (see Part IV). It appears that most companies will need the services of a banker or other lender at some time in this respect. The decision also can involve how a banker or other lender can serve as an advisor.

As with other advisors, the banker or other lender needs to be a partner, not a difficult minority shareholder. First and foremost, therefore, an entrepreneur will be well advised to pick the *right banker or lender*, rather than to pick just a bank or a financial institution, although picking the bank or institution is also important. Different bankers and lenders have reputations ranging from "excellent" to "just OK" to "not OK" in how they work with entrepreneurial companies. Their institutions also have reputations for how well they work with entrepreneurial compa-

[22] Ketchum, "You and Your Attorney," p. 52.
[23] Stevenson and Sahlman, "How Small Companies Should Handle Advisers," p. 297.

nies. Ideally, an entrepreneur needs an excellent banker or lender with an excellent financial institution, although an excellent banker or lender with a just OK institution is preferable to a just OK banker or lender with an excellent institution.

For an entrepreneur to know clearly what he or she needs from a lender is an important starting point. Some will have needs that are asset-based, such as money for equipment, facilities, or inventory. Others may need working capital to fund short-term operating needs.

Having a business plan is invaluable preparation for selecting and working with a lender. Also, since a banker or other lender is a "partner," it is important to invite him or her to see the company in operation, to avoid late financial statements (as well as late payments and overdrafts), and to be honest and straightforward in sharing information.

Selection Criteria: Add Value with Know-How and Contracts

Bankers and other lenders are known to other entrepreneurs, lawyers, accountants that provide general business advisory services, and venture capitalists. Starting with their recommendations is ideal. From among four to seven or so possibilities, an entrepreneur will find the right lender and the right institution.

Today's banking and financial services marketplace is much more competitive than in the past. There are more choices, and it is worth the time and effort to shop around.

Accountants

The Decision

The accounting profession has come a long way from the "green eyeshades" stereotype one hears reference to occasionally. Today, virtually all of the larger accounting firms have discovered the enormous client potential of new and entrepreneurial ventures, and a significant part of their business strategy is to cater specifically to these firms. In the Boston area, for instance, leading Big Six accounting firms have located new offices for their small business groups on Route 128 in the heart of entrepreneurs' country.

Accountants often are unfairly maligned. As one author put it:

> It is hard for entrepreneurs to fully appreciate accounting and what it can do for them. In fact, many tend to view the accountant as a bean counter, a sort of scorekeeper sitting on the sidelines, rather than as a player on the first team. This is a great mistake.[24]

Accountants who are experienced as advisors to emerging companies can provide, in addition to audits and taxation, other valuable services. An experienced general business advisor can be invaluable in helping to think through strategy, in helping to find and raise debt and equity capital, in mergers and acquisitions, in locating directors, and in helping to balance business decisions with important personal needs and goals. For a listing of how five small companies use their accountants, see *Exhibit 10.3*.

EXHIBIT 10.3

How Do You Use Your CPA?

Company	How Often Does CEO Consult CPA?	What's CEO Looking for in a CPA?	How Often Has Company Switched CPAs?
Coastal Production Service; operates oil and gas platforms	Once a month	Audit proficiency, so CEO chose a firm that employs a former IRS auditor.	Twice
UniLink Software; software developer	Weekly	Computer literacy, since CEO especially tailors his cash flow and other statements.	Never
Pro-Tec Industries; manufacturer of truck parts	Quarterly	Ability to analyze numbers quickly, especially during expansion activities.	Never
Vance International; protective services	Quarterly	Red-flag warnings on issues like insurance costs or financial ratios.	Twice
Roadshow Services; theatrical transportation management	Once every two months	Reality checks to keep fast-growing company's profit and other margins in line.	Twice

Source: Adapted from Susan Greco and Christopher Caggiano, "Advisors: How Do You Use Your CPA?" *INC.*, September 1991, p. 136.

---

[24]Gordon Baty, *Entrepreneurship for the 80s* (Reston, VA: Reston Publishing, 1982), p. 107.

Selection Criteria: Add Value with Know-How and Contacts

In selecting accountants, the first step is for the venture to decide whether to go with a smaller local firm, a regional firm, or one of the Big Six accounting firms. Although each company should make its own decision, it is noteworthy that in an informal survey of companies with sales between $4 million and $20 million, "More than 85 percent of the CEOs preferred working with smaller regional accounting firms, rather than the Big Six, because of lower costs and what they perceived as better personal attention."[25] In making this decision, you will need to address several factors:[26]

- **Service.** Levels of service offered and the attention likely to be provided need to be evaluated. Chances are, for most startups, both will be higher in a small firm than a large one. But, if an entrepreneur of a higher-potential firm seeking venture capital or a strategic partner has aspirations to go public, a Big Six firm is a good place to start.

- **Needs.** Needs, both current and future, have to be weighed against the capabilities of the firm. Larger firms are more equipped to handle highly complex or technical problems, while smaller firms may be preferable for general management advice and assistance because the principals are more likely to be involved in handling the account. However, if the goal of the firm is to go public, a series of audits from one of the larger firms is preferable.

- **Cost.** Most Big Six firms will offer very cost-competitive services to startups with significant growth and profit potential. If a venture needs the attention of a partner in a larger firm, services of the larger firm are more expensive. However, if the firm requires extensive technical knowledge, a larger firm may have more experience and therefore be cheaper.

- **Chemistry.** Always, chemistry is an important consideration.

Of course, the right accountant is competent, as evidenced by the fact that he or she does not always adopt the government's point of view on tax matters, does not need to look up information often, and seems interested and informed on managerial issues.[27] Sources of reference for good attorneys are also sources of reference for accountants, and trade groups are also valuable sources.

Once a firm has reached any significant size, it will have many choices. The founders of one firm, which had grown to about $5 million in sales and had a strong potential to reach $20 million in sales in the next five years and eventually go public, put together a brief summary of the firm, including its background and track record, and a statement of needs for both banking and accounting services. The founders were quite startled at the time at the aggressive response they received from several banks and Big Six accounting firms.

The accounting profession is straightforward enough. Whether the firm is small or large, they sell time, usually by the hour. In a 1990 survey, the hourly partner rates were reported to be between $235, for one of the Big Six firms, to $117, for a small, local firm.[28]

Consultants

The Decision [29]

Consultants are hired to solve particular problems and to fill gaps not filled by the management team. There are many skilled consultants who can be of invaluable assistance and a great source of "other people's resources." Advice needed can be quite technical and specific or quite general or far ranging. Problems and needs also vary widely, depending upon whether the venture is just starting up or is an existing business.

Startups usually require help with critical one-time tasks and decisions that will have lasting impact on the business. In a recent study of how consultants are used and their impact on venture formation, Karl Bayer, of Germany's Institute for Systems and Innovation Research of the Fraunhofer-Society, interviewed 315 firms. He found that 96 used consultants and that consultants are employed by startups for the following reasons:

1. To compensate for a lower level of professional experience.

2. To target a wide market segment (possibly to do market research for a consumer goods firm).

3. To undertake projects which require a large startup investment in equipment.[30]

[25] Susan Greco and Christopher Caggiano, "Advisors: How Do You Use Your CPA?" *INC.*, September 1991.
[26] Neil C. Churchill and Louis A. Werbaneth, Jr., "Choosing and Evaluating Your Accountant," in *Growing Concerns*, ed. David E. Gumpert (New York: John Wiley & Sons and *Harvard Business Review*, 1984), p. 265.
[27] Ibid., p. 263.
[28] Survey was conducted by *Accounting Today* (New York, 1990) and published in *INC.* (November 1991), p. 196.
[29] The following is excerpted in part from David E. Gumpert and Jeffry A. Timmons, *The Encyclopedia of Small Business Resources* (New York: Harper & Row, 1984), pp. 48–51.
[30] Karl Bayer, "The Impact of Using Consultants during Venture Formation on Venture Performance," in *Frontiers of Entrepreneurship Research 1991*, ed. Neil H. Churchill et al. (Babson Park, MA: Babson College, 1991), pp. 298–99.

These tasks and decisions might include assessing business sites, evaluating lease and rental agreements, setting up record- and bookkeeping systems, finding business partners, obtaining startup capital, and formulating initial marketing plans.

Existing businesses face ongoing issues resulting from growth. Many of these issues are so specialized that rarely is this expertise available on the management team. Issues of obtaining market research, evaluating when and how to go about computerizing business tasks, whether to lease or buy major pieces of equipment, and whether to change inventory valuation methods can be involved.

While it is not always possible to pinpoint the exact nature of a problem and sometimes simply an unbiased and fresh view is needed, a new venture is usually well advised to try to determine the broad nature of its concern, such as whether it involves a personnel problem, manufacturing problem, or marketing problem, for example. Observations in the *Harvard Business Review* by a consultant are revealing:

> Management consultants are generally hired for the wrong reasons. Once hired, they are generally poorly employed and loosely supervised. The result is, more often than not, a final report that decorates an executive's bookshelf with as much usefulness as "The Life and Mores of the Pluvius Aegiptus" would decorate his coffee table—and at considerably more expense.[31]

Confirming these observations, Bayer reported that the use of consultants had a negative effect on sales three to five years later. Additionally, his surveys overwhelmingly reported (two-thirds of the 96) that "the work delivered by the consultants . . . [was] inadequate for the task."[32] So how can entrepreneurs fill gaps and solve problems? Bayer suggests that the entrepreneur can find and adequately prepare a consultant, so that the firm benefits in the long run. His advice includes:

- Use a coentrepreneurial approach with a high degree of interaction between entrepreneur and consultant.
- Make sure the consultant states the results of his or her work in terms easily accessible to the founder.
- Insist that the consultant demonstrate a readiness to check the plausibility of the entrepreneur's statements and to inform the entrepreneur if those statements and assumptions are not correct.[33]

Selection Criteria: Add Value with Know-How and Contacts

Unfortunately, nowhere are the options so numerous, the quality so variable, and the costs so unpredictable as in the area of consulting. The number of people calling themselves management consultants is large and growing steadily. By 1989, there were an estimated 50,000 to 60,000 private management consultants around the country. It is estimated that approximately 2,000 or more are added annually. Further, somewhat more than half the consultants were found to work on their own, while the remainder work for firms. In addition, government agencies (primarily the Small Business Administration) employ consultants to work with businesses; various private and nonprofit organizations provide management assistance to help entrepreneurs; and others, such as professors, engineers, and so forth, provide consulting services part time. Such assistance also may be provided by other professionals, such as accountants and bankers.

Again, the right chemistry is critical. One company president who was asked what he had learned from talking to clients of the consultant he finally hired said, "They couldn't really pinpoint one thing, but they all said they would not consider starting and growing a company without him!"

As unwieldy and risky as the consulting situation might appear, there are ways of limiting the choices. For one thing, consultants tend to have specialties; while some consultants claim wide expertise, most will indicate the kinds of situations they feel most comfortable with and skillful in handling. Some of the desirable qualities in a consulting firm are summarized below:[34]

- A shirtsleeve approach to the problems.
- An understanding attitude toward the feelings of managers and their subordinates.
- A modest and truthful offer of services and an ability to produce results.
- A reasonable and realistic charge for services.
- A willingness to maintain a continuous relationship.

Three or more potential consultants can be interviewed about their expertise and approach and their references checked. Candidates who pass this initial screening then can be asked to prepare specific proposals.

A written agreement, specifying the consultant's responsibilities and objectives of the assignment, the

---

[31] Jean Pierre Frankenhuis, "How to Get a Good Consultant," *Harvard Business Review*, November–December 1977, p. 133.
[32] Bayer, "The Impact of Using Consultants," p. 301.
[33] Bayer, "The Impact of Using Consultants," pp. 302–03.
[34] Harvey C. Krentzman and John N. Samaras, "Can Small Business Use Consultants," in *Growing Concerns*, ed. David E. Gumpert (New York: John Wiley & Sons and *Harvard Business Review*, 1984), pp. 243–62.

length of time the project will take, and the type and amount of compensation, is highly recommended. Some consultants work on an hourly basis, some on a fixed-fee basis, and some on a retainer-fee basis. Huge variations in consulting costs for the same services exist. At one end of the spectrum is the Small Business Administration, which provides consultants to small businesses without charge. At the other end of the spectrum are well-known consulting firms that may charge large amounts for minimal marketing studies or technical feasibility studies.

While the quality of many products roughly correlates with their price, this is not so with consulting services. The point is that it is difficult to judge consultants solely on the basis of the fees they charge.

Financial Resources

Analyzing Financial Requirements

Once the opportunity has been assessed, once a new venture team has been formed, and once all resources needs have been identified, *then* is the time for a new venture to evaluate what financial resources are required and when. (Sources of financing and how to obtain funding are covered in detail in Part IV.)

As has been noted before, there is a temptation, in this area particularly, to place the cart before the horse. Entrepreneurs are tempted to begin their evaluation of business opportunities—and particularly their thinking about formal business plans—by analyzing spreadsheets, rather than focusing first on defining the opportunity, deciding how to seize it, and then preparing the financial estimates of what is required.

However, when the time comes to analyze financial requirements, it is important to realize that cash is the life's blood of a venture. As James Stancill, professor of finance at the University of Southern California's business school, has said: "Any company, no matter how big or small, moves on cash, not profits. You can't pay bills with profits, only cash. You can't pay employees with profits, only cash."[35] Financial resources are almost always limited, and important and significant trade-offs need to be made in evaluating a company's needs and the timing of those needs.

Spreadsheets Computers and spreadsheet programs are tools that save time and increase productivity and creativity enormously. Spreadsheets are nothing more than pieces of accounting paper adapted for use with a computer. *Exhibit 10.4* shows a sample spreadsheet analysis done using Lotus 1-2-3 and Robert Morris Associates (RMA) data. (See Appendix I for information on using RMA data.)

The origins of the first spreadsheet program, VisiCalc, reveal its potential relevance for entrepreneurs. It was devised by an MBA student while he was attending Harvard Business School.[36] The student was faced with analyzing pro forma income statements and balance sheets, cash flows, and breakeven for his cases. The question "*What if* you assumed such and such?" was inevitably asked.

The major advantage of using spreadsheets to analyze capital requirements is having the ability to answer what-if questions. This takes on particular relevance also when one considers, as James Stancill points out:

> Usual measures of cash flow—net income plus depreciation (NIPD) or earnings before interest and taxes (EBIT)—give a realistic indication of a company's cash position only during a period of steady sales.[37]

Take cash flow projections. An entrepreneur could answer a question such as: What if sales grow at just 5 percent, instead of 15 percent, and what if only 50 percent, instead of 65 percent, of amounts billed are paid in 30 days? The impact on cash flow of changes in these projections can be seen.

The same what-if process also can be applied to pro forma income statements and balance sheets, budgeting, and break-even calculations. To illustrate, by altering assumptions about revenues and costs such that cash reaches zero, break-even can be analyzed. Thus, for example, RMA assumptions could be used as comparative boundaries for testing assumptions about a venture.

An example of how computer-based analysis can be of enormous value is the experience of a colleague who was seriously considering starting a new publishing venture. His analysis of the opportunity was encouraging, and important factors such as relevant experience and commitment by the lead entrepreneur were there. Assumptions about fixed and variable costs, market estimates, and probable startup resource requirements had also been assembled. What needed to be done next was to generate detailed monthly cash flows to determine more precisely the economic character of the venture, including the impact of the quite seasonal nature of the business, and to determine the amount of money needed to launch the business and the amount and timing of potential rewards. In less than three hours, the assumptions about revenues and expenditures associated with the

---

[35] Reprinted by permission of *Harvard Business Review.* An excerpt from "When Is There Cash in Cash Flow?" by James M. Stancill, March–April 1987, p. 38. Copyright © 1987 by the President and Fellows of Harvard College.
[36] Dan Bricklin.
[37] Stancill, "When Is There Cash in Cash Flow?" p. 38.

EXHIBIT 10.4

Sample Spreadsheet Analysis

OUTPUT GENERATED:

```
# # # # # # # # # # # # # # # # # #
#            Cash Budget          #
# # # # # # # # # # # # # # # # # #
```

	Months											
	1	2	3	4	5	6	7	8	9	10	11	12
CASH BALANCE (Opening)	$50,000	$31,235	$9,073	($18,917)	($50,811)	($85,583)	($122,252)	($173,852)	($228,743)	($293,067)	($359,823)	($431,361)
Plus RECEIPTS: Sales Collections	$2,725	6,000	$9,675	$13,350	$17,025	$20,700	$24,375	$28,050	$34,350	$38,775	$42,750	$46,425
Other Proceeds	$0	$0	$2,000	$0	$2,000	$5,000	$0	$4,000	$0	$0	$0	$0
Total	$2,725	$6,000	$11,675	$13,350	$19,025	$25,700	$24,375	$32,050	$34,350	$38,775	$42,750	$46,425
Less DISBURSEMENTS: Raw Material Payables	$16,875	$20,625	$26,260	$31,875	$37,500	$43,125	$50,625	$60,000	$67,500	$71,250	$76,875	$82,500
Other Expenses (Accruals)	$4,494	$6,806	$9,169	$11,531	$13,894	$16,256	$19,313	$22,369	$25,706	$28,069	$30,431	$32,794
Fixed Asset Additions	$0	$0	$3,000	$0	$0	$0	$2,400	$0	$0	$0	$0	$0
Lease Expense	$0	$80	$80	$80	$80	$80	$80	$80	$80	$80	$80	$80
Long Term Debt Payments	$5	$5	$5	$5	$5	$5	$5	$5	$5	$5	$5	$5
Other Expenses (Itemized)	$0	$30	$0	$60	$20	$0	$0	$500	$0	$0	$0	$0
"Other Asset" Additions	$0	$0	$10	$0	$0	$0	$0	$0	$0	$0	$0	$0
Federal Taxes (Operations)	$238	$645	$1,048	$1,430	$1,863	$2,285	$2,678	$2,840	$3,915	$4,328	$4,740	$5,153
Total	$21,611	$28,191	$39,561	$44,981	$53,361	$61,751	$75,100	$85,794	$97,206	$103,731	$112,131	$120,531
Net Cash Gain (Loss)	($18,886)	($22,191)	($27,886)	($31,631)	($34,336)	($36,051)	($50,725)	($53,744)	($62,856)	($64,956)	($69,381)	($74,106)
Cumulative Cash Balance	$31,114	$9,044	($18,813)	($50,548)	($85,147)	($121,634)	($172,977)	($227,595)	($291,599)	($358,023)	($429,205)	($505,467)
Financial Income (Expense), net of tax	$121	$29	($104)	($263)	($436)	($618)	($875)	($1,148)	($1,468)	($1,800)	($2,156)	($2,537)
ENDING CASH BALANCE	$31,235	$9,073	($18,917)	($50,811)	($85,583)	($122,252)	($173,852)	($228,743)	($293,067)	($359,823)	($431,361)	($508,004)
Desired Cash Level	$2,000	$2,000	$2,000	$2,000	$2,000	$2,000	$2,000	$2,000	$2,000	$2,000	$2,000	$2,000
Loan Required to Maintain Minimum Cash Level	$0	$0	$20,813	$52,548	$87,147	$123,634	$174,977	$229,595	$293,599	$360,023	$431,205	$507,467
Cash Surplus	$29,114	$7,044	$0	$0	$0	$0	$0	$0	$0	$0	$0	$0

(Continued)

EXHIBIT 10.4 (continued)

Sample Spreadsheet Analysis

OUTPUT GENERATED:

```
# # # # # # # # # # # # # # # # # #
#            Cash Budget          #
# # # # # # # # # # # # # # # # # #
```

		Months											
		1	2	3	4	5	6	7	8	9	10	11	12
NET SALES		$5,000	$10,000	$15,000	$20,000	$25,000	$30,000	$35,000	$40,000	$50,000	$55,000	$60,000	$65,000
Allowance for Slippage of Sales Forecast		$1,250	$2,500	$3,750	$5,000	$6,250	$7,500	$8,750	$10,000	$12,500	$13,750	$15,000	$16,250
GROSS SALES		$3,750	$7,500	$11,250	$15,000	$18,750	$22,500	$26,250	$30,000	$37,500	$41,250	$45,000	$48,750
Less: Materials Used		$1,875	$3,750	$5,625	$7,500	$9,375	$11,250	$13,125	$15,000	$18,750	$20,625	$22,500	$24,375
Direct Labor		$375	$750	$1,125	$1,500	$1,875	$2,250	$2,625	$3,000	$3,750	$4,125	$4,500	$4,875
Other Manufactoring Expense		$159	$319	$478	$638	$797	$956	$1,116	$1,275	$1,594	$1,753	$1,913	$2,072
Indirect Labor		$159	$319	$479	$638	$797	$956	$1,116	$1,275	$1,594	$1,753	$1,913	$2,072
COST OF GOODS SOLD		$2,569	$5,138	$7,706	$10,275	$12,844	$15,413	$17,981	$20,550	$25,688	$28,256	$30,825	$33,394
GROSS PROFIT		$1,181	$2,363	$3,544	$4,725	$5,906	$7,088	$8,269	$9,450	$11,813	$12,994	$14,175	$15,356
Less: Sales Expense		$188	$375	$563	$750	$938	$1,125	$1,313	$1,500	$1,875	$2,063	$2,250	$2,438
General and Administrative Expense		$94	$188	$281	$375	$469	$563	$656	$750	$938	$1,031	$1,125	$1,219
Bad Debt Expense		$75	$150	$225	$300	$375	$450	$525	$600	$750	$825	$900	$975
Depreciation Expense, Fixed Assets		$250	$250	$300	$300	$300	$300	$340	$340	$340	$340	$340	$340
Lease Expense		$0	$80	$80	$80	$80	$80	$80	$80	$80	$80	$80	$80
Other Expenses (Itemized Above)		$0	$30	$0	$60	$20	$0	$0	$500	$0	$0	$0	$0
OPERATING PROFIT		$575	$1,290	$2,095	$2,860	$3,725	$4,570	$5,355	$5,680	$7,830	$8,655	$9,480	$10,305
Income Taxes on Operations		$238	$645	$1,048	$1,430	$1,863	$2,285	$2,678	$2,840	$3,915	$4,328	$4,740	$5,153
OTHER FINANCIAL REVENUE (EXPENSES)		$243	$59	($208)	($525)	($871)	($1,236)	($1,750)	($2,296)	($2,936)	($3,600)	($4,312)	($5,075)
Income Tax Provision		$121	$29	($104)	($263)	($436)	($618)	($875)	($1,148)	($1,468)	($1,800)	($2,156)	($2,537)
NET PROFIT		$459	$674	$944	$1,167	$1,427	$1,667	$1,803	$1,692	$2,447	$2,528	$2,584	$2,615

(Continued)

EXHIBIT 10.4 (continued)

Sample Spreadsheet Analysis

LIST OF ASSUMPTIONS:

	Months 1	2	3	4	5	6	7	8	9	10	11
Net Sales $	$5,000	$10,000	$15,000	$20,000	$25,000	$30,000	$35,000	$40,000	$50,000	$55,000	$60,000
Projected Sales, net of slippage	$3,750	$7,500	$11,250	$15,000	$18,750	$22,500	$26,250	$30,000	$37,500	$41,250	$45,000

	YEAR 1984	1985	1986	1987	1988
Slippage of Sales Forecast, % of sales . . . What if?	25.0%	15.0%	10.0%	10.0%	5.0%
Material Costs, as % of sales	50.0%	48.0%	46.0%	45.0%	45.0%
Direct Labor, as % of sales	10.0%	10.0%	9.0%	9.0%	9.0%
Other expense (overhead, etc., but exclude depreciation), as % of sales	4.3%	4.3%	4.3%	4.3%	4.3%
Indirect Labor, as % of sales	4.3%	4.3%	4.3%	4.3%	4.3%
Sales expense, as % of sales	5.0%	4.0%	4.0%	4.0%	4.0%
General and administrative, $	2.5%	2.5%	2.5%	2.5%	2.5%
Federal income tax rate, % of Profit before Tax	50.0%				
What month does this analysis begin (1–12)	1				
What is the present year?	1984				
Schedule B—Accounts Receivable Aging					
% Collections 0–30 Days	70%	70%	70%	80%	80%
% Collections 30–60 Days	20%	20%	20%	19%	19%
% Collections 60–90 Days	8%	8%	8%	0%	0%
% Uncollectable—Bad Debts	2%	2%	2%	1%	1%
Schedule C—Accounts Payable Aging (Raw Materials)					
% Payments 0–30 Days	100%	100%	80%	80%	80%
% Payments 30–60 Days	0%	0%	20%	20%	20%
% Payments 60–90 Days	0%	0%	0%	0%	0%
Schedule E—Direct Labor, Indirect Labor, M'fg Expense, Selling and G & A Expense, Accruals Aging					
% Payments 0–30 Days	100%	100%	90%	90%	90%
% Payments 30–60 Days	0%	0%	10%	10%	10%
Schedule F—Inventory Assumptions					
What is desired cash level? ($)	$2,000	$5,000	$7,000	$10,000	$10,000
How many months of finished goods inventory on hand?	2	2	3	3	3
How many months of raw materials inventory on hand?	3	3	4	4	4
Schedule G—Financial Revenue and Term Debt Assumptions					
What interest is paid on outstanding loans to maintain desired cash level?	12%	12%	12%	15%	15%
What is your return on a cash surplus?	10%	10%	10%	11%	11%

(Continued)

EXHIBIT 10.4 (Continued)

Sample Spreadsheet Analysis

Schedule H—Beginning Balances, period one

ASSETS:

Cash Balance	$50,000
Accounts Receivable	$100
Raw Materials Inventory	$100
Finished Goods Inventory	$300
Fixed Assets, Depreciable	$3,000
Accumulated Depreciation	$50
Other Assets, net	$200
Total Assets	$53,650

LIABILITIES:

Raw Materials payable	$100
Accruals Payable	$50
Notes Payable—Banks	$100
Long-Term Debt	$100
Contributed Capital	$500
Retained Earnings	$52,800
Total Liabilities + Equity	$53,650
Other—Present Loss Carryforward (−)	($100)

Schedule I—Cash Budget, Income Statement Monthly Changes $$

Months	1	2	3	4	5	6	7	8	9	10	11	12
Receipts (Cash Basis):												
Other proceeds (LTD)	$0	$2,000	$0	$2,000	$0	$0	$4,000	$0	$0	$0	$0	$0
Contributed Capital Additions	$0	$0	$0	$0	$5,000	$0	$0	$0	$0	$0	$0	$0
Disbursements (Cash Basis):												
Long-Term Debt Payments	$5	$5	$5	$5	$5	$5	$5	$5	$5	$5	$5	$5
Other Expenses	$30	$0	$60	$20	$0	$0	$500	$0	$0	$0	$0	$0
"Other Asset" Additions, non- depreciable	$0	$10	$0	$0	$0	$0	$0	$0	$0	$0	$0	$0

Schedule J—Fixed Asset Additions

	Asset 1	Asset 2	Asset 3
CURRENT ASSETS:			
Amount	$3,000		
Depreciation Period	1		
YEAR 1:			
Amount	$2,400	$3,000	$2,400
Month Bought (1–12)	2	3	7
Depreciation Period or Lease Term	3	5	5
Cash Basis = 1 / Lease = 2	2	1	1
YEAR 2:			
Amount	$3,600		$3,600
Month Bought (1–12)	1	6	6
Depreciation Period or Lease Term	5	5	5
Cash Basis = 1 / Lease = 2	1	1	1
YEAR 3:			
Amount	$4,000		$5,000
Date Bought	2	3	3
Depreciation Period or Lease Term	3	3	3
Cash Basis = 1 / Lease = 2	2	2	1

NOTE: YEARS FOUR AND FIVE ASSUMPTIONS SAME AS ABOVE

(Continued)

336

EXHIBIT 10.4 (concluded)

OUTPUT GENERATED:

```
# # # # # # # # # # # # # # # #
#                              #
#        Balance Sheet         #     Months
#                              #
# # # # # # # # # # # # # # # #
```

(End of Month)	1	2	3	4	5	6	7	8	9	10	11	12
ASSETS: Cash	$31,135	$8,973	$0	$0	$0	$0	$0	$0	$0	$0	$0	$0
Receivables	$1,125	$2,625	$4,200	$5,850	$7,575	$9,375	$11,250	$13,200	$16,350	$18,825	$21,075	$23,400
Less: Allowance for doubtful accts.	($75)	($225)	($450)	($750)	($1,125)	($1,575)	($2,100)	($2,700)	($3,450)	($4,275)	($5,175)	($6,150)
Net Receivables	$1,050	$2,400	$3,750	$5,100	$6,450	$7,800	$9,150	$10,500	$12,900	$14,550	$15,900	$17,250
Finished Goods Inventory (Net)	$13,144	$31,125	$54,244	$82,500	$115,894	$154,425	$200,663	$254,606	$313,688	$377,906	$447,263	$521,756
Raw Materials Inventory (Net)	$5,625	$9,375	$13,125	$16,875	$20,625	$24,375	$28,125	$33,750	$39,375	$43,125	$46,875	$50,625
CURRENT ASSETS	$50,954	$51,873	$71,119	$104,475	$142,969	$186,600	$237,938	$298,856	$365,963	$435,581	$510,038	$589,631
Fixed Assets	$3,000	$3,000	$6,000	$6,000	$6,000	$6,000	$8,400	$8,400	$8,400	$8,400	$8,400	$8,400
Accumulated Depreciation	$300	$550	$850	$1,150	$1,450	$1,750	$2,090	$2,430	$2,770	$3,110	$3,450	$3,790
Net Fixed Assets	$2,700	$2,450	$5,150	$4,850	$4,550	$4,250	$6,310	$5,970	$5,630	$5,290	$4,950	$4,610
Other Assets	$200	$200	$210	$210	$210	$210	$210	$210	$210	$210	$210	$210
TOTAL ASSETS	$53,854	$54,523	$76,479	$109,535	$147,729	$191,060	$244,458	$305,036	$371,803	$441,081	$515,198	$594,451
LIABILITIES: Notes Payable—Banks	$0	$0	$19,017	$50,911	$85,683	$122,352	$173,952	$228,843	$293,167	$359,923	$431,461	$508,104
Raw Materials Payable	$0	$0	$0	$0	$0	$0	$0	$0	$0	$0	$0	$0
Accruals Payable	$0	$0	$0	$0	$0	$0	$0	$0	$0	$0	$0	$0
Income Tax Payable	$0	$0	$0	$0	$0	$0	$0	$0	$0	$0	$0	$0
Total Current Liabilities	$0	$0	$19,017	$50,911	$85,683	$122,352	$173,952	$228,843	$293,167	$359,923	$431,461	$508,104
Total Long-Term Debt	$95	$90	$85	$2,080	$2,075	$4,070	$4,065	$4,060	$8,055	$8,050	$8,045	$8,040
TOTAL LIABILITIES	$95	$90	$19,102	$52,991	$87,758	$126,422	$178,017	$232,903	$301,222	$367,973	$439,506	$516,144
CAPITAL STOCK: Contributed Capital	$500	$500	$500	$500	$500	$5,500	$5,500	$5,500	$5,500	$5,500	$5,500	$5,500
Retained Earnings	$53,259	$53,933	$56,877	$56,044	$59,471	$59,138	$60,941	$66,633	$65,080	$67,608	$70,192	$72,807
TOTAL LIABILITIES AND NET WORTH	$53,854	$54,523	$76,479	$109,535	$147,729	$191,060	$244,458	$305,036	$371,803	$441,081	$515,198	$594,451

startup were entered into a computer model. Within another two hours, he had been able to see what the venture would look like financially over the first 18 months and then to see the impact of several different what-if scenarios. The net result was that the new venture idea was abandoned, since the amount of money required appeared to outweigh the potential.

The strength of computer-based analysis is also a source of problems for entrepreneurs who place the "druther" before the fact. With so many moving parts, analysis that is not grounded in sound perceptions about an opportunity is most likely to be confused.

General Sources of Information

There are *many* sources of information in the area of resources, including magazines such as *INC.* and *Venture*. Online database services mentioned in Chapter 3 are good sources of information. A book written by the author with David Gumpert puts together, under one cover, basic sources of information. It is called *The Encyclopedia of Small Business Resources* (Harper & Row, 1984). See the Annotated Bibliography for a summary of "best selections" of interest to entrepreneurs, as well as John Tracy's article "How to Read Financial Reports."

Chapter Summary

1. Successful entrepreneurs use ingenious bootstrapping approaches to marshaling and minimizing resources.
2. Control of resources—not necessarily ownership—is the key to this "less is more" resource strategy.
3. Entrepreneurs are also creative in identifying other people's money and resources, thereby spreading and sharing the risks.
4. Selecting outside advisors, directors and other professionals boils down to one key criterion: Do they add value through their know-how and networks?
5. Today, access to financial and nonfinancial resources is greater than ever before and is increasing because of the Internet.

Study Questions

1. Entrepreneurs think and act ingeniously when it comes to resources. What does this mean and why is it so important?
2. Describe at least two creative bootstrapping resources you know of.
3. Why will the Internet become an increasingly important gateway to controlling resources?
4. In selecting outside advisors, a board, consultants and the like, what are the most important criteria, and why?

MIND STRETCHERS
Have You Considered?

1. Many successful entrepreneurs and private investors say it is just as bad to start out with too much money, as it is too little. Why is this so? Can you find some examples?
2. It is said that money is the least important part of the resource equation and of the entrepreneurial process. Why is this so?
3. What bootstrapping strategies do you need to devise?

Exercise—How Entrepreneurs Turn Less into More

Entrepreneurs are often creative and ingenious in bootstrapping their ventures and in getting a great deal out of very limited resources. This assignment can be done alone, in pairs or in trios. Identify at least two or three entrepreneurs whose companies exceed $3 million in sales and are less than 10 years old and who have started their companies with less than $25,000 to $50,000 of initial seed capital. Interview them with a focus on their strategies and tactics which minimize and control (not necessarily own) the necessary resources.

1. What methods, sources, and techniques did they devise to acquire resources?
2. Why were they able to do so much with so little?
3. What assumptions, attitudes, and mind sets seemed to enable them to think and function in this manner?
4. What patterns, similarities, and differences exist among the entrepreneurs you interviewed?
5. What impact did these minimizing bootstrapping approaches have on their abilities to conserve cash and equity and to create future options or choices to pursue other opportunities?
6. How did they devise unique incentive structures in the deals and arrangements with their people, suppliers, and other resource providers (their first office space or facility, brochures, etc.)?
7. In lieu of money, what other forms of currency did they use, such as bartering for space, equipment, or people or giving an extra day off or an extra week's vacation?

8. Can they think of examples of how they acquired (gained control of) a resource which they could afford to pay for with real money and did not?

9. Many experienced entrepreneurs say that for first-time entrepreneurs it can be worse to start with too much money rather than too little. How do you see this and why?

10. Some of the strongest new companies are started during an economic recession, among tight credit and capital markets. It is invaluable to develop a lean-and-mean, make-do, less-is-more philosophy and sense of frugality and budgetary discipline. Can you think of any examples of this? Do you agree or disagree? Can you think of opposite examples, such as companies started at or near the peak of the 1990s economic boom with more capital and credit than they needed?

You will find as very useful background reading the feature articles on bootstrapping, in *INC.* magazine, *Success* magazine, *Fast Company*, and others.

Case

FAX International, Inc.*

Preparation Questions

1. Evaluate the opportunity and the FAX International business plan.
2. What fund-raising and financial strategy should Douglas Ranalli pursue?
3. What should Doug do?

FAX International, Inc., Business Plan

Executive Summary

FAX International, Inc., was founded in June 1990 by Mr. Douglas J. Ranalli and Dr. Thomas P. Sosnowski, PhD. The goal of the company is to build an international communications network that will be seven times more efficient at transmitting fax documents than the switched-voice networks of AT&T, MCI, and Sprint. The company's year-long design and development effort has been extremely successful. As a result the network will be ready for demonstration by the end of July 1991, and ready for full-scale implementation during October 1991. The opportunity now exists to offer business customers a vastly superior facsimile transmission service between the United States and major international city centers like Tokyo, London, Paris, and so on. Service is superior because it is both easier to use than direct-dial service from AT&T and 50 percent less expensive. For example, customers currently paying an average of $1.40/minute for service to Tokyo will pay only $.69 with FAX International, Inc. The FAX International network is so efficient that it will provide business customers 50 percent savings over current rates while earning 50 percent gross margins on the service once a minimum efficient volume level has been achieved.

The international telecommunications market has historically been closed to competition due to the presence of monopoly carriers in almost every country. The regulatory situation, however, is changing rapidly as countries all over the world look for ways to make their telecommunications industries more competitive. In June 1990, the European Commission directed members of the European Economic Community to begin deregulating all enhanced telecommunications services. Similarly, the United States and Japan negotiated the International Value Added Network Services (IVANS) agreement, which guarantees U.S. value-added network service providers like FAX International fair and equal access to the Japanese market. The actions of the European Commission and the signing of the IVANS agreement between the United States and Japan have created an opportunity for a variety of international enhanced-communications services between the United States, Europe, and Japan. The opportunities have yet to be exploited due to the time required for companies to understand the recent regulatory changes and to develop appropriate technologies. An article in the June 15 issue of *EMMS* (Electronic Mail and Micro Systems) summed up the opportunity as follows:

> What is the magic formula for success in enhanced fax service? Whoever figures it out may turn out to be the William McGowan (MCI) success story of the 1990s . . . Conceivably, a fax from [the United States] could travel via private lines to Tokyo, or London and be delivered with a local call—completely eliminating the need for the international switched network. The economic incentive is so strong that over the next two to three years, hundreds of millions of dollars/year of international facsimile traffic are likely to migrate from the switched voice networks of AT&T, MCI, and Sprint to dedicated facsimile networks.

*Reprinted with the permission of Douglas J. Ranalli, Founder and President of FAX International.

FAX International, Inc., is prepared with the technology, the management team, and the regulatory approvals necessary to capitalize on this exciting international opportunity.

FAX International's initial objective is to establish a leadership position in the United States-to-Tokyo market during the first 12 months of operation. Expansion into two more markets, London to the United States and Paris to the United States, will follow soon afterwards. The United States–Tokyo market has been targeted first for three reasons:

1. It is the highest-volume international facsimile route in the world (390 million fax minutes/year in both directions between the United States and Japan in 1990; 175 million fax minutes/year in one direction from just the United States to Tokyo). See "Market Size."

2. It is the fastest growing route (growth rate projected at over 30 percent/year).

3. Potential customers are highly concentrated in a few major U.S. city centers and are easy to identify. Of the 9,000 Japanese affiliated firms operating in the United States, over 50 percent are located in Los Angeles, San Francisco, and New York.

FAX International has succeeded in assembling the technology, the business support systems, and the management team necessary to provide a full scale service between the United States, Tokyo, and other major international city centers. The next step is to complete a second round of financing which will be used to install the network and bring the company to a cash-positive position within the first 12 months of operations. An equity investment of $1,000,000 combined with equipment lease loans representing assets worth $1,500,000 will be required to achieve the following projected financial results:

	Year 1	Year 2	Year 3
Revenue:	$2,200,000	$8,800,000	$14,800,000
EBIT:	$ (950,000)	$1,950,000	$ 4,200,000

Table of Contents

Market Development Strategy

FAX International's market development strategy is based on expanding into one international market at a time and building traffic to an efficient economy of scale before moving into the next market. FAX International has chosen this conservative strategy based on an analysis of the economic, regulatory, and competitive environments the company is likely to encounter over the next several years. The company's board of advisors has played an instrumental role in providing detailed market and competitive information during the formulation of this strategy.

- **Economics.** The economics of the store-and-forward facsimile business are driven by the need to achieve substantial traffic volume along each selected international route (i.e., the United States to Tokyo, or the United States to London). This economic environment results from the high cost of setting up a digital circuit between two points and the low cost of carrying additional traffic on an already established circuit. Efficient operation of FAX International's network results from carrying 7,000,000 minutes of traffic/year on any given route. For example, variable costs on the United States–Tokyo route drop from $.61/minute to $.31/minute as traffic volume grows from 0 minutes/year to 7,000,000 minutes/year. (See "Market Size" and "Network Economics.") The economics of this industry heavily favor a strategy focused on achieving high traffic volume on each individual route.

- **Regulatory Complexity.** The international regulatory environment has eased dramatically in the last two years. However, the regulatory issues associated with carrying international telecommunications traffic are still complex, cumbersome, and specific to each international market. Each new market represents a commitment of time, money, and management resources to a process that is fraught with uncertainty and delays.

- **Competition.** FAX International anticipates the emergence of a large number of small competitors in the international store-and-forward business as the market develops. The world market for this type of service is large enough to support dozens of small niche players operating on the multiple international routes. In the long run, however, the economics of the industry dictate that the only competitive companies will be those that reach the minimum required economy of scale along a given route. Consolidation is almost guaranteed to occur since increasing volume leads to decreasing variable costs. Those firms which fail to achieve the minimum scale will be faced with an increasingly competitive environment and an inferior cost structure.

In summary, FAX International's analysis reveals that although the opportunity exists to launch a service in multiple markets, the fastest and most conservative route to profitability lies in concentrating on one market at a time. FAX International has decided to address the markets in the order outlined below based on an analysis of each market's size, growth rate, cost of entry, cost of customer acquisition, and short- and long-term profit potential.

- United States to Tokyo.
- Tokyo to the United States.
- London and Paris to the United States.

Market Entry Strategy: The United States to Tokyo

FAX International will utilize a low-price, fast-growth strategy to enter the United States–Tokyo market. This strategy was chosen based on FAX International's analysis of the US telecommunications market and an analysis of MCI's success against AT&T in a similar competitive situation.

The objective is to reach 7,000,000 minutes of traffic per year from the United States to Tokyo as quickly as possible. FCC statistics show that fax traffic on the United States–Japan route has been growing at 30 percent per year and reached 250 million minutes per year in 1990. Traffic on the United States-to-Tokyo route alone is estimated at 175 million minutes per year. FAX International's business plan is based on winning just 4 percent of this clearly defined and highly focused United States–Tokyo market segment (source: FCC Statistics, "International Message Telephone Service between the United States and Selected Countries, 1957–1989").

MCI successfully proved that business customers in the United States are willing to test new telecommunications services if the cost savings are attractive enough. MCI started in the United States as an unknown and unproven company, but its aggressive offer of 30 to 50 percent discounts prompted potential customers to take a chance. MCI's low-price, fast-growth strategy allowed it to quickly capture the market share necessary to reach an efficient scale of operations. FAX International will apply a nearly identical strategy in entering the facsimile transmission market.

The FAX International network has been designed from the ground up to meet the needs of U.S.-based customers identified through market research and field interviews. Potential customers have stated they will test and utilize the service if it can deliver the following features:

- 40–60 percent cost savings for business customers of all sizes on calls from the United States to Tokyo.
- No risk trial offer:
  —No installation fees or up-front costs.
  —No change in long-distance carrier required.
  —No employee training needed to use the service.
  —No change in fax equipment required.
  —Free 100-minute test period for every potential customer.

The recessionary economic environment in the United States is the ideal time for FAX International to launch a low-price, fast-growth strategy. The facsimile market between the United States and Tokyo is huge and growing at 30 percent per year. Breaking into a new market is never easy, but the opportunity is clear, the cost savings are clear, the customers are easy to identify, and the timing is perfect.

Japanese Market Entry Strategy

The Japanese telecommunications market is completely different than the U.S. market in terms of customer willingness to test a service from a new and unproven competitor. Japanese customers prefer to work with established Japanese organizations. Breaking into the Japanese market as a small U.S. company has proven over and over again to be almost impossible.

FAX International's strategy for breaking into the Japanese market is to enter into a joint venture agreement with a large Japanese firm that already has access to the target customers in Japan. FAX International is in a position to offer an extremely attractive joint venture opportunity because the network has been designed to carry traffic in both directions simultaneously between the United States and Japan. Once a steady flow of traffic has been developed from the United States to Tokyo, return traffic can be carried at an extremely low variable cost ($.13/minute). By succeeding in the United States–Tokyo market first, FAX International will be in a position to provide a Japanese firm with a complete franchiselike opportunity for carrying fax traffic from Tokyo back to the United States. The Japanese partner will be responsible for marketing the service in Tokyo and providing all customer support. Business customers in Tokyo currently pay $1.20 to $1.60 per minute for facsimile transmission service to the United States. FAX International's current plan is to offer the Japanese partner an opportunity to carry traffic on the network at a cost of just $.35/minute. At this rate, the Japanese partner will be in a position to mark up its cost of goods sold by 100 percent and still offer customers a 40–60 percent savings. At a rate of $.35/minute, FAX International will earn 60 percent gross margins on all return traffic from Tokyo. The profit opportunity is extremely attractive for all parties involved.

FAX International will begin searching for a joint venture partner in early 1992 once the network has been successfully established between the United States and Tokyo. Several options for identifying joint venture partners have already been presented. One option under serious consideration is to hire Mr. Douglas Fine to negotiate and manage the joint venture. Doug Fine has had specific experience in negotiating joint ventures for U.S. firms interested in entering the Japanese market while working for the venture capital arm of Nomura Securities in Tokyo. Doug holds a BS and master's degree in electrical engineering from Stanford University, is a graduate of the Harvard Business School, and is fluent in Japanese.

FAX International's activities in Japan to date have been coordinated through two key relationships that have developed over the past year:

- *Coopers & Lybrand.* The consulting office of Coopers & Lybrand in Tokyo has been responsible for working with FAX International personnel to secure the necessary operating licenses for the company in Japan.

- *KDD.* KDD is Japan's largest international telecommunications carrier. KDD has been selected to provide FAX International's digital communications lines between the United States and Japan in coordination with AT&T. In addition, FAX International's network equipment will be housed in Tokyo within the KDD facilities. The KDD facility provides FAX International with 24-hour network monitoring, 24-hour security, climate control, guaranteed power backup, and other emergency control measures.

London/Paris Market Strategy

FAX International anticipates an opportunity to enter the London and Paris markets simultaneously with a low-price, fast-growth approach identical to the strategy employed in the United States. The geographic proximity of London and Paris will allow these two major markets to be serviced from a single business support office located in London. International facsimile traffic in and out of Great Britain and France is highly concentrated within London and Paris. Rough estimates provided by the consulates of each country show 70 percent or more of each country's international traffic tied to these two cities. Each city will have its own sales office and customer support office, but will share a common business systems office providing billing, accounting, and network management services.

The economic opportunity in both London and Paris is extremely attractive.

In addition to carrying traffic from London and Paris to the United States, the network will be capable of carrying traffic in all directions between London, Paris, and Tokyo. The economic opportunity along all of these routes is equally attractive to the opportunity outlined above.

	London	Paris
Current business rates to United States:	$1.08/minute	$1.58/minute
FAX International variable cost:	$0.30*	$0.30*
FAX International rate/minute:	$0.60	$0.60
Customer savings:	44%	62%

*Variable costs based on traffic volume of $5 million/year from each city.

Market Size

The Federal Communications Commission keeps track of the number of direct dial international calls placed every year over the public switched networks. (AT&T, MCI, Sprint, etc.) An analysis of the statistics shows the following trends:

1. Switched international voice traffic is growing at 15–20 percent per year worldwide.
2. Switched international facsimile traffic is growing at more than twice the pace of voice traffic (30–40 percent).
3. Facsimile traffic already accounts for up to 70 percent of the calls on the United States–Japan route and 33 percent on the United States–United Kingdom route. These statistics are estimates and are unavailable for most international routes.
4. International traffic is highly concentrated between major U.S. city centers and major international city centers. For example, Tokyo represents almost 70 percent of the traffic in and out of Japan. Similar traffic concentrations exist in London, Paris, Hong Kong, and so forth.

International Direct Dial Calls—Voice and Fax 1990

	Voice and Fax Traffic	Percent Fax	Fax Market
U.S./Japan (both directions)	560 million minutes/year	70%	390 million
U.S./Great Britain	1,150 million minutes/year	33	380 million
U.S./France	390 million minutes/year	N/A	N/A
U.S./West Germany	700 million minutes/year	N/A	N/A

N/A = not available.

Note: Unlike most telecommunications equipment, the FAX International network has been designed to meet the regulatory requirements of every international phone system. The opportunity exists to expand the service to all of the countries listed above plus many others.

Sources: FCC and June 15, 1990 issue of *EMMS* (Electronic Mail and Micro Systems)

How the Network Works

The FAX International network can be broken down into four functional components:

1. Interface with the customer.
2. Collect and distribute documents within a country.
3. Transmit documents to a foreign country.
4. Monitor the status of every document on the network.

Customer Interface

The goal of the customer interface is to allow customers to utilize the FAX International network without changing their current behavior. The expectations of the 100 customers interviewed to date were clear and straightforward. Customers want to dial a phone number into their fax machine and know that the document is going to reach its destination. If the document is destined for Tokyo, then it should be invisibly routed over the FAX International network. If the document is destined for a city not served by FAX International then it should be transmitted via the customer's primary long-distance carrier (AT&T, MCI, Sprint, etc.). FAX International has achieved this goal of invisible performance by incorporating an intelligent auto-dialer into the system. Every fax machine that is signed onto the network will have a programmable auto-dialer attached to the back of the machine. The auto-dialer will determine which fax calls should be routed over FAX International. For example, if a customer enters a phone number destined for Tokyo, the dialer will intercept the call, dial an access number to reach FAX International, and then pass along the following information:

- Customer account number.
- Password.
- Other control information.
- Phone number entered by the customer.

The network will read in the information from the auto-dialer, check to make sure the customer is authorized to use the network, and then issue a fax receive tone to the customer's fax machine. The document will be received into the FAX International network and then forwarded to the appropriate destination country. The auto-dialer is able to perform the tasks outlined above in less time than it takes AT&T to connect an average international call. The customer experiences no delay as a result of the auto-dialer's activities.

Collect and Distribute Documents within a Country

Customers located anywhere in the United States will be able to access the FAX International network. The capability has been built in to send or receive a document from any fax machine in the United States, but over time the communications assets utilized to accomplish the task will change.

1. *Initial approach.* FAX International will start with a single network node (central node) located in Boston. When a customer in New York City dials a number destined for Japan, the auto-dialer attached to the customer's fax machine will reach FAX International by dialing an 800 number. This type of 800 number access will cost FAX International $.15/minute on average.

2. *Network expansion.* Once the volume of traffic in and out of a given city like New York exceeds 500 minutes per day, a separate network node will be installed in that city. The auto-dialers located in New York City will then be reprogrammed to access FAX International by dialing a local call in New York to reach the network. The document will be received into the New York City node and then transmitted to the central node in Boston over a high-speed digital line. The cost of collecting a document from New York City will then drop to only $.05/minute.

Over time, FAX International will expand the network to include remote nodes all over the country. The same type of expansion will take place in Japan thus allowing the company to reach customers more efficiently. Since the auto-dialers installed at the customer sites can be programmed remotely, customers will not be affected as the network configuration changes and grows.

Transmit Documents to a Foreign Country

Once a document has reached the central node in the United States it will be transmitted to its foreign destination over a dedicated high speed digital line. Dedicated fiber optic based circuits between the United States and Tokyo can be leased from a variety of international carriers, including AT&T, MCI, and Sprint. These lines are billed on a flat monthly charge basis. The line will be dedicated to FAX International and available for simultaneous use in both directions 24 hours a day. The average cost of sending a fax document from the United States to Tokyo over one of these lines depends on two factors:

1. *Size of the fiber optic lines.* Substantial economies of scale result from leasing high-volume lines known as full T1 circuits. A full T1 circuit consists of 24 smaller channels which can be leased one at a time. The first channel between the United States and Tokyo costs $14,500/month to lease. The cost per channel drops consistently as channels are added until the average cost per channel reaches $5,000/month on a full T1 circuit. A traffic volume of 7 million minutes/year is required to efficiently utilize a full T1 circuit between any two points.

2. *Utilization of the T1 line in each direction.* The international T1 circuit utilized by FAX International can carry traffic in both directions simultaneously. The average cost per minute of traffic carried on the circuit will depend on the volume of traffic flowing in each direction. In order to be conservative, the FAX International business plan is based on the full cost of the circuit being covered by traffic running from the United States to Tokyo.

Monitor the Status of Every Document on the Network

Customers demand perfectly accurate, up-to-the-minute information on the status of their documents as they move through the network. The FAX International network has been designed to provide a status update on every document once every five minutes. The information will be used to provide high-quality customer service and to provide customers with up-to-the-minute status on all of the documents entered into the network.

Document status information will be collected at the central node in the United States and forwarded to the company's customer service office. The customer service office can be located anywhere in the United States. Initially it will be located in the Boston area, but if necessity dictates a move to a different location, the operation can be easily relocated.

Network Economics

The economics of the FAX International network are based on two issues, hardware costs and communications costs. Outlined below is an introduction to the variables which drive these two cost centers. Surprisingly, the network hardware is quite inexpensive when measured by the revenue it produces. The financial plan will show that hardware lease costs end up representing less than 5 percent of gross revenue once the network achieves an efficient operating volume. Communications costs on the other hand are quite expensive since they represent the network's cost of goods sold. Variable communications costs will eventually stabilize to represent 50 percent or less of gross revenue. The hardware costs and communications costs are connected to the extent that the deployment of hardware assets has a direct bearing on the cost of collecting or distributing a fax document within the United States or Japan.

Hardware Costs

The network hardware can be broken into three pieces:

- Fixed/core network hardware and software.
- Variable network hardware and software.
- Customer-based auto-dialers.

The hardware block diagram provides a graphic representation of the central processing nodes that will be installed in both the United States and Tokyo (see *Exhibit A*). All of the equipment shown will be leased rather than purchased by FAX International. The company is currently working with a leasing operation located in Boston called TLP Leasing Programs, Inc.

Fixed Network Hardware/Software A fixed core investment is required to allow the company to function properly. The core system includes all of the hardware and software necessary to provide the following system features:

- Efficient document transmission.
- Critical asset redundancy.
- Customer service and support system.
- Sales support and Customer Installation system.
- Network management system.
- Business management software (includes automated billing).
- Core system investment: $300,000.

Variable Network Hardware The second component of the network varies depending on the volume of traffic carried daily. As traffic volume increases, additional fax lines will be added to the central node and to the remote city nodes around the United States and Japan. Additional capacity can be added in units of 5,000 traffic minutes per day.

- Additional investment required for each additional 5,000 minutes/day: $45,000.

Customer Site Auto-dialers FAX International will be using programmable auto-dialers produced by MITEL Electronics. Purchased in volume, they cost $125/dialer. The auto-dialers provide the following capabilities:

- *Fraud prevention.* Each auto-dialer will be given a unique password to use when dialing into the FAX International network.
- *Invisible access to the network.* The auto-dialer will allow customers to utilize the FAX International network without changing their current routine. A customer simply dials a destination phone number on a fax machine and hits the start button. Documents destined for Tokyo will be intercepted by the auto-dialer and passed on to the FAX International network automatically. The process is completely invisible to the customer.

Customers will be provided with a certain number of free auto-dialers based on their average daily volume of traffic. A free auto-dialer will be provided for every 10 minutes of traffic per day. This policy is designed to deter customers from asking FAX International to install auto-dialers on fax machines that are rarely used for international transmissions. At the customer's request, additional auto-dialers will be provided for a rental fee rate of $10/month per auto-dialer. For planning purposes, the company has planned to provide a free auto-

EXHIBIT A

Central Node: Hardware Block Diagram

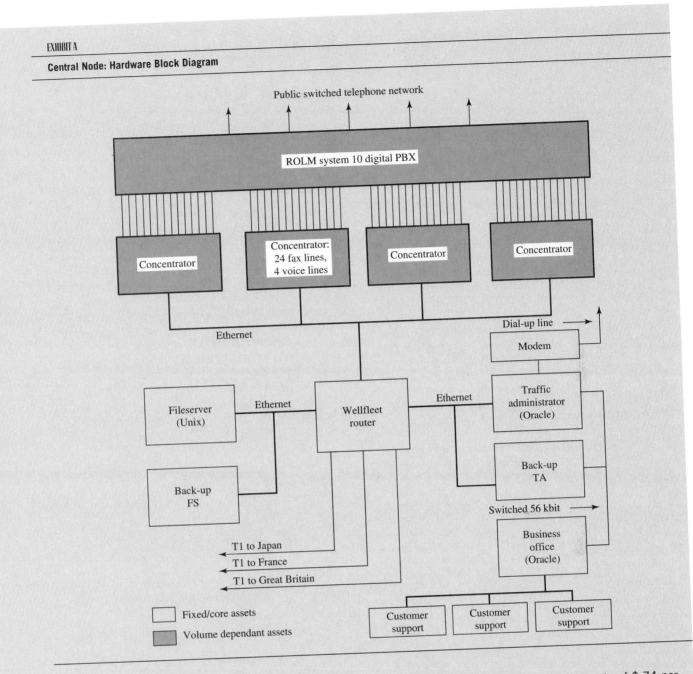

dialer for every 10 minutes/day of additional traffic that is signed onto the network.

Auto-dialers will be purchased in units of 500 dialers. If each dialer represents 10 minutes per day of traffic and costs $125 then the following cost structure results.

- Auto-dialer investment for each 5,000 minutes/day of traffic: $62,500.

Hardware Utilization Analysis

Each additzional 5,000 minutes per day of traffic that is added to the FAX International network requires a hardware investment of $45,000 in network hardware and $62,500 in customer auto-dialers, for a total in-

vestment of $107,500. At an average rate of $.74 per minute to Tokyo, 5,000 minutes of traffic per day represents $890,000 per year of revenue, assuming 20 business days per month.

An investment of $107,500 in hardware and software that has a useful life of at least three years will generate $890,000 per year in incremental revenue. The asset intensity of this network is extremely low.

Communications Costs

FAX International has the option to purchase its fiber optic communications lines from a variety of common carriers, including AT&T, MCI, Sprint, Cable & Wireless, and many other less well-known carriers. Transmitting a document between the United States and Tokyo involves three types of communications costs:

1. Local reception or delivery in the United States:
   a. Minimum $.09/minute.
   b. Maximum $.15/minute
   c. Average cost will drop as volume grows.
2. Transmission from the United States to Tokyo:
   a. Minimum $.20/minute.
   b. Maximum $.43/minute.
   c. Average cost will drop as volume grows.
3. Local reception or delivery in Tokyo: Average $.03/minute regardless of volume.

Substantial economies of scale result from reaching a minimum volume of 7 million minutes of traffic/year on the network. A company operating in this market at a low volume (less than 1 million minutes/year) will be faced with variable costs of $.61/minute. Alternatively, a company operating at a volume of 7 million minutes per year will face a variable cost of just $.31/minute. These variable cost figures are based on carrying traffic in one direction only. The international leased circuit between the United States and Tokyo is capable of carrying traffic in two directions simultaneously. As a result, once traffic has been developed in one direction, the network is capable of carrying return traffic at very low variable cost.

The following *Exhibit B* and *Exhibit C* summarize the variable cost structure that FAX International will face at different levels of traffic volume.

Technology

Dr. Thomas P. Sosnowski, PhD, is responsible for the network design and development effort. Dr. Sosnowski (Tom), age 54, has worked his entire career in telecommunications development, including 13 years at AT&T's Bell Labs.

Network Systems

The following network systems are currently under development at FAX International:

1. *Communications network.* A fiber optic based network that can move a fax document between the United States and any foreign country seven times as efficiently as the AT&T switched voice network.
2. *Customer interface.* A system that will allow FAX International to invisibly route specific documents from a customer's fax machine onto the network. The goal is to ensure that the process of using the FAX International network is completely invisible to a customer sending a fax to Tokyo.
3. *Sales support.* A sales rep support system based on a portable PC platform that will dramatically increase the efficiency of the field sales force.
   a. Lead management and tracking software.
   b. Automated customer installation system.
   c. Automated proposal generation.

EXHIBIT B

Variable Costs—United States to Tokyo

Traffic Volume	U.S. Reception	Transmit to Tokyo	Local Delivery in Tokyo	Total
<500,000 min/yr	$.15	$.43	$.03	$.61
<1,000,000	$.15	$.34	$.03	$.52
<3,000,000	$.09	$.28	$.03	$.40
<5,000,000	$.09	$.24	$.03	$.36
<7,000,000	$.09	$.20	$.03	$.32

EXHIBIT C

Return Traffic Variable Costs—Tokyo to the United States

Traffic Volume	Tokyo Reception	Transmit to the United States	Local Delivery in the United States	Total
<500,000 min/yr	Free	Free	$.14	$.14
<1,000,000	Free	Free	$.13	$.13
<3,000,000	Free	Free	$.13	$.13
<5,000,000	Free	Free	$.13	$.13
<7,000,000	Free	Free	$.13	$.13

4. *Customer service.* A system that will automatically identify service problems, suggest solutions, and assist service reps in contacting the affected customers before the customer even knows a problem exists.

5. *Network management.* A system to allow an operator to sit at a terminal in Boston and monitor the behavior of every piece of network equipment worldwide.

6. *Business management.* A system to provide the FAX International management team with access to the following information on a daily basis:

   a. Network asset utilization.
   b. Customer behavior statistics.
   c. Sales rep productivity.
   d. Customer service rep productivity.
   e. Billing/accounting data.

7. *Integrated billing and accounting system.* A system to automate the entire billing and accounting cycle under the ORACLE relational database management program. Customer bills will be generated automatically by the network and entered into the integrated accounting system.

Development Philosophy

Tom Sosnowski and his development team are dedicated to producing a network that is capable of meeting the full range of business objectives set out for FAX International. Outlined below are some of the design tenets that have been used to guide the development process:

1. Utilize standard off-the-shelf technology wherever possible. Never make what you can buy.

2. Efficient technical development results from extensive planning. Project costs are projected based on an average of 80 percent planning and 20 percent implementation.

3. The design and construction of the network should be focused on meeting the specific needs of the customers, the sales force, and the customer service reps, not on potential technological capabilities.

4. Develop a hardware and software architecture that can incorporate frequent changes in customer demands.

5. Build the network in a modular fashion so that it can grow as quickly as the business requires.

Sales Strategy

The FAX International sales strategy has been designed around one primary goal:

Make it easy for customers of all sizes to say yes to a free test of the service. Once customers have tested the network, they will sign up for the service if it successfully provides the following features and benefits:

- High quality, reliable service.
- 40 percent to 60 percent savings.
- No up front fees.
- No training or change in behavior.
- No change in equipment.
- No change in long-distance carrier.

The FAX International sales organization will be based around a sales force of six field sales reps located in Los Angeles, San Francisco, and New York City. Although the FAX International sales presentation is simple enough to be delivered via a telemarketing operation, a field sales force approach has been selected for the following reasons:

1. *On-site installations required.* Signing up a customer to use the network involves attaching auto-dialers to each of the customer's fax machines and entering information about each user into the FAX International database. Gathering accurate information during the installation process is crucial to the efficient operation of the business. FAX International explored several opportunities to use third-party organizations for installation work but opted against this approach.

2. *Highly concentrated customer base.* FAX International sales reps will be pursuing leads provided by a directory, *Japanese Affiliated Companies in the U.S.,* published by the Japanese External Trade Organization. This directory lists 9,000 Japanese-affiliated firms in the United States. Over half of these leads are located in New York City, Los Angeles, and San Francisco. FAX International further estimates that over 80 percent of the decision makers for the 9,000 listed organizations are located in these three cities. The definition of a Japanese-affiliated firm is one that is at least 10 percent owned by a Japanese firm.

Convincing customers to accept a free, no-risk test of the network is the primary job of the field sales organization. Once a customer has agreed to a free test, the network will sell itself based on the performance of the system. Convincing customers to test the service is dependent on FAX International's cutting through the confusion and clutter created by the intense competition in the United States between MCI, Sprint, and AT&T.

FAX International is not offering a typical long-distance service, and the company cannot afford to let customers categorize the service as being similar to MCI, Sprint, and so on. FAX International is offering a totally different service concept which offers customers both superior service and superior price with no risk to the customer's organization. FAX International's sales presentation and promotional material have been designed to transmit the following five points:

1. *Totally different communications concept.* The FAX International network is seven times more efficient at transmitting a fax document than the voice network of AT&T, MCI, or Sprint. Comparing a highly specialized service like FAX International to AT&T, MCI, or Sprint is like comparing Federal Express to the U.S. Post Office.

2. *Better service.* The FAX International network has been designed to simplify life for heavy fax users:

   —Automatic redialing of busy numbers.
   —Delayed delivery and priority delivery options.
   —Broadcast distribution.
   —Enhanced billing functions.

3. *Better price.* FAX International's introductory offer of $.69 per minute to Tokyo represents a 40–60 percent cost savings for customers of all sizes. AT&T, MCI, Sprint, and others charge between $1.80 and $2.75 for the first minute of a call to Tokyo and $.90 to $1.15 for each additional minute during business hours.

4. *No-risk decision.* FAX International customers do not have to change their primary long-distance carrier. Only those fax calls destined for Tokyo or other cities serviced by FAX International will be routed over the network. All other fax calls will be transmitted by the customer's primary long-distance carrier. In most situations the customer's primary long-distance carrier won't even know that FAX International exists.

5. *Free test opportunity for qualified customers.* Customer interviews have shown that the biggest barrier to accepting the service is a fear that the network will not function as advertised. To combat this primary objection, FAX International will offer customers 100 free minutes of digital fax service to Tokyo from a single fax machine, with no strings attached.

Price Comparison

FAX International, Inc. pricing structure:

- *Small customers* (below $500/month): $.79/minute (billed in six-second increments).
- *Large customers* (above $500/month): $.69/minute.
- *Auto-dialer rental fee:* Customers will receive a free auto-dialer for every fax machine that transmits an average of 10 minutes of traffic/business day over the network. Additional auto-dialers will be provided at a rental rate of $10/month. Note: Auto-dialers cost FAX International $125/unit.

EXHIBIT D

Price/minute comparison for an average three-minute fax call to Tokyo

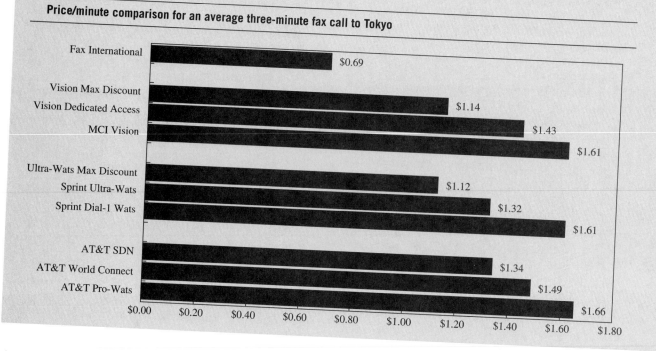

Fax International	$0.69
Vision Max Discount	$1.14
Vision Dedicated Access	$1.43
MCI Vision	$1.61
Ultra-Wats Max Discount	$1.12
Sprint Ultra-Wats	$1.32
Sprint Dial-1 Wats	$1.61
AT&T SDN	$1.34
AT&T World Connect	$1.49
AT&T Pro-Wats	$1.66

Sales Expectations

FAX International field sales reps will be responsible for qualifying accounts, setting up network demonstrations, installing free tests, and closing sales. The sales cycle is short and clearly defined. The profile of an ideal sales rep for FAX International is a young, successful sales person who has proven abilities to qualify accounts, set up meetings, and close sales. Top performers in the telecommunications industry in similar sales environments earn $40,000, including bonuses and commissions. FAX International's goal is to take six of these superior performers and offer them a base salary of $36,000 with an opportunity to earn $60,000 or more.

Monthly sales goals have been set with the following expectations in mind:

1. *5 to 10 new accounts per month.* The definition of an account is a single customer location that sends at least 25 minutes of traffic per day to Tokyo. Most of the customers contacted by FAX International will operate out of multiple offices in the United States. As a result, each sales presentation has the potential to result in sales to multiple locations.

2. *350 minutes/day of new traffic each month.* An average customer office location is expected to generate between 35 and 70 minutes of traffic per day. Interviews with 100 customers showed a range of 10 to 500 minutes of traffic per day from a single customer location.

3. *$700,000 in net new business per year.* The aggregate goal for the year is to sign up at least 4,000 minutes/day of new traffic. The potential exists to sign up a single customer that represents 1,000 minutes/day or more from a combination of multiple locations. For example, Nippon Express is one of the companies that has expressed great interest in testing the service. The Boston office of Nippon Express sends 125 pages per day to Tokyo, and they represent just 1 of 17 U.S. offices.

Field sales reps will be responsible for working with accounts located within driving distance of their assigned metropolitan area. All sales contacts made outside of the assigned area will be passed on to corporate headquarters. Installations at remote customer sites will be handled by a sales rep working out of the Boston office and traveling around the country.

Competition

FAX International's business plan has been developed with the assumption that competition will develop over the next few years from two sources: Small niche players similar to FAX International and full-service common carriers like AT&T, MCI, and Sprint. In the near term a large number of small companies are likely to enter the market with a variety of technical approaches and service offerings. All of these companies will be able to move fax documents more efficiently than the international switched voice networks, and most of these competitors will succeed in winning customers. AT&T, MCI, and Sprint are expected to enter the market once FAX International and others have proven that a large market exists for store and forward fax networks. In the interim, AT&T, MCI, and Sprint are expected to maintain the status quo since they currently control almost 100 percent of the international facsimile market and any reduction in price would come directly off their bottom lines.

Niche players: The international store and forward fax market has the potential to support dozens of small niche players operating on the multiple international routes. The opportunity has just recently been defined and as a result no standards of excellence have been established. FAX International anticipates the emergence of a large number of entrants each applying a different technology, service, and marketing approach in an attempt to find out what the customers are willing to buy. A limited number of these companies will enjoy great success and as a result will define standards for the industry. Success will be based on how well the networks function, how closely the service offerings meet the needs of the customers, and the efficiency of the sales/marketing approach applied. FAX International has designed a network and series of business support systems that will allow the company to refine its approach quickly to meet the needs of the market.

AT&T, MCI, and Sprint: All three of these companies have the technology and resources required to dominate this new market, but none of these companies has the incentive. All three companies know that if one enters the market the other two will follow immediately. The result will be a quick drop in revenue for all three companies with no change in market share or competitive advantage. FAX International anticipates that all three competitors will prepare the necessary technology to compete in the market but will avoid entry until FAX International and several other players develop the market and capture substantial market share.

AT&T, MCI, and Sprint represent both a threat and an opportunity to FAX International. Once FAX International reaches 7,000,000 minutes ($5,000,000) of traffic/year on the United States–Tokyo route, the company will be in a position to operate profitably no matter who enters the market. FAX International expects to grow far beyond this minimum required level in several markets before any major competitor presents a competing offer. If AT&T, MCI, and Sprint enter the market, a furious fight for market share is likely to ensue. All of those niche players that failed to reach the minimum required economy of scale will be forced out of the market. FAX International on the other hand should be in the enviable position of being able to sell out at a premium to one of several companies eager to build market share quickly.

FAX International Team

- *Douglas J. Ranalli:* president/founder, age 30. Mr. Ranalli brings a combination of marketing, entrepreneurial, and engineering skills to the organization. Past experience includes five years as the Founder/Publisher of *Student Life* magazine. Mr. Ranalli built *Student Life* to a national circulation of 1,200,000 copies per issue before selling to Time, Inc., in 1987 for a multiple of 1.3 times revenue. Educational background: MBA, Harvard Business School (Baker Scholar); BS, Cornell University, industrial engineering.
- *Dr. Thomas P. Sosnowski:* vice president and director of engineering, age 54. Dr. Sosnowski is an engineering project management and product development specialist in the communications industry. Tom's background in telecommunications includes 13 years in R&D at Bell Laboratories.
- *Steven Lanzilla:* U.S. sales manager, age 37. Mr. Lanzilla brings 17 years of sales experience in telecommunications to the FAX International team. In particular, Steven's experience includes four years of sales, sales management, and product development experience at U.S. Sprint. Currently Steven is a telecommunications consultant in Boston.
- *Steven Orr:* UNIX system designer, age 38. Mr. Orr is a UNIX systems development consultant on PC platforms. Steve is responsible for system design, testing, and redundancy analysis.
- *Tom Flaherty:* database development and administration, age 32. Mr. Flaherty is a relational database programming expert specializing in the ORACLE RDMS. Tom is responsible for all database management, which includes information for billing, accounting, customer service, network management, and sales support.
- *Michael Landino:* database development, age 26. Michael is an ORACLE programmer specializing in SQL Forms 3.0 development.

- *Bradlee T. Howe:* chief financial officer (CFO), age 50. Mr. Howe is the president of Financial Managers Trust of Cambridge, Massachusetts, a company which serves as the part-time CFO for high-tech startups and smaller corporations.
- *James O. Jacoby, Jr.:* finance consultant, age 28. Mr. Jacoby is employed full-time by the Corporate Finance Department of Chemical Bank in New York City. Jim will be assisting FAX International in the two critical areas of fund-raising and bank relationship management. Jim's background includes a financial degree from Notre Dame and an MBA from Harvard.
- *Barry Nearhos:* accountant, Coopers & Lybrand. Mr. Nearhos is a partner in the Emerging Business Group in the C&L Boston office.
- *Steve Snyder:* lawyer. Mr. Snyder is a partner at O'-Connor, Broude, and Snyder in Waltham, Massachusetts, specializing in high-tech startups.

FAX International Advisory Board

- *Mike Williams:* age 53. Mr. Williams retired from AT&T in 1990 after a 29-year career and now resides in Tucson, Arizona. Recent positions within AT&T included president of the AT&T–Americas subsidiary, and chief negotiator for AT&T's first joint venture in Japan.
- *Kurt Weidenhaupt:* age 52. Mr. Weidenhaupt is a German national and president of AEG of North America, a subsidiary of Daimler-Benz. Mr. Weidenhaupt's career has encompassed numerous international assignments, including 13 years in London.
- *Robert Casale:* age 52. Mr. Casale's career has included senior executive positions in both the communications and financial services industry. Currently, Mr. Casale is the president of ADP's Brokerage Information Services Group in Journal Square, New Jersey.
- *Jerry Johnson:* age 54. A retired AT&T mergers and acquisitions executive, Mr. Johnson is now managing partner of the MJI consulting firm in Stamford, Connecticut. MJI specializes in forming strategic alliances within the telecommunications industry.
- *Bob Petzinger:* age 51. Mr. Petzinger retired from AT&T in 1990 and now resides in Naples, Florida. Mr. Petzinger's most recent position was as director of AT&T's operations in the United Kingdom.

Financial Projections: Year 1 Statement of operations

	1991					1992							Total year
	Aug.	Sept.	Oct.	Nov.	Dec.	Jan.	Feb.	Mar.	Apr.	May	June	July	
Net sales	$0	$0	$0	$73,260	$114,286	$155,311	$196,337	$237,362	$278,388	$319,414	$377,939	$431,215	$2,183,512
Operating expenses:													
Cost of communications	500	1,000	2,000	64,500	85,680	107,060	129,490	127,120	143,800	158,680	182,010	197,815	1,199,655
Administrative expenses	38,850	10,050	10,050	10,100	10,100	10,150	10,200	10,250	10,250	10,300	10,300	10,350	150,950
Billing and accounting expenses	500	5,520	5,520	7,487	7,580	8,023	13,067	13,660	13,753	13,847	13,940	14,033	116,930
Sales expenses	11,750	64,500	50,500	54,163	56,214	58,266	60,317	62,368	64,419	66,471	68,522	70,573	688,063
Japanese J/V expenses	0	0	0	0	0	10,000	0	10,000	20,000	10,000	10,000	10,000	70,000
Customer service	2,500	2,500	2,500	5,000	5,000	7,500	9,000	10,500	10,500	12,000	12,000	13,500	92,500
Lease expense	1,656	31,356	13,967	24,498	17,942	24,047	26,461	23,596	29,700	32,114	34,529	36,943	296,809
Technical expenses	21,700	21,700	143,200	33,200	33,200	34,700	39,700	36,200	36,200	36,200	36,200	36,200	508,400
Total expenses	77,456	136,626	227,737	198,947	215,717	259,746	288,235	293,694	328,623	339,612	367,501	389,415	3,123,307
EBITDA	(77,456)	(136,626)	(227,737)	(125,687)	(101,431)	(104,434)	(91,898)	(56,331)	(50,235)	(20,198)	10,438	41,800	(939,796)
Depreciation/amortization	0	0	0	0	0	0	0	0	0	0	0	0	0
Corporate expenses	0	0	0	0	0	0	0	0	0	0	0	0	0
EBIT	(77,456)	(136,626)	(227,737)	(125,687)	(101,431)	(104,434)	(91,898)	(56,331)	(50,235)	(20,198)	10,438	41,800	(939,796)
Other income (expense):													
Cash interest income	0	0	0	0	0	0	0	0	0	0	0	0	0
Revolver interest (11%)	0	0	0	0	0	0	0	0	(14)	(567)	(847)	(904)	(2,332)
Extraordinary items	0	0	0	0	0	0	0	0	0	0	0	0	0
Other (expenses) income	0	0	0	0	0	0	0	0	0	0	0	0	0
Total other income (expenses)	0	0	0	0	0	0	0	0	(14)	(567)	(847)	(904)	(2,332)
EBT	(77,456)	($136,626)	($227,737)	($125,687)	($101,431)	($104,434)	($91,898)	($56,331)	($50,249)	($20,765)	$9,591	$40,896	($942,128)
Income taxes	0	0	0	0	0	0	0	0	0	0	0	0	0
Net income	($77,456)	($136,626)	($227,737)	($125,687)	($101,431)	($104,434)	($91,898)	($56,331)	($50,249)	($20,765)	$9,591	$40,896	($942,128)
Cumulative NOLs	(77,456)	(214,083)	(441,819)	(567,507)	(668,938)	(773,372)	(865,270)	(921,601)	(971,849)	(992,615)	(983,024)	(942,128)	

EBITDA = earnings before interest, tax, depreciation, and amortization; EBIT = earnings before interest and tax; NOL = net operating loss.

Year 1 Balance sheet

	1991 Aug.	Sept.	Oct.	Nov.	Dec.	1992 Jan.	Feb.	Mar.	Apr.	May	June	July
Assets												
Current assets:												
Cash	$923,037	$786,904	$560,153	$427,516	$312,226	$196,181	$95,759	$10,000	$10,000	$10,000	$10,000	$10,000
Invested cash	0	0	0	0	0	0	0	0	0	0	0	0
Accounts receivable	0	0	0	72,256	112,720	153,184	193,647	234,111	274,574	315,038	372,762	425,308
Total current assets	923,037	786,904	560,153	499,773	424,946	349,364	289,406	244,111	284,574	325,038	382,762	435,308
Long-term assets:												
Capital leases costs, net	0	0	0	0	0	0	0	0	0	0	0	0
Net property, plant, and equipment	0	0	0	0	0	0	0	0	0	0	0	0
Intangibles	0	0	0	0	0	0	0	0	0	0	0	0
Organizational expenses	150,000	150,000	150,000	150,000	150,000	150,000	150,000	150,000	150,000	150,000	150,000	150,000
Total assets	$1,073,037	$936,904	$710,153	$649,773	$574,946	$499,364	$439,406	$394,111	$434,574	$475,038	$532,762	$585,308
Liabilities												
Accounts payable	$493	$986	$1,973	$63,616	$84,506	$105,593	$127,716	$125,379	$141,830	$156,506	$179,517	$195,105
Accrued expenses	0	0	0	3,663	9,377	17,143	26,960	38,828	52,747	68,718	87,615	109,176
Revolving facility	0	0	0	0	0	0	0	1,505	61,847	92,429	98,654	73,155
Other current/CMLTD	0	0	0	0	0	0	0	0	0	0	0	0
Total current liabilities	493	986	1,973	67,279	93,884	122,736	154,676	165,712	256,424	317,653	365,785	377,436
Total liabilities	$493	$986	$1,973	$67,279	$93,884	$122,736	$154,676	$165,712	$256,424	$317,653	$365,785	$377,436
Shareholders' equity												
Founders' invested capital	150,000	150,000	150,000	150,000	150,000	150,000	150,000	150,000	150,000	150,000	150,000	150,000
Additional paid-in capital	1,000,000	1,000,000	1,000,000	1,000,000	1,000,000	1,000,000	1,000,000	1,000,000	1,000,000	1,000,000	1,000,000	1,000,000
Retained earnings	(77,456)	(214,083)	(441,819)	(567,507)	(668,938)	(773,372)	(865,270)	(921,601)	(971,849)	(992,615)	(983,024)	(942,128)
Total shareholders' equity	1,072,544	935,918	708,181	582,493	481,062	376,628	284,730	228,399	178,151	157,385	166,976	207,872
Total liabilities and shareholders' equity	$1,073,037	$936,904	$710,153	$649,773	$574,946	$499,364	$439,406	$394,111	$434,574	$475,038	$532,762	$585,308

Year 1 Statement of cash flow

	Aug. 1991	Sept.	Oct.	Nov.	Dec.	Jan. 1992	Feb.	Mar.	Apr.	May	June	July	Total Year
Net income	($77,456)	($136,626)	($227,737)	($125,687)	($101,431)	($104,434)	($91,898)	($56,331)	($50,249)	($20,765)	$9,591	$40,896	($942,128)
Depreciation/amortization	0	0	0	0	0	0	0	0	0	0	0	0	0
Other adjustments	0	0	0	0	0	0	0	0	0	0	0	0	0
Gross cash flow	(77,456)	(136,626)	(227,737)	(125,687)	(101,431)	(104,434)	(91,898)	(56,331)	(50,249)	(20,765)	9,591	40,896	(942,128)
Changes in working capital													
Accounts receivable	0	0	0	(72,256)	(40,464)	(40,464)	(40,464)	(40,464)	(40,464)	(40,464)	(57,724)	(52,546)	(425,308)
Accounts payable	493	493	986	61,644	20,890	21,087	22,123	(2,338)	16,452	14,676	23,010	15,588	195,105
Accrued commissions	0	0	0	3,663	5,714	7,766	9,817	11,868	13,919	15,971	18,897	21,561	109,176
Other current liabilities	0	0	0	0	0	0	0	0	0	0	0	0	0
Cash flow from operations	(76,963)	(136,133)	(226,750)	(132,637)	(115,290)	(116,045)	(100,422)	(87,264)	(60,341)	(30,582)	(6,225)	25,499	(1,063,155)
Capital expenditures	0	0	0	0	0	0	0	0	0	0	0	0	0
Operating cash flow	(76,963)	(136,133)	(226,750)	(132,637)	(115,290)	(116,045)	(100,422)	(87,264)	(60,341)	(30,582)	(6,225)	25,499	(1,063,155)
Changes in nonoperations items	0	0	0	0	0	0	0	0	0	0	0	0	0
Changes in capital stock	1,000,000	0	0	0	0	0	0	0	0	0	0	0	1,000,000
Cash available	$923,037	($136,133)	($226,750)	($132,637)	($115,290)	($116,045)	($100,422)	($87,264)	($60,341)	($30,582)	($6,225)	$25,499	($63,155)
Cumulative cash	923,037	786,904	560,153	427,516	312,226	196,181	95,759	8,495	(51,847)	(82,429)	(88,654)	(63,155)	(63,155)
Maintenance cash level	10,000	10,000	10,000	10,000	10,000	10,000	10,000	10,000	10,000	10,000	10,000	10,000	10,000

Year 1 Assumptions and ratios

	1991 Aug.	Sept.	Oct.	Nov.	1992 Dec.	Jan.	Feb.	Mar.	Apr.	May	June	July
Income statement:												
Net monthly sales growth				N/A	56%	36%	26%	21%	17%	15%	18%	14%
Current gross margin				12%	25%	31%	34%	46%	48%	50%	52%	54%
Current EBITDA margin				−172%	−89%	−67%	−47%	−24%	−18%	−6%	3%	10%
Communication as percentage of sales				88%	75%	69%	66%	54%	52%	50%	48%	46%
Administrative as percentage of sales				14%	9%	7%	5%	4%	4%	3%	3%	2%
Sales expense as percentage of sales				74%	49%	38%	31%	26%	23%	21%	18%	16%
Customer service as percentage of sales				7%	4%	5%	5%	4%	4%	4%	3%	3%
Leases as percentage of sales				33%	16%	15%	13%	10%	11%	10%	9%	9%
Technical costs as percentage of sales				45%	29%	22%	20%	15%	13%	11%	10%	8%
Balance sheet:												
A/R days	30.0	30.0	30.0	30.0	30.0	30.0	30.0	30.0	30.0	30.0	30.0	30.0
A/P days	30.0	30.0	30.0	30.0	30.0	30.0	30.0	30.0	30.0	30.0	30.0	30.0
Revolver as percentage of receivable base				0.00%	0.00%	0.00%	0.00%	0.64%	22.52%	29.34%	26.47%	17.20%

Year 1 Revenue breakdown

United States:
Avg price/minute: $0.74
Monthly growth rate: 350 minutes/salesrep

	1991 Aug.	Sept.	Oct.	Nov.	Dec.	1992 Jan.	Feb.	Mar.	Apr.	May	June	July	Total Year
Free minutes/day	0	0	0	1,000	1,000	1,000	1,000	1,000	1,000	1,000	1,000	1,000	
Net new minutes/day	0	0	0	5,000	2,800	2,800	2,800	2,800	2,800	2,800	2,800	2,800	
Total paid minutes/day	0	0	0	5,000	7,800	10,600	13,400	16,200	19,000	21,800	24,600	27,400	
Total minutes/month (20 days)	0	0	0	100,000	156,000	212,000	268,000	324,000	380,000	436,000	492,000	548,000	2,916,000
Monthly gross revenue	0	0	0	74,000	115,440	156,880	198,320	239,760	281,200	322,640	364,080	405,520	2,157,840
Uncollectables (1%)	0	0	0	740	1,154	1,569	1,983	2,398	2,812	3,226	3,641	4,055	21,578
Net monthly U.S. revenue	$0	$0	$0	$73,260	$114,286	$155,311	$196,337	$237,362	$278,388	$319,414	$360,439	$401,465	2,138,262
Japan joint venture:													
Avg price/minute	$0.35												
Total minutes/month	0	0	0	0	0	0	0	0	0	0	50,000	85,000	135,000
Net Japanese revenue	$0	$0	$0	$0	$0	$0	$0	$0	$0	$0	$17,500	$29,750	47,250
Total U.S./Japan revenues	$0	$0	$0	$73,260	$114,286	$155,311	$196,337	$237,362	$278,388	$319,414	$377,939	$431,215	$2,183,512

Year 1 Expense Breakdown

	1991 Aug.	Sept.	Oct.	Nov.	Dec.	1992 Jan.	Feb.	Mar.	Apr.	May	June	July	Total Year
Technical development:													
Dr. Tom Sosnowski	$6,000	$6,000	$6,000	$6,000	$6,000	$6,000	$6,000	$6,000	$6,000	$6,000	$6,000	$6,000	$72,000
Tom Flaherty (Oracle)	4,200	4,200	4,200	4,200	4,200	4,200	4,200	4,200	4,200	4,200	4,200	4,200	50,400
Steve Orr (UNIX)	6,000	6,000	6,000	6,000	6,000	7,500	7,500	7,500	7,500	7,500	7,500	7,500	82,500
Michael Landino (Oracle)	3,500	3,500	3,500	3,500	3,500	3,500	3,500	3,500	3,500	3,500	3,500	3,500	42,000
Contact programmers	0	0	0	0	0	0	0	0	0	0	0	0	0
Tokyo engineer	0	0	1,500	1,500	1,500	1,500	1,500	1,500	1,500	1,500	1,500	1,500	15,000
Equipment housing expenses	0	0	0	10,000	10,000	10,000	10,000	11,500	11,500	11,500	11,500	11,500	97,500
Installation expenses	0	0	120,000	0	0	0	5,000	0	0	0	0	0	125,000
Other expenses	2,000	2,000	2,000	2,000	2,000	2,000	2,000	2,000	2,000	2,000	2,000	2,000	24,000
Subtotal	21,700	21,700	143,200	33,200	33,200	34,700	39,700	36,200	36,200	36,200	36,200	36,200	508,400
Sales expenses:													
Doug Ranalii	0	5,000	5,000	5,000	5,000	5,000	5,000	5,000	5,000	5,000	5,000	5,000	55,000
Steve Lanzilla—VP sales	5,000	5,000	5,000	5,000	5,000	5,000	5,000	5,000	5,000	5,000	5,000	5,000	60,000
LA sales reps (2)	0	6,000	6,000	6,000	6,000	6,000	6,000	6,000	6,000	6,000	6,000	6,000	66,000
San Francisco reps (2)	0	6,000	6,000	6,000	6,000	6,000	6,000	6,000	6,000	6,000	6,000	6,000	66,000
NYC sales reps 92	0	6,000	6,000	6,000	6,000	6,000	6,000	6,000	6,000	6,000	6,000	6,000	66,000
National accounts sales rep	0	3,000	3,000	3,000	3,000	3,000	3,000	3,000	3,000	3,000	3,000	3,000	33,000
Sales commissions (5%)	0	0	0	3,663	5,714	7,766	9,817	11,868	13,919	15,971	18,022	20,073	106,813
Sales office space	750	4,500	4,500	4,500	4,500	4,500	4,500	4,500	4,500	4,500	4,500	4,500	50,250
Sales expenses	6,000	14,000	14,000	14,000	14,000	14,000	14,000	14,000	14,000	14,000	14,000	14,000	160,000
Marketing/office supplies	0	5,000	1,000	1,000	1,000	1,000	1,000	1,000	1,000	1,000	1,000	1,000	15,000
Headhunter fees	0	10,000	0	0	0	0	0	0	0	0	0	0	10,000
Total sales personnel	1	8	8	8	8	8	8	8	8	8	8	8	
Subtotal	11,750	64,500	50,500	54,163	56,214	58,266	60,317	62,368	64,419	66,471	68,522	70,573	688,063
Japanese joint venture:													
Doug Fine	0	0	0	0	0	0	0	5,000	5,000	5,000	5,000	5,000	25,000
Chuo Coopers & Lybrand	0	0	0	0	0	0	0	0	5,000	5,000	5,000	5,000	20,000
Performance Bonuses	0	0	0	0	0	0	0	0	0	0	0	0	0
Expenses	0	0	0	0	0	0	0	0	0	0	0	0	0
Subtotal	0	0	0	0	0	0	0	5,000	10,000	10,000	10,000	10,000	45,000
Network assets:													
Network hardware lease	0												70,000
Japanese J/V hardware	1,500	9,600	9,600	12,480	12,480	13,920	15,360	15,360	16,800	18,240	18,240	19,680	163,260
Auto-dialer lease	0	0	0	0	0	0	0	0	0	0	1,440	1,440	2,880
Up-front lease deposits	0	0	1,600	2,347	3,093	3,840	4,587	5,333	6,080	6,827	7,573	8,320	49,600
Extended service contract	0	8,100	1,600	3,627	746	2,186	2,187	747	2,186	2,186	2,187	2,186	27,940
Import duties	117	750	875	1,158	1,217	1,388	1,558	1,617	1,788	1,958	2,129	2,300	16,855
Equipment insurance	0	12,656	0	4,500	0	2,250	2,250	0	2,250	2,250	2,250	2,250	30,656
Operating leases	39	250	292	386	406	463	519	539	596	653	710	767	5,618
Network asset value	1,656	31,356	13,967	24,498	17,942	24,047	26,461	23,596	29,700	32,114	34,529	36,943	296,809
	46,875	300,000	350,000	463,333	486,667	555,000	623,333	646,667	715,000	783,333	851,667	920,000	

(continued)

Year 1 Expense breakdown (concluded)

	1991 Aug.	Sept.	Oct.	Nov.	Dec.	1992 Jan.	Feb.	Mar.	Apr.	May	June	July	Total Year
Communications expenses:													
Network Demonstrations	$500	$1,000	$2,000	$0	$0	$0	$0	$0	$0	$0	$0	$0	$3,500
Avg Variable Cost/Min	$0.18	$0.18	$0.18	$0.18	$0.18	$0.18	$0.18	$0.13	$0.13	$0.13	$0.13	$0.13	$0.13
Monthly U.S. Variable Costs	0	0	0	21,600	31,680	41,760	51,840	44,720	52,000	59,280	66,560	73,840	443,280
Monthly Japanese JV Costs	0	0	0	0	0	0	0	0	0	0	6,750	11,475	18,225
Number of 64kbps Channels	0	0	0	4	6	8	10	11	13	15	17	18	
Fractional T1	0	0	0	30,400	41,800	52,250	64,600	69,350	77,900	85,500	93,100	96,900	611,800
Switched Digital Service	0	0	0	4,800	4,800	4,800	4,800	4,800	4,800	4,800	4,800	4,800	43,200
Local Loop Service	0	0	0	4,700	6,400	7,250	7,250	7,250	8,100	8,100	9,800	9,800	68,650
Installation Expenses				3,000	1,000	1,000	1,000	1,000	1,000	1,000	1,000	1,000	11,000
Subtotal	500	1,000	2,000	64,500	85,680	107,060	129,490	127,120	143,800	158,680	182,010	197,815	1,199,655
Customer Service:													
Carla Ferrara (CSR)	2,000	2,000	2,000	2,000	2,000	2,000	2,000	2,000	2,000	2,000	2,000	2,000	24,000
Add'l full-time reps	0	0	0	0	0	0	1,000	2,000	2,000	3,000	3,000	4,000	14,000
Peak period service reps	0	0	0	0	0	2,000	1,000	2,000	2,000	2,000	3,000	2,000	15,000
Evening service rep	0	0	0	2,000	2,000	2,000	2,000	2,000	2,000	2,000	2,000	3,000	18,000
Expenses	500	500	500	1,000	1,000	1,500	2,000	2,500	2,500	3,000	3,000	3,500	21,500
Number of service personnel	1	1	1	2	2	3	4	5	5	6	6	7	
Subtotal	2,500	2,500	2,500	5,000	5,000	7,500	9,000	10,500	10,500	12,000	12,000	13,500	92,500
Administrative expenses:													
Headquarters office space	350	2,550	2,550	2,600	2,600	2,650	2,700	2,750	2,750	2,800	2,800	2,850	29,950
Furniture lease	0	1,000	1,000	1,000	1,000	1,000	1,000	1,000	1,000	1,000	1,000	1,000	11,000
Legal and accounting consultants	30,000	2,000	2,000	2,000	2,000	2,000	2,000	2,000	2,000	2,000	2,000	2,000	52,000
Financial consulting	2,000	2,000	2,000	1,000	1,000	1,000	1,000	1,000	1,000	1,000	1,000	1,000	24,000
Office supplies, etc.	5,000	1,000	1,000	1,000	1,000	1,000	1,000	1,000	1,000	1,000	1,000	1,000	16,000
Other expenses	1,500	1,500	1,500	1,500	1,500	1,500	1,500	1,500	1,500	1,500	1,500	1,500	18,000
Subtotal	38,850	10,050	10,050	10,100	10,100	10,150	10,200	10,250	10,250	10,300	10,300	10,350	150,950
Billing and accounting:													
Payroll expenses	0	5,020	5,020	5,320	5,320	5,670	6,120	6,620	6,620	6,620	6,620	6,620	65,570
Bookkeeper	500	500	500	1,500	1,500	1,500	3,000	3,000	3,000	3,000	3,000	3,000	24,000
Credit collections person	0	0	0	0	0	0	3,000	3,000	3,000	3,000	3,000	3,000	18,000
Bill preparation/mailing	0	0	0	167	260	353	447	540	633	727	820	913	4,860
Errors/omissions insurance	0	0	500	500	500	500	500	500	500	500	500	500	4,500
Subtotal	500	5,520	5,520	7,487	7,580	8,023	13,067	13,660	13,753	13,847	13,940	14,033	116,930
Total expenses	$77,456	$136,626	$227,737	$198,947	$215,717	$259,746	$288,235	$293,694	$328,623	$339,612	$367,501	$389,415	$3,123,307

Year 2 Statement of operations

	1992 Aug.	Sept.	Oct.	Nov.	Dec.	1993 Jan.	Feb.	Mar.	Apr.	May	June	July	Total Year
Net sales	$454,592	$505,096	$555,600	$606,103	$656,607	$707,110	$757,614	$808,118	$858,621	$909,125	$959,628	$1,010,132	$8,788,340
Operating expenses:													
Cost of communications	222,970	240,675	259,130	278,185	302,340	324,145	346,950	366,055	389,760	411,615	431,670	447,275	4,020,770
Administrative expenses	15,350	15,400	15,450	15,450	15,500	15,500	15,550	15,600	15,600	15,650	15,650	15,700	186,400
Billing and accounting expenses	15,547	15,640	15,733	15,827	15,920	16,013	16,107	16,200	16,293	16,387	16,480	16,573	192,720
Sales expenses	77,130	75,042	75,684	75,684	75,684	75,684	75,684	75,684	75,684	75,684	75,684	75,684	909,012
Japanese J/V expenses	14,463	12,713	13,325	13,938	14,550	15,163	15,775	16,388	17,000	17,613	18,225	18,838	187,988
Customer service	14,100	15,600	17,100	17,100	18,600	18,600	20,100	21,600	21,600	23,100	23,100	24,600	235,200
Lease expense	39,358	41,772	49,467	42,911	49,016	56,710	50,154	61,539	54,983	61,088	68,782	62,227	638,007
Technical expenses	40,300	40,300	40,300	40,300	40,300	40,300	40,300	40,300	40,300	40,300	40,300	40,300	483,600
Total operating expenses	439,217	457,142	486,189	499,394	531,910	562,115	580,620	613,365	631,221	661,436	689,891	701,197	6,853,696
EBITDA	15,376	47,954	69,411	106,709	124,697	144,996	176,994	194,752	227,401	247,689	269,737	308,935	1,934,650
Depreciation/amortization	0	0	0	0	0	0	0	0	0	0	0	0	0
Corporate expenses	0	0	0	0	0	0	0	0	0	0	0	0	0
EBIT	15,376	47,954	69,411	106,709	124,697	144,996	176,994	194,752	227,401	247,689	269,737	308,935	1,934,650
Other income (expense):													
Cash interest income	0	0	0	0	0	0	0	0	0	0	0	0	0
Revolver interest (11%)	(671)	(311)	0	0	0	0	0	0	0	0	0	0	
Extraordinary items	0	0	0	(1,034)	(349)	0	0	0	0	0	0	0	
Other (expenses) income	0	0	0	0	0	0	0	0	0	0	0	0	(2,365)
Total other income (expense)	(671)	(311)	0	(1,034)	(349)	0	0	0	0	0	0	0	0
EBT	14,705	47,643	69,411	105,675	124,348	144,996	176,994	194,752	227,401	247,689	269,737	308,935	1,932,285
Income taxes	0	0	0	0	0	0	0	0	55,691	84,214	91,711	105,038	336,653
Net income	$14,705	$47,643	$69,411	$105,675	$124,348	$144,996	$176,994	$194,752	$171,710	$163,475	$178,027	$203,897	$1,595,632
Cummulative NOL's	(927,423)	(879,780)	(810,370)	(704,694)	(580,347)	(435,351)	(258,357)	(63,605)	0	0	0	0	0

EBITDA = earnings before interest, tax, depreciation, and amortization; EBIT = earnings before interest and tax; NOL = net operating loss.

Year 2 Balance sheet

	1992 Aug.	Sept.	Oct.	Nov.	Dec.	1993 Jan.	Feb.	Mar.	Apr.	May	June	July
Assets												
Current Assets:												
Cash	$10,000	$16,581	$10,000	$10,000	$70,240	$186,930	$336,604	$500,388	$645,667	$780,885	$928,880	$1,098,357
Invested cash	0	0	0	0	0	0	0	0	0	0	0	0
Accounts receivable	448,365	498,177	547,989	597,800	647,612	697,424	747,236	797,047	846,859	896,671	946,483	996,295
Total current assets	458,365	514,758	557,989	607,800	717,852	884,354	1,083,840	1,297,436	1,492,526	1,677,556	1,875,363	2,094,652
Long-term assets:												
Capital leases, costs, net	0	0	0	0	0	0	0	0	0	0	0	0
Net property, Plant, and equipment	0	0	0	0	0	0	0	0	0	0	0	0
Intangibles	0	0	0	0	0	0	0	0	0	0	0	0
Organizational expenses	150,000	150,000	150,000	150,000	150,000	150,000	150,000	150,000	150,000	150,000	150,000	150,000
	150,000	150,000	150,000	150,000	150,000	150,000	150,000	150,000	150,000	150,000	150,000	150,000
Total assets	$608,365	$664,758	$707,989	$757,800	$867,852	$1,034,354	$1,233,840	$1,447,436	$1,642,526	$1,827,556	$2,025,363	$2,244,652
Liabilities												
Accounts payable	$219,916	$237,378	$255,580	$274,374	$298,198	$319,705	$342,197	$361,041	$384,421	$405,976	$425,757	$441,148
Accrued expenses	131,905	157,160	0	0	0	0	0	0	0	0	0	0
Revolving facility	33,967	0	112,778	38,121	0	0	0	0	0	0	0	0
Other current/CMLTD	0	394,538	368,358	312,495	298,198	319,705	342,197	361,041	384,421	405,976	425,757	441,148
Total current liabilities	385,788	394,538	368,358	312,495	298,198	319,705	342,197	361,040	384,421	405,976	425,757	441,148
Total liabilities	$385,788	$394,538	$368,358	$312,495	$298,198	$319,705	$342,197	$361,040	$384,421	$405,976	$425,757	$441,148
Shareholders' equity												
Founders' invested capital	150,000	150,000	150,000	150,000	150,000	150,000	150,000	150,000	150,000	150,000	150,000	150,000
Additional paid-in capital	1,000,000	1,000,000	1,000,000	1,000,000	1,000,000	1,000,000	1,000,000	1,000,000	1,000,000	1,000,000	1,000,000	1,000,000
Retained earnings	(927,423)	(879,780)	(810,370)	(704,694)	(580,347)	(435,351)	(258,357)	(63,605)	108,105	271,580	449,606	653,504
Total shareholders' equity	222,577	270,220	339,630	445,306	569,653	714,649	891,643	1,086,395	1,258,105	1,421,580	1,599,606	1,803,504
Total liabilities and shareholders' equity	$608,365	$664,758	$707,989	$757,800	$867,852	$1,034,354	$1,233,840	$1,447,436	$1,642,526	$1,827,556	$2,025,363	$2,244,652

Year 2 Statement of Cash Flow

	1992 Aug.	Sept.	Oct.	Nov.	Dec.	1993 Jan.	Feb.	Mar.	Apr.	May	June	July	Total Year
Net income	$14,705	$47,643	$69,411	$105,675	$124,348	$144,996	$176,994	$194,752	$171,710	$163,475	$178,027	$203,897	$1,595,632
Depreciation/amortization	0	0	0	0	0	0	0	0	0	0	0	0	0
Other adjustments	0	0	0	0	0	0	0	0	0	0	0	0	0
Gross cash flow	14,705	47,643	69,411	105,675	124,348	144,996	176,994	194,752	171,710	163,475	178,027	203,897	1,595,632
Changes in working capital:													
Accounts receivable	(23,057)	(49,812)	(49,812)	(49,812)	(49,812)	(49,812)	(49,812)	(49,812)	(49,812)	(49,812)	(49,812)	(49,812)	(570,987)
Accounts payable	24,810	17,462	18,202	18,794	23,824	21,506	22,493	18,843	23,380	21,556	19,780	15,391	246,043
Accrued commissions	22,730	25,255	(157,160)	0	0	0	0	0	0	0	0	0	(109,176)
Other current liabs	0	0	0	0	0	0	0	0	0	0	0	0	
Cash flow from operations	39,188	40,548	(119,359)	74,657	98,360	116,690	149,675	163,784	145,279	135,218	147,995	169,477	1,161,512
Capital expenditures	0	0	0	0	0	0	0	0	0	0	0	0	0
Operating cash flow	39,188	40,548	(119,359)	74,657	98,360	116,690	149,675	163,784	145,279	135,218	147,995	169,477	1,161,512
Changes in non-operating items	0	0	0	0	0	0	0	0	0	0	0	0	0
Change in capital stock	0	0	0	0	0	0	0	0	0	0	0	0	0
Cash available	$39,188	$40,548	($119,359)	$74,657	$98,360	$116,690	$149,675	$163,784	$145,279	$135,218	$147,995	$169,477	$1,161,512
Cumulative cash	(23,967)	16,581	(102,778)	(28,121)	70,240	186,930	336,604	500,388	645,667	780,885	928,880	1,098,357	0
Maintenance cash level	10,000	10,000	10,000	10,000	10,000	10,000	10,000	10,000	10,000	10,000	10,000	10,000	

Year 2 Assumptions and ratios

	1992 Aug.	Sept.	Oct.	Nov.	Dec.	1993 Jan.	Feb.	Mar.	Apr.	May	June	July
Income statement:												
Net monthly sales growth	5%	11%	10%	9%	8%	8%	7%	7%	6%	6%	6%	5%
Current gross margin	51%	52%	53%	54%	54%	54%	54%	55%	55%	55%	55%	56%
Current EBITDA margin	3%	9%	12%	18%	19%	21%	23%	24%	26%	27%	28%	31%
Communication as percentage of sales	49%	48%	47%	46%	46%	46%	46%	45%	45%	45%	45%	44%
Administrative as percentage of sales	3%	3%	3%	3%	2%	2%	2%	2%	2%	2%	2%	2%
Sales expense as percentage of sales	17%	15%	14%	12%	12%	11%	10%	9%	9%	8%	8%	7%
Customer service as percentage of sales	3%	3%	3%	3%	3%	3%	3%	3%	3%	3%	2%	2%
Leases as percentage of sales	9%	8%	9%	7%	7%	8%	7%	8%	6%	7%	7%	6%
Technical costs as percentage of sales	9%	8%	7%	7%	6%	6%	5%	5%	5%	4%	4%	4%
Balance sheet:												
A/R days	30.0	30.0	30.0	30.0	30.0	30.0	30.0	30.0	30.0	30.0	30.0	30.0
A/P days	30.0	30.0	30.0	30.0	30.0	30.0	30.0	30.0	30.0	30.0	30.0	30.0
Revolver as percentage receivable	7.58%	0.00%	20.58%	6.38%	0.00%	0.00%	0.00%	0.00%	0.00%	0.00%	0.00%	0.00%

Year 2 Revenue breakdown

United States:

Avg price/minute	$0.69	
Monthly Growth Rate	350 Minutes/rep	

	1992 Aug.	Sept.	Oct.	Nov.	Dec.	1993 Jan.	Feb.	Mar.	Apr.	May	June	July	Total Year
Free minutes/day	1,000	1,000	1,000	1,000	1,000	1,000	1,000	1,000	1,000	1,000	1,000	1,000	1,000
Net new minutes/day	2,800	2,800	2,800	2,800	2,800	2,800	2,800	2,800	2,800	2,800	2,800	2,800	2,800
Total paid minutes/day	30,200	33,000	35,800	38,600	41,400	44,200	47,000	49,800	52,600	55,400	58,200	61,000	
Total minutes/month (20 days)	604,000	660,000	716,000	772,000	828,000	884,000	940,000	996,000	1,052,000	1,108,000	1,164,000	1,220,000	10,944,000
Monthly gross revenue	416,760	455,400	494,040	532,680	571,320	609,960	648,600	687,240	725,880	764,520	803,160	841,800	7,551,360
Uncollectables (1%)	4,168	4,554	4,940	5,327	5,713	6,100	6,486	6,872	7,259	7,645	8,032	8,418	75,514
Net monthly U.S. revenue	$412,592	$450,846	$489,100	$527,353	$565,607	$603,860	$642,114	$680,368	$718,621	$756,875	$795,128	$833,382	7,475,846
Japan joint venture:													
Avg price/minute	$0.35												
	35,000												
Total minutes/month	120,000	155,000	190,000	225,000	260,000	295,000	330,000	365,000	400,00 0	435,000	470,000	505,000	3,750,000
Net Japanese Revenue	$42,000	$54,250	$66,500	$78,750	$91,000	$103,250	$115,500	$127,750	$140,000	$152,250	$164,500	$176,750	$1,312,500
Total U.S. Japan revenues	$454,592	$505,096	$555,600	$606,103	$656,607	$707,110	$757,614	$808,118	$858,621	$909,125	$959,628	$1,010,132	$8,788,346

Year 2 Expense breakdown

	1992 Aug.	Sept.	Oct.	Nov.	Dec.	1993 Jan.	Feb.	Mar.	Apr.	May	June	July	Total Year
Technical development:													
Dr. Tom Sosnowski	$7,000	$7,000	$7,000	$7,000	$7,000	$7,000	$7,000	$7,000	$7,000	$7,000	$7,000	$7,000	$84,000
Tom Flaherty (Oracle)	4,800	4,800	4,800	4,800	4,800	4,800	4,800	4,800	4,800	4,800	4,800	4,800	57,600
Steve Orr (UNIX)	7,500	7,500	7,500	7,500	7,500	7,500	7,500	7,500	7,500	7,500	7,500	7,500	90,000
Michael Landino (Oracle)	4,000	4,000	4,000	4,000	4,000	4,000	4,000	4,000	4,000	4,000	4,000	4,000	48,000
Contract programmers	2,000	2,000	2,000	2,000	2,000	2,000	2,000	2,000	2,000	2,000	2,000	2,000	24,000
Tokyo engineer	1,500	1,500	1,500	1,500	1,500	1,500	1,500	1,500	1,500	1,500	1,500	1,500	18,000
Equipment housing expenses	11,500	11,500	11,500	11,500	11,500	11,500	11,500	11,500	11,500	11,500	11,500	11,500	138,000
Installation expenses	0	0	0	0	0	0	0	0	0	0	0	0	0
Other expenses	2,000	2,000	2,000	2,000	2,000	2,000	2,000	2,000	2,000	2,000	2,000	2,000	24,000
Subtotal	40,300	40,300	40,300	40,300	40,300	40,300	40,300	40,300	40,300	40,300	40,300	40,300	483,600
Sales expenses:													
Doug Ranalli	7,000	7,000	7,000	7,000	7,000	7,000	7,000	7,000	7,000	7,000	7,000	7,000	84,000
Steve Lanzila-VP Sales	5,000	5,000	5,000	5,000	5,000	5,000	5,000	5,000	5,000	5,000	5,000	5,000	60,000
LA sales reps (2)	6,000	6,000	6,000	6,000	6,000	6,000	6,000	6,000	6,000	6,000	6,000	6,000	72,000
San Francisco reps (2)	6,000	6,000	6,000	6,000	6,000	6,000	6,000	6,000	6,000	6,000	6,000	6,000	72,000
NYC sales reps (2)	6,000	6,000	6,000	6,000	6,000	6,000	6,000	6,000	6,000	6,000	6,000	6,000	72,000
National accounts sales rep	3,000	3,000	3,000	3,000	3,000	3,000	3,000	3,000	3,000	3,000	3,000	3,000	36,000
Sales commissions (5%)	20,630	22,542	23,184	23,184	23,184	23,184	23,184	23,184	23,184	23,184	23,184	23,184	275,012
Sales office space	4,500	4,500	4,500	4,500	4,500	4,500	4,500	4,500	4,500	4,500	4,500	4,500	54,000
Sales expenses	14,000	14,000	14,000	14,000	14,000	14,000	14,000	14,000	14,000	14,000	14,000	14,000	168,000
Marketing/office supplies	5,000	1,000	1,000	1,000	1,000	1,000	1,000	1,000	1,000	1,000	1,000	1,000	16,000
Headhunter fees	0	0	0	0	0	0	0	0	0	0	0	0	0
Total sales personnel	77,130	75,042	75,684	75,684	75,684	75,684	75,684	75,684	75,684	75,684	75,684	75,684	909,012
Japanese joint venture:													
Doug Fine	5,000	5,000	5,000	5,000	5,000	5,000	5,000	5,000	5,000	5,000	5,000	5,000	60,000
Chuo Coopers & Lybrand	4,463	2,713	3,325	3,938	4,550	5,163	5,775	6,388	7,000	7,613	8,225	8,838	67,988
Performance bonuses	5,000	5,000	5,000	5,000	5,000	5,000	5,000	5,000	5,000	5,000	5,000	5,000	60,000
Subtotal	14,463	12,713	13,325	13,938	14,550	15,163	15,775	16,388	17,000	17,613	18,225	18,838	187,988
Network assets:													
Network Hardware Lease	19,680	21,120	22,560	22,560	24,000	25,440	25,440	26,880	26,880	28,320	29,760	29,760	302,400
Japanese J/V Hardware	2,880	2,880	4,320	4,320	4,320	5,760	5,760	7,200	7,200	7,200	8,640	8,640	69,120
Auto-dialer Lease	9,067	9,813	10,560	11,307	12,053	12,800	13,547	14,293	15,040	15,787	16,533	17,280	158,080
Up-front Lease Deposits	2,187	2,187	3,627	747	2,187	3,627	747	3,627	747	2,187	3,627	747	26,240
Extended Service Contract	2,471	2,642	2,925	2,983	3,154	3,438	3,496	3,779	3,838	4,008	4,292	4,350	41,375
Import Duties	2,250	2,250	4,500	0	2,250	4,500	0	4,500	0	2,250	4,500	0	27,000
Equipment Insurance	824	881	975	994	1,051	1,146	1,165	1,260	1,279	1,336	1,431	1,450	13,792
Operating leases	39,358	41,772	49,467	42,911	49,016	56,710	50,154	61,539	54,983	61,088	68,782	62,227	638,007
Network asset value	988,333	1,056,667	1,170,000	1,193,333	1,261,667	1,375,000	1,398,333	1,511,667	1,535,000	1,603,333	1,716,667	1,740,000	

(Continued)

Year 2 Expense breakdown (concluded)

	1992					1993							
	Aug.	Sept.	Oct.	Nov.	Dec.	Jan.	Feb.	Mar.	Apr.	May	June	July	Total Year
Communications expenses:													
Network demonstrations													
Avg variable cost/min	$0	$0	$0	$0	$0	$0	$0	$0	$0	$0	$0	$0	$0
Monthly U.S. variable costs	$0.13	$0.13	$0.13	$0.13	$0.13	$0.13	$0.13	$0.13	$0.13	$0.13	$0.13	$0.13	$0.13
Monthly Japanese JV costs	81,120	88,400	95,680	102,960	110,240	117,520	124,800	132,080	139,360	146,640	153,920	161,200	1,453,920
Number of 64kbps channels	16,200	20,925	25,650	30,375	35,100	39,825	44,550	49,275	54,000	58,725	63,450	68,175	506,250
Fractional T1	20	22	24	25	27	29	31	32	34	36	38	39	
Switched digital service	103,550	109,250	114,000	121,050	133,200	141,300	152,100	157,500	169,299	178,200	185,400	189,000	1,753,750
Local loop service	9,600	9,600	9,600	9,600	9,600	9,600	9,600	9,600	9,600	9,600	9,600	9,600	115,200
Installation expenses	11,500	11,500	13,200	13,200	13,200	14,900	14,900	16,600	16,600	17,450	18,300	18,300	179,650
	1,000	1,000	1,000	1,000	1,000	1,000	1,000	1,000	1,000	1,000	1,000	1,000	12,000
Subtotal	222,970	240,675	259,130	278,185	302,340	324,145	346,950	366,055	389,760	411,615	431,670	447,275	4,020,770
Customer service:													
Carla Ferrara (CSR)	2,200	2,200	2,200	2,200	2,200	2,200	2,200	2,200	2,200	2,200	2,200	2,200	26,400
Add'l full-time reps	2,200	2,200	2,200	2,200	2,200	2,200	2,200	2,200	2,200	2,200	2,200	2,200	26,400
Peak period service reps	4,000	5,000	6,000	6,000	7,000	7,000	8,000	9,000	9,000	10,000	10,000	11,000	92,000
Evening service rep	2,200	2,200	2,200	2,200	2,200	2,200	2,200	2,200	2,200	2,200	2,200	2,200	26,400
Expenses	3,500	4,000	4,500	4,500	5,000	5,000	5,500	6,000	6,000	6,500	6,500	7,000	64,000
Number of service personnel	7	8	9	9	10	10	11	12	12	13	13	14	
Subtotal	14,100	15,600	17,100	17,100	18,600	18,600	20,100	21,600	21,600	23,100	23,100	24,600	235,200
Administrative expenses:													
Headquarters office space	2,850	2,900	2,950	2,950	3,000	3,000	3,050	3,100	3,100	3,150	3,150	3,200	36,400
Furniture lease	1,000	1,000	1,000	1,000	1,000	1,000	1,000	1,000	1,000	1,000	1,000	1,000	12,000
Legal and accounting consultants	2,000	2,000	2,000	2,000	2,000	2,000	2,000	2,000	2,000	2,000	2,000	2,000	24,000
Financial consulting	7,000	7,000	7,000	7,000	7,000	7,000	7,000	7,000	7,000	7,000	7,000	7,000	84,000
Office supplies, etc.	1,000	1,000	1,000	1,000	1,000	1,000	1,000	1,000	1,000	1,000	1,000	1,000	12,000
Other expenses	1,500	1,500	1,500	1,500	1,500	1,500	1,500	1,500	1,500	1,500	1,500	1,500	18,000
Subtotal	15,350	15,400	15,450	15,450	15,500	15,500	15,550	15,600	15,600	15,650	15,650	15,700	186,400
Billing and accounting:													
Payroll expenses	7,790	7,790	7,790	7,790	7,790	7,790	7,790	7,790	7,790	7,790	7,790	7,790	93,480
Bookkeeper	3,000	3,000	3,000	3,000	3,000	3,000	3,000	3,000	3,000	3,000	3,000	3,000	36,000
Credit/collections person	3,000	3,000	3,000	3,000	3,000	3,000	3,000	3,000	3,000	3,000	3,000	3,000	36,000
Bill preparation/mailing	1,007	1,100	1,193	1,287	1,380	1,473	1,567	1,660	1,753	1,847	1,940	2,033	18,240
Errors/omissions insurance	750	750	750	750	750	750	750	750	750	750	750	750	9,000
Subtotal	15,547	15,640	15,733	15,827	15,920	16,013	16,107	16,200	16,293	16,387	16,480	16,573	192,720
Total expenses	$439,217	$457,142	$486,189	$499,394	$531,910	$562,115	$580,620	$613,365	$631,221	$661,436	$689,891	$701,197	6,853,696

Revenue and Expense Assumptions

Detailed Revenues

United States:

Average price/minute:

The average price assumes that new account traffic will be split evenly between large and small accounts. Accounts billing over $500/month will be billed at $.69/minute. Small accounts will be billed at $.79/minute.

- **Year 1:** The average price is projected to drop to $.69/minute in Year 2 and $.62/minute in Year 3 as the percentage of large customers increases and as competition enters the market.
- **Year 2 and Year 3:** Average price is projected to drop to $.69/minute in Year 2 and $.62/minute in Year 3 as the percentage

Monthly growth rate: Each sales rep is expected to generate 350 new minutes/day of traffic each month. A detailed explanation of this item is provided in the business plan under "Sales Expectations."

Free minutes/day: Sales reps are expected to give away 100 free minutes of service to three times as many accounts as they are expected to close.

Net new minutes/day: Multiplication of the number of sales reps times the monthly growth rate figure addressed above.

Uncollectible accounts: One percent uncollectibles based on statistics generated by AT&T.

Japan joint venture:

Average price/minute: Average price per minute charged to the Japanese partner for use of the network is a combination of $.30/minute to cover transmission costs and $.05/minute to cover the equipment dedicated to the Japanese joint venture.

Total minutes/month: Aggregate number of minutes transmitted by the Japanese partner each month. Traffic growth rate is estimated to be 60% of the rate achieved by the U.S. sales force. The 60% number was selected with the intention of being conservative. Initial sales from Japan are not scheduled to begin until six months after a list of qualified joint venture partners has been developed. Initial sales volume from Japan will be bolstered by the actions of U.S. sales reps introducing the return service to Japanese companies already using FAX International in the United States.

Detailed Expenses

Technical development:

Personnel: All salary figures reflect actual agreements for full-time employment. All four full-time network development personnel are tied into three-year stock vesting programs. Dr. Sosonowski and Steve Orr have each accepted salary reductions equal to $6,000/month in return for their stock positions.

Contract programmers: No additional consulting work is anticipated in Year 1. A small budget has been set aside for Years 2 and 3 to deal with intermittent needs.

Tokyo engineer: Ministry of Post and Telecommunications (MPT) in Japan requires that FAX International employ a certified senior telecommunications engineer to be responsible for meeting all regulatory approvals.

Equipment housing expenses: FAX International's network hardware will be housed at KDD's main international switching facility in Tokyo. All hardware and communications lines will be monitored and maintained on a 24-hour basis. Similar arrangements have been negotiated in the U.S. with Teleport Communications in Boston and New York, and M.F.S. in Los Angeles and San Francisco.

Installation expenses: Budget for installation of all network hardware and communications lines in Tokyo and Boston. The majority of the cost will go towards custom installation work performed by KDD to provide security, 24-hour maintenance, earthquake protection, guaranteed back-up power supply, and so on.

Sales expenses:

Sales office space: Field sales reps in Los Angeles, New York, and San Francisco will share an office in an executive office suite. The budget for each shared office has been set at $1,500/month. Offices will include furniture, limited secretarial support, answering service, voice mail, copy facilities, mail facilities, and so on.

Sales expenses: Field sales reps will be responsible for covering all accounts within driving distance of their assigned metropolitan area. Expenses for each field sales rep are projected at $500/month to cover local travel expenses and local phone expenses. An additional $10,000/month has been allocated to cover travel expenses and long distance phone expense for Ranalli, Lanzilla, and the national accounts installation rep.

Japanese joint venture:

Chuo Coopers & Lybrand: C&L has submitted a proposal for a $20,000 three-month project to identify and prequalify a list of joint venture candidates. No decision has been made but a budget has been set aside beginning in January 1992.

Network assets:

Network hardware lease: All lease payments are based on three-year contracts at a monthly lease rate of 3.2% per month calculated on the purchase price of the assets. The lease rate assumption is based on the current rates being paid by FAX International.

Japanese J/V hardware: Hardware purchased specifically to handle return traffic from Japan.

Import duties: 10 percent import duty paid on all network hardware equipment purchased in the United States and shipped to Japan for use in the Tokyo network node.

(Continued)

Revenue and Expense Assumptions (concluded)

Communications expenses:

Network demonstrations: FAX International sales reps will be able to provide full-function network demonstrations to potential customers before the system is actually installed between the United States and Tokyo. Expenses cover the cost of placing international telephone calls to Tokyo to deliver the demonstration documents.

Average variable cost per minute: Combination of $.15/minute to collect a document in the United States via an 800 number and $.03/minute to deliver a document via a local call in Tokyo. Average variable cost drops to $.13 in March once the U.S. network is expanded to include remote collection nodes in Los Angeles, San Francisco, and New York City. Documents received at a remote collection node cost only $.05/minute to collect. Business plan assumes half of all documents will always be received via an 800 number.

Monthly Japanese JV costs: Documents received from the Japanese partner will be delivered in the United States via a long-distance call from Boston to the destination fax machine. Average cost per minute will be a maximum of $.135.

Number of 64kbps channels: Calculation of the total bandwidth required on the international private line between Boston and Tokyo.

Fractional T1: Monthly fee for an international private line with the number of active channels shown in the row above.

Local loop service: Cost of fiber optic communications access from the FAX International network nodes in the United States and Tokyo into the AT&T and KDD facilities.

Installation expenses: Fees paid for adding capacity to the communications facilities outlined above.

Customer service: FAX International will employ both full-time customer service reps (CSR) and part-time reps to cover peak demand periods. CSR staffing levels are based on the assumption that 5% of all documents handled by the network will require special handling by a CSR. Each CSR is expected to be able to handle a maximum of 20 problem documents per hour. Note: Research conducted by Cable & Wireless shows that 98% of all fax documents get delivered within three attempts.

Administrative expenses:

Legal and accounting consulting: $30,000 charge in the first month of operations is an estimate of the cost to negotiate and close a deal for the second round of financing. Monthly budget of $2,000 is intended to cover all ongoing legal and accounting consulting fees.

## Chapter Eleven

The Business Plan

Madame, enclosed please find the novel you commissioned. It is in two volumes. If I had had more time I could have written it in one.

Voltaire

Results Expected

Upon completion of this chapter, you will have:

1. Examined a model of a business plan proven and refined over 25 years of actual use.
2. Determined what needs to be included in the plan, why, and for whom.
3. Identified some of the pitfalls in the business plan preparation process and how to avoid these.
4. Analyzed a complete business plan developed by a young entrepreneur to raise capital for a new telecommunications venture.
5. Concluded what has to be done to develop and complete a business plan for your proposed venture.
6. Analyzed the "Douglas Ranalli and Shae Plimley" case.

Developing the Business Plan

The business plan itself is the culmination of a usually lengthy, arduous, creative, and iterative process that, as we explored in Chapters 3 and 4, can transform the caterpillar of a raw idea into the magnificent butterfly of an opportunity. The plan will carefully articulate the merits, requirements, risks, and potential rewards of the opportunity and how it will be seized. It will demonstrate how the four anchors noted in Chapter 4 will reveal themselves to the founders and investors by converting all the research, careful thought, and creative problem solving from the Venture Opportunity Screening Guide into a thorough plan:

1. They create or add significant value to a customer or end user.
2. They do so by solving a significant problem, or meeting a significant want or need for which someone is willing to pay a premium.
3. They therefore have robust market, margin, and money-making characteristics: large enough ($50+ million), high growth (20 percent-plus), high margins (40 percent-plus), strong and early free cash flow (recurring revenue, low assets and working capital), high profit potential (10–15 percent-plus after tax), and offer attractive realizable returns for investors (25–30 percent-plus IRR).
4. They are a good *fit* with the founder(s) and management team at the time and marketspace, and with the risk/reward balance.

The plan becomes the point of departure for prospective investors to begin their due diligence in order to ascertain the various risks and potential of the venture: technology risks, market risks, management risks, competitive and strategic risks, and financial risks. Even if you do not intend to raise outside capital, this homework is vital. The collisions between founders and investors that occur during meetings, discussions, and investigations reveal a great deal to all parties and begin to set the code for their relationship and negotiations. Getting to know each other much more closely is a crucial part of the evaluation process. Constantly on all minds will be such issues as: are these intelligent people; can we work well with them during thick but especially thin times; are they creative; do they listen; can they add value to the venture; is this the right management; do I want them as business partners; are they honest; are we having fun yet?

The investors who can bring the most insight, know-how, and contacts to the venture, and thus add the greatest value, will reveal themselves as well. The most valuable investors will see weaknesses, even flaws, in how the market is viewed, the technology or service, the strategies, the proposed size and structure of the financing, and the team, and will propose strategies and people to correct these. If it is the right investor, it can make the difference between an average and a good or great venture.

The Plan Is Obsolete at the Printer

The author has argued for three decades that the plan is obsolete the instant it emerges from the printer. Indeed, in today's Internet time, it is obsolete before it goes into the printer! The pace of technological and information-age change, and the dynamism of the global marketplace, shorted the already brief life expectancy of any business plan. It is nearly impossible to find a year-old venture today that is identical in strategy, market focus, products or services, and team as it was described in its original business plan.

Work in Progress—Bent Knees Required

In such a rapidly changing environment, flexibility and responsiveness become critical survival skills. The process of developing an idea into a business, and articulating how this will be done via a business plan, requires an open mind and "bent knees," along with clear focus, commitment, and determination.

The business plan can be thought of as a work in progress. Though it must be completed, if you are try-ing to raise outside capital, attract key advisors, directors, or team members, and the like, it can never be completed. Like a cross-country flight plan, many unexpected changes can occur along the way—a thunderstorm, smoke impaired visibility, fog, or new powerful winds pop up. One has to be prepared to continually adjust course to minimize risk and ensure successful completion of the journey. Such risk/reward management is inherent in the business planning process.

The Plan Is Not the Business

Developing the business plan is one of the best ways to define the blueprint, strategy, resource, and people requirements for a new venture. The vast majority of *INC.*'s 500 fastest growing companies had business plans at the outset. Without a business plan it is exceedingly difficult to raise capital from informal or formal investors.

Yet, all too often first time entrepreneurs jump to a simplistic conclusion: All that is needed is a fat, polished, and enticing business plan and the business will automatically be successful. They confuse the plan and building the business. Paradoxically, some of the most impressive business plans never become great businesses. And some of the weakest plans lead to extraordinary businesses. Such was the case with Lotus Development Corporation, creator of the leading 1-2-3 spreadsheet. Mitch Kapor's original business plan was a brief letter, some descriptions of the personal computer market, a description of nearly 10 separate products, a one-year monthly startup budget, and a five-year goal of $30 million in revenue, which would require about $200–$300 thousand of capital. Venture capital backers Sevin–Rosen basically discarded the entire plan, the strategy, the product mix, the capital requirements, the launch plan, and the vision for the venture's first five years. They concluded the opportunity was much bigger, that $1 million of startup capital was required, that the company would either be several hundred million in revenue in five years, or would not be in business, even at $30 million in sales. The first-mover advantage of a warp-speed launch strategy was vital, and the rocket needed to be lit. The rest is history. Lotus Development reached $500 million in revenue in the first five years.

The message here is two-edged. The odds can be shaped in your favor through the development of a business plan. But, just because you have a plan does not mean the business will be an automatic success. Unless, the fundamental opportunity is there, along with the requisite resources and team needed to pursue it, the best plan in the world won't make much difference. Some helpful tips in preparing a business plan are summarized in *Exhibit 11.1.*

Some Tips from the Trenches

The most valuable lessons about preparing a business plan and raising venture capital come from entrepreneurs who have succeeded in these endeavors. Tom Huseby[1] is founder and head of SeaPoint Ventures outside Seattle, a venture capital firm allied with Venrock Venture Capital, Oak Venture Partners, and Sevin–Rosen Venture Partners. An engineering graduate of Columbia University and a Stanford MBA, Huseby spent 18 years with Raychem Corporation of California, first working in sales and eventually developing and managing new businesses, then running Raychem's businesses in several countries. Tom is a remarkable entrepreneur who has raised over $80 million of venture capital as CEO of two telecommunications startup companies in the early and mid-1990s that subsequently became publicly traded companies: Innova Corporation (NASDAQ: INNV) and Metawave Corporation (NASDAQ: MWAV). Consider the following wisdom Tom gleaned from his own experience on both sides of the negotiating table: entrepreneur/CEO and venture capitalist:

RE: Venture Capitalists—

- There are a lot of venture capitalists. Once you meet one you could end up meeting all 700+ of them.
- Getting a "no" from venture capitalists is as hard as getting a yes; qualify your targets and force others to say no.
- Be vague about what other venture capitalists you are talking to.
- Don't ever meet with an associate or junior member twice without a partner.

RE: The Plan—

- Stress your business concept in the executive summary.
- The numbers don't matter; but the economics (e.g., value proposition and business model) really matter.
- Make the business plan look and feel good; don't use any filler—you'll need it later.
- Prepare lots of copies of published articles, contracts, market studies, purchase orders, and the like.
- Prepare very detailed resumés and reference lists of key players in the venture.

- If you can't do the details, make sure you hire someone who can.

RE: The Deal—

- Make sure your current investors are as desperate as you are.
- Create a market for your venture.
- Never say no to an offer price.
- Use a lawyer who has closed lots of venture deals.
- Don't stop selling until the money is in the bank.
- Make it a challenge—never lie.

RE: The Fund Raising Process—

- It is much harder than you ever thought it could be.
- You can last much longer than you ever thought you could.
- The venture capitalists have to do this for the rest of their lives!

This is particularly valuable advice for any entrepreneur seeking outside capital and anticipating dealing with investors.[2]

Sell, Sell, Sell! Myopia

One of the most frequently missed opportunities in the entire process of developing a business plan and trying to convince outside investors to part with their cash is a consequence of sell-sell-sell! myopia by the founders. Obviously, the founder(s) will rarely if ever succeed in raising money or growing the business if she or he is not effective at selling. Selling ability is one of the most common denominators among successful entrepreneurs.

All too often, however, entrepreneurs—typically out of cash, or nearly so—become so obsessed with selling to prospective investors that they fail to ask great questions and do little serious listening. As a result, these founders learn very little from these prospects, even though they probably know a great deal about the technology, market, and competitors. After all, *that* is the investor's business.

Entrepreneurs who not only succeed at developing a great business concept but also attract the right investors who can add a great deal of value to the venture through their experience, wisdom, and

---

[1] The author is extremely grateful to Tom Huseby, a long-time friend, fellow fly fisherman, and wilderness explorer, for sharing his extraordinary wit and insights over the years in my classes at Babson College, Harvard Business School, and with the Kauffman Fellows Program, and for his contribution here.

[2] See "How to Write a Great Business Plan," William A. Sahlman, *Harvard Business Review*, July–August, 1997, pp. 98–108, for an excellent recent article on business plans.

networks, are usually very savvy listeners. They use the opportunity, beyond presenting their plan and selling themselves, to carefully query prospective investors: You've seen our concept, our story and our strategies, what have we missed? Where are we vulnerable? How would you knock us off? Who will knock us off? How would you modify our strategy? What would you do differently? Who do we need with us to make this succeed? What do you believe has to happen to make this highly successful? Be as blunt as you wish.

Two powerful forces are unleashed in this process. First, as a founder, you will begin to discern just how smart, knowledgeable, and, most importantly, creative the investors are about the proposed business. Do they have creative ideas, insights, and alternative ways of thinking about the opportunity and strategy that you and your team may not have thought of? This enables you, the founder, to ascertain just what value the investors might add to the venture and whether their approach to telling you and your team that you are "all wet" on certain things is acceptable. Would

the relationship be likely to wear you out over time and demoralize you? In the process you will learn a great deal about your plan and the investors.

The second powerful force is the message implicitly sent to the investors when you make such genuine queries and listen, rather than become argumentative and defensive (which they may try to get you to do): We have given this our best shot. We are highly committed to our concept and believe we have the right strategy, but our minds are open. We listen, we learn, we have bent knees; we adapt and change when the evidence and ideas are compelling; we are not granite heads. Investors are much more likely to conclude that you are a founder and a team that they can work with.

The Dehydrated Business Plan

A dehydrated business plan usually runs from 4 to 10 pages, but rarely more. It covers key points, such as those suggested for the executive summary in the

---

EXHIBIT 11.1

Do's and Don'ts

Do

Do involve all of the management team in the preparation of the business plan.

Do make the plan logical, comprehensive, and *readable*—and as short as possible.

Do demonstrate commitment to the venture by investing a significant amount of time and some money in preparing the plan.

Do articulate what the critical risks and assumptions are and how and why these are tolerable.

Do disclose and discuss any current or potential problems in the venture.

Do identify several alternative sources of financing.

Do spell out the proposed deal—how much for what ownership share—and how investors will win.

Do be creative in gaining the attention and interest of potential investors.

Do remember that the plan is not the business and that an ounce of can-do implementation is worth two pounds of planning.

Do accept orders and customers that will generate a positive cash flow, even if it means you have to postpone writing the plan.

Do know your targeted investor group (e.g., venture capitalist, angel, bank, or leasing company) and what they really want and what they dislike, and tailor your plan accordingly.

Do let realistic market and sales projections drive the assumptions underlying the financial spreadsheets, rather than the reverse.

Don't

Don't have unnamed, mysterious people on the management team (e.g., a "Mr. G" who is currently a financial vice president with another firm and who will join you later).

Don't make ambiguous, vague, or unsubstantiated statements, such as estimating sales on the basis of what the team would like to produce.

Don't describe technical products or manufacturing processes using jargon or in a way that only an expert can understand, because this limits the usefulness of the plan. For example, a venture capitalist will not invest in what he or she does not understand—or what he or she thinks the team does not understand—because it cannot explain these to such a smart person as he or she is.

Don't spend money on developing fancy brochures, elaborate slide show presentations, and other "sizzle"—instead, show the "steak."

Don't waste time writing a plan when you could be closing sales and collecting cash.

Don't assume you have a done deal when you have a handshake or verbal commitment but no money in the bank. (The deal is done when the check clears!)

Business Planning Guide that follows. Essentially, such a plan documents the analysis of and information about the heart of the business opportunity, competitive advantages the company will enjoy, and *creative insights* that an entrepreneur often has.

Since it can usually be prepared in a few hours, it is preferred by entrepreneurs who find it difficult to find enough slack time while operating a business to write a complete plan. In many instances investors prefer a dehydrated plan in the initial screening phase.

It is important to note that such a plan is not intended to be used exclusively in the process of raising or borrowing money, and it is not useful in guiding the operations of a business over time.

Who Develops the Business Plan

Consideration often is given to hiring an outside professional to prepare the business plan, so the management team can use its time to obtain financing and start the business.

There are two good reasons why it is *not* a good idea to hire outside professionals. First, in the process of planning and of writing the business plan, the consequences of different strategies and tactics and the human and financial requirements for launching and building the venture can be examined, before it is too late. For example, one entrepreneur discovered, while preparing his business plan, that the major market for his biomedical product was in nursing homes, rather than in hospital emergency rooms, as he and his physician partner had previously assumed. This realization changed the focus of the entire marketing effort. Had he left the preparation to an outsider, this might not have been discovered, or, at the very least, it is unlikely he would have had the same sense of confidence and commitment to the new strategy.

the management team. They now need to ask about the most significant risks and problems involved in launching the enterprise, the long-term profit prospects, and the future financing and cash flow requirements. They must also ask about the demands of operating lead times, seasonality, and facility location, as well as about marketing and pricing strategy needs, and so forth, so they can take action.

These questions now need to be answered convincingly and the evidence for them shown *in writing*. The planning and the development of such a business plan is neither quick nor easy. In fact, effective planning is a difficult and demanding process and demands time, discipline, commitment and dedication, and practice. However, it also can be stimulating and fun as innovative solutions and strategies to solve nagging problems are found.

The skills to write a business plan are not necessarily the ones needed to make a venture successful (although some of these skills are certainly useful). The best single point of departure for, and an anchor during, the planning process is the motto on a small plaque in the office of Paul J. Tobin, president of Cellular One, a company that was a pioneer in the cellular car phone business in America. The motto says CAN DO, and is an apt one for planning and for making sure that a plan serves the very practical purpose for which it is intended.

Further, if a venture intends to use the business plan to raise capital, it is important for the team to do the planning and write the plan itself. Investors attach great importance to the quality of the management team *and* to their complete understanding of the business they are preparing to enter. Thus, investors want to be sure that what they see is what they get— that is, the team's analysis and understanding of the venture opportunity and its commitment to it. They are going to invest in a team and a leader, not in a consultant. Nothing less will do, and anything less is usually obvious.

A Closer Look at the What

The Relationship between Goals and Actions

Consider a team that is enthusiastic about an idea for a new business and has done a considerable amount of thinking and initial work evaluating the opportunity (such as thoroughly working through the Venture Opportunity Screening Guide in Chapter 4). Team members believe the business they are considering has excellent market prospects and fits well with the skills, experience, personal goals and values, and aspirations of its lead entrepreneur and

Segmenting and Integrating Information

In the task of planning and writing a business plan, it is necessary to organize information in a way that it can be managed and that is useful.

An effective way to organize information with the idea of developing a business plan is to segment the information into sections, such as one about the target market, a section about the industry, one about competition, one about the financial plan, and so on, and then integrate the information into a business plan.

This process works best if sections are discrete and the information within them digestible. Then the order in which sections are developed can vary, and different sections can be developed simultaneously. For example, since the heart and soul of a plan lies in the analysis of the market opportunity, of the competition, and of a resultant competitive strategy that can win, it is a good idea to start with these sections and integrate information along the way. Since the financial and operations aspects of the venture will be driven by the rate of growth and the magnitude and specific substance of the market revenue plans, these can be developed later.

The information is then further integrated into the business plan. For example, the executive summary is prepared last.

Establishing Action Steps

The following steps, centered around actions to be taken, outline the process by which a business plan is written. Note these action steps are then presented in an exercise, "The Business Plan Guide."

- Segmenting information. An overall plan for the project, by section, needs to be devised and needs to include priorities, who is responsible for each section, the due date of a first draft, and the due date of a final draft.

- *Creating an overall schedule.* A list of specific tasks, their priorities, who is responsible for them, when they will be started, and when they will be completed needs to be made. This list needs to be as specific and detailed as possible. Tasks need to be broken down into the smallest possible component (e.g., a series of phone calls may be necessary before a trip). The list then needs to be examined for conflicts and lack of reality in time estimates. Peers and business associates can be asked to review the list for realism, timing, and priorities.

- *Creating an action calendar.* Tasks on the *do* list then need to be placed on a calendar. When the calendar is complete, the calendar needs again to be examined for conflicts or lack of realism.

- *Doing the work and writing the plan.* The necessary work needs to be done and the plan written. Adjustments need to be made to the *do* list and the calendar, as necessary. As part of this process, it is important to have a plan reviewed by an attorney to make sure that it contains no misleading statements and unnecessary information and caveats, and also reviewed by an objective outsider, such as an entrepreneurially minded executive who has significant profit and loss responsibility, or a venture capitalist who would not be a potential investor. No matter how good the lead entrepreneur and his or her team are in planning, there will be issues that they will overlook and certain aspects of the presentation that are inadequate or less than clear. Few entrepreneurs are good at both planning and communication. A good reviewer also can act as a sounding board in the process of developing alternative solutions to problems and answers to questions investors are likely to ask.

Preparing a Business Plan

A Complete Business Plan

It may seem to an entrepreneur who has completed the Opportunity Screening Guide in Chapter 4 and who has spent hours of thinking and planning informally that all that now needs to be done is to jot down a few things. *However, there is a great difference between screening an opportunity and developing a business plan.*

There are two important differences in the way these issues need to be addressed. First, a business plan can have two uses: (1) inducing someone to part with maybe $500,000 to $2 million, or even more, and (2) guiding the policies and actions of the firm over a number of years. Therefore, strategies and statements made need to be well thought out, unambiguous, and capable of being supported.

Another difference is that more detail is needed. (The exception to this is the "Dehydrated Business Plan" discussed earlier in this chapter.) This means that the team needs to spend more time gathering detailed data, interpreting it, and presenting it clearly. For example, for the purpose of screening an opportunity, it may be all right to note (if one cannot do any better) that the target market for a product is in the $30–$60 million range and the market is growing over 10 percent per year. For purposes of planning to launch an actual new enterprise, determining strategy, and so forth, this level of detail would not get by. The size range would need to be narrowed considerably; if it were not narrowed, those reading or using the plan would have little confidence in this critical number. And saying the target market is growing at over 10 percent is too vague. Does that mean the market grew at the stated rate between last year and the year before, or does it mean that the market grew on average by this amount over the past three years? Also, a statement phrased in terms of "over 10 percent" smacks of imprecision. The actual growth rate needs to be known and needs to be stated. Whether the rate will or will not remain the same, and why, needs to be explained also.

Preparing an effective business plan for a startup can easily take 200 to 300 hours. Squeezing that amount of time into evenings and weekends can make the process stretch over 3 to 12 months.

A business plan for a business planning expansion or for a situation such as a leveraged buyout typically can take half this effort. The reason is that the knowns about the business, including the market, its competition, financial and accounting information, and so on, at this point are greater.

Exhibit 11.2 is a sample table of contents for a business plan. The information shown is included in most effective business plans. The way information is presented in this exhibit is a good framework to follow. First, organizing the material into sections makes dealing with the information more manageable. Second, while the amount of detail and the order of presentation may vary for a particular venture according to its particular circumstances, most effective business plans contain this information in some form. (Note that the amount of detail and the order in which information is presented is important. These can vary for each particular situation, and will depend upon the purpose of the plan and the age and stage of the venture, among other factors.)

Exercise—The Business Plan Guide

The Business Plan Guide follows the order of *presentation* outlined in *Exhibit 11.2*. Based on a guide originally developed at Venture Founders Corporation by Leonard E. Smollen and the late Brian Haslett, and on over 20 years of observing and working with entrepreneurs and actually preparing and evaluating hundreds of plans, it is intended to make this challenging task easier.

Certainly, there is no single best way to write a business plan, and there are many ways to approach the preparation for and writing of a business plan. It is recommended that you begin with the market research and analysis sections. In the final analysis, the task will evolve in a way that suits you and your situation.

In writing your plan, you should remember that although one of the important functions of a business plan is to influence investors, rather than preparing a fancy presentation, you and your team need to prove to yourselves and others that your opportunity is worth pursuing, and to construct the means by which you will do it. Gathering information, making hard decisions, and developing plans come first.

The plan guide that follows shows how to present information succinctly and in a format acceptable to investors. While it is useful to keep in mind who your audience is, and that information not clearly presented will most likely not be used, it also is important not to be concerned *just* with format.

In the Business Plan Guide, issues are indicated. The intent is to show you what needs to be included in a business plan and why.

Further, you may feel as though you have seen much of this before. You should. The guide is based on the analytical framework described in the book and builds upon the Opportunity Screening Guide in Chapter 4. If you have not completed the Opportunity Screening Guide, it will help you to do so before proceeding. It is assumed in the Business Plan Guide that you will be able to draw on data and analysis developed in the Opportunity Screening Guide to help you prepare your business plan.

As you proceed through the Business Plan Guide, remember that statements need to be supported with data where possible. Note also that it is sometimes easier to present data in tabular form. Include the source of all data, the methods and/or assumptions used, and the credentials of people doing research. If data on which a statement is based is available elsewhere in the plan, be sure to indicate where it can be found.

Finally, it is important to remember that the Business Plan Guide is just that—a guide. It is intended to be applicable to a wide range of product and service businesses. For any particular industry or market, certain critical issues are unique to that industry or market. In the chemical industry, for example, some special issues of significance currently exist, such as increasingly strict regulations at all levels of government covering the use of chemical products and the operation of processes, diminishing viability of the high-capital-cost, special-purpose chemical processing plants serving a narrow market, and long delivery times of processing equipment. In the electronics industry, the special issues may be the future availability and price of new kinds of large-scale integrated circuits.

Common sense should rule in applying the guide to your specific venture.

EXHIBIT 11.2

Business Plan

Table of Contents

Exercise
The Business Plan Guide

Name:

Venture:

Data:

STEP 1

Segment Information into Key Sections and Set Priorities For Each Section, Who Is Responsible, and Due Dates for Drafts and Final Versions. When you segment your information, it is vital to keep in mind that the plan needs to be logically integrated and that information should be consistent. Note that since the market opportunity section is the heart and soul of the plan and, most likely, the most difficult, it is best to assign it a high priority and to begin work there first. Remember to include such tasks as printing in the list.

Section or Task	Priority	Person(s) Responsible	Date to Begin	First Draft Due Date	Date Completed or Final Version Due Date

STEP 2

Devise an Overall Schedule for Preparing the Plan and List Tasks That Need to Be Completed, Priorities, Who Is Responsible, When the Task Is to Be Started, and When It Is to Be Completed. It is helpful to break larger items (field work to gather customer and competitor intelligence, trade show visits, etc.) into the small, manageable components (such as phone calls required before a trip can be taken) and to include the components as a task. Be as specific as possible.

Task	Priority	Person Responsible	Date to Begin	Date of Completion

STEP 3

Combine the List of Segments and the List of Tasks and Create a Calendar. In combining your list, consider if anything has been omitted and whether you have been realistic in what people can do, when they can do it, what needs to be done, and so forth. To create your calendar, place an *X* in the week when the task is to be started and an *X* in the week it is to be completed and then connect the *X*s. When you have placed all tasks on the calendar, look carefully again for conflicts or lack of realism. In particular, evaluate if team members are overscheduled.

							Week									
Task	1	2	3	4	5	6	7	8	9	10	11	12	13	14	15

STEP 4

Develop and Write a Business Plan Using the Following As a Framework. As has been discussed, the framework follows the order of presentation of the table of contents shown in *Exhibit 11.2.* While preparing your own plan, you will most likely want to consider sections in a different order from the one presented in *Exhibit 11.2.* (Also, when you integrate your sections into your final plan, you may choose to present material somewhat differently.)

Cover

The cover page includes the name of the company, its address, its telephone number, the date, and the securities offered. Usually, the name, address, telephone number, and the date are centered at the top of the page and the securities offered are listed at the bottom. Also suggested on the cover page at the bottom is the following text:

This business plan has been submitted on a confidential basis solely for the benefit of selected, highly qualified investors in connection with the private placement of the above securities and is not for use by any other persons. Neither may it be reproduced, stored, or copied in any form. By accepting delivery of this plan, the recipient agrees to return this copy to the corporation at the address listed above if the recipient does not undertake to subscribe to the offering. Do not copy, fax, reproduce, or distribute without permission.

Table of Contents

Included in the table of contents is a list of the sections, any appendices, and any other information and the pages on which they can be found. (See *Exhibit 11.2.*)

I. Executive Summary

The first section in the body of the business plan is usually an executive summary. The summary is usually short and concise (one or two pages). The summary articulates what the opportunity conditions are and why they exist, who will execute the opportunity and why they are capable of doing so, how the firm will gain entry and market penetration, and so on. Essentially, the summary for your venture needs to mirror the criteria shown in *Exhibit 3.5* and the Venture Opportunity Screening Guide.

The summary is usually prepared after the other sections of the business plan are completed. It is therefore helpful, as the other sections are drafted, to note one or two key sentences, and some key facts and numbers from each.

The summary is important for those ventures trying to raise or borrow money. Many investors, bankers, managers, and other readers use the summary to determine quickly whether the venture the plan describes is of interest. Therefore, unless the summary is appealing and compelling, it may be the only section read, and you may never get the chance to make a presentation or discuss your business in person.

Therefore, leave plenty of time to prepare the summary. (Successful public speakers have been known to spend an hour of preparation for each minute of their speech.) The executive summary usually contains a paragraph or two covering each of the following:

A. *Description of the business concept and the business.* Describe the business concept for the business you are or will be in. For example, Outdoor Scene, Inc. wanted to produce tents, but the concept was "to become a leader in providing quality, service, and on-time delivery in outdoor leisure products." Be sure the description of your concept explains how your product or service will fundamentally change the way customers currently do certain things. For example, Arthur Rock, the lead investor in Apple Computer and Intel, has stated that he focuses on concepts that will change the way people live and/or work. You need to identify when the company was formed, what it will do, what is special or proprietary about its product, service, or technology, and so forth. Include summary information about any proprietary technology, trade secrets, or unique capabilities that give you an edge in the marketplace. If the company has existed for a few years, a brief summary of its size and progress is in order. Try to make your description 25 words or less, and mention the specific product or service.

B. *The opportunity and strategy.* Summarize what the opportunity is, why it is compelling, and the entry strategy planned to exploit it. This information may be pre-sented as an outline of the key facts, conditions, competitors' vulnerabilities ("sleepiness," sluggishness, poor service, etc.), industry trends, and other evidence and logic that define the opportunity. Note plans for growth and expansion beyond the entry products or services and into other market segments (such as international markets) as appropriate.

C. *The target market and projections.* Identify and briefly explain the industry and market, who the primary customer groups are, how the product(s) or service(s) will be positioned, and how you plan to reach and service these groups. Include information about the structure of the market, the size and growth rate for the market segments or niches you are seeking, your unit and dollar sales estimates, your anticipated market share, the payback period for your customers, and your pricing strategy (including price versus performance/value/benefits considerations).

D. *The competitive advantages.* Indicate the significant competitive edges you enjoy or can create as a result of your innovative product, service, and strategy; advantages in lead time; competitors' weaknesses and vulnerabilities; and other Industry conditions.

E. *The economics, profitability, and harvest potential.* Summarize the nature of the "forgiving and rewarding" economics of the venture (e.g., gross and operating margins, expected profitability and durability of those profits); the relevant time frames to attain break-even and positive cash flow; key financial projections; the expected return on investment; and so on. Be sure to include a brief discussion of your contribution analysis and the underlying operating and cash conversion cycle. Use key numbers whenever possible.

F. *The team.* Summarize the relevant knowledge, experience, know-how, and skills of the lead entrepreneur and any team members, noting previous accomplishments, especially those involving profit and loss responsibility and general management and people management experience. Include significant information, such as the size of a division, project, or prior business with which the lead entrepreneur or a team member was the driving force.

G. *The offering.* Briefly indicate the dollar amount of equity and/or debt financing needed, how much of the company you are prepared to offer for that financing, what principal use will be made of the capital, and how the targeted investor, lender, or strategic partner will achieve its desired rate of return.

II. The Industry and the Company and Its Product(s) or Service(s)

A major area of consideration is the company, its concept for its product(s) and service(s), and its interface with the industry in which it will be competing. This is the context into which the marketing information, for example, fits. Information needs to include a description of the industry, a description of the concept, a description of your company, and a description of the product(s) or service(s) you will offer, the proprietary position of these product(s) or service(s), their potential advantages, and entry and growth strategy for the product(s) or service(s).

A. *The industry:*
— Present the current status and prospects for the industry in which the proposed business will operate. Be sure to consider industry structure.
— Discuss briefly market size, growth trends, and competitors.
— Discuss any new products or developments, new markets and customers, new requirements, new entrants and exits, and any other national or economic trends and factors that could affect the venture's business positively or negatively.

B. *The company and the concept:*
— Describe generally the concept of the business, what business your company is in or intends to enter, what product(s) or service(s) it will offer, and who are or will be its principal customers.
— By way of background, give the date your venture was incorporated and describe the identification and development of its products and the involvement of the company's principals in that development.
— If your company has been in business for several years and is seeking expansion financing, review its history and cite its prior sales and profit performance, and if your company has had setbacks or losses in prior years, discuss these and emphasize current and future efforts to prevent a recurrence of these difficulties and to improve your company's performance.

C. *The product(s) or service(s):*
— Describe in some detail each product or service to be sold.
— Discuss the application of the product or service and describe the primary end use as well as any significant secondary applications.
— Emphasize any unique features of the product or service and how these will create or add significant value; also, highlight any differences between what is currently on the market and what you will offer that will account for your market penetration. Be sure to describe how value will be added and the payback period to the customer—that is, discuss how many months it will take for the customer to cover the initial purchase price of the product or service as a result of its time, cost, or productivity improvements.
— Include a description of any possible drawbacks (including problems with obsolescence) of the product or service.
— Define the present state of development of the product or service and how much time and money will be required to fully develop, test, and introduce the product or service. Provide a summary of the functional specifications and photographs, if available, of the product.
— Discuss any head start you might have that would enable you to achieve a favored or entrenched position in the industry.

— Describe any features of the product or service that give it an "unfair" advantage over the competition. Describe any patents, trade secrets, or other proprietary features of the product or service.
— Discuss any opportunities for the expansion of the product line or the development of related products or services. (Emphasize opportunities and explain how you will take advantage of them.)

D. *Entry and growth strategy:*
— Indicate key success variables in your marketing plan (e.g., an innovative product, timing advantage, or marketing approach) and your pricing, distribution, advertising, and promotion plans.
— Summarize how fast you intend to grow and to what size during the first five years and your plans for growth beyond your initial product or service.
— Show how the entry and growth strategy is derived from the opportunity and value-added or other competitive advantages, such as the weakness of competitors.

III. Market Research and Analysis

Because of the importance of market analysis and the critical dependence of other parts of the plan on this information, you are advised to prepare this section of the business plan before any other. Take enough time to do this section very well and to check alternative sources of market data.

Information in this section needs to support the assertion that the venture can capture a substantial market in a growing industry in the face of competition.

This section of the business plan is one of the most difficult to prepare, yet it is one of the most important. Other sections of the business plan depend on the market research and analysis presented here. For example, the predicted sales levels directly influence such factors as the size of the manufacturing operation, the marketing plan, and the amount of debt and equity capital you will require. Yet most entrepreneurs seem to have great difficulty preparing and presenting market research and analyses that show that their ventures' sales estimates are sound and attainable.

A. *Customers:*
— Discuss who the customers for the product(s) or service(s) are or will be. Note that potential customers need to be classified by relatively homogeneous groups having common, identifiable characteristics (e.g., by major market segment). For example, an automotive part might be sold to manufacturers and to parts distributors supplying the replacement market, so the discussion needs to reflect two market segments.
— Show who and where the major purchasers for the product(s) or service(s) are in each market segment. Include regional and foreign countries, as appropriate.
— Indicate whether customers are easily reached and receptive, how customers buy (wholesale, through

manufacturers' representatives, etc.), where in their organizations such buying decisions are made, and how long such decisions take. Describe customers' purchasing processes, including the bases on which they make purchase decisions (e.g., price, quality, timing, delivery, training, service, personal contacts, or political pressures) and why they might change current purchasing decisions.

— List any orders, contracts, or letters of commitment that you have in hand. These are far and away *the most powerful data* you can provide. List also any potential customers who have expressed an interest in the product(s) or service(s) and indicate why; also list any potential customers who have shown no interest in the proposed product or service and explain why they are not interested and explain what you will do to overcome negative customer reaction. Indicate how fast you believe your product or service will be accepted in the market.

— If you have an existing business, list your principal current customers and discuss the trends in your sales to them.

B. *Market size and trends:*

— Show for five years the size of the current total market and the share you will have, by market segment and/or by region and/or country, for the product or service you will offer, in units, dollars, and potential profitability.

— Describe also the potential annual growth for at least three years of the total market for your product(s) or service(s) for each major customer group, region, or country, as appropriate.

— Discuss the major factors affecting market growth (e.g., industry trends, socioeconomic trends, government policy, and population shifts) and review previous trends in the market. Any differences between past and projected annual growth rates need to be explained.

C. *Competition and competitive edges:*

— Make a realistic assessment of the strengths and weaknesses of competitors. Assess the substitute and/or alternative products and services and list the companies that supply them, both domestic and foreign, as appropriate.

— Compare competing and substitute products or services on the basis of market share, quality, price, performance, delivery, timing, service, warranties, and other pertinent features.

— Compare the fundamental value that is added or created by your product or service, in terms of economic benefits to the customer and to your competitors.

— Discuss the current advantages and disadvantages of these products and services and say why they are not meeting customer needs.

— Indicate any knowledge of competitors' actions that could lead you to new or improved products and an advantageous position. For example, discuss whether competitors are simply sluggish or nonresponsive or are asleep at the switch.

— Review the strengths and weaknesses of the competing companies and determine and discuss the share of the market of each competitor, its sales, its distribution methods, and its production capabilities.

— Review also the financial position, resources, costs, and profitability of the competition and their profit trend. Note that you can utilize Robert Morris Associates data for comparison (see Appendix I on this book's Web site).

— Indicate who are the service, pricing, performance, cost, and quality leaders. Discuss why any companies have entered or dropped out of the market in recent years.

— Discuss the three or four key competitors and why customers buy from them, and determine and discuss why customers *leave* them.

— From what you know about the competitors' operations, explain why you think that they are vulnerable and you can capture a share of their business. Discuss what makes you think it will be easy or difficult to compete with them. Discuss, in particular, your competitive advantages gained through such "unfair" advantage as patents.

D. *Estimated market share and sales:*

— Summarize what it is about your product(s) or service(s) that will make it saleable in the face of current and potential competition. Mention, especially, the fundamental value added or created by the product(s) or service(s).

— Identify any major customers (including international customers) who are willing to make, or who have already made, purchase commitments, and indicate the extent of those commitments and why they were made, and discuss which customers could be major purchasers in future years and why.

— Based on your assessment of the advantages of your product or service, the market size and trends, customers, the competition and their products, and the trends of sales in prior years, estimate the share of the market and the sales in units and dollars that you will acquire in each of the next three years. Remember to show assumptions used.

— Show how the growth of the company sales in units and its estimated market share are related to the growth of its industry and customers and the strengths and weaknesses of competitors. Remember, the assumptions used to estimate market share and sales need to be clearly stated.

— If yours is an existing business, also indicate the total market, your market share, and sales for two prior years.

E. *Ongoing market evaluation:*

— Explain how you will continue to evaluate your target markets so as to assess customer needs and service and to guide product-improvement programs and new-product programs, plan for expansions of your production facility, and guide product/service pricing.

IV. The Economics of the Business

The economic and financial characteristics, including the apparent magnitude and durability of margins and profits generated, need to support the fundamental attractiveness of the opportunity. The underlying operating and cash conversion cycle of the business, the value chain, and so forth, need to make sense in terms of the opportunity and strategies planned.

A. *Gross and operating margins:*
  — Describe the magnitude of the gross margins (i.e., selling price less variable costs) and the operating margins for each of the product(s) and/or service(s) you are selling in the market niche(s) you plan to attack. Include results of your contribution analysis.

B. *Profit potential and durability:*
  — Describe the magnitude and expected durability of the profit stream the business will generate—before and after taxes—and reference appropriate industry benchmarks, other competitive intelligence, or your own relevant experience.
  — Address the issue of how perishable or durable the profit stream appears to be. Provide reasons why your profit stream is perishable or durable, such as barriers to entry you can create, your technological and market lead time, and so on.

C. *Fixed, variable, and semivariable costs:*
  — Provide a detailed summary of fixed, variable, and semivariable costs, in dollars and as percentages of total cost as appropriate, for the product or service you offer and the volume of purchases and sales upon which these are based.
  — Show relevant industry benchmarks.

D. *Months to breakeven:*
  — Given your entry strategy, marketing plan, and proposed financing, show how long it will take to reach a unit breakeven sales level.
  — Note any significant stepwise changes in your breakeven that will occur as you grow and add substantial capacity.

E. *Months to reach positive cash flow:*
  — Given the above strategy and assumptions, show when the venture will attain a positive cash flow.
  — Show if and when you will run out of cash. Note where the detailed assumptions can be found.
  — Note any significant stepwise changes in cash flow that will occur as you grow and add capacity.

V. Marketing Plan

The marketing plan describes how the sales projections will be attained. The marketing plan needs to detail the overall marketing strategy that will exploit the opportunity and your competitive advantages. Include a discussion of sales and service policies; pricing, distribution, promotion, and advertising strategies; and sales projections. The marketing plan needs to describe *what* is to be done, *how* it will be done, *when* it will be done, and *who* will do it.

A. *Overall marketing strategy:*
  — Describe the specific marketing philosophy and strategy of the company, given the value chain and channels of distribution in the market niche(s) you are pursuing. Include, for example, a discussion of the kinds of customer groups that you already have orders from or that will be targeted for initial intensive selling effort and those targeted for later selling efforts; how specific potential customers in these groups will be identified and how will they be contacted; what features of the product or service, such as service, quality, price, delivery, warranty, or training, will be emphasized to generate sales; if any innovative or unusual marketing concepts will enhance customer acceptance, such as leasing where only sales were previously attempted; and so forth.
  — Indicate whether the product(s) or service(s) will initially be introduced internationally, nationally, or regionally; explain why; and if appropriate, indicate any plans for extending sales at a later date.
  — Discuss any seasonal trends that underlie the cash conversion cycle in the industry and what can be done to promote sales out of season.
  — Describe any plans to obtain government contracts as a means of supporting product development costs and overhead.

B. *Pricing:*
  — Discuss pricing strategy, including the prices to be charged for your product and service, and compare your pricing policy with those of your major competitors, including a brief discussion of payback (in months) to the customer.
  — Discuss the gross profit margin between manufacturing and ultimate sales costs and indicate whether this margin is large enough to allow for distribution and sales, warranty, training, service, amortization of development and equipment costs, price competition, and so forth—and still allow a profit.
  — Explain how the price you set will enable you (1) to get the product or service accepted, (2) to maintain and increase your market share in the face of competition, and (3) to produce profits.
  — Justify your pricing strategy and differences between your prices and those for competitive or substitute products or services in terms of economic payback to the customer and value added through newness, quality, warranty, timing, performance, service, cost savings, efficiency, and the like.
  — If your product is to be priced lower than those of the competition, explain how you will do this and maintain profitability (e.g., through greater value added via effectiveness in manufacturing and distribution, lower labor costs, lower material costs, lower overhead, or other component of cost).
  — Discuss your pricing policy, including a discussion of the relationship of price, market share, and profits.

For example, a higher price may reduce volume but result in a higher gross profit.

— Describe any discount allowance for prompt payment or volume purchases.

C. *Sales tactics:*

— Describe the methods (e.g., own sales force, sales representatives, ready-made manufacturers' sales organizations, direct mail, or distributors) that will be used to make sales and distribute the product or service and both the initial plans and longer-range plans for a sales force. Include a discussion of any special requirements (e.g., refrigeration).

— Discuss the value chain and the resulting margins to be given to retailers, distributors, wholesalers, and salespeople and any special policies regarding discounts, exclusive distribution rights, and so on, given to distributors or sales representatives and compare these to those given by your competition. (See the Venture Opportunity Screening Guide.)

— Describe how distributors or sales representatives, if they are used, will be selected, when they will start to represent you, the areas they will cover and the build-up (a head count) of dealers and representatives by month, and the expected sales to be made by each.

— If a direct sales force is to be used, indicate how it will be structured and at what rate (a head count) it will be built up; indicate if it is to replace a dealer or representative organization and, if so, when and how.

— If direct mail, magazine, newspaper, or other media, telemarketing, or catalog sales are to be used, indicate the specific channels or vehicles, costs (per 1,000), and expected response rates and yield (as percentage) from the various media, and so on, used. Discuss how these will be built up.

Show the sales expected per salesperson per year and what commission, incentive, and/or salary they are slated to receive, and compare these figures to the average for your industry.

— Present a selling schedule and a sales budget that includes all marketing promotion and service costs.

D. *Service and warranty policies:*

— If your company will offer a product that will require service, warranties, or training, indicate the importance of these to the customers' purchasing decisions and discuss your method of handling service problems.

— Describe the kind and term of any warranties to be offered, whether service will be handled by company servicepeople, agencies, dealers and distributors, or returns to the factory.

— Indicate the proposed charge for service calls and whether service will be a profitable or break-even operation.

— Compare your service, warranty, and customer training policies and practices to those of your principal competitors.

E. *Advertising and promotion:*

— Describe the approaches the company will use to bring its product or service to the attention of prospective purchasers.

— For original equipment manufacturers and for manufacturers of industrial products, indicate the plans for trade show participation, trade magazine advertisements, direct mailings, the preparation of product sheets and promotional literature, and use of advertising agencies.

— For consumer products, indicate what kind of advertising and promotional campaign is contemplated to introduce the product and what kind of sales aids will be provided to dealers, what trade shows, and so forth, are required.

— Present a schedule and approximate costs of promotion and advertising (direct mail, telemarketing, catalogs, etc.), and discuss how these costs will be incurred.

F. *Distribution:*

— Describe the methods and channels of distribution you will employ.

— Indicate how sensitive shipping cost is as a percent of the selling price.

— Note any special issues or problems that need to be resolved, or present potential vulnerabilities.

— If international sales are involved, note how these sales will be handled, including distribution, shipping, insurance, credit, and collections.

VI. Design and Development Plans

The nature and extent of any design and development work and the time and money required before a product or service is marketable need to be considered in detail. (Note that design and development costs are often underestimated.) Such design and development might be the engineering work necessary to convert a laboratory prototype to a finished product; the design of special tooling; the work of an industrial designer to make a product more attractive and salable; or the identification and organization of employees, equipment, and special techniques, such as the equipment, new computer software, and skills required for computerized credit checking, to implement a service business.

A. *Development status and tasks:*

— Describe the current status of each product or service and explain what remains to be done to make it marketable.

— Describe briefly the competence or expertise that your company has or will require to complete this development.

— List any customers or end users who are participating in the development, design, and/or testing of the product or service. Indicate results to date or when results are expected.

B. *Difficulties and risks:*
— Identify any major anticipated design and development problems and approaches to their solution.
— Discuss the possible effect on the cost of design and development, on the time to market introduction, and so forth, of such problems.

C. *Product improvement and new products:*
— In addition to describing the development of the initial products, discuss any ongoing design and development work that is planned to keep product(s) or service(s) competitive and to develop new related product(s) or service(s) that can be sold to the same group of customers. Discuss customers who have participated in these efforts and their reactions, and include any evidence that you may have.

D. *Costs:*
— Present and discuss the design and development budget, including costs of labor, materials, consulting fees, and so on.
— Discuss the impact on cash flow projections of underestimating this budget, including the impact of a 15 to 30 percent contingency.

E. *Proprietary issues:*
— Describe any patent, trademark, copyright, or intellectual property rights you own or are seeking.
— Describe any contractual rights or agreements that give you exclusivity or proprietary rights.
— Discuss the impact of any unresolved issues or existing or possible actions pending, such as disputed rights of ownership, relating to proprietary rights on timing and on any competitive edge you have assumed.

VII. Manufacturing and Operations Plan

The manufacturing and operations plan needs to include such factors as plant location, the type of facilities needed, space requirements, capital equipment requirements, and labor force (both full- and part-time) requirements. For a manufacturing business, the manufacturing and operations plan needs to include policies on inventory control, purchasing, production control, and which parts of the product will be purchased and which operations will be performed by your workforce (called make-or-buy decisions). A service business may require particular attention to location (proximity to customers is generally a must), minimizing overhead, and obtaining competitive productivity from a labor force.

A. *Operating cycle:*
— Describe the lead/lag times that characterize the fundamental operating cycle in your business. (Include a graph similar to the one found in the Venture Opportunity Screening Guide.)
— Explain how any seasonal production loads will be handled without severe dislocation (e.g., by building to inventory or using part-time help in peak periods).

B. *Geographical location:*
— Describe the planned geographical location of the business. Include any location analysis, and so on, that you have done.
— Discuss any advantages or disadvantages of the site location in terms of such factors as labor (including labor availability, whether workers are unionized, and wage rates), closeness to customers and/or suppliers, access to transportation, state and local taxes and laws (including zoning regulations), access to utilities, and so forth.

C. *Facilities and improvements:*
— For an existing business, describe the facilities, including plant and office space, storage and land areas, special tooling, machinery, and other capital equipment currently used to conduct the company's business, and discuss whether these facilities are adequate. Discuss any economies to scale.
— For a startup, describe how and when the necessary facilities to start production will be acquired.
— Discuss whether equipment and space will be leased or acquired (new or used) and indicate the costs and timing of such actions and how much of the proposed financing will be devoted to plant and equipment.
— Explain future equipment needs in the next three years.
— Discuss how and when, in the next three years, plant space and equipment will be expanded to the capacities required by future sales projections and any plans to improve or add to existing plant space or move the facility; indicate the timing and cost of such acquisitions.

D. *Strategy and plans:*
— Describe the manufacturing processes involved in production of your product(s) and any decisions with respect to subcontracting of component parts, rather than complete in-house manufacture.
— Justify your proposed make-or-buy policy in terms of inventory financing, available labor skills, and other nontechnical questions, as well as production, cost, and capability issues.
— Discuss who potential subcontractors and/or suppliers are likely to be and any information about, or any surveys which have been made of, these subcontractors and suppliers.
— Present a production plan that shows cost/volume information at various sales levels of operation with breakdowns of applicable material, labor, purchased components, and factory overhead, and that shows the inventory required at various sales levels.
— Describe your approach to quality control, production control, inventory control, and explain what quality control and inspection procedures the company will use to minimize service problems and associated customer dissatisfaction.

E. *Regulatory and legal issues:*

— Discuss here any relevant state, federal, or foreign regulatory requirements unique to your product, process, or service, such as laws or other regulatory compliance unique to your business and any licenses, zoning permits, health permits, environmental approvals, and the like, necessary to begin operation.

— Note any pending regulatory changes that can affect the nature of your opportunity and its timing.

— Discuss any legal or contractual obligations that are pertinent as well.

VIII. Management Team

This section of the business plan includes a description of the functions that will need to be filled, a description of the key management personnel and their primary duties, an outline of the organizational structure for the venture, a description of the board of directors, a description of the ownership position of any other investors, and so forth. You need to present indications of commitment, such as the willingness of team members to initially accept modest salaries, and of the existence of the proper balance of technical, managerial, and business skills and experience in doing what is proposed.

A. *Organization:*

— Present the key management roles in the company and the individuals who will fill each position. (If the company is established and of sufficient size, an organization chart needs to be appended.)

— If it is not possible to fill each executive role with a full-time person without adding excessive overhead, indicate how these functions will be performed (e.g., using part-time specialists or consultants to perform some functions), who will perform them, and when they will be replaced by a full-time staff member.

— If any key individuals will not be on board at the start of the venture, indicate when they will join the company.

— Discuss any current or past situations where key management people have worked together that could indicate how their skills complement each other and result in an effective management team.

B. *Key management personnel:*

— For each key person, describe in detail career highlights, particularly relevant know-how, skills, and track record of accomplishments, that demonstrate his or her ability to perform the assigned role. Include in your description sales and profitability achievements (budget size, numbers of subordinates, new product introductions, etc.) and other prior entrepreneurial or general management results.

— Describe the exact duties and responsibilities of each of the key members of the management team.

— Complete resumes for each key management member need to be included here or as an exhibit and

need to stress relevant training, experience, and concrete accomplishments, such as profit and sales improvement, labor management success, manufacturing or technical achievements, and meeting of budgets and schedules.

C. *Management compensation and ownership:*

— State the salary to be paid, the stock ownership planned, and the amount of their equity investment (if any) of each key member of the management team.

— Compare the compensation of each key member to the salary he or she received at his or her last independent job.

D. *Other investors:*

— Describe here any other investors in your venture, the number and percentage of outstanding shares they own, when they were acquired, and at what price.

E. *Employment and other agreements and stock option and bonus plans:*

— Describe any existing or contemplated employment or other agreements with key members.

— Indicate any restrictions on stock and vesting that affect ownership and disposition of stock.

— Describe any performance-dependent stock option or bonus plans that are contemplated.

— Summarize any incentive stock option or other stock ownership plans planned or in effect for key people and employees.

F. *Board of directors:*

— Discuss the company's philosophy about the size and composition of the board.

— Identify any proposed board members and include a one- or two-sentence statement of the member's background that shows what he or she can bring to the company.

G. *Other shareholders, rights, and restrictions:*

— Indicate any other shareholders in your company and any rights and restrictions or obligations, such as notes or guarantees, associated with these. (If they have all been accounted for above, simply note that there are no others.)

H. *Supporting professional advisors and services:*

— Indicate the supporting services that will be required.

— Indicate the names and affiliations of the legal, accounting, advertising, consulting, and banking advisors selected for your venture and the services each will provide.

IX. Overall Schedule

A schedule that shows the timing and interrelationship of the major events necessary to launch the venture and realize its objectives is an essential part of a business plan. The underlying cash conversion and operating cycle of the business will provide key inputs for the schedule. In addition to being a planning aid, by showing deadlines critical to a venture's success, a well-presented schedule can be extremely valuable in convincing potential investors that the management team is able to plan for venture growth in a way that recognizes obstacles and minimizes investor risk. Since the time to do things tends to be underestimated in most business plans, it is important to demonstrate that you have correctly estimated these amounts in determining the schedule. Create your schedule as follows:

Step 1: Lay out (use a bar chart) the cash conversion cycle in the business to capture for each product or service expected the lead and elapsed times from an order to the purchase of raw materials or inventory to shipping and collection.

Step 2: Prepare a month-by-month schedule that shows the timing of such activities as product development, market planning, sales programs, production, and operations, and that includes sufficient detail to show the timing of the primary tasks required to accomplish an activity.

Step 3: Show on the schedule the deadlines or milestones critical to the venture's success, such as:

— Incorporation of the venture.
— Completion of design and development.
— Completion of prototypes.
— Obtaining of sales representatives.
— Obtaining product display at trade shows.
— Signing up of distributors and dealers.
— Ordering of materials in production quantities.
— Starting of production or operation.
— Receipt of first orders.
— Delivery on first sale.
— Receiving the first payment on accounts receivable.

Step 4: Show on the schedule the "ramp up" of the number of management personnel, the number of production and operations personnel, and plant or equipment and their relation to the development of the business.

Step 5: Discuss in a general way the activities most likely to cause a schedule slippage, what steps will be taken to correct such slippages, and the impact of schedule slippages on the venture's operation, especially its potential viability and capital needs.

X. Critical Risks, Problems, and Assumptions

The development of a business has risks and problems, and the business plan invariably contains some implicit assumptions about them. You need to include a description of the risks and the consequences of adverse outcomes relating to your industry, your company and its personnel, your product's market appeal, and the timing and financing of your startup. Be sure to discuss assumptions concerning sales projections, customer orders, and so forth. If the venture has anything that could be considered a fatal flaw, discuss why it is not. The discovery of any unstated negative factors by potential investors can undermine the credibility of the venture and endanger its financing. Be aware that most investors will read the section describing the management team first and then this section.

It is recommended that you *not omit* this section. If you do, the reader will most likely come to one or more of the following conclusions:

1. You think he or she is incredibly naive or stupid, or both.
2. You hope to pull the wool over his or her eyes.
3. You do not have enough objectivity to recognize and deal with assumptions and problems.

Identifying and discussing the risks in your venture demonstrate your skills as a manager and increase the credibility of you and your venture with a venture capital investor or a private investor. Taking the initiative on the identification and discussion of risks helps you to demonstrate to the investor that you have thought about them and can handle them. Risks then tend not to loom as large black clouds in the investor's thinking about your venture.

1. Discuss assumptions and risks implicit in your plan.
2. Identify and discuss any major problems and other risks, such as:
   — Running out of cash *before* orders are secured.
   — Potential price cutting by competitors.
   — Any potentially unfavorable industrywide trends.
   — Design or manufacturing costs in excess of estimates.
   — Sales projections not achieved.
   — An unmet product development schedule.
   — Difficulties or long lead times encountered in the procurement of parts or raw materials.
   — Difficulties encountered in obtaining needed bank credit.
   — Larger-than-expected innovation and development costs.
   — Running out of cash *after* orders pour in.
3. Indicate what assumptions or potential problems and risks are most critical to the success of the venture, and describe your plans for minimizing the impact of unfavorable developments in each case.

XI. The Financial Plan

The financial plan is basic to the evaluation of an investment opportunity and needs to represent your best estimates of financial requirements. The purpose of the financial plan is to indicate the venture's potential and to present a timetable for financial viability. It also can serve as an operating plan for financial management using financial benchmarks. In preparing the financial plan, you need to look creatively at your venture and consider alternative ways of launching or financing it.

As part of the financial plan, financial exhibits need to be prepared. To estimate *cash flow needs,* use cash-based, rather than an accrual-based, accounting (i.e., use a real-time cash flow analysis of expected receipts and disbursements). This analysis needs to cover three years. Included also are current- and prior-year income statements and balance sheets, if applicable; profit and loss forecasts for three years; pro forma income statements and balance sheets; and a break-even chart. On the appropriate exhibits, or in an attachment, assumptions behind such items as sales levels and growth, collections and payables periods, inventory requirements, cash balances, cost of goods, and so forth, need to be specified. Your analysis of the operating and cash conversion cycle in the business will enable you to identify these critical assumptions.

Pro forma income statements are the plan-for-profit part of financial management and can indicate the potential financial feasibility of a new venture. Since usually the level of profits, particularly during the start-up years of a venture, will not be sufficient to finance operating asset needs, and since actual cash inflows do not always match the actual cash outflows on a short-term basis, a cash flow forecast that will indicate these conditions and enable management to plan cash needs is recommended. Further, pro forma balance sheets are used to detail the assets required to support the projected level of operations and, through liabilities, to show how these assets are to be financed. The projected balance sheets can indicate if debt-to-equity ratios, working capital, current ratios, inventory turnover, and the like are within the acceptable limits required to justify future financings that are projected for the venture. Finally, a break-even chart showing the level of sales and production that will cover all costs, including those costs that vary with production level and those that do not, is very useful.

A. *Actual income statements and balance sheets:* For an existing business, prepare income statements and balance sheets for the current year and for the prior two years.

B. *Pro forma income statements:*
— Using sales forecasts and the accompanying production or operations costs, prepare pro forma income statements for at least the first three years.
— Fully discuss assumptions (e.g., the amount allowed for bad debts and discounts, or any assumptions made with respect to sales expenses or general and administrative costs being a fixed percentage of costs or sales) made in preparing the pro forma income statement and document them.
— Draw on Section X of the business plan and highlight any major risks, such as the effect of a 20 percent reduction in sales from those projected or the adverse impact of having to climb a learning curve on the level of productivity over time, that could prevent the venture's sales and profit goals from being attained, plus the sensitivity of profits to these risks.

C. *Pro forma balance sheets:* Prepare pro forma balance sheets semiannually in the first year and at the end of each of the first three years of operation.

D. *Pro forma cash flow analysis:*
— Project cash flows monthly for the first year of operation and quarterly for at least the next two years, detailing the amount and timing of expected cash inflows and outflows; determine the need for and timing of additional financing and indicate peak requirements for working capital; and indicate how needed additional financing is to be obtained, such as through the equity financing, through bank loans, or through short-term lines of credit from banks, on what terms, and how it is to be repaid. Remember they are based on cash, not accrual, accounting.
— Discuss assumptions, such as those made on the timing of collection of receivables, trade discounts given, terms of payments to vendors, planned salary and wage increases, anticipated increases in any operating expenses, seasonality characteristics of the business as they affect inventory requirements, inventory turnovers per year, capital equipment purchases, and so forth. Again, these are real time (i.e., cash), not accrual.
— Discuss cash flow sensitivity to a variety of assumptions about business factors (e.g., possible changes in such crucial assumptions as an increase in the receivable collection period or a sales level lower than that forecasted).

E. *Break-even chart:*
— Calculate breakeven and prepare a chart that shows when breakeven will be reached and any stepwise changes in breakeven which may occur.
— Discuss the breakeven shown for your venture and whether it will be easy or difficult to attain breakeven, including a discussion of the size of break-even sales volume relative to projected total sales, the size of gross margins and price sensitivity, and how the break-even point might be lowered in case the venture falls short of sales projections.

F. *Cost control:* Describe how you will obtain information about report costs and how often, who will be responsible for the control of various cost elements, and how you will take action on budget overruns.

G. *Highlights:*
— Highlight the important conclusions, such as what the maximum amount of cash required is and when it will be required, the amount of debt and equity needed, how fast any debts can be repaid, etc., that can be drawn.

XII. Proposed Company Offering

The purpose of this section of the plan is to indicate the amount of any money that is being sought, the nature and amount of the securities offered to the investor, a brief description of the uses that will be made of the capital raised, and a summary of how the investor is expected to achieve its targeted rate of return. It is recommended that you read the discussion about financing in Part IV.

It is important to realize the terms for financing your company that you propose here are the *first step* in the negotiation process with those interested in investing, and it is very possible that your financing will involve different kinds of securities than originally proposed.

A. *Desired financing.* Based on your real-time cash flow projections and your estimate of how much money is required over the next three years to carry out the development and/or expansion of your business as described, indicate how much of this capital requirement will be obtained by this offering and how much will be obtained via term loans and lines of credit.

B. *Offering:*
— Describe the type (e.g., common stock, convertible debentures, debt with warrants, debt plus stock), unit price, and total amount of securities to be sold in this offering. If securities are not just common stock, indicate by type, interest, maturity, and conversion conditions.
— Show the percentage of the company that the investors of this offering will hold after it is completed or after exercise of any stock conversion or purchase rights in the case of convertible debentures or warrants.
— Securities sold through a private placement and that therefore are exempt from SEC registration should include the following statement in this part of the plan:

The shares being sold pursuant to this offering are restricted securities and may not be resold readily. The prospective investor should recognize that such securities might be restricted as to resale for an indefinite period of time. Each purchaser will be required to execute a Non-Distribution Agreement satisfactory in form to corporate counsel.

C. *Capitalization:*
— Present in tabular form the current and proposed (postoffering) number of outstanding shares of common stock. Indicate any shares offered by key management people and show the number of shares that they will hold after completion of the proposed financing.
— Indicate how many shares of your company's common stock will remain authorized but unissued after the offering and how many of these will be reserved for stock options for future key employees.

D. *Use of funds.* Investors like to know how their money is going to be spent. Provide a brief description of how the capital raised will be used. Summarize as specifically as possible what amount will be used for such things as product design and development, capital equipment, marketing, and general working capital needs.

E. *Investors' return.* Indicate how your valuation and proposed ownership shares will result in the desired rate of return for the investors you have targeted and what the likely harvest or exit mechanism (IPO, outright sale, merger, MBO, etc.) will be.

XIII. Appendixes

Include pertinent information here that is too extensive for the body of the business plan but which is necessary (product specs or photos; lists of references; suppliers of critical components; special location factors, facilities, or technical analyses; reports from consultants or technical experts; and copies of any critical regulatory approval, licenses, etc).

STEP 5

Integrate Your Discrete Sections into a Coherent and Logical Business Plan That Can Be Used for the Purpose For Which It Is Created.

STEP 6

Get Feedback; if Your Plan Is to Be Submitted to Outside Investors, Have Your Plan Reviewed By Your Attorney. Once written, it is recommended that you get the plan reviewed. No matter how good you and your team are, you will most likely overlook issues and treat aspects of your venture in a manner that is less than clear. A good reviewer can give you the benefit of an outside objective evaluation. Your attorney can make sure that there are no misleading statements in your plan and that it contains all the caveats and the like.

Chapter Summary

1. The business plan is more of a process and work in progress than an end in itself.
2. Given today's pace of change in all areas affecting an enterprise, the plan is obsolete the moment it emerges from the printer.
3. The business plan is a blueprint and flight plan for a journey that converts ideas into opportunities, articulates and manages risk and reward, and articulates the likely *fit* and timing for a venture.
4. Ironically, the numbers in a business plan don't matter, but the economics of the business model and value proposition matter enormously.
5. The plan is not the business; in fact, some of the most successful ventures ever were launched without a formal business plan or with one that would be considered weak or flawed.
6. Preparing and presenting the plan to prospective investors is one of the best ways for the team to have a trial marriage, to learn about the venture strategy, and to determine who can add the greatest value.
7. The dehydrated business plan can be a valuable shortcut in the process of creating, shaping, and molding an idea into a business.

Study Questions

1. What is a business plan, for whom is it prepared, and why?
2. What should a complete business plan include?

3. Who should prepare the business plan?

4. How is the plan used by potential investors, and what are the four anchors they are attempting to validate?

5. What is a "dehydrated business plan," and when and why can it be an effective tool?

6. What does this mean: The numbers in the plan don't matter? Please explain.

7. How can entrepreneurs use the business plan process to identify the best team members, directors, and value-added investors?

8. Prepare an outline of a business plan tailored to the specific venture you have in mind.

MIND STRETCHERS

Have You Considered?

1. You have sell-sell-sell, but it has to be tempered with listening, inquiry, and learning. Can you think of a time when you have oversold? What did you learn from that experience?

2. Under what conditions and circumstances is it not to your advantage to prepare a business plan?

3. Identify three businesses that exceed $10 million in sales, are profitable, and did not have a business plan at launch. Why, and what did you learn from this?

4. Some of the most valuable critiques and inputs on your venture will come from outside your team. Who else should review your plan; who knows the industry/market/technology/competitors?

5. A good friend of yours offers a look at a business plan. It turns out that you are a director of a company who is a potential competitor of the venture proposed in the plan. What would you do?

Case

Douglas Ranalli and Shae Plimley*

Preparation Questions

1. Evaluate the opportunity and FAX International's performance and financing requirements.

2. What financing strategies and capital structure should FAX International pursue?

3. What would you recommend to Ranalli for a deal proposal? The minimum number of shares and what share price Ranalli should accept?

4. What should Doug do? Why?

Douglas J. Ranalli

As he left the office March 23, 1992, Doug Ranalli, founder and president of FAX International (FI), said goodnight to the engineers and salespeople that were working late again. It was the end of another long and exhausting day. He began the 20-minute drive from his Burlington, Massachusetts, office to his home in Cambridge with a lot on his mind. Ranalli knew he had some important decisions to make, and soon. He had to decide whether or not to launch the FI service, now several weeks overdue, with its imperfections. He also needed to decide how much money to raise and under what terms.

Ranalli had begun building FI some 18 months earlier after he came up with the idea of starting a private telecommunications network exclusively for facsimile traffic between the United States and Tokyo. The last year had been spent assembling the management team, designing and building the network, and recruiting and training the sales and service groups. After more than two months of identifying potential customers, the sales force had finally commenced selling the service on March 9, promising the customers a start date during the next week to 10 days.

However, the network, originally scheduled for a February 1 start date, was still experiencing technical difficulties and thus was not yet operational. Certain bugs in the software and in the vendor hardware were causing periodic shutdowns and the loss of test documents. The customers who had been sold in the first week had now waited two weeks for the network to go online and the sales force was running out of excuses. To make matters worse, due to the length of this unexpected delay, FI was out of money. The private investors Ranalli had lined up

*Benjamin Campbell (MBA 1992) prepared this case under the supervision of Professor Jeffry A. Timmons as the basis for class discussion, rather than to illustrate either effective or ineffective handling of an administrative situation. Copyright © 1993 by the President and Fellows of Harvard College.

for the next round of financing were all waiting for an operational network before they invested.

Ranalli was faced with a serious dilemma. On the one hand, he could bring the imperfect network online to get the much needed cash infusion, yet he ran the risk of losing customers and demoralizing the sales and service people if the system experienced shutdowns. On the other hand, he could wait until the system was fully debugged before going online, which could take weeks. And he was already running on fumes financially. The costs in lost momentum would be tremendous if he had to slow or stop operations due to lack of funds.

In addition, Ranalli wondered how much money he should raise in this round of financing and at what price. The sales in minutes of traffic/day seemed to be holding at twice the projected business plan assumptions. (See *Exhibits A* through *D* for pro forma assumptions.) If this kept up, FI would be able to finance operations from internally generated funds sooner than expected. In fact, Ranalli hoped that this would be the last financing round FI would need before he expanded to other international locations later in the year.

Company History

Ranalli started his first business, *Student Life* magazine, while studying industrial engineering at Cornell University. After selling *Student Life* to Time, Inc., in 1987, he worked at Time, Inc., for one year, after which he entered the Harvard Business School (HBS). While at HBS he searched for new business ideas to pursue upon graduation. Given the fast pace of growth in information technology industries and his background in engineering, he decided to focus on areas involving information technology. Ranalli firmly believed that he could start a successful entrepreneurial venture in an area in which he had little or no experience, as long as he researched the industry and the idea thoroughly.

Throughout his second year at HBS, Ranalli tried to think of ideas and either prove or disprove their viability by researching them in his spare time. He came up with eight possible ventures that he thought were worthy of pursuit but proceeded to discard each of them. In his last semester (spring 1990) he completed an independent research report on his most promising idea to date, only to conclude at the end of the study that it, too, was not viable.

Ranalli graduated as a Baker Scholar with the HBS class of 1990 and still had no business to pursue. He had spent the summer after his first year working for a prominent consulting firm that had given him a very lucrative employment offer. Determined to launch an entrepreneurial venture, Ranalli decided to dedicate the summer to finding a viable business idea. He informed the firm that he would begin work in September if he was unsuccessful. The firm was supportive, due in part to their skepticism regarding his chances of success.

In late July, while reading through an AT&T technology journal, Ranalli believed he had found the concept he had been searching for. The article described the different types of information that people were sending over telephone lines. It explained that the phone companies had no idea whether the open line was being used for voice or data. More importantly, it revealed that data travels on a phone line seven times more efficiently than voice traffic. Thus, when a fax is sent over the telephone line, only one-seventh of the line is being used, yet the phone company must dedicate an entire line to the call since it has no idea whether voice or data traffic is on the line. The business, in its most basic form, was born. Ranalli knew that if he could build a network exclusively for facsimile traffic, then he could, with the right equipment, send seven times the amount of data that a normal fax machine could send in a given time period. A quick phone call to the author of the article verified his assumption about the fundamental viability of such a business.

Ranalli spent the next several days calling the valuable contacts he had made in the industry while researching ideas over the past year and a half. His initial questions were very simple. Will the idea work? Is anyone else already doing it? Are there any regulations against it?

Over the course of the next month, Ranalli was able to work out enough of the basic details, including the decision to focus on high-cost international traffic, to feel comfortable turning down the consulting offer and pursuing FAX International. He recalled:

> Before I felt comfortable writing a business plan or asking anyone to invest, I needed to know a lot more and I needed a director of engineering. I searched for three months before I found someone. I soon discovered I was mistaken and had to fire him after only a month. That was a very difficult decision. It was not until the next February [1991] that I found Tom Sosnowski.

At age 52, Tom Sosnowski, PhD, the new vice president and director of engineering, had spent most of his adult life in either engineering project management or product development, including 12 years at AT&T Bell Labs and 4 years at GTE. He had been an engineering management consultant for the last six years prior to joining Ranalli at FI. (*Exhibit E* contains Ranalli's and Sosnowski's resumes.) Sosnowski was a true expert in this field. Ranalli commented later:

> It was a very difficult decision for me. Although I don't feel comfortable discussing the details, let's just say I had to give up more of the company than I had originally intended in order to get him. But in the end, I knew that he could get the job done. I knew that I needed his expertise. I knew that he shared the vision. And I knew that he was a good man and that we would get along well.
>
> It just doesn't pay to be greedy. Sure, I could have fought tooth and nail and held on to a few extra percent of the company, but what's a few extra percent of nothing if the business doesn't fly because I was too focused on the money and not on getting the job done?

From the Original Business Plan (December 1991) Pro Forma Revenue/Expense Breakdown (Year 1)

Detailed Revenue

United States:

Average price/minute	$0.75	
Monthly growth rate	500 minutes/sales rep	

1992	Jan.	Feb.	Mar.	Apr.	May	June	July	Aug.	Sept.	Oct.	Nov.	Dec.	Total Year
Free minutes/day	0	1,000	1,000	1,000	1,000	1,000	1,000	1,000	1,000	1,000	1,000	1,000	
Net new minutes/day	0	500	1,500	2,000	2,500	2,500	2,500	2,500	2,500	2,500	2,500	2,500	
Total paid minutes/day	0	500	2,000	4,000	6,500	9,000	11,500	14,000	16,500	19,000	21,500	24,000	
Total minutes/month (month = 20 days)	0	10,000	40,000	80,000	130,000	180,000	230,000	280,000	330,000	380,000	430,000	480,000	2,570,000
Monthly traffic revenue	0	$7,500	$30,000	$60,000	$ 97,500	$135,000	$172,500	$210,000	$247,500	$285,000	$322,500	$360,000	$1,927,500
Uncollectibles (1%)	0	(75)	(300)	(600)	(975)	(1,350)	(1,725)	(2,100)	(2,475)	(2,850)	(3,225)	(3,600)	(19,275)
Autodialer rental revenue	0	333	1,333	2,667	4,333	6,000	7,667	9,333	11,000	12,667	14,333	16,000	85,667
Net monthly U.S. revenue	0	$7,758	$31,033	$62,067	$100,858	$139,650	$178,442	$217,233	$256,025	$294,817	$333,608	$372,400	$1,993,892

Japan joint venture: *

Average price/minute:	$0.35	
Monthly growth rate:	1,500 minutes/day	

	Jan.	Feb.	Mar.	Apr.	May	June	July	Aug.	Sept.	Oct.	Nov.	Dec.	Total Year
Total paid minutes/day	0	0	0	0	0	0	0	500	2,000	3,500	5,000	6,500	
Total minutes/month	0	0	0	0	0	0	0	10,000	40,000	70,000	100,000	130,000	350,000
Net Japanese revenue	0	0	0	0	0	0	0	3,500	14,000	24,500	35,000	45,500	122,500
Total U.S./Japan revenues	0	$7,758	$31,033	$62,067	$100,858	$139,650	$178,442	$220,733	$270,025	$319,317	$368,608	$417,900	$2,116,392

*The Japan joint venture was part of Ranalli's original plan to have a partner in Japan to sell traffic from Japan to the United States. As of September 1992, a joint venture partner had not been found.

(Continued)

EXHIBIT A (continued)

Detailed Expenses

	1992 Jan.	Feb.	Mar.	Apr.	May	June	July	Aug.	Sept.	Oct.	Nov.	Dec.	Total Year
Technical development:													
Salaries	$30,000	$30,000	$30,000	$30,000	$30,000	$30,000	$30,000	$30,000	$30,000	$30,000	$30,000	$30,000	$360,000
Other expenses	2,000	2,000	2,000	2,000	2,000	2,000	2,000	2,000	2,000	2,000	2,000	2,000	24,000
Subtotal:	$32,000	$32,000	$32,000	$32,000	$32,000	$32,000	$32,000	$32,000	$32,000	$32,000	$32,000	$32,000	$384,000
Sales expenses:													
Douglas Ranalli	5,000	5,000	5,000	5,000	5,000	5,000	5,000	5,000	5,000	5,000	5,000	5,000	60,000
Number of sales reps	5	5	5	5	5	5	5	5	5	5	5	5	
Base salaries	15,000	15,000	15,000	15,000	15,000	15,000	15,000	15,000	15,000	15,000	15,000	15,000	180,000
Sales commissions	0	388	1,552	3,103	5,043	6,983	8,922	10,862	12,801	14,741	16,680	18,620	99,695
Sales expenses	6,000	10,500	10,500	10,500	10,500	10,500	10,500	10,500	10,500	10,500	10,500	10,500	121,500
Office supplies	5,000	1,000	1,000	1,000	1,000	1,000	1,000	1,000	1,000	1,000	1,000	1,000	16,000
Headhunter fees	8,000	0	0	0	0	0	0	0	0	0	0	0	8,000
Subtotal:	$39,005	$31,893	$33,057	$34,608	$36,548	$38,548	$40,427	$42,367	$44,306	$46,246	$48,185	$50,125	$485,255
Japanese joint venture:													
Country manager	0	0	0	0	0	0	0	0	0	0	0	0	0
Chuo Coopers & Lybrand	2,500	2,500	2,500	2,500	2,500	2,500	2,500	2,500	2,500	2,500	2,500	2,500	30,000
Subtotal:	$ 2,500	$ 2,500	$ 2,500	$ 2,500	$ 2,500	$ 2,500	$ 2,500	$ 2,500	$ 2,500	$ 2,500	$ 2,500	$ 2,500	$ 30,000
Network hardware:	12,800	14,240	14,240	15,680	15,680	17,120	17,120	18,560	18,560	20,000	21,440	21,440	206,880
Network hardware lease	0	0	0	0	0	0	0	1,440	1,440	1,440	2,880	2,880	10,080
Japanese J/V hardware	2,000	2,000	2,000	2,080	2,773	3,467	4,160	4,853	5,547	6,240	6,933	7,627	49,680
Auto-dialer lease	1,000	1,000	1,000	1,000	1,000	1,000	1,000	1,000	1,000	1,000	1,000	1,000	12,000
Tokyo engineer	0	6,500	6,500	6,500	10,000	10,000	10,000	10,000	10,000	10,000	10,000	10,000	99,500
Equipment housing	25,000	0	0	0	10,000	0	45,000	0	0	25,000	0	0	105,000
Installation	0	1,440	0	1,520	693	2,133	693	3,573	693	2,133	3,573	693	17,147
Up-front deposits	0	0	0	0	0	0	0	0	0	0	0	0	
Extended service contract	1,156	1,269	1,269	1,388	1,442	1,608	1,663	1,942	1,996	2,163	2,442	2,496	20,831
Equipment insurance	385	423	423	463	481	536	554	647	665	721	814	832	6,944
Subtotal:	$ 42,342	$ 26,872	$ 25,432	$ 28,630	$ 42,069	$ 35,864	$ 80,190	$ 42,016	$ 39,901	$ 68,697	$ 49,082	$ 46,968	$528,062
Network asset value	$462,500	$507,500	$507,500	$555,000	$576,667	$643,333	$665,000	$776,667	$798,333	$865,000	$976,667	$998,333	

(Continued)

EXHIBIT A (concluded)

	1992 Jan.	Feb.	Mar.	Apr.	May	June	July	Aug.	Sept.	Oct.	Nov.	Dec.	Total Year
Communications:													
Average variable cost (per minute)	$ 0.18	$ 0.18	$ 0.18	$ 0.18	$ 0.13	$ 0.13	$ 0.13	$ 0.13	$ 0.13	$ 0.13	$ 0.13	$ 0.13	
U.S. variable costs	0	500	500	500	500	500	500	500	500	500	500	500	6,500
Japanese JV costs	0	5,400	10,800	18,000	19,500	26,000	32,500	39,000	45,500	52,000	58,500	65,000	372,200
Number of kbps channels	0	0	0	0	0	0	0	1,350	5,400	9,450	13,500	17,550	47,250
Fractional T1	0	1	2	4	5	7	8	10	11	13	15	16	
Digital service	1,500	9,700	15,400	23,800	31,150	37,750	37,750	49,800	49,800	58,800	58,800	58,800	431,550
Local loop service	2,100	1,200	2,400	4,800	4,800	4,800	4,800	4,800	4,800	4,800	4,800	4,800	48,300
Installation	1,000	2,100	2,100	3,100	3,100	3,100	4,100	5,300	5,300	6,300	7,500	8,500	52,600
Subtotal	$ 4,600	$ 18,900	$ 31,200	$ 50,200	$ 59,050	$ 72,650	$ 79,650	$100,750	$111,300	$131,850	$143,600	$155,150	$ 958,400
Account management:													
VP account management	3,500	3,500	3,500	3,500	3,500	3,500	3,500	3,500	3,500	3,500	3,500	3,500	42,000
Full-time AMs	2,000	4,000	4,000	4,000	4,000	4,000	4,000	4,000	4,000	4,000	4,000	4,000	46,800
Peak period reps	0	0	0	0	0	0	1,000	1,000	2,000	2,000	3,000	3,000	12,000
Evening AM	0	2,000	2,000	2,000	2,000	2,000	2,000	2,000	2,000	2,000	2,000	2,000	22,000
Other expenses	2,000	2,000	2,000	2,000	2,000	2,000	2,000	2,000	2,000	2,000	2,000	2,000	58,000
Number of AMs	2	4	4	4	4	4	5	5	6	6	7	7	
Subtotal	4,000	10,000	10,000	10,000	10,000	10,000	12,000	12,000	14,000	14,000	16,400	16,400	138,800
Administrative:													
Headquarters office	2,500	5,500	5,500	5,500	5,500	5,500	5,500	5,500	5,500	5,500	5,500	5,500	63,000
Furniture lease	1,000	1,000	1,000	1,000	1,000	1,000	1,000	1,000	1,000	1,000	1,000	1,000	12,000
Legal and accounting	2,000	2,000	2,000	2,000	2,000	2,000	2,000	2,000	2,000	2,000	2,000	2,000	24,000
Financial consulting	2,000	2,000	2,000	2,000	2,000	2,000	2,000	2,000	2,000	2,000	2,000	2,000	24,000
Office supplies, etc.	5,000	1,000	1,000	1,000	1,000	1,000	1,000	1,000	1,000	1,000	1,000	1,000	16,000
Office expenses	1,500	1,500	1,500	1,500	1,500	1,500	1,500	1,500	1,500	1,500	1,500	1,500	18,000
Subtotal	14,000	13,000	13,000	13,000	13,000	13,000	13,000	13,000	13,000	13,000	13,000	13,000	157,000
Billing and accounting:													
Payroll expenses	5,720	6,300	6,300	6,300	6,300	6,300	6,600	6,600	6,600	6,600	6,640	6,640	76,900
Bookkeeper	1,700	3,500	3,500	3,500	3,500	3,500	3,500	3,500	3,500	3,500	3,500	3,500	40,200
Credit/collections	0	0	0	0	0	0	3,000	3,000	3,000	3,000	3,000	3,000	18,000
Bills/mailings	0	25	100	200	325	450	575	700	825	950	1,075	1,200	6,425
Omissions Insurance	500	500	500	500	500	500	500	500	500	500	500	500	6,000
Subtotal	7,920	10,325	10,400	10,500	10,625	10,750	14,175	14,300	14,425	14,550	14,715	14,840	147,525
Total expenses	$ 146,367	$ 145,490	$ 157,588	$ 181,438	$ 205,792	$ 214,752	$ 273,942	$ 258,932	$ 271,432	$ 322,843	$ 319,483	$ 330,983	$2,829,041
Net cash result	$(147,367)	$(137,731)	$(126,555)	$(119,372)	$(104,933)	$ (75,102)	$ (95,500)	$ (41,699)	$ (15,407)	$ (28,026)	$ 14,126	$ 41,417	$ (835,150)
Total cash loss	$(890,693)												

From the Original Business Plan (December 1991) Pro Forma Statement of Income (Year 1)

	1992 Jan.	Feb.	Mar.	Apr.	May	June	July	Aug.	Sept.	Oct.	Nov.	Dec.	Total Year
Net sales	$ 0	$ 7,758	$ 31,033	$ 62,067	$ 100,858	$ 139,650	$ 178,442	$ 220,733	$ 270,025	$ 319,317	$ 368,608	$ 417,900	$ 2,116,392
Operating expenses:													
Communications	4,600	18,900	31,200	50,200	59,050	72,150	79,650	100,750	111,300	131,850	143,600	155,150	958,400
Administrative	14,000	13,000	13,000	13,000	13,000	13,000	13,000	13,000	13,000	13,000	13,000	13,000	157,000
Billing and accounting	7,920	10,325	10,400	10,500	10,625	10,750	14,175	14,300	14,425	14,550	14,715	14,840	147,525
Sales expenses	39,005	31,893	33,057	34,608	36,548	38,488	40,427	42,367	44,306	46,246	48,185	50,125	485,255
Japanese J/V	2,500	2,500	2,500	2,500	2,500	2,500	2,500	2,500	2,500	2,500	2,500	2,500	30,000
Customer service	4,000	10,000	10,000	10,000	10,000	10,000	12,000	12,000	14,000	14,000	16,400	16,400	138,800
Network expenses	42,342	26,872	25,432	28,630	42,069	35,864	80,190	42,016	39,901	68,697	49,082	46,968	528,062
Technical expenses	32,000	32,000	32,000	32,000	32,000	32,000	32,000	32,000	32,000	32,000	32,000	32,000	384,000
Operating expenses	$ 146,367	$ 145,490	$ 157,588	$ 181,438	$ 205,792	$ 214,752	$ 273,942	$ 258,932	$ 271,432	$ 322,843	$ 319,483	$ 330,983	$ 2,829,041
EBIT	(146,367)	(137,731)	(126,555)	(119,372)	(104,933)	(75,102)	(95,500)	(38,199)	(1,407)	(3,526)	49,126	86,917	(712,650)
Other income:													
Cash interest	0	0	0	0	0	0	0	0	(284)	(872)	(1,395)	(1,520)	(4,071)
Revolver interest	0	0	0	0	0	0	0	0	0	0	0	0	0
Extraordinary items	0	0	0	0	0	0	0	0	0	0	0	0	0
Other income	0	0	0	0	0	0	0	0	0	0	0	0	0
Other income	$ 0	$ 0	$ 0	$ 0	$ 0	$ 0	$ 0	$ 0	$ (284)	$ (872)	$ (1,395)	$ (1,520)	$ (4,071)
EBT	(146,367)	(137,731)	(126,555)	(119,372)	(104,933)	(75,102)	(95,500)	(38,199)	(1,691)	(4,398)	47,730	85,397	(716,721)
Income taxes	0	0	0	0	0	0	0	0	0	0	0	0	0
Net income	$(146,367)	$(137,731)	$(126,555)	$(119,372)	$(104,933)	$(75,102)	$(95,500)	$(38,199)	$(1,691)	$(4,398)	$ 47,730	$ 85,397	$(716,721)
Cumulative NOL's	$(146,367)	$(284,098)	$(410,653)	$(530,025)	$(634,958)	$(710,060)	$(805,560)	$(843,759)	$(845,450)	$(849,849)	$(802,118)	$(716,721)	

EXHIBIT C

From the Original Business Plan (December 1991) Pro Forma Balance Sheet (Year 1)

	1992 Jan.	Feb.	Mar.	Apr.	May	June	July	Aug.	Sept.	Oct.	Nov.	Dec.
Assets												
Current assets:												
Cash	$158,170	$23,065	$624,207	$477,663	$324,068	$204,496	$59,003	$10,000	$10,000	$10,000	$10,000	$10,000
Invested cash	0	0	0	0	0	0	0	0	0	0	0	0
Accounts receivable	0	11,478	45,912	91,825	149,215	206,605	263,996	326,564	399,489	472,414	545,338	618,263
Total current assets	$158,170	$34,543	$670,120	$569,488	$473,283	$411,102	$322,998	$336,564	$409,489	$482,414	$555,338	$628,263
Long-term assets:												
Capital leases costs	0	0	0	0	0	0	0	0	0	0	0	0
Net property and equipment	0	0	0	0	0	0	0	0	0	0	0	0
Intangibles	0	0	0	0	0	0	0	0	0	0	0	0
Organizational expense	450,000	450,000	450,000	450,000	450,000	450,000	450,000	450,000	450,000	450,000	450,000	450,000
Total assets	$608,170	$484,543	$1,120,120	$1,019,488	$923,283	$861,102	$772,998	$786,564	$859,489	$932,414	$1,005,338	$1,078,263
Liabilities												
Accounts payable	4,537	18,641	30,773	49,512	58,241	71,162	78,558	99,370	109,775	130,044	141,633	153,025
Revolving facility	0	0	0	0	0	0	0	0	0	0	0	0
Other current/CML TD	0	0	0	0	0	0	0	30,954	95,164	152,218	165,824	141,959
Total current liabilities	$4,537	$18,641	$30,773	$49,512	$58,241	$71,162	$78,558	$130,324	$204,939	$282,262	$307,457	$294,984
Total liabilities	4,537	18,641	30,773	49,512	58,241	71,162	78,558	130,324	204,939	282,262	307,457	294,984
Shareholders' Equity												
Founders' capital	150,000	150,000	150,000	150,000	150,000	150,000	150,000	150,000	150,000	150,000	150,000	150,000
Add'l paid-in capital	600,000	600,000	1,350,000	1,350,000	1,350,000	1,350,000	1,350,000	1,350,000	1,350,000	1,350,000	1,350,000	1,350,000
Retained earnings	(146,367)	(284,098)	(410,653)	(530,025)	(634,958)	(710,060)	(805,560)	(843,759)	(845,450)	(849,849)	(802,118)	(716,721)
Total shareholders' equity	$603,633	$465,902	$1,089,347	$969,975	$865,042	$789,940	$694,440	$656,241	$654,550	$650,151	$697,882	$783,279
Total liabilities and shareholders' equity	$608,170	$484,543	$1,120,120	$1,019,488	$923,283	$861,102	$772,998	$786,564	$859,489	$932,414	$1,005,338	$1,078,263
Assumptions and Ratios												
Income statement:												
Net monthly sales growth	N/A		300%	100%	63%	38%	28%	24%	22%	18%	15%	13%
Current gross margin		-144%	-1	19	41	48	55	54	59	59	61	63
Current EBITDA margin		-1775	-408	-192	-104	-54	-54	-17	-1	-1	13	21
Communication as percent of sales		244	101	81	59	52	45	46	41	41	39	37
Administration as percent of sales		168	42	21	13	9	7	6	5	4	4	4
Sales expense as percent of sales		411	107	56	36	28	23	19	16	14	13	12
Account management as percent of sales		129	32	16	10	7	7	5	5	4	4	4
Equipment lease as percent of sales		346	82	46	42	26	45	19	15	22	13	11
Technical costs as percent of sales		412	103	52	32	23	18	14	12	10	9	8
Revolver as percent of receivable base	0	0	0	0	0	0	0	9	24	32	30	23

From the Original Business Plan (December 1991) Pro Forma Statement of Cash Flow (Year 1)

	1992 Jan.	Feb.	Mar.	Apr.	May	June	July	Aug.	Sept.	Oct.	Nov.	Dec.	Total Year
Net income	$(146,367)	(137,731)	(126,555)	(119,372)	(104,933)	(75,102)	(95,500)	(38,199)	(1,691)	(4,398)	47,730	85,397	(716,721)
Gross cash flow	(146,367)	(137,731)	(126,555)	(119,372)	(104,933)	(75,102)	(95,500)	(38,199)	(1,691)	(4,398)	47,730	85,397	(716,721)
Changes in working capital:													
Accounts receivable	0	(11,478)	(34,434)	(45,912)	(57,390)	(57,390)	(57,390)	(62,568)	(72,925)	(72,925)	(72,925)	(72,925)	(618,263)
Accounts payable	4,537	14,104	12,132	18,740	8,729	12,921	7,397	20,811	10,405	20,268	11,589	11,392	153,025
Other current liabilities	0	0	0	0	0	0	0	0	0	0	0	0	0
Cash flow from operations	$(141,830)	$(135,105)	$(148,858)	$(146,544)	$(153,595)	$(119,572)	$(145,494)	$(79,956)	$(64,210)	$(57,054)	$(13,605)	$23,864	$(1,181,959)
Operating cash flow	(141,830)	(135,105)	(148,858)	(146,544)	(153,595)	(119,572)	(145,494)	(79,956)	(64,210)	(57,054)	(13,605)	23,864	(1,181,959)
Changes in non-operating items:													
Change in capital	300,000	0	750,000	0	0	0	0	0	0	0	0	0	0
Cash available	$158,170	$(135,105)	$601,142	$(146,544)	$(153,595)	$(119,572)	$(145,494)	$(79,956)	$(64,210)	$(57,054)	$(13,605)	$23,864	
Cumulative cash	158,170	23,065	624,207	477,663	324,068	204,496	59,003	(20,954)	(85,164)	(142,218)	(155,824)	(131,959)	
Maintenance cash level	10,000	10,000	10,000	10,000	10,000	10,000	10,000	10,000	10,000	10,000	10,000	10,000	

Resumes of Douglas J. Ranalli and Thomas J. Sosnowski

DOUGLAS J. RANALLI

Education

1988–1990   **Harvard Graduate School of Business Administration**

Candidate for Master in Business Administration degree, June 1990. General management curriculum.   Boston, MA

1979–1983   **Cornell University**

Ithaca, NY

Awarded Bachelor of Science in Operations Research and Industrial Engineering, with distinction, in May 1983. Member Tau Beta Pi National Engineering Honor Society. Elected President of Cornell University Senior Class, and President of the 1983 Alumni Class. Member Phi Sigma Kappa social fraternity. Elected social chairman 1981.

Experience

1987–1988   **Time, Inc.**

Publisher, *Student Life* magazine   New York, NY

Student Life is a national publication for college students delivered twice a year, by direct mail, to 1,200,000 students living on 600 campuses nationwide. Founded *Student Life* in 1981, published it independently for six years, and sold it to Time, Inc. in 1987. (Details below)

1983–1987   **Student Life Magazine**

Founder and President   Upper Saddle River, NJ

Launched Student Life in 1981 as an undergraduate at Cornell. Raised $200,000 in equity/loan financing after graduating in 1983 to fund national development. Expanded circulation to over 1,000,000 per issue within four years. Negotiated the sale of *Student Life* to Time, Inc., in January 1987 for a multiple of 17 times earnings. Continued as publisher at the request of Time, Inc.

Experiences and accomplishments include:

- Personally sold $250,000 of advertising in the first national issue published Sept. 1984. Clients included: AT&T, Ford, Revlon, General Foods, Anheuser-Busch, U.S. Army, Marines, etc. Increased sales to a maximum of $750,000/issue by September 1987.
- Hired and trained full-time staff including: Editor, Circulation Director, Sales Director, and salespeople. All art, photography, and production positions managed on a contract basis.
- Negotiated printing and production contracts worth $600,000 per year.
- Managed media/public relations. Quoted or featured in: *The Wall Street Journal, Venture, Entrepreneur, Advertising Age, Ad Week, Marketing and Media Decisions, Manhattan Inc.*

Summers

1982   **AT&T Communications**

Summer management development program.   New York, NY

1981   **COMEX Futures Exchange**

Runner on commodities exchange for Continental Grain.   New York, NY

Personal   Married. Favorite activities include golf, skiing, and tennis.

November 1988

(Continued)

In hindsight, one of the best decisions I made during the early stages of the business was to tie the entire engineering group into the company with three-year stock vesting agreements.

Reflecting on this period, Sosnowski commented:

Doug initially wanted me to consult for the company but he couldn't afford my rates so I told him that I'd let him take me to lunch when he needed to bounce his ideas off someone. Eventually, I did do some consulting for him. And after his first head of engineering did not work out, he asked me to come on full-time.

Virtually every company I consulted for had asked me to join them full-time. Doug's offer was the first I even considered. The reason I decided to accept goes beyond the ob-vious opportunity I saw in the Fax International concept. It had to do with how I felt about Doug and his philosophy of treating people. I believe that there is an enormous gulf in our society between what is known about how people should be treated and the way most managers actually treat people in practice. Doug and I see eye to eye on the importance of treating and rewarding people fairly. One doesn't find that kind of match very often.

When I first met Doug, I don't think he fully appreciated the importance or the worth of the engineering side of this business. This value was more clear to me, not just from my years in the industry but from the fees I charged in my private consulting practice. We had many discussions about it and I think we are much more in agreement today.

In some industries, once a product is designed and built, the engineers can just go home. That's not the case here.

THOMAS P. SOSNOWSKI

Summary

Senior manager with experience spanning basic research through product development. Thorough understanding of the role of research in the product development process. Expertise in strategic and tactical planning, project analysis, allocation of resources, program proposal review and evaluation, manufacturability, negotiation with subcontractors and vendors, and policy development. Substantial knowledge of a broad range of technologies, including telephone switching and terminal systems, gas lasers, holography, optical waveguides, and microcomputer-based systems.

Selected Professional Highlights

As a consultant, aided numerous companies in restructuring their engineering organizations. Clients include Fortune 100 companies but the majority are small entrepreneurial organizations. As part of the restructuring, often assume control of the engineering organization and assist in the selection of new engineering management. Products involved range from sophisticated microcomputer-controlled optical systems to high-volume automotive components in which manufacturability and reliability are paramount concerns.

Organized the commercial engineering section of a small high-tech company; oversaw expansion to over 50 professional and support staff with a $3.8 million annualized budget in less than two years. Structured interfaces with marketing to assure proper product configuration and with manufacturing to provide smooth transition into production. Created policies and procedures which established the orderly development of new products. Initiated and directed redesign of product lines; results included reduction in product costs while increasing functionality, quality, and aesthetic design.

Created, staffed, and managed a new department to research new products and services for telecommunications. Initiated construction of an image processing facility to explore new services. Demonstrated the utility of several new communication systems including an innovative visual telephone system for use by the deaf. Research efforts in local area networks contributed to the specialized voice and data networks required to meet future business objectives.

Conceived and implemented many new devices and system concepts, including: An interactive visual communication system which used standard voice-grade telephone lines for interconnection, one of the first systems to contain a microcomputer for system control and signal processing; a mechanism to implement voice conferencing using digital technology, which served as the basis for experimental PABX systems and was later incorporated into toll telephone switches; several new techniques to control light in optical waveguides; mechanisms to improve He-Cd gas lasers, allowing for the first time continuous wave operation in the ultraviolet; new holographic devices including a means to improve single tube color television cameras.

(Continued)

The engineering side of this business is an ongoing thing in a big way. The operation of the network, as well as the design, assembly, and expansion of it, is and will continue to be very engineering intensive.

Commenting on the period following Sosnowski's hiring, Ranalli explained:

Even with Tom's expertise it still took us five to six more months to find the other five members of the engineering team, transfer the vision, find a suitable headquarters, and get moving. Only then was I comfortable enough about what we knew and where we were headed to write a business plan and ask people to give me their money. [*Exhibit F* contains excerpts from the business plan "Executive Summary."]

It was funny—when I first thought of the idea, I actually believed I could get a working prototype up between August and the end of 1990. As it turned out, it was almost a full year later [the following June] before I felt knowledgeable enough about what I was doing even to sit down and write the plan. Planning and budgeting are very difficult in an entrepreneurial venture. And it changes daily in the early stages. No matter how closely you try to calculate a timetable, it always takes longer than you think. There are just too many unknowns.

Financing

As with his approach toward finding a venture, Ranalli's approach toward raising money was unconventional. His initial position was reasonably secure due to the fact that he had saved most of the money from the sale of his first business. However, he was determined to use no more than half of this nest egg. His attitude throughout the financing was that if he could not convince people to invest in the company, then either the idea was simply not viable or he had not yet earned the right to use their money.

Initially Ranalli tried to follow the advice he had heard at HBS, "Raise as much as you can up front." Yet, as hard as he tried, Ranalli found this to be impossible. Several venture capital companies were interested but each insisted on taking the majority of the company. Ranalli was unwilling to do this as long as he thought he could raise the money through private investors. The problem he encountered was that no wealthy individuals were willing to invest in the seed round. They all seemed interested but were not willing to take the risk at the embryonic stage. They wanted to see more than

EXHIBIT E (concluded)

T. P. Sosnowski (Cont.)

EXPERIENCE

Management and Engineering Consultant
Self-Employed   (Jan 1986–Present)

Director of Product Development
Elkonix Corporation, Bedford, MA   (Jan 1984–Jan 1986)

Department Manager
Advanced Communication Techniques   (Jun 1980–Jan 1984)
GTE Laboratories, Waltham, MA

Team Leader, Member of Technical Staff
Computer Systems Research   (Feb 1968–Jun 1980)
Bell Telephone Laboratories, Holmdel, NJ

SKILLS

Management—Highly creative yet pragmatic problem solver and decision maker. Known for logical, practical, and cost-effective project planning and implementation strategies. Exceptional ability to evaluate projects. Good negotiator. Excellent verbal and written communication skills. A thorough understanding of the innovation process, including the transition of ideas from research into product development; a highly developed sense for recognizing the time to terminate development and finalize engineering design. Participative management style. Regarded as a team player with an ability to attract high-quality staff.

Technical—Excellent understanding of a wide range of technical disciplines. Broad experience with devices and systems, hardware and software. A hands-on individual with an exceptional ability to "make things work." Highly creative with superior conceptual skills. Author of 22 publications in reviewed technical journals; holds nine patents with one pending.

EDUCATION

PhD Engineering, Case-Western Reserve University   1967
MS Engineering, Case-Western Reserve University   1965
BS Engineering Science, Penn. State University   1962

Professional Associations

Senior Member, IEEE
Member, IEEE Management Society
Former Officer, IEEE Multimedia Services and Terminals Committee
Listed in *American Men and Women in Science*
Adjunct Professor of Management Science, Wentworth Institute of Technology

---

just the idea. It soon became clear to Ranalli that he was not going to be able to raise the money he needed up front. If he wanted to keep the company, he would have to use his own and the management team's money as seed capital. They would have to take all the up-front risk alone. No one else was willing to share it yet. Ranalli commented:

I decided that the only way I was going to succeed at raising the money on my own was to structure the first round (after the seed round) financing in stages. I figured if I could lay out the startup process in definite stages where each would be complete once a hurdle was met (such as working prototype completed or certain government approval received), then I could convince investors to invest more in each subsequent stage if I had proven to them that I was able to achieve the preestablished goal.

I told them point-blank that if I cannot reach this goal, then I have not earned the right to your money. Thus, it was only as the project became less risky that I was able to gradually find investors to share in the risk. I know I was taking

a chance by raising money in this manner, but the way I see it is that I had no choice. I did not want to scrap the idea and I did not want to give the company away. So I took it as I could get it.

Ranalli found raising the money easier and easier as he got closer to actually turning on the network. (*Exhibit G* summarizes the financing rounds.) Once he was able to actually set a date to close the first round, then most of the investors that had been undecided made up their minds to invest, due mostly to the fact that the price per share was scheduled to increase the day the network became operational. In February 1992, Ranalli commented:

People are as afraid of missing an opportunity to make money as they are of losing money. Once you have delivered on your promises and once you've convinced them that the odds are reasonably good that your concept really will work, then raising money is less of a problem.

Ranalli conceded that the resulting business had become a much larger and more expensive enterprise than

The Business Plan (Excerpts from the "Executive Summary," dated December 1991)

FAX International, Inc., was founded in June 1990 by Mr. Douglas J. Ranalli and Dr. Thomas P. Sosnowski. The goal of the company is to build an international communications network that is six times more efficient at transmitting fax documents than the switched voice networks of AT&T, MCI, and US Sprint.

FAX International's tremendous efficiency results from designing a network with special technology for transmitting fax documents only. A standard international telephone circuit is capable of transmitting data at 64 kbps (kilo bits per second). A standard fax machine however is only capable of transmitting data at 9.6 kbps. Since AT&T and the other major carriers don't know in advance whether a customer is going to place a voice or fax call when they pick up the phone, each call is allocated a full 64 kbps channel. The result is that each fax call utilizes less than 1/6th of the capability of the circuit. FAX International knows in advance that every call carried by the network is a fax call and hence the network has been designed to carry six fax calls on the same circuit that AT&T, MCI, and Sprint currently use to transmit a single fax call.

FAX International's year-long design and development effort has been extremely successful. As a result, the network went into full-scale testing in November 1991, and is scheduled for installation in January 1992. The opportunity now exists to offer business customers a vastly superior facsimile transmission service between the United States and major international city centers like Tokyo, London, Paris, and so on. Superior because it is just as easy to use as direct dial service from AT&T, MCI, or Sprint at half the price. For example, business customers who are currently paying an average of $1.50/minute for service to Tokyo will pay only $.75 with FAX International, Inc. The FAX International network is so efficient that it will provide business customers with 50 percent savings over current rates while earning 50 percent gross margins on the service once a minimum efficient volume level has been achieved.

Minimum efficient volume is defined by FAX International as the traffic volume necessary to utilize a full TI circuit between the United States and any single international city center. (A TI circuit is equivalent to 24 standard 64 kbps voice circuits.) Seven million minutes of traffic per year are required to efficiently utilize a TI circuit. To reach this minimum volume on FAX International's first route between the United States and Tokyo, the company will have to win 3 percent of market for fax calls in one direction from the United States to Tokyo.

The international telecommunications market has historically been closed to competition due to the presence of monopoly carriers in almost every country. But, the regulatory situation is changing rapidly as countries all over the world look for ways to make their telecommunications industries more competitive. In June 1990, the European Commission directed members of the European Economic Community to begin deregulating all enhanced telecommunications services. Similarly, the United States and Japan negotiated an agreement known as the International Value Added Network Services (IVANS) agreement which guarantees U.S. Value-added network service providers like FAX International fair and equal access to the Japanese market. The actions of the European Commission coupled with the signing of the IVANS agreement between the United States and Japan have created an opportunity for a variety of international enhanced communication services between the United States, Europe, and Japan. The opportunities have yet to be exploited due to the time required for companies to understand the recent regulatory changes and the time required to develop appropriate technologies. An article in the June 15 issue of *EMMS* (Electronic Mail and Micro Systems) summed up the opportunity as follows:

What is the magic formula for success in enhanced fax service? Whoever figures it out may turn out to be the William McGowan (MCI) success story of the 1990s . . . Conceivably, a fax from the United States could travel via private lines to Tokyo or London and be delivered with a local call—completely eliminating the need for the international switched network.

FAX International, Inc., is prepared with the technology, the management team, and the regulatory approvals necessary to capitalize on this exciting international opportunity.

he had originally envisioned. By the time he had finished hiring the initial sales team (February 1992), FI was rapidly running out of money. (See *Exhibit H*.)

The FI Network

A user-friendly, bug-free system was a critical factor in determining the success or failure of the venture. User-friendly in this case meant invisible. The less the customer had to change his or her current fax habits, the more likely they would be to use the service. Thus, the concept of the auto-dialer (called FAXLINK) was born. The Sosnowski team designed a device which could be easily plugged into a fax machine, exactly as an answering machine plugs into a telephone line, which would scan every outgoing call. The FAXLINK would reroute only those calls destined for Tokyo over the FI network. (See *Exhibit I* for a FAXLINK diagram.) The call would first go over regular phone lines to the FI node in San Francisco. There it would wait (five-minute maximum) to be sent on the international leg of its journey simultaneously with other faxes bound for Tokyo. Once received in Tokyo, the faxes would be sent to their local destinations over regular telephone lines again. (See *Exhibit J* for a description of the FI network.)

Everyone involved understood the importance of the network functioning properly. If the system was not fully debugged by startup time, many of the customers trying the service for the trial period would probably become

Capitalization

Round	Percentage of Total Ownership Fully Diluted	Number of Shares CS	Number of Shares Convertible Pref. @ $1/share	Debt @ 12% ($)	Total $ Raised
Seed financing (Ranalli, Sosnowski, management team)	71.3%	3,250,000		$200,000	$ 335,000
Reserved shares for future directors/employees	3.3	150,000			
First round—closed February 1992 (private investors)	14.4		655,500		655,500
Second round—proposed to close May 1992 (private investors)	11		500,000	500,000	1,000,000
Total	100%	3,400,000	1,155,500	$700,000	2,010,500

Monthly Burn Rate (000)

Salaries	$ 60
Asset expenses	16
Office operating expenses	15
Expenses in Japan	20
Fixed communication expenses	25
Miscellaneous start-up expenses (lawyers, network installation, equipment, travel)	39
Total	$175

discouraged and decide not to join the network. It was this factor that had delayed the startup from February 1 to late March after the appearance of last-minute minor glitches in the software. In the last week of February Sosnowski commented:

I have never told anyone this . . . but it wasn't until just about a week ago that I really started to believe that this monster was really actually going to work the way we designed it. I knew that it would send faxes as we wanted . . . but it had to be error-free. Up until last week, when we found that burned-out card in the switch at the San Francisco node, we were running tests with failure rates of 30 percent. If we were not able to get them down below 1 or 2 percent then I knew we were out of business. For a while there I was really worried. Now we're running it with almost zero errors and I've shifted my worry to whether or not we'll be able to sell it.

Customer Service

Ranalli understood the importance of outstanding service to FI's survival. It was with this in mind that the network was designed as a total service concept and not just as a discount alternative alone. To aid them in this critical area, Ranalli made yet another move that many would consider unconventional. In February 1992, he hired his wife Shae, also an engineer from Cornell, to design and run their service department. Ranalli spoke candidly about this decision.

Shae had worked closely with me in my first business, *Student Life* magazine. Not only did I find that she was extremely capable but we didn't experience any of the problems that many couples seem to encounter in similar situations. With respect to Fax International, I knew that I would have to search months in order to find anyone as qualified. Even then it would take months more still before they understood the business or the vision the way she already did.

I found that having her in the business gave us another added advantage—better communication with the other employees. No matter how open I try to be with everyone here, there would always be things that the employees would be reluctant to tell the boss. Shae was very close with everyone. And they all knew that if something was bothering them they could share it with her and that it would get back to me right away. This was very helpful in terms of keeping the culture and the communication open and understanding.

Shae's first action in building the service department was to create the position of 24-hour account manager (AM). She designed the role of the AM as the focal point of FI's strategy to compete by offering outstanding customer service. The AMs were responsible for notifying customers of nondeliverable documents. In addition, they were in charge of walking customers through the installation process and monitoring customer accounts for any sudden decline in usage. Furthermore, in an effort to achieve the idea of total service, the FI system was designed so that a user could send a fax on the first try every time. Never again would a customer have to wait by the machine until the number at the other end was no longer busy. Every customer had a choice as to the length of time that would be allowed to pass before they were to be notified that a fax was undeliverable due to a wrong or busy number, or a broken machine at the fi-

EXHIBIT 1

FAXLINK diagram

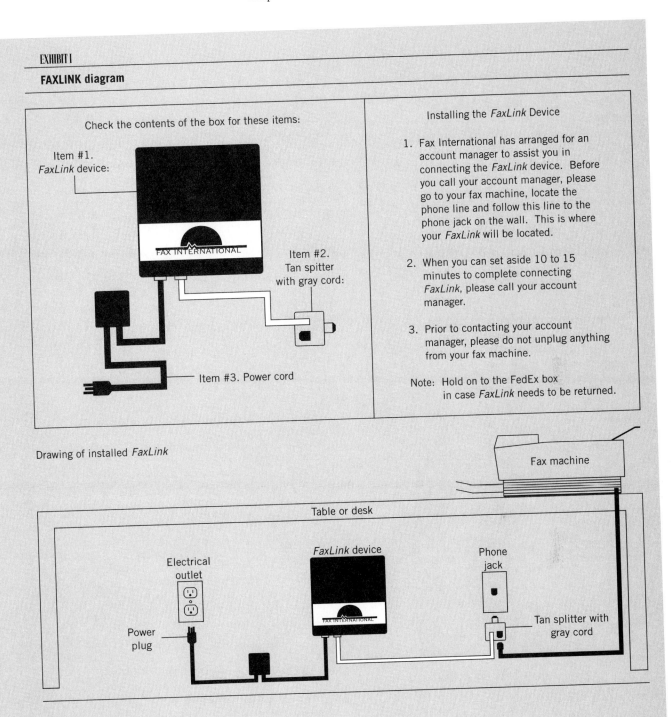

Check the contents of the box for these items:

Item #1.
FaxLink device:

FAX INTERNATIONAL

Item #2.
Tan splitter
with gray cord:

Item #3. Power cord

Installing the *FaxLink* Device

1. Fax International has arranged for an account manager to assist you in connecting the *FaxLink* device. Before you call your account manager, please go to your fax machine, locate the phone line and follow this line to the phone jack on the wall. This is where your *FaxLink* will be located.

2. When you can set aside 10 to 15 minutes to complete connecting *FaxLink*, please call your account manager.

3. Prior to contacting your account manager, please do not unplug anything from your fax machine.

Note: Hold on to the FedEx box in case *FaxLink* needs to be returned.

Drawing of installed *FaxLink*

Fax machine

Table or desk

Electrical
outlet

FaxLink device

Phone
jack

Power
plug

Tan splitter with
gray cord

nal destination. The network would store the fax and attempt delivery continuously until it was either successful or the predetermined time had elapsed, at which time a 24-hour AM would notify the sender and request additional instructions.

Sales

Considering that FI was a new concept, Ranalli found himself faced with the question of how and where to look for customers. He decided early on that he did not want to spend large sums of money on an advertising campaign. First, he did not have a great deal of faith in the effectiveness of such an approach for this concept. Second, he did not want to alert the world and would-be competitors to the idea any sooner than he had to, especially considering the infant state of the company.

Ranalli believed that the service could be sold over the phone via telemarketers. To qualify as a lead, a company had to send a minimum of 10 pages per day. In December 1991, approximately three months before

The FAX International Network

How are these savings possible?

Documents are received into the Fax International network at one of six network nodes within the United States. Once a document enters the network it is converted from the standard fax transmission speed of 9.6 kbps to 64 kbps. This six-fold increase in the transmission speed allows Fax International to use its communications link between the United States and Tokyo far more efficiently than the switched networks of AT&T, MCI, or Sprint.

"Technology is available to build networks that are far more efficient at serving high volume international communications routes. Fax International is dedicated to utilizing this new technology to dramatically lower the cost of international fax communication."

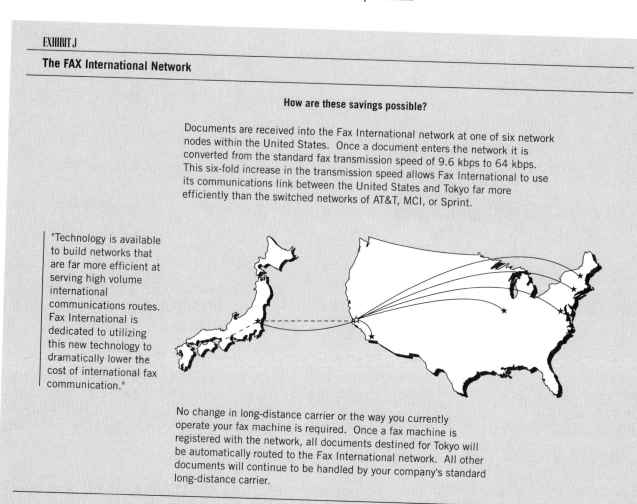

No change in long-distance carrier or the way you currently operate your fax machine is required. Once a fax machine is registered with the network, all documents destined for Tokyo will be automatically routed to the Fax International network. All other documents will continue to be handled by your company's standard long-distance carrier.

the network was scheduled to become operational, two members of the sales team conducted a day-long test to determine the usefulness of the *Directory of Japanese-Affiliated U.S. Companies* as a lead generator. They called 100 of the companies listed in the directory to ascertain the number of pages faxed to Tokyo per day and the key decision maker with respect to long-distance service. Forty percent of the companies called faxed at least the minimum 10 pages daily to Tokyo; many were faxing over 100.

Great care was taken to teach the salespeople to position the service as a fax network only, a totally new concept with a two-week/unlimited-usage free trial. They wanted to completely dissociate themselves in the customer's mind from the long-distance carrier wars that were currently raging. It was decided early on that the service would be priced 50 percent less than the average discount package offered by any of the big three carriers. (See *Exhibit K* for the FI marketing material which compared AT&T, MCI, and Sprint to FI.)

Ranalli found himself facing a variety of strategic issues on several different fronts. As mentioned, one issue was rate of growth. A decision as to how fast he could safely grow would clearly affect strategy in a variety of areas. He had to decide whether or not to focus on just high-volume accounts for fast growth or on many small to medium-sized accounts for better entrenchment. His initial impulse told him that since he had no proprietary technology, he should grow as fast as possible in order to gain scale economies early and enhance his competitive position. On the other hand, if he grew too fast, he could run into two very real problems. The first was the risk of being noticed by, and angering, AT&T or MCI for taking too many big customers. This could easily result in predatory pricing and the loss of critical volume in a very short period of time. The second was the danger of overloading the capacity of the entire operation before new capital could be raised to finance the necessary expansion.

Overall, the primary strategic concern was creating barriers to entry and a strong competitive advantage. Ranalli intended to do this by providing outstanding service through a very user-friendly system and a very efficient service department. This in turn should generate a greater customer base that would allow him to achieve further scale economies on which to compete. What he did not know was how the competition would react to his entry in the marketplace, particularly with respect to FI's ultra-low price.

EXHIBIT K

Marketing Material for FAX International

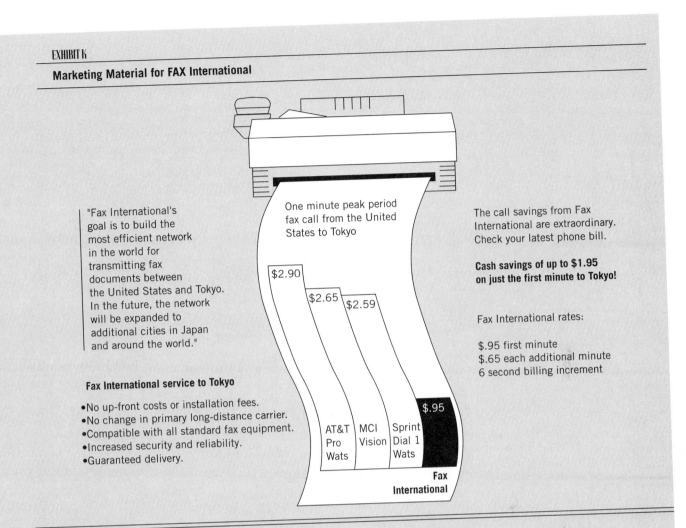

"Fax International's goal is to build the most efficient network in the world for transmitting fax documents between the United States and Tokyo. In the future, the network will be expanded to additional cities in Japan and around the world."

Fax International service to Tokyo

- No up-front costs or installation fees.
- No change in primary long-distance carrier.
- Compatible with all standard fax equipment.
- Increased security and reliability.
- Guaranteed delivery.

One minute peak period fax call from the United States to Tokyo

$2.90
AT&T Pro Wats

$2.65
MCI Vision

$2.59
Sprint Dial 1 Wats

$.95
Fax International

The call savings from Fax International are extraordinary. Check your latest phone bill.

Cash savings of up to $1.95 on just the first minute to Tokyo!

Fax International rates:

$.95 first minute
$.65 each additional minute
6 second billing increment

Competition

Unfortunately, Ranalli was not the first to think of this concept. There were already three direct competitors, each backed by powerful companies, offering almost exactly the same service.

Graphnet, Inc., was a Global Telecommunications company that started in the messaging services business in the late 1960s. In 1979 they received FCC authorization to compete directly with Western Union in the public record message services business. By the late 1980s Graphnet was offering text fax services and integrated packet switched services to its customers. In 1991 they began offering the MEGAFAX service. MEGAFAX was a fax network almost identical to FI in concept. In addition to each of the FI services mentioned above, MEGAFAX offered a voice prompted user menu, document broadcast capability (to send the same document to many different locations), a fax mailbox feature that allowed customers receiving faxes to store them in a confidential mailbox and retrieve them all at once at their discretion, and a special user phone number that allowed customers away from home to retrieve their faxes from any telephone in the world. Further-more, unlike FI, MEGAFAX did not transmit exclusively to Tokyo. Their worldwide network covered all major U.S. cities for domestic transmissions, as well as four major European cities, three major South American cities, the Philippines, Seoul, South Korea, and Osaka, Japan. The savings offered by MEGAFAX over the big three carriers ranged from 33 percent to 45 percent. (See *Exhibit L* for a comparison of direct competitor prices versus FI.)

K-NET was owned by a consortium of major companies (mostly Japanese) such as Matsushita Electric, Mitsubishi, Nippon Life Insurance, Sumitomo, and British Telecom. The K-NET service was called SUPER-Fax and was essentially a network identical to that of FI. The only significant service differences were a broadcast function and a mailbox feature, both similar to MEGAFAX. However, SUPERFax was different from the others in that it offered a range of prices depending on the time of day, much like the three time periods offered by the big three long-distance carriers. In addition, SU-PERFax charged a monthly subscription charge of $15 per terminal and a per-page add-on price for most of their service options that came standard with the other competitors. SUPERFax savings over the big three carriers ranged from 30 percent to 57 percent.

EXHIBIT L

Comparison of Direct Competitor Prices

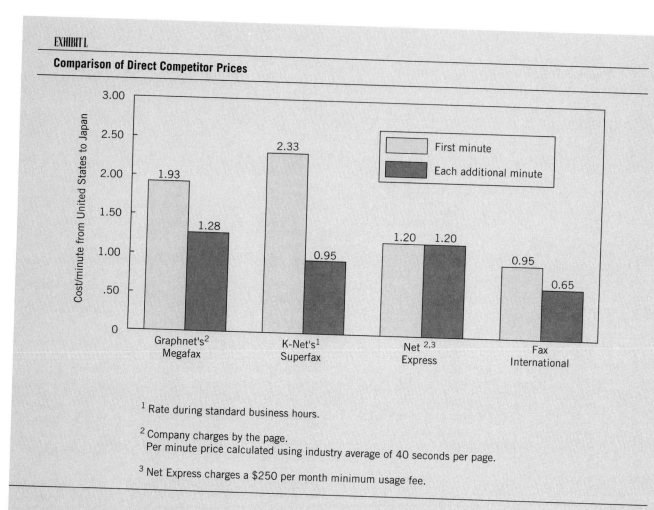

[1] Rate during standard business hours.

[2] Company charges by the page.
Per minute price calculated using industry average of 40 seconds per page.

[3] Net Express charges a $250 per month minimum usage fee.

Net Express, Inc., was founded in 1982 by two entrepreneurs in association with DHL worldwide express and Canon, Inc. DHL, as a major international courier, and Canon, as a major maker of fax machines, each had obvious reasons for being interested in this market. Net-Express was slightly different in the way it functioned. The user had to first dial a special phone number with each fax sent in order to access the network. Other than this, the services offered were roughly the same as the other FI competitors. However, the network could send documents to virtually every country in the world. The rate per page varied depending on country of destination, but estimates put savings over the Big Three ranging between 30 percent and 75 percent.

Ranalli was uncertain as to how these different and powerful competitors would react as FI tried to enter the market. (See business plan estimate of market size, *Exhibit M.*)

Current Situation

By March 1992, Ranalli had succeeded in raising close to $1 million in the seed and first private placement round of financing. His biggest concern, based on the current and projected sales figures, was not whether or not he was going to meet the plan but by how much was he going to exceed the plan. He had been conservative in his projections. Now he was concerned that the possibility of explosive growth was very real. What would this mean in terms of his financial needs? Would the $1 million second round be enough?

On March 24, 1992, Ranalli and Sosnowski made the decision to "light the fuse" and bring the network on-line. Customers were informed that their service had been installed, and traffic flowed without incident for the remainder of the day. The next morning, March 25, the network experienced a total shutdown. Fortunately, the system was designed so that all FAXLINKs automatically deactivate during a shutdown. This means that customers' fax transmissions were simply carried over their normal long-distance carrier rather than being routed over the FI network. However, the service department was flooded with calls from customers wondering why their machines indicated AT&T and MCI had carried the calls rather than the far less expensive FI network. The FI account managers assured the customers that it was only a routine "software enhancement" procedure and that service would be back on shortly.

The FI engineers worked all through the night and finally discovered that the failure had come from a defect

---

EXHIBIT M

Market Size Estimate

The Federal Communications Commission keeps track of the number of direct-dial international calls placed every year over the public switched networks (AT&T, MCI, Sprint, etc.). An analysis of the statistics shows the following trends.

1. Switched international voice traffic is growing at 15–20% per year worldwide.
2. Switched international facsimile traffic is growing at more than twice the pace of voice traffic (30–40 % per year). During the past five years annual traffic growth for all types of international direct dial calls has grown an average of 20%. Japan in particular has averaged growth rates of almost 25% per year while Great Britain has averaged close to 15% per year.
3. Facsimile traffic already accounts for up to 70% of the calls on the United States/Japan route and 33% on the United States/United Kingdom route. These statistics were not found for any other international routes.
4. International traffic is highly concentrated between major U.S. city centers and major international city centers. For example, Tokyo represents almost 70% of the traffic in and out of Japan. Similar traffic concentrations exist in London, Paris, Hong Kong, etc.

International Direct Dial Calls (1990)

	Voice and Fax Traffic (minutes per year)	Percent Fax	Fax Market (minutes per year)
United States/Japan	560 million	70%	392 million
United States/Great Britain	1,150 million	33%	380 million
United States/France	390 million	N/A	N/A
United States/West Germany	700 million	N/A	N/A

Note: Unlike most telecommunications equipment, the FAX International network has been designed to meet the regulatory requirements of every international phone system. The opportunity exists to expand the service to all of the countries listed above plus many others.

Sources: Adapted from FCC and *Electronic Mail and Micro Systems.* June 15, 1990.

---

in the leased line and not the FI system. The next morning the system was back on and the company was back to business as usual. The most important lesson had actually been a positive one. The network worked properly in terms of deactivating the FAXLINKs so that not a single customer's fax was lost.

Ranalli believed he had cleared a major hurdle. The network was now operational and working properly. The possibility of a shutdown was still very real but he felt that any damage that could be caused was survivable. It was time to turn his full attention to his desperate financial situation. He had a host of investors waiting only for the network to come online to write their checks. Therefore, Ranalli immediately issued an "investor update" (see *Exhibit N*) and opened the next round of financing.

Only days after this announcement, Ranalli was introduced to Jeff Parker, a successful entrepreneur Ranalli had read about in several HBS cases. At a lunch meeting the following day, much to Ranalli's surprise, Parker, along with a large family investment fund (Family A) led by Mr. Gulee Arshad, expressed an interest in investing the full $1 million for the coming round. Of course they would want a slightly better deal than the proposed $500,000 in debt and 500,000 shares of convertible preferred stock. They would also need a seat on the FI board of directors.

Ranalli felt he was faced with yet another dilemma; the trade-offs were relatively obvious. On the one hand, one single, very sophisticated investor would make the fund-raising simple and quick. He could be back doing the important job of running the company and planning the future in a much shorter period of time with fewer headaches than he would encounter dealing with a dozen or more smaller investors. Yet, even though Parker seemed a perfectly reasonable individual at their first meeting, he couldn't help but remember the cases he had read concerning a few of Parker's earlier investments. Were Ranalli to accept this investment offer, then Parker would clearly be the most powerful private investor in the company. How much would Parker want? What should Ranalli do about the other investors waiting to write their checks? How much should he raise? He wanted to be sure that they had enough not to have to worry about returning to the well. Yet, he did not want to unnecessarily dilute the value of the stock either. He wanted to be sure to consider all his options. (See *Exhibit O* for information on the capital market environment.) One thing was clear—FI was out of cash. He would have to make a decision soon.

Investor Update (March 1992)

I. Network Start Date

FAX International officially began marketing its service between the United States and Tokyo on March 9th and began carrying traffic between the United States and Tokyo on March 24, 1992. A list of the customers who began using the service on March 24th is attached. The sales organization has done an outstanding job over the past two weeks of bringing on a large number of highly desirable Japanese customers. Based on the initial customer response, it appears that the sales organization will substantially exceed the growth rate projected in the Business Plan, dated December 1991. The first two weeks of selling experience seem to indicate that the potential customer base is much larger and more receptive to the service offering than originally anticipated.

II. Financing

February 28, 1992: FAX International closed its Series A preferred stock financing offer after substantially exceeding the original goal of $600,000. The Series A offer finished $125,000 oversubscribed. Many thanks to all of the investors who have helped to make FAX International's vision a reality.

March 10, 1992: TLP Leasing Programs, Inc. provided FAX International with the final installment of a $450,000 equipment lease package. The TLP lease combined with a $130,000 loan from Douglas Ranalli has allowed FAX International to install sufficient network capacity to meet the growth needs of the company for a period of three to six months.

March 24, 1992: FAX International announced a $1,000,000 Series B preferred stock offering. The initial closing date for the offering has been set at April 10, 1992. The company has been preparing for this round of financing since November and we expect the round to proceed smoothly. Funds will be raised from accredited investors in units of $50,000. Each Unit is comprised of 25,000 shares of convertible preferred stock and a $25,000 subordinated two-year debenture paying 12% cumulative annual interest. At the conclusion of this round of financing the company will have approximately 4,600,000 shares of common and convertible preferred stock outstanding. Series B investors will own approximately 11% of the fully diluted shares of the company.

III. Japanese Approval Process

On January 23, 1992, FAX International received its license from the Ministry of Post and Telecommunications in Japan to operate as a Special Type II International Telecommunications Carrier. FAX International is the first American firm which was not an existing telecommunications carrier to receive this license.

IV. Key Indicators to Watch

In order to simplify the process of tracking FAX International's progress, each investor will receive a bimonthly growth rate report during 1992. The report will contain a growth rate chart which will present information in the format outlined below. The numbers shown represent the section of the Business Plan under Year 1 Detailed Revenues. Please note that the Business Plan shows the company starting on February 1. For simplicity and clarity, all future analysis will be presented with a start date of April 1, 1992.

	April Month 1	May Month 2	June Month 3	July Month 4
Business plan	500*	1,500	2,000	2,500
New projections	1,000	3,000		
Actual results	(provided at the end of each month)		(to be projected one month in advance)	

*Net new minutes per day

EXHIBIT 0

Capital Markets Environment (1980–1992)

FAX INTERNATIONAL
Selected Macroeconomic Data

	1980	1981	1982	1983	1984	1985	1986	1987	1988	1989	1990	1991	1992 1st Q
Macroeconomic data													
Nominal gross national product ($B)	2,732	3,053	3,166	3,406	3,772	4,010	4,235	4,524	4,881	5,201	5,463	5,720	n/a
Percent change in real GNP	−0.2%	1.9%	−2.5%	3.6%	6.4%	2.7%	2.5%	3.7%	4.4%	2.5%	0.9%	−0.7%	3.2%
Consumer price inflation	12.4%	8.9%	3.9%	3.8%	4.0%	3.8%	1.1%	4.4%	4.4%	4.6%	6.1%	4.2%	7.3%
Unemployment rate	7.1%	7.6%	9.7%	9.6%	7.5%	7.2%	7.0%	6.1%	5.4%	5.2%	5.8%	6.7%	n/a
Federal government surplus (deficit)	−73.8	−78.9	−127.9	−207.8	−185.3	−212.3	−221.2	−149.7	−155.1	−152.0	−220.4	−268.7	n/a
Balance of trade (current account)	1.5	8.1	−7.0	−44.0	−104.0	−112.0	−133.2	−143.7	−126.5	−110.0	−102.3	−8.1	n/a
Yen/dollar	226.6	220.6	249.1	237.6	237.5	238.5	168.4	144.6	128.2	138.1	135.0	129.5	134.1
German marks/dollar	1.82	2.26	2.43	2.55	2.85	2.94	2.17	1.80	1.76	1.88	1.50	1.63	1.67
Financial markets data													
Prime Rate	15.3%	18.9%	14.9%	10.8%	12.0%	9.9%	8.3%	8.2%	9.3%	10.9%	10.0%	8.5%	6.5%
S&P 500 (end of year)	135.8	122.6	140.6	164.9	167.2	211.3	242.2	247.1	277.1	348.8	326.5	417.1	412.7
S&P 500 price/earnings ratio	6.0	8.4	8.6	12.0	10.0	12.3	16.4	18.2	10.4	13.7	15.3	20.5	25.8
Venture 100 index (end of year)	655.7	569.8	715.7	842.6	536.3	626.4	567.6	534.9	546.5	589.8	515.2	922.6	1071.3
Average Aaa corporate bond rate	11.9%	14.2%	13.8%	12.0%	12.7%	11.4%	9.0%	9.4%	9.7%	9.3%	9.3%	8.7%	8.6%
Treasury bill total return	11.2%	14.7%	10.5%	8.8%	9.8%	7.7%	6.2%	5.5%	6.0%	8.4%	7.8%	5.4%	3.9% est.
Venture capital and IPO activity													
Net new commitment to the venture capital industry ($mil)	700	1,300	1,800	4,500	4,200	3,300	4,500	4,900	2,100	3,330	1,520	1,350 est.	n/a
Initial Public Offerings (all Co.s) Number	237	448	222	884	548	362	717	541	280	247	209	393	143
Amount raised ($mil)	1,397	3,215	1,446	12,619	3,832	8,625	22,382	24,200	23,750	13,827	10,122	24,300	7,850

PART FOUR

Financing Entrepreneurial Ventures

A financing strategy should be driven by corporate and personal goals, by resulting financial requirements, and ultimately by the available alternatives. In the final analysis, these alternatives are governed by the entrepreneur's relative bargaining power and skill in managing and orchestrating the fund-raising moves. In turn, that bargaining power is governed to a large extent by the cruelty of *real time*. It is governed by when the company will run out of cash given its current cash burn rate.

There are more numerous alternatives for financing a company than ever before. Many contend that money remains plentiful for well-managed emerging firms with the promise of profitable growth. Yet, savvy entrepreneurs

remain vigilant for the warnings noted here to avoid the myopic temptation to "take the money and run."

While some of these alternatives look distinct and separate, a financing strategy probably will encompass a combination of both debt and equity capital.

In considering which financial alternatives are best for a venture at any particular growth stage, it is important to draw on the experience of others who have already been there. This includes other entrepreneurs, professional investors, lenders, accountants, and other professionals.

In their search for either debt or equity capital, it is important that entrepreneurs take a professional approach to selecting and presenting their ventures to investors and lenders.

Chapter Twelve

Entrepreneurial Finance

Happiness to an entrepreneur is a positive cash flow.

Fred Adler
Venture Capitalist

Results Expected

Upon completion of this chapter, you will have:

1. Examined critical issues in financing new ventures.
2. Studied the difference between entrepreneurial finance and conventional administrative or corporate finance.
3. Examined the process of crafting financial and fund-raising strategies and the critical variables involved, including identifying the financial life cycles of new ventures, a financial strategy framework, and investor preferences.
4. Analyzed the Fax International Japan case.

Venture Financing: The Entrepreneur's Achilles' Heel[1]

There are three core principles of entrepreneurial finance: (1) more cash is preferred to less cash, (2) cash sooner is preferred to cash later, and (3) less risky cash is preferred to more risky cash. While these principles seem simple enough, entrepreneurs, chief executive officers, and division managers often seem to ignore them. To these individuals, financial analysis seems intimidating, regardless of the size of the company. Even management teams, comfortable with the financial issues, may not be adept at linking strategic and financial decisions to their companies' challenges and choices. Take, for example, the following predicaments:

- Reviewing the year-end results just handed to you by your chief financial officer, you see no sur-

prises—except that the company loss is even larger than you had projected three months earlier. Therefore, for the fourth year in a row, you will have to walk into the boardroom and deliver bad news. A family-owned business since 1945, the company has survived and prospered with average annual sales growth of 17 percent. In fact, the company's market share has actually increased during recent years despite the losses. With the annual growth rate in the industry averaging less than 5 percent, your mature markets offer few opportunities for sustaining higher growth. How can this be happening? Where do you and your company go from here? How do you explain to the board that for four years you have increased sales and market share but produced losses? How will you propose to turn the situation around?

---

[1] This section is drawn from Jeffry A. Timmons, "Financial Management Breakthrough for Entrepreneurs."

- During the past 20 years, your cable television company has experienced rapid growth through the expansion of existing properties and numerous acquisitions. At your company's peak, your net wealth reached $25 million. The next decade of expansion was fueled by the high leverage common in the cable industry and valuations soared. Ten years later, your company had a market value in the $500 million range. You had a mere $300 million in debt, and you owned 100 percent of the company. Just two years later, your $200 million net worth is an astonishing zero! Additionally, you now face the personally exhausting and financially punishing restructuring battle to survive; personal bankruptcy is a very real possibility. How could this happen? Can the company be salvaged?[2]

- At mid-decade, your company was the industry leader, meeting as well as exceeding your mid-decade business plan targets for annual sales, profitability, and new stores. Exceeding these targets while doubling sales and profitability each year has propelled your stock price from $15 at the initial public offering to the mid $30s. Meanwhile, you still own a large chunk of the company. Then the shocker—at decade's end your company loses $78 million on just over $90 million in sales! The value of your stock plummets. A brutal restructuring follows in which the stock is stripped from the original management team, including you, and you are ousted from the company you founded and loved. Why did the company spin out of control? Why couldn't you as the founder have anticipated its demise? Could you have saved the company in time?

- As the chairman of a rapidly growing telecommunications firm, you are convening your first board meeting after a successful public stock offering. As you think about the agenda, your plans are to grow the company to $15 million in sales in the next three years, which is comfortable given the $5 million in sales last year, the $3.5 million of cash in the bank, and no debt on the balance sheet. Early in the meeting one of the two outside directors asks the controller and the chief financial officer his favorite question, "When will you run out of cash?" The chief financial officer is puzzled at first, then he is indignant, if not outraged, by what he considers to be an irrelevant question. After all, he reasoned, our company has plenty of cash and we won't need to use our bank line. However, 16 months later, without

warning from the chief financial officer, the company is out of cash and has overdrawn its $1 million credit line by $700,000 and the hemorrhaging may get worse. The board fires the president, the chief financial officer, and the senior audit partner from a major accounting firm. The chairman has to take over the helm and must personally invest half a million dollars in the collapsing company to keep it afloat. At this point, it's the bank that is indignant and outraged. You have to devise an emergency battle plan to get on top of the financial crisis. How can this be done?

Financial Management Myopia: It Can't Happen to Me

All of these situations have three things in common. First, they are real companies and these events actually happened. Second, each of these companies was led by successful entrepreneurs who knew enough to prepare audited financial statements.[3] Third, in each example, the problems stemmed from financial management myopia, a combination of self-delusion and just plain not understanding the *complex dynamics* and *interplay between financial management and business strategy*. Why is this so?

Getting Beyond "Collect Early, Pay Late"   During my 30 years as an educator, author, director, founder, and investor in entrepreneurial companies, I have met a few thousand entrepreneurs and managers, including executives participating in an executive MBA program, MBA students, company founders, presidents, members of the Young Presidents Organization, and the chief executive officers of middle-market companies. By their own admission, they felt uniformly uncomfortable if not downright intimidated and terrified, by their lack of expertise in financial analysis and its relationship to management and strategy. No doubt about it, the vast majority of entrepreneurs and nonfinancial managers are disadvantaged. Beyond "collect early, pay late," there is precious little sophistication and an enormous level of discomfort when it comes to these complex and dynamic financial interrelationships. Even good managers who are reveling in major sales increases and profit increases often fail to realize until it's too late the impact increased sales have on the cash flow required to finance the increased receivables and inventory.

---

[2] For more detail, see Burton C. Hurlock and William A. Sahlman, "Star Cablevision Group: Harvesting in a Bull Market," HBS Case 293-036, Harvard Business School, 1992.

[3] Their outcomes as of this writing have ranged from demise to moderate success to radical downsizing followed by dramatic recovery to still being in the midst of a turnaround.

EXHIBIT 12.1

The Crux of It: Anticipation and Financial Vigilance

To avoid some of the great tar pits like the ones described earlier, entrepreneurs need answers to questions that link strategic business decisions to financial plans and choices. The crux of it is anticipation: *What is most likely to happen? When? What can go right along the way? What can go wrong? What has to happen to achieve our business objectives and to increase or to preserve our options?* Financially savvy entrepreneurs know that such questions trigger a process that can lead to creative solutions to their financial challenges and problems. At a practical level financially astute entrepreneurs and managers maintain vigilance over numerous key strategic and financial questions:

- What are the financial consequences and implications of crucial business decisions such as pricing, volume, and policy changes affecting the balance sheet? How will these change over time?
- How can we measure and monitor changes in our financial strategy and structure from a management, not just a GAAP, perspective?
- What does it mean to grow too fast in our industry? How fast can we grow without requiring outside debt or equity? How much capital is required if we increase or decrease our growth by X percent?
- What will happen to our cash flow, profitability, return on assets, and shareholder equity if we grow faster or slower by X percent?
- How much capital will this require? How much can be financed internally and how much will have to come from external sources? What is a reasonable mix of debt and equity?
- What if we are 20% less profitable than our plan calls for?
- What should be our focus and priorities? What are the cash flow and net income break-even points for each of our product lines? For our company? For our business unit?
- What about our pricing, our volume, and costs? How sensitive is our cash flow and net income to increases or decreases in price, variable costs, or volume? What price/volume mix will enable us to achieve the same cash flow and net income?
- How will these changes in pricing, costs and volume affect our key financial ratios and how will we stack up against others in our industry? How will our lenders view this?
- At each stage—startup, rapidly growing, stagnating, or mature company—how should we be thinking about these questions and issues?

The Spreadsheet Mirage   It is hard to imagine any entrepreneur who would not want ready answers to many financial vigilance questions. (See *Exhibit 12.1*.) Until now, however, getting the answers to these questions was a rarity. If the capacity and information are there to do the necessary analysis (and all too often they are not), it can take up to several weeks to get a response. In this era of spreadsheet mania, more often than not, the answers will come in the form of a lengthy report with innumerable scenarios, pages of numbers, backup exhibits, and possibly a stand-up presentation by a staff financial analyst, controller, or chief financial officer.

Yet, all too often the barrage of spreadsheet exhibits is really a *mirage*. What is missing? Traditional spreadsheets can only report and manipulate the data. The numbers may be there, the trends may be identified, but the connections and interdependencies between financial structure and business decisions inherent in key financial questions may be missed. As a result, gaining true insights and getting to creative alternatives and new solutions may be painfully slow, if not interminable. By themselves, spreadsheets cannot model the more complex financial and strategic interrelationships that entrepreneurs need to grasp. And for the board of directors, failure to get this information would be fatal and any delay would mean too little and too late. Such a weakness in financial know-how becomes life-threatening for entrepreneurs such as those noted earlier, when it comes to anticipating the financial and risk-reward consequences of their business decisions. During a period of financial crisis such a weakness can make an already dismal situation even worse.

Time and again, the financially fluent and skillful entrepreneurs push what would otherwise be an average company toward and even beyond the brink of greatness. What many entrepreneurs may fail to consider is their competitor CEOs who *are* knowledgeable. No doubt about it, such adversaries enjoy a secret competitive weapon that can yield a decisive edge over less financially skilled entrepreneurs.

Critical Financing Issues

Exhibit 12.2 illustrates the central issues in entrepreneurial finance. These include the creation of value, how the value pie is sliced and divided among those who have a stake or have participated in the venture, and the handling of the risks inherent in the venture. Developing financing and fund-raising strategies, knowing what alternatives are available, and obtaining funding are tasks vital to the survival and success of most higher potential ventures.

EXHIBIT 12.2

Central Issues in Entrepreneurial Finance

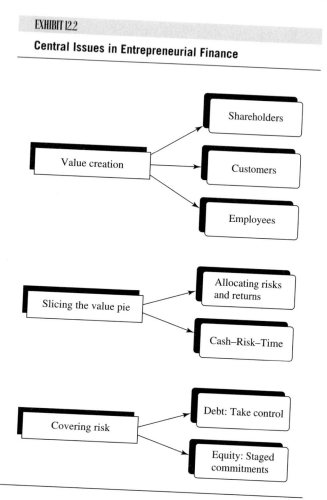

As a result, entrepreneurs face certain critical issues and problems, which bear on the financing of entrepreneurial ventures, such as:

- *Creating value.* Who are the constituencies for whom value must be created or added to achieve a positive cash flow and to develop harvest options?
- *Slicing the value pie:*
  —How are deals, both for startups and for the purchases of existing ventures, structured and valued, and what are the critical tax consequences of different venture structures?
  —What is the legal process and what are the key issues involved in raising outside risk capital?
  —How do entrepreneurs make effective presentations of their business plans to financing and other sources?
  —How can entrepreneurs apply the microcomputer and applications software to the financial analysis and evaluation inherent in the above questions?

  —What are some of the nastier pitfalls, minefields, and hazards that need to be anticipated, prepared for, and responded to?
  —How critical and sensitive is timing in each of these areas?

- *Covering risk:*
  —How much money is needed to start, acquire, or expand the business, and when, where, and how can it be obtained on acceptable terms?
  —What sources of risk and venture capital financing—equity, debt, and other innovative types—are available, and how is appropriate financing negotiated and obtained?
  —Who are the financial contacts and networks that need to be accessed and developed?
  —How do successful entrepreneurs marshall the necessary financial resources and other financial equivalents to seize and execute opportunities, and what pitfalls do they manage to avoid, and how?

A clear understanding of the financing requirements is especially vital for new and emerging companies, because new ventures go through financial hell compared to existing firms, both smaller and larger, that have a customer base and revenue stream. In the early going, new firms are gluttons for capital, yet are usually not very debt-worthy. To make matters worse, the faster they grow, the more gluttonous is their appetite for cash.

This phenomenon is best illustrated in *Exhibit 12.3* where loss as a percentage of initial equity is plotted against time.[4] The shaded area represents the cumulative cash flow of 157 companies from their inception. For these firms, it took 30 months to achieve operating breakeven and 75 months (or going into the *seventh* year) to recover the initial equity. As can be seen from the illustration, *cash goes out for a long time before it starts to come in.* This phenomenon is at the heart of the financing challenges facing new and emerging companies.

Entrepreneurial Finance: The Owner's Perspective

If an entrepreneur who has had responsibility for financing in a large established company and in a private emerging firm is asked whether there are differences between the two, the person asking will get quite an earful. While there is, of course, some common ground, there are both stark and subtle differences, both in theory and in practice, between

[4] Special appreciation is due to Bert Twaalfhoven, founder and chairman of Indivers, the Dutch firm that compiled this summary and that owns the firm on which the chart is based. Mr. Twaalfhoven was also a leader in the Class of 1954 at Harvard Business School and has been active in supporting the Entrepreneurial Management Interest Group and research efforts there.

EXHIBIT 12.3

Initial Losses by Small New Ventures

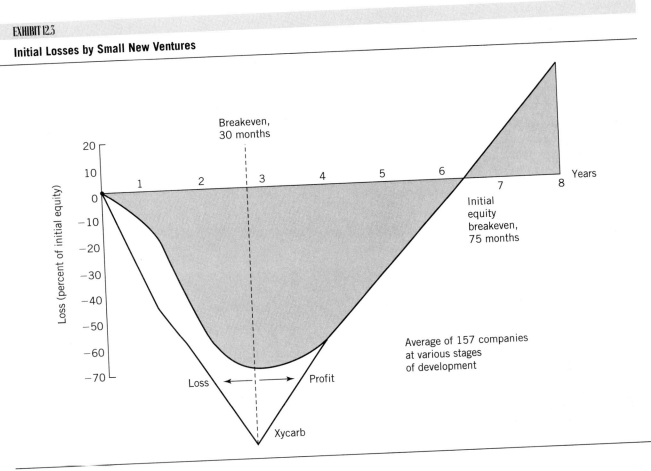

Source: Indivers.

entrepreneurial finance as practiced in higher potential ventures and corporate or administrative finance, which usually occurs in larger publicly traded companies. Further, there are important limits to some financial theories as applied to new ventures.

Students and practitioners of entrepreneurial finance have always been dubious about the reliability and relevance of much of so-called modern finance theory, including the capital asset pricing model (CAPM), beta, and so on. Apparently, this skepticism is gaining support from a most surprising source, corporate finance theorists. As reported in a *Harvard Business Review* article:

One of the strongest attacks is coming from a man who helped launch modern finance, University of Chicago Professor Eugene Fama. His research has cast doubt on the validity of a widely used measure of stock volatility—beta. A second group of critics is looking for a new financial paradigm; they believe it will emerge from the study of nonlinear dynamics and chaos theory. A third group, however, eschews the scientific approach altogether, arguing that investors aren't always rational and

that managers' constant focus on the markets is ruining corporate America. In their view, the highly fragmented U.S. financial markets do a poor job of allocating capital and keeping tabs on management.[5]

Challenging further the basic assumptions of corporate finance, the author continued: "These three concepts, the efficient market hypothesis, portfolio theory, and CAPM, have had a profound impact on how the financial markets relate to the companies they seek to value. . . . They have derailed and blessed countless investment projects."[6] The author, Nancy Nichols, concluded that "despite tidy theories, there may be no single answer in a global economy."[7]

Acquiring knowledge of the limits of financial theories, of differences in the domain of entrepreneurial finance, and of understanding the implications is a core task for entrepreneurs. In order to begin to appreciate the character and flavor of these limits and differences, consider the following sampling:

- **Cash flow and cash.** Cash flow and cash are king and queen in entrepreneurial finance. Accrual-based

---

[5] Nancy A. Nichols, "In Question: Efficient? Chaotic? What's the New Finance?" *Harvard Business Review*, March–April 1993, p. 50.
[6] Ibid. p. 52.
[7] Ibid., p. 60.

accounting, earnings per share, or creative and aggressive use of the tax codes and rules of the Securities and Exchange Commission are not.

- **Time and timing.** Financing alternatives for the financial health of an enterprise are often more sensitive to, or vulnerable to, the time dimension. In entrepreneurial finance, time for critical financing moves often is shorter and more compressed, the optimum timing of these moves changes more rapidly, and financing moves are subject to wider, more volatile swings from lows to highs and back.

- **Capital markets.** Capital markets for over 95 percent of the financing of private entrepreneurial ventures are relatively imperfect, in that they are frequently inaccessible, unorganized, and often invisible. Virtually all the underlying characteristics and assumptions that dominate such popular financial theories and models as the capital asset pricing model simply do not apply, even up to the point of a public offering for a small company. In reality, there are so many and such significant information, knowledge, and market gaps and asymmetries that the rational, perfect market models suffer enormous limitations.

- **Emphasis.** Capital is one of the least important factors in the success of higher potential ventures. Rather, higher potential entrepreneurs seek not only the best deal but also the backer who will provide the most value in terms of know-how, wisdom, counsel, and help. In addition, higher-potential entrepreneurs invariably opt for the value added (beyond money), rather than just the best deal or share price.

- **Strategies for raising capital.** Strategies that optimize or maximize the amount of money raised can actually serve to increase risk in new and emerging companies, rather than lower it. Thus, the concept of "staged capital commitments," whereby money is committed for a 3- to 18-month phase and is followed by subsequent commitments based on results and promise, is a prevalent practice among venture capitalists and other investors in higher potential ventures. Similarly, wise entrepreneurs may refuse excess capital when the valuation is less attractive and when they believe that valuation will rise substantially.

- **Downside consequences.** Consequences of financial strategies and decisions are eminently more personal and emotional for the owners of new and emerging ventures than for the managements of large companies. The downside consequences for such entrepreneurs of running out of cash or failing are monumental and relatively catastrophic, since personal guarantees of bank or other loans are common. Contrast these situations with that of the president of RJR Nabisco. His bonus for signing and his five-year employment package guarantees him a total of $25 million, and he could earn substantially more based on his performance. However, even if he does a mediocre or lousy job, his downside is $25 million.

- **Risk/reward relationships.** While the high-risk/high-reward and low-risk/low-reward relationship (a so-called law of economics and finance) works fairly well in efficient, mature, and relatively perfect capital markets (e.g., those with money market accounts, deposits in savings and loan institutions, widely held and traded stocks and bonds, certificates of deposit), just the opposite occurs all too often in entrepreneurial finance to permit much comfort with this law. Time and again, some of the most profitable, highest return venture investments have been quite *low-risk* propositions from the outset. Many leveraged buyouts using extreme leverage are probably much more risky than many startups. Yet, the way the capital markets price these deals is just the reverse. The reasons are anchored in the second and third points noted above—timing and the asymmetries and imperfections of the capital markets for deals. Entrepreneurs or investors who create or recognize lower risk/very high-yield business propositions, before others jump on the Brink's truck, will defy the laws of economics and finance.

- **Valuation methods.** Established company valuation methods, such as those based on discounted cash flow models used in Wall Street megadeals, seem to favor the seller, rather than the buyer, of private emerging entrepreneurial companies. A seller loves to see a recent MBA or investment banking firm alumnus or alumna show up with an HP-12C calculator or the latest laptop personal computer and then proceed to develop "the 10-year discounted cash flow stream." The assumptions normally made and the mind-set behind them are irrelevant or grossly misleading for valuation of smaller private firms.

- **Conventional financial ratios.** Current financial ratios are misleading when applied to most private entrepreneurial companies. For one thing, entrepreneurs often own more than one company at once and move cash and assets from one to another. For example, an entrepreneur may own real estate and equipment in one entity and lease it to another company. Use of different fiscal years compounds the difficulty of interpreting what the balance sheet really means and the possibilities for aggressive tax avoidance. Further, many of the most important value and equity builders in the business are off the balance sheet or are hidden assets: the excellent management team; the best scientist, technician, or designer; know-how and business relationships that cannot be bought or sold, let alone valued for the balance sheet.

■ *Goals.* Creating value over the long term, rather than maximizing quarterly earnings, is a prevalent mind-set and strategy among highly successful entrepreneurs. Since profit is more than just the bottom line, financial strategies are geared to build value, often at the expense of short-term earnings. The growth required to build value often is heavily self-financed, thereby eroding possible accounting earnings.

Determining Capital Requirements

How much money does my venture need? When is it needed? How long will it last? Where and from whom can it be raised? How should this process be orchestrated and managed? These are vital questions to any entrepreneur at any stage in the development of a company. In the next two sections these questions are answered.

Financial Strategy Framework

The financial strategy framework shown in *Exhibit 12.4* is a way to begin the crafting of financial and fund-raising strategies.[8] The exhibit provides a flow and logic with which an otherwise confusing, if not befuddling task, can be attacked. *The opportunity leads and drives the business strategy, which in turn drives the financial requirements, the sources and deal structures, and the financial strategy.* (Again, unless and until this part of the exercise is well-defined, developing spreadsheets and "playing with the numbers" is just that—playing.)

Once the core of the market opportunity and the strategy for seizing it are well defined as well as possible (of course, these may well change, even dramatically), an entrepreneur can then begin to examine the financial requirements in terms of (1) operating needs (i.e., working capital for operations) and (2) asset needs (for startup or for expansion facilities, equipment, research and development, and other

EXHIBIT 12.4

Financial Strategy Framework

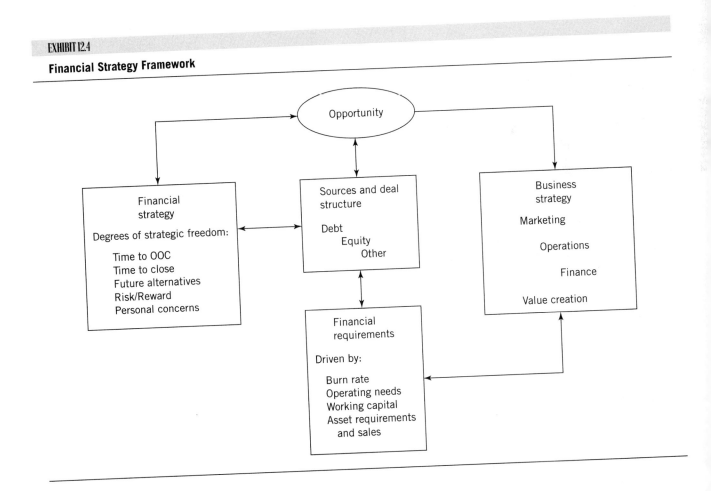

apparently one-time expenditures). This framework leaves ample room for crafting a financial strategy, for creatively identifying sources, for devising a fund-raising plan, and for structuring deals.

Each *fund-raising strategy,* along with its accompanying deal structure, commits the company to actions that incur actual and real-time costs and may enhance or inhibit future financing options. Similarly, each *source* has particular requirements and costs—both apparent and hidden—that carry implications for both financial strategy and financial requirements. The premise is that successful entrepreneurs are aware of potentially punishing situations, and that they are careful to "sweat the details" and proceed with a certain degree of wariness as they evaluate, select, negotiate, and craft business relationships with potential funding sources. In doing so, they are more likely to find the right sources, at the right time, and on the right terms and conditions. They are also more likely to avoid potential mismatches, costly sidetracking for the wrong sources, and the disastrous marriage to these sources that might follow.

Certain changes in the financial climate, such as the aftershocks felt after October 1987, can cause repercussions across financial markets and institutions serving smaller companies. These take the form of greater caution by lenders and investors alike as they seek to increase their protection against risk. When the financial climate becomes harsher, an entrepreneur's capacity to devise financing strategies and to effectively deal with financing sources can be stretched to the limit and beyond. Also, certain lures of cash that come in unsuspecting ways turn out to be a punch in the wallet. (The next chapter covers some of these potentially fatal lures and some of the issues and considerations needed to recognize and avoid these traps while devising a fund-raising strategy and evaluating and negotiating with different sources.)

Free Cash Flow: Burn Rate, OOC, and TTC

The core concept in determining the external financing requirements of the venture is free cash flow. Three vital corollaries are the *burn rate* (projected or actual), time to *OOC* (when will the company be out of cash), and *TTC,* or the time required to close the financing—and have the check clear! These are critical since they have major impact on the entrepreneur's choices and relative bargaining power with various sources of equity and debt capital, which is represented in *Exhibit 12.5.* Chapter 14, "The Deal: Valuation, Structure, and Negotiation," addresses the details of deal structuring, terms, conditions, and covenants.

The message is clear: If you are out of cash in 90 days or less, you are at a major disadvantage. OOC even in six months is perilously soon. But if you have a year or more, the options, terms, price, and covenants that you will be able to negotiate will improve dramatically. The implication is clear: Ideally, raise money when you do not need it.

The cash flow generated by a company or project is defined as follows:

	Earnings before interest and taxes (EBIT)
Less	Tax exposure (tax rate times EBIT)
Plus	Depreciation and other noncash charges
Less	Increase in operating working capital
Less	Capital expenditures

EXHIBIT 12.5

Entrepreneur's Bargaining Power Based on Time to OOC

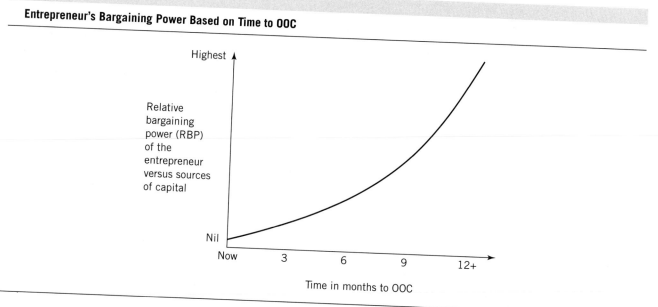

Economists call this figure free cash flow. The definition takes into account the benefits of investing, the income generated, *and* the cost of investing, the amount of investment in working capital and plant and equipment required to generate a given level of sales and net income.

The definition can fruitfully be refined further. Operating working capital is defined as:

	Transactions cash balances
Plus	Accounts receivable
Plus	Inventory
Plus	Other operating current assets (e.g., prepaid expenses)
Less	Accounts payable
Less	Taxes payable
Less	Other operating current liabilities (e.g., accrued expenses)

Finally, this expanded definition can be collapsed into a simpler one:[9]

	Earnings *before interest* but *after taxes* (EBIAT)
Less	Increase in net total operating capital (FA + WC)

where the increase in net total operating capital is defined as:

	Increase in operating working capital
Plus	Increase in net fixed assets

Crafting Financial and Fund-raising Strategies

Critical Variables

When financing is needed, a number of factors affect the availability of the various types of financing, and their suitability and cost:

- Accomplishments and performance to date.
- Investor's perceived risk.
- Industry and technology.
- Venture upside potential and anticipated exit timing.
- Venture anticipated growth rate.
- Venture age and stage of development.

- Investor's required rate of return or internal rate of return.
- Amount of capital required and prior valuations of the venture.
- Founders' goals regarding growth, control, liquidity, and harvesting.
- Relative bargaining positions.
- Investor's required terms and covenants.

Certainly, numerous other factors, especially an investor's or lender's view of the quality of a business opportunity and the management team, will also play a part in a decision to invest in or lend to a firm.

Generally speaking, a company's operations can be financed through debt and through some form of equity financing.[10] Moreover, it is generally believed that a new or existing business needs to obtain both equity and debt financing if it is to have a sound financial foundation for growth without excessive dilution of the entrepreneur's equity.

Usually, short-term debt (i.e., debt incurred for one year or less) is used by a business for working capital and is repaid out of the proceeds of its sales. Longer-term borrowings (i.e., term loans of one to five years or long-term loans maturing in more than five years) are used for working capital and/or to finance the purchase of property or equipment that serve as collateral for the loan. Equity financing is used to fill the nonbankable gaps, preserve ownership, and lower the risk of loan defaults.

However, a new venture just starting operations will have difficulty obtaining either short-term or longer-term bank debt without a substantial cushion of equity financing or long-term debt that is subordinated or junior to all bank debt.[11] As far as a lender is concerned, a startup has little proven capability to generate sales, profits, and cash to pay off short-term debt and even less ability to sustain profitable operations over a number of years and retire long-term debt. Even the underlying protection provided by a venture's assets used as loan collateral may be insufficient to obtain bank loans. Asset values can erode with time; in the absence of adequate equity capital and good management, they may provide little real loan security to a bank.[12]

A bank may loan money to a startup to some maximum debt-to-equity ratio. As a rough rule of thumb, a startup *may* be able to obtain debt for working capital purposes that is equal to its equity and subordinated

---

[9] This section is drawn directly from "Note on Free Cash Flow Valuation Models," HBS 288-023, p. 2–3.

[10] In addition to the purchase of common stock, equity financing is meant to include the purchase of both stock and subordinated debt, or subordinated debt with stock conversion features or warrants to purchase stock.

[11] For lending purposes, commercial banks regard such subordinated debt as equity. Venture capital investors normally subordinate their business loans to the loans provided by the bank or other financial institutions.

[12] The bank loan defaults by the real estate investment trusts (REITs) in 1975 are examples of the failure of assets to provide protection in the absence of sound management and adequate equity capital.

debt. A startup can also obtain loans through such avenues as the Small Business Administration, manufacturers and suppliers, or through leasing.

An existing business seeking expansion capital or funds for a temporary use has a much easier job obtaining both debt and equity. Sources like banks, professional investors, and leasing and finance companies often will seek out such companies and regard them as important customers for secured and unsecured short and term loans or as good investment prospects. Furthermore, an existing and expanding business will find it easier to raise equity capital from private or institutional sources and to raise it on better terms than the startup.

A key message from the above is that awareness of criteria used by various sources of financing—whether for debt, equity, or some combination of the two—that are available for a particular situation is central to devise a time-effective and cost-effective search for capital.

Financial Life Cycles

One useful way to begin the process of identifying equity financing alternatives, and when and if certain alternatives are available, is to consider what can be called the financial life cycle of firms. *Exhibit 12.6* shows the types of capital available over time for different types of firms at different stages of development (i.e., as indicated by different sales levels).[13] It also summarizes, at different stages of development (research and development, startup, early growth, rapid growth, and exit), the principal sources of risk capital and costs of risk capital.

As can be seen in the exhibit, sources have different preferences and practices, including how much money they will provide, when in a company's life cycle they will invest, and the cost of the capital or expected annual rate of return they are seeking. The available sources of capital change dramatically for companies at different stages and rates of growth, and there will be variations in different parts of the country.

Thus, one can see that many of the sources of equity are not available until a company progresses beyond the earlier stages of its growth. Conversely, some of the sources available to early-stage companies, especially personal sources, friends, and other informal investors or angels, will be insufficient to meet the financing requirements generated in later stages, if the company continues to grow successfully.

One also can see that another key factor affecting the availability of financing is the upside potential of a company. Consider that of the three million plus new businesses of all kinds expected to be launched in the United States in 1999, probably 5 percent or less will achieve the growth and sales levels of high-potential firms. Foundation firms will total around 8–12 percent of all new firms, which will grow more slowly but exceed $1 million in sales and may grow to $5 million to $15 million. Remaining are the traditional, stable lifestyle firms. What have been called high-potential firms (those that grow rapidly and are likely to exceed $20 million to $25 million or more in sales) are strong prospects for a public offering and have the widest array of financing alternatives, including combinations of debt and equity and other alternatives (which are noted later on), while foundation firms have fewer, and lifestyle firms are limited to the personal resources of their founders and whatever net worth or collateral they can accumulate.

In general, investors believe the younger the company, the more risky the investment. This is a variation of the old saying in the venture capital business: The lemons ripen in two-and-a-half years, but the plums take seven or eight.

While the timeline and dollar limits shown are only guidelines, they do reflect how these money sources view the riskiness, and thus the required rate of return, of companies at various stages of development.

Investor Preferences

It is important to realize that precise practices of investors or lenders may vary between individual investors or lenders in a given category, may change with the current market conditions, and may vary in different areas of the country from time to time.

Identifying realistic sources and developing a fund-raising strategy to tap them depend upon knowing what kinds of investments investors or lenders are seeking. While the stage, amount, and return guidelines noted in *Exhibit 12.6* can help, doing the appropriate homework in advance on specific investor or lender preferences can save months of wild goose chases and personal cash, while significantly increasing the odds of successfully raising funds on acceptable terms.

---

[13] William H. Wetzel, Jr., of the University of New Hampshire, originally showed the different types of equity capital that are available to three types of companies. The exhibit is based on a chart by Wetzel, which the author has taken the liberty of updating and modifying. See William H. Wetzel, Jr., "The Cost of Availability of Credit and Risk Capital in New England," in *A Region's Struggling Savior: Small Business in New England*, ed. J. A. Timmons and D. E. Gumpert (Waltham, MA: Small Business Foundation of America, 1979).

EXHIBIT 12.6

Financing Life Cycles

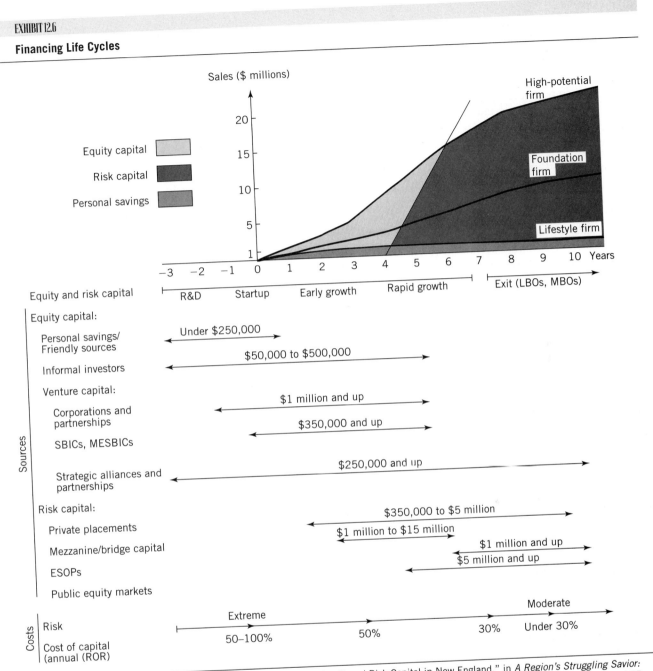

Source: Adapted from W. H. Wetzel, Jr., "The Cost of Availability of Credit and Risk Capital in New England," in *A Region's Struggling Savior: Small Business in New England*, ed. J. A. Timmons and D. E. Gumpert (Waltham, MA: Small Business Foundation of America, 1979), p. 175.

Chapter Summary

1. *Cash* is King and Queen. Happiness is a positive cash flow. More cash is preferred to less cash. Cash sooner is preferred to cash later. Less risky cash is preferred to more risky cash.

2. Financial know-how, issues, and analysis are often the entrepreneurs Achilles' heels.

3. Entrepreneurial finance is the art and science of quantifying value creation, slicing the value pie, and managing and covering financial risk.

4. Determining capital requirements, crafting financial and fund-raising strategies, and managing and orchestrating the financial process are critical to new venture success.

5. Harvest strategies are as important to the entrepreneurial process as value creation itself. Value that is unrealized may have no value.

Study Questions

1. Can you define the following and explain why they are important: burn rate, fume date, free cash flow, OOC, TTC, financial management myopia, spreadsheet mirage?

2. Why is entrepreneurial finance simultaneously both the least and most important part of the entrepreneurial process? Explain this paradox.

3. What factors affect the availability, suitability, and cost of various types of financing? Why are these factors critical?

4. What is meant by free cash flow, and why do entrepreneurs need to understand this?

5. Why do financially savvy entrepreneurs ask the financial and strategic questions in Exhibit 12.1? Can you answer these questions for your venture?

MIND STRETCHERS

Have You Considered?

1. To what extent might you be suffering from financial myopia and spreadsheet mirage?

2. People who believe that you first have to have money, in large amounts, to make money are naive and ignorant. Why is this so? Do you agree?

3. Who do you need to get to know well to strengthen the entrepreneurial finance know-how on your team?

4. Assume that in five years you are financially successful beyond your wildest dreams as a result of the business plan you are now working on. So what?

Case

Fax International Japan (A)

"This is a great story isn't it? It's the bottom of the ninth, two outs, men on first and third, Fax International comes to the plate and . . ."

Doug Ranalli

Introduction

Fax International Japan (FIJ) had come a long way since February 1993, when company President Doug Ranalli held his first meetings in Japan looking for minority partners to invest $10,000,000 in the startup of Fax International's Japanese subsidiary, FIJ. By the middle of August 1993, FIJ had landed the Nichimen Corporation as a lead investor with an agreement to purchase 30 percent of FIJ for 600,000,000 yen (see *Exhibit A*). Doug Ranalli said in his original business plan for Fax International, written during the spring and summer of 1991, "Japanese customers prefer to work with established Japanese organizations. Breaking into the Japanese market as a small U.S. company has proven over and over again to be almost impossible." It seemed that Ranalli had achieved the impossible.

The whole idea of Fax International depended upon opening up Japan-to-U.S. fax transmission. The U.S.-to-Japan route had already been established and was in working order, but only two-way telecommunications would make the business as profitable as Ranalli envisioned. Succeeding in Japan would be Ranalli's go-ahead to open offices around the world. See *Exhibit B* for the proposed structure of Fax International. For background on Fax International, see the Fax International Business Plan in *New Venture Creation*, 4th edition, by Jeffry A. Timmons.

By late fall 1993 Ranalli was entering a new, more challenging and exhausting phase of the FIJ deal. He had won the approval of Nichimen, but was torn between multiple conflicting demands and opportunities. He wondered how best to balance these, at times overwhelming, pressures. Would he be able to seize the op-

Research Assistant Rebecca W. Voorheis prepared this case under the supervision of Professor Jeffry A. Timmons as the basis for class discussion rather than to illustrate either effective or ineffective handling of an administrative situation. Copyright © 1994 by the President and Fellows of Harvard College.

EXHIBIT A

Nichimen Proposal

Nichimen

Nichimen Corporation

13-1, KYOBASHI 1-CHROME, CHUO-KU, TOKYO, 10-4 JAPAN C.P.O. BOX 1138, TOKYO 100-91, JAPAN

August 12, 1993

Mr. Douglas J. Ranalli
President
Fax International, Inc.
60 Mall Road, Burlington
MA. 01803.4517

Dear Mr. Ranalli:

We wish to inform you that we will invest maximum six hundred million Yen for 30% of Fax International. Japan on the following conditions.

1) There is or are minority partner(s) who commit investment for the remaining 19% or more, before we make investment.

2) A market survey by both you and us is to be performed to confirm there are enough users for our planned services to make our business plan realistic and feasible.

3) All other details of conditions to be discussed to reach final agreement between you and us.

We thank you for your cooperation and patience and hope that we can build up a good company together to gain customers satisfaction.

Very truly yours,

Nichimen Corporation

Y.TO
Depart. Senior General Manager
Electronics Division

portunities in both countries without jeopardizing the survival and upside of Fax International? As Ranalli boarded his next flight for Tokyo to begin meeting with investors again, he contemplated his next move and the future of Fax International. The lesson he had learned in the past few years weighed heavily on his mind: Everything takes longer than you think.

At the same time Ranalli was devoting his time and efforts to getting FIJ off the ground, operations in the United States were at their maximum pace. Fax International in the United States (FIUS) would soon be out of cash. The abundance of opportunities, along with shortages of cash and time, proved to be a destabilizing combination (for losses to date, see *Exhibit C*). While Ranalli was in Japan, he was spending time and money that FI couldn't afford. Therefore, he was eager to make a deal and launch FIJ as soon as possible, without compromising commitments to his people and existing investors.

EXHIBIT B

The Corporate Structure of Fax International, Inc.

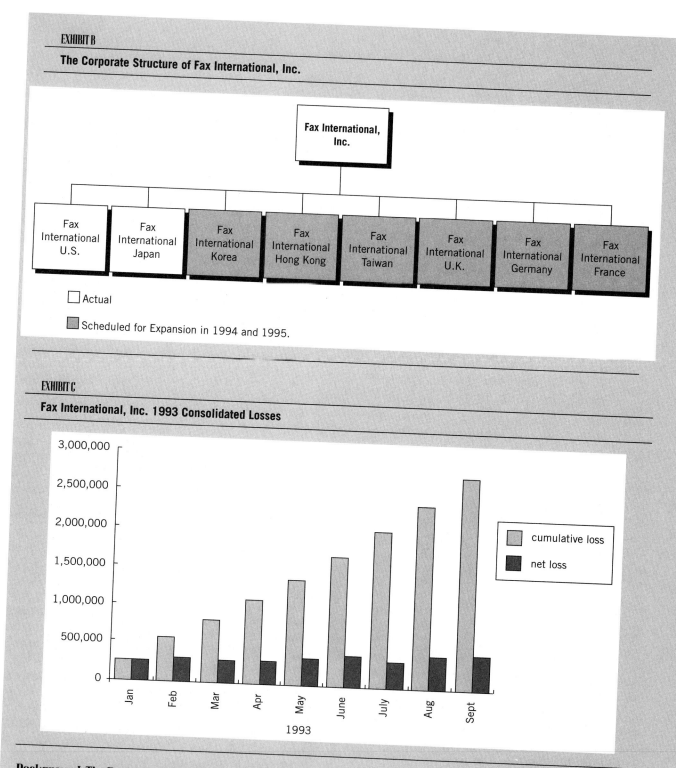

EXHIBIT C

Fax International, Inc. 1993 Consolidated Losses

Background: The Beginning of Fax International Japan

In September of 1992, Ranalli began to develop the strategy for the startup of Fax International Japan. Several expansion strategies were considered: Finance the startup through a franchise approach, allow a local partner to own a large part of the business, demand that FI own a majority and control the business or finance the startup through FI as a holding company. When Ranalli decided to work with Japanese companies as partners while maintaining majority ownership, he began to look for advisors and consultants to help in the process of locating a partner.

In October 1992, while Sachio Semmoto was in transit between Tokyo and Atlanta on business, he received a fax from his Tokyo office. As co-founder and senior vice president of DDI, the Japanese equivalent of MCI, he had to keep in close contact with Tokyo in order to receive information constantly and give instructions regularly. The fax was from Doug Ranalli, a 1990 Harvard Business School graduate and the founder of Fax International, Inc.

Sachio Semmoto was introduced to Doug Ranalli in October 1992 (by his former professor of entrepreneurial finance at Harvard Business School) as a potentially important contact while Doug began the process of building Fax International Japan. FIJ was designed to be the corollary to FIUS that would allow Japanese businesses to send faxes to the United States, and soon around the world for a fraction of current costs. The return lines for FI would be used, which were currently used in one direction only—from the United States to Japan. Two way utilization was economically vital and one of the premises behind Fax International. Since traffic had already been developed in one direction, the network was capable of carrying return traffic at a very low variable cost. The following tables are taken from the Fax International Business Plan (see *New Venture Creation*, 4th edition).

Variable Costs, United States to Tokyo

Traffic Volume	U.S. Reception	Transmit to Tokyo	Local Delivery in Tokyo	Total
<500,000 min/yr	$.15	$.43	$.03	$.61
<1,000,000	$.15	$.34	$.03	$.52
<3,000,000	$.09	$.28	$.03	$.40
<5,000,000	$.09	$.24	$.03	$.36
<7,000,000	$.09	$.20	$.03	$.32

Return Traffic Costs, Tokyo to the United States

Traffic Volume	Tokyo Reception	Transmit to U.S.	Local Delivery in U.S.	Total
<500,000 min/yr	Free	Free	$.14	$.14
<1,000,000	Free	Free	$.13	$.13
<3,000,000	Free	Free	$.13	$.13
<5,000,000	Free	Free	$.13	$.13
<7,000,000	Free	Free	$.13	$.13

Substantial economies of scale would exist in this business by completing the route to include Japan-to-U.S. traffic.

Semmoto immediately understood the importance of Fax International, being a telecommunications entrepreneur himself. Along with Kazuo Inamori, one of Japan's most successful entrepreneurs, Semmoto created DDI in 1984. Commonly equated with MCI, DDI is a long distance company that was created to challenge the established giants, namely N.T.T. In Japanese, DDI's name translates as the "second telegraph and telephone company." An article in the *New York Times* describes DDI:

With its long-distance rates high to offset cheap local phone rates, N.T.T. was somewhat easy prey. DDI grew explosively, following much the same path as the MCI Corporation in challenging AT&T in the United States. It is now the largest of three alternative long-distance providers.[1]

With a successful experience like this in telecommunications, Semmoto was a logical connection for Ranalli.

Ranalli sent a fax to Semmoto's Tokyo office to request a meeting in Japan, during which he would explain his vision for Fax International Japan and get feedback from Semmoto, as a successful entrepreneur and someone who knew the Japanese telecommunications business well. Semmoto was quick to respond to Ranalli's request, telling Ranalli that he could meet with him in Atlanta while he was in the United States. Semmoto, however, didn't expect Ranalli to actually come down to Atlanta. He was sure that the short notice he gave Ranalli and the fact that Ranalli wanted to meet in Japan would be disincentive enough. Semmoto believed, though, that if Ranalli had a "good passion" for this business he would come. "If he hadn't come to Atlanta," stated Sachio Semmoto, "we wouldn't have met."

Sachio Semmoto was immediately impressed by the enthusiasm of Ranalli. Semmoto strongly believed that this type of enthusiasm is necessary for an entrepreneur to take advantage of every opportunity that arises. In addition to being impressed with the man behind FIJ, Semmoto also agreed with the idea of FIJ itself. He had always thought that future telecommunications should be shifted to fax traffic. This is especially true on an international basis, considering the barriers that exist in cross-country voice communication. In fact, the majority of Semmoto's own international business dealings are conducted through fax transmission.

Impressed with the combination of a clearly defined idea and an entrepreneurial spirit, Sachio Semmoto agreed to help Ranalli enter the Japanese telecommunications market. Semmoto explained to Ranalli that he has excellent telecommunications connections. "The top people in this area in Japan are either my customers or sales agents," Semmoto explained. He could introduce many potential partners to Doug Ranalli. In January 1993 Ranalli assembled his negotiating team with Akira Odani, who runs a consulting firm in New York called Odani Research, as the negotiation/communication consultant and Sachio Semmoto as the main source of high level contacts.

Ironically, at the same time Ranalli was preparing to launch Fax International Japan, FI was out of cash again, as expected. Ranalli knew this was coming and planned to raise additional funding from existing investors. He thought these investors would be prepared to invest again if the business looked good. However, FI had to show some form of positive results before asking for the money. Luckily, FI had managed to post a company record sales month during December 1992 due to

---

[1]Andrew Pollack, "In Japan, One Public Offering, Many Consequences," *New York Times*, September 2, 1993, pg. D1.

the efforts of the sales staff during the fall of 1992. FI got through the January crunch by raising another $1 million from existing investors to cover the $250,000 per month burn rate and $50,000 per month necessary hardware financing.

Aside from capital, one of Ranalli's biggest needs was encouragement. Semmoto believed that one of the most important contributions he made to Doug Ranalli was spiritual support. "My role in the process was to give advice," stated Semmoto, "You have to be patient, giving support and encouragement." He realized that the majority of Ranalli's energy would be spent on fighting and protecting himself from attack. Semmoto knew this well from his own entrepreneurial experiences in Japan. He said whenever he would come up with a new idea at N.T.T., his former employer, "I had to devote 90 percent of my energy persuading my associates, while 10 percent was used for actual output." Semmoto and others lent Ranalli emotional support during this demanding pre-startup period.

Doug had tremendous flexibility, said Semmoto, and would spend whole days at the hotel analyzing changed conditions. Additionally, he would go to Japan without specific return dates in an atypical American business style. This way he had the slack to cope with twelfth hour changes in previously agreed upon conditions. Semmoto also observed that Ranalli paid very good attention to each personal detail, like saying hello and greeting others properly. "A chief executive needs a hearty collaboration, a personal, human touch" said Sachio Semmoto, "which Doug Ranalli has."

Neither Ranalli nor Semmoto believed the service of FIJ would be difficult to sell considering its quality. Fax International's network carries fax documents 15 times more efficiently than the voice networks of telecommunications giants like AT&T, Kokusai Denshin Denwa Co., Ltd. (KDD) and British Telecommunications. FI's proprietary telecommunications network would allow FIJ to charge a significantly lower price for fax transmission from Japan to the United States than currently existed. This network is, as of yet, unduplicated. FIJ would enter the Tokyo market with guaranteed document delivery at a price of 120 Yen per minute (approximately 80 Yen per page), while existing carriers charge between 140 Yen per minute and 240 Yen per minute. At this price, FIJ planned to attain gross margins in excess of 65 percent and pretax earnings of over 30 percent (see *Exhibit D*). FIJ's cost advantage coupled with the potential size of the market makes for impressive possibilities. For Fax International, Inc.'s 1992 and 1993 revenues, see *Exhibit E*.

Estimates indicate there will be at least 250 million minutes per year of fax traffic from Japan to the top five world markets in 1995. Already, 30 percent to 50 percent of Japan's international telecommunications traffic is facsimile. With the combination of higher quality and lower price, Ranalli expects FIJ to capture 10 percent to 15 percent of this market within the next few years. FI is already the largest provider of dedicated fax traffic from the United States to Japan and hopes to complete this circuit by dominating the Japan-to-U.S. fax market. Ranalli would need the help of an insider to accomplish his goals, though, and saw Sachio Semmoto as an ideal advisor in the arena of Japanese telecommunications.

While other advisors had tried to prepare Ranalli for doing business in Japan, a successful and well respected Japanese businessman that would support Ranalli, sell his idea and introduce him to powerful and well-connected investors was invaluable. This was especially necessary since a joint venture like this was rare

EXHIBIT D

Fax International Gross Margins

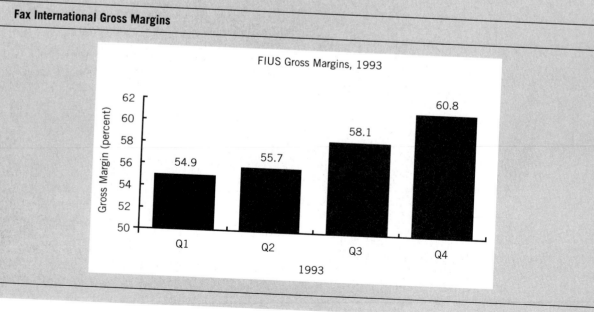

FIUS Gross Margins, 1993

EXHIBIT E

Fax International Quarterly Revenues

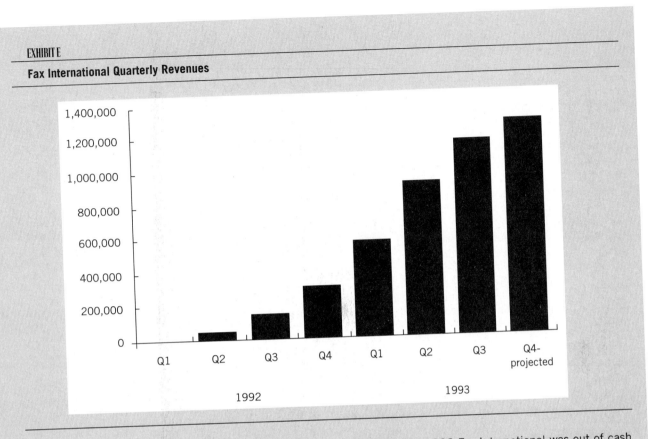

in Japan, as Sachio Semmoto explained. The theory, he said, of doing business in Japan is "if you want to create a new business, follow past examples." Semmoto would have to act as the external stimulant to get potential investors to reexamine their strategies. Akira Odani also played a crucial role as a member of the FI negotiating team during 1993. Odani filled the role of Japanese business associate in the negotiations, with strong consulting and negotiation skills, and was a member Ranalli said he couldn't have done without.

Finding a Lead Investor

In February 1993, Ranalli held the first set of meetings with prospective investors in Japan. He insisted that FI pursue multiple companies simultaneously. The FIJ team met with eight companies on the first trip, although only four expressed sufficient interest to warrant serious consideration. These were Eiko, Nichimen, OCS and ORIX.

In April 1993, Ranalli and his FIJ team held the second set of meetings in Tokyo. These meetings were intended to follow up with several of the first round companies, plus hold initial meetings with four new companies. At this point, only KDD was added to the list of potential investors. In May 1993, Ranalli held the third round of meetings with companies that expressed serious interest in FIJ from the first two months. This was a three week trip, which ended in early June.

During May 1993 Fax International was out of cash once again. The FI team again knew this was coming. Ranalli made the following statement:

Our strategy was to count on the strength of our sales results in the U.S. and good news from the negotiations in Japan to help boost our price per share and our ability to raise additional cash. Once again, we were planning on going back to the well with the existing investors. During the first four months of 1993 we were selling to customers like crazy. You can see the results from our 1993 financial summary. Although the Japan deal was not close to closing at that point in time I was able to generate excitement by keeping everyone informed of my specific results with each potential partner. By the way, my use of detailed investor updates on a regular basis played a key role in my ability to keep going back to the well with the existing investors.

In the end, however, Ranalli decided not to go with the existing investors. He needed to raise the FI price per share since the valuation of FI based on the existing $1 per share price actually put a higher valuation on the Japanese subsidiary than the worldwide holding company. Ranalli was having difficulty in Japan explaining why he wanted $20 million for FIJ when the entire holding company was worth $6 million. As a result, he asked the existing investors to pay $2.50 per share and they refused, though they agreed to pay $1.50 per share—a 50 percent increase.

Ranalli was disappointed in this response. FI needed cash, though, so he decided to offer the $1.50 per share price in a "friends and family" financing round. He specifically excluded the existing investors because he wanted to be able to tell the potential partners in Japan that the $1.50 per share price was actually a substantial discount off the "real" valuation of the company. "This offer was extremely well received," told Ranalli, "Counting the existing investors who also asked to participate, we received requests for $3,000,000 but the SEC limited us to just $1,000,000 based on the type of investors involved in the deal. This solved our problems for another four months." Ranalli had to deal with this financial distraction at the same time he was putting all his effort into making a deal in Japan.

Between each round of meetings in Tokyo, Fax International was constantly corresponding with each potential investor, through either fax or Federal Express. FI provided additional information and visits were scheduled for each of the potential partners to visit FI's office in the United States. Nichimen visited four times In total while the others visited once each.

In early June of 1993, at the end of the third set of meetings, Doug Ranalli returned to the President Hotel in Tokyo and sat down to write an update for his board of directors and investors. How could he sound optimistic? Now that the May meetings were over, Ranalli was left with probable rejections (he quickly found that the Japanese businessmen he worked with never said no straight out) from two possible Japanese investors in FIJ. July 1993 was Ranalli's decision-date goal for securing a partner in Japan. Not much time was left. As he reviewed the performance of FI, Ranalli wondered if he could close a deal in Japan soon enough. Fax International's U.S. operations were out of cash once again, while Ranalli had to invest his time and energy in Japan.

Ranalli believed he needed to secure a major Japanese investor in order for FIJ to enter the Japanese market in fax transmission to the United States. A powerful Japanese investor would give FIJ access to a large customer base in Japan, hiring power and the capital to start up a business that Ranalli fully expected to take off. Unfortunately, two of the potential investors he was introduced to, and negotiated with, were not convinced of the future success of FIJ.

Neither KDD nor Eiko joined with Doug Ranalli or bought into the FIJ idea. Although KDD was very diplomatic and gracious (complete with a dinner banquet for Ranalli and his partners), FIJ would have been very small for KDD. Also, almost all of KDD's new ventures were failures and it had decided to not make any new investments—with no exceptions. Therefore, the negotiations with KDD as lead investor ended. Negotiations, however, turned to the possibility of KDD becoming a sales agent for FIJ, then later to KDD as minority investor. KDD couldn't bring itself to give Ranalli an unequivocal rejection. The negotiations never looked positive to Ranalli, but he wasn't given a clear and formal "no."

Likewise, Eiko didn't take advantage of the opportunity to become FIJ's lead investor, despite spending a long time studying the potential of this business. Eiko & Company, unlike KDD, has been very successful with its new investments, but was still extremely cautious with a new concept like FIJ. Eiko decided for internal reasons that it couldn't support FIJ. Eiko & Company, however, never came out and said "no" explicitly. By the time FIJ received a letter of intent from a lead investor in August of 1993, Eiko & Company was still passively allowing itself to be pursued. Ranalli stated, "Eiko never said no. We just let these discussions die on the vine." Both KDD and Eiko were receptive to meeting with Ranalli and hearing about the FIJ concept, but neither thought it was a worthwhile risk.

Sachio Semmoto arranged the meetings with top executives at KDD and Eiko. Semmoto told Ranalli not to give up and encouraged him to begin the search for another partner. Ranalli didn't need much persuasion, though. He had suffered more setbacks than this while setting up Fax International in the United States. His commitment and perseverance allowed him to keep going. Semmoto applauds the patience and flexibility of Ranalli, demonstrated from the outset.

Could Ranalli have been prepared for the rejections of KDD and Eiko? They weren't even rejections in the style Ranalli was used to. Both KDD and Eiko strung FIJ along in one way or another, not intending to say "yes" but not prepared to say "no." The courtship with these two Japanese companies was always ambiguous.

Strategy

It seemed all of the Japanese companies agreed that FIJ had the best technology and service they had come across. The combination of reduced price, guaranteed document delivery service, a 24-hour bilingual fax delivery staff, high profit margins and dramatically increased efficiency made it hard to argue with Ranalli. The Japanese investors held other concerns that Ranalli did not anticipate, though: 1) The average customer was smaller than expected. 2) The Japanese government might not approve FIJ's low pricing plan. 3) Service to the U.S. only was insufficient. 4) Customers don't like dialing access digits. Ranalli considered the first two of these issues as the necessary topics to address, while he believed the others would work themselves out once potential investors understood the natural advantages of FIJ.

He needed to convince potential investors of FIJ's ability to sell to thousands of small customers and the advantage of this strategy in creating barriers to entry. Ranalli also needed to gain approval from the Japanese government. Based on these concerns, Ranalli revised his business strategy for future negotiations. Ranalli's revised strategy included winning support of the government; convincing either KDD or N.T.T. to act as Sales Agent for FIJ; and closing a deal with a lead partner for a least $3 million of initial funding. In sum, FIJ needed capital and credibility, and needed each to get the other.

Dealing with the Government

Meeting and negotiating with the Japanese Ministry of Post and Telecommunications (MPT) was relatively easy. The MPT was very gracious to FIJ and was in fact far more accepting of FIJ than anyone expected. All of the potential partners in Japan were seriously afraid of the MPT's reaction to FI's proposed low prices. However, after hearing of FI's plan, the MPT responded by saying, "We wish you the best of luck with this strategy and we hope that you get started as quickly as possible." Ranalli exclaimed, "I wish I could have video-taped this meeting for everyone back in the United States!"

Ranalli surmised that the MPT made an internal risk reward analysis on the entry of FIJ into the Japanese market and concluded that very little risk to the Japanese market would come from this small company, but there existed a very high risk of a public relations disaster if FI felt that it was being unfairly blocked in Japan. Ranalli stated:

> Imagine the press coverage if the MPT tells FI that we can't lower the price even though our technology is superior and our business operates with 50 percent gross margins: 'Japanese Government Blocks Superior Technology From the U.S.: Once Again, the Japanese Government Proves That They Lie About Open Markets.'

In fact, FIJ received its license from the MPT in just four months in 1991. Other established telecommunications companies have had a much more difficult time in gaining approvals from the MPT. One of the major telecommunications carriers in the United States spent three years getting the same license. The difference was one of approach—FI's advantage was gained from its small size.

Now that the support of the Japanese government was won, Ranalli's next step in his business strategy was to secure a sales agent in either KDD or N.T.T.

Finding a Sales Agent

Experience with Japanese companies told Ranalli that the Japanese view the sales process as being extremely difficult in Japan due to the reluctance of customers to change their existing vendor relationships. Ranalli states, "This is one of the reasons why Japanese companies join together into a family of companies who tend to buy from each other." It was only natural, then, that potential investors would be wary of Ranalli's confidence in securing customers. Despite the Japanese companies' concern, Ranalli was convinced that the success of FIJ depended upon selling the service to thousands of small companies. This would create a barrier to entry in the future since it is easy to steal a few big customers from an existing competitor, but extremely difficult to steal thousands of small customers.

To convince potential Japanese investors of the sales strength of FIJ, Ranalli decided to secure a sales agent in Japan. His two targets were KDD, the dominant international telephone carrier, and N.T.T., the dominant domestic carrier. Ranalli gave the following information in a May 28, 1993 update letter from Tokyo to the board of directors and investors:

KDD: Annual Sales = $2.5 billion
        Size of sales force = 745

N.T.T.:   Annual Sales = $50.0 billion
           Size of sales force = 30,000

Securing either KDD or N.T.T. would establish an impressive sales power, give credibility to FIJ and make Japanese companies less wary of investing. Ranalli extended his June 1993 trip to Tokyo to engage in discussions with KDD and N.T.T. and try to gain a commitment from either one to act as sales agent for FIJ.

Ranalli met with KDD on Friday, May 28th, 1993. Although KDD was interested in the project, nothing definitive came of the discussion. Ranalli described the discussions;

> Our meeting on Friday afternoon with KDD didn't go well. They are still interested in the project, but my assessment of the situation is that they might take another year to make a decision. It appears that KDD is tied up in an internal debate. Half the company wants to cooperate with competitors like Fax International and half the company wants to bury its head in the sand. I don't hold out a great deal of hope for the KDD deal but I am going to keep it alive until we close a deal.

Although KDD had engaged in negotiations with FIJ before (as a potential lead investor), it still couldn't offer a positive response to FIJ.

Ranalli's meeting with N.T.T., on the other hand, was "astounding." Discussions were held on Monday, May 31st—two days after the meeting with KDD. N.T.T. reacted with enthusiasm and expressed a desire to move forward as FIJ's sales agent immediately, both in Japan and the United States. Ranalli told his board of directors and investors, "I realize that this sounds a little hard to believe. I didn't believe it myself so I asked them to write me a 'letter of interest.'" N.T.T. delivered a letter to Ranalli the next morning. The following statements were made:

> N.T.T. has been watching FI's progress in the United States over the past year and it is very impressed with the competitive advantages of FI's service.

> N.T.T. wants to become a full service vendor to Japanese companies in Japan and abroad. Since N.T.T. is prevented by law from operating its own international services it would like to act as Sales Agent for the best international services available in each market. It believes FI meets its requirements.

> N.T.T. has 28,000 account executives in Tokyo alone. N.T.T. believes that it can be the most effective Sales Agent possible for FI and it is willing to move forward immediately with negotiating a contract.

Although the letter of interest from N.T.T. did not guarantee that N.T.T. and FIJ would ever reach a final agreement on a Sales Agent contract, the indication of interest by N.T.T. was extremely exciting. Ranalli had to provide N.T.T. with a "high quality product that works perfectly, has a very attractive price and is easy to sell. FIJ needed an influential Sales Agent and N.T.T. needed a product that would enhance its own image—the partnership was perfect.

Securing a Lead Investor

Now Ranalli could continue looking for a lead investor, this time with some more leverage. Ranalli's goal was to secure a lead investor that would put up at least $3 million in initial funding. KDD and Eiko were still wavering, but other companies also had serious negotiations going with FIJ. The remaining companies included Nichimen Corporation and Overseas Courier Service (OCS).

Ranalli had been meeting with Overseas Courier Service (OCS) in the Spring of 1993. OCS would be an effective partner since much of its business is conducted through fax transmission, therefore it would also be a captive customer. A follow-up meeting with OCS was scheduled for May 28, 1993. Although Ranalli felt this meeting went well, he stated;

> I am afraid that OCS does not represent a viable lead partner for FIJ. During the meeting we learned that OCS is only willing to go forward if they can be the sole investor in FIJ. They are not interested in sharing the project with anyone else, and they are not interested in working with N.T.T. on a Sales Agent basis. OCS has 3,000 existing customers and they believe they can convince all of these customers to use FIJ's service. As a result, they don't want to share commissions with N.T.T. In general, I don't think OCS really understands this business and I feel they are thinking too small. But, I don't want to kick a gift horse in the mouth. The way I left it with OCS is that they are going to spend the next two weeks developing their own financial model for FIJ and then they will make a final decision on June 11th.

A lead partner deal with OCS didn't work out. Ranalli felt his other options were much more appealing, though he was careful to keep communication open with OCS.

Perhaps the most promising candidate for lead investor was Nichimen, a Japanese trading company. Sachio Semmoto had suggested looking into the largest ten trading companies in Japan. The one picked as a target was Nichimen. Nichimen is a very respectable and stable worldwide trading company with $50 billion in business a year, though it is at the smaller end of the largest ten Japanese trading companies.

Nichimen was the choice for a number of reasons. It had consistently engaged in business with DDI, it had no investments in new entrants in telecommunications, and Sachio Semmoto knew the Senior Managing Director of the Electronics Division, Mr. Nagayama, very well. Not only did Semmoto know Nagayama well, he also knew that Nichimen had a strong interest in the telecommunications business. Ranalli described Nichi-

men in a June 2, 1993, update to the FI board of directors and investors, "They are sophisticated, they speak English perfectly, they understand our business, and they are a pleasure to deal with. Given an option, I would greatly enjoy working with Nichimen." Ranalli, therefore, began to focus his efforts on attaining a partnership with Nichimen.

Sachio Semmoto talked to Mr. Nagayama in early February 1993 and introduced Nichimen as a potential lead investor. Having explained all of the details of FIJ, Semmoto was told that FIJ would be allowed to proceed to the next step in negotiations. Nagayama agreed that the project is worth pursuing. Because of Semmoto, FIJ's proposal was reviewed at the highest levels within Nichimen. Although the first step in getting to Nichimen was accomplished, there were still two other large steps to be taken. Ranalli described the necessary steps in an August 2, 1993, update to staff, investors and directors;

> First, the highest ranking person within the Electronics Division has to agree that the project is worth pursuing. This was accomplished by Dr. Semmoto during our first visit to Nichimen back in early February. The Senior Managing Director of the Electronics Division is Mr. Nagayama.
>
> Second, the Electronics Division assigns a manager to take responsibility for the project. This manager is then responsible for assembling a team to review the project and make a recommendation. Mr. Toi is the manager in charge of our project. We are lucky that Mr. Toi speaks perfect English and he has lived in the United States for seven years so he understands the differences between the two cultures.
>
> Third, once the Electronics Division decides to pursue a project they must first gain the approval of the remainder of the Nichimen organization before committing funds. This is the consensus building process in Japan that gets so much attention and criticism from the U.S. business press. This is a slow and painful process but it is absolutely necessary if our goal is to get Nichimen to provide all the financing necessary to fund our startup in Japan. Patience is critical during this process.

These deliberate and well-defined steps were necessary to take in order to gain Nichimen as lead investor. The second step was finished on June 3rd, 1993, when Mr. Toi said he liked the FIJ project and was prepared to recommend the project to the Nichimen Board of Directors.

Yasuoki Toi was chosen as the director of the FIJ case, responsible for completing the second step on Nichimen's side. Semmoto commented that Toi, a manager in his middle fifties, was chosen for this position because he was a "competent and exceptional type of person within a trading house." Toi formed a special team to review the possibilities of the FIJ deal. Semmoto found this team exceptionally effective at analyzing the FIJ business plan and adapting it to a Japanese environment. Toi worked closely with Semmoto and Ranalli in order to review the FIJ plan, then to sell FIJ to Nichimen and, later, attain minority investors. Like

Semmoto, Ranalli was also very impressed with Yasuoki Toi. He said;

> One of the major reasons that I focused my efforts on getting Nichimen to join the project is because I developed a great relationship with Mr. Toi. One of the key issues in selecting a partner is finding an individual, or individuals, who you can trust and who share your vision for the business. Mr. Toi and I built a strong relationship of trust and respect during the year-long negotiation process which allowed us to deal with many difficult negotiating issues.

Nichimen's board followed the discussions between Toi and FIJ all along. In June, they gave Toi the authorization to move forward. Toi called Semmoto in early June and told him that he wanted to move forward with the deal. He then asked for Semmoto's assistance in winning the final approval of the Nichimen Board. Semmoto had several good personal friends on the Nichimen Board. Ranalli, Semmoto and Toi began to compile a Term Sheet to present to the Nichimen Board. Ranalli stated in his June 6, 1993, investors' and directors' update, "Once we finish negotiating the Term Sheet with Mr. Toi, I believe that Semmoto has the ability to close the deal with one phone call."

The first Term Sheet meeting was scheduled for June 7. Ranalli had to, once again, extend his trip to Japan. He hoped to gain agreement from Nichimen on the following points:

- FI keeps 51 percent and control of the Board of Directors.
- Nichimen puts up three million dollars as an initial investment.
- FI gets a 5 percent gross revenue royalty.

Large disagreements between FIJ and Nichimen weren't expected.

On August 12, 1993, Doug Ranalli received a fax from Nichimen in his Burlington, Massachusetts, office, in which Mr. Toi detailed the conditions of the deal. Nichimen had decided to become FIJ's lead investor by purchasing 30 percent of FIJ for 600,000,000 Yen.

Soon after Ranalli received this fax from Nichimen, FI was out of cash again. Therefore, he initiated a bridge financing round which was based on convertible debt. The effective price was $2.75 per share. From August to October FI raised $1.5 million under this bridge while simultaneously continuing the negotiations in Japan. This was enough to make it through the fall. Ranalli made the following statement:

> By the way, just in case you think everything was going smoothly with the base business during this period, it wasn't. We had to remove our Director of Sales in July. The sales organization that was so successful in the first six months of the year absolutely fell apart in July. Morale was at an all time low, they had no strategy and no confidence in the existing Director. The reason for this failure was that the Director of Sales failed to anticipate a breakdown in our lead generation process. The result was that we ran out of leads in June and the organization literally ground to a halt. We sold to 270 customers in February and just 100 in July.

Sales success was necessary in gaining confidence from investors. A new Director of Sales gave FI confidence that the sales organization was going to come back onto track and the letter from Nichimen gave FI credibility.

Extra Pressure of U.S. Operations

Now that the lead investor was decided upon, Ranalli rethought his strategy for Fax International. He chose the following general strategy:

Step I: Prove the success of our business concept in the United States. We can move onto Stage II once we exceed 30,000 minutes per day of traffic, but the process of improving our U.S. operation is an ongoing responsibility. The U.S. operation is the proving ground for all of the technology, service concepts, and business strategies that we will use all over the world. The long-term success of our entire worldwide operation is dependent on Fax International U.S. maintaining a competitive lead in the United States.

Step II: Transfer everything that we've learned in the United States to our operation in Japan. Use this as the opportunity to develop our skills in setting up and supporting an operation outside of the United States. Place our network into multiple markets around the world just like we did two years ago in Japan and carry one-way traffic from the United States to these new markets. This will have the impact of dramatically expanding the number of customers we can sell to in the United States.

Step III: Establish operations in the top 10 markets around the world, just like we are trying to do in Japan. Once we complete the process in Japan, I will ask the company to try and set up the next three markets simultaneously, and then at least five more after that. Continue to get better and better at operating our business in the United States so that we can pass on these skills to our operations outside the United States.

Step IV: Develop new communications products and services to sell to our large customer base all over the world.

How could Ranalli be sure he had proven the success of FI in the United States? While Ranalli was in Japan searching for a minority investor, operations in the United States still needed his leadership.

While Ranalli was trying to establish FIJ, news from the United States was daunting. At the time Nichimen joined the FIJ team, FI was out of cash and was surviving on "friends and family financing," which caused great anxiety and shifted energy from operations and development of FI to emergency financing. FI was eating up more and more capital as its growth accelerated. The aggressive growth strategy back in the United States had boosted the net monthly revenue of FI to $348,974 per month in June 1993, but the net negative cash flow rate had grown to $250,000 per month. The break even point grew at an equally aggressive pace to $502,155 per month. Ranalli stated, "I don't believe that we ever had more than two months of cash in the bank at any point in time during all of 1993. This might sound either impossible, or extremely strange, but it was reality. While negotiating this deal in Japan we were constantly involved in the process of raising money."

The FI team was beginning to question whether they could keep this business under control as burn rates and break even points steadily grew. Shae Plimley, Director of Service and Customer Accounts for FI, and Ranalli's wife, joked that while most businesses talk of "creeping" breakevens, FI experienced "leaping" breakevens. FI was supposed to break even in November 1992 (see Fax International (A) case), but by June 1993, the break even point was still out of reach, and growing.

The expenses of FI were also increasing as FI was growing. The monthly expenses on a consolidated basis had increased from $175,000 per month in February 1992 to about $600,000 per month in July 1993. Actual revenue was far below FI's annualized run rate (see Exhibit F).

Also during this time, Ranalli had compiled a daunting list of all the tasks that had to be accomplished for FIUS. These included hiring more people, moving into a larger office, dealing with the backlog of projects within Engineering, modifying the sales and service division to allow FI to operate in multiple markets, improving customer retention, selling more customers, upgrading network quality, writing a new business plan, purchasing more network hardware and raising an additional $5–$10 million of equity with the range of $3–$5 per share.

Fax International had come a long way since the original idea by Doug Ranalli, but was now eating up resources faster than anyone had expected and investors were becoming more and more wary of investing. Ranalli was determined to find a minority investor for FIJ, though.

EXHIBIT F

Actual FI Revenue and Annualized Run Rate

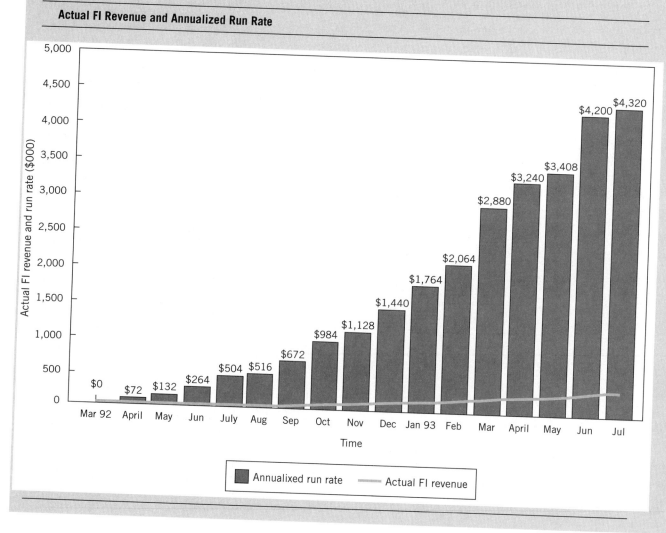

The Search for a Minority Investor

The three steps Ranalli had defined—approval from the Japanese government, getting a Sales Agent and securing a lead investor—were completed. The process took longer than expected, but Semmoto explained, "To Americans this is a long time, but for Japanese (especially in the case of a joint venture) this is a short time and a tremendous achievement. Doug was very patient and did a magnificent job." Ranalli's struggle to get FIJ off the ground, though, was hardly over. Nichimen agreed to be FIJ's lead investor only if Ranalli could find one or more minority investors. The process of searching for investors would have to start all over again.

Nichimen insisted upon finding minority investors that would purchase 19 percent of FIJ for 380,000,000 Yen. Ranalli stated in an investment proposal on August 30, 1993, "We are now looking for minority investors who can provide additional funding for FIJ, plus, assistance in locating high quality personnel, and assistance in winning market share through Sales Agent agreements." This would help reach Ranalli's goal of gaining Japanese partners who could contribute 1) cash to fund operations within Japan, 2) access to high quality personnel, and 3) sales agent capabilities. Nichimen was in, but FIJ needed to close the necessary second investor.

During the week of September 13–17, 1993, Doug Ranalli and Yuki Yamamoto, a 30-year-old Japanese graduate of Tokyo University and Columbia University Business School, took a trip to Japan to identify potential minority investors. Yuki Yamamoto would be the person responsible for the successful establishment of FIJ. Ranalli hired Yamamoto one year out of business school from a position in strategic consulting in order to take over the role that Akira Odani had been providing on a part-time basis. Yamamoto would help Ranalli in the negotiations, then continue on with the project as FI's representative to FIJ. Five possible minority investors were identified and contacted.

Kokusai Denshin Denwa Co., Ltd. (KDD)

KDD once again entered the scene as a prospect for FIJ. Ranalli had previously negotiated with KDD to become a lead investor, then a Sales Agent. Both attempts to get KDD to join the FIJ team had failed. The deals were always given serious consideration by KDD, but it had hedged and stalled too much to allow a deal to go through. KDD had been FIJ's telecommunications provider for the past two years and is the dominant international phone company of Japan. It would be a valuable player for FIJ to have on its side, in terms of capital, credibility and a large customer pool.

As a result of the week Ranalli and Yamamoto spent in Japan, KDD was seriously considering an investment of 10 percent in FIJ, under the same terms and conditions as the Nichimen deal. Although partnership talks over the past few months hadn't gone well, FIJ had gained some credibility in KDD's eyes since the Nichimen deal went through. Ranalli and Yamamoto believed, at this time, that the potential for an investment by KDD was over 50 percent. With this in mind, Ranalli and Yamamoto asked KDD to make a decision by November 1, with December 15 as an absolute deadline. Ranalli stated in a September 18, 1993, update on Japan and other corporate issues, "If we can succeed in closing a deal with KDD then FIJ will be viewed as one of the strongest telecommunications carriers in Japan. The impact of having KDD as an investor in FIJ will be enormous due to the power of KDD's name within worldwide telecommunications."

ORIX Corporation

ORIX is the largest equipment leasing company in Japan, having leasing relationships with 250,000 companies in Japan and operations in all of the key Asian markets. ORIX would be a good minority investor because it has contacts all over Japan through its existing business. As minority investor it would represent a large captive customer pool. Akira Odani first attempted to contact ORIX by submitting a proposal and information to middle managers. Although the lower level managers had a mild interest, the report stayed down low with the middle staff and nothing was accomplished. Because of the potential internal pressures that exist in Japanese corporations when a new project is undertaken, information never filtered up.

Luckily, Sachio Semmoto happened to know the CEO, Mr. Miyauchi, well. Semmoto, therefore, set up a meeting with Miyauchi, Ranalli and himself. He explained the importance of a business like this to Miyauchi. Semmoto informed Miyauchi that investment in FIJ would expand his own business in the future. This meeting lasted almost two hours, with constant questioning from Miyauchi. Semmoto stated, "Miyauchi is very smart—he could pinpoint many good issues. Miyauchi is a tough guy, and would ask tough questions, but if he said 'yes', the whole company would come along."

Although Semmoto thought Miyauchi had an interest in the business, Ranalli assessed, "The two companies [ORIX and Nichimen] are interested in working together but there does not appear to be a perfect fit on this project. The CEO, Mr. Miyauchi, was very honest in his assessment of the situation. He felt that we had an exciting opportunity but he wasn't sure that it fit with his business strategy." Miyauchi gave orders to his staff to study the prospects of FIJ in more detail, while Toi at Nichimen and Semmoto were assigned to following up on the ORIX lead.

Between September 30 and November 27, ORIX and FIJ met 10 times.

3iBJ Investments

The 3i Corporation of Great Britain and the Industrial Bank of Japan formed a joint venture to create the Japanese venture capital company, 3iBJ. Yuki Yamamoto identified this company as a potential minority investor and was responsible for setting up a meeting. After meeting with 3iBJ twice during the week of September 13–17, 1993, Ranalli said, "The results were excellent . . . From our end, the next step is to provide 3iBJ with detailed business plan projections for both FIUS and FIW."

Yuki Yamamoto was responsible for bringing this company through the learning process. After a period of review, David Wilson, one of the 3iBJ partners, decided to visit the Fax International office in Burlington, Massachusetts on November 29, 1993. 3iBJ additionally expressed interest in being a minority partner along with JAFCO, another Japanese venture capital firm.

Japan Affiliated Finance Company (JAFCO)

JAFCO is Japan's largest venture capital company, which operates in the United States and Japan. During the week in September that Ranalli and Yamamoto were in Japan looking for minority investors, JAFCO America visited the Fax International office in Burlington, Massachusetts to learn more about the company and its operations. Shae Plimley, Director of Sales and Customer Accounts, conducted the presentation to JAFCO on FI's service capabilities. During the same week, Ranalli and Yamamoto met with JAFCO in Japan. Ranalli stated, "Our meeting was productive but difficult to read."

JAFCO would most likely want to include another venture capital company in the deal if it chose to take the offer. In the first week of November 1993, JAFCO told FIJ that it would only be willing to invest if it could get a large discount off the price being paid by Nichimen for the same investment. JAFCO thought that the current valuation of FIJ was too high.

JAFCO announced that it would present the FIJ project to its Board of Directors the week of December 13.

Daimaru Trading Company

Daimaru's main line of business is a chain of department stores under the same name. Daimaru has no experience in telecommunications and knows nothing about the industry. Regardless of this fact, Daimaru was very interested in the FIJ project because, as Ranalli said, "FIJ looks like it is going to be an absolute money tree once it gets past breakeven in Japan. The gross margins on FIJ's recurring revenue are projected to be 70 percent or greater even if you include the full costs of all the network hardware and equipment housing fees in the calculation."

Despite the intense interest of Daimaru, the negotiations were difficult since the company and its leaders had no technical knowledge and couldn't accurately evaluate the quality of FIJ's network technology. Ranalli stated in late November, "Luckily, they [Daimaru] are willing to put a great deal of faith in Nichimen's review of our operation. I have to say that it has been very helpful having Nichimen as part of our negotiating team while looking for a minority partner in Japan. Having one large Japanese corporation already committed to the project has given us a great deal of credibility."

Daimaru told FIJ in late November that all of its questions had been answered and it was about to embark on preparing a report for its Board of Directors. Daimaru was, at this time, about two weeks away from completing a final report and presenting to the Board. Daimaru, however, expressed its intent to consciously lag behind ORIX and JAFCO in making its final decision.

Closing the Deal

Which of the above companies would be the most suited to become FIJ's minority investor and how would the deal be closed before Nichimen grew impatient? While Ranalli tried to answer this question for himself, the U.S. operations were out of cash again. The FIJ deal was taking longer than Doug originally estimated. Was Ranalli sacrificing his first priority for FI? Ranalli was eager to close a deal. However, he didn't want to miss an investment opportunity with the right company in order to buy time, nor did he want to do a deal that was not favorable for his existing investors.

With this in mind, Ranalli outlined the challenges that would face his company over the next few weeks:

- Sell to customers as quickly as possible and drive the company toward the 30,000 minutes per day breakeven point. Show investors that we are selling to customers at a constantly increasing rate/month (i.e.: 175 in September, 210 in October, 250+ in November).

- Install our new customers as quickly as possible, while increasing the level of traffic from the existing customers, and continuing to improve the quality of our service.

- Continue to expand the capabilities of our technology so that we are prepared to support multiple destination countries along with return traffic from Japan by the middle of 1994.

- Prepare for our move to new offices at the end of January.

- Reach agreement with a minority investor in Japan so that we are prepared to fund the startup of FIJ after the first of the year.

Ranalli summarized the delicate, even fragile, balancing act he faced in solidifying the future of Fax International:

> What does it take to make the U.S. operation profitable as a separate operating unit? How much money are we prepared to risk on the Fax International World (FIW) staff that is focused on worldwide expansion and has no source of immediate revenue?
>
> We can either be a small U.S.-based operation, or we can be a worldwide telecommunications company, but we can't be somewhere in between. The U.S. operation alone can't support a big FIW staff that doesn't generate any revenue.
>
> The FIW staff that is needed to grow the business is way too big to support without setting up operations in multiple countries quickly. This is a case of either grow fast or scale way back. There is no middle ground for FI.
>
> Our goal is not to be profitable at this point in time, our goal is to grow as fast as possible while trying to raise money at higher and higher prices per share so that we protect the investors. There is a constant balancing act going on between the desire that people have to see profits and the desire that people have to see growth. The real trick lies in balancing these two needs within the real limitation of constantly running out of cash as you try to grow.

Chapter Thirteen

Obtaining Venture and Growth Capital

Money is like a sixth sense without which you cannot make a complete use of the other five.

W. Somerset Maugham
Of Human Bondage

Results Expected

At the conclusion of this chapter, you will have:

1. Considered the implications of an equity investment.
2. Identified informal and formal investment sources of equity capital.
3. Learned how to find, contact, and deal with equity investors.
4. Discovered how venture capital investors make decisions.
5. Analyzed a case, "Hindman & Company," about an entrepreneur's multifaceted fund-raising strategies to launch and grow a new franchising company in the quick-lube industry.

Cover Your Equity

One of the toughest trade-offs for any young company is to balance the need for startup and growth capital with preservation of equity. Holding on to as much as you can for as long as you can is generally good advice for entrepreneurs. As was readily evident in *Exhibit 12.6*, the earlier the capital enters, regardless of the source, the more costly it is. Creative bootstrapping strategies can be great preservers of equity, as long as such parsimony does not slow down the venture's progress so much that the opportunity weakens or disappears altogether.

There are three central issues to consider when beginning to think about obtaining risk capital:

(1) Does the venture *need* outside equity capital? (2) Do the founders *want* outside equity capital? and finally, (3) *Who* should invest? While these three issues should be at the center of the management team's thinking, it is also important to remember that a smaller percentage of a larger pie is preferred to a larger percentage of a smaller pie. Or as one entrepreneur stated, "I would rather have a piece of a watermelon than a whole raisin."[1]

After reviewing the Venture Opportunity Screening Guide in Chapter 4, the Business Plan you prepared in Chapter 11, and the free cash flow equations (including OOC, TTC, and breakeven) from Chapter 12, it may be easier to assess the *need* for additional capital. Deciding whether the capital infusion will be

---

[1] Taken from a lecture on March 4, 1993, at the Harvard Business School, given by Paul A. Maeder and Robert F. Higgins of Highland Capital Partners, a Boston venture capital firm.

debt or equity is situation specific, and it may be helpful to be aware of the trade-offs involved; see Chapter 15 for an introduction to debt capital. In the majority of the high-technology startups and early-stage companies, some equity investment is normally needed to fund research and development.

Once the *need* for additional capital has been identified and quantified, the management team must consider the desirability of an equity investment. As was mentioned in Chapter 10, bootstrapping continues to be an attractive source of financing. For instance, *INC.* magazine suggested that entrepreneurs in certain industries "tap vendors"[2] by getting them to extend credit.

Other entrepreneurs interviewed by *INC.* suggested getting customers to pay fast.[3] These options, and others, exist if the management team members feel that a loss of equity would adversely impact the company and their ability to manage it effectively. An equity investment requires that the management team firmly believe that investors can and will add value to the venture. With this belief, the team can begin to identify those investors who bring expertise to the venture.

Deciding *who* should invest is a process more than a decision. The management team has a number of sources to consider. There are both informal and formal investors, private and public markets. The single most important criterion for selecting investors is what they can contribute to the value of the venture—beyond just capital. Angels or wealthy individuals are often sought because the amount needed may be less than the minimum investment required by formal investors (i.e., venture capitalists and private placements). Whether a venture capitalist would be interested in investing can be determined by the amount needed and the required rate of return expected.

Recently, as classic venture capitalists apparently are becoming a rare breed and as the banks exercise serious credit restraint, syndicated private offerings are meeting the needs of younger companies.[4] Take Symbus Technology, for instance. When this Massachusetts-based software company was in need of cash, their options were limited. The *Boston Globe* reported that a bank loan was out of the question. Venture capital meant the loss of both equity and control, and the public markets would not have responded to Symbus Technology's $2 million in 1992 revenue.[5] Thus, a syndicated private offering was pursued by Richard Tabor, the president and chief executive officer. The company successfully raised $3.1 million in August 1992. Yet, entrepreneurs should be cautioned that "only 30 to 40 percent of the companies seeking private equity actually wind up getting it at the end of the process."[6] Additionally, the fees due the investment bankers and attorneys involved in writing up the prospectus and other legal documents must be paid whether or not the company raises capital.

Timing

Timing is also critical. It is important that a venture not delay looking for capital until it has a serious cash shortage. For a startup, especially one with no experience or success in raising money, it is unwise to delay looking for capital since it is likely to take six months or more to raise money. In addition to the problems with cash flow, the lack of planning implicit in waiting until there is a cash shortage can undermine the credibility of a venture's management team and negatively impact its ability to negotiate with investors; recall *Exhibit 12.5.*

On the other hand, if a venture tries to obtain equity capital too early, the equity position of the founders may be unnecessarily diluted and the discipline instilled by financial leanness may be eroded inadvertently.

Angels and Informal Investors

Who They Are

Wealthy individuals are probably the single most important source of capital for startup and emerging businesses in America today.[7] According to William Wetzel, there are 250,000 or more such wealthy individuals, or angels, in the United States, 100,000 of whom are active.[8] In total, Wetzel believes angels invest $5 billion to $10 billion annually in 20,000 to 30,000 companies, an amount which is staggering in comparison to the 3,000 to 3,500 investments made

---

[2] Robert A. Mamis, "The Secrets of Bootstrapping," *INC.*, September 1992, p. 72.

[3] Ibid., p. 76.

[4] Andrew D. Myers, "Syndicated Private Offerings Add Equity to Emerging Companies," *Corporate Cashflow*, December 1992, p. 47.

[5] Judy Temes, "When the venture capital dries up . . . small firms look to private placement," *Boston Globe*, May 16, 1993, pp. 76–77.

[6] Ibid.

[7] G. Baty, *Initial Financing of the New Research Based Enterprise in New England*, Federal Reserve Bank of Boston research Report No. 25, Boston, MA, 1964; and G. Baty, *Entrepreneurship: Play to Win* (Reston, VA: Reston Publishing, 1974), p. 97.

[8] William H. Wetzel, Jr., "Angels and Risk Capital," *Sloan Management Review* 24, no. 4 (Summer 1984), pp. 23–34. The information in the text about angels is based on Wetzel's work.

each year by the United States venture capital industry. Typical investments are in the $20,000–$50,000 range, with 36 percent involving less than $10,000 and 24 percent over $50,000. These amounts are usually too small for professional venture capital sources.

Wetzel has found that these angels are mainly American self-made entrepreneur millionaires. They have made it on their own, have substantial business and financial experience, and are likely to be in their 40s or 50s. They are also well educated; 95 percent hold college degrees from four-year colleges, and 51 percent have graduate degrees. Of the graduate degrees, 44 percent are in a technical field and 35 percent are in business or economics.

Since the typical informal investor will invest from $10,000 to $50,000 in any one venture, informal investors are particularly appropriate for the following:[9]

- Ventures with capital requirements of between $50,000 and $500,000.
- Ventures with sales potential of between $2 million and $20 million within 5 to 10 years.
- Small, established, privately held ventures with sales and profit growth of 10 percent to 20 percent per year, a rate which is not rapid enough to be attractive to a professional investor, such as a venture capital firm.
- Special situations, such as very early financing of high-technology inventors who have not developed a prototype.

These investors may invest alone or in syndication with other wealthy individuals, may demand considerable equity for their interests, or may try to dominate ventures. They also can get very impatient when sales and profits do not grow as they expected.

Usually, these informal investors will be knowledgeable and experienced in the market and technology areas they invest in. If the right angel is found, he or she will add a lot more to a business than just money. As an advisor or director, his or her savvy, know-how, and contacts that come from having "made it" can be far more valuable than the $20,000 to $50,000 invested. Generally, the evaluations of potential investments by such wealthy investors tend to be less thorough than those undertaken by organized venture capital groups, and such noneconomic factors as the desire to be involved with entrepreneurship may be important to their investment decisions. For example, a successful entrepreneur may want to help other entrepreneurs get started, or a wealthy individual may want to help build new businesses in his or her community.

Finding Informal Investors

Finding these backers is not easy. One expert noted: "Informal investors, essentially individuals of means and successful entrepreneurs, are a diverse and dispersed group with a preference for anonymity. Creative techniques are required to identify and reach them."[10]

Invariably, they are found by tapping an entrepreneur's own network of business associates and other contacts. Other successful entrepreneurs know them, as do many tax attorneys, accountants, bankers, and other professionals. Apart from serendipity, the best way to find informal investors is to seek referrals from attorneys, accountants, business associates, university faculty, and entrepreneurs who deal with new ventures and are likely to know such people. Since such investors learn of investment opportunities from their business associates, fellow entrepreneurs, and friends, and since many informal investors invest together, more or less regularly, in a number of new venture situations, one informal investor contact can lead the entrepreneur to contacts with others.

In most larger cities, there are law firms and private placement firms that syndicate investment packages as Regulation D offerings to networks of private investors. They may raise from several hundred thousand dollars to several million. Directories of these firms are published annually by *Venture* magazine and are written about in magazines such as *INC*.

Contacting Investors

If an entrepreneur has obtained a referral, he or she needs to get permission to use the name of the person making a referral when the investor is contacted. A meeting with the potential investor then can be arranged. At this meeting, the entrepreneur needs to make a concise presentation of the key features of the proposed venture.

However, entrepreneurs need to avoid meeting with more than one informal investor at the same time. Meeting with more than one investor often results in any negative viewpoints raised by one investor being reinforced by another. It is also easier to deal with negative reactions and questions from only one investor at a time. Like a wolf on the hunt, if an entrepreneur isolates one target "prey" and then concentrates on closure, he or she will increase the odds of success.

Whether or not the outcome of such a meeting is continued investment interest, the entrepreneur needs to try to obtain the names of other potential investors from this meeting. If this can be done, the

---

[9] William H. Wetzel, Jr., "Informal Investors—When and Where to Look," in *Pratt's Guide to Venture Capital Sources*, 6th ed., ed. Stanley E. Pratt (Wellesley Hills, MA: Capital Publishing, 1982), p. 22.
[10] Ibid.

entrepreneur will develop a growing list of potential investors and will find his or her way into one or more networks of informal investors.

If the outcome is positive, often the participation of one investor who is knowledgeable about the product and its market will trigger the participation of other investors.

Evaluation Process

An informal investor will want to review a business plan, meet the full management team, see any product prototype or design that may exist, and so forth. The investor will conduct background checks on the venture team and its product potential, usually through someone he or she knows who knows the entrepreneur and the product. The process is not dissimilar to the due diligence of the professional investors (see below) but may be less formal and structured.

The new venture entrepreneur, if given a choice, would be wise to select an informal investor who can be a useful advisor and whose objectives are consistent with those of the entrepreneur.

The Decision

If the investor decides to invest, he or she will have some sort of investment agreement drafted by an attorney. This agreement may be somewhat simpler than those used by professional investors, such as venture capital firms. All the cautions and advice about investors and investment agreements that are discussed later on in the chapter apply here as well.

Most likely, the investment agreement with an informal investor will include some form of a "put," whereby the investor has the right to require the venture to repurchase his or her stock after a specified number of years at a specified price. If the venture is not harvested, this put will provide an investor with a cash return.

Venture Capital: Gold Mines and Tar Pits

There are only two classes of investors in new and young private companies: value-added investors and all the rest. If all you receive from an investor, especially a venture capitalist or a substantial private investor, is money, then you may not be getting much of a bargain at all. One of the keys to raising risk capital is to seek investors who will truly add value to the ven-

ture well beyond the money. Research and practice show that investors may add or detract value in a young company. Therefore, carefully screening potential investors to determine how specifically they might fill in some gaps in the founders' know-how and networks can yield significant results.

A young founder of an international telecommunications venture landed a private investor who also served as an advisor. The following are examples of how this private investor provided critical assistance: introduced the founder to other private investors, to foreign executives (who became investors and helped in a strategic alliance), to the appropriate legal and accounting firms; served as a sounding board in crafting and negotiating early rounds of investments; identified potential directors and other advisors familiar with the technology and relationships with foreign investors and cross-cultural strategic alliances.

Numerous other examples exist of venture capitalists' being instrumental in opening doors to key accounts and vendors that otherwise might not take a new company very seriously. They may also provide valuable help in such tasks as negotiating OEM agreements, licensing or royalty agreements, making key contacts with banks and leasing companies, finding key people to build the team, helping to revise or to craft a strategy. It is always tempting for an entrepreneur desperately in need of cash to go after the money that is available, rather than wait for the value-added investor. These quick solutions to the cash problem usually come back to haunt the venture.

What Is Venture Capital?[11]

The word *venture* suggests that this type of capital involves a degree of risk and even something of a gamble. Specifically, "the venture capital industry supplies capital and other resources to entrepreneurs in business with high growth potential in hopes of achieving a high rate of return on invested funds."[12] The whole investing process involves many stages, which are represented in *Exhibit 13.1*. Throughout the investing process, venture capital firms seek to add value in several ways: identifying and evaluating business opportunities, including management, entry, or growth strategies; negotiating and closing the investment; tracking and coaching the company; providing technical and management assistance; and attracting additional capital, directors, management, suppliers, and other key stakeholders and resources. The process begins with

[11] Unless otherwise noted, this section is drawn from William D. Bygrave and Jeffry A. Timmons, Venture Capital at the Crossroads (Boston: Harvard Business School Press, 1992.), pp. 13–14. Copyright © 1992 by William D. Bygrave and Jeffry A. Timmons.

[12] "Note on the Venture Capital Industry (1981)," HBS Case 285-096, Harvard Business School, 1982, p. 1.

EXHIBIT 13.1

Classic Venture Capital Investing Process

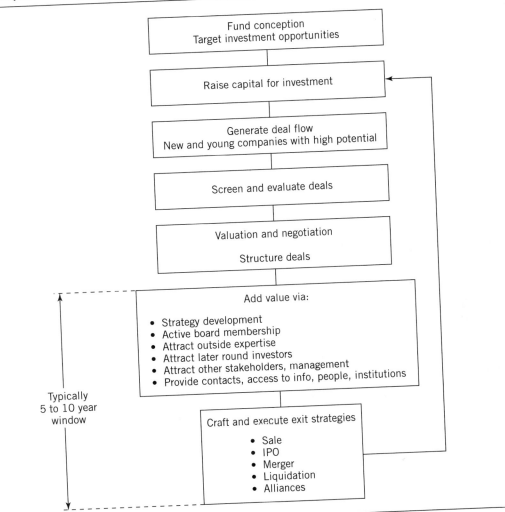

Source: William D. Bygrave and Jeffry A. Timmons, *Venture Capital at the Crossroads* (Boston: Harvard Business School Press, 1992), Figure 1–4.

the conception of a target investment opportunity or class of opportunities, which leads to a written proposal or prospectus to raise a venture capital fund. Once the money is raised, the value creation process moves from generating deals to crafting and executing harvest strategies and back to raising another fund. The process usually takes up to 10 years to unfold, but exceptions in both directions often occur. (See *Exhibit 13.2*.)

The Venture Capital Industry[13]

Although the roots of venture capital can be traced from investments made by wealthy families in the 1920s and 1930s, most industry observers credit Ralph E. Flanders, then president of the Federal Reserve Bank of Boston, with the idea. In 1946, Flanders joined a top-ranked team to found American Research and Development Corporation, the first firm, as opposed to individuals, to provide risk capital for new and rapidly growing firms, most of which were manufacturing and technology oriented.

Despite the success of American Research & Development, the venture capital industry did not experience a growth spurt until the 1980s, when the industry "went ballistic." See *Exhibit 13.3* for the capital commitments between 1969 and 1990.

[13] Bygrave and Timmons, *Venture Capital at the Crossroads*, pp. 16–28.

EXHIBIT 13.2 (A)

Venture Capital Industry

**Estimated Capital Under Management and Disbursements
(Millions of Dollars)
1969 to 1992**

Year	New Capital Committed to Independent Private Venture Capital Firms Only	Total Venture Capital Under Management*	Disbursements to Portfolio Companies
1992	$2,550	$31,074	$2,540
1991	1,388	32,870	1,348
1990	1,800	35,950	1,922
1989	2,400	34,430	3,395
1988	2,900	31,100	3,847
1987	4,200	29,000	3,977
1986	3,300	24,100	3,242
1985	2,300	19,600	2,681
1984	3,200	16,300	2,771
1983	3,400	12,100	2,581
1982	1,400	7,600	1,454
1981	867	5,800	1,155
1980	661	4,500	608
1979	170	3,800	457
1978	216	3,500	288
1977	—	2,500–3,000	159
1976	—		107
1975	—		92
1974	—		100
1973	—		201
1972	—		128
1971	—		134
1970	—		83
1969	—	2,500–3,000	not available

*Total venture capital under management remained static from 1969 through 1977 at approximately $2.5 to $3.0 billion with new funding more or less equal to withdrawals (Venture Economics' policy is to withdraw dollars invested in the industry after eight years).

NOTE: Some numbers may be affected by rounding.

Source: Venture Economics National Venture Capital Association Annual Report

(Continued)

Before 1980, venture capital investing activities could be called dormant; just $460 million was invested in 375 companies in 1979. But at its peak in 1987, the industry had ballooned to more than 700 venture capital firms, which invested $3.94 billion in 1,729 portfolio companies. The sleepy, cottage industry of the 1970s was transformed into a vibrant, at times frenetic, occasionally myopic, and dynamic market for private risk and equity capital in the 1980s. "After shrinking by an average of 25 percent a year for four years, new venture capital raised in 1992 more than doubled over 1991."[14] Yet, industry observers attributed the increase to "repeat fund raisers assembling partnerships of more than $100 million."[15]

By the late 1980s, not only had the commitments changed, but a new structure was emerging, increasingly specialized and focused. See *Exhibit 13.4.* This chart summarized some of the important changes in the industry, which have implications for entrepreneurs seeking money and for those investing it.

[14] Michael Vachon, "Venture Capital Reborn," *Venture Capital Journal*, January 1993, p. 32.
[15] Ibid.

EXHIBIT 13.2 (B)

Total Venture Capital Under Management

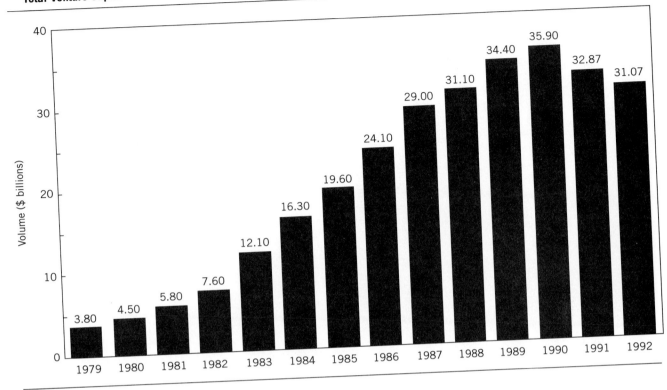

Source: Venture Economics.

EXHIBIT 13.3

United States Commitments (1969–1992)

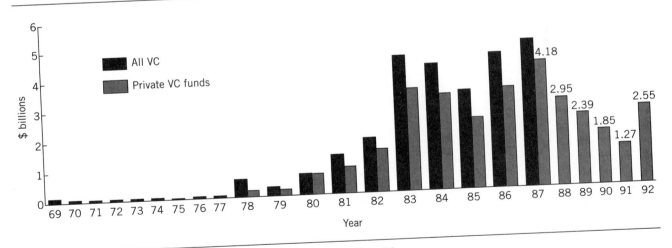

Source: Venture Economics Publishing, *Venture Capital Journal*, January 1993, p. 32.

The Venture Capital Process

Exhibit 13.5 represents the core activities of the venture capital process. At the heart of this dynamic flow is the collision of entrepreneurs, opportunities, investors, and capital.[16] Because the venture capitalist brings, in addition to money, experience, networks, and industry contacts, a professional venture capitalist can be very attractive to a new venture. Moreover, a venture capital firm has deep pockets and contacts with other groups that can facilitate the raising of money as the venture develops.

---

[16] Bygrave and Timmons, *Venture Capital at the Crossroads*, p. 11.

EXHIBIT 15.4

New Heterogeneous Structure of the Venture Capital Industry

	Megafunds	Mainstream	Second Tier	Specialists and Niche Funds	Corporate Financial and Corporate Industrial
Estimated number and type (1988)	100+; Predominately private, independent funds	125–150; Predominately private and independent; some large institutional SBICs and corporate funds	150–175; Mostly SBICs; some private independent funds	50–75; Private, independent	150–175
Size of funds under management	$150+	$50M–$150M	Below $50M	$3–$15M	$25–$50M+
Typical investment (1st round)	$5–$10M+	$1M–$3M	$500K–$1M	$50K–$200K	Larger $10M–$15M deals possible
Stage of investment	Later expansion, LBOs, startups	Later expansion, LBOs, some starts; mezzanine	Later stages; few starts; specialized areas	Seed and startup	Later
Strategic focus	Technology; national and international markets; capital gains; broad focus	Technology and manufacturing; national and regional markets; capital gains; more specialized focus	Eclectic—more regional than national; capital gains, current income; service business	Technology or market focus High-technology national and international links; "feeder funds" capital gains	Windows on technology; direct investment in new markets and suppliers; diversification; strategic partners; capital gains
Balance of equity and debt	Predominately equity	Predominately equity; convertible preferred	Predominately debt: about 91 SBICs do equity principally	Predominately equity	Mixed
Principal sources of capital	Mature national and international institutions; own funds; insurance company and pension funds; institutions and wealthy individuals; foreign corporation and pension funds; universities		Wealthy individuals; some smaller institutions	Institutions and foreign companies; wealthy individuals	Internal funds
Main investing role	Active lead or colead; frequent syndications; board seat	Less coinvesting with some solo investing	Initial or lead investor; outreach; shirtsleeves involvement	Later stages, rarely startups; direct investor in funds and portfolio companies	

Note: Target rates of return vary considerably, depending on stage and market conditions. Seed and startup investors may seek compounded after-tax rates of return in excess of 50 to 100 percent; in mature, later stage investments they seek returns in the 30–40 percent range. The rule of thumb of realizing gains of 5 to 10 times the original investment in 5 to 10 years is a common investor expectation.

EXHIBIT 13.5

Flows of Venture Capital

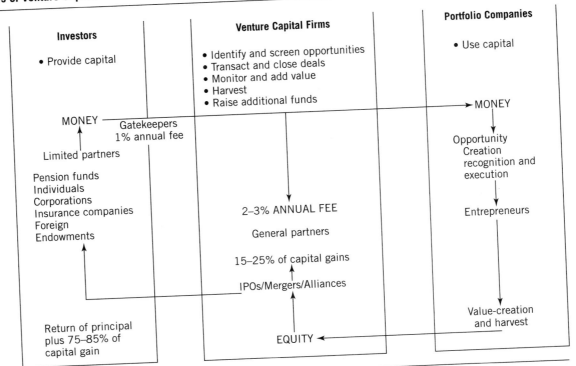

Source: William D. Bygrave and Jeffry A. Timmons, *Venture Capital at the Crossroads* (Boston: Harvard Business School Press, 1992), Figure 1–3.

The venture capital process occurs in the context of mostly private, quite imperfect capital markets for new, emerging, and middle-market companies (i.e., those companies with $5 million to $100 million in sales). The availability and cost of this capital depend on a number of factors:

- Perceived risk, in view of the quality of the management team and the opportunity.
- Industry, market, attractiveness of the technology, and fit.
- Upside potential and downside exposure.
- Anticipated growth rate.
- Age and stage of development.
- Amount of capital required.
- Founders' goals for growth, control, liquidity, and harvest.
- Fit with investors' goals and strategy.
- Relative bargaining positions of investors and founders.

However, no more than 2 to 4 percent of the ventures contacting venture capital firms receive financing from them; see *Exhibit 13.6* for the number of companies and the types of investments made.

Despite the increase in funds in 1992, observers comment that the repeat fund-raisers "stay away from seed and early-stage investments largely because those deals tend to require relatively small amounts of capital and the megafunds, with $100 million-plus to invest, like to make larger commitments."[17] Further, an entrepreneur may give up 25 to 75 percent of his or her equity for seed/startup financing. Thus, after several rounds of venture financing have been completed, an entrepreneur may own no more than 10 to 20 percent of the venture.

It is the venture capitalists' stringent criteria for their investments that limit the number of companies receiving venture capital money. Venture capital investors look for ventures with very high growth potential where they can quintuple their investment in five years; they place a very high premium on the quality of management in a venture; and they like to see a management team with complementary business skills headed by someone who has previous entrepreneurial or profit-and-loss (P&L) management experience. In fact, these investors are searching for the "superdeal." Superdeals meet the investment criteria outlined in *Exhibit 13.7*.

---

[17] Vachon, "Venture Capital Reborn," p. 35.

EXHIBIT 15.6

USA Venture Capital Investment by Year (1979–1989)

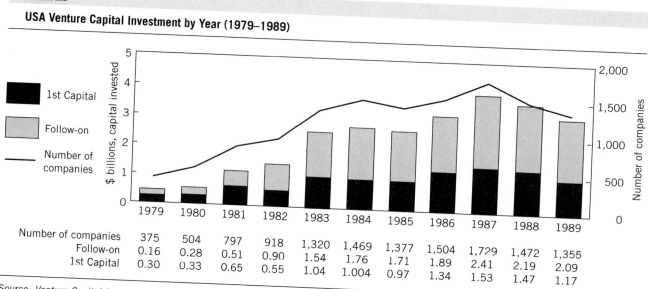

	1979	1980	1981	1982	1983	1984	1985	1986	1987	1988	1989
Number of companies	375	504	797	918	1,320	1,469	1,377	1,504	1,729	1,472	1,355
Follow-on	0.16	0.28	0.51	0.90	1.54	1.76	1.71	1.89	2.41	2.19	2.09
1st Capital	0.30	0.33	0.65	0.55	1.04	1.004	0.97	1.34	1.53	1.47	1.17

Source: *Venture Capital Journal*, July 1990, p. 14.

EXHIBIT 15.7

Characteristics of the Classic Superdeal from the Investor's Perspective

Mission

- Build a highly profitable and industry-dominant company.
- Go public or merge within four to seven years at a high price–earnings (P/E) multiple.

Complete Management Team

- Led by industry "superstar."
- Possess proven entrepreneurial, general management, and P&L experience in the business.
- Have leading innovator or technologies/marketing head.
- Possess complementary and compatible skills.
- Have unusual tenacity, imagination, and commitment.
- Possess reputation for high integrity.

Proprietary Product

- Has significant competitive lead and "unfair" advantages.
- Has product or service with high value-added properties resulting in early payback to user.
- Has or can gain exclusive contractual or legal rights.

Large and Rapidly Growing Market

- Will accommodate a $50 million entrant in five years.
- Has sales currently at $100 million, or more, and growing at 25% per year.
- Has no dominant competitor now.
- Has clearly identified customers and distribution channels.
- Possesses forgiving and rewarding economics, such as:
    - —Gross margins of 40% to 50%, or more.
    - —10 percent of more profit after tax.
    - —Early positive cash flow and break-even sales.

Deal Valuation and ROR

- Has "digestible" first-round capital requirements (i.e., greater than $1 million and less than $10 million).
- Able to return 10 times original investment in five years at P/E of 15 times or more.
- Has possibility of additional rounds of financing at substantial markup.
- Has antidilution and IPO subscription rights.

Source: William D. Bygrave and Jeffry A. Timmons, *Venture Capital at the Crossroads* (Boston: Harvard Business School Press, 1992), Figure 1–2.

Identifying Venture Capital Investors

Venture capital corporations or partners have an established capital base and professional management. Their investment policies cover a range of preferences in investment size and the maturity, location, and industry of a venture. Capital for these investments can be provided by one or more wealthy families, one or more financial institutions (e.g., insurance companies or pension funds), and wealthy individuals. Most are organized as limited partnerships, in which the fund managers are the general partners and the investors are the limited partners. Today, most of these funds prefer to invest from $500,000 to $1 million or more. Although some of the smaller funds will invest less, most of their investments are in the range of $500,000 to $1.5 million. Some of the so-called megafunds with upwards of $100 million to invest do not consider investments of less than $1 million to $2 million. The investigation and evaluation of potential investments by venture capital corporations and partnerships are thorough and professional. Most of their investments are in high-technology businesses, but a good number will consider investments in other areas.

Sources and Guides. If an entrepreneur is searching for a venture capital investor, a good place to start is with *Pratt's Guide to Venture Capital Sources,* published by Venture Economics, one of several directories of venture capital firms. Entrepreneurs also can seek referrals from accountants, lawyers, investment and commercial bankers, and business people who are knowledgeable about professional investors. Especially good sources of information are other entrepreneurs who have recently tried, successfully or unsuccessfully, to raise money.

Sometimes professional investors find entrepreneurs. Rather than wait for a deal to come to them, a venture capital investor may decide on a product or technology it wishes to commercialize and then put its own deal together. Kleiner Perkins used this approach to launch Genentech and Tandem Computer Corporation, as did Greylock and J. H. Whitney in starting MassComp.

What to Look For. Entrepreneurs are well advised to screen prospective investors to determine the appetites of such investors for the stage, industry, technology, and capital requirements proposed. It is also useful to determine which investors have money to invest, which are actively seeking deals, and which have the time and people to investigate new deals. Depending on its size and investment strategy, a fund which is a year or two old will generally be in an active investing mode.

Early-stage entrepreneurs need to seek investors who (1) are considering new financing proposals and can provide the required level of capital; (2) are interested in companies at the particular stage of growth; (3) understand and have a preference for investments in the particular industry (i.e., market, product, technology, or service focus); (4) can provide good business advice, moral support, and contacts in the business and financial community; (5) are reputable and ethical and with whom the entrepreneur gets along; and (6) have successful track records of 10 years or more advising and building smaller companies.[18]

Entrepreneurs can expect a number of value-added services from an investor. Ideally, the investor should define his or her role as a coach, thoroughly involved, but not a player. In terms of support, investors should have both patience and bravery. The entrepreneur should be able to go to the investor when he or she needs a sounding board, counseling, or an objective, detached perspective. Investors should be helpful with future negotiations, financing, private and public offerings, as well as in relationship building with key contacts.

What to Look Out For. There are also some things to be wary of in finding investors. These warning signs are worth avoiding unless an entrepreneur is so desperate that he or she has no real alternatives:

- *Attitude.* Entrepreneurs need to be wary if they cannot get through to a general partner in an investment firm and keep getting handed off to a junior associate, or if the investor thinks he or she can run the business better than the lead entrepreneur or the management team.
- *Overcommitment.* Entrepreneurs need to be wary of lead investors who indicate they will be active directors but who also sit on the boards of six to eight other startup and early-stage companies or are in the midst of raising money for a new fund.
- *Inexperience.* Entrepreneurs need to be wary of dealing with venture capitalists who have an MBA; are under 30 years of age; have worked only on Wall Street or as a consultant; have no operating, hands-on experience in new and growing companies; *and* have a predominantly financial focus.
- *Unfavorable reputation.* Entrepreneurs need to be wary of funds that have a reputation for early and frequent replacement of the founders or those where over one-fourth of the portfolio companies are in trouble or failing to meet projections in their business plans.

Dealing with Venture Capitalists[19]

It is important to keep in mind that venture capitalists see lots of business plans and proposals, sometimes one hundred or more a month. Typically, they invest in only one to three of these. The following suggestions may be helpful in working with them.

If possible, obtain a personal introduction from someone that is well-known to the investors (a director or founder of one of their portfolio companies, a limited partner in their fund, a lawyer or accountant who has worked with them on deals) and who knows

[18] For more specifics see Harry A. Sapienza and Jeffry A. Timmons, "Launching and Building Entrepreneurial Companies: Do the Venture Capitalists Build Value?" in *Proceedings of the Babson Entrepreneurship Research Conference, May 1989,* Babson Park, MA. See also Jeffry A. Timmons, "Venture Capital: More than Money," in *Pratt's Guide to Venture Capital Sources,* 13th ed., ed. Jane Morris (Needham, MA: Venture Economics, 1989), p. 71.

[19] The author expresses appreciation to Mr. Thomas Huseby, of SeaPoint Ventures, in Washington, for his valuable insights in the following two sections.

you well. After identifying the best targets, you should create a market for your company by marketing it. Have several prospects. Be vague about who else you are talking with. The problem is, you can end up with a rejection from everyone if the other firms know who was the first firm that turned you down. It is also much harder to get a yes than to get a no. You can waste an enormous amount of time before getting there.

Most investors who have serious interest will have some clear ideas about how to improve your strategy, product line, positioning, and a variety of other areas. This is one of the ways they can add value—if they are right. Consequently, you need to be prepared for them to take apart your business plan and to put it back together. They are likely to have their own format and their own financial models. Working with them on this is a good way to get to know them.

Never lie. As one entrepreneur put it, "You have to market the truth, but do not lie." Do not stop selling until the money is in the bank. Let the facts speak for themselves. Be able to deliver on the claims, statements, and promises you make or imply in your business plan and presentations. Tom Huseby adds some final wisdom: "It's much harder than you ever thought it could be. You can last much longer than you ever thought you could. They have to do this for the rest of their lives!" Finally, never say no to an offer price. There is an old saying that your first offer may be your best offer.

Due Diligence: A Two-way Street

It usually takes several weeks or months to complete the due diligence on a startup, although if the investors know the entrepreneurs, it can go much more quickly. The verification of facts, backgrounds, and reputations of key people, market estimates, technical capabilities of the product, proprietary rights, and the like, is a painstaking investigation for investors. They will want to talk with your directors, advisors, former bosses, and previous partners. Make it as easy as possible for them by having very detailed resumes, lists of 10 to 20 references (with phone numbers and addresses) such as former customers, bankers, vendors, and so on, who can attest to your accomplishments. Prepare extra copies of published articles, reports, studies, market research, contract, or purchase orders, technical specifications, and the like, that can support your claims.

One recent research project examined how 86 venture capital firms nationwide conducted their intensive due diligence. In order to evaluate the opportunity, the management, the risks, the competition, and weigh the upside against the downside, firms spent from 40 to 400 hours, with the typical firm spending 120 hours. That is nearly three weeks of full-time effort. At the extreme, some firms engaged in twice as much due diligence.[20] Central to this investigation were careful checks of the management's references, and verification of track record and capabilities.

While all this is going on, do your own due diligence on the venture fund. Ask for the names and phone numbers of some of their successful deals, some that did not work out, and the names of any presidents they ended up replacing. Who are their legal and accounting advisors? What footprints have they left in the sand vis-à-vis their quality, reputation, and record in truly adding value to the companies in which they invest? Finally, the chemistry between the management team and the general partner that will have responsibility for the investment and, in all likelihood, a board seat is crucial. If you do not have a financial partner you respect and can work closely with, then you are likely to regret ever having accepted the money.

Other Equity Sources

Small Business Administration's 7(a) Guaranteed Business Loan Program

Promoting small businesses by guaranteeing long-term loans, the Small Business Administration's 7(a) Guaranteed Business Loan Program has been supporting startup and high-potential ventures since 1953. Between 1980 and 1991, the SBA guaranteed $31 billion[21] in loans through the 7(a) program. The 7(a) program is almost exclusively a guarantee program, but under this program the Small Business Administration also makes direct loans to the handicapped, veterans, and Minority Enterprise Small Business Investment Companies (MESBICs). Eligible activities under 7(a) include acquisition of borrower-occupied real estate, fixed assets such as machinery and equipment, and working capital for items such as inventory or to meet cashflow needs.[22]

The $500,000 guarantees, the largest of all the SBA's programs, have helped many entrepreneurs

[20] Geoffrey H. Smart, "Management Assessment Methods in Venture Capital," unpublished doctoral dissertation, 1998; (Claremont, CA: The Claremont Graduate University), p. 109.

[21] "SBA Loans Spur Start-Up Growth," *INC.*, November 1992, p. 66.

[22] Daniel R. Garner, Robert R. Owen, and Robert P. Conway, *The Ernst & Young Guide to Raising Capital* (New York: John Wiley & Sons, 1991), pp. 165–66.

start, stay in, expand, or purchase a business. In fact, a recent Price Waterhouse study found that "the SBA-backed companies showed a higher survival rate than the nonrecipients. Four years after receiving the loans, more than three-quarters of the SBA recipients were still in business, versus fewer than two-thirds of the comparison group."[23]

Small Business Investment Companies[24]

SBICs (small business investment companies) are licensed by the SBA and can obtain from it debt capital—four dollars in loans for each dollar of private equity. An SBIC's equity capital is generally supplied by one or more commercial banks, wealthy individuals, and the investing public. In 1990, there were about 450 SBICs in the United States, of which about 137 had active venture capital rather than just loan programs; some of these SBICs are affiliates of venture capital firms.

SBICs are limited by law to taking minority shareholder positions and can invest no more than 20 percent of their equity capital in any one situation. Because SBICs borrow much of their capital from the SBA and must service this debt, they prefer to make some form of interest-bearing investment.

Four common forms of financing are long-term loans with options to buy stock, convertible debenture, straight loans, and in some cases, preferred stock. A typical financing is in the range of $100,000 to $300,000. Also, because of their SBA debt, SBICs tend not to finance startups and early-stage companies but to make investments in more mature companies. SBICs have been an important small business financing source and in over 20 years have invested $3 billion in more than 50,000 businesses. At this writing, major changes are being proposed to improve the operating regulations and structure of the SBIC program.

Mezzanine Capital[25]

At the point where the company has overcome many of the early-stage risks, it may be ready for mezzanine capital. The term *mezzanine financing* refers to capital that is between senior debt financing and common stock. In some cases it takes the form of redeemable preferred stock, but in most cases it is subordinated debt which carries an equity "kicker" consisting of warrants or a conversion feature into common stock.

This subordinated-debt capital has many characteristics of debt but also can serve as equity to underpin senior debt. It is generally unsecured, with a fixed coupon and maturity of 5 to 10 years. A number of variables are involved in structuring such a loan: the interest rate, the amount and form of the equity, exercise/conversion price, maturity, call features, sinking fund, covenants, and put/call options. These variables provide for a wide range of possible structures to suit the needs of both the issuer and the investor.

Offsetting these advantages are a few disadvantages to mezzanine capital compared to equity capital. As debt, the interest is payable on a regular basis, and the principal must be repaid, if not converted into equity. This is a large claim against cash and can be burdensome if the expected growth and/or profitability does not materialize and cash becomes tight. In addition, the subordinated debt often contains covenants relating to net worth, debt, and dividends.

Mezzanine investors generally look for companies that have a demonstrated performance record, with revenues approaching $10 million or more. Since the financing will involve paying interest, the investor will carefully examine existing and future cash flow and projections.

Mezzanine financing is utilized in a wide variety of industries, ranging from basic manufacturing to high technology. As the name implies, however, it focuses more on the broad middle spectrum of business, rather than on high-tech, high-growth companies. Specialty retailing, broadcasting, communications, environmental services, distributors, and consumer or business service industries are more attractive to mezzanine investors.

Private Placements

Private placements are an attractive source of equity capital for a private company that for whatever reason has ruled out the possibility of going public. If the goal of the company is to raise a specific amount of capital in a short period of time, this equity source may be the answer. In this transaction, the company offers stock to a few private investors, rather than to the public as in a public offering. A private placement requires little paperwork compared to a public offering, in addition to the fact that this private transaction can take a small amount of time.

If the company's management team knows of enough investors, then the private placement could be distributed among a small group of friends, family,

---

23 "SBA Loans Spur Start-Up Growth," p. 66.
24 This section was drawn from Jeffry A. Timmons, *Planning and Financing the New Venture* (Acton, MA: Brick House Publishing Company, 1990), pp. 49–50.
25 This section was drawn from Donald P. Remey, "Mezzanine Financing: A Flexible Source of Growth Capital," in *Pratt's Guide to Venture Capital Sources*, ed. D. Schutt (New York: Venture Economics Publishing, 1993), pp. 84–86.

relatives, or acquaintances. Or the company may decide to have a broker circulating the proposal among a few investors who have expressed an interest in small companies. The following four groups of investors might be interested in a private placement:[26]

1. Let us say you manufacture a product and sell to dealers, franchisors, or wholesalers. These are the people who know and respect your company. Moreover, they depend on you to supply the product they sell. They might consider it to be in their interest to buy your stock if they believe it will help assure continuation of product supply, and perhaps give them favored treatment if you bring out a new product or product improvement. One problem is when one dealer invests and another does not; can you treat both fairly in the future? Another problem is that a customer who invests might ask for exclusive rights to market your product in a particular geographical area, and you might find it hard to refuse.

2. A second group of prospective buyers for your stock are those professional investors who are always on the lookout to buy a good, small company in its formative years, and ride it to success. Very often, these sophisticated investors choose an industry and a particular product or service in that industry they believe will become hot and then focus 99 percent of their attention on the caliber of the management. If your management, or one key individual, has earned a high reputation as a star in management, technology, or marketing, these risk-minded investors tend to flock to that person. (The high-tech industry is an obvious example.) Whether your operation meets their tests for stardom as a hot field may determine whether they find your private placement a risk to their liking.

3. Other investors are searching for opportunities to buy shares of smaller growth companies in the expectation that the company will soon go public and they will benefit as new investors bid the price up, as often happens. For such investors, news of a private placement is a tip-off that a company is on the move and worth investigating, always with an eye on the possibility of its

going public. These investors usually have no fear of losing control or suffering their interference.

4. Private placements also often attract venture capitalists who hope to benefit when the company goes public or when the company is sold. To help assure that happy development, these investors get seriously active at the level of the board of directors, where their skill and experience can help the company reach its potential.

Initial Public Stock Offerings

Commonly referred to as an IPO, an initial public offering raises capital through federally registered and underwritten sales of the company's shares. Numerous federal and state securities laws and regulations govern these offerings; thus, it is important that management consult with lawyers and accountants who are intimately familiar with the current regulations.

In the past, such as during the strong bull market for new issues that occurred in 1983, 1986, and 1992, it was possible to raise money for an early-growth venture or even for a startup. These boom markets are easy to identify because the number of new issues jumped from 281 in 1980 to an astounding 888 in 1983, representing a jump from $1.4 billion in 1980 to about three times that figure in 1983 (see *Exhibit 13.8*). Another boom came three years later, in 1986, when the number of new issues reached 727. While in 1992, the number of new issues (595) did not exceed the 1986 record, a record $39.4 billion was raised in IPOs.[27] Accounting for this reduction in the number of new issues and the increase in the amounts raised, one observer commented that "the average size of each 1983 deal was a quarter of the $70 million average for the deals done."[28]

In other, more difficult financial environments, most dramatically, following the stock market crash on October 19, 1987, the new-issues market became very quiet for entrepreneurial companies, especially compared to the hot market of 1986. As a result, exit opportunities were limited. In addition, it was very difficult to raise money for early-growth or even more mature companies from the public market. The following examples are typical:

An entrepreneur spent a dozen years building a firm in the industrial mowing equipment business from scratch to $50 million in sales. The firm had a solid record of profitable growth in recent years. Although the firm is

---

[26] The following examples are drawn directly from Daniel R. Garner, Robert R. Owen, and Robert P. Conway, *The Ernst & Young Guide to Raising Capital* (New York: John Wiley & Sons, 1991), pp. 51–52.

[27] Sara Calian, "IPOs Raise Record $39.4 Billion for '92," *The Wall Street Journal*, January 4, 1993, p. C1.

[28] Thomas N. Cochran, "IPOs Everywhere: New Issues Hit a Record in the First Quarter," *Barrons*, April 19, 1993, p. 14. Though softened in 1997, the IPO market by any prior standard remains very robust.

EXHIBIT 13.8

Initial Public Offerings (1980–1992)

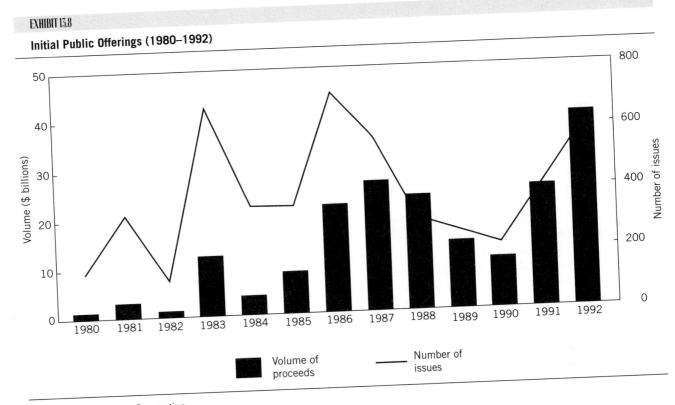

Source: Securities Data Corporation.

still small by Fortune 500 standards, it was the dominant firm in the business in mid-1987. Given the firm's plans for continued growth, the entrepreneur, the backers, and the directors decided the timing was right for an IPO, and the underwriters agreed. By early 1987, everything was on schedule and the "road show," which was to present the company to the various offices of the underwriter, was scheduled to begin in November. The rest is history. Nearly two years later, the IPO was still on hold.

In 1991, as the IPO market began to heat up, a Cambridge-based biotech firm was convinced by its investors and investment bankers to take the company public. In the spring, the IPO window opened as medical and biotechnology stocks were the best performing of all industry groups. By May, they had the book together; in June, the road show started in Japan, went through Europe and ended in the United States in mid-July. As the scheduled IPO date approached, so did the United Nations deadline for Saddam Hussein. After U.S. involvement, the new issues market turned downward, as the management of the biotech company watched their share price decline from $14 to $9 per share.[29]

The more mature a company is when it makes a public offering, the better the terms of the offering. A higher valuation can be placed on the company, and less equity will be given up by the founders for the required capital.

There are also a number of reasons why an entrepreneurial company would want to go public. The following are some of the advantages

- To raise more capital with less dilution than occurs with private placements or venture capital.
- To improve the balance sheet and/or to reduce or to eliminate debt, thereby enhancing the company's net worth.
- To obtain cash for pursuing opportunities that would otherwise be unaffordable.
- To access other suppliers of capital and to increase bargaining power, as the company pursues additional capital when it needs it least.
- To improve credibility with customers, vendors, key people, and prospects. To give the impression that "You're in the big leagues now."
- To achieve liquidity for owners and investors.
- To create options to acquire other companies with a tax-free exchange of stock, rather than having to use cash.
- To create equity incentives for new and existing employees.

[29] This synopsis is drawn from "Rational Drug Design Corporation," HBS Case 293-102, Harvard Business School, 1992.

Notwithstanding the above, IPOs can be disadvantageous for a number of reasons:

- The legal, accounting, and administrative costs of raising money via a public offering are more disadvantageous than other ways of raising money.
- A large amount of management effort, time, and expense are required to comply with SEC regulations and reporting requirements and to maintain the status of a public company. This diversion of management's time and energy from the tasks of running the company can adversely affect its performance and growth.
- Management can become more interested in maintaining the price of the company's stock and computing capital gains than in running the company. Short-term activities to maintain or increase a current year's earnings can take precedence over longer-term programs to build the company and increase its earnings.
- The liquidity of a company's stock achieved through a public offering may be more apparent than real. Without a sufficient number of shares outstanding and a strong "market maker," there may be no real market for the stock and, thus, no liquidity.
- The investment banking firms willing to take a new or unseasoned company public may not be the ones with whom the company would like to do business and establish a long-term relationship.

Private Placement after Going Public[30]

Sometimes a company goes public and then, for any number of reasons that add up to bad luck, the high expectations that attracted lots of investors in the first place turn sour. Your financial picture worsens; there is a cash crisis; down goes the price of your stock in the public marketplace. You find that you need new funds to work your way out of difficulties, but public investors are disillusioned and not likely to cooperate if you bring out a new issue.

Still, other investors are sophisticated enough to see beyond today's problems; they know the company's fundamentals are sound. While the public has turned its back on you, these investors may well be receptive if you offer a private placement to tide you over. In such circumstances, you may use a wide variety of securities—common stock, convertible preferred stock, convertible debentures. There are several types of exempt offerings. They are usually described by reference to the securities regulation that applies to them.

Regulation D is the result of the first cooperative effort by the SEC and the state securities associations to develop a uniform exemption from registration for small issuers. A significant number of states allow for qualification under state law in coordination with the qualification under Regulation D. Heavily regulated states, such as California, are notable exceptions. However, even in California, the applicable exemption is fairly consistent with the Regulation D concept.

Although Regulation D outlines procedures for exempt offerings, there is a requirement to file certain information (Form D), with the SEC. Form D is a relatively short form that asks for certain general information about the issuer and the securities being issued, as well as some specific data about the expenses of the offering and the intended use of the proceeds.

Regulation D provides exemptions from registration when securities are being sold in certain circumstances. The various circumstances are commonly referred to by the applicable Regulation D rule number. The rules and their application are as follows:

Rule 504. Issuers that are not subject to the reporting obligations of the Securities Exchange Act of 1934 (nonpublic companies) and that are not investment companies may sell up to $1,000,000 worth of securities over a 12-month period to an unlimited number of investors.

Rule 505. Issuers that are not investment companies may sell up to $5 million worth of securities over a 12-month period to no more than 35 nonaccredited purchasers, and to an unlimited number of accredited investors. Such issuers may be eligible for this exemption even though they are public companies (subject to the reporting requirements of the 1934 Act).

Rule 506. Issuers may sell an unlimited number of securities to no more than 35 unaccredited but sophisticated purchasers, and to an unlimited number of accredited purchasers. Public companies may be eligible for this exemption.

Employee Stock Option Plans (ESOPs)

ESOPs are another potential source of funding used by existing companies that have high confidence in the stability of their future earnings and cash flow. An ESOP is a program in which the employees become investors in the company, thereby creating an internal source of funding. An ESOP is a tax-qualified retirement benefit plan. In essence, an ESOP borrows money, usually from a bank or insurance company, and uses the cash proceeds to buy the

---

[30] Garner, Owen, and Conway, *The Ernst & Young Guide to Raising Capital*, pp. 52–54.

company's stock (usually from the owners or the treasury). The stock then becomes collateral for the bank note, while the owners or treasury have cash that can be used for a variety of purposes. For the lender, 50 percent of the interest earned on the loan to the ESOP is tax exempt. The company makes annual tax-deductible contributions—of *both* interest and principal—to the ESOP in an amount needed to service the bank loan. "The combination of being able to invest in employer stock and to benefit from its many tax advantages make the ESOP an attractive tool."[31]

Keeping Current about Capital Markets

One picture is vivid from all this: Capital markets, especially for closely held, private companies right through the initial public offering, are very dynamic, volatile, asymmetrical, and imperfect. Keeping abreast of what is happening in the capital markets in the 6 to 12 months prior to a major capital infusion can save invaluable time and hundreds of thousands and occasionally millions of dollars. Below are listed the best sources currently available to keep you informed:

- William D. Bygrave and Jeffry A. Timmons, *Venture Capital at the Crossroads* (Boston: Harvard Business School Press, 1992).
- Daniel R. Garner, Robert R. Owen, and Robert P. Conway, *The Ernst & Young Guide to Raising Capital* (New York: John Wiley & Sons, 1991).
- David Schutt ed., *Pratt's Guide to Venture Capital Sources* (New York: Venture Economics Publishing, 1993).
- *Venture Capital Journal* (published monthly by Venture Economics Publishing).
- *Venture Finance.*
- *IPO Reporter.*
- *INC.*
- *Red Herring,* a Silicon Valley magazine.
- *Venture One,* database and reports on venture capital from California.

Chapter Summary

1. Entrepreneurs have to determine the *need* for outside investors, whether they *want* outside investors, and if so whom.

2. America's unique capital markets include a wide array of private investors, from "Angels" to venture capitalists.

3. The search for capital can be very time consuming, and whom you obtain money from is more important than how much.

4. It is said that the only thing that is harder to get from a venture capitalist than a "yes" is a "no."

5. Fortunately for entrepreneurs, the booming rebirth of classic venture capital in the 1990s has raised the valuations and the sources available.

6. Entrepreneurs who know what and whom to look for—and look out for—increase their odds for success.

Study Questions

1. What is meant by the following, and why are these important: cover your equity; angels; venture capital; valuation; due diligence; IPO; mezzanine; SBIC; private placement; Regulation D; Rules 504, 505, and 506; and ESOP?

2. What does one look for in an investor, and why?

3. How can the founders prepare for the due diligence and evaluation process?

4. Describe the venture capital investing process and its implications for fund raising.

5. Most venture capitalists say: There is too much money chasing too few deals. Why is this so?

6. What other sources of capital are available and how are these accessed?

MIND STRETCHER
Have You Considered?

1. Some entrepreneurs say you shouldn't raise venture capital unless you have no other alternative. Do you agree or disagree, and why?

2. Identify a founder/CEO who has raised outside capital, and was later fired by the Board of Directors. What are the lessons here?

3. How do venture capitalists make money? What are the economics of venture capital as a business?

---

[31] Ibid., p. 281.

Preparation Questions

1. Evaluate the business opportunity for the franchisee and the franchisor. How do they make money in this business?
2. Evaluate the company's growth and financial strategy. What have been the consequences?
3. Evaluate the current strategy, both for growth and for financing. How much money is needed and when?
4. What should Hindman do?

Dismal Friday

It is March 10, 1983, another "Dismal Friday" for Jiffy Lube, Inc., and Jim Hindman, president and founder. Today's layoffs are the latest in a series of cutbacks that have reduced Jiffy Lube's payroll by over 40 percent since the beginning of February. The layoffs and other cost reductions are painful, but Hindman realizes that things can still get worse.

Jim Hindman founded Jiffy Lube in 1979. Now, in March 1983, it is the largest franchisor of quick oil change and lubrication service centers in the United States. Jiffy Lube service centers perform a "14 point fluid maintenance program" on automobiles in approximately 10 minutes. Customers pay $18–$20 for the basic service (optional services also are provided for an additional charge).

Background

After graduating from the University of Minnesota with a master's degree in health care administration, Hindman worked 10 years as a hospital administrator. In 1967, he started his own health care business, Hindman & Associates. The company built 32 nursing homes and eventually diversified into several unrelated businesses. By the mid-1970s, Hindman's ownership interests in these ventures were worth several million dollars, and he was bored and looking for new challenges.

In the early 1970s, Hindman began coaching football in his free time, eventually taking over as head coach of Western Maryland College in 1977. By 1979, Hindman was again restless and looking for new business opportunities. One of the factors that prompted Hindman to start another business was a comment made by one of his students, who claimed that: "There are no opportunities left. You couldn't make a million dollars in America today."

"I was really perplexed at how in the hell he could come away from college believing that," recalls Hind-

man. "That really was a major, triggering, emotional event that caused me to start looking around for a new business." Joining him were Ed Kelley and Steve Spinelli. Kelley had worked for Hindman in the health care business and was an assistant coach at Western Maryland.

The fast oil change business quickly caught Hindman's attention. Research revealed that in the prior 10 years, the number of full-service gas stations had been reduced by almost half. Most had been replaced by self-service stations, which didn't do oil changes or other minor maintenance. Hindman's brother-in-law knew a man who operated a "Jiffy Lube" franchise (part of a chain of oil change centers headquartered in Utah). After several meetings with Jiffy Lube's owner in Utah, Hindman purchased the Jiffy Lube trademark and the rights to seven franchises.

Early Strategy

Jim Hindman describes Jiffy Lube's early progress after acquiring the first seven units in May 1979:

> We spent most of the first year putting together a formal policy and procedure manual for the franchises and developing a standard design for the service centers. E&W assisted us in the development of our franchise audit program and in setting up our accounting system. We also did a complete market study; we were trying to develop a system that would be responsive to the customer.

Jiffy Lube's early strategy is summarized in excerpts from a business plan prepared in the first year of operation (see *Exhibit A*).

Ed Kelley sums up their early strategy:

> Our goal was to get to 100 units as quickly as possible. We were trying to reach a level of respectability. That would allow us to go out and do some of the things we needed to do, which was primarily to attract capital, and attract people to buy our franchises.

Expansion . . . and Losses

The Jiffy Lube network of service centers has grown rapidly from its original seven units (*Exhibit B*). The growth has come from the acquisition of four small chains of service centers (approximately 30 units in total), the acquisition of individual centers, and the sale of new franchises.

Jiffy Lube has successfully expanded its network of service centers, but it has incurred cumulative losses of more than $5 million since inception (*Exhibit C*). The entire network of service centers is projected to generate over $15 million in sales for fiscal 1983. However, as the

EXHIBIT A

Business Plan

Over 100 Jiffy Lube Service centers will be in operation by the end of 1982. Expansion will be accomplished through:

1. Sales of new franchises.
2. Acquisition of existing service centers or small franchise chains which meet the company's specifications.

Franchising will be used as the primary means of expanding the Jiffy Lube network. Franchising will attract qualified managers to each individual center because of the ownership opportunity offered them. Franchising will also accelerate growth because it eliminates many of the managerial and financial requirements that would be necessary to develop and maintain a large network of company-operated centers.

Franchises will be positioned to create blocks of service centers in targeted cities. "Clustering" these centers in large blocks will build name recognition and make advertising cost-effective.

The overall image of Jiffy Lube is not yet at the point where all franchisees will be willing to pay up front the $250K–$300K required to purchase land and develop a new center. In many situations it may be necessary for Jiffy Lube to provide the real estate development financing.

Reaching 100 units by the end of 1982 will require the sale of 40 to 60 new franchises (depending on the number of units acquired from existing chains). The company may find it necessary to provide real estate financing for half, or 20 to 30, of these units. Based on a cost of $300K per unit, Jiffy Lube will need to obtain real estate financing of $6 million to $9 million to achieve the projected level of new franchise sales.

EXHIBIT B

Jiffy Lube Service Center Network (includes statistics for both franchised and company-owned centers)

	Year Ending March 31			
	1980	1981	1982	1983 (projected)
Total gross sales for network (millions)	$1.5	$2.5	$7.1	$15.6
Total centers in operation:				
Franchised	7	19	40	96
Company owned	1	10	30	0

EXHIBIT C

Jiffy Lube, Inc., Operating Results

	Year Ended March 31 (in millions)			
	1980	1981	1982	1983 (projected)
Revenues	$.2	$2.0	$3.5	$5.5
Net loss	$(0.4)	$(0.7)	$(1.4)	$(2.6)

See *Exhibit G* for projected 1983 financial statements.

franchisor, Jiffy Lube shares in only a portion of this total. Jiffy Lube's revenues are made up of the following:

- Royalty fees from franchisees (approximately 5 percent of each franchisee's gross sales).
- Rental income on property leased or subleased to franchisees.
- Initial fees from new franchises (approximately $20,000 per new service center).
- Sales by company-owned centers (however, as described in a later section, all company-owned centers were disposed of in fiscal 1983).

The majority of franchisees are individuals who operate one or two franchises.

Early Financing

Jiffy Lube was financed during its startup and first several years of growth largely through Jim Hindman's personal resources. During the first three years of operation Hindman contributed over $1.5 million in the form of cash, assumptions of debt, and forgiveness of personal loans made to Jiffy Lube. Hindman also personally guaranteed certain transactions Jiffy Lube entered into, including lines of credit with banks, loans relating to the purchase or development of service centers, and real estate lease obligations. Ernst & Whinney provided introductions to several banks and, at Hindman's request, participated in key meetings with the bankers.

Financing also was obtained through the sale of stock to directors, officers, employees, and other investors. The most significant sale was a private placement of $530K in preferred stock, the majority of which was sold to a small group of Midwest investors. In addition, Jiffy Lube used its common stock in several acquisitions, the largest being the purchase of Speedy Lube, a franchisor and operator of seven oil change centers.

In addition to the above, the need for real estate financing outlined in Jiffy Lube's business plan resulted in the company's most significant financing transaction to date, its 1981 agreement with Pennzoil.

Pennzoil Agreement

In December 1980, Hindman and Kelley attended a trade meeting put on by Pennzoil for its regional sales people and major distributors. Pennzoil was the oil supplier for the majority of Jiffy Lube centers and believed that the quick oil change business could become a new major distribution channel for oil products. Pennzoil saw the quick change industry as an opportunity to gain market share from Quaker State, the leading oil distributor in the eastern United States. Pennzoil's national sales manager told Hindman that the oil company planned on building 100 quick oil change centers in the East.

Hindman spent the night writing a proposal to convince Pennzoil to work with Jiffy Lube, rather than compete against it. In October 1981, the two companies signed an agreement (*Exhibit D*). For $1 million Jiffy Lube sold convertible preferred stock representing 29 percent of the company to Pennzoil. The agreement allowed Pennzoil to place four members on Jiffy Lube's board of directors. Pennzoil agreed to guarantee $6.3 million of real estate financing. Service centers developed with the financing guaranteed by Pennzoil were required to purchase the majority of their oil products from Pennzoil.

Pennzoil's financing allowed Jiffy Lube to initiate its aggressive expansion plan. The agreement also strengthened Jiffy Lube's financial credibility, and enabled it to increase its bank line of credit from $300K to over $1.2 million.

The relationship with Pennzoil was far from perfect, however. The two companies apparently had different objectives, which resulted in different strategies for Jiffy Lube's expansion. Jiffy Lube's business plan emphasized "clustering" and "franchising"; Pennzoil advocated "wide coverage" and "assured distribution channel" (company-owned service centers).

Jiffy Lube quickly discovered that Pennzoil's "right to approve the selection of new sites" as outlined in the agreement really meant that the oil company would select the new sites. Pennzoil used a "scattergun" approach to site selection. To create maximum exposure for the Pennzoil name, the oil company wanted service centers to be developed in as many markets as possible. "It seemed like we had one center in every major city from Miami to Boston," recalls Hindman.

EXHIBIT D

Pennzoil Agreement

Pennzoil will purchase 10,000 shares of Jiffy Lube Convertible Preferred Stock for $1,000,000.

Cumulative dividends of $12 per preferred share are payable quarterly. Any deficiency must be paid or declared before setting aside any funds for any junior stock. These shares are redeemable by Jiffy Lube at any time after November 17, 1985, upon payment in cash of $110 per share plus an amount equal to all accrued dividends. They can be converted at the option of Pennzoil into common stock at a conversion price of $0.553 per share of each $1.00 Preferred Stock value.

Pennzoil shall have the option of electing the greater of 3 or 30 percent of the members of the board of directors of Jiffy Lube.

Jiffy Lube agrees to furnish Pennzoil certain financial information, including audited financial statements within 150 days after the close of each fiscal year, and unaudited statements within 45 days after the close of the first three fiscal quarters.

Jim Hindman, and then Jiffy Lube, shall have the right of first refusal should Pennzoil desire to sell any of its shares of Jiffy Lube stock. Pennzoil has the right of first refusal should Jim Hindman decide to sell any of his shares of Jiffy Lube stock.

Pennzoil agrees to issue a commitment to guarantee $6,250,000 worth of indebtedness to be incurred in connection with the financing of real estate site acquisition and construction cost in connection with the erection of Jiffy Lube centers. These units are to be built east of the Mississippi River and generally along the eastern seaboard.

Pennzoil agrees to guarantee an additional $1,000,000 in order to finance Jiffy Lube's purchase from Pennzoil of four units which Pennzoil has financed under its "Build to Suit" program.

Any units built using financing guaranteed by Pennzoil will be required to enter into a Lube Center Sales Agreement and to execute a Pennzoil Sign Agreement. Pennzoil will have the right to approve the selection of new sites to be financed under this agreement.

In addition, Pennzoil did not believe that franchising should be relied on to provide all of the growth. Jim Hindman:

> As soon as we signed the agreement and walked out of their corporate offices, they took me by the hand and got us involved in the acquisition of service centers which we were to operate. This was despite the fact that our business plan specifically stated that we were going to go out and franchise.

Under Pennzoil's direction, Jiffy Lube acquired three chains of oil change centers (23 units in total) in late 1981 and early 1982. Hindman felt that Pennzoil's strategy ran counter to Jiffy Lube's own strategy and that "our business plan had been trashed. We were not capitalized to operate these centers, and we didn't have the management team." Why did Jiffy Lube go along? "They were supplying the money. I felt that we just got married to these guys; we've got to go along to get along."

The acquired stores quickly became a burden to Jiffy Lube. By the end of fiscal 1982, 30 of the 70 Jiffy Lube centers were owned and operated by the company. These required a large commitment of Jiffy Lube's managerial and financial resources and resulted in significant overhead costs. And sales at many of the new centers were not growing as fast as expected. "Every market where we had just one unit we were dying," recalls Hindman. Jiffy Lube lost $1.4 million in the year ended March 31, 1982, and was expected to lose $2.6 million for fiscal 1983.

By April 1982 Hindman made three major decisions:

1. All company-owned centers would be sold to franchisees.
2. Hindman was going to buy Pennzoil's Jiffy Lube stock.
3. Jiffy Lube would have to find other sources of financing to continue its growth plans.

Between May 1982 and February 1983, Jiffy Lube sold all of its company-owned centers to franchisees. In most cases, to expedite the sale, Jiffy Lube retained ownership of the service center's real estate and sold only the rights to operate the franchise. The real estate was then leased to the franchisee.

Hindman had also tried to resolve the conflict with Pennzoil:

> We tried to convince Pennzoil that (1) we had to cluster and (2) we had to have a different relationship. They were a giant and they took too long. They had 10 committees, and everything required 10 sign-offs. We needed to move fast to get back to our original strategy. Our only solution was to buy them out. We had to move carefully, though. We wanted to end up with a good relationship with Pennzoil. Even if they sold us the stock back, they were still our largest supplier, and had guaranteed over $5 million in real estate financing for us.
>
> From October 1982 to February 1983, I didn't put any money into the company even though we were hurting. I knew that if I started putting money in, it would just give Pennzoil an incentive to want to keep their stock. So we let our payables build up and let a large part of our staff go.

In February 1983, Pennzoil agreed to sell Hindman its stock for $435K. Jiffy Lube's worsening financial status during fiscal 1983 made it easier for Hindman to buy out Pennzoil: "They wanted out. Maybe they thought we were going bankrupt, and they could pick up the service centers after we went under."

The split with Pennzoil was reasonably amicable. Hindman:

> They recognized that the arrangement wasn't working. Pennzoil still believed in the concept of quick oil change centers, though. They believed that regardless of whether we survived or not, a large amount of oil was going to be sold through the quick change centers. Pennzoil kept their real estate guarantees in place.

Current Situation: 1983

Now, in 1983, Jiffy Lube feels that it is well positioned for the future, despite the past losses and current cash crises. Jiffy Lube has 96 units and is the largest franchisor of quick oil change centers in the United States. The company has reached a respectable size and feels it can take advantage of the name recognition being generated in some areas.

In addition, the company has gotten back to its original strategy of franchising, rather than operating service centers. The sale of all company-owned stores has cut costs and freed management to spend more time selecting and selling new franchise sites. The company expects to open at least 25 new franchises in the coming year. Jiffy Lube also expects improvements in the units it recently sold, as franchised centers have historically outperformed the company-owned centers. *Exhibit E* summarizes the financial characteristics of the typical franchise.

Fiscal 1983 is coming to a close, and management's analysis of future operations has been prepared, along with projected financial statements based on the first 11 months of operation (Exhibits F, G, H, I, and J). Jiffy Lube is now dependent on franchise royalties and rental income, because of the sale of the company stores.

Because of its dependence on franchise royalties, Jiffy Lube needs to quickly increase the number of franchises. Much of the growth to date has come through the acquisition of existing chains. Franchise agreements for new units are typically made with individuals for one or two service centers. Experience to date has proven that the sale and development of new franchises can be accelerated when Jiffy Lube offers to provide or arrange for real estate and construction financing.

Possible Alternatives

Hindman has already used the majority of his liquid assets in his prior contributions to Jiffy Lube and in the purchase of the Pennzoil stock. His major remaining assets are his interests in W. James Hindman, Ltd. (75 percent

---

EXHIBIT E

Financial Characteristics of Typical Jiffy Lube Franchise

Real estate requirements	15,000 square feet of land (building interior covers 2,500 square feet)
Cost of land and building	$300,000
Startup costs (equipment, etc.)	$100,000
Monthly fixed costs	$8,000
Variable costs	57% of sales
Breakeven car count/day	28–35 cars
Typical months to breakeven	7–8 months

A "typical" mature unit (approximately two years old) will service between 60–70 cars per day, producing annual revenues of about $400,000–$500,000 and $75,000–$100,000 of pretax income.

Depending on whether the franchisee owns or leases the real estate, the monthly fixed costs include a charge for either:

1. Rent ($3,000–$4,000) paid to Jiffy Lube or to a 3rd party lessor, or
2. A similar charge for mortgage interest.

The 96 franchises currently in operation have the following real estate arrangements:

Real estate owned by Jiffy Lube and rented to the franchisee	20
Real estate owned by Jiffy Lube and subleased to the franchisee	4
Real estate owned or leased by the franchisee. (Approximately 30 of these were part of chains to which Jiffy Lube acquired the franchise rights. In these cases the franchisees already had their own real estate arrangements before Jiffy Lube became involved.)	72

EXHIBIT F

Management's Analysis of Future Operations

Management has made the following projections of future operations:

Service Centers in Operation

Fiscal Year	At Year End	On Average during the Year	Total Gross Sales for Network
1983	96	83	$16 million
		(based on 11 months of actual operations)	
1984	125	111	$28 million
1985	200	163	$49 million
1986	300	250	$75 million

In addition to projecting the future revenues, management has reviewed current expenditures and made the following prognosis for the upcoming year:

1. All expenses related to the company-operated centers have been eliminated.
2. Management believes that because of the recent restructuring, selling, general, and administrative expenses can be held to approximately $2.1 million during fiscal 1984. To achieve the growth projected for fiscal 1985 and 1986, it is anticipated that selling, general, and administrative (S, G, & A) expenses will have to increase to $2.6 million and $3.1 million respectively.
3. The only other significant expenses expected are interest on the outstanding debt and real estate lease commitments.

---

ownership), and several other nursing home partnerships (these might be worth as much as $3 million).

Hindman has considered disposing of his partnership interests to provide cash for Jiffy Lube. However, Hindman's tax basis in these (approximately $200K) is far less than the current market value, and he views the outright sale of them as a last resort because of the tax conse-

quences. Several other investors in W. James Hindman, Ltd., are also shareholders in Jiffy Lube and seem willing to use their investments to raise cash for Jiffy Lube.

Another source Jiffy Lube has considered is a second private placement with existing shareholders. Specific terms haven't been discussed, and it is unknown how much these investors would be willing to contribute.

EXHIBIT G

Projected Statement of Operations and Balance Sheet

Projected Statement of Operations

	Year Ended March 31, 1983 (projected)
Revenues:	
Sales by company-operated units	$3,877,000
Initial franchise fees	685,000
Franchise royalties	542,000
Rental income from franchisees	276,000
Net gain on sales of company-operated units	40,000
Miscellaneous	41,000
Total revenues	5,461,000
Expenses:	
Company-operated units:	
Cost of products sold	1,300,000
Salaries and wages	1,090,000
Depreciation and amortization	180,000
Interest	258,000
Rent	308,000
Other	1,250,000
Total units expenses	4,386,000
Commissions	136,000
Selling, general, and administrative expenses	2,749,000
Interest expense	762,000
Total expenses	8,033,000
Net loss	$(2,572,000)

Projected Balance Sheet

	March 31, 1983 (projected)
Assets	
Current assets:	
Cash	$139,000
Accounts receivable	962,000
Prepaid expenses	23,000
Total current assets	1,124,000
Accounts receivable from future franchises	636,000
Property and equipment:	
Land	2,372,000
Buildings and improvements	3,913,000
Automobiles, furniture, and equipment	255,000
Construction in progress	682,000
	7,222,000
Less allowances for depreciation	203,000
	7,019,000
Intangible assets—trademarks, franchise rights, and deferred finance costs	815,000
Deferred franchise costs	199,000
Other assets	103,000
Total assets	$9,896,000

(Continued)

EXHIBIT G (concluded)

Liabilities and Stockholders' Equity

Current liabilities:	
Accounts payable and accrued expenses	
Due to officers, directors, and employees	$1,252,000
Notes payable	696,000
Current portion of long-term debt	2,211,000
Current portion of capital lease obligations	86,000
Total current liabilities	4,000
Long-term debt, less current portion	4,249,000
Capital lease obligations, less current portion	6,577,000
Deferred franchise fees	359,000
Stockholders' equity:	1,143,000
Series A 12% cumulative convertible preferred stock	
$12.00 cumulative convertible preferred stock	1,307,000
Common stock	1,000,000
Capital in excess of par value	166,000
Retained-earnings deficit	880,000
	(5,238,000)
Less cost of common stock held in treasury	(1,885,000)
Total stockholders' equity	(547,000)
Total liabilities and stockholders' equity	(2,432,000)
	$9,896,000

EXHIBIT H

Long-Term Debt/Rent Commitments at March 1983

Description	March 1983 Balance	Interest Rate	Payment Terms/ Comments
Construction loans:			
NA mortgage	$5,372,000	16.5%	Monthly payments of approximately $75,000 are required in fiscal 1984. Requires increasing monthly payments for interest and maturity through February 1994. Guaranteed by Pennzoil.
Maryland National Bank	524,000	Prime	Monthly payments of approximately $7,000, varying based on the prime interest rate.
Notes relating to acquisitions of service center chains:			
Benchmark/Archeo	250,000	Prime + 1%	Due 6/85
Browns Quick Lube	117,000	13%	Due 2/87
Joe Wilkerson	117,000	13%	Due 2/87
Stock repurchase—John Lindholm	104,000	Prime	Annual payments of approximately $50,000.
Others	179,000	Vary from 12% to 18%	Mature at various times through 1987.
	$6,663,000		
Rent commitments:			
Fiscal 1984 commitments *payable* under capital and operating leases ($150K represents real estate subleased to franchisees; the remainder is office building, etc., included in S, G & A)	$ 230,000		
Rentals *receivable* in fiscal 1984 from franchises already in operation, land, buildings, and improvements rented to franchisees	$ 775,000		

EXHIBIT I

Notes Payable and Amounts Due to Officers, Directors, and Employees at March 1983

Description	March 1983 Balance	Interest Rate	Payment Terms/Comments
Notes payable:			
Bank lines of credit:			Minimum interest rate of 12%. The notes become payable at various times between 6/83 and 3/84. Jiffy Lube has drawn the full amount of each line.
Maryland National Bank	$499,000	Prime + 1%	
Savings Bank	500,000	Prime + 1%	
1st National	250,000	Prime + 1%	
Jiffy Lube International Partnership #1	675,000	Prime + 1/2%	Due on demand. Hindman owns 27% of partnership. Another 56% is owned by four individuals who are directors (or former directors) of Jiffy Lube.
Notes to four accounts payable vendors	287,000	0–10%	All due by 6/83.
	$2,211,000		
Due to officers, directors, and employees:			
Jim Hindman	$550,000	Prime + 1%	Due on demand.
Others	146,000		Majority are noninterest-bearing demand notes to J. Hindman.
	$696,000		

EXHIBIT J

Ownership at March 1983

	Shares	Percent
Common stock	2,133,333	69%
Jim Hindman, president/CEO	285,710	9
Gilbert Campbell, director	675,775	22
Others (less than 5%)	3,094,818	100%
Series A 12% cumulative preferred stock:	7,255	66%
Jim Hindman	5,815	44
Others (less than 5%)	13,070	100%

(Convertible at the option of the holders into approximately 1,568,000 shares of common stock.)

	Shares	Percent
$12.00 cumulative convertible preferred stock:		
Jim Hindman	10,000	100%

(Convertible at the option of the holders into approximately 1,808,000 shares of common stock.)

Chapter Fourteen

The Deal: Valuation, Structure, and Negotiation

Always assume the deal will not close and keep several alternatives alive.

James Hindman
Founder, Chief Executive Officer, and Chairman
Jiffy Lube International

Results Expected

Upon completion of this chapter, you will have:

1. Determined methodologies used by venture capitalists and professional investors to estimate the value of a company.
2. Examined how equity proportions are allocated to investors.
3. Examined how deals are structured, including critical terms, conditions, and covenants.
4. Examined key aspects of negotiating and closing deals.
5. Characterized good versus bad deals and identified some of the sand traps entrepreneurs face in venture financing.
6. Analyzed an actual deal presented to an entrepreneur in the Bridge Capital Investors case.

The Art and Craft of Valuation

Entrepreneurial Value versus Corporate Finance Value[1]

Entrepreneurial finance differs from corporate finance in a number of dimensions. First the players and markets that are explored are different; corporate finance deals primarily with decisions confronting chief financial officers of publicly traded companies. Entrepreneurial finance deals primarily with decisions confronting the chief executive officer of private companies. The suppliers of capital to each are very different. Also, the nature of the contracts between suppliers and users of capital is very different. Finally, the typical projects, companies, industries, and stages of development are very different. Corporate finance deals with more mature situations than entrepreneurial finance; in the latter, the context of decision making is more often characterized by rapid change and great uncertainty.

Determinants of Value

The message here is simple. The criteria and methods applied in corporate finance to value companies traded publicly in the capital markets, when cavalierly

---

[1] The following paragraph is adapted from "Entrepreneurial Finance—Course Introduction," by William A. Sahlman. HBS Note 9-288-004, Harvard Business School, 1988, p. 6. Copyright © 1988 by the President and Fellows of Harvard College.

applied to entrepreneurial companies, have severe limitations. The ingredients to the entrepreneurial valuation are cash, time, and risk. In Chapter 12 you determined the burn rate, OOC, and the TTC for your venture, so it is not hard to infer that the amount of cash available and the cash generated will play an important role in valuation. Similarly, if you recall *Exhibit 12.5*, "The Entrepreneur's Bargaining Power Based on Time to OOC," you'll remember that time also plays an influential role. Finally, risk or perception of risk contributes to the determination of value. The old adage "The greater the risk, the greater the reward" plays a considerable role in how investors size up the venture. A useful theoretical way of understanding how risk levels are perceived by the capital markets is shown in *Exhibit 14.1*. Consider for a moment that you are thinking about investing $1,000 and your options are to invest in a startup company or in a mutual fund. Where would you expect the greater return? Why?

Long-term Value Creation versus Quarterly Earnings

The core mission of the entrepreneur is to build the best company possible and, if possible, a great company. This is the single surest way of generating long-term value for all the stakeholders and society. Such a mission has quite different strategic imperatives than one aimed solely at maximizing quarterly earnings in order to attain the highest share price possible given price/earnings ratios at the time. More will be said about this in Chapter 18, "The Harvest and Beyond."

Psychological Factors Determining Value

Time after time companies are valued at preposterous multiples of any sane price/earnings or sales ratios. In the best years, for example, the 1992–93 bull market, the New York Stock Exchange Index was trading at nearly 20 times earnings; it sank to around 8 after the stock market crash of October 19, 1987. Even 12 to 15

EXHIBIT 14.1

Risk versus Rate of Return

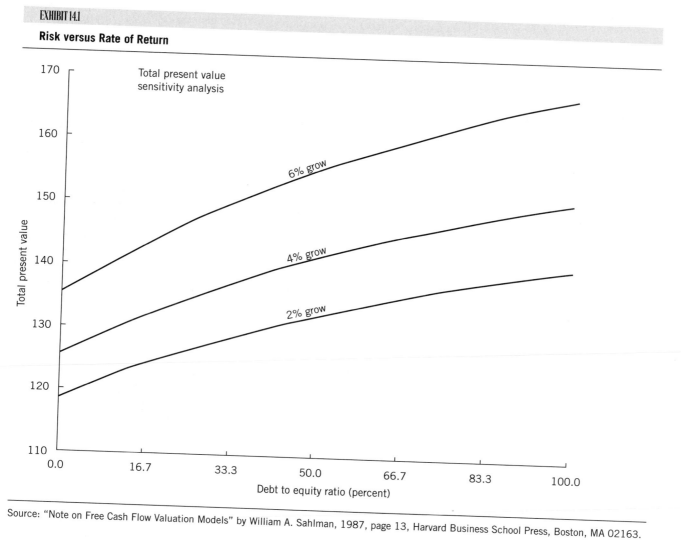

Source: "Note on Free Cash Flow Valuation Models" by William A. Sahlman, 1987, page 13, Harvard Business School Press, Boston, MA 02163.

would be considered good in many years. In contrast, consider a recent survey of the top one hundred public companies in Massachusetts. The stocks of many of these companies were being traded at 50 or more times earnings and several were at 95 to 100 times earnings and six to seven times sales!

Often what is behind extraordinarily high valuations is a psychological wave, a combination of euphoric enthusiasm for a fine company, exacerbated by greed and fear—of missing the run up. The same psychology can also drive prices to undreamed of heights in private companies. In the late 1960s, for instance, Xerox bought Scientific Data Systems, then at $100 million in sales and earning $10 million after taxes, for $1 billion: 10 times sales and 100 times earnings! Value is also in the eye of the beholder.

A Theoretical Perspective

Establishing Boundaries and Ranges, Rather than Calculating a Number. Valuation is much more than science, as can be seen from the examples just noted. As will be seen shortly, there are at least a dozen different ways of determining the value of a private company. A lot of assumptions and a lot of judgment calls are made in every valuation exercise. In one case, for example, the entrepreneur consulted 13 different experts to determine how much he should bid for the other half of a $10 million in sales company. The answers ranged from $1 million to $6 million. He subsequently acquired the other half for $3.5 million.

It can be a serious mistake, therefore, to approach the valuation task in hopes of arriving at a single number or even a quite narrow range. All you can realistically expect is a range of values with boundaries driven by the different methods and underlying assumptions for each. Within that range the buyer and the seller need to determine the comfort zone of each. At what point are you basically indifferent to buying and selling? Determining your point of indifference can be an invaluable aid in preparing you for negotiations to buy or sell.

Investor's Required Rate of Return (IRR)

Various investors will require a different rate of return (ROR) for investments in different stages of development and will expect holding periods of various lengths. For example, *Exhibit 14.2* summarizes, as ranges, the annual rates of return that venture capital investors seek on investments in firms by stage of development and how long they expect to hold these investments. Several factors underlie the required ROR on a venture capital investment, including premium for systemic risk, illiquidity, and value added. Of course, these can be expected to vary regionally and from time to time as market conditions change, because these investments are in what are decidedly imperfect capital market niches to begin with.

Investor's Required Share of Ownership

The rate of return required by the investor determines the investor's required share of the ownership, as *Exhibit 14.3* illustrates. The future value of our $1 million investment at 50 percent compounded is $1 million $\times (1.5)^5 = $1 million $\times 7.59 = 7.59$ million. The future value of the company in Year 5 is profit after tax $\times$ price/earnings ratio = $1 million $\times 15 = $15 million. Thus, the share of ownership required in year five is:

$$\frac{\text{Future value of the investment}}{\text{Future value of the company}} = \frac{\$7.59 \text{ million}}{\$15.00 \text{ million}} = 51\%$$

As a final note, one can readily see that by changing any of the key variables, the results will change accordingly.

If the venture capitalists require the RORs mentioned earlier, the ownership they also require is determined as follows: In the startup stage, 25–75 percent for investing all of the required funds; beyond the startup stage, 10–40 percent, depending on the amount invested, maturity, and track record of the venture; in a seasoned venture in the later rounds of investment, 10–30 percent to supply the additional funds needed to sustain its growth.

EXHIBIT 14.2

Rates of Return Sought by Venture Capital Investors

Stage	Annual ROR%	Typical Expected Holding Period (years)
Seed and startup	50–100% or more	More than 10
First stage	40–60	5–10
Second stage	30–40	4–7
Expansion	20–30	3–5
Bridge and mezzanine	20–30	1–3
LBOs	30–50	3–5
Turnarounds	50+	3–5

EXHIBIT 14.3

Investor's Required Share of Ownership under Various ROR Objectives

Assumptions:

Amount of initial startup investment = $1 million
Holding period = 5 years
Required rate of return = 50%

Year 5 after-tax profit = $1 million
Year 5 Price/earnings ratio = 15

Calculating the required share of ownership:

Price / Earnings Ratio	Investor's Return Objective Percent / Year Compounded			
	30%	40%	50%	60%
10 X	37%	54	76	106
15 X	25	36	51	70
20 X	19	27	38	52
25 X	15	22	30	42

Valuation Methods

The Venture Capital Method [2]

This method is appropriate for investments in a company with negative cash flows at the time of the investment, but which in a number of years is projected to generate significant earnings. As discussed in Chapter 13, venture capitalists are the most likely professional investors to partake in this type of an investment, thus the reference to the venture capital method. The steps involved in this method are as follows:

1. Estimate the company's *net income* in a number of years, at which time the investor plans on harvesting. This estimate will be based on the sales and margin projections presented by the entrepreneur in his or her business plan.

2. Determine the appropriate *price-to-earnings ratio,* or P/E ratio. The appropriate P/E ratio can be determined by studying current multiples for companies with similar economic characteristics.

3. Calculate the projected *terminal value* by multiplying net income and the P/E ratio.

4. The terminal value can then be discounted to find the *present value* of the investment. Venture capitalists use discount rates ranging from 35 percent to 80 percent, because of the risk involved in these types of investments.

5. To determine the investor's *required percentage of ownership,* based on their initial investment, the initial investment is divided by the estimated present value.

To summarize the above steps the following formula can be used:

$$\text{Final ownership required} = \frac{\text{Required future value (investment)}}{\text{Total terminal value}}$$

$$= \frac{(1 + \text{IRR})^{\text{years}} (\text{investment})}{\text{P/E ratio (terminal net income)}}$$

6. Finally, the number of shares and the share price must be calculated by using the following formula:

$$\text{New shares} = \frac{\text{Percentage of ownership required by investor}}{1 - (\text{Percentage ownership required by investor} \times \text{Old shares})}$$

By definition, the share price equals the price paid divided by the number of shares.

This method is commonly used by venture capitalists because they make equity investments in industries often requiring a large initial investment with significant projected revenues; in addition to the fact that in the negotiations, the percentage of ownership is a key issue.

The Fundamental Method

This method is simply the present value of the future earnings stream (see *Exhibit 14.4*).

The First Chicago Method [3]

Another alternative valuation method, developed at First Chicago Corporation's venture capital group, employs a lower discount rate, but applies it to an *expected* cash flow. That expected

---

[2] The venture capital method of valuation is adapted from William A. Sahlman, "A Method for Valuing High-Risk, Long-Term Investments: The "Venture Capital Method," Note 9-288-006, Harvard Business School, 1988, pp. 2–4. Copyright © 1988 by the President and Fellows of Harvard College.
[3] This paragraph is adapted from Sahlman, "A Method for Valuing High-Risk, Long-Term Investments: The Venture Capital Method," p. 56.

EXHIBIT 14.4

Example of the Fundamental Method

		Hitech, Inc.				
Year	Percentage growth of revenue	Revenue (millions)	After-Tax Margin	After-Tax Profit (millions)	Present Value Factor	PV of Each Year's Earnings (millions)
1	50%	$ 3.00	-0-	-0-	1.400	-0-
2	50	4.50	4.0%	$+0.18	1.960	$0.09
3	50	6.75	7.0	0.47	2.744	0.17
4	50	10.13	9.0	0.91	3.842	0.24
5	50	15.19	11.0	1.67	5.378	0.31
6	40	21.26	11.5	2.45	7.530	0.33
7	30	27.64	12.0	3.32	10.541	0.32
8	20	33.17	12.0	3.98	14.758	0.27
9	15	38.15	12.0	4.58	20.661	0.22
10	10	41.96	12.0	5.04	28.926	0.17
Total present value of earnings in the supergrowth period						$2.12
Residual future value of earnings stream				$ 63.00	28.926	2.18
Total present value of company						$4.30

Source: QED.

cash flow is the average of three possible scenarios, with each scenario weighted according to its perceived probability. The equation to determine the investor's required final ownership is:

$$\text{Required final ownership} = \frac{\text{Future value of investment} - \text{Future value of non-IPO cash flow}}{\text{Probability (Success)} \left(\text{Forecast terminal value} \right)}$$

This formula[4] differs from the original basic venture capital formula in two ways: (1) the basic formula assumes that there are no cash flows between the investment and the harvest in Year 5. The future value of the immediate cash flows is subtracted from the future value of the investment because the difference between them is what must be made up for out of the terminal value; (2) the basic formula does not distinguish between the *forecast* terminal value and the *expected* terminal value. The traditional method uses the forecast terminal value, which is adjusted through the use of a high discount rate. The formula employs the expected value of the terminal value. *Exhibit 14.5* is an example of using this method.

Ownership Dilution[5]   The previous example is unrealistic because in most cases, several rounds of investments are necessary to finance a high-potential venture. Take for instance the pricing worksheet presented in

Exhibit 14.6, in which three financing rounds are expected. In addition to estimating the appropriate discount rate for the current round, the first-round venture capitalist must now estimate the discount rates that are most likely to be applied in the following rounds, which are projected for Years 2 and 4. Although a 50 percent rate is still appropriate for Year 0, it is estimated that investors in HI-Potent, Inc., will demand a 40 percent return in Year 2, and a 25 percent return in Year 4. The final ownership that each investor must be left with, given a terminal price/earnings ratio of 15, can be calculated using the basic valuation formula:

Round 1:

$$\frac{\text{Future value (Investment)}}{\text{Terminal value (Company)}} = \frac{1.50^5 \times \$1.5 \text{ million}}{15 \times \$2.5 \text{ million}} = 30.4\% \text{ ownership}$$

Round 2:

$$(1.40^3 \times 1 \text{ million}) / (15 \times \$2.5 \text{ million}) = 7.3\%$$

Round 3:

$$(1.25^1 \times \$1 \text{ million}) / (15 \times \$1.5 \text{ million}) = 3.3\%$$

Discounted Cash Flow   In a simple discounted cash flow method, three time periods are defined: (1) Years 1–5, (2) Years 6–10, and (3) Years 11–infinity.[6] The necessary operating assumptions for each period are initial sales, growth rates, EBIAT/sales, and (net fixed

---

[4] Ibid., pp. 58–59.
[5] Ibid., p. 24.
[6] Jeffry A. Timmons, "Valuation Methods and Raising Capital," lecture, Harvard Business School, March 2, 1993.

EXHIBIT 14.5

Example of the First Chicago Method

	Success	Sideways Survival	Failure
1. Revenue growth rate (from base of $2 million)	60%	15%	0%
2. Revenue level after 3 years	$8.19 million	$3.04 million (liquidation)	$2 million
3. Revenue level after 5 years	$20.97 million (IPO)	$4.02 million	
4. Revenue level after 7 years		$5.32 million (acquisition)	
5. After-tax profit margin and earnings at liquidity	15% $3.15 million	7% $.37 million	
6. Price-earnings ratio at liquidity	17	7	
7. Value of company liquidity	$53.55 million	$2.61 million	$.69 million
8. Present value of company using discount rate of 40%	$9.96 million	$.25 million	$.25 million
9. Probability of each scenario	.4	.4	.2
10. Expected present value of the company under each scenario	$3.98 million	$.10 million	$.05 million
11. Expected present value of the company		$4.13 million	
12. Percentage ownership required to invest $2.5 million		60.5%	

EXHIBIT 14.6

Example of a Three-Stage Financing

Hi-Potent, Inc. (000)						
	Year 0 1989	Year 1 1990	Year 2 1991	Year 3 1992	Year 4 1993	Year 5 1994
Revenues	500	1,250	2,500	5,000	8,000	12,800
Net income	(250)	(62)	250	750	1,360	2,500
Working capital @ 20%	100	250	500	1,000	1,600	2,560
Fixed assets @ 40%	200	500	1,000	2,000	3,200	5,120
Free cash flow	(550)	(512)	(500)	(750)	(440)	(380)
Cumulative external financial need	500	1,653	1,543	2,313	2,753	3,133
Equity issues	1,500	0	1,000	0	1,000	0
Equity outstanding	1,500	1,500	2,500	2,500	3,500	3,500
Cash balance	950	436	938	188	748	368
Assume: long-term IRR required each round by investors	50%	45%	40%	30%	25%	20%

assets + operating working capital)/sales. While using this method, one should also note relationships and trade-offs. With these assumptions, the discount rate can be applied to the weighted average cost of capital (WACC).[7] Then the value for free cash flow (Years 1–10) is added to the terminal value. This terminal value is the growth perpetuity.

Other Rule-of-Thumb Valuation Methods Several other valuation methods are also employed to estimate the value of a company. Many of these are based on similar most recent transactions of similar firms, established by a sale of the company, or a prior investment. Such comparables may look at several different multiples, such as earnings, free cash flow, rev-

---

[7] Note that it is WACC, not free cash flow, because of the tax factor.

enue, EBIT, and book value. Knowledgeable investment bankers and venture capitalists make it their business to know the activity on the current market place for private capital and how deals are being priced. These methods are used most often to value an existing company, rather than a startup, since there are so many more knowns about the company and its financial performance.

Tar Pits Facing Entrepreneurs

Inherent Conflicts Between Users and Suppliers of Capital [8]

There are several inherent conflicts between entrepreneurs or the users of capital and investors or the suppliers of capital. Whereas the entrepreneur wants to have as much time as possible for the financing, the investors want to supply capital just in time or to invest only when the company needs the money. Entrepreneurs should be thinking of raising money when they do not need it, while preserving the option to find another source of capital.

Similarly, users of capital want to raise as much money as possible, while the investors want to supply just enough capital in staged capital commitments. The investors, such as venture capitalists, use staged capital commitments to manage their risk exposure over 6- to 12-month increments of investing.

In the negotiations of a deal, the entrepreneur sometimes becomes attracted to a high valuation with the sentiment "My price, your terms." The investors will generally attempt to change this opinion, because after all it is their capital. The investors will thus focus on a low valuation, with the sentiment, "My price *and* my terms."

This tension applies not only to financial transactions but to the styles of the users versus the styles of the suppliers of capital. The users value their independence and treasure the flexibility their own venture has brought them. However, the investors are hoping to preserve their options as well. These options usually include both reinvesting and abandoning the venture.

These points of view also clash in the composition of the board of directors, where the entrepreneur seeks control and independence, and the investors want the right to control the board if the company does not perform as well as was expected. This sense of control is an emotional issue for most entrepreneurs, who want to be in charge of their own destiny. Prizing their autonomy and self-determination, many of these users of capital would agree with the passion Walt Disney conveyed in this statement: "I don't make movies to make money. I make *money* to make movies." The investors may believe in the passions of these users of capital, but they still want to protect themselves with first refusals, initial public offering rights, and various other exit options.

The long-term goals of the users and suppliers of capital may also be contradictory. The entrepreneurs may be content with the progress of their venture and happy with a single or double. It is their venture, their baby; if it is moderately successful, many entrepreneurs feel that they have accomplished a lot. Yet, the investors will not be quite as content with moderate success, but instead want their capital to produce extraordinary returns—they want a home run from the entrepreneur. Thus, the pressures put on the entrepreneur may seem unwarranted to the entrepreneur, yet necessary for the investor.

These strategies contradict each other when they are manifested in the management styles of the users and providers of capital. When the entrepreneur is willing to take a calculated risk or is working to minimize and avoid unnecessary risks, the investor has bet on the art of the exceptional and thus is willing to bet the farm everyday.

Entrepreneurs possess the ability to see opportunities and, more importantly, to seize those opportunities. They possess an instinctual desire to change, to adapt, or to decommit in order to seize new opportunities. Yet, the investors are looking for clear steady progress, as projected in the business plan, which leaves little room for surprises.

Finally, the final goals may differ. As the entrepreneur who continues to build his or her company may find operating a company enjoyable. At this point, the definition of success both personally and for the company may involve long-term company building, such that a sustainable institution is created. But the investors will want to cash out in two to five years, so that they can reinvest their capital in another venture.

Staged Capital Commitments [9]

Venture capitalists rarely, if ever, invest all the external capital that a company will require to accomplish its business plan; instead, they invest in companies at distinct stages in their development. As a result, each company begins life knowing that it has only enough capital to reach the next stage. By staging capital, the venture capitalists preserve the right to abandon a project whose prospects look dim. The right to abandon is essential because an entrepreneur will almost never stop investing in a failing project as long as others are providing capital.

---

[8] Jeffry A. Timmons, "Deals and Deal Structuring," lecture, Harvard Business School February 23, 1993.
[9] The following section was adapted from W. A. Sahlman, "Structure of Venture Capital Organizations," *Journal of Financial Economics* 27(1990), pp. 506–7. Reprinted with permission.

Staging the capital also provides incentives to the entrepreneurial team. Capital is a scarce and expensive resource for individual ventures. Misuse of capital is very costly to venture capitalists but not necessarily to management. To encourage managers to conserve capital, venture capital firms apply strong sanctions if it is misused. These sanctions ordinarily take two basic forms. First, increased capital requirements invariably dilute management's equity share at an increasingly punitive rate. Second, the staged investment process enables venture capital firms to shut down operations completely. The credible threat to abandon a venture, even when the firm might be economically viable, is the key to the relationship between the entrepreneur and the venture capitalist. By denying capital, the venture capitalist also signals other capital suppliers that the company in question is a bad investment risk.

Short of denying the company capital, venture capitalists can discipline wayward managers by firing or demoting them. Other elements of the stock purchase agreement then come into play. For example, the company typically has the right to repurchase shares from departing managers, often at prices below market value, and vesting schedules limit the number of shares employees are entitled to if they leave prematurely. Finally, noncompete clauses can impose strong penalties on those who leave, particularly if their human capital is closely linked to the industry in which the venture is active.

Entrepreneurs accept the staged capital process because they usually have great confidence in their own abilities to meet targets. They understand that if they meet those goals, they will end up owning a significantly larger share of the company than if they had insisted on receiving all of the capital up front.

Structuring the Deal

What Is a Deal?[10]

Deals are defined as economic agreements between at least two parties. In the context of entrepreneurial finance, most deals involve the allocation of cash flow streams (with respect to both amount and timing), the allocation of risk, and hence the allocation of value between different groups. For example, deals can be made between suppliers and users of capital, or between management and employees of a venture.

A Way of Thinking about Deals over Time   To assess and to design long-lived deals, Professor William A. Sahlman suggests the following series of questions as a guide for deal makers in structuring and in understanding how deals evolve over time:[11]

- Who are the players?
- What are their goals and objectives?
- What risks do they perceive and how have these risks been managed?
- What problems do they perceive?
- How much do they have invested, both in absolute terms and relative terms, at cost and at market value?
- What is the context surrounding the current decision?
- What is the form of their current investment or claim on the company?
- What power do they have to act? To precipitate change?
- What real options do they have? How long does it take them to act?
- What credible threats do they have?
- How and from whom do they get information?
- How credible is the source of information?
- What will be the value of their claim under different scenarios?
- How can they get value for their claims?
- To what degree can they appropriate value from another party?
- How much uncertainty characterizes the situation?
- What are the rules of the game (e.g., tax, legislative)?
- What is the context (e.g., state of economy, capital markets, industry specifics) at the current time? How is the context expected to change?

The Characteristics of Successful Deals[12]   While deal making is ultimately a combination of art and science, it is possible to describe some of the characteristics of deals that have proven successful over time:

- They are simple.
- They are robust (they do not fall apart when there are minor deviations from projections).

---

[10] The following paragraph was adapted from "Note on Financial Contracting: Deals," by William A. Sahlman. HBS Note 288-014, Harvard Business School, 1988, p. 1. Copyright © 1988 by the President and Fellows of Harvard College.

[11] Ibid., pp. 35–36.

[12] Ibid., p. 43.

- They are organic (they are not immutable).
- They take into account the incentives of each party to the deal under a variety of circumstances.
- They provide mechanisms for communications and interpretation.
- They are based primarily on trust rather than on legalese.
- They are not patently unfair.
- They do not make it too difficult to raise additional capital.
- They match the needs of the user of capital with the needs of the supplier.
- They reveal information about each party (e.g., their faith in their ability to deliver on the promises).
- They allow for the arrival of new information before financing is required.
- They do not preserve discontinuities (e.g., boundary conditions that will evoke dysfunctional behavior on the part of the agents of principals).
- They take into account the fact that it takes time to raise money.
- They improve the chances of success for the venture.

The Generic Elements of Deals   There are a number of terms governing value distribution, as well as basic definitions, assumptions, performance incentives, rights, and obligations. The deal should also cover the basic mechanisms for transmitting timely, credible information. Representations and warranties, plus negative and positive covenants will also be part of the deal structure. Additionally, default clauses and remedial action clauses are appropriate in most deals.

Tools for Managing Risk/Reward   In a deal the claims on cash and equity are prioritized by the players. Some of the tools available to the players are common stock, partnerships, preferred stock (dividend and liquidation preference), debt (secured, unsecured, personally guaranteed, or convertible), performance conditional pricing (ratchets or positive incentives), puts and calls, warrants, and cash. Some of the critical aspects of a deal go beyond just the money:

- Number, type, and mix of stocks (and perhaps of stock and debt) and various features that may

go with them (such as puts) which affect the investor's rate of return.

- The amounts and timing of takedowns, conversions, and the like.
- Interest rates on debt or preferred shares.
- The number of seats, and who actually will represent investors, on the board of directors.
- Possible changes in the management team and in the composition of the board.
- Registration rights for investor's stock (in the case of a registered public offering).
- Right of first refusal granted to the investor on subsequent private placements or an IPO.
- Employment, noncompete, and proprietary rights agreements.
- The payment of legal, accounting, consulting, or other fees connected with putting the deal together.
- Specific performance targets for revenues, expenses, market penetration, and the like, by certain target dates.

Understanding the Bets

Deals, because they are based on cash, risk, and time, are subject to interpretation. The players' perceptions of each of these factors contribute to the overall valuation of the venture and the subsequent proposed deal. As was described earlier, there are a number of different ways to value a venture, and these various valuation methods contribute to the complexity of deals. Consider, for instance, the following term sheets:[13]

- A venture capital firm proposes to raise $150 million to $200 million to acquire and build RSA Cellular Phone Properties. The venture capital firm will commit between $15 million and $30 million in equity and will lead in raising senior and subordinated debt to buy out licenses. Licensees will have claim to 30 percent of the future equity value in the new company, the venture capital firm will claim 60 percent (subordinated debt claim is estimated at 10 percent), and management will get 5–10 percent of the future equity but only after all prior return targets have been achieved. The venture capital firm's worst-case scenario will result in 33 percent ROR to their firm, 9 percent ROR to licensees, and 0 percent for management. The noncompete agreements extend for 12 years, in addition to the vesting and the like.
- An entrepreneur must decide between two deals:

---

13 Timmons, "Deals and Deal Structuring."

- —Deal A: A venture capital firm will lead a $3 million investment and requires management to invest $1 million. Future gains are to be split fifty-fifty after the venture capital firm has achieved a 25 percent ROR on the investment. Other common investment provisions also apply (vesting, employment agreements, etc.). The venture capital firm has the right of first refusal on all future rounds and other deals management may find.

- —Deal B: Another venture capital firm will lead a $4 million investment. Management will invest nothing. The future gains are to be split 75 percent for the venture capital firm and 25 percent for management on a side-by-side basis. Until the venture achieves positive cash flow, this venture capital firm has the right of first refusal on future financing and deals management may find.

- A group of very talented money managers is given $40 million in capital to manage. The contract calls for the managers to receive 20 percent of the excess return on the portfolio over the Treasury bond return. The contract runs for five years. The managers cannot take out any of their share of the gains until the last day of the contract (except to pay taxes).

While reading and considering these deals, try to identify the underlying assumptions, motivations, and beliefs of the individuals proposing the deals. These are some questions that may help in identifying the bets of the players:

- What is the bet?
- Who is it for?
- Who is taking the risk? Who receives the rewards?
- Who should be making these bets?
- What will happen if the entrepreneurs exceed the venture capitalists' expectations? If they fall short?
- What are the incentives for the money managers? Consequences of their success or failure to perform?
- How will the money managers behave? What will be their investing strategy?

Some of the Lessons Learned: The Dog in the Suitcase

A few years ago a friend, living in a New York City high-rise, called in great distress. Her beloved barkless dog had died in the middle of the night. She wanted a decent burial for the dog, but since it was the dead of winter, she did not know what to do. It was suggested that she contact a pet cemetery on Long Island and take the dog there. It would be frozen until spring, at which time it would be properly buried. After all, such things are common in the Big Apple!

She gathered her courage, placed the dog in a suitcase, and headed down the elevator to the outdoors. As she struggled toward the nearest intersection a block away to catch a cab, a young man noticed her struggle and offered to help. Puffing by now, she sized up the young man quickly and accepted his offer to carry the bag. In no time, she turned to find the young man sprinting down the street with her suitcase. Now, imagine the look on the faces of the young man and his buddies when they opened the suitcase and discovered the loot!

The moral of this story is that raising capital can have all the surprises of a dog in the suitcase for the entrepreneur. The following tips may help to minimize many of these surprises:

1. Raise money when you do not need it.
2. Learn as much about the process and how to manage it as you can.
3. Know your relative bargaining position.
4. If all you get is money, you are not getting much.
5. Assume the deal will never close.
6. Always have a backup source of capital.
7. The legal and other experts can blow it—sweat the details yourself.
8. Users of capital are invariably at a disadvantage in dealing with suppliers of capital.
9. If you are out of cash when you seek to raise capital, suppliers of capital will eat your lunch.
10. Startup entrepreneurs are raising capital for the first time; suppliers of capital have done it many times, everyday, for a living.

Negotiations

Negotiations have been defined by many experts in a variety of ways, as the following examples demonstrate. Herb Cohen, the author of *You Can Negotiate Anything*, defines negotiations as "a field of knowledge and endeavor that focuses on gaining the favor of people from whom we want things"[14] or, similarly,

---

[14] Herb Cohen, *You Can Negotiate Anything* (New York: Bantam Books, 1982), p. 15.

as "the use of information and power to affect behavior within a 'web of tension.' "[15] Other experts in the field of negotiations, Roger Fisher and William Ury, assert that negotiations are a "back-and-forth communication designed to reach an agreement when you and the other side have some interests that are shared and others that are opposed."[16]

What Is Negotiable?

Far more is negotiable than entrepreneurs think.[17] For instance, a normal ploy of the attorney representing the investors is to insist, matter of factly, that "this is our boilerplate" and that the entrepreneur should take it or leave it. Yet, it is possible for an entrepreneur to negotiate and craft an agreement that represents his or her needs.

During the negotiation, the investors will be evaluating the negotiating skills, intelligence, and maturity of the entrepreneur. The entrepreneur has precisely the same opportunity to size up the investor. If the investors see anything that shakes their confidence or trust, they probably will withdraw from the deal. Similarly, if an investor turns out to be arrogant, hot-tempered, unwilling to see the other side's needs and to compromise, and seems bent on getting every last ounce out of the deal by locking an entrepreneur into as many of the "burdensome clauses" as is possible, the entrepreneur might well want to withdraw.

Throughout the negotiations, entrepreneurs need to bear in mind that a successful negotiation is one in which both sides believe that they have made a fair deal. The best deals are those in which neither party wins and neither loses, and such deals are possible to negotiate. This approach is further articulated in the works of Roger Fisher and William Ury, who have focused neither on soft nor hard negotiation tactics, but rather on principled negotiation, a method developed at the Harvard Negotiation Project. This method asserts that the purpose of negotiations is "to decide issues on their merits rather than through a haggling process focused on what each side says it will and won't do. It suggests that you look for mutual gains wherever possible, and that where your interests conflict, you should insist that the result be based on some fair standards independent of the will of either side."[18] They continue to describe principled negotiations in the following four points:

- *People:* Separate the people from the problem.
- *Interests:* Focus on interests, not positions.
- *Options:* Generate a variety of possibilities before deciding what to do.
- *Criteria:* Insist that the result be based on some objective standard.

Others have spoken of this method of principled negotiation, for example, Bob Woolf of Bob Woolf Associates, a Boston-based firm that represents everyone from Larry Bird to Gene Shalit. Woolf states simply that "you want the other side to be reasonable, not defensive—to work *with* you. You'll have a better chance of getting what you want. Treat someone the way that you would like to be treated, and you'll be successful most of the time."[19]

The Specific Issues Entrepreneurs Typically Face[20]

Whatever method you choose in your negotiations, chances are that the primary focus will be on how much the entrepreneur's equity is worth and how much is to be purchased by the investor's investment. Even so, numerous other issues involving legal and financial control of the company and the rights and obligations of various investors and the entrepreneur in various situations may be as important as valuation and ownership share. Not the least of which is the value behind money—such as contacts and helpful expertise, additional financing when and if required, and patience and interest in the long-term development of the company—that a particular investor can bring to the venture. The following are some of the most critical aspects of a deal that go beyond "just the money":

- Number, type, and mix of stocks (and perhaps of stock and debt) and various features that may go with them (such as puts) which affect the investor's rate of return.
- The amounts and timing of takedowns, conversions, and the like.
- Interest rate in debt or preferred shares.
- The number of seats, and who actually will represent investors, on the board of directors.
- Possible changes in the management team and in the composition of the board of directors.
- Registration rights for investor's stock (in case of a registered public offering).

[15] Ibid., p. 16.

[16] Roger Fisher and William Ury, *Getting to Yes* (New York: Penguin Books, 1991), p. xvii.

[17] See, for example, H. M. Hoffman and J. Blakey, "You Can Negotiate with Venture Capitalists," *Harvard Business Review,* March–April 1987, pp. 16–24.

[18] Fisher and Ury, p. xviii.

[19] Quoted in Paul B. Brown and Michael S. Hopkins, "How to Negotiate Practically Anything." Reprinted with permission. *Inc.* magazine, (February 1989) p. 35. Copyright © 1989 by Goldhirsh Group, Inc. 38 Commercial Wharf, Boston, MA 02110.

[20] Jeffry A. Timmons, from Deals and Valuation lecture, Feb. 1993.

- Right of first refusal granted to the investor on subsequent private or initial public stock offerings.
- Stock vesting schedule and agreements.
- Employment, noncompete, and proprietary rights agreements.
- The payment of legal, accounting, consulting, or other fees connected with putting the deal together.

Entrepreneurs may find some subtle but highly significant issues negotiated. If they, or their attorneys, are not familiar with these, they may be missed as just boilerplate when, in fact, they have crucial future implications for the ownership, control, and financing of the business. Some issues that can be burdensome for entrepreneurs are:

- *Cosale provision.* This is a provision by which investors can tender their shares of their stock before an initial public offering. It protects the first-round investors but can cause conflicts with investors in later rounds and can inhibit an entrepreneur's ability to cash out.
- *Ratchet antidilution protection.* This enables the lead investors to get for free additional common stock if subsequent shares are ever sold at a price lower than originally paid. This protection can create a "dog-in-the-manger syndrome," whereby first-round investors can prevent the company from raising additional necessary funds during a period of adversity for the company. While nice from the investors' perspective, it ignores the reality that in distress situations, the last money calls the shots on price and deal structure.
- *Washout financing.* This is a strategy of last resort, which wipes out all previously issued stock when existing preferred shareholders will not commit additional funds, thus diluting everyone.
- *Forced buyout.* Under this provision, if management does not find a buyer or cannot take the company public by a certain date, then the investors can proceed to find a buyer at terms they agree upon.
- *Demand registration rights.* Here, investors can demand at least one IPO in three to five years. In reality, such clauses are hard to invoke since the market for new public stock issues, rather than the terms of an agreement, ultimately governs the timing of such events.
- *Piggyback registration rights.* These grant to the investors (and to the entrepreneur, if he or she insists) rights to sell stock at the IPO. Since the underwrit-

ers usually make this decision, the clause normally is not enforceable.

- *Mandatory redemption of preferred stock.* Under mandatory redemption, the company is required to buy out investors if an IPO fails to occur. However, if a company is not attractive enough to go public, it will most likely be attractive enough to raise other cash for a buyout.
- *Key-person insurance.* This requires the company to obtain life insurance on key people. The named beneficiary of the insurance can be either the company or the preferred shareholders.

Sand Traps [21]

Strategic Circumference

Each fund-raising strategy sets in motion some actions and commitments by management that will eventually *scribe a strategic circumference* around the company in terms of its current and future financing choices. These future choices will permit varying degrees of freedom as a result of the previous actions. Those who fail to think through the consequences of a fund-raising strategy and the effect on their degrees of freedom fall into this trap.

While it is impossible to avoid strategic circumference completely, and while in some cases scribing a strategic circumference is clearly intentional, others may be unintended and, unfortunately, unexpected. For example, a company that plans to remain private or plans to maintain a 1.5 to 1.0 debt-to-equity ratio has intentionally created a strategic circumference.

Legal Circumference

Many people have an aversion to becoming involved in legal or accounting minutiae. Many believe that since they pay sizeable professional fees, their advisors should and will pay attention to the details.

Legal documentation spells out the terms, conditions, responsibilities, and rights of the parties to a transaction. Since different sources have different ways of structuring deals, and since these legal and contractual details come at the *end* of the fund-raising process, an entrepreneur may arrive at a point of no return, facing some very onerous conditions and covenants that are not only very difficult to live with but also create tight limitations and constraints—legal circumference—on future choices that are potentially

---

[21]Copyright © 1990 by Jeffry A. Timmons.

disastrous. Entrepreneurs cannot rely on attorneys and advisors to protect them in this vital matter.

To avoid this trap, entrepreneurs need to have a fundamental precept: "The devil is in the details." It is very risky for an entrepreneur *not* to carefully read final documents and very risky to use a lawyer who is *not* experienced and competent. It also is helpful to keep a few options alive and to conserve cash. This also can keep the other side of the table more conciliatory and flexible.

Attraction to Status and Size

It seems there is a cultural attraction to higher status and larger size, even when it comes to raising capital. Simply targeting the largest or the best-known or most-prestigious firms is a trap entrepreneurs often fall into.

These are often the most visible firms because of their size and investing activity and because they have been around a long time. Yet, as the venture capital industry has become more heterogeneous, as well as for other reasons, such firms may or may not be a good fit.

Take, for example, an entrepreneur who had a patented, innovative device that was ready for use by manufacturers of semiconductors. He was running out of cash from an earlier round of venture capital investment and needed more money for his device to be placed in test sites and then, presumably, into production. Although lab tests had been successful, his prior backers would not invest further since he was nearly two years behind the schedule in his business plan. For a year, he concentrated his efforts on many of the largest and most well-known firms and celebrities in the venture capital business, but to no avail. With the help of outside advice, he then decided to pursue an alternative fund-raising strategy. First, he listed those firms that were mostly likely prospects as customers for the device. Next, he sought to identify investors who already had investments in this potential customer base, because it was thought that these would be the most likely potential backers, since they would be the most informed about his technology, its potential value-added properties, and any potential competitive advantages the company could achieve. Less than a dozen venture capital firms were identified (from among a pool of over 700), and none had been contacted previously by this entrepreneur. In fact, many were virtually unknown to him, even though they were very active investors in the industry. In less than three months, offers were on the table from three of them and the financing was closed.

It is best to avoid this trap by looking for financial backers, whether debt or equity, who have intimate knowledge and first-hand experience with the technology, marketplace, and networks of expertise and intelligence in the competitive arena and to focus on the relevant know-how that would characterize a good match.

Unknown Territory

Venturing into unknown territory is another problem. Entrepreneurs need to know the terrain in sufficient detail, particularly the requirements and alternatives of various equity sources. If they do not, they may make critical strategic blunders and waste time.

For example, a venture that is not a "mainstream venture capital deal" may be overvalued and directed to investors who are not a realistic match, rather than being realistically valued and directed to small and more specialized funds, private investors, or potential strategic partners. The preceding example is a real one. The founders went through nearly $100,000 of their own funds, strained their relationship to the limit, and nearly had to abandon the project.

Another illustration of a fund-raising strategy that was ill conceived and, effectively, a lottery—rather than a well-thought-out and focused search—is a company in the fiberoptics industry called Opti-Com.[22] Opti-Com was a spin-off as a startup from a well-known public company in the industry. The management team was entirely credible but members were not considered superstars. The business plan suggested the company could achieve the magical $50 million in sales in five years, which the entrepreneurs were told by an outside advisor was the minimum size that venture capital investors would consider. The plan proposed to raise $750,000 for about 10 percent of the common stock of the company. Realistically, since the firm was a custom supplier for special applications, rather than a provider of a new technology advance with a significant proprietary advantage, a sales estimate of $10 million to $15 million in five years would have been more plausible. The same advisor urged that their business plan be submitted to 16 blue-ribbon mainstream venture capital firms in the Boston area. Four months later they had received 16 rejections. The entrepreneurs then were told to "go see the same quality of venture capital firms in New York." A year later, the founders were nearly out of money and had been unsuccessful in their search for capital. When redirected away from mainstream venture capitalists to a more suitable source, a small fund specifically created in Massachusetts—to provide risk capital for emerging firms

---

[22] This is a fictional name for an actual company.

that might not be robust enough to attract conventional venture capital but would be a welcome addition to the economic renewal of the state—the fit was right. Opti-Com raised the necessary capital, but at a valuation much more in line with the market for startup deals.

Opportunity Cost

The lure of money often leads to a most common trap—the opportunity cost trap. After all, an entrepreneur's optimism leads him or her to the conclusion that with good people and products (or services), there has to be a lot of money out there with "our name on it!" In the process, entrepreneurs tend to grossly underestimate the real costs of getting the cash in the bank. Further, entrepreneurs also underestimate the real time, effort, and creative energy required. Indeed, the degree of effort fund-raising requires is perhaps the least appreciated aspect in obtaining capital. In both these cases, there are opportunity costs in expending these resources in a particular direction when both the clock and the calendar are moving.

For a startup company, for instance, founders can devote nearly all of their available time for months to seeking out investors and telling their story. It may take six months or more to get a yes and up to a year for a no. In the meantime, a considerable amount of cash and human capital has been flowing out, rather than in, and this cash and capital might have been better spent elsewhere.

One such startup began its search for venture capital in 1984. A year later the founders had exhausted $100,000 of their own seed money and had quit their jobs to devote themselves full time to the effort. Yet they were unsuccessful after approaching over 35 sources of capital. The opportunity costs are clear.

There are opportunity costs, too, in existing emerging companies. In terms of human capital, it is common for top management to devote as much as half of its time trying to raise a major amount of outside capital. Again, this requires a tremendous amount of emotional and physical energy as well, of which there is a finite amount to devote to the daily operating demands of the enterprise. The effect on near-term performance is invariably negative. In addition, if expectations of a successful fund-raising effort are followed by a failure to raise the money, morale can deteriorate and key people can be lost.

Significant opportunity costs are also incurred in forgone business and market opportunities that could have been pursued. Take, for example, the startup firm just noted. When asked what level of sales the

company would have achieved in this past year had it spent the $100,000 of the founders' seed money on generating customers and business, the founder answered without hesitation, "We'd be at $1 million sales by now, and would probably be making a small profit."

Underestimation of Other Costs

Entrepreneurs tend to underestimate the out-of-pocket costs associated with both raising the money and living with it. For instance, there are incremental costs after a firm becomes a public company. The Securities and Exchange Commission requires regular audited financial statements and various reports, there are outside directors' fees and liability insurance premiums, there are legal fees associated with more extensive reporting requirements, and so on. These can add up quickly, often to $100,000 or more annually.

Another "cost" that can be easily overlooked is of the disclosure that may be necessary to convince a financial backer to part with his or her money. An entrepreneur may have to reveal much more about the company and his or her personal finances than he or she ever imagined. Thus, company weaknesses, ownership and compensation arrangements, personal and corporate financial statements, marketing plans and competitive strategies, and so forth may need to be revealed to people whom the entrepreneur does not really know and trust and with whom he or she may eventually not do business. In addition, the ability to control access to the information is lost.

Greed

The entrepreneur—especially one who is out of cash, or nearly so—may find the money irresistible. One of the most exhilarating experiences for an entrepreneur is the prospect of raising that first major slug of outside capital, or obtaining that substantial bank line needed for expansion. If the fundamentals of the company are sound, however, then there is money out there.

Being Too Anxious

Usually, after months of hard work finding the right source and negotiating the deal, another trap awaits the hungry but unwary entrepreneur, and all too often, the temptation is overwhelming. It is the trap of believing that the deal is done and terminating discussions with others too soon. Entrepreneurs fall into this trap because they want to believe the deal is done with a handshake (or perhaps with an accompanying letter of intent or an executed term sheet).

The following is a good illustration of a masterful handling of such a situation. An entrepreneur and a key vice president of a company with $30 million in sales had been negotiating with several venture capitalists, three major strategic partners, and a mezzanine source for nearly six months. The company was down to 60 days' worth of cash, and the mezzanine investors knew it. The offer from the mezzanine investors of $10 million was a take-it-or-leave-it proposition. The vice president, in summarizing the company's relative bargaining position, said, "It was the only alternative we had left; everything else had come to rest by late last month; and the negotiations with the three major companies had not reached serious stages. We felt like they were asking too much, but we needed the money." Yet the two had managed to keep this weakness from being apparent to the mezzanine investors. Each time negotiations had been scheduled, the entrepreneur had made sure he also had scheduled a meeting with one of the other larger companies for later that afternoon (a good two-hour plane ride away). In effect, he was able to create the illusion that these discussions with other investors were far more serious than they actually were. The deal was closed on terms agreeable to both. The company went public six months later and is highly successful today.

Impatience

Yet another trap is being impatient when an investor does not understand quickly and because each deal has velocity and momentum.

Take, as an example, the effort of one group to acquire a firm in the cellular car phone business for whom they were employed. As the management team, they became the first to know in May that the company was going to be sold by its owners. By early July, the investment bankers representing the sellers were expected to have the offering memorandum ready for the open market. To attempt to buy the company privately would require the management team to raise commitments for about $150 million in three to four weeks, hardly enough time to put together even a crude business plan, let alone raise such a substantial sum. The train was moving at 140 miles per hour and gaining speed each day. The founders identified five top-notch, interested venture capital and leveraged buy-out firms and sat down with representatives of each to walk through the summary of the business plan and the proposed financing. One excellent firm sent an otherwise very experienced and

capable partner. One of his main questions about how the company prevented its phones from being stolen revealed that he knew little about the business. Car phones are not stolen like CB radios, because they cannot be used without an authorized installation and activation of service. The group looked elsewhere.

Had the group fallen into this trap of being impatient because the train was moving quickly, it would have exposed itself to risk. The investor had a serious lack of elementary knowledge of the industry and the business and had not done his homework in advance. By the time this investor became knowledgeable about the business, it would be too late.

Take-the-Money-and-Run Myopia

A final trap in raising money for a company is a take-the-money-and-run myopia that invariably prevents an entrepreneur from evaluating one of the most critical longer-term issues—that is, to what extent can the investor add value to the company beyond the money? Into this trap falls the entrepreneur who does not get a clear sense that his or her prospective financial partner possesses the relevant experience and know-how in the market and industry area, the contacts he or she needs but does not have, the savvy and the reputation that adds to his or her association with the investor—and yet takes the money.

As has been said before, the successful development of a company can be critically impacted by the interaction of the management team and the financial partners. If an effective relationship can be established, the value-added synergy can be a powerful stimulant for success. Many founders overlook the high value-added contributions that some investors are accustomed to making and erroneously opt for a "better deal."

Chapter Summary

1. There is rarely a "fair fight" between users (entrepreneurs) and suppliers of capital (investors). Entrepreneurs need to be prepared by learning how the capital markets determine valuation and risk.

2. Several valuation methods are used to arrive at value for a company, the venture capital method being most common.

3. Investors prefer to stage their capital commitments, thereby managing and containing the risk, and preserving their options to invest further or cease.

4. Numerous potential conflicts exist between users and suppliers of capital, and these require appreciation and managing.

5. Successful deals are characterized by careful thought and sensitive balance among a range of important issues.

6. Deal structure can make or break an otherwise sound venture.

7. Negotiating the deal is both art and science, and also can make or break the relationship.

8. The entrepreneur encounters numerous strategic, legal, and other "sand traps" during the fund-raising cycle and needs awareness and skill in coping with them.

6. What are some of the inherent conflicts between investors and entrepreneurs, and how and why can these affect the venture's odds for success?

7. What are the most important questions and issues to consider in structuring a deal? Why?

8. What issues can be negotiated in a venture investment, and why are these important?

9. What are the pitfalls and sand traps in fund raising, and why do entrepreneurs sometimes fail to avoid them?

Study Questions

1. Why can there be such wide variations in the valuations investors and founders place on companies?

2. What are the determinants of value?

3. Define and explain why the following are important: long-term value creation, investor's required IRR, investor's required share of ownership, DCF, deal structure, and sand traps in fund-raising.

4. Explain five prevalent methods used in valuing a company and their strengths and weaknesses, given their underlying assumptions.

5. What is a staged capital commitment, and why is it important?

MIND STRETCHERS

Have You Considered?

1. Who should and should not have outside investors in their companies?

2. It is said that a good deal structure cannot turn a bad business into a good one, but many a good business has been killed by a bad deal structure. Can you find an example of each? Why is this so?

3. What beliefs and assumptions are revealed by the "bets" made in different deals?

4. What is a good deal? Why?

Case

Bridge Capital Investors, Inc.

Preparation Questions

1. Evaluate the situation and financing alternatives Hindman is now facing. What is his strategy?

2. Is the $10 million Bridge investment enough money? How long will it last? What is Hindman's relative bargaining position? BCIs? Be prepared to represent both the company and BCI in a meeting to negotiate the proposed financing.

3. What are the consequences for JLI of the proposed financing? Calculate the consequences of the "put."

4. What should Hindman do? What should Bridge do?

Bridge Capital Investors, Inc.*

"Local Savings & Loan Collapses, State Takes Over."

The morning headline on May 6, 1985, highlighted what was more than just a local-interest story to Jiffy Lube. Old Court Savings & Loan was the company's primary real estate lender, and its collapse left the development of 37 new service centers, and Jiffy Lube's future, at risk.

Throughout the summer of 1985, the Jiffy Lube team battled the crises through short-term borrowings and other stopgap measures. It is now November 1985, and time is running out. Construction costs have depleted the company's finances, and Jim Hindman's personal resources are running out. Serious competition has also

*Copyright © 1987 by Curtis-Palmer & Co., Inc., Harvard, MA. This case was prepared by Dale Sander (of Ernst & Whinney's national office, Privately Owned Emerging Business Services Group, Cleveland, Ohio) and Jeffry A. Timmons.

EXHIBIT A

EXHIBIT A

Jiffy Lube, Inc., Operating Results (year ended March 31; dollars in millions)

	1983	1984	1985	1986 (projected)
Revenue	$ 5.5	$6.0	$14.5	$29.8
Net income	$(2.6)	$ .3	$ .6	$ 1.9
Service centers (franchised/ company owned)	96/0	120/1	208/23	361/23

See *Exhibit I* and *Exhibit J* for 1984 and 1985 financial statements.

appeared. In August, Quaker State Oil bought Minit Lube, the number two company in the quick change industry, for $35 million. As Jim Hindman notes, "This puts us up against the big boys for the first time."

However, not all is bleak. Since March 1983, Jiffy Lube has rapidly expanded and recorded its first operating profits (see *Exhibit A*). Despite the current problems, Jiffy Lube's number one position in the industry creates a number of alternatives. Last month, Shearson Lehman Brothers proposed a $10 million private debt placement. Also, five major oil companies are showing varying degrees of interest in Jiffy Lube, ranging from outright purchases to strategic partnerships.

Jiffy Lube's recent growth (and survival) were made possible by creative financing obtained in early 1983 and a major change in strategy.

1983 Financing

In March 1983, Jim Hindman and a group of other investors contributed their interests in W. James Hindman, Ltd., and two other nursing home partnerships to Jiffy Lube in an exchange for common stock. These interests had a combined fair market value of over $3.4 million. For some time Hindman had considered the idea of using the value of his partnership interests to help finance Jiffy Lube. Selling the partnership interests to raise cash represented a second-rate alternative. Hindman had almost no tax basis in his interests, and income taxes would have consumed a significant portion of the proceeds from a sale.

After reviewing the available options, Ernst & Whinney helped Hindman and a small group of investors structure the transaction as a tax-free exchange under Internal Revenue Code Section 351. The group transferring the assets represented a controlling group (i.e., they owned over 80 percent of Jiffy Lube's stock after the transfer). As a controlling group they were able to transfer their interests to the company at the existing tax basis without realizing any gain for tax purposes.

The partnership interests were sold by Jiffy Lube to third parties during the following year and raised much needed cash. A tax gain of over $3 million was recognized from the sales but was offset by the massive net operating loss carry forwards from prior years.

Also part of the "351 transaction" was the contribution of an additional $1.9 million in cash from the Midwest individuals and other shareholders in exchange for common stock.

New Corporate Strategy

During its first several years of operation, the majority of Jiffy Lube's franchises were sold one unit at a time. But individual sales of franchises did not saturate areas quickly enough to achieve name recognition and make advertising cost effective. In early 1983, Neal O'Shea, vice president for franchise sales, suggested that Jiffy Lube stop selling franchises on a unit-by-unit basis.

Instead, Jiffy Lube began selling "area development rights" to investors and entrepreneurs. In return for an up-front nonrefundable fee, Jiffy Lube gave investors the exclusive right to build a certain number of franchises within a specified geographical location. Fees have varied depending on the potential of the market (e.g., Tampa—$150K, San Francisco—$250K). As Jiffy Lube continued to grow, management expected the rights to become more valuable, eventually selling for as much as $1 million in some larger markets (such as Los Angeles).

In addition to the up-front fee, Jiffy Lube also collected an initial franchise fee ($20,000–$25,000) for each individual franchise developed. If investors failed to complete the required number of units within the agreed-upon time, they forfeited their exclusive rights to the area.

The area development concept increased growth, advanced the clustering concept, and attracted more sophisticated franchisees. The up-front fees also were a significant source of cash for Jiffy Lube. Earnings also dramatically improved as the development fees went straight to the bottom line. In fiscal 1984, Jiffy Lube was in the black for the first time.

At the same time, management recognized that the area development fees were going to decline and eventually fade away as the rights to all of the major metropolitan areas were sold. Royalty fees collected from franchisees (originally 5 percent of gross franchise sales) would progressively become a more important source of revenue and key determinant of profitability.

In 1984, Jiffy Lube took advantage of its growing leadership position in the industry to enhance its royalty agreement with new franchisees. Under these newer agreements, Jiffy Lube collected a 6 percent royalty after the franchise had been operating for one year. Jiffy Lube also achieved some vertical integration in its business by acquiring its major supplier of automotive supplies, Heritage Merchandising.

Jiffy Lube's goals and strategy for the future are summarized in this excerpt from its business plan prepared in the late summer of 1985:

> The company's goal is to become the nation's dominant supplier of fast oil changes, with approximately 1,300 service centers by 1990. Its strategy for achieving this goal is to cluster centers in the 30 major metropolitan markets, thereby realizing economies of scale in operations, advertising, and the distribution of auto supplies. As the company becomes a nationwide firm and undertakes national advertising and promotional campaigns, it should be able to capture an increasingly large market share.

Jim Hindman summarized Jiffy Lube's plan with the following comparison: "We will become the 'McDonald's' of the quick oil change business." With approximately 270 service centers currently open in late 1985, these goals require the opening of over 1,000 new centers by 1990.

Construction Financing

Jiffy Lube's growth and the sale of the large area development rights increased the need for real estate financing. Purchasing real estate today for a new center generally costs between $100K and $275K, while construction typically costs an additional $225K. Even with more sophisticated investors, it is often necessary to provide real estate and construction financing to speed the development of the new franchises (approximately 50 percent of the franchisees have required assistance with their real estate and construction financing). Jiffy Lube funds real estate purchases and construction costs through two main sources.

"Permanent real estate financing" consists of mortgages on properties owned by the company and rented to franchisees. The mortgage payments are offset by rental income received from the franchisees. The other source is "construction financing," used to develop centers to be sold to franchisees. Upon sale of the centers, Jiffy Lube uses the proceeds to retire the debt, while the franchisees obtain their own permanent financing.

In 1983, Jiffy Lube signed an agreement with Old Court Savings & Loan to provide $16 million in construction financing for the purchase and development of 37 new centers (see *Exhibit B*). In addition, Old Court agreed to supply permanent financing to a partnership purchasing these centers from Jiffy Lube.

By May 1985, other projects were also in process, and the company had 60 new service centers in various stages of development. Jiffy Lube determined that its growth pace would require additional capital, and it researched the possibility of a private placement. Management hoped to raise up to $10 million and began working with Shearson Lehman Brothers in April 1985 to organize a deal.

May 1985: Crisis

In May 1985, as the morning headlines announced, the state declared Old Court Savings & Loan insolvent and appointed a conservator. The state had been investigating the S&L since early in the year, but there had been no warning that the situation was this serious and Jiffy Lube's management was caught off guard. All loan activity was halted, including the funding on Jiffy Lube's development projects. Before the collapse, partial financing (approximately $6.3 million) on only 25 of the 37 service centers had been provided.

Jiffy Lube quickly found that obtaining substitute financing from another lender was unlikely. Old Court had liens on the partially funded properties; because of the existing liens, no lenders were willing to fund the completion of these units.

As Jim Hindman describes:

> Whatever could go wrong, did go wrong. We had one bank lined up who seemed ready to continue the financing. On Monday, we went down to Old Court to show the bank the records detailing the loans, property liens, and so forth. During the weekend, the state had moved some of Old Court's records to another location, and lost all the Jiffy Lube documents! The bank we had lined up got nervous and said "see you later." (The records were eventually located.)

In late May, Shearson Lehman also backed away and progress on the private placement stopped. "It was a case of guilt by association," notes Hindman. The state's investigation had turned up allegations of improprieties at Old Court, including charges of falsified appraisals on certain loans. Although Jiffy Lube was not involved or implicated in any of the allegations, the shadow of Old Court appeared to scare off potential backers.

Another investment banker, Alex Brown & Sons, proposed raising $10 million in equity for a real estate partnership. The partnership would then obtain $40 million in debt from a savings and loan. The money would be used to replace Old Court and fund the development of Jiffy Lube centers.

Hindman was confident that the deal would go through, but Alex Brown's final review committee turned down the proposal. The Ernst & Whinney CSE phoned a contact at Alex Brown and determined that the deal had been rejected because of the Old Court situation. Old Court's key officers were under investigation for improper activities and "no one wanted to touch anything Old Court has been involved with."

Short-Term Solutions

Management decided immediately after the May 6 announcement of Old Court's collapse that Jiffy Lube could not wait for funding from the S&L to resume (particularly since this did not appear to be a likely possibility). Development of the service centers involved a series of events which could not be put on hold. Jiffy Lube would default on a number of real estate purchases if

---

EXHIBIT B

Old Court Savings & Loan Master Commitment

OLD COURT SAVINGS AND LOAN   May 24, 1983

Jiffy Lube, Inc.
   RE: Various Sites—Jiffy Lube—Master Commitment

Gentlemen:

   Please be advised that Old Court Savings & Loan, Inc., will provide construction funds, on various sites, for buildings to be built by your company. As your request draws on specific sites Old Court will issue individual commitments to you. The following is a general outline of our understanding of your request and Old Court's commitment to you:

BORROWER:	Jiffy Lube, Inc.
TOTAL COMMITMENT AMOUNT:	Not to exceed sixteen million ($16,000,000) dollars.
INTEREST RATE:	Two (2%) percent over Union Trust prime.
TERM OF EACH INDIVIDUAL LOAN:	Six (6) months after closing, with one six month extension.
LOAN FEES:	One and one-half (1 1/2) points for first (1st) six (6) months, one (1%) percent additional if additional six month extension is used.

SPECIAL CONDITIONS:

1. Subject to satisfactory appraisal on each site.
2. Subject to satisfactory financial statements, to be updated from time to time.
3. Review and approval of all loan documents by Old Court's attorney.
4. Subject to availability of funds for loan.

   Please indicate your acceptance of this general outline of terms and conditions by signing the bottom of this letter and returning it to me.

Sincerely,

David Falco
Executive Vice President

---

cash payments were not made by specified dates. Contractors were lined up, and individuals expecting to earn their livelihood operating franchises were depending on the service centers' being completed.

In addition, significant delays would damage the company's strategy. Jim Hindman:

> I really believe that the guy that gets his distribution system in place first is going to have the chance of being the "McDonald's" of the industry. Speed is the most critical element; we have to get out there before anyone else does. It's like Patton's rush across Europe in World War II; go until you run out of fuel. Once you take territory, you never have to give it back.
>
> There have been many times when we could have pulled back and been just a regional company. A couple of our directors have always pushed for us to slow down and concentrate more on short-term profits. Look at what is happening now, though. The small firms are being snapped up—like all of the local chains we've bought. And now Minit Lube has been acquired by Quaker State. If we maintain our growth, we will be the only independent company in the industry with the ability to go on national television, and the smaller chains will see their car counts go down.

Jiffy Lube decided to proceed with construction of the centers and to fund the costs itself out of its limited operating capital. Construction draws required approximately $150K–$200K per week, and Jiffy Lube's cash reserves were quickly used up. Hindman lent Jiffy Lube $865K.

Franchisees also rallied behind Jiffy Lube. Jiffy Lube had recognized from the start that the franchisees were the parties responsible for actually selling and providing the quick lube service to consumers. They were the key link to the success or failure of Jiffy Lube. Acknowledging their importance, Jiffy Lube had worked hard to create a "partnership" relationship between it and the franchisees. Shortly after the crises began, franchisees combined with employees to make $1.2 million in short-term unsecured loans to Jiffy Lube.

The cash drain continued, however, and by July Jiffy Lube was again out of cash. John Sasser, the CFO, walked into Hindman's office on a Wednesday and told him that they needed a million dollars by Monday if Jiffy Lube was to meet all its commitments. With no apparent sources of cash immediately available, Hindman consulted with his attorney, Jacques Schlenger, about the options available, including the potential benefits of filing Chapter 11.

Schlenger happened to represent two entrepreneurs who had recently cashed out of a business. Schlenger set up a 45-minute meeting between Hindman and one of the men on Thursday. By Monday, Jiffy Lube had a loan for the $1 million it needed.

In the late summer of 1985, the state of Maryland determined that Old Court was not salvageable and placed the S&L in receivership for the purpose of liquidation. Ed Kelley, senior vice president, describes the decision Jiffy Lube had to make:

> We didn't know if we should join the bandwagon and threaten suits against Old Court and the state, or try diplomacy. We decided that the best approach was to be nice guys, and told them, "Look, we understand you've got a problem and we want to cooperate with you to work it out. We want to pay you back everything that we've borrowed, but we can't do that until these units are completed."

In September, the receiver of Old Court agreed to allow the S&L to extend a $4 million line of credit to Jiffy Lube for temporary construction financing on the units Jiffy Lube could not complete on its own (16 units). The key points of this agreement are summarized in *Exhibit C*.

Decision-making Time: Long-Term Alternatives

By late summer, Shearson Lehman became convinced that Jiffy Lube was not going to suffer any more fallout as a result of the Old Court disaster, and again became interested in putting together a private placement. At the same time a number of major oil companies demonstrated an interest in Jiffy Lube.

The environment Jiffy Lube faced in late 1985 is summarized in the excerpts from the company's business plan: (see *Exhibit D*):

Since the Old Court collapse, Jiffy Lube has followed through on its business strategy by using a variety of the short-term financing sources available to it. The new agreement with Old Court, though, requires Jiffy Lube to quickly pay off $2.5 million of the $6.3 million construction loans outstanding. Jiffy Lube has committed to paying this amount with the proceeds from the private placement proposed by Shearson or through other means.

Personal loans and other short-term borrowings are also coming due (see *Exhibit E* for a summary of the outstanding debt). And, additional financing is needed if the company is to execute its long-term growth plan. Jiffy Lube, with the assistance of Ernst & Whinney, prepared a projection of its operations for fiscal 1986 and for the five years following. A summary of the projections is included in *Exhibit F*.

EXHIBIT C

Old Court Savings & Loan: Amended Master Commitment

On September 12, 1985, Jiffy Lube signed an agreement with Old Court Savings and Loan:

Amended Master Commitment for Real Estate Acquisition and Construction Financing on Sixteen (16) Jiffy Lube Locations

The agreement is summarized in the excerpts below:

Financing shall consist of no more than sixteen (16) loans (collectively the "loan," and individually, the "individual loan"). Proceeds of each loan to be used to defray a portion of the acquisition and construction costs for the purchase of each individual property.

Terms and conditions:

Loan Amount. *On each individual loan the amount of the total advance shall be equal to eighty percent (80%) of the appraised fair market value of the real estate, including the improvements to be constructed thereon. In no event, however, shall the amount of the loan exceed the sum of four million dollars ($4,000.000).*

Interest Rate. *A floating rate two percent (2%) over the prime rate charged by the Union Trust Company of Maryland, but in no event shall the rate be less than thirteen percent (13%) per annum.*

Interest Payments: *Interest only is payable on the first (1st) day of the seventh (7th) calendar month following closing. Borrower shall have the option to extend the maturity of each individual loan to the first (1st) day of the tenth (10th) calendar month following closing.*

Special Conditions:

This commitment letter supersedes the May 24, 1983, master commitment. Borrower releases and holds harmless the Bank for any claims arising out of the master agreement or any alleged defaults by the bank thereunder.

All existing notes and mortgages will be modified to provide for payment in full on the first (1st) day of the seventh (7th) month following execution of this commitment letter. Borrower will have the right, upon payment of an extension fee equal to one (1%) percent of the loan amount, to extend the maturity date of the loans to first day of the thirteenth (13th) month following the date of the commitment.

Bank's obligation to perform hereunder is expressly conditioned upon:

(i) the delivery by Borrower to Bank a letter from Shearson Lehman Brothers wherein Shearson agrees that it will use its best efforts to market not less than nine million dollars ($9,000,000) of subordinated notes with warrants of Jiffy Lube International, Inc., of which two and one-half million dollars ($2,500,000) will be paid to Bank within five days of Borrower's closing under its agreement with Shearson.

(ii) the delivery by Borrower to Bank a letter from Reality Income Corporation (RIC) wherein RIC agrees that it will purchase eighteen (18) Jiffy Lube locations which are secured by mortgages to Bank.

(Note: Both letters referred to above were delivered to the bank at the time the agreement was signed.)

EXHIBIT D

Industry Trends and Current Developments

Fast oil change specialists currently perform approximately 3.5 percent of the 367 million oil changes estimated annually for automobiles and light trucks. The company believes the market share should grow rapidly due to the decline in the number of full-service gas stations. According to the 1985 National Petroleum News Factbook Annual Issue, the number of gas stations offering oil changes decreased to fewer than 137,000 in 1985 from 226,000 in 1973. A recent Pennzoil study concluded that quick oil change centers would become one of the major distribution channels for oil lubrication products by the early 1990s.

The company currently has approximately 270 service centers operating, and estimates that the other major fast oil change operators have the following numbers of centers:

Minit Lube	90
Grease Monkey	45
Rapid Oil Change	26
Kwik Change	19
McQuick Oilube	16
Lube Pit Stop	14

On August 1, 1985, Quaker State Oil Refining Corporation announced that it had signed a letter of intent to acquire Arctic Circle, Inc., for $35 million in stock. Arctic Circle, Inc., is the parent company of Minit Lube, and holds over 100 Arctic Circle restaurants in addition to the oil change centers.

EXHIBIT E

Debt Outstanding at September 30, 1985

Description	September 30, 1985, Balance (000's)	Interest Rate	Payment Terms/Comments
Financing for centers under construction:			
Old Court Savings & Loan	$6,300	Prime + 2%	See "Amended Master Commitment" (*Exhibit C*)
James McDonagh and Robert Vogel	1,000	11%	Due 8/86.
Jim Hindman	865	15%	Five notes, maturing between 9/85 and 1/86.
Other directors, employees, and franchisees	1,185	15%	Due 3/86.
	9,350		
Permanent real estate financing:			Requires increasing monthly payment through 2/94. Current payments are approximately $80,000.
INA Mortgage	5,250	16.5%	Monthly payments of approximately $40,000. All mature by 1993.
Other mortgages	2,052	Prime + 1 to 2%	
	7,302		
Funds borrowed to acquire companies or assets:			
Pennzoil	1,800	14.25%	Due 2/86.
			Borrowed under line of credit agreement and due on demand. Under an oral agreement with the bank, the loan can be paid over five years, beginning in 12/85, if necessary.
Maryland National Bank	1,300	Prime + 1%	
Others (included notes payable to selling shareholders of chains acquired, and debts assumed in acquistions)	2,900	8%–18%	Mature over the next four years.
	6,000		
Total at September 30, 1985	$22,652		

EXHIBIT F

Jiffy Lube, Inc., Projected Operations

	1986	1987	1988	1989	1990	1991
Revenue:						
Sales by company-operated units	$ 7,683	$10,169	$14,218	$18,840	$22,210	23,954
Initial franchise fees	3,630	4,527	4,735	5,048	5,215	2,706
Area development fees	2,000	500				
Franchise royalties	5,280	9,946	16,062	23,405	32,162	41,014
Sales of automotive products	8,880	15,789	24,489	34,623	46,169	56,561
Rental income from franchisees	2,328	3,010	3,701	4,440	5,137	5,442
Total revenues	29,801	43,941	63,205	86,356	110,893	129,677
Costs and expenses:						
Company-operated units	6,377	8,440	11,801	15,637	18,434	19,882
Cost of sales of automotive products	7,548	13,420	20,816	29,429	39,243	48,077
Expenses related to rental properties, including interest	1,711	1,546	1,502	1,433	1,341	1,332
Selling, general, and administrative expenses	8,880	14,399	20,341	26,163	31,694	35,221
Total costs and expenses	24,516	37,805	54,460	72,662	90,712	104,512
Income from operations	5,285	6,136	8,745	13,694	20,181	25,165
Other income (expense):						
Interest expense	(2,798	(3,423	(2,650)	(2,827	(2,883)	(2,259)
Other	315	324	97	68	439	1,286
Income before income taxes	2,802	3,037	6,192	10,935	17,737	24,192
Income tax expense	951	1,518	3,096	5,465	8,868	12,096
Net income	$ 1,851	$ 1,518	$ 3,096	$ 5,467	$ 8,868	$ 12,096
Service centers in operation:						
Franchised	361	578	805	1,047	1,297	1,427
Company-operated	23	31	39	47	47	47

These projections were prepared assuming that Jiffy Lube obtains $10 million in debt financing.

November 1985 Alternatives

Bridge Capital Investors

As the Old Court episode cooled down toward the end of August, Shearson Lehman again proposed putting together a private placement. Shearson worked through the rest of August and September searching for parties interested in a $10 million private debt placement. By early October 1985, Shearson had identified four interested parties, and key management from Jiffy Lube flew to New York to meet with each of them.

One of the four, Bridge Capital Investors, expressed an immediate interest in Jiffy Lube. Bridge Capital Investors, a mezzanine capital partnership, proposed providing financing through the purchase of $10 million in subordinated notes with warrants attached to purchase 10 percent of Jiffy Lube. The proposed terms are summarized in *Exhibit G*.

Don Remey, general partner, described Bridge Capital as a "$50 million partnership financed by pension funds and insurance companies. We specialize in financing growing companies, using debt with equity kickers." Remey also indicated that "unlike venture capital, we do not seek control or a major share of ownership." The personal chemistry between Hindman and Remey was positive from the first meeting on.

Quaker State

The president of Quaker State called in August and said, "Look, we just bought Minit Lube and I think we should talk." After some preliminary meetings, Jiffy Lube agreed to let Quaker State perform "due diligence" on the company as a prelude to a possible purchase offer. In September, Quaker State made an offer to purchase Jiffy Lube. The purchase price is contingent on future earnings as described in the purchase offer summarized in *Exhibit H*.

Details of Quaker State's Arctic Circle/Minit Lube acquisition are now available (these were outlined in the

EXHIBIT G

Bridge Capital Investors: Proposed Private Placement

12% Senior Subordinated Notes Due 1992 with Warrants

NOTES

Amount	$10,000,000
Issue price	97.254%
Maturity	December 15, 1992 (7 years)
Interest rate	12%, payable quarterly

Mandatory sinking fund

Beginning during the fourth year, the Company will make eight equal semiannual payments of $1,250,000.

In the event of an initial public offering of $20 million or more, the Company shall prepay at par 50% of the Notes from the proceeds of the offering.

Subordination

The notes will be subordinate in payment of principal and interest to senior debt, and senior to all subsequent subordinated debt.

WARRANTS

Amount

549,218 warrants to purchase 10% of the fully diluted, pro forma shares of common stock. After six months there will be an adjustment for any new shares or warrants issued to maintain 10%.

Issue price	$0.50 per warrant
Exercise price	$6 per share
Term	Seven years

Put Provision

If during five years from issuance, the Company's common stock has not traded publicly at levels set forth in the table that follows, the Purchasers may put the warrants and/or underlying stock to the Company. The price will be determined by the calculation of the amount necessary to result in a 30% per annum internal rate of return to the Purchasers on that proportion of warrants not previously sold, taking into account all interest premium and principal repayment on the proportionately related notes.

If (i) the Company completes one or more public offerings of common stock with aggregate proceeds to the Company of at least $15 million and (ii) the average closing price for 60 consecutive trading days exceeds:

6 months ending	6/88—	$17.50
6 months ending	12/88—	$20.00
6 months ending	6/89—	$25.00
6 months ending	12/89—	$30.00
6 months ending	6/90—	$35.00
6 months ending	12/90—	$40.00

then the put provision will expire.

In the event the Company is unable to pay the amount due, the Purchasers have the right to nominate a majority of the Board of Directors.

Merger/Sale

If prior to December 21, 1987, the Company is sold or merged into another company the Purchasers shall be entitled to not less than $15 per warrant share.

BOARD OF DIRECTORS

Donald P. Remey to be elected as Director.

S-14 filing related to the transaction and in the company's September 30, 1985, 10-Q). The shareholders of Arctic Circle received 1,425,000 shares of Quaker State common stock; the stock was trading at $24⅞ at the time of the transaction; Arctic Circle had sales and net income of $31 million and $1.4 million, respectively, for the year ended March 31, 1985. Minit Lube accounted for 47 percent and 57 percent of the sales and net income, respectively.

Financial details of debt and operation are in *Exhibits I* and *J*; Jiffy Lube's master agreement for real estate and construction is in *Exhibit K*.

EXHIBIT H

Quaker State Purchase Offer

PURCHASE PRICE

Quaker State will purchase the outstanding shares of Jiffy Lube for $13 per share, contingent on Jiffy Lube's meeting the earnings requirements detailed below. The total potential purchase price is as follows:

Total shares (shares outstanding, warrants, and options)	
Purchase price per share	4,144,681
Total	× $13
	$53,880,853

$5 million will be paid in cash at closing, the remainder is payable June 30, 1989, based on Jiffy Lube's net income for the three years ending March 31, 1989 (in aggregate):

Aggregate Net Income for 3 Years Ending March 31, 1989	Purchase Price Per Share	Purchase Price Total
Exceeding $10 million	$13.0	$53,880,853
8	10.4	43,104,682
6	7.8	32,328,512
4	5.2	21,552,341
2	2.6	10,776,171
$2 million or less	1.2	5,000,000

An additional $25 million will be paid to management as bonuses based on Jiffy Lube's net income for the five years ending March 31, 1991 (in aggregate):

Aggregate Net Income for 5 Years Ending March 31, 1991	Total Bonus
Exceeding $25 million	$25 million
20	20
15	15
10	10
5	5
$5 million or less	0

TRANSACTIONS PRIOR TO CLOSE OF SALE

Upon signing of a contract of sales, Quaker State will loan Jiffy Lube $10 million. If negotiations break down or are stopped for antitrust reasons, Jiffy Lube will repay the debt one year after the formal break off of negotiations.

Jiffy Lube management will be independent of Quaker State from signing until closing except that no new stock, warrants, or options shall be issued until the deal is closed, canceled, or one year passes.

ORGANIZATION AND CONTINUING OPERATIONS

Jiffy Lube will operate as a separate subsidiary, reporting directly to the President or CEO of Quaker State. Jiffy Lube will have a separate board composed of Jiffy Lube and Quaker State management.

The name "Jiffy Lube" shall be maintained on all units in the system.

In any market where Jiffy Lube has sold the exclusive area rights or where Jiffy Lube units and Minit Lube units have conflicting franchise or territorial rights, the Minit Lube system must be kept separate until an agreement is reached between the Jiffy Lube and Minit Lube franchises.

REAL ESTATE FINANCING

Quaker State commits to provide at least $50 million of real estate financing to Jiffy Lube per year for the next four (4) years at competitive rates. Such debt will be used to build quick lubrication centers, all of which will, as a condition of the lease, use at least 80 percent of their motor oil from Quaker State.

INA debt guaranteed by Pennzoil is to be repaid or assumed.

EXHIBIT I

Consolidated Balance Sheet

	March 31	
	1985	1984
Assets		
Current assets:		
Cash	$ 1,476,889	$ 510,282
Accounts receivable, less allowance of $164,800 in 1985 and $47,000 in 1984	1,933,576	1,181,396
Current portion of fees receivable from franchises in development	1,311,000	143,500
Current portion of loans and notes receivable and net investment in direct financing leases	1,215,825	628,824
Current portion of loans and notes receivable from related parties	411,221	219,177
Inventory	985,554	467,351
Real estate held for resale	6,510,781	1,516,492
Prepaid expenses	122,178	181,449
Total current assets	13,967,024	4,848,471
Fees receivable from franchises in development	1,232,500	975,000
Loans and notes receivable, less current portion	898,805	642,876
Loans and notes receivable from related parties, less current portion		261,000
Net investment in direct financing leases	1,006,057	
Investments in and advances to affiliates	306,204	
Property and equipment:		
Land	2,854,344	2,371,679
Buildings and improvements	6,868,768	3,998,741
Automobiles, furniture, and equipment	1,205,801	335,600
	10,928,913	6,706,020
Less allowances for depreciation	761,455	433,686
Intangible assets, less accumulated amortization:		
Franchise rights	5,246,583	461,918
Other	913,628	549,185
	6,160,211	1,011,103
Deferred franchise costs	335,050	144,780
Other assets	206,870	23,374
Total assets	$34,280,179	$14,178,938
Liabilities and Stockholders' Equity		
Current liabilities:		
Accounts payable and accrued expenses	$ 5,129,510	$ 1,387,460
Notes payable	1,679,470	300,000
Construction advances for real estate held for resale	5,936,682	1,506,015
Current portion of long-term debt and capital lease obligations	864,312	165,506
Total current liabilities	13,609,974	3,358,981
Long-term debt, less current portion	10,196,905	5,639,701
Capital lease obligations, less current portion	2,341,217	417,353
Deferred franchise fees	3,595,250	1,302,500
Minority interest	36,498	
Stockholders' equity:		
Common stock, par value $0.05:		
Authorized—5,000,000 shares		
Issued—3,499,521 shares in 1985	174,974	162,198
—3,243,996 shares in 1984		
Capital in excess of par value	9,648,965	8,875,764
Retained-earnings deficit	(4,427,524)	(5,030,730)
Less: Cost of common stock held in treasury—22,808 shares	546,829	546,829
Due from officers for purchase of common stock	349,251	
Total stockholders' equity	4,500,335	3,460,403
Total liabilities and stockholders' equity	$34,280,179	$14,178,938

EXHIBIT J

Consolidated Statement of Operations

	Year Ended March 31	
	1985	1984
Revenue:		
Sales by company-operated units		
Initial franchise fees	$ 2,037,325	$ 80,118
Area development fees	1,177,875	672,500
Franchise royalties	2,208,125	1,219,500
Sales of automotive products	2,141,600	1,294,617
Rental income from franchisees	5,811,421	1,839,270
Total revenues	1,108,852	909,597
	14,485,198	6,015,602
Costs and expenses:		
Company-operated units		
Cost of sales of automotive production	1,714,645	59,585
Costs and expenses related to rental properties, including interest of $966,894 in 1985 and $928,974 in 1984	4,985,386	1,779,658
Selling, general, and administrative expenses	1,413,794	1,250,485
Total costs and expenses	5,908,195	2,821,181
Income (loss) from operations	14,022,020	5,910,909
Other income (expense):	463,178	104,693
Other income		
Interest expense	339,663	203,810
Minority interest in loss of subsidiary	(212,702)	(304,062)
Income (loss) before income taxes	13,067	
Income tax expense	603,206	4,441
Income (loss) before disposal of partnership interests and	301,603	
extraordinary item	301,603	4,441
Income from operations and disposition of partnership interests, net of tax of $115,906		190,933
Income (loss) before extraordinary item	301,603	195,374
Extraordinary reduction of income tax expense arising from the utilization of prior year's net operating losses	301,603	115,906
Net income (loss)	$ 603,206	$ 311,280

Pennzoil

Jiffy Lube had maintained a good relationship with Pennzoil despite Hindman's repurchase of the oil company's investment. Pennzoil was Jiffy Lube's largest supplier of oil products, and it had arranged financing for the development and acquisition of some Jiffy Lube centers. Jiffy Lube was a major channel of distribution, and Pennzoil had much to lose if Jiffy Lube was acquired by another oil company.

Pennzoil told Hindman: "We don't think we should buy you. You don't want to be owned by a large oil company. Your biggest need is for real estate financing. Let's cut a deal whereby we can arrange a financing vehicle that will allow you to grow. With enough money for real estate development you can attract equity on your own." The two parties agreed to continue to discuss this possibility.

Other Options

In the summer, Ashland Oil (the makers of Valvoline) contacted Jiffy Lube to see if the two companies had any interest in each other (e.g., investment, joint venture, purchase). A team of Ashland executives and attorneys came out to do their own due diligence on Jiffy Lube, but the talks have not yet moved beyond the conceptual stage.

Exxon also expressed an interest because of surplus properties it was holding. No serious discussions have been held.

Working for Amoco, Boston Consulting Group had tried to put together a deal whereby Amoco would acquire both Jiffy Lube and Minit Lube. Now, after Quaker State's purchase of Minit Lube, Boston Consulting was working on a proposal for Amoco to purchase Jiffy Lube. No serious discussions have been held yet.

EXHIBIT K

Old Court Savings & Loan: Amended Master Commitment

On September 12, 1985, Jiffy Lube signed an agreement with Old Court Savings and Loan:

Amended Master Commitment for Real Estate Acquisition and Construction Financing on Sixteen (16) Jiffy Lube Locations

The agreement is summarized in the excerpts below:

Financing shall consist of no more than sixteen (16) loans (collectively the "Loan," and individually, the "Individual Loan"). Proceeds of each loan to be used to defray a portion of the acquisition and construction costs for the purchase of each individual property.

Terms and conditions:

Loan Amount. On each individual Loan the amount of the total advance shall be equal to eighty percent (80%) of the appraised fair market value of the real estate, including the improvements to be constructed thereon. In no event, however, shall the amount of the loan exceed the sum of Four Million Dollars ($4,000,000).

Interest Rate. A floating rate two percent (2%) over the prime rate charged by the Union Trust Company of Maryland, but in no event shall the rate be less than thirteen percent (13%) per annum.

Interest Payments: Interest only is payable on the first (1st) day of each month following closing and upon payment in full of each individual loan.

Maturity: Each individual loan shall mature on the first (1st) day of the seventh (7th) calendar month following closing. Borrower shall have the option to extend the maturity of each individual loan to the first (1st) day of the tenth (10th) calendar month following closing.

Special Conditions:

This commitment letter supersedes the May 24, 1983, Master Commitment. Borrower releases and holds harmless the Bank for any claims arising out of the Master agreement or any alleged defaults by the bank thereunder.

All existing notes and mortgages will be modified to provide for payment in full on the first (1st) day of the seventh (7th) month following execution of this commitment letter. Borrower will have the right, upon payment of an extension fee equal to one (1%) percent of the loan amount, to extend the maturity date of the loans to first day of the thirteenth (13th) month following the date of the commitment.

Bank's obligation to perform hereunder is expressly conditioned upon:

(i) the delivery by Borrower to Bank a letter from Shearson Lehman Brothers wherein Shearson agrees that it will use its best efforts to market not less than Nine Million Dollars ($9,000,000) of subordinated notes with warrants of Jiffy Lube International, Inc., of which Two and One-half Million Dollars ($2,500,000) will be paid to Bank within five days of Borrower's closing under its agreement with Shearson.

(ii) the delivery by Borrower to Bank a letter from Reality Income Corporation (RIC) wherein RIC agrees that it will purchase eighteen (18) Jiffy Lube locations which are secured by mortgages to Bank.

(Note: Both letters referred to above were delivered to the bank at the time the agreement was signed.)

Opportunities or "Vultures"?

In Ed Kelley's words, Jiffy Lube is in the middle of a "feeding frenzy." Management has little time to do anything other than contend with the parties interested in arranging a deal with the company.

Jiffy Lube is an enigma; it is the largest quick lube franchisor in the United States but is continually fighting for survival. Hindman feels that the oil companies, especially Quaker State, are "playing hardball" because they don't expect Jiffy Lube to last much longer on its own. Sometimes it seems like Jiffy Lube is surrounded by vultures waiting to pick up the pieces.

15

Obtaining Debt Capital

Leveraging a company is like driving your car with a sharp stick pointed at your heart through the steering wheel. As long as the road is smooth it works fine. But hit one bump in the road and you may be dead.

Warren Buffet

Results Expected

The 1990s ushered in a new era in credit availability—or lack thereof—for emerging companies. Many old rules disappeared and a newer, harsher banking climate has evolved. This chapter is aimed at preparing you to cope better with the new realities in the debt capital markets. Upon completion of this chapter, you will have:

1. Identified sources of debt and how to access them in the 1990s capital markets.
2. Examined the lender's perspective and criteria in making loans, how to prepare a loan proposal, and how to negotiate a loan.
3. Gained a knowledge to help you in managing and orchestrating the acquisition of debt capital.
4. Determined how lenders estimate the debt capacity of a company.
5. Identified some tar pits entrepreneurs need to avoid in considering debt.
6. Analyzed the Jiffy Lube International case.

The New Millenium: The Good Old Days Return

Fortunately, for entrepreneurs and their investors, the punishing credit crunch and stagnant equity markets of the early 1990s gave way to the most robust capital markets in U.S. history as we approached the end of the millenium. Declining interest rates reached historical lows and the credit environment was much friendlier, mimicking the heady days of precrash 1987. Not only have interest rates declined, the availability of bank loans and competition among banks have increased dramatically from the dormant days of the early 1990s.

Enhancing this improved credit environment is a greater marketing awareness by lenders of the potential represented by the growth companies in the new entrepreneurial economy. Bank presidents and loan officers are aggressively seeking out entrepreneurial companies as prospective clients. They work with local universities and entrepreneurial associations to sponsor seminars, workshops, and business fairs, all to cultivate entrepreneurial customers. This is welcome change in the credit climate for entrepreneurs.

A Word of Caution

Even though it is a quite favorable credit environment just now, history suggests that this can change with suddenness. Entrepreneurs who are mindful of this can appreciate just how onerous lending can become. What can be expected should the credit climate reverse itself? For one thing, personal guarantees would be back. Even the most creditworthy companies with enviable records for timely repayment of interest and principal would be asked to provide personal guarantees by the owners. As if this were not onerous enough, there would be an additional phenomenon which can only be called a perversion of the debt capital markets. As the credit crunch becomes more severe, banks would face their own illiquidity and insolvency problems, which would result in the failure of many more banks, including giants such as those that crashed in the early 1990s, like the Bank of New England. To cope with their own balance sheet dissipation, banks would commonly *call the best loan first!* Thousands of high-quality smaller companies would be stunned and debilitated by such actions. After all, given their excellent credit records, it would be easy for them to assume their loans will not be terminated. Yet, a bank can run out of cash, too, and have few choices when its own survival is at stake. The net effect of such a credit crunch would be a massive reduction of balance sheets. Debt reduction would become a dominant financial strategy of small and large companies alike.

The Lender's Perspective

Lenders have always been wary capital providers. Understandably, since banks may earn a 1 percent net profit on total assets, they are especially sensitive to the possibility of a loss. Imagine writing off a $1 million loan to a small company. The bank has to turn around and write an incremental $100 million in profitable loans just to recover the loss. Additionally, given the mayhem of the decade, they are even more sensitive.

Yet, they are businesses and seek to grow and improve profitability as well. They can do this only if they find and bet on successful, young, growing companies. Historically, points and fees charged for making the loan have been a major contributor to bank profitability. The opportunity to entice banks to make loans by offering various sweeteners may be reviving. Take, for instance, a recent lending proposal for a company seeking a $15 million five-year-term loan. In addition to the up-front origination fees and points, the bank further proposed a YES, or yield enhancement security, as a part of the loan. This additional requirement would entitle the bank to receive an additional $3 million payment from the company once its sales exceeded $10 million and it was profitable, or if it was sold, merged, or taken public. The loan was closed in mid-1993, and management and existing investors were happy and would have been willing to pay more.

Sources of Debt Capital[1]

The principal sources[2] of borrowed capital for new and young businesses are trade credit, commercial banks, finance companies, factors, and leasing companies. Admittedly, startups have more difficulty borrowing money than existing businesses. Nevertheless, startups managed by an entrepreneur with a track record and with significant equity in the business who can present a sound business plan can borrow money from one or more sources. But if little equity or collateral exists, the startup won't have much success with banks.

The availability of such debt depends, in part, on where the business is located. Debt and leases as well as equity capital are more available to startup companies in such hotbeds of entrepreneurial activity as eastern Massachusetts and Silicon Valley in California than, say, in the Midwest. Also, in the hotbed areas there is close contact between venture capital firms and the high-technology lending officers of banks. This contact tends to make it easier for startups and early-stage companies to borrow money.

The advantages and disadvantages[3] of these sources, summarized in *Exhibit 15.1*, are basically determined by such obvious dimensions as the interest rate or cost of capital, the key terms, conditions and covenants, and the fit with the owner's situation and the company's needs at the time. How good a deal you can strike is a function of your relative bargaining position and the competitiveness among the alternatives.

What is ultimately most important, given a deal at or above an acceptable threshold, is the person you will be dealing with, rather than the amount, terms, or institution. In other words, you will be better off seeking the right banker (or other provider of capital) than just the right bank. Once again, the industry and market characteristics, stage and health of the firm in terms of cash flow, debt coverage, and collateral are central to the evaluation process. *Exhibit 15.2* summarizes the term of financing available from these different sources. Note the difficulty in finding sources for more than one year of financing.

Finally, an enduring question entrepreneurs ask is, What is bankable? How much money can I expect to borrow based on my balance sheet? *Exhibit 15.3* summarizes some general guidelines in answer to this question. Since most loans and lines of credit are asset-based loans, knowing the guidelines employed by lenders to determine how much to lend the

---

[1] This section is drawn from Jeffry A. Timmons, *Financing and Planning the New Venture* (Acton, MA: Brick House Publishing Company, 1990).
[2] Ibid., p. 68.
[3] Ibid., p. 33.

EXHIBIT 15.1

Debt Financing Sources for Types of Business

Source	Startup Company	Existing Company
Trade credit	Yes	Yes
Commercial banks	Occasionally, with strong equity	Yes
Finance companies	Rare (if assets are available)	Yes
Factors	Rare	Yes
Leasing companies	Difficult, except for startups with venture capital	Yes
Mutual savings banks and savings & loans	Rare	Real estate and other asset based companies
Insurance companies	Rare, except alongside venture capital	Yes

Source: Jeffry A. Timmons, *Financing and Planning the New Venture* (Acton, MA: Brick House Publishing Company, 1990), p. 34.

EXHIBIT 15.2

Debt Financing Sources by Term of Financing

Source	Term of Financing		
	Short	Medium	Long
Trade credit	Yes	Yes	Possible
Commercial banks	Most frequently	Yes (asset-based)	Rare (depends on asset)
Factors	Most frequently	Rare	No
Leasing companies	No	Most frequently	Some
Mutual savings banks, savings & loans	No	No	Real estate and other asset-based companies
Insurance companies	Rare	Most frequently	Yes

Source: Jeffry A. Timmons, *Financing and Planning the New Venture* (Acton, MA: Brick House Publishing Company, 1990), Table 3, p. 34.

EXHIBIT 15.3

What Is Bankable? Specific Lending Criteria

Security	Credit Capacity
Accounts receivable	70%–80% of those less than 90 days
Inventory	40%–60% depending on obsolescence risk
Equipment	70%–80% of market value (less if specialized)
Chattel mortgage	100%–150% or more of auction appraisal value
Conditional sales contract	60%–70% or more of purchase price
Plant improvement loan	60%–80% of appraised value or cost

Source: Jeffry A. Timmons, *Financing and Planning the New Venture* (Acton, MA: Brick House Publishing Company, 1990), Table 1, p. 33.

company is very important. When you observe the percentages of key balance sheet assets that are often allowable as collateral, note that these are only ranges and will vary from region to region and for different types of businesses. For instance, nonperishable consumer goods versus technical products that may have considerable risk of obsolescence would be treated very differently in making a loan collateral computation. If the company already has significant debt and has pledged all of its assets, there may not be a lot of room for negotiations. A bank with full collateral in hand for a company having cash flow problems is unlikely to give up such a position in order to enable the company to attract another lender, even though the collateral is more than enough to meet these guidelines.

Trade Credit[4]

Trade credit is a major source of short-term funds for small businesses. In fact, trade credit represents 30–40 percent of the current liabilities of nonfinancial companies, with generally higher percentages in smaller companies. Trade credit is reflected on the balance sheets as accounts payable.

If a small business is able to buy goods and services and be given, or take, 30, 60, or 90 days to pay for them, that business has essentially obtained a loan of 30 to 90 days. Many small and new businesses are able to obtain such trade credit when no other form of debt financing is available to them. Suppliers offer trade credit as a way of getting new customers, and often build the bad debt risk into their prices.

The ability of a new business to obtain trade credit depends on the quality and reputation of its management and the relationships it establishes with its suppliers. A word of warning: continued late payment or nonpayment may cause suppliers to cut off shipments or ship only on a COD basis. Also, the real cost of using trade credit can be very high, for example, the loss of discounts for prompt payment. Because the cost of trade credit is seldom expressed as an annual amount, it should be analyzed carefully, and a new business should shop for the best terms.

Trade credit may take some of the following forms: extended credit terms; special or seasonal datings, where a supplier ships goods in advance of the purchaser's peak selling season and accepts payment 90–120 days later during the season; inventory on consignment, not requiring payment until sold; and loan or lease of equipment.

Commercial Bank Financing

Commercial banks prefer to lend to existing businesses that have a track record of sales, profits, satisfied customers, and a current backlog. Their concern about the high failure rates in new businesses can make them less than enthusiastic about making loans to such firms. They like to be no-risk lenders. For their protection, they look first to positive cash flow and then to collateral, and in new and young businesses they are likely to require personal guarantees of the owners' business. Like equity investors, they place great weight on the quality of the management team.

Notwithstanding these factors, banks do not make loans to startups or young businesses that have strong equity financings from venture capital firms. This is especially true in such centers of entrepreneurial and venture capital activity as Silicon Valley, Boston, and Los Angeles.

Commercial banks are the primary source of debt capital for existing (not new) small and medium-sized businesses, those with less than $5 million in sales. Small business loans may be handled by a bank's small business loan department. Larger loans may require the approval of a loan committee. If a loan exceeds the limits of a local bank, part or all of the loan will be offered to "correspondent" banks in neighboring communities and nearby financial centers. This correspondent network enables the smaller banks in rural areas to handle loans that otherwise could not be made.

Most of the loans made by commercial banks are for one year or less. Some of these loans are unsecured and others are secured by receivables, inventories, or other assets. Commercial banks also make a large number of intermediate-term loans (or term loans) with a maturity of one to five years. On about 90 percent of these term loans, the banks require collateral, generally consisting of stocks, machinery, equipment, and real estate. Most term loans are retired by systematic payments over the life of the loan. Apart from real estate mortgages and loans guaranteed by the SBA or a similar organization, commercial banks make few loans with maturities greater than five years.

Banks also offer a number of services to the small business, such as computerized payroll preparation, letters of credit, international services, lease financing, and money market accounts.

There are almost 14,000 commercial banks in the United States. A complete listing of these banks can be found, arranged by states, in the *American Bank Directory* (McFadden Business Publications), published semiannually.

Line of Credit Loans

A line of credit is a formal or informal agreement between a bank and a borrower concerning the maximum loan balance a bank will allow the borrower for a one-year period. Often the bank will charge a fee of a certain percent of the line of credit for a definite commitment to make the loan when requested.

Line of credit funds are used for such seasonal financings as inventory buildup and receivable financing. It is general practice to repay these loans from the sales and liquidation of short-term assets that they financed. Lines of credit can be unsecured, but often

---

[4] Ibid., pp. 68–80.

a bank will require a pledge of inventory, receivables, equipment, or other acceptable assets. Unsecured lines of credit have no lien on any asset of the borrower and no priority over any trade creditor, but the banks do require that all debt to the principals and stockholders of the company be subordinated to the line of credit debt.

The line of credit is executed through a series of renewable 90-day notes or through an installment loan to be paid within the year. The renewable 90-day note is the more common practice, and the bank will expect the borrower to pay off his or her open loan within a year and to hold a zero loan balance for one to two months. This is known as "resting the line." Commercial banks may also generally require that a borrower maintain a checking account at the bank with a minimum ("compensating") balance of 15 to 20 percent of the outstanding loan.

For a large, financially sound company, the interest rates for a "prime risk" line of credit will be quoted at about 1 to 2 percent over the rediscount rate charges by the Federal Reserve. A small firm may be required to pay a higher rate. It should be noted that the true rate of interest will depend on the method of charging interest. If the bank deducts interest in advance (discounts the loan) or the loan is prepaid in installments, the effective rate of interest will be higher than the quoted figure. Any compensating-balance or resting-the-line requirements will also increase effective interest rates.

Accounts Receivable Financing

Accounts receivable financing is short-term financing that involves either the pledge of receivables as collateral for a loan or the sale of receivables (factoring). Accounts receivable loans are made by commercial finance companies and factoring concerns. Only a very limited number of banks do factoring.

Accounts receivable bank loans are made on a discounted value of the receivables pledged. Invoices that do not meet the bank's credit standard will not be accepted as collateral. (Receivables more than 90 days old are not normally accepted.) A bank may inform the purchaser of goods that the account has been assigned to the bank, and payments are made directly to the bank, which credits them to the borrower's account. This is called a notification plan. Alternatively, the borrower may collect the accounts as usual and pay off the bank loan; this is a nonnotification plan.

Accounts receivable loans can make it possible for a company to secure a loan that it might not otherwise get. The loan can be increased as sales and receivables grow. However, receivables loans do have drawbacks. They can be expensive, and receivable financing is sometimes regarded by trade creditors as evidence of a company in financial difficulty.

Time–Sales Finance

Many dealers or manufacturers who offer installment payment terms to purchasers of their equipment cannot themselves finance installment or conditional sales contracts. In such situations, they sell and assign the installment contract to a bank or sales finance company. (Some very large manufacturers do their own financing through captive finance companies. Most very small retailers merely refer their customer installment contracts to sales finance companies, which provide much of this financing, and on more flexible terms.)

From the manufacturer's or dealer's point of view, time-sales finance is, in effect, a way of obtaining short-term financing from long-term installment accounts receivable. From the purchaser's point of view, it is a way of financing the purchase of new equipment.

Under time–sales financing, the bank purchases installment contracts at a discount from their full value and takes as security an assignment of the manufacturer/dealer's interest in the conditional sales contract. In addition, the bank's financing of installment note receivables includes recourse to the seller in the event of loan default by the purchaser. Thus, the bank has the payment obligation of the equipment purchaser, the manufacturer/dealer's security interest in the equipment purchased, and recourse to the manufacturer/dealer in the event of default. The bank also withholds a portion of the payment (5 percent or more) as a dealer reserve until the note is paid. Since the reserve becomes an increasing percentage of the note as the contract is paid off, an arrangement is often made when multiple contracts are financed to ensure that the reserve against all contracts will not exceed 20 percent or so.

The purchase price of equipment under a sales financing arrangement includes a "time-sales price differential" (e.g., an increase to cover the discount, typically 6–10 percent) taken by the bank that does the financing. Collection of the installments may be made directly by the bank or indirectly through the manufacturer/dealer.

Unsecured Term Loans

Bank term loans are generally made for periods of one to five years, and may be unsecured or secured. Most of the basic features of bank term loans are the same for secured and unsecured loans. Secured term loans are described below under chattel mortgages and collateral loans.

Term loans provide needed growth capital to companies that could not obtain such capital from the sale of stock. They are also a substitute for a series of short-term loans made with the anticipation of renewal by both the borrower and the lender.

Term loans have three distinguishing features: They are made by banks for periods of up to five years (and occasionally more). Periodic repayment is required. Term loan agreements are designed to fit the special needs and requirements of the borrower (e.g., payments can be smaller at the beginning of a loan term and larger at the end).

Because term loans do not mature for a number of years, during which time there could be a significant change in the situation and fortunes of the borrower, the bank must carefully evaluate the prospects and management of the borrowing company. Even the protection afforded by initially strong assets can be wiped out by several years of heavy losses. Term lenders place particular stress on the entrepreneurial and managerial abilities of the borrowing company. The bank will also carefully consider such things as the long-range prospects of the company and its industry, its present and projected profitability, and its ability to generate the cash required to meet the loan payments.

To lessen the risks involved in term loans, a bank will require some restrictive covenants in the loan agreement. These covenants might prohibit additional borrowing, merger of the company, payment of dividends, sales of assets, and the like.

Chattel Mortgages and Equipment Loans

Assigning an appropriate possession (chattel) as security is a common way of making secured term loans. The chattel is any machinery, equipment, or business property that is made the collateral of a loan in the same way as a mortgage on real estate. The chattel remains with the borrower unless there is default, in which case the chattel goes to the bank. Generally, credit against machinery and equipment is restricted primarily to new or highly serviceable and salable used items.

It should be noted that in many states, loans that used to be chattel mortgages are now executed through the security agreement forms of the Uniform Commercial Code (UCC). However, chattel mortgages are still used in many places, and from custom, many lenders continue to use that term even though the loans are executed through the UCC's security agreements. The term *chattel mortgage* is typically from one to five years; some are longer-term.

Conditional Sales Contracts

Conditional sales contracts are used to finance a substantial portion of the new equipment purchased by businesses. Under a sales contract, the buyer agrees to purchase a piece of equipment, makes a nominal down payment, and pays the balance in installments over a period of from one to five years. Until the payment is complete, the seller holds title to the equipment. Hence, the sale is conditional upon the buyer's completing the payments.

A sales contract is financed by a bank that has recourse to the seller should the purchaser default the loan. This makes it more difficult to finance a purchase of a good piece of used equipment at an auction. No recourse to the seller is available if the equipment is purchased at an auction; the bank would have to sell the equipment if the loan goes bad. Occasionally, a firm seeking financing on existing and new equipment will sell some of its equipment to a dealer and repurchase it, together with new equipment, in order to get a conditional sales contract financed by a bank.

The effective rate of interest on a conditional sales contract is high, running to as much as 15–18 percent if the effect of installment features is considered. The purchaser/borrower should thus make sure that the interest payment is covered by increased productivity and profitability resulting from the new equipment.

Plant Improvement Loans

Loans made to finance improvements to business properties and plants are called plant improvement loans. They can be intermediate- and long-term and are generally secured by a first mortgage on that part of the property or plant that is being improved.

Commercial Finance Companies

The commercial bank is generally the lender of choice for a business. From whom does a business seek loans when the bank says no? Commercial finance companies, which aggressively seek borrowers. They frequently loan money to companies that do not have positive cash flow—although they will not make loans to companies unless they consider them viable.

The primary factors in a bank's loan decision are the continuing successful operation of a business, and its generation of more than enough cash to repay a loan. By contrast, commercial finance companies lend against the liquidation value of assets (receivables, inventory, equipment) that it understands, knows how and where to sell, and whose liquidation value is sufficient to repay the loan.

In the case of inventories or equipment, liquidation value is the amount that could be realized from an auction or quick sale. Finance companies will generally *not* lend against receivables more than 90 days old, federal or state government agency receivables (because they are slow payers), or any receivables whose collection is contingent on the performance of a delivered product.

Because of the liquidation criteria, finance companies prefer readily salable inventory items such as electronic components, or metal in such commodity forms as billets or standard shapes. Generally, a finance company will not accept inventory as collateral unless it also has receivables. As for equipment loans, these are made only by certain finance companies and against such standard equipment as lathes, milling machines, and the like.

How much of the value of collateral will a finance company lend? Generally, 70–80 percent of acceptable receivables under 90 days old, 42–50 percent of the liquidation value of raw materials and/or finished goods inventory that are not obsolete or damaged, and 60–70 percent of the liquidation value of equipment, as determined by an appraiser. Receivables and inventory loans are for one year, while equipment loans are for three to seven years.

All of these loans have tough prepayment penalties: Finance companies do not want to be immediately replaced by banks when a borrower has improved its credit image.

The data required for a loan from a finance company includes all that would be provided to a bank, plus additional details for the assets being used as collateral. For receivables financing this includes detailed aging of receivables (and payables) and historical data on sales, returns, and collections.

For inventory financing, it includes details on the items in inventory, how long they have been there and their rate of turnover. Requests for equipment loans should be accompanied by details on the date of purchase, cost of each equipment item, and appraisals, if available. If not, the finance company will have such an appraisal made.

The advantage of dealing with a commercial finance company is that it will make loans that banks will not, and it can be flexible in lending arrangements. The price a finance company exacts for this is an interest rate anywhere from 2 to 6 percent over that charged by a bank, prepayment penalties, and in the case of receivables loans recourse to the borrower for unpaid collateralized receivables.

Because of their greater risk taking and asset-based lending, finance companies usually place a larger reporting and monitoring burden on the borrowing firm in order to stay on top of the receivables and inventory serving as loan collateral. Personal guarantees will generally be required from the principals of the business. The finance company will generally reserve the right to reduce the percentage of the value lent against receivables or inventory if it gets nervous about the borrower's survivability.

Factoring

Factoring is a form of accounts receivable financing. However, instead of borrowing and using receivables as collateral, the receivables are sold, at a discounted value, to a factor. Some commercial finance companies do factoring. The factor provides receivables financing for the company unable to obtain such financing from a bank.

In a standard factoring arrangement, the factor buys the client's receivables outright, without recourse, as soon as the client creates them by shipment of goods to customers. Although the factor has recourse to the borrowers for returns, errors in pricing, and so on, the factor assumes the risk of bad debt losses that develop from receivables it approves and purchases.

Cash is made available to the client as soon as proof is provided (old-line factoring) or on the average due date of the invoices (maturity factoring). With maturity factoring, the company can often obtain a loan of about 90 percent of the money a factor has agreed to pay on a maturity date. Most factoring arrangements are for one year.

Factoring fits some businesses better than others. For a business that has annual sales volume in excess of $300,000 and a net worth over $50,000 that sells on normal credit terms to a customer base that is 75 percent credit rated, factoring is a real option. Factoring has become almost traditional in such industries as textiles, furniture manufacturing, clothing manufacturing, toys, shoes, and plastics.

The same data required from a business for a receivable loan from a bank is required by a factor. Because a factor is buying receivables with no recourse, it will carefully analyze the quality and value of a prospective client's receivables. It will want a detailed aging of receivables plus historical data on bad debts, return, and allowances. It will also investigate the credit history of customers to whom its client sells and establish credit limits for each customer. The business client can receive factoring of customer receivables only up to the limits so set.

The cost of financing receivables through factoring is higher than that of borrowing from a bank or a finance company. The factor is assuming the credit risk, doing credit investigations and collections, and advancing funds. A factor generally charges up to 2 percent of the total sales factored as a service charge.

There is also an interest charge for money advanced to a business, usually 2–6 percent above prime. A larger, established business borrowing large sums will command a better interest rate than the small borrower with a one-time, short-term need. Finally, factors withhold a reserve of 5 to 10 percent of the receivables purchased.

Factoring is not the cheapest way to obtain capital, but it does quickly turn receivables into cash. Moreover, although more expensive than accounts receivable financing, factoring saves its users credit agency fees, salaries of credit and collection personnel, and bad debt write-offs.

Leasing Companies

The leasing industry has grown substantially in recent years, and lease financing has become an important source of medium-term financing for businesses. There are about 700 to 800 leasing companies in the United States. In addition, many commercial banks and finance companies have leasing departments. Some leasing companies handle a wide variety of equipment, while others specialize in certain types of equipment—machine tools, electronic test equipment, and the like.

Common and readily resalable items such as automobiles and trucks, typewriters and office furniture can be leased by both new and existing businesses. However, the startup will find it difficult to lease other kinds of industrial, computer, or business equipment without providing a certificate of deposit to secure the lease or personal guarantees from the founders or from a wealthy third party.

An exception to this condition is high-technology startups that have received substantial venture capital. Some of these ventures have received large amounts of lease financing for rather special equipment from equity-oriented lessors, who receive some form of stock purchase rights in return for providing the startup's lease line. Two companies doing this sort of venture leasing are Equitec of Oakland, California, with offices in Boston, New York, and Dallas, and Intertec of Mill Valley, California.

Generally, industrial equipment leases have a term of three to five years, but in some cases may run longer. There can also be lease renewal options for 3 to 5 percent per year of the original equipment value. Leases are usually structured to return the entire cost of the leased equipment plus finance charges to the lessor, although some so-called operating leases do not, over their term, produce revenues equal to or greater than the price of the leased equipment.

Typically, an up-front payment is required of about 10 percent of the value of the item being leased. The interest rate on equipment leasing may be more or less than other forms of financing, depending on the equipment leased, the credit of the lessee, and the time of year.

Leasing credit criteria are very similar to the criteria used by commercial banks for equipment loans. Primary considerations are the value of the equipment leased, the justification of the lease, and the lessee's projected cash flow over the lease term.

Should a business lease equipment? Leasing has certain advantages. It enables a young or growing company to conserve cash, and can reduce its requirements for equity capital. Leasing can also be a tax advantage, because payments can be deducted over a shorter period than depreciation.

Finally, leasing provides the flexibility of returning equipment after the lease period if it is no longer needed or if it has become technologically obsolete. This can be a particular advantage to companies in high-technology industries.

Leasing no longer improves a company's balance sheet, because accounting practice now requires that the value of the equipment leased be capitalized and a lease liability shown.

Managing and Orchestrating the Banking Relationship

Before the Loan Decision[5]

Choosing a bank and, more specifically, a banker is one of the more important decisions a new or young business will make. (See *Exhibit 15.4*). A good lender relationship can sometimes mean the difference between the life and death of a business during difficult times. There have been cases where, other things being equal, one bank has called its loans to a struggling business, causing it to go under, and another bank has stayed with its loans and helped a business to survive and prosper. (Although I refer specifically to banks and banking relationships, much of what follows on lending practices and decisions applies as well to commercial finance company lenders.)

Some banks and bankers will make loans to startups and early-stage ventures and others will not. Those that will not generally cite the lack of operating track record as the reason for turning down a loan. Lenders that make such loans usually do so for previously successful entrepreneurs of means or for firms backed by investors with whom they have had prior relationships and whose judgment they trust—established venture capital firms, for example.

---

[5] Ibid., pp. 81–82.

What to Look for in a Bank

Banking Knowledge: Few bankers will intentionally lead you astray. But Dan Lang, co-owner of Nature's Warehouse, a $6 million baked-goods business in Sacramento, recently discovered that some bankers have a tighter grip than others on what's possible on a given situation. Lang and his partner recently met with lending officers at several banks to try to get $1 million in financing to help buy Nature's Warehouse. But only one, the lending officer at Sacramento Commercial Bank, "said right away he could do it as a 10-year SBA loan. Without hesitating, he knew what he could and couldn't do."

Sense of Urgency: "Banker's hours" may be a fading notion, but a CEO's and a banker's ideas of a "quick turnaround" are often days, even weeks, apart. Tom Kinder, co-owner of Pure Patience, a bedding-products mail-order business in Sharon, Vermont, found that his bankers at Vermont National Bank were able—and extremely willing—to meet his compressed timetable for a recent $100,000 loan. Kinder says he even got calls during evening at home, updating him on the progress.

Teaching Talent: Many bankers can't—or don't want to—articulate what they expect from customers and how the bank makes its decisions. But Dwight Mulch, president of three-year-old Preferred Products Corp., a building-materials distributor in Burlington, Iowa, says he gets both types of information from his leading officer at First Star Bank and has benefitted greatly. "When I was starting," says Mulch, "he practically led me around by the nose. He showed me what to put in the plan, and he still tells me how the system works."

Industry Knowledge: Whatever industry you're in, it helps to have a banker who has had some exposure to your type of business, says Dave Sanger, president of Resource Solution Group, a computer-consulting business in Southfield, Michigan. Sanger's lending officer at Manufacturer's Bank in Detroit "knows we don't have the same kind of assets as a retailer or a manufacturer," Sanger says, "and she knows the terminology."

Financial Stability: Given a choice, Kevin Whalen, chief financial adviser of Twin Modal, Inc., a Minneapolis transportation-brokerage firm, didn't pick the bank that was offering the most aggressive deal. And it's a good thing too, he says: "that bank has had real problems with regulators and has pulled way back." Before selecting Marquette Bank, in 1989, Whalen, a former banker himself, did spreadsheet comparisons of several banks, comparing returns on assets, capital-to-asset ratios, and so on. "I felt that in the long run, we'd be better off with the most conservative bank around."

Manager with Backbone: Banks have policies, notes Mike Walker, president of Walker Communications Inc., a public relations firm in Scottsdale, Arizona, "But you want to have a manager with the courage to override them if it makes sense to do so." Walker's branch manager at First Interstate Bank of Arizona, for instance, allows him to draw on checks immediately after they're deposited and often acts as a troubleshooter for him within the bank. "I don't know what the manual says," offers Walker, "but I think you need somebody who can take a stand."

In centers of high technology and venture capital, the main officers of the major banks will have one or more high-technology lending officers who specialize in making loans to early-stage, high-technology ventures. Through much experience, these bankers have come to understand the market and operating idiosyncrasies, problems, and opportunities of such ventures. They generally have close ties to venture capital firms and will refer entrepreneurs to such firms for possible equity financing. The venture capital firms, in turn, will refer their portfolio ventures to the bankers for debt financing.

What should an entrepreneur consider in choosing a lender? What is important in a lending decision? How should entrepreneurs relate to their lenders on an ongoing basis? In many ways, the lender's decision is similar to that of the venture capitalist. The goal is to make money for his or her company, through interest earned on good loans. The lender fears losing money by making bad loans to companies that default on their loans. To this end, he or she avoids risk by building in every conceivable safeguard. The lender is concerned with the client company's loan coverage,

its ability to repay, and the collateral it can offer. Finally, but most important, he or she must judge the character and quality of the key managers of the company to whom the loan is being made. *Exhibit 15.5* outlines the key steps.

Choosing a Value-added Banker

Because of the importance of a banking relationship, an entrepreneur should shop around before making a choice. The criteria for selecting a bank should be based on more than just loan interest rates. Equally important, entrepreneurs should not wait until they have a dire need for funds to try to establish a banking relationship. The choice of a bank and the development of a banking relationship should begin when you do not urgently need the money. When an entrepreneur faces a near-term financial crisis, the venture's financial statements are at their worst and the banker has good cause to wonder about management's financial and planning skills—all to the detriment of the entrepreneur's chances of getting a loan.

EXHIBIT 15.5

Key Steps in Obtaining a Loan

Before choosing and approaching a banker or other lender, the entrepreneur and his or her management team should go through the following steps in preparing to ask for a loan.

- Decide how much growth they want, and how fast they want to grow, observing the dictum that financing *follows* strategy.
- Determine how much money they require, and when they need to have it. To this end, they must:
  —Develop a schedule of operating and asset needs.
  —Prepare a real-time cash flow projection.
  —Decide how much capital they need.
  —Specify how they will use the funds they borrow.
- Revise and update the "corporate profile" in their business plan. This should consist of:
  —The core ingredients of the plan in the form of an executive summary.
  —A history of the firm (as appropriate).
  —Summaries of the financial results of the past three years.
  —Succinct descriptions of their markets and products.
  —A description of their operations.
  —Statements of cash flow and financial requirements.
  —Descriptions of the key managers, owners, and directors.
  —A rundown of the key strategies, facts and logic that guide them in growing the corporation.
- Identify potential sources for the type of debt they seek, and the *amount, rate, terms, and conditions* they seek.
- Select a bank or other lending institution, solicit interest, and prepare a presentation.
- Prepare a *written loan request.*
- Present their case, negotiate, and then close the deal.
- After the loan is granted, it is important that the borrowers maintain an effective relationship with the lending officer.

Source: Jeffry A. Timmons, *Financing and Planning the New Venture* (Acton, MA: Brick Housing Publishing Co., 1990), pp. 82–83. Also see Bruce G. Posner, "The One-Page Loan Proposal," *INC.,* September 1991.

G. B. Baty and J. M. Stancill describe some of the factors that are especially important to an entrepreneur in selecting a bank.[6]

- The bank selected should be big enough to service a venture's foreseeable loans but not so large as to be relatively indifferent to your business.
- Banks differ greatly in their desire and capacity to work with small firms. Some banks have special small business loan officers and regard new and early-stage ventures as the seeds of very large future accounts. Other banks see such new ventures loans as merely bad risks.
- Does the bank tend to call or reduce its loans to small businesses that have problems? When they have less capital to lend will they cut back on small business loans and favor their older, more solid customers?
- Are they imaginative, creative, and helpful when a venture has a problem? To quote Baty, "Do they just look at your balance sheet and faint or do they try to suggest constructive financial alternatives?"

- Has the bank had lending experience in your industry, especially with young, developing companies? If they have, your chances of getting a loan are better, and the bank will be more tolerant of problems and better able to help you exploit your opportunities.
- Is there good personal chemistry between you and your prospective lending officer? Remember, the person you talk to and deal with is the bank. Does this person know your industry and competition? Can this officer competently explain your business, technology, and uniqueness to other loan officers? Is he or she experienced in administering loans to smaller firms? Can you count on this person consistently? Does he or she have a good track record? Does his or her lending authority meet or exceed your needs? Does he or she have a reputation for being reasonable, creative, and willing to take a sound risk?

How does an entrepreneur go about evaluating a bank? First, the entrepreneur should consult accountants, attorneys, and other entrepreneurs who have

---

[6] G. B. Baty, *Entrepreneurship: Playing to Win* (Reston, VA: Reston Publishing Company, 1974); J. M. Stancill, "Getting the Most from Your Banking Relationship," *Harvard Business Review,* March–April 1980.

had dealings with the bank. The advice of entrepreneurs who have dealt with a bank through good and bad times can be especially useful. Second, the entrepreneur should meet with loan officers at several banks and systematically explore their attitudes and approaches to their business borrowers. Who meets with you, for how long, and with how many interruptions can be useful measures of a bank's interest in your account. Finally, ask for small business references from their list of borrowers and talk to the entrepreneurs of those firms. Throughout all of these contacts and discussions, check out particular loan officers as well as the viability of the bank itself; they are a major determinant of how the bank will deal with you and your venture.

Approaching and Meeting the Banker

Obtaining a loan is a sales job. Many borrowers tend to forget this. An entrepreneur with an early-stage venture must sell himself or herself as well as the viability and potential of the business to the banker. This is much the same situation that the early-stage entrepreneur faces with a venture capitalist.

The initial contact with a lender will likely be by telephone. The entrepreneur should be prepared to describe quickly the nature, age, and prospects of the venture; the amount of equity financing and who provided it; the prior financial performance of the business; the entrepreneur's experience and background; and the sort of bank financing desired. A referral from a venture capital firm or a business associate who knows the banker can be very helpful.

If the loan officer agrees to a meeting, he or she may well ask that a summary loan proposal, business plan, and financial statements be sent ahead of time. A well-prepared business plan and a reasonable amount of equity financing should pique a banker's interest—even for a startup venture.

The first meeting with a loan officer will likely be at the venture's place of business. The banker will be interested in meeting the management team, seeing how they relate to the entrepreneur, and getting a sense of the financial controls and reporting used and how well things seem to be run. The banker may also want to meet one or more of the venture's equity investors. Most of all, the banker is using this meeting to evaluate the integrity and business acumen of those who will ultimately be responsible for the repayment of the loan.

Throughout meetings with potential bankers, the entrepreneur must convey an air of self-confidence and an optimistic but realistic view of the venture's prospects. If the banker is favorably impressed by what has been seen and read, he or she will ask for further documents and references and begin to discuss the amount and timing of funds that the bank might lend to the business.

What the Banker Wants to Know[7]

What are you going to do with the money? Does the use of the loan make business sense? Should some or all of the money required be equity capital rather than debt? For new and young businesses, lenders do not like to see total debt-to-equity ratios greater than one. The answers to this question will also determine the type of loan (e.g., line of credit or term).

How much do you need? You must be prepared to justify the amount requested and describe how the debt fits into an overall plan for financing and developing the business. (See *Exhibit 15.6*.) Further, the amount of the loan should have enough cushion to allow for unexpected developments.

When and how will you pay it back? This is an important question. Short-term loans for seasonal inventory build-ups or for financing receivables are easier to obtain than long term loans, especially for early-stage businesses. How the loan will be repaid is the bottom-line question. Presumably you are borrowing money to finance activity that will throw off enough cash to repay the loan. What is your contingency plan if things go wrong? Can you describe such risks and indicate how you will deal with them? Is there a secondary source of repayment, a guarantor of means?

When do you need the money? If you need the money tomorrow, forget it. You are a poor planner and manager. On the other hand, if you need the money next month or the month after, you have demonstrated an ability to plan ahead, and you have given the banker time to investigate and process a loan application. Typically, a lending decision can be made in one to three weeks.

One of the best ways for all entrepreneurs to answer these questions is by providing the bankers with a well-prepared business plan. This plan should contain projections of cash flow, profit and loss, and balance sheets that will demonstrate the need for a loan and how it can be repaid.

A well-prepared business plan is vital for the startup seeking loans. Particular attention will be given by the lender to such financial ratios as current assets to current liabilities, gross margins, net worth to debt, accounts receivable and payable periods, inventory turns, and net profit to sales. The ratios for

---

[7] Timmons, *Financing and Planning the New Venture*, pp. 85–88.

EXHIBIT 15.6

Sample of a Summary Loan Proposal

Date of request:	May 30, 1994	
Borrower:	Curtis-Palmer & Company, Inc.	
Amount:	$4,200,000	
Use of proceeds:	A/R, up to	
	Inventory, up to	$1,600,000
	WIP, up to	824,000
	Marketing, up to	525,000
	Ski show specials	255,000
	Contingencies	105,000
	Officer loans dues	50,000
		841,000
		$4,200,000
Type of loan:	Seasonal revolving line of credit	
Closing date:	June 15, 1994	
Term:	One year	
Rate:	Prime + 1 percent, no compensating balances, no points or origination fees.	
Takedown:	$500,000 at closing	
	1,500,000 on August 1, 1994	
	1,500,000 on October 1, 1994	
	700,000 on November 1, 1994	
Collateral:	70 percent of A/R	
	50 percent of inventory	
Guarantees:	None	
Repayment schedule:	$4,200,000 or balance on anniversary of note	
Source of funds for repayment:	a. Excess cash from operations (see cash flow).	
	b. Renewable and increase of line if growth is profitable.	
	c. Conversion to three-year note.	
Contingency source:	a. Sale and leaseback of equipment.	
	b. Officer's loans.	

Source: Jeffry A. Timmons, *Financing and Planning the New Venture* (Acton, MA: Brick House Publishing Co., 1990), p. 86.

the borrower's venture will be compared to averages for competing firms to see how the potential borrower measures up to them.

For an existing business, the lender will want to review financial statements from prior years prepared or audited by a CPA, a list of aged receivables and payables, the turnover of inventory, and lists of key customers and creditors. The lender will also want to know that all tax payments are current. Finally, he or she will need to know details of fixed assets and any liens on receivables, inventory, or fixed assets.

The entrepreneur–borrower should regard his or her contacts with the bank as a sales mission and provide data that are required promptly and in a form that can be readily understood. The better the material entrepreneurs can supply to demonstrate their business credibility, the easier and faster it will be to obtain a positive lending decision.

The Lending Decision

One of the significant changes in today's lending environment is the centralized lending decision. Traditionally, loan officers might have up to several million

dollars of lending authority and could make loans to small companies. Besides the company's creditworthiness as determined by analysis of its past results via the balance sheet, income statement, cash flow, and collateral, the lender's assessment of the character and reputation of the entrepreneur was central to the decision. As loan decisions are made increasingly by loan committees, this face-to-face part of the decision process has given way to deeper analysis of the company's business plan, cash flow drivers and dissipators, competitive environment, and the cushion for loan recovery given the firm's game plan and financial structure.

The implication for entrepreneurs is a demanding one: You can no longer rely on your salesmanship and good relationship with your loan officer alone to continue to get favorable lending decisions. You, or the key team member, needs to be able to prepare the necessary analysis and documentation to convince people you may never meet that the loan is a good one. You also need to know the financial ratios and criteria used to compare your loan request with industry norms and to defend the analysis. Such a presentation can make it easier and faster to obtain approval of a loan.

Lending Criteria

First and foremost, as with equity investors, the quality and track record of the management team will be a major factor. Historical financial statements which show three and five years of profitability are also essential. A well-developed business plan which articulates the company's sales estimates, market niche, cash flow, profit projections, working capital, capital expenditure uses of proceeds, and evidence of competent accounting and control systems is essential.

In its simplest form, what is needed is analysis of the available collateral based on guidelines such as those shown in *Exhibit 15.3* and of debt capacity determined by analysis of the coverage ratio once the new loan is in place. Interest coverage is calculated as *earnings before interest and taxes divided by interest* (EBIT/interest). A business with steady, predictable cash flow and earnings would require a lower coverage ratio (say, in the range of two) than would a company with a volatile, unpredictable cash flow stream, for example, a high-technology company with risk of competition and obsolescence (which might require a coverage ratio of five or more). The bottom line, of course, is the ability of the company to repay both interest and principal on time.

After the Loan Decision[8]

Loan Restrictions

A loan agreement defines the terms and conditions under which a lender provides capital. With it, lenders do two things: protect their position as creditor, and try to assure repayment of the loan as agreed. Within the loan agreement (as in investment agreements) there are negative and positive covenants. Negative covenants are restrictions on the borrower, for example, no further additions to the borrower's total debt, no pledge to others of assets of the borrower, and no payment of dividends.

Positive covenants define what the borrower must do. Some examples are maintenance of some minimum net worth or working capital, prompt payment of all federal and state taxes, adequate insurance on key people and property, repayment of the loan and interest according to the terms of the agreement, and provision to the lender of periodic financial statements and reports.

Some of these restrictions can hinder a company's growth—for example, a flat restriction on further borrowing. Such a borrowing limit is often based on the borrower's assets at the time of the loan. However, rather than stipulating an initially fixed limit,

the loan agreement should recognize that as a business grows and increases its total assets and net worth, it will need and be able to carry the additional debt required to sustain its growth. Similarly, covenants that require certain minimums on working capital or current ratios may be very difficult, for example, for a highly seasonal business to maintain at all times of the year. Only analysis of past financial monthly statements can indicate whether such a covenant can be met.

Covenants to Look out For

Before borrowing money, an entrepreneur should decide what sorts of restrictions or covenants are acceptable. Attorneys and accountants of the company should be consulted before any loan papers are signed. Some restrictions are negotiable, and an entrepreneur should negotiate to get terms that the venture can live with next year as well as today. Once loan terms are agreed upon and the loan is made, the entrepreneur and the venture will be bound by them. If the banks says, "Yes, but . . ."

- Wants to put constraints on your permissible financial ratios.
- Would not allow any new borrowing.
- Wants a veto on any new management.
- Would not allow new products or new directions.
- You cannot acquire or sell any assets.
- Would not allow any new investment or new equipment.

Personal Guarantees and the Loan

When to Expect Them:
- If you are undercollateralized.
- If you have had a poor or erratic performance.
- If you have management problems.
- If your relationship with your banker is strained.
- If you have a new loan officer.
- If there is turbulence in the credit markets.
- If there has been a wave of bad loans made by the lending institution, and a crackdown is in force.

How to Avoid Them:
- Good to spectacular performance.
- Conservative financial management.
- Adequate collateral.
- Careful management of the balance sheet.

8 Ibid., pp. 90–94.

How to Eliminate Them
(if you already have them):

- See previous list, "How to Avoid Them."
- Develop a financial plan with performance targets and a timetable.
- Negotiate elimination *up front* when you have some bargaining chips.
- Stay active in the search for back-up sources of funds.

Building a Relationship

After obtaining a loan, entrepreneurs should cultivate a close working relationship with their bankers. Too many business people do not see their lending officers until they need a loan. The astute entrepreneur will take a much more active role in keeping a banker informed about the business, thereby improving the chances of obtaining larger loans for expansion, and cooperation from the bank in troubled times.

Some of the things that should be done to build such a relationship are fairly simple.[9] In addition to monthly and annual financial statements, bankers should be sent product news releases and any trade articles about the business or its products. The entrepreneur should invite the banker to the venture's facility, review product development plans and the prospects for the business, and establish a personal relationship with him or her. If this is done, when a new loan is requested, the lending officer will feel better about recommending its approval.

What about bad news? Never surprise a banker with bad news; make sure he or she sees it coming as soon as you do. Unpleasant surprises are a sign that an entrepreneur is not being candid with the banker or that management does not have the business under the proper control. Either conclusion by a banker is damaging to the relationship.

If a future loan payment cannot be met, entrepreneurs should not panic and avoid their bankers. On the contrary, they should visit their banks and explain why the loan payment cannot be made and say when it will be made. If this is done before the payment due date and the entrepreneur–banker relationship is good, the banker will go along. After all, what else can he or she do? If an entrepreneur has convinced a banker of the viability and future growth of a business, the banker really does not want to call a loan and cause bankruptcy. The real key to communicating with a banker is candidly to inform but not to scare. In other words, entrepreneurs must indicate that they are aware of adverse events and have a way of dealing with them.

To build credibility with bankers further, entrepreneurs should borrow before they need to and then repay the loan. This will establish a track record of borrowing and reliable repayment. Entrepreneurs should also make every effort to meet the financial targets they set for themselves and have discussed with their banker. If this cannot be done, there will be an erosion of the credibility of the entrepreneur, even if the business is growing.

Bankers have a right to expect an entrepreneur to continue to use them as the business grows and prospers, and not to go shopping for a better interest rate. In return, entrepreneurs have the right to expect that their bank will continue to provide them with needed loans, particularly during difficult times when a vacillating loan policy could be dangerous for businesses' survival.

The TLC of a Banker or Other Lender

1. Your banker is your partner, not a difficult minority shareholder.
2. Be honest and straightforward in sharing information.
3. Invite the banker to see your business in operation.
4. Always avoid overdrafts, late payments, and late financial statements.
5. Answer questions frankly and honestly. *Tell the truth.* Lying is illegal and undoubtedly violates loan covenants.

What to Do When the Bank Says No

What do you do if the bank turns you down for a loan? Regroup, and review the following questions.

1. Does the company really need to borrow now? Can cash be generated elsewhere? Tighten the belt. Are some expenditures not really necessary? Sharpen the financial pencil: Be lean and mean.
2. What does the balance sheet say? Are you growing too fast? Compare yourself to published industry ratios to see if you are on target.
3. Does the bank have a clear and comprehensive understanding of your needs? Did you *really* get to know your loan officer? Did you do enough homework on the bank's criteria and their likes and dislikes? Was your loan officer too busy to give your borrowing package proper consideration? A loan officer

---

[9] Baty, *Entrepreneurship: Playing to Win.*

may have 50 to as many as 200 accounts. Is your relationship with the bank on a proper track?

4. Was your written loan proposal realistic? Was it a normal request, or something that differed from the types of proposals the bank usually sees? Did you make a verbal request for a loan, without presenting any written backup?

5. Do you need a new loan officer, or a new bank? If your answers to the above questions put you in the clear, and your written proposal was realistic, call the head of the commercial loan department and arrange a meeting. Sit down and discuss the history of your loan effort, the facts, and the bank's reasons for turning you down.

Tar Pits: Entrepreneurs Beware

Modern corporate financial theory has preached the virtues of zero cash balances and the use of leverage to enhance return on equity. Such thinking applied to closely held companies whose dream is to last forever can be extremely destructive. If you judge by the 1980s, the excessive leverage used by so many larger companies apparently simply is not worth the risk: Two-thirds of the LBOs done in the 1980s have ended up in serious trouble, and the jury is still out on others. It is no accident that the serious erosion of IBM began about the same time as the company acquired debt on its balance sheet for the very first time, in the early 1980s.

Beware of Leverage: The ROE Mirage

According to the theory, one can significantly improve return on equity (ROE) by utilizing debt. Thus, the present value of a company would also increase significantly as the company went from a zero debt-to-equity ratio to 100 percent, as shown in *Exhibit 15.7*. On closer examination, however, such an increase in debt only improves the present value, given the 2 percent to 8 percent growth rates, shown by 17 to 26 percent. If the company gets into any trouble at all—and the odds of that happening sooner or later are very high—its options and flexibility become very seriously constrained by the covenants of the senior lenders. Leverage creates an unforgiving capital structure and the potential additional ROI often is not worth the risk. If the upside is worth risking the loss of the entire company should adversity strike, then go ahead. This is easier said than survived, however.

Ask any entrepreneur who has had to deal with the workout specialists in a bank and you will get a sobering, if not frightening, message: It is hell and you will not want to do it again.

IRS: Time Bomb for Personal Disaster

There is a much lesser known tar pit that entrepreneurs need to be aware of when considering leveraging their companies. Once the company gets into

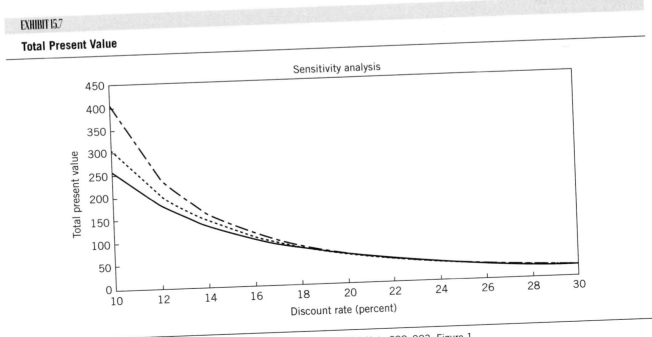

EXHIBIT 15.7

Total Present Value

Source: William A. Sahlman, "Note on Free Cash Flow Valuation Models," HBS Note 288–023, Figure 1.

serious financial trouble, a subsequent restructuring of debt is often part of the survival and recovery plan. The problem becomes, in such a restructuring, principal and interest due to lenders may be forgiven in exchange for warrants, direct equity, or other considerations. Unfortunately, such forgiven debt becomes *taxable income* for the entrepreneur who owns the company and who has personally had to guarantee the loans. In one restructuring of a midwestern cable television company, the founder at one point faced a possible $12 million personal tax liability, which would have forced him into personal bankruptcy, and possibly worse. In this case, fortunately, the creative deal restructuring enabled him to avoid such a calamitous outcome, but many other overleveraged entrepreneurs from the 1980s have not fared as well.

Neither a Lender nor a Borrower Be, But If You Must . . .

In Garrison Keillor's radio program, "A Prairie Home Companion," he describes the mythical town of Lake Wobegon, Minnesota. Inscribed in granite over the entrance to the Bank of Lake Wobegon is the motto Neither a Lender Nor a Borrower Be, which is actually very good advice for early-stage entrepreneurs. Thus, the following may serve as useful tips if you must borrow:

1. Borrow when you do not need it (which is the surest way to accomplish No. 2).
2. Avoid personal guarantees, put caps and time limits on the amounts based on performance milestones, such as achieving certain cash flow, working capital, and equity levels.
3. The devil is in the details. Read each loan covenant and requirement carefully—only the owner can truly appreciate their consequences.
4. Do not accept so-called hair-trigger covenants, such as: If there is any change or event of any kind that can have any material adverse effect on the future of the company, the loan shall become due and payable.
5. Be conservative and prudent.

Chapter Summary

1. Entrepreneurs are benefiting from a much kinder and gentler credit environment during the late 1990s.
2. Startups are candidates for bank credit but numerous sources of debt capital are available once profitability and a decent balance sheet are established.
3. Managing and orchestrating the banking relationship before and after the loan decision is a key task for entrepreneurs.
4. Knowing the key steps in obtaining a loan, and selecting a banker who can add value—not a bank—can improve your odds.

5. Loan covenants can have profound impact on how you can and cannot run the business. The devil is in the details of the loan agreement.
6. For the vast majority of small companies, leverage only works during the most favorable economic booms of credit availability. Leverage is a disaster if business turn sour.
7. The IRS also places a time bomb for personal disaster with every entrepreneur who borrows money: Even if your bank debt is forgiven in a restructuring it becomes *taxable income* to the borrower!
8. When the bank says no to a loan request, several key questions need to be addressed in an effort to reverse the decision.

Study Questions

1. Define and explain the following, and why they are important: sources of debt financing, trade credit, line of credit, accounts receivable financing, time–sales factoring, commercial finance company.
2. What security can be used for a loan, and what percentage of its value do banks typically lend?
3. What are the things to look for in evaluating a lender, and why are these important?
4. What is meant by value-added banker, and how and why is this crucial?
5. What criteria do lenders use to evaluate a loan application, and what can be done before and after the loan decision to facilitate a loan request?
6. What restrictions and covenants might a lender require, and how and why should these be avoided whenever possible.
7. What issues need to be addressed to deal with a rejection of a loan request?
8. Why do entrepreneurs in smaller companies need to be especially wary of leverage?
9. Why is there an IRS time bomb any time one borrows money?
10. When should a company borrow money?

MIND STRETCHERS
Have You Considered?

1. You have been married nearly 30 years and love your spouse and family. A credit crunch leads to defaults on your loans, and the lenders forgive $50 million of debt. The IRS tells you that you owe them $15 million. Your lawyers say you should get divorced to protect other assets. What would you do?
2. Why is Warren Buffet so wary about leverage?
3. Can you calculate the debt capacity of your proposed venture three to four years hence, if it achieves positive cash flow and profitability?

Case

Jiffy Lube International, Inc.

Preparation Questions

1. Evaluate Jiffy Lube International's performance, opportunities, and financial strategy.
2. What should Hindman do now?
3. What should Don Remey do in order to realize his investment objectives?
4. As a new outside director to Jiffy Lube International, what questions would you raise and what recommendations would you offer to management?

Jiffy Lube International, Inc.

In the summer of 1987, Jiffy Lube International, Inc., faced some of the most critical issues in its young life. Preparing for a strategy meeting with some board members, management, and franchisees, Jim Hindman paced the room in the same way he had paced the locker room before a football game. Booz, Allen & Hamilton had recently completed a study of the quicklube industry; their findings indicated a fragmented, rapidly growing market. These market findings encouraged Hindman, who had projected a market of 6,000 units by 1990. The study indicated demand for 12,000 units. Additionally, the study revealed that Jiffy Lube International had a competitive advantage with a large number of mature units and the resources to sustain a national promotional campaign.

Jim Hindman and Jiffy Lube International (JLI) had come a long way from the acquisition of seven centers in Utah in 1979. By 1987 JLI had exceeded its projections for the last four years. (See Exhibits G, H, and I.) The company's growth included a larger management team and a more formal relationship with franchisees.

Hindman went over the agenda for the meeting. He wanted to review JLI's progress and to evaluate the op-

erational and financial strategy going forward. He wondered about the credibility of Booz, Allen & Hamilton's findings. Was JLI taking enough risk to capture the potentially huge reward that Booz, Allen & Hamilton envisioned, or was the company on the verge of overextending itself?

The Quicklube Industry

Since 1979, the quicklube market had legitimized itself, as many Americans changed how they maintain their automobiles. As Jim Hindman stated:

The "quicklube" industry was the fastest growing in the automotive aftermarket, due in part to the way more and more Americans live today. Because both spouses are employed in the majority of families, car dependency is higher than ever. Women are now faced with more of the responsibility in seeking car service, too. Greater work demands have created the need for prompt attention to car care matters. Leaving the car for a day at a typical car care facility becomes a serious time strain for many. People are also keeping cars longer these days. While many drivers understand the importance of frequent oil changes, more are coming to appreciate the importance of complete fluid maintenance.

Additionally, JLI conservatively estimated that the number of passenger cars and small trucks on the road would grow at a rate of 1 to 2 percent annually. Also, the smaller engines in automobiles would require more frequent oil changes. The combined effects of these factors suggested, at the very least, a 2 percent increase in the quicklube market annually. (See Exhibit A.) Indeed, according to investment banker Alex Brown & Sons, "as consumer awareness and service availability improve, there was no reason why market share in new areas could not approach the [20 percent market share] level reached in Salt Lake City."[1]

[1] Alex Brown & Sons, "Industry Note," October 30, 1986.

EXHIBIT A

Automobile Oil Change and Lubrication Market

	1985 Actual	1990 Estimated
Number of oil changes (millions)	360	397
Average price:	$ 19.00	$ 22.00
Subtotal ($ millions)	$6,840	$8,734
Related supplies ($ millions)	821	1,048
Total ($ millions)	$7,661	$9,782
Quicklube market share	4.6%	11.5%
Quicklube sales ($ millions)	$ 352	$1,125
Number of centers	2,000	5,500

Sources: Jiffy Lube and Alex Brown & Sons estimates.

EXHIBIT B

Major Quicklube Center Operators (October 1986)

Operator	Number of Centers in Operation		Total	Market Share	Ownership
	Company	Franchised			
Jiffy Lube	21	401	422	63%	Private
Minit Lube	70	63	133	20%	Quaker State
Grease Monkey	0	75	75	11%	Public
Rapid Oil	42	0	42	6%	Valvoline
			672		

Source: Alex Brown & Sons, Industry Report (October 30, 1986).

EXHIBIT C

Financial Characteristics of Typical Jiffy Lube Franchise

Real estate requirements	15,000 square feet of land
Cost of land and building	$300,000
Startup costs (equipment, etc.)	$100,000
Monthly fixed costs	$8,000
Variable costs	57% of sales
Break-even car count/day	28–35 cars
Typical Months to breakeven	7–8 months

A typical mature unit (approximately two years old) will service between 60 and 70 cars per day, producing annual revenues of about $400,000–$500,000 and $75,000–$100,000 of pre-tax income.

Depending on whether the franchisee owns or leases the real estate, the monthly fixed costs include a charge for either:

1. Rent ($3,000–$4,000) paid to Jiffy Lube or to a third party lessor.
2. A similar charge for mortgage interest.

Source: Jiffy Lube International, Inc., annual reports, 1985–1987.

Within the quicklube industry, this growth opportunity attracted competition. (See *Exhibit B*.) Major oil companies invested in the quicklube market to increase their market share, to increase brand awareness, and to take advantage of this growing distribution channel. In the summer of 1985, Quaker State became a major competitor, having purchased Minit Lube for $29 million. In 1986, Valvoline purchased Rapid Lube and also planned to develop centers in the quicklube market. In addition, many small, local, and regional, chains were being developed by entrepreneurs.

JLI's Financial Strategy

In December 1985, Bridge Capital Investors (BCI) led a private placement group that invested $10 million in JLI. The investment fueled the effort to build out rapidly and for JLI to be the first quicklube company to advertise nationally. Capital contributed to expenses, new franchisees, and acquisitions. (See *Exhibit C*.)

Pennzoil and Jiffy Lube shared a mutually beneficial relationship. JLI was the largest purchaser of Pennzoil oil; Pennzoil provided the necessary financial backing for JLI to acquire real estate and to develop centers. In December 1985, the $100 million Pennzoil/Jiffy Lube Real Estate Partnership was established. Each party contributed $15 million in cash or properties valued at actual cost incurred over the next three years, with an additional $70 million in seven-year notes. The agreement provided for the development of 325 units over the next three years. Additionally, all the independent quicklubes affiliated with Pennzoil were to be converted into Jiffy Lube centers.

Jiffy Lube pursued its strategy by acquiring independent quicklube centers. In March 1985, JLI acquired 26 centers from Chicago's BW Oil Change chain and 5 centers from Indiana's Pit Stop '500 chain. The Chicago centers were franchised and the Indiana centers were operated by the new Company Operated Stores division. At the same time, on the franchisee level, JLI offered a "growth-oriented real estate program, targeting individual locations with third-party landowners. 'We are interested in talking to anyone who's interested in us,' Hindman said."[2] Expansion was not limited to the United States. In 1986, Jiffy Lube began to investigate international markets in Canada, Great Britain, and France.

[2] "Jiffy Lube Buyouts Bolster Market Lead," *National Petroleum News*, March 1985, p. 35.

EXHIBIT D

Excerpt from Bridge Capital Investors: Private Placement

12% Senior Subordinated Notes Due 1992 with Warrants

Put Provision
If during five years from issuance, the Company's Common Stock has not traded publicly at levels set forth in the table that follows, the Purchase may put the warrants and/or underlying stock to the Company. The price will be determined by the calculation of the amount necessary to result in a 30% per annum internal rate of return to the Purchasers on that proportion of warrants not previously sold, taking into account all interest premium and principal repayment on the proportionately related Notes.

If (i) the Company completes one or more public offerings of Common Stock with the aggregate proceeds to the Company of at least $15 million and (ii) the average closing price for 60 consecutive trading days exceeds:

> 6 months ending 6/88—$17.50
> 6 months ending 12/88—$20.00
> 6 months ending 6/89—$25.00
> 6 months ending 12/89—$30.00
> 6 months ending 6/90—$35.00
> 6 months ending 12/90—$40.00

then the put provision will expire.
In the event the Company is unable to pay the amount due, the Purchasers have the right to nominate a majority of the Board of Directors.

In the United States, internal operations were developed to meet the challenges that accompany growth. As units were added, some organizational structure was needed to establish communication avenues for both the franchisee and the franchisor. Franchisees were organized into three geographic locations, with regional presidents for each area. The Association of Franchisees, of which all franchisees were a part, increased its prestige within the national organization by securing a seat on the board of directors. The president of the Association of Franchisees worked as a liaison between JLI management, the board, and the franchisees.

At the board's recommendation, Hindman brought in a professional manager as president. Bringing someone into JLI from the outside was not an easy transition for Hindman. He remembered his response to their request: "Some of these Wall Street types, the first thing that they wanted to do was to get a search committee to get someone to run this business. I thought: What am I doing so terribly wrong? I am telling you—I took that request personally."

In April 1986, J. Richard Breen was appointed president and chief operating officer. Hindman found Breen himself and had confidence in his appointment based on Breen's experience as the executive vice president of international for Tenneco Automotive, a $500 million business, and as executive vice president of Fram Corporation, where he was in charge of the sales of Autolite Spark Plug Corporation and the Bentrix Brake Company.

Going Public

With the put provision on the $10 million private replacement by BCI in December 1985 and the need for more capital for expansion, an initial public offering (IPO) was inevitable. As Stephen Spinelli, the president of the Association of Franchisees, recalled:

> From the first meeting, Don Remey of BCI said, "When we go public . . ."—he never allowed any alternative to be introduced. He got everyone to naturally believe that we were going public. Negotiations focused on when we were going public and what the return would be on the put. (See *Exhibit D.*)

In addition to BCI's incentive to achieve liquidity, other members of the board and investors wanted to see JLI go public. Prior investors wanted cash or a cash equivalent. The management of JLI had obligations to meet and wanted to reduce debt. In 1986, the Old Court Savings and Loan financing for the construction of centers would finally be paid. Pennzoil's earlier investment of $1.6 million was also due. Management realized that the company was highly leveraged and that the proceeds of an offering would reduce the large interest and principal obligations.

Hindman saw the IPO as a chance to attract a large amount of capital, possibly JLI's largest investment ever, at a cheap price. Beyond the lower cost of money the IPO offered, Hindman felt that the IPO would generate name recognition. As a public company, Hindman believed that the units would profit from added publicity, advertising, and credibility. The parent company, JLI, would be more visible as a public company, which would help the franchisees in obtaining real estate financing. Acquisitions would also benefit because stock, rather than cash, could be used to purchase independent units and chains.

A major pressure on Hindman was the put, which compounded at a 30 percent internal rate of return. Depending on the timing of a public offering or a sale of the company, the put represented a major obligation of $9.1 million to $17.1 million. (See *Exhibit E.*)

EXHIBIT E

Possible Outcomes of the Put

Likelihood of Reaching Minimum Stock Prices as Outlined in the BCI proposal

	FY 1988	FY 1989	FY 1990
Projected Net Income	$3,096	$5,467	$8,868
Earnings Per Share	$.56	$.99	$1.61
Minimum Market Price	$17.5	$25	$35
Price/Earnings Ratio	31x	25x	22x

Potential Amounts due under the Put Option

Three Possible Scenarios Amount Payable

No public offering, notes are outstanding for entire term	$17.1 million
Public offering after two years, $5 million worth of notes are prepared	$13.1 million
Entire $10 million of notes are prepaid after two years	$ 9.1 million

FY = fiscal year.

Hindman had begun discussing the possibility of a public offering shortly after the closing of the $10 million private placement. By the spring of 1986, Alex Brown & Sons, a major Baltimore-based investment banker, indicated that a public offering might be possible later that year. They were impressed by the company's recent success and the growth opportunity for quicklubes. Shearson Lehman Hutton, which had acted as the agent on the $10 million private offering, was also supportive of an IPO. Preliminary pricing was discussed in the $8 to $12 per share range which was over 30 times estimated 1986 earnings per share. Hindman worked hard to produce company results and to develop underwriters' interest for an IPO.

The company filed a registration statement to sell 2,030,000 shares, in July 1986. The IPO market was increasingly receptive and the offering generated significant retail investor demand. The "road show" meetings in 10 cities in the United States and Canada gave Hindman and John Sasser, the chief financial officer, the opportunity to share their enthusiasm with hundreds of prospective investors.

The investment bankers priced the issue at $10 to $12 per share, or more than 30 times fiscal 1986 earnings per share. Interest created by the road show pushed the actual price to $15. And when Jiffy Lube finished its first day on the ticker—carrying the stock ticker JLUB—it had risen to $21.25.[3]

In its final review of the registration statement, the Securities and Exchange Commission ruled that the put could be a significant claim against future stockholders'

equity. BCI and the other investors agreed, just prior to the offering, to give up the put, in consideration for the pending stock offering at $15 versus their warrants at $6. The IPO was over subscribed by 300 percent and the aftermarket was very robust.

Further Expansion

The $28 million of IPO proceeds fueled JLI's continued expansion. Hindman was convinced that Jiffy Lube would "*never* be 'just another company.' " The IPO investors had shown their confidence in the company. In fiscal 1987, ending in March, the average number of cars serviced was 42 daily, with 5.4 million customers serviced annually. Hindman attributed the success of the individual units to the JLI philosophy: Integrity. Intensity. And Intimacy. The number of Jiffy Lube centers increased from 348 in 1986 to 561 in 1987, and 54 service centers had been acquired by JLI. "An internal acquisitions team had been formed and was headed by an acquisition manager,"[4] according to John Sasser, chief financial officer. Neal D. Borden, the executive vice president and secretary, added that JLI

represented, by virtue of our acquisitions and conversions, not just Jiffy Lube but also a lot of the pioneers in this business. We were far ahead of our competition and we wouldn't let them catch us. Our goal was to maintain rapid growth, to stay ahead. We were getting close to 600 stores. Our nearest competitor only had around 200.[5]

---

[3] Michael Yockel, "Striking It Rich: Fast Oil Changes Have Made Jim Hindman and Jiffy Lube a Nice Piece of Change: Is This the McDonald's of the Oil Industry?" *Baltimore Business Monthly,* October 1988, p. 89.

[4] Joseph E. McCann and William G. Cornelius, "How Acquisitions Fit Strategies of Young Firms," *Mergers & Acquisitions,* July–August 1987, pp. 39–44.
[5] Jiffy Lube International, Inc., Annual Report, March, 1987, p. 11.

EXHIBIT F

Jiffy Lube International, Inc., Franchisee Agreement (1986)

"A company is only as strong as its weakest link. At Jiffy Lube, our links are our franchisees. They are the people doing the ultimate selling and are indispensable, invaluable company representatives." (Jiffy Lube International, Inc., Annual Report, 1986, p. 10)

Area Development Fee

Franchisee purchased the exclusive right to develop and operate a number of centers within a geographic location for an initial, nonrefundable area development fee. Fees varied based on the number of centers to be developed, the difficulty of development, and the demographics of the area.

Franchisee signed a master license agreement. Licensees were obligated to find the site, to finance the real estate, and to construct the units. Construction had to be completed in 12 months. Licensee had the option of fixed payments or payments as development occurs. A full-time executive had to be hired within 30 days of the application acceptance.

Initial Franchisee Fee

The average initial franchisee fee was $20,000 for the development of each center. Initial deposit was $10,000 (to be cashed when the applicant was accepted) and the balance of the fee was due 10 business days after the receipt of building permits.

Royalty Fee

The royalty fee for the initial year was 5% of gross sales; thereafter, the royalty fee was 6%. No minimum royalty fee existed.

Support Services

National Advertising Fund: The required contribution was 1% of gross sales. A required total advertising commitment per unit was established as at least 6% of gross sales.

Quality Control: Jiffy Lube International monitored and inspected the centers at least once a year to ensure that company-approved programs and practices were in use and being followed. An accountant, an advertising agency, and other support services inspected the centers annually.

Default Procedures: Default occurred when timely payments had not been made in any 12 month period, after JLI had given 30 days notice that such failure has already occurred. JLI provided reimbursements to franchisees who have defaulted and who had their units taken by JLI for tools, equipment, etc. at fair market value.

Not only had JLI covered 29 out of 30 media markets in the United States, international agreements for development had been secured in England and France.

At the same time, JLI broadened the scope of services to the franchisees. Training and maintenance of company programs and policies were high priorities. (See *Exhibit F.*) A certification program for technicians was developed and run by JLI. Formal procedures were established for employee selection. To ensure that individual centers were following company procedures, a "mystery shopper" paid surprise visits to the units. John Sasser initiated a centralized cash management system to monitor the franchisees. Hindman created a quality award, "The Best There Is," for the franchisees. Stephen Spinelli, president of the Association of Franchisees, explained that

> there are always points of contention in a franchise relationship and we had our fair share. However, Hindman had an ability to intercede personally at strategic moments and to force communication between top management and franchisees. His open door policy included making sure our door was open too.

The results were dramatic: 1987 sales revenues exceeded the original business plan. (See *Exhibit G*). By March 1987, JLI became the first quicklube company

to advertise nationally. Touting the slogan, "We'll take care of you like family," a $5 million television campaign featured Dick Van Patten's family. Additionally, regional and local franchisees planned to spend $15 million on a localized advertising effort. Just as Hindman had expected, the IPO raised public awareness. By February 1987, the stock had risen to $38 per share, which prompted management to declare a two-for-one stock split. Profits after tax more than doubled earlier projections, reaching $3.4 million of sales on $44 million. (see *Exhibit H.*)

As JLI's appetite for cash grew in July 1987, the company made a second public offering of 2,900,000 shares at $14.75 per share. The second offering raised $35 million. Most of the proceeds from the July offering went toward debt payments rather than fueling growth. (See *Exhibit I.*)

Financing was aided by a license from the Small Business Administration (SBA) to form the Jiffy Lube Capital Corporation (JLCC), a small business investment company. JLCC became a financing vehicle to purchase real estate and to develop more centers. JLI was entitled to borrow $4 of capital from the government, at a nominal interest rate, for each $1 of capital contributed to JLCC.

EXHIBIT G

Jiffy Lube International, Inc., Projected Operations

	1986	1987	1988	1989	1990	1991
Revenue:						
Sales by company-operated centers	$7,683	$10,169	$14,218	$18,840	$22,210	$23,954
Initial franchisee fees	3,630	4,527	4,735	5,048	5,215	2,706
Area development fees	2,000	500	0	0	0	0
Franchisee royalties	5,280	9,946	16,062	23,405	32,162	41,014
Sales of automotive products	8,880	15,789	24,489	34,623	46,169	56,561
Rental income from franchisees	2,328	3,010	3,701	4,440	5,137	5,442
Total revenues	$29,801	$43,941	$63,205	$86,356	$110,893	129,677
Costs and expenses:						
Company-operated centers	6,377	8,440	11,801	15,637	18,434	19,882
Sales of automotive products	7,548	13,420	20,816	29,429	39,243	48,077
Rental expenses (interest)	1,711	1,546	1,502	1,433	1,341	1,332
General and administrative	8,880	14,399	20,341	26,163	31,694	35,221
Total costs and expenses	$24,516	$37,805	$54,460	$72,662	$90,712	104,512
Income from operations	$5,285	$6,136	$8,745	$13,694	$20,181	$25,165
Other income (expense):						
Interest expense	(2,798)	(3,423)	(2,650)	(2,827)	(2,883)	(2,259)
Other	315	324	97	68	439	1,286
Income before income taxes	$2,802	$3,037	$6,192	$10,935	$17,737	$24,192
Income tax expense	951	1,518	3,096	5,465	8,868	12,096
Net income	$1,851	$1,519	$3,096	$5,470	$8,869	$12,096
Service centers in operation:						
Franchised	361	578	805	1,047	1,297	1,427
Company-operated	23	31	39	47	47	47

EXHIBIT H

Jiffy Lube International, Inc., Consolidated Statement of Operations (OOO)

	1987	1986
Revenue:		
Franchising:		
United States	$14,634	$8,546
International	1,457	0
Automotive products	13,505	8,792
Financing activity	6,495	4,288
Sales by cooperated centers	8,079	7,825
Total revenues	$44,170	$29,451
Costs and expenses:		
Franchising		
United States	10,168	9,281
International	411	0
Automotive products	12,415	7,492
Financing activities	5,670	4,065
Company-operated centers	8,172	6,548
Provision for credit losses	681	271
Total costs and expenses	$37,517	$27,657
Income from operations	$6,653	$1,794
Other income (expense):		
Other income	1,727	865
Corporate interest expense	(1,362)	(1,197)
Income before income taxes	$7,018	$1,462
Income tax (expense)	(3,333)	(720)
Income (loss) before extraordinary item	$3,685	$742
Extraordinary item	(219)	470
Net income (loss)	$3,466	$1,212
Earnings per share	$0.28	$0.16
Service centers	561	348
Company-operated	29	14

EXHIBIT I

Jiffy Lube International, Inc., Consolidated Balance Sheet (000)

	1987	1986
Assets		
Current assets:		
Cash and cash equivalents	$1,277	$2,474
Accounts and fees receivable	7,584	6,771
Notes receivable	4,682	1,811
	12,266	8,582
Less allowance for doubtful accounts	935	299
	11,331	8,283
	1,217	752
Inventory	1,130	2,977
Other current assets	14,955	14,486
Total current assets	10,549	3,792
Notes and fees receivable	2,663	0
Assets of centers held for resale	2,217	237
Investments in/advances to affiliates	57,383	7,694
Assets leased to franchisees	1,885	16,297
Property and equipment	9,104	6,228
Intangible assets	3,687	1,958
Other assets	87,488	36,206
Total assets	$102,443	$50,692
Liabilities and Stockholders' Equity		
Current liabilities:		
Accounts Payable/Accrued expenses	$9,167	$3,905
Notes Payable	1,981	2,403
Construction advances	0	2,331
Current portion of long-term debt	1,047	1,355
Total current liabilities	12,195	9,994
Long-term debt	26,684	19,707
Capital lease obligations	18,969	9,586
Other liabilities	5,099	4,646
	50,752	33,939
Stockholders' equity:		
Preferred stock, par value $50;		
46,140 authorized shares,		
no shares issues or outstanding		
Common stock, par value $.025;		
Authorized—100,000,000 shares;	294	
Issued—11,760,828 shares (1987);		180
—3,602,912 shares (1986)		
Capital in excess of value	39,479	10,221
Retained earnings (deficit)	(277)	(3,467)
	39,496	6,934
Less cost of common stock held in treasury	0	175
Total stockholders' equity	39,496	6,759
Total liabilities and stockholders' equity	$102,443	$50,692

Plotting a Future Course

In the summer of 1987, the prospects for Jiffy Lube International never seemed brighter. If Booz, Allen & Hamilton's estimates were correct, management and the board had significantly underestimated the quicklube market potential. The distinction between Booz, Allen & Hamilton's and Hindman's projections held enormous implications for the company and investors alike. Hindman and his team wondered whether their growth strategy was aggressive enough. Could it be too ambitious? Were the 1987 financial statements indicators of the future growth in the quicklube industry and JLI? Hindman paced the room one more time; the meeting was about to begin.

## PART FIVE

Startup and After

Under conditions of rapid growth, entrepreneurs face unusual paradoxes and challenges as their companies grow and the management modes required by these companies change.

Whether they have the adaptability and resiliency in the face of swift developments to grow fast enough as managers and whether they have enough courage, wisdom, and discipline to balance controlled growth with growing fast enough to keep pace with the competition and industry turbulence will become crystal clear.

There are enormous pressures and physical and emotional wear and tear that entrepreneurs will face during the rapid growth of their companies. It goes with the territory. Entrepreneurs after startup find that "it" has to be done now, that there is no room to falter, and that there are no "runners up." Clearly, those who have a personal entrepreneurial strategy, who are healthy, who have their lives in order, and who know what they are signing up for fare better than those who do not.

Among all the stimulating and exceedingly difficult challenges entrepreneurs face—and can meet successfully—none is more liberating and exhilarating than a harvest. Perhaps the point is made best in one of the final lines of the musical *Oliver:* "In the end all that counts, is in the bank, in large amounts!"

Obviously, money is not the only thing, or everything. But money is the vehicle that can ensure both independence and autonomy to do what you want to do, mostly on your terms, and can significantly increase the options and opportunities at your discretion. In effect, for entrepreneurs, net worth is the final score card of the value creation process.

## Chapter Sixteen

Managing Rapid Growth

Bite off more than you can chew, and then chew it!

Roger Babson
Founder, Babson College

Results Expected

Upon completion of the chapter you will have:

1. Examined how higher potential, rapidly growing ventures have invented new organizational paradigms to replace Brontosaurus Capitalism.
2. Studied how higher potential ventures "grow up big" and the special problems, organization, and leadership requirements of rapid growth.
3. Examined new research on the leading management practices that distinguish high growth companies.
4. Explored concepts of organizational culture and climate, and how entrepreneurial leaders foster favorable cultures.
5. Identified specific signals and clues that can alert entrepreneurial managers to impending crises and approaches to solve these.
6. Analyzed the "Quick Lube Franchise Corporation" case.

Inventing New Organizational Paradigms

We saw in Chapter 1 the chronicle of the demise of brontosaurus capitalism. It is the nimble and fleet-footed entrepreneurial firms that have supplanted the aging giants with new leadership approaches, a passion for value creation, and an obsession with opportunity that has been unbeatable in the marketplace for talent and ideas. These entrepreneurial ventures have experienced rapid to explosive growth and have become the investments of choice of the U.S. venture capital community.

Because of their innovative nature and competitive breakthroughs, entrepreneurship ventures have demonstrated a remarkable capacity to invent new paradigms of organization and management. They have abandoned the organizational practices and structures typical of the industrial giants from the post-World War II era to the 1990s. One could characterize those brontosaurus approaches thus: What they lacked in creativity and the flexibility to deal with ambiguity and rapid change, they made up for with rules, structure, hierarchy, and quantitative analysis.

The epitome of this pattern is the Hay System, which by the 1980s became the leading method of defining and grading management jobs in large companies. Scoring high with "Hay points" was the key to more pay, a higher position in the hierarchy, and greater power. The criteria for Hay points include: number of people who are direct reports, value of assets under management, sales volume, number of products, square feet of facilities, total size of one's operating and capital budget, and the like. One can easily see who gets ahead in such a system: Be bureaucratic, have the most people and largest budget, increase head count and levels under your control, and think up the largest capital projects. Note that missing in the criteria are all the basic components of entrepreneurship we have seen in the book: value creation, opportunity creation/seeking/seizing, frugality with resources, bootstrapping strategies, staged capital commitments, team building, achieving better fits, and juggling paradoxes.

Contrast the multilayered, hierarchical, military-like levels of control and command that characterize brontosaurus capitalism with the common patterns among entrepreneurial firms, they are flat—often only one or two layers deep, adaptive, and flexible; they look like interlocking circles rather than ladders; they are integrative around customers and critical missions; they are learning and influence based, rather than rank and power based. People lead more through influence and persuasion, which are derived from knowledge and performance rather than through formal rank, position, or seniority. They create a perpetual learning culture. They value people and share the wealth with people who help create it.

Entrepreneurial Leaders Aren't Administrators or Managers

Consider the following quotes from two distinguished business leaders, based on their experiences with MBAs in the 1960s–80s. First, Fred Smith, founder, chairman, and CEO of Federal Express:

> MBAs are people in Fortune 500 companies who make careers out of saying no!

General George Doriot, father of American venture capital and for years a professor at Harvard Business School, said:

> There isn't any business that a Harvard MBA cannot analyze out of existence!

Those are profound statements, given the sources. These perceptions also help to explain the stagnancy and eventual demise of brontosaurus capitalism. After all, legions of MBAs in the 1950s, 60s, 70s, and early 1980s were taught the brontosaurus model of management. Until the 1980s, virtually all of the cases, problems, and lectures in MBA programs were about large, established companies.

Breakthrough Strategy: Babson's F.W. Olin Graduate School

The first MBA program in the world to break the lockstep of the prior 50 years was the Franklin W. Olin Graduate School of Business at Babson College, in 1992. Practicing what they teach, the faculty completely discarded the traditional, functional approach to an MBA education, consisting of individual courses in accounting, marketing, finance, information technology, operations, and human resources in stand-alone sequence, with too many lectures.

In its place, a revolutionary new curriculum for the first year of the MBA: An entirely new and team-taught curriculum in a series of highly integrative modules anchored conceptually in the model of the entrepreneurial process from *New Venture Creation*.[1] MBAs now experience a unique learning curve that immerses them for the first year in cases, assignments, and content that has immediate and relevant applicability to the entrepreneurial process. Emerging entrepreneurial companies are the focal points for most case studies, while larger, established companies seeking to recapture their entrepreneurial spirit and management approach are examined in others. The new program has been characterized as a resounding success by students, employers, and faculty. (See the Babson College web site: www.babson.edu.)

Leading Practices of High Growth Companies[2]

Earlier in Chapter 2, (Exhibit 2.13) we examined a summary of research conducted on fast-growth companies to determine the leading practices of these firms. Having completed much of the book at this time, this research will likely take on new meaning to the reader. As one examines each of these four practice areas—marketing, financial, management, and planning—one can see the practical side of how fast-growth entrepreneurs pursue opportunities; devise, manage and orchestrate their financial strategies; build a team with collaborative decision making; and plan with vision, clarity, and flexibility. Clearly, rapid growth is a different game, requiring an entrepreneurial mind-set and skills.

---

[1] See William Glavin, *The President's report—1996*, Babson College, Babson Park, MA.
[2] Special appreciation is given to Ernst & Young LLP and The Kauffman Center for Entrepreneurial Leadership for permission to include the summary of their research here.

(EXHIBIT 2.13 repeated)

Leading Marketing Practices *of Fast Growth Firms:*

- Deliver products and services that are perceived as highest quality to expanding segments.
- Cultivate pace-setting new products and services that stand out in the market as best of the breed.
- Deliver product and service benefits that demand average market or higher pricing.
- Generate revenue flows from existing products and services that typically sustain approximately 90 percent of the present revenue base while achieving flows from new products and services that typically expand revenue approximately 20 percent annually.
- Generate revenue flows from existing customers that typically sustain approximately 80 percent of the ongoing revenue base while achieving flows from new customers that typically expand revenue flows by about 30 percent annually.
- Create important new product and service improvements with development expenditures that typically account for no more than approximately 6 percent of revenues.
- Use a high-yielding sales force that typically accounts for approximately 60 percent of marketing expenditures.
- Rapidly develop broad product and service platforms with complementary channels to expand a firm's geographic marketing dimensions.

Leading Financial Practices of Fast Growth Firms:

- Anticipate multiple rounds of financing (on average every 2.5 years).
- Secure funding sources capable of significantly expanding their participation amounts.
- Utilize financing vehicles that retain the entrepreneur's voting control.
- Maintain control of the firm by selectively granting employee stock ownership.
- Link the entrepreneur's long-term objectives to a defined exit strategy in the business plan.

Leading Management Practices of Fast Growth Firms:

- Use a collaborative decision-making style with the top management team.
- Accelerate organizational development by assembling a balanced top management team with and without prior experience of working together.
- Develop a top management team of three to six individuals with the capacity to become the entrepreneur's entrepreneurs.
- Align the number of management levels with the number of individuals in top management.
- Establish entrepreneurial competency first in the functional areas of finance, marketing and operations.
- Assemble a balanced board of directors composed of both internal and external directors.
- Calibrate strategies constantly with regular board of directors meetings.
- Involve the board of directors heavily at strategic inflection points.

Leading Planning Practices of Fast Growth Firms:

- Prepare detailed written monthly plans for each of the next 12 to 24 months and annual plans for three or more years.
- Establish functional planning and control systems that tie planned to actual performance and adjust management compensation accordingly.
- Share with employees periodic planned versus actual performance data that is directly linked to the business plan.
- Link job performance standards that have been jointly set by management and employees to the business plan.
- Prospectively model the firm based on benchmarks that exceed industry norms, competitors, and the industry leader.

Growing up Big

Stages of Growth Revisited

Higher potential ventures do not stay small very long. While an entrepreneur may have done a good job of assessing an opportunity, forming a new venture team, marshalling resources, planning, and so forth, managing and growing such a venture is, simply put, a different managerial game.

Ventures in the high-growth stage face the problems discussed in Chapter 6. These include forces that limit the creativity of founders and team; that cause confusion and resentment over roles, responsibilities, and goals; that call for specialization and therefore erode collaboration; that require operating mechanisms and controls; and the like.

Recall also that managers of rapidly growing ventures are usually relatively inexperienced in launching a new venture and yet face situations where time and change are compounded and where events are nonlinear and nonparametric. Usually, structures, procedures, and patterns are fluid, and decision making needs to follow counterintuitive and unconventional patterns.

That companies experience stages or phases during their growth was discussed in Chapter 6. Recall that the first three years before startup are called the *research-and-development* (R&D) *stage;* the first three years, the *startup stage;* years 4 through 10, the *early-growth stage;* the 10th year through the 15th or so, *maturity;* and after the 15th year, *stability stage.* Remember that these time estimates are approximate and may vary somewhat in particular cases.

Various life cycle models, and our previous discussion, depicted the life cycle of a growing firm as a smooth curve with rapidly ascending sales and profits and a leveling off toward the peak and then dipping toward decline.

In truth, however, very very few, if any, new and growing firms experience such smooth and linear phases of growth. By and large, if the actual growth curves of new companies are plotted over their first 10 years, the curves will look far more like the ups and downs of a roller-coaster ride than the smooth progressions usually depicted. Over the life of a typical growing firm, there are periods of jerks, bumps, hiccups, indigestion, and renewal interspersed with periods of smooth sailing. Sometimes there is continual upward progress through all this, but with others, there are periods where the firms seem near collapse or at least in considerable peril.

Core Management Mode

As was noted earlier, changes in several critical variables determine just how frantic or easy transitions from one stage to the next will be. As a result, it is possible to make some generalizations about the main management challenges and transitions that will be encountered as the company grows. The core management mode is influenced by the number of employees a firm has, which is in turn related to its dollar sales.[3]

Recall, as shown in *Exhibit 6.4* in Chapter 6, that until sales reach approximately $3 million and employees number 30, the core management mode is one of *doing.* Between $3 million and $10 million in sales and 30 to 75 employees, the core management mode is *managing.* When sales exceed $10 million and employees number over 75, the core management mode is *managing managers.* Obviously, these revenue and employment figures are broad generalities. The number of people is a better indicator of the increasing complexity of the management task, and suggest a new wall to be scaled, rather than a precise point. To illustrate just how widely sales per employee

can vary, consider *Exhibit 16.1.* Typically, in 1992, established firms generated $125,000 to $175,000 in sales, but Reebok's $671,000 (due to having relatively few employees because of a great deal of subcontracting of shoe manufacture) was nearly 35 times larger than Sonesta International Hotel's $19,700. Thus, these numbers are boundaries, constantly moving as a result of inflation and competitive dynamics.

The central issue facing entrepreneurs in all sorts of businesses is this: As the size of the firm increases, the core management mode likewise *changes from doing to managing to managing managers.*

During each of the stages of growth of a firm, there are entrepreneurial crises, or hurdles, that most firms will confront. *Exhibit 16.2,* as well as the following discussion, considers by stage some indications of crisis.[4] As the exhibit shows, for each fundamental driving force of entrepreneurship, there are a number of "signals" that crises are imminent. While the list is long, these are not the only indicators of crises new ventures can and most likely will see—only the most common. Of course, each of these signals does not necessarily indicate that particular crises will happen to every company at each stage, but when the signals are there, serious difficulties cannot be too far behind.

EXHIBIT 16.1

1992 Sales per Employee

Company	(000)
Raytheon Company	$141.8
Digital Equipment Corporation	138.7
Data General Corporation	159.5
Stratus Computer, Inc.	185.5
Wang Laboratories, Inc.	164.8
Well Fleet Communications	226.9
Lotus Development Corporation	204.6
Gillette	167.6
Biogen, Inc.	309.4
Genetic Institute	158.1
Picture Tel Corporation	199.2
Augat, Inc.	92.7
Ground Round Restaurants	23.4
Sonesta International Hotels	19.7
Mediplex Group, Inc.	40.8
Neiman Marcus Group	170.0
Stop & Shop Company	118.5
Reebok International Ltd.	691.7

Source: *Boston Globe,* June 8, 1993, p. 60.

---

[3] Harvey "Chet" Krentzman described this phenomenon to the author many years ago. The principle still applies.
[4] The crises discussed here are the ones the author considers particularly critical. Usually, failure to overcome even a few can seriously imperil a venture at a given stage. There are, however, many more, but a complete treatment of all of them is outside the scope of this book.

EXHIBIT 16.2

Crises and Symptoms: Pre-Startup (Years−3 to−1)

Entrepreneurs:

- *Focus.* Is the founder really an entrepreneur, bent on building a company, or an inventor, technical dilettante, or the like?
- *Selling.* Does the team have the necessary selling and closing skills to bring in the business and make the plan—on time?
- *Management.* Does the team have the necessary management skills and relevant experience, or is it overloaded in one or two areas (e.g., the financial or technical areas)?
- *Ownership.* Have the critical decisions about ownership and equity splits been resolved, and are the members committed to these?

Opportunity:

- *Focus.* Is the business really user-, customer-, and market-driven (by a need), or is it driven by an invention of a desire to create?
- *Customers.* Have customers been identified with specific names, addresses, and phone numbers, and have purchase levels been estimated, or is the business still only at the concept stage?
- *Supply.* Are costs, margins, and lead times to acquire supplies, components, and key people known?
- *Strategy.* Is the entry plan a shotgun and cherry-picking strategy, or is it a rifle shot at a well-focused niche?

Resources:

- *Resources.* Have the required capital resources been identified?
- *Cash.* Are the founders already out of cash (OOC) and their own resources?
- *Business plan.* Is there a business plan, or is the team "hoofing it"?

Startup and Survival (Years 0−3)

Entrepreneurs:

- *Leadership.* Has a top leader been accepted, or are founders vying for the decision role or insist on equality in all decisions?
- *Goals.* Do the founders share and have compatible goals and work styles, or are these starting to conflict and diverge once the enterprise is underway and pressures mount?
- *Management.* Are the founders anticipating and preparing for a shift from doing to managing and letting go—of decisions and control—that will be required to make the plan on time?

Opportunity:

- *Economics.* Are the economic benefits and payback to the customer actually being achieved, and on time?
- *Strategy.* Is the company a one-product company with no encore in sight?
- *Competition.* Have previously unknown competitors or substitutes appeared in the marketplace?
- *Distribution.* Are there surprises and difficulties in actually achieving planned channels of distribution on time?

Resources:

- *Cash.* Is the company facing a cash crunch early as a result of not having a business plan (and a financial plan)? That is, is it facing a crunch because no one is asking: When will we run out of cash? Are the owners' pocketbooks exhausted?
- *Schedule.* Is the company experiencing serious deviations from projections and time estimates in the business plan? Is the company able to marshall resources according to plan and on time?

Early Growth (Years 4−10)

Entrepreneurs:

- *Doing or managing.* Are the founders still just *doing,* or are they managing for results by a plan? Have the founders begun to delegate and let go of critical decisions, or do they maintain veto power over all significant decisions?
- *Focus.* Is the mind-set of the founders operational only, or is there some serious strategic thinking going on as well?

Opportunity:

- *Market.* Are repeat sales and sales to new customers being achieved on time, according to plan, and because of interaction with customers, or are these coming from the engineering, R&D, or planning group? Is the company shifting to a marketing orientation without losing its killer instinct for closing sales?
- *Competition.* Are price and quality being blamed for loss of customers or for an inability to achieve targets in the sales plan, while customer service is rarely mentioned?
- *Economics.* Are gross margins beginning to erode?

Resources:

- *Financial control.* Are accounting and information systems and control (purchasing orders, inventory, billing, collections, cost and profit analysis, cash management, etc.) keeping pace with growth and being there when they are needed?
- *Cash.* Is the company always out of cash—or nearly OOC, and is no one asking when it will run out or is sure why or what to do about it?
- *Contacts.* Has the company developed the outside networks (directors, contacts, etc.) it needs to continue growth?

(Continued)

EXHIBIT 16.2   (concluded)

Maturity (Years 10–15 plus)

Entrepreneurs:

- *Goals.* Are the partners in conflict over control, goals, or underlying ethics or values?
- *Health.* Are there signs that the founders' marriages, health, or emotional stability are coming apart (i.e., are there extramarital affairs, drug and/or alcohol abuse, or fights and temper tantrums with partners or spouses)?
- *Teamwork.* Is there a sense of team building for a "greater purpose," with the founders now managing managers, or is there conflict over control of the company and disintegration?

Opportunity:

- *Economics/competition.* Are the products and/or services that have gotten the company this far experiencing unforgiving economics as a result of perishability, competitor blind sides, new technology, or off-shore competition, and is there a plan to respond?
- *Product encore.* Has a major new product introduction been a failure?
- *Strategy.* Has the company continued to cherry-pick in fast-growth markets, with a resulting lack of strategic definition (which opportunities to say no to)?

Resources:

- *Cash.* Is the firm OOC again?
- *Development/information.* Has growth gotten out of control, with systems, training, and development of new managers failing to keep pace?
- *Financial control.* Have systems continued to lag behind sales?

Harvest/Stability (Years 15–20 plus)

Entrepreneurs:

- *Succession/ownership.* Are there mechanisms in place to provide for management succession and the handling of very tricky ownership issues (especially family)?
- *Goals.* Have the partners' personal and financial goals and priorities begun to conflict and diverge? Are any of the founders simply bored or burned out, and are they seeking a change of view and activities?
- *Entrepreneurial passion.* Has there been an erosion of the passion for creating value through the recognition and pursuit of opportunity, or are turf-building, acquiring status and power symbols, and gaining control favored?

Opportunity:

- *Strategy.* Is there a spirit of innovation and renewal in the firm (e.g., a goal that half the company's sales come from products or services less than five years old), or has lethargy set in?
- *Economics.* Have the core economics and durability of the opportunity eroded so far that profitability and return on investment are nearly as low as that for the Fortune 500?

Resources:

- *Cash.* Has OOC been solved by increasing bank debt and leverage because the founders do not want—or cannot agree—to give up equity?
- *Accounting.* Have accounting and legal issues, especially their relevance for wealth building and estate and tax planning, been anticipated and addressed? Has a harvest concept been part of the long-range planning process?

The Problem in Rate of Growth

Difficulties in anticipating these shifts by recognizing signals and developing management approaches are compounded by rate of growth itself. The faster the rate of growth, the greater the potential for difficulty; this is because of the various pressures, chaos, confusion, and loss of control. It is not an exaggeration to say that these pressures and demands increase geometrically, rather than in a linear way (see discussion in Chapter 6).

Growth rates affect all aspects of a business. Thus, as sales increase, as more people are hired, and as in-ventory increases, sales outpace manufacturing capacity. Facilities are then increased, people are moved between buildings, accounting systems and controls cannot keep up, and so on. The cash burn rate accelerates, and such acceleration continues. Learning curves do the same. Worst of all, cash collections lag behind, as shown in *Exhibit 16.3*.

For example, distinctive issues caused by rapid growth were considered at seminars at Babson College with the founders and presidents of rapidly growing companies—companies with sales of at least $1 million and growing in excess of 30 percent per year.[5] These founders and presidents pointed to the following:

---

[5] These seminars were held at Babson College near Boston in 1985 and 1986. A good number of the firms represented had sales over $1 million, and a good number were growing at greater than 100 percent per year.

EXHIBIT 16.3

Spend-Rate/Orders/Collection Leads and Lags

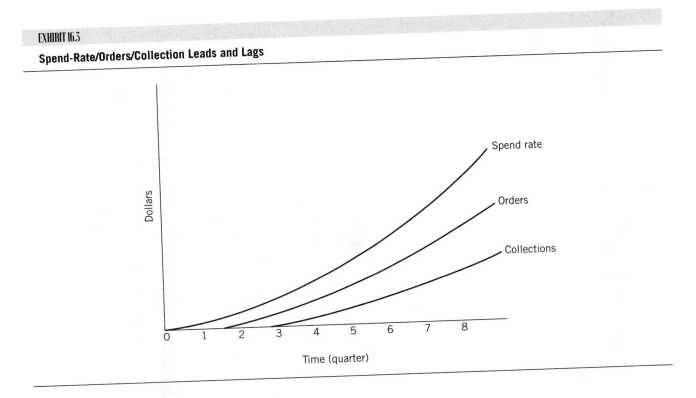

- *Opportunity overload.* Rather than lacking enough sales or new market opportunities, a classic concern in mature companies, these firms faced an abundance. Choosing from among these was a problem.
- *Abundance of capital.* While most stable or established smaller or medium-sized firms often have difficulties obtaining equity and debt financing, most of the rapidly growing firms were not constrained by this. The problem was, rather, how to evaluate investors as "partners" and the terms of the deals with which they were presented.
- *Misalignment of cash burn and collection rates.* These firms all pointed to problems of cash burn rates racing ahead of collections. They found that unless effective integrated accounting, inventory, purchasing, shipping, and invoicing systems and controls are in place, this misalignment can lead to chaos and collapse. One firm, for example, had tripled its sales in three years from $5 million to $16 million. Suddenly, its president resigned, insisting that, with the systems which were in place, the company would be able to grow to $100 million. However, the computer system was disastrously inadequate, which compounded other management weaknesses. The generation of any believable financial and accounting information that could be relied upon was not possible for many months. Losses of more than $1 million annually mounted, and the company's lenders panicked. To make matters worse, the auditors failed to stay on top of the situation until it was too late and were replaced. While

the company has survived, it has had to restructure its business and has shrunk to $6 million in sales, to pay off bank debt and to avoid bankruptcy. Fortunately, it is in the process of recovering.

- *Decision making.* Many of the firms succeeded because they executed functional day-to-day and week-to-week decisions, rather than strategizing. Strategy had to take a back seat. Many of the representatives of these firms argued that in conditions of rapid growth it was only about 10 percent of the story.
- *Surprises and the like.* Expansion of space or facilities is a problem and one of the most disrupting events during the early explosive growth of a company. Managers of many of these firms were not prepared for the surprises, delays, organizational difficulties, and system interruptions that are spawned by such expansion.

Industry Turbulence

The problems just discussed are compounded by the amount of industry turbulence surrounding the venture. Firms with higher growth rates usually are found in industries that are also developing rapidly. In addition, there are often many new entrants, both with competing products or services and with substitutes.

The effects are many: Often, prices fluctuate. The turbulence in the semiconductor industry in the 1980s is a good example. From June 1984 to June 1985, the price to original equipment manufacturers (OEMs) of 64K memory chips fell from $2.50 each to 50 cents. The price to OEMs of 256K chips fell from $15 to $3. The disruption this caused in marketing and sales projections, in financial planning and cash forecasting, and the like, for firms in the industry can be imagined. Often, too, there are rapid shifts in cost and experience curves.

The Importance of Culture and Organizational Climate

Six Dimensions

The organizational culture and climate, either of a new venture or of an existing organization, are critical in how well the organization will deal with growth. A number of studies of performance in large business organizations that used the concept of organizational climate (i.e., the perceptions of people about the kind of place it is to work in) have led to two general conclusions.[6] First, the climate of an organization can have significant impact on performance. Further, climate is created both by the expectations people bring to the organization and the practices and attitudes of the key managers.

The climate notion has relevance for new ventures, as well as for entrepreneurial efforts in large organizations. An entrepreneur's style and priorities—particularly, how he or she manages tasks and people—is well known by the people being managed and affects performance. Recall the entrepreneurial climate described by Enrico of Pepsi, where the critical factors included setting high-performance standards by developing short-run objectives that do not sacrifice long-run results, providing responsive personal leadership, encouraging individual initiative, helping others to succeed, developing individual networks for success, and so forth. Or listen to the tale of Gerald H. Langeler, the president of the systems group of Mentor Graphics Corporation, who explained what the "vision trap" was.[7] Langeler described the vision of his company's entrepreneurial climate as simply to "Build Something People Will Buy."[8] The culture of Mentor Graphics was definitely shaped by the founders' styles because "there were perhaps 15 of us at the time—we could not only share information very quickly, we could also create a sense of urgency and purpose without the help of an articulated vision."[9]

Evidence suggests that superior teams operate differently in terms of setting priorities, in resolving leadership issues, in what and how roles are performed by team members, in attitudes toward listening and participation, and in dealing with disagreements. Further, evidence suggests that specific approaches to management can impact the climate of a growing organization. For example, gains from the motivation, commitment, and teamwork, which are anchored in a consensus approach to management, while not immediately apparent, are striking later on. At that time there is swiftness and decisiveness in actions and in follow-through, since the negotiating, compromising, and accepting of priorities are history. Also, new disagreements that emerge generally do not bring progress to a halt, since there is both high clarity and broad acceptance of overall goals and underlying priorities. Without this consensus, each new problem or disagreement often necessitates a time-consuming and painful confrontation and renegotiation simply because it was not done initially.

Organizational climate can be described along six basic dimensions:

- *Clarity.* The degree of organizational clarity in terms of being well organized, concise, and efficient in the way that tasks, procedures, and assignments are made and accomplished.
- *Standards.* The degree to which management expects and puts pressure on employees for high standards and excellent performance.
- *Commitment.* The extent to which employees feel committed to the goals and objectives of the organization.
- *Responsibility.* The extent to which members of the organization feel individual responsibility for accomplishing their goals without being constantly monitored and second-guessed.
- *Recognition.* The extent to which employees feel they are recognized and rewarded (nonmonetarily) for a job well done, instead of only being punished for mistakes or errors.
- *Esprit de corps.* The extent to which employees feel a sense of cohesion and team spirit, of working well together.

Approaches to Management

In achieving the entrepreneurial culture and climate described above, certain approaches to management (also discussed in Chapter 6) are common across core management modes.

[6] See Jeffry A. Timmons, "The Entrepreneurial Team: Formation and Development," a paper presented at the Academy of Management, annual meeting, Boston, August 1973.
[7] Gerald H. Langeler, "The Vision Trap," *Harvard Business Review,* March–April 1992 reprint 92204.
[8] Ibid., p. 4.
[9] Ibid., p. 5.

Leadership

No single leadership pattern seems to characterize successful ventures. Leadership may be shared, or informal, or a natural leader may guide a task. Common, however, is the pattern whereby a manager defines and gains agreements on who has what responsibility and authority and who does what with and to whom. Roles, tasks, responsibilities, accountabilities, and appropriate approvals are defined.

There is no competition for leadership in these organizations, and leadership is based on expertise, not authority. Emphasis is placed on performing task-oriented roles, but someone invariably provides for "maintenance" and group cohesion by good humor and wit. Further, the leader does not force his or her own solution on the team or exclude the involvement of potential resources. Instead, the leader understands the relationships among tasks and between the leader and his or her followers and is able to lead in those situations where it is appropriate, including managing actively the activities of others through directions, suggestions, and so forth.

This approach is in direct contrast to the commune approach, where two to four entrepreneurs, usually friends or work acquaintances, leave unanswered such questions as who is in charge, who makes the final decisions, and how real differences of opinion are resolved. While some overlapping of roles and a sharing in and negotiating of decisions are desirable in a new venture, too much looseness is debilitating.

This approach also contrasts with situations where a self-appointed leader takes over, where there is competition for leadership, or where one task takes precedence over other tasks.

Consensus Building

Leaders of most successful new ventures define authority and responsibility in a way that builds motivation and commitment to cross-departmental and corporate goals. Using a consensus approach to management requires managing and working with peers and with the subordinates of others (or with superiors) outside formal chains of command and balancing multiple viewpoints and demands.

In the consensus approach, the manager is seen as willing to relinquish his or her priorities and power in the interests of an overall goal, and the appropriate people are included in setting cross-functional or cross-departmental goals and in making decisions. Participation and listening are emphasized.

The most effective managers, in addition, are committed to dealing with problems and working problems through to agreement by seeking a reconciliation of viewpoints, rather than emphasizing differences, and by blending ideas, rather than playing the role of hard-nose negotiator or devil's advocate to force their own solution. There is open confrontation of differences of opinion and a willingness to talk out differences, assumptions, reasons, and inferences. Logic and reason tend to prevail, and there is a willingness to change opinions based on consensus.

Communication

The most effective managers share information and are willing to alter individual views. Listening and participation are facilitated by such methods as circular seating arrangements, few interruptions or side conversations, and calm discussion versus many interruptions, loud or separate conversations, and so forth, in meetings.

Encouragement

Successful managers build confidence by encouraging innovation and calculated risk-taking, rather than by punishing or criticizing what is less than perfect, and by expecting and encouraging others to find and correct their own errors and to solve their own problems. They are perceived by their peers and others as accessible and willing to help when needed, and they provide the necessary resources to enable others to do the job. When it is appropriate, they go to bat for their peers and subordinates, even when they know they can't always win. Further, differences are recognized and performance is rewarded.

Trust

The most effective managers are perceived as trustworthy and straightforward. They do what they say they are going to do; they are not the corporate rumor carriers; they are more open and spontaneous, rather than guarded and cautious with each word; and they are perceived as being honest and direct. They have a reputation of getting results and become known as the creative problemsolvers who have a knack for blending and balancing multiple views and demands.

Development

Effective managers have a reputation for developing human capital (i.e., they groom and grow other effective managers by their example and their mentoring). As noted in Chapter 6, Bradford and Cohen distinguish between the heroic manager, whose need to be in control in many instances actually may stifle cooperation, and the postheroic manager, a developer who actually brings about excellence in organizations by developing entrepreneurial middle management. If a company puts off developing middle management until price competition appears and its margins erode, the organization may come unraveled. Linking a plan to grow human capital at the middle management and the supervisory levels with the business strategy is an essential first step.

Entrepreneurial Management for the 21st Century: Three Breakthroughs

Three extraordinary companies have been built or revolutionized in the past two decades: Marion Labs, Inc., of Kansas City; Johnsonville Sausage of Cheybogan, Wisconsin; and Springfield Remanufacturing Corporation of Springfield, Missouri. Independently and unbeknownst to each other, these companies created what I describe as "High Standard, Perpetual Learning Cultures," which create and foster a "Chain of Greatness." The lessons from these three great companies provide a blueprint for entrepreneurial management in the twenty-first century. They set the standard and provide a tangible vision of what is possible. Not surprisingly, the most exciting, faster growing, and profitable companies in America today have striking similarities to these firms.

Ewing Marion Kauffman and Marion Labs

As described in Chapter 1, Marion Labs, founded in Ewing Marion Kauffman's garage in 1950, had reached $2.5 billion in sales by the time it merged with Dow-Merrel in 1989. Its market capitalization was $6.5 billion. Over 300 millionaires and 13 foundations were created from the builders of the company, including the Ewing Marion Kauffman Foundation. In sharp contrast, RJR Nabisco, about 10 times larger than Marion Labs at the time of the KKR leveraged buyout, generated only 20 millionaires. Clearly, these were very different companies. What was central to this phenomenal success story was the combination of a high-potential opportunity with management execution based on core values and management philosophy ahead of its time. These principles are simple enough, but difficult to inculcate and sustain through good times and bad:

1. Treat everyone as you would want to be treated.
2. Share the wealth with those who have created it.
3. Pursue the highest standards of performance and ethics.

As noted earlier the company had no organizational chart, referred to all its people as associates, not employees, and had widespread profit-sharing and stock participation plans. Having worked for a few years now with Mr. K and the top management that built Marion Labs and that now runs the foundation, I can say that they are genuine and serious about these principles. They also have fun while succeeding, but they are highly dedicated to the practice of these core philosophies and values.

Jack Stack and Springfield Remanufacturing Corporation

The truly remarkable sage of this revolution in management is Jack Stack, and his book, *The Great Game of Business*, is a must-read for any entrepreneur. In 1983, Stack and a dozen colleagues acquired a tractor engine remanufacturing plant from the failing International Harvester Corporation. With an 89-to-1 debt-to-equity ratio and 21 percent interest, they acquired the company for 10 cents a share. In 1993, the company's shares were valued near $20 for the employee stock option plan (ESOP), and the company had completely turned around with sales approaching $100 million. What had happened?

Like Ewing Marion Kauffman, Jack Stack created and implemented some management approaches and values radically opposite to the top-down, hierarchical, custodial management commonly found in large manufacturing enterprises. At the heart of his leadership was creating a vision. *The Big Picture: Think and act like owners, be the best we can be, and be perpetual learners. Build teamwork as the key by learning from each other, open the books to everyone, and educate everyone so they can become responsible and accountable for the numbers, both short- and long-term.* Stack puts it this way:

> We try to take ignorance out of the workplace and force people to get involved, not with threats and intimidation but with education. In the process, we are trying to close the biggest gaps in American business—the gap between workers and managers. We're developing a system that allows everyone to get together and work toward the same goals. To do that, you have to knock down the barriers that separate people, that keep people from coming together as a team.[10]

At Springfield Remanufacturing Corporation, everyone learns to read and interpret all the financial statements, including an income statement, balance sheet, and cash flow, and how his or her job affects each line item. This open-book management style is

---

[10] Jack Stack, *The Great Game of Business* (New York: Currency/Doubleday Books, 1991), p. 5.

linked with pushing responsibility downward and outward, and to understanding both wealth creation (i.e., shareholder value) and wealth sharing through short-term bonuses and long-term equity participation. Jack describes the value of this approach thus: "The payoff comes from getting the people who create the numbers to understand the numbers. When that happens, the communication between the bottom and the top of the organization is just phenomenal."[11] The results he has achieved in 10 years are nothing short of astounding. What is more amazing is that he has found the time to share this approach with others. To date, over 150 companies have participated in seminars that have enabled them to adopt this approach.

Ralph Stayer and Johnsonville Sausage Company[12]

In 1975, Johnsonville Sausage was a small company with about $5 million in sales and a fairly traditional, hierarchical, and somewhat custodial management. In just a few years, Ralph Stayer, the owner's son, created a radical transformation of the company, a management revolution whose values, culture, and philosophy are remarkably similar to the principles of Ewing Marion Kauffman and Jack Stack.

The results are astonishing: By 1980 the company had reached $15 million in sales; by 1985, $50 million; and by 1990, $150 million. At the heart of the changes he created was the concept of *total learning culture: everyone is a learner, seeking to improve constantly, finding better ways. High performance standards accompanied by an investment in training, and performance measures that made it possible to reward fairly both short- and long-term results* were critical to the transition. Responsibility and accountability was spread downward and outward. For example, instead of forwarding complaint letters to the marketing department, where they are filed and the standard response is sent, they go directly to the front-line sausage stuffer responsible for the product's taste. They are the ones who respond to customer complaints now. Another example is the interviewing, hiring, and training process for new people. A newly hired woman pointed out numerous shortcomings with the existing process and proposed ways to improve it. As a result, the entire responsibility was shifted from the traditional human resources/personnel group to the front line, with superb results.

As one would guess, such radical changes do not come easily. After all, how do such changes ever become initiated in the first place? Consider Ralph's insight:

In 1980, I began looking for a recipe for change. I started by searching for a book that would tell me how to get people to care about their jobs and their company. Not surprisingly, the search was fruitless. No one could tell me how to wake up my own workforce; I would have to figure it out for myself . . . The most important question any manager can ask is: "In the best of all possible worlds what would I really want to happen?"[13]

Even having taken such a giant step, Jack was ready to take the next, equally perilous steps:

Acting on instinct, I ordered a change. "From now on," I announced to my management team, "you're all responsible for making your own decision." . . . I went from authoritarian control to authoritarian abdication. No one had asked for more responsibility; I had forced it down their throats.[14]

Further insight into just how challenging it is to transform a company like Johnsonville Sausage is revealed in another Stayer quote:

I spent those two years pursuing another mirage as well—detailed strategic and tactical plans that would realize my goals of Johnsonville as the world's greatest sausage maker. We tried to plan organizational structure two to three years before it would be needed . . . Later I realized that these structural changes had to grow from day-to-day working realities; no one could dictate them from above, and certainly not in advance.[15]

Exhibit 16.4 summarizes the key steps in the transformation of Johnsonville Sausage over several years. Such a picture undoubtedly oversimplifies the process and understates the extraordinary commitment and effort required to pull it off, but it does show how the central elements weave together.

The Chain of Greatness

As we reflect on these three great companies, we can see that there is clearly a pattern here, with some common denominators in both the ingredients and the process. This chain of greatness becomes reinforcing and perpetuating (see *Exhibit 16.5*). Leadership that instills across the company a vision of

---

[11] Ibid., p. 93.
[12] For an excellent discussion of this transformation, see "The Johnsonville Sausage Company," HBS Case 387-103, rev. June 27, 1990. Copyright © 1990 by the President and Fellows of Harvard College. See also Ralph Stayer, "How I Learned to Let My Workers Lead," *Harvard Business Review*, November–December 1990. Copyright © 1990 by the President and Fellows of Harvard College.
[13] Stayer, "How I Learned to Let My Workers Lead," p. 1.
[14] Ibid., pp. 3–4.
[15] Ibid., p. 4.

EXHIBIT 16.4

Summary of the Johnsonville Sausage Company

The critical aspects of the transition:

1. Started at the top: Ralph Stayer recognized that he was the heart of the problem and recognized the need to change—the most difficult step.
2. Vision was anchored in human resource management and in a particular idea of the company's culture:
   - Continuous learning organization.
   - Team concept—change players.
   - New model of jobs (Ralph Stayer's role and decision making).
   - Performance- and results-based compensation and rewards.
3. Stayer decided to push responsibility and accountability downward to the front-line decision makers:
   - Front-liners are closest to the customer and the problem.
   - Define the whole task.
   - Invest in training and selection.
   - Job criteria and feedback = development tool.
4. Controls and mechanisms make it work:
   - Measure performance, not behavior, activities, and the like.
   - Emphasize learning and development, not allocation of blame.
   - Customize to you and the company.
   - Decentralize and minimize staff.

EXHIBIT 16.5

The Chain of Greatness

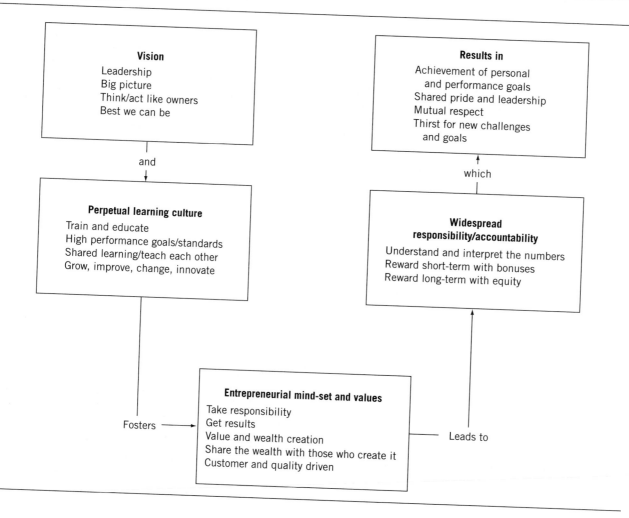

greatness and an owner's mentality is a common beginning. A philosophy of perpetual learning throughout the organization accompanied by high standards of performance is key to the value-creating entrepreneurial cultures at the three firms. A culture that teaches and rewards teamwork, improvement, and respect for each other provides the oil and glue to make things work. Finally, a fair and generous short- and long-term reward system, as well as the necessary education to make sure that everyone knows and can use the numbers, creates a mechanism for sharing the wealth with those who contributed to it. The results speak for themselves: extraordinary levels of personal, professional, and financial achievement.

Chapter Summary

1. The demands of rapid growth have led to the invention of new organizational paradigms by entrepreneurs.

2. The entrepreneurial organization today is flatter, faster, more flexible and responsive, and copes readily with ambiguity and change. It is the opposite of the hierarchy, layers of management, and the more-is-better syndrome prevalent in brontosaurus capitalism.

3. Entrepreneurs in high growth firms distinguish themselves with leading entrepreneurial practices in marketing, finance, management, and planning.

4. As high-potential firms "grow up big" they experience stages, each with its own special challenges and crises, which are compounded the faster the growth.

5. Establishing a culture and climate conducive to entrepreneurship is a core task for the venture.

6. A chain of greatness characterizes some breakthrough approaches to leadership and management in entrepreneurial ventures.

Study Questions

1. Why have old hierarchical management paradigms given way to new organizational paradigms?

2. What special problems and crises can new ventures expect as they grow? Why do these occur?

3. Explain the stages many ventures experience and why these are unique.

4. What role does the organizational culture and climate play in a rapidly growing venture? Why are many large companies unable to create an entrepreneurial culture?

5. What is the *chain of greatness* and why can entrepreneurs benefit from the concept?

6. Why is the rate of growth the central driver of the organizational challenges a growing venture faces?

MIND STRETCHERS
Have You Considered?

1. Many large organizations are now attempting to reinvent themselves. What will be the biggest challenge in this process, and why?

2. How fast should a company grow? How fast is too fast, organizationally and financially?

3. In your ideal world how would you describe what it is like to live and work within the perfect entrepreneurial organization?

4. Who should *not* be an entrepreneur?

Case

Quick Lube Franchise Corporation (QLFC)

Preparation Questions

1. What grounds might QLFC have for filing a lawsuit against Huston?

2. Why do you think Huston has asked for a meeting with Herget?

3. What advice would you give Herget as he considers Huston's request for a meeting with QLFC?

4. As part of that advice, how much is QLFC worth?

5. Does your answer to Question 4 depend on how QLFC is harvested?

It had been a year since Huston, a major oil company, had bought 80 percent of Super Lube, Inc., the number one franchisor of quick lubrication and oil-change service

This case was prepared by Professors Stephen Spinelli and William Bygrave. © Copyright Babson College, 1991. All rights reserved.

centers in the United States with 1,000 outlets. As a result of that takeover, Super Lube's largest franchisee, Quick Lube Franchise Corporation (QLFC) found itself in the position where its principal supplier, lead financing vehicle, and franchisor were the same entity. Was this an opportunity or a disaster? In April 1991, Frank Herget, founder, chairman, and CEO of QLFC was faced with one of the most important decisions of his life.

Historical Background

Super Lube was the innovator of the quick lube concept, servicing the lube, motor oil, and filter needs of motorists in a specialized building with highly refined procedures. It was founded in March 1979 by Jeff Martin. Frank Herget was one of the four founding members of Martin's team. After a few years, Herget became frustrated with life at the franchisor's headquarters in Dallas. He believed that the future of the Super Lube was in operating service centers. That put him at odds with founder, Chairman, and CEO Jeff Martin who was passionately committed to franchising service centers as fast as possible. Martin and Herget had known each other for a long time so they sought a mutually acceptable way to resolve their differences. Their discussions quickly resulted in the decision that Herget would buy a company-owned service center in northern California by swapping his Super Lube founder's stock valued at $64,000, which he had purchased originally for $13,000. Quick Lube Franchise Corporation was founded.

Early Success and Growth

Success in his first service center inspired growth. Eventually, QLFC controlled service center development and operating rights to a geographic area covering parts of California and Washington with the potential for over 90 service centers. Herget's long-term goal was to build QLFC into a big chain of Super Lube service centers that would have a public stock offering or merge with a larger company (Exhibits A and B).

Herget financed QLFC's growth with both equity and debt (Exhibits C and D). Most of the additional equity came from former Super Lube employees who left the franchisor to join QLFC in senior management positions. They purchased stock in QLFC with cash realized by selling their stock in Super Lube. A key member of Herget's team was Mark Roberts, who had been Super Lube's CFO until 1986. He brought much needed financial sophistication to QLFC.

The primary debt requirement was for financing new service centers. In 1991, the average cost of land acquisition and construction had risen to $750,000 per service center from about $350,000 10 years earlier.

Growth was originally achieved through off-balance-sheet real estate partnerships. An Oregon bank lent about $4 million and a Texas bank lent almost $3 million. However, rapid growth wasn't possible until QLFC struck a deal with Huston Oil for $6.5 million of subordinated debt. The Huston debt was 8 percent interest—only for 5 years and then amortized on a straight line basis in years 6 through 10. The real estate developed with the Huston financing was kept in the company. QLFC was contractually committed to purchasing Huston products.

Super Lube's Relationship with Its Franchisees

Despite bridge financing of $10 million at the end of 1985 followed by a successful initial public offering, Super Lube's growth continued to outpace its ability to finance it. At the end of the 1980s, Super Lube was in technical default to its debt holders. Huston struck a deal to acquire 80 percent of the company in a debt restructuring scheme. However, during the time of Super Lube's mounting financial problems and the subsequent Huston deal, franchisees grew increasingly discontented.

A franchise relationship is governed by a contract called a license agreement. As a "business format" franchise, a franchisor offers a franchisee the rights to engage in a business system by using the franchisor's trade name, trademark, service marks, know-how, and method of doing business. The franchisee is contractually bound to a system of operation and to pay the franchisor a royalty in the form of a percentage of top-line sales.

The Super Lube license agreement called for the franchisor to perform product development and quality assurance tasks. Super Lube had made a strategic decision early in its existence to sell franchises on the ba-

EXHIBIT A

QLFC Growth

	82	83	84	85	86	87	88	89	90	91
Service Centers	2	3	4	7	16	25	34	44	46	47
Sales ($ Mill.)	.5	1.6	2.1	3.8	8.5	15.5	19	27	28	30

EXHIBIT B

Quick Lube Franchise Corp.: FY 1991 Budget Worksheet*

	Apr	May	Jun	Jul	Aug	Sep	Oct	Nov	Dec	Jan	Feb	Mar	Total
Sales	2,424,718	2,444,629	2,756,829	2,816,765	2,872,074	2,358,273	2,619,415	2,435,022	2,494,696	2,733,469	2,464,172	2,795,804	31,215,866
Cost of sales	544,689	549,348	613,728	626,809	639,126	529,542	588,628	547,137	573,063	627,574	565,836	642,144	7,047,624
Variable expenses[1]	805,251	826,956	894,782	914,080	943,260	790,276	893,236	819,709	844,626	911,313	826,811	949,576	10,419,876
Fixed expenses	358,640	349,858	351,828	363,917	371,498	366,260	371,988	391,686	378,485	388,381	399,375	393,974	4,485,890
Real estate cost	320,377	337,372	340,652	341,353	352,053	352,053	372,030	372,030	392,337	392,452	392,452	410,552	4,375,713
Store operating income	395,761	381,095	555,839	570,606	566,137	320,142	393,533	304,460	306,185	413,749	279,698	399,558	4,886,763
Overhead	255,515	261,573	245,083	241,089	263,458	278,333	258,655	274,724	277,974	269,551	279,819	275,440	3,181,214
Operating income	140,246	119,522	310,756	329,517	302,679	41,809	134,878	29,736	28,211	144,198	(121)	124,118	1,705,549
Other income	7,392	7,392	7,392	7,392	7,392	7,392	7,392	7,392	7,392	7,392	7,392	7,392	88,704
Dropped site expense	(8,333)	(8,333)	(8,333)	(8,333)	(8,333)	(8,333)	(8,333)	(8,333)	(8,333)	(8,333)	(8,333)	(8,333)	(99,996)
Minority interest	686	613	(2,610)	(3,254)	(3,145)	2,065	511	4,529	4,346	1,290	6,564	2,459	14,054
Interest expense	(5,495)	(5,495)	(5,495)	(5,495)	(5,495)	(5,495)	(5,495)	(5,495)	(5,495)	(5,495)	(5,495)	(5,495)	(65,940)
Taxable income	134,496	113,699	301,710	319,827	293,098	37,438	128,953	27,829	26,121	139,052	7	120,141	1,642,371
Income tax expense	54921	47253	119971	126613	115680	17885	53211	17790	16727	58652	6880	51779	687,362
Net income	79,575	66,446	181,739	193,214	177,418	19,553	75,742	10,039	9,394	80,400	(6,873)	68,362	955,009

* Budget revised March 21, 1990

[1] Royalties to the franchisor equal 7% of gross sales

EXHIBIT C

Quick Lube Franchise Corp.: Consolidated Balance Sheets

	Year Ended March 31	
	1991	1990
Assets		
Current Assets		
Cash		
Accounts receivable, net doubtful accounts of $61,000 in 1991 and $44,000 in 1990	$ 740,551	$ 665,106
Construction advances receivable	518,116	309,427
Due from government agency	508,168	137,412
Inventory		407,678
Prepaid expenses other	1,093,241	1,074,513
Total Current Assets	407,578	401,562
Property and Equipment	3,267,654	2,995,698
Land		
Buildings	351,772	351,772
Furniture, fixtures and equipment	3,171,950	2,519,845
Leasehold improvements	2,988,073	2,644,801
Property under capital leases	242,434	183,635
Construction in progress	703,778	703,778
	68,138	531,594
Less accumulated deprec and amort	7,526,145	6,935,425
	(1,290,565)	(854,473)
Other Assets	6,235,580	6,080,952
Area development and license agreements, net of accumulated amortization		
Other intangibles, net accumulated amort	923,970	988,314
Other	273,737	316,960
	151,604	208,898
	$10,852,545	$10,590,822
Liabilities and Shareholders' Equity		
Current Liabilities		
Accounts payable & accrued expenses		
Income taxes payable	$ 3,085,318	$ 3,198,694
Note payable	37,224	256,293
Current portion - LTD		250,000
Current portion of capital lease	203,629	174,134
Total Current Liabilities	19,655	17,178
Long-Term Debt, less current	3,345,826	3,896,299
Capital Lease Obligations, less current	2,848,573	3,052,597
Other Long-Term Liabilities	628,199	648,552
Minority Interest	731,783	483,534
Total Long-Term Liabilities	2,602	13,821
Shareholders' Equity	4,211,157	4,198,504
Common stock, par value $.01/share authorized 10,000,000 shares; issued 1,080,000 shares		
Additional paid-in capital	10,800	10,800
Retained earnings	1,041,170	774,267
	2,243,592	1,710,952
	3,295,562	2,496,019
	$10,852,545	$10,590,822

EXHIBIT D

Quick Lube Franchise Corp.: Consolidated Cash Flow

	Year Ended March 31		
	1991	**1990**	**1989**
Operating Activities			
Net Income	$ 532,640	$ 764,794	$ 524,211
Adjustments to reconcile net income to net cash provided by operating activities:			
Depreciation and Amortization	612,063	526,750	414,971
Provision for losses on accounts receivable	16,615	30,510	5,559
Provision for deferred income taxes	(15,045)	12,519	50,388
Minority interest in losses of subsidiaries	(11,217)	(129,589)	(83,726)
Loss (gain) on disposition of property and equipment	33,301	(420)	N/A
Changes in operating assets and liabilities:			
Accounts Receivable	(225,304)	(58,700)	(135,585)
Inventory	(18,728)	(273,559)	(286,037)
Prepaid expenses and other	(6,016)	(102,117)	(34,334)
Accounts payable and accrued expenses	(113,376)	559,456	1,409,042
Income taxes payable	(219,069)	404,068	(620,434)
Due from shareholders and affiliates	N/A	N/A	(43,742)
Other long-term liabilities	263,294	167,501	84,697
Net Cash Provided by Operating Activities	849,158	1,901,213	1,285,010
Investing Activities			
Purchases of property and equipment	(599,327)	(1,922,892)	(1,922,852)
Proceeds from sale of property and equipment	374,592	8,523	782,519
Acquisition of license agreements	(44,000)	(127,000)	(117,000)
Acquisition of other intangibles	(2,615)	(327,549)	(2,500)
Change in construction advance receivable	(370,756)	593,017	(601,525)
Change in other assets	43,894	(138,816)	11,908
Net Cash Used in Investing Activities	(598,212)	(1,914,717)	(1,849,450)
Financing Activities			
Proceeds from long-term borrowings and revolving line of credit	4,940,000	4,026,441	2,448,071
Proceeds from borrowings from related parties	N/A	N/A	19,600
Principal payments on long-term borrowings	(5,364,529)	(3,463,693)	(2,658,534)
Principal payments on borrowings from related parties		(19,600)	(7,216)
Principal payments on capital lease obligations	(17,876)	(38,048)	N/A
Proceeds from sale of Common Stock and capital contributions	266,903	97,201	19,600
Net Cash Provided by (Used in) Financing Activities	(175,502)	602,301	(178,479)
Increase (Decrease) in Cash	75,444	588,797	(742,919)
Cash at beginning of year	665,106	76,309	819,228

sis of area development agreements. These franchisees had grown to become a group of sophisticated, fully integrated companies. As the franchisees grew with multiple outlets and became increasingly self-reliant, the royalty became difficult to justify. When the franchisor failed to perform its contractually obligated tasks as its financial problems grew more and more burdensome toward the end of the 1980s, a franchisee revolt began to surface.

The Huston Era Begins

The new owners, Huston Oil, quickly moved to replace virtually the entire management team at Super Lube. The new CEO was previously a long-term employee of a Kmart subsidiary. He took a hard-line position on how the franchise system would operate and that Huston motor oil would be an important part of it. The first national convention after the Huston takeover was a disaster. The franchisees, already frustrated, were dismayed by the focus of the franchisor on motor oil sales instead of service center-level profitability.

Herget decided to make a thorough analysis of the historical relationship between Quick Lube Franchise Corporation and Super Lube. Three months of research and documentation led to Quick Lube Franchise Corporation calling for a meeting with Huston to review the findings and address concerns.

The meeting was held at the franchisor's offices with Herget and the franchisor's CEO and executive vice president. Herget described the meeting:

> The session amounted to a three-hour monologue by me followed by Super Lube's rejection of the past as relevant to the relationship. I was politely asked to trust that the future performance of the franchisor would be better and to treat the past as sunk cost. In response to my concern that Huston might have a conflict of interest in selling me product as well as being the franchisor and having an obligation to promote service center profitability, they answered that Huston bailed Super Lube out of a mess and the franchisees should be grateful, not combative.

Litigation

The QLFC board of directors received Herget's report and told him to select a law firm and to pursue litigation against Huston. QLFC's three-months of research was supplied to the law firm. A suit against Huston was filed three months after the failed QLFC/Huston "summit."

Huston denied the charges and filed a countersuit. Document search, depositions, and general legal maneuvering had been going on for about three months when QLFC's attorneys received a call from Huston requesting a meeting. Herget immediately called a board meeting, and prepared to make a recommendation for QLFC's strategic plan.

Preparation Questions

1. What grounds might QLFC have for filing a lawsuit against Huston?

2. Why do you think Huston has asked for a meeting with Herget?

3. What advice would you give Herget as he considers Huston's request for a meeting with QLFC?

4. As part of that advice, how much is QLFC worth?

5. Does your answer to Question 4 depend on how QLFC is harvested?

17

The Entrepreneur and the Troubled Company

Yes, I did run out of time on a few occasions, but I never lost a ball game!
Bobby Lane, great quarterback in the 1950s and 1960s of the Detroit Lions and the Pittsburgh Steelers

Results Expected

Upon completion of this chapter,[1] you will have:

1. Examined the principal causes and danger signals of impending trouble.
2. Discussed both quantitative and qualitative symptoms of trouble.
3. Examined the principal diagnostic methods used to devise intervention and turnaround plans.
4. Identified remedial actions used for dealing with lenders, creditors, and employees.
5. Analyzed the "Paul J. Tobin" case.

When the Bloom Is off the Rose

This chapter is about the entrepreneur and the troubled company. It traces the firm's route into and out of crisis and provides some insight into how a troubled company can be rescued by a turnaround specialist.

As was seen in Chapter 1, sooner or later the competitive dynamics of the free enterprise system catch up with many smaller companies. This is a natural process of birth, growth, and death of firms. Even firms in the Fortune 500 are not immune to such forces. Today, over one-third of the Fortune 500 companies of 1970 no longer exist. Some have failed and gone bankrupt, others have been absorbed by larger firms, and still others have been acquired and dismantled.

Although there are similarities in the experiences of new and emerging companies and large companies that experience trouble, there are important differences. New and emerging firms need to approach crises more quickly and have less in the way of financial resources to help them. New and emerging firms deal with simpler strategic and organizational issues. Yet, these firms are more likely to commit errors in the area of financial planning and policy, to manage working capital poorly, to underutilize assets, and to have weak information systems. Finally, these firms are often too insignificant in the eyes of government to qualify for the kind of help Chrysler received.

There is a saying among horseback riders that the rider who has never been thrown from a horse probably has never ridden one! This insight

[1] Special credit is due to Robert Bateman, Scott Douglas, and Ann Morgan for the material in this chapter. The material is the result of research and interviews with turnaround specialists and was submitted in a paper as a requirement for the author's Financing Entrepreneurial Ventures course in the MBA program at Babson College.
The author is especially grateful to two specialists, Leslie B. Charm, chairman of Doktor Pet Centers, and Leland Goldberg, of Coopers & Lybrand, Boston, who contributed enormously to the efforts of Bateman, Douglas, and Morgan and to the material.

captures the essence of the ups and downs that can occur during the growth and development of a new venture.

Getting into and out of Trouble

Troubled companies face a situation similar to that described by Winston Churchill in *While England Slept*, "descending inconstantly, fecklessly, the stairway which leads to dark gulf. It is a fine broad stairway at the beginning, but after a bit the carpet ends, a little farther on there are only flagstones, and a little farther on still these break beneath your feet."

If a firm has in sight a good opportunity, crisis for such a firm is usually the result of management error, although external uncontrollable factors (such as the oil embargo of 1973) can precipitate crisis. In these management errors are found part of the solution to problems of the troubled company. It is pleasing to see that many companies—even companies that are insolvent or have negative net worth or both—can be rescued and restored to profitability.

The causes and signals of trouble described below, as well as the process of developing an action plan for turnaround, are usually more readily recognized by outsiders than those insiders who are immersed as part of the problem. However, the best single insurance policy to avoid such trouble, or at least to minimize the painful consequences, is to keep the company entrepreneurial in mind-set, culture, and management action.

Causes of Trouble

Trouble can be caused by external forces not under the control of management. Among the most frequently mentioned are recession, interest rate changes, changes in government policy, inflation, the entry of new competition, and industry/product obsolescence.

However, those who manage turnarounds find that while such circumstances define the environment to which a troubled company needs to adjust, they rarely account by themselves for an individual company failure. External shocks impact all companies in an industry, and only some of them fail. Others can survive and prosper.

Most causes of failure can be found within company management. Although there are many causes of trouble, the most frequently cited fall into three broad areas: inattention to strategic issues, general management problems, and poor financial/accounting systems and practices. There is striking similarity between these causes of trouble and the causes of startup failure given in Chapter 1.

- **Strategic issues:**

  —*Misunderstood market niche.* The first of these issues is a failure to understand the company's market niche and to focus on growth without considering profitability. Instead of developing a strategy, these firms take on low-margin business and add capacity in an effort to grow. They then can find they run out of cash.

  —*Mismanaged relationships with suppliers and customers.* Related to the issue of not understanding market niche is the failure to understand the economics of relationships with suppliers and customers. Some firms allow practices in the industry to dictate payment terms, and so forth, when in fact they may be in a position to dictate their own terms.

  —*Diversification into an unrelated business area.* A common failing of cash-rich firms that suffer from the growth syndrome is diversification into unrelated business areas. These firms use the cash flow generated in one business to start another without good reason. As one turnaround consultant said, "I couldn't believe it. There was no synergy at all. They added to their overhead but not to their contribution. No common sense!"

  —*Mousetrap myopia.* Related to the problem of starting a firm around an idea, rather than an opportunity, is the problem of firms that have "great products" looking for other markets where they can be sold. This is done without analyzing opportunities.

  —*The big project.* The company gears up for a "big project" without looking at the cash flow implications. Cash is expended by adding capacity and hiring personnel. When sales do not materialize or take longer than expected to materialize, there is trouble. Sometimes the "big project" is required by the nature of the business opportunity. An example of this would be the high-technology startup that needs to capitalize on a "first-mover" advantage. The company needs to prove the product's "right to life" and grow quickly, to the point where it can achieve a public market or become an attractive acquisition candidate for a larger company, so that a larger company cannot use its advantages in scale and existing distribution channels, after copying the technology, to achieve dominance over the startup.

  —*Lack of contingency planning.* As has been stated over and over, the path to growth is not a smooth curve heading up. Firms need to be geared to think about what happens if things go sour—if sales fall or if collections slow. There needs to be plans in place for layoffs and capacity reduction.

- **Management issues:**
  —*Lack of management skills, experience, and know-how.* As was mentioned in Chapter 6, while companies grow, managers need to change their management mode from doing to managing to managing managers.
  —*Weak finance function.* Often, in a new and emerging company the finance function is nothing more than a bookkeeper. One company was five years old, with $20 million in sales, before the founders hired a financial professional.
  —*Turnover in key management personnel.* Although turnover of key management personnel can be difficult in any firm, it is a critical concern in businesses that deal in specialized or proprietary knowledge. For example, one firm lost a bookkeeper who was the only one who really understood what was happening in the business.
  —*Big-company influence in accounting.* A mistake that some companies often make is to focus on accruals, rather than cash.

- **Poor planning, financial/accounting systems, practices, and controls:**
  —*Poor pricing, overextension of credit, and excessive leverage.* These causes of trouble are not surprising and need not be elaborated. Some of the reasons for excess use of leverage are interesting. Use of excess leverage can result when growth outstrips the company's internal financing capability. The company then relies increasingly on short-term notes until a cash flow problem develops. Another reason is the use of guaranteed loans in place of equity for either startup or expansion financing. One entrepreneur remarked that the guaranteed loan "looked just like equity when we started, but when trouble came it looked more and more like debt."
  —*Lack of cash budgets/projections.* This is a most frequently cited cause of trouble. In small companies cash budgets/projections are often not done.
  —*Poor management reporting.* While some firms have good financial reporting, they suffer from poor management reporting. As one turnaround consultant stated, the general ledger system "just tells where the company has been. It doesn't help *manage* the business. If you look at the important management reports—inventory analysis, receiv-

ables agings, sales analysis—they're usually late or not produced at all. The same goes for billing procedures. Lots of emerging companies don't get their bills out on time."

—*Lack of standard costing.* Poor management reporting extends to issues of costing, too. Many emerging businesses have no standard costs against which they can compare the actual costs of manufacturing products. The result is they have no variance reporting. The company cannot identify problems in process and take corrective action. The company will know only after the fact how profitable a product is.

Even when standard costs are used, it is not uncommon to find that engineering, manufacturing, and accounting each has its own version of the bill of material. The product is designed one way, manufactured a second way, and costed a third.

—*Poorly understood cost behavior.* Companies often do not understand the relationship between fixed and variable costs. For example, one manufacturing company thought it was saving money by closing on Saturday. In this way, management felt it would save paying overtime. It had to be pointed out to the lead entrepreneur by a turnaround consultant that "he had a lot of high-margin product in his manufacturing backlog that more than justified the overtime."

It is also important for entrepreneurs to understand the difference between theory and practice in this area. The turnaround consultant mentioned above said, "Accounting theory says that all costs are variable in the long run. In practice, almost all costs are fixed. The only truly variable cost is a sales commission."

The Gestation Period of Crisis

Crisis rarely develops overnight. The time between the initial cause of trouble and the point of intervention can run from 18 months to five years. Rarely does intervention occur in less than a year.

What happens to a company during the gestation period has implications for the later turnaround of the company. Thus, how management reacts to crisis and what happens to morale determine what will need to happen in the intervention. A situation that usually develops is a demoralized and unproductive organization whose members think only of survival, not turnaround, and an entrepreneur who has lost credibility. Further, the company has lost valuable time.

The Paradox of Optimism

A typical scenario for a troubled company is as follows: The first signs of trouble (such as declining margins, customer returns, or falling liquidity) go unnoticed or are written off as teething problems of the new project or as the ordinary vicissitudes of business. For example, one entrepreneur saw increases in inventory and receivables as a good sign, since sales were up and the current ratio had improved. However, although sales were up, margins were down, and he did not realize he had a liquidity problem until cash shortages developed.

Although management may miss the first signs, outsiders usually do not. Banks, board members, suppliers, and customers see trouble brewing. They wonder why management does not respond. Credibility begins to erode.

Soon management has to admit that trouble exists, but valuable time has been lost. Furthermore, requisite actions to meet the situation are anathema. The lead entrepreneur is emotionally committed to people, to projects, or to business areas. Further, to cut back in any of these areas goes against instinct, because the company will need these resources when the good times return.

The company continues its downward fall, and the situation becomes stressful. Turnaround specialists mention that stress can cause avoidance on the part of an entrepreneur. Others have likened the entrepreneur in a troubled company to a rabbit caught in a car's headlights: The entrepreneur is frozen and can take no action. Avoidance has a basis in human psychology. One organizational behavior consultant who has worked on turnarounds said that, when a person under stress does not understand the problem and does not have the skills to deal with it, the person will tend to replace the unpleasant reality with fantasy. The consultant went on to say that the outward manifestation of this fantasy is avoidance. This consultant noted it is common for an entrepreneur to deal with pleasant and well-understood tasks, such as selling to customers, rather than dealing with the trouble. The result is that credibility is lost with bankers, creditors, and so forth. (Of course, these are the very people whose cooperation needs to be secured if the company is to be turned around.)

Often, the decisions the entrepreneur does make during this time are poor and accelerate the company on its downward course. To illustrate, the accountant or the controller may be fired with the result that the company is then "flying blind." One entrepreneur, for example, running a company that manufactured a high-margin product, announced across-the-board cuts in expenditures, including advertising, without stopping to think that cutting advertising on such a product only added to the cash flow problem.

Finally, the entrepreneur may make statements that are untrue or may make promises that cannot be kept. This is the death knell of his or her credibility.

Decline in Organizational Morale

Among those who notice trouble developing are the employees. They deal with customer returns, calls from creditors, and the like, and they wonder why management does not respond. They begin to lose confidence in management.

Despite troubled times, the lead entrepreneur talks and behaves optimistically. Employees hear of trouble from each other and from other outsiders. They lose confidence in the formal communications of the company. The grapevine, which is always exaggerated, takes on increased credibility. Company turnover starts to increase. Morale is eroding.

It is obvious there is a problem and that it is not being dealt with. Employees wonder what will happen, whether they will be laid off, and whether the firm will go into bankruptcy. With their security threatened, employees lapse into "survival mode." As an organizational behavior consultant explains:

> The human organism can tolerate anything except uncertainty. It causes so much stress that people are no longer capable of thinking in a cognitive, creative manner. They focus on survival. That's why in turnarounds you see so much uncooperative, finger-pointing behavior. The only issue people understand is directing the blame elsewhere.

At last, crisis can force intervention. The occasion is usually forced by the board of directors or a lender. For example, the bank may call a loan, or the firm may be put on cash terms by its suppliers. Perhaps creditors try to put the firm into involuntary bankruptcy.

Predicting Trouble

Since crises develop over time and typically result from an accumulation of fundamental errors, the question can be asked whether crisis can be predicted. The obvious benefit of being able to predict crisis is that the entrepreneur, employees, and significant outsiders, such as investors, lenders, trade creditors—and even customers—could see trouble brewing in time to take corrective actions.

There have been several attempts to develop predictive models. Two are presented below and have been selected because each is easy to calculate and uses information available in common financial reports. Since management reporting in emerging companies is often inadequate, the predictive model needs to use information available in common financial reports.

Each of the two approaches below uses easily obtained financial data to predict the onset of crisis as much as two years in advance. For the smaller public company, these models can be used by all interested observers. With private companies, they are useful only to those privy to the information and are probably only of benefit to such nonmanagement outsiders as lenders and boards of directors.

In considering the two models, it is important to note that the most frequently used denominator in all these ratios is the figure for total assets. This figure often is distorted by "creative accounting," with expenses occasionally improperly capitalized and carried on the balance sheet or by substantial differences between tangible book value and book value (i.e., overvalued or undervalued assets).

Net-Liquid-Balance-to-Total-Assets Ratio

This model, shown in *Exhibit 17.1*, was developed by Joel Shulman, a Babson College professor, to predict loan defaults.[2] Shulman found that his ratio can predict loan defaults with significant reliability as much as two years in advance.

Shulman's approach is noteworthy because it explicitly recognizes the importance of cash. Among current accounts, Shulman distinguishes between operating assets (such as inventory and accounts receivable) and financial assets (such as cash and marketable securities). The same distinction is made among liabilities, where notes payable and contractual obligations are financial liabilities and accounts payable are operating liabilities.

Shulman then subtracts financial liabilities from financial assets to obtain a figure known as the net liquid balance (NLB). NLB can be thought of as "uncommitted cash," cash the firm has available to meet contingencies. Because it is the short-term margin for error should sales change, collections slow, or interest rates change, it is a true measure of liquidity. The

NLB is then divided by total assets to form the predictive ratio.

Nonquantitative Signals

Discussed in Chapter 16 were patterns and actions that could lead to trouble, indications of common trouble by growth stage, and critical variables that can be monitored.

There are also some nonquantitative signals that turnaround specialists use as indicators of the possibility of trouble. As with the signals discussed in Chapter 16, the presence of a single one of these does not necessarily imply an immediate crisis. However, once any of these does surface and if the others follow over the ensuing days and weeks, then trouble is likely to mount.

- Change in management or advisors, such as directors, accountants, or other professional advisors.
- Inability to produce financial statements on time.
- Accountant's opinion that is qualified and not certified.
- Changes in behavior of the lead entrepreneur (such as avoiding phone calls or coming in later than usual).
- New competition.
- Launching of a "big project."
- Lower research and development expenditures.
- Writing off of assets.
- Lowering of credit line.

The Threat of Bankruptcy

It is unfortunate that the heads of most troubled companies usually do not understand the benefits of bankruptcy law. To them, bankruptcy carries the stigma of failure; however, the law merely defines the priority of creditors' claims when the firm is liquidated.

EXHIBIT 17.1

Net-Liquid-Balance-to-Total-Assets Ratio

Net-Liquid-Balance-to-Total-Assets Ratio = NLB/Total assets

Where

NLB = (Cash + Marketable securities) − (Notes Payable + Contractual obligations)

---

[2] A working paper by Joel Shulman, Wayne State University, Detroit, Michigan.

Although bankruptcy can provide for the liquidation of the business, it also can provide for its reorganization. Bankruptcy is not an attractive prospect for creditors because they stand to lose at least some of their money, so they often are willing to negotiate. The prospect of bankruptcy also can be a foundation for bargaining in a turnaround.

Voluntary Bankruptcy

When bankruptcy is granted to a business under bankruptcy law (called *Chapter 11*), the firm is given immediate protection from creditors. Interest payments are suspended, and creditors must wait for their money. A trustee is appointed (sometimes the entrepreneur), and creditor committees are formed.

The great benefit of Chapter 11 is that it buys time for the firm. The firm has 120 days to come up with a reorganization plan and 60 days to obtain acceptance of the plan by creditors.

Under the reorganization plan, debt can be extended. Debt also can be restructured (composed). Interest rates can be increased, and convertible provisions can be introduced to compensate debt holders for any increase in their risk as a result of the restructuring. Occasionally, debt holders need to take part of their claim in the form of equity. Trade creditors can be asked to take equity as payment, and they occasionally need to accept partial payment. If liquidation is the result of the reorganization plan, partial payment is the rule, with the typical payment ranging from zero to 30 cents on the dollar, depending on the priority of the claim.

Involuntary Bankruptcy

In involuntary bankruptcy, creditors force a troubled company into bankruptcy. Although this is regarded as a rare occurrence, it is important for an entrepreneur to know the conditions under which creditors can force a firm into bankruptcy.

A firm can be forced into bankruptcy by any three creditors whose total claim exceeds the value of assets held as security by $5,000, and by any single creditor who meets the above standard when the total number of creditors is less than 12.

Bargaining Power

For creditors, having a firm go into bankruptcy is not particularly attractive. *Bankruptcy, therefore, is a tremendous source of bargaining power for the troubled company.* The reasons bankruptcy is not attractive to creditors are the following: Once protection is granted to a firm, creditors must wait for their money. Further, they are no longer dealing with the troubled company but with a trustee, as well as with other creditors. Even if creditors are willing to wait for their money, they may not get full payment and may have to accept payment in some unattractive form. Last, the legal and administrative costs of bankruptcy, which can be substantial, are paid before any payments are made to creditors.

Faced with these prospects, many creditors conclude that their interests are better served by negotiating with the firm. Since the law defines the priority of creditors' claims, an entrepreneur can use it to determine who might be willing to negotiate.

Since the trade debt has the lowest claim (except for owners), these creditors are often the most willing to negotiate. In fact, the worse the situation, the more willing they may be. If the firm has negative net worth but is generating some cash flow, the trade debt creditors should be willing to negotiate extended terms or partial payment, or both.

However, the secured creditors, with their higher priority claims, may be less willing to negotiate. Many factors affect the willingness of secured creditors to negotiate. Two are the strength of their collateral and their confidence in management. Yet, bankruptcy is still something they wish to avoid for the reasons cited above.

Bankruptcy can free a firm from obligations under executory contracts. This has caused some firms to file for bankruptcy as a way out of union contracts. Since bankruptcy law in this case conflicts with the National Labor Relations Act, the law has been updated and a good-faith test has been added. The firm must be able to demonstrate that a contract prevents it from carrying on its business. While most lawyers say that using bankruptcy law in this way is a questionable practice, some entrepreneurs have used it in this manner.

Intervention

A company in trouble usually will want to use the services of an outside advisor who specializes in turnarounds.

The situation the outside advisor usually finds at intervention is not encouraging. The company is often technically insolvent or has negative net worth. It already may have been put on a cash basis by its suppliers. It may be in default on loans, or if not, it is probably in violation of loan covenants. Call provisions may be exercised. Creditors may be trying to force the company into bankruptcy, and the organization is demoralized.

The critical task is to quickly diagnose the situation, develop an understanding of the company's bargaining position with its many creditors, and produce a detailed cash flow business plan for the turnaround of the organization.

To this end, a turnaround advisor usually quickly signals that change is coming. He or she will elevate the finance function, putting the "cash person" (often the consultant himself) in charge of the business. All payments are put on hold until problems can be diagnosed and remedial actions decided upon. Creditors are called and informed that the company is experiencing difficulties.

Diagnosis

The task of diagnosis can be complicated by the mixture of strategic and financial errors. For example, for a company with large receivables, questions need to be answered about whether receivables are bloated because of poor credit policy or because the company is in a business where liberal credit terms are required to compete.

Diagnosis takes place in three areas: the appropriate strategic posture of the business, analysis of management, and "the numbers."

Strategic Analysis

The purpose of this analysis in a turnaround is to identify the markets in which the company is capable of competing and deciding on a competitive strategy. With small companies, turnaround experts state that most strategic errors relate to the involvement of firms in unprofitable product lines, customers, and geographic areas.

It is outside the scope of this book to cover strategic analysis in detail. (See the many texts in the area.)

Analysis of Management

Analysis of management consists of interviewing members of the management team and coming to a subjective judgment of who belongs and who does not. Turnaround consultants can give no formula for how this is done except that it is the result of judgment that only comes from experience.

The Numbers

Involved in "the numbers" is a detailed cash flow analysis, which will reveal areas for remedial action. The task is to identify and quantify the profitable core of the business.

- *Determine available cash.* The first task is to determine how much cash the firm has available in the near term. This is accomplished by looking at bank balances, receivables (those not being used as security), and the confirmed order backlog.

- *Determine where money is going.* This is a more complex task than it appears to be on the surface. A common technique is called *subaccount analysis,* where every account that posts to cash is found and accounts are arranged in descending order of cash outlays. Accounts then are scrutinized for patterns. These patterns can indicate the functional areas where problems exist. For example, it was noticed that one company had its corporate address on its bills, rather than the lock box address at which checks were processed. The result was that the practice was adding two days to its dollar days outstanding.

- *Calculate percent-of-sales ratios* for different areas of a business and then analyze trends in costs. Typically, several of the trends will show "flex points," where relative costs have changed. For example, for one company that had undertaken a big project, an increase in cost of sales, which coincided with an increase in capacity and in the advertising budget, was noticed. Further analysis revealed this project was not producing enough in dollar contribution to justify its existence. Once the project was eliminated, excess capacity could be reduced to lower the firm's break-even point.

- *Reconstruct the business.* After determining where the cash is coming from and where it is going, the next step is to compare the business as it should be to the business as it is. This involves reconstructing the business from the ground up. For example, a cash budgeting exercise can be undertaken and collections, payments, and so forth determined for a given sales volume. Or the problem can be approached by determining labor, materials, and other direct costs and the overhead required to drive a given sales volume. What is essentially a cash flow business plan is created.

- *Determine differences.* Finally, the cash flow business plan is tied into pro forma balance sheets and income statements. The ideal cash flow plan and financial statements are compared to the business's current financial statements. For example, the pro forma income statements can be compared to existing statements to see where expenses can be reduced. The differences between the projected and actual financial statements form the basis of the turnaround plan and remedial actions.

The most commonly found areas for potential cuts/improvements are these: (1) working capital management, from order processing and billing to receivables, inventory control, and, of course, cash management; (2) payroll; and (3) overcapacity and underutilized assets. It is interesting to note that over 80 percent of potential reduction in expenses can usually be found in workforce reduction.

The Turnaround Plan

The turnaround plan not only defines remedial actions, but because it is a detailed set of projections, provides a means to monitor and control turnaround activity. Further, if the assumptions about unit sales volume, prices, collections, and negotiating success are varied, it can provide a means by which worst-case scenarios—complete with contingency plans—can be constructed.

Since short-term measures may not solve the cash crunch, a turnaround plan gives a firm enough credibility to buy time to put other remedial actions in place. For example, one firm's consultant approached its bank to buy time with the following:

> By reducing payroll and discounting receivables, we can improve cash flow to the point where the firm can be current in five months. If we are successful in negotiating extended terms with trade creditors, then the firm can be current in three months. If the firm can sell some underutilized assets at 50 percent off, it can become current immediately.

The turnaround plan helps address organizational issues. The plan replaces uncertainty with a clearly defined set of actions and responsibilities. Since it signals to the organization that action is being taken, it is of great help in getting employees out of their survival mode. An effective plan breaks tasks into the smallest achievable unit, so successful completion of these simple tasks soon follows and the organization begins to experience success. Soon the downward spiral of organizational morale is broken.

Finally, the turnaround plan is an important source of bargaining power. By identifying problems and providing for remedial actions, the turnaround plan enables the firm's advisors to approach creditors and tell them in very detailed fashion how and when they will be paid. If the turnaround plan proves that creditors are better off working with the company as a going concern, rather than liquidating it, they will most likely be willing to negotiate their claims and terms of payment. Payment schedules can then be worked out that can keep the company afloat until the crisis is over.

Quick Cash

Ideally, the turnaround plan has established enough creditor confidence to buy the turnaround consultant time to raise additional capital and turn underutilized assets into cash. It is imperative, however, to raise cash quickly. The result of the actions described below should be an improvement in cash flow. The solution is far from complete, however, because suppliers need to be satisfied.

For the purpose of quick cash, the working capital accounts hold the most promise.

Accounts receivable is the most liquid noncash asset. Receivables can be factored, but negotiating such arrangements takes time. The best route to cash is discounting receivables. How much receivables can be discounted depends on whether they are securing a loan. For example, a typical bank will loan up to 80 percent of the value of receivables that are under 90 days. As receivables age past the 90 days, the bank needs to be paid. New funds are advanced as new receivables are established as long as the 80 percent and under-90-day criteria are met. Receivables under 90 days can be discounted no more than 20 percent, if the bank obligation is to be met. Receivables over 90 days can be discounted as much as is needed to collect them, since they are not securing bank financing. One needs to use judgment in deciding exactly how large a discount to offer. A common method is to offer a generous discount with a time limit on it, after which the discount is no longer valid. This provides an incentive for the customer to pay immediately. Consultants agree it is better to offer too large a discount than too small a one. If the discount is too small and needs to be followed by further discounts, customers may hold off paying in the hope that another round of discounts will follow.

Inventory is not as liquid as receivables but still can be liquidated to generate quick cash. An inventory "fire sale" gets mixed reviews from turnaround experts. The most common objection is that excess inventory is often obsolete. The second objection is that since, for the small manufacturer, much inventory is work in process, it is therefore not in salable form and requires money to put in salable form. The third is that discounting finished-goods inventory may generate cash but is liable to create customer resistance to restored margins after the company is turned around. The sale of raw materials inventory to *competitors* is generally considered the best route.

One interesting option to the company with a lot of work-in-process inventory is to ease credit terms. It often is possible to borrow more against receivables than against inventory. By easing credit terms, the company can increase its borrowing capacity to perhaps enough to get cash to finish work in process. This option may be difficult to work out because, by the time of intervention, the firm's lenders are likely following the company very closely and may veto the arrangements.

Also relevant to generating quick cash is the policy regarding current sales activity. Increasing the total dollar value of margin, generating cash quickly, and keeping working capital in its most liquid form need to be guiding criteria. Prices and cash discounts need to be increased and credit terms eased. Easing credit terms, however, can conflict with the receivables policy described above. Obviously, care needs to be taken to maintain consistency of policy. Easing credit is really an "excess inventory" policy. The overall idea is to leverage policy in favor of cash first, receivables second, and inventory third.

Putting all accounts payable on hold is the next option. Clearly, this eases the cash flow burden in the near term. Although some arrangement to pay suppliers needs to be made, the most important uses of cash at this stage are meeting payroll and paying lenders. Suppliers may not like this solution, but a company with negative cash flow simply needs to "prioritize" its use of cash. Suppliers are the least likely to force the company into bankruptcy because, under the law, they have a low priority claim.

Dealing with Lenders

The next step in the turnaround is to negotiate with lenders. Lenders need to be satisfied that there is a workable long-term solution, if they are to continue to do business with the company.

However, at the point of intervention, the company is most likely in default on its payments. Or, if payments are current, the financial situation has probably deteriorated to the point where the company is in violation of loan covenants. It also is likely that many of the firm's assets have been pledged as collateral. To make matters worse, it is likely that the troubled entrepreneur has been avoiding his or her lenders during the gestation period and has demonstrated that he or she is not in control of the situation. Credibility has been lost.

It is important for a firm to know that it is not the first ever to default on a loan, that the lender is usually willing to work things out, and that it is still in a position to bargain.

Strategically, there are two sources of bargaining power. The first is that, to a lender, despite its senior claims, bankruptcy is an unattractive result. A low-margin business cannot absorb large losses easily. (Recall that banks typically earn 0.5 percent to 1.0 percent total return on assets.)

The second is credibility. The firm that, through its turnaround specialist, has diagnosed the problem and produced a detailed turnaround plan with best case/worst case scenarios, the aim of which is to prove to the lender that the company is capable of paying, is in a better bargaining position. The plan details specific actions (e.g., layoffs, assets plays, changes in credit policy, etc.) which will be taken.

There are also two tactical sources of bargaining power. First, there is the strength of the lender's collateral. The second is the bank's inferior knowledge of aftermarkets—and the entrepreneur's superior ability to sell.

The following example illustrates that, when the lender's collateral is poor, it has little choice but to look to the entrepreneur for a way out without incurring a loss. It also shows that the entrepreneur's superior knowledge of his business and ability to sell got himself and the lender out of trouble. One turnaround company in the leather business overbought inventory one year, and, at the same time, a competitor announced a new product that made his inventory almost obsolete. Since the entrepreneur went to the lender with the problem, it was willing to work with him. The entrepreneur had plans to sell the inventory at reduced prices and also to enter a new market that looked attractive. The only trouble was he needed more money to do it, and he was already over his credit limit. The lender was faced with the certainty of losing 80 percent of its money and putting its customer out of business or the possibility of losing money by throwing good money after bad. The lender decided to work with the entrepreneur. It got a higher interest rate and put the entrepreneur on a "full following mechanism," which meant that all payments were sent to a lock box. The lender processed the checks and reduced its exposure before it put money in his account.

Another example illustrates the existence of bargaining power with a lender who is undercollateralized and stands to take a large loss. A company was importing look-alike Cabbage Patch dolls from Europe. This was financed with a letter of credit. However, when the dolls arrived in this country, the company could not sell the dolls because the Cabbage Patch doll craze was over. The dolls, and the bank's collateral, were worthless. The company found that the doll heads could be replaced, and with the new heads, the dolls did not look like Cabbage Patch dolls. It found also that one buyer of dolls would buy all the inventory. The company needed $30,000 to buy the new heads and have them put on, so it went back to the bank. The bank said that, if the company wanted the money, key management had to give liens on their houses. When this was refused, the banker was astounded. But what was he going to do? The company had found a way for him to get his money out, so it got the $30,000.

In addition, lenders are often willing to advance money for a company to meet its payroll. This is largely a public relations consideration. The other reason is that, if a company does not meet its payroll, a crisis may be precipitated before the lender can consider its options.

However, it is important to be aware that, when the situation starts to improve, a lender then may call the loan. Such a move will solve the lender's problem but may put the company under. While many bankers will deny this ever happens, some will concede that such an occurrence "depends on the loan officer."

Dealing with Trade Creditors

In dealing with trade creditors, the first step is to understand the strength of the company's bargaining position. Trade creditors have the lowest priority claims should a company file for bankruptcy and, therefore, are often the most willing to deal. In bankruptcy, trade creditors often are left with just a few cents on the dollar.

Another aspect of the bargaining power a firm has with trade creditors is the existence of a turnaround plan. As long as a company demonstrates that it can offer a trade creditor a better result as a going concern than it can in bankruptcy proceedings, the trade creditor should be willing to negotiate.

Also, trade creditors have to deal with the customer relations issue. Trade creditors will work with a troubled company if they see it as a way to preserve a market.

The relative weakness in the position of trade creditors has allowed some turnaround consultants to negotiate impressive deals. For example, one company got trade creditors to agree to a 24-month payment schedule for all outstanding accounts. In return, the firm pledged to keep all new payables current. The entrepreneur was able to keep the company from dealing on a cash basis with many of its creditors and to convert short-term payables into what amounted to long-term debt. The effect on current cash flow was very favorable.

The second step is to prioritize trade creditors according to their importance to the turnaround. The company then needs to take care of those creditors that are most important. For example, one entrepreneur told his controller never to make a commitment he could not keep. The controller was told that, if the company was going to miss a commitment, he was to get on the phone and call. The most important suppliers were told that if something happened and they really needed payment sooner than had been agreed, they were to let the company know and it would do its best to come up with the cash.

The third step in dealing with trade creditors is to switch vendors if necessary. Inevitably, the lower priority suppliers will put the company on cash terms or refuse to do business at all. The troubled company needs to be able to switch suppliers, and its relationship with its priority suppliers will help it to do this, because they can give credit references. One firm said, "We asked our best suppliers to be as liberal with credit references as possible. I don't know if we could have established new relationships without them."

The fourth step in dealing with trade creditors is to communicate effectively. "Dealing with the trade is as simple as telling the truth," said one consultant. If a company is honest, there is not much a creditor can do, and at least it can plan.

Work-Force Reductions

With work-force reduction representing 80 percent of the potential expense reduction, layoffs are inevitable in a turnaround situation.

A number of turnaround consultants use the following guidelines: Turnaround specialists recommend that layoffs be announced to an organization as a one-time reduction in the work force and be done all at one time. They recommend further that layoffs be accomplished as soon as possible, since employees will never regain their productivity until they feel some measure of security. Finally, they recommend that a firm cut deeper than seems necessary. The reason for this is that if other remedial actions turn out to be difficult to implement, the difference may have to be made up in further reductions in the work force. For example, it is one thing to set out to reduce capacity by half and quite another thing to sell or sublet half a plant.

Longer-term Remedial Actions

If the turnaround plan has created enough credibility and has bought the firm time, longer-term remedial actions can be implemented.

These actions will usually fall into three categories:

- *Systems and procedures.* Systems and procedures that contributed to the problem in the first place can be improved, or they can be implemented.
- *Asset plays.* Assets that could not be liquidated in a shorter time frame can be liquidated. For example, real estate could be sold. Many smaller companies, particularly older ones, carry real estate on their balance sheet at far below market value. This could be sold and leased back or could be borrowed against to generate cash.
- *Creative solutions.* Creative solutions that depend, of course, on the situation need to be found. For example, one firm had a large amount of inventory that was useless in its current business. However, it found that if the inventory could be assembled into parts, there would be a market for it. The company shipped the inventory to Jamaica, where labor rates

were low, for assembly, and it was able to sell very profitably the entire inventory.

As was stated at the beginning of the chapter, many companies—even companies that are insolvent or have negative net worth or both—can be rescued and restored to profitability. It is perhaps helpful to recall another quote from Winston Churchill: "I have nothing to offer but blood, toil, tears, and sweat."

Chapter Summary

1. An inevitable part of the entrepreneurial process is that firms are born, grow, get ill, and die.
2. Numerous signals of impending trouble—strategic issues, poor planning and financial controls, and running out of cash—invariably point to a core cause: top management.
3. Crises don't develop overnight. Often it takes 18 months to five years before the company is sick enough to trigger a turnaround intervention.
4. Both quantitative and qualitative signals can predict patterns and actions that could lead to trouble.
5. Bankruptcy, usually an entrepreneur's nightmare, can actually be a valuable tool and source of bargaining power to help a company survive and recover.
6. Turnaround specialists begin with a diagnosis of the numbers—cash, strategic market issues, and management—and develop a turnaround plan.
7. The turnaround plan defines remedial action to generate cash, deal with lenders and trade creditors, begin long-term renewal, and is a way to monitor progress.

Study Questions

1. What do entrepreneurs need to know about how companies get into and out of trouble? Why?
2. Why do most turnaround specialists invariably discover that it is management that is at the root cause of trouble?
3. Why is it difficult for existing management to detect and to act early on signals of trouble?
4. What are some of the key predictors and signals that warn of impending trouble?
5. Why can bankruptcy be the entrepreneur's ally?
6. What diagnosis is done to detect problems, and why and how does cash play the central role?
7. What are the main components of a turnaround plan and why are these so important?

MIND STRETCHERS
Have You Considered?

1. In the 1970s, IBM had more cash on its balance sheet than the total sales of the rest of the computer industry. Why, and how, did IBM get into so much trouble 10 years later?
2. Talk in person to an entrepreneur who has personal loan guarantees and has been through bankruptcy. What lessons were learned?
3. Can Microsoft become a troubled company? When, and why?

Case
Paul J. Tobin

Preparation Questions

1. Evaluate the situation, and harvest options for BCGI.
2. How should Paul think about the process? What should he do with the RFQ (Exhibit N)?
3. Evaluate the deals struck in 1990 and 1992 (Exhibits H and K).
4. What do investment bankers do? How do they make money?
5. What should Paul do, and why?

Paul Tobin, founder, CEO, and chairman of Boston Communications Group, Inc. (BCGI) had already been through a venture-backed harvest, but this situation was quite different than anything he'd faced before. As he prepared for his board meeting in early November 1995, Paul wondered whether this was the right time to harvest BCGI, a provider of support services to the

©1996, Jeffry A. Timmons. This case was prepared by Dan D'Heilly and Andrea Alyse, under the direction of Jeffry A. Timmons, Franklin W. Olin Professor, Babson College, Babson Park, MA. Funding provided by the Ewing Marion Kauffman Foundation. All rights reserved.

wireless carrier industry, and how best to handle the process. The board had enthusiastically encouraged him at its August meeting to test the waters for a possible strategic sale, but the board also believed substantial value in the company was in the future. Should he wait? Given BCGI's product lines and strategy, both the board and management felt that a cash sale to a large corporate strategic buyer probably made the most sense. Recent projections indicated that the company would exceed $100 million in revenue by the end of the decade. If this was achieved, the company could conceivably be valued in the $150–250 million range by the year 2000, but today he felt fortunate to have a prospective buyer willing to pay $60–75 million.

An eventual harvest was a given. After all, that is what an entrepreneur signs up for when accepting a venture capital investment: the only issues were when and how. One of Paul's outside directors and a founding shareholder was a professor at a nearby college widely considered the world's leading school in entrepreneurship. He suggested a dual strategy in order to maximize the company's terminal value: Create a competition among investment banks to determine whether a strategic sale or an initial public offering (IPO) made the most sense. This strategy would best enable the capital markets to value the company at its maximum while determining which harvest mechanism would be the best overall fit, given the company's strategy, stage of development, and future opportunities.

Paul's team had done it before with a venture capital-backed company in only two years: launch, grow, and harvest. This time around it had taken five years, a capital investment of nearly $12 million, major strategic changes, deal restructuring, and at least one false start in the paging business to create enough value to make the harvest attractive. By the late summer of 1995, it appeared that BCGI had become the high potential venture Paul and his partners had envisioned. The prospect for a harvest was, for the first time, becoming a reality. One corporate buyer, GTE Corp., was showing serious interest, and while initial contact was a cautious, cat-and-mouse exercise, early indications seemed to suggest a valuation of as much as $75 million for the company. There was considerable joy at this possibility among the management team, founding shareholders, and investors.

The Wireless Telecommunications Communications Industry

The consumer wireless telecommunications industry was divided into three segments: paging devices, enhanced specialized mobile radio communications (ESMR), and cellular phoning. Cellular phoning first emerged in the early 1980s when the Federal Communications Committee (FCC) granted frequency concessions for wireless telephony. After dividing the country

into 734 potential geographic market segments, two frequencies per segment were granted, resulting in duopolistic competition between carriers.

In the 1980s the cellular industry underwent significant consolidation as cellular carriers sought to achieve greater market coverage and economies of scale in operations, marketing, and customer service. As of mid-1995, the majority of cellular licenses were held by a small number of companies, with the remaining cellular licenses divided between approximately 200 others (See *Appendix A* for a listing of the top 50 cellular companies.)

Between 1985 and 1995, wireless phoning was considered one of the fastest growing areas of the telecommunications industry. The Cellular Telecommunications Industry Association (CTIA) projected that the number of cellular subscribers in the United States would continue to rise dramatically: It had gone from 340,000 in 1985, to a projected 34 million in 1995, and the number of subscribers was projected to grow to 116 million by the year 2005. Aggregate annual service revenues from cellular subscribers were expected to grow from approximately $482 million in 1985 to a projected $19 billion in 1995 (See *Exhibit A* for industry forecast). A number of factors contributed to this growth, including the build-out of the cellular network infrastructure, the decreasing cost of cellular telephones, technological improvements in the size and battery life of cellular telephones, and greater acceptance of wireless phones.

One important source of revenues for cellular carriers were subscribers that used their phones outside their home service areas. These users, known as "roamers," were projected to be billed nearly $2.5 billion in 1995, or 13 percent of total revenues. From 1990 to 1995, roaming revenues grew at a compounded annual rate of 41 percent compared to 33 percent for aggregate wireless service revenues (See *Exhibit B*). Roaming revenues were generated when an agreement was in place between cellular carriers, and a roamer made a call from the non-home carrier's territory. Under these agreements, home carriers billed subscribers on behalf of the servicing carrier whose territory the subscriber was roam-

EXHIBIT A

Wireless Revenue Forecast ($ billions)

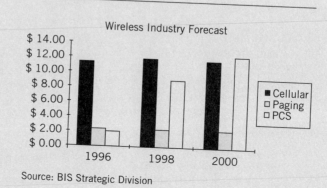

Source: BIS Strategic Division

EXHIBIT B

Cellular Industry Revenues (billions)

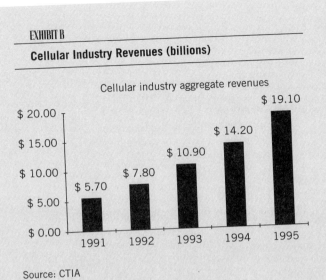

Cellular industry aggregate revenues

Source: CTIA

ing. The home carrier often did not retain any revenues, yet still bore all collection and fraud risks associated with the call. Increasing amounts of fraud, projected at over $400 million for 1995, caused some carriers to terminate roaming agreements in markets with high incidents of fraud. In addition, both the home and the servicing carrier bore costs associated with the inter-carrier roaming agreement. These costs related primarily to managing the authorized-user databases and to validating roaming calls. No carrier had licenses or agreements in every market, so roamers were limited in their ability to place and receive cellular telephone calls.

Cellular carriers were also developing strategies to penetrate untapped market segments. Due to relatively high marketing and service costs, cellular carriers had generally only accepted subscribers who met certain credit, volume, and use standards. There were many people who didn't qualify for cellular service: people with credit problems, low-volume users, temporary subscribers, and people who wanted to authorize multiple users for one account were often denied service by both carriers in their region.

Although the subscriber base was increasing rapidly, profitability lagged. This was primarily due to a high customer turnover rate and to low revenue per customer. The average revenue per subscriber was steadily declining due to an increasing number of lower-volume cellular subscribers. Cellular carriers looked to reduce the subscriber churn rate, historically between 26 percent and 36 percent per year, through increased customer satisfaction. Customer retention was linked to a carrier's ability to respond promptly to subscriber inquiries regarding billing matters, rate plans, service problems and other related issues, but the demands of hiring, training, and retaining a large number of customer service representatives made it difficult to provide high-quality, 24-hour, 7-day service on a cost-effective basis.

It was expected that the wireless communication industry would change significantly with the introduction of Personal Communication System (PCS) technology (See Appendix B for PCS industry overview) and the termination of the duopolistic market structure. While PCS offerings would vary by carrier, a likely set of services would include local cellular-like voice service combined with data messaging, wireless data service, and wireless office telephony. The FCC planned to auction three to six PCS licenses in most markets across the United States. Analysts predicted that the wireless industry would become increasingly fragmented with the introduction of PCS, and that market share would come to be dominated by multiple-service providers, each with a variety of service packages offered at different price points.

Acquiring Relevant Entrepreneurial Experience

Paul Tobin began his career as a securities analyst at Chase Manhattan Bank after receiving his undergraduate degree in economics from Stonehill College. He earned his MBA in marketing/finance through the full-time program at Northeastern University in 1970 and launched U.S. Glass with two partners. U.S. Glass was a middleman connecting large retail chains and franchises with reputable glaziers from New England to the mid-Atlantic region. When a window was broken, the local manager had a phone number to call for fast, reliable, and economical service.

The U.S. Glass partnership dissolved in 1978 when Paul sold his interest to his former partners. Next, Paul tried his hand at light-industrial manufacturing and chemicals brokering. Then in 1980, he joined Satellite Business Systems (a joint venture of IBM, Comsat, and Aetna) as a salesman. Paul was quickly promoted to regional sales and marketing manager at this telecom joint venture (launched with nearly $1 billion in startup capital). Then in 1984, Paul was recruited by a headhunter to interview for the position of president for Metromedia's cellular telephone operation in Boston and Worcester, Massachusetts. He got the job. Under Paul Tobin's leadership, the Boston CellularOne operation gained a 75 percent market share in a region that achieved a 1 percent market penetration in the first three years of the embryonic cellular car phone industry.

Creating a Venture–backed Wireless Company

In 1987, John Kluge, chairman of Metromedia, put his telecom holdings up for sale: Cellular and paging operations in Boston, Dallas, Chicago, New York, Philadelphia, and many other markets across the country. Having led the launch and development of CellularOne in Boston, Paul knew that the market still had significant potential. He put together a team of his top executives at CellularOne, and introduced himself to the venture capital community.

After a series of meetings, Paul secured an agreement with Boston Ventures. One of a select number of firms known for doing deals of this magnitude (See *Exhibit C: Size Structure of the VC Industry*). Boston Ventures had also handled many of Kluge's telecom purchases. They had taken Metromedia public, then private through a leveraged buy-out, so they had both access and credibility. Paul presented an offer to purchase Boston CellularOne for $130 million, but SW Bell offered to acquire John Kluge's entire telecom portfolio for $1.65 billion. The game was over. However, Paul had also formed a relationship with the people at the Boston venture capital firm of Burr, Egan, Deleage, & Co., and they decided to back Paul's team in a cellular venture. Paul was concerned that SW Bell would want to put their own people into executive management at Boston CellularOne and he did not intend to wait around for the takeover.

That spring, they acquired the Portsmouth cellular license (Southern Maine and Southeastern New Hampshire) for $2 million, or $9 per pop,[1] and Paul tendered his resignation to SW Bell. However, Boston CellularOne was a model operation, and SW Bell knew that Paul would take his team with him, so instead of letting him go, they made him an unusual offer. They allowed him to stay on as president of Boston CellularOne with the stipulation that he operate Portsmouth CellularOne, located an hour and a half north of Boston, through a remote management team.

Over the next 18 months, the Boston CellularOne team successfully provided remote executive manage-ment for the Portsmouth operation. Then in 1989, Paul managed to obtain an offer for Portsmouth Cellular worth just over $37 million, or $148 per pop, at an industry seminar. The lead venture capital investor, Burr, Egan, Deleage, & Co., received proceeds of $16.9 million, for a 132.5 percent IRR (including a later-stage subordinated-debt investment of $3 million). When Paul announced his intention to create another venture in the cellular industry, they were interested in leading a syndicate to fund his next deal.

Creating Another Venture–backed Wireless Company

Three members of the management team that built and sold Portsmouth Cellular left SW Bell and formed a new company in 1989, Boston Communications Group, Inc. Paul Tobin, Bob Sullivan, and Fritz von Mering planned to purchase cellular licenses when possible, and to pursue other wireless businesses as opportunities appeared.

Paul was pleased that Brion Applegate of Burr, Egan, Deleage, & Co. was able to put together a syndicate with Highland Capital Partners. They were well-respected firms with knowledgeable partners, and he anticipated that BCGI would benefit from their contributions as members of his Board of Directors. Although pleased with the investors, Paul was not entirely pleased with the terms of the investment. The venture capital market was being squeezed in 1989: The IPO window was tight and venture capitalists were having difficulty raising new funds. (See *Exhibits D, E* and *F* for venture market information)

However, the demand for cellular licenses peaked in 1989 (See *Exhibit G*, Price per Pop), and the most enticing opportunities in cellular were rural service areas (RSA), but even that market was overpriced. In 1990, they purchased the RSA license for Franklin county in southern Massachusetts for $6 million, or $90 per pop. BCGI paid $1.5 million in cash and the seller took paper for the rest. The Franklin county license had not been developed; Paul and his team installed an infrastructure and grew the business from the ground up.

BCGI launched three other new companies in 1990: Cellular Service of Washington DC, a sales and service company; BeeperPlus, a paging company in upstate New York; and ROAMER*plus* (aka Cellular Express), a company based in the Boston area that processed remote transactions for cellular carriers. BeeperPlus and the Franklin county license were sold in 1992, for just under a million dollars, and for $8 million ($120 per pop), respectively. In 1995, Cellular Service of Washington, D.C., was also sold for less than a million dollars. Paul recalled the situation:

> Our objective was to acquire, build and operate cellular licenses. But the price of cellular licenses skyrocketed so we had to divert our strategy and try a couple of different things.

EXHIBIT C

Size-Structure of the Venture Capital Industry

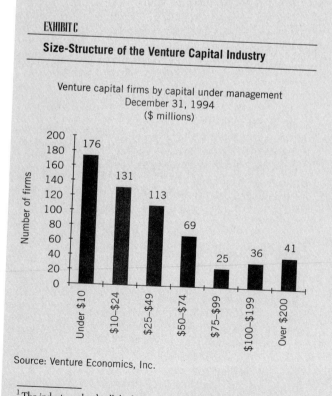

Venture capital firms by capital under management
December 31, 1994
($ millions)

Number of firms:
- Under $10: 176
- $10–$24: 131
- $25–$49: 113
- $50–$74: 69
- $75–$99: 25
- $100–$199: 36
- Over $200: 41

Source: Venture Economics, Inc.

---

[1] The industry valued cellular licenses based on the population—per pop—in the area under license.

EXHIBIT D

Venture Capital Resources by Type of Firm ($ millions)

Type of Firm	Average Capital/Firm		Median Size of Firm		Number of Firms	
	1990	1995*	1990	1995*	1990	1995*
Independent Private	$56.1	$ 61.0	$21.2	$29.9	514	424
Corporate Financial	67.6	103.7	22.3	16.0	68	39
Corporate Industrial	30.5	37.8	20.0	26.7	82	63
Totals	$54.1	$ 61.7	$21.0	$20.0	664	521

*projected

Source: Venture Economics, Inc.

EXHIBIT E

Venture Capital Market

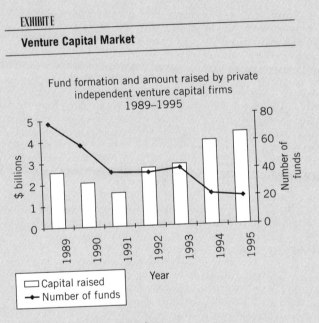

Fund formation and amount raised by private independent venture capital firms 1989–1995

☐ Capital raised
◆ Number of funds

Source: Venture Economics, Inc.

Fortunately, ROAMER*plus* was a winner. ROAMER*plus* allowed carriers to profit from customers traveling outside of their cellular service area: These customers were called roamers. The FCC duopoly system had created a fragmented service industry, so roamers were sometimes unable to make calls. ROAMER*plus* processed calls placed by unregistered roamers.

To complete a call, the carrier simply forwarded unregistered users to BCGI's automated call processing system and the carrier was compensated directly by BCGI for the airtime. The majority of calls did not require an operator, but operators were available as needed. Carriers were attracted to this service because it provided additional revenues with little additional cost. BCGI bore a substantial collection risk and reserved 15 percent of gross revenues for uncollectible ROAMER*plus* charges. However, BCGI needed funding to build a nationwide telecom network, for working capital, and to develop the software to make it work.

Paul's investors had originally agreed to supply $10 million, but had staged the investment so that disbursements were linked to specific acquisitions (See *Exhibit H*, 1990 Term Sheet). BCGI had received $6 million for the Franklin county acquisition, starting the cellular service company, the paging company, and the roaming service. The other $4 million was committed to acquire 20 ground-to-air frequencies from NYNEX, but that deal fell through when the New England wireless market weakened in 1990.

In lieu of the NYNEX deal, the investors committed to funding the purchase of a paging company in Rhode Island that had 15,000 subscribers. After weeks of negotiations, an intent to purchase agreement was executed. However, adverse developments in the credit and capital markets raised strong enough doubts that Paul decided to terminate the agreement. Final first-round funding totaled $6 million for acquisitions and working capital; unfortunately, BCGI had already spent the entire amount.

In 1990, Paul went back to his investors with a new strategy and a request for additional funding. He repositioned the company to focus on the ROAMER*plus* market, providing services to cellular carriers. Burr, Egan, Deleage, & Co. and Highland Capital Partners brought Hancock Venture Partners into the syndicate (See *Exhibit I*, Venture Firm Summaries), and renegotiated the deal with management. The syndicate invested an additional $4 million, and the management team contributed $900,000 to provide the rest of the financing. However, the recapitalization came with a price: The investors wanted a five-year put[2] clause that would rapidly transfer ownership of the

---

[2] A put (called a "mandatory redemption" in the 1990 term sheet) is a contract allowing the holder to sell a given number of securities back to the issuer of the contract at a fixed price for a given period of time.

EXHIBIT F

Trends in the IPO Market

Firm commitment IPOs

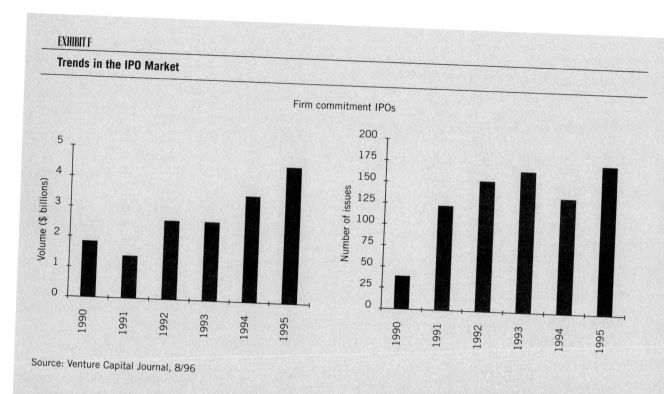

Source: Venture Capital Journal, 8/96

EXHIBIT G

Cellular License Price per Pop

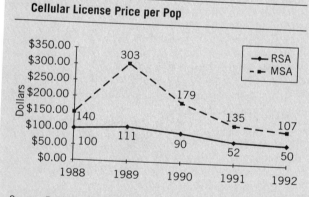

Source: Paul Kagan & Associates

case we were unable to come up with the capital to pay off the venture guys, their money would stay in. From then on, it would accrue at an additional 25 percent interest a year. We wanted a call because we believed in ourselves and thought it was fair. I probably should have been tougher in the negotiations.

Hockey Stick Growth

By late 1992, the company was growing rapidly (See *Exhibit J* for financial statement) as ROAMER*plus* gained momentum. Bill Egan, a partner at Burr, Egan, Deleage, & Co., suggested that he would like to renegotiate the deal because the original note lacked the proper management incentives. (See *Exhibit K* for 1992 Term Sheet which governed the restructuring) Relations with the investors had remained positive, though occasionally strained, as the company underperformed its original plan. In particular, Brion Applegate had worked closely with Paul's team since the mid-1980s and was held in the highest regard as a partner, advisor, and friend.

Another opportunity arose in 1993 when Ameritech asked for off-hour customer service support. BCGI already offered 24-hour, 7-day service for ROAMER*plus* customers, operators just needed additional training to service Ameritech customers. BCGI called this new business Carrier Support Services. This service was labor intensive and was characterized by high personnel turnover. Several carriers soon followed Ameritech and outsourced off-hour customer service activities to BCGI.

In 1994, cellular industry leader Brian Boyle (See *Exhibit L* for biographical sketches) joined the BCGI team. In the mid-1980s, Brian had founded APPEX

company to the syndicate if BCGI could not provide liquidity. BCGI agreed, with the condition that there also be a call. Paul recalled that the investors readily agreed.

We structured the original deal to be 50/50 after a 25 percent annual rate of return for the investors. Then we converted it to preferred and we got a 50/50 split on the returns after a 35 percent rate of return. They also got to pick three people for the board, and I only had one seat, then the four of us picked the fifth member of the board, so they had control. It sounded pretty onerous at the time, but we were in no position to argue. We could renegotiate if things went well, if not, then who cares?

The put was to protect the venture guys. The terms were that they could put their interest to us at fair market value [e.g., forcing BCGI to buy-back the investors' shares] as determined by a jury of three; one of theirs, one of mine and one independent chosen by the first two, at five years. In

EXHIBIT H

Excerpts[6] from Summary of Terms for Proposed Private Placement, 2/27/90

Radio Telephone Systems (dba BCGI)

Current Outstanding Securities

100 shares of Common Stock (Common) sold to Burr, Egan, Deleage & Co. (BED); 100 shares of Common Stock issuable to Highland Capital Partners Limited Partnership (HCP) upon conversion of $305,000 demand convertible note; and shares of Common and/or options to purchase Common representing an aggregate of up to 28 shares issued to or reserved for issuance to Management (as defined below).

At or prior to the Closing (as defined below, each share of Common held by BED will be converted into 100 shares of Class A Common Stock (Class A Common); HCP will convert its $305,000 demand convertible note into 100 shares of Common and each such share of Common will be converted into 100 shares of Class A Common; and each share (and/or option to purchase a share of) Common held by Management will be converted into 100 shares of (and/or options to purchase 100 shares of) Class B Common Stock (Class B Common).

Investors

Entities affiliated with BED will invest an aggregate of $4,445,000; HCP will invest $4,445,000; and $2,500,000 will come from other investors. Management may invest up to $125,000 of the remaining $2,500,000 at the initial closing (the Closing), and the balance will be invested by Fidelity Ventures (Fidelity).

Type of Security and Amount of Investment

An aggregate of $10,800,000 of Non-Convertible Preferred Stock (Preferred) and an aggregate of $590,000 of Class A Common. The Preferred and the Class A Common (the Securities) will be sold in two closings. The initial Closing will involve an aggregate of approximately $4,746,000 of Securities, and will be conditioned on the obtaining of all necessary approvals for the acquisition of certain radio paging systems from NYNEX as well as on the obtaining of all necessary regulatory approvals for the change in control of the Company resulting from this financing.

	First Closing		Second Closing	
	P.S.	Cl.A.C.S	P.S.	Cl.A.C.S
BED	$1,781,250*	$ 70,833	$2,493,750	$ 99,166
HCP	1,781,250*	70,833	2,493,750	99,166
Others	937,500	104,167	1,312,500	145,834

*Payment will be in cash and surrender of demand notes: all other payments will be in cash.

Cellular Express, Inc.

Prior to the Closing, an accommodation will be reached among the Company, BED and HCP with respect to Cellular Express, Inc.

Bank Line of Credit

Prior to the second closing, the Company shall use its best efforts to obtain a bank line of credit in an amount of at least $2 million on terms approved by the Board. If such line of credit cannot be obtained, the Company and Investors will negotiate for the Investors to provide additional financing on mutually agreeable terms.

Post-Second Closing Capitalization

Preferred		$10,800,000
Class A Common:		39,400 shares
Class B Common:	Committed to Management	2,800 shares
	Uncommitted Shares	8,313 shares
Total		50,513 shares

Bridge Advances

Any bridge advances made by Highland prior to Closing will be structured to bring Highland's position into line with BED, subject to FCC and other regulatory requirements. Additional bridge advances will be conditioned on Management preparing cash budgets for the existing business of the Company for the approval of the Investors.

---

[6] The non-excerpted areas of this term sheet cover important boilerplate deal points including voting, default, liquidation, stock options, anti-dilution, key-man insurance, and other protective provisions.

Price per Share

$1,000 per share of Preferred and $30.50 per share of Class A Common.

Description of Preferred

1) <u>Dividend Provisions:</u> A cumulative dividend will accrue at a rate of 10 percent per annum on the original purchase price and any accrued but unpaid dividends of the Preferred. Such dividend will be payable only if (a) as, and when declared by the Board of Directors (Board) or (b) upon a Liquidation Event (as defined below) or redemption of the Preferred.

2) <u>Mandatory Redemption:</u> On the fifth (5th) anniversary of the Closing the Company shall redeem the Preferred by paying in cash the Preferred Liquidation Amount. If the Company fails to redeem the Preferred when due, the per annum dividend of the Preferred shall thereafter increase by $10 on the first day of each calendar quarter; provided, however, that the Preferred dividend rate shall not in any event exceed 15 percent per annum.

3) <u>Optional Redemption:</u> The Company may redeem the Preferred in whole or in part at any time, without penalty or premium, by paying in cash the Preferred Liquidation Amount.

Description of Class A Common

1) <u>Dividend Provisions:</u> A cumulative dividend on the Class A Common will accrue at the rate of $2,745 per share per annum. Such dividend will be payable only (a) if, as, and when determined by the Board or (b) upon a Liquidation Event.

2) <u>Liquidation Preference:</u> Upon any Liquidation Event, the holder of Class A Common will be entitled to receive in preference to the holders of Class B Common an amount per share (Class A Liquidation Amount) equal to the greater of (a) $30.50 plus any dividends accrued on the Class A Common but not paid, or (b) the amount they would have received had they converted the Class A Common to Class B Common immediately prior to such Liquidation Event.

3) <u>Conversion:</u> A holder of Class A Common will have the right to convert the Class A Common, at the option of the holder, at any time, into shares of Class B Common. The total number of shares of Class B Common into which the Class A Common may be converted initially will be determined by dividing by $30.50. The conversion price will be subject to adjustment as provided in paragraph (5) below.

4) <u>Automatic Conversion:</u> The Class A Common will be automatically converted into Class B Common, at the then applicable conversion price, in the event of an underwritten public offering of shares of the Class B Common at the public offering price per share that is not less than $90.00 in an offering of not less than $10,000,000.

5) <u>Voting Rights:</u> Except with respect to election of directors and certain protective provisions, the holders of Class A Common will have the right to that number of votes equal to the number of shares of Class B Common issuable upon conversion of the Class A Common. Election of directors and the protective provisions will be as described under "Board Representation and Meetings" and "Protective Provisions," respectively, below.

6) <u>Protective Provisions:</u> Consent of the holders of at least two-thirds of the Class A Common will be required for (i) any sale by the company of all or substantially all of its assets, (ii) any merger or consolidation of the company with another entity, (iii) any liquidation or winding up of the Company, (iv) any amendment of the Company's charter or by-laws, (v) any dividend on, or repurchase of, any security other than the Preferred or Class A Common in accordance with their respective terms, or (vi) certain other actions materially affecting the Class A Common.

Description of Class B Common

Upon a Liquidation Event, after payment of the Preferred Liquidation Amounts and the Class A Liquidation Amounts, the remaining net assets of the Company will be distributed pro-rata to the holders of Class B Common. The Class B Common shall have one vote per share on all matters presented to the stockholders of the Company generally.

Board Representation and Meetings

The charter will provide that the authorized number of directors is five. The Class A Common (voting as a class) will elect three directors; the Class B Common (voting as a class) will elect one director; and the fifth director will be elected by the Class A Common and Class B Common, voting as separate classes.

Corporation and grew it to $16 million in annual revenues before selling to EDS for $48 million. In 1989, he founded Credit Technology, Inc., a developer of custom software for the cellular industry. Credit Technology generated approximately $10 million in 1994. Brian and Paul negotiated a merger between BCGI and Credit Technology which essentially combined the companies with a 50/50 stock split. The merger passed the BCGI board, but stalled in the Credit Technology board meeting. Brian became vice chairman in charge of developing new wireless services.

EXHIBIT I

Summary of Venture Firm Activities

Burr, Egan, Deleage, & Co.

Burr, Egan, Deleage, & Co., founded in 1979, is based in Boston, Massachusetts, with one additional office located in San Francisco, California. This is a private venture capital firm which invests its own capital and functions either as a deal originator or as an investor in deals created by others. Current capital under management is $600 million. The company provides financing for projects needing seed, startup, first-stage, second-stage, or mezzanine capital, and projects focused on leveraged buyouts, control-block purchases or other, special situations. The minimum investment made is $1 million, to companies located in the United States. Industry preferences for investment from Burr, Egan, Deleage, & Co. are communications, computer-related, distribution, electronic components and instrumentation, genetic engineering, industrial products and equipment, medical and health-related, and education-related. The company will not consider investing in oil and gas exploration and production or real estate. Return on investment is the company's primary concern and there are no additional fees charged for their services.

Highland Capital Partners

Highland Capital Partners, founded in 1988, is located in Boston, Massachusetts. This private venture capital firm invests its own capital and prefers to function as a deal originator but will consider investing in deals created by others. Current capital under management is $280 million. The company provides financing for projects needing seed, research and development, startup, first-stage, second-stage, or mezzanine capital, and projects focused on control-block purchases or other, special situations. The minimum investment made is $500,000 to companies located in the United States. Industry preferences for investment from Highland Capital Partners are communications, computer-related, electronic components and instrumentation, genetic engineering, and medical and health-related. The company will not consider investing in real estate. Return on investment is the company's primary concern and there are additional closing and service fees.

Hancock Venture Partners, Inc.

Hancock Venture Partners, Inc., founded in 1982, is located in Boston, Massachusetts with one additional office located in London, United Kingdom. This venture capital subsidiary of John Hancock will function either as a deal originator or as an investor in deals created by others. Current capital under management is $2 billion. The company provides financing for projects needing first-stage, second-stage, or mezzanine capital, and projects focused on leveraged buyouts. The minimum investment made is $2 million to companies located in the United States. Industry preferences for investment from Hancock Venture Partners, Inc., are communications, computer-related, distribution, electronic components and instrumentation, energy and natural resources, industrial products and equipment, finance and insurance, and publishing. The company will not consider investing in oil and gas exploration and production or real estate. Return on investment is the company's primary concern and there are no additional fees charged for their services.

Source: Pratt's Guide to Venture Capital, 1996 Edition.

EXHIBIT J

BCGI Financials

Boston Communications Group
Pro Forma Financials
Year Ended December 31,

	1991	1992	1993	1994	1995E(5)	CAGR 1991–1994	CAGR 1994–1995
Revenues	$ 1,447	$7,557	$10,244	$21,520	$35,500	145.9%	65.0%
Costs and expenses (1)	1,838	6,504	9,684	20,184	32,602		
EBITDA	(391)	1,053	560	1,336	2,898	12.6%(6)	116.9%
Depreciation and amortization (2)	629	613	681	600	926		
Income (loss from operations)	(1,020)	440	(121)	736	1,972		168.0%
Interest expense (3)	100	100	100	100	100		
Pre-tax income (loss)	(1,120)	340	(221)	636	1,872		
Assumed net income after taxes (4)	$(1,120)	$ 204	$ (221)	$ 382	$ 1,123		194.4%

(Continued)

EXHIBIT J

BCGI Financials (continued)

Boston Communications Group
Pro Forma Financials
Year Ended December 31,

	1991	1992	1993	1994	1995E(5)	CAGR 1991–1994	CAGR 1994–1995
Growth Rates							
Revenues	—	422.3%	35.6%	110.1%	65.0%		
EBITDA	—	NM	−46.8%	138.4%	116.9%		
EBIT	—	NM	NM	NM	168.0%		
Pre-tax	—	NM	NM	NM	194.4%		
Net income	—	NM	NM	NM	194.4%		
Margin Analysis							
EBITDA	−27.0%	13.9%	5.5%	6.2%	8.2%		
EBIT	−70.5%	5.8%	−1.2%	3.4%	5.6%		
Pre-tax	−77.4%	4.5%	−2.2%	3.0%	5.3%		
Net income	−77.4%	2.7%	−2.2%	1.8%	3.2%		

Source: Company's projections as of June, 1995. Pro forma to exclude discontinued operations.

(1) Corporate overhead allocated as a percentage of Cellular Express revenues
(2) Assumes all depreciation and amortization attributable to Cellular Express
(3) Assumes historical interest expense of $100,000 for Cellular Express
(4) Assumes a 40% tax rate
(5) Excludes $2,500 in revenue and $250 in operating income which is assumed to be from discontinued operations
   Assumes $100,000 of interest expense attributable to continuing operations
(6) CAGR from 1992–1994

EXHIBIT K

Summary of Terms for Proposed Restructuring, 12/31/92

1. The new capital structure for Boston Communications Group (BCGI or the Company) will consist of the following:

   a. Common Stock—One vote per share.

   b. Redeemable Preferred Stock—These shares have no voting rights. The shares will be subject to redemption at the option of either the BCGI or the holder thereof on the earlier to occur of (i) 6/30/97 or (ii) the sale of BCGI's Roamer Plus business, at their purchase price, plus unpaid dividends. The shares may also be redeemed, on a pro-rata basis, with the proceeds of bank financing at any time without penalty. The shares will have an 8 percent cumulative dividend and a liquidation purchase price, plus unpaid dividends.

   c. Convertible Preferred Stock—These shares may be converted to Common Stock at any time, and the Class B may be converted to Class A at any time, subject in each case to the prior receipt of any necessary approvals of the FCC or State regulatory bodies. The holders of the Convertible Preferred will be entitled to convert their shares into 75 percent of the total Common Stock which may be outstanding from time to time at and after the date of restructuring, assuming the exercise or conversion of all options, warrants, and other securities which are convertible into or exchangeable for Common Stock. Conversion of the Class B Convertible Preferred to Class A Convertible Preferred will be on a one-for-one basis. These shares will have a liquidation preference in the amount of their purchase price, junior to the Redeemable Preferred Stock and will have no dividend. The shares will be subject to put/call provisions at fair market value following the redemption of the redeemable Preferred Stock, but not before 6/30/97. There will be two classes of Convertible Preferred Stock:
   Class A—Voting—Each share shall be entitled to that number of votes equal to the number of shares of Common Stock into which it is then convertible.
   Class B—Nonvoting.

2. The funds managed by Burr, Egan, Deleage & Company (BEDCO) will exchange the 375 shares of old Class A Common Stock for 375 shares of the new Class A Convertible Preferred Stock.

3. Highland Capital Partners L.P. (Highland) will exchange its Convertible Note (Class A Common Stock) in the principal amount of $275,000 for 275 of the new Class B Convertible Preferred Stock.

4. BEDCO, Highland, Hancock Venture Partners III and Paul Tobin (the Investors) will exchange their Convertible Notes (Class B Common Stock) in the principal amount of $400,000 for 200 shares of the new Class B Convertible Preferred Stock.

5. The management group (consisting of Paul Tobin, Robert Sullivan, Frederick von Mering, Jeffry Timmons, Clifford Tallman and Robin Leonard) (Management) will exchange their stock options to acquire 850 shares of the old Class C Common Stock for 283.3 shares of the new Common Stock, which shall constitute 25 percent of the total Common Stock which may be outstanding from time to time at and after the date of restructuring, assuming the exercise or conversion of all options, warrants, and other securities which are convertible into or exchangeable for Common Stock.

6. The holders of Senior Subordinated Notes (except the holders of the rollover notes) will exchange their notes, in the total amount of $9,991,118, plus accrued interest (for 1991) in the total amount of $1,855,900, for Redeemable Preferred Stock.

7. The holders of the rollover notes (except Kim Mayyasi) will exchange their notes in the total principal amount of $865,934, plus accrued interest (for 1991) in the total amount of $158,100, for Redeemable Preferred Stock.

8. As a result of these exchanges, the Company will be held as follows:

BEDCO	375.0	Shares of Class A Convertible Preferred Stock
BEDCO	71.0	Shares of Class B Convertible Preferred Stock
Highland	333.5	Shares of Class B Convertible Preferred Stock
Hancock	62.5	Shares of Class B Convertible Preferred Stock
Tobin	7.5	Shares of Class B Convertible Preferred Stock
Mgmt.	283.8	Shares of Common Stock
Total	1,133.3	

BEDCO	$5,991,857	Redeemable Preferred Stock
Highland	4,517,861	Redeemable Preferred Stock
Hancock	1,337,300	Redeemable Preferred Stock
Tobin	412,466	Redeemable Preferred Stock
Sullivan	171,440	Redeemable Preferred Stock
BCGI	440,128	Redeemable Preferred Stock

The Company will use its best reasonable effort to raise bank debt of $2 million to $5 million by December 31, 1992 for the purpose of redeeming the Redeemable Preferred Stock, on a pro-rata basis.

9. Upon sale of the Beeper One (New York State) paging system, the Company will pay the Senior Subordinated Note in the principal amount of $144,900 held by Kim Mayyasi in full, including any accrued interest. Following the sale of assets of the Massachusetts One RSA (Franklin County) cellular system or Beeper One, the Company shall pay the following from the net proceeds of sale, to the extent received, on a pro-rata basis:

BEDCO Redeemable Preferred	928,100
Highland Redeemable Preferred	715,500
Hancock Redeemable Preferred	212,300
BCGI Redeemable Preferred	67,600
Tobin Redeemable Preferred	64,200
Sullivan Redeemable Preferred	26,300
BCGI Redeemable Preferred	372,528
Tobin Redeemable Preferred	348,266
Sullivan Redeemable Preferred	145,140
	$2,879,934

10. There will be no payment of accrued interest for 1992 on the Senior Subordinated Notes or the Convertible Notes.

11. Management will establish a management company to provide management services to BCGI. BCGI and the management company will enter into a management agreement, containing such terms and conditions as may be agreed upon by BCGI and the management company. The fee for the management company's services will be based upon the current BCGI G&A expenses.

12. Management will devote sufficient time, energy and skills to the proper performance of the duties of the Company.

13. Immediately following the restructuring, the board of directors shall consist of five members: Brion B. Applegate, William J. Boyce, Paul J. Tobin, Clifford P. Tallman and Jeffry A. Timmons.

14. In the event that the internal rate of return to the investors on their $12,897,018 of invested capital, as measured from January 1, 1992, exceeds 35 percent per annum at the time of any complete or partial liquidation or sale of the Company or a major portion of its assets, then the excess above 35 percent shall be divided equally between the investors and management.

15. Preemptive rights to purchase, on a pro-rata basis, new issues of securities by the Company (as in the current Articles of Organization, as amended) shall be granted to the holders of the Convertible Preferred Stock and the Common Stock.

EXHIBIT L

Executive Officers and Directors

The executive officers and directors of the Company and their ages as of September 31, 1995, are as follows:

Name	Age	Position
Paul J. Tobin	53	Chairman, President, and Chief Executive Officer
Brian E. Boyle	48	Vice Chairman
Frederick E. von Mering	43	Vice President, Finance and Administration, Director
Jeffry A. Timmons	53	Director
Clifford Tallman	52	Director
Craig L. Burr	51	Director
James L. McLean	35	Director

Mr. Tobin has served as Chairman of the Board of Directors of the Company since February 1996 and served as the Company's President and Chief Executive Officer from 1990 until February 1996. Prior to joining the Company, Mr. Tobin served as President of CellularOne Buston/Worcester from July 1984 to January 1990 and as a Regional Marketing Manager for Satellite Business Systems, a joint venture of IBM, Comsat Corp. and Aetna Life & Casualty from April 1980 to June 1984. Mr. Tobin received his undergraduate degree in economics from Stonehill College and his MBA, in marketing and finance, from Northeastern University. Mr. Tobin also serves as a member of the Board of Trustees at Stonehill College.

Mr. Boyle has served as Vice Chairman of the Company since February 1996 and as Chairman, New Wireless Services of the Company from January 1994 to February 1996. From July 1990 to September 1993, Mr. Boyle served as Chief Executive Officer of Credit Technologies, Inc., a supplier of customer application software for the cellular telephone industry. Prior to 1990, Mr. Boyle founded and operated a number of ventures servicing the telecommunications industry, including APPEX Corp. (now EDS Personal Communications Division of EDS Corporation, a global telecommunications service company) and Leasecomm Corp., a micro-ticket leasing company. Mr. Boyle earned his BA in mathematics from Amherst College and his BS, MS and Ph.D. in electrical engineering and operations research from M.I.T. Mr. Boyle is also a Director of Saville Systems PLC, a provider of customized billing solutions to telecommunications providers, as well as of several private companies.

Mr. von Mering has served as the Company's Vice President, Finance and Administration since 1989. Prior to joining the Company, Mr. von Mering served as Regional Vice President and General Manager for the paging division of Metromedia, Inc., a communications company, from 1980 to 1986. From 1975 to 1979, Mr. von Mering was employed at Coopers & Lybrand LLP. Mr. von Mering earned his BA in accounting from Boston College and his MBA from Babson College.

Dr. Timmons has served as Director of the company since 1989. He is director of CellularOne in Boston and was co-founder and director of CellularOne in both Maine and New Hampshire. He is an advisor to Ernst & Young's National Entrepreneurial Service Group, BCI Advisors, Inc., Chemical Venture Partners, and Fax International. Dr. Timmons is internationally recognized for his work in entrepreneurship and venture capital, has authored and co-authored many books, and has been a trustee of Colgate University since 1991. In 1989 he became the first to hold a joint appointment with Harvard University as the MBA Class of 1954 Professorship of New Ventures and first to hold the Frederic C. Hamilton Professorship for Free Enterprise Studies at Babson College.

Mr. Tallman has served as Director of the company since 1989. Prior to joining the Company, Mr. Tallman was an associate with Highland Capital Partners from 1984 to 1988. Mr. Tallman received his AB from Harvard College and his MBA from Harvard Graduate School of Business Administration.

Mr. Burr has served as a Director of the Company since April 1993. Mr. Burr has been a Managing General Partner of Burr, Egan, Deleage & Co., a venture capital firm, since 1979. Mr. Burr received his AB from Harvard College and his MBA from Harvard Graduate School of Business Administration. Mr. Burr is a director of several privately-held companies affiliated with Burr, Egan, Deleage & Co.

Mr. McLean has served as a Director of the Company since May 1995. Mr. McLean has been a general partner of Highland Capital Partners, Incorporated, a venture capital firm, since December 1994. From December 1993 to December 1994, he was an associate with Highland Capital Partners. Prior to that, Mr. McLean was an associate with Accel Partners, a venture capital firm, from October 1990 to December 1993. Mr. McLean received his BS from Harvard University and his MBA from the University of California, Berkeley.

Robert Sullivan, Vice President of Engineering at Boston Communications Group, is responsible for development of telecommunications systems and service supporting the cellular telephone industry. Mr. Sullivan is also technical advisor for all telephony related products and services. As a co-founder of BCGI, Mr. Sullivan came to the partnership with over 20 years experience in engineering and construction of communications systems. After graduating from Northeastern University, Mr. Sullivan was employed by Raytheon, Inc. in Norwood, MA in the Microwave Radio Delay Department. From there Mr. Sullivan took a position with ZipCall, Inc. in Boston, MA where he became a Chief Engineer and worked to develop the largest radio paging system in New England. ZipCall was sold to Metromedia Telecommunications, Inc. in 1993. At CellularOne Boston, Mr. Sullivan became Vice President of Operations and was responsible for startup construction and operation of cellular telephone systems in the Boston/Worcester, Massachusetts, and Portsmouth, New Hampshire markets.

Each officer serves at the discretion of the Board of Directors. There are no family relationships among any of the directors and executive officers of the Company.

BCGI, 1995

By mid-1995, BCGI provided services exclusively to cellular carriers and their subscribers. BCGI's largest source of revenue was ROAMER*plus.* This calling service was so widely used by cellular carriers, that further growth was more likely to be from general growth in the roaming market, than from the addition of new carrier clients.

A significant portion of these revenues came from a limited number of carriers. Although ROAMER*plus* served almost 100 carriers, net revenues attributable to the ten largest customers accounted for approximately 85 percent, 81 percent, and 85 percent of BCGI's total revenues in 1993, 1994, and the first half of 1995, respectively. Similarly, two carriers accounted for 75 percent of BCGI's Carrier Support Services business in the first half of 1995, with the remaining 25 percent contributed by four other carriers.

The contracts for both ROAMER*plus* and Carrier Support Services were generally for a period of one year, and except for certain support contracts, had no minimum payment obligation to BCGI. In addition to being vulnerable to fluctuations within its key-account customer base, BCGI's calling services were affected by a number of relatively unpredictable factors: The frequency of temporary suspensions of intercarrier roaming agreements, competitive developments, changes in regulations affecting the wireless industry, general economic conditions, and changes in the technological landscape.

BCGI was recognized for developing leading-edge technology and services, setting the pace of change in the wireless telephone industry. The company hired some of the best software engineers in the industry and its ability to compete was partially dependent upon proprietary technology. BCGI relied primarily on a combination of statutory and common law copyright, trademark and trade secret laws, customer licensing agreements, employee and third-party nondisclosure agreements to protect its intellectual property rights. BCGI also entered into confidentiality agreements with employees, consultants, clients, and potential clients to protect its proprietary knowledge. In spite of these precautions, all proprietary advantages had to be considered temporary due to vulnerability to reverse engineering and to the high quality R&D being conducted in the wireless communications industry. Despite these vulnerabilities, Paul was optimistic because BCGI had the plan (See *Exhibit M* for Pro Forma projections), the people, and the strategy to succeed in this industry.

EXHIBIT M

BCGI Pro Forma Financials

	Boston Communications Group Projected Financials Year Ended December 31,					CAGR	CAGR
	1995E(1)	1996E	1997E	1998E	1999E	1995–1996	1996–1998
Revenues	$35,500	$54,000	$77,000	$109,000	$153,000	52.1%	41.5%
Cost and expenses	32,602	48,530	66,740	91,776	125,226		
EBITDA	2,898	5,470	10,260	17,224	27,774	88.8%	71.9%
Depreciation and amortization	926	1,270	2,360	2,724	2,974		
Income (loss from operations)	1,972	4,200	7,900	14,500	24,800	113.0%	80.7%
Interest expense	100	300	400	500	600		
Loss (gain) on sale of furniture and equipment	—	—	—	—	—		
Pre-tax income (loss)	1,872	3,900	7,500	14,000	24,200		
Assumed net income after taxes @ 40% tax rate	$ 1,123	$ 2,340	$ 4,500	$ 8,400	$ 14,520	108.3%	83.8%
Growth Rates							
Revenues	—	52.1%	42.6%	41.6%	40.4%		
EBITDA	—	88.8%	87.6%	67.9%	61.3%		
EBIT	—	113.0%	88.1%	83.5%	71.0%		
Pre-tax	—	108.3%	92.3%	86.7%	72.9%		
Net income	—	108.3%	92.3%	86.7%	72.9%		
Margin Analysis							
EBITDA	8.2%	10.1%	13.3%	15.8%	18.2%		
EBIT	5.6%	7.8%	10.3%	13.3%	16.2%		
Pre-tax	5.3%	7.2%	9.7%	12.8%	15.8%		
Net income	3.2%	4.3%	5.8%	7.7%	9.5%		

Source: Company's projections

(1) Excludes discontinued operations

Strategy

BCGI was focused on developing, marketing and providing high quality, innovative call processing and customer support services to wireless carriers. Paul believed that wireless telephone service would continue to be one of the fastest growing segments of the telecommunications industry and that wireless carriers would be under increasing competitive pressure. As a result, he believed there would be significant opportunities to provide wireless carriers with services that enabled them to focus internal resources on their core business activities while simultaneously increasing revenues, improving service quality, and reducing costs. In addition to focusing on the wireless carrier services industry, BCGI's strategy included the following elements:

■ *Identify and Develop Additional Value-added Services*
BCGI sought to create innovative value-added services that wireless telephone carriers either had not identified or had found difficult or uneconomical to provide on their own. It was particularly focused on developing and providing services that created incremental revenue and profit for wireless carriers, such as its ROAMER*plus* service and a new prepaid wireless service BCGI called C2C. C2C would allow carriers to offer cellular service to prospective customers who did not qualify for credit approval. Many people who wanted cellular service were turned away, but very few would be ineligible for C2C because service was prepaid. BCGI planned to introduce C2C in the fall of 1995. Paul believed that such services would be increasingly attractive to wireless telephone carriers seeking innovative ways to respond to a highly competitive and evolving industry.

■ *Develop and Maintain Long-term Customer Relationships*
BCGI established and maintained long-term relationships with carriers to enable it to understand customer needs and continue to develop new service offerings to meet those needs. They regularly solicited feedback from customers regarding the challenges they faced in order to identify potential new service offerings. Paul's team sought to build upon its existing customer relationships and distribution channels by integrating and cross-selling its different service offerings. Paul believed that focus on building customer relationships was an important factor in developing customer loyalty and expanding existing customer relationships over time.

■ *Provide Services on a Recurring Revenue Basis*
BCGI focused on offering services that generated recurring revenues. Paul wanted to provide ongoing services to align BCGI's interests with those of its customers and maximize the potential benefit to those customers. BCGI provided its call processing and Carrier Support Services on a per-minute or per-call basis,

or in combination. These pricing methods minimized up-front costs and focused on the revenue enhancement potential for the carriers.

■ *Offer Premium Quality Services*
Paul believed that providing high quality service was critical to BCGI's ability to satisfy customers. BCGI's Carrier Support Services were designed to be indistinguishable from the services provided by the cellular carrier's own customer support personnel. BCGI provided extensive inhouse classroom and on-the-job training programs for its personnel, including carrier-specific training programs designed in collaboration with the applicable carrier.

■ *Expand into New Wireless Telephone Markets*
Paul believed there were significant opportunities to leverage BCGI's experience to penetrate new wireless telephone markets. First, he believed there would be opportunities for BCGI to provide services to PCS carriers similar to those which it provided to cellular carriers. Second, the management team was exploring ways to expand into new international markets, primarily through the establishment of joint ventures and strategic alliances.

By mid-1995, BCGI was on track to generate $38 million, so Paul was not surprised when GTE Sylvania approached to discuss a buyout.

In this industry, there were a number of service providers to the cellular carriers, and there are three majors: EDS, GTE, and Cincinnati Bell. The fourth largest in terms of revenues and name recognition was BCGI. We were on a much lower tier, but we probably provided more services to more carriers than anyone. They just get more revenue out of it. So it was natural for someone who wanted to be a supplier to the cellular industry to wind up at our door pretty fast.

Determining a Harvest Strategy

Paul began considering his harvest options in mid-1995, about the time that he was approached by the acquisition group at GTE. He liked the idea of a buyout because of the intense burdens of going public (e.g., insider trading rules, competitive and personal disclosures, SEC regulations, etc.), so he was attentive to GTE's approach. However, the discussions progressed slowly.

We had three or four meetings and each one was more aggressive than the last. The discussion went back and forth, "What do you guys think you're worth?" "I don't know, you tell me." "No, you tell me first." Over the past couple of years it had dawned on them that we were a pretty good management group, and that they didn't want to compete with us in the marketplace. They had more money and more resources to throw at it, but we had a better reputation. Given an equal service, we were going to sell more than they would. Part of their motivation was to buy distribution, but another part was to buy out a competitor.

GTE provided a number of the same services to the wireless industry that we did. We had a great sales and marketing group; about 25 people who started in the cellular industry in 1984–1985. These people had 10-year relationships with cellular people all across the country. So our marketing strength was much better, or we like to think that it was much better, than this $20 billion corporation.

GTE's interest was part of the impetus to thinking, maybe it is time. In addition to that, we were funded by three different firms. Burr, Egan, Deleage, & Co., Highland Capital Partners, and Hancock Venture Partners. The life cycle of a venture fund is generally ten years, then you can get a two-year extension on top of that, and maybe another year or two after that. We were the last investment in one of these funds, and they were in the two-year extension period. So there was some pressure from our venture guys to come up with liquidity because they don't like to go back and ask for another extension. A third reason we looked at GTE was that the venture guys had the put. It was time for us to start looking for liquidity.

Another option was an IPO. Paul held meetings with people familiar with the IPO process, particularly R. Douglas Kahn, a Boston-area entrepreneur whose company was the first to go public following the invasion of Kuwait in August, 1990. Kahn had been remarkably thorough and perceptive in developing his approach to the harvest process.[3] Tobin was particularly intrigued with a letter sent by Kahn to "The Four Horsemen"[4] (See *Exhibit N* for a copy of the letter). This request for quotation (RFQ) posed a number of tough questions to the investment banks. Although the IPO market of late-1995 was very different than mid-1990, Paul was better able to understand the bank selection process after meeting with Kahn. Paul settled on a strategy and contacted investment bankers at the Four Horsemen:

> Our venture partners gave me names at each of the four firms—the people they did business with on a regular basis. So I called, and then the venture guys called them. We had a couple of meetings with each of them before they drew up their proposals.
>
> When you are talking to investment bankers, you want to project your company in the best light to get the best valuation. You need to make sure they understand your company, but everybody's selling: we're selling them, they're selling us, and both of us are trying to sell the public or a deal guy.

Generally, the bankers sent two or three guys, an analyst and a couple of salespeople called managing directors. They tell you what it costs and then they try to sell you on why they are the best. The guy from Alex Brown said, "We know a lot about communications and we can do an M&A deal, but we think it would be crazy. You're leaving too much money on the table—you should do an IPO," because that was their expertise. DLJ also does a lot of telecommunications deals. They said, "We have a good M&A department and this should be an M&A deal." It depends on the bank, but it also has a lot to do with the bias of the managing director, whether he's an M&A guy or an IPO guy.

[3] See Jeffry A. Timmons, "EASEL Corporation," *New Venture Creation, 4th edition,* 1994.
[4] The investment banking firms of Alex Brown & Sons, Donaldson, Luftkin & Jennette, Hambrecht & Quist, and Robertson, Stephens & Company.

EXHIBIT N

EASEL Corp., Request for Quotation Summary (condensed)

July 18, 1990

Dear _____:

We appreciate the interest you have expressed in providing investment banking services to EASEL. In order to provide us with the information to help us in the investment banker selection process, we would appreciate your written response to the following questions.

I. IPO Timing
- When would be the best time, given current market conditions? Why?
- What financial performance would need to be achieved in order to feel comfortable with an IPO in the September time frame? Would you require an audit of interim financials in order to go public in 1990?
- How does your "commitment committee" operate and at what point in the process is the "commitment" obtained?

II. Pricing
- What offering price range would you select if the IPO were today? Please explain how you determined this price.
- How would you position EASEL among comparable software companies? Please indicate which companies you would add or delete from the list of companies which we believe to be comparable to EASEL.

III. IPO Process
- Please provide the names of the proposed investment banking team and describe specific involvement of each person (drafting sessions, due diligence sessions . . .)
- Which law firm would you select and who would be the lead attorney from the firm?
- Would you market the offering outside of the United States? Why or why not?
- What is your recommended mix of institutional versus retail buyers and why?
- Describe your recommended "road show" process. Please note anything unique or unusual relative to other investment banks.

(Continued)

EASEL Corp., Request for Quotation Summary (condensed), (continued)

IV. Research

- Who within your firm will be responsible for research? How long have they been with your firm? Is there any information that we should be aware of that would provide us comfort that this person will remain with your firm in the future? Please attach some reports developed by this individual in the past year.
- How would the analyst describe EASEL (positioning statement)? What is the analyst's opinion of the company's strategy? Will EASEL be included in the "universe" of software companies your firm tracks?
- When would you release the first research report?
- How often would research reports be released?

V. Fees

- Please provide a schedule of fees expected to be incurred.

VI. The Offering

- What percentage of shares would you feel comfortable allocating to existing investors? To management? What are your policies on selling stockholder indemnification? What are your policies on company reimbursement of selling stockholder expenses?
- What "lockup" provisions would you want to place for investors, management and employees?
- Management has received proposals from counsel as to the implementation of anti-takeover provisions prior to an IPO, including poison pill defense and a staggered board. What is your position on these provisions?

VIII. Support

- Describe the scope of your trading operation and how you would support our stock in the market. Will you act as market-maker? Who else would you recommend as additional market-makers?
- What type and level of support would we receive after an IPO?

VIII. Other Information

- Please provide examples of the last five technology company IPOs you have managed or comanaged. Please provide IPO price and 30-day post IPO price. Please also provide prospectus copies, and CEO and CFO names and telephone numbers.
- Please provide any other information you would like us to consider.

We would appreciate six copies of your response to this request by April 30 which we will share with our IPO committee and Board of Directors. We may ask you to make a formal presentation to this committee at a later date.

Thank you for your continued interest and feel free to contact me if you would have any questions.

Sincerely,

John McDonough
Vice President and
Chief Financial Officer

Source: Jeffry A. Timmons, "EASEL Corporation," *New Venture Creation*, 4th edition, 1994.

November Board of Directors Meeting

Three of the Four Horsemen responded to Paul's request for a proposal. Working with the rest of the management, Paul prepared a summary evaluation of the bankers' proposals for the next board meeting (see *Exhibit O* for Proposal Matrix). He recalled the board's discussions.

Our board thought an IPO was better money. There is a structural conflict between the venture guys and management here: On a sale everybody cashes in, but on an IPO the venture guys do better because of the lock up. Not only are they cashing in on the IPO, but then you have rule 144 restrictions.[5] So there is a potential conflict of objectives, but we always had a great relationship with our venture guys. They said, "It's your deal. Do what you think is right—here is our best advice."

To further complicate his recommendation to the board, the bankers were split on their recommendations: Alex Brown & Sons recommended an IPO (See Appendix C: Excerpts from Alex Brown Proposal), while Donaldson, Luftkin & Jenrette (See Appendix D: Excerpts from Donaldson, Luftkin & Jenrette Proposal) and Robertson, Stephens recommended a sale of the company. To his pleasant surprise, valuations also covered a higher range than Paul had expected, $45–125 million. Clearly, BCGI had created a significant amount

---

[5] Rule 144 governs securities sold through interstate commerce and mail. It is designed to prevent fraud by mandating that all securities provide adequate information to consumers. It also limits the amount and timing of securities that can be sold by individuals involved in the deal.

EXHIBIT 0

BCGI Evaluation of Investment Bankers: Underwriting Proposal Summaries

	Alex Brown	Donaldson, Lufkin, & Jenrette	Robertson, Stephens & Company
Strategic Alternatives	1. IPO 2. Sale to Strategic/Financial Buyer 3. Hedged Approach (approach select group of potential buyers to gauge interest) 4. Status Quo	1. IPO 2. Sale to Strategic/Financial Buyer 3. Strategic Investor/Partner	1. IPO 2. Sale of Company (partial to 100%) 3. Joint Venture/Merger 4. Recapitalization (in anticipation of acquisitions) 5. Status Quo
Recommended Pricing	$80–120 million	1. $90–$125 million	$70–$95 million
Pricing Method	1–3.4x Revenues(*) 7.8–31.4x EBITDA 10.1–60.9x EBIT 17.4–105.3x NI	Discounted Cash Flows(**) Modification of BCGI's Projections	Discounted Cash Flows
Recommended Pricing			
Pricing Method			
Recommended Pricing		2. $65–$95 million	
Pricing Method		Comparable Acquisitions	
Pricing Comparables	Physician Billing, Inc. Genex Services, Inc. Advacare, Inc. EPS/National Card System Medical Management Resources, Inc. Consolidated Medical Services, Inc. Northwest Creditors Service, Inc. Datamedic Corporation Alpha Beta Daya Services, Inc. General Electric Information Services CyCare Systems Financial Processors, Inc. Vantage Computer Systems, Inc. Winsbury Co. LP	3. $45–$60 million Comparable Public Companies Cellular Technical Services Global Telecom. Solutions Midcom Communications Racotek Tel-Save Holdings Tele-Matic Corp.	Affiliated Computer Services, Inc. AMNEX, Inc. Brite Voice Systems, Inc. Business Records Corporation Holding Company Shared Technologies, Inc. Transition Network Services, Inc.

EXHIBIT 0

BCGI Evaluation of Investment Bankers: Underwriting Proposal Summaries (continued)

Range of Selected Market Multiples for Public Companies

1. Transaction Processing(**)
   - 2.3–7.4X Trailing Revenues
   - 13.9–31.9X Trailing Cash Flow
   - 18.7–38.6X Trailing EBIT

2. Specialty Business Service Providers(**)
   - .4–5.4X Trailing Revenues
   - 6.9–24.8X Trailing Cash Flow
   - 10.2–28.7X Trailing EBIT

3. Wireless Communication
   - (227.5)–319.6X LTM EPS
   - 1.6–19.6X Book Value

4. Information Processing
   - 11.4–145.8 P/E Ratio
   - .7–4.1 Enterprise Value/Revenue (LTM)
   - 12.7–28.1 Enterprise Value/EBIT (LTM)
   - 20.0–35.0 Equity Value/LTM Net Income
   - 13.1–33.3 NI/LTM
   - 1.0–8.2 Book Value/LTM
   - .5–3.8 Revenue/LTM
   - 6.5–18.8 EBIT/LTM

Range of Selected Recent Transaction Multiples(***)
   - .5–8.4X Trailing Revenues
   - 7.0–33.4X LTM EBITDA
   - 8.3–53.2X LTM EBIT
   - 9.6–54.1X LTM EPS
   - 4.5–11.8X Book Value

Primary Offering Size
   - $30 million
   - Not Specified

Preferred Strategy
   - IPO to maximize value
   - If sale, use auction among candidates. Identified 12 potential acquirers, strong on transaction processing.
   - Sale with auction; should get a higher Value with control premium vs. potential IPO discount. Identified 36 potential acquirers, good mix, includes most of our potentials
   - Sale of 100% of the Company
   - Sale with "controlled competitive offering"

Timing
   - Immediate
   - Not Specified
   - Immediate—Closing in 1996

Strengths/Weaknesses
   - Oriented toward equity underwriting: #1 in venture backed IPOs; strong sales & distribution channels
   - MEDIUM focus on wireless
   - 14 analysts for media, Communications & technology
   - Ranked #1 in cellular underwriting 1990–1994
   - Very focused on technology players
   - 18 analysts in the technology sector, 4 in communication
   - LOW focus on wireless
   - STRONG focus on wireless
   - Dennis Leibowitz ranked #2 wireless analyst #1 cable; long DLJ tenure

(*)Calculated using 1995–1997 est. Revenues, EBITDA, EBIT, and NI.

(**)Cash flow analysis is based on company projections and a 10X exit multiple discounted at 25% to 35%.

(***)An adjusted market value was calculated using the market value of equity plan total debt less cash and equivalents. Multiples are expressed in relation to this adjusted market value.

of value in a fairly short period of time. In addition, the robust capital and IPO markets were influencing valuations. The trick was: How long would it last? On balance, it appeared that the company might bring $75–90 million, if one assumed the banks more optimistic estimates were part of their own selling process. As Paul reviewed the summary of management's evaluations, he pondered his choices.

Table of Appendices

APPENDIX A

The Top 50 Wireless Operators

	Operator Name	Mkts	Population		Operator Name	Mkts	Population
1	AT&T Wireless Services, Inc.*	142	175,296,174	26	Cellular Communications, Inc.	22	8,189,198
2	Nextel Communications	311	158,183,228	27	American Personal Communications	1	7,777,875
3	Sprint Spectrum	29	144,938,590	28	Comcast Cellular Com.	9	7,629,202
4	Geotek Communications	25	69,045,270	29	ALLTEL Mobile Communications	53	7,524,952
5	GTE Mobilnet*	127	68,704,157	30	Century Cellunet	37	7,333,411
6	PCS PrimeCo	11	57,191,542	31	Activated Com.	1	7,261,176
7	Bell Atlantic NYNEX Mobile	79	57,043,488	32	Vanguard Cellular Systems, Inc.	26	6,869,771
8	AirTouch Communications	100	55,228,917	33	SNET Mobility, Inc.	12	5,609,227
9	Southwestern Bell Mobile Systems*	72	54,576,997	34	CommNet Cellular, Inc.	55	4,008,766
10	BellSouth Corp.	94	47,417,568	35	Wireless One Network	19	3,788,988
11	Ameritech Cellular Services*	44	35,428,615	36	Palmer Wireless, Inc.	18	3,569,247
12	Pacific Bell Mobile Services	2	31,036,409	37	Centennial Cellular Corp.—PCS	1	3,522,037
13	American Portable Telecommunications	8	26,439,502	38	Puerto Rico Telephone Co.	12	3,522,037
14	OmniPoint Corporation	1	26,410,597	39	B.C. Tel Mobility Cellular, Inc.	1	3,221,600
15	Rogers Cantel Mobile, Inc.	11	26,293,388	40	Horizon Cellular Group	15	3,098,508
16	Western Wireless	75	24,245,556	41	PriCellular Corporation	19	2,858,249
17	US Cellular	136	21,034,955	42	Frontier Corporation	12	2,765,286
18	Cox Com	2	20,804,505	43	AGT Mobility, Inc.	2	2,479,956
19	Pittencrieff Communications	68	20,052,039	44	Cellular Com of Puerto Rico	4	2,466,350
20	360° Communications	94	19,536,870	45	Poka Lambro Telecommunications	5	2,218,905
21	GTE Macro Communications	4	19,366,561	46	Lincoln Telecommunications	13	1,706,625
22	Bell Mobility	2	16,849,800	47	Centennial Cellular	9	1,610,342
23	BellSouth Personal Communications	2	11,474,228	48	Radiofone, Inc.	4	1,504,908
24	Powertel PCS Partners, L.P.	3	8,984,235	49	Cellular South	11	1,407,371
25	PhillieCo	1	8,927,748	50	Pacific Telecom Cellular	8	1,246,908

*Market and population figures reflect the combined cellular and PCS holdings for these companies. Source: CTIA

Personal Communications Services

Personal Communications Services (PCS) are a wide range of wireless mobile technologies, including two-way paging and cellular-like calling services, which are transmitted at lower power and higher frequencies than regular cellular services. The PCS spectrum is comprised of three sections: one for operating narrowband services, one for broadband services, and a third reserved for unlicensed devices.

Narrowband: In July of 1994, the Federal Communication Commission (FCC) auctioned its first group of PCS licenses. Six companies, with combined bids totaling more than $617 million, were awarded rights to provide nationwide, narrowband PCS paging services. In late 1994, nine other companies with bids totaling $491 million, were awarded rights to provide regional, narrowband PCS services.

Broadband: In March of the following year, 18 companies bid more than $7 billion for broadband PCS licenses. Broadband PCS will consist of cellular-like services including new categories of wireless voice and data transmissions, including enhanced privacy and antifraud security features, over both local and wide areas using low power, lightweight pocket phones and hand-held computers.

Unlicensed: The area between the narrowband and broadband blocks is allocated for unlicensed PCS device use, including short-distance wireless voice and data devices (e.g., local area networks and Private Branch Exchanges). Previously, unlicensed short distance wireless voice and data applications had been relegated to industrial, scientific, or medical bands and were often plagued by interference.[7]

There are 2,074 licenses in 51 Major Trading Areas and 493 Basic Trading Areas in the United States. As of December 1995, 18 percent of these had been auctioned. Three of them were awarded to companies designated by the FCC as holders of "pioneer's preferences," a category for awarding licenses to parties that have developed new communications services and technologies.[8] The FCC also created a "designated entities" category for small, rural, women, or minority-owned businesses. Businesses in this category have race or gender-based preferences.

"The PCS industry is expected to compete with existing cellular and private advanced mobile communications services, thereby yielding lower prices for existing users of those services," according to the FCC. Additionally, PCS will promote the development of other services and devices (e.g., private branch exchanges, smaller, lighter, multi-function portable phones, multichannel cordless phones, and portable facsimiles and other imaging equipment.[9]

[7] Mathias and Rysavy, "The ABCs of PCS," *Network World,* March 1995.
[8] The pioneer's preference regulations are codified at 47 C.F.R. §§ 1.402, 5.207. *Establishment of Procedures to Provide a Preference,* Report and Order, 6 FCC Rcd 3488 (1991), 7 FCC Rcd 1808 (1992), further recon. pending.
[9] See FCC Gen Docket No. 90-314, *Amendment of the Commissions Rules to Establish New Personal Communications Services,* Second Report and Order, October 22, 1993, page 11.

Excerpts from Alex Brown Proposal, Free Cash Flow Analysis

($ 000s)	Fiscal Year Ending December 31,					CAGR 1995–1999
	1995E[4]	1996E	1997E	1998E	1999E	
Total Revenue	$35,500	$54,000	$77,000	$109,000	$153,000	44.1%
Operating Expenses	32,602	48,530	66,740	91,776	125,226	
Operating Cash Flow	2,898	5,470	10,260	17,224	27,774	75.9%
Less: Deprec. & Amortization	926	1,270	2,360	2,724	2,974	
Operating Income	1,972	4,200	7,900	14,500	24,800	88.3%
Less: Interest Expense	100	300	400	500	600	
Pre-Tax Expense	1,872	3,900	7,500	14,000	24,200	
Income Tax Expense[1]	749	1,560	3,000	5,600	9,680	
Earnings After Tax	1,123	2,340	4,500	8,400	14,520	89.6%
Plus: Deprec. & Amortization	926	1,270	2,360	2,724	2,974	
Less: Capital Expenditures[2]	1,000	1,000	1,000	1,000	1,000	
Increase/(Decrease) in WC[3]	86	370	460	640	880	
Free Cash Flow	$ 963	$ 2,240	$ 5,400	$ 9,484	$ 15,614	100.6%
Revenue Growth	13.7%	52.1%	42.6%	41.6%	40.4%	
Operating Cash Flow Margin	8.2%	10.1%	13.3%	15.8%	18.2%	
Operating Income Margin	5.6%	7.8%	10.3%	13.3%	16.2%	
Free Cash Flow Margin	2.7%	4.1%	7.0%	8.7%	10.2%	

[1] Assumes a 40% tax rate
[2] Assumes annual $1,000 capital expenditure
[3] Assumes working capital = 2% of revenues
[4] Excludes discontinued operations

APPENDIX C2

Discounted Cash Flow Analysis from Alex Brown Proposal

Disc Rate	($000s)	1.75 X	2.00 X	2.25 X	8.0 X	10.0 X	12.0 X	22.0 X	24.0 X	26.0 X
18%	PV of Cash Flow	$ 19,602	$ 19,602	$ 19,602	$ 19,602	$ 19,602	$ 19,602	$ 19,602	$ 19,602	$ 19,602
	PV of Terminal Value	$138,102	157,831	177,560	114,604	143,255	171,906	164,764	179,742	194,721
	Total Market Value	157,705	177,434	197,163	134,206	162,857	191,509	184,366	199,344	214,323
20%	PV of Cash Flow	18,635	18,635	18,635	18,635	18,635	18,635	18,635	18,635	18,635
	PV of Terminal Value	129,123	147,569	166,016	107,153	133,941	160,729	154,051	168,056	182,060
	Total Market Value	147,758	166,204	184,651	125,788	152,576	179,364	172,686	186,691	200,695
22%	PV of Cash Flow	17,735	17,735	17,735	17,735	17,735	17,735	17,735	17,735	17,735
	PV of Terminal Value	120,862	138,128	155,394	100,297	125,372	150,446	144,195	157,304	170,412
	Total Market Value	138,597	155,863	173,129	118,032	143,107	168,181	161,930	175,039	188,147

To December 31, 1995

APPENDIX C3

Excerpts from Alex Brown Proposal Valuation Summary[10]

Firm Value* Value as a Multiple	($ mil.)	$80	$90	$100	$110	$120
Revenues						
1995E	$38.0	2.1X	2.4X	2.6X	2.9X	3.2X
1995E-Adj.	35.5	2.3	2.5	2.8	3.1	3.4
1996E	54.0	1.5	1.7	1.9	2.0	2.2
1997E	77.0	1.0	1.2	1.3	1.4	1.6
EBITDA						
1995E	$3.1	25.4X	28.6X	31.8X	34.9X	38.IX
1995E-Adj.	2.9	27.6	31.1	34.5	38.0	41.4
1996E	5.5	14.6	16.5	18.3	20.1	21.9
1997E	10.3	7.8	8.8	9.7	10.7	11.7

Equity Market Value Multiple

Net Income	($ mil.)	$80	$90	$100	$110	$120
1995E	$1.2	65.2X	73.5X	81.8X	90.2X	98.5X
1995E-Adj.	1.1	69.6	78.5	87.4	96.3	105.3
1996E	2.3	33.4	37.7	42.0	46.2	50.5
1997E	4.5	17.4	19.6	21.8	24.0	26.3

* Firm Value defined as equity value plus debt less cash and equivalents.

[10] This analysis is based upon data drawn from the following sectors: 1) transaction processing companies such as Paycheck, Inc.; 2) specialty service providers such as Mead Data Central; and 3) cellular companies like Nationwide Cellular.

APPENDIX C4

Excerpts from Alex Brown Proposal, IPO Valuation Analysis: Pro Forma Income Statement for Initial Public Offering

	Pre-IPO 1995[1]	Post-IPO 1995[1]	Post-IPO 1996
Revenues	$35,500	$35,500	$54,000
Cost and expenses	32,602	32,602	48,530
EBITDA	2,898	2,898	5,470
Depreciation and amortization	926	926	1,270
Income (loss) from operations	1,972	1,972	4,200
Pro forma interest expense[2]	100	0	0
Pro forma interest income[3]	0	1,026	966
Pro forma pre-tax income (loss)	2,838	2,998	5,166
Assumed net income @ 40% tax rate	$ 1,703	$ 1,799	$ 3,100
Growth Rates			
Revenues	—	—	52.1%
EBITDA			88.8%
EBIT			113.0%
Pre-tax			82.0%
Net income			82.0%
Margin Analysis			
EBITDA	8.2%	8.2%	10.1%
EBIT	5.6%	5.6%	7.8%
Pre-tax	8.0%	8.4%	9.6%
Net income	4.8%	5.1%	5.7%

[1] Excludes discontinued operations

[2] Assumes debt repayment of $ 1,000 with offering proceeds in 1995 and assumes 10% interest rate and the use of $2,000 in cash to pay down debt in 1996

[3] Assumes 6% interest rate on cash proceeds from offering

APPENDIX C5

Excerpts from Alex Brown Proposal, Selected Potential Buyers

1) Alltel Corp.	4) British Telecom.	7) Cincinnati Bell	10) First Data Corp.
2) AT&T	5) Cable Data	8) Concord EFS	11) First Financial Mgmt.
3) Automatic DP	6) Cable & Wireless	9) EDS	12) GTE Corp.
			13) Nat'l. Dispatch Center

Excerpts from Donaldson, Luftkin & Jenrette Proposal

APPENDIX D1

Effect of Growth on Future Trading Value

	1996	1997	1998
Projected EBITDA	$ 5.5	$ 10.3	$ 17.2
Assumed Trading Multiple	10.0x	10.0x	10.0x
Future Trading Value	$55.0	$103.0	$172.0
Discount Rate	17.5%	20.5%	22.5%
Discounted Enterprise Value[1]	$46.8	$ 70.9	$ 93.6

(1) Discounted based on respective discount rates presented above.

APPENDIX D2

The M&A Sales Process

The Company. In order to properly position the Company for sale, the DLJ team will identify:
—Strengths and weaknesses of BCGI's competitive position;
—Growth opportunities; and
—Synergy and cost saving opportunities that may be available to potential purchasers.

Financial Presentation. In order to maximize the value that can be obtained for the Company, the DLJ team will:
—Develop a complete understanding of BCGI's business and financial performance; and
—Prepare adjusted financial statements for the Company which restate BCGI's performance exclusive of non-recurring charges and, if appropriate, after giving effect to the cost saving programs which have been implemented.

Potential Purchasers. DLJ will work with BCGI's management to identify the most complete universe of potential purchasers
—DLJ has well established North American and International relationships in the telecommunications industries.
—DLJ is the leading investment bank to financial buyers.

Valuation. After fully understanding the competitive position and financial performance of BCGI, DLJ will deliver a preliminary valuation of the Company in order to provide BCGI with a useful basis for analyzing offers received for the Company.

Selling Memorandum. DLJ will work with the Company's management to prepare a confidential information memorandum for delivery to potential purchasers which reflects the attractive investment opportunity that BCGI represents.

Management Presentations. DLJ will work with the management to tailor a presentation and outlook by management which presents BCGI in the most defensible and the best light.

Sale Procedures. After fully understanding the strengths and weaknesses of the Company and developing a view of the likely purchasers and valuation range, DLJ will design and implement a sale process which is designed to achieve the highest price.
—Because several potential strategic buyers exist, an auction/sale process designed to maximize price competition for the Company will likely yield the highest price.

Negotiations with Interest Parties. DLJ has negotiated over 350 transactions since 1990. Given this expertise, DLJ will work with BCGI and potential purchasers to negotiate and structure a transaction which provides the highest value to BCGI's shareholders.

APPENDIX D5

Proposed Time Schedule

Organizational Meeting
- Preliminary Valuation of the Company
- Prepare Offering Memo
- Create Buyer List

  - Marketing Call Program
  - Draft Purchase Agreements
  - Prepare Management Presentation
  - Prepare Data Room

    Preliminary Indications of Interest
    - Management Presentations
    - Plant Visits and Due Diligence
    - Supplemental Information
      - Bidding Procedures Letter
      - Purchase Agreement Distributed

        Final Bid Date
        - Evaluation of Bids & Contracts
        - Contract Negotiation & Execution
        - Hart-Scott[11] Filing

												Close
0	2	4	6	8	10	12	14	16	18	20	22	24 weeks

[11] The Hart-Scott-Rodino Act requires notification before a merger takes place if the acquiring person will hold 15% or more of the voting securities and assets or an aggregate total of the amount of the voting securities in excess of $15,000,000.

Selected M&A Transaction Multiples Wireless Communications Industry

Announcement Date	Target/ Acquirer	Equity Purchase Price	Adjusted Purchase Price	Last Twelve Months (LTM) Revenue	LTM EBITDA	LTM EBIT	LTM Net Income	Target Business Description
14 May 93	LDDS Communications, Inc./ Resurgens Communications Group	$ 2,044.4	$ 2,480.7	3.0x	13.6x	19.8x	35.9x	Provides telecommunications services
1 Jun. 93	OCOM Corp. International CableTel., Inc.	$ 77.6	$ 47.3	4.4x	12.1x	NM	NM	Provides radio/telephone communication services
16 Aug. 93	McCaw Cellular Communications, Inc./ AT&T	$15,229.9	$20,039.8	10.2x	26.9x	NM	NM	Largest cellular telephone company in the U.S.
19 Aug. 93	Celutel, Inc./ Century Telephone Enterprises	$ 62.3	$ 101.9	4.2x	NM	NM	NM	Provides cellular telephone services
23 Sep. 93	Telematics International, Inc./ ECI Telecom, Ltd.	$ 305.4	$ 286.8	4.1x	22.2x	35.5x	41.7x	Manufacturers high-performance networking and communication products
31 Jan. 94	Radiation Systems, Inc./ COMSTAT Corp.	$ 154.0	$ 165.5	1.5x	9.7x	12.3x	17.6x	Designs and manufactures communication systems
24 Feb. 94	Associated Communications Corp./ SBC Communications Inc.	$ 674.2	$ 440.0	0.5x	2.6x	NM	NM	Operator of six domestic cellular telephone systems
15 Mar. 94	Centex Telemanagement Inc./ MFS Communications Co. Inc.	$ 210.6	$ 189.9	1.0x	13.2x	17.6x	30.8x	Provides telecommunications services
13 Jul. 94	IDB Communications Group/ LDDS Communications, Inc.	$ 659.8	$ 829.6	1.9x	13.7x	23.0x	NM	Provider of international telecommunications services as well as specialized broadcasting services
22 Jul. 94	Keptel, Inc./ ANTEC Corp.	$ 89.2	$ 84.5	1.8x	8.8x	11.8x	20.4x	Manufacturers telecommunications and transmission equipment for residential and commercial applications
9 Aug. 94	Network Systems Corporation/ Storage Technology Corporation	$ 314.2	$ 278.8	1.2x	8.8x	32.1x	33.1x	Manufacturer of high-performance data communication systems, hubs, bridges and routers
10 Oct. 94	WCT Communications/ Rochester Telephone Corp.	$ 79.6	$ 109.3	0.9x	NM	NM	NM	Provider of telephone services
19 Jan. 95	Confertech International, Inc./ ALC Communications Corp.	$ 64.0	$ 63.2	1.5x	10.6x	24.4x	38.6x	Manufacturer of teleconferencing systems
	Summary:							
	High			10.2x	26.9x	35.5x	47.1x	
	Low			0.5x	2.6x	11.8x	17.6x	
	Average[1]			2.5x	13.4x	22.9x	32.4x	

(1) Average excludes high and low.

Comparison of Selected Publicly Held, Value-added Companies

	AVG.	HIGH	LOW	CELLULAR TECHNICAL SERVICE	GLOBAL TELECOM. SOLUTIONS	MIDCOM COMMUNICATIONS	RACOTEK	TEL-SAVE HOLDINGS	TELE-MATIC CORP.
Fiscal Year End				12/94	12/94	12/94	12/94	12/94	7/95
Last Financial Statement				6/95	5/95	6/95	6/95	6/95	4/94
BUSINESS DESCRIPTION				Software development co. specializing in facilitating wireless communications, namely, switching, billing.	Produces, markets, and sells prepaid phone cards.	Switchless reseller, with a focus on small businesses.	Develops, markets, and supports software and related products for wireless mobile transmission.	Long-distance telecom. services to small and med.-sized businesses (reseller); now building its own network.	Specialized call processing services on a transaction fee basis for use in correctional facilities.
MARKET DATA									
Symbol/Where Traded				CTSC/OTC	GTST/OTC	MCCI/OTC	RACO/OTC	TALK/OTC	TMAT/OTC
Stock Price (10/24/95)				$17.73	$5.95	$14.25	$5.88	$13.75	$13.25
Shares Outstanding				10.0	3.1	13.5	23.8	12.6	7.6
Equity Market Capitalization				$176.7	$18.7	$192.6	$139.8	$172.6	$100.1
Enterprise Value				$167.7	$15.3	$239.6	$117.3	$162.3	$104.8
LTM Price Range				$12.25-$31.00	$3.88-$7.00	$11.25-$16.75	$3.00-$7.88	$13.75-$16.50	$7.38-$15.00
OPERATING DATA									
LTM Revenues				$14.7	$2.2	$145.6	$5.8	$135.3	$23.3
LTM Operating Cash Flow (EBDAIT)				3.9	(2.6)	5.6	(11.6)	15.8	6.3
LTM Operating Earnings (EBIT)				3.4	(2.6)	(1.5)	(12.2)	15.0	3.4
LTM EPS				$0.33	($1.05)	($0.79)	($0.51)	$1.44	$0.31
Book Value per Share				$1.49	$1.03	$0.41	$1.30	$1.84	$2.57
1995 Projected EPS				$0.57	$0.22	($0.60)	($0.51)	$1.62	$0.59
1996 Projected EPS				$0.64	$0.11	$0.28	($0.35)	$1.82	$0.66
MARKET CAP MULTIPLES Price/									
LTM EPS	14.4x	54.1x	9.6x	54.1x	NM	NM	NM	9.6x	43.1x
1995 Projected EPS	22.5	30.9	8.5	30.9	NM	NM	NM	8.5	22.5
1996 Projected EPS	32.8	54.0	7.6	27.5	54.0x	50.9x	NM	7.6	20.0
Book Value	6.1	11.8	4.5	11.8	5.8	34.5	4.5	7.5	5.2
Enterprise Value/LTM Revenues	6.1x	20.4x	1.2x	11.4x	6.9x	1.6x	20.4x	1.2x	4.5x
LTM EBDAIT	25.6	45.6	10.3	45.6	NM	NM	NM	10.3	16.6
LTM EBIT	31.3	49.6	10.8	49.6	NM	NM	NM	10.8	31.1
THREE YEAR AVG. MARGINS									
Gross Margin	28.2%	49.5%	12.8%	49.5%	12.8%	32.7%	40.6%	16.1%	23.5%
LTM EBDAIT	-71.1%	10.1%	-298.3%	-5.1%	-267.1%	4.2%	-298.3%	10.1%	-16.3%
LTM EBIT	-75.7%	9.8%	-311.0%	-11.6%	-270.0%	1.4%	-311.0%	9.8%	-22.6%
Net Margin	-81.2%	9.8%	-317.5%	-7.9%	-284.2%	-1.7%	-317.5%	9.8%	-30.9%
THREE YEAR GROWTH RATES									
LTM Revenues	111.4%	222.7%	41.8%	41.8%	222.7%	106.1%	132.5%	116.5%	90.7%
LTM EBDAIT	74.3%	160.4%	51.3%	51.3%	83.4%	65.2%	51.3%	160.4%	NM
LTM EBIT	157.4%	157.4%	157.4%	157.4%	NM	NM	NM	NM	NM
LTM EPS	148.5%	148.5%	148.5%	148.5%	NM	NM	NM	NM	NM

Comparison of Publicly Held Wireless Communication Companies

	AVG.	HIGH	LOW	PALMER WIRELESS	ROGER CANTEL	VANGUARD	VODAFONE GROUP
Last Statement/Fiscal Year End				12/94...6/95	12/94...6/95	12/94...6/95	3/95...3/95
BUSINESS DESCRIPTION				Construction/operation of cellular phone systems in Southeast; recently acquired GTE's GA cellular assets.	In Canada, largest cellular, 2nd largest paging company; chain of communications stores.	Owns/operates cellular phone systems primarily in the eastern US; under trademark of CellularOne.	UK operator os analog/digital cellular radio network; paging, value-added services.
MARKET DATA							
Symbol/Where Traded				PWIR/OTC	RCMIF/OTC	VCELA/OTC	VOD/NYSE
Stock Price (10/24/95)				$22.75	$22.38	$24.00	$41.50
Fully Diluted Shares				24.0	93.9	42.9	307.3
Equity Market Capitalization				$546.0	$2,101.0	$1,029.6	$12,753.0
LTM Price Range				$24.50–$14.25	$31.88–$22.25	$29.63–$21.50	$45.00–$41.50
OPERATING DATA							
LTM Revenues				$86.6	$711.0	$202.7	$1,866.1
LTM Operating Cash Flow (EBDAIT)				30.9	249.7	46.5	733.3
LTM Operating Earnings (EBIT)				18.0	126.9	16.9	583.9
LTM EPS				($0.10)	$0.07	($0.58)	$1.25
Book Value per Share				$12.45	($3.50)	$0.78	$4.34
1995 Projected EPS				$0.12	$0.03	($0.18)	$1.59
1996 Projected EPS				$0.51	$0.51	$0.41	$2.12
1995 Projected Cellular EBITDA				51.1	233.1	69.7	843.9
1996 Projected Cellular EBITDA				70.8	286.8	116.8	1,047.4
Subscribers at 6/30/95 (thousands)				141.9	840.7	314.0	2,040.0
Total Proportionate POPs				3.1	23.6	7.5	104.9
MARKET MULTIPLES: Price/							
LTM EPS	48.9x	319.6x	(227.5)x	(227.5)x	319.6x	(41.2)x	33.3x
1995 Projected EPS	48.3	745.8	(133.3)	189.6	745.8	(133.3)	26.1
1996 Projected EPS	36.7	64.4	(11.6)	44.6	43.9	58.5	19.6
Book Value	4.2	19.6	1.6	1.8	NM	NM	9.6
Enterprise Value/LTM Revenues	7.7x	34.4x	4.3x	8.4	4.3	7.3	7.0x
LTM EBDAIT	23.3	43.5	11.8	23.3x	11.8x	30.1x	14.4x
1995 Projected Cellular EBDAIT	14.8	20.1	12.5	14.1	12.6	20.1	12.5
1996 Projected Cellular EBDAIT	10.8	12.6	10.1	10.2	10.3	12.0	10.1
Per POP/Pager	170.1x	322.6x	66.4x	232.4	124.9	186.8	100.9
LEVERAGE RATIOS							
Debt/LTM EBDAIT	5.4x	10.2x	0.4x	6.1x	3.7x	9.9x	0.4x
Debt+Preferred/LTM	5.4	15.3	0.4	6.1	3.7	9.9	0.4
Valuation							
Equity Market Capitalization				$546.0	$2,101.0	$1,029.6	$12,753.0
Plus: Long Term Debt				187.3	925.4	459.1	284.8
Less: Cash and Equivalents				(3.4)	0.0	(5.7)	(25.7)
Less: Option/Warrant Proceeds				(9.3)	0.0	(53.0)	0.0
Less: Int Value at 70% PMV				0.0	0.0	0.0	(2,077.6)
Less: Other Value at 70% PMV				0.0	(79.2)	(29.1)	(350.0)
Implied Enterprise Value				$720.6	$2,947.2	$1,400.9	$10,584.4

Chapter Eighteen

The Harvest and Beyond

And don't forget: Shrouds have no pockets.

The late Sidney Rabb
Chairman Emeritus,
Stop & Shop, Boston

Results Expected

After completing the chapter, you will have:

1. Examined the importance of first building a great company and thereby creating harvest options.
2. Examined why harvesting is an essential element of the entrepreneurial process and does not necessarily mean abandoning the company.
3. Identified the principal harvest options, including going public.
4. Analyzed the "Boston Communications Group, Inc." case.

A Journey, Not a Destination

A common sentiment among successful entrepreneurs is that it is the challenge and exhilaration of the journey that gives them the greatest kick. Perhaps Walt Disney said it best: "I don't make movies to make money. I make money to make movies." It is the thrill of the chase that counts.

These entrepreneurs also talk of the venture's incredibly insatiable appetite for not only cash but also time, attention, and energy. Some say it is an addiction. Most say it is far more demanding and difficult than they ever imagined. Most, however, plan not to retire and would do it again, usually sooner. What's more, they also say it is more fun and satisfying than any other career they have had.

For the vast majority of entrepreneurs it takes 10, 15, even 20 years or more to build a significant net worth. According to the popular press and government statistics, there are more millionaires than ever in America. In 1998, as many as 3.5 million persons in the United States (or nearly 3 percent of the working population) will be millionaires—their net worth exceeding $1 million. While these numbers may be true, a million dollars, sadly, is not really all that much money today, as a result of high inflation, and while lottery and sweepstakes winners become instant millionaires, entrepreneurs do not. The number of years it usually takes to accumulate such a net worth is a far cry from the instant millionaire, the get-rich-quick impression associated with lottery winners or in fantasy TV shows.

The Journey Can Be Addictive

In addition, the total immersion required, the huge workload, the many sacrifices for a family, and the burnout often experienced by an entrepreneur are real. Maintaining the energy, enthusiasm, and drive to get across the finish line, to achieve a harvest, may be, when the time comes, exceptionally difficult. For instance, one entrepreneur in the computer software

573

business, after working alone for several years, developed highly sophisticated software. Yet, he was the first one to insist that he could not stand the computer business for another day. Imagine trying to position a company for sale effectively and to negotiate a deal for a premium price after such a long battle.

Some entrepreneurs, even with what most of us would agree has been raging success, wonder if the price of victory is too high. One very successful entrepreneur put it this way: "What difference does it make if you win, have $20 million in the bank—I know several who do—and you are a basket case, your family has been washed out, and your kids are a wreck?"

The opening quote of the chapter is a sobering reminder and its message is clear: Unless an entrepreneur enjoys the journey and thinks it is worthy, he or she may end up on the wrong train to the wrong destination.

First Build a Great Company

One of the simplest but most difficult principles for nonentrepreneurs to grasp is that wealth and liquidity are *results*—not causes—of building a great company. They fail to recognize the difference between making money and spending money. Most successful entrepreneurs possess a clear understanding of this distinction; they get their kicks from growing the company. They know the payoff will take care of itself if they concentrate on the money-making part of the process.

Create Harvest Options

Here is yet another great paradox in the entrepreneurial process: Build a great company but do not forget to harvest. This apparent contradiction is difficult to reconcile, especially among entrepreneurs with several generations in a family-owned enterprise. Perhaps a better way to frame this apparent contradiction is to keep harvest options open and to think of harvesting as a vehicle for reducing risk and for creating future entrepreneurial choices and options, not simply selling the business and heading for the golf course or the beach, although these options may appeal to a few entrepreneurs. To appreciate the importance of this perspective, consider the following actual situations.

In the first instance, an entrepreneur in his 50s, Nigel, reached an agreement with a young entrepreneur in his 30s, Brian, to join the company as marketing vice president. Their agreement also included an option for Brian to acquire the company in the next five years for $1.5 million. At the time, the firm, a small biscuit maker, had revenues of $500,000 per year. By the end of the third year, Brian had built the company to $5 million in sales and substantially improved profitability. He notified Nigel of his intention to exercise his option to buy the company. Nigel immediately fired Brian, who had no other source of income, had a family, and a $400,000 mortgage on a house whose fair market value had catapulted to $275,000. Brian learned that Nigel had also received an offer from a company for $6 million. Thus, Nigel wanted to renege on his original agreement with Brian. Unable to muster the legal resources, Brian settled out of court for less than $100,000. When the other potential buyer learned how Nigel had treated Brian, it withdrew the $6 million offer. Then, there were no buyers. Within two years, Nigel drove the company into bankruptcy. At that point, he called Brian and asked if he would now be interested in buying the company. Brian suggested that Nigel go perform certain unnatural anatomical acts on himself!

In a quite different case, a 100-year-old family business was approached by a buyer who was willing to pay $100 million for the business, a premium valuation by any standard. Yet, the family insisted, it would never sell the business under any circumstances. Two years later, market condition changes and the credit crunch transformed slow-paying customers into nonpaying customers. The business was forced into bankruptcy, which wiped out 100 years of family equity.

It is not difficult to think of a number of alternative outcomes for these two firms and many others like them, who have erroneously assumed that the business will go on forever. By stubbornly and steadfastly refusing to explore harvest options and exiting as a natural part of the entrepreneurial process, owners may actually increase their overall risk and deprive themselves of future options. Innumerable examples exist whereby entrepreneurs sold or merged their companies and then went on to acquire or to start another company and pursued new dreams:

- Robin Wolaner founded *Parenting Magazine* in the mid 1980s and sold it to Time-Life.[1] Wolaner then joined Time and built a highly successful career there, and in July of 1992, she became the head of Time's Sunset Publishing Corporation.[2]
- After college, Douglas Ranalli[3] founded and built a student magazine, which he sold to a major publisher. After returning to school to get his MBA, he

[1] This example is drawn from "Parenting Magazine," Harvard Business School Case 291-015.
[2] Lawrence M. Fisher, "The Entrepreneur Employee," The *New York Times*, August 2, 1992, p. 10.
[3] For a more detailed description of Douglas Ranalli's first venture, as well as some of his thoughts on opportunity analysis, see "Doug Ranalli," Harvard Business School Case 391-027.
[4] See Chapter 12 case on his second venture.

launched a second company, FAX International.[4] Ranalli was able to conserve his equity by having capital from his first venture.

- Jeff Parker built and sold two companies, including Technical Data Corporation,[5] by the time he was 40. His substantial gain from these ventures has led to an entire new career as a private investor who works closely with young entrepreneurs to help them build their companies.

- In mid-1987, George Knight, founder and president of Knight Publications,[6] was actively pursuing acquisitions in order to grow his company into a major force. Stunned by what he believed to be exceptionally high valuations for small companies in the industry, he concluded that this was the time to be a seller rather than a buyer. Therefore, in 1988, he sold Knight Publications to a larger firm, within which he could realize his ambition of contributing as a chief executive officer to the growth of a major company. Having turned around the troubled divisions of this major company, he is currently seeking a small company to acquire and to grow into a large company.

One could fill a book with numerous other examples. The entrepreneurial process is endless.

A Harvest Goal

Having a harvest goal and crafting a strategy to achieve it are indeed what separate successful entrepreneurs from the rest of the pack. Many entrepreneurs seek only to create a job and a living for themselves. But it is quite another thing to grow a business that creates a living for many others, including employees and investors, by creating value—value that can result in a capital gain.

Setting a harvest goal achieves many purposes, not the least of which is helping an entrepreneur get after-tax cash out of an enterprise and enhancing substantially his or her net worth. Such a goal also can create high standards and a serious commitment to excellence over the course of developing the business. It can provide, in addition, a motivating force and a strategic focus that does not sacrifice customers, employees, and value-added products and services just to maximize quarterly earnings.

There are other good reasons as well. The workload demanded by a harvest-oriented venture versus one in a venture that cannot achieve a harvest may actually be less and is probably no greater. Such a business, in fact, may be less stressful than managing a business that is not oriented to harvest. Imagine the plight of the 46-year-old entrepreneur, with three children in college, whose business is overleveraged and on the brink of collapse. Contrast that frightful pressure with the position of the founder and major stockholder of another venture who, at the same age, sold his venture for $15 million. Further, the options open to the harvest-oriented entrepreneur seem to rise geometrically in that investors, other entrepreneurs, bankers, and the marketplace respond. There is great truth in the old cliche that "success breeds success."

There is a very significant societal reason as well for seeking and building a venture worthy of a harvest. These are the ventures that provide enormous impact and value added in a variety of ways. These are the companies that contribute most disproportionately to technological and other innovations, to new jobs, to returns for investors, and to economic vibrancy.

Also, within the process of harvest, the seeds of renewal and reinvestment are sown. Such a recycling of entrepreneurial talent and capital is at the very heart of our system of private responsibility for economic renewal and individual initiative. Entrepreneurial companies organize and manage for the long haul in ways to perpetuate the opportunity creation and recognition process and thereby to ensure the process of economic regeneration, innovation, and renewal.

Thus, a harvest goal is not just a goal of selling and leaving the company. Rather, it is a long-term goal to create real value added in a business. (It is true, however, that if real value added is not created, the business simply will not be worth very much in the marketplace.)

Crafting a Harvest Strategy: Timing Is Vital

Consistently, entrepreneurs avoid thinking about harvest issues. In a survey of the computer software industry between 1983 and 1986, Steven Holmberg found that 80 percent of the 100 companies surveyed had only an informal plan for harvesting. The rest of the sample confirmed the avoidance of harvest plans by entrepreneurs—only 15 percent of the companies had a formal written strategy for harvest in their business plans and the remaining 5 percent had a formal harvest plan written after the business plan.[7] When a company is first launched, then struggles for survival, and finally begins its ascent, the farthest thing from its founder's mind usually is selling out. Selling out is often viewed by the entrepreneur as the equivalent to complete abandonment of his or her very own "baby."

---

[5] For TDC's business plan, see "Technical Data Corporation Business Plan," Harvard Business School Case 283-973, Revised November 1987. For more on TDC's progress and harvest strategy, see "Technical Data Corporation," Harvard Business School Case 283-072, Revised December 1987.
[6] For a detailed description of this process, see Harvard Business School Case 289-027, revised February 1989.
[7] Steven R. Holmberg, "Value Creation and Capture: Entrepreneurship Harvest and IPO Strategies," in *Frontiers of Entrepreneurship Research: 1991*, ed. Neil C. Churchill et al. (Babson Park, MA: Babson College, 1991), pp. 191–205.

Thus, time and again, a founder does not consider selling out until terror, in the form of the possibility of losing the whole company, is experienced. Usually, this possibility comes unexpectedly: New technology threatens to leapfrog over the current product line, a large competitor suddenly appears in a small market, or a major account is lost. A sense of panic then grips the founders and shareholders of the closely held firm, and the company is suddenly for sale—for sale at the wrong time, for the wrong reasons, and thus for the wrong price. Selling at the right time, willingly, involves hitting a strategic window, one of the many strategic windows that entrepreneurs face.

Entrepreneurs find that harvesting is clearly a non-issue until something begins to sprout, and again there is a vast distance between creating an existing revenue stream of an ongoing business and ground zero. Most entrepreneurs agree that securing customers and generating continuing sales revenue are much harder and take much longer than even they could have imagined. Further, the ease with which those revenue estimates can be cast and manipulated on a spreadsheet belie the time and effort necessary to turn those projections into cash.

At some point, with a higher potential venture, it becomes possible to realize the harvest. In terms of the strategic window, it is wiser to be selling as it is opening than as it is closing. Bernard Baruch's wisdom is as good as it gets on this matter. He has said, "I made all my money by selling too early." For example, in 1986, a private candy company with $150 million in sales was not considering selling. After contemplating advice to sell early, the founders recognized a unique opportunity to harvest and sold the firm for 19 times earnings, an extremely high valuation. Another example is that of a cellular phone company that was launched and built from scratch and began operations in late 1987. Only 18 months after purchasing the original rights to build and operate the system, the founders decided to sell the company, even though the future looked extremely bright. They sold because the sellers' market they faced at the time had resulted in a premium valuation—30 percent higher on a per capita basis (the industry valuation norm) than that for any previous cellular transaction to date. The harvest returned over 25 times the original capital in a year and a half. (Interestingly, the founders had not invested a dime of their own money.)

If the window is missed, disaster can strike. For example, at the same time as the harvests described above were unfolding, another entrepreneur saw his real estate holdings rapidly appreciate to nearly $20 million, resulting in a personal net worth, *on paper*, of nearly $7 million. The entrepreneur used this equity to refinance and leverage existing properties (to more than 100 percent in some cases) to seize what he perceived as further prime opportunities. Unfortunately,

after changes in the federal tax law in 1986 and the 1987 stock market crash, there was a major softening of the real estate market in 1988. As a result, in early 1989, half of the entrepreneur's holdings were in bankruptcy, and the rest were in a highly precarious and vulnerable position because prior equity in the properties had evaporated, leaving no collateral as increasing vacancies and lower rents per square foot turned a positive cash flow into a negative one.

Shaping a harvest strategy is an enormously complicated and difficult area. Thus, crafting such a strategy cannot begin too early. For example, HTC, Inc., a company that became a leading innovator in developing vapor-phase technology for soldering printed circuit boards, began crafting its harvest strategy in 1977, when it was basically a one-person garage-shop venture with no marketable product, and when it had been able to raise venture capital of just $10,000 for 10 percent of the venture from a firm that was very reluctant to invest a dime. An advisor worked closely with the lead entrepreneur from the beginning, and he thus knew the intricacies of the market, the industry, the competitors, the customers, and the internal management capabilities of the firm intimately. In 1984, the company had grown to nearly $7 million in sales and was subsequently sold for $15 million cash to a larger firm.

In shaping a harvest strategy, some guidelines and cautions can help:

- *Patience.* As has been shown, several years are required to launch and build most successful companies; therefore, patience can be invaluable. A harvest strategy is more sensible if it allows for a time frame of at least 3 to 5 years and as long as 7 to 10.

- *Vision.* The other side of the patience coin is not to panic as a result of precipitate events. Selling under duress is usually the worst of all worlds.

- *Realistic valuation.* If impatience is the enemy of an attractive harvest, then greed is its executioner. For example, an excellent, small firm in New England, which was nearly 80 years old and run by the third generation of a line of successful family leaders, had attracted a number of prospective buyers and had obtained a bona fide offer for over $25 million. The owners, however, had become convinced that this "great little company" was worth considerably more, and they held out. Before long, there were no buyers, and market circumstances changed unfavorably. In addition, interest rates skyrocketed. Soon thereafter, the company collapsed financially, ending up in bankruptcy. Greed was the executioner.

- *Outside advice.* It is difficult but worthwhile to find an advisor who can help craft a harvest strategy while the business is growing and, at the same time, maintain objectivity about its value and have the patience and skill to maximize it. A major problem seems to be that people who sell businesses, such as investment bankers or business brokers, are performing the same economic role and function as real estate brokers; in essence, their incentive is their commissions during a quite short time frame, usually a matter of months. However, an advisor who works with a lead entrepreneur for as much as five years or more can help shape and implement a strategy for the whole business so that it is positioned to spot and respond to harvest opportunities when they appear.

Harvest Options

There are seven principal avenues by which a company can realize a harvest from the value it has created. Described below, these most commonly seem to occur in the order in which they are listed. No attempt is made here to do more than briefly describe each avenue, since there are entire books written on each of these, including their legal, tax, and accounting intricacies.

Capital Cow

A "capital cow" is to the entrepreneur what a "cash cow" is to a large corporation. In essence, the high-margin profitable venture (the cow) throws off more cash for personal use (the milk) than most entrepreneurs have the time and uses or inclinations for spending it.

The result is a capital-rich and cash-rich company with enormous capacity for debt and reinvestment. Take, for instance, a health care–related venture that was started in the early 1970s that realized early success and that went public. Several years later, the founders decided to buy the company back from the public shareholders and to return it to its closely held status. Today the company has sales in excess of $100 million and generates extra capital of several million each year. This capital cow has enabled its entrepreneurs to form investing entities to invest in several other higher potential ventures, which included participation in the leveraged buy out of a $150 million sales division of a larger firm and in some venture capital deals.

Employee Stock Ownership Plan

Employee stock ownership plans (ESOPs) have become very popular among closely held companies as a valuation mechanism for stock for which there is no formal market. They are also vehicles through which founders can realize some liquidity from their stock by sales to the plan and other employees. And since an ESOP usually creates widespread ownership of stock among employees, it is viewed as a positive motivational device as well.

Management Buy Out

Another avenue, called a management buy out (MBO), is one by which a founder can realize a gain from a business by selling it to existing partners or to other key managers in the business. If the business has both assets and a healthy cash flow, the financing can be arranged via banks, insurance companies, and financial institutions that do leveraged buy outs (LBOs) and MBOs. Even if assets are thin, a healthy cash flow that can service the debt to fund the purchase price can convince lenders to do the MBO.

Usually, the problem is that the managers who want to buy out the owners and remain to run the company do not have the capital. Unless the buyer has the cash up front—and this is rarely the case—such a sale can be very fragile, and full realization of a gain is questionable. MBOs typically require the seller to take a limited amount of cash up front and a note for the balance of the purchase price over several years. If the purchase price is linked to the future profitability of the business, the seller is totally dependent on the ability and integrity of the buyer. Further, the management, under such an arrangement, can lower the price by growing the business as fast as possible, spending on new products and people, and showing very little profit along the way. In these cases, it is often seen that after the marginally profitable business is sold at a bargain price, it is well positioned with excellent earnings in the next two or three years. As can be seen, the seller will end up on the short end of this type of deal.

Merger, Acquisition, and Strategic Alliance

Merging with another firm is still another way for a founder to realize a gain. For example, two founders who had developed high-quality training programs for the rapidly emerging personal computer industry consummated a merger with another company. These entrepreneurs had backgrounds in computers, rather than in marketing or general management, and the results of the company's first five years reflected this gap. Sales were under $500,000, based on custom programs and no marketing, and they had been unable to attract venture capital, even during the market of 1982 to 1983. The firm with which they merged was a $15 million company that had an excellent reputation for its management training programs, had a Fortune-1000 customer base, had repeat sales of 70 percent, and had requests from the field sales force for programs to train managers in the use of personal computers. The buyer obtained 80 percent of the shares of the smaller firm, to consolidate the revenues and earnings from the merged company into its own financial statements, and the two founders of the smaller firm retained a 20 percent ownership in their firm. The two founders also obtained employment contracts, and the buyer provided nearly $1.5 million of capital advances during the first year of the new business. Under a put arrangement, the founders will be able to realize a gain on their 20 percent of the company, depending upon performance of the venture over the next few years.[8] The two founders now are reporting to the president of the parent firm, and one founder of the parent firm has taken a key executive position with the smaller company, an approach common for mergers between closely held firms.

In a strategic alliance, founders can attract badly needed capital, in substantial amounts, from a large company interested in their technologies. Such arrangements often can lead to complete buyouts of the founders downstream.

Outright Sale

Outright sale is viewed by most advisors as the ideal route to go because up-front cash is preferred over most stock, even though the latter can result in a tax-free exchange.[9] In a stock-for-stock exchange, the problem is the volatility and unpredictability of the stock price of the purchasing company. Many entrepreneurs have been left with a fraction of the original purchase price when the stock price of the buyer's company declined steadily. Often the acquiring company wants to lock key management into employment contracts for up to several years. Whether this makes sense depends on the goals and circumstances of the individual entrepreneur.

Public Offering

Probably the most sacred business school cow of them all—other than the capital cow—is the notion of taking a company public.[10] The vision or fantasy of having one's venture listed on one of the stock exchanges, even over-the-counter, arouses passions of greed, glory, and greatness. For many would-be entrepreneurs, this aspiration is unquestioned and enormously

appealing. Yet, for all but a chosen few, taking a company public, and then living with it, may be far more time and trouble—and expense—than it is worth.

After the stock market crash of October 1987, the market for new issues of stock shrank to a fraction of the robust IPO market of 1986 and a fraction of those of 1983 and 1985, as well. The number of new issues and the volume of IPOs did not rebound—instead they declined between 1988 to 1991. Then in 1992 and into the beginning of 1993 the IPO window opened again after a long dormant period (see *Exhibit 18.1*). During this IPO frenzy, "small companies with total assets under $500,000 issued more than 68 percent of all IPOs."[11] Previously, small companies had not been as active in the IPO market. (Companies such as Lotus, Compaq, and Apple Computer do get unprecedented attention and fanfare, but these firms were truly exceptions.) Recently, however, the SEC has been trying "to reduce issuing costs and registration and reporting burdens on small companies The SEC began by simplifying the registration process by adopting Form S-18, which applies to offerings of less than $7,500,000, and reduced disclosure requirements."[12] Similarly, Regulation D created "exemptions from registration up to $500,000 over a twelve-month period."[13]

There are several advantages to going public, many of which relate to the ability of the company to fund its rapid growth. Public equity markets provide access to long-term capital, while also meeting subsequent capital needs. Companies may use the proceeds of an IPO to expand the business in the existing market or to move into a related market. The founders and initial investors might be seeking liquidity, but it is important to note that SEC restrictions limiting the timing and the amount of stock that the officers, directors, and insiders can dispose of in the public market are increasingly severe. As a result, it can take several years after an IPO before a liquid gain is possible. Additionally, as Jim Hindman believed, a public offering not only increases public awareness of the company but also contributes to the marketability of the products, including franchises.

However, there are also some disadvantages to being a public company. For example, 50 percent of the computer software companies surveyed by Holmberg agreed that the focus on short-term profits and performance results was a negative attribute of being a

---

[8] This is an arrangement whereby the two founders can force (the put) the acquirer to purchase their 20 percent at a predetermined and negotiated price.

[9] See several relevant articles on selling a company in *Growing Concerns,* ed. David E. Gumpert (New York: John Wiley & Sons, 1984), pp. 332–98.

[10] The Big Six accounting firms, such as Ernst & Young, publish information on deciding to take a firm public. See also Richard Salomon, "Second Thoughts on Going Public," in *Trials and Rewards of the Entrepreneur,* ed. David E. Gumpert (Boston: Harvard Business Review, 1983); and Safi U. Quereshey, "How I Learned to Live with Wall Street," *Harvard Business Review,* reprint No. 91309.

[11] Seymore, Jones, M. Bruce Cohen, and Victor V. Coppola, "Going Public," in William A. Sahlman and Howard H. Stevenson, eds., *The Entrepreneurial Venture* (Boston: Harvard Business School Publications, 1992), p. 394.

[12] Ibid., p. 395.

[13] Ibid.

EXHIBIT 18.1

Initial Public Offerings

EXHIBIT 18.1

Initial Public Offerings

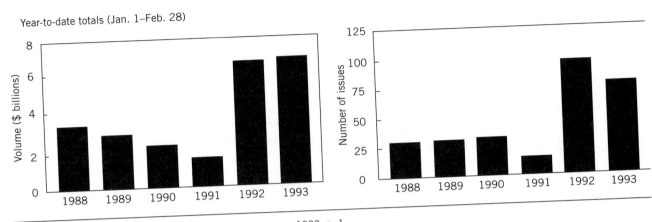

Firm commitment IPOs

Source: Adapted from *Going Public: The IPO Reporter*, February 1993, p. 1.

public company.[14] Also, because of the disclosure requirements, public companies lose some of their operating confidentiality, not to mention having to support the ongoing costs of public disclosure, audits, and tax filings. With public shareholders, the management of the company has to be careful about the flow of information because of the risk of insider trading. Thus, it is easy to see why companies need to think about the positive and negative attributes of being a public company. When considering this decision, you may find it useful to review Boston Communications Group, Inc., to identify the key components of the IPO process and to assess which investment bankers, accountants, lawyers, and advisors might be useful in making this decision.

Wealth-building Vehicles

The 1986 Tax Reform Act severely limited the generous options previously available to build wealth within a private company through large deductible contributions to a retirement plan. To make matters worse, the administrative costs and paperwork necessary to comply with federal laws have become a nightmare. Nonetheless, there are still mechanisms that can enable an owner to contribute up to 25 percent of his or her salary to a retirement plan each year, an amount which is deductible to the company and grows tax free. Entrepreneurs who can contribute such amounts for just a short time will, having Uncle Sam as a financial partner, build significant wealth.

Beyond the Harvest

A majority of highly successful entrepreneurs seem to accept a responsibility to renew and perpetuate the system that has treated them so well. Somehow they are keenly aware that our unique American system of opportunity and mobility depends in large part upon a self-renewal process.

There are many ways in which this happens. Some of the following data often surprise people:

- *College endowments.* It was shown a few years ago that over half of MIT's endowment comes from gifts of stock and other assets made by the founders of companies. A recent study of Babson College alumni showed that up to eight times as many entrepreneurs, compared to other graduates, made large gifts to the college.[15] Among the most generous and enthusiastic contributors to the Harvard Business School are the graduates of the Smaller Company Management Program, a short nondegree course for the heads of smaller firms. Among Harvard Business School alumni, entrepreneurs lead the way.

- *Community activities.* Entrepreneurs who have harvested their ventures very often reinvest their leadership skills and money in such community activities as symphony orchestras, museums, and local colleges and universities. These entrepreneurs lead fund-raising campaigns, serve on boards of directors, and devote many hours to other voluntary work. One Swedish couple, after spending six months working

14 Steven R. Holmberg, "Value Creation and Capture: Entrepreneurship Harvest and IPO Strategies," in *Frontiers of Entrepreneurship Research: 1991*, ed. Neil Churchill et al., (Babson Park, MA: Babson College, 1991), p. 203.
15 John A. Hornaday, "Patterns of Annual Giving," in *Frontiers of Entrepreneurship Research: 1984*, ed. J. Hornaday et al. (Babson Park, MA: Babson College, 1984).

with venture capital firms in Silicon Valley and New York, was "astounded at the extent to which these entrepreneurs and venture capitalists engage in such voluntary, civic activities." This couple found this pattern in sharp contrast to the Swedish pattern, where paid government employees perform many of the same services as part of their jobs.

- *Investing in new companies.* Postharvest entrepreneurs also reinvest their efforts and resources in the next generation of entrepreneurs and their opportunities. Successful entrepreneurs behave this way since they seem to know that perpetuating the system is far too important, and too fragile, to be left to anyone else. They have learned the hard lessons.

The innovation, the job creation, and the economic renewal and vibrancy are all results of the entrepreneurial process. The complicated and little understood process is *not caused* by government, though it is facilitated and/or impeded by it. Nor is it caused by the stroke of a legislative pen, though it can be ended by such a stroke. Rather, it is created by entrepreneurs, investors, and hard-working people in pursuit of opportunities.

Fortunately, entrepreneurs seem to accept a disproportionate share of the responsibility to make sure the process is renewed. And, judging by the new wave of entrepreneurship in the United States, both the marketplace and society once again are prepared to allocate the rewards to entrepreneurs that are commensurate with their acceptance of responsibility and delivery of results.

Seven Secrets of Success

The following seven secrets of success are included for your contemplation and amusement:

- There are no secrets. Understanding and practicing the fundamentals discussed here, along with hard work, will get results.
- As soon as there is a secret, everyone else knows about it, too. Searching for secrets is a mindless exercise.
- Happiness is a positive cash flow.
- If you teach a person to work for others, you feed him or her for a year, but if you teach a person to be an entrepreneur, you feed him or her, and others, for a lifetime.
- Do not run out of cash.
- Entrepreneurship is fundamentally a human process, rather than a financial or technological process. *You* can make an enormous difference.
- Happiness is a positive cash flow.

Chapter Summary

1. Entrepreneurs thrive on the challenges and satisfactions of the game: It is a journey, not a destination.
2. First and foremost, successful entrepreneurs strive to build a great company; wealth follows that process.
3. Harvest options mean more than simply selling the company, and these options are an important part of the entrepreneur's know-how.
4. Entrepreneurs know that to perpetuate the system for future generations, they must give back to their communities and invest time and capital in the next E-Generation.

Study Questions

1. Why did Walt Disney say, "I don't make movies to make money; I make money to make movies"?
2. Why is it essential to focus first on building a great company, rather than on just getting rich?
3. Why is a harvest goal so crucial for entrepreneurs and the economy?
4. Define the principal harvest options, the pros and cons of each, and why each is valuable.
5. Beyond the harvest, what do entrepreneurs do to "give back," and why is this so important to their communities and the nation?

MIND STRETCHERS
Have You Considered?

1. The Outdoor Scene (case in Chapter 1) became the largest independent tent manufacturer in North America, but eventually went out of business. The founder never realized a dime of capital gain. Why?
2. When Steve Pond sold his company in the late 1980s, he wrote checks for hundreds of thousands of dollars to several people who had left the company up to several years previously, but who had been real contributors to the early success of the company. What are the future implications for Steve, for you?
3. Dorothy Stevenson, the first woman to earn a ham radio license in Utah, said, "Success is getting what you want. Happiness is wanting what you get." What does this mean? Why should you care?
4. How will you personally define success in 5, 10, and 25 years? Why?
5. Assume that at age 40–50 years you have achieved a net worth of $25–$50 million in today's dollars. So what? Then what?

Case

Boston Communications Group, Inc.

Preparation Questions

1. Evaluate the investment bank proposals and options facing the company in early February 1996.
2. What should be the company's valuation? Why?
3. Which underwriter would you select? Why?
4. As a venture capital director, what would you do?
5. As a founder? As an outside director?
6. What will happen?

As Paul Tobin headed across Boston's Nahant Causeway on the cold morning of February 6, 1996, for a breakfast meeting with a director on his board, he reviewed his agenda for the board meeting afterwards. Two things stuck in his mind; one was a surprise, the other was not. First, the best harvest option at this point was clearly an IPO. But what had been a substantial, albeit most pleasant, surprise was the new valuations (See *Paul J. Tobin* case study in Chapter 17.) Instead of the $50 to $90 million range originally suggested by the investment bankers known as the Four Horsemen, they now concluded that the company might have a post-money IPO market cap as high as $290 million, and at least $200 million. Assuming the board voted later this morning to pursue an IPO, the major decision now was: Who should be the underwriter?

In the discussion over breakfast, the director confirmed what Paul had suspected all along; he would step down from the board this morning, as he had a personal policy of not being on the board of new public companies.

Strategic Revelations: The Paradox of Dry Powder[1]

The delicate balancing act between optimistic versus conservative financial forecasts in a business plan can be befuddling for entrepreneurs and investors alike. The more aggressive the business plan, the less likely the management team will be able to achieve it and as a consequence of underperforming, the company will likely suffer dilution. On the other hand, the more conservative the estimates, the more likely management will achieve its business plan projections, but may fail to attract investors at all since the company just won't be large enough nor profitable enough. Further, at the harvest window overly conservative estimates lead to the ultimate "dry powder paradox" as the depressed values come back to haunt the conservative estimator.

Paul Tobin faced this paradox of dry powder, since one of his core entrepreneurial philosophies had always been: "Commit to a business plan you know you can make or exceed. Make it aggressive, but make sure you achieve the plan." He had consistently demonstrated his capacity to do this in building CellularOne in eastern Massachusetts from the launch to $100 million in sales in five years, and

again in Maine and New Hampshire with Portsmouth Cellular. This had been a key to creating long-term credibility with potential investors, and had enabled him to both attract venture capital and to negotiate favorable terms, given the capital market conditions at the time. Further, this same philosophy, backed by performance, had enabled him to renegotiate the BCGI deal in 1992 and significantly improve management's ownership position. Ironically, his strategy of preserving their ambitious R&D plans for the new C2C prepaid service targeted at the antifraud market as dry powder (which would have been appropriate if preparing for a future round of venture capital), resulted in a quite different set of comparable companies and valuation analysis by the investment bankers.

It was just this paradoxical situation that had revealed itself to Paul over the past three months. Fortunately, he was able to show the investment bankers that the company's future services—not just R&D, but a product already in trials—would significantly change both how one would perceive the company's future and the fundamental strategic businesses it was pursuing. BCGI was not a plain vanilla transaction processing company, such as defined in one valuation report, but rather a company whose future business also encompassed the antifraud/antitheft arena.

How does the entrepreneur discover such things? In the case of BCGI, one outside board member was uncomfortable with the initial valuations and the profile of the company articulated in the valuation reports. In seeking to understand possible misconceptions embedded in the valuation studies, he talked to Janet Green, who headed up Ernst & Young's Corporate Finance activities. A brief discussion revealed that, based on the hundreds of telecommunications transactions over the past year that she was familiar with, companies in the cellular-related antifraud arena were often valued at 5 to 10 times revenue, and some outliers commanded as much as 15 to 20 times trailing revenues (See *Exhibit A*). This was a stunning contrast to everything the company had heard up to this point. The director immediately put Paul in touch with Janet. This resulted in a quite different view of the business, a new five-year business plan, and some significantly more robust valuations from the investment bankers.

© Copyright 1996, Jeffry A. Timmons. This case was prepared by Dan D'Heilly and Andrea Alyse, under the direction of Jeffry A. Timmons, Franklin W. Olin Professor, Babson College, Babson Park, MA. Funding provided by the Ewing Marion Kauffman Foundation. All rights reserved.

[1] "Dry powder" is an expression from the Colonial days of flintlock muskets, which were fired by pouring a small charge of gun powder into a flashpan which would ignite from the sparks of the flint striking a metal piece once the trigger was pulled. If one's powder became damp the musket would not fire. Thus, having a cushion or back-up reserve of "dry-powder" was a must for survival. Having "dry powder" in business plan forecasts simply describes a conservative philosophy of estimating.

EXHIBIT A

Data of Selected Telecommunications Companies

	1995 Average Price	1994 Average Price	Common Shares Out (mil)	Total Debt ($ mil)	1995 Revenues ($ mil)	1994 Revenues ($ mil)	1995 EPS	1994 EPS	Market Cap ($ mil)	Multiple
Airtouch Communications	29.80	25.25	498.57	1,075	1,619	1,235	0.27	0.20	14,857	9
MFS Communications	20.65	15.55	130.26	1,334	583	286	1.21	2.21	2,690	5
Mobile Telephone Technology	27.60	20.45	54.13	364	246	148	1.19	0.76	1,494	6
Nextel Communications	15.60	30.05	193.55	2,285	225	83	2.31	1.25	3,019	13
U.S. Cellular	32.15	28.85	82.97	359	492	332	0.52	0.21	2,667	5
Vanguard Cellular	24.70	23.65	41.31	542	236	168	0.17	0.36	1,020	4

Source: Value Line, Inc. October 11, 1996.

A New Service, A New Valuation

BCGI launched C2C, a prepaid wireless telephone carrier support service, in the fall of 1995. Although prepaid calling was relatively new to North America, many parts of the world depended upon it. For example, Japan's NTT[2] sold over 2 billion prepaid phone cards between 1985 and 1995. Annual revenues for the prepaid wireless market in the United States were $1 billion in 1995; however this market was still considered to be in its infancy. BCGI created a nationwide service that benefited from the expertise developed with ROAMER*plus* and found rapid market acceptance. BCGI anticipated that at least four of the regional Bell operating companies would be C2C clients by the end of the first quarter of 1996.

The synergy between ROAMER*plus* and C2C was considerable. ROAMER*plus* was in 1,100 markets nationwide, and C2C could be rolled out using much of the same infrastructure and many of the same relationships. As a result, BCGI would be the only company able to offer a national prepaid roaming service in early 1996.

Providing prepaid services had many advantages over offering credit-based services for wireless vendors. One of the biggest expenses in credit operations was fraud. Losses from wireless fraud in the United States ran at over $1 million a day. Prepaid services almost eliminated this cost (See *Exhibit B*, Relative Cost Model).

A New Business Plan

The revised business plan did not show a major increase in projected revenues and profits (See *Exhibit C* for new projections), but rather conveyed a new strategic definition and positioning of BCGI's products and services. Paul still wanted to hold back some dry powder. The difference was that the bankers used a different set of comparable companies to determine BCGI's marketability.

The new comparables provided a rationale for the investment bankers to offer higher valuation estimates: One bank thought the company could be worth as much as $290 million, post-IPO, and all thought it would reach or exceed $200 million. This was about three to four times greater than the valuation offered at the last board meeting in November, just two-and-a-half months earlier.

Paul hoped that his next business plan would have another important addition: A new CEO, George Hertz. Paul wanted to step down before BCGI became a public company. George had been in the wireless and paging business in various capacities since 1982. He was currently serving as president of Advanced MobilComm, Inc., a wholly owned subsidiary of Fidelity Investments. George previously worked at Zip-Call, Inc., where he developed a nationwide multi-city paging program utilizing radio frequencies and worked on cellular license applications for four major New England markets. From 1979 to 1982 he served as budget director for the Commonwealth of Massachusetts. George earned both his undergraduate and graduate degrees from the University of Massachusetts.

Paul and George had been friends for over a decade, and when it became apparent that an IPO would be the preferred harvest strategy, Paul contacted him immediately. By the time of the board meeting, George's appointment was assured. An agreement had been reached between the principals over the preceding months. George's experience managing a cellular company in a public environment would be invaluable in both growing the business and operating as a public company. The board would vote to offer George the position of president immediately following the vote to go public.

Selecting An Underwriter

Three of the Four Horsemen were enthusiastic about taking BCGI to market. Hambrecht and Quist didn't respond with much enthusiasm and were quickly eliminated from consideration. Paul had to make a recommendation to the board as to which one to hire (See Exhibits D-1 and D-2 for ratings of investment bankers). Paul and his team had spent most of January reviewing the proposals (See Exhibit E for typical proposal terms), comparing track records (See *Exhibits F-1* and *F-2* for 1995 IPOs managed by Robertson, Stephens, and Alex Brown), and talking to advisors.

EXHIBIT B

Relative Prepaid vs. Credit Cost Model*

Post-Paid Billing $$ Cost	Prepaid Service $ Cost
Fraud Losses	Usage Inquiry
Fraud Staff	C2C Service
Uncollectible Accounts	Card Production
Collection Agencies	Access Facilities
Collection Staff	
Billing Inquiry (Customer Service)	
Postage	
Billing Staff	
Billing System	

*Not drawn to scale

Source: C2C White Paper

---

[2] NTT was the largest telecommunications company in the world in 1996.

EXHIBIT C

Five Year Financial Plan (February 1, 1996) (000s)

	1991	1992	1993	1994	1995(e)	1996	1997	1998	1999	2000
Revenues:										
Cellular Express, Inc.										
Call Processing Services	$1,001	$7,557	$9,786	$18,712	$29,896	$34,200	$41,707	$50,056	$59,109	$68,660
Carrier Support Services			458	2,330	8,774	13,650	17,745	22,536	28,170	34,650
Network Services	446					3,198	15,747	36,405	62,214	98,381
Other Services										
Total Cellular Express	1,447	7,557	10,244	21,042	38,670	51,048	75,199	108,995	149,493	201,691
Cellular Services of WA	5,433	7,642	7,556	9,455	1,000					
Franklin County Cellular, Inc.	11	440	646	717						
Radio Telephone Systems, Inc.	737	228	544							
Total Revenue	7,628	15,867	18,990	31,214	39,670	51,048	75,199	108,995	149,493	201,691
Direct Operating Income:										
Cellular Express Inc.	-225	1,461	1,247	2,305	4,283	4,787	14,382	29,657	47,415	70,370
Cellular Services of WA	331	-187	317	337	-110					
Franklin County Cellular, Inc.	-78	182	406	455						
Radio Telephone Systems, Inc.	-97	-295	509							
Corporate	-873	-856	-1,273	-1,503	-1,267					
Total Operating Income	-942	305	1,206	1,594	2,906	4,787	14,382	29,657	47,415	70,370
Depreciation and Amortization	629	613	681	588	907	1,660	3,180	4,020	5,000	6,120
Interest Exp. (net of income)	2,361	526	590	558	142	54				
Other	346	103	359	-1,402	45					
Income (Loss) Before Taxes	-4,278	-937	-424	1,850	1,812	3,073	11,202	25,637	42,415	64,250
Income (Loss) After Taxes	($4,278)	($937)	($424)	$1,795	$1,726	$2,923	$7,281	$16,664	$27,570	$41,763

EXHIBIT II-1

Analyst Rankings

Overall Rankings

Firm	1993	1994	1995
Bear Stearns	16	15	11
C.J. Lawrence/Deutsche Bank Securities	16	18	20
Cowen & Co.	18	16	12
CS First Boston	6	7	7
Dean Witter Reynolds	15	14	16
Donaldson, Lufkin & Jenrette	4	3	2
Gerald Klauer Mattison	—	—	20
Goldman Sachs	2	1	3
Kidder Peabody	11	—	—
Lehman Brothers	1	9	13
Merrill Lynch	1	2	1
Montgomery Securities	19	18	6
Morgan Stanley	5	6	—
NatWest Securities	20	—	15
Oppenheimer & Co.	14	17	5
Paine Webber	8	8	8
Prudential Securities	9	10	6
Salomon Brothers	10	4	10
Sanford C. Bernstein	13	11	—
Smith Barney	7	5	—
Wertheim Schroder	12	13	—

1995 All American Research Team Rankings

Rank	Telecommunications Equipment
1	Joseph Bellace, Merrill Lynch
2	Anthony Langham, NatWest Securities
3	James Kedersha, Cowen & Co.
4	Mary Henry, Goldman Sachs

Rank	Telecommunications Services
1	Daniel Reingold, Merrill Lynch
2	Jack Grubman, Salomon Brothers
3	Frank Governali, CS First Boston
4	Charles Schelke, Smith Barney

Rank	Wireless Communications
1	Linda Runyon, Merrill Lynch
2	Dennis Leibowitz, DLJ
3	Susan Passoni, Cowen & Co.
4	Barry Kaplan, Goldman Sachs

1994 Information Tech./Software and Data Services Analyst Rankings

First-Team	Richard Sherlund, Goldman Sachs
Second-Team	Stephen McClellan, Merrill Lynch
Third-Team	Scott Smith, Donaldson, Lufkin & Jenrette

Source: *Institutional Investor*, October 1995.

EXHIBIT D–2

Most Active Lead Managers, 1995 Venture-backed IPOs

Underwriter	No. of Companies Managed	Total Co. Offering Size($ mil)	Avg. Price Change*	No. of Issues That Increased	No. of Issues That Decreased
Alex Brown & Sons	33	$1,681	72%	28	5
Hambrecht & Quist	36	1294	73	27	8
Robertson Stephens & Co.	28	1059	57	21	7
Cowen & Co.	27	946	48	20	7
Montgomery Securities	21	945	62	17	4
Morgan Stanley	15	891	91	12	3
Smith Barney	16	814	30	11	5
DLJ	13	796	42	12	1
Goldman, Sachs	15	771	83	13	2
CS First Boston	9	643	26	7	2
Volpe, Welty & Co.	15	531	55	12	3
Needham & Co.	16	498	36	12	4
Wessels, Arnold	12	445	78	10	2
Merrill Lynch & Co.	7	395	10	3	4
Bear Stearns	6	369	70	3	2

*From date of IPO to December 31, 1995.
Source: Securities Data Co., Venture Economics.

EXHIBIT E

Details of a Typical Proposal

Valuation Matrix

NI = $1.22 million

Calendar Year 1995 P/E Multiple	Implied Post Offering Valuation ($ millions) Valuation
65.2	80.0
73.5	90.0
81.8	100.0
90.2	110.0
98.5	120.0

Written Reports
- Memo/Internal Report (2–6 pages)
  - After quiet period expires
  - After each quarter's results are announced (8 per 24 months)
- Spot Report (2–6 pages)
  - As appropriate (4 per 12 months)
- Full Company Report
  - Approximately every 12 months after IPO
  - Investor contact (beyond reports)
- Sales Force
  - Regular updates from analyst at daily capital market reports
  - Direct access by management
  - Software focus, experience, and credibility
- Analysts Contracts
  - Interactive relationship with investment community
  - Media and trade press exposure
- Investor Meetings
  - Informal road shows arranged by underwriter
  - Sponsorship at New York Society of Securities Analysts
- High-Tech Company Conferences
  - Institutional investor attendance
  - Breakout sessions for detailed question and answer
  - Company-sponsored dinners
  - Exposure to other corporate clients

EXHIBIT F-1

Public Offerings Managed By Robertson Stevens & Co.

Issue[a]	Date	Managing Underwriters[b]	Total Dollar Value of Underwriting[c]	Number of Shares[c]	Offer Price per Share
Enterprise Systems, Inc.*	10/9	RS & Co., Volpe Welty, Wessels Arnold	$38,800,000	2,425,000	$16.00
Platinum Technology, Inc.	10/18	DLJ, H&Q, RS & Co	182,500,000	10,000,000	18.25
Tegal Corporation*	10/18	Merrill Lynch, RS & Co., Soundview Financial	49,200,000	4,100,000	12.00
Alteon, Inc.	10/17	RS & Co., Lehman, Montgomery	18,000,000	2,000,000	9.00
Logic Works, Inc.*	10/16	Morgan Stanley, H&Q, RS & Co.	35,200,000	3,200,000	11.00
VTEL Corp.	10/16	Piper Jaffray, RS & Co., Cowen	60,000,000	3,000,000	20.00
Intertape Polymer Group	10/10	First Marathon, Dean Witter, RS & Co., RBC Dominion First Analysis, Midland Weyland	43,800,000	1,500,000	29.20
Microwave Power Devices*	9/29	RS & Co., J.P. Morgan	31,200,000	3,900,000	8.00
Supreme International Corp.	9/28	Oppenheimer, RS & Co., Josephthal	24,700,000	1,300,000	19.00
Spectrum Holobyte, Inc.[d]	9/26	RS & Co., Jeffries, Piper Jaffray	50,000,000	50,000	100.00
Cannondale Corp.	9/20	Hambrecht & Quist, Montgomery, RS & Co.	43,987,500	2,550,000	17.25
Information Storage Devices	9/19	Alex Brown, RS & Co.	63,000,000	3,150,000	20.00
Alkermes, Inc.	9/19	RS & Co., Cowen	14,000,000	2,000,000	7.00
CBT Group, PLC	9/13	Alex Brown, RS & Co.	91,579,500	2,070,000	44.25
Opta Food Ingredients, Inc.	8/24	Wessels, RS & Co., Adams, Harkness & Hill	30,000,000	2,000,000	15.00
P-COM, Inc.	8/18	RS & Co., Paine Webber	49,875,000	1,500,000	33.25
Mackie Designs, Inc.*	8/17	Piper Jaffray, RS & Co.	30,000,000	2,500,000	12.00
Neurogen Corporation	8/17	Smith Barney, RS & Co., Pacific Growth	40,000,000	2,500,000	16.00
Gilead Sciences, Inc.	8/17	RS & Co., Hambrecht & Quist	81,956,250	3,525,000	23.25
The Vantive Corporation*	8/14	Hambrecht & Quist, RS & Co.	24,000,000	2,000,000	12.00
Northfield Laboratories, Inc.	8/10	RS & Co., Alex Brown	51,918,750	2,925,000	17.75
Trimble Navigation, Limited	8/3	Smith Barney, Needham, RS & Co.	57,750,000	2,000,000	28.88
The Men's Warehouse, Inc.	8/3	Bear Stearns, Montgomery, Paine Webber, RS & Co.	64,000,000	2,000,000	32.00
Cephalon, Inc.	8/1	Cowen, Hambrecht & Quist, RS & Co.	74,508,998	3,311,511	22.50
ON Technology Corporation*	8/1	RS & Co., Wessels	42,000,000	2,800,000	15.00
U.S. Office Products Company	7/28	RS & Co., Furman Selz, Rodman & Renshaw	49,875,000	3,500,000	14.25
Ascend Communications, Inc.	7/27	Morgan Stanley, RS & Co., Wessels	222,956,250	3,162,500	70.50
PRI Automation, Inc.	7/15	RS & Co., Hambrecht & Quist	42,550,000	1,150,000	37.00
Exogen, Inc.*	7/20	RS & Co., Cowen, Piper Jaffray	31,625,000	2,875,000	11.00
Project Software & Development, Inc.	7/13	RS & Co., Montgomery, First Albany	43,470,000	2,070,000	21.00
Legato Systems, Inc.*	7/6	RS & Co., Hambrecht & Quist, Punk, Siegel & Knoell	43,700,000	2,300,000	19.00
Discreet Logic Inc.*	6/30	RS & Co., Volpe Welty	74,865,000	3,565,000	21.00
Metra Biosystems, Inc.*	6/30	RS & Co., Cowen, Furman Selz	34,500,000	3,450,000	10.00
Applied Materials, Inc.	6/28	Morgan Stanley, Lehman, Cowen, Needham, RS & Co.	333,068,750	4,025,000	82.75
Tower Semiconductor Ltd.	6/27	Bear Stearns, RS & Co., Furman Selz	92,958,050	3,205,450	29.00
PhyCor, Inc.	6/23	Alex Brown, RS & Co., Smith Barney, Equitable	122,687,500	3,250,000	27.75
Spine-Tech, Inc.*	6/22	RS & Co., Piper Jaffray	36,225,000	4,025,000	9.00
HNC Software, Inc.*	6/20	Morgan Stanley, RS & Co.	36,225,000	2,587,500	14.00
Datalogix International, Inc.*	6/15	RS & Co., Alex Brown, UBS Securities	64,515,000	3,795,000	17.00
TransSwitch Corporation*	6/14	RS & Co., Hambrecht & Quist	28,875,000	2,875,000	9.00
American Oncology Resources*	6/13	Alex Brown, RS & Co., Volpe Welty	114,712,500	5,462,500	21.00

(Continued)

EXHIBIT F-1 (concluded)

Public Offerings Managed By Robertson Stevens & Co.

Issue[a]	Date	Managing Underwriters[b]	Total Dollar Value of Underwriting[c]	Number of Shares[c]	Offer Price per Share
ResMed, Inc.*	6/2	RS & Co., William Blair, Nomura	$ 37,950,000	3,450,000	11.00
Eltrom International, Inc.	5/31	RS & Co., Cruttenden Roth	42,000,000	2,000,000	21.00
Computer Learning Centers, Inc.*	5/31	RS & Co., Piper Jaffray	18,320,000	2,290,000	8.00
Number Nine Visual Technology Corporation*	5/25	RS & Co., Cowen, Unterberg Harris	45,712,635	3,047,509	15.00
ITI Technologies, Inc.	5/24	Piper Jaffray, RS & Co., Dain Bosworth	82,800,000	3,450,000	24.00
Nexgen, Inc.*	5/24	Paine Webber, Alex Brown, RS & Co.	53,250,000	3,550,000	15.00
VideoServer, Inc.*	5/24	Goldman Sachs, RS & Co.	49,725,000	2,925,000	17.00
ADFlex Solutions, Inc.	5/24	RS & Co., Paine Webber	61,582,500	2,415,000	25.50
Finlay Enterprises*	4/6	Goldman Sachs, DLJ, RS & Co.	36,610,000	2,615,000	14.00
Pairgain Technologies, Inc.	3/20	H & Q, Lehman, RS & Co., Furman Selz	88,977,656	3,766,250	23.63
PacificCare Health Systems, Inc.	3/16	Dean Witter, Salomon, Dillon Read, Lehman, RS & Co.	351,900,000	5,175,000	68.00
Horizon Mental Health Management, Inc.*	3/13	RS & Co., Raymond James	23,920,000	2,392,000	10.00
National Instruments Corporation*	3/13	RS & Co., Lehman	56,695,000	3,910,000	14.50
Tivoli Systems, Inc.*	3/10	Goldman Sachs, RS & Co.	40,652,500	2,903,750	14.00
McAfee Associates, Inc.	3/8	RS & Co., Bear Stearns, Alex Brown	64,009,000	2,909,500	22.00
P-COM, Inc.*	3/2	RS & Co., Paine Webber	29,325,000	1,955,000	15.00
Software Artistry, Inc.*	3/2	RS & Co., Cowen	30,348,500	2,167,750	14.00
Information Storage Devices, Inc.*	2/9	Alex Brown, RS & Co.	34,500,000	2,300,000	15.00
TheraTx, Inc.	2/9	RS & Co., DLJ, Morgan Stanley	100,000,000	100,000	100.00

[a] Asterisk indicates company's initial public offering.
[b] Bold lettering indicates managing underwriter who handled the books.
[c] Total amounts reflect the over-allotment option in the offerings in which it was exercised.
[d] A private placement of securities.
Note: All numbers reflect 6.5% convertible subordinated notes due September 15, 2002.

The most important factors for Paul were the recommendations of his board. Paul reasoned that they had experience with IPOs and he had none, so he was careful to heed their advice; however, the board was not unanimous. While all favored a rigorous examination of quantitative and qualitative data, it was common for venture capitalists to form close working relationships with investment bankers. On the BCGI Board, Highland had a long-standing relationship with DLJ, and Burr Egan Deleage with Alex Brown. Both these firms came highly recommended.

A complicating factor arose when Alex Brown lost its key wireless analyst, Mark Roberts, to competitor Montgomery Securities. This was a difficult decision. Fritz described the dilemma:

When Burr Egan recommended Alex Brown, Paul decided they would take us public. But when they lost Mark Roberts to Montgomery, it was a big loss.

The IPO Environment

Timing was another crucial issue. The IPO market, though decidedly uncertain at year-end, was holding up reasonably well through January 1996. (See *Exhibits G-1, G-2*, and *G-3* for IPO aftermarket data.) In January, 32 small companies had succeeded with new issues (see *Exhibits H* and *I* for examples of IPO registration announcements). This nearly 400-per-year pace would be considered a very strong year, even though it might not match the extremely robust IPO markets of 1993–1995. (See *Exhibits J* and *K* for stock performance by industry.) The trick was, given the four to five month lead time required from the filing to the offering, would the IPO window stay open, and how robust would it be when the day arrived? (See *Exhibit L* for VC-backed companies in registration.) No one claimed much predictive capacity to provide accurate answers to such elusive matters.

EXHIBIT F–2

Alex Brown & Sons, 1995 IPOs

Issue[a]	Date	Managing Underwriters[b]	Total Dollar Value of Underwriting[c]	Number of Shares[c]	Offer Price per Share
Discreet Logic, Inc.*	6/30	**RS & Co.**, Volpe Welty	$ 74,865,000	3,566,000	$21.00
Metra Biosystems, Inc.*	6/30	**RS & Co.**, Cowen, Furman Selz	34,500,000	3,450,000	10.00
Applied Materials, Inc.	6/28	**Morgan Stanley**, Lehman, Cowen, Needham, RS & Co.	333,068,750	4,025,000	82.75
Tower Semiconductor Ltd.	6/27	**Bear Stearns**, RS & Co., Furman Selz	92,958,050	3,205,450	29.00
PhyCor, Inc.	6/23	**Alex Brown**, RS & Co., Smith Barney, Equitable	122,687,500	3,250,000	27.75
Spine-Tech, Inc.*	6/22	**RS & Co.**, Piper Jaffray	36,225,000	4,025,000	9.00
HNC Software, Inc.*	6/20	**Morgan Stanley**, RS & Co.	36,225,000	2,587,500	14.00
Datalogix International, Inc.*	6/15	**RS & Co.**, Alex Brown, UBS Securities	64,515,000	3,795,000	17.00
TransSwitch Corporation*	6/14	**RS & Co.**, Hambrecht & Quist	28,875,000	2,875,000	9.00
American Oncology Resources, Inc.*	6/13	**Alex Brown**, RS & Co. Volpe Welty	114,712,500	5,462,500	21.00
ResMed, Inc.*	6/2	**RS & Co.**, William Blair, Nomura	37,950,000	3,450,000	11.00
Eltrom International, Inc.	5/31	**RS & Co.**, Cruttenden Roth	42,000,000	2,000,000	21.00
Computer Learning Centers, Inc.*	5/31	**RS & Co.**, Piper Jaffray	18,320,000	2,290,000	8.00
Number Nine Visual Technology Corporation*	5/25	**RS & Co.**, Cowen, Unterberg Harris	45,712,635	3,047,509	15.00
ITI Technologies, Inc.	5/24	**Piper Jaffray**, RS & Co., Dain Bosworth	82,800,000	3,450,000	24.00
Nexgen, Inc.*	5/24	**Paine Webber**, Alex Brown, RS & Co.	53,250,000	3,550,000	15.00
VideoServer, Inc.*	5/24	**Goldman Sachs**, RS & Co.	49,725,000	2,925,000	17.00
ADFlex Solutions, Inc.	5/24	**RS & Co.**, Paine Webber	61,582,500	2,415,000	25.50
Firefox Communications, Inc.*	5/4	**RS & Co.**, Montgomery, Cowen	47,610,000	2,645,000	18.00
Photronics, Inc.	4/18	**RS & Co.**, Prudential, Needham	29,400,000	1,400,000	21.00
CBT Group PLC*	4/13	**Alex Brown**, RS & Co.	42,320,000	2,645,000	16.00
Finlay Enterprises*	4/6	**Goldman Sachs**, DLJ, RS & Co.	36,610,000	2,615,000	14.00
Pairgain Technologies, Inc.	3/20	**H&Q**, Lehman, RS & Co., Furman Selz	88,977,656	3,766,250	23.63
McAfee Associates, Inc.	3/8	**RS & Co.**, Bear Stearns, Alex Brown	64,009,000	2,909,500	22.00
P-COM, Inc.*	3/2	**RS & Co.**, Paine Webber	29,325,000	1,955,000	15.00
Software Artistry, Inc.*	3/2	**RS & Co.**, Cowen	30,348,500	2,167,750	14.00
Information Storage Devices, Inc.*	2/9	**Alex Brown**, RS & Co.	34,500,000	2,300,000	15.00
TheraTx, Inc.	2/9	**RS & Co.**, DLJ, Morgan Stanley	100,000,000	100,000	100.00

[a] Asterisk indicates company's initial public offering.
[b] Bold lettering indicates managing underwriter who handled the books.
[c] Total amounts reflect the over-allotment option in the offerings in which it was exercised.
Note: All numbers reflect 6.5% convertible subordinated notes due September 15, 2002.

Decision Time: The February 1996 Board Meeting

Paul knew his board would in all likelihood accept his recommendation to pursue an IPO and would honor his recommendation as to which underwriter to hire, so the burden of decision was squarely on his shoulders. He had occasional nagging thoughts about the risks of an IPO versus a sale to a strategic buyer. He also worried about timing. Although the signs of an improving IPO market looked good for the moment, the IPO window could slam shut in short order, such as in mid-1983 and after the stock market crash of 1987. (See Exhibit M for annual IPO data.) The risks were significant: $500,000 or so in out-of-pocket expenses, a demoralizing impact on the company, and potentially, a long delay before the market would be favorable again. He also knew that picking the right underwriter for the company was a subtle task, and the outcome could make a major difference in the company's future.

These and other thoughts circled his mind as he entered the Callahan tunnel for his office next to Quincy Market.

EXHIBIT G-1

A Review of the IPO Aftermarket

Company/Location	Offering Date	Offering Size ($ mil)	Offering Price Per Share	Closing Price 12/31/95	Price Change (%)	Post Offering Valuation ($ mil)
AMISYS Managed Care, Rockvill, MD	12/20/95	29.0	$14.5	$19	31%	106.2
Adept Technology, San Jose, CA	12/15/95	22.8	71.3	9.5	10.5%	57.5
BENCHMARQ, Dallas, TX	12/1/95	8.0	8	8.125	18.9%	51.4
CapMAC Holding, New York, NY	12/31/95	74.2	20	25.125	25.6%	309.6
Cardiovascular, Raleigh, NC	12/11/95	23.4	11	11	0 %	70.9
Castelle, Santa Clara, CA	12/19/95	7.0	7	7.75	10.7%	24.3
Celeritek, Santa Clara, CA	12/20/95	15.0	7.5	10.625	41.7%	49.6
Citrix, Coral Springs, FL	12/7/95	37.5	15	32.5	116.7%	170.9
DeltaPoint, Greenville, SC	12/20/95	6.6	6	8.75	45.8%	12.2
Ergo Science, Charlestown, MA	12/14/95	22.5	9	14.25	58.3%	87.9
Fuisz Technologies, Chantilly, VA	12/14/95	33.0	12	15.25	27.1%	144.3
META Group, Stamford, CT	12/1/95	43.2	18	30.625	70.1%	90.0
Mecon, San Ramon, CA	12/6/95	33.2	13	15.875	22.1%	71.9
MetaTools, Carpinteria, CA	12/12/95	43.2	18	26	44.4%	202
Molecular Devices, Sunnyvale, CA	12/12/95	25.3	11	10.5	4.5%	95.2
Pharmacopeia, Princeton, NJ	12/5/95	41.6	16	24.25	51.6%	154.4
Physio-Control, Redmond, WA	12/12/95	135.4	14.5	17.875	23.3%	242.9
Raytel Medical, San Mateo, CA	12/1/95	20.0	8	8.5	6.3%	58.0
Schlotzsky's, Austin, TX	12/15/95	24.8	11	10.25	6.8%	60.7
Spacehab, Arlington, VA	12/20/95	45.0	12	12.25	2.1%	128.4
Synaptic Pharmaceutical, Paramus, NJ	12/13/95	20.5	12.5	13.25	6 %	91.6
United TransNet, Roswell, GA	12/14/95	56.9	14.5	15.125	4.3%	125.8
Visioneer, Palo Alto, CA	12/11/95	48.0	12	22.25	85.4%	217.6

Source: *Venture Capital Journal*, February 1996.

EXHIBIT G-2

Communications Equipment and Service IPO Aftermarket

Company	P/E Ratio	60-Month High	60-Month Low	11/30/95 Close or Bid Price	Change from 10/31/95
Brooktree	18	21 3/4	5 3/4	13 1/8	1 1/8
CMC Industries	d	10 1/2	2	4 7/16	3/16
Global Village Communication	40	24 1/8	5 3/4	22 3/4	5 3/4
LCI International	100	45 1/2	13 1/2	18 1/2	1/2
Metricom	d	33 3/4	4	15 3/4	-7/8
Microcom	40	26 5/8	1 17/32	25 1/4	3 3/8
Octel Communications	24	42 1/8	10 1/2	32 7/8	−1 1/4
PairGain Technologies	58	50 3/8	7	50 3/8	7 5/8
Racotek	d	14	3/16	5 3/4	−3/8
Signal Technology	94	10	2 7/8	5 5/8	5/8
Tricord Systems	d	29 1/8	2 7/8	3 1/8	−5/8
Trimble Navigation	31	35	6 3/4	20 3/8	5/8
Xircom	d	27 3/4	7 1/4	12 1/4	3 1/4

d = Deficit
Source: *Venture Capital Journal*, January, 1996.

Venture-backed IPOs, December 1995

Company Location	Offering Date	Size	Offering Price	Bid Price (per share)	Post Offering Valuation	Earnings per Share	Period	Underwriters	Business
Benchmarq Micro (Dallas, TX)	12/1/95	$ 8M	$ 8	$ 8.13	$ 51.3M	$ 0.35	12 Months 12/31/94	Needham & Co.	Integrated Circuits
Meta Group (Stamford, CT)	12/1/95	$ 43.2M	$18	$30.63	$ 91.69M	$(0.99)	12 months 12/31/94	RS & Co. DLJ	Market Assessment Services
Raytel Medical (San Mateo, CA)	12/1/95	$ 20M	$ 8	$ 8.50	$ 57.89M	$ 0.69	12 months 9/30/94	Vector Securities Van Kasper & Co.	Cardiovascular Heathcare Services
Pharmacopeia (Princeton, NJ)	12/5/95	$ 41.6M	$16	$24.25	$154.42M	$(3.15)	12 months 3/31/94	Alex Brown & Sons Cowen & Co. UBS Securities	Drug Discovery Technologies
Mecon (San Ramon, CA)	12/6/95	$ 33.15M	$13	$15.88	$ 71.94M	$(0.06)	12 months 3/31/95	Montgomery Securities Cowen & Co.	Health care Information Systems
Citrix (Coral Springs, FL)	12/7/95	$ 37.5M	$15	$32.50	$170.86M	$ 0.02	12 months 12/31/94	Hambrecht & Quist RS & Co	Multi-User Server Products
Visioneer (Palo Alto, CA)	12/7/95	$ 48M	$12	$22.25	$217.57M	$(0.76)	12 months 12/31/94	RS & Co Montgomery Securities Paine Webber	Paper Input Systems
Cardiovascular Diagnostic (Raleigh, NC)	12/7/95	$ 23.38M	$11	$11.00	$ 70.92M	$(0.35)	12 months 12/31/94	Bear Stearns & Co. Scott & Stringfellow	Cardiovascular Diagnostic Test System

Source: *Venture Capital Journal*, February 1996.

EXHIBIT H

IPOs in Registration, Celeritek, Inc.—Actual

SANTA CLARA, Calif.—Celeritek, which makes transceivers, completed an initial public offering on December 20, 1995. The company sold two million shares at $7.50 per share. The shares priced well below the company's $10 to $12 filing range.

Selling shareholders sold 400,000 of the total shares offered. Venture investors Sutter Hill Ventures, Greylock Management, Venrock Associates, and Mayfield Fund V did not reduce their positions in the offering. Venture investors Burr, Egan, Deleage & Co. and Technology Funding sold shares.

Oppenheimer & Co. and Needham & Co. served as underwriters of the initial public offering. The IPO left 6,608,035 shares outstanding.

The company plans to use a portion of the funds to pay debt. Remaining proceeds are slated for working capital.

Founded in 1984, Celeritek has been profitable every year since 1991, according to its prospectus. It earned $0.06 per share for the year ending March 31, 1995.

Celeritek makes transceivers for military and wireless communications applications. The company's devices operate via its integrated circuit and proprietary gallium arsenide process technologies.

William Younger, general partner of Sutter Hill Ventures, and Charles Waite, general partner of Greylock Management, have served on Celeritek's board since 1984.

Celeritek Inc.—Selected Financials*

(in thousands, except per share amounts)

	Year ending March 31					Six Months Ended Sept 30	Six Months Ended Sept 30
	1991	1992	1993	1994	1995	1994	1995
Sales	$18,016	$22,476	$30,751	$36,029	$32,667	$16,614	$16,734
NI (Loss)	1,944	3,851	1,836	1,925	284	205	599
NI per share	0.40	0.74	0.36	0.36	0.06	0.04	0.11

*Unaudited

Source: *Venture Capital Journal*, February 1996.

EXHIBIT I

IPOs in Registration, CSG Systems International—Projected

ENGLEWOOD, Colo.—CSG Systems International, a provider of services to communication companies, plans to go public on February 28, 1996. CSG Systems plans to sell 2.9 million shares at $12 to $14 per share.

The initial public offering is being underwritten by Alex Brown & Sons and Hambrecht & Quist. The IPO will leave 25 million shares outstanding.

The Company plans to use approximately $40 million of the IPO's proceeds to reduce its debt and pay dividends on its preferred stock.

CSG Systems was formed in October 1994 to acquire First Data Corp.'s Cable Services Group division. The purchase price was approximately $137 million, according to the Company's filing document.

Although CSG's revenue was a record $96.4 million at year-end December 31, 1995, it lost $0.86 per share during that period, according to its prospectus.

The company's software and support services enable its clients to manage such functions as billing, sales and order processing, invoice production, management reporting and customer analysis.

Morgan Stanley Capital Partners III, its affiliate Morgan Stanley Venture Partners II, and Trident Capital Partners Fund I are the venture investors.

Frank Sica, a vice chairman of Morgan Stanley Capital Partners, Robert Loarie, vice president of Morgan Stanley Venture Partners, Rockwell Schnabel, co-chairman of Trident Capital and Donald Dixon, president of Trident Capital, all have served as board members since CSG's inception. Andrew Cooper, also a vice president of Morgan Stanley Venture Partners, became a director of the company in November 1994.

CSG Systems International Inc.—Selected Financials

(In thousands, except per share amounts)

	Predecessor				Company	
				Eleven Months Ended Nov. 30, 1994	One Month Ended Dec. 31, 1994	Year Ended Dec. 31, 1995
	1991*	1992	1993			
Revenue	$65,206	$71,258	$75,578	$76,081	$7,757	$96,404
NI	3,609	6,727	8,347	8,610	(40,704)	(19,180)
NI per share	-	-	-	-	(1.81)	(.86)

*Unaudited

Source: *Venture Capital Journal*, April 1996.

EXHIBIT J

1994–1995 Venture-backed IPO Performance by Industry

Industry	1995 No.	1995 %	1994 No.	1994 %	5-Year Total No.	5-Year Total %
Computer Software & Services	56	31.0%	17	11.9%	131	16.7%
Medical/Health-related	27	14.9%	27	18.9%	149	19.0%
Other Electronics-related	23	12.7%	15	10.5%	80	10.1%
Telephone & Data Com.	16	8.9%	21	14.7%	85	10.9%
Other	15	8.3%	21	14.7%	66	8.4%
Biotechnology	12	6.6%	10	7.0%	91	11.6%
Consumer-related	12	6.6%	10	7.0%	77	9.8%
Computer Hardware	8	4.4%	9	6.3%	49	6.3%
Industrial Machines & Eqpt.	6	3.3%	8	5.6%	31	4.0%
Industrial Automation	3	1.7%	2	1.4%	9	1.2%
Commercial Communications	2	1.0%	3	2.0%	9	1.2%
Energy-related	1	0.6%	0	0.0%	6	0.8%
TOTAL	181	100.0%	143	100.0%	783	100.0%

Source: Securities Data Co./Venture Economics, *Venture Capital Journal*, February 1996.

EXHIBIT K

Telecommunications Stock Market Indices

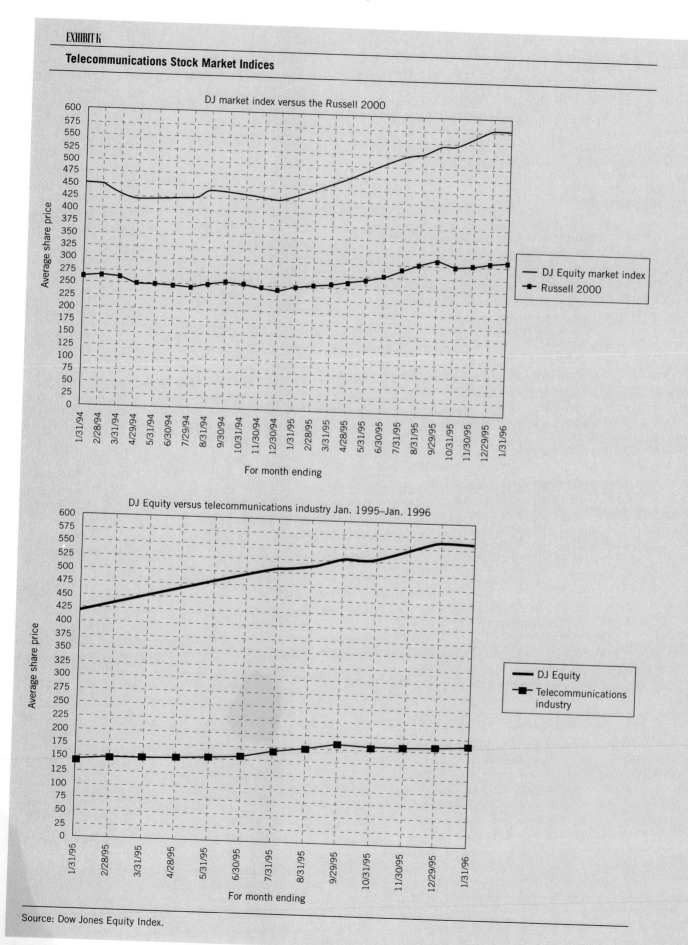

EXHIBIT L

Venture-backed Companies in Registration, 12/29/95

Date Filed	Issuer	Low Filing Price	High Filing Price	Shares Filed	Book Manager
9/8/95	RAC Financial Group	13.00	15.00	3,000,000	Bear Stearn
9/11/95	Grand Junction Network*	12.00	14.00	3,000,000	Goldman Sachs
9/27/95	Red Brick Systems	8.00	10.00	1,800,000	Morgan Stanley
10/26/95	IC Works	7.00	9.00	3,500,000	Prudential
10/27/95	Pharmavene	10.00	12.00	2,000,000	Lehman Brothers
11/2/95	Impath	11.00	13.00	1,950,000	Salomon Brothers
11/06/95	Hybridon	9.00	11.00	2,500,000	Lehman Brothers
11/7/95	Advanta Systems	11.50	13.50	2,000,000	ABS
11/7/95	Fast Multimedia	7.00	9.00	2,500,000	ABS
11/13/95	Aavid Thermal Technologies	10.00	12.00	2,300,000	Montgomery Securities
11/22/95	TresCom International	11.00	13.00	4,166,667	Morgan Stanley
11/22/95	Wilmar Industries	10.00	12.00	4,000,000	ABS
12/1/95	Heartstream	—	13.00	3,000,000	UBS
12/1/95	Iron Mountain	16.00	18.00	4,800,000	Prudential Securities
12/1/95	Optical Sensors	11.00	13.00	2,500,000	ABS
12/4/95	Associated Building, Systems	12.00	13.00	2,100,000	George K. Baum
12/5/95	K&G Men's Center	11.00	13.00	1,700,000	Robinson-Humphrey
12/8/95	Connective Therapeutics	11.00	13.00	2,500,000	Smith Barney
12/8/95	Digital Generation Systems	—	—	3,000,000	Hambrecht & Quist
12/12/95	Platinum Entertainment	12.00	14.00	2,650,000	DLJ
12/14/95	Arthrocare	11.00	13.00	2,000,000	RS & Co
12/15/95	Caribiner International	15.00	17.00	3,000,000	Merrill Lynch
12/18/95	EndoVascular Technologies	11.00	13.00	2,000,000	Hambrecht & Quist
12/18/95	Preferred Networks	14.00	16.00	3,300,000	Paine Webber
12/18/95	Premiere Technologies	12.00	14.00	650,000	ABS
12/18/95	Trident	15.00	17.00	2,700,000	Prudential
12/19/95	Micro Enhancement	5.00	7.50	1,000,000	J.E. Liss
12/21/95	Gensym	9.00	11.00	2,000,000	Hambrecht & Quist
12/21/95	Landec	11.00	13.00	2,500,000	Smith Barney
12/21/95	Neose Technology	12.50	14.50	2,250,000	Smith Barney
12/22/95	Diacrin	14.00	16.00	2,500,000	Paine Webber
12/22/95	Health VISION	12.00	14.00	3,850,000	Montgomery

*has agreed to be acquired by Cisco Systems

Source: Securities Data Company.

EXHIBIT M

Venture-backed IPOs, 1985–1995

Year of IPO	No. of IPOS	Total Offered ($ mil)	Average Offering Size ($ mil)	Median Offering Size ($ mil)	Average Offering Valuation ($ mil)	Median Age of Co. at IPO (years)
1985	47	$843	$17.9	$15.2	$69.7	3
1986	98	2,128	21.7	16.3	86.7	5
1987	81	1,840	22.7	17.6	85.1	5
1988	36	789	21.9	17.0	91.8	5
1989	39	996	25.5	16.5	100.0	5
1990	42	1,188	28.3	23.8	109.3	6
1991	127	3,732	29.4	25.4	110.0	6
1992	160	4,317	26.9	23.1	98.7	6
1993	172	5,034	29.3	23.0	97.7	7
1994	243	3,582	25.1	22.8	87.8	7
1995	282	6,737	37.2	32.0	136.0	7

Source: Securities Data Co., *Venture Economics.*

Index